Management of Company Finance

D0528196

Management of Company Finance

J.M. SAMUELS
Professor of Business Finance
Birmingham Business School
University of Birmingham, UK

F.M. WILKES
Professor of Business Investment and Management
Birmingham Business School
University of Birmingham, UK

R.E. BRAYSHAW
Senior Lecturer in the Department of Accounting and Finance
Birmingham Business School
University of Birmingham, UK

SIXTH EDITION

INTERNATIONAL THOMSON BUSINESS PRESS
I⊕P An International Thomson Publishing Company

London • Bonn • Boston • Johannesburg • Madrid • Melbourne • Mexico City • New York • Paris
Singapore • Tokyo • Toronto • Albany, NY • Belmont, CA • Cincinnati, OH • Detroit, MI

Management of Company Finance

Copyright © 1990, 1995 J.M Samuals and F.M Wilkes
Copyright © 1971, 1975, 1980, 1986 J.M Samuals, F.M Wilkes and R.E Brayshaw

I(T)P   A division of International Thomson Publishing Inc.
         The ITP logo is a trademark under licence

All rights reserved. No part of this work which is copyright may be reproduced or used in any form or by any means – graphic, electronic, or mechanical, including photocopying, recording, taping or information storage and retrieval systems – without the written permission of the Publisher, except in accordance with the provisions of the Copyright Designs and Patents Act 1988.

Whilst the Publisher has taken all reasonable care in the preparation of this book the Publisher makes no representation, express or implied, with regard to the accuracy of the information contained in this book and cannot accept any legal responsibility or liability for any errors or omissions from the book or the consequences thereof.

Products and services that are referred to in this book may be either trademarks and/or registered trademarks of their respective owners. The Publisher/s and Author/s make no claim to these trademarks.

British Library Cataloguing-in-Publication Data
A catalogue record for this book is available from the British Library

First edition printed by Chapman & Hall 1971
Reprinted by Chapman & Hall 1972
Second edition printed by Chapman & Hall 1975
Third edition printed by Chapman & Hall 1980
Reprinted by Chapman & Hall 1981 (twice), 1982, 1983, 1985
Fourth edition printed by Chapman & Hall 1986
Reprinted by Chapman & Hall 1987, 1989
Fifth edition printed by Chapman & Hall 1990
Sixth edition printed by Chapman & Hall 1995
Reprinted by International Thomson Business Press 1996

Typeset by SetAll, Clifton Hampden
Printed in the UK by Unwin Brothers Limited, Old Woking

ISBN 0-412-60810-3

International Thomson Business Press
Berkshire House
168–173 High Holborn
London WC1V 7AA
UK

International Thomson Business Press
20 Park Plaza
13th Floor
Boston MA 02116
USA

http://www.thomson.com/itbp.html

Short contents

	Preface	xv
1	The financial environment	1
2	Flow of funds and taxation	21
3	Finance and accounting	39
4	Investment appraisal: basic methods	73
5	Investment appraisal: further topics	102
6	Capital rationing and risk analysis in imperfect capital markets	144
7	Corporate strategy and high-technology investments	212
8	Introduction to risk and return	235
9	Portfolio theory and capital asset pricing model	251
10	Capital budgeting and the capital asset pricing model	270
11	Introduction to derivatives and option theory	297
12	Stock markets and equity share capital	320
13	Stock market efficiency	385
14	Long-term debt finance	427
15	Share price valuation and the cost of capital	492
16	Short- and medium-term sources of finance	558
17	The dividend decision	610
18	Gearing and company cost of capital	634
19	Financial planning	676
20	Cash and interest rate management	708
21	Foreign exchange markets	766
22	Management of debtors	797
23	Management of inventory	821
24	Mergers and acquisitions	855
25	Company restructuring, refinancing and liquidation	908
26	International financial management	935
27	Small business finance	992

Long contents

Short Contents   v
Preface   xv

1   The financial environment   1
    1.1   Introduction   1
    1.2   Objectives of the company   2
    1.3   The shareholders   5
    1.4   Corporate governance   7
    1.5   The capital market   13
    1.6   Conclusions   17
    1.7   Key terms   18
    1.8   Revision questions   18
    1.9   References   19
    1.10 Further reading   19
    1.11 Problems   19

2   Flow of funds and taxation   21
    2.1   The flow of funds   21
    2.2   The personal sector   24
    2.3   The business sector   27
    2.4   The public sector   28
    2.5   Taxation policy   30
    2.6   Corporation tax   31
    2.7   Small company taxation   33
    2.8   Capital allowances   34
    2.9   Capital gains tax   35
    2.10 Taxation and decision-making   36
    2.11 Key terms   37
    2.12 Further reading   37
    2.13 Problems   37

3   Finance and accounting   39
    3.1   Introduction   39
    3.2   Accounting policies   41
    3.3   Cash flow versus accrual accounting   47
    3.4   Financial ratios   50
    3.5   The use of ratios to forecast company failure   63
    3.6   Conclusions   65
    3.7   Key terms   66
    3.8   Revision questions   66
    3.9   References   66

| | 3.10 | Further reading | 67 |
| | 3.11 | Problems | 67 |

4		**Investment appraisal: basic methods**	**73**
	4.1	Introduction	73
	4.2	Compound interest	74
	4.3	Discounting and present values	75
	4.4	The net present value decision rule	77
	4.5	Terminal value	79
	4.6	Yield: the internal rate of return	79
	4.7	The multiple yield problem	83
	4.8	Comparing alternative investments	85
	4.9	The modified internal rate of return	87
	4.10	Interest rate changes and discounted cash flow	90
	4.11	Different interest rates for borrowing and lending	91
	4.12	Theoretical justification for net present value	92
	4.13	The separation theorem	94
	4.14	Computer program	96
	4.15	Conclusions	98
	4.16	Key concepts	98
	4.17	Revision questions	99
	4.18	References	99
	4.19	Further reading	99
	4.20	Problems	100

5		**Investment appraisal: further topics**	**102**
	5.1	Annuities	103
	5.2	Perpetuities	103
	5.3	Yield to maturity	105
	5.4	Sinking funds	106
	5.5	Annual equivalent annuities	108
	5.6	Repair or replace	109
	5.7	Annuities with growth	113
	5.8	Make or buy	115
	5.9	Discounted cash flows and tax payments	116
	5.10	Investment appraisal and inflation	118
	5.11	Capital project commencement and termination dates	120
	5.12	Non-standard cash flows and other methods of compounding	123
	5.13	Formulae	129
	5.14	Computer programs	131
	5.15	Key concepts	134
	5.16	Revision questions	135
	5.17	References	135
	5.18	Further reading	136
	5.19	Problems	136
	5.20	Appendix: Arithmetic and geometric series	138

6		**Capital rationing and risk analysis in imperfect capital markets**	**144**
	6.1	Introduction	144
	6.2	Capital rationing: overview	145
	6.3	Single-constraint problems	146
	6.4	Multi-constraint problems	152
	6.5	Financial planning models	158
	6.6	Risk: some general considerations	160
	6.7	Payback	160
	6.8	Return on capital measures	163

	6.9	Risk premiums	165
	6.10	Sensitivity analysis	166
	6.11	Simulation	173
	6.12	Single investment risk analysis	178
	6.13	Multiple investment risk analysis	187
	6.14	Mean-variance analysis	195
	6.15	Spreadsheets and what-if analysis	198
	6.16	Key concepts	202
	6.17	Revision questions	203
	6.18	References	204
	6.19	Further reading	204
	6.20	Problems	205
	6.21	Appendix: Basic program	208
7		*Corporate strategy and high-technology investments*	212
	7.1	Introduction	212
	7.2	Strategic planning	213
	7.3	Models of strategic management	214
	7.4	Profit impact of market strategy	216
	7.5	Investment decisions in advanced manufacturing technology	218
	7.6	AMT investment: payback and present values	218
	7.7	Discount rates and time horizons	220
	7.8	Relevant costs and revenues	223
	7.9	An appraisal methodology for strategic investments	226
	7.10	The decision environment	227
	7.11	Key concepts	230
	7.12	Revision questions	231
	7.13	References	232
	7.14	Further reading	233
	7.15	Problems	233
8		*Introduction to risk and return*	235
	8.1	Introduction	235
	8.2	Measurement of investor return and risk	236
	8.3	Choosing between risky alternatives	241
	8.4	Return and risk of combining investments	243
	8.5	Summary and conclusions	247
	8.6	Key terms	248
	8.7	Revision questions	248
	8.8	References	248
	8.9	Further reading	249
	8.10	Problems	249
9		*Portfolio theory and capital asset pricing model*	251
	9.1	Introduction	251
	9.2	Analysis of a two-asset portfolio	252
	9.3	Extension to a multi-asset portfolio	256
	9.4	Risk-free asset combined with risky securities	258
	9.5	Capital asset pricing model	261
	9.6	Implications of the capital asset pricing model	264
	9.7	Summary and conclusions	265
	9.8	Key terms	265
	9.9	Revision questions	265
	9.10	References	266

	9.11	Further reading	266
	9.12	Problems	266
	9.13	Appendix: The capital asset pricing model	268
10		*Capital budgeting and the capital asset pricing model*	270
	10.1	Introduction	270
	10.2	Project risk and return	271
	10.3	Measuring equity betas and beta books	273
	10.4	Ungearing equity betas	282
	10.5	Multi-activity companies	283
	10.6	Single-company cost of capital and the capital asset pricing model	285
	10.7	Realism of the capital asset pricing model	287
	10.8	Arbitrage pricing model	289
	10.9	Summary and conclusions	290
	10.10	Key terms	290
	10.11	Revision questions	291
	10.12	References	291
	10.13	Further reading	291
	10.14	Problems	292
11		*Introduction to derivatives and option theory*	297
	11.1	Introduction	297
	11.2	Types of options	300
	11.3	Simple option strategies	306
	11.4	Call options and futures compared	308
	11.5	Factors affecting option values	309
	11.6	Binomial valuation formula	312
	11.7	Black-Scholes option valuation formula	313
	11.8	Application of option pricing theory to corporate finance	315
	11.9	Summary and conclusions	316
	11.10	Key terms	317
	11.11	Revision questions	317
	11.12	References	317
	11.13	Further reading	318
	11.14	Problems	318
12		*Stock markets and equity share capital*	320
	12.1	Introduction	320
	12.2	The global equity market	322
	12.3	Stock markets around the world	323
	12.4	The London Stock Exchange	325
	12.5	Types of company	339
	12.6	Types of equity share	341
	12.7	Methods of raising equity capital	345
	12.8	Financial terminology	349
	12.9	Scrip dividends and scrip issues	354
	12.10	Stock splits	358
	12.11	Rights issues	359
	12.12	Preference shares	373
	12.13	Venture capital	375
	12.14	Key terms	376
	12.15	Revision questions	376
	12.16	References	377
	12.17	Further reading	377
	12.18	Problems	378

13 Stock market efficiency 385
13.1 Introduction 385
13.2 The efficient market hypothesis 386
13.3 Tests of the efficient market hypothesis 389
13.4 Fads and bubbles 399
13.5 Insider dealing 400
13.6 Doubts about stock market efficiency 404
13.7 Market anomalies 407
13.8 Implications of the efficient market hypothesis 411
13.9 Summary 419
13.10 Key terms 420
13.11 Revision questions 420
13.12 References 420
13.13 Further reading 423
13.14 Problems 424

14 Long-term debt finance 427
14.1 Introduction 427
14.2 Debentures and bonds 428
14.3 Medium-term notes 430
14.4 Long-term bank and institutional borrowing 432
14.5 Register of charges 433
14.6 Corporate bond market 434
14.7 Mezzanine finance and junk bonds 436
14.8 The value of fixed-interest securities 438
14.9 The cost of debt capital 443
14.10 Bonds: a variety of features 445
14.11 Securitization 447
14.12 Redemption of bonds 448
14.13 Call provision 449
14.14 Special-purpose transactions 452
14.15 Long-term versus short-term borrowing 455
14.16 Interest-rate swaps 461
14.17 Debt equity swaps 464
14.18 Repayment of loans 464
14.19 Convertible loan stock 468
14.20 Warrants 477
14.21 Revision questions 483
14.22 References 483
14.23 Further reading 483
14.24 Problems 484

15 Share price valuation and the cost of capital 492
15.1 Share valuation 492
15.2 Dividends and share values 494
15.3 Valuation based on earnings? 504
15.4 The capital asset pricing model and share values 507
15.5 Valuation based on free cash flow 512
15.6 Country differences in valuation methods 513
15.7 Does it pay to manipulate earnings? 513
15.8 Pricing new issues 517
15.9 The valuation of a company 521
15.10 The cost of equity capital 540
15.11 Key terms 549
15.12 Revision questions 549
15.13 References 549

	15.14	Further reading	550
	15.15	Problems	551
16	**Short- and medium-term sources of finance**		558
	16.1	Short-term bank borrowing	558
	16.2	Bank overdrafts	559
	16.3	Revolving underwriting facility	566
	16.4	Medium-term bank borrowing	566
	16.5	Bills of exchange	567
	16.6	Acceptance credits	567
	16.7	Trade credit	570
	16.8	Factoring	572
	16.9	Invoice discounting and credit insurance	573
	16.10	Deferred tax payments	574
	16.11	Government guaranteed loans	574
	16.12	Merchant banks	574
	16.13	Export finance	576
	16.14	Project finance	581
	16.15	Hire purchase	582
	16.16	Sale and lease-back	584
	16.17	Mortgaging property	585
	16.18	Leasing	585
	16.19	British government sources	597
	16.20	European sources	599
	16.21	Revision questions	601
	16.22	References	601
	16.23	Further reading	602
	16.24	Problems	602
17	**The dividend decision**		610
	17.1	Introduction	610
	17.2	Dividend irrelevancy in perfect capital markets	612
	17.3	Dividend payments may increase shareholder wealth	614
	17.4	Dividend payments may reduce shareholder wealth	617
	17.5	Dividend payments and taxation	617
	17.6	Practical issues in dividend policy	619
	17.7	Share repurchase and scrip dividends	622
	17.8	Empirical evidence on dividend payments	624
	17.9	Summary and conclusions	627
	17.10	Key terms	627
	17.11	Revision questions	628
	17.12	References	628
	17.13	Further reading	629
	17.14	Problems	629
18	**Gearing and company cost of capital**		634
	18.1	Introduction	634
	18.2	Capital structure implications	635
	18.3	Overall cost of capital: weighted-average cost approach	639
	18.4	Adjusted present value method	645
	18.5	Traditional view of capital structure	648
	18.6	Capital structure in perfect capital markets	649
	18.7	Capital structure and corporate and personal taxes	653
	18.8	Capital structure and financial distress	658
	18.9	A target debt/equity ratio?	660
	18.10	Summary and conclusions	663
	18.11	Key terms	664

	18.12	Revision questions	664
	18.13	References	664
	18.14	Further reading	665
	18.15	Problems	665

19 Financial planning — 676

	19.1	Strategic planning	676
	19.2	Long-term and medium-term financial planning	678
	19.3	Financial modelling	680
	19.4	Short-term financial planning	684
	19.5	Working capital requirements	687
	19.6	From rule of thumb to planning models	689
	19.7	The operating cycle	694
	19.8	Funds flow and cash flow statements	696
	19.9	Key terms	700
	19.10	Revision questions	701
	19.11	References	701
	19.12	Further reading	701
	19.13	Problems	701

20 Cash and interest-rate management — 708

	20.1	Introduction	708
	20.2	The management of cash	711
	20.3	The collection and payment cycles	712
	20.4	Cash transmission techniques	713
	20.5	Cash budget	714
	20.6	Cash cycle	720
	20.7	Cash flow statements	722
	20.8	Planning the cash balance	725
	20.9	Interest-rate risk management	729
	20.10	Interest-rate futures contracts	733
	20.11	Interest-rate swaps	742
	20.12	Treasury organization and control	748
	20.13	Key terms	750
	20.14	Revision questions	750
	20.15	Further reading	751
	20.16	Problems	751
	20.17	Appendix: Cash management models	758
	20.18	References	765

21 Foreign exchange markets — 766

	21.1	Introduction	766
	21.2	Meaning of quotations	767
	21.3	Factors influencing exchange rates	770
	21.4	Managing transaction risk	777
	21.5	Currency futures contracts	784
	21.6	Foreign exchange risk	788
	21.7	Key terms	789
	21.8	Revision questions	790
	21.9	Reference	790
	21.10	Further reading	790
	21.11	Problems	790

22 Management of debtors — 797

| | 22.1 | The problem | 797 |
| | 22.2 | Deciding an acceptable level of risk | 799 |

22.3	Investigating the credit applicant	802
22.4	Terms of sale	803
22.5	Policy on the collection of debts	809
22.6	Credit insurance	811
22.7	A technical approach	811
22.8	Concluding remarks	814
22.9	Key terms	814
22.10	Revision questions	814
22.11	References	814
22.12	Further reading	814
22.13	Problems	815

23	**Management of inventory**	821
23.1	Introduction	821
23.2	The classical model	823
23.3	Variable re-order costs	826
23.4	Cash management model	827
23.5	Lead time	828
23.6	Production for stock	829
23.7	Buffer stocks	830
23.8	Random demand	831
23.9	Random lead time	836
23.10	A service level approach	839
23.11	Periodic review models	842
23.12	The ABC classification scheme	844
23.13	Lot size inventory management	845
23.14	Material requirements planning and just-in-time management	846
23.15	Basic program	848
23.16	Conclusions	849
23.17	Key concepts	849
23.18	Revision questions	850
23.19	References	851
23.20	Further reading	851
23.21	Problems	851

24	**Mergers and acquisitions**	855
24.1	Introduction	855
24.2	Merger and takeover activity	857
24.3	Motives for individual mergers	860
24.4	Management motives	866
24.5	Takeover tactics	867
24.6	Financing acquisitions	879
24.7	The results – who wins?	885
24.8	Win at what price? a case study	893
24.9	Key terms	895
24.10	Revision questions	896
24.11	References	896
24.12	Further reading	897
24.13	Problems	897

25	**Company restructuring, refinancing and liquidation**	908
25.1	Divestment	909
25.2	Sell-off	911
25.3	Spin-off (demerger)	912
25.4	Management buyout	913
25.5	Going private	918

25.6	Buy-in	919
25.7	Increase the amount of borrowing	920
25.8	Share re-purchase	920
25.9	Reverse takeover	921
25.10	Business failure	921
25.11	Refinancing	923
25.12	Insolvency/liquidation	925
25.13	Key terms	929
25.14	Revision questions	929
25.15	References	930
25.16	Further reading	930
25.17	Problems	930

26	**International financial management**	**935**
26.1	The international (global) financing markets	935
26.2	Sources of funds for overseas subsidiaries	951
26.3	The cost of capital	957
26.4	The foreign investment decision	963
26.5	Managing risk	967
26.6	Internal hedging techniques	971
26.7	Political risk	976
26.8	Taxation	978
26.9	Key terms	985
26.10	Revision questions	986
26.11	Further reading	986
26.12	Problems	986

27	**Small business finance**	**992**
27.1	Introduction	992
27.2	The small business sector	993
27.3	Financing problems of small firms	995
27.4	The life-cycle of a firm	998
27.5	Company failures	999
27.6	Equity finance	1002
27.7	Specialist institutions	1007
27.8	Loan finance	1008
27.9	Conclusions	1012
27.10	Key terms	1012
27.11	Revision questions	1012
27.12	References	1012
27.13	Further reading	1013
27.14	Problems	1013

| Tables and programs | | 1014 |

| Index | | 1037 |

Preface

Our aim in this extensively upgraded and revised edition is twofold: to provide a framework of knowledge which will assist the financial manager in making decisions, and to provide the student of finance and accounting with a text which will not only be of assistance in preparing for examinations but which will also be of help in developing the student's skills and career in management.

The book is designed for use both by the student needing a theoretical rationale for decision making and to the practising manager interested in techniques and ideas to help solve the problems he or she meets every day.

There are four aspects which, we believe, make it of special interest. First, we have attempted to balance advanced analytical approaches to financial management with the more traditional approaches still often employed in practice. Many of the problems in finance can be approached through a rigorous type of analysis; other problems, however, are still solved by more intuitive methods or rules of thumb. Second, we have based both text and examples on the financial situation in the UK. Third, where relevant, the empirical findings related to the theories and folk-lore of financial management are discussed. Fourth, the book emphasizes the importance of the links between company financial management and the financial community. The reactions of the stock market and the financial institutions to a company's decisions are especially important to the company, and the future of the management of a company can depend upon the stock market. A text on financial management should, therefore, attach considerable importance to the workings of the financial community.

It is surprising how rapidly the subject of company finance alters. What is appropriate at the time of one economic situation becomes outdated by new circumstances. The theory of the subject does not, of course change so quickly, but tends to evolve as new ideas and techniques emerge over time. It is in the day-to-day problems faced by financial managers that most changes occur.

Change takes place at a rapid rate in the organization and control of the financial institutions. Governments make frequent changes to tax policy, to economic policy and to the financial support they make available to companies. New financial instruments are created and the Financial Markets become more international.

When the first edition of this book appeared in 1971, the United Kingdom was in the midst of a merger and take-over boom which, we were assured by those involved, would revitalize industry. British Leyland had recently been created following the merger of two companies. By the time of the second edition in 1975, financial managers were more concerned with survival than with growth through acquisition. Many companies had severe liquidity problems and it was to the banks and the Government that companies were turning for help. The restructuring of British industry did not appear to have led to many improvements. British Leyland, short of funds, were to be taken over by the Government. By the time of the fourth edition, the Government was engaged in privatizing British Leyland.

The first edition of the book had leaned in the direction of policies for growth; the fourth edition appeared at a time of uncertainty, but at a time when, some commentators claimed the structural changes that have taken place in the early 1980s (following the structural changes of the 1970s) offered prospects of growth in the 1980s. Many new companies were being established. Barriers were being removed and regulations being relaxed.

At the time of the fifth edition in 1990 there were unfortunately signs that the enterprise culture was not working out as hoped. During the 1980s many small businesses had been set up, but by the end of the decade they were experiencing financial problems. There were also signs that some of the success stories of the 1980s were not as successful as first appeared. The expression 'creative accounting' was much used. Companies such as Polly Peck, Queens Moat and Maxwell Communications were being linked to such practices. Questions were being asked as to whether or not the financial community had been fooled by such companies. By the time of the fifth edition British Leyland had been purchased by British Aerospace and were now called Rover. The fifth edition included a chapter for the first time on restructuring.

By the time of the sixth edition, Rover, the last major British owned car manufacturer had been sold off to BMW and the early 1990s had seen a record number of company failures. The sixth edition for the first time includes a section on liquidation. The government are, however, once again assuring us that conditions are right for future growth. The next few years will doubtless present us with new material for analysis and comment.

We would like to express our thanks for help we have received over the various editions of the book, in particular to Scott Goddard, whose imaginative questions have often been used to enliven a particular section. We would also like to thank the Institute of Chartered Accountants in England & Wales and the Chartered Association of Certified Accountants for permission to reproduce a number of their examination questions. We would also like to thank Mr Manpuria for helpful comments, and Margaret Watson and Karen Hanson for valuable assistance in the preparation of this edition.

1 The financial environment

1.1	Introduction	1	1.7	Key terms	18
1.2	Objectives of the company	2	1.8	Revision questions	18
1.3	The shareholders	5	1.9	References	19
1.4	Corporate governance	7	1.10	Further reading	19
1.5	The capital market	13	1.11	Problems	19
1.6	Conclusions	17			

In this chapter we shall examine the objectives of the firm. Are the decisions made by those who manage the firm designed to maximize the wealth of the owners of the firm? How are the interests of the other parties involved in a firm taken into account?

We then introduce the theory of business finance. We consider the shareholders, the interest group who are legally the owners of the company, and examine the financial aspects of the relationship between shareholders and managers. By focusing on this relationship we are not suggesting that it is more or less important than that between any of the other interested parties and the company, but these other relationships are subjects for other primarily non-financial books. Finally, we introduce some of the problems that exist in the relationship between the investment community and companies, problems in the financial environment in which companies have to operate.

1.1 Introduction

A company has a responsibility towards employees, customers, shareholders, creditors and society. Each of these interest groups sees the role of that company in a slightly different way. This book is concerned with the financial aspects of companies, with the optimal use of their financial resources. Sound financial management is necessary for a company's survival and for its growth. All interest groups benefit from good financial management.

The types of questions that financial management seeks to answer are as follows.

1. What percentage of funds needed by a business should be obtained from borrowing and what percentage from the owners?
2. What percentage of the annual profits should be paid out to shareholders as dividends?
3. Is it worth while for the company to replace its existing manufacturing machines with a new computer-integrated system?
4. The earnings per share figure for the company is falling, despite the fact that the

manufacturing facilities have been recently modernized. Should a shareholder be concerned?

5. A potential customer has enquired whether the company will sell goods to him or her now, and allow the customer six months to pay. Is it profitable to do so?

6. The bank keeps offering me new types of business loans, but I like the traditional overdraft arrangement. Should I, as Financial Manager, change my policy?

1.2 Objectives of the company

One of the long-term objectives of a company must be to make money for its owners, and its future is guaranteed or jeopardized according to the satisfaction, or lack of it, that the shareholders exhibit regarding its performance on their behalf. There are of course other long-term objectives of a company, in particular those involving employee and customer satisfaction, but it is not possible to compromise on the financial objective.

During particular periods of time it may seem rather optimistic to think in terms of making money for the owners, and in the short term all efforts may have to be devoted to keeping the company liquid and to maintaining the value of the owners' investment. These are, however, only short-term situations, and in the long run the owners of capital must be encouraged to invest in companies by the prospect of gains which are at least as great as those they can obtain from investing elsewhere.

The last century and a half has seen the rise and fall of more than one business philosophy dedicated to the problem of a company's rationale. When enlightened self-interest was a notion dear to the hearts of nineteenth-century capitalists, it was fashionable to justify the company almost exclusively as a quasi-benevolent institution satisfying a yawning social need by generously providing employment and other opportunities. Today, cynicism permits us to recognize this as a half-truth inspired by some real benevolence and more real guilt. The fact is, and was, that a company must make sufficient money to be able to offer the providers of its capital an attractive return. This is not to deny that it must also attempt to provide all its employees, from directors down, with the means to enjoy an attractive life.

All who agree with some form of the capitalist system should not find anything contentious in the preceding paragraphs. However, when we start to consider whether the owners' position should be maximized and the employees' position satisfied, or the shareholders' position satisfied and the employees' position maximized, we immediately enter into the political arena – as we do when we start to consider whether the employees of the firm should receive a 2% annual pay rise and the directors of the firm a 20% increase.

The classical view of the firm is that it should be operated so as to maximize profits. Hayek states: 'the only specific purpose which corporations ought to serve is to secure the highest long-term return on their capital' [1]. Milton Friedman states: 'there is one and only one social responsibility of business – to use its resources and to engage in activities designed to increase its profits as long as it stays within the rules of the game' [2].

According to this classical approach, the objective of the firm should be to maximize the shareholders' wealth, subject to a number of constraints. However, this might not be satisfactory to the changing attitudes and values of society. Why should the providers of the capital have all the rewards that are left over after the other interests have been merely satisfied? Why, for example, should it not be the providers of labour who have their rewards maximized, who have all that is left over after the other parties (including the shareholders) have been satisfied? This is of course what the representatives of the providers of labour, the unions, might like to see as the accepted company objective. There are many interests represented in a company, and the importance attached to each interest depends on the political system, the attitudes of the community at a particular time, and the bargaining power of the interests at the time.

The theory of business finance is based on the assumption that the company should seek to maximize the wealth of the shareholder. The shareholders own the company and there is therefore some logic in the idea that it should be run in their interests.

Although this is the theory, it is recognized that in practice most companies do not always make decisions based on this assumption.

A difficulty arises in that in large and medium-sized companies control and investment are usually in different hands. The shareholders have to leave the decision-making to the top management of the company, who may well be looking for rewards other than through returns on the small number of shares that they own. Top management are concerned with salaries, pensions, executive life style and security. Top management is in a good position to look after its own interests.

The top managers are acting as agents of the shareholders. Shareholders may attempt to bring about 'goal congruence' through share option schemes. But with other rewards to take into account there is no reason to believe that top management will always be seeking to maximize shareholders' wealth. It is not easy for the owners to monitor the actions of the top managers, and it is expensive to try to do so. In using the funds they manage, to look after their own position and/or that of the shareholders, it is often said that in the UK this leads to 'short-termism'. The environment in which they manage gives greater rewards for short-term performance than for long-term performance. They are motivated to take advantage of any short-term opportunities that arise.

One point that should be appreciated is that part of the return to shareholders is in the form of dividend payments. These dividends have to be paid out of profits; in legal terminology they are an appropriation of profits. The fact that dividends are paid out of profits does not mean that the shareholders are taking out of the business something that they are not entitled to. They are as entitled to some return as are the other interested parties in the company: the employees to wages, the bank to interest payments or the providers of land to rent. The fact that the shareholders' return is treated as an appropriation of profits rather than as a cost, as are wages and interest payments, is purely a legal point. To think that all the profits of a company are available for 'grabs' by all interested parties is to misunderstand the nature of the term 'profits'.

All interested parties in a company are entitled to some income, and the income flowing from the company to the shareholder is the dividend which has to be paid out of profits. If dividends could be thought of as a normal cost of being in business, that has to be paid to encourage those with capital and those with savings to risk their money by investing in a company, then a lot of the emotional reaction to paying out profits to shareholders would disappear. The argument whether the shareholders' position should be maximized or satisfied should be an argument concerning the distribution of profits that remain after the shareholder has received a fair return.

Whether the directors maximize or satisfy the shareholders' interests, at least they must be aware of the share price, for it is through capital gains, i.e. increases in share price, that the shareholders receive much of their return. They must be aware of how the decisions they take will influence the share price.

Not only must a company earn a return on its shareholders' funds, it must ensure that its earning power is reflected in its share price. It is possible to have two companies with identical profit performance and potential, and yet for one to have a higher stock market value than the other simply because one group of directors is more concerned than the other group about their stock market image.

The stock market price is possibly the most important single criterion by which the company is judged. An increasing share price, or one that is falling less quickly than the market index, will keep the shareholders content, and the management will have little reason to worry about survival or a takeover. If the company is prospering nicely but failing to reflect the fact in its share price, it becomes of course an ideal candidate for a takeover, and in the event of being swallowed up – or fired – the management would have no one to blame but themselves for neglecting the shareholders' interests by failing to ensure that the company's true earning ability was reflected in its share price.

There are (or were) economic systems where the objectives of the production units are not expressed in terms of the providers of capital. There may be a time when, in the capitalist world, the objectives of companies are not expressed in terms of the shareholders' interests, when all shareholders will be satisfied with a reasonable return on their money. But we are not at that time. Investors can buy and sell the shares of whichever company they like, influenced by the returns they expect. They will move their funds to where they expect the highest returns, which may not even be in equity investments. This means that, as long as some companies see their objectives as the maximization of shareholders' wealth, it is difficult for other companies to survive, or at least to expand, with more socially minded objectives. It means that if the corporate sector cannot earn a return on shareholders' money which is, after taking risk into account, at least as high as shareholders can obtain from investing in some other form of asset, then equity capital may not continue to flow into the corporate sector.

If the management of a company fails to recognize the fact that in the long run it is in competition for funds with other companies and other forms of investment, it can, particularly at certain times, put its own position and possibly that of the employees of the company, in danger. When the stock market is active, especially when prices are rising, a company that is not financially aware must live with the possibility of a takeover bid from a company that will offer the shareholders a considerably improved future under new management. When the stock market is declining, it is difficult for such a non-aware company to obtain new equity capital and, with constraints on a company's level of borrowing and possibly on its profit margins, liquidity problems can result which can endanger the company's future.

Recent literature on the theory of the firm does, however, view the company as a team whose members act in their own self-interest, but who realize that their well-being depends on the survival of the team in its competition with other teams. This approach is referred to as 'agency theory', or the recognition of 'property rights' [3]. Each agent, each interest group in the firm, behaves to maximize its own position, being motivated by self-interest. The firm is viewed as a set of contracts among the different factors of production, with the contracts recognizing the rights of the different agents. This approach can help to explain why on occasions the financial actions that a company takes do not conform to the action that would be expected if the company was seeking to maximize shareholders' wealth.

Balanced score-card

In the 1990s the expression 'balanced scorecard' came into use. This refers to a new technique that can be used to evaluate the overall performance of a company. It seeks to balance the short-term financial performance goals with other long-term drivers of growth and financial performance.

Companies have been urged to focus on quality, and on the education and training of its employees. These are clearly desirable objectives. They help generate growth and long-term economic value. It is possible to produce performance measures which indicate how a company is performing against targets in these areas. The problem is: how does a company balance these long-term objectives against the short-term need to produce profits? Quality, training and customer satisfaction can result in good financial results in the long run but not necessarily improve short-term financial results.

The balanced scorecard seeks to balance the short-run and long-run goals. Kaplan and Norton identified corporate performance measures from four perspectives.

Financial   – Profits
Customers   – What do customers value from a company?
Internal   – In what processes must the company excel?
Innovation and learning – How can a company create future value?

This is a comparatively new idea and is being used in some companies to translate its strategic objectives into operational measures.

The importance ascribed to the role of the shareholders has changed in recent years. It was once common to play down their influence; though legally the owners of the business, it was assumed that they did not much concern themselves with the way that the company was run. Some of them might make their opinions known at the annual general meeting, but usually few of them attend, and in any case the directors could well have obtained enough proxy votes to overcome any opposition.

This position has changed, partly because of a change in the type of shareholder, partly as a result of takeover activity and partly because of social pressure.

The characteristics of the typical shareholder have changed. No longer can he or she be regarded as an individual afflicted with a comforting inability to read a balance sheet. The growth of shareholding by institutions has been dramatic, and these institutions employ experts to advise on the investment of their funds. The financial performance of a company is thus judged by a knowledgeable body of people who may be either existing or potential shareholders. The company must accordingly be run in a way that guarantees the satisfaction of the shareholder – an increasingly sophisticated shareholder, who will be both competent and keen to assess the truth behind any optimistic statements.

In the UK, as in many other countries with a developed financial system, institutions now own the majority of shares. In the UK they now own nearly 70% of listed equity shares. The main institutional holders are the insurance companies, the pension funds, the investment trusts and the unit trusts. This ownership pattern results from the savings of individuals flowing to pension funds and insurance companies partly because of the tax advantages arising from contractual savings schemes. The unit trusts have also been successful in attracting the savings of private investors.

Table 1.1 *Beneficial ownership of UK equities (in percentages) 1963–93*

	1963	1969	1975	1981	1990	1993
Pension funds	6.4	9.0	16.8	26.7	31.6	34.2
Insurance companies	10.0	12.2	15.9	20.5	20.4	17.3
Unit trusts	1.3	2.9	4.1	3.6	6.1	6.6
Banks	1.3	1.7	0.7	0.3	0.7	0.6
Investment trusts, and other financial institutions	11.3	10.1	10.5	6.8	2.3	3.1
Individuals	54.0	47.4	37.5	28.2	20.3	17.7
Other personal sector	2.1	2.1	2.3	2.2	1.9	1.6
Public sector	1.5	2.6	3.6	3.0	2.0	1.3
Industrial and commercial sector	5.1	5.4	3.0	5.1	2.8	1.5
Overseas	7.0	6.6	5.6	3.6	11.8	16.3
Total	100	100	100	100	100	100

Source: Central Statistical Office.

Table 1.1 shows the estimated ownership of UK equity shares by different categories. The points to observe are:

1. The dramatic increase in the percentage of total shares held by the pension funds and to a lesser extent by the insurance companies. Although these institutions only account for a small percentage of the total bargains conducted on the Stock Exchange, the average bargain size with which they are involved makes them the major players in the markets.

2. The growth of overseas ownership of UK equities. The increase has been particularly fast in recent years; it increased from 11.8% in 1990 to 13.1% in 1992 and then

to 16.3% in 1993. This growth reflects the globalization of financial markets with portfolio funds moving around the world seeking high returns.

It should be appreciated that most of this investment is by institutional investors. The US accounted for 41.8% of the known origin of this investment, with European Union countries responsible for only 15%.

3. The considerable decline in the percentage of shares held by individuals. The importance of the individual investor declined, but not the number of investors.

4. The banks in the UK only own a very small percentage of the equity of companies. This contrasts with the position in many other countries, for example Germany. It reflects a deliberate policy on the part of banks.

Table 1.2 lists the major shareholders in Signet Group plc. The extract is taken from the Report of the Directors in the Annual Report and Accounts for 1994. It is typical of the information now being disclosed by companies in their annual reports. It will be seen that they have more than one class of share.

Table 1.2 *Major shareholders in Signet Group plc 1994*

Name of interested person	Number of shares	Percentage
a Ordinary shares:		
Schroder Investment Management Limited	35 545 000	12.13
Robert Fleming Holdings Limited	30 447 273	10.39
Barclays Bank PLC	17 726 210	6.04
Bank of New York	11 601 258	3.96
b 6.875p convertible preference shares:		
Schroder Investment Management Limited	5 295 649	15.32
Everest Capital Limited	1 825 000	5.28
c US$0.01 convertible preference shares:		
UK Active Value Fund Inc.†	2 852 000	23.14
Goldman Sachs Group, LP*	1 559 911	12.66
Joerg G Bucherer	1 622 901	13.17
Everest Capital limited	1 378 000	11.18
Brown Bros Harriman & Co	1 009 005	8.13
Swiss American Securities Inc	804 881	6.53
Second Aspern Limited	600 304	4.87
Morgan Guaranty Trust Co NY	550 000	4.46
N C Lombard Street Nominees Ltd	500 000	4.00
National City Bank	449 485	3.66

* Includes notified interest of Goldman Sachs Equity Securities UK in 1 559 911 shares.
† Includes interests of other persons (not shown separately above) notified on their behalf by UK Active Value Fund Inc., some of which are interests arising under s.203 and s.204 Companies Act 1985.

Despite the dominant position of the institutional shareholders, there has been a trend in the UK over the last decade for the number of private shareholders to increase. The number of private shareholders rose from under three million in 1979 to over 11 million in 1990, with the result that the proportion of the population of the United Kingdom holding shares was similar to that of the United States – a higher proportion than is the case in Japan. The main reason for this increase has been the privatization issues. The significance of private shareholding should not, however, be exaggerated; most of such holders own only a few shares with over half only owning shares in one company. Another factor is that many buy privatization issues to make a quick profit; they are not interested in long-term investment.

This trend in institutional holdings has caused concern because of the increasing levels of concentration of ownership. It has also caused problems because, as a result of the channelling of the funds available for investment into a few hands, certain classes of business have found it difficult to obtain finance. The institutions have shown a preference for listed shares and, in particular, for the shares of the very large companies.

The reasons are perfectly understandable. The institutions wish to hold investments that are easily marketable, and it can be difficult to dispose of shares in unquoted companies. It is easy for them to obtain information on the large publicly quoted companies. The administrative costs are reduced if an institution invests in a few large shareholdings rather than holding a few shares in many companies. It is not necessary to hold shares of a large number of companies in order to spread risk. It has been shown that most of the advantages of diversification can be obtained from holding the shares of 30–40 companies. Yet another reason, if another is needed, is that the institutions wish to be in a position to unload a large number of shares on the stock market quickly without moving the share price by more than a few pence, and this would not be possible if the shares were those of a smaller company where the one holding would be a large proportion of the total company shares.

The attitude towards investing in smaller and medium-sized companies has changed slightly, however. Partly because of political pressure, partly because of changes in the capital market and partly because of tax changes, the equity shares of smaller companies have begun to attract investors. The Unlisted Securities Market (USM) attracted both newer, smaller companies seeking funds and the institutional investors supplying funds. High-technology companies have become sought after by investors, and many financial institutions have set up venture capital funds. These developments will be discussed at various points throughout the book.

The power that the institutional shareholders have over a company rests on the effect that their investment decisions can have on the share price of a company, on the fact that at times of a takeover bid the decision of a few shareholders can have a major influence on whether the bid succeeds or fails, and on the fact that the institutions have large amounts of funds that can be made available to a company. The type of shareholder and the way that shareholders behave is changing. Traditional relationships are altering. The institutions need the companies, as they need good investment opportunities in a healthy economic climate, in order to be able to meet their future pension and assurance obligations. The relationship between the shareholders of a company and the management is one which is complex.

1.4 Corporate governance

This topic which became of increasing interest in the late 1980s is concerned with who governs a company and in whose interest it is run. In small private companies there is usually no conflict of interest. The owners of the company are the same people who make the key management decisions and who control the company. But with larger companies there has been for a long time a 'divorce' of ownership and control. Those who provide the funds are not the same people as those who control the company.

The various Companies Acts are explicit, in that the directors of a company are supposed to run the company in the interests of the shareholders. However, when ownership and control become separated there are situations in which there is a potential conflict of interest between shareholders and managers. Managers may be motivated to behave in a way which from the shareholders' point of view is sub-optimal. In 1989 Charkham in a Bank of England discussion paper raised the question of whether there is the possibility that our system (the UK system), 'so excellent when viewed in isolation, may put us at a disadvantage in international competition by those who have superior linkages and lines of accountability within it, and a greater sense of patience?' [4]

The governance debate centres on whether the relationship between the owners and the controllers of a business that exists in the UK puts us at a disadvantage to our European and Japanese competitors. A similar concern exists in the USA. The UK and

US systems are similar in that they rely on the market to exercise control (an external control system). This contrasts with the more flexible relationship between providers of finance and managers to be found with many of our major competitors, who have stronger internal control systems.

Internal control means that within the structure of the company through committees and boards, the top management of the company is subject to control. Top management is accountable. External control means that investors in the market place control top management. If they do not like decisions being made by the directors of a company or are dissatisfied with the performance of the company they let their feelings be known. They can do this either by voting at annual general meetings (using their voice) or they can take an 'exit' route by selling their shares (voting with their feet). With external control top management might not be strongly controlled within the company, but they are aware they are ultimately accountable in the market place. We will briefly examine (a) what has gone wrong with the system in the UK, (b) how the system of corporate governance in the UK differs from that in our 'competitor' countries and (c) what is being done to change the position in the UK.

The ideal model for accountability in the UK is:

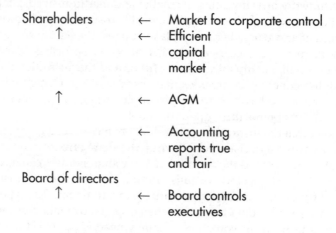

Some of the things that are alleged to have gone wrong with the system in the UK are:

- shareholders pursue own goals (portfolio investors);
- directors act in own interests;
- boards dominated by executive directors;
- non-executive directors in weak position/not independent;
- AGMs do not work (shareholders keep arm's length relationship);
- market for corporate control (takeovers and mergers):
  - expensive;
  - good and bad managers both suffer;
- poor accounting standards (poor monitoring);
- stock market not always efficient.

These failings in the UK system have allegedly resulted in what is known as short-termism. The owners of the company, the vast majority in the UK being institutional shareholders, have been accused of avoiding a long-term involvement with a company. The institutions are themselves under pressure to show good financial performance, so they need to be able to buy and sell the shares of a company as the opportunity for profits arise. They are portfolio investors rather than long-term stakeholders in a company.

There are pressures on institutional investment managers to show good relative returns each quarter in the funds they manage. If they find the performance on their portfolios amongst the lower rankings of the performance league tables they themselves will be removed.

The problem is not just the way in which institutional investment managers' performance is judged, but also the fact that the top managers of companies can find themselves in a position where the maximization of performance during their periods of control is not consistent with the maximization of a company's long-term performance. The directors of a company are sometimes accused of being motivated by short-term considerations. The fear of takeovers means that investment decisions have to take into account the need to show profits early in a project's life. The financial rewards of directors are sometimes linked to short-term profit or share price movements. The length of directors' service contracts and the age of most directors again have contributed towards short-term thinking.

Similar criticisms have been made about the system in the USA. Donaldson [5] and Jensen [6] have pointed to a number of possible areas of conflict in the financial field. One problem is that shareholders and managers have different attitudes towards risk. Shareholders can spread their risks by investing their money in a number of companies; one company may go into liquidation but a diversified shareholders' financial security is not threatened. A manager's financial security, however, usually depends on what happens to the one company that employs him or her. The manager could therefore be less inclined than the shareholder to invest the company's funds in a risky investment. The manager is interested in the total risk position of the company, whereas a diversified shareholder is interested in the systematic risk. These terms will be explained later in the book.

When capital investment decisions are analysed from a financial point of view, it is the net present value of the cash flow that is to be maximized. Managers are, however, interested in their own promotion possibilities, and so if they are to be responsible for a project they might well prefer it to be one with a shorter life rather than one with a longer life, as this will enable them to show their ability more quickly. Donaldson suggests that this may help to explain the popularity of the payback criterion as an investment criterion among managers.

The differences in the interests of managers and shareholders may help to explain a number of other aspects of finance where the practice does not conform to what financial theory would predict, e.g. acquisitions undertaken for diversification purposes to reduce the risk of the company (whereas in fact the shareholders could undertake their own diversification), levels of gearing below the theoretical optimum and dividend policies resulting in lower levels of dividends than theory would suggest.

A further situation in which conflict can arise is when a company is the subject of a takeover bid. It has been shown in many studies that the shareholders of acquired firms very often receive above normal gains in share price. However, shareholders of companies that have been the subject of unsuccessful takeover bids do not receive such gains. It can therefore be argued that it is not always in the shareholders' interests for the managers of sought-after companies to put up such a defence as to drive the bidder away. Yet many managers lose either their jobs or their status if the company that employs them is taken over. In whose interests, therefore, do the managers act when their company is the subject of a takeover bid?

Jensen wrote an article entitled 'The eclipse of the public corporation' [7]. He expressed the view that in certain industries for a variety of reasons the present relationship between owners and managers is out of date. He believes it is changing and needs further change. He argues that the clear separation of ownership and control has worked against efficiency and growth. His views are representative of those who want fundamental change. He makes the point that many investors are dissatisfied, and that managers have been putting their own interests first over the last 10–20 years. Golden parachute-type contracts and other perks have shown that managers are not taking the interest of the investor seriously enough.

Rappaport, disagreeing with Jensen, argues against fundamental change. He believes that the existing system will be improved when the USA (and UK) move to a 'governance system that provides effective monitoring of and checks on managerial authority' [8]. It seems to be agreed that the present system in the UK and USA, with a strong emphasis on external control, is not an effective monitoring system.

There are significant differences between countries within the EC in the form of ownership and control of companies. The UK system is based on the promotion of free markets, and close links between investors and managers, are discouraged by law and stock exchange rules. A major concern is the prevention of insider dealing and the protection of minority interest shareholders. One result is that with an arm's length relationship between owners and managers the annual financial reports take on a greater significance. Also there is less opportunity for owners to monitor the decisions and policies of managers.

In France and Germany, traditionally far less emphasis has been placed on the operations of the stock markets. There are therefore less restrictions on the closeness of the relationship between owners and managers. More information is exchanged informally. The financial reports are therefore of less significance, with a more established informal communication system.

Another important difference between countries within the European Community arises because of the different structure of financing by companies. As is well known, UK companies have traditionally worked with lower levels of gearing than companies in other European countries. Debt and equity lead to different forms of corporate governance. Debt governance works mainly through rules, with covenants and other legal restraints restricting the actions of those who manage companies. Equity governance on the other hand allows much greater discretion. With a greater proportion of funds being provided through equity, those who run UK companies are more concerned than management in other European countries in creating a favourable impression in the stock market. With an over-active market in corporate control (takeovers and mergers) the short-term survival of the UK manager depends on it.

In Germany, companies have a two-tier board structure. The supervisory board consists of representatives of many interest groups, with far more outside directors involved than is found in a UK company. Most countries have some criticisms of their own system. In Germany the minority shareholders feel their interests are not represented. It is the power and influence of the large banks – through (a) their direct shareholdings in companies, (b) the loans advanced to companies and (c) the votes they can control through the proxy system – that worries many people.

Cadbury Report

In the UK in response to increasing concern about the system of corporate governance, a committee was set up by the Council of the London Stock Exchange and the accountancy profession to examine the financial aspects of corporate governance (known as the Cadbury Committee) [9]. They concluded that the basic system of corporate governance in the UK was sound, but did recommend a number of changes.

Two key areas where they thought that changes were necessary were in connection with making the board of directors more effective and increasing the long-term commitment to a company of its institutional shareholders.

They were concerned to prevent a board of directors being dominated by a powerful person, who was both the chairman and chief executive. They wished to ensure that the views of non-executive directors (NEDs) carry weight in board decisions. They recommend that there will be at least three NEDs on a board, and that the people appointed to such positions be of independent minds who could represent the shareholders' interests.

They wished the NEDs to take a leading role in the remuneration committee and audit committees to be set up within companies. They wished to improve the system of internal control that existed in some companies.

The recommendations of the Cadbury Committee were accepted by the Stock Exchange and quoted companies are now required to make a statement in their annual reports on whether or not they comply with the best practices recommended by the Committee.

Key recommendations of the Cadbury Report

- Corporate board authority should be divided between the chairman and the chief executive.
- Non-executives should be persons of a high calibre and be appointed in sufficient numbers to give their views weight on the board.
- Boards should establish audit committees composed entirely of non-executive directors, the majority of whom are completely independent.
- Audit committees should meet at least annually with the outside auditors with no member of the executive present.
- Directors' pay should be set by a remuneration committee, consisting entirely of non-executives.
- The pay of the chairman and the highest paid director should be fully disclosed in the annual report and split into their salary and performance related earnings.
- Institutional investors should disclose their policies on the use of voting rights.

As major shareholders in many quoted companies, the institutions have for many years been in a position to influence company management. In the past they chose not to do so, preferring not to interfere but to remain at arm's length. They were then free to buy and sell a particular company's shares as they saw fit; not being involved in the management of the company, they could sell when for investment reasons they thought it best to do so.

Partly as a result of the large amount of funds institutions have available and partly as a result of the comparatively unhappy state of UK industry, pressure has increased on the institutions to encourage them to influence management decision-making. This was by no means a new idea. In 1928 Keynes also suggested that shareholders should do more to influence managers.

The Blue Arrow Case

This is a case in which the stock market was deliberately misled, and the rules of the Companies Act were broken.

Blue Arrow, a UK recruitment agency which was launched on the USM in 1984, was able to take over a US agency (Manpower) in 1987, even though the price paid, over £720 million, was twice the pre-acquisition value of Blue Arrow (£350 million).

How was it able to fund the acquisition? Not by selling junk bonds, but by making a rights issue which raised £837 million. At the time this was the largest rights issue that had been made in the UK. Unfortunately the issue was not a success, and shareholders took up only 48.9% of the shares offered them. It was a difficult time; the stock market was weakening prior to the October 1987 collapse. The result was that £435 million of shares had to be placed with financial institutions. In order to assist in raising the necessary finance, the investment bankers handling the issue, County Nat West, purchased in their own right a considerable number of the shares. They finished up owning 9.6% of the total shares of Blue Arrow.

The impression had to be given to the market that the placing of shares was easy, not that the bankers had themselves needed to purchase a large block of shares costing over £100 million. The bank did not disclose the full extent of their holding. If they had done so the market would have realized the extent to which the rights issue had failed and the price of Blue Arrow shares would have fallen, with a resulting loss to holders of the shares and particularly large losses to a holder of 9.6% of the total.

Phillips and Drew, who were brokers to Blue Arrow, even went as far as to announce that the shares had been placed at a premium. A Department of Trade and Industry (DTI) report subsequently revealed that Phillips and Drew wrote a letter to the Stock Exchange which contained five statements which were either untrue or misleading. In fact, Phillips and Drew and their parent company, the Union Bank of

Switzerland (UBS), finished up owning 9% of Blue Arrow through their purchase of rights. It later transpired that County Nat West indemnified UBS against any losses resulting from acquiring these shares. Unfortunately for County Nat West, with the subsequent collapse of the stock market, this indemnity cost them £20 million.

Section 209 of the Companies Act requires all holders of over 5% of the shares of a company to disclose their holding. But the Act does allow a market-maker to avoid disclosing shares acquired in the normal course of its buying and selling business. County Nat West claimed that 4.6% of Blue Arrow's shares were held by its market-making activity. It argued that these were a different holding from the 5% in the hands of its corporate finance subsidiary. The 9.6% was split up into two separate holdings, and therefore it was claimed that it was not necessary to disclose the holding. The DTI was not convinced and launched an investigation, which they are entitled to do if there are circumstances suggesting that a company's affairs have been conducted for a fraudulent or unlawful purpose.

The fact that County Nat West held 9.6% of the shares might never have been known but for the stock market collapse at the end of 1987. In its financial accounts the bank had to admit losing £49 million from its two Blue Arrow holdings. (This was in addition to the £20 million loss from the UBS indemnity.)

The National Westminster Bank, the parent company of County Nat West, conducted an investigation to see what had gone wrong. The results were passed to the DTI who decided to conduct their own investigation. Unfortunately, County Nat West's argument that their two holdings were separate, and so did not need to be disclosed, suffered a setback when it came to light that the share-dealing subsidiary (the market-making arm of County Nat West) was indemnified against losses on its Blue Arrow shares by the corporate finance subsidiary. This indemnity, a form of compensation, undermined the claim that the market-maker held shares in the normal course of its activities.

Important aspects of self-regulation in the City are the internal controls within a bank or other financial institution and the role of The Securities Association (TSA). Part of the internal control mechanism is for a bank to operate a compliance office to ensure that the provisions of the regulatory acts are being followed in its day-to-day activities. TSA is the self-regulatory body responsible for ensuring that the securities industry conducts itself properly. Ironically, at the time that the market was being misled over the rights issue the head of the compliance office at County Nat West was a member of TSA, and had chaired its Conduct of Business Rules Committee.

The DTI report revealed that it was this compliance officer who had approached the share-dealing subsidiary to see whether they would take some of the shares in return for an indemnity. Such a holding by a share-dealing subsidiary in the normal course of their business would be exempt from disclosure, but pressure was being exerted on the share-dealing subsidiary and incentives were being offered. No legal advice was taken on whether such a holding needed disclosure. The DTI report commented that the conduct of the responsible compliance officer was below that to be expected.

The surprise to some was that those responsible in the largest bank in the UK should have had such little regard for the regulations, and that those responsible for the effective working of the self-regulation system should be so willing to turn a blind eye to the rules. It is the belief of some that people dealing in the market should tell the truth and follow the spirit of the law, and not try to devise policies which squeeze through legal loopholes.

The Blue Arrow-County Nat West case was examined by inspectors from the Department of Trade and Industry. They issued a report in 1989, which criticized aspects of the affair. The Serious Fraud Office took a case to court against a number of the senior officials involved.

On 23rd July 1989, the Observer newspaper had commented, 'Ten senior city figures, including three Nat West main board directors have their conduct (in the DTI report) described as "falling well below that expected from responsible executives" . . . The City's self regulation is once again firmly in the spotlight.'

The case against a number of the executives was dismissed when the case got to court, for lack of evidence.

Undoubtedly the financial institutions could use their position as major shareholders to good effect. They could use their financial expertise to assist managers, and by reducing financial uncertainties they could enable management to take a long-term attitude towards investment. Managers, of course, would not necessarily welcome such interference from shareholders.

The information system between the company, its shareholders and its potential shareholders is far from perfect. Even a company's bankers, who are usually in a better position to obtain information from the company than the shareholders, can misinterpret the financial position of a company. Those who operate in the capital markets do not have all the information about a company that they would like. Each company supplies them with a certain amount of information, and they attempt to find out more about its future prospects by discussions with those involved and by studying the statements of the company and the performance of companies in similar industries. The capital markets are faced with incomplete information, and they are influenced by the statements and actions of a company or its directors.

The investors can make two types of error. One is to believe that a company is performing better than it actually is, with the result that funds are channelled into this company, whereas if the truth were known the funds could have been better used elsewhere. The second type of error is to fail to provide financial support for a company that is in fact in a healthy and promising position.

The first of these types of error can be caused by companies deliberately setting out to mislead the financial community.

There is nothing new about this. There have been many occasions when the capital markets have been misled by the opportunistic representations of individuals and companies. Many of these cases subsequently received much publicity. The heroes of one year became the villains of the next. In 1973 Mr Heath, the then Prime Minister, described certain of the financial practices that were being employed at the time as the unpleasant and unacceptable face of capitalism. This summed up the feelings of many who were becoming disillusioned with certain practices of some of those who operated in the financial system.

As the unacceptable practices of one decade are blocked, a new set of practices develops in the next. In the 1980s a new set of creative accounting 'techniques' emerged. These were adopted not just by companies quoted on the stock exchanges, but by public sector bodies such as local authorities and no doubt by central government itself. As the regulatory bodies and the accounting profession struggled to close one set of creative practices, a new set emerged. For example, the second half of the 1980s saw 'special purpose financial transactions' emerge.

Whether or not investors are fooled by these creative techniques is a subject of debate. There are empirical studies that suggest that the stock market, as a whole, is not misled, and that at least some investors can unravel the true underlying cash flow figures and are not misled by the 'apparent' earnings per share figures. Not all would agree with the conclusions of these studies.

There is a view that it is possible to mislead many investors by creative accounting techniques. These issues will be discussed later in the book in connection with the 'efficiency of the capital market'.

Regulation of the City

One worry in any stock exchange is the extent of insider dealing. This is trading by certain individuals who are in possession of what is known as price-sensitive information. It means that the person possessing this information is able to gain from trading with an individual who is not aware of the significant information. In the UK such practice is against the law, but it is hard to detect. It is not new: the practice and attempts to stop it have been going on for over 200 years.

In London there is a Stock Exchange surveillance department. This monitors all deals and attempts to detect unusual and suspicious trading. The department looks for large volumes of trading, and unexpected price movements. The Exchange has the power to question the people taking part in any deal to try to ascertain on what basis the investment decisions were made. It is possible that such questioning can lead to prosecution. Unfortunately in the vast majority of the suspicious cases the surveillance department finds there is insufficient evidence to make a prosecution.

The surveillance department identifies between 500 and 2000 deals a day that are unusual, but well over 99% of these turn out to be innocent.

The Financial Services Act 1986 and the Banking Act 1986 are the two key pieces of legislation for the control of the City of London. Both introduced radical new changes in the system of control, although there are many critics who do not feel the Acts are strict enough.

The legislation of the investment business is based on the self-regulation approach. This is now based on the following.

1. A clear legislative framework.
2. A central controlling body (an umbrella body), the Securities and Investment Board (SIB), which oversees the authorization and regulation of all investment business in the UK.
3. The SIB functions largely through a number of self-regulating organizations (SROs), each of which is responsible for a section of the investment industry.
4. Authorization and enforcement of the SRO rules by practitioners, i.e. those involved in the City, with some lay people involvement.
5. Each firm involved in the investment business polices its own activities through good management and an adequate system of controls. Firms are required to set up their own compliance offices, with a named director taking responsibility.
6. The external auditors of the investment firms have a role to play, checking that the rules are being followed.

The banks are regulated according to the legislation of the Banking Act 1986, which established a Board of Banking Supervision to assist the Bank of England with its banking supervisory responsibilities. The Bank of England is in fact the key to the control of many of the activities of the financial system. Its responsibilities cover the wholesale money market, the foreign exchange markets and the gilt markets as well as the banking system. There are separate Acts covering the regulation of building societies, insurance companies and Lloyds of London.

We now turn to the Financial Services Act. This aims to provide protection for investors by making it a criminal office to carry on investment business in the UK without authorization. When authorized the business has to follow the rules of the appropriate SRO.

The SIB is designated statutory powers by the Secretary of State for Trade. It is responsible for authorizing and controlling those involved in the investment business. Its powers are wide-ranging and enable the SIB to investigate and prosecute firms practising without authorization. Proper appeal procedures are provided for, and should an investor, the complainant, not receive a satisfactory response from the relevant SRO, there is an ombudsman for investors who will take complaints further.

The following activities are classified as investment business:

1. dealing in investments;
2. arranging deals in investments (arranging for others to buy and sell);
3. managing investment belonging to others;
4. giving investment advice;
5. acting in connection with a collective investment scheme.

There are a number of ways in which a firm may be authorized to do investment business. These include the following

1. membership of a recognized SRO;
2. membership of a recognized professional body (RPB), e.g. for lawyers and accountants, in which case the RPB would effectively perform the function of an SRO;
3. direct authorization by the SIB;

4. authorization by another member state of the European Community (EC) with equivalent standards of investor protection.

The general philosophy of the regulations is to allow healthy competition, but to identify and measure the risks. The Financial Services Act is concerned with issues such as the following:

1. capital adequacy, i.e. maintaining minimum levels of capital to support the perceived risks of security trading;
2. the status of individual firms within a group of companies (following the 'big bang' many financial institutions became just subsidiaries of large companies; the financial position of the overall group is important);
3. the control of clients' money by firms;
4. the conduct of business rules, including
   (a) disclosure – telling counter-parties about the firm's relationship with the securities being traded
   (b) share dealing
   (c) warning customers of the risks of particular securities
   (d) putting customers' interests ahead of the firm's interest;
5. compliance, records and reporting (appropriate records must be maintained and be available for inspection by the SRO).

Whether all these good intentions are carried out depends on the effectiveness of the self-regulation system. There is a danger that self-regulating bodies can become anti-competitive in nature. The SRO could become more concerned with protecting the interests of its members than with looking after the interests of companies and investors. There is always a danger that bodies representing the interests of one group begin to believe that what is good for their members is good for everyone.

A further danger is that, at the very time when large financial conglomerates are being formed that can deal with all aspects of finance, the regulatory bodies are becoming fragmented. The Department of Trade and Industry does not have the time or experience to be able to handle detailed consideration of the competing interests of the different SROs and to monitor the changes taking place within each aspect of the securities and investment industry. The SIB needs to be strong in order to prevent the numerous tails wagging the dog.

The self-regulation system in the UK is expensive and not particularly effective. There are many critics of the Financial Services Act. It has not stopped the many financial scandals. As well as big name company frauds, there have been investors tricked by BCCI and Barlow Clowes, and in 1993 it was revealed that as many of 90% of private pension schemes that had recently been sold to the public had been sold on inappropriate advice.

Serious Fraud Office

A key aspect of the system of regulation in the UK is the Serious Fraud Office (SFO). It is this office that is responsible for bringing cases of fraud to court. They have to build up the evidence against the likes of BCCI. It was they who made the case against Blue Arrow, a case in which the legal fees were in excess of £50 million.

The SFO is a very large operation. Unfortunately it has been criticized as being too slow, too expensive and not particularly effective. As at mid 1994, it was handling over 60 cases. Its biggest enquiry, against BCCI, employs more than 60 people. The amount of fraud is increasing: fraud cases are extremely complex, requiring many accounting, legal and banking experts. In the Blue Arrow case a number of defendants were acquitted because the judge believed the evidence brought to the court by the SFO was too flimsy. Changes have been proposed in the way the SFO operates and whether or not changes are introduced, more money is required to support this office. Fraud in the City and financial community is a serious problem.

Ways in which certain individuals are able to make money for themselves without benefiting either the investor who provides the funds or the companies that use the funds come to light with monotonous regularity. The authorities take steps to eliminate misleading practices. It is good that things are put right where they are wrong. The trouble is that not enough people realize that things are wrong until the full publicity machine is turned on to the offending practices.

Clearly, company directors and shareholders have to follow the provisions of the relevant Acts, but it is in the area where there are gaps or no legislation that problems of reporting, interpretation and financial behaviour give cause for concern. Company legislation only changes at infrequent intervals and, by necessity, changes in the law tend to lag behind changes in practice.

The financial community in the UK prefers self-regulation to the more formal legal regulations that exist in the USA. The arguments for self-regulatory bodies are based on the idea that experts know best. The workings of the City of London are complicated and it is argued that there is a danger that if outsiders try to interfere they could destroy the intricate mechanisms and delicate working relationships. Also, because practices in the securities industry change quickly, any regulating authority must possess the flexibility to respond to these changes. It can be argued that any statutory authority would be too cumbersome and possibly not sufficiently knowledgeable to meet these demands. It is possible, however, that an intermediary body consisting of experts, but acting in the public interest, could meet the needs.

Those involved in the financial system need to be regulated. Savers need to be confident that those who handle their funds, whether financial intermediaries or companies, are abiding by a fair set of rules. Undoubtedly financial scandals do occur and when this happens it tends to undermine investors' confidence in the system. Therefore laws and rules are required that ensure that scandals occur as infrequently as possible and that when they do occur those that are at fault are caught and seen to be punished.

In the UK the system of control is a mixture of law and 'self-regulation'. The various Companies Acts define the relationship between a company, its shareholders and those who lend money to the company.

The Big Bang

The Rules, Regulations and Methods of operating in the city are continuously changing. One of the most dramatic set of changes occurred in 1986, the year of the 'big bang' in the City. The changes had a considerable effect on the structure of the city institutions.

One of the most significant changes that took place was in the method of share dealing in the Stock Exchange. It resulted in the ending of the single-capacity system and the introduction of dual capacity. Under the single-capacity system, which came in for much criticism, the stockbrokers dealt with the buyers and sellers of securities but they did not trade directly with other stockbrokers. The brokers had to deal through jobbers who made the market in the shares of listed companies. If one stockbroker represented an investor who wanted to buy the shares of a particular company, he approached a jobber who dealt in the shares of that company. Jobbers either owned shares in the company themselves or knew brokers who had clients who wished to sell. The brokers and jobbers had separate functions which they operated in a single capacity.

We now have the dual-capacity system, in which the same firm can deal with the buyer or seller of shares and also make a market in the shares. Making a market means that the firm can buy shares on its own account and keep them until the price is attractive enough for them to be sold. Market-makers help to smooth fluctuations in the price of a share. The more market-makers there are dealing in the shares of a particular company, the greater is the competition and the better the position from the point of view of an investor. Other changes introduced in 1986 included the ending of a minimum rate of commission on buying and selling shares.

It should be pointed out that the Stock Exchange did not agree willingly to introduce such changes. It fought a case against the Office of Fair Trading who argued that the old practices were against the public interest. The case never reached court, as in 1983 the Minister of Trade and Industry came to an agreement with the Stock Exchange Council whereby he would stop the case proceedings on condition that certain practices were changed.

One large change that came about following the 'big bang' was the growth of 'supermarket' financial conglomerates. Whereas before the changes the City consisted of many small specialist firms, following the changes there were many mergers, with merchant banks, jobbers and brokers coming together in single firms. Many of these firms are international in scope, with much foreign ownership and many of the traditional British jobbers, brokers and banks were taken over by large foreign financial institutions. Following the 'big bang' the city was opened up to free international competition. This was necessary in order for London to maintain its position as a leading financial centre. It is the job of the regulators to ensure that all who take part in this global market are competent to do so.

1.6 Conclusions

Traditionally it has been possible to divide the subject of company finance into three subgroups, which has been convenient at a theoretical, practical and teaching level. But, as Weston points out, 'the traditional trinity of money and capital markets, business finance, and investment is no longer meaningful at the theoretical level and of questionable use for descriptive and empirical study' [10]. For example, it is not always possible to separate the finance decision from the investment decision as anybody will know who has faced a decision in a lease or buy situation . It is necessary in such a situation to decide on the method of financing before calculating the present value of the cash flow resulting from the investment and it is not easy to calculate the cost of capital until one has decided whether the company will lease or buy the asset.

The directors of a company are interested in the financial expectations of the shareholders, in how long they are prepared to hold the shares and in whether institutional holders behave differently from private holders. In making corporate investment decisions, it is becoming increasingly common, at least at a theoretical level, to take into account the goals and wishes of those who have provided the finance through the money and capital markets. As explained in this chapter, the trend is in the direction of an increasing proportion of the shares of a company being held by institutions and a declining proportion being held by directors.

This divorce of ownership and control has important implications for decision-making. Competent financial management requires, therefore, the technical expertise appropriate to all deployment of current and fixed assets, solving problems of capital costs and so forth. It also demands awareness of the various factors that determine or influence share price. The subject of finance spreads itself wider and wider; behavioural factors are clearly of importance and need to be studied.

The money and capital markets and the financial intermediaries are of key importance in determining the allocation of funds. One can even go as far as to say that one cannot study corporate finance at an aggregate level without considering the flow of funds between the sectors of the economy because the savings behaviour of the household sector and the involvement of the public sector help to determine the supply of funds for companies and the terms on which they are made available. This flow of funds will be examined in the next chapter.

A company is part of the financial community. Its financial management can be fully interpreted only within the context created by the workings of the financial institutions and markets. The theory of investment and the theory of business finance are intimately interdependent. No activity in the one area can fail to have repercussions, to a greater or lesser degree, in the other.

In broad terms, financial management entails constructing a conceptual framework within which one can establish a meaningful interrelationship of three main variables:

1. the financial goals of the company;

2. the valuation of the company, and the extent to which this valuation is influenced by company decisions;
3. the means of measuring the performance of the company – when its goals have been identified and the method of valuation chosen, the company's performance must be monitored and assessed.

The necessary subdivision of this wide field produces many specific areas in which important decisions have to be made – in capital budgeting, optimum financing, financial reporting, short-term cash management and so on. But no decision in these areas can have any validity until the three basic problems have been resolved and reconciled.

A company is both part of a system and a system in itself. The larger system, the environment in which it operates, will both affect its goals and influence its results.

Within the company itself there will be individuals and groups whose own goals deviate to a greater or lesser extent from those of the company. All this means that the company will no doubt find it difficult to achieve its desired goals. But despite this – or rather, because of it – the company must have a clear conception of what it is trying to achieve. A list of objectives is an easy, not to say glib, answer to the problem, but until some weight is attached to the different objectives, they are of no use in decision-making. A decision almost always involves conflicting objectives, and it is vital to know where priorities lie.

Clearly a multiplicity of factors, inside and outside the firm, determine its fortunes. However, this crude conceptual approach with its network of inherent linkages and feedback loops is not particularly helpful when formulating the company's overall objectives in operational terms. The concepts of planning and control are meaningful only to the extent that they can be related to some specific or quantifiable objective or operational goal. A company has responsibilities to a number of interests. But this plurality of responsibilities cannot be neatly embodied in a corporate objective at an operational level.

Since, however, financial activities surround and permeate all corporate action and provide the opportunities for and limitations on a company, the financial interests of the company should be the key factor, i.e. the chief operational objective of a limited company given the existing legal, political and economic environment.

This is not to suggest that the other elements of input and output in the conceptual model are not important; when the environment has no further need for the organization in its existing form, either it will cease to exist or the management, in response to the outside pressure, will ensure that it adapts.

1.7 Key terms

Agency theory
Balanced scorecard
The capital market
Corporate governance
Goal congruence
Institutional shareholders

Market for corporate control
Maximization of profits
Self-regulation
Serious Fraud Office
SIB

1.8 Revision questions

1. What is the relevance of agency theory to the ownership and control of companies?
2. How can shareholders attempt to achieve goal congruence?
3. Is it meaningful to think of the goal of a company as the maximization of shareholders' wealth?
4. What are the reasons for the decline in the percentage ownership of shares by individuals?
5. What is self-regulation in respect of capital markets?
6. What is the role of the Securities and Investment Board?

1. Hayek, F. (1960) The corporation in a democratic society – in whose interests ought it and should it be run? In *Management and Corporations* (eds M. Asher and C.L. Bach), McGraw-Hill, New York, 1960.
2. Freidman, M. (1970) The social responsibility of business is to increase its profits. *New York Magazine*, 30 September.
3. Fama, E.F. and Jensen, M.C. (1983) Separation of ownership and control. *Journal of Law and Economics*, June.
4. Charkham, J. (1989) *Corporate Governance and the Market for Companies: Aspects of the Shareholders Role*. Bank of England Discussion Paper, London.
5. Donaldson, G. (1963) Financial goals: management v stockholders. *Harvard Business Review*, May–June.
6. Jensen, M.C. (1976) Theory of the firm: managerial behaviour, agency costs and ownership structure, *Journal of Financial Economics*, **3**.
7. Jensen, M.C. (1989) The eclipse of the public corporation, *Harvard Business Review*, Sept.–Oct.
8. Rappaport, A. (1990) The staying power of the public corporation, *Harvard Business Review*, Jan.–Feb.
9. *Report of the Committee on the Financial Aspects of Corporate Governance*, Gee, London, 1992.
10. Weston, F. (1974) New themes in finance, *Journal of Finance*, March.

There is a vast and growing literature on this topic. Those listed here give a flavour. The *Harvard Business Review*, *Corporate Governance* and *The Bank of England Quarterly Bulletin* are all good sources of up-to-date articles.

Benson, J.R. (1985) The self-serving management hypothesis: some evidence. *Journal of Accounting and Economics*, 67–84.
Charkham, J. (1994) *Keeping Good Company*, Clarendon Press, Oxford.
Clarke, M. (1986) *Regulating the City*, Open University Press.
Grinyer, J.R. (1986) Alternatives to maximisation of shareholders wealth. *Accounting and Business Research*, Autumn.
Hamilton, A. (1986) *The Financial Revolution*, Penguin Books.
Kaplan, R. S. and Norton, D. P. (1992) The balanced scorecard: measures that drive performance, *Harvard Business Review*, Jan.–Feb.
Miles, D. (1992) Testing for short-termism in the UK Stock Market. Bank of England Working Paper Series, Oct.
Pozen, R.C. (1994) Institutional investors: the reluctant activist. *Harvard Business Review*, Jan.–Feb., 140–9.
Sheridan, T. and Kendall, N. (1992) *Corporate Governance*, Financial Times/Pitman Publishing London.
Tricker, R. (1984) *Corporate Governance Around the World*, Gower Press, Vermont.
Whitley, R. (1986) The transformation of business finance into financial economics, *Accounting, Organizations and Society*, **11**(2), 171–92.

1. To what extent is it in the interests of the shareholders of publicly quoted companies to link the rewards of managers to the financial performance of the company?
2. One of the most important elements of any decision is the specification of goals or objectives which the decision-maker seeks to achieve. The capital budgeting literature generally assumes the goal of the firm to be 'maximization of owner's welfare'. Discuss the rationale for this assumption, highlighting the disadvantages of alternative proposals.
3. 'Whereas the proportion of personal wealth held in land and buildings doubled over the 15 years 1960–1974, the proportion held in company securities halved although the average proportions had originally been the same at 23 per cent' (Royal Commission on the Distribution of Incomes and Wealth, Report No. 5, 1977,

Cmnd 6999). Suggest reasons for this shift and discuss the implications for the activities of industrial and commercial entities.

4. For the purpose of the exposition of financial management techniques, the assumed single objective of commercial entities is often taken to be the maximization of firm and equity valuation. Comment on the extent to which this assumed single objective is realistic and explain why corporate management needs to be concerned with firm valuation. How can financial management techniques assist in meeting actual corporate objectives?

5. What are the arguments for and against self-regulation in City institutions?

6. Discuss what objectives might be important to a company other than shareholder wealth maximization. Are such objectives likely to be consistent with shareholder wealth?

7. Discuss how managers' objectives might differ from those of shareholders, especially if managers are not closely monitored by shareholders and are not subject to constraints and/or incentives imposed by shareholders. Illustrate for these differing objectives the policies that managers might adopt that are likely to be sub-optimal.   *ACCA, 1987*

8. Within a financial management context discuss the problems that might exist in the relationships (sometimes referred to as agency relationships) between (a) shareholders and managers, and (b) shareholders and creditors. How might a company attempt to minimize such problems?   *ACCA, December 1986*

9. Critically examine the view that *'voice'* based corporate governance mechanisms are likely to have a greater positive impact on enterprise efficiency than mechanisms which rely on *'exit'*.

10. Discuss what objectives might be important to a company other than shareholder wealth maximization. Are such objectives likely to be consistent with shareholder wealth maximization?

11. 'Change can be viewed by some as a problem and by others as an opportunity. So what has been the result of the Cadbury Committee's report on corporate governance – opportunities or new problems for the accounting profession and business community?' Discuss and reach a conclusion.   *ICAEW, July 1993*

2 *Flow of funds and taxation*

2.1	The flow of funds	21
2.2	The personal sector	24
2.3	The business sector	27
2.4	The public sector	28
2.5	Taxation policy	30
2.6	Corporation tax	31
2.7	Small company taxation	33

2.8	Capital allowances	34
2.9	Capital gains tax	35
2.10	Taxation and decision-making	36
2.11	Key terms	37
2.12	Further reading	37
2.13	Problems	37

One objective of this chapter is to show that corporate finance cannot be considered in isolation from the rest of the economy. Businesses compete for funds with other sectors, and the availability and cost of funds for a business depends to a large extent upon decisions being made in other sectors.

It should be appreciated that businesses, whether companies, partnerships or sole traders, constitute only one sector of an economy. To study any sector in isolation means that the analysis is incomplete and that factors that help to explain what is happening within a sector are being ignored.

Another objective of the chapter is to provide an introduction to corporation tax. This may be particularly valuable for those not studying taxation as a separate subject.

2.1 The flow of funds

For the national income accounting purposes, the economy is divided, for convenience, into four sectors: the business sector, the public sector, the personal (household) sector and the overseas sector. Funds flow within each of these sectors (for example, from one company to another) and between the sectors. Some of the movements of funds are contractual, for example companies paying wages to their employees who are classed as being in the personal sector, and the payment of taxes by the corporate and personal sector to the public sector. Other movements of funds depend upon savings and investment decisions.

The financial markets and financial intermediates help mobilize financial resources. Financial intermediaries, such as banks, pension funds and insurance companies, move funds from where they are available to where they can be best used. In the complex financial environment that now exists, it is necessary to understand the interrelationship of these sectors. Figure 2.1 illustrates the movement of funds between sectors. It is a very simplified diagram, dealing only with the items which are of direct relevance to company finance. It ignores many of the items classified as current account items, for

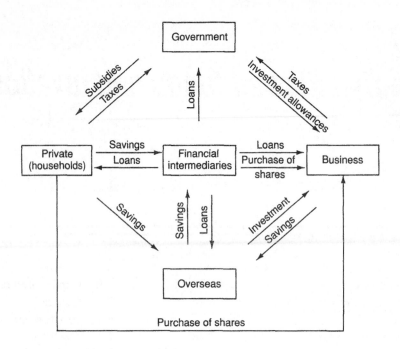

Figure 2.1 *Flow of funds between sectors*

example the payment of wages by the business sector to the private sector and the funds that flow to the business sector as a result of the purchase of goods and services.

Flow of funds accounting at the national level is an extension of national income accounting. To those trained in accounting, the concept is easy to understand. National income accounts are for a country what a profit and loss account is for a company, or to use the terminology of North America, what the income account is for a company. Another way of showing the financial activities of a company in a year is by means of a sources and applications of funds statement. At this national level, it is helpful to produce such funds flow statements for each sector. These show for each sector where its funds came from and how they are used, and so indicate the extent of the interdependence of the sectors. The statements help identify both the role of finance in the generation of incomes, savings and expenditure and the influence of economic activity on the financial markets. Some knowledge of this form of economic analysis is important to accountants and company financial managers. The level of savings in each sector and where the savings are invested is vital for the health of the business sector and the economy.

Unfortunately, owing to the limitations of existing statistics, each of the sectors cannot be as clearly defined as would be ideal. The public sector consists of central government, local government and public corporations, where the latter are mainly nationalized industries. The business sector covers most of the privately owned part of business and can be divided between the non-financial side, usually referred to as industrial and commercial, and the financial side including the banks and institutions. It is usual in published statistics to separate these two elements of the business sector, as the financial institutions clearly have a special role to play in the financial system very different from that of the industrial and commercial enterprises. Unfortunately, figures for unincorporated businesses, i.e. partnerships and sole traders, are not included in this business sector. Because of statistical problems, the figures for these forms of business, which include, among others, farmers, lawyers and small shopkeepers, are included in the personal sector.

The personal sector should ideally just cover the transactions of all the individuals in the country when acting in their own right as consumers, as opposed to when they act as businessmen or businesswomen.

Unfortunately, the statistics for the personal sector also include figures for the unincorporated businesses, charities and other non-profit-making bodies. Fortunately, the individual personal element predominates. On occasions the personal sector is referred to, even in official publications, as the household sector. This name can be misleading as there are, of course, individuals in the personal sector who are not householders.

The overseas sector is more or less self-explanatory; the financial surplus or deficit of this sector on the current account is equivalent to the much discussed balance of payments. The flow of funds of the overseas sector represents all dealings by the public, personal or business sector with anybody outside the UK whether the transactions are of a capital or current nature.

UK flow of funds figures are to some extent confusing. One problem is that there exists a residual error, i.e. unidentified items, which can in any year account for as much as 10% of the total funds available. To accountants trained in industry, commerce or the profession, it may be disturbing to see accounts published with such a large unidentified balancing item. However, to those who have tried to wrestle with the problem of national income accounting, it is not surprising. The residual figures, however, can bedevil anyone hoping to draw policy conclusions from national income accounts, including unfortunately the government!

The black hole

It is not just the UK that has problems with national income accounts. An example of a statistical problem is the so-called black hole in the aggregated national income accounts for the world. These aggregate figures are produced by the IMF. Technically the aggregate of all countries' imports and interest payments should equal the total of all their exports and interest received. Somebody's exports are somebody's imports; somebody's payments are somebody's receipts. The world's current account in total should be in balance, but it is not; it is in deficit! The value of goods and services imported plus interest paid exceeds the value received from exports and interest. The deficit is rising each year.

Goods are being imported and paid for, yet the records do not show that anybody is receiving payment. Where is this money going? Some of it is statistical error but much of it is secret money. This is an intriguing subject; there is great demand for secret money, not just from criminals and political dictators but also from companies and elected governments. Many financial centres in the world are willing to provide a home for secret money.

In the case of the black hole, it is money paid for goods and services that is never recorded by the company or individual receiving it. It may not be recorded in order to avoid tax, or because the payment (a bribe) is illegal.

The Single European Act states that the internal market shall comprise an area without internal frontiers in which the free movement of goods, persons, services and capital is ensured in accordance with the provisions of this Treaty. The supporters of the single market believe that efficient and competitive financial markets are essential for the achievement of a genuine Single Market. This requires full freedom for capital movements and the liberalization of the financial services field, but with efficient regulation of the markets.

A directive removing controls from all capital movement within the Community was adopted in June 1988. It applied to most Member States from 1 July 1990. However some countries were given additional time in which to implement the directive.

The directive hopes it will be possible for the liberalization to extend beyond the Community. This means free capital movements to and from non-Community countries.

It is believed that the opening of national financial markets will enhance competition and choice in financial services within the Community. It should therefore lead to a more efficient and less costly channelling of savings into investment. Savers will be offered a wider range of financial assets, and borrowers will have access to more diverse and cheaper financing.

As barriers to the provision of financial services throughout the Community are dismantled, the financial sector is exposed to new competitive pressure. The effect of these changes should be to strengthen the Community economy generally as well as the financial sector. The benefits for UK firms could well be significant.

When the Single Market is complete, there will, for example, be no restrictions on French residents opening bank accounts in the UK, Greek residents will be able to borrow from a UK bank without needing authorization, and an Irish firm will be free to place its excess funds on the UK money market. UK firms will be able to borrow in, and use the financial services of, any member country.

With the liberalization of controls, savings would move from countries offering low real interest rates to countries offering high real interest rates. On the other hand borrowers would be looking for the lowest interest rates.

2.2 The personal sector

Saving is the difference between current income and current expenditure. The amount of funds that the personal sector releases for investment in other sectors depends upon savings habits and upon the amount invested in physical assets, mainly housing. Savings represents the money received that is not spent on consumption of goods. It represents the funds that the personal sector has available to invest either in physical assets or in financial assets such as pension funds, equity shares and bank accounts.

Each year the personal sector makes decisions similar to the business sector on how much of its income is to be spent on consumption (the current account or profit and loss account) and how much it can save and transfer to the capital account (the balance sheet). These savings add to the wealth of the sector (the equity). The savings can be invested in physical assets or financial assets.

Savings of the personal sector in the UK

The savings ratio of the personal sector, i.e. savings as a percentage of disposable income, fell over the 1980s, but increased in the 1990s. (Disposable income consists of wages, salaries and government grants, less income tax and national insurance contributions.) If the household sector is spending its income and not saving, it means that there are less funds flowing to the other sectors. Certain payments made by the household sector do flow to the financial sector; these are termed contractual savings. These are payments that have to be made each year by individuals to life assurance and superannuation schemes, and these contractual payments figures have increased dramatically over the last 30 years. Traditionally, those individuals who saved would use their available funds to buy the shares or debentures of companies. However, for the last 30 years or so the household sector has been a disinvestor in terms of company securities. Each year the household sector has sold more company securities than it has purchased. What has happened is that increasingly the savings of the household sector have been collected by the financial institutions: householders, rather than investing on their own behalf, have entered into contractual savings schemes.

Membership of compulsory and contractual savings schemes has increased considerably. This reduces both the need and the resources available for private investment. Savings schemes involve a minimum of trouble and expense as far as the individual pension fund member or policy-holder is concerned and there are usually guaranteed minimum values for both pensions and life assurance policies. On occasions membership of such a scheme is a condition of employment, and so the employee does not have a choice of private or institutional investment.

There are also many tax advantages to saving through a contractual savings scheme. When an individual pays into a pension scheme, the whole of the contribution is a deductible expense in arriving at the amount of his income that is subject to tax. If the person concerned earns £20 000 a year and £2000 of this is paid into a pension scheme, then the income subject to tax will be at the most £18 000. The pension fund will be able, if it wishes, to buy £2000 of company securities. If the same individual wishes to use his savings to buy an insurance policy, again there are tax savings to the individual. An individual wishing to buy shares on the stock market on his own behalf would have to obtain his £2000 of funds out of after-tax income, i.e. after tax had been deducted from the full £20 000.

As well as tax advantages to the individual in channelling savings into financial intermediaries, there are also tax advantages enjoyed by the financial intermediaries over the individual as investors. Most individuals have to pay more tax on the income they receive from owning a share or debenture than would an institution receiving the same income from owning the same investment. With the comparative costs of buying shares and the returns from owning shares so heavily in favour of using a financial intermediary rather than buying directly, it is not surprising that the household sector has been disinvesting in company shares over the last three decades and channelling its savings into financial intermediaries. The level of funds flowing into life insurance companies and pension funds from the personal sector can be seen clearly in Table 2.1. This table summarizes the financial transactions of the personal sector. One large collector of household savings is the building societies, but they do not usually use their funds to buy company shares or make loans to companies. Most of their money is lent for house purchase, with investment of surplus funds in the capital or money markets on a short-term basis.

Table 2.1 *Sources and uses of capital funds in the personal sector (£ billion)*

	1989	1993
Sources		
Savings	25.5	52.7
Capital transfers	2.6	5.5
Bank borrowing	20.4	8.3
Building society borrowing	24.0	9.8
Other borrowing	4.1	–(0.6)
Accruals adjustment	–(3.9)	–(2.5)
Total identified sources	72.7	73.2
Uses		
Investment in fixed assets and stocks	30.3	24.4
Deposits with banks	21.4	1.5
Deposits with building societies	17.6	8.9
Other liquid assets	–(0.7)	4.1
Purchase of:		
British government securities	–(3.3)	5.4
Other public sector debt	–(0.4)	0.2
Company securities	–(20.0)	1.3
Life assurance and pension funds	28.5	29.7
Capital transfers	3.2	2.0
Total identified uses	76.6	77.5
Balancing item	3.9	4.3

There are four dramatic changes in the financial policies of the personal sector that are illustrated by the figures in this table. They are:

1. The increase in the level of savings of the personal sector. Such savings have more than doubled over four years.
2. The decline in personal borrowing over this period. This is one of the factors leading to the problems of the banking sector.
3. The decline in investment in fixed assets and stocks. This contrasts with the continued relatively high level of investment of personal savings in life assurance policies and pension funds. This helped contribute to the slump in house prices.
4. The decline in deposits in banks and building societies.

The flow of funds accounts for the personal sector in the UK for 1993 (Table 2.1) show a 'balancing' item of £4.3 billion. This represents an outflow of funds in excess of the inflow for this sector that at the time the statistics were prepared could not be accounted for.

Flow of funds after 1992

We are concerned within a country and between countries with the flow of funds. With a free market funds can flow from individuals and companies in one country to individuals and companies in other countries. With government restrictions this movement of funds is limited. Since the adoption of deregulation policies in many countries the flow of funds across borders has increased dramatically. In this chapter we are using the UK economy to illustrate the way the system works. It should however be appreciated that from 1992 technically the position within Europe changed.

The European Community envisages the free movement of capital among the member states as an essential complement to the free movement of goods, people and services. But progress on removing controls has varied from one state to another. The UK abolished all exchange controls in 1979. Germany, the Netherlands and Denmark also have full freedom of capital movements.

Italy made substantial progress in the late 1980s towards complete liberalization. French residents were, at the beginning of the 1990s, generally permitted to hold bank accounts abroad or to open foreign currency accounts in France, but there have been restrictions on the amount banks can lend to non-residents.

Personal savings habits vary very much from country to country (Table 2.2). In Japan and West Germany the annual average level of personal savings as a percentage of disposable income has for many years been comparatively high. For a long time this benefited the companies in these countries. Before the restrictions on the transfer of personal funds out of these countries was lifted, these funds could only be invested within Japan and Germany respectively. This high supply of savings helped keep down interest rates in these countries, with a resulting low cost of borrowing for companies.

Table 2.2 *Average annual personal savings as % of disposable income, 1992*

Japan	15.0%
West Germany	14.0%
UK	12.0% (1988 = 6.0%)
France	12.0%
USA	5.0%

Source: OECD Economic Outlook

A sources and uses of capital funds account for industrial and commercial companies is shown in Table 2.3. The internal funds figure represents profits after paying tax, dividends and interest, but before providing for depreciation and additions to reserves. The government has an influence on the size of this amount through taxation policy. If the government has a policy of not taxing companies heavily, then the companies can retain more of their income and finance their investment this way. The public sector, however, raises its income partly through taxation. If less is collected in taxation, then the government may well need to borrow more to finance its needs. More borrowing by the government means that there are less funds available in the capital markets for companies to borrow. This is a simplified version of fiscal policy, but it does illustrate the interrelationships.

As can be seen from Table 2.3, corporate investment is primarily financed out of internally generated funds. One element of internally generated funds is retained profit; the other element is depreciation. Over time a variety of financial incentives, most of which operate through the tax system, and in particular through the capital allowances, have been offered to companies to encourage them to invest. Depreciation is deducted before arriving at taxable profits, and the size of the depreciation deduction that is allowed in a year will influence the tax paid and hence the amount of funds that a company has to invest.

The figures in Table 2.3 reveal a number of important points about the financing of industrial and commercial companies in the early 1990s.

1. Internal funds became of increasing importance as a source of finance. In 1989 they provided 33% of the total, and 64% in 1993. This move to internal finance in the 1990s

Table 2.3 *Industrial and commercial companies: sources and uses of funds (£ billion)*

	1989	1993
Sources		
Internal funds	35.7	50.6
Bank borrowing	34.0	–(11.9)
Other loans and mortgages	10.1	4.4
UK capital issues	8.0	17.4
Capital issues	7.8	6.7
Capital issues overseas	11.0	11.0
Credit received	0.8	0.3
Capital transfers (receipts)	0.6	0.4
	108.0	78.9
Uses		
Gross domestic fixed capital formation	52.5	48.6
Increase in value of stocks	9.3	2.2
Investment in UK company securities	18.0	2.5
Direct investment in overseas securities	8.3	2.3
Other investment overseas	2.0	3.9
Credit given	–(0.4)	–(0.5)
Liquid assets	11.6	8.0
Other financial assets	4.7	7.3
Capital transfers	1.5	0.7
	107.5	75.0
Balancing item	0.5	3.9

was the result of two factors, (a) increasing levels of profitability, and (b) a reduction in the levels of investment, both in physical and financial assets. Because less funds were needed there was not the need to go outside the business to borrow. Although this was the position in the early 1990s it should be appreciated that the self-financing ratio of companies can be very volatile. It depends on the stage of the economic business cycle.

2. The decline in the level of bank borrowing by industrial and commercial companies. As already mentioned a similar trend exists in the personal sector.

3. There has been a steady increase in capital issues in the UK by industrial and commercial companies. The figures in Table 2.3 represent new money raised by issues of company securities on the UK Stock Exchange and the issues of unlisted companies in the UK that can be identified. It is not easy for those compiling the statistics to be able to ascertain capital issues in small unlisted public and private companies, where all that happens is that a few shareholders transfer money into the company in return for more shares. New capital issues are a minor source of funds, although as can be seen they began to take on a greater significance during the 1990s.

4. The overseas figure requires some explanation. The overseas sources figure includes funds moved into the UK by overseas companies wishing to invest here. It includes that part of the profits of UK subsidiaries of overseas companies that is not sent out of the UK, but is retained here and so is a source of funds in this country. It also includes the purchase of shares and loan capital of UK subsidiaries and associates by overseas parents and capital issues raised by UK companies overseas, import credits and advance payments on exports. Overseas uses of funds comprise intracompany investment by UK companies overseas, which includes the unremitted portion of the profits of overseas subsidiaries of UK companies (the profits which are not returned to the UK). Other uses included suppliers export credits, advance payments on imports and the acquisition of commercial short-term overseas assets.

5. There was no increase during the early 1990s in the level of investment in fixed assets, in stock, nor in financial assets.

Table 2.4 shows the level of profits of UK industrial and commercial companies, and how these profits are used. The important points to note are as follows.

1. It can be seen that the level of dividends increased between 1989 and 1993. This is in fact a long-term trend. The total amount of dividends paid to shareholders began to increase from the early 1980s.

2. Because the level of borrowing declined, as did the level of interest rates, the total interest paid fell.

3. The total amount of taxes paid fell. This figure of course varies year by year depending on the level of company profitability. There has, however, been a trend to lower levels of taxation.

2.4 The public sector

One source of finance for the corporate sector is money made available by the public sector, i.e. by the government. In taking on this role, the government is acting as a financial intermediary. Traditionally, funds flow between the different sectors of the economy, with the financial institutions collecting savings and allocating them where they believe they can be most profitably used. However, in recent years governments have been of the opinion that there are gaps in the provision of finance for investment in industry.

It is accepted that for many years there has not been enough investment in fixed assets in manufacturing industry in the UK. Successive governments have responded to this point by taking steps to provide industry with the finance necessary for such investment.

Governments, through taxation, can take funds from the household sector, the sector that saves the most, and channel this into approved business investment, or alternatively they can themselves borrow in the capital and money markets and make these

Table 2.4 *Appropriation account of industrial and commercial companies (£ billion)*

	1989	1993
Income arising in UK		
• gross trading profit	80.1	91.6
• rent and non trading income	12.5	9.9
Income from abroad*	18.1	16.1
	110.7	117.6
Dividends on ordinary and preference shares	16.2	22.6
Interest and other current transfer payments	25.9	21.6
Profits due abroad	8.7	6.3
UK taxes on income	19.0	13.1
	69.8	63.6
Balance of undistributed income	40.9	54.0
Less net unremitted profits	–5.2	–4.6
Internally generated funds (as per Table 2.3)	35.7	50.4

*Net of taxes paid abroad

funds available to industry. This is the government supplementing the normal private market mechanism for the allocation of savings.

Before considering some of the schemes whereby government funds are channelled into the business sector, we should point out that the other side of the picture is that the government competes with the business sector for the savings that are available. Much is written about the public sector borrowing requirement (PSBR). This is the amount that the three branches of the public sector, central and local government and public (state owned) corporations, need to borrow. In borrowing they are competing for scarce funds, and by increasing the demand for these funds without increasing the supply they are forcing up the price, i.e. the interest rate. They borrow in domestic markets and in international markets, and in both markets they are competing for funds with the business sector. The fact that two of the branches of the public sector, central government and local government, are not required to earn a profit means that they can afford to be less conscious of the price of borrowed funds than the business sector; the public corporations are required to earn a surplus.

Table 2.5 shows an income and expenditure account for UK central government for 1993. As explained the public sector can be divided into three components: central government, local government and public corporations – the nationalized industries. As it is central government that is the most involved with the finances of industrial and commercial companies, it is on this relationship that we shall concentrate. We have shown a detailed current account for this one part of the public sector, so that the contribution of the different forms of income and expenditure can be seen. The table clearly shows the following:

1. the importance of taxation, both on income (of personal and business sectors) and expenditure (value-added tax, customs and excise duties, petroleum tax etc.);
2. the importance of national insurance contributions, which are a form of taxation;

Table 2.5 *Central government current account 1993*

	(£ billion)
Receipts	
Taxes on income	72.6
Taxes on expenditure	91.0
National insurance contributions	33.9
National health contributions	4.7
Rents and royalties	1.1
Interest and dividends	8.4
Other	1.9
	213.6
Expenditures	
Final consumption	
Military defence	22.3
National health	35.6
Other	29.1
Subsidies	7.1
Social insurance benefits	71.7
Other grants to personal sector	4.1
Grant to local authorities	54.6
Current grants paid abroad	4.8
Debt interest	18.0
	247.3
Balance – deficit	33.7

3. the high level of interest that has to be paid on the PSBR; this relates only to the central government debt. The size of the annual borrowing requirement of the public sector declined over the 1980s. One reason for this was because of the income generated from the privatization programme.

Funds flow from one sector to another. If the public sector borrows it means that less funds are available elsewhere in the economy. In the 1980s it was government policy to reduce the level of public sector borrowing.

The relationship between the public sector and the business sector is complex. From a financial point of view the public sector performs the following services.

1. It takes funds from the business sector through taxation and employers' national insurance contributions.
2. It puts money back into industry through various schemes of financial support for certain regions and certain industries. These will be discussed elsewhere in the book. It should also be appreciated that the most important form of government assistance to industry is through tax allowances.

2.5 Taxation policy

The problems of corporate taxation have reached proportions of Olympian grandeur and it would be unwise to pretend that anything but the barest outline could be offered adequately within the scope of this chapter. The object of this section is to explain a little of the system as it operates at present, to explain how it has changed over time and to indicate some of the effects that fiscal policy is having on firms.

Fiscal policy, i.e. taxation policy, must be considered in the light of the overall economic policy of the government of the time, for together with monetary policy it is used to regulate and direct the economy in the paths of political righteousness. It is generally accepted that the aims of recent economic policy are to increase the national income, to avoid excessive inflation, to limit the level of unemployment and to achieve a satisfactory balance of payments position. However, there will be shifts of emphasis in this policy as and when political and economic expediencies dictate them.

The taxation policy is designed to help achieve economic goals. In particular the ways in which it can be used to achieve such goals are as follows:

1. to raise money for the government to spend;
2. to stimulate private sector investment;
3. to help combat inflation;
4. to redistribute income and wealth.

It is a fact that taxation results in a transfer of funds away from the individual or company that has earned the income into the hands of the government. At times this transfer has been justified in that it is the opinion of many people that decisions made by the government on the use of these funds are made in the so-called national interest. This leads to a 'better' society than if the decisions are left in private hands. At other times this transfer has been criticized in that it is a disincentive to individuals and companies to work and earn money when it is to be taken away from them. Many people believe that greater prosperity results if decisions on how money is spent are left in the hands of individuals, rather than if made by governments or economic planners.

Taxation means the taking away of money from the taxpayer, money which he would otherwise have spent either on consumption or investment. The government may itself spend the revenue it raises on consumption or investment. National income largely depends upon the volume of investment, and investment is a function of a number of variables, two of which are the rate of interest and the marginal efficiency of capital. The government can manipulate the interest rates and it can affect the marginal efficiency of capital. If the profits on investment earned by companies are reduced through taxation, the marginal efficiency of investment will decline and this will mean a fall in investment. However, it can be argued that through negative taxation (i.e. by way of grants, subsidies and other transfers from the public sector to the private sector) the government may be able to stimulate investment in the private sector.

The government can also use fiscal policy to help combat inflation. Through the manipulation of the levels of government expenditure and taxation, it can either put money into the economy or take it out. It can therefore help balance the current level of output of goods and services in the economy with the current effective demand in the economy.

In an inflationary atmosphere, therefore, the government aims to maintain and increase the level of investment which is necessary if the national income is to grow, and yet it must also siphon off what it considers to be surplus spending power in order to balance output and effective demand and so contain inflation. Taxation has become an all-important instrument of policy; it is not merely a means of raising revenue.

2.6 Corporation tax

A brief description follows of the taxes and allowances under the corporation tax system. The system was introduced in 1966. However, an important change took place in 1973 in the method of applying corporation tax; the UK moved to what is known as the imputation system. Table 2.6 shows the rates of corporation tax that have been in operation from 1966 to 1995.

Under the system that was introduced in 1966 one rate of tax was to be charged on the taxable profits of companies. If a company wished to distribute dividends, the individual shareholders incurred a further deduction of income tax on the amount of the

Table 2.6 *Rates of corporation tax (%)*

1966–8	42.5
1968–70	45.0
1970–1	42.5
1971–3	40.0
1973–83	52.0
1983–4	50.0
1984–5	45.0
1985–6	40.0
1986–90	35.0
1990–1	34.0
1991–5	33.0

dividends. If a company did not wish to distribute its profits as dividends, the profits were not subject to any further tax after the deduction of the corporation tax.

Under the corporation tax system that existed from 1966 to 1973 all profits were subject to one form of taxation, and then the proportion distributed was subject to additional tax. It was thought that the introduction of this system would encourage firms to retain profits. Undoubtedly in any year less tax was paid in total if profits were not distributed, but whether this tax system meant that companies were likely to reduce their dividends depended on the company dividend policy.

The imputation system

In 1973 the UK moved to the imputation system. Under this system, a company pays corporation tax at a certain rate on the profits it earns, and the shareholders do not necessarily have to pay any further tax on dividends distributed. The shareholder is allowed to have part of the tax that the company paid 'imputed' to him or her to offset against tax that would otherwise have to be paid on any dividends received. If the shareholder pays income tax at a rate above the basic rate, the amount he or she is allowed to 'impute' will not be sufficient to discharge all his or her tax liability on the income received. If he or she is paying tax at the basic rate then, after taking credit for the 'imputed' amount, there will be no further tax to pay on the dividends received.

One aspect of the imputation tax system is that, near the time dividends are distributed to the shareholders, the company has to make an advance payment of corporation tax (advance corporation tax (ACT)). The amount of ACT that has to be paid depends upon the amount of dividends being distributed and the rates of income tax.

To illustrate we shall take the corporation tax rate as 33% and the lower income tax rate as 20% (the rates in effect for 1994/95). The rate of ACT for the year to 5 April 1995 was 25% of the net dividend. This means that for any dividends distributed in 1994/95 the ACT that had to be paid to the tax authorities was 20/80ths of the amount distributed. If for example a company decided that after six months of trading it wished to pay to its shareholders an interim dividend of £8,000 net, then the ACT to be paid by the company would be £2000 (i.e. 1/4 × £8000).

It can be seen that using this 1/4 fraction to calculate ACT gives the same result as if the gross dividend were being taxed in the shareholders' hands at the lower tax rate. The company is in fact acting as a tax collector for the government; it is taxing the dividend at source.

ACT has to be handed to the tax authorities approximately three months after the company pays dividends. When the company eventually is required to settle its total corporation tax bill at some time in the future, the advance payment that is has made will be offset.

Although not increasing the monetary total of the tax that has to be paid by a company, ACT effectively increases the real cost. This ACT has to be paid ahead of the normal date for tax payment. It should be appreciated that normally there is a delay between the time when a company earns profit and when it pays the tax on those profits.

There is a limit to the amount of ACT that can be offset against the total UK tax liability. This can result in what is known as unrelieved ACT. It arises when the tax bill is relatively low compared with the dividends that have been paid. The maximum ACT that can be reclaimed is the ACT that would be paid on a full distribution of the company's taxable income.

As an example let us assume that a company's taxable income is £2 000 000 and the corporation tax rate is 33%. The maximum amount of ACT that a company may set against its liabilities for corporation tax for the year to 5 April 1995 is 20% of taxable profits. This gives a maximum amount in our example of £400 000. If an interim dividend of £1 800 000 is paid, the ACT would be 25% of this amount, namely £450 000. Not all this can be set off against tax: only the maximum amount can be claimed, resulting in unrelieved ACT of £50 000.

One case of companies that have in the past experienced difficulties with the imputation system of corporation tax are companies with a high proportion of their profits earned overseas in countries with high tax rates. These companies have suffered in comparison with companies earning a similar level of profit from UK operations, particularly if they have a policy of distributing a high proportion of their profits to shareholders. This is because they have not been able to receive full credit for their profits which have borne foreign tax. The position has however changed and in certain circumstances they can pay dividends out of foreign income. This issue is returned to in Chapters 12 and 16.

2.7 Small company taxation

A reduced rate of corporation tax applies to companies with low levels of profits. This rate is usually thought of as being the rate applicable to small companies. This is in fact the justification for lower rates. However, it is based on the level of profits and not the size of the company. It is also the tax rate that applies to a large company that suffers a decline in profits. The actual rate of tax has varied over time with the variations in the full rate of corporation tax. The Finance Act 1989 introduced a rate of 25% for the year 1989–90 applicable to companies whose taxable profits did not exceed £150 000. This rate was the same at the time as the basic rate of income tax.

For the year 1994/95 the rate remained at 25%. By 1994 the upper and lower limits for calculating marginal relief had risen to £300 000 and £1 500 000. The marginal relief fraction was 1/50th.

Marginal relief is necessary so that companies are not unfairly taxed as their profits grow beyond the £200 000 level.

The way the system works is as follows:

Case A Profits £200 000
  Tax payable (25%)   £50 000
  _____

Case B Profits £500 000
  Full tax (33%)   165 000
  Less abatement
    1/50 (1 500 000 – 500 000)   –20 000
  _____
      145 000
  _____

Average tax rate 29%

Case C Profits £1 000 000

Full tax (33%)	£330 000
Less abatement	
1/50 (1 500 000 – 1 000 000)	–10 000
	320 000

Average tax rate 32%

As can be seen the average rate of tax is 25% in Case A, 29% in Case B, and 32% in Case C.

The abatement is based on the level of income tax, the level of corporation tax and the size of the abatement band. Consequently it can vary from one tax year to another.

It can be seen that the difference in tax payable between Case A and Case B is £95 000. This is on an increase in profits of £300 000. Therefore this increase is being taxed at a marginal rate of 31.66%, which is lower than the normal corporation tax rate.

2.8 Capital allowances

When computing their taxable profit, companies provide for depreciation by means of capital allowances. These allowances are based on rates laid down by the Inland Revenue, which are not necessarily the same as those used by a company when computing its own profit in its profit and loss account. For tax purposes, depreciation of plant and machinery is normally based on the use of a specific percentage of the balance (although an alternative straight-line method can be used if the Commissioners of Inland Revenue agree). Buildings are depreciated using a straight-line method, by which an equal absolute amount is written off each year. Once computed, the various allowances are deducted from profit as computed for tax purposes, to give net taxable profit.

The computation of net taxable profits allows for the deduction of annual writing-down allowances and in very rare cases an initial allowance. The annual writing-down allowance on plant and machinery, cars and vehicles, and mines is 25% of the reducing balance, and on such items as industrial buildings and hotels it is 4% of the cost. In the case of investment in scientific research (excluding land) the whole of the expenditure can be deducted from profits in the year in which the expenditure is incurred. With this 100% write-off in the first year there is no need for an annual writing-down allowance. The book value of the asset, for tax purposes, is zero at the end of the first year.

Tax rates and capital allowance rates have varied considerably over time. Different governments have different policies. Companies were, in fact, allowed to adopt for tax purposes a free depreciation policy on plant and machinery purchased between March 1972 and March 1984. The company could claim a 100% initial allowance in the first year or it could take credit for a lower figure in the first year and obtain credit for the balance in subsequent years through the normal annual writing-down allowance.

The system of 100% initial allowances on plant and machinery was brought to an end by the 1984 Finance Act.

Closely controlled companies

Closely controlled companies are companies controlled by a small number of individuals. The tax legislation defines such a company as one that is controlled by five or fewer participants. A 'participator' is not the same as a shareholder. It is possible to have many shareholders, but only five 'participators'. If a number of members of a family own shares, a husband, his wife and each of his children, there is judged to be only one 'participator'. It is assumed that the 'participator' has the power of his associates, and associates do not just include immediate family, but also close relatives, fellow trustees and any business partners.

The legislation is designed to deal with family businesses. It specifically excludes a company owned by another company that is not itself a close company. It also excludes companies that are quoted on a stock exchange with 35% or more of their shares held by the public.

It is thought necessary to treat family businesses differently for tax purposes because, as the directors and shareholders are the same people or are from within the same families, they could organize the affairs of the company to avoid taxation. The particular concern is with the level of profits that they distribute. When personal tax rates were very high, 60% at the margin, it was tempting to keep the profits in the family business and so only be taxed at the corporation tax rate of 35%. The family would try to obtain returns from the business in forms other than dividends. The close company rules tax the company and its shareholders as if it has distributed a certain percentage of its profits as dividends, whether or not this is what has happened in fact. With top income tax rates at 40%, the difference is not so important. It should also be remembered that many family businesses retain a large percentage of profits earned because they need finance to enable them to grow. It is not necessarily to avoid tax.

2.9 Capital gains tax

Normally an individual or a company will be charged capital gains tax on any chargeable gain that accrues in a particular tax year as a result of disposing of an asset. An asset can be disposed of either by a sale or a transfer. It is possible to deduct capital losses from capital gains in arriving at the amount subject to tax in a particular year.

The rate of capital gains tax for 1994–95 was as follows: for the individual, as if the gain is income and so chargeable at the individual's marginal income tax rate; for companies, at normal corporation tax rates. For individuals capital gains below a certain figure are exempt from tax. The tax-free level in 1994–95 was £5800. This exemption for small gains does not apply to companies.

Chargeable assets include all forms of property, stocks and shares, land and buildings, goodwill, certain debts and options. There are various exceptions and these include certain UK government securities held for more than 12 months, and the gain on the disposal of a person's main residence.

A chargeable gain is one which accrues after 6 April 1965; this is the base date. If the asset was owned prior to that date, the gain between the date of acquisition and 6 April 1965 is not subject to tax. If it is not clear how much of a gain accrued prior to that date and how much after, it can be assumed that the asset increased in value at a uniform rate over time and the taxpayer is relieved of tax on the gain that arose prior to the base date. If the amount is known, the taxpayer has the option of using the market value of the asset at 6 April 1965 as the base from which to calculate the gain instead of the time apportionment method.

The rule for valuing assets is to take the market value of the assets at the time of the sale or transfer. Market value is the price which the assets might reasonably be expected to fetch on a sale in the open market. It is necessary to value only the assets actually being disposed of.

In calculating the chargeable gain on the disposal of assets held for over 12 months, a deduction is allowed to take account of inflation (as reflected by movements in the Retail Price Index in periods of ownership in excess of 12 months, after March 1982) on the cost of the asset. This adjustment cannot create an allowable loss nor can it be applied to increase an allowable loss.

Subject to conditions, losses arising on the disposal by an individual of ordinary shares he has acquired by way of subscription in an unquoted UK trading company can be relieved against taxable income rather than against capital gains; any unrelieved balance can be offset against capital gains in the normal way.

The abandonment of a traded option to buy or sell shares in a company or in gilt edged securities, bonds or loan stock is treated as a disposal of an asset for capital gains tax purposes. It can produce an allowable loss. The definition of a traded option includes options quoted on the London International Financial Futures Exchange.

A company would normally be liable to gains tax in respect of the sale of any one of its business assets. However, it is possible to obtain relief from such tax if the business asset is to be replaced. If a company sells, say, machinery, with the object of replacing it with better machinery, it could be considered unjust if it was taxed on any capital gains on the asset being sold, as the object of the transaction is to improve performance, not to make a capital gain. The tax concession is that if further business assets are purchased within one year preceding or three years after the sale, 'roll-over' relief can be obtained, with the result that the gain on the disposal is for tax purposes deducted from the cost of the new business assets. The relief is therefore rolled over and no tax is paid on the gain until the newly acquired asset is disposed of, and then it is again possible to roll over any gain then arising by making another replacement. The old and new assets must be used in the same business, and to obtain the full relief the entire sale proceeds must be reinvested. This roll-over relief from capital gains tax can benefit shareholders in family companies. The way in which this concession works is that when business assets of such companies are transferred, any capital gains that may arise will not have to be taxed at the time of transfer, but can be rolled over. The capital gains tax will not have to be paid unless the business is actually sold; it will not be paid on transfer.

Another way in which the roll-over concept benefits shareholders, in quoted as well as unquoted companies, is at the time of a takeover or merger. A shareholder disposing of his holding through the takeover or merger can at such times postpone paying any tax on capital gains which may have accrued on his own shares if he accepts new shares in exchange for the old shares. If he accepts cash he has to pay tax immediately on any capital gains. By accepting shares, he is delaying paying tax, rolling it over until he sells for cash the new shares he has received. This relief only applies if the new company in which the shareholder receives shares is acquiring at least 25% of the shareholder's old company.

There are numerous other aspects of capital gains tax. This section has only attempted to give the reader a flavour of these forms of taxation. The emphasis has been on the way in which they affect companies, and the availability of finance.

2.10 Taxation and decision-making

There are many situations in which the tax rules and regulations affect the decisions being made by management. The tax rules and changes in the rules have economic consequences. Of course, the government is aware of this and so uses the fiscal system in an attempt to influence decisions.

The areas in which the taxation position influences decisions include the following.

1. The decision whether to form a company or operate as a partnership is affected.
2. The decision whether to use capital-intensive or labour-intensive methods is similarly affected. The capital allowance system has at times been used to encourage companies to invest in new equipment. In 1984 important changes were made in the UK with regard to the system of capital allowances relating to company investments. The corporation tax rate was reduced, and the phasing out of first year allowances began. The Chancellor expressed the belief that the Budget offered exciting opportunities for expansion with rewards for enterprise stimulating innovation and the creation of jobs. Most analysts concluded that the Budget would not help capital-intensive manufacturing companies, although it would help the retail and service sectors. The Budget introduced greater neutrality in the taxation treatment of different types of capital investment, but it did this at the expense of investment in manufacturing industry.
3. The decision as to where to locate a new factory can be influenced by the grants or tax concessions available. The corporation tax system has a significant influence on the cost of one form of finance relative to another. The tax system favours debt finance against equity finance. Interest payments have for many years been deductible against profits. They are not seen as an appropriation of profits.

4. Decisions as to whether to lease or purchase an asset are affected by the taxation position.
5. Decisions by multinational companies as to where to locate their registered office and in which countries to locate manufacturing facilities are influenced by such factors as transfer pricing rules, double taxation agreements, tax havens etc.

Undoubtedly the subject of taxation is extremely complex. All we have attempted to do in this chapter is to cover some of the basic points that will assist in an understanding of the rest of the book.

2.11 Key terms

Business sector
Capital allowances
Capital gains tax
Capital transfers
Corporation tax
Enforced savings

Financial institutions
Household savings ratio
Imputation tax
Public sector
Sector surpluses/deficits
Tax burdens

The books below divide into those concerned with flow of funds and those concerned with taxation. There are of course many specialist publications on the taxation of companies. Flow of funds is often covered in general economics textbooks.

2.12 Further reading

Bain, A.D. (1973) Flow of funds analysis: A survey. *Economic Journal*, December, pp. 1055–93.
Bain, A.D. (1981) *The Economics of the Financial System*, Martin Robertson.
Bank of England (1972) *An Introduction to Funds Flow Accounting: 1952–70*, August.
Bank of England (1978) *UK Flow of Funds Accounting, 1963–76*, May.
Bank of England (1994) Company profitability and finance. *Bank of England Quarterly Bulletin*, **34**(3), Aug.
Central Statistical Office, *Financial Statistics* (monthly editions), HM Stationery Office.
Central Statistical Office, *National Income and Expenditure* (annual editions), HM Stationery Office.
Hancock, P.J. *An Introduction to Taxation: Policy and Practice*, Chapman & Hall.
James, S. and Nobes, C. (1992) *The Economics of Taxation*, 4th edn, Prentice Hall.
Kay, J.A. and King, M.A. (1986) *The British Tax System*, Oxford University Press.
Mason, S. (1976) *The Flow of Funds in Britain*, Elek Books.
Moon, P. and Hodges, S. (1989) Implications of the recent tax changes for corporate capital investment. *J. Bus. Finance and Accounting*, Spring.
Peasnell, K.V. and Ward, C.W.R. (1985) *British Financial Markets and Institutions*, Prentice Hall.

2.13 Problems

1. (a) Describe and explain the pattern of the flow of funds that occurs between the major sectors of an economy, and identify the sectors that are normally in surplus and those that are normally in deficit. (6 marks)
   (b) Many borrowers wish to borrow large sums of money for long periods of time. Many savers wish to invest small sums of money for short periods of time. Explain how financial intermediaries can help to satisfy the needs of both borrowers and lenders and describe the nature and functions of five major types of financial intermediary. (13 marks)
   (c) Discuss the role of government in channelling funds to the public sector.

2. Outline the major government activities that influence financial management and briefly illustrate how government activities affect companies in achieving their financial objectives.
3. Must the total savings and the total investment of a country be equal?

3 Finance and accounting

3.1	Introduction	39
3.2	Accounting policies	41
3.3	Cash flow versus accrual accounting	47
3.4	Financial ratios	50
3.5	The use of ratios to forecast company failure	63

3.6	Conclusions	65
3.7	Key terms	66
3.8	Revision questions	66
3.9	References	66
3.10	Further reading	67
3.11	Problems	67

There is a close link between finance and accounting, a link that should often be closer than it is. The theories and concepts in the subject of finance are usually developed by economists who have an inadequate knowledge of the technical details of accounting, whilst accountants are often not sufficiently aware of the theories of finance and the economic consequences of accounting reports. In this chapter, and in Chapters 8, 13, 14 and 15, we try to bring the subjects closer together.

We attempt to introduce the reader to accounting concepts and policies. It is necessary to understand these in order to be able to analyse accounting statements.

We then examine the technique of financial ratio analysis. This is a starting point in the financial analysis of any company. It is necessary to understand not only what it can offer, but also its limitations.

It is important to clarify the relationship between accounting and finance. One role of accounting is what is referred to as the 'stewardship' role. This involves the record keeping activity and the internal and external audit function with the object of ensuring that the financial resources of the business are spent on legitimate purposes. This is part of the 'accountability' process; those who run the business, the directors and managers, are accountable to the owners of the business, and in fact to a wider social constituency.

An important part of the accountability process is the production of financial reports. These are of particular concern to those who provide finance as the reports enable an analysis to be made of a firm's past actions to assess its current standing and possibly to form opinions about its likely future performance. The fundamental object of financial reports, of the financial statements, 'is to communicate economic measurements of, and information about resources and performance of the reporting entity useful to

3.1 Introduction

those having reasonable rights to such information' [1]. Shareholders, creditors, financial analysts and providers of debt finance are clearly groups with a right to such information.

It is not easy to be able to assess the performance and value of a company on the basis of its published financial reports. There is more to it than just looking at the earnings per share figures. The annual report usually contains an optimistic statement from the Chairman, some spectacular photographs of the company operations, photographs of an acceptable group of people who are the directors and a boring looking set of numbers (although Burtons PLC have been known to liven up the actual pages on which the financial accounts appear with distracting photographs of female models – wearing Burtons clothes of course).

The standard technique used to analyse financial reports is what is known as ratio analysis. But to do this meaningfully it is necessary to understand a few things about accounting practices and conventions. We shall deal with a few of the difficulties before moving on to ratio analysis.

Undoubtedly the complexity of, and amount of disclosure in, accounting statements has increased as bodies which set accounting standards have tried to improve the communication process between the users and the preparers of accounts.

The preparation of financial reports costs a great deal of money. Nevertheless a question that needs to be considered is how useful these statements are to the financial community. We shall consider this from three points of view: the first is whether knowledge of past performance can ever be a guide to future performance, the second is the effects of the actual earning announcements and publication of the accounts of the company, and the third is whether an efficient capital market is able to detect the 'correct' signals from a set of accounts that has been designed to 'create' a favourable impression. At this stage we shall deal with the issues only briefly. They will be considered in greater depth later in the book. The issues are being considered at this stage only in relation to the usefulness of accounting reports to those involved with the financing function.

Financial accounts relate to the past; they enable users to assess past performance. One of the main principles of finance is that the economic value of a business is the discounted sum of the firm's expected future cash flows. To what extent can knowledge of accounts relating to the past assist in forecasting future cash flows?

The market receives a large amount of information that is relevant to a particular company. In addition to the annual report of the company, there might be press releases put out by the company, interim financial statements and reports on the prospects for the economy and the industry in which the company is engaged. There are also meetings between investment analysts and directors of the company, and of course rumours. At one level therefore it could be said that the annual financial report is just one piece of information that will enable the market to form opinions on the financial strength of a company and its potential for taking advantage of future opportunities. Investors value shares on the basis of the expected future position of a firm. When the financial accounts are produced, investors can ascertain whether or not their expectations relating to the year just completed have been realized. The annual accounting report can confirm or refute the expectations of investors. It provides an opportunity to reassess future expectations. It might be thought therefore that share prices would rise or fall following the annual earnings announcement. This is not necessarily the case.

There has been much empirical work analysing how the stock markets respond to accounting numbers. There is considerable evidence supporting the view that, whilst much of the share price change that will result from a difference between expected and actual company earnings occurs before the announcement, there is still a significant movement in the share price on the day of the announcement [2]. Some of the information will have been anticipated before the announcement. But there is convincing evidence that movements in accounting earnings have a strong correlation with movements in stock prices [3].

There is another question that needs to be considered in this context. Financial accounts are prepared on the accruals basis, but in finance valuations are based on cash flows. The two are not necessarily the same; the earnings per share figure is not the same as the cash flow per share. On average it can be shown that reported earnings are highly correlated with cash flows. But this is on average; there are cases of companies where the two can differ significantly. The user of accounts has to be aware of these possible differences.

At times some companies have changed their accounting policies in order to attempt to create a favourable impression. There is no one profit figure for a company that is correct, with all others wrong! Many assumptions have to be made to produce a profit figure. On a number of issues a firm has to decide what assumptions to make and which of the possible accepted accounting practices it will follow. If the capital market is efficient it will see through changes designed to boost performance; cosmetic increases in reported profits should not result in increases in share price. There are many studies that show that the market is not misled, and that manipulating reported profit figures is a waste of time [4]. The market is able to read the financial statements and ascertain the 'true' position. This is of course on average. Undoubtedly there are individual cases where the market has been misled by a company. It is therefore important for the users of accounting statements to understand something about accounting. It is important to understand what lies behind each of the numbers that are used to produce financial ratios. If the numbers are unreliable the ratio will be unreliable. If one company produces its accounting numbers based on one set of assumptions and policies and another company produces its numbers according to a different set, there is no point in comparing the ratios of the two companies.

Financial accounting has existed for many centuries, even with no agreement on theory and objectives. We shall consider what are sometimes called the 'principles', 'rules', 'concepts' or 'conventions' that underlie the accounting reports that are actually produced.

3.2 Accounting policies

The accounting standard on the disclosure of accounting policies tries to explain the general principles that are being employed to cope with the practical problems faced every day in producing financial reports [5]. The statement begins by explaining that it is not attempting to develop a basic theory of accounting, but is mainly concerned with ensuring that companies disclose in their financial reports the accounting policies followed. It seeks to clarify what is meant by the world 'policies'. It differentiates between fundamental accounting concepts, accounting bases and accounting policies.

Fundamental concepts, it is explained, are 'working assumptions having general acceptance' at a point in time. They underlie the financial accounts produced by a business enterprise at a point in time. In no way are accounting concepts the same as accounting theory; they are just broad assumptions. They are practical rules which are adopted generally but can be varied and possibly changed over a time.

The accounting standard singles out four particular concepts for special mention: the going concern concept, the consistency concept, the prudence concept and the accruals concept. The standard requires that 'any material differences from the four fundamental concepts as well as the critical accounting policies must be disclosed in the annual accounts and suitably explained. If financial reports are to be valuable as communicators of information, these disclosures are important, clarifying which, of a spectrum of available methods, have been utilized.'

The four concepts mentioned in the standard are as follows.

• Going concern. This postulate, which is sometimes referred to as 'continuity', is introduced to cope with the problem of periodic reporting for an entity having a life extending beyond the current period. It represents the assumption that, provided that there is no significant evidence to the contrary, the entity will be assumed to continue in existence long enough to carry out its commitments, sell its stock in trade in an orderly manner and derive the use from its assets not purchased for resale. A machine held to provide production capacity will be valued for the use that can be made by operating it rather that what it would fetch in the open market. If continuity is not expected, a different approach to valuation and reporting must be taken.

- Consistency. Reflecting the user need of comparability, this principle requires the accounting treatment to be consistent both within a particular period and between different periods. Where changes occur, there is a need to provide information to help the user understand the effects, possibly by quantifying the change and/or adjusting results already reported.

- Prudence. It is often recommended that, in accounting, pessimism should be adopted in preference to optimism, given the uncertainty that necessarily exists in the reporting of financial results. This conservative approach implies that revenue and profit should not be anticipated, but provision should be made for any expected liabilities; assets should be valued at the lowest of several possible values, while liabilities and expenses should be valued at their highest. This approach is justified by assuming that overstatement is more dangerous than understatement, and that a businessman's optimism needs to be tempered with the accountant's pessimism. However, it is a defective method of dealing with uncertainty, as it is not free from bias. Understatement can lead to poor decisions just as overstatement can; it supports the concealment and distortion of data considered 'optimistic' and can have indirect effects that run totally counter to its main objective. The understatement of asset values may result in an overstatement of profit owing to the reduction in the associated depreciation charge.

- Accruals. When considering the performance of a business the need to produce reports for particular periods needs to be considered. From an economic point of view, the income measurement adopted in accounting concentrates on recording events leading to increases or decreases in capital values, rather than on comparing opening and closing values. For this, a means must be given for matching events to periods. The nature of income is such that the revenues of a period are not always the receipts of that period and the expenses are not always the outlays. Sales are recognized in the period in which they are invoiced; payments made in one period that produce benefits in another are treated as expenses of the period in which the benefits are derived. Although this may not represent the legal or physical position, substance over form is invoked and the financial reality is represented by tracing events to the appropriate period. This approach is known as an 'accruals approach' and involves the process known as 'matching'.

Before examining matching, it is necessary to mention a feature of income reporting that stems from the accruals approach but is not always explicitly recognized. This is **income smoothing**. If future changes in value are anticipated fully, as suggested by the *ex ante* economic concept of income, the effects of such changes will be spread over a number of periods and the resulting income figures will show a smoother trend than without that anticipation. To the extent that accrual allows the reporting of receipts and outlays to be spread or allocated to 'appropriate' periods, it permits smoothing. Some would argue that this is desirable if it produces an income figure that projects the general trend of progress, rather than fluctuations caused by uneven cash flows, while highlighting any major deviation from this trend as a cause for special concern. Smoothing is given effect in many accounting practices; depreciation and amortization spread expenditure of a capital or unusually 'lumpy' nature, the treatment of taxation involves smoothing, and extraordinary and exceptional items are separated in an attempt to remove distortions from a smooth recurring trend of reported income.

Another concept is substance over form. This supports the idea of reporting to reflect financial reality in preference to the legal position. There are many examples of this, including the reporting of assets acquired on a long-term lease as if they were, in fact, owned, and the treatment of associated (related) companies where the group's share of the earnings of the associate are reflected in group accounts and not merely the dividends to which there is a legal right.

Accounting bases and policies

Accounting bases are methods which have been developed for expressing or applying fundamental accounting concepts to financial transactions and items.

Accounting bases are diverse since they have evolved in response to the variety and complexity of types of business and business transactions, and for this reason there may justifiably exist more than one recognized accounting basis for dealing with particular items. In the course of practice a variety of accounting bases have developed designed to provide consistent, fair and as nearly as possible objective solutions to these problems in particular circumstances; these include bases for calculating such items as depreciation, the amounts at which stocks and work in progress are to be stated and deferred taxation. The significance of accounting bases is that they provide limits to the area subject to the exercise of judgement, and a check against arbitrary, excessive or unjustifiable adjustments where no other objective yardstick is available. By definition it is not possible to develop generalized rules for the exercise of judgement, although practical working rules may be evolved on a pragmatic basis for limited use in particular circumstances.

Accounting policies are the specific accounting bases selected and consistently followed by a business enterprise as being, in the opinion of the management, appropriate to its circumstances and best suited to present its results and financial position fairly.

In circumstances where more than one accounting basis is acceptable in principle, the accounting policy followed can significantly affect a concern's reported results and financial position and the view presented can be properly appreciated only if the policies followed in dealing with material items are also explained. For this reason, adequate disclosure of the accounting policies is essential to the fair presentation of financial accounts, but it has to be recognized that the complexity and diversity of business renders total and rigid uniformity of bases impracticable.

In a following section we shall analyse the accounts of Guinness PLC. The balance sheet and profit and loss account of the company are given in Tables 3.1 and 3.2. The point is being made that the numbers by themselves are of limited value. The user of the annual accounts needs to know the accounting policies on which they are based and also to refer to the notes to the accounts. Table 3.3 gives information on some of the policies adopted by Guinness in preparing the accounts.

Valuation of assets

A major problem that companies face when preparing accounts is the changing price level. Fixed assets have traditionally been valued at cost, with revaluation taking place when, in the opinion of the directors, historic cost values are out of line with market values. As prices change, a choice arises not only in the valuation of the assets that make up the capital value, but also in the comparability of the opening and closing valuations, and there are even alternatives for the units in which the valuations are expressed. As a result any system of accounting for profit must adopt a policy on three basic dimensions: 'the units of measurement', 'the valuation model' and 'the concept of capital maintenance'.

In the present-day economy, money plays a major role as a common medium of exchange. It is therefore appropriate, in any aggregation of economic values, to adopt money as a common unit of measurement. However, prices change, which means not only that the value of particular goods changes in relation to money, but also that the value of money changes in relation both to particular goods and to collections of goods; money is not a stable unit of value.

In tackling another of these dimensions, the valuation model, there is a need to consider the fact that values change over time (requiring the selection of a point or points of time at which the value is current), and also that more than one value exists at a given time. A current market value may differ depending on whether the viewpoint of a buyer or a seller is taken, and there could be an array of anticipated future values for different owners depending on their perceptions of the future and the uses to which they are variously able to put the particular asset.

Measuring profit for a business in terms of the maximum distribution that could be made before the capital value is reduced has been expressed as the maximum

Table 3.1 *Guinness PLC, group profit and loss account for the year ended 31 December 1993*

	Notes	1993 (£ million)	1992 (£ million)	Growth %
Turnover	1	4663	4363	7
Net trading costs	2	(3725)	(3340)	
Reorganization costs	3	–	(125)	
Total operating costs	2	(3725)	(3465)	
Profit before interest and taxation (excluding LVMH)	1	938	898	4
Share of profit before taxation of LVMH	4	125	101	
Provision against investment in LVMH	5	(173)	–	
Profit before interest and taxation		890	999	(11)
Net interest charge	8	(188)	(204)	
Profit on ordinary activities before taxation		702	795	(12)
Taxation on profit on ordinary activities	9	(247)	(242)	
Profit on ordinary activities after taxation		455	553	(18)
Minority interests		(22)	(28)	
Preference dividends		–	(1)	
Profit for the financial year		433	524	(17)
Dividends	10	(258)	(237)	
Retained earnings	23	175	287	
Earnings per share	11			
Basic		22.9p	28.1p	(18)
Diluted – before exceptional items		31.7p	33.0p	(4)
Effect of provision against investment in LVMH		(8.8)p		
Effect of reorganization costs		–	(5.2)p	
Diluted earnings per share		22.9p	27.8p	(18)
Dividends per share	10			
Paid or payable		12.80p	11.85p	8
Gross equivalent		16.00p	15.09p	
Interest cover (times, before exceptional items)		5.7	5.5	
Dividend cover (times, before exceptional items)		2.5	2.8	

distribution while maintaining capital intact. In applying this to business in times of changing values, the questions 'Which capital?' and 'In what terms is it maintained?' become relevant; the answers are to be supplied by the adoption of a concept of capital maintenance.

To answer the first of these questions, the extent of the capital of the business must be established. Among suitable definitions are the shareholders' capital or, alternatively, all long-term investment by shareholders and lenders. The second question addresses itself to the manner in which the capital is considered to be maintained. Debate has centred on two major concepts, physical capital and economic capital. An extreme interpretation of the former would recognize profit only after ensuring that the same physical assets could be provided from capital allowing for them to be in the same condition as at the beginning of the period. This interpretation which views the business as

Table 3.2 *Guinness PLC, group balance sheet at 31 December 1993*

	Notes	1993 (£ million)	1993 (£ million)	1992 (£ million)	1992 (£ million)
Net Assets					
Fixed Assets					
Acquired brands at cost	13		1395		1395
Tangible assets	14		1725		1719
Investments	15		1439		1436
			4559		4550
Current Assets					
Stocks	16	1822		1810	
Debtors	17	1239		1244	
Cash at bank and in hand		399		635	
		3460		3689	
Creditors (amounts falling due within one year)					
Short term borrowings	18	(907)		(1116)	
Other creditors	19	(1455)		(1440)	
		(2362)		(2556)	
Net current assets			1098		1133
Total assets less current liabilities			5657		5683
Creditors (amounts falling due after more than one year)					
Long term borrowings	18		(1366)		(1548)
Other creditors	20		(171)		(184)
Provisions for liabilities and charges	21		(282)		(299)
Total net assets	12		3838		3652
Equity					
Capital and reserves					
Called up share capital	22 (B)		503		500
Share premium account	22 (B)		522		498
			1025		998
Other reserves	23 (A)		3933		3900
Goodwill	23 (B)		(1229)		(1327)
Shareholders' funds			3729		3571
Minority interests			109		81
Total equity			3838		3652

a stagnant entity is inappropriate, particularly when physical assets are rapidly becoming obsolete and anachronistic in a world of technological change. A modified interpretation of the physical capital maintenance concept, which is more consistent with such change, can be described as operating capital maintenance. Here, the capital base from which profit is measured is that which enables the same output to be achieved.

Even this operating concept fails to reflect the full dynamism of economic change, since not only are methods of manufacture modified over time, but the nature, range and desirability of the products themselves are always likely to undergo major changes. The economic capital maintenance concept seeks a full response to change, requiring capital to be measured in terms of its current real value, maintaining its purchasing power.

The idea of maintaining capital intact has been given considerable importance, but it

Table 3.3 *Guinness PLC, accounting policies*

Basis of accounting
The accounts are prepared under the historical cost convention, modified to include the revaluation of land and buildings, and in accordance with applicable accounting and financial reporting standards.

Basis of consolidation
The Group accounts include the accounts of the Company and its subsidiary undertakings together with the Group's share of the profits and retained post-acquisition reserves of associated those of the Group undertakings. Associated undertakings are those in which the Group holds a long- term equity interest and over which it is in a position to exercise a significant influence.

Where the Group's interest in unincorporated joint venture partnerships is determined on the basis of the contribution to the results of the partnership from the sale of the Group's products, the attributable results and the related underlying net assets and borrowings are consolidated.

Brands
The fair value of businesses acquired and of interests taken in associated undertakings includes brands, which are recognized where the brand has a value which is substantial and long term. Acquired brands are only recognized where title is clear, brand earnings are separately identifiable, the brand could be sold separately from the rest of the business and where the brand achieves earnings in excess of those achieved by unbranded products.

Amortization is not provided except where the end of the useful economic life of the acquired brand can be foreseen. The useful economic lives of brands and their carrying value are subject to annual review and any amortization or provision for permanent impairment would be charged against the profit for the period in which they arose.

Tangible fixed assets and depreciation
Land and buildings are stated at cost or valuation less depreciation. In the case of distilleries, breweries and related specialized properties, valuations are principally on a depreciated replacement cost basis. Hotel and leisure business properties are valued on the basis of an open market valuation for existing use.

Freehold land is not depreciated. Other tangible fixed assets are depreciated on a straight line basis at annual rates estimated to write off their book values over their expected useful lives.

Stocks
Stocks are stated at the lower of cost and net realizable value. Cost includes raw materials, duties where applicable, direct labour and expenses, and the appropriate proportion of production and other overheads, including financing costs in respect of whisky and other spirit stocks during their normal maturation period.

Accounting for acquisitions and disposals
(a) **Results** The results of businesses acquired or disposed of are consolidated from or to the effective dates of acquisition or disposal.
(b) **Fair value adjustments and acquisition provisions** On the acquisition of a business or of an interest in an associated undertaking the acquisition cost is allocated to the fair value of net tangible assets and the fair value of significant brands acquired, after adjustments to bring accounting policies into line with
(c) **Goodwill** The goodwill arising on the acquisition of businesses and interests in associated undertakings is calculated by reference to the fair value of net assets acquired and is deducted from reserves. Where merger relief is taken under Section 131 of the Companies Act 1985, the difference between the fair value and the nominal value of shares issued as purchase consideration is treated as a merger reserve. Goodwill realized on disposals is included in the calculation of the gain or loss on disposal.

Foreign currencies
The profit and loss accounts and cash flows of overseas subsidiary and associated undertakings are translated into Sterling at average rates of exchange. Balance sheets are translated at closing rates. When hedging arrangements are in place, the transactions to which they relate are translated at the rate achieved under those arrangements.

Exchange differences arising on the retranslation at closing rates of the opening balance sheets of overseas subsidiary and associated undertakings, together with the year end adjustment to closing rates of profit and loss accounts translated at average rates, are taken to reserves.

Exchange differences arising in the normal course of trading and on the translation of monetary assets and liabilities are dealt with in the profit and loss account. Differences arising on the translation of foreign currency borrowings are taken directly to reserves where there is a corresponding exchange difference on the translation of the related net investment in overseas

Turnover
Turnover represents invoiced amounts inclusive of excise duties but excluding value added tax.

Deferred taxation
Deferred taxation on differences between the treatment of certain items for accounting and taxation purposes, whisky and other spirit stocks during including financing costs in respect of within the foreseeable future.their normal maturation period, is accounted for to the extent that a liability or an asset is expected to crystallize

Pensions and other post-retirement benefits
The cost of providing pensions and other post-retirement benefits is charged against profits on a systematic basis, with pension surpluses and deficits arising allocated over the expected remaining service lives of current employees. Differences between the amounts charged in the profit and loss account and payments made to pension or other schemes are treated as assets or liabilities.

---

must be qualified. Economics provides no absolute justification for maintaining capital intact; it is not necessarily unethical to fail to maintain capital. Capital maintenance has been employed as a theoretical construct, a point of reference from which measurement can take place. Legal rules regarding dividends have been drawn up in terms of profit, which may offer some protection for creditors, although it must be recognized that the rules take on the imprecision associated with profit measurement.

3.3 Cash flow versus accrual accounting

In the next chapter we discuss investment decision-making which, in theory and most of practice, is based on cash flow data. It is important to understand the difference between cash flow accounting and accrual accounting. The accounting ratios we are about to consider are not usually based on cash flow data but on accrual accounting data. A company is judged by the profits it discloses in its profit and loss account and by the strength of its balance sheet, and these statements are prepared on the accrual basis.

Even though from a finance point of view decisions need to be made based on cash flows, the results of these decisions will be reported in the annual financial accounts. Therefore the impact of the results of the decisions on the accruals-based financial accounts cannot be ignored. As argued above, it is necessary for the student of finance to understand something about accounting and accounting conventions, otherwise he or she could be led astray by a 'good' set of creative accounts, or an investment decision could be made that has a disastrous effect on the balance sheet.

We shall illustrate the difference between cash flow accounting and the accrual system which is used to measure profit with a simple example. A typical examination question is to give details of the transactions of a business over a period of time and to require the production of a cash flow statement. As an example we shall produce such a statement for Hampton Ltd (see Table 3.4) and then use the same data to produce a balance sheet and a profit and loss account.

Hampton Ltd commences in business on 1 January. The founders of the business invest capital of £100 000, and negotiate with a bank to obtain an overdraft facility which enables them to borrow up to £40 000. On 1 January the business purchases a machine for £96 000; it has a life of three years and is to be depreciated on the straight-line basis.

In January 1000 units are produced. The business is successful and in each succeeding month an additional 250 units are produced, so that during June 2500 units are produced. The direct cost of producing a unit is £5.00. The payment (the cash flow) of these production costs occurs in the month following production.

The goods are sold in the month following production, i.e. all the goods produced in January are sold in February, and so on. The selling price of a unit is £10.00. Goods are sold on credit and Hampton have to wait two months following sales for the customers to pay. Goods sold in February are therefore paid for in April. The company has to rent premises; payment in advance is required, and £20 000 is paid on 1 January for the first year's rent.

In addition to a cash flow statement, the company produces quarterly balance sheets and profit and loss accounts. The company adopts a policy of valuing inventory on the basis of the direct costs of production plus a depreciation charge allocated on a time basis. The company wishes to make provisions for taxation that will have to be paid on the profits earned at a rate of 33%.

The resulting statements are as shown. The cash flow statement is straightforward and does not require explanation. The time lag in the payment of production costs and the receipt of sales revenue can clearly be seen. The overdraft reaches a level of £27 250 at the end of March and then falls.

The balance sheet as at 31 March shows this peak level of borrowing. The company does not look too healthy at that date; it appears to have liquidity problems. Its current liabilities equal £34 750 (creditors plus overdraft) and its current assets are £47 670 (stock, payments in advance and debtors). Nevertheless, the company is trading at a small profit. The significance of this comparison will be seen in the next section when we produce financial ratios to analyse a company's performance. It is a well-known fact that a company can be profitable and have liquidity problems.

One or two figures in the financial statements need explanation. The production costs for the first quarter cover the goods produced during that period, but it can be seen from the cash flow statement that the March production has not been paid for at that date. Hence the amount involved appears as a creditor. The sales figure in the profit and loss account reflects the fact that the sales of £10 000 in February and £12 500 in March have been recognized. However, the cash has not been collected, and hence the amounts are shown as debtors.

The inventory at 31 March is valued based on the direct production cost plus one month's depreciation, i.e. 1500 units at £5.00 each plus one-twelfth of £32 000.

This simple example illustrates a number of ways in which accounting policies and conventions, relating to recognition of income, matching of expenses with income, accruals and prudence, enable estimates to be made of profits earned over periods of time and valuations placed on the net assets of a business. If the company adopted different policies and there were different accounting conventions, different profit figures would be produced.

The example illustrates a number of ways in which accruals accounting differs from cash flow accounting. These include the following:

1. Income is recognized at the time of sale, not when cash is received.
2. The matching convention means that through depreciation the cost of the asset is related to the time when the income is earned. Depreciation is not a cash flow. The cash flow occurs at the time when the asset is paid for.
3. Expenses which are paid for in advance are charged to the accounting periods in which the benefits are received. This is not necessarily the same period as when the cash is paid.
4. Items may be charged against the profits of a period, even though the cash payment is not to be made until some time in the future. Even though strictly it is not a liability, a provision is made for tax that may have to be paid in the future.

Table 3.4 *Accounting data for Hampton Ltd*

(a) Cash flow statement £000

	Opening	Jan	Feb	Mar	Apr	May	Jun
Cash sources							
Capital	100						
From sales		–	–	–	10	12.5	15.0
Cash uses							
Machinery	96						
Production costs		–	5	6.25	7.5	8.75	10.0
Rental of premises		20					
Cumulative balance	+4	–16	–21	–27.25	–24.75	–21	–16

(b) Profit and loss account for

	1st Quarter		2nd Quarter	
Sales				
Cost of goods sold		22.50		52.50
Opening inventory	0		10.17	
Production costs	18.75		30.00	
Depreciation	8.00		8.00	
	26.75		48.17	
Less Closing inventory	10.17	16.58	13.92	34.25
Rent of premises		5.00		5.00
Profit before tax		0.92		13.25
Provision for tax (33%)		0.30		4.37
Profit after tax		0.62		8.88

(c) Balance sheet as at

	1 January	31 March	30 June
Capital	100 000	100 000	100 000
Profit		620	9 500
Provision for tax		300	4 670
Creditors		7 500	11 250
	100 000	108 420	125 420
Machinery (net depreciation)	96 000	88 000	80 000
Stock		10 170	13 920
Payments in advance		15 000	10 000
Debtors		22 500	37 500
Cash/overdraft	4 000	(27 250)	(16 000)
	100 000	108 420	125 420

It is necessary to be able to assess whether or not a company has performed well over a period of time. From its profit and loss account we can observe the profits it has made, but are these as high as they should be when considering the amount of money that has been invested in the business? Are they equivalent to the level earned by major competitors? We need to know whether the company is in a healthy short-term financial position, and whether it is in a good financial position for long-term expansion.

We need to know the answers to these and many other questions. The most common method of analysing accounts is by use of financial ratios. These ratios are used by analysts outside the company when making investment decision and by managers within the company when comparing the performance of one division with another. They can be used by management for interpreting the performance of the past or for setting targets against which future performance will be measured.

A ratio by itself is not particularly useful: it has to be compared with something. The basis for comparison can be with any one or all of the following:

1. a predetermined target, with the ratio being used within a firm for planning and management control purposes;
2. the level of the ratio in the past, with the trend being observed to see whether or not it is favourable;
3. the level of the ratio in similar firms, perhaps either in the same industry or the same risk class;
4. a norm, i.e. a standard that experts, bankers or analysts consider to be acceptable or, in other words, normal.

Ratios can be divided into at least four categories: those measuring profitability, those measuring liquidity, those measuring overall financial strength and those involving stock market data.

Definitions

An early problem we face is that we have different measures of profits. These include profit before interest and taxation (PBIT), profit on ordinary activities after taxation (PAT) and profit attributable to shareholders shown in the accounts as profit for the financial year. The exact profit figure we use in any ratio needs to be appropriate to which capital invested figure we are interested in. Some of the profits are distributed to the providers of loan capital as interest. Some of the profits belong to shareholders. It is essential to relate the correct profit figure to the appropriate source of finance.

Table 3.5 illustrates how the distribution of profit (earnings) is related to the sources of finance. Basically, interest is the return paid to the providers of loan capital, and any profits remaining after the deduction of interest and after deduction of tax on profits belongs to the providers of the equity finance (the shareholders). As can be seen from the profit and loss account, interest is deducted in arriving at the profits subject to tax. The taxation rules of most countries recognize interest as a tax-deductible expense. In addition interest has to be paid whether or not the company makes a profit.

The funds to purchase fixed and current assets typically come from sources such as those listed in Table 3.5. One item needs explanation: provisions. This item represents funds that have been set aside out of profits to meet future commitments. The funds do not need to be paid to outsiders, or spent on a specific need in the near future, so they can be used to acquire liquid assets which can be realized when the anticipated payments need to be made. In the case of Guinness this item mainly comprises deferred taxation and provisions made on acquisitions. Technically as at 31 December 1993 these funds belong to the shareholders, but they have been put aside for special purposes. As mentioned they will, most likely, have been invested in short-term assets.

An important point to appreciate is that there are no agreed definitions for each ratio. There are certainly no accounting or stock market standards on the subject. One company can, in its annual report, refer to its profits-to-assets ratio and use a different def-

Table 3.5 *Distribution of returns to sources of finance, Guinness 1993 (£m)*

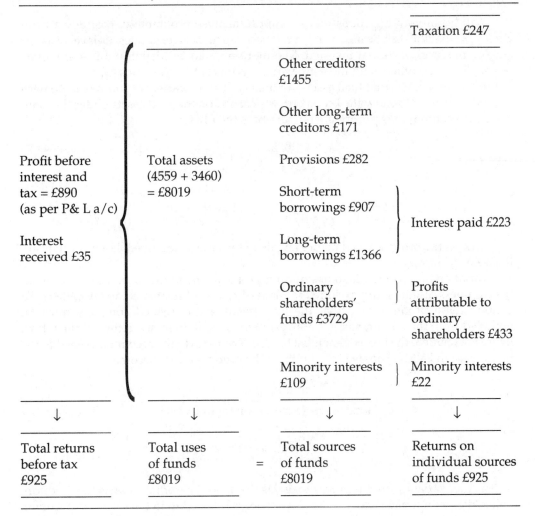

			Taxation £247
		Other creditors £1455	
		Other long-term creditors £171	
Profit before interest and tax = £890 (as per P& L a/c)	Total assets (4559 + 3460) = £8019	Provisions £282	
		Short-term borrowings £907	Interest paid £223
Interest received £35		Long-term borrowings £1366	
		Ordinary shareholders' funds £3729	Profits attributable to ordinary shareholders £433
		Minority interests £109	Minority interests £22
↓	↓	↓	↓
Total returns before tax £925	Total uses of funds £8019	=	Total sources of funds £8019	Returns on individual sources of funds £925

inition of profits and/or assets to another company using the same title to illustrate its performance. One textbook can use a different definition to another textbook. This is unfortunate for the student of the subject, who would like a precise definition. The important thing is for the user of the ratios to ensure that he or she is comparing like with like. The important thing is to be consistent. No one definition is right and the other wrong. But it is certainly wrong to compare two ratios, each prepared with a slightly different definition.

Financial ratios can be based on the numbers appearing in the accounting statements, i.e. the balance sheet and profit and loss account, the projection of cash flows and stock market statistics.

We shall illustrate the most important financial ratios with the figures taken from the 1993 Annual Report and Accounts of Guinness PLC. A summary of the balance sheet and profit and loss account was given in Tables 3.1 and 3.2. As with other companies not all the useful relevant information is shown on the face of these two statements, but is hidden away in the notes to the accounts. It is not possible to perform a meaningful analysis of the performance of any company without considering the details given in the notes to the accounts.

Profitability

We shall begin with the ratios that attempt to analyse profitability. Basically a company's profitability can be measured in relationship to its level of sales, its level of assets and/or the level of capital invested. The more popular profitability ratios are given below. There are others, and there are variations on each of the ratios given.

Table 3.5 illustrates that total assets are finances from a variety of sources. If we wish to produce a ratio to show the pre-tax profits earned on the total assets under the management's control, the appropriate numerator is the PBIT:

(a)
$$\frac{\text{PBIT}}{\text{total assets}} \times 100$$

$$= \frac{890}{8019} \times 100 = 11.10\%$$

This reflects the profits earned before tax on all the assets employed, however they are financed.

A variation on this ratio is to use trading profits as the numerator. If this is done in the Guinness case it would exclude the share of results of related company LVMH. To exclude these profits means that the investment in the related company must be excluded from the denominator. An investment is made to earn a return; if the return figure is excluded, the investment must be also. The notes to the accounts reveal that the investment in LVMH equals £1282 million. The ratio therefore becomes

(b)
$$\frac{\text{trading profits}}{\text{total assets less investment in LVMH}}$$

$$= \frac{938}{6737} \times 100 = 13.92\%$$

A further variation on this ratio is to use as the denominator total assets less creditors falling due within one year. This asset measure is referred to in the Guinness accounts as 'total assets less current liabilities', and is sometimes called 'capital employed'. It reflects the long-term capital investment in the business, and therefore those assets financed by 'creditors – amounts falling due within one year' are excluded.

It must be remembered that some of the total interest payable figure relates to short-term borrowings which are included in this 'creditors falling due within one year' figure. If the denominator in the ratio excludes short-term borrowings, the numerator must be the figure obtained before deducting interest paid on long-term loans but after interest paid on short-term borrowings. With this alternative approach, if this is not done, one is ignoring the cost of some of the short-term funds being used and exaggerating what is available to pay for long-term funds.

In the case of Guinness the profit and loss account shows a net interest charge of £188 million. This is the net charge, i.e. the difference between interest paid and interest received. The total payable is £223 million, and the interest received is £35 million. The appropriate note to the accounts only divides the interest figure between that paid on 'loans wholly repayable within five years' and that paid on 'loans of which any portion is due after five years'. Therefore it is not possible to ascertain the interest paid on the borrowings that have to be repaid within one year.

The alternative ratio is

(c)
$$\frac{\text{profit before tax and interest on bank loans and loan stock repayable after longer than one year}}{\text{total net assets (capital employed)}}$$

The above ratios have been calculated based on the total assets at the close of the accounting period. Yet another variation of this approach would be to use the average level of total assets employed over the accounting year as a denominator. The profits were in fact not necessarily earned on the level of assets on the last day of the accounting year. This point could be particularly important if a major acquisition of assets had been made near the year end.

A popular ratio is

(d)
$$\frac{\text{profit on ordinary activities after taxation}}{\text{total equity}}$$

$$= \frac{455}{3838} \times 100 = 11.85\%$$

It is measuring the return on the equity funds employed in the business, including those associated with minority interests. Because assets financed from current liabilities and longer-term loans are excluded from the denominator, the interest paid to the providers of loan funds has to be excluded from the numerator. This ratio could be based on profits before or after tax. Similarly, the total equity figure could include or exclude the minority interest figure. If it is excluded in the denominator, then of course the return belonging to minority interests (shown in the profit and loss account) has to be deducted from the numerator.

Another profit ratio is

(e)
$$\frac{\text{profit attributable to ordinary shareholders}}{\text{ordinary shareholders' funds}}$$

$$= \frac{433}{3729} \times 100 = 11.61\%$$

The numerator shows the after-tax profit figure attributable to the shareholders of Guinness PLC.

One issue that in the past made financial statement analysis comparisons difficult was the treatment of extraordinary items. These items which might have been unusual or non-recurring items were often treated differently by similar companies or even by the same company in successive years. Following the issue of FRS 3 by the ASB [6] extraordinary items have effectively been outlawed; financial statements now contain few such items. However, this process has produced its own problems in that, by proposing an all-inclusive approach to profit disclosure, comparisons are still difficult where companies have unusual income or costs arising. Many companies are now showing two earnings per share figures which is what Guinness has done. The first basic earnings per share figure of 22.9p gives an all-inclusive figure while the company also includes a figure of 31.7p which is the earnings per share before the exceptional provision for the investment in LVMH. Note 11 to the accounts states that this relates to non-recurring reorganization costs; the idea behind this is that analysts using the accounts will be doing so to try and predict future profits and cash flows. By highlighting continuing and normal activities it is hoped to provide more useful information to analysts and others using the accounts. The UK investment analysts association, the IIMR, have themselves issued recommendations on this and databases are now tending to use 'headline earnings per share' figures as recommended by the IIMR [7]. In our second profitability ratio we did in fact exclude the results and assets of LVMH.

A further important profit ratio is

(f)
$$\frac{\text{PBIT}}{\text{sales}} \times 100 = \frac{890}{4663} \times 100 = 19.09\%$$

This gives the profit margin on sales. It can be calculated on profit before or after tax, depending again on what one wishes to show.

The activity ratio

Asset turnover

The asset turnover indicates the number of times in a year that the firm's assets are being turned over; it shows how the assets are being used. The level of the ratio will of course vary from one industry to another. With a retailing company, for example, where the level of investment in assets does not need to be high, the asset turnover ratio will be much higher than in a heavy engineering or petrochemical company. For Guinness it is

$$\frac{\text{sales}}{\text{total assets}} = \frac{4663}{8019} = 0.58$$

In fact this ratio is one of the key ratios which indicates how a company is able (or is unable) to generate profits. Three key ratios, this one and (a) and (f) above, are linked by the following formula:

$$\frac{\text{PBIT}}{\text{total assets}} \times 100 = \frac{\text{PBIT} \times 100}{\text{sales}} \times \frac{\text{sales}}{\text{total assets}}$$

$$11.1\% = 19.09 \times 0.58$$

Investors want a level of profit to total assets commensurate with the level of risk. If the risks are the same in retailing as in heavy engineering then they will expect the same level of profitability. The fact that the asset turnover in heavy engineering is relatively low means that they need to obtain a higher profit margin on sales to give the same profit on assets as in retailing. In retailing they can get away with a low profit margin on sales, relying on their fast turnover of assets. If the retailer pushes up his profit margin, lowering the level of sales, he will reduce his asset turnover. Of course, these points are generalizations. But they indicate the way in which ratio analysis can be used.

This type of ratio analysis enables relevant questions to be asked. They focus attention on points where differences from expectations occur, and they indicate possible problem areas.

Problems with financial ratio analysis

Three points should be emphasized. One is that all ratios are imperfect and imprecise, and should only be treated as guidelines. Whilst users of financial statements should take account of these ratios, they ought not to regard them as providing the final word on all aspects of financial management and performance. For example, it can be dangerous to judge the liquidity and gearing position of a company on the basis of the balance sheet information, which relates to only one day in the year. The impression can be misleading, particularly if the company is engaged in a business subject to cyclical variations.

A second problem relates to comparisons. What are the targets for these ratios? No two companies are identical. Care has to be exercised when comparing the performance and financial position of one company with another. Of course, this is an even more difficult problem when comparing companies in different countries. Accounting conventions and practices differ from one country to another.

A third weakness is that the ratios are only as reliable as the accounting numbers on which they are based. The accounts of a company are prepared on the basis of a number of accounting conventions and assumptions. The users of ratios must be aware of what lies behind the accounting numbers.

Liquidity ratios

Perhaps the most important short-term ratio is the current ratio, i.e. the ratio of current assets to current liabilities, where current liabilities are creditors' amounts falling due within one year'. A second working capital ratio, referred to as the acid test, is the ratio of quick assets (cash plus money at short call plus debtors) to current liabilities. Other ratios include debtors to net sales, which shows the average speed of collection, and inventory to sales, which shows the number of days' sales held in inventory.

The financial manager must watch these ratios because any noticeable movement from one annual report to the next can encourage observers to draw conclusions about the liquidity position and creditworthiness of the company. Whether ratios such as these actually merit the practical importance ascribed to them as guides in financial decision-making is, of course, a debatable point.

While the theoreticians occupy themselves with the debate, the financial manager must be aware of the ratios and ensure that they do not move too far from the line of acceptable standards. The company does not exist in a vacuum, it coexists in a financial community, and while the 'arbitrary' standards of outsiders may have a low rating in company opinion, these constraints must nevertheless be acknowledged in the shaping of internal financial policy. In assessing the liquidity position of a company, outsiders use the current ratio and the liquidity ratio as two of their key indicators, and few companies can afford to ignore this fact entirely.

The current ratio

The current ratio is the ratio of current assets to current liabilities. The ratio for Guinness PLC, as at 31 December 1993, was 3460:2362 i.e. 1.46:1.

Traditionally the satisfactory norm accepted for the current ratio was 2:1 which was taken to indicate that the company's short-term financial position was healthy. With the financial problems of the 1970s and 1980s coupled with improved cash management techniques the acceptable level for this ratio has been reduced.

The current assets of a manufacturing company need to be well in excess of the current liabilities for a company to be classified as safe by anyone furnishing it with credit or a short-term loan. The reason for this cover is that one of the current assets – usually the largest – is the inventory. This is far from being the safest form of asset since the money it represents is not necessarily realizable in the short term, and even if it is, the actual returns from a hurried sale may amount to considerably less than valuation (cost or market value, whichever is lower) would suggest. Furthermore, inventory can deteriorate or become obsolete. Hence cover is required on the current assets over current liabilities.

The 'quick' ratio

The quick ratio is the ratio of current assets less inventory to current liabilities. For Guinness the ratio was 1638:2362, i.e. 0.69:1.

Inventory is excluded because it is not usually regarded as an asset that can quickly be turned into cash. There are of course items of inventory to which this does not apply, e.g. commodity stocks. The 'rule of thumb' for this ratio used to be 1:1, but again in the more difficult liquidity conditions of the 1970s and 1980s a lower ratio was found to be acceptable. The typical ratio declined from 0.9:1 in the early 1970s to 0.8:1 in the mid-1980s, and lower levels are now regarded as acceptable.

This reduction in the ratio can be achieved partly as a result of tighter credit control. If some companies reduce their net trade credit (debtors – creditors) it means that somebody else has to provide more. Often it is the smaller companies that lose, for they lack the financial power and bargaining strength of the largest companies. The financial manager has to steer the ratios along a route determined partly by the accepted lower limit below which suppliers may be unwilling to grant credit and banks to lend. It is not, of course, a matter of a single absolute level inviting approval or disapproval: there exists a range of values, certain regions of which are considered less desirable than others. It is considered bad financial management to allow the ratio to become too high. For example, a current ratio of 2.5:1 would make a company a very sound client for anyone thinking of giving it credit – but the company's shareholders might reasonably be less happy with the situation. It could mean that the company has not made the best use of its borrowing possibilities. It could mean that too many resources are tied up in current assets.

Such a situation needs to be remedied. This might call for the company to operate with lower levels of inventory, although the short-term effect of this policy may not lead to an improvement in the current ratio, for if the sale of the finished goods in inventory is speeded up, this will lead, if the goods are sold on credit, to an increase in debtors. The company may try to attempt to improve the situation by speeding up the collection of debts, although in the short run this will not necessarily improve the ratio, for as the debtors pay, cash is received which increases the level of one of the other current assets. It is only when the increased cash, made available through reducing current assets or increasing the current liabilities, is invested in long-term assets that the current ratio of the company will move nearer a normal level. The investment must, of course, be profitable to justify such action.

Liquidity ratios such as the two referred to above have two important limitations. First, any thorough assessment of a company's working capital position should take into account the bank overdraft ceiling. This is not usually shown in the annual accounts, but the freedom to borrow from the bank can put a remarkably different complexion on the recorded liquidity position. It could be perfectly safe to supply goods on credit to a company whose quick ratio is far below 1:1, if it had adequate overdraft facilities to call on. It is, of course, difficult to find out about these standby arrangements.

Secondly, these liquidity ratios are all static; they do not reflect the flux or potentially rapid changeability of a company's financial situation. If the current liabilities of the company exceed its liquid assets (i.e. if the quick ratio is less than 1:1), it is relevant to know how quickly the situation could be remedied without drastic measures. Earnings would be the important factor here.

As with many accounting ratios, acceptable levels of ratios will be linked to the type of industry or business being analysed. With Guinness we are dealing with a company which manufactures products and also keeps long-term inventories of maturing liquor. Its sales will be made on credit to customers who will pay at the end of their account period. Guinness is likely to have a high profit mark-up but slow turnover of stock. We can contrast this with a good retailer where nearly all sales will be for cash, inventories will be turned over quickly (particularly fresh foods) and credit will be taken from suppliers who will often be paid after the cash has been received for the sale of their product. These businesses may at first sight appear to be hopelessly insolvent as short-term liabilities may exceed short-term assets; however, because of the nature of the business they are able to operate successfully with these very low levels of liquidity. This emphasizes the point made earlier that comparisons need to be made with companies in similar industries or with industry-based norms or averages.

Cash ratio

The cash ratio compares the cash and marketable securities with the level of current liabilities. It indicates whether a firm has enough liquid resources on hand or nearly on hand to meet its current liabilities. It is an even stronger 'acid' test or quick ratio than the one referred to above. It is not of much importance. It ignores any borrowing facilities or lines of credit that the firm may have negotiated. It is concerned with the immediate payment of creditors, but ignores the payments to be received from debtors.

Financial efficiency ratios

The collection period is a well-used ratio. It indicates the period of time from when a sale is made to when the cash is received. In the Guinness example it equals

$$\frac{\text{debtors}}{\text{sales}} \times 365 = \frac{953}{4663} \times 365 = 75 \text{ days}$$

This period of time is not out of line with other manufacturing companies in the UK. Clearly it should be much lower for companies such as retail stores, for whom most of the sales are for cash and not on credit terms. The debtors figure used was obtained from the notes to the accounts and represents trade debtors. The balance sheet figure includes other debts not directly related to trading.

The other side of the coin to the collection period is the payments period. How long does it take a company to pay its creditors? If it takes longer to pay them than it does to collect from debtors it is on balance taking credit from other businesses. If it is the other way round it is supplying credit. Unfortunately very often it is the smaller company that ends up supplying credit because of its weak bargaining position.

The ratio that we need to ascertain the average payment period in days is

$$\frac{\text{creditors (relating to the supply of materials and goods)}}{\text{purchases of materials and goods}} \times 365$$

Unfortunately we cannot obtain this ratio from an analysis of published accounts. The creditors figure that is published covers all payments to be made, which includes wages and salaries, payments for the supply of electricity and gas, and even payments to be made on the purchase of assets. Some of these have to be paid within short periods of time, for example wages and salaries. To aggregate all the different types of creditors together and to ascertain their relationship with the cost of goods sold is not therefore a particularly useful exercise. If this is done it should certainly show a period less than the collection period, but that is hopefully because wages can at the most have a one week delay and salaries a one month delay.

There are three principal financial ratios that management can employ to indicate when questions should be asked about the level of stocks. There may be perfectly good reasons why a high level of inventory is being maintained. Nevertheless, at a broad-brush level the financial ratios can provide a starting point for enquiry.

The inventory-to-sales ratio estimates the number of days stock that the company has on hand:

$$\frac{\text{inventory}}{\text{cost of sales}} \times 365$$

Management can observe the movement of the ratio over time to see if any dangerous trends develop that cannot be explained by justifiable causes. It should be noted that it is the cost of sales figure which should be used as the denominator, rather than the sales revenue figure. This is because inventory is valued at cost price, as is the cost of sales. The sales revenue, however, includes profits.

In the Guinness example, if we take net trading costs as approximating to cost of sales, the number of days stock on hand becomes

$$\frac{1822}{3725} \times 365 = 178 \text{ days}$$

This is a particular high level of stock because of the large quantities of maturing spirits. For most manufacturing companies the stock on hand is in the region of 90 days. The ratio is obviously more useful if separate values are obtained for the different categories of inventory. This can easily be determined by management, but again the information is not available to an outsider as companies in the UK are not required to show the breakdown of inventories in their accounts.

Instead of expressing the inventory figure as the number of days' sales on hand, it is sometimes shown in the following form:

$$\frac{\text{sales}}{\text{inventory}}$$

This is the inventory-to-turnover ratio, and is again intended to indicate whether a company's inventories are justifiable in relation to its sales. In this case a high ratio indicates that management can move its inventory quickly. However, caution is necessary in the use of these ratios, for in many businesses the inventory figure can vary considerably with the date of the balance sheet. It might be satisfactory for a company to consider the movement of its own ratio over time, but if it starts to compare this ratio with that of other companies in the same industry, it must ensure that the balance sheets are for comparable dates. Another danger is to read too much into the expression 'number of days' inventory on hand'. As mentioned above, for the typical company this figure is about 90 days, but this does not mean that there is sufficient inventory to be able to meet 90 days sales if no more production takes place. This conclusion could only be drawn if the inventory was all finished goods, but the aggregate figure includes inventory not in a saleable form.

The third ratio that is concerned with inventory expresses inventory as a percentage of total assets, namely the inventory-to-assets ratio:

$$\frac{\text{inventory}}{\text{total assets}} \times 100$$

This ratio can also be affected by the closing date of the company's financial year, and is dependent upon the way that assets are valued.

In summary, the ratios at a highly aggregated level can point to the need for enquiry into how well the company's stock control policy is functioning.

Gearing (leverage) ratios

The guides or rules for determining the amount of funds that can be raised from loans are somewhat confusing. Perhaps the best known rule of thumb is the ratio of total debt to total assets:

$$\text{debt ratio} = \frac{\text{total debt}}{\text{total assets}} \times 100$$

where total debt includes all the current liabilities plus long- and medium-term loans, leasing obligations and tax liabilities. 'Total assets' is self-explanatory; it includes all fixed and current assets. Sometimes it is suggested that only tangible assets should be included in the calculations. This means excluding assets such as goodwill, patents and any capitalized expenses that are normally considered to have no commercial value. Very often the goodwill arises because upon the purchase of a company more was paid for the acquired assets than their book value; in such a case it could be argued that their real value was the price paid. Therefore a more realistic valuation of the assets of a company would include intangibles.

The rule of thumb in the UK for an acceptable ratio of total debt to total assets is 50% (or 1:2). This implies that it is reasonable to finance half the assets of the company by debt. Total debt always includes tax payments due in the next accounting period and sometimes deferred tax. The justification for including these last two items is that the amounts represent somebody else's money which is being used to finance the business and in time these liabilities will have to be paid.

The ratio for Guinness PLC as at 31 December 1993 was

$$\frac{2362 + 1366 + 171}{8019} = 48.6\%$$

There are two points to make about this ratio. One is a general point: the provisions for liabilities and charges (£282 million) have not been included as part of the total debt as at 31 December 1993. In this company's case it comprises a provision for deferred taxation and provision made on acquisitions. The second point is specific to Guinness. The company appears to have an average level of borrowing, with shareholders' funds financing 51.4% of the total assets:

$$\frac{3838 + 282}{8019} = 51.4\%$$

We have not yet considered in detail the composition of Guinness's fixed assets. If this is done it will be seen that the major asset is 'Acquired brands at cost' which amounts to £1395 million. This is about 30% of the total of fixed assets. The recognition and valuation of brand names is a controversial subject in accounting. There is a large problem in valuing a brand name. To be fair to Guinness the value that they show in their balance sheet is the price that they paid to purchase their brand names. Guinness were engaged in a controversial takeover of Distillers PLC in 1986 and did have to pay a 'high' price to acquire many brand names.

The brands the company owns are well-known whisky names like Bells, Johnnie Walker and White Horse and also include well-known gin and brandy names. In fact when we consult the notes to the accounts we find that the 'investments' figure is mainly represented by an investment in LVMH, the French company, which itself owns many famous brands some of which are capitalized on the LVMH balance sheet.

Two lessons can be learned from this for those engaged in analysing the accounts of companies:

1. the importance of footnotes and the statement of accounting policies given with the accounts;
2. the difficulty of comparison. If one were looking at the movement in the debt ratio of Guinness over time, one would have to allow for this dramatic change in valuation policy. If one were comparing Guinness's debt ratio with that of another company in the same industry one would need to ensure that the other company included the value of its brand names as an asset.

A slightly different way of looking at the borrowing position of a company is by means of the borrowing ratio:

$$= \frac{\text{long- and short-term borrowing}}{\text{capital employed (including short-term borrowing)}}$$

The calculation of this ratio needs some explanation. Bank overdrafts have traditionally been regarded as short-term debt and so have been included in the balance sheet under the heading of current liabilities. Certainly a bank has the legal right to recall an overdraft at comparatively short notice, and so it may be thought prudent always to treat the item as if it were a short-term liability. However, a number of companies tend to use overdrafts as if they were a continuing source of finance.

To obtain the total level of borrowing it is clearly necessary to add together overdrafts and longer-term loans. To obtain the figure of capital employed is a little more contentious. Traditionally capital employed (total net assets) was taken to be total assets minus current liabilities, where, as explained, current liabilities included overdrafts. However, to obtain comparable statistics for capital employed in different companies, it is necessary not to deduct the assets financed by overdrafts.

It should be emphasized that this approach to determining borrowing potential is dependent on the correct valuation of assets. It is not possible to compare the ratio for a company that has recently revalued its assets, and one that has a historical valuation. Often the comparatively simple act of revaluing assets can reveal increased borrowing possibilities.

The debt ratio is sometimes expressed in a slightly different form, namely total debt to shareholders' funds, where shareholders' funds are the sum of ordinary capital, preference capital and all reserves. The rule of thumb for the total debt to total asset ratio implied that half the assets could be financed by debt. The other half of the assets must be financed from the sum of ordinary capital, preference capital and reserves, namely shareholders' funds. Therefore the rule of thumb for this total debt to shareholders' funds ratio is 1:1. This means that the assets could decline in value or be reduced in value by up to 50% before threatening the security of the funds provided from loans. If the debt to shareholders' funds ratio is higher than the norm, say 2:1, the claims of the debt holders and the creditors are not so safe; assets need to fall in value by only a third before their claims are threatened.

Debt capacity is here being expressed as the relationship between the balance sheet assets financed by debt and those financed by equity. The ratio for Guinness is as follows:

$$\text{total debt : equity}$$
$$3899 : 3838$$
$$1.02 : 1$$

A problem with the use of such ratios as a guide to levels of debt is that the measure is static. Risk levels change over time, with the risk being the possible inability of the company to pay the interest or repay the debt. The balance sheet data on which the gearing ratios are based relate to one point of time, and do not reflect the cash flow and funds flow which can affect the level of risk.

A further problem arises because of new types of financial security that have been developed. These are called complex capital instruments. It is not always clear whether they should be treated as debt or equity. One such instrument is a 'convertible redeemable preference share'. Under certain conditions it is equity, under other conditions debt.

The method of valuing assets, and depreciation policy, will affect the debt-to-asset ratio. These accounting policies should have no bearing on the ability to repay debt.

A better measure of risk might be the interest cover, namely the number of times by which earnings exceed interest payments. Interest cover shows whether a company is capable of servicing a level of debt. The importance of this ratio became apparent when in 1988 a number of companies adopted accounting practices that made it more difficult to interpret their debt-to-equity ratio. Some companies, including Guinness and Grand Metropolitan, valued brand names and included these intangibles as assets in their balance sheet. This increased the reserves, which are shareholders' funds, and so improved the debt-to-equity ratio. Other companies, including Tube Investments, at the same time showed goodwill as a negative reserve in the balance sheet. Instead of adding goodwill to the asset side of the balance sheet it was deducted from the liabilities side, i.e. from equity. This reduces the debt-to-equity ratio. Tube Investments PLC presented debt-to-equity ratio calculations in their accounts, measuring equity both before and after deduction of goodwill. However, the company emphasized that in their opinion the number of times that profits cover the annual interest bill was a better indication of the level of gearing than the debt-to-equity ratio. The ratio that shows interest cover is

$$\frac{\text{profits available to pay interest}}{\text{interest payable}}$$

For Guinness in 1993 this was

$$\frac{890}{223} = 4.0$$

The interest payable figure is obtained from the notes to the accounts. The profit and loss account often only shows net interest, i.e. the difference between interest paid and interest received. An interest cover of 4.0 would be considered healthy.

Of course, the amount of cover that is required depends on the economic conditions of the time. If the level of economic activity is expected to grow or at least remain stable, then less cover would be required than if the economy was expected to decline. On an unsecured loan, at the present time, interest cover of about five times would be required. It is obviously possible to obtain a loan with less cover, but the risks are greater, and it would be more difficult and probably more expensive. The measure shows how much earnings can fluctuate before the interest payments are threatened. It is a good measure, but it does have limitations. The earnings figure is not the same as cash flow. The ability to make payments depends upon cash flow. Also one can ask what guide past earnings are to future earnings, with the risk depending on future earnings. A meaningful attempt to determine risk should study the cash flow patterns of the company, particularly during recession periods. It is these data that would give some guide to the possibilities of default, i.e. the possibility that the company will not be able to meet its fixed cash commitments.

In order to determine its own debt capacity, the management of a company should study its cash flow position. It should then attempt to persuade the institutions to accept these cash flow figures as the basis for determining its debt capacity and not merely to adopt the usual rules of thumb. By showing the cash flow that it can maintain, even in the worst circumstances, the company should be able to encourage sufficient confidence to obtain the level of debt it seeks.

Financial ratios as a measure of market risk

A number of studies have been undertaken to see whether ratios produced from a company's financial statements can be used to provide a proxy for capital market risk. The rate of return an investor expects on an equity share depends on the level of its market risk (its beta). Can accounting numbers be used to estimate this variable? Beaver *et al.* [8] calculated an accounting measure of earnings sensitivity risk which measures the relationship between the change in earnings of an individual company and movements in aggregate earnings of all companies. This measure of earnings sensitivity for a company, together with its level of gearing and payment ratio, provided a useful measure of market risk. Other researchers have obtained similar results, supporting the usefulness of financial ratios.

Cash flow ratios

The use of cash flow ratios to ascertain the financial strength of a company is quite common in certain industries. It is a normal part of credit analysis. Situations arise in which banks will provide medium-term loans, not on the basis of asset cover, but on the basis of projected cash flows. This position occurs with companies in the following industries or sectors:

- oil and gas
- mining
- property/real estate
- leasing.

Occasionally projected cash flows will also be used to ascertain the creditworthiness of a borrower in manufacturing industry. The bank will want statements of expected future cash flows provided by independent experts (for example mining engineers) rather than the in-house 'experts' of the potential borrower. Most project financing (i.e. North Sea Oil and Eurotunnel) is based on projected cash flow estimates.

Usually the banks will have their own rule of thumb as to the ratios based on cash flow that they consider desirable. One is a 'loan collateral value'. This could be written in a form such that the outstanding loans at any one time are always to be less than 50% of the discounted present value of the net cash flows from proven developed reserves. This is similar to the total debt cover ratio referred to in the Eurotunnel prospectus (see below). It can be used to determine at the outset how much borrowing will be allowed, and to monitor during the life of the investment whether adequate security is being provided.

A second common ratio is the debt service cover ratio. The typical wording of this ensures that the borrower will not allow the ratio of annual historic and projected cash flows (whichever is appropriate) to annual fixed charges to be less than 1.3–1.0 at any time.

These ratios would be monitored. They would normally be written into what is referred to as the 'borrower's negative covenants' which accompany any loan agreement. The banks are of course still taking risks when lending on the security of proven oil and mineral reserves. The cash flow depends not just on quantity but also on price. Commodity prices are very volatile over time.

An interesting use of financial ratios based not on accounting estimates of profits or asset values but on estimates of cash flow figures was shown in the original Eurotunnel prospectus. The tunnel is being financed mainly by funds obtained from a syndicate of banks. The level of drawings obtained from this syndicate may be in the form of cash or letters of credit issued to secure loans from third parties including the European Investment Bank and the Credit National. Under the credit agreement the funds made available could be drawn over a period of approximately seven years. A 'regular repayment schedule is designed to ensure repayment in full by 15th November 2005.'

The credit agreement contained a number of warranties and covenants by Eurotunnel in favour of the banks. The agreement listed a number of events, the occurrence of which would entitle the banks to take various actions, for example preventing further borrowing and going as far as allowing the banks to assume management of the project. These events included failing to achieve certain agreed target financial ratios.

The terms of the credit agreement provided for the banks to monitor the progress and expected cash flows of the project.

Extract from Eurotunnel Prospectus

Cash flow forecasts, . . . will be used in the calculation of cover ratios which are relevant in determining Eurotunnel's ability to make drawings under the facilities, to refinance the facilities, and to pay dividends and in determining the occurrence of an event of default. The ratios are as follows:

1. Bank debt cover ratio
This is the present value of forecast net cash flow (after deducting, *inter alia*, payments to refinancing creditors and, once the letters of credit in its favour have been released, the European Investment Bank) to 15th November, 2005 or (for certain purposes) to the current estimated maturity date of the facilities, and certain cash balances and a proportion of the interest reserve mentioned above, divided by the expected maximum amount of debt due to the banks lending under the Credit Agreement, all calculated as at a particular date.

Eurotunnel will not be entitled to make drawings under the facilities if, at the relevant time, the bank debt cover ratio is below 1.2, or to refinance borrowings under the facilities if the ratio is less than 1.3, or to pay dividends if the ratio is less than 1.25. If the ratio remains below 1.0 for 90 days or more this will be an event of default.

2. Total debt cover ratio
This is the present value of forecast net cash flow to 31st December, 2020 and certain cash balances and the interest reserve divided by the aggregate expected maximum amount of debt due to the banks, refinancing creditors and (once the letters of credit in its favour have been released) the European Investment Bank, all calculated as at a particular date.

Eurotunnel will not be entitled to make drawings under the facilities if, at the relevant time, the total debt cover ratio is below 1.9, or to refinance borrowings under the facilities if the ratio is less than 1.95. If the ratio remains below 1.3 for 90 days or more this will be an event of default.

3. Debt service cover ratio

This is the ratio of forecast net cash flow during any annual period to the estimated interest and principal repayments on both the credit facilities and refinancing debt during the same year. A ratio of at least 1.1 must be satisfied to permit refinancing to take place.

4. Dividend restrictions

The Credit Agreement imposes certain restrictions on dividend payments. Eurotunnel will not generally be permitted to pay dividends until after the last day upon which drawings may be made under the Credit Agreement and unless certain conditions are satisfied at the time of the declaration of the dividend. Broadly, these are that: (i) the interest reserve account referred to above is fully established; (ii) the aggregate repayments made up to that time (and projected for the next year) are not less than the aggregate amounts required by the repayment schedule; and (iii) the bank debt cover ratio (referred to above) is not less than 1.25. (Prospectus, Eurotunnel PLC)

A particularly interesting feature of the first two ratios is that, although they are calculated at particular dates, the numerator is not the actual cash flow for a past period, or even the forecast cumulative cash flow to the year 2005 or 2020, but the present value of the estimates of the future cash flow. We shall discuss the present value concept in Chapter 4.

One major difficulty of course is to forecast future cash flows. These forecasts will depend upon assumptions made about 'capital expenditure, operating expenditure, traffic and revenue, taxation, inflation, future interest rates and other economic factors. These variable assumptions will be determined on the basis of information supplied by Eurotunnel, the Maître d'Oeuvre and Eurotunnel's traffic and revenue consultants and reports commissioned by the banks. They will be discussed between Eurotunnel and the banks but, in the event of dispute, will be determined by the banks' (Prospectus, Eurotunnel PLC, 1987).

Financial ratios are an indication of the financial strength of a company. However, they are only an indication; they do not prove anything. They are a trigger mechanism; if a ratio is out of the ordinary, questions need to be asked. There might be perfectly satisfactory explanations for the particular size of the ratio, but the ratio does need an explanation.

A number of researchers have attempted to forecast company failure based on the levels of the company's financial ratios. One distinguished writer on this topic in the USA is Altman [9]. In one of his studies he examined characteristics of a number of companies that became bankrupt over a period, and the characteristics of a sample of companies that remained solvent over the period. He used a statistical technique known as multiple discriminant analysis in an attempt to differentiate between the two groups. Initially he considered 22 potentially helpful variables (ratios), but from this list five variables were selected 'as doing the best overall job together in the prediction of corporate bankruptcy'. Of these five, the liquidity variable which was found to be more useful for discrimination purposes than either the current ratio or the liquidity ratio was:

$$\frac{\text{working capital}}{\text{total assets}}$$

where working capital equals current assets minus current liabilities. The other four ratios were

$$\frac{\text{retained earnings}}{\text{total assets}}$$

$$\frac{\text{earnings before interest and taxes}}{\text{total assets}}$$

$$\frac{\text{market equity value}}{\text{book value of total debts}}$$

$$\frac{\text{sales}}{\text{total assets}}$$

The discriminant ratio model proved to have some success, with correct predictions in 94% of the bankrupt cases. Altman claims that 'investigation of the individual ratio movements prior to bankruptcy corroborated the model's findings that bankruptcy can be accurately predicted up to two years prior to actual failure'.

The one ratio that made the largest contribution to differentiating between the two groups was the current profitability ratio: earnings to total assets. In fact there was no evidence of bankruptcy in companies earning profits. This may seem an undramatic observation, but it does underline the importance of considering liquidity ratios in a dynamic context. A company may have a current liquidity problem, but if it is profitable, the flow of funds should be able to remedy the liquidity position. This explains the importance of considering the ratios in conjunction with the current flow of funds.

Altman found that the Z score model was a good forecaster of failure two years prior to bankruptcy. The model was able to predict with 95% accuracy one year prior to bankruptcy and with 72% accuracy two years prior to bankruptcy. The accuracy diminished substantially as the lead time to bankruptcy extended beyond two years. The model was not used to examine its usefulness in predicting the failure of small firms.

Following Altman, numerous studies attempted to improve and extend the bankruptcy classification process. One was a zeta model, which is claimed to be quite accurate at predicting bankruptcy up to five years prior to failure. This model used seven financial variables, covering return on assets, stability of earnings, interest cover, cumulative profitability, the current ratio, size and a gearing ratio. The most significant variable was found to be cumulative profitability, which is measured by the ratio of retained earnings to total assets.

There are two types of error that can arise with such predictions. One is that the model will fail to identify a company that is in financial distress, and the other is that the model will identify a company as having a high probability of failure when in fact it is sound.

It should be appreciated that all accounting numbers can do is indicate something has gone wrong within a company. The cause of the financial distress is usually bad management, and the mistakes have already been made before that fact is revealed in the financial accounts. Those investing in companies and those making credit available may well have left it too late if they wait for the publication of the annual accounts in order to assess the company's strengths and weaknesses. Analysts should look for the symptoms of failure. Such issues are discussed in Chapter 25 and 27.

A number of other researchers have used a similar technique to that of Altman. Multiple discriminant analysis attempts to find the combination of variables which best discriminates between two or more groups. This involves attributing weights to each variable such that the distribution of scores obtained for each group have the least overlap. In the application of this technique in the financial distress area one group consists of those companies that became bankrupt during the period of study, and the other group consists of those companies that survived. The variables used to discriminate are of course the financial ratios. Having determined the relative importance of each ratio, these weights can then be used to predict the chance of failure for any company.

Research in the UK in this area has been led by Taffler [10]. In his 1982 paper he reports that as a result of testing the usefulness of 50 ratios the five most significant from a discrimination point of view were

$$\frac{\text{earnings before interest and tax}}{\text{total assets}}$$

$$\frac{\text{total liabilities}}{\text{net capital employed}}$$

$$\frac{\text{quick assets}}{\text{total assets}}$$

$$\frac{\text{working capital}}{\text{net worth}}$$

$$\frac{\text{cost of sales}}{\text{stock}}$$

The first two of these five ratios were found to be the most significant. The first ratio is a measure of the flow of funds into the business resulting from the company's own operations. It was also found to be important in Altman's study. The second ratio shows the outside claims on the resources of the business. The fifth ratio indicates stock turnover.

The Bank of England has looked at the potential of this technique [11]. Their model did not show results that were particularly encouraging. The Bank concluded that 'careful analysis of accounts over a long period together with scrutiny of other published information is likely to provide the best, indeed the only basis for any adequate assessment by an outsider of the financial position of a company'.

The discriminant approach is still used, however, to indicate companies at financial risk. A financial data service is available in which figures are produced that indicate the chance of a particular company failing.

There are many theoretical problems with this type of statistical analysis. There are also problems with the accounting data. Nevertheless, the results of these studies and other similar types of work are used by financial analysts and bankers.

Many of the studies have only used financial ratios. A few studies used mixed models (with some cash flow variables and some financial ratios). The cash flow ratio most often used in such studies is cash flow to total debt. Other cash flow statistics used in the prediction of failure are cash to sales, cash to current liabilities and cash flow from operations.

It is hoped that there is more to the use of this approach than just 'self-fulfilling prophesies'. If bankers and analysts use the technique and believe in it, then any company that ranks badly as a result of the analysis might well find its funds cut off. As a result the company will fail and the technique will have been said to have worked!

3.6 Conclusions

A very popular way of analysing the performance of a business is through the use of financial ratio analysis. Impressions formed on the basis of this analysis can affect decisions as to whether to supply the business with goods on credit, whether bank loans will be made available, whether a company will be given a stock market listing, and whether or not to buy the company's shares.

Accounting by its nature has to be an inexact subject. It is necessary to make many assumptions in preparing a set of financial accounts. All attempts to value a company must be estimated, whether based on measuring asset values or based on expected future cash flows. Nevertheless, those operating in the stock market must make decisions every day on what they believe should be the value of a company's shares.

There is a major debate as to whether those who operate in the stock market are or are not fooled by attempts to manipulate accounting earnings figures. There is much literature on how capital markets respond to accounting numbers. There is also concern as to how the system of rewarding managers affects reported earnings. These issues will be returned to later in the book.

3.7 Key terms

Accounting concepts
Accounting policies
Accruals accounting
Capital maintenance
Cash flow

Financial gearing
Financial ratios
Profitability versus liquidity
Valuation basis

3.8 Revision questions

1. What is the fundamental objective of financial reports?
2. What are accounting standards? Why are they important to a financial analyst?
3. What is the difference between cash flow accounting and accrual accounting, and which is most useful to the financial analyst?
4. Before embarking on the preparation of a set of financial ratios, which are the key areas of the accounting policy of the company that you would enquire into?
5. What are the limitations of financial ratios?
6. What are the weaknesses of gearing ratios?
7. A large amount of research has been undertaken attempting to use financial ratios to predict bankruptcy. Is there not a danger that if this work is successful it will result in self-fulfilling prophecies?

3.9 References

1. Accounting Standards Committee (1975) *The Corporate Report*, Accounting Standards Committee, London.
2. Ball, R.J. and Brown, P.B. (1968) An empirical evaluation of accounting income numbers. *Journal of Accounting Research*, Autumn.
   Beaver, W.H. (1968) The information content of annual earnings announcements. *Journal of Accounting Research*, 67–92.
3. Beaver, W.H., Clarke, R. and Wright, W. (1979) The association between unsystematic security returns and the magnitude of the earnings forecast error. *Journal of Accounting Research*, Autumn.
4. Kaplan, R.S. and Roll, R. (1972) Investor evaluation of accounting information; some empirical evidence. *Journal of Business*, April.
   Watts, R. (1986) Does it pay to manipulate EPS? In *The Revolution in Corporate Finance* (eds J.M. Stern and D.H. Chew, Basil Blackwell).
5. Accounting Standards Committee (1972) *Disclosure of Accounting Policies*, Accounting Standards Committee, London.
6. Accounting Standards Board (1992) Financial Reporting Standard No. 1: *Reporting Financial Performance*, October.
7. Statement of Investment Practice No. 1 (1993) *The definition of headline earnings*, Institute of Investment Management and Research, September.
8. Beaver, W.H., Kettler, P. and Scholes, M. (1970) Association between market determined and accounting determined risk measures. *Accounting Review*, October.
9. Altman, E.I. (1968) Financial ratios, discriminant analysis and the prediction of corporate bankruptcy. *Journal of Finance*, September.
   Altman, E.I. (1974) Evaluation of a company as a going concern. *Journal of Accounting*, December.
10. Taffler, R.J. (1982) Forecasting company failure in the UK using discriminant analysis and financial ratio data. *Journal of the Royal Statistical Society*, Series A, **146** (3), 342–58.
    Taffler, R.J. (1983) The Z-score approach to measuring company solvency. *Accountants Magazine*, 91–6, March.

Taffler, R.J. and Tisshaw, H. (1977) Going, going, gone – four factors which predict. *Accountancy*, 50–4, March.
11. Techniques for assessing corporate financial strength (1982) *Bank of England Quarterly Bulletin*, 221–3, June.

There are many textbooks on financial accounting and some on financial statement analysis. Those below are the main texts dealing with the latter topic. The Altman book shows what can happen when things go wrong.

Altman, E.I. (1992) *Corporate Financial Distress: A Complete Guide to Predicting, Avoiding and Dealing with Bankruptcy*, John Wiley, New York.
Foster, G. (1986) *Financial Statement Analysis*, 2nd edn, Prentice Hall.
Holmes, G. and Sugden, A. (1994) *Interpreting Company Reports and Accounts*, 5th edn, Woodhead-Faulkner, London.
Parker, R.H. (1994) *Understanding Company Financial Statements*, 4th edn, Penguin.
Rees, W. (1990) *Financial Analysis*, Prentice Hall.
Samuels, J.M., Brayshaw, R.E. and Craner, J.M. (1994) *Financial Statement Analysis in Europe*, Chapman & Hall.

Note: Certain of the following problems are concerned with dividend yields and price earnings ratios. These topics are dealt with in Chapter 12.

1. (a) Complete the balance sheet and sales information shown for Jones Software Company using the following financial data:
   Quick assets ratio, 0.8:1
   Total assets turnover, 1.5×
   Average collection period, 36.5 days
   Inventory turnover, 5×
   Net return on shareholders' funds, 20%

   Balance sheet and sales data

	£		£
Equity		Fixed	
shares	—	assets	—
Retained		Inventories	—
earnings	65 000	Amounts	
Long-term		receivable	—
debt	40 000	Cash	—
Creditors	—		
		Total	
		assets	200 000
		Profit after	
		interest	
Sales	—	and tax	20 000

   (b) C. Barngrover and Company had earnings per share of £4 last year, and it paid a £2 dividend. The book value per share at year-end was £40, while the total retained earnings increased by £12 million during the year. Barngrover has no preferred stock, and no new equity shares were issued during the year. If Barngrover's year-end debt (which equals its total liabilities) was £120 million, what was the company's year-end debt-to-assets ratio?

   (c) What are the limitations of ratio analysis?

2. A friend of yours who has invested in the equity shares of Baxter PLC has recently received a copy of its annual report. He enjoys looking at the pictures in the early

part of the report, but finds the financial accounts confusing. This is the first time that he has seen a set of published accounts. He seeks your advice and asks the following questions.

(a) How, if at all, can these accounts give him any guidance as to the future profitability of the company?

(b) In the ten year summary, many financial ratios are shown; these look impressive. Are there any dangers in relying on the numbers shown in these ratios?

(c) From the profit and loss account he can see that the company has made a profit but, given the circumstances in which the firm operates, how can he tell if this profit is satisfactory?

(d) He has read in the newspaper that although Baxter PLC is profitable it is experiencing liquidity problems. He asks how this can be – the company is either doing well or it is not – and you are asked to explain.

(e) Finally, he asks what figures in the accounts he should look at in order to see whether the company has liquidity problems, and at what figures he should look to see whether there could be long-term financing problems.

You are required to answer your friend's questions.

3. The following is an extract from the annual accounts of Madness Ltd, an unquoted limited company, for the year ended 31 May 1989.

Profit and loss account

	£000	£000
Turnover		5600
Profit for the year after deducting:		1200
Bank interest	300	
Less: Corporation tax liability		200
Profit after tax		1000
Less: Dividends on preference shares	400	
Proposed dividend on ordinary shares	500	900
Retained profit		100

Balance sheet

	£000	£000
Fixed assets at cost		9400
Less: Aggregate depreciation		2400
		7000
Current assets		
Stock/inventory	3800	
Debtors	1200	
Shares held in quoted companies	650	
Bank and cash	350	
	6000	

Less: Current liabilities

Creditors	2300	
Corporation tax 1988–9	200	
Proposed dividends	500	
	3000	3000
		10 000

Authorized and issued capital

2000k ordinary shares of £1 each	2000
4000k preference shares of £1 each	4000
	6000
Retained profit	1000
Bank loan repayable 1996	3000
	10 000

You are required to write a report for a prospective investor regarding the profitability and financial stability of this company. Your report should be written around appropriate ratios and include reference to the earnings per share, the return on capital, the working capital and liquidity position, the gearing/leverage, a suitable price for each ordinary share, given that the price-to-earnings ratio of comparable quoted companies is about 7.

4. The trading and profit and loss accounts and the balance sheets for X Ltd and Y Ltd for the year ended 31 March 1988 are as shown below.

Trading and profit and loss accounts for the year ended 31 March 1988

	X Ltd £	Y Ltd £		X Ltd £	Y Ltd £
Opening stock	15 000	5 000	Sales	100 000	100 000
Purchases	80 000	86 000	Closing stock	25 000	11 000
Gross profit	30 000	20 000			
	125 000	111 000		125 000	111 000
Overheads	10 900	800			
Interest	2 000	7 000			
Dividends	3 000	5 000			
Taxation	6 000	—			
Net profit before extraordinary items	8 100	7 200	Gross profit	30 000	20 000
	30 000	20 000		30 000	20 000
Extraordinary items	2 000	(5 000)			

Balance sheets as at 31 March 1988

	X Ltd £	Y Ltd £		X Ltd £	Y Ltd £
Share capital (£1 shares)	50 000	50 000	Fixed assets	80 000	99 000
Profit and loss account	40 000	10 000	Current assets		
			Stocks	25 000	11 000
Shareholders' capital			Debtors	10 000	7 500
employed	90 000	60 000	Cash at bank	5 000	3 500
Loans	20 000	50 000			
Current liabilities	10 000	11 000			
	120 000	121 000		120 000	121 000

Both companies are quoted on the Stock Exchange. At 30 June 1988 the share price of X Ltd was £3.24 and the share price of Y Ltd was £2.16.

You are required (a) to calculate the liquidity, profit and gearing ratios of the two companies that would be of interest to investors, and (b) to calculate the price-to-earnings ratios of the two companies and give the reasons that might explain the difference in the market's evaluation of them.

5. You have been asked by a client to assess the financial position of Everrett PLC. The books for the year ended 31 December 1987 have been closed, but the profit and loss account and the balance sheet have not yet been prepared.

Before answering a number of questions raised by the client it is necessary for you to prepare the profit and loss account for the year and the closing balance sheet. You are given the following trial balance as at 31 December 1987.

	£	£
Ordinary shares (£1 par value)		6 000
Reserves as at 1 January 1987		1 900
Turnover		15 000
Distribution costs	750	
Interest paid	200	
Stock at 1 January 1987	4 000	
Purchases	8 800	
Debtors	5 000	
Prepayments	200	
Bank overdraft		600
Preference dividends	100	
Creditors		2 100
Cash in hand	500	
Fixed assets (net)	9 050	
Debenture loan		2 000
Preference shares		1 000
	28 600	28 600

Additional information:
stock at 31 December 1987, £3800
corporation tax on 1987 profits, £890
depreciation to be provided, £1000
dividends payable out of this year's profits, £600
the share price at 1 January 1987 was £5.00
and at 31 December 1987 was £5.60.

(a) For each of the following, calculate ratios (two in each case) that will be helpful in appraising the company.
  (i) How liquid is the company?
  (ii) How well is it managing its short-term assets?
  (iii) How profitable is the company?
  (iv) From a long-term point of view does the company appear to have the ability to raise funds for investment without seeking new funds from shareholders?

(b) What rate of return was earned by an ordinary shareholder of the company over the last year, assuming that he purchased his shares at 1 January 1987? What was the dividend cover?

(c) What was the dividend yield as at 31 December 1987? What was the price-to-earnings ratio as at 31 December 1987?

(d) What does the price-to-earnings ratio of a company indicate about the market's expectations? What explanation can you offer for the fact that in the Drapery and Stores sector Bodyshop International had a price-to-earnings ratio of 50:1 and Marks and Spencer a price-to-earnings ratio of 17:1?

6. Shown below are the profit and loss account for Hopkins Ltd for the year ending 31 December 1988 and the balance sheets for the company as at 31 December 1988 and 31 December 1989.

Profit and loss account for year ended 31 December 1989

	£	£
Sales		85 000
Cost of goods sold		40 000
		45 000
Depreciation	5000	
Interest paid	5000	10 000
		35 000
Extraordinary item		10 000
		25 000
Dividend proposed		15 000
		10 000

Balance sheets as at 31 December

	1988	1989
	£	£
Equity	100 000	110 000
Reserves	70 000	80 000
Loans	50 000	30 000
Creditors	35 000	40 000
Dividends proposed	5 000	15 000
	260 000	275 000
Fixed assets (net)	150 000	170 000
Stock	30 000	15 000
Debtors	20 000	50 000
Cash	60 000	40 000
	260 000	275 000

(a) Calculate the cash collected from customers.

(b) Calculate the cost of goods purchased during the year.

(c) Calculate the payments made to suppliers of goods.

(d) Give a cash flow statement analysing the changes between the opening and the closing cash balances.

(e) Explain to a businessman why the profit performance of a company over a one year period might bear little relationship to the cash flow position.

Investment appraisal: basic methods

4.1	Introduction	73
4.2	Compound interest	74
4.3	Discounting and present values	75
4.4	The net present value decision rule	77
4.5	Terminal value	79
4.6	Yield: the internal rate of return	79
4.7	The multiple yield problem	83
4.8	Comparing alternative investments	85
4.9	The modified internal rate of return	87
4.10	Interest rate changes and discounted cash flow	90
4.11	Different interest rates for borrowing and lending	91
4.12	Theoretical justification for net present value	92
4.13	The separation theorem	94
4.14	Computer program	96
4.15	Conclusions	98
4.16	Key concepts	98
4.17	Revision questions	99
4.18	References	99
4.19	Further reading	99
4.20	Problems	100

The methods of investment appraisal as an essential part of the capital budgeting process have a wide scope and range of application. In this chapter and those that follow we examine techniques that are used extensively in business, industry and government and which also apply to individual investors in personal financial management. A range of models and topics are included to reflect the varying circumstances of the users of the techniques.

Capital budgeting aims to make the best use of the investor's resources. The methods must take into account the differences between a major public company, a small private firm and an individual person in terms of fund-raising opportunities, the conditions on which money is supplied and the ability to bear risk. But there are also common features between these cases, most notably in the logical structure of the problems, and we shall be studying principles that apply to all of them.

By the end of the chapter you will have seen the importance of the discounted cash flow approach and will have learnt to use discounting to assess investment proposals in three ways. You will also be able to take account of complicating factors and make judgements between competing projects.

4.1 Introduction

Corporate investment decision-making is set in the context of the company's capital budgeting process and its overall aims, culture and environment. Capital budgeting involves decisions on the sources and scale of funding as well as the selection of investment projects. The natural environmental effects and regional and national economic impacts of the larger investment decisions will be taken into account by senior management in the decision process as a whole. This is best accomplished if management are armed with appropriate and accurate financial information from the investment appraisals. The objective is to provide management with the best possible quantitative basis on which to ground the final decision. At less significant levels of investment expenditure, the appraisal methods can generate rules that can be applied routinely by middle management. Most importantly it should be noted that decision rules and processes can only be applied to those projects that have been developed to the proposal stage or otherwise sought out.

An investment can be thought of as an action which changes the cash flow of the decision-maker. The forms that corporate investment takes include expenditures on buildings, equipment, land, research and development, changes in stock level, shares, deposits at financial institutions and the extension of credit. Major public sector investments include economic development projects, schools, highways and other components of infrastructure. Private individuals make investment decisions when purchasing a house and major durable goods such as cars. Making such investments requires the outlay of funds at certain times, usually including the present, while income (or less tangible benefits) are produced at other times (usually in the future). Income benefits from private sector investments are usually more readily identifiable than those from within the public sector. In the corporate realm, major investments not only change a company's cash flow, they also affect its financial position measured by key financial ratios and other statistics. Changes in several measures of performance may need to be taken into account and this topic is considered in a later chapter.

Here we appraise investment possibilities in terms of the **cash flow** alterations that they bring about. This involves both the timing of returns and costs and an appropriate rate or rates of interest. Cash flow items are **discounted** (multiplied by a factor less than one) according to their distance from the present and the rate of discount used. All increases or decreases in revenues and costs (including tax payments) brought about by a project are *relevant* to the calculations. Note that the process of depreciation does not itself change the project's cash flow, and is therefore not included. But depreciation allowances may affect cash flow through taxation payments. This topic is discussed in Chapter 5. The study of these **discounted cash flow** (DCF) methods of investment appraisal begins with a description of compound interest.

4.2 Compound interest

The concept of compound interest underlies all financial transactions involving time delayed receipts and payments. For commercial reasons some loans are quoted in terms of simple interest, but the packages are constructed following calculations in compound terms.

Consider a deposit account paying interest at 10% annually compounded. Suppose that the sum deposited initially, the **principal**, is £1. At the end of one year the investor has £1.10 in the account. If this amount is left on deposit there is no reason to treat this investor less well than a new customer making a deposit of £1.10 at this time. So the entire £1.10 (made up of the principal of £1 and the first year's interest of £0.10) is available to earn interest in the second year. This is the key point of compounding – **interest itself gains interest**.

Interest in the second year is 10% of £1.10 (£0.11) so the total in the account after two years is £1.21. The 'pound's progress' is shown in Table 4.1.

At 10% compound interest, after n years the principal of £1 becomes $£(1 + 0.1)^n$. Generalizing, £1 invested for n years at $100r\%$ becomes $£(1 + r)^n$. Table 1 (page 1015) gives these *future* or *terminal values* for various r and n. So £1 invested at 10% for seven years grows to £1.9487 while £1 invested for 15 years at 25% becomes £28.4217.

From Table 1 we can see the substantial consequences of quite small changes in interest rates when long periods of time are involved. For example, at 20% compound £1 becomes £38.3376 after 20 years, but at 21% the original £1 produces £45.2593 after 20 years. A 5% increase in the rate of interest (which has risen one percentage point from

Table 4.1 *Growth of £1 at 10%*

Principal	After one year	After two years	After three years
1	1 + 0.1(1) = 1.1	1.1 + 0.1(1.1) = 1.1(1 + 0.1) = $(1 + 0.1)^2$ = 1.21	1.21 + 0.1(1.21) = 1.21(1 + 0.1) = $(1 + 0.1)^3$ = 1.331

20 to 21) has produced a much larger proportional increase in the end result – over 18%. If the horizon alters when high rates of interest are applied there will be large changes in the terminal sum. For example, at 30% £1 becomes £190 after 20 years or £705 after 25 years. This highlights future dangers in debt rescheduling under high rates of interest.

If the principal sum is more than £1, the future value is found by multiplication of the principal by the appropriate factor from Table 1 as illustrated in the following problem.

Problem 4.1

Find the future value of £75 invested for 12 years at 8%.

Answer

For $r = 0.08$ and $n = 12$ the compound interest factor given in Table 1 is 2.5182. Thus the original £75 would accumulate to £75(2.5182) = £188.87.

It can on occasion be necessary to find the principal required to generate a particular future value. An illustration is given in the following problem.

Problem 4.2

How much would have to be invested originally in order to produce £250 after 16 years at 14%?

Answer

For $r = 0.14$ and $n = 16$ the compound interest factor is 8.1372. So if the initial sum invested is £S, then it is required that £S(8.1372) = £250. Thus:

$$S = \frac{250}{8.1372} = 30.72$$

This problem leads to consideration of present values.

The required principal in Problem 4.2 is the discounted present value or simply the **present value** of the future sum. The present value of £1 depends on the number of years – or, more generally, the number of compounding periods – and the rate of discount that are involved. The relationship is:

4.3 Discounting and present values

$$PV = \frac{1}{(1 + r)^n} \qquad (4.1)$$

for if PV is invested now, its future value after n years compound interest at $100r\%$ will be $PV(1 + r)^n = 1$. Table 2 (page 1018) gives present value or **discount factors** for various values of r and n. For instance, £1 due after 16 years at 14% has a present value of £0.1229 and £250 due at this time has a present value of $250 \times 0.1229 = £30.72$. All the entries in this table are the reciprocals of the corresponding entries in Table 1, hence 0.1229 is the reciprocal of 8.1372.

The present value of a stream of receipts or payments is found by adding the present values of the individual items. So if receipts of £100, £150 and £200 occur at the end of each of three consecutive years, then the present value of this income stream at 10% interest will be:

$$PV = \frac{100}{(1 + 0.1)} + \frac{150}{(1 + 0.1)^2} + \frac{200}{(1 + 0.1)^3}$$

or, more conveniently, using the discount factor table:

$$PV = 100 \times 0.9091 + 150 \times 0.8264 + 200 \times 0.7513$$
$$= 364.93$$

Problem 4.3

Find the present value of £450 to be received four years from the present at an interest rate of 8%.

Answer

The discount factor given by Table 2 for $r = 0.08$ and $n = 4$ is 0.7350. So the present value is:

$$£450 \times 0.7350 = £330.75$$

Problem 4.4

Using a 15% discount rate, find the present value of the cash flow:

$t=0$	$t=1$	$t=2$	$t=3$
−600	750	−150	1050

Answer

A convenient layout for the workings is:

Year	Sum	Discount factor	PV
0	−600	1	−600
1	750	0.8696	652.20
2	−150	0.7561	−113.42
3	1050	0.6575	690.38
		Total	629.16

The −600 which is the **initial outlay** of 600 on the project generating the cash flow has a discount factor of unity since it is assumed payable at once and so is its own present value. The loss of 150 in the second year might be caused by a cyclical recession in the market, the entry of a competitor or overhaul of equipment. The figure 629.16 is the **net present value**.

Investment projects typically generate a series of returns S_t where the subscript t is the timing of the return. If there are n returns in all, they could be written out in full as S_1, S_2, S_3, S_4, ..., where S_1 is the return after one year, S_2 is the return after two years and so on. It is assumed that cash flow components arise at equally spaced intervals (adjustment can be made in cases where this is not so).

The present value of the entire n year stream is

$$PV = \frac{S_1}{(1+r)} + \frac{S_2}{(1+r)^2} + \frac{S_3}{(1+r)^3} + \ldots + \frac{S_n}{(1+r)^n}$$

This can be written more concisely in **summation** or **sigma notation** as:

$$PV = \sum_{t=1}^{n} S_t(1+r)^{-t} \tag{4.3}$$

The symbol Σ 'sigma' in equation (4.3) tells us to sum all terms which follow, the form of these terms in this case being $S_t(1+r)^{-t}$ over the range of values of t from $t = 1$ up to and including $t = n$.

The terms S_t might not all be positive. In order to secure the returns it will usually be necessary to invest money in one or more years. If an investment of £K now is required to secure the returns S_t then (4.3) is said to be the **gross present value** (GPV) of the investment, and the GPV minus K (the initial outlay) gives the **net present value** (NPV):

$$NPV = \sum_{t=1}^{n} S_t(1+r)^{-t} - K \tag{4.4}$$

For an individual investment, the single-project NPV decision rule is:

Invest in the project if the NPV is positive. Do not invest if the NPV is negative.

If NPV = 0 the rule is inconclusive; it makes no difference to the investor in terms of present value whether the project is accepted or rejected. The rule can be summarized in tabular form:

Outcome	Decision
NPV > 0	Accept
NPV < 0	Reject
NPV = 0	Inconclusive

A rationale for the rule is as follows. GPV is an amount of money which is equivalent to all the returns in that if it was invested now at $100r\%$ it would just generate the returns. That is, it would allow amounts S_t to be withdrawn in each year t. £K is the sum of money which has to be paid now to secure the returns S_t, so if this price, K, is less than GPV then the deal is good. To illustrate this point consider the returns:

$t = 1$	$t = 2$
220	363

At a 10% rate of discount GPV is 500. Now consider an investment of £500 at $t = 0$. By $t = 1$ this becomes 500(1.1) = 550, so if 220 is then withdrawn, 330 remains on deposit and becomes 330(1.1) = 363 by $t = 2$. So if GPV > K (and therefore NPV > 0) this means that the present value of the stream of returns exceeds the present value of the money required to secure them. If, however, GPV < K, then the initial outlay exceeds the value now of the returns that the outlay brings. Consequently the proposed investment is rejected. GPV is the single-figure equivalent of the stream of net returns and the NPV decision rule compares like with like.

We shall frequently refer to the 'correctness' of the NPV decision rule, and while detailed justification of this view is given in sections 4.11 and 4.12 some general remarks are appropriate here.

The reason that NPV gives the most appropriate – the 'correct' – decision for investors is that when one rate of interest applies to all financial transfers, the higher the value of

NPV achieved the greater are the cash sums that can be spent in **every** time period. This is because the returns can be redistributed through time at the uniform rate of interest to suit the requirements of the investor. (Cases where there is not a uniform rate of interest are considered in section 4.11.) Financial markets allow consumption decisions to be made separately from the choice of investment, subject only to limits given by the value of NPV (the present value of consumption expenditures must not exceed NPV).

To illustrate the NPV decision rule, consider the investment in the following problem.

Problem 4.5

A company can purchase a machine at the price of £2200. The machine has a productive life of three years and the net additions to cash flows (after tax and including scrap value at the end of the third year) at the end of each of the three years are £770, £968 and £1331. The company can buy the machine without having to borrow and the best alternative is investment elsewhere at an interest rate of 10%. Should the machine be bought?

Answer

If the company chooses the investment it loses the chance to earn 10% compound interest. This provides the rate (in this context) to be used in the discount calculations. Putting the data into (4.4) gives the NPV as:

$$NPV = \frac{770}{(1.1)} + \frac{968}{(1.1)^2} + \frac{1331}{(1.1)^3} - 2200 = 300$$

The investment is worthwhile and the machine should be bought. It can be convenient to put the workings into a table:

Year	Sum	Discount factor	PV
0	−2200	1	−2200
1	770	0.9091	700
2	968	0.8264	800
3	1331	0.7513	1000
		NPV =	+300

The discount rate is very important to the NPV decision rule. For example, if the discount rate used to evaluate the investment in the machine had been 20% ($r = 0.2$) instead of 10% ($r = 0.1$), then the NPV of the project would have been negative. The workings in this case are:

Year	Sum	Discount factor	PV
0	−2200	1	−2200.00
1	770	0.8333	641.64
2	968	0.6944	672.18
3	1331	0.5787	770.25
		NPV =	−115.93

and the project should be rejected because although the investment in the machine is profitable in a sense (the undiscounted sum of the returns exceeds the cost of the machine) **it is not profitable enough** when there is the chance to earn 20% on the money needed to buy the machine. The discount rate represents the *opportunity cost* of the investment.

Sometimes *net terminal value* (NTV), or as it is sometimes called **net future value**, is a convenient yardstick for projects and it gives the same accept or reject decision as NPV. NTV is what the investor will end up with over and above the sum if the project was rejected. NTV is the **end-of-project excess**. The NTV decision rule for a single investment can be expressed as follows:

Outcome	Decision
NTV > 0	Accept
NTV < 0	Reject
NTV = 0	Inconclusive

Suppose that the firm in Problem 4.5 had £3000 available for investment. If the machine is bought, £800 remains and can be invested at 10%, becoming £880 after one year when it is added to the first receipt from the project, £770, and carried forward at 10%. After three years of this reinvestment process, at the end of the project the investor will have:

$$\{[(3000 - 2200) \times 1.1 + 770] \times 1.1 + 968\} \times 1.1 + 1331 = 4392.3$$

Subtract from this sum the amount that would have been obtained if the machine had not been bought:

$$3000 \times (1.1)^3 = 3993$$

the result is the NTV of the project:

$$NTV = 4392.3 - 3993 = 399.3$$

Recall that the NPV was 300 and note that the NTV is $300 \times (1.1)^3$ which shows the link between NTV and NPV. In the one discount rate case, for an n period project:

$$NTV = NPV (1 + r)^n$$

$$= \sum_{t=1}^{n} S_t(1 + r)^{n-t} - K(1 + r)^n \tag{4.5}$$

The example illustrates an important point about NPV. For the NPV formula to be appropriate money coming in should be reinvested at the rate of discount. This also applies to the case of finance by borrowing, with returns being used to repay capital and interest on the borrowed sum. In NTV the reinvestment process is clear, and NPV is obtainable from NTV by dividing by $(1 + r)^n$. If the returns are held as cash and if the £3000 would also be held as cash, then the appropriate discount rate is 0%.

Occasionally it may be necessary to assess a project at a point **within** its life rather than at its beginning or end. This can be done in a way that is consistent with NPV. If the assessment point is at $t = m$ (where $0 \leq m \leq n$) then the net value, $NV(m)$, of the project at this point in the future is:

$$NV(m) = \sum_{t=1}^{n} S_t(1 + r)^{m-t} - K(1 + r)^m \tag{4.6}$$

Equation (4.6) includes NPV as a special case (if $m = 0$) and NTV as a special case (if $m = n$). In fact it may be that $m > n$. This may occur when projects with different lives are being compared. Also if $t = 0$ is defined as the point when cash flow begins, conceivably $m < 0$ and an optimal starting date is being sought at a future time. Note from (4.6) that the value of m cannot affect the sign of $NV(m)$, only its magnitude and the accept/reject decision is unaffected.

Net present value represents the financial outcome of a project as an **amount** of return. The performance of an investment can also be measured as a *rate* of return. The **yield** of a project, known also as the **internal rate of return** (IRR) or DCF rate of return or simply rate of return, is the discount rate required to equate the present value of future returns with the outlay needed to secure them. That is, yield is the rate of discount for which NPV is zero. This is 100i% where i is given by:

$$\sum_{t=1}^{n} S_t(1 + i)^{-t} - K = 0 \qquad (4.7)$$

The project's IRR is the maximum interest rate that the investor can afford calculated in the declining balance manner (as in overdrafts). The returns to the investment, paid in as they occur, would just be enough to eliminate all liability. The overdraft interest rate in such a case represents the **cost of capital** to the investor. In general, ascertaining the appropriate cost-of-capital figure can be a complex task.

If project evaluation is based on yield, the yield is compared with a preplanned threshold or 'hurdle' rate which will usually be the cost of capital. The single-project **yield decision rule** is:

If the yield of the project exceeds the comparison rate (cost of capital) accept the investment; if the IRR is less than the comparison rate, reject the investment.

That is, with a comparison rate of 100r%:

Outcome	Decision
$i > r$	Accept
$i < r$	Reject
$i = r$	Inconclusive

The inconclusive case, where the yield is equal to the comparison rate, is of little practical importance. It is not usually easy to find the yield of an investment by hand, but most spreadsheets and a number of other software packages will provide a yield figure for a specified cash flow. The packages vary in their ability to handle unconventional cash flows containing negative returns. All work satisfactorily for the conventional pattern of an initial outlay followed by positive returns. For manual work a method of approximation is employed which is relatively simple and gives answers accurate to one decimal place in the percentage figure. This will usually be sufficient. Consider the project in Problems 4.5 and 4.6 (with cash flow: –2200, 770, 968, 1331) and plot the NPV of this investment against the discount rate used. As the rate rises, the NPV of a project with all positive returns will fall. This relationship is shown in Fig. 4.1.

The point where the NPV graph crosses the horizontal axis is the project's IRR. At a zero discount rate NPV is the sum of the undiscounted returns less the outlay: 869. At 10% we saw that the NPV was +300 and at 20% it was –116. Zero NPV is thus at a rate of discount somewhere between 10% and 20%. Greater accuracy can be achieved by a process of trial and error in which the whole number rates of discount either side of the

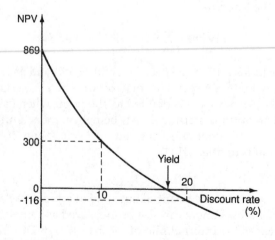

Figure 4.1 *Graph of net present value*

yield are determined, followed by **interpolation** between these values. Workings are shown in Table 4.2.

Table 4.2 *Interpolation exercise*

| | | 15% | |
Year	Sum	Discount factor	PV
0	−2200	1	−2200.00
1	770	0.8696	669.59
2	968	0.7561	731.90
3	1331	0.6575	875.13
		NPV =	+76.62

| | | 16% | |
Year	Sum	Discount factor	PV
0	−2200	1	−2200.00
1	770	0.8621	663.83
2	968	0.7432	719.42
3	1331	0.6407	852.77
		NPV =	+36.01

| | | 17% | |
Year	Sum	Discount factor	PV
0	−2200	1	−2200.00
1	770	0.8475	652.58
2	968	0.7305	711.48
3	1331	0.6244	831.08
		NPV =	−4.86

A rate of 15% might be guessed to start with, producing an NPV of +76.62 and so, since the NPV graph still lies above the horizontal axis, 15% is too low. A rate of 16% is then tried which gives NPV = +36.01, still too low. A rate of 17% gives NPV = −4.86, from which it is clear that the yield is between 16% and 17% but nearer to the higher figure. The linear interpolation proceeds as follows. As shown in Fig. 4.2, a straight line is drawn between the point on the NPV graph above 16% and the point on the NPV graph below 17%. Where this line crosses the axis is the estimated yield.

As can be seen from the figure, the approximation will be a slight overestimate – but not so much as might appear from the diagram (in which the curvature of the NPV graph is exaggerated for clarity). For the calculations note that the ratio of distance C to D is the same as the ratio of A to B so the straight line cuts the discount axis a proportion 36.01/(36.01 + 4.86) of the way along the 1% interval from 16% to 17% so the estimated internal rate of return is:

$$\left\{16 + \frac{36.01}{40.87}\right\}\% = 16.88\%$$

in which 16.88% might well be rounded to 16.9%. (The true yield correct to three decimal places is 16.905 so in this case interpolation has apparently produced a slight **underestimate** of the yield. This is due to rounding errors in the discount factors. If the

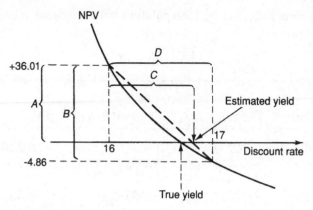

Figure 4.2 *Estimating yield by linear interpolation*

discount factors were taken to enough decimal places no such 'underestimate' would arise.)

Where there is a uniform discount rate, the yield and NPV rules give the same accept/reject decision for a single project, technical problems caused by possible multiple-yield figures notwithstanding (see section 4.7). In Fig. 4.3 the NPV of a project with a unique IRR is plotted against the discount rate.

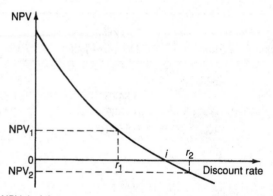

Figure 4.3 *Yield and NPV decisions*

The figure shows that the yield and present value (and also terminal value) decision rules are consistent in the single project case. If the cost of capital was $100r_1\%$, then the project's NPV is NPV_1 which is positive indicating acceptance. The yield of the project, $100i\%$, exceeds the cost of capital so the yield rule also indicates acceptance. If the cost of capital was $100r_2\%$, NPV would be NPV_2 which, being negative, signals rejection. Since the project's yield is less than $100r_2\%$ the project is also rejected by the yield rule.

Care is required in using the yield rule when the cash flow does not follow the pattern of an initial outlay (negative cash flow item) with positive returns thereafter. Consider a loan and repayments cash flow:

$t = 0$	$t = 1$	$t = 2$	$t = 3$
+1000	−475	−475	−475

The present value of this cash flow is shown in Fig. 4.4.

If the 'hurdle rate' is **less** than the yield figure in a case such as this the project is **not** worthwhile. This is because one of the two following situations obtains. If the hurdle rate is given by an alternative source of borrowing, the loan represented by the cash flow is a more expensive source of funds as the yield (about 20%) is the true cost of this

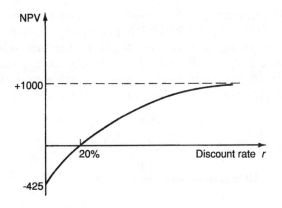

Figure 4.4 *Loan and repayment example*

loan. But if the hurdle rate represents the return available on £1000 invested, this rate is not enough to cover the £475 annual repayments. If the comparison rate exceeds the yield figure, then either the project loan is a cheaper source of funds or the £1000 can be invested at a rate of return that will cover the £475 repayments.

This case is an example where care is needed in the interpretation and use of the yield figure. There are other cash flow patterns that can cause technical problems in the form of more than one yield figure, but such difficulties can be overcome and the conclusions about the use of yield still apply.

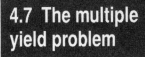

4.7 The multiple yield problem

We define a **well-behaved** project as one for which the present value graph cuts the discount rate axis once only and from above. All projects which make an 'accounting profit' (the undiscounted returns exceed the outlay) and in which an initial cash flow out is followed by non-negative returns are well behaved. But if a project has a cash flow which includes more than one negative and positive returns, there **may** be a multiple-yield problem: the internal rate of return is ambiguous, equation (4.7) may solve for more than one value of i. For instance the project

$t = 0$	$t = 1$	$t = 2$	$t = 3$
–1000	3600	–4310	1716

has yields of 10%, 20% and 30% as can be verified by discounting at these rates. The project is plotted in Fig. 4.5.

To use a yield approach here, the cash flow must be modified to produce a single yield figure but without changing the project's NPV. The **extended yield method** brings negative returns towards the present, discounted appropriately, to be absorbed by earlier positive returns or, if a negative value still remains at $t = 1$, to be added to the

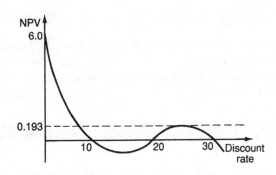

Figure 4.5 *Multiple yields*

outlay. This process produces a cash flow with an unchanged net present value but which has only one possible figure for IRR. (There are other ways in which the cash flow may be modified to the same effect. The crucial point is that any redistribution of negative values is carried out at the NPV rate of discount.) Consider the application of the extended yield method to the multiple-yield project above. Suppose that the cost of capital is 15%. First bring the year 2 figure back to year 1 discounted at 15%. The following cash flow pattern results:

$$
\begin{array}{cccc}
t = 0 & t = 1 & t = 2 & t = 3 \\
-1000 & 3600 - \dfrac{4310}{1.15} & 0 & 1716 \\
= -1000 & -147.83 & 0 & 1716
\end{array}
$$

This still contains a negative value at $t = 1$, which is now moved at the 15% discount rate to $t = 0$. This produces the cash flow:

$$
\begin{array}{cccc}
t = 0 & t = 1 & t = 2 & t = 3 \\
-1000 - \dfrac{147.83}{1.15} & 0 & 0 & 1716 \\
= -1128.54 & 0 & 0 & 1716
\end{array}
$$

which can only have one figure for yield. Since the negative return was redistributed using the cost of capital, the modified cash flow –1128.54, 0, 0, 1716 will have the same NPV as the original cash flow, which is slightly negative. The yield on the modified project is slightly under 15% (a fact disguised by rounding if four-figure tables of discount factors are used) so both the NPV and yield rules reject the project.

Multiple yields

The practical significance of multiple yields is limited, but theoretical interest is considerable and some startling examples can be constructed. For instance, consider the project with the cash flow:

$t=0$	$t=1$	$t=2$	$t=3$	$t=4$	$t=5$
−100	240	1944	−4370	−6988	11856

The project has no less than five yields: 30%, 200%, 300%, −300% and −480%. The separation between the yield values is enormous and at once raises questions about the meaning of yield in such cases.

Even more extreme examples can be constructed – witness the following cash flow data:

$t=0$	$t=1$	$t=2$	$t=3$	$t=4$	$t=5$
−1000	21 100	1 000 001 889	−110 010 330	−3 108 988 447	2 221 995 778

Which produces yield values of:

1%   10%   100 000%   −300%   and   −100 000%

So in terms of one of the calculated internal rates of return, this project could claim to be equivalent to an El Dorado investment transforming £100 000 into £10 000 million in the space of a year. Alas, in terms of one of the other yield values, it could also be seen as equivalent to an investment able to transform a mountain of silk into a very small sow's ear – in which the same £100 000 shrinks to less than £1 during the same period!

Physical projects giving cash flow patterns with multiple roots are uncommon, since very large fluctuations in cash flow either side of zero are required. The phenomenon is more likely to arise when separate cash flows are being combined as in the **incremental yield method** to be discussed in the following section. A further point is that the NPV of the projects **between** the multiple yield rates is usually trivial when taken as a proportion of the outlay. So for practical purposes the NPV of multiple yield projects can usually be approximated to zero over the range of the multiple yields.

A consequence of the small variation in NPV over the range of multiple yield values is that such projects are insensitive to interest rate variability within, and some way beyond, this range. So there is the possibility of the decision-makers having the rare luxury to put interest rate uncertainties on one side and focus attention on other aspects of the decision. This may not seem worthwhile for a project with almost zero NPV, but multiple-yield projects are members of a broader class of projects which have positively sloped sections in their graph of NPV and will have an almost flat and interest rate insensitive interval. Such projects may be attractive when interest rates are highly volatile. An example is found by reducing the outlay in one of the multiple yield cases above. As may be verified, the project:

$$\begin{array}{cccc} t=0 & t=1 & t=2 & t=3 \\ -850 & 3600 & -4310 & 1716 \end{array}$$

has NPV almost constant around 150 through an interval of over 23 percentage points.

The NPV and yield rules give the same accept/reject decision for a single project. But where several investments are involved there can appear to be conflict and yield should be used in a particular way to give decisions consistent with NPV.

Two distinct situations will be distinguished:

4.8 Comparing alternative investments

1. Selection of all worthwhile projects;
2. Selection between mutually exclusive projects.

In both situations it is assumed that there are no financial or other constraints on choice, the subject of a later chapter. When NPV is used in case 1 all projects with positive NPV are selected. In case 2 the projects with the greater NPVs are preferred – so long as these are positive. In case 1 the yield approach selects (correctly) all projects with yields above the NPV discount rate. But in case 2 it is *not* correct to select those projects with the greatest yields. Decisions taken on this basis may conflict with NPV decisions which, as is shown in section 4.12, are formally correct. Where cost is to be minimized, the alternatives producing the least present value of costs should be selected. If the revenue stream is the same in each case, the problem can be expressed in maximization terms by subtracting the cost alternatives from the revenues and selecting the option producing the greatest net present value.

Consider the four projects shown in Table 4.3. In situation 1 with a 10% discount rate projects A, C and D should be accepted and project B should be rejected as clearly indicated by NPV. In situation 2, if only two projects were to be chosen these should be the two with greatest NPV, namely A and C.

If the 25% discount rate is appropriate, the NPV rule would still identify A, C and D as being worthwhile, but if only two projects were required these should now be C and D. The fact that NPV gives different decisions at 25% and 10% in the latter case reflects the changed conditions of the decision. A change in the discount rate has different effects across the projects. Projects which produce their best returns in the distant future will be more severely affected by a rise in interest rates than those with their larger returns nearer to the present, a point developed in the chapter on high-technology investments.

Now suppose that a straight choice between A and C is required. The projects may be a mutually exclusive pair – perhaps different ways of doing the same thing. The NPV rule selects project A if the discount rate is 10%. Fig. 4.6 illustrates the choice situation.

The two PV graphs intersect at 20.7%. At costs of capital below this figure project A is preferable, and for costs of capital above 20.7% project C is superior. The yields of the

Table 4.3 *Selecting projects by net present value*

Project	Cash flow			NPV (10%)	NPV (25%)	NPV (30%)	NPV (35%)
A	−100	80	60	22.3	2.4	−3.1	−7.8
B	−120	40	100	−1.0	−24.0	−30.1	−35.5
C	−60	40	50	17.7	4.0	0.4	−2.9
D	−30	30	20	13.8	6.8	4.9	3.2

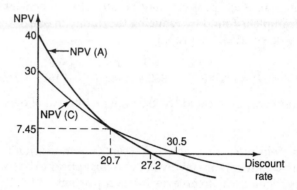

Figure 4.6 *Yield and comparison of investments*

two projects are 27.2% for A and 30.5% for C. A naive extension of the single-project yield rule would prefer C to A on grounds of greater yield. In the comparison between the yield figures no account is taken of the cost of capital, and this fact alone should arouse suspicions about the process. Consider the case where the NPV decision and the naive yield approach clash directly – when the cost of capital is less than 20.7%. NPV then selects A and naive yield selects C. The NPV decision is correct and the yield rule has to be modified. Why?

One weakness of the yield rule is that it considers only the **rate** of return on projects and not the **scale** of the benefit to be obtained. For instance, the projects −6, 4, 5 and −600, 400, 500 have equal yields, although the second project gives much greater total value. But scale is not the whole story; the naive yield rule can be shown to contradict itself.

Consider the problem of choice between A and C with an external discount rate of 10%. Suppose that a decision-maker chooses C in preference to A simply because C has the greater yield. Now offer an additional choice of C **plus** a further project E with cash flow:

$$\text{E:} \quad −40 \quad 40 \quad 10$$

Would C alone be preferred or C plus E? Since E has a yield of 20.7% – well above the cost of capital – this yield-oriented decision-maker would presumably accept E in addition to C and consider themselves better off as a result. But now add up the outlay and returns on C + E:

$$\text{C + E:} \quad −100 \quad 80 \quad 60$$
$$= \quad \text{project A}$$

So this decision-maker should be happier with project A rather than C, contradicting the original choice. The point is that the extra outlay required for project A is money well spent since it gives a yield greater than the cost of capital. The project E: −40, 40, 10 (the difference between A and C) is called the **incremental project**.

To make a decision between two mutually exclusive projects using yield, the incremental project should be formed by subtracting the cash flows of the project with the lower initial outlay from the other project. If the yield on the incremental project exceeds the cost of capital the project with greater outlay should be selected. If the yield on the incremental project is less than the cost of capital then the project with lower outlay should be selected. This is the **incremental yield method**. The incremental project A – B is plotted in Fig. 4.7. The yield of the incremental project is the rate of discount at which the NPV graphs cross. More complicated pictures than Fig. 4.7 can arise, for example the incremental project could have multiple yields even if A and B individually did not.

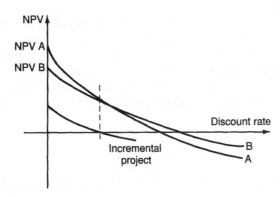

Figure 4.7 *The incremental project A – B*

Consider a further example involving two projects: first A, with a constant return of £100 for ten years and costing £502 initially, and B with a constant return of £144 also for ten years but costing £780 initially. The IRR of A is 15% and the IRR of B is 13%. With a cost of capital of 8% the NPV of A is £169 and the NPV of B is £185, indicating a preference for B. The incremental project here costs £278 and gives a return of £44 in each of ten years. The IRR of this project is 9.6% which is greater than the cost of capital, so B is the better investment.

The incremental yield method is impractical if many projects are involved since many incremental projects may need to be evaluated. For example, suppose that two projects were to be chosen from the four projects in Table 4.3. Not only would the incremental yields of A, B and C over D be required, but we would also need to find the incremental yields of A – B and A – C, the result being a decision obtained much faster using NPV. Outside the two-project case if a statement in terms of yield is required, the choice should be made using NPV, and the results can then be presented in terms of yield.

One of the points advanced in favour of the yield/IRR approach is that IRR is expressed as a percentage and many business decision-makers prefer to think in percentage terms. This, to the extent that it is true, is fair enough; decision-making tools are made to fit people and not the other way about. But the IRR approach has also been criticized on the grounds that it is a percentage – that it contains the implicit assumption that returns are invested (and outstanding debt carried forward) at a rate equal to the IRR.

There has been much discussion about this point. If the existence – not to say *discovery* – of investment opportunities themselves having yields equal to any and every project that the company might consider was an essential precondition for the use of IRR for decision-making, then the method would indeed be fatally flawed. But the argument is a red herring.

For **decision-making** purposes yield can be seen as one number to be compared with another – the discount rate. In this context the discount rate can be regarded as a hurdle

4.9 The modified internal rate of return

rate that must be cleared for project viability. A project accepted on the basis of its IRR does *not* require the decision-maker to find other projects with identical internal rates of return to absorb surpluses. An infinite regress would be created: if such projects did exist, they should themselves be accepted since their IRRs exceed the discount rate, but on the basis of the reinvestment argument acceptance would require the identification of yet further projects with the same IRR . . .

For consistency with NPV, a project accepted on the basis of yield should have its returns invested at the NPV rate of discount. This is the opportunity cost of the funds, the most effective 'non-project' use of money and is the rate at which returns should be invested regardless of the decision rule used to select the investment. The reinvestment may take the form of deposits with financial institutions or the repayment of borrowing as circumstances dictate.

However, analysts favouring the use of IRR but concerned about the impact of the reinvestment debate have provided a modified device, also consistent with NPV, which circumvents any reinvestment worries. This is called the **modified internal rate of return** (MIRR) or the terminal rate of return. The MIRR of an investment is that rate of compounding which if applied to the initial outlay produces the terminal value of the project returns. For example, consider the project of Problem 4.5 in section 4.4. The cash flow was:

$$
\begin{array}{cccc}
t = 0 & t = 1 & t = 2 & t = 3 \\
-2200 & 770 & 968 & 1331
\end{array}
$$

The terminal value of the returns (which is the terminal value analogue to gross present value) at 10% will be:

$$770(1.1)^2 + 968(1.1) + 1331 = 3327.5$$

The modified internal rate of return is $100m\%$ found from:

$$2200(1 + m)^3 = 3327.5 \tag{4.8}$$

The value of m can be obtained exactly by use of a scientific calculator or from a simple Basic program. Linear interpolation can also be used. From (4.8):

$$(1 + m)^3 = \frac{3327.5}{2200} = 1.5125$$

Using the future values in Table 1 we see that at 14% for three years, £1 becomes 1.4815 while at 15% for three years £1 becomes 1.5208. So using linear interpolation over the 1% interval, the modified internal rate of return is:

$$\text{MIRR} \approx 14 + \frac{1.5125 - 1.4815}{1.5208 - 1.4815}$$

$$= 14.79\%$$

which is accurate to the two decimal places given. The project is acceptable on grounds of the MIRR since MIRR > 10% (the discount rate in this case).

There are significant differences between MIRR and IRR although as we shall see later on, they are similar in one important respect. As can be seen from equation (4.8) multiple values of MIRR will not arise so there will not be a need for an equivalent of the extended yield method. Unlike IRR, for projects lasting more than one compounding period, the value of MIRR for a project depends on the discount rate used in the compounding calculations. (Since this is influenced by considerations external to the project, the 'I' in MIRR is partly compromised.) In the example above, if a rate of 30% had been appropriate, the terminal value of the returns would be:

$$770(1.3)^2 + 968(1.3) + 1331 = 3890.7$$

and MIRR as given by:

$$(1 + m)^3 = \frac{3890.7}{2200} = 1.7685$$

is 20.93%. Note that in this case the project would, correctly, be rejected since MIRR < 30%.

In the single project case, MIRR will always give a decision consistent with NPV or NTV. This can be shown as follows; if NTV is positive, i.e.

$$\Sigma R_t (1 + r)^{n-t} - K(1 + r)^n > 0 \qquad (4.9)$$

In (4.9) the project runs for n years, the initial outlay is K, the discount rate is $100r\%$ and the return in year t is R_t. The information in (4.9) can be re-presented as:

$$\Sigma R_t(1 + r)^{n-t} = K(1 + r)^n + D \qquad (4.10)$$

where in (4.10), D is a positive number. So in the MIRR calculation:

$$K(1 + m)^n = \Sigma R_t(1 + r)^{n-t}$$

we can replace the term $\Sigma R_t(1 + r)^{n-t}$ with the right hand side of (4.10) to obtain:

$$K(1 + m)^n = (1 + r)^n + D$$

which in turn can be re-expressed as:

$$K[(1 + m)^n - (1 + r)^n] = D$$

that is:

$$(1 + m)^n - (1 + r)^n = \frac{D}{K} \qquad (4.11)$$

where in (4.11) the value of D/K is positive (assuming that $K > 0$) so that:

$$(1 + m)^n > (1 + r)^n$$

and hence $m > r$ whenever NTV > 0. In other words, the MIRR of a project must be greater than the discount rate if NTV is positive. Recall that NTV is $NPV(1 + r)^n$ so if NTV is positive, so must NPV be positive (at any interest rate greater than –100%!).

We now come to the important similarity between MIRR and IRR referred to above. This concerns mutually exclusive projects. The project with the greater MIRR will not always have the greater NPV or NTV. This can be shown by an example. For the mutually exclusive projects:

	$t = 0$	$t = 1$
A:	–1000	1331
B:	–10	110

with a discount rate of 10% results are as follows:

	NPV(10%)	NTV(10%)	IRR(%)	MIRR(%)
A:	210	231	33.1	33.1
B:	90	99	1100	1100

So in this case the project with the greater NPV has the lesser MIRR. In other particular cases, the result could, of course, have been that NPV and MIRR happened to give consistent rankings. The use of MIRR for selection between mutually exclusive projects to guarantee consistency with NPV would involve the formation of incremental projects as was the case with yield. These complexities are quite unnecessary and it is preferable to perform the selections on the basis of NPVs and, if desired, state the MIRRs of the selected projects as additional management information.

Interest rates change over time. If the pattern of these changes is known, the information can be used in calculating present values. Consider a case involving a series of one-period interest rates. If $100r_1\%$ is the rate for year 1 (from $t = 0$ to $t = 1$) and if $100r_2\%$ is appropriate in year 2, and in general $100r_t\%$ in year t, then the expression for GPV becomes:

$$\text{GPV} = \frac{S_1}{(1 + r_1)} + \frac{S_2}{(1 + r_1)(1 + r_2)} + \frac{S_3}{(1 + r_1)(1 + r_2)(1 + r_3)}$$

$$+ \frac{S_4}{(1 + r_1)(1 + r_2)(1 + r_3)(1 + r_4)} + \dots$$

$$= \sum_{t=1}^{n} S_t \prod_{s=1}^{t} (1 + r_s)^{-s} \qquad (4.12)$$

where the notation Π signifies the product of the relevant discount factors. As an example, suppose that the NPV of the project:

$t = 0$	$t = 1$	$t = 2$	$t = 3$
−500	300	400	200

was needed and where $r_1 = 0.10$ (a first-year discount rate of 10%), $r_2 = 0.13$ and $r_3 = 0.11$. Substituting into (4.12) and subtracting the outlay gives:

$$\text{NPV} = \frac{300}{1.1} + \frac{400}{(1.1)\,(1.13)} + \frac{200}{(1.1)\,(1.13)\,(1.11)} - 500 = 239.5$$

If, as an approximation, the project had been discounted at the average of the three rates: $(1.10 + 1.13 + 1.11)/3 = 1.113$ the resulting NPV is little changed at 237.5, an error of only 0.84%. As a percentage, the error in NPV depends on the initial outlay and it is better to take the percentage error in GPV, which is 0.24%.

In this example the inaccuracy due to the use of an average rate is small. In view of the difficulties of estimation an approximate average rate is usually justified in practice. But it should be noted that significant biases can occur. The size of the error depends on the nature of the interest rate changes – whether there is a trendless pattern or a declining or rising trend in the rates – and the cash flow pattern (rising, falling or trendless). With no trend in either cash flow or interest rates the use of an average discount rate produces 'small' percentage errors in GPV and is satisfactory in practice. But consider the effects of definite trends in interest rates or cash flow. Begin by assuming that a project returns 100 in each of three years with interest rates of 30% in the first year, 20% in the second year and 10% in the third year. GPV is:

$$\text{GPV} = \frac{100}{(1.3)} + \frac{100}{(1.3)\,(1.2)} + \frac{100}{(1.3)\,(1.2)\,(1.1)} = 199.30$$

Whereas if an average 20% rate is used:

$$\text{GPV} = \frac{100}{(1.2)} + \frac{100}{(1.2)^2} + \frac{100}{(1.2)^3} = 210.65$$

and if the interest rates had been rising:

$$\text{GPV} = \frac{100}{(1.1)} + \frac{100}{(1.1)\,(1.2)} + \frac{100}{(1.1)\,(1.2)\,(1.3)} = 224.94$$

Given an even distribution of cash flow, the use of an average rate when the time trend of interest rates is down will bias GPV and NPV upwards. There is an opposite bias when the time trend of interest rates is downwards.

These effects can be amplified, neutralized or reversed depending on the cash flow pattern. For instance we saw that with a declining trend of rates the use of an average figure would bias up the GPV figure in a project with equal returns. In an extreme case this effect can be neutralized, for example:

$$\frac{10}{(1.3)} + \frac{1000}{(1.3)(1.2)} + \frac{100\,000}{(1.3)(1.2)(1.1)} = 58\,924$$

and with an average rate of 20% employed:

$$\frac{10}{(1.2)} + \frac{1000}{(1.2)^2} + \frac{100\,000}{(1.2)^3} = 58\,573$$

so very little difference is shown here. But if the cash flow is reversed:

$$\frac{100\,000}{(1.3)} + \frac{100}{(1.3)(1.2)} + \frac{10}{(1.3)(1.2)(1.1)} = 77\,570$$

whereas using 20%:

$$\frac{100\,000}{(1.2)} + \frac{1000}{(1.2)^2} + \frac{10}{(1.2)^3} = 84\,034$$

In the latter case, use of the average rate causes GPV to be overstated by 8.33%. In the earlier example (with even cash flows of 100) the overstatement was 5.69%. Longer time scales could have produced more marked biases, but the quite extreme examples above produced only single figure percentage biases. In practical terms these are 'margin of error' phenomena and the use of multiple interest rates in DCF calculations is the exception rather than the rule.

4.11 Different interest rates for borrowing and lending

DCF methods are most often used with a single interest rate. This gives good approximations even when interest rates change over time. The approximation will be especially good if the company is not constantly changing from being a debtor to a creditor and back again as the cash flow items come in. But if the company is constantly moving into and out of debt and if there are different rates of interest for borrowing and lending, these different rates should ideally be applied to the cash flow items. This can make significant differences to the small investor but is less likely to be important for the larger company. Where exact working is justified it is necessary to use a terminal value formulation. This is illustrated in the following example.

An investor has reserves of £4000 and is considering undertaking an investment costing £10 000. The investment returns £8200 at $t = 1$ and a further £5000 at $t = 2$. Money can be borrowed at 20% and surpluses are invested at 10%. We shall compare the investor's situation at $t = 2$ with and without the project. If the project is undertaken, the investor must borrow £6000 initially on which 20% is payable. At $t = 1$ the return of £8200 more than cancels the debt of £7200 and the balance of £1000 is invested at 10% to which is added the £5000 return at $t = 2$. So at $t = 2$ the investor's cash position is:

$$[(4000 - 10\,000)(1.2) + 8200](1.1) + 5000 = 6100$$

Without the project, the investor could earn 10% over two years giving:

$$4000(1.1)^2 = 4840$$

The NTV of the investment is thus:

$$6100 - 4840 = 1260$$

and using the NTV decision rule the investment should be accepted. Two things should be noted however. The initial sum held by the investor does not cancel out in the NTV calculation if it is smaller than the initial outlay. So the project, strictly speaking, cannot be assessed independently of the investor's initial cash position. Secondly, although the NTV calculation is not difficult, a formula cannot be written down in advance of knowing which interest rate applies between any two years. This is also true of NPV for which there is no unambiguous definition in this case. The nearest approach to a general formula in this case is:

$$NTV = \sum_{t=0}^{n} R_t (1 + i)^{y(t)} (1 + j)^{z(t)}$$

where the R_t are the returns (R_0 is initial funds less outlay), the borrowing rate is $100i\%$, the lending rate is $100j\%$, $y(t)$ is the number of periods including and beyond t in which the investor is a net borrower, and $z(t)$ is the number of periods including and beyond t in which the investor is a net creditor. However, it is interesting to note the result of applying an unweighted average interest rate of 15% to the project's cash flows. The outcome is:

$$-10\,000\,(1.15)^2 + 8200\,(1.15) + 5000 = 1205$$

an error of under 4.4%. As with the case of varying interest rates over time, it is usually reasonable to work with a uniform rate.

4.12 Theoretical justification for net present value

We stated that NPV is the 'correct' means by which to assess and compare investment projects. We now produce the theoretical support for this claim. The argument is that, under certain conditions, a project can produce a superior cash flow in **every** period compared to a project with lower NPV. So whether the investor is a private individual or a company with shareholders, the selection of the alternative with greatest NPV is preferred and the selection of any project with positive NPV will increase wealth (which in the case of a company will be reflected in share price).

A sufficiently strong condition for the project with greater NPV to produce, or to be convertible to, a superior cash flow at all times is that a uniform rate of interest prevails throughout the time horizon of the projects at which all financial transactions (borrowing and lending) can take place. If this perfect capital market applies, it is only necessary to assume that at all points in time more cash is preferred to less – a very plausible assumption!

Consider an example. Two dissimilar projects are shown below:

	$t = 0$	$t = 1$	$t = 2$
A	−200	176	121
B	60	198	−242

At 10% project A has an NPV of 60 and project B has an NPV of 40. Because of the greater NPV, by moving funds around at 10% the cash flow of A can be transformed into the cash flow of B with no less available at any point in time and more available at some (or all) times. For example, with all the additional cash concentrated at $t = 0$, A can be transformed into:

$$80 \quad 198 \quad -242$$

or, with all the extra money available at time $t = 1$:

$$60 \quad 220 \quad -242$$

or concentrated at time $t = 2$:

$$60 \quad 198 \quad -217.8$$

or as one possible arrangement with more at all times:

$$70 \quad 203.5 \quad -235.95$$

Project A can generate any cash flow:

$t = 0$	$t = 1$	$t = 2$
$60 + D_0$	$220 + D_1$	$-242 + D_2$

such that:

$$D_0 + \frac{D_1}{(1.1)} + \frac{D_2}{(1.1)^2} = 20 \qquad (4.10)$$

where in (4.10), 20 is the difference between the NPVs of the two projects.

The result can be graphed in a one-period case. In Fig. 4.8 the coordinates of points A and B are the cash flows of two rather attractive projects:

	$t = 0$	$t = 1$
A	90	132
B	100	110

The two lines A_0A_1 and B_0B_1 show the cash combinations that each project can produce at time 0 and time 1 by movements of cash at a rate of interest determined by the slope of the lines.

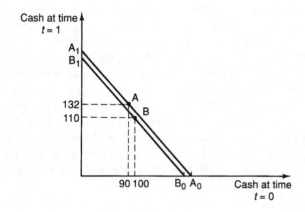

Figure 4.8

A_0 and B_0 are the NPVs of the projects and A_1 and B_1 are the NTVs. With a uniform interest rate of $100r\%$, the slope of the lines is $-(1 + r)$. With the slope shown, A offers superior options to B. A will be preferred to B for interest rates up to 120% (which gives a line passing through A and B). Above this rate B is preferred to A. Note that whatever the interest rate, the decision between A and B is never dependent on when the cash is required, and the NPV or NTV decision rules can be used with confidence.

Things may be different if there are distinct interest rates for borrowing (moving cash from $t = 1$ to $t = 0$) and lending ($t = 0$ to $t = 1$ transfers). Fig. 4.9 shows a case where the choice between A and B may depend upon the balance the investor wishes to achieve between cash at time 0 and cash at time 1.

The frontier of possibilities is no longer a straight line but is given by B_0BCAA_1. Different points along the frontier correspond to different choices between A and B. There will still be cases in which one or other project is definitely superior. Criteria for identifying such cases are given on in Wilkes (1983). In Fig. 4.9 the difference between the borrowing rate (the slope of the steeper sections) and the lending rate (flatter sections) is exaggerated for purposes of illustration. In practice the difference is less dramatic and the consequences of the use of a single composite rate are correspondingly reduced.

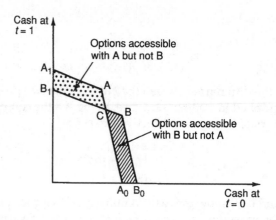

Figure 4.9

4.13 The separation theorem

The preceding discussion presumed that it is possible to transfer money from one period to another at an appropriate rate of interest, i.e. that a **capital market** exists. Here we consider investment appraisal in the absence of a capital market and then see the consequences of its introduction. Fig. 4.10 shows the classical model with no capital market. The line AB is the **investment opportunity line**, a transformation curve showing the combinations of expenditure possible in the two periods. If the investor starts at point B (has an **endowment** of OB) they may choose to locate anywhere on AB by investing in unspecified 'physical' processes to arrive at the desired point. In the case shown, the investor's best point is at E on the highest attainable **indifference curve** U2. All points along any one indifference curve have the same utility for the decision-maker. All points on a higher indifference curve are preferred to all points on any lower curve.

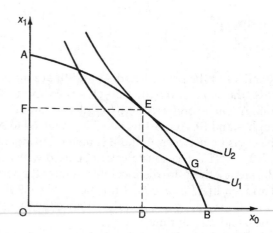

Figure 4.10

A sum BD is invested at $t = 0$ and generates OF at $t = 1$. The slope of the indifference curves is the investor's marginal rate of time preference for cash, and at equilibrium, E, this is equal to the slope of the investment opportunity line. The classical description of this slope is the **marginal efficiency of capital** which is the yield on an infinitesimal investment at point E.

The investment opportunity line consists of continuously divisible independent investments arranged to exhibit diminishing IRR in moving from one investment to the next, starting at point B. To use this approach the investor compares yield at the margin with his or her marginal rate of time preference. In operational terms, a yield-based decision rule would have the investor's marginal rate of time preference as the comparison or cut-off rate. Equivalently, the investor could discount the future return on an investment at the marginal rate of time preference. If point G had been arrived at, the next investments would pass the yield hurdle (using the marginal rate of time preference at this point) and show positive NPV. The optimum E is a point from which all remaining investments have negative NPV when discounted at the marginal rate of time preference at E. NPV is a purely subjective concept here since other investors have different rates of time preference and hence different discount rates.

Now extend this Fisherian analysis to include a perfect capital market where all financial transactions over time take place at a uniform rate of interest. Fig. 4.11 shows the situation.

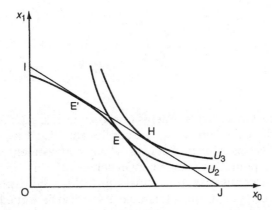

Figure 4.11 *Perfect capital market enhances opportunities*

E is the previous optimum. The investor now uses the physical investments up to E′ and then operates on the capital market (in this case by borrowing) to achieve the superior position H. The rate of interest is given by the slope of the line IJ:

$$100 \left\{ \frac{OI - OJ}{OJ} \right\}\%$$

Projects beyond E′ have negative NPV when discounted at the market rate of interest – they will not pass the yield test with the market rate as a whole. NPV is now an objective calculation, it is the same for all investors. Everyone would use the market rate of interest in their calculations and invest up to E′. They differ according to how much they wish to borrow or lend to obtain their own points of tangency along IJ.

These transactions equate the marginal efficiency of capital (yield) with the market rate of interest which is in turn equated with the investor's own marginal rate of time preference. The investor decides the optimal level of physical investment (up to E′) and then, separately, determines the optimal amount of borrowing or lending on the capital market (moves from E′ to H in the case shown). This is the essence of the **separation theorem** – financial decisions are made independently of investment in assets.

The separation theorem has the important consequence of allowing unambiguous decisions by multi-owner firms. The company as a whole first determines the optimal level of physical investment and then, given the distribution policy, shareholders determine the differing extents to which they as individuals will use the capital market. The separation of management and ownership is in this sense unimportant in the case of a perfect capital market.

This result is also known as the Hirschleifer separation theorem after its originator. The fly in the ointment is the presence in reality of distinct rates of interest for borrowing and lending, in which event the separation theorem does not hold. The frontier of

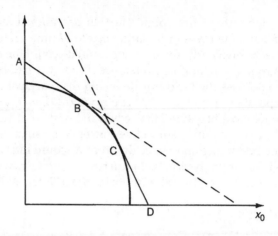

Figure 4.12

possibilities now contains three segments as shown in Fig. 4.12: AB where the lending rate applies, CD where the borrowing rate applies and BC where neither rate applies.

It now depends on investor preferences whether investment in physical processes proceeds to point C, point B or somewhere in between. but it can be argued that, given the number of compromises with exactness in reality, the degree of approximation implied by use of a composite rate is tolerable. It can also be argued that companies tend to attract investors of a particular type, so that if management knows the ownership they will know on which section of ABCD they should be.

4.14 Computer program

The program below, VALUES.BAS, finds gross and net present values and net terminal values. It is written in Basic and will run in Microsoft QBasic as supplied with MS-DOS 5.0 or later. (The program will also run in various other versions of Basic – for example the various versions of QuickBasic, Visual Basic for Dos or, with the addition of line numbers, GW-Basic.) The program has limited objectives and is written in an unsophisticated style so that the intent of each line will be easier to discern. Even so, the program is useful in calculating present or future values when there are several cash flow elements.

The program first clears the screen (when the program is run) of any previous output (CLS) and prints (PRINT) a heading and request to enter the problem data. The INPUT statements print the messages inside the quotation marks as a prompt and wait for the user to key in values for the variables *outlay* and *n*. (The semicolon keeps the cursor on the present line.) A PRINT statement by itself will introduce a blank line. The DIM (for dimension) allows the entry of *n* returns Ret(t) in the FOR . . . NEXT loop that follows. The discount rate is then entered as a percentage. The first calculation converts the discount rate to a decimal. The variable **tempsum** is initiated at zero and is the temporary sum of the discounted returns which is added to at each pass through the following loop. (The line 'tempsum = 0' could be omitted but it is usually a good idea to put such a line in if the program is later extended to allow further calculations to be made. The symbol '*' represents the operation of multiplication while the caret symbol '^' represents exponentiation.) The gross present value GPV is the final value of tempsum. NPV and NTV are then calculated in an obvious fashion. The program then clears the screen and displays the cash flow data and the results.

NPV.BAS

```
CLS

PRINT "Present and Future Value Programme."
PRINT "----------------------------------"
PRINT

PRINT "Please enter the cash flow data . . ."
PRINT

INPUT "Initial Outlay"; outlay
PRINT

INPUT "Number of years"; n
PRINT

DIM Ret(n)

For t = 1 TO n

    PRINT "Return in year"; t;
    INPUT Ret(t)

NEXT t

PRINT
INPUT "Discount rate as percentage"; percentrate

r = percentrate / 100

tempsum = 0

FOR t = 1 TO n

    tempsum = tempsum + Ret(t) * (1 + r) ^ −t

NEXT t

GPV = tempsum

NPV = GPV − outlay

NTV = NPV * (1 + r) ^ n

CLS

PRINT "For the cash flow:"
PRINT

PRINT −outlay;

FOR t = 1 TO n

    PRINT " ";
    PRINT Ret(t);

Next t

PRINT

PRINT

PRINT "With a discount rate of"; percentrate; "%"; "the results are:"
PRINT
PRINT "Gross Present Value  = "; GPV
PRINT "Net Present Value    = "; NPV
PRINT "Net Terminal Value   = "; NTV

END
```

4.15 Conclusions

The NPV decision rule with a uniform rate of discount gives reasonable results in most circumstances. Where several interest rates apply, precise calculations can be carried out if warranted. Yield gives consistent decisions with NPV in the single project case and can be made consistent with NPV when several projects are involved. NPV has strong theoretical underpinning and should be the method of choice in assessing investment projects.

4.16 Key concepts

The **present value** (PV) of £1 received in t years' time is:

$$PV = \frac{1}{(1 + r)^t} = (1 + r)^{-t}$$

where the discount rate is $100r\%$.

The **gross present value** (GPV) of a stream of returns S_t, is:

$$NPV = \sum_{t=1}^{n} S_t(1 + r)^{-t}$$

The **net present value** (NPV) is GPV less the **initial outlay** K:

$$NPV = \sum_{t=1}^{n} S_t(1 + r)^{-t} - K$$

The **NPV decision rule** in the single project case is:

Outcome	Decision
NPV > 0	Accept
NPV < 0	Reject
NPV = 0	Inconclusive

The **net terminal value** (NTV) is the end of project excess that the investment creates. This is:

$$NTV = \sum_{t=1}^{n} S_t (1 + r)^{n-t} - K(1 + r)^n$$

The NTV decision rule is the same as that for NPV.

Yield is the rate of discount for which NPV = 0. This is also known as **internal rate of return** (IRR) or **DCF rate of return**. Yield is $100i\%$ where:

$$\sum_{t=1}^{n} S_t(1 + i)^{-t} - K = 0$$

With a comparison rate of $100r\%$ the yield decision rule for a single investment is:

Outcome	Decision
i > r	Accept
i < r	Reject
i = r	Indeterminate

Yield, NPV and NTV decision rules give the same result for a single investment when there is one rate of interest for all transactions.

The **extended yield method** is used for projects having some negative returns. Multiple rates of return are avoided by bringing forward the negative returns at the comparison rate and absorbing them in the positive returns or adding to the outlay.

Where several projects are involved, if there are no constraints, any project with positive NPV is worthwhile. If m projects only may be taken from a group of n, the NPV rule *ranks* projects by size of NPV. The m projects at the top of the ranking are accepted and the remainder are rejected.

The **incremental yield method** is used to choose between projects using yield. If yield on the **incremental project** A – B exceeds the cost of capital (comparison rate) accept A.

If the incremental yield is less than the cost of capital, accept B.

Where interest rates change over time, PV expressions can take the anticipated changes into account. With a rate of $100r_s\%$ prevailing in the sth year, the PV of a stream of returns R_t is:

$$\text{TV} = \sum_{t=1}^{n} R_t \prod_{s=1}^{t} (1 + r_s)^{-s}$$

Where there are different borrowing and lending rates of interest, NTV is a convenient model for appraising projects.

Where a uniform interest rate applies to borrowing and lending (perfect capital markets) the greater is NPV the greater can be the cash sum available in every year, implying greater shareholder wealth or consumption possibilities. A capital market enhances possibilities for all investors, and where the capital market is perfect the separation theorem applies – financial decisions can be made independently of investment decisions in assets.

4.17 Revision questions

1. What expression shows the future value of a principal sum P, n years hence when the interest rate is $100r\%$ compound?
2. What dangers may be involved in rescheduling debts over longer repayment periods without compensating reductions in interest charges?
3. Distinguish between net and gross present values.
4. Explain how NTV and NPV give the same accept/reject decision for an individual project with a uniform interest rate.
5. Explain what is meant by the yield of an investment.
6. Using a diagram, show how yield and NPV give consistent decisions in the single-project case.
7. How can the multiple-yield problem be overcome?
8. How should a yield approach be used to compare alternative investments?
9. What perceived shortcomings of yield are addressed by MIRR?
10. How can the NPV decision rule be adjusted to take into account known changes in interest rates over time?
11. Show how the NTV decision rule can be used when there are different borrowing and lending rates of interest.
12. Give a theoretical justification for the NPV decision rule.
13. What is the separation theorem?
14. What is the impact on the separation theorem of different borrowing and lending rates of interest?

4.18 References

Hirschleifer, J. (1958) On the theory of optimal investment decisions. *Journal of Political Economy*, August.

Wilkes, F.M. and Brayshaw, R.E. (1986) *Company Finance and its Management*, Van Nostrand Reinhold.

Wilkes, F.M. (1980) On multiple rates of return. *Journal of Business Finance and Accounting*, **7** (4).

Wilkes, F.M. (1983) Dominance Criteria for the ranking of projects with an imperfect capital market. *Journal of Business Finance and Accounting*, **10** (1).

4.19 Further reading

This section contains a reference to a classical work on the subject of interest (Fisher), articles on specific technical subjects (Arditti, Beidelman, Emery, Jean) and three UK-oriented books from among the many works covering capital budgeting. The approach of Bromwich is mainly literal; Lumby is a text on a similar level to this book; and Drury introduces the topics in the context of management accounting. An introductory text on programming in structured Basic is also included.

Arditti, F.D. (1973) The reinvestment assumptions in the internal rate of return. *Journal of Business Finance*, **5** (1).

Beidleman, C.R. (1984) DCF reinvestment rates assumptions. *Engineering Economist*, Winter.

Bromwich, M. (1976) *The Economics of Capital Budgeting*, Penguin.

Drury, C. (1992) *Management and Cost Accounting*, 3rd edn, Chapman & Hall.

Emery, G.M. (1982) Some guidelines for evaluating capital investment alternatives with unequal lives. *Financial Management*, Spring.

Fisher, I. (1930) *The Theory of Interest*, Macmillan.

Jean, W.H. (1971) Terminal value or present value in capital budgeting programmes. *Journal of Financial and Quantitative Analysis*, **6**, January.

Lumby, S. (1994) *Investment Appraisal and Financing Decisions*, 5th edn, Van Nostrand Reinhold.

Venit, S.M. (1991) *Programming in QuickBasic*, West Publishing Company.

4.20 Problems

1. Using a 12% rate of discount, find the net present value of the project with cash flow:

$t = 0$	$t = 1$	$t = 2$	$t = 3$
−400	500	−100	700

2. The next receipts and outlays (including tax payments) for a project are:

	Year					
	0	1	2	3	4	5
Outlay	500					
Net receipts		100	150	250	200	150

The receipt in year 5 includes the residual value of the project at that time. Show that while the project is acceptable at a 10% discount rate on the basis of the net present value criterion, it should be rejected at a discount rate of 20%.

3. Find the net **terminal** value of the investment in question 1.

4. Find the yield of the project:

$t = 0$	$t = 1$	$t = 2$	$t = 3$
−1400	600	700	400

5. (a) Verify that the project with cash flow:

$t = 0$	$t = 1$	$t = 2$
−10 000	24 000	−14 375

has yields of 15% and 25%.

(b) Apply the extended yield method with a cost of capital of 20%.

(c) Sketch the graph of NPV against discount rate. Would the owner of such an investment wish to see a rapid decline in interest rates?

6. With no restriction on expenditure, and with the following projects available:

	$t = 0$	$t = 1$	$t = 2$
A	−60	60	40
B	−120	80	100
C	−200	160	120

(a) which project would be chosen on the basis of NPV at:
  (i) 10%
  (ii) 25%

(b) Which project has the greatest yield?

(c) Use the incremental yield method to select one of projects B and C when the interest rate is 10%.

7. (a) With a 15% cost of capital, find the modified internal rate of return (MIRR) for the investment with the cash flow:

$t = 0$	$t = 1$	$t = 2$	$t = 3$	$t = 4$
−1000	360	330	300	270

Would the project be acceptable on the basis of the MIRR criterion?

   (b) Would the project have been accepted on the basis of its **unmodified** internal rate of return?

8. (a) Find the net present value of the project:

$t = 0$	$t = 1$	$t = 2$	$t = 3$
−1000	600	800	400

when the first year discount rate is 5%, the second year discount rate is 15% and the third year discount rate is 10%.

   (b) Compare the result in (a) with the net present value when there is a uniform discount rate of 10% in all three years.

9. (a) Find the net terminal value (NTV) of a project having the cash flow:

$t = 0$	$t = 1$	$t = 2$
−12 000	10 050	4000

where the investor has £5000 available at $t = 0$, the borrowing rate of interest is 15% and the lending rate is 5%.

   (b) How much would the investor obtain at $t = 2$ if the investment is not undertaken?

   (c) Would the same decision have been arrived at on the basis of NTV if a uniform rate of 10% had been used throughout the calculations?

10. Show that, with a uniform rate of interest of 10% applying throughout, the project with cash flow:

	$t = 0$	$t = 1$	$t = 2$
A	−1500	1320	1210

can be converted to a stream of returns which is superior in every year to the project:

	$t = 0$	$t = 1$	$t = 2$
B	−1400	880	1331

5 Investment appraisal: further topics

5.1	Annuities	103
5.2	Perpetuities	103
5.3	Yield to maturity	105
5.4	Sinking funds	106
5.5	Annual equivalent annuities	108
5.6	Repair or replace	109
5.7	Annuities with growth	113
5.8	Make or buy	115
5.9	Discounted cash flows and tax payments	116
5.10	Investment appraisal and inflation	118
5.11	Capital project commencement and termination dates	120
5.12	Non-standard cash flows and other methods of compounding	123
5.13	Formulae	129
5.14	Computer programs	131
5.15	Key concepts	134
5.16	Revision questions	135
5.17	References	135
5.18	Further reading	136
5.19	Problems	136
5.20	Appendix: Arithmetic and geometric series	138

In this chapter we consider how annuities are calculated, the forms they may take and the uses to which they are put. An annuity is a cash flow, either income or outgoings, involving the same sum in each period. There are many examples of annuities at governmental, corporate and personal finance levels. For example when a company sets aside a fixed sum each year to meet a future obligation, it is using an annuity. Consols are a UK government stock, the interest payments on which are a never-ending annuity. A personal loan from a bank is a familiar fixed-term annuity. Other examples include mortgages (assuming a steady interest rate), leasing arrangements and fixed-interest coupons.

We shall calculate the present values of annuities of finite and unlimited durations and find the redemption yield on loan stock with a fixed maturity date. The possibility of growth will also be taken into account. We show how to compute the annual payments necessary to retire debt and apply annuities to important business problems.

We also examine the inclusion of tax payments in cash flow calculations and how factors such as depreciation are best taken into account. The effects of inflation on cash flow components and overall project viability are investigated. The question of the best starting and finishing dates for projects and associated end of project costs are considered. Alternative methods of compounding are explained and corresponding formulae and associated programs are provided.

The present value of an annuity **could** be found by discounting each return individual, but there is a better method. Consider an annuity of £100 for four years at 10% interest. Assume that the first payment will be made after one year. Using the discount factor table the PV is:

100(0.9091) + 100(0.8264) + 100(0.7513) + 100(0.6830)
= 100 (0.9091 + 0.8264 + 0.7513 + 0.6830)
= 100(3.1699)
= 316.99

The most significant line in the workings above is the second in which the annual amount, £100, is multiplied by the sum of the first four discount factors: 3.1699. (The last digit of this sum is nine rather than eight because of the rounding of the discount factors.) Table 3 is the annuity table and shows the sum of the discount factors up to n years. The entries are the present values of annuities of £1 and are given by:

$$\sum_{t=1}^{n} (1 + r)^{-t} = \frac{1 - (1 + r)^{-n}}{r} \tag{5.1}$$

See the Appendix for further discussion of the basis of this formula.

An annuity where the first payment is made after one year (as assumed by (5.1)) is an **immediate annuity**. Where the first payment occurs at once this is an **annuity due** – for which the entries of Table 3 must be increased by one to obtain the present value. Where the first payment is delayed beyond one year, the annuity is called a **deferred annuity**. Now consider an example.

Problem 5.1

(a) Find the present value of an immediate annuity of £125 running for six years at 11%.
(b) Use Table 3 to find the present value at 12% of the cash flow:

$t=1$	$t=2$	$t=3$	$t=4$	$t=5$	$t=6$
1400	1400	1400	600	600	600

Answer

(a) PV = 125(4.2305) = 528.81
(b) The cash flow can be seen as the sum of two annuities: an immediate annuity of 600 for six years plus an immediate annuity of 800 for three years. (It could also be seen as the sum of an immediate annuity of £1400 for three years plus an annuity of £600 for three years deferred by three years.) Seen as the sum of two immediate annuities, the present value is found as follows:

$$
\begin{aligned}
800(2.4018) &= 1921.44 \\
600(4.1114) &= 2466.84 \\
\hline
\text{Total PV} &= 4388.28
\end{aligned}
$$

Consider a company which leases a building for ten years for £10 000 a year, the first payment to be made after one year. At a 16% rate of interest, what is the present cost of the contract? This is £10 000(4.8332) = £48 332. The present cost of under £50 000 shows the impact of discount factors on distant payments.

A special case of an annuity is where a contract runs indefinitely, there being no end to the payments. This is called a **perpetuity**. Perpetuities are rare in the private sector, but some government securities are undated – for instance Consols and War Loan – and it is unlikely that the principal on these securities will be repaid. There is a simple formula for the present value of a perpetuity. This is the value of (5.1) as n goes to infinity, so the present value of a perpetuity of £1 is:

$$PV = \lim_{n \to \infty} \left| \frac{1 - (1 + r)^{-n}}{r} \right| = \frac{1}{r} \qquad (5.2)$$

The present value of a perpetuity is the annual sum divided by the interest rate as a decimal. Although the income stream is infinite the present value is finite (for $r > 0$). If the annual sum is £S and the interest rate is $100r\%$, then:

$$PV = \frac{S}{r}$$

So at a 10% rate of interest a perpetuity of £50 has a present value of £500, and if it can be sold this should be its approximate price. For instance, what should be the price of a unit of 3½% War Loan stock if the market rate of interest for this kind of very low-risk security is 12%? War Loan is quoted in units of £100 nominal value and the annual interest payment is 3½% of this figure, i.e. £3.50. If for simplicity, a single annual payment is assumed, the price should be the present value:

$$PV = \frac{3.5}{0.12} = £29.17$$

The interest in interest

In *The Sleeper Awakes* H.G. Wells dramatized the extreme results of compound interest operating over very long periods. In the story a skilful investor falls into a centuries-long sleep to find on waking that the accumulated value of his investments had made him the master of the world! Although this caused much popular strife, at least it showed confidence in the stability of financial institutions! In reality, interest, the price charged for the use of money over time, has long been a contentious subject. In the Industrial Revolution the view prevailed that interest was one amongst many prices, and this seems to have been the view in Roman times. But at other times and in other places the practice of charging interest has been viewed less dispassionately.

There are legal provisions against excessive charges for the use of money (usury) on the statute book in some states in the USA. Recent borrowers would be interested in the view that charges over 8% were usurious! Officially, the Islamic world goes further in declaring overt charges for the use of money to be sinful in certain circumstances, but even so this does not make it impossible for banking to flourish. In contrast, in Victorian times in Britain and elsewhere, thrift, saving and by implication the **receiving** of interest was seen as a virtue. In the credit-conscious world of today the consumer, bombarded with offers of loans and 'easy payments', risks looking odd if he or she does not **pay** interest. Indeed behind the view that interest rate cuts will stimulate demand is the presumption that individual consumers are typically in this position. Since the 1970s governments in much of the western world have attached great significance to interest rates as an economic regulator, in some cases as **the** overt regulator. In other times interest rates were seen as one among many policy instruments.

There is no doubt, however, that interest rates have profound significance for economies, companies and individuals. But the **level** of interest rates is not the only important factor, it is the **compound** nature of interest charges that can cause ever-increasing additions to national, corporate or personal indebtedness where prudence is lacking or circumstances overwhelming. For example, at 15% compound, without repayments an initial debt more than doubles over five years and quadruples over ten. Sustained breaks or 'holidays' in interest payments should therefore be viewed with caution, particularly when interest rates are high.

The consequences of **changes** in interest rates when long periods of time are involved can be enormous. At 15%, an initial £100 would become £1636.65 after 20 years, but at 20% the principal of £100 would have produced £3833.76 after 20 years. A 33% increase in the rate of interest, has produced a much larger proportional increase in the end result – over 134%. If the horizon date changes there will be substantial changes in the terminal sum due particularly if the rate of interest is high. For example, at 30% £100 becomes £19 005 after 20 years but no less than £261 999.60 after 30 years – illustrating the danger of inappropriate debt rescheduling under high rates of interest. Restructuring of international debt or personal liabilities has to be carefully constructed if it is not to make matters worse for the debtors involved.

While 30% is an unlikely rate for international borrowings, rates of return of this order have been not infrequently required for potential industrial investments in the UK, particularly in the 1980s. This is one of the ways in which 'short-termism' can operate to the disadvantage of manufacturing industry since 30% instead of 15% as the discount rate has an enormous effect on present values and the outcome of financial appraisals. At 15% a return ten years hence has a discount factor of 0.2472, and so would add 24.72% of its nominal value to NPV. With a discount rate of 30%, the ten-year discount factor is 0.0725 and the contribution to present value is just 7¼% of the nominal amount. And the effects get worse. With discounting at 30% the present value in 1990 of £1 000 000 received each year for the **whole of the 21st century** was just £242 000!

Reasonable rates of interest are also important at the personal level. Personal loan rates from banks and hire purchase rates of 25% to 30% have been commonplace in recent times. But far higher effective annual rates have been and are still charged, quite legally, by other organizations in the UK. A survey carried out in 1987 showed effective annual percentage rates (APRs) of over 100% to be quite common. With no repayments, at 100% indebtedness doubles annually. The survey revealed loans with implied true compound rates of over 1000% per annum, at which rate a repayment 'holiday' increases the debt **tenfold** in a year. There was one case of a loan with a true annual rate of 4822%! To illustrate the financial enslavement that could result from this appalling usury, the liability arising from a pound borrowed now, in the absence of repayment would within seven years exceed the UK gross national product! Unpleasant dreams indeed for the sleeping borrower.

Figure 5.1 shows the graph of the present value of an annuity of £1 as the duration of the annuity increases.

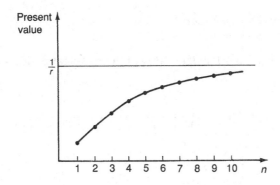

Figure 5.1

The higher the rate of interest, the more rapidly the value of $1/r$ is approached. For example, in the case of a 25% rate of interest, a 20-year annuity has almost 99% of the value of a perpetuity at the same rate, whereas at 1% interest, a 20-year annuity has less than 19% of the value of a perpetuity. When interest rates are changing, there can be significant effects on the value of perpetuities – a topic discussed in the following section.

Here we consider securities given a constant return for a fixed number of years, but in the final year the bond is redeemed. So in addition to the fixed annual payment the nominal issue price of the bond is refunded. The nearer is the redemption date to

5.3 Yield to maturity

the present, the greater will be the effect on the yield and the price of the bond As the redemption date nears the price of the bond rises to bring the yield on the bond, the **yield to maturity** or **redemption yield**, to a level appropriate to the terms of the bond. Special tables can be prepared, but yield to maturity can also be found by interpolation using the annuity table (Table 3) and the present value table (Table 2). For instance, consider a security currently priced at £900 (ex-interest) which gives an annual interest payment of £100 with a redemption value of £1000 after five years. The cash flow on the investment is then:

$t = 0$	$t = 1$	$t = 2$	$t = 3$	$t = 4$	$t = 5$
−900	100	100	100	100	100 + 1000

Using the factors in the tables, the workings are:

	At 12%	At 13%
PV of interest:	360.48	351.72
PV of lump sum:	567.4	542.8
	927.88	894.52

and the yield to maturity is estimated as:

$$\left(12 + \frac{27.88}{33.36}\right)\% = 12.48\%$$

in which $27.88 = 927.88 - 900$ and $33.36 = 927.88 - 894.52$.

An important difference between long-dated and short-dated stock is sensitivity to interest rate changes. The price of short-dated stock is much less variable when interest rates are changing than is the price of long-dated stock. This exposure to price changes (and so to possible capital losses or gains) is called **interest rate risk**. To illustrate interest rate risk consider two sharply contrasting securities – a two-year bond and a perpetuity. Suppose that each is priced at £100 at a 10% rate of interest. The cash flows are:

	$t = 1$	$t = 2$	$t \geq 3$
Two year bond:	10	10 + 100	0
Perpetuity:	10	10	10

The value of the perpetuity is $10/r$. The value of the two-year bond as a function of the interest rate is:

$$PV = 10\left(\frac{1 - (1 + r)^{-2}}{r}\right) + \frac{100}{(1 + r)^2}$$

which reduces to:

$$PV = \frac{10r + 120}{(1 + r)^2} \tag{5.3}$$

Values of (5.3) for various r are given in Table 5.1 from which it is seen that when the interest rate rises from 10% to 15% the two-year bond falls in price by 8.13% while the perpetuity experiences a 33⅓% price fall. If the interest rate falls to 5% the two-year bond rises in price by 9.3% while the perpetuity doubles in value.

5.4 Sinking funds

Where a constant annual sum is saved – possibly to provide for the payment of a future debt – it is useful to know the **terminal** value of the annuity. If £1 is set aside at the end of each of four years, how much will be on hand after four years, with interest at $100r\%$ per annum? The first pound attracts interest for three years and becomes $(1 + r)^3$, the second pound is interest earning for two years and so becomes $(1 + r)^2$, the third pound

Table 5.1 *Perpetuity and two-year bond prices*

Interest rate %	Two-year bond price	Perpetuity price
1	117.73	1000.00
2	115.53	500.00
3	113.39	333.33
4	111.32	250.00
5	109.30	200.00
6	107.33	166.67
7	105.42	142.86
8	103.57	125.00
9	101.76	111.11
10	100.00	100.00
11	98.29	90.91
12	96.62	83.33
13	95.00	76.92
14	93.41	71.43
15	91.87	66.67
16	90.37	62.50
17	88.90	58.82
18	87.47	55.56
19	86.08	52.63
20	84.72	50.00

becomes $(1 + r)$ and the fourth pound is placed in the account at the day of reckoning so that the terminal value at $t = 4$ is:

$$(1 + r)^3 + (1 + r)^2 + (1 + r) + 1$$

At a 10% rate of interest this is:

$$1.331 + 1.21 + 1.1 + 1 = 4.641$$

Table 4 gives these terminal values of an annuity of £1 for various interest rates and number of years. Now consider a specific problem.

Problem 5.2

(a) Find the terminal value at eight years of £375 placed annually into an account starting after one year with interest at 6%.

(b) A company sets aside the following sum at the stated times:

$t = 0$	$t = 1$	$t = 2$	$t = 3$
10 000	5000	5000	20 000

Using Tables 1 and 4 and an interest rate of 9% find how much the company would have at $t = 3$.

Answer

(a) £375 × 9.8975 = £3711.56.

(b) Rather like Problem 1(b) the payments can be separated out as follows:

	$t=0$	$t=1$	$t=2$	$t=3$
Stream 1	10 000	—	—	—
Stream 2	—	5000	5000	5000
Stream 3	—	—	—	15 000
Total	10 000	5000	5000	20 000

Using Table 1 the terminal value of stream 1 at $t = 3$ is £10 000 × 1.2950 = £12 950; using Table 4 the terminal value of stream 2 is £5000 × 3.2781 = £16 390.50 to which is added the £15 000 deposited at $t = 3$. The total is £44 340.50.

The closely related idea of a **sinking fund** is useful. Table 5 shows how much must be set aside each year to get a terminal value of £1. The numbers in the table are the reciprocals of the corresponding entries in Table 4. With a 12% rate of interest £0.0813 would need to be saved annually to produce £1 after eight years. Consider an example. A company has loan stock of £750 000 due to mature in seven years. The company wishes to pay off the debt rather than make an issue of fresh stock at this time. At an interest rate of 10% how much is needed annually to meet the liability? To give a terminal value of £1 after seven years at 10% £0.1054 must be saved each year, so to finish with £750 000 the annual sum required is £750 000(0.1054) = £79 050. This process of **amortization** is one example of the 'conversion' of a one-off charge to a recurrent sum. In the following section we consider another way in which this capital-to-revenue transformation can be useful.

5.5 Annual equivalent annuities

The conversion of a capital sum to an annuity with the same present value is helpful in many financial problems. It is useful to know what annuity gives a present value of £1 given the length of time the annuity would run and the rate of discount. The **annual equivalent** annuity table (Table 6), shows the annuity required to give a present value of £1 for various rates of interest and numbers of years. Thus a lump sum of £1 is equivalent to an immediate annuity for two years at 10% of £0.5762.

Suppose that the capital cost of a machine tool is £25 000 and that the expected life of the equipment is ten years. At an interest rate of 8% the capital cost is equivalent in present-value terms to an annual charge of £25 000(0.1490) = £3725. The £3725 could be compared with the annual cost of alternative financing arrangements and also represents the gross amount of the depreciation charged on the equipment using the annuity method of depreciation. Entries in Table 6 are the reciprocals of corresponding entries in Table 3. Annual equivalents can be used in project appraisal and are useful in repair–replace problems. For the moment consider an exercise in the conversion of an irregular cash flow to annuity form (Problem 5.3).

Problem 5.3

Using Tables 2 and 6 find the annual equivalent annuity for two years at 10% for a project with the cash flow:

	$t=0$	$t=1$	$t=2$
	−700	650	800

Answer

First find the project's net present value in the usual manner:

Year	Sum	Discount factor	Present value
0	−700	1	−700
1	650	0.9091	590.92
2	800	0.8264	661.12
		NPV =	552.04

Second, convert the 'lump-sum' NPV to the annual equivalent figure for two years at 10%. This is £552.04(0.5762) = £318.09.

This two-stage process – the capitalization of an irregular cash flow and amortization of the resultant capital sum over a standard term – forms the basis of an effective method for finding the best strategy for equipment replacement. It is to this subject that we now turn.

5.6 Repair or replace

When should an asset be scrapped and with what, if anything, should it be replaced? As an asset ages, the operating and maintenance costs are likely to rise, and in some cases quality of output may fall, causing reduced revenues. But the longer an asset is kept the more the capital outlay associated with replacement is postponed. When capital equipment is to be replaced by financially identical equipment when it is scrapped, the problem is to determine the optimal interval between the installation of new machinery – the length of the replacement cycle. 'Financially identical' means that the cash flows produced by the new and old equipment are the same.

There may be data problems because not only do future cash flows need to be estimated, interdependencies must be untangled. For instance some of the costs may be joint costs, machines may compete for resources, or may be complementary or competitive on the revenue side. The data that are required are as follows:

1. a table of the net residual values of the asset;
2. the capital cost of the new asset;
3. operating and maintenance costs (O and M);
4. the revenues produced in each period.

The objective is the maximization of the present value of net revenues or the minimization of the present value of costs. The cost formulation is more convenient and any differences in revenue produced by machines of different ages are included in operating costs as **opportunity costs**. Given the cost-based formulation there still remain several ways of expressing the problem:

1. the annual equivalent annuity (AE) method;
2. the lowest common multiple (LCM) method;
3. the finite-horizon (FH) method.

First consider the **annual equivalent annuity method** – also known as the equivalent annual cost method. Suppose that a firm operates one machine of a certain type and that all such machines (existing asset and replacements) have a maximum life of four years with the financial data shown in Table 5.2. The cost of capital is 10% and the objective is to choose the length of replacement cycle which minimizes the present value of costs.

First compute the total present values of costs (some will be negative) associated with keeping the first machine for different lengths of time. Workings are shown in Table 5.3.

Table 5.2

Time t (years)	0	1	2	3	4
Initial outlay (£)	10 000				
O and M (£)		3000	4000	5000	6000
Residual Value (£)		6000	4500	3000	1000

Table 5.3

t	1 year	2 years	3 years	4 years
0	10 000	10 000	10 000	10 000
1	–3 000	3 000	3 000	3 000
2		–500	4 000	4 000
3			2 000	5 000
4				5 000
PV at 10%	7 272.72	12 314.05	17 535.69	23 204.70

The one-year column in Table 5.3 contains the cash flows associated with keeping the initial asset for one year. An outlay of £10 000 is required at $t = 0$ but at $t = 1$ the machine is scrapped for £6000 and only incurs O and M costs of £3000. Thus the net figure for costs is –£3000. Similarly in the two-year column at $t = 2$, O and M costs are £4000, but scrapping at this point produces £4500, a new inflow of £500 (hence the 'cost' of –£500). Other entries are found in the same way and the present value of each cash flow is then calculated.

The numbers in the last row of Table 5.3 represent the costs to the firm for different periods of time. Where the machine is retained for just one year a new machine is required at $t = 1$ which will again (if kept for one year) produce a stream of costs giving a 'present value' at $t = 1$ of 7272.72. One way to compare these different length cycles is to find the constant annual sum (annual equivalent annuity) which would give a present value at $t = 0$ equal to indefinitely repeated cycles of the given lengths. For instance, in the case of a cycle length of one year a payment of £8000 at $t = 1$ has a present value of 7272.72, and an annual payment of £8000 is equivalent in present value to the actual cash flow produced by a one-year cycle as shown in Table 5.4. In the case of a two-year cycle length the AE for two years at 10% giving a present value of 12 314.05 is 7095.24. In each case the AE figure is found by multiplying the present value entry in Table 5.3 by the AE factor for £1 at $100r\%$ for n years which is obtained from Table 6. The results are shown in Table 5.5(a). So a three-year cycle length is optimal; each machine is scrapped and replaced by a financially identical machine after three years. The calculations as a whole can be summarized as in Table 5.5(b).

Over an infinite horizon the total present value of costs with the optimal option is £70 511 which is the lowest figure achievable. The actual costs produced by the three-year cycle are:

$$10\,000 \quad 3000 \quad 4000 \quad 12\,000 \quad 3000 \quad 4000 \quad 12\,000 \quad \text{etc.}$$

After the initial 10 000 there are triennial perpetuities of 3000, 4000 and 12 000 and the figure of 70 511 can be obtained (difference due to rounding) as:

$$\frac{12\,000}{0.331} + \frac{4000(1.1)}{0.331} + \frac{3000(1.1)^2}{0.331} + 10\,000 = 70\,514$$

Table 5.4

	$t = 0$	$t = 1$	$t = 2$	$t = 3$	$t = 4$	$t = 5$
Machine 1	10 000	−3 000				
Machine 2		10 000	−3 000			
Machine 3			10 000	−3 000		
Machine 4				10 000	−3 000	
Machine 5					10 000	−3 000
Machine 6						10 000
etc						
Net cash flow:	10 000	7 000	7 000	7 000	7 000	7 000

Table 5.5(a)

Cycle length	PV of one cycle	AE factor	AE annuity
1	7 272.72	1.1000	8000.00
2	12 314.05	0.5762	7095.36
3	17 535.69	0.4021	7051.10
4	23 204.70	0.3155	7321.08

Table 5.5(b)

Cycle length	Net cash flow					NPV	AE Fac	AE Ann
	$t = 0$	$t = 1$	$t = 2$	$t = 3$	$t = 4$			
1 yr	10 000	−3000				7 273	1.10 000	8000
2 yr	10 000	3000	−500			12 314	0.57 619	7095
3 yr	10 000	3000	4000	2000		17 536	0.40 211	7051
4 yr	10 000	3000	4000	5000	5000	23 205	0.31 547	7320

The 4000 and 3000 flows begin at $t = 1$ and $t = 2$ respectively rather than at $t = 3$. However, a triennial flow of 4000 starting at $t = 2$ has the same present value as a triennial flow of 4000(1.1) starting at $t = 3$. A triennial flow of 3000 starting at $t = 1$ has the same present value as a triennial flow of $3000(1.1)^2$ starting at $t = 3$. With these adjustments we can consider all flows (apart from the original 10 000) as being triennial and starting at $t = 3$. In calculating the present value, the discount factors would be $1/(1.1)^3$, $1/(1.1)^6$, $1/(1.1)^9$ and so on, which are equivalent to $1/1.331$, $1/(1.331)^2$, $1/(1.331)^3$ etc. This explains the division by 0.331 above.

Finally, we can obtain the figure of 70 514 in one more slightly different way. If we consider the costs in the three-year case to be equivalent to a sum of 17 535.69 every third year, starting at $t = 0$, the total present value works out as:

$$\frac{17\ 535.69 \times 1.331}{0.331} = 70\ 514$$

Implicit in the AE method is the presumption that there is a sufficiently long time horizon over which to compare the alternative cycle lengths. This is made explicit in the

lowest common multiple method where the cycle-length alternatives are compared by the present value of the costs that they produce over a horizon equal to the lowest common multiple of the cycle lengths. In the above example the horizon is 12 years. The AE method is preferable in all but near trivial cases, although with careful use of standard tables the LCM method is not as bad as may appear from a case with 8-, 9-, and 10-year cycle alternatives and an LCM of 360 years!

What is a 'sufficiently long' horizon for the AE method? Ideally, for complete accuracy, this is the lowest common multiple of the cycle lengths so that there is a whole number of replacements under each policy alternative. As we have seen, this may be *very* long, but since discount factors decay exponentially a cut-off point – the **finite horizon** – can be determined with minor, and in realistic terms frequently negligible, effects on present value (though the effects are not necessarily negligible on the environment of future generations). In practice it is quite legitimate to use the AE approach when it is clear that a long view is being taken. To illustrate the practical validity of this standpoint, with a 10% discount rate, a cost or return is discounted by over 95% of its value at 32 years from the present. In the case of a 20% interest rate a discount of similar magnitude applies after 17 years, while with a 30% discount rate this position is reached after just 12 years. This fact is recognized by the **finite-horizon method** which calculates and compares the present values of the cash flows produced by the alternatives over a predetermined, long horizon in the knowledge of the fact that the degree of approximation implied by not necessarily having whole numbers of cycle lengths is slight. The FH method has been used to assess cycles of road maintenance and upgrading in the USA. Other US public utility investments have been appraised using a 50 year horizon.

An interesting theoretical issue with the finite-horizon method is the treatment of posthorizon cash flows. In practice these are usually consolidated into a single figure at the horizon date. This issue becomes more significant the shorter is the horizon, and it may be necessary to work with a time horizon that is neither very long nor the LCM of the cycle lengths. This situation, which from the decision-maker's point of view is just a plain **fact**, could occur for example with plant and equipment specific to a major construction project for which they are the contractor and which is to be completed in a set length of time. In this case the finite horizon, although undesirably short, is imposed and the NPVs of the costs over this period are found inclusive of any residual value of the plant and equipment at the horizon date which may have worth in other uses or as scrap.

Now consider the replacement of an existing machine by a new and different type of machine. The problem is when to break into the cycle for the existing type of equipment and introduce the **optimal** cycle with the new machines. An enumerative approach (considering all possible alternatives) is again employed. Consider an example. A firm's existing machine of an old design has operating and maintenance costs and scrap value as follows:

Time (years) t	0	1	2	3
O and M (£)	0	3600	4800	6000
Residual value (£)	3500	2000	1000	0

Column 0 shows that if the old machine was scrapped at once there would be no O and M costs and a scrap value would be £3500. If scrapping occurred after one year there would be a single net outflow of £1600 at $t = 1$. The old machine can be scrapped at any of the four values of t and replaced permanently by machines with costs as shown in Table 5.2 for which we have seen that a three-year replacement cycle is optimal. The total present value of costs for the new machines was £70 511 **from the date of introduction of these machines**. So if the new cycle began at $t = 2$ (scrapping the old machine at this time), the present value of costs on the new machines at $t = 0$ would be £70 511(0.8264) = £58 270. The whole picture is presented in Table 5.6.

So the optimal policy is to keep the old machine for two years and then replace it with the three-year cycle on the new machines. The figure of 64 683 is obtained as:

$$3600(0.9091) + (3800 + 70\,511)(0.8264)$$

Table 5.6

Replace at	Cash flow				Total PV
	$t = 0$	$t = 1$	$t = 2$	$t = 3$	
	–3 500				
$t = 0$	70 511				67 011
	0	1 600			
$t = 1$		70 511			65 556
	0	3 600	3 800		
$t = 2$			70 511		64 683
	0	3 600	4 800	6 000	
$t = 3$				70 511	64 722

with remaining figures in the PV column obtained in a similar fashion. There is little practical difference between the two-year and three-year options – just £39 in present-value terms.

The AE method can be modified to take into account anticipated inflation at a uniform rate as long as the underlying structure of cost (to which the inflation applies) remains unchanged. The necessary revisions to the method are detailed in Wilkes (1983). When the underlying structure of costs does change – as is normally the case under conditions of technical progress – the AE method cannot be modified to give exact answers unless the technical progress is reflected in alterations to the original costs at a constant percentage rate (as would be the case with a **negative** inflation rate). As things are rarely this convenient, either the AE method can be applied to give approximate answers sufficient for practical purposes or the LCM or FH approaches must be used.

5.7 Annuities with growth

So far we have been considering regular cash flows in which the sum involved is the same in each year. But a known cash flow may exhibit other forms of regularity than constancy. For example, some agreements to provide central financial support for public-sector responsibilities involve a 'taper' requirement where the sums transferred are reduced year by year in a structured way. The number of years involved in these arrangements is usually quite small so that special formulae will not normally be required to compute present values. In other areas of activity, growth may be involved and it is on these cases that we shall concentrate.

Consider the case where a cash flow instead of being of constant value in each year grows at a constant compound rate from year to year. What is the present value of such 'annuities with growth'? Suppose that the base payment is £S (set at $t = 0$) but that the actual sum payed in year t is £$S(1 + g)^t$. Here the growth is at $100g\%$ per annum compound. If $S = 1$, the stream of payments over n years would be:

$$
\begin{array}{cccccc}
t = 1 & t = 2 & t = 3 & t = 4 & \ldots\ldots & t = n \\
(1 + g) & (1 + g)^2 & (1 + g)^3 & (1 + g)^4 & \ldots\ldots & (1 + g)^n
\end{array}
$$

The present value of this stream at a rate of discount of $100r\%$ would be:

$$
PV = \sum_{t=1}^{n} \frac{(1 + g)^t}{(1 + r)^t}
$$

A formula can be found for an expression of this form. (The sum represents a geometric series. The result given uses the well known formula for the sum to n terms of a geometric series. See for example Wilkes (1994).) The formula is:

$$PV = \frac{\frac{(1+g)}{(1+r)}\left[1 - \frac{(1+g)^n}{(1+r)^n}\right]}{1 - \frac{(1+g)}{(1+r)}} \qquad (5.4)$$

where in (5.4) it is assumed that r is not equal to g. If $r = g$ then the present value is simply:

$$PV = n$$

In usage, expression (5.4) may be slightly more convenient when rearranged as:

$$PV = \frac{(1+g)\left[1 - \frac{(1+g)^n}{(1+r)^n}\right]}{r - g} \qquad (5.5)$$

Consider a numerical example: what is the present value of an annuity of £150 for 10 years growing at 3% per annum (from a baseline of $t = 0$) when the discount rate is 8%?

Using formula (5.5) with $g = 0.03$, $r = 0.08$, $n = 10$ and multiplying by 150 gives:

$$PV = 150 \frac{(1.03)\left[1 - \frac{(1.03)^{10}}{(1.08)^{10}}\right]}{0.08 - 0.03}$$
$$= 1166.50$$

While tables could be prepared for values of (5.5) since three parameters are involved here, they would be rather extensive.

How does the present value of an 'annuity with growth' compare with the case of an immediate annuity (no growth)? The formula for the present value of an immediate annuity is obtained in a similar fashion to (5.4) and reduces to the form given in the Tables. The formula is:

$$PV = \frac{\frac{1}{(1+r)}\left[1 - \frac{1}{(1+r)^n}\right]}{1 - \frac{1}{(1+r)}} \qquad (5.6)$$

It is clear from a comparison of (5.6) and (5.4) that $1/(1 + r)$ in (5.6) replaces $(1 + g)/(1 + r)$ in (5.4). This means that a 'growing annuity' with a given discount rate is equivalent to a fixed annuity at the original level (i.e. £S) but at a lower discount rate. This lower discount rate is $100e\%$ where:

$$(1 + e) = \frac{(1 + r)}{(1 + g)}$$

So, for example, in a case where payments were growing at 3% p.a. and where the discount rate was 10% the annuity (£S at $t = 0$) with growth is equivalent in present value to an annuity of £S at approximately 6.8% since:

$$(1 + 0.06796) \approx \frac{(1 + 0.1)}{(1 + 0.03)}$$

In the case of a perpetuity with growth, it is clear that for a finite present value, the rate of growth must be strictly less than the discount rate. Given that $g < r$ then in (5.5) it is evident that the term:

$$\frac{(1+g)^n}{(1+r)^n}$$

approaches zero as n increases. This being the case, (5.5) will simplify to:

$$PV = \frac{(1 + g)}{r - g}$$

So, for example, a perpetuity based on £100 (i.e. $S = 100$) at $t = 0$ growing at 3½% per annum, with a discount rate of 8% has a present value of:

$$PV = \frac{100}{0.08 - 0.035} \approx 2222.22$$

There is another way of looking at annuities with growth. They can be seen as the sum of annuities with receding commencement dates. For example if $S = 100$ and growth was at 10% p.a. compound, then the cash flow involved would be:

$t = 1$	$t = 2$	$t = 3$	$t = 4$	$t = 5$	
110	121	133.1	146.41	161.051	.....

which can be seen as the sum of the following annuities:

$t = 1$	$t = 2$	$t = 3$	$t = 4$	$t = 5$	
110	110	110	110	110	.....
	11	11	11	11	.....
		12.1	12.1	12.1	.....
			13.31	13.31	.....
				14.461	.....
					.....

5.8 Make or buy

A classic problem in the application of discounted cash flow (DCF) methods is the **make or buy** problem which also illustrates the way that opportunity costs can be taken into account within a single project DCF framework. The make or buy problem arises when a company has the choice of making an item it needs or buying in supplies manufactured elsewhere. The costs in each case usually have a different structure. The make or buy decision can often be formulated as an investment appraisal problem, although there may be some important factors that are not readily quantifiable – for instance, the benefits of any extra security of supply if the 'make' decision is taken.

Consider the case where the 'make' decision requires an outlay of K now for equipment lasting n years; where $M_1, M_2, \ldots M_n$ represent the costs of producing the required quantities of the item in each year and where $B_1, B_2, \ldots, B_n$ are the costs of buying. The cash flow to be evaluated is:

$$-K \quad B_1 - M_1 \quad B_2 - M_2 \quad B_3 - M_3 \ldots \ldots B_n - M_n + S_n \qquad (5.7)$$

where S_n is the scrap value of equipment at time n. This basic framework can be expanded. If the make decision displaces other projects, then the returns to the forgone opportunities should be deducted throughout (5.7). In terms of taxation, the effects of any writing-down allowance would need to be taken into account.

Suppose that a firm is considering making for itself a component that it needs in an assembly operation. The manufacturing requires equipment costing £400 000 which would last for four years with a residual value of £200 000. Manufacturing costs in each year would be £500 000, £700 000, £800 000 and £900 000 respectively. If the firm buys the components from a supplier the costs are £900 000, £1 000 000, £1 100 000 and £1 400 000 in each year. However, the equipment would occupy floor space which could have been put to other uses generating £200 000 net in each of the four years. This opportunity is lost if the make option is adopted. If the cost of capital is 13% should the company make or buy the component?

The cost cash flow from manufacture (net of the residual value in the final year) is:

$$t = 0 \quad t = 1 \quad t = 2 \quad t = 3 \quad t = 4$$
$$400\ 000 \quad 500\ 000 \quad 700\ 000 \quad 800\ 000 \quad 700\ 000$$

while the costs associated with buying in the components are

$$t = 0 \quad t = 1 \quad t = 2 \quad t = 3 \quad t = 4$$
$$0 \quad 900\ 000 \quad 1\ 000\ 000 \quad 1\ 100\ 000 \quad 1\ 400\ 000$$

Thus the *gross* savings in costs if the component is made rather than bought are:

$$t = 0 \quad t = 1 \quad t = 2 \quad t = 3 \quad t = 4$$
$$-400\ 000 \quad 400\ 000 \quad 300\ 000 \quad 300\ 000 \quad 700\ 000$$

The income forgone if the make decision is taken is now deducted from these savings. This leaves the cash flow changes due to making the component as:

$$t = 0 \quad t = 1 \quad t = 2 \quad t = 3 \quad t = 4$$
$$-400\ 000 \quad 200\ 000 \quad 100\ 000 \quad 100\ 000 \quad 500\ 000$$

The net present value of this stream is now found. Workings are:

Year	Cash flow	Discount factor	Present value
0	−400 000	1	−400 000
1	200 000	0.8550	177 000
2	100 000	0.7831	78 310
3	100 000	0.6931	69 310
4	500 000	0.6133	306 650
		Total	231 270

Since the net present value is positive the decision to make is confirmed. The make or buy problem is a particular example of sourcing problems seen as investments.

5.9 Discounted cash flows and tax payments

The tax environment in which capital budgeting decisions are taken varies through time for any given country and also, of course, between nations. This section shows in general terms how, with a given tax structure, the tax payments should be taken into account. We are not concerned with the finer points of corporate tax law or methods of tax assessment and for illustration will use a simple and adaptable framework.

Ideally, after-tax cash flows and costs should be used in discounted cash flow calculations, but netting the data of tax may be quite a difficult problem. For instance, consider one of the returns to an investment – say the return R_3 in the third year. If the company is in profit, R_3 is added to taxable earnings. There is then a cash outflow of $t(R_3)$ (where t is the rate of profits tax) when the tax is payable. If $R3$ is negative (representing a loss) then if the company is earning a profit on other activities the tax bill in total will be reduced by $t(R_3)$. But if the company was not making taxable profits and if R_3 was not large enough to change this, then the project adds the full R_3 to earnings with no offsetting additions to tax. A further complicating factor is that liability for taxation depends on how the project is financed – tax relief on debt interest should be taken into account if this means of financing is an option.

The basic principle is that tax payments represent cash out and should be treated in the same way as other cash flows. The next present value of a project is therefore calculated after tax in the case of companies with shareholders, private firms or individuals. Apart from the financing question, the following example shows how taxation can be taken into account in a discounted cash flow calculation.

A company has an opportunity to buy a machine for £10 000. Net returns (revenues minus operating costs) are £5000 in each of the next four years. The question to be decided is whether or not the investment is worthwhile after tax and after allowing for provision for working capital. (Working capital allows for minor cash flows too small and unpredictable to include explicitly in the NPV calculation.) The rate of discount is 12% and £500 cash is set aside by the company as working capital for its day-to-day contingencies. This sum is taken from other uses in year zero and replaced at the end of the final year. Suppose that the tax regime is that tax payable is 35% of net return less a writing down allowance (WDA) on a straight line basis of 20% of the initial capital expenditure for five years. Tax payments are lagged by one year. (Depreciation is relevant to discounted cash flow financial appraisals only in circumstances where it affects the tax payments of the decision-maker.) Workings for this example are then as shown in Table 5.7.

Table 5.7

				Year			
	0	1	2	3	4	5	6
1 Outlay/returns	−10 000	5000	5000	5000	5000	0	0
2 Working capital	−500	0	0	0	500	0	0
3 WDA*		2000	2000	2000	2000	2000	0
4 Taxable profit*		3000	3000	3000	3000	−2000	0
5 Taxation at 35%			−1050	−1050	−1050	−1050	700
6 Net cash flow	−10 500	5000	3950	3950	4450	−1050	700
7 Discount factor	1.0000	0.8929	0.7972	0.7118	0.6355	0.5674	0.5066
8 Present value	−10 500	4464	3149	2812	2828	−596	355
9 Net present value	2512						
10 Yield	23.4%						

*Not cash flow items

Note how the net cash flow data in line 6 that are used for the discounted cash flow calculations differ from the original outlay and return figures both in respect of the figure in any given year and in terms of the number of years over which the project would affect cash flow. The yield of the project is 23.4% and at 12% the net present value is £2512 so the opportunity to invest in the machine should be taken up. Note (for reference shortly) that the NPV at a discount rate of 24% is −110.

The solution above assumed a writing down allowance of 20% over five years. Suppose that this is changed by the tax authorities to 25% over four years. With no other changes, the workings would then have been as shown in Table 5.8.

From Table 5.8 the overall effect of the change both on yield and net present value is seen to be small. In this case therefore the changed way in which the writing down allowance is calculated does not alter the company's decision to invest in the project at the current discount rate. However, if the discount rate was double the present level, an NPV of −110 in the five-year WDA case is turned into a marginally acceptable +36 in the four-year case. Alternative schemes (such as 'free depreciation' or the use of declining balances) and the associated taxation and cash flow consequences could be accommodated within a similar framework, the principle of determining post-tax cash flows being unchanged. The reader is referred to Chapter 3 or to Drury (1992) for further discussion of taxation considerations.

Table 5.8

				Year			
		0	1	2	3	4	5
1	Outlay/returns	−10 000	5000	5000	5000	5000	0
2	Working capital	−500	0	0	0	500	0
3	WDA*		2500	2500	2500	2500	0
4	Taxable profit*		2500	2500	2500	2500	0
5	Taxation at 35%			−875	−875	−875	−875
6	Net cash flow	−10 500	5000	4125	4125	4625	−875
7	Discount factor	1.0000	0.8929	0.7972	0.7118	0.6355	0.5674
8	Present value	−10 500	4464	3288	2936	2939	−496
9	Net present value	2632					
10	Yield	24.2%					

*Not cash flow items

5.10 Investment appraisal and inflation

How should account be taken of inflation in discounted cash flow calculations and investment decision-making? In answering this question it is important to distinguish between **anticipated** inflation – which can be taken into account within the framework of a deterministic model – and **unanticipated** inflation. Unanticipated inflation is one of a number of sources of uncertainty, and methods which address this situation are discussed in the following chapter.

The focus here is on anticipated inflation, and a given rate of inflation will refer to the annual rate of change of an appropriate group or index of prices. The returns and costs of a particular investment project may or may not inflate at the same rate as prices overall. Whatever the circumstances, discounted cash flow calculations should be performed using the best available estimates of actual (i.e. **nominal**) cash flows and the discount rate. An investment decision made on the basis of present value calculated in this fashion maximizes the net cash sum available to the investor (at whatever point in time this is desired). As was seen in Chapter 4, this is the case when the discount rate applies to all interperiod transfers of funds and the NPV criterion is valid for all investors regardless of individual time preferences. The presence of inflation would erode the purchasing power of the cash sums but would not alter the **relative** sizes of cash sums made possible by the competing projects. So diminished purchasing power should not affect the choice between projects – including the choice between an individual project and the null project (not investing at all) – as long as the same rate of discount is applied before and after inflation.

This said, for any given actual discount rate or yield figure a 'real' or inflation-adjusted discount rate could be computed, if desired, where:

$$(1 + e)(1 + a) = (1 + i) \tag{5.8}$$

in which the nominal interest rate is $100i\%$, the rate of inflation is $100a\%$ and the 'real' rate is $100e\%$. Of course, if a is greater than i then the real rate is negative. This would have no bearing on any accept/reject decision for the reasons stated earlier. If the decision-maker prefers to use a real rate of discount in the NPV calculations (as defined by (5.8)) this can be done as long as the cash flow elements are also deflated at $100a\%$ per annum. The two sets of workings – actual and real – are then formally identical. What is *not* justifiable is to mix 'real' and nominal data in the present value calculations. Unfortunately however, this confusion still occurs in practice. A survey by Drury *et al.* in 1992 showed that almost half of the firms responding to the survey had discounted real returns at a nominal rate, while about one firm in nine had discounted nominal returns at the real rate.

In practice not all costs and revenues will inflate at the same rate, in which event while the use of real values with appropriate deflators is still possible – and Drury's survey indicated that a small number of firms do in fact employ this approach – nominal values having the double advantage of simplicity and accuracy. When different components of a cash flow inflate at different rates projective sensitivity analysis can be helpful in assessing the consequences for present values. We shall consider this approach in Chapter 6. But even in the case where all prices and costs are inflating or deflating at the same rate, there is still a reason for preferring the use of nominal rather than real values in DCF calculations. This is because taxation payments typically depend in part on writing down allowances related to a given initial sum, and will therefore be damped in their movements.

Consider a numerical example of a case where all prices and costs move in a similar fashion. A firm can invest in a project costing £3 250 000 in 1996. At 1996 prices the project would return £1 000 000 net at the end of each of four years. However, prices are inflating at 6% generally and the magnitude of the net returns in cash would be affected accordingly. The nominal rate of interest is 11.3%. Should the project be undertaken? The NPV of the investment can be found by discounting the cash net returns at the nominal rate of interest. Thus the cash flow to be discounted at 11.3% is:

$t = 0$	$t = 1$	$t = 2$	$t = 3$	$t = 4$
–3 250 000	1 060 000	1 123 600	1 191 016	1 262 477

which has a net present value of £295 951 and the project is therefore worthwhile. Alternatively, the NPV could be found by discounting the price deflated returns at the 'real' interest rate. The real rate as given by (5.8) is $100e\%$ where:

$$(1 + e)\,(1.06) = (1.113)$$

so that:

$$e = \frac{1.113}{1.06} - 1 = 0.05$$

and the cash flow for discounting at this 5% rate is:

$t = 0$	$t = 1$	$t = 2$	$t = 3$	$t = 4$
–3 250 000	1 000 000	1 000 000	1 000 000	1 000 000

which gives the £295 951 value for NPV obtained above. Note that if, quite incorrectly, the 'real' returns of £1 000 000 had been discounted at the nominal rate of 11.3% the resulting figure for NPV would have been –£167 322 which is a false value that would lead to unjustified rejection of the project.

When a uniform rate of interest does not apply to both positive and negative interperiod financial transfers, not only do the particular investor's time preferences now count, as was seen in Chapter 4, but the choice between competing alternative projects can be affected by the presence or absence of inflation even if their cash flows are influenced in the same ways. (This result is of mainly theoretical interest (see Wilkes (1972)) and in practice projects should continue to be compared at uniform discount rates.)

There are several other significant consequences of inflation. For example, there can be acute liquidity problems if the inflated costs are incurred before the inflated revenues arrive. These cash flow crises arise under unanticipated inflation. The consequences of counter-inflation policy need also to be taken into account. For example, if the primary instrument of macroeconomic policy is interest rates, the decision between projects can be changed (as was seen in Chapter 4). But the choice between projects should still be determined on the basis of actual cash sums discounted at actual discount rates. For multinational companies, differential inflation rates between countries and consequent variations in exchange rates as well as domestic interest rates are further complicating factors. But if the eventual corporate objective is in terms of repatriated monies, these cash sums should be the relevant units of account here.

5.11 Capital project commencement and termination dates

The date at which a capital project of given duration is commenced can have an important influence on the present value and viability of the investment. So can the timing of the end of a project when the duration is variable. As regards start date, one is not here speaking of operational matters, the capital spend having begun (as for example with the Channel Tunnel) but of the decision as to when the project and the capital spend is to begin. On the issue of termination dates, net cash flow may become erratic with negative as well as positive elements – with possibly crucial end of project costs such as decommissioning.

First consider the question of starting date. The present value of a project may change if the commencement date is altered because the outlay and returns maybe affected asymmetrically by the changed timing. For example, postponement will affect the present value of the initial outlay as well as any decommissioning costs at the end of the project. Up to a point, these reductions may more than offset the reduction in the present value of the positive cash inflows. Consider a numerical example.

A company is considering the installation of a power generation plant with a life expectancy of 15 years. If undertaken in 1995, the capital cost would be £295m with estimated net revenues of £50m in each of the first five years of operation, £60m for the next five years, and £80m p.a. in the last five years of the operating life of the plant. There would then follow decommissioning costs of £300m in year 16. There is the option of commencement in 2000 at which point capital cost would be £350m with annual net revenues of £60m, £80m and £110m for the five-year periods and end of project costs of £400m in year 16. Finally there is the option of commencement in 2005 at a capital cost of £450m and net revenues of £80m, £110m and £140m for the five-year periods with decommissioning costs of £500m in year 16. Cost of capital is 10%. Which starting date should be selected on the basis of net present value in 1995?

The mutually exclusive cash flows are as follows. For the 1995 start:

1995	1996–2000	2001–2005	2006–2010	2011
–295	50	60	80	–300

For the 2000 start:

2000	2001–2005	2006–2010	2011–2015	2016
–350	60	80	110	–400

For the 2005 start:

2005	2006–2010	2011–2015	2016–2020	2021
–450	80	110	140	–500

At 10% the NPVs of the options are £87.4m, £86.6m and £80.2m respectively, so that although there is relatively little in it given likely uncertainties, a 1995 start date would be preferred. But further analysis shows the importance of the discount rate that is applied to the calculations. Table 5.9 gives results from 1% to 20% rates of discount. At low rates of discount the 2005 start date would be preferred, at 8% or 9% the 2000 start had the edge, at 10% and 11% the 1995 start comes out best, in the range 12% to 15% the 2000 start date again comes to the fore while for higher rates the 2005 option regains its edge. The reason for the switching is that different components of the cash flows are differentially affected by the changing discount rate.

In general, the present value of a project may change in both magnitude and sign as a result of a changed starting date. The graph of NPV against starting date may have any shape, and one possibility is illustrated in Figure 5.2. In this figure it can be seen that the NPV of the project if started in 1995 is negative, and that the optimum starting date is 1999.

Now consider the optimum termination date for a project. It may be desirable to wind up an operation even though it would have continued to yield **some** positive net returns beyond the date of termination. Less obviously, in certain circumstances it may pay to proceed into a period of all negative returns. This matter may be considered at the time that the investment decision is taken or at a later point in the light of new information

Table 5.9 *Present value of project with alternative start dates*

Discount rate	1995 start	2000 start	2005 start
1.00%	320.40	430.84	574.82
2.00%	287.62	369.80	470.71
3.00%	256.68	316.06	384.27
4.00%	227.56	268.85	312.61
5.00%	200.21	227.44	253.28
6.00%	174.56	191.18	204.22
7.00%	150.54	159.47	163.70
8.00%	128.06	131.78	130.30
9.00%	107.04	107.63	102.79
10.00%	87.40	86.60	80.18
11.00%	69.04	68.30	61.64
12.00%	51.88	52.40	46.46
13.00%	35.84	38.61	34.08
14.00%	20.85	26.66	24.00
15.00%	6.83	16.34	15.84
16.00%	−6.28	7.43	9.25
17.00%	−18.56	−0.24	3.97
18.00%	−30.06	−6.82	−0.23
19.00%	−40.84	−12.45	−3.55
20.00%	−50.94	−17.25	−6.13

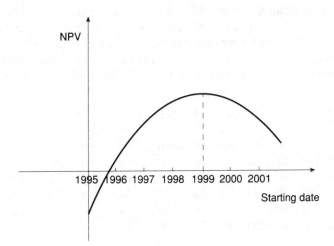

Figure 5.2

on cash flow. The optimum termination date is that for which the NPV of the project is maximized. As a first example, and with a discount rate of 10%, consider the cash flow:

$t=0$	$t=1$	$t=2$	$t=3$	$t=4$	$t=5$	$t=6$	$t=7$	$t=8$	$t=9$	$t=10$
−60	90	−50	70	−40	30	−40	50	20	−30	30

It is fairly clear that unless there are specific constraints on the decision-maker's freedom of action, a project should not be terminated on grounds of cash flow immediately prior to a positive return. Possible termination dates therefore precede negative returns, of which a special case is the initial outlay itself. The possible dates and associated NPVs are then as shown in Table 5.10.

Table 5.10

Date	Cash flow	NPV	Comment
$t = 0$	n/a	0	rejects project
$t = 1$	–60 90	21.82	precedes neg return
$t = 3$	–60 90 –50 70	33.09	precedes neg return
$t = 5$	–60 90 –50 70 –40 30	24.40	precedes neg return
$t = 8$	–60 90 –50 70 –40 30 –40 50 20	36.80	precedes net return
$t = 10$	whole project	35.65	accept in entirety

In this case, the optimum termination date is at $t = 8$ immediately on receipt of the return of 20. Inspection of the cash flow reveals that the $t = 5$ option could be ruled out without calculating overall NPV since what it adds to the $t = 3$ option: –40 30 cannot have a positive present value, assuming that the discount rate is not negative, but as the result for the $t = 8$ option shows, it is possible to add to present value by going on beyond $t = 3$. The criterion of maximizing NPV can be re-stated as choosing that cut-off point starting from which there are no cash flow streams of any length that have positive present value. In general, the optimum termination date will depend on the rate of discount as well as the cash flow data. See problem 18 for an illustration of this point.

Another scenario of variable length of life for a project may be described as that of 'putting off the evil day' at which substantial end of project costs are incurred. One example would be that of decommissioning costs for nuclear power stations. Clearly, in this case there are many wider considerations to be taken into account. But we shall consider here only the cash flow and the associated present value implications. Suppose that a project costs £80m to initiate with first-year net revenues of £70m and where net revenues decline by £10m in each subsequent year as maintenance and operating costs increase. (Obviously, we are compressing the time scales likely to be found in a practical context.) There is no fixed lifespan for the project but when the venture is terminated there are substantial end of project costs of £160m. The cash flows associated with various lengths of life would then be:

5 years	–80	70	60	50	40	30	–160					
6 years	–80	70	60	50	40	30	20	–160				
7 years	–80	70	60	50	40	30	20	10	–160			
8 years	–80	70	60	50	40	30	20	10	0	–160		
9 years	–80	70	60	50	40	30	20	10	0	–10	–160	
10 years	–80	70	60	50	40	30	20	10	0	–10	–20	–160
11 years	–80	70	60	50	40	30	20	10	0	–10	–20	–30 –160
12 years	–80	70	60	50	40	30	20	10	0	–10	–20	–30 –40 –160

Clearly, in terms of NPV it is worth continuing the project so long as positive returns are coming in. Note that this statement would not necessarily be true in a context where the end of project costs increased as the termination date receded. However, it applies here. Although the net inflow in year 8 is zero, the move from 7 to 8 years is beneficial in present value terms since at any positive discount rate the postponement of the –160 penalty reduces its value at any earlier date. The present values for the 7–11 year horizons are:

Duration	NPV (10%)	NPV (15%)
7	58.52	57.00
8	65.30	63.82
9	67.23	66.91
10	65.13	67.13
11	59.71	65.17

Note that at 10% it is worth accepting the loss of 10 in year 9 since the gain in present value from a further postponement of the −160 penalty exceeds 10. At 10% it is not worth proceeding further than this, and the optimum duration (exclusive of the −160 penalty year) is 9 years. However, at 15% it is worth putting of the day of reckoning for a further year, since NPV increases. The loss of 20 taken in year 10 is a price worth paying at 15% to postpone the loss of 160. Note too that the present value of the project is actually **greater** at the higher discount rate for the greater project durations. This apparently perverse effect results from the fact that the loss years at the end of the project are affected more than the revenue producing years by the higher discount rate. The importance of using a discount rate which reflects true costs and opportunities is well illustrated by this example.

5.12 Non-standard cash flows and other methods of compounding

It is usually assumed that the cash flow and method of discounting are in the conventional form of discrete returns at the end of discrete and equal length compounding periods. This is our normal practice in this text. In reality, detailed departures from this standard model will be quite frequent, but the standard model will also be a sufficiently good approximation most of the time. On occasion, however, it may be worth reformulating the model to correspond more closely to an exceptional practical situation. It is also as well to be aware of the degree of approximation that is implied by the standard model. (This can be significant. See Wilkes (1983). Tariq (1994) has surveyed UK businesses on the question of continuous returns.)

A common exception to the year's end case is the half-yearly payment of interest on bank deposit accounts and government securities. Discounting formulae can be adjusted to allow for more frequent payments. If the quoted rate of interest was $100x\%$ but in fact interest was paid half yearly at $100(x/2)\%$, the result is two compounding periods a year and, for investors, an example of benign understatement. In these circumstances, £1 on deposit for one year at $100x\%$ nominal becomes:

$$\left(1 + \frac{x}{2}\right)^2 = 1 + x + \frac{x^2}{4} > 1 + x$$

So future value is increased if this is worked out using half the nominal interest rate compounded twice as frequently. For example, if a declared 12% annual interest is in practice implemented as twice yearly compounding at 6%, the end of year value of £1 will be:

$$(1 + 0.12/2)^2 = 1.1236$$

which is equivalent to an annually compounded rate of 12.36%. But what if interest was compounded quarterly? At 12% the result would be:

$$(1 + 0.12/4)^4 = 1.1255 \text{ or } 12.55\%$$

If interest was compounded monthly, as with most credit cards, the result would be:

$$(1 + 0.12/12)^{12} = 1.1268 \text{ or } 12.68\%$$

Credit card companies normally quote interest rates per month. The equivalent annual rate is *more* than 12 times the monthly rate. For example, the annual rate equivalent to 2% per month is given by $(1.02)^{12} = 1.2682$; that is, 26.82%.

In some major financial transactions interest is charged on a daily basis, so the equivalent annual rate in this case would be given by:

$$(1 + 0.12/365)^{365} = 1.1275 \text{ or } 12.75\%$$

So for example, a sum of £850 borrowed initially at a nominal 12% but with daily compounding would, by the end of the year, have grown to:

$$850(1 + 0.12/365)^{365} \approx 958$$

What would happen if interest was compounded more frequently still? The answer is provided by the limiting value of:

$$\left\{1 + \frac{x}{n}\right\}^{n} \qquad (5.9)$$

as n increases without limit. In so doing, **continuous compounding** is approached. In working towards a value for (5.9), we start with the simpler case where $x = 1$. Table 5.11 shows values of $(1 + 1/n)^{n}$ for selected values of n.

Table 5.11

n	0	1	2	5	10	25	100
$(1 + 1/n)^{n}$	1	2	2.25	2.48 832	2.59 374	2.66 584	2.70 481
n	500		1000	10 000	100 000	500 000	1 000 000
$(1 + 1/n)^{n}$	2.715 57		2.716 92	2.718 15	2.718 27	2.718 28	2.718 28

From Table 5.11 it is seen that the value of $(1 + 1/n)^{n}$ approaches 2.71 828 (to five decimal places) as n continues to increase. When stated as a **limit** (a value that an expression approaches ever more closely as the independent variable increases) this is written as:

$$\lim_{n \to \infty} (1 + 1/n)^{n} = 2.718\ 281\ 828\ 459\ 045 \ldots = e$$

The number e is known as the **natural number**. What of $(1 + x/n)^{n}$? It can be shown that the limit of this term as n increases is e raised to the power of x. That is:

$$\lim_{n \to \infty}\left(1 + \frac{x}{n}\right)^{n} = e^{x} \qquad (5.10)$$

An answer can now be given to the question of to where the process of ever more frequent compounding would lead: 12% continuous compounding gives an end of year result for a principal of £1 of:

$$e^{0.12} \approx 1.1275 \text{ or } 12.75\%$$

Two years of continuous compounding at $100x\%$ per annum produces a future value of e^{2x}. So for example with $x = 0.12$, after two years £1 would become:

$$£e^{2(0.12)} \approx £1.2712$$

In general, if a principal of £P is invested at $100r\%$ per annum continuously compounded, with no withdrawals, the future value after t years is:

$$Pe^{rt}$$

So for example, a principal of £500 deposited for two years at 12% continuously compounded, would produce a future value of:

$$500e^{0.24} = 635.62$$

while over five years, the future value would be:

$$500e^{0.6} = 911.06$$

Similarly, the present value of £1 to be received t years in the future with continuous compounding at $100r\%$ would be:

$$e^{-rt}$$

and the present value of an n period cash flow with a return of R_t in period t is:

$$PV = \sum_{t=1}^{n} R_t e^{-rt}$$

Note that for any continuously compounded interest rate there is a unique equivalent discretely compounded rate. To illustrate, the equivalent rate to 12% continuously compounded, with once yearly compounding is $100r\%$ where, for example at two years:

$$(1 + r)^2 = 1.2712$$

which solves for $r = 1.1275$ or 12.75% per annum. Table 5.12 gives a comparison of the discount factors at 10% for discrete and continuous compounding. Note that the difference is more marked in the later years.

Table 5.12

n	Discrete $(1 + r)^{-n}$	Continuous e^{-nr}
1	0.9091	0.9048
2	0.8264	0.8187
3	0.7513	0.7408
4	0.6830	0.6703
5	0.6209	0.6065
6	0.5645	0.5488
7	0.5132	0.4966
8	0.4665	0.4493
9	0.4241	0.4066
10	0.3855	0.3679
11	0.3505	0.3329
12	0.3186	0.3012
13	0.2897	0.2725
14	0.2633	0.2466
15	0.2394	0.2231
20	0.1486	0.1353
30	0.0573	0.0498
40	0.0221	0.0183
50	0.0085	0.0067

Consider a numerical example. A project gives the following net returns at the end of five successive years:

$t = 1$	$t = 2$	$t = 3$	$t = 4$	$t = 5$
100	150	200	100	80

The initial outlay is 300 and interest is compounded continuously at 10%. What is the net present value of the project? Using the discount factors of Table 5.12, the net present value is:

NPV = 100(0.9048) + 150(0.8187) + 200(0.7048) + 100(0.6703) + 80(0.6065) − 300
     = 177.00

Now consider the case of annuities under continuous compounding, in particular that of an immediate annuity with discrete sums at the end of each year but with continuous compounding within the year. It can be shown that the present value of such an annuity of £1 over n years is given by:

$$PV = \frac{1 - e^{-nr}}{e^r - 1} \qquad (5.11)$$

Consider a numerical example. What is the present value of a discrete annuity of £100 for 12 years when interest is compounded continuously at 10%? Using formula (5.11), with $n = 12$ and $r = 0.1$, the present value will be:

$$PV = 100 \frac{(1 - e^{-1.2})}{(e^{0.1} - 1)}$$

which, by use of a suitable calculator or program emerges as:

$$PV = 100 \,(6.6445) = 664.45$$

For comparison, the present value under discrete compounding at 10% would be £681.37. Comparisons over a number of years are given in Table 5.13.

Table 5.13

n	Discrete $\dfrac{1 - (1 + r)^{-n}}{r}$	Continuous $\dfrac{1 - e^{-nr}}{e^r - 1}$
1	0.9091	0.9048
2	1.7355	1.7236
3	2.4869	2.4644
4	3.1699	3.1347
5	3.7908	3.7412
6	4.3553	4.2900
7	4.8684	4.7866
8	5.3349	5.2360
9	5.7590	5.6425
10	6.1446	6.0104
11	6.4951	6.3433
12	6.8137	6.6445
13	7.1034	6.9170
14	7.3667	7.1636
15	7.6061	7.3867
20	8.5136	8.2215
30	9.4269	9.0349
40	9.7791	9.3342
50	9.9148	9.4443

Since in formula (5.11), e^{-nr} approaches zero as n increases for positive r, the present value of a discrete perpetuity with continuous compounding is seen to be:

$$PV(\text{perpetuity}) = \frac{1}{e^r - 1} \qquad (5.12)$$

which compares with the familiar $1/r$ when discounting as well as receipts are continuous. As an example, a perpetuity of £100 with continuous compounding at 10% would be:

$$PV = 100 \frac{1}{e^{0.1} - 1}$$

$$= 100(9.5083) = 950.83$$

In comparison, the present value of a perpetuity of £100 with discrete compounding at 10% would be $100/0.1 = 1000$.

The case of continuous receipts but discrete compounding in which there are no other arrangements as regards interest payments is, in the present context, equivalent to the discrete receipts and discrete compounding case since no interest advantage is gained by the earlier receipts. (Considerations such as risk would of course given an edge to the continuous receipts case.) In practice financial institutions may adopt a hybrid approach where, say, interest is compounded twice yearly but where deposits made between compounding points attract simple interest up to the time at which compounding occurs. In any given case the decision-maker would have to determine whether the additional precision of adjusting the discounting process to reflect a very particular scenario was genuinely worthwhile.

Now suppose that the future cash flow as well as the compounding is continuous. It can be shown that the present value of an n year cash flow, with $£R_t$ received evenly throughout year t is given by:

$$PV = \frac{1 - e^{-r}}{r} \sum R_t \, e^{-(t-1)r} \tag{5.13}$$

which is a considerably less convenient expression than that for the discrete returns discrete compounding case. Nevertheless it can be used. Consider a numerical example. Find the present value of the stream of returns:

$$
\begin{array}{lcccc}
\text{Time } t: & 0-1 & 1-2 & 2-3 & 3-4 \\
\text{Return:} & 10\,000 & 30\,000 & 20\,000 & 10\,000
\end{array}
$$

where the returns are regarded as arriving through each year in an effectively continuous fashion – for example as takings at a counter – and where interest is compounded continuously at 15%. Fitting the data into expression (5.13), the present value is given by:

$$PV = \frac{(1 - e^{-0.15})}{0.15} [10\,000 + 30\,000e^{-0.15} + 20\,000e^{-0.3} + 10\,000e^{-0.45}]$$

$$= 52\,943.88$$

If both the returns and the compounding had been discrete, the familiar present value formula would give a comparative figure of £50 247.82.

A comparison of the discount factors between the conventional discrete returns and discrete compounding case and the continuous returns and continuous compounding case is revealing. Table 5.14 gives selected values of the factors for a discount rate of 10% in each case.

In Table 5.14 note the large difference in the **earlier** years. For instance £10 000 received as a lump sum at the end of year 1 is worth £9091 with discrete compounding. If a total of £10 000 was received evenly throughout the year, the present value would be £9516, an increase of 4.67%.

However, note that beyond ten years the continuous factors are **less** than the discrete factors. In the early years the greater size of the continuous factors is due to the significantly earlier receipt of some of the money – 8.33% of the first year's return coming in the first month of the year instead of at the end. But in much later years the differences in timing between the two schemes have only marginal effects which are outweighed by the increased impact of compounding continuously. It is interesting to note that over an infinite horizon the two arrangements give the same value for a perpetuity. The more severe discounting is exactly compensated by the earlier receipts.

Let us follow up this point by considering an annuity, continuously received and with continuous compounding. In the continuous analogue of the discrete case of an annuity of £R, payment would be at the *rate* of £R per year. If in formula (5.13) $R_t = R$ for all values of t, the summation has the following closed form:

Table 5.14

n	$(1 + r)^{-n}$	$\dfrac{1 - e^{-t}}{r} e^{-(n-1)r}$
1	0.9091	0.9516
2	0.8264	0.8611
3	0.7513	0.7791
4	0.6830	0.7050
5	0.6209	0.6379
6	0.5645	0.5772
7	0.5132	0.5223
8	0.4665	0.4726
9	0.4241	0.4276
10	0.3855	0.3869
11	0.3505	0.3501
12	0.3186	0.3168
13	0.2897	0.2866
14	0.2633	0.2593
15	0.2394	0.2347
20	0.1486	0.1423
30	0.0573	0.0524
40	0.0221	0.0193
50	0.0085	0.0071

$$PV = \frac{R}{r} \; (1 - e^{-nr}) \tag{5.14}$$

As a numerical example of a continuous annuity with continuous discounting, we shall find the present value of an annuity of £1000 received evenly throughout each of 15 years and with an interest rate of 12%. Using formula (5.14) with $n = 15$ and $r = 0.12$ we have:

$$PV = \frac{1000}{0.12} (1 - e^{-15(0.12)})$$

$$= 6955.84$$

For comparison, if both returns and discounting had been discrete, the present value would have been £6810.86.

Values of formula (5.14) for the case of a 10% discount rate ($r = 0.1$) are given in Table 5.15.

From Table 5.15 it will be noted that while there is a considerable difference in present value for shorter annuities, as the time horizon lengthens the two values come nearer to coincidence. As may be seen from formula (5.14) since e^{-nr} approaches zero as n increases without limit, the value of a continuous perpetuity of £1 continuously discounted is $1/r$.

Table 5.15

n	Discrete $\dfrac{1-(1+r)^{-n}}{r}$	Continuous $\dfrac{1-e^{-nr}}{r}$
1	0.9091	0.9516
2	1.7355	1.8127
3	2.4869	2.5918
4	3.1699	3.2968
5	3.7908	3.9347
6	4.3553	4.5119
7	4.8684	5.0341
8	5.3349	5.5067
9	5.7590	5.9343
10	6.1446	6.3212
11	6.4951	6.6713
12	6.8137	6.9881
13	7.1034	7.2747
14	7.3667	7.5340
15	7.6061	7.7687
20	8.5136	8.6466
30	9.4269	9.5021
40	9.7791	9.8168
50	9.9148	9.9326

5.13 Formulae

There is a wide variety of ways in which cash flows are formed in practice. Frequently, simplifying assumptions can be made that will allow the use of the familiar, straight-forward formulae and calculations. But if precision is required, non-standard calculations will be necessary. It is not practical to include all likely possibilities here, but the existence of alternative formulae should be noted. These expressions don't exist in isolation, and this section presents various compounding formulae with information as to how they relate to each other.

Formulae (F1) to (F8) presume discrete cash flow and compounding (i.e. the standard situation with cash flow occurring and discounting taking place at end of each equal length period). The interest rate is $100r\%$.

(F1) Present value of an annuity of £1 $\quad \dfrac{1-(1+r)^{-n}}{r}$

(F2) Present value of a perpetuity of £1 $\quad \dfrac{1}{r}$

(F3) Terminal value of an annuity of £1 $\quad \dfrac{(1+r)^n - 1}{r}$

(F4) Sinking fund: annual sum required to achieve £1 at $t=n$ $\quad \dfrac{r}{(1+r)^n - 1}$

(F5) Annual equivalent annuity $\quad \dfrac{r}{1-(1+r)^{-n}}$

(F6) Present value of annuity of £1 (with growth at $100g\%$)

$$\frac{(1+g)}{(r-g)}\left(1-\frac{(1+g)^n}{(1+r)^n}\right)$$

(F7) Present value of a perpetuity of £1 (with growth at $100g\%$ where $g < r$) $\dfrac{(1+g)}{(r-g)}$

(F8) Terminal value of an annuity of £1 (with growth at $100g\%$) $\dfrac{(1+g)\,[(1+r)^n-(1+g)^n]}{(r-g)}$

Formulae (9) to (12) presume continuous compounding:

(F9) Present value of discrete annuity of £1* $\dfrac{1-e^{-nr}}{e^r-1}$

(F10) Present value of a discrete perpetuity of £1* $\dfrac{1}{e^r-1}$

(F11) Present value of a continuous annuity of £1 $\dfrac{1-e^{-nr}}{r}$

(F12) Present value of a continuous perpetuity of £1 $\dfrac{1}{r}$

*Note: 'Discrete' means the normal situation with receipts at period end.

The relationships between these formulae can be expressed in a variety of ways. For example:

(F3) is (F1) multiplied by $(1 + r)^n$
(F2) is the limiting value of (F1) as $n \to \infty$
(F4) is the reciprocal of (F3)
(F5) is the reciprocal of (F1)

The relationships between (F1), (F3), (F4) and (F5) can be stated as:

(F3) = (F1) $(1 + r)^n$

(F4) = $\dfrac{1}{(F1)\,(1 + r^n)}$

(F5) = $\dfrac{1}{F1}$

To continue:

(F1) is a special case of (F6) in which $g = 0$
(F7) is the limiting value of (F6) as $n \to \infty$
(F2) is a special case of (F7) in which $g = 0$
(F3) is a special case of (F8) in which $g = 0$
(F10) is the limiting value of (F9) as $n \to \infty$
(F12) is the limiting value of (F11) as $n \to \infty$
(F2) is the same as (F12)

Many other formulae could be produced – as most building societies, insurance companies and other financial institutions will have done. The selection of formulae above can be used as approximations to some of the wide variety of situations that the corporate or individual investor may encounter.

The first program below, NPVMULT. BAS, finds the net present value for a project where the rates of discount may be different in different compounding periods. It is written in Basic and will run in Microsoft QBasic as supplied with MS-DOS 5.0 or later. (The program will also run in various other version of Basic – for example the various versions of QuickBasic, Visual Basic for Dos or, with the addition of line numbers, GW-Basic.) As in Chapter 4, this program is intentionally written in an unsophisticated style.

The program title is given as a remark (REM) and the label 'start:' marks a point that may be returned to if the user wishes to input revised data. The program then clears the screen and prints a heading and request to enter the problem data starting with the number of periods, n. REDIM (for redimension) allows the entry of n cash flow elements $R(t)$ in the loop that follows. (Re-dimension here because the user may later re-input data for a different number of time periods.) Note that $R(0)$ represents the initial outlay which should be entered as a negative number. Returns and the discount rate in each period are then entered (discount rates as percentages). 'LOCATE' positions the cursor for somewhat more user friendly data input. The next loop calculates the product of the discount rates up to each point in time ($h(t)$). Overall present value is then calculated in the usual way, and the result stated. Finally, the user is given the option of inputting fresh data. (The 'DO WHILE' loop with INKEY\$ is a method of putting the computer on hold so long as no key has been pressed.) The program code is as follows:

```
REM                NPVMULT.BAS
start:
CLS
PRINT "Present Value Calculator."
PRINT
PRINT "Different discount rate in each period allowed."
PRINT
PRINT "Discount rate t covers period t–1 to t."
PRINT "--------------------------------------"
PRINT
PRINT "Please input data as requested..."
PRINT

INPUT "Number of periods"; n

REDIM R(n + 1)
REDIM f(n + 1)
REDIM h(n + 1)

PRINT
PRINT "Please enter actual cash flow data (ie outflows are negative)"
PRINT "and discount rates as percentages..."

LOCATE 15, 5

PRINT "R(0) = "

FOR row = 16 TO n + 15

    LOCATE row, 5

    PRINT "R("; row – 15; ") = "

    LOCATE row, 30

    PRINT "Disc rate("; row – 15; ") = "

NEXT

LOCATE 15, 20
```

```
INPUT "", R(0)
FOR i = 16 TO n + 15
    LOCATE i, 20
    INPUT "", R(i – 15)
    LOCATE i, 55
    INPUT "", f(i – 15)
NEXT i
PRINT
FOR t = 1 TO n
    temp = 0
    w = 1
    FOR i = 1 TO t
        temp = (1 + f(i) / 100)
        w = temp * w
    NEXT i
    h(t) = w
NEXT t
h(0) = 1
z = 0
For j = 0 TO n
    z = z + R(j) / h(j)
NEXT j
NPV = z
PRINT
PRINT "NPV = "; NPV
PRINT
INPUT "recalculate NPV for new data, y/n"; C$
IF C$ = "y" OR C$ = "Y" THEN
    GOTO start
ELSE
    PRINT
    PRINT "Press any key to leave the program..."
    DO WHILE INKEY$ = ""
    LOOP
END IF
END
```

The Basic program used to generate Tables 5.12, 5.14 and 5.15 may be of interest. For on-screen display of results the program is:

```basic
REM ch5table.bas generates tables 5.12, 5.14 and 5.15
CLS
PRINT "Table 5.12"
PRINT "------------------------------------------------"
PRINT TAB(2); "n"; TAB(20); "Discrete"; TAB(40); "Continuous"
PRINT TAB(20); "(1 + r)^–n"; TAB(43); "e^–nr"
PRINT
FOR i = 1 TO 10
  PRINT i;
  PRINT TAB(20); USING "#.####"; (1.1) ^ –i;
  PRINT TAB(40); USING "#.####"; EXP(–.1 * i)
NEXT i
PRINT
PRINT "------------------------------------------------"
PRINT
PRINT
REM Table 5.14 follows
DEF fnf (i) = ((1 – EXP(–1.1)) / .1) * EXP(–(i – 1) * .1)
PRINT "Table 5.14"
PRINT "------------------------------------------------"
PRINT TAB(2); "n"; TAB(20); "(1 + r)^ –n"; TAB(40); "1–e^–t"
PRINT TAB(40); "———— e^–(n–1)r"
PRINT TAB(42); "r"
PRINT
FOR i = 1 TO 15
  PRINT i;
  PRINT TAB(20); USING "#.####"; (1.1) ^ –i;
  PRINT TAB(40); USING "#.####"; fnf(i)
NEXT i
FOR i = 20 TO 50 STEP 10
  PRINT i;
  PRINT TAB(20); USING "#.####"; (1.1) ^ –i;
  PRINT TAB(40); USING "#.####"; fnf(i)
NEXT i
PRINT
PRINT "------------------------------------------------"
PRINT
PRINT
REM Table 5.15 follows
DEF fng (i) = ((1 – (1.1 ^ –i)) / .1)
DEF fnh (i) = (1 – EXP(–.1 * i)) / .1
PRINT "Table 5.15"
PRINT "------------------------------------------------"
```

```
PRINT TAB(20); "Discrete"; TAB(40); "Continuous"
PRINT TAB(2); "n"; TAB(20); "1–(1+r)^–n"; TAB(40); "1–e^–nr"
PRINT TAB(20); "————"; TAB(40); "————"
PRINT TAB(22); "r"; TAB(42); "r"
PRINT
FOR i = 1 TO 15
    PRINT i;
    PRINT TAB(20); USING #.####'; fng(i);
    PRINT TAB(40); USING "#.####"; fnh(i)
NEXT i
FOR i = 20 to 50 STEP 10
    PRINT i;
    PRINT TAB(20); USING "#.####'; fng(i);
    PRINT TAB(40); USING "#.####"; fnh(i)
NEXT i
PRINT
PRINT "-------------------------------------------"
END
```

In order to send the program output to the printer, the PRINT statement in the program should be replaced with:

```
LPRINT
```

In order to send the output to a text file (for incorporation into a word processor for example) then add (near the beginning of the program) a line similar to:

```
OPEN "c:\tables5.txt" FOR OUTPUT AS #1
```

and replace the PRINT statements with:

```
PRINT #1,
```

including the comma. A plain text file named tables5.txt will be created in the root directory of the C drive when the program is run.

5.15 Key concepts

A cash flow with the same amount each year is called an **annuity**. Where the first return or payment occurs after one year the stream is an **immediate annuity**. Where the first cash flow item occurs at once this is an **annuity due**. A **perpetuity** is an annuity that continues indefinitely. A **growth** factor can be included in annuity calculations.

Yield to maturity or **redemption yield** is the current yield on a security which provides a fixed return for a given number of years with the nominal value of the bond being paid back in the final year. Short-dated stocks are less sensitive to interest rate variability than stocks with a distant redemption date; they have less **interest-rate risk**.

A sinking fund is a form of annuity where a given sum is set aside each year so that a given terminal value is achieved. An **annual equivalent annuity** converts a lump sum to a series of equal annual payments with the same present value.

Repair–replace problems can be solved by the **annual equivalent annuity** method of converting the cash flows of various schemes to annuity form. The scheme which gives the lowest per year equivalent cost is preferred. In the **lowest common multiple** method, different arrangements are compared over a horizon length such that a whole number of cycles can be completed in each case. In the **finite horizon** method a long horizon value is chosen and the schemes are compared by NPV over the given horizon.

The **make or buy** problem can be structured as a single-project investment appraisal exercise. The present value of the savings achieved by manufacture are set against the capital cost of the equipment.

Whenever possible, **tax payments** should be included as cash flow items in discounted cash flow calculations. Computer-based tax planning models are available for complex corporate situations.

With anticipated **inflation**, projects should be evaluated using actual cash (nominal) returns discounted at the nominal (rather than the 'real') discount rate.

There may be a best **starting date** for a project, one for which the net present value of the project is maximized. Similarly, if there is flexibility regarding the time at which a project is terminated, the net present value of a project can be optimized.

There are alternatives to the conventional pattern of discrete cash flow at evenly spaced compounding points. One example is that of **continuous compounding** which represents a limiting case of very short compounding periods.

1. What is an annuity? Distinguish between deferred annuities, immediate annuities and annuities due.
2. What is a perpetuity? How does the value of a perpetuity vary with the interest rate?
3. What is the redemption yield on a security?
4. What is meant by interest rate risk?
5. What is a sinking fund? How does this relate to the terminal value of annuities?
6. What are annual equivalent annuities? How are they useful in addressing repair–replace problems?
7. What are the main methods available for assessing different repair or replace possibilities?
8. To what extent can the possibility of growth be accommodated within the framework of annuities?
9. How can the make or buy problem be expressed in the form of a single project?
10. How should tax payments be included in discounted cash flow calculations?
11. How should the present values of projects be calculated under anticipated inflation?
12. By what means can the optimal starting date for a project be found?
13. What issues are raised by variability of the termination date for a project and how might a best value of this date be chosen?
14. What are some of the alternatives to the conventional end of period return and compounding cash flow pattern?

Drury, C., Braund, S., Osborne, P. and Tayles, M. (1992) *A Survey of Management Accounting Practices in UK Manufacturing Companies*, ACCA Research Occasional Paper, Chartered Institute of Certified Accountants.

Kay, J.A. and King, M.A. (1990) *The British Tax System*, 5th edn, Oxford University Press.

5.17 References

Wilkes, F.M. (1972) Inflation and capital budgeting decisions. *Journal of Business Finance*, Autumn.

Wilkes, F.M. (1983) *Capital Budgeting Techniques*, 2nd edn, John Wiley and Sons.

Wright, M.G. (1973) *Discounted Cash Flow*, 2nd edn, McGraw-Hill.

5.18 Further reading

This section includes references discussing the treatment of deferred tax liabilities in discounted cash flow calculations (Nurnberg, Wolk and Tearney) and an article on the use of the incremental principle in capital budgeting (Coulhurst). Texts giving broadly parallel coverage to the present volume on annuities (Drury, Lumby) are also cited. Further technical material and numerical examples on several topics covered in this chapter can be found in Wilkes (1983).

Coulhurst, N.J. (1986) The application of the incremental principle in capital investment project evaluation. *Accounting and Business Research*, Autumn.

Drury, C. (1992) *Management and Cost Accounting*, 3rd edn, Chapman & Hall.

Lumby, S. (1994) *Investment Appraisal and Financial Decisions*, 5th edn, Chapman & Hall.

Nurnberg, H. (1972) Discounting deferred tax liabilities. *Accounting Review*, Oct.

Wolk, H. and Tearney, M. (1980) Discounting deferred tax liabilities: review and analysis. *Journal of Business Finance and Accounting*, **7** (1).

5.19 Problems

1. Use the appropriate formula to find the present value of an immediate annuity of £100 for six years at 10% interest annually compounded.

2. What is the present value of a perpetuity of £200 p.a. with a discount rate of 4%?

3. A security is currently priced at £1200 (ex interest) and gives an annual interest payment of £150. It has a redemption value of £1500 five years in the future. Estimate the yield to maturity on the security.

4. Find the terminal value achieved at ten years if £700 is placed annually into an account – starting after one year. Interest is compounded at 10%.

5. A company has loan stock of £5 000 000 due to mature in nine years time. At an interest rate of 15% how much should be set aside annually in order to meet the liability when it falls due?

6. (a) Determine the net present value of the cash flow:

$t = 1$	$t = 2$	$t = 3$	$t = 4$	$t = 5$
1500	1500	1500	500	500

   at a discount rate of 12%.

   (b) how might the calculations be carried out using only a table of annuity factors (Table 3)?

7. Making use of Tables 2 and 6 find the annual equivalent annuity (for 2 years) at 15% of the cash flow:

$t = 0$	$t = 1$	$t = 2$
1200	350	500

8. A company puts the following sums of money into an account at the stated times:

$t = 0$	$t = 1$	$t = 2$	$t = 3$
24 000	12 000	12 000	35 000

   Using Tables 1 and 4 and an interest rate of 10% find the sum of money that the company would have at $t = 3$.

9. A minor road costs £400 a year to maintain. These maintenance costs can be reduced if capital expenditure is made to provide a new road surface. What is the maximum expenditure for a new surface that would be justified if no maintenance would then be required for the first 5 years, £100 per year for the next 10 years and £400 a year thereafter? Assume that money costs 5%.

10. A new machine can be bought for £15 000 with an economic life of 10 years and salvage value at that time of £3000. Its operating costs are £8000 a year. The existing machine has operating costs of £10 000 a year, but could be sold now for £3000. If the machine is not replaced now, it would continue in service for ten years with zero salvage value. Alternatively, the existing machine can be overhauled and modernized for £4000, which would change the operating costs to £9000 a year, give a salvage value of £1500 but would not change the economic life. The minimum required rate of return is 25%. Which course of action should be selected?

11. For a machine with the financial data given below, determine the optimal length of replacement cycle when the appropriate interest rate is 12%.

Time	$t = 0$	$t = 1$	$t = 2$	$t = 3$	$t = 4$
Outlay	5000				
Operating costs		1400	1500	1600	1700
Maintenance costs			300	400	500
Scrap value		3400	2000	800	600

12. A firm uses a machine for which the operating costs and maintenance expenditures and residual value are:

Time	Operating costs	Maintenance	Residual value
0	0	0	1500
1	2500	500	1000
2	3000	1000	600
3	3500	1500	100
4	4000	1700	0

The machine is to be replaced by one of a new type for which financial data are:

Time	$t = 0$	$t = 1$	$t = 2$	$t = 3$	$t = 4$
Outlay	7000				
Operating costs		1800	2200	2600	2800
Maintenance costs		200	500	900	1200
Residual value		4000	3000	2000	1000

The discount rate is 8%. At what time should the existing machine be replaced?

13. What is the present value of an annuity of £250 per annum for eight years growing at 4% per annum from a baseline of $t = 0$ when the discount rate is 10%?

14. What is the present value of a perpetuity of £175 per annum growing at 2% from a baseline of $t = 0$ when the discount rate is 7%?

15. A firm has to make the decision as to whether to make a component itself or buy it in. In the manufacturing option, the capital cost of the equipment is £1 000 000 incurred immediately. The equipment would last for four years with no residual value. Manufacturing costs would be £1 300 000 in year one, £1 400 000 in year two, £1 700 000 in year three and £1 800 000 in year four. These costs reflect all considerations and no other opportunities are foregone if the decision to manufacture is taken. If the component is bought in there would be no immediate outlay and the costs would be £1 700 000 in years one and two and £2 200 000 in years three and four. A discount rate of 15% is appropriate and apart from the outlay all costs may be assumed to occur at year end. Should the component be made in house or bought in?

16. A firm can invest in a project costing £520 000 in 1996. At 1996 prices the project would return £200 000 net at the end of each of three years. However, prices are inflating at 5% generally and the magnitude of the net returns in cash would be affected accordingly. The nominal rate of interest is 9.2%. Should the project be undertaken?

17. A company is considering a capital project with a life expectancy of 10 years. If undertaken in 1995, the capital cost would be £250m with estimated net revenues of £50m in each of the first five years of operation and £60m for each of the last five

years of the operating life of the plant. There would then follow winding up costs of £200m in year 11. The company has the option of commencement in 2000 at which point capital cost would be £300m with annual net revenues of £60m and £80m for the five-year periods respectively and end of project costs of £300m eleven years after commencement. With a discount rate of 10%, which starting date should be selected on the basis of net present value in 1995?

18. If carried to its conclusion, a project would have the cash flow:

$t=0$	$t=1$	$t=2$	$t=3$	$t=4$	$t=5$	$t=6$	$t=7$	$t=8$	$t=9$	$t=10$	$t=11$
−100	80	70	−80	70	−90	130	−100	100	10	−70	80

However, the project may be terminated at any time with the effect of eliminating subsequent cash flow.

(a) What is the optimum date to conclude the project if the discount rate is 10%?
(b) What is the optimum date to conclude the project if the discount rate is 20%?
(c) With the 10% discount rate, what would the best termination date be if the year 11 return was 75 instead of 80 (all else unchanged)?

19. (a) Using the data of Table 5.7 with a discount rate of 12%, show the effects of an increase in the tax rate to 45% of returns net of the writing down allowance.
(b) Would the project still be worthwhile in the new tax environment if the discount rate was 20%?

20. A project has the following cash flow with the net returns at the end of each of four years:

$t=0$	$t=1$	$t=2$	$t=3$	$t=4$
−150	80	50	60	40

Interest is compounded continuously at 10%. What is the net present value of the project?

21. What is the present value of:

(a) A discrete annuity of £100 for five years under continuous compounding at 8%?
(b) A discrete perpetuity of £250 under continuous compounding at 6%?

22. What is the present value of the stream of returns:

Time t:	0 − 1	1 − 2	2 − 3	3 − 4
Return:	20 000	30 000	40 000	20 000

where the returns arrive through each year in a continuous fashion and where interest is compounded continuously at 12%? What would the present value have been if both returns and discounting had been discrete?

23. Find the present value of an annuity of £2000 received evenly throughout each of ten years with a continuously compounded interest rate of 14%? What would be the comparable figure if both returns and discounting had been discrete?

24. What is the present value of a continuous perpetuity of £350 when interest is compounded continuously at 7½%? How does this figure compare with the discrete returns and discrete compounding case?

5.20 Appendix: Arithmetic and geometric series

In financial arithmetic the decision-maker frequently encounters sequences of numbers – for example the quarterly interest payments on an investment. With their elements taken in succession, each of these collections of numbers represents a **sequence** – an ordered set of numbers that is either finite or is denumerable. The set of cash returns to a 20-year project:

$$R_1, R_2, R_3, \ldots R_t, \ldots, R_{19}, R_{20}$$

is a sequence. R_t, indicating the return in year t, represents the typical member of the sequence and is called the **general term**. Where successive terms of a sequence are related in the same way, the sequence is called a **progression**. The way in which pairs of terms are related defines a particular kind of progression. Because of their importance in finance, we focus here on **arithmetic progressions** and **geometric progressions**.

In an arithmetic progression, consecutive terms differ by a fixed amount. So, for example, the sequence:

$$50, 60, 70, 80, 90, 100$$

is an arithmetic progression. So is the sequence:

$$13, 10, 7, 4, 1, -2, -5, \ldots$$

In the first of the progressions above, the **common difference** between successive terms is 10 and the first term is 50. In the second example, the first term is 13 and the common difference is –3. In general, if the first term is represented by a and the common difference by d, any arithmetic progression containing n terms will have the form:

$$a, a + d, a + 2d, a + 3d, \ldots a + (n - 1)d \tag{A.1}$$

The example progressions above have, respectively:

$$a = 50, d = 10 \; n = 6$$

and:

$$a = 13, d = -3 \; n = \infty$$

Using the first example to check the value of the last term as given by (A.1), this should be:

$$50 + (6 - 1)10 = 100$$

which is correct. A financial example of arithmetic progression is provided by **simple interest**. Under simple interest, the same fixed payment is made in each period regardless of the amount on deposit or the sum outstanding. Thus if £100 is banked on 1 January 1994 at 12.5% simple interest per annum, the amount on deposit will increase by £12.50 each year, and a running record of these amounts makes up an arithmetic progression shown as follows:

1994	1995	1996	1997	1998	1999
100	112.5	125	137.5	150	162.5

The value of the investment after n years can be obtained by use of (A.1) but care is required. The value after one year is the **second** term in the progression and in general the value after n years is given by the $(n + 1)^{\text{th}}$ term in the progression: $a + nd$. So, since a = 100 and $d = 12.5$, the value after 20 years will be:

$$a + nd = 100 + 20(12.5)$$

$$= 350$$

A further illustration of the use of arithmetic progressions is provided by **straight line depreciation**. In this method, the book value of an asset in any year will be its book value of the preceding year less a constant amount. If an asset is initially valued at £50 000 and is written off over ten years at £5000 per year, its book value over time will form an arithmetic progression:

	Initial value	1 year	2 years	3 years
Book value:	£50 000	£45 000	£40 000	£35 000

The nth term of this progression gives the book value after $(n - 1)$ years. Thus, since a = 50 000 and $d = 5000$, the book value after seven years (corresponding to term eight in the series) will be:

$$50\,000 + (8 - 1)(-5000) = 15\,000$$

As we have seen, it is often useful to know the sum of a number of terms in a sequence. Such a sum is called a *series*. The sum of a sequence can be written concisely in sigma notation. So for example:

$$\sum_{t=1}^{t=20} R_t$$

represents the sum of a sequence of 20 terms where the general term is R_t. Where the sequence has a finite number of terms the series is said to be a **finite series** otherwise it is an infinite series. The number of terms is the **length** of the series. The sum, S_n, of an arithmetic progression containing n terms could be written out in full as:

$$S_n = a + (a + d) + (a + 2d) + (a + 3d) + \ldots + [a + (n-1)d]$$

but it is possible to develop a formula for this sum by noting the result of adding the terms in a particular way. (Assume for what follows that the value of n is even. The result holds good if n is odd.) If the first and last terms are added, the result will be:

$$a + [a + (n-1)d] = 2a + (n-1)d$$

and if the second and second last terms are added:

$$(a + d) + [a + (n-2)d] = 2a + (n-1)d$$

similarly, if the third and third last term are added:

$$(a + 2d) + [a + (n-3)d] = 2a + (n-1)d$$

Terms can be paired so that the sum of each pair is $2a + (n-1)d$. Since there are $n/2$ pairs all told, the total must be:

$$S_n = \frac{n}{2}[2a + (n-1)d] \qquad\qquad (A.2)$$

(A.2) is a great timesaver! For example, to find the sum to 100 terms of the arithmetic progression:

$$10, 15, 20, 25, 30, \ldots$$

note that $a = 10$, $d = 5$ and, of course, $n = 100$. So using the formula, the sum is:

$$S_{100} = 50[20 + (99)5]$$

$$= 27\,750$$

For the progression:

$$100, 95, 90, 85, \ldots$$

the value of a = 100 and $d = -5$. So, from (A.2), the sum to 31 terms will be:

$$S_{31} \quad = 15.5[200 + 30(-5)]$$

$$= 775$$

while the sum to 100 terms is:

$$S_{100} = 50[200 + 99(-5)]$$

$$= -14\,750$$

The formula can also be used in a different way to solve problems such as finding the value of n required to make the sum to n terms reach zero for the progression:

$$-200, -190, -180, -170, \ldots$$

In this case, $a = -200$ and $d = 10$. Therefore, the value of n is required for which:

$$S_n = \frac{n}{2}[-400 + (n-1)10] = 0$$

i.e.

$$\frac{n}{2}[-410 + 10n] = 0$$

so, discounting the trivial case in which n itself is zero, the sum is zero when:

$$-410 + 10n = 0$$

that is, after 41 terms.

A formula such as (A.2) stating the required sum in terms of known parameters is a **closed form expression**. Where closed form expressions can be obtained they are extremely useful. Note that (A.2) will work even if the number of terms is odd. In the case of odd n, the solitary middle term will be the $[(n + 1)/2]^{th}$ term with a value of:

$$a + \{[(n + 1)/2] - 1\}d$$

which is one half of $2a + (n - 1)d$.

Now apply (A.2) to a simple interest calculation. Suppose that someone is in the habit of borrowing £100 annually at 5% simple interest. What would be the total interest that they would pay over a 20-year period? The interest payments in each year form an arithmetic progression as can be seen from the Σ row in Table 5.A1.

Table 5.A1

£100 invested at:	Interest payable at:				
	$t = 1$	$t = 2$	$t = 3$	$t = 4$	$t = 5$
$t = 0$	5	5	5	5	5
$t = 1$		5	5	5	5
$t = 2$			5	5	5
$t = 4$				5	5
$t = 5$					5
Σ	5	10	15	20	25

The total of interest payments over the 20-year period is found from (A.2) with the values: $a = 5$, $d = 5$ and $n = 20$. The result is:

$$\frac{20}{2}[2(5) + 19(5)] = 1050$$

A further example of the use of the formula is provided by a common system of royalty payments. Suppose that a firm of publishers have decided on a print run of 5000 copies of a particular book for which no reprint is envisaged. The book will sell at £10 per copy. Royalty payable to the author is expressed as percentages of the sales price and is calculated on a sliding scale as follows:

First 1000 copies	10%
Next 1000 copies	11.25%
Third 1000 copies	12.5%
Fourth 100 copies	13.75%
Fifth 1000 copies	15%

If the book sells out, what will be the total royalty payment to the author? The royalty payments form an arithmetic progression in which the first term is 10% of £10(1000) = £1000. Each successive tranche is greater than its predecessor by 1.25% of £10 000, so the common difference is £125. Application of formula (A.2) produces:

$$S_n = \frac{5}{2}[2000 + (5 - 1)125]$$

$$= 6250$$

In a **geometric progression** it is the **ratio** of each term to the preceding term that is constant throughout. In other words, the terms differ by a constant multiplier. The following progressions are geometric:

$$5, \quad 10, \quad 20, \quad 40, \quad 80, \quad 160, \quad \ldots$$
$$128, \quad 32, \quad 8, \quad 2, \quad 0.5, \quad 0.125, \quad \ldots$$

Successive terms in each of these progressions take the following form:

$$a, \quad ad, \quad ad^2, \quad ad^3, \quad ad^4, \quad ad^5, \ldots, ad^{n-1}$$

where the first term is a, the constant factor of difference between adjacent terms, the **common ratio**, is d and the nth term is ad^{n-1}. The number of terms in a geometric progression must be finite or else denumerable. In the first illustration, $a = 5$ and $d = 2$ while in the second case $a = 128$ and $d = 0.25$.

There are many examples of the use of geometric progressions in finance. In accounting, under the **declining balance** method of depreciation, the first term, a, represents the asset's original book value, the factor of difference, d (which must be less than one) gives the proportionate change in value from year to year, and the $(n + 1)^{\text{th}}$ term of the progression gives the value of the asset after n years. For example, if a car depreciates in value by 20% each year, then the common ratio will be:

$$d = 1 - 0.2 = 0.8$$

and the value of the car after n years of depreciation is given by the $(n + 1)^{\text{th}}$ term of the geometric progression. Thus the value of a car bought initially for £9000 would, after three years be:

$$ad^n = £9000(0.8)^3 = £4608$$

Geometric progressions are used in compound interest calculations and the sum to n terms is of particular importance. As was the case with arithmetic progressions, it is possible to obtain a closed form expression for the sum, S_n:

$$S_n = a + ad + ad^2 + ad^3 + ad^4 + \ldots + ad^{n-1}$$

Note that:

$$dS_n = ad + ad^2 + ad^3 + ad^4 + \ldots + ad^{n-1} + ad^n$$

from which it is clear that S_n and dS_n have all but their first and last terms in common. That is:

$$S_n - dS_n = a - ad^n$$

so:

$$S_n(1 - d) = a - ad^n = a(1 - d^n)$$

so that:

$$S_n = \frac{a(1 - d^n)}{(1 - d)} \tag{A.3}$$

Many instances of the use of (A.3) are found in business finance, where it is one of the most useful of all expressions. We saw that an **annuity** consists of the receipt (or payment) of a fixed amount each year. The **present value** of an annuity is the lump sum to which the future receipts are presently equivalent. If the **discount rate** that is appropriate is $100r\%$, then the present value of an annuity of £1 received at the end of each of n years will be:

$$\frac{1}{(1+r)} + \frac{1}{(1+r)^2} + \frac{1}{(1+r)^3} + \frac{1}{(1+r)^4} + \ldots + \frac{1}{(1+r)^n} = \sum_{t=1}^{t=n}(1+r)^{-t} \tag{A.4}$$

The constant difference in the annuity sum is $1/(1 + r)$ and the first term is also $1/(1 + r)$.

Use of this information in (A.3) produces:

$$S_n = \frac{(1+r)^{-1}[1-(1+r)^{-n}]}{1-(1+r)^{-1}}$$

$$= \frac{1-(1+r)^{-n}}{r} \qquad (A.5)$$

Expression (A.5) allows rapid calculation of the present value of any annuity. For example, with a discount rate of 10% ($r = 0.1$) an annuity of £50 for six years would have a present worth of:

$$£50 \; \frac{[1-(1+0.1)^{-6}]}{0.1}$$

$$= £282.24$$

An important property of (A.3) is that if $d < 1$ the series has a bound on its value even if the number of terms is infinite. In this case as n increases without limit, d^n approaches zero. This can be written as:

$$\text{as } n \to \infty \; d^n \to 0$$

So:

$$\text{as } n \to \infty \; S_n \to \frac{a}{(1-d)} \qquad (A.6)$$

As we have seen, (A.6) is very important in financial calculations and can be used to give the present value of undated stocks such as Consols.

6 Capital rationing and risk analysis in imperfect capital markets

6.1	Introduction	144	6.12	Single investment risk analysis	178
6.2	Capital rationing: overview	145	6.13	Multiple investment risk analysis	187
6.3	Single-constraint problems	146	6.14	Mean-variance analysis	195
6.4	Multi-constraint problems	152	6.15	Spreadsheets and what-if analysis	198
6.5	Financial planning models	158			
6.6	Risk: some general considerations	160	6.16	Key concepts	202
6.7	Payback	160	6.17	Revision questions	203
6.8	Return on capital measures	163	6.18	References	204
6.9	Risk premiums	165	6.19	Further reading	204
6.10	Sensitivity analysis	166	6.20	Problems	205
6.11	Simulation	173	6.21	Appendix: Basic program	208

In Chapters 4 and 5 we considered investment appraisal methods when the decision-maker's success in achieving their objective was limited only by the range of opportunities that were open and where outcomes were not subject to random variability. For practical purposes the cash flow and discount rate/s were certain and capital availability was limited only by the ability to repay.

In this chapter a range of methods are introduced that can be useful to management when the ability to undertake possible projects is restricted by limits on financial or other resources and where there is appreciable uncertainty concerning important data.

By the end of the chapter you will have learnt how to solve capital budgeting problems in which there is a constraint on the initial capital outlay. You will see how the approach can be developed to involve several restrictions that may involve physical as well as financial resources. The models will allow the inclusion of acceptable ranges for key financial statistics.

A critical review of the traditional (and still used) methods for dealing with risk is followed by discussion of methods which derive and present information for investment decision-making by company management under risk and uncertainty.

6.1 Introduction

The two subjects addressed in this chapter, capital shortage and risk that is not washed through into yield rates, can both be considered as departures from a near-perfect market in capital assets. If managers in search of funds and the market itself function sufficiently well, it is arguable that no absolute shortage of capital will occur; it should always be available – at a price. Where this is so, all well and good. Where it is not so, useful analytical tools are available.

The appropriate treatment of risk also depends on how well the market functions. Some parts of the market, like the proverbial curate's egg, may be better than others and it is as well to have available methods relevant to either case. So in this book we consider the subject of risk in two stages. In this chapter we present methods for cases where the ownership of the company is not fully diversified. The techniques apply when the impact of investments on the total risk of the enterprise is a consideration and where managerial judgement can play a decisive rôle.

Methods based on the capital asset pricing model are introduced in Chapter 8. This is the appropriate framework when a fully diversified company ownership can be presumed and where there are no substantial and lasting departures from a well-functioning capital market.

We now consider the first of the market imperfections; rationing of capital. The methods also apply where **any** key resource – physical as well as financial – restricts the investor's ability to undertake projects. So the relevance of this topic is not just a question of how well **financial** markets function. The functioning of commodity and labour markets make methods for handling restricted resources relevant.

6.2 Capital rationing: overview

Capital rationing (or the shortage of other key resources) may arise in many ways. Funds for investment may not be unlimited at all points in time and there may be limitations on the availability of factors of production such as skilled labour, raw materials or machinery. Constraints are also defined by interdependencies between investments such as projects being contingent and upper limits on the investment levels themselves. There may also be acceptable limits to values taken by key financial ratios and management may try to avoid cash flow patterns producing large fluctuations in year to year profits or which would inhibit the firm's ability to declare an adequate dividend. We shall use problems in which the constraints are financial, but the same principles apply whatever the scarce resource or constraint.

A **capital rationing** problem is defined as a situation where there are insufficient funds to finance all *prima facie* profitable projects. Where wider considerations are incorporated, a **financial planning model** is produced. A distinction is often made between **hard** and **soft** capital rationing. **Hard capital rationing** arises when the constraints are **externally** determined. **Soft capital rationing** arises with **internal**, management imposed, limits on investment expenditure. In a perfect capital market, hard capital rationing would not occur while soft capital rationing would be irrational. In the real world both situations do arise – frequently with good reason. Borrowing limits are imposed by banks, particularly in the cases of smaller companies and individuals, while publicly funded organizations are keenly aware of cash limited budgets and of spending restrictions on both capital and revenue programmes. Self-imposed restrictions are often prudential in character and can relate to questions of control within, and of, an organization. For example, there may be a reluctance to issue further equity by management fearful of losing control of the company.

The distinction between hard and soft rationing is in some cases one of perspective. From the point of view of a department, cost centre or wholly owned subsidiary, the budgetary constraints determined by head office are external, while from the boardroom they can be seen as internal. In both hard and soft rationing the limits are usually negotiated (in the first instance at least) and to an extent may be renegotiable, and the solution methodology should provide valuable input to such processes. Indeed, it can be argued that the **existence** of either form of rationing represents some kind of managerial failure: failure to convince the supplier of funds of the true worth of the investments under consideration. Although there is something in this argument, it would in practice usually represent a harsh judgement. Furthermore, even if there were no limits on the total **amounts** of available finance in reality the price may vary with the size as well as the term of the loan. If this variation takes the form of discrete tranches, a rationing or programming formulation is still appropriate since finance at **each price** is rationed. Surveys suggest that a minimum of three out of five companies experience capital rationing and we begin with consideration of the single constraint case.

6.3 Single-constraint problems

Rationing problems involving a single constraint can take a variety of forms. We shall consider those problems in which the constraint limits initial capital expenditure rather than outlay in a subsequent time period or a resource other than capital. A simple solution procedure can be applied to many single constraint problems. The method is best explained in the context of an example.

A company is considering investment in up to six projects and has £215 000 for the total initial outlay. The cost of capital is 10%, there are no other investment opportunities available and no constraints other than on initial outlay. Each investment can be accepted or rejected in its entirety or accepted on a partial basis. (The consequences of imperfect divisibility of investments are considered at a later point.) No investment is repeatable. The company has the objective of maximizing present value overall. (The arguments in support of net present value in section 4.11 also apply under capital rationing as long as a uniform interest rate applies to transfers between time periods.) Details of the investments are shown in Table 6.1.

Table 6.1

	Investment					
Year	1	2	3	4	5	6
0	−25 000	−60 000	−90 000	−100 000	−120 000	−35 000
1	7 500	17 500	25 000	0	75 000	40 000
2	7 500	17 500	25 000	0	75 000	0
3	7 500	17 500	25 000	50 000	0	0
4	7 500	17 500	25 000	50 000	0	0
5	7 500	17 500	25 000	50 000	0	0
NPV	3 431	6 339	4 770	2 759	10 163	1 364
Yield	15.2	14.1	12.1	11.6	16.3	14.3

As evident from Table 6.1, **all** projects would be accepted on the grounds of NPV or yield **if it were not for the capital rationing situation**. But which projects should be selected given the constraint on outlay?

First consider what would seem to be the obvious extension of the NPV rule to the rationing case, namely: **rank projects by size of NPV and accept them in this order until the budget is exhausted**. The results of this process are shown in Table 6.2.

Table 6.2

Project	NPV	Outlay	Total outlay
5	10 163	120 000	120 000
2	6 339	60 000	180 000
7/18 of 3	1 855	35 000	215 000
1			
4			
6			
Total NPV =	18 357		

A net present value of £18 357 results from the selection of 5, 2 and 38.89% of project 3.

Now consider the selection of projects and the NPV that results if the investments are ranked by **size of yield**. The outcome is shown in Table 6.3.

Table 6.3

Project	Yield	NPV	Outlay	Total outlay
5	16.3	10 163	120 000	120 000
1	15.2	3 431	25 000	145 000
6	14.3	1 364	35 000	180 000
7/12 of 2	14.1	3 698	35 000	215 000
3	12.1			
4	11.6			
Total NPV =		18 656		

The resulting total NPV of £18 656 is superior to that produced by the ranking by size of NPV. So the unconstrained NPV decision rule does not generalize to the rationing case. But the better result produced by yield is merely a feature of the present problem. The outcome could have been better or worse than the ranking by NPV. *Neither* process produces the optimal selection of investments.

The correct procedure is to rank the alternatives according to **the ratio of NPV to initial outlay**. This ratio is sometimes called the *benefit cost ratio*. The justification for the method will be given presently, but first consider the outcome of this process as shown in Table 6.4.

Table 6.4

Project	Ratio	NPV	Outlay	Total outlay
1	0.137	3 431	25 000	25 000
2	0.106	6 339	60 000	85 000
5	0.085	10 163	120 000	205 000
1/9 of 3	0.053	530	10 000	215 000
6	0.039			
4	0.028			
Total NPV =		20 463		

A substantial improvement has resulted from ranking by benefit–cost ratio. The total NPV is 9.7% higher than from the yield ranking and 11.5% greater than the result produced by ranking by NPV itself. The optimal group of projects produces the cash flow:

$$\begin{array}{ccc} t = 0 & t = 1 & t = 2 \\ -215\,000 & 102\,778 & 107\,778 \end{array}$$

which gives a yield of slightly over 15%. The maximal outcome is achieved because the project at the top of the benefit–cost ratio list has the **highest achievement of objective per unit of scarce resource**. Once project 1 has been accepted in full, the maximum gain in the objective for the next unit of resource spent is achieved through investment in project 2. When project 2 is fully accepted, project 5 produces the best increase in NPV per pound spent ... and so on.

We have been assuming that projects cannot be repeated. It is worth examining the full impact of this restriction. Had it been possible to repeat project 1, no other project would have been selected and the outcome would have been as shown in Table 6.5.

Table 6.5

Project	Ratio	NPV	Outlay	Total outlay
1	0.137	3 431	25 000	50 000
1	0.137	3 431	25 000	75 000
1	0.137	3 431	25 000	100 000
1	0.137	3 431	25 000	125 000
1	0.137	3 431	25 000	150 000
1	0.137	3 431	25 000	175 000
1	0.137	3 431	25 000	200 000
6/10 of 1	0.137	2 059	15 000	215 000
Total NPV =		29 507		

A total NPV of £29 507 would have been achieved by investment in 8.6 units of project 1. This is an increase of 44.2% on the maximum when projects cannot be repeated.

If project 1 was not repeatable, but project 2 was repeatable, the outcome would have been as shown in Table 6.6.

Table 6.6

Project	Ratio	NPV	Outlay	Total outlay
1	0.137	3 431	25 000	25 000
2	0.106	6 339	60 000	85 000
2	0.106	6 339	60 000	145 000
2	0.106	6 339	60 000	205 000
1/6 of 2	0.106	1 057	10 000	215 000
Total NPV =		23 505		

So the non-repeatability of project 1 results in a drop of £6002 in NPV if project 2 is repeatable. The present value consequences of the non-repeatability of projects 2 and 5 can be found in a similar manner.

The use of benefit–cost ratios can be illustrated graphically. Figure 6.1 plots the level of total NPV achievable against the total availability of funds.

In Figure 6.1, the benefit–cost ratios are the slopes of the line segments of the NPV graph. As available funds expand, the successive investments taken show a decreasing rate of increase of NPV per pound spent. This continues until project 4, the last project that could be undertaken, is completed. An overall NPV of £28 826 could be achieved if £430 000 was available for outlay and no project was repeatable.

The ratio of **gross** present value (GPV) to outlay can also be used to obtain the optimum. This ratio, the **profitability index** (PI), always gives the same ranking as the benefit cost ratio. If, for two projects A and B, project A has the greater benefit–cost ratio, then:

$$\frac{NPV_A}{K_A} > \frac{NPV_B}{K_B}$$

which could equally well be written as:

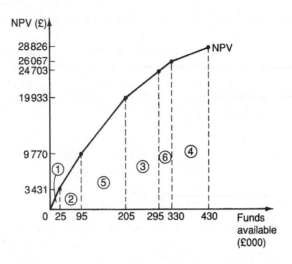

Figure 6.1

$$\frac{GPV_A - K_A}{K_A} > \frac{GPV_B - K_B}{K_B}$$

that is:

$$\frac{GPV_A}{K_A} - 1 > \frac{GPV_B}{K_B} - 1$$

so:

$$\frac{GPV_A}{K_A} > \frac{GPV_B}{K_B}$$

All worthwhile projects must have PI > 1 corresponding to NPV > 0 and a positive benefit–cost ratio.

Now consider the question of the marginal value of funds in the rationing problem with non-repeatability of all projects. If further funds beyond the original £215 000 were available, at a price, what rate of interest would it be worth paying to get the funds? Consider the uncompleted marginal project 3 and its yield of 12.1%. If further money was available at a rate of interest between 10% and 12.1% the remaining 8/9 of project 3 would have a positive present value and increase the NPV achieved overall. But care must be exercised. It is not correct to say that 12.1% is the maximum rate worth paying for extra funds, nor is it correct to state that if extra funds are obtainable at less than 12.1% project 3 should be completed.

Suppose that a further £35 000 was available at 12%. If this was used to take a further ⁷⁄₁₈ of project 3, discounting at 12% gives an additional present value of £46.7. However, if the £35 000 was used in Project 6 the increase in NPV would be £714.3. What has occurred is that the benefit–cost ratios of projects 3 and 6 now have different relative sizes. At 12% the ratio for project 6 is 1.0204 and for project 3 it is 1.0013. So if further funds are available the ratios for unused or uncompleted projects should be recalculated at the higher rate and, in effect, a separate problem must be solved. The maximum rate of interest worth paying for extra funds will be the highest yield on any of the projects or part projects which are still available. In the present case this is given by project 6 which has a yield of 14.3%.

There are two distinct situations here. If, after a commitment has been made to the original group of investments, it is then discovered that further funds are available, the above procedure is correct. If it is known **in advance** that the first £215 000 is available at 10% and a further £35 000 is available at 12%, then a more complex problem results in which a terminal value formulation is appropriate as unambiguous individual NPVs cannot be defined.

Now resume the simpler framework of the single constraint single interest rate model and consider mutually exclusive investments. Care is needed in using the ratio method. Consider the following problem in which the profitability index form is used.

A company has four investment possibilities, all of which are divisible as necessary. The outlays required and the PI value in each case are as follows:

	Outlay	PI
A	£1 million	1.40
B	£0.1 million	1.45
C	£1 million	1.10
D	£0.1 million	1.35

The company has £1.10 million available for investment. Projects A and B are mutually exclusive. All projects are divisible. Which group of projects maximizes NPV and what is the NPV obtained? First note that it would be incorrect to eliminate project A to start with on the grounds that B has the greater PI. If this was done the projects selected would be B, D and 9/10 of C, and the total NPV achieved would be:

$$100\ 000 \times 0.45 + 100\ 000 \times 0.35 + 0.9 \times 1\ 000\ 000 \times 0.1 = 170\ 000$$

The optimal solution is to take A and D, producing an NPV of £435 000. When there is a mutually exclusive pair, two sub-problems have to be solved, one containing A and the other B:

Sub-problem 1	Sub-problem 2
A	B
C	C
D	D

Sub-problem 1 produces the £435 000 result and sub-problem 2 gives £170 000. The solution is the best result from either sub-problem. With several mutually exclusive pairs, many sub-problems would be formed and the procedure would become rather complicated.

So far we have assumed that a fractional share in an investment is a practical possibility – as will often be the case. But what of the problem where this is not so, and projects must be accepted or rejected in their entirety? The result is an **integer linear programming** problem in two-state variables (zero or one). A combinatorial element is introduced and a large number of different combinations of investments may arise. For instance, in an extreme case with just 20 all or nothing investments there are 184 756 different combinations of ten projects that could be made up. But the number of different combinations to identify and evaluate directly or indirectly will be nothing like this level if the size of initial outlay on a typical project is large relative to the budget available.

For instance, if ten projects are available and the outlays are such that no more than three can be taken within budget, there is a maximum of 120 groups of size three to consider. Some solution procedures for such problems are given by Wilkes (1983) but it is preferable to get round the whole-number requirement if possible. There are two ways in which this could be done. It may be possible to 'stretch' the budget. If this can be done at the existing cost of capital it is optimal to **round off the project at the margin**. (There will be no more than one fractional project in a problem with a single constraint.)

Stretching the budget may be more likely under soft capital rationing than hard capital rationing. If the budget can be stretched, but at an increased price for the extra funds, this leads to further complications as we have seen. But if the budget is invariant, there is an alternative approximation method. The method often produces an optimal result and is likely to be within one or two percentage points of maximum NPV – although a different combination of projects may be involved. The procedure is as follows.

First select the project with the greatest PI (if its outlay does not exceed the limit), then take the project with next greatest PI (if the two outlays do not exceed the limit) and so on until the project with the next greatest PI would exceed the budget. Projects with lower PIs are then examined and the one with the greatest PI **that can be afforded** is chosen. The list is then searched for the project with the greatest PI that can be afforded from the funds which then remain. Selection is completed when the cheapest project (of those remaining) cannot be financed from remaining funds.

Now apply this method to the six project example. Projects 1, 2 and 5 are selected giving an NPV of £19 933. This is the optimal solution in integers, verifiable in this case by listing all feasible combinations of projects (of which there are nine). The results are shown in Table 6.7.

Table 6.7

Project combinations	Net present value
5, 3	14 933
5, 2, 6	17 866
5, 2, 1	29 933
5, 6, 1	14 958
4, 3, 1	10 960
4, 2, 6	10 462
4, 2, 1	12 529
4, 6, 1	7 554
3, 2, 6, 1	15 904

Each combination listed in Table 6.7 is such that insufficient funds remain for the acceptance of another complete project. Seven are three-project combinations, and there is one example each of a two-project and a four-project combination. The combination of projects 5, 2 and 1 turns out to be optimal (and is identified by the approximation procedure) for budget levels between £205 000 and £240 000. When the budget available reaches £240 000 the optimal combination of projects is 5, 2, 1 and 6. This too is identified by the approximation procedure, which is a practical method for manual solution of single constraint rationing problems with indivisible projects.

The ratio method applies to single-constraint problems. However, in those multi-constraint problems in which the capital inputs at each time retain the same relative sizes in every constraint (projects are 'large' or 'small' throughout) the ratio approach can still be used. But such problems are not representative, and systematic solution requires linear programming.

Before we look at multi-constraint problems, it makes a useful link to express the single-constraint problem with divisible and non-repeatable projects in programming form. These problems are known as **Lorie-Savage problems** after the authors of a milestone paper that gave formal consideration to them. Suppose there are n possible investments, and X_j is the proportion of investment j accepted, N_j is the NPV per unit of the jth investment and N is total NPV achieved, K_j is the initial outlay per unit of investment j and L is the budget limit. The problem can be written as:

$$\text{maximize } N = \sum_{j=1}^{n} N_j X_j \tag{6.1}$$

$$\text{subject to:} \quad \sum_{j=1}^{n} K_j X_j \leq L \tag{6.2}$$

$$X_j \leq 1 \text{ for all } j \tag{6.3}$$

$$X_j \geq 0 \text{ for all } j \tag{6.4}$$

(6.1) is the **objective function**, (6.2) is a resource **constraint**, (6.3) are **upper bound** constraints and (6.4) are **sign requirements**. Such problems can be solved by the simplex method of linear programming. Consider a Lorie-Savage problem with three investments. Full investment in project 1 requires a capital outlay of £5000 and gives an NPV of £9000. A unit of investment 2 requires an outlay of £10 000 and gives an NPV of £17 000. A unit of investment 3 requires an outlay of £6000 and gives an NPV of £12 000. A total of £11 000 is available. There are no other financial or physical constraints. No more than one full unit of any investment can be taken, but investments can be scaled down with equal proportionate effects on outlay and present value. What levels of investment maximize net present value overall?

Using the framework of (6.1) to (6.4) the problem can be stated as:

$$\text{maximize: } N = 9x_1 + 17x_2 + 12x_3$$
$$\text{subject to:} \quad 5x_1 + 10x_2 + 6x_3 \le 11$$
$$x_1 \qquad\qquad\quad \le 1$$
$$x_2 \qquad\quad \le 1$$
$$x_3 \le 1$$
$$x_1, x_2, x_3 \ge 0$$

The optimal solution (which can be checked by the ratio method) is to accept projects 1 and 3 in full ($x_1 = 1$ and $x_3 = 1$) and to ignore investment 2 ($x_2 = 0$). This plan exhausts the budget and produces a total net present value of $N = 21$.

In a problem of this scale it is easy to find the effect of variations in the budget. At present there is £11 000 available. A further £1000 would enable one-tenth of investment 2 to be undertaken ($x_2 = 0.1$). This would increase N by 1.7. If £1000 *less* was available ($L = 10$) then either x_1 or x_3 would have to be reduced. The best choice is to reduce x_1 by one-fifth (new level of $x_1 = 0.8$) which will reduce N by 1.8. The complete picture of the impact on N of variations in L is shown in Figure 6.2.

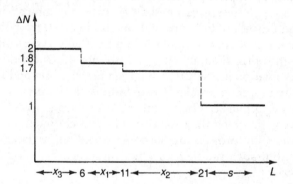

Figure 6.2

The step pattern in Figure 6.2 results from the upper bounds on the projects and the fact that the steps are down shows a declining marginal product for additional funds. (The effects shown on N include the additions to L.) Further analysis of this problem and its dual solution may be found in Wilkes (1983).

6.4 Multi-constraint problems

Multi-constraint capital rationing problems can be expressed in linear programming form and normally require LP methods for solution. But advanced methods are not **always** needed and we begin with a simplified stock market investment problem in which a number of 'institutional' constraints are represented in addition to a single expenditure constraint. A financial manager has to decide on the percentages of a given sum to invest in various companies. The yields per pound invested in each company are as follows:

	Unit trusts		Chemicals		Stores		Mines	
Company no.	1	2	3	4	5	6	7	8
Yield (%)	4.8	5.4	7.5	8.5	9	10	15	18

Company policy does not give the investment manager a completely free hand. At least 30% of any portfolio must be in unit trusts, no more than 25% may be invested in mining, at least 10% must be in chemicals and no more than 20% of the portfolio may be invested in any one company. Given these constraints, the objective is to maximize overall yield. How should the sum available be divided among the companies?

Let x_j represent the percentage of the portfolio invested in the jth company. The yield on the total sum is a weighted average on the individual yields. The problem can be expressed as:

$$\text{maximize } F = 4.8x_1 + 5.4x_2 + 7.5x_3 + 8.5x_4 + 9x_5 + 10x_6 + 15x_7 + 18x_8$$

$$
\begin{aligned}
\text{subject to:} \quad x_1 + x_2 + x_3 + x_4 + x_5 + x_6 + x_7 + x_8 &= 100 \\
x_1 + x_2 &\geq 30 \\
x_7 + x_8 &\leq 25 \\
x_3 + x_4 &\geq 10 \\
x_1 &\leq 20 \\
x_2 &\leq 20 \\
x_3 &\leq 20 \\
x_4 &\leq 20 \\
x_5 &\leq 20 \\
x_6 &\leq 20 \\
x_7 &\leq 20 \\
x_8 &\leq 20
\end{aligned}
$$

and where $x_1, x_2, x_3, x_4, x_5, x_6, x_7, x_8 \geq 0$

The structure of this problem allows informal solution. Company 8 is the most lucrative investment and x_8 is set at 20. Company 7 is the next most attractive, but x_7 may not exceed 5 because of constraint 3. The best way of satisfying constraint 2 is to set x_2 equal to 20 and x_1 equal to 10. Constraint 3 is met by setting x_4 equal to 10. Constraint 1 then allows x_6 to be set at 20 and x_5 at 15. So the solution in full is:

$$x_1 = 10 \quad x_2 = 20 \quad x_3 = 0 \quad x_4 = 10 \quad x_5 = 15 \quad x_6 = 20 \quad x_7 = 5 \quad x_8 = 20$$

The yield overall is 10.11%. Analysis on the predetermined policy elements reveals the effects of relaxing the constraints. For example, if the policy was changed so that 35% of the portfolio could be in mining, the new optimal levels of x_5 and x_7 would be 5 and 15 respectively and the average yield would increase to 10.71%. The framework of this model can be built upon for more complex modelling, as for example in the Chemical Bank model described in section 20.17.

The constraints of the problem in a modest way try to take into account the riskiness of investments. Management required at least a minimum investment in the relatively safe unit trust while a maximum was specified for the higher-risk mining industry. Furthermore the eggs had to be divided among at least five baskets. In this instance risk itself was not quantified. The succeeding example includes a simple measure of risk. More sophisticated considerations of risk are deferred until later chapters.

A finance of company is considering lending up to a total of £900 000 to five prospective clients. The rates of interest that the potential customers will pay and the finance company's estimate of the default risk in each case are as follows:

Company	1	2	3	4	5
Interest rate (%)	6.5	7	8.5	9.5	11.5
Default probability:	0.006	0.008	0.013	0.015	0.024

In the event of default, the entire loan is written off. The objective is to maximize the rate of interest on the £900 000 if there are no defaulters subject to the **expected loss** not exceeding 1% of available funds, i.e. £9000. If x_j is the amount advanced to each company, the expected loss constraint is:

$$0.006x_1 + 0.008x_2 + 0.013x_3 + 0.015x_4 + 0.024x_5 \leq 9000$$

The total lending constraint is:

$$x_1 + x_2 + x_3 + x_4 + x_5 \leq 900\ 000$$

and the objective is to maximize:

$$F = 6.5x_1 + 7x_2 + 8.5x_3 + 9.5x_4 + 11.5x_5$$

The normal solution procedure would be to use the simplex method of linear programming. Graphical solution is possible if either the number of variables or the number of constraints (as here) does not exceed two. The solution shows that:

$$x_1 = 500\ 000 \text{ and } x_4 = 400\ 000$$

with all other variables zero. So only two of the five possible client companies should be lent money. An average rate of just over 7.83% is earned. Some evaluation of the risk policy of the finance company can be made. For example, for every £100 by which the expected loss figure is raised, loans to company 4 increase by 100 000/9, loans to company 1 decrease by 100 000/9 and overall yield rises by 0.037 percentage points.

We now consider cases where finance is limited in more than one time period. There are many possible objectives for investing companies in these circumstances but we shall consider the most common case where the objective is the maximization of equity value. This is a measurable proxy for shareholders' utility. The **discounted dividend model** is followed in which equity is measured by the present value of future dividend payments with discounting at the cost of equity capital. Undertaking an investment programme means changes in the stream of dividends. These changes are of two kinds. There may be years in which dividend is reduced because of higher retentions to help finance the investments. But there will be years in which increased dividends can be paid because of the returns from the investments. The present value of the set of dividend changes must be positive for an investment programme to be worthwhile. The requirement is:

$$\Delta D_0 + \frac{\Delta D_1}{(1+e)} + \frac{\Delta D_2}{(1+e)^2} + \ldots + \frac{\Delta D_n}{(1+e)^n} > 0 \qquad (6.5)$$

where in (6.5) the ΔD_t are the dividend changes over an n year horizon and $100e\%$ is the cost of equity. The objective is to choose a group of investments, affordable in all years, to maximize the left-hand side of (6.5). Consider an example.

A company is settling its capital budget for 1996 and 1997 against a background which suggests a likely shortage of cash during the period. The company's existing activity will generate a cash surplus of £250 000 on 1 January 1996 ($t = 0$) and £240 000 on 1 January 1997 ($t = 1$). These sums are available for dividend payment and for financing new investments. Market conditions effectively rule out raising additional capital from external sources during the period, but things are expected to improve during 1998 and it is expected that the company will from that point no longer experience capital rationing. Six continuously divisible but not repeatable investments are available. The financial data are:

| | Project number | | | | | |
	1	2	3	4	5	6
Outlay at:						
$t = 0$	30	40	20	40	60	0
$t = 1$	0	0	40	40	40	80
Return at:						
$t = 2$	72	72	96	132	168	144

The objective is to maximize equity value $t = 0$, equity value being determined by the discounted dividend model. The cost of equity capital is 20%. The company can invest unused funds elsewhere at 15%. The previously determined dividends at £100 000 at $t = 0$ and £105 000 at $t = 1$ can be added to but not decreased. There is no restriction on dividend at $t = 2$ nor are the relative sizes of dividend payments restricted.

Let ΔD_t be the increase, if any, in the dividend at $t = 0$, $t = 1$ and $t = 2$. The increase in current value of equity that would result is then:

$$\Delta V = \Delta D_0 + \frac{\Delta D_1}{1.2} + \frac{\Delta D_2}{(1.2)^2} \qquad (6.6)$$

and it is desired to maximize ΔV. This is one way in which the objective function can be written.

For the constraints, expenditure on the investments at $t = 0$ must not exceed £150 000. This is because while £250 000 is available at this time £100 000 has already been earmarked for dividend. So:

$$30x_1 + 40x_2 + 20x_3 + 40x_4 + 60x_5 + 0x_6 + S_0 + \Delta D_0 = 150 \qquad (6.7)$$

where x_1 to x_6 are the number of units taken of each investment and where S_0, a *slack variable*, is unused funds if any at $t = 0$ which will be carried forward at 15%.

At $t = 1$, funds outlaid on the projects must not exceed £135 000 (i.e. £240 000 – £105 000) plus any unused funds from $t = 0$ invested at 15%. The constraint is then:

$$0x_1 + 0x_2 + 40x_3 + 40x_4 + 40x_5 + 80x_6 + \Delta D_1 \leq 135 + S_0(1.15)$$

When this is re-expressed with variables on the left hand side only and with slack variables included, we have:

$$0x_1 + 0x_2 + 40x_3 + 40x_4 + 40x_5 + 80x_6 - 1.15S_0 + S_1 + \Delta D_1 = 135 \qquad (6.8)$$

in which S_1 will be carried forward at 15% to $t = 2$. The extra dividends that can be paid at time $t = 2$ are limited. The increase in dividend possible at that time depends on the returns from the investments and any surplus from $t = 1$ invested at 15%. This means that ΔD_2 is limited by:

$$72x_1 + 72x_2 + 96x_3 + 132x_4 + 168x_5 + 144x_6 + 1.15S_1 - \Delta D_2 = 0 \qquad (6.9)$$

Finally there are upper bounds on the xs:

$$x_1 \leq 1 \quad x_2 \leq 1 \quad x_3 \leq 1 \quad x_4 \leq 1 \quad x_5 \leq 1 \quad x_6 \leq 1 \qquad (6.10)$$

The problem is to maximize (6.6), subject to (6.7) to (6.10) and the sign requirements on all variables. From (6.9) we can obtain ΔD_2 in terms of the xs and S_1:

$$\Delta D_2 = 72x_1 + 72x_2 + 96x_3 + 132x_4 + 168x_5 + 144x_6 + 1.15S_1 \qquad (6.11)$$

But S_1 cannot be positive at an optimum since if S_1 is positive, funds are being transferred from $t = 1$ to $t = 2$ at 15%. The xs are being cut back or ΔD_2 is being increased at the expense of ΔD_1. Reductions in the xs as a result of positive S_1 may have even more serious consequences in terms of V. At best, £1 transferred from $t = 1$ to $t = 2$ causes V to fall by $1/1.2 - 1.15/1.44$ hence S_1 is zero at an optimum. Using this information simplifies the problem. With ΔD_2 given by (6.11) and with $S_1 = 0$ we can substitute for ΔD_2 in (6.6) producing the objective function:

$$V = 50x_1 + 50x_2 + 66\tfrac{2}{3}x_3 + 91\tfrac{2}{3}x_4 + 116\tfrac{2}{3}x_5 + 100x_6 + \Delta D_0 + \frac{\Delta D_1}{1.2} \qquad (6.12)$$

which is to be maximized subject to:

$$30x_1 + 40x_2 + 20x_3 + 40x_4 + 60x_5 + 0x_6 + S_0 + \Delta D_0 = 150$$

$$0x_1 + 0x_2 + 40x_3 + 40x_4 + 40x_5 + 80x_6 - 1.15S_0 + 0\Delta D_0 + \Delta D_1 = 135$$

$$x_1 \leq 1 \quad x_2 \leq 1 \quad x_3 \leq 1 \quad x_4 \leq 1 \quad x_5 \leq 1 \quad x_6 \leq 1$$

$$x_1, x_2, x_3, x_4, x_5, x_6, S_0, \Delta D_0, \Delta D_1 \geq 0 \tag{6.13}$$

If any surpluses could be transferred from $t = 0$ to $t = 1$ at 20% instead of 15% then both ΔD_0 and ΔD_1 could be substituted out of the objective function and the resulting coefficients of the xs would be the project NPVs at a 20% discount rate. But since more than one interest rate applies here this substitution cannot be made.

Now find the solution without upper bounds on the xs. At once six constraints go from (6.13) and some of the xs can be eliminated when repeatability is allowed. x_1 **dominates** x_2 since it has the same objective function coefficient as x_2 but requires a smaller outlay. Less obviously x_4 is dominated by $x_3 + \frac{2}{3}x_1$, the combination requires the same outlays as one unit of x_4 but yields 100 in the objective function in comparison with 91$\frac{2}{3}$. Also, x_5 is dominated by $x_3 + 1\frac{1}{3}x_1$ while x_3 is itself inferior to $\frac{1}{2}x_6 + \frac{2}{3}x_1$. The problem has now been reduced to:

$$\text{maximize } \Delta V = 50x_1 + 100x_6 + \Delta D_0 + 0.833\Delta D_1$$

$$\text{subject to:} \quad 30x_1 + S_0 + \Delta D_0 = 150$$
$$80x_6 - 1.15S_0 + \Delta D_1 = 135$$
$$x_1, x_6, S_0, \Delta D_0, \Delta D_1 \geq 0$$

Furthermore, ΔD_0 is dominated by $x_1/30$ and ΔD_1 is dominated by $x_6/80$ so that all that is left is:

$$\text{maximize } \Delta V = 50x_1 + 100x_6$$

$$\text{subject to:} \quad 30x_1 + S_0 = 150$$
$$80x_6 - 1.15S_0 = 135$$
$$x_1, x_6, S_0, \geq 0$$

From the first of the constraints:

$$S_0 = 150 - 30x_1$$

and substitution into the second gives:

$$80x_6 - 1.15(150 - 30x_1) = 135$$

which on rearrangement becomes:

$$80x_6 + 34.5x_1 = 307.5$$

Solving this for x_6 produces:

$$x_6 = 3.84375 - 0.43125x_1 \tag{6.14}$$

and substituting into the objective function gives:

$$\Delta V = 50x_1 + 384.375 - 43.125x_1$$
$$= 6.875x_1 + 384.375 \tag{6.15}$$

The important thing about the objective function in (6.15) is that the coefficient of x_1 is positive. The constraints are implicitly included, which means that for each unit that x_1 is raised **after allowing for the changes in the other variables** ΔV will increase by 6.875. So the optimum requires x_1 to be as large as possible. The largest value that x_1 can take is when $S_0 = 0$ and $x_1 = 5 \; (= 150/30)$ and by substitution into (6.14) $x_6 = 1.6875$. Substituting these values into (6.15) produces $\Delta V = 418.75$. This implies that $\Delta D_0 = 0 \; \Delta D_1 = 0$ (as we have seen ΔD_0 and ΔD_1 are dominated) and substitution of the optimal values of x_1 and x_6 into (6.11) (everything else in the equation is zero) gives $\Delta D_2 = 603$. As a check, substituting these dividend increases into (6.6) gives:

$$\Delta V = 0 + \frac{0}{1.2} + \frac{603}{(1.2)^2} = 418.75$$

So without upper limits on investment size, the optimal policy would be to take five units of the first investment, nothing of the second to fifth investments, take 1.6875 units of investment six, transfer no money from 1 January 1996 to 1 January 1997, pay the minimum dividends of £100 000 in 1996 and £105 000 in 1997 and increase dividend by £603 000 in 1998. If this is an unacceptable dividend policy, further constraints on ΔD_0, ΔD_1 and ΔD_2 should be included. The value of the firm's equity will rise by £418 750.

Now consider the upper bounds. If no more than one unit of each investment is possible we cannot eliminate any of the investments *ex ante*. The solution procedure, the simplex method of linear programming, is not within the scope of this text. We shall state and interpret the solution. The optimal solution is:

$$x_1 = 1 \quad x_2 = 1 \quad x_3 = 0 \quad x_4 = 0.44 \quad x_5 = 1 \quad x_6 = 1 \quad S_1 = 2.33$$

$$\Delta D_0 = 0 \quad \Delta D_1 = 0 \quad \Delta D_2 = 514.33 \quad \Delta V = 357.17$$

So the optimum requires full acceptance of investments 1, 2, 5 and 6, an approximate 44% share in investment 4 and no investment in project 3. A sum of £2330 is transferred from 1 January 1996 to 1 January 1997. No dividend increases are scheduled for January 1996 or January 1997; the entire impact of the investments is to increase dividend in January 1998 by £514 330 producing an increase in the value of equity of £357 170. The upper bounds cut the equity value increase by £61 580.

In the optimal solution to the problem with upper bounds a 'loan' was made for one period which **apparently** yielded less than the cost of capital. This can happen in capital rationing situations. The **nominal** yield on £1 invested at 15% in these conditions is 15%, but the **true** yield is much greater. Investing at 15% at $t = 0$ makes money available at $t = 1$ when it is more valuable. This enables a better investment programme with larger returns and $t = 2$ dividend. The implied yield on the marginal £1 invested at the nominal 15% at $t = 0$ can be worked out from the linear programming output. This is no less than 43.87% which is well in excess of the cost of equity. An interperiod transfer of funds would *not* be made if this implied yield was less than the objective function discount rate.

The programming solution gives still more information. The maximum period to period borrowing interest rates at $t = 0$ and $t = 1$ can be found. At $t = 0$ this is 15% for the one year to $t = 1$. But it would be worth paying up to 53.49% to obtain a further £1 from outside sources at $t = 1$. So a project with the cash flow:

$$
\begin{array}{cc}
t = 1 & t = 2 \\
100 & -140
\end{array}
$$

would bring about an improvement in the present value of divided payments despite the fact that it has a negative NPV calculated in isolation at either the 15% or 20% external rates. The cash inflow of 100 at the crucially restricted $t = 1$ time period enables highly lucrative opportunities to be taken which repay more than the 140 liability at $t = 1$. There is no unambiguous figure that can be said to be the present or terminal value of a project in a multi-project context with multi-period constraints. The effect of a given stream of costs and returns on present or terminal value depends on the cash flow of other projects and the capital constraints. Any given 'present value' will change if a project is added to a different set of other possible projects or a different set of constraints. The consequence of this is that under capital rationing an asset cannot be valued in isolation from other assets to which it may be joined or from the capital or other constraints which may apply.

Returning to the numerical example, still further information could be obtained regarding the value of relaxing the upper bound constraints. It is a valuable feature of the simplex method that such information is provided *gratis*. It is interesting to work out the overall yield obtained on the sums invested. With the upper bounds imposed, the yield achieved is $100e\%$ given by:

$$150(1 + e)^2 + 135(1 + e) - 514.33 = 0$$

which solves for $e = 0.4556$, i.e. the equivalent annually compounded rate of interest is 45.56%. Without the upper bounds, the yield is obtained by solving:

$$150(1 + e)^2 + 135(1 + e) - 603 = 0$$

which gives a yield of 60.49%. So the effect of the upper bounds is to cut the yield by almost 25% (fifteen percentage points).

Capital rationing problems with more than two constraints can be expressed as in (6.12) and (6.13). Programming methods are needed for solution and several software packages are now available.

Linear programming can also be used in short-term financial management. A model developed by Srinivasan (1974) applies a highly efficient transportation algorithm to the problem of the management of cash and short-term investments. The model optimizes investment of cash inflows and optimal financing for outflows, simultaneously producing payment schedules for the incurred liabilities. The model allows distinction between four decision variables: securities transactions, payment schedules, short-term financing and cash balance. (See also the Chemical Bank Model described in section 20.17).

6.5 Financial planning models

One approach to the interrelated problems of capital investment, financing and short-term management of funds is through a financial planning model. These models are a development of the programming approach to capital rationing. A financial planning model brings together the sub-problems and seeks a complementary set of solutions.

Normative models, based on mathematical programming, look for an ideal set of consistent decisions in all the sub-problem areas. These can be vast models even though uncertainties are dealt with indirectly. The models can be used in a number of ways, for example financial modelling could be applied first to a restricted area and a well-specified problem. Optimization models can also be 'a way of sifting through alternative strategies, identifying good ones, and projecting their consequences' (Myers, 1976).

Simulating models are positive in that they are based on accounting practice. Simulating models produce the results that would follow given courses of action under stated assumptions about the future. The models use as inputs forecasts and decisions from company departments and then produce the financial statements that would follow. The models can be used to provide management with derived information – rather as in **sensitivity analysis** (see section 6.10). The relative emphasis placed upon the financial statistics produced and the final decision is left to the executives of the company.

We shall not attempt to develop a full-scale financial planning model here. Rather, we shall give illustrations of the type of constraint that a financial planning context adds on to the capital rationing framework. Typically, corporate management will wish to take account of the way that the use of investment funds affects other published financial results as well as cash flows. The changes that potential investments can cause in financial statistics based on accounts rather than cash flow cannot always be neglected. What are seen by the ownership as reasonable bounds for key financial ratios can be built into a model that represents the actual situation of a company. When the model is run, data will be produced which show the effects of the chosen bounds on achievement of corporate objectives. This information can provide powerful arguments for change. Such **marginal values** or **dual values** are part of standard LP output.

As an example of a constraint related to the value of a financial statistic, consider the **current ratio** defined as:

$$\frac{\text{current assets}}{\text{current liabilities}}.$$

Management decides an acceptable minimum for the ratio. Let this be M. To include the constraint in the model, current assets and current liabilities are expressed as functions of the investment levels. It is simplest to write current assets in year t, V_t, as:

$$V_t = V_t^0 + \sum_{j=1}^{n} \sum_{s=0}^{t} V_{js} x_j \qquad (6.16)$$

where V_t^0 is current assets in year t attributed to the existing activities of the company and V_{js} is the increase in current assets in the sth period per unit of investment j. The summation in (6.16) is the unweighted sum of the increase in current assets due to the new investments in all periods from zero up to and including period t. Current liabilities B_t can be defined as:

$$B_t = B_t^0 + \sum_{j=1}^{n} \sum_{s=0}^{t} B_{js} x_j \qquad (6.17)$$

where B_t^0 is current liabilities generated by existing activities and B_{js} is the increase in current liabilities in the sth period per unit of project j. With the requirement that

$$\frac{V_t}{B_t} \geq M \qquad (6.18)$$

substitution of (6.16) and (6.17) into (6.18) and rearrangement produces:

$$\sum_{j=1}^{n} \sum_{s=0}^{t} (MB_{js} - V_{js}) x_j \leq V_t^0 - MB_t^0 \qquad (6.19)$$

where the right-hand side of (6.19) is a constant (the value of which would be data). Similarly the coefficients of the x_j on the left-hand side are constants and the whole of (6.19) is a linear constraint.

Other requirements in financial planning models may include a minimum value for return on gross assets, minimum requirements for earnings net of tax and depreciation and requirements relating to minimum values for dividend payments in each year. For example, it may be required that dividends in any year are a given proportion of earnings net of tax and depreciation. All these provisions, and other similar ones, can be handled in ways similar to the current ratio, and they result in further linear constraints to be added to the model.

The objective function may be of discounted dividend form and, since a definite horizon will need to be employed, must include some assessment of wealth at the horizon. This will usually be the discounted value at the horizon of post-horizon cash flow from both new and existing investments.

When the financial planning model is run, solution values for the investment levels (the x_j) will result. In addition, information will be provided within the solution as to the effects of varying key parameters (such as the size of the current ratio, M). The model could be run with different sets of values of the parameters for different possible **states of the world** or hypothetical scenarios and there may be a core of projects that would be accepted in all scenarios. These could be implemented, while more detailed studies of the likelihood of the different states of the world are carried out, for example, forecasting interest rates or inflation.

Financial planning models enable the balance sheet impact of major investment decisions to be projected – indeed the entire balance sheet can be forecast. Because the required constraints are built into the model, the optimal investment programme will produce acceptable values of the selected balance sheet measures. Further possibilities for the use of the models include assessment of the effects of alternative dividend policies on the optimal investment programme and examination of alternatives that would make published results more consistent from year to year if this was not already included as a requirement within the model.

Within the same organization it is possible to link models addressing particular aspects of the company's operations. Within a conglomerate enterprise a model-based approach may be used for control purposes as far as subsidiary companies are concerned. Financial planning models can be constructed that encompass virtually all corporate activities, and this was a particularly fashionable approach 10 or 15 years ago. But there is much to commend financial planning models of relative simplicity. The flexibility of such models, their adaptability in changing circumstances, their lower development costs and lower development times are an advantage in managerial decision-making. Clearly, there is a wide variety of situations in which financial planning models are of considerable practical value. Further details are given by Bryant (1987).

6.6 Risk: some general considerations

Most investment decisions are made in the face of some degree of uncertainty about the outcome. Project revenues may be lower or higher than initial estimates suggest. Costs, although usually estimated with more confidence than revenues, can also be subject to considerable variability. Even if costs and revenues were guaranteed in amount, if relative timings are altered this may give rise to substantial liquidity (cash flow) problems.

There are many approaches to risk from the theoretical standpoint. But in practice the range of methods used is narrow, with traditional methods such as **payback** still in widespread usage. One way to account for the variety of approaches to risk is to take the view that there is no single approach that is best for all companies or individual investors in all circumstances. There is much to commend this opinion.

Sometimes a distinction is drawn between **risk** and **uncertainty**; risk meaning a situation in which cash flow values follow known probability distributions. In contrast, uncertainty is said to exist when various outcomes are possible but where probabilistic information is incomplete or does not exist at all. However, except where explicitly stated, we shall use the words interchangeably.

Following the capital rationing discussion it is appropriate that the first of the traditional methods of allowing for risk that we consider is **payback**. This is because apologists for payback have justified the method on the grounds that it is supposed to generate cash quickly in periods of shortage. In the following section we consider whether this view can be sustained.

6.7 Payback

The **payback** period for an investment is the number of years required for the undiscounted sum of the returns to equal or exceed the initial outlay – in other words to pay it back. To appraise an individual investment by this means, the project's payback period is calculated and compared with a predetermined threshold figure. If the project's payback is less than or equal to the pre-assigned value it is acceptable – otherwise it is rejected. Projects with shorter payback periods would be preferred.

For example, suppose that a company determines that acceptable projects should pay back within six years. The project (no. 1):

$t = 0$	$t = 1$	$t = 2$	$t = 3$	$t = 4$	$t = 5$	$t = 6$	$t = 7$
−20 000	11 000	5000	2000	1000	2000	7000	9000

would be acceptable since the cumulative total of the returns after five years is 21 000 and the outlay has been more than repaid within the specified period. If project 1 is compared with an alternative project 2 with the cash flow:

$t = 0$	$t = 1$	$t = 2$	$t = 3$	$t = 4$	$t = 5$	$t = 6$	$t = 7$
−20 000	1000	3000	5000	11 000	5000	3000	1000

then if the payback rule is rigidly applied, project 2 which returns its outlay in four years would be preferred as it has the shorter payback period. A convenient layout for the workings is shown in Table 6.8.

The disadvantages of payback are obvious. It takes no account of the cost of capital, cash flows outside the payback period are ignored and the distribution of cash flow both within and beyond the payback period are ignored. However, companies using payback may apply a degree of discretion so that the post payback returns are 'taken into account' in an informal fashion. Consider the point about the distribution of returns within the payback period. Project 1 pays back a large proportion of the outlay (55%) in

Table 6.8

Year	Project 1 cash flow	Cumulative net flow	Project 2 cash flow	Cumulative net flow
0	–20 000	–20 000	–20 000	–20 000
1	11 000	–9 000	1 000	–19 000
2	5 000	–4 000	3 000	–16 000
3	2 000	–2 000	5 000	–11 000
4	1 000	–1 000	11 000	0
5	2 000	1 000	5 000	5 000
6	7 000	8 000	3 000	8 000
7	9 000	17 000	1 000	9 000

Table 6.9 Percentage of outlay paid back

Year	Project 1	Project 2
1	55	5
2	80	20
3	90	45
4	95	100
5	105	125
6	140	140
7	185	145

the first year whereas project 2 pays back only 5% at this point. The percentages of outlay returned (undiscounted) are showing Table 6.9.

It is only around years 4 and 5 that project 2 has any advantage in respect of the proportion of outlay returned. Figure 6.3 illustrates the advantage of project 1 in the early and later years.

While the S-shaped track of project 2 in Figure 6.3 is more common than the early take-off, flat period and pick-up of project 1, the question arises as to what is special abut the particular figure of 100% payback?

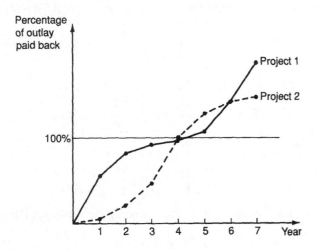

Figure 6.3

Payback will tend to be less wide of the mark in cases where returns to competing projects always tail off over time in comparable fashions, and the rule can be made more sophisticated in a number of ways. For example, minimum payback percentages can be set at various points in time or discounted returns can be used. (With the use of discounting payback can at least decide whether or not a project will become profitable in its own right, but it still cannot say *how* profitable nor make decisions between mutually exclusive projects.) Such adaptations go some way towards meeting the criticisms of payback on theoretical grounds, but also remove some of the grounds on which payback is said to be preferred. There are three main justifications offered in defence of payback:

1. it is simple to use and easy to understand;
2. projects which return their outlay quickly leave the investor less exposed to risk and uncertainty;
3. under capital rationing, the sooner the money is returned the sooner can other profitable investments be undertaken.

It is tempting to argue that reason (1) ought not to carry much weight but in practice it often does. Reason (1) is less vulnerable to rational attack when, as under uncertainty, the theoretical underpinning of the more sophisticated methods is often less than perfect. The more that uncertainty increases with time, the more force there is in reason (2). In industries where the pace of technological change is extremely fast, the use of arbitrary and quite short horizons can be made more convincing. A good example is provided by the personal computer sector of the IT industry, in particular IBM compatible 'clone' manufacturers. However, the criticisms of lack of discounting or allowance for interest charges and lack of consideration for the cash flow pattern within the payback period remain. Reason (3) also has something in it, but this does not justify ignoring the more precise methods for dealing with capital rationing. For example if year 1 was the point of most acute capital shortage, it is highly likely that project 1 would be preferred.

As regards net present values for the projects of Table 6.9, project 1 has a greater NPV than project 2 at **any** discount rate. This suggests that if a large part of the uncertainty related to interest rates rather than cash flow components there would be a strong case for project 1.

Where the projects being compared have more or less constant returns, decision by payback approximates to decision by yield. For example, in the case of two perpetuities, suppose that perpetuity 1 gives an annual return of R against an outlay of K_r. The yield $100i\%$ is given by:

$$\frac{R}{i} = K_r$$

Let perpetuity 2 give an annual inflow of S against an outlay of K_s. It has a yield of $100j\%$ given by:

$$\frac{S}{j} = K_s$$

so:

$$i = \frac{R}{K_r} \text{ and } j = \frac{S}{K_s}$$

Hence if $i > j$:

$$\frac{R}{K_r} > \frac{S}{K_s}$$

The payback periods for the alternatives are P_r and P_s periods respectively where:

$$P_r = \frac{K_r}{R} \text{ and } P_s = \frac{K_s}{S}$$

But if $i > j$:

$$\frac{K_r}{R} < \frac{K_s}{S}$$

Therefore:

$$P_r < P_s$$

so that the yield and payback rules give the same outcome in the case of perpetuities.

On balance, the greater the uncertainty, the more the uncertainty increases with time and the poorer the quality of information available to the decision-makers, the less there is to be said against the use of payback. But is the use of payback ever completely justified? The answer can only be yes if the need for simplicity overrides all other considerations. Where useful information exists concerning probabilities, cash flow data, times of acute capital shortage etc., the more there is to be said for a DCF-based rationing or risk-analysis approach.

A method of investment appraisal with some similarities to payback period but which employs discounting is the **finite-horizon** (FH) method where cash flows after a predetermined time are ignored. As we saw in Chapter 4, for long horizons and/or high interest rates, returns beyond a reasonable cut-off point are unlikely to make much difference to present values. Where uncertainty and risk increase with time, weight is added to the argument for not counting on (or counting in) the distant cash flow. But there is also the danger of ignoring a possibly problematic legacy for future generations.

If in the use of the FH method a 'short' horizon was selected, some assessment would have to be made of the value of post-horizon returns at the horizon date. This can be done – for example by finding the discounted value of post-horizon cash flow at the horizon – but if this is done with sufficient accuracy, the method ceases to have a meaningful 'finite horizon'. Occasionally circumstances suggest a natural horizon as, for example, in the case of Hong Kong where the transfer of sovereignty in 1997 is a point beyond which there is a significant increase in uncertainty.

6.8 Return on capital measures

Investment appraisal methods based on return on capital begin with the disadvantage that the number of possible meanings for this concept is the product of the number of definitions of 'return' and the number of definitions of 'capital'. A measure of capital associated with a project is divided into a measure of return or profit and the result is expressed as a percentage. Consider projects 1 and 2 of Table 6.8 if the 'rate' of return on capital is expressed as the ratio of average return to 'average' capital. If average capital is taken to be half of initial capital (initial outlay) in each case, and the average return is taken as the total of undiscounted cash flow returns divided by project duration, then this measure of return on (average) capital for the two projects gives:

$$\frac{100(5286)}{10\,000}\% = 52.9\%$$

for project 1 and:

$$\frac{100(4143)}{10\,000}\% = 41.4\%$$

for project 2. The **accounting rate of return** divides a measure of annual **profit** (rather than net cash flow) defined as net returns less depreciation by the average investment defined as:

$$0.5(\text{initial outlay} + \text{residual value})$$

if straight line depreciation is used. For example, with the assumption of zero residual value, for project 1 in Table 6.8, the average net return is the total of returns, 37 000, divided by the number of years, 7, with the result of 5286. From this is subtracted one-seventh of the cost of the investment, i.e. 20 000/7 = 2857 to give an annual profit figure of:

$$5286 - 2857 = 2429$$

and an accounting rate of return of:

$$100 \ \frac{2429}{10\ 000} \ \% = 24.3\%$$

Similar calculations for project 2 give an accounting rate of return of:

$$100 \ \frac{29\ 000/7 - 20\ 000/7}{10\ 000} \ \% = 12.9\%$$

Decision rules based on accounting rate of return would accept an individual project if its return exceeded the target figure, and in the case of a mutually exclusive pair would select the project with the greater accounting rate of return figure. Thus project 1 would be selected here. Arguments advanced in favour of return on capital measures are similar to those made in support of payback period. As with payback there is no theoretical underpinning.

In a comparison between projects of unequal duration giving similar total returns for similar outlay, accounting rate of return and other measures of return on capital will favour the shorter project. Although accounting rate of return and return on capital measures generally do at least consider returns over the whole lifetime of projects, the timing of returns, as with payback, is ignored. Equal value is effectively given to a return of £100 after one year and the same return after ten years. These measures are conservative if the larger returns come near the start of the project, when the averaging of returns understate the value of the project and thus provide a margin of safety. But on the whole, the averaging of undiscounted return obscures important differences between otherwise similar projects in respect of the timing of larger returns. This is important if, as is usually the case, uncertainty increases with distance from the present. Consider for example the projects:

	$t = 0$	$t = 1$	$t = 2$	$t = 3$	$t = 4$
A	−1400	800	600	400	200
B	−1400	500	500	500	500
C	−1400	200	400	600	800

for which the following measures may be confirmed:

	A	B	C
Accounting rate of return	21.43	21.43	21.43
Return on capital (average)	71.43	71.43	71.43
Payback period	2	3	4
Internal rate of return	20.53	15.97	12.91
Net present value (15%)	126.70	27.49	−71.72

The three projects appear identical in terms of accounting rate of return and return on capital, but are clearly distinguished by all the other methods – including, in this case, payback. A is preferred to B which is preferred to C. There can be little doubt which is the more attractive project.

In practice, accounting rate of return may be one of a number of criteria the values of which are 'taken into account', though this does not mean that the decision-maker can trust to the deficiencies of one approach being compensated by other methods. Most UK firms use several methods – around three typically. About nine out of ten use payback but upwards of eight out of ten use a DCF method (yield somewhat more than NPV). Only around four out of ten use accounting rate of return. (See Wilkes *et al.* (1994), Pike (1993) or Sangster (1993) for further details.)

In the risk premium approach a number of percentage points (a premium) is added to the discount rate on grounds of risk. Although this very old pragmatic response to uncertainty in banking and money lending can draw some support from the capital asset pricing model if appropriate project-specific risk premia are used, in practice premia tend to be judgemental and can be lacking in consistency.

The risk-discounted present value can be written as:

$$\text{NPV} = \sum_{t=1}^{n} R_t (1+r+p)^{-t} - K \tag{6.20}$$

where the risk premium is $100p\%$ and where r is an estimate of the risk-free discount rate, for example, the yield to maturity on long-term government bonds. Historically the average extra return demanded from equities in the UK has been around 8% or 9% above the risk-free rate. The risk-adjusted discount rate in (6.20) is $100(r + p)\%$. For example, the project:

$t = 0$	$t = 1$	$t = 2$	$t = 3$	$t = 4$
–100	40	50	60	70

has an NPV of 70.6 at a discount rate of 10% ($r = 0.1$). The use of a 5% risk premium ($p = 0.05$) produces an NPV figure of 52.1. The use of the 'risk adjusted' discount rate causes a higher discount factor to be applied to all returns, but the further away a return is from the present, the larger is the increase in the discount factor. This increasing impact is shown in Table 6.10 where for the project data above it is seen that the 15% risk-adjusted rate cuts the contribution to present value of the year 1 return by 4.35% but the present value of the year 4 return is reduced by 16.29%. Correspondingly larger impacts would be made on the present values of the more distant returns in longer running projects.

Table 6.10

Time	Return	10%PV	15%PV	Reduction %
1	40	36.36	34.78	4.35
2	50	41.32	37.81	8.51
3	60	45.08	39.45	12.48
4	70	47.81	40.02	16.29

A more sophisticated variant of the basic risk premium approach makes a distinction between investments with different perceived levels of risk by applying banded premia according to the risk category of a project. A typical categorization is a three-tier split into low-risk, medium-risk and high-risk classes, with a different risk premium applying within each class. For example, against the background of a 7% risk-free rate, management may determine risk premiums of 4, 9 and 15 percentage points as shown in Table 6.11.

Management then assesses the various factors involved in a project and places the project in one of the categories.

An extension of this approach determines an individual risk premium for each project. Each investment then has its own risk-adjusted discount rate. At this level, the risk premium approach begins to gain some theoretical support from the capital asset pricing model. In this case the risk considered must be that component of project-specific risk that cannot be diversified away (**systematic risk**). A more ambitious approach can be applied to large-scale complex projects if the components of the cash flow can be disentangled and different risk premia applied to the distinguishable types of income. Empirical support should be provided for the differential premia, the logical basis for which would be the capital asset pricing model described in Chapter 9.

Table 6.11

Risk class	Premium	Risk adjusted discount
Low	4	11
Medium	9	16
High	15	22

6.10 Sensitivity analysis

In sensitivity analysis the viability of an investment is examined in relation to each uncertain parameter. An acceptable range of variation or tolerance interval is found for each parameter under investigation or two or for more parameters jointly.

Consider a numerical example. A company is considering a project that would involve the production of a commodity for six years. The initial estimates of the parameter values are as shown in Table 6.12.

Table 6.12

Initial outlay (K)	40 000
Selling price (p)	20
Unit cost (c)	15
Discount rate (r)	10
Lifetime (L)	6
Sales volumes: Year 1	2 000
Year 2	2 000
Year 3	3 000
Year 4	3 000
Year 5	1 500
Year 6	1 500

The return received in any year will be the unit profit $p - c$ multiplied by the sales volume v. Thus on the basis of the initial estimates the cash flow would be:

$t = 0$	$t = 1$	$t = 2$	$t = 3$	$t = 4$	$t = 5$	$t = 6$
−40 000	10 000	10 000	15 000	15 000	7500	7500

Applying the 10% discount rate:

$$\text{GPV} = 47\ 761 \text{ and NPV} = 7761$$

The threshold for acceptability of the project is non-negative NPV. We now use single-parameter sensitivity analysis to determine the individual percentage variation in each parameter (p, c, v, K, r and L) that would produce zero NPV.

First consider the unit profit on the product. This is $p - c$ and is currently £5. Any variation in this figure would have equal proportionate effect on each return and hence on GPV as a whole, so that as long as unit profit is not less than:

$$£5 \, \frac{40\ 000}{47\ 761} = £4.19$$

with the other data unchanged, NPV will not become negative.

Thus on the income side with unchanged unit costs, as long as the selling price is not less than £19.19, the project will still be viable. In other words the price must not drop by more than 4.05%.

On the cost side, with unchanged selling price, if unit costs remain below £15.81 then NPV will be positive, so that any increase must not exceed 5.40%.

On the sales volume front, if unit profits are unchanged but sales are:

$$100 \frac{40\,000}{47\,761} \% = 83.75\%$$

of the original estimates in each year the project remains viable. Put another way, with other things equal, sales volume figures must not fall by more than 16.25%.

For the remaining parameters, again considered individually, NPV will become zero for an initial outlay of £47 761 or 19.40% above the original figure. As regards the discount rate, the yield of the project turns out to be 16.57% so that a 65.7% increase over the original value for the discount rate is tolerable.

Variation in project lifetime is somewhat more difficult to allow for as an approximating assumption will be necessary if reductions in life involving a fraction of a year are involved. If the project's life is four years, i.e. if the last two returns of £7500 are ignored, the GPV would be £38 870, a decrease of £8891. To make the gross present value exactly £40 000 the contribution to present value of returns in the fifth year needs to be £1130. Suppose that if the project runs for some fraction, f, of the fifth year then the return that arises is $7500f$ to be received at time $t = 4 + f$. Thus if the truncated fifth year is to produce a return giving a present value of £1130 then f must be such as to satisfy:

$$\frac{7500f}{(1.1)^{4+f}} = 1130$$

that is:

$$750f = 113(1.1)^{4+f}$$

The object is to choose a value of f so as to equate the two sides of the equation. This is accomplished for $f = 0.2254$ with example workings as shown in Table 6.13.

Table 6.13

f	$750f$	$113(1.1)^{4+f}$
0.2000	150.00	168.63
0.2200	165.00	168.95
0.2250	168.75	169.03
0.2251	168.82	169.03
0.2252	168.90	169.03
0.2253	168.98	169.03
0.2254	169.05	169.04
0.2255	169.13	169.04

Thus with $f = 0.2254$, the breakeven life time is 4.2254 years, a reduction of 1.7746 years or 29.58% on the original value.

The full results of the single parameter breakeven exercise are shown in Table 6.14.

Table 6.14

Datum	Percentage change
Selling price	4.05
Unit cost	5.40
Sales volume	16.25
Initial outlay	19.40
Discount rate	65.70
Project lifetime	29.58

Entries in the percentage change column of Table 6.14 are the unfavourable changes (decrease or increase) which, if occurring individually, would reduce NPV to zero. It is evident that NPV is much more sensitive to changes in sales price and unit costs than to any other datum.

Calculations of sales volume sensitivity could have been performed for each year individually. For example consider the year 3 figure. With all else unchanged, the level of sales in year 3 necessary to produce an NPV of zero is V_3 where:

$$-40\,000 + 10\,000(0.9091) + 10\,000(0.8264) + 5V_3(0.7513)$$

$$+\,15\,000(0.6830) + 7500(0.6209) + 7500(0.5645)$$

$$= 0$$

so that:

$$V_3 = 934.1$$

a percentage reduction of up to 68.9% in this individual figure. The full results for all sales volumes figures, each stated individually, are shown in Table 6.15.

Table 6.15

Year	Original sales	Minimum	Percent variation
1	2000	292.63	85.37
2	2000	121.90	93.91
3	3000	934.09	68.86
4	3000	727.49	75.75
5	1500	−999.76	166.65
6	1500	−1249.73	183.32

Some of the figures in Table 6.15 may, at first sight, seem surprising. The negative minimum values for sales volume in years 5 and 6 produced by the arithmetic simply indicate that if there were no sales at all in either of those years there would, with other data unchanged, still be a positive net present value – an outcome consistent with our findings for minimum length of life. The required minimum falls between years 1 and 2 and years 3 and 4 because the greater discount applied to the second of each pair of figures reduces its significance to present value.

As regards the initial outlay, a variation of almost 20% would be somewhat unusual in a one-off cost at a given time. However, had these costs been spread over a period, more variability might be expected.

While the tolerable adverse variation in discount rate is the largest of any parameter in percentage terms, rates of interest are typically more volatile than are finished goods prices or manufacturing costs. Thus, despite the apparent robustness of the NPV figure in respect of this parameter, due caution should still be exercised.

Similar caveats apply to interpretation of the tolerable change in project lifetime – the second largest percentage figure. Should demand for the end product be overtaken by technological progress or change in taste, then a variation in anticipated lifetime of around one-third is not that unlikely.

Multi-parameter sensitivity analysis considers simultaneous changes in a number of values. For example, correlated movements in prices are likely if many are affected by common factors such as exchange-rate movements or general inflation. Consider selling price and unit cost in the present example. If these are the only parameters varying, then the project remains viable as long as unit profit is at least 4.19. That is:

$$c \leq p - 4.19$$

Suppose that the percentage increase in price in all years is $100x_p\%$ and the percentage increase in unit cost (all years) is $100x_c\%$. Then, for viability:

$$p(1 + x_p) - c(1 + x_c) \geq \frac{40\ 000(5)}{47\ 761}$$

Therefore, with the original values of $p = 20$ and $c = 15$ as the baseline for viability, the percentage changes must satisfy:

$$x_p \geq 0.75x_c - 0.0406$$

An alternative approach when a number of parameters change is to specify particular sets of changes and deduce the consequences for present value. The specific changes might correspond to certain states of the world or **scenarios**, and could represent for example the choice by a national government of alternative economic targets or methods of regulation. For illustration consider three possible inflation scenarios.

In scenario 1, suppose that competitive conditions and exchange rate variations mean that product selling price would rise by 10% per annum while unit costs would rise at 15%. Assume that both sets of rises begin right away at $t = 0$. First we need to find out what selling price and unit costs will be at the end of each year; then unit profit is obtained as the difference between them. Unit profit is then multiplied by sales volume and discounted in the usual way. The results, with price in year t, p_t, given by:

$$p_t = 20(1.1)^t$$

and costs in year c, c_t given by:

$$c_t = 15(1.15)^t$$

are shown in Table 6.16.

Table 6.16

Year	Price	Cost	Unit profit	Sales	Revenue	PV
1	22.00	17.25	4.75	2000	9 500.00	8 636.36
2	24.20	19.84	4.36	2000	8 725.00	7 210.75
3	26.62	22.81	3.81	3000	11 420.63	8 580.49
4	29.28	26.24	3.05	3000	9 140.72	6 243.23
5	32.21	30.17	2.04	1500	3 059.76	1 899.87
6	35.43	34.70	0.74	1500	1 102.96	622.59
					GPV =	33 193.29
					NPV =	−6 806.71

The end result of the different rates of inflation has been to turn a positive net present value of £7761 into a loss of £6807. Note that the major impact of the different rates of inflation is in the later years. In the first and second years there are relatively minor reductions in unit profit, but this figure is rapidly approaching zero by $t = 6$.

Now consider inflation scenario 2. In this case severe inflation at 23% in selling price and 28% of unit cost is expected. With a similar layout to Table 6.16, the results are displayed in Table 6.17.

In this case the end result is an **increase** of 38% in the net present value of the project. This is due to the increase in unit profit in money terms in the earlier years. This illusion of prosperity is due to the fact that, although the escalation of selling price is slower than that of unit cost, it works from a larger base. This is sufficient at first to more than counteract the difference of five percentage points in the inflation rates. However, as is seen from Table 6.17, the chickens are coming home to roost in the later years of the project

Table 6.17

Year	Price	Cost	Unit profit	Sales	Revenue	PV
1	24.60	19.20	5.40	2000	10 800.00	9818.18
2	30.26	24.58	5.68	2000	11 364.00	9391.73
3	37.22	31.46	5.76	3000	17 280.18	12 982.85
4	45.78	40.27	5.51	3000	16 536.03	11 294.33
5	56.31	51.54	4.77	1500	7 149.76	4 439.44
6	69.26	65.97	3.29	1500	4 928.74	2 782.15

GPV = 50 708.68
NPV = 10 708.68

Table 6.18

Year	Price	Cost	Unit profit	Sales	Revenue	PV
1	21.00	16.20	4.80	2000	9 600.00	8 533.33
2	22.05	17.50	4.55	2000	9 108.00	7 196.44
3	23.15	18.90	4.26	3000	12 770.46	8 969.10
4	24.31	20.41	3.90	3000	11 708.38	7 309.48
5	25.53	22.04	3.49	1500	5 228.57	2 901.48
6	26.80	23.80	3.00	1500	4 498.20	2 218.83

GPV = 37 128.67
NPV = –2 871.33

with unit profit falling rapidly (it would have become negative by year eight). The example suggests that differences in inflation rates between prices and costs can be 'got away with' for a while, provided that the project is profitable to begin with. The corrosive effect of the inflation becomes evident at a later stage.

Thus far we have worked with the original discount rate of 10%. However, where other prices are moving upwards the price of money will not usually remain constant for long. In inflation scenario 3 suppose that costs rise by 8% while product prices increase at 5% and where interest rates rise such that the discount rate becomes 12.5%. The results are shown in Table 6.18.

Here the apparently modest difference between the cost and price inflation rates, three percentage points, eats into unit profits from the outset. This is not surprising in view of the fact that the rate of cost inflation is 60% greater than the rise in selling prices. The rise in discount rate adds to the damage and the investment would no longer be undertaken if this scenario were assured.

Now consider scenario 4 in which inflation of both revenues and costs has been constrained to 3% in each case. The policies that achieved this have also produced low interest rates reflected in a 7% discount rate for the project. The one downside is that the level of activity has fallen and sales volumes are down 10% in each year. Table 6.19 gives the results.

Despite the fact that the level of economic activity has fallen, net present value in cash terms is greater than the original value. The increase in money values of unit profit com-

Table 6.19

Year	Price	Cost	Unit profit	Sales	Revenue	PV
1	20.60	15.45	5.15	1800	9 270.00	8 663.55
2	21.22	15.91	5.30	1800	9 548.10	8 339.68
3	21.85	16.39	5.46	2700	14 751.81	12 041.87
4	22.51	16.88	5.63	2700	15 194.37	11 591.71
5	23.19	17.39	5.80	1350	7 825.10	5 579.19
6	23.88	17.91	5.97	1350	8 059.85	5 370.62

GPV = 51 586.63

NPV = 11 586.63

Table 6.20

Year	Price	Cost	Unit profit	Sales	Revenue	PV
1	20.40	15.60	4.80	1800	8 640.00	8 000.00
2	20.81	16.22	4.58	1800	8 251.20	7 074.08
3	21.22	16.87	4.35	2700	11 748.24	9 326.13
4	21.65	17.55	4.10	2700	11 072.07	8 138.30
5	22.08	18.25	3.83	1350	5 172.96	3 520.63
6	22.52	18.98	3.54	1350	4 783.67	3 014.53

GPV = 39 073.66

NPV = −926.34

bined with the lower rate of discount in this case more than offset the depressed state of sales and produce the financial improvement.

Things are however, rather delicately balanced in scenario 4. In scenario 5, sales are still assumed to be 10% down, but the inflation and discount rate figures are also off their previous values by an adverse 1 percentage point in each case. So sales prices increase by 2%, costs rise by 4% and the discount rate is 8%. The outcome for the project is shown in Table 6.20.

Here the picture is very different to that for scenario 4. Overall net present value is now negative and the decline in physical activity represented by the depressed sales volumes is now matched by a financial loss. It is hard to see how, in practice, economic regulation could fine-tune outcomes to produce scenario 4 rather than scenario 5.

There are many other possible futures that could be projected, for example with inflation first rising and then falling, varying interest rates, different patterns of initial cash flow and more subtle differences in sales volumes. The sensitivity analysis approach could be used in all these cases to project the outcomes for net present values. This is all the more easy to do with an appropriate computer program or use of a spreadsheet. Tables 6.16 to 6.20 were generated with programs written in Basic. (The Basic dialect used here is Microsoft QuickBasic. The program will run under Q-Basic as supplied with MS-DOS versions 5.0 or later and under VisualBasic for Dos. With line numbers added it should run under older variants such as the GW-Basic supplied with earlier versions of MS-DOS.) That for Table 6.16 is:

```
'CH6614.BAS
n = 6
DIM p(n), c(n), dif(n), v(n), rev(n), pv(n)
K = 40000
priceinf = .1
costinf = .15
r = .1
FOR i = 1 TO n
   READ v(i)
NEXT i
FOR i = 1 TO n
   p(i) = 20 * (1 + priceinf) ^ i
   c(i) = 15 * (1 + costinf) ^ i
   diff(i) = p(i) – c(i)
   rev(i) = diff(i) * v(i)
   pv(i) = rev(i) * (1 + r) ^ –i
NEXT i
temp = 0
FOR i = 1 TO n
   temp = temp + pv(i)
NEXT
gpv = temp
npv = gpv – K
CLS
PRINT
PRINT STRING$(72, "–")
PRINT TAB(30); "unit"
PRINT "year"; TAB(10); "price"; TAB(20); "cost"; TAB(30); "profit";
PRINT TAB(40); "sales"; TAB(51); "revenue"; TAB(69); "PV"
PRINT STRING$(72, "–")
FOR i = 1 TO n
   PRINT i;
   PRINT TAB(10); USING "##.##"; p(i);
   PRINT TAB(20); USING "##.##"; c(i);
   PRINT TAB(30); USING "##.##"; diff(i);
   PRINT TAB(40); USING "####"; v(i);
   PRINT TAB(50); USING "#####.##"; rev(i);
   PRINT TAB(65); USING "#####.##"; pv(i)
```

```
NEXT i
PRINT TAB(66); STRING$(7, "–")
PRINT TAB(59); "GPV = ";
PRINT USING "#####.##"; gpv
PRINT TAB(59); "NPV = ";
PRINT USING "#####.##"; npv
PRINT STRING$(72, "–")
END
DATA 2000,2000,3000,3000,1500,1500
```

The program is easily modified through alteration of the values for the inflation and discount rates. The program reads in the original sales data, which values can also be altered. If the number of periods differs from 6, the value of *n* should be adjusted accordingly.

In general terms, there are three main uses to which management can put the results of a sensitivity analysis:

1. as derived information to be taken into account in an initial assessment of the project;
2. as a pointer to where more detailed data and estimates would be most valuable;
3. as an aid in the preparation of contingency plans should key parameters show unfavourable variation *ex post*.

Sensitivity analysis is not itself a *decision rule*. Management must weigh the information provided by the analysis in deciding whether the investment is worthwhile. As we have pointed out, sensitivity analysis is most valuable under conditions of uncertainty where probabilistic information is inadequate. Any hard and fast decision rule proposed for such circumstances would rightly be treated with some reserve. The due exercise of managerial judgement is most important. In other approaches, numerical values are attached to subjective elements and included in calculations with objective data. There may be some merit in this, but there is a strong case for keeping judgemental elements separate (a point that is developed further in the following chapter) and avoiding what may be seen as spurious quantification.

In respect of the second possible use, the acquisition of data takes time and costs money. If, on the basis of relatively inexpensive initial estimates, it is found that the project is particularly sensitive to the selling price of the product, a more detailed investigation of demand conditions can be carried out on this parameter. Conversely if a project is relatively insensitive to discount rate changes, the costs of more detailed work in this area can be escaped.

In respect of use (3) above, it is important to remember that with the exception of some purely paper investments the managerial function does not cease once a decision has been taken to accept an investment project. Management will not be passive in the face of unfavourable variation from estimated values of parameters. For example, if unit costs are working out at a higher level than at first anticipated, it would be helpful to know that the project is sensitive to this parameter and to have had contingency plans drawn up to deal with this eventuality.

6.11 Simulation

Where reasonable probabilistic information is available on variable elements in a project's cash flow, the technique of **simulation** can be of considerable value. The simulation procedure involves taking samples from these distributions and computing present values. This process is repeated a sufficiently large number of times for a reliable distribution of present value to be obtained. The purpose of the exercise in this form is to estimate the mean and variance of the distribution of net present value or yield when analytical results are unobtainable. A decision is then taken on the basis of the simulated results. Needless to say, computers have much to offer in this context and most simulation models will be computer based.

Simulation is so highly malleable an instrument that the temptation is, if anything, to over-use the technique in situations where random variables are related in complex ways. A caveat is that the number of variables with independent uncertainty must not be too great, as computation time can increase rapidly. The five or six cash flow parameters studied in the sensitivity analysis example would be a reasonable number of independent variables in the context of investment appraisal.

There is no clear dividing line between where sensitivity analysis ends and where simulation can be said to begin. For example, sensitivity analysis of the 'scenario' variety has been called **deterministic simulation**. Balance sheet projections, giving values of financial statistics if particular investment projects were undertaken, are an example of deterministic simulation or projective sensitivity analysis. However, simulation is usually taken to mean that random variables are involved.

Simulation is not usually employed as an optimizing technique. It **can** be used in an accept or reject manner – for example accepting a project only if it has a predetermined probability of achieving a positive net present value. Simulation provides a highly convenient representation of reality and, in some cases, can be used to **improve** performance by adjusting certain variables under the decision-maker's control. The art of the process is at two levels, the construction of the model and the judgement of changes to be made to controllable variables.

Consider a simple exercise that can be carried out manually. (This exercise is in fact simple enough for direct calculation to be performed by other means, but the purpose here is to illustrate a basic procedure that could be extended to more complex examples.) Suppose that it is known with certainty that the outlay on a project will be £65 000, the discount rate is 10% and the project will run for five years. Only the returns in each year are subject to random variability as described in Table 6.21.

Table 6.21

Probability	Return
0.1	10 000
0.2	15 000
0.4	20 000
0.2	25 000
0.1	30 000

The returns in each year are assumed to follow the distribution of Table 6.21 and independence is assumed between years. The first step in the manual exercise allocates single-digit numbers to each value of return. In each case the numbers of digits allocated must correspond to the probabilities above.

The ten numbers it is necessary to use will be 0, 1, 2, 3, . . . 9. For the 10 000 return, having probability 0.1, we assign one of the numbers (a proportion 0.1 of the total of ten numbers) to this outcome. In principle *any* one of the numbers would do, but for convenience we shall select 0. The 15 000 return has probability 0.2 so that 20% of the numbers are assigned to this outcome. Again these 2 could by any of the remaining 9 numbers, but we shall employ 1 and 2. The procedure is applied in a similar fashion to the remaining returns with the results shown in Table 6.22.

The next step is to obtain a series of random digits – for example by use of a computer program, a scientific calculator or a table of random numbers. Suppose that the sequence of digits is:

Table 6.22

Numbers allocated	Corresponding return
0	10 000
1,2	15 000
3,4,5,6	20 000
7,8	25 000
9	30 000

1 8 7 5 6 3 4 0 9 7 9 3 2 1 4 4 4 9 2 0
6 0 3 4 0 2 9 2 6 6

A digit is selected and for convenience let this be the first one: 1. This number is used to generate a value for the first-year return in run 1 of the exercise. The number falls in the group 1,2 so that the first return is 15 000. The second return is then given by the next digit. This is 8 and as it is in the group 7, 8 it gives a value of 25 000 for the return in year 2. In similar fashion the third-, fourth- and fifth-year returns generated are 25 000, 20 000 and 20 000 by using the numbers 7, 5 and 6. This completes the data generation for the first run, the simulated cash flow being:

$t = 0$	$t = 1$	$t = 2$	$t = 3$	$t = 4$	$t = 5$
–65 000	15 000	25 000	25 000	20 000	20 000

for which the net present value at 10% is 14 159. It is important to note that this cash flow pattern is **not** a prediction of what would happen if the project was accepted. It is a simulated sample drawn according to the appropriate probabilities.

Continuing to make use of the random numbers in the same fashion, with a total of six runs the overall results are as shown in Table 6.23.

Table 6.23

	Run number					
	1	2	3	4	5	6
1	15 000	20 000	30 000	20 000	20 000	15 000
2	25 000	20 000	20 000	20 000	10 000	30 000
3	25 000	10 000	15 000	30 000	20 000	15 000
4	20 000	30 000	15 000	15 000	20 000	20 000
5	20 000	25 000	20 000	10 000	10 000	20 000
GPV	79 159	78 237	77 735	73 705	61 342	75 778
NPV	14 159	13 237	12 735	8 705	–3 658	10 778

In practice a much larger number of runs would be carried out, but for this illustration we shall restrict ourselves to six runs. Later on, the results from a thousand run exercise will be given. The important row of Table 6.23 is the last one, with six values of NPV. From these numbers we obtain the simulation estimate of the **expected net present value**, ENPV, as the arithmetic mean of the NPV figures generated. Thus:

$$\Sigma \, \text{NPV} = 14\,159 + 13\,237 + 12\,735 + 8705 - 3658 + 10\,778 = 55\,956$$

so the six run simulation estimate of expected net present value for the project is:

Table 6.24

Run no.	Average NPV
1	10 239
2	10 775
3	10 679
4	11 124
5	10 716
6	10 482
7	10 644
8	10 552
9	10 987
10	10 536

$$\text{ENPV} \approx \frac{55\ 956}{6} = 9326$$

Of course, this figure is an **estimate** of ENPV and a different value would have been obtained if different random digits had been drawn to start with. The important point is that the larger is the number of runs, the smaller will these differences tend to be. To illustrate this point ten trials of 1000 runs each were carried out and the results were as shown in Table 6.24.

From Table 6.24 it is reasonable to conclude that the true value of ENPV is between £10 000 and £11 000, so the estimate we obtained from our particular six run case, 9326, turns out to be a little low. (The average of the values in Table 6.24, 10 673, is also a little low. In this case a precise value for ENPV can be calculated. This is 10 816.)

Other useful data can be obtained from a simulation exercise. In the present case the standard deviation of net present value can be estimated. This figure can then be used to estimate the probability that NPV will be within a given range of values – for example above zero. To find an estimate for the standard deviation of NPV in the six run simulation, proceed as follows.

$$sd_{\text{NPV}} = \sqrt{\left(\frac{\Sigma(\text{NPV} - \text{ENPV})^2}{n-1} \right)}$$

where n is the number of runs of the simulation (the observations of the variable NPV). Workings are shown in Table 6.25. Thus

Table 6.25

NPV	NPV –ENPV	(NPV – ENPV)²
14 159.09	4 833	23 358 304
13 237.33	3 911	15 298 152
12 735.01	3 409	11 621 041
8 704.602	–621	386 189
–3 657.938	–12 984	168 583 744
10 778.17	1 452	2 108 678
		221 356 112

Using the formula above, from Table 6.25, the estimate of standard deviation from the six run simulation therefore emerges as:

$$sd_{\text{NPV}} \approx \sqrt{\left(\frac{221\ 356\ 112}{5} \right)}$$
$$= 6654$$

This estimate based on six runs of the model only turns out to be significantly low. For a particular 10 000 run comparison the figure that emerged from sd_{NPV} was 9392. This is much nearer the true figure of 9369. (Recall that in actual usage it will not usually be possible (or necessary) to calculate the true value of the standard deviation.) For illustrative purposes we will continue to work with the figure obtained for the six runs, bearing in mind that a much larger number of runs would be used in practice.

The standard deviation of net present value can be used to produce a confidence interval for NPV. For example, there is a 95% chance that in the event of the acceptance of the project, the actual net present value will be within 1.96 standard deviations of the mean. Using the six run estimate, this means inside the range:

$$9326 \pm 1.96(6654)$$

Even with the admittedly low estimate of standard deviation, from this range there is clearly a significant risk of the project producing a negative NPV. This probability can be calculated using methods set out in the following section. The investor may wish to estimate the probability of achieving at least some minimal level of NPV – for example zero. This can be estimated directly by setting up the simulation exercise to count the occasions as a proportion of the total when the specified level of NPV is reached. A value can be estimated indirectly by using the standard deviation and a table of values of areas under a normal curve when it is reasonable to suppose that NPV values are approximately normally distributed. For example, in the present case zero NPV is $9326/6654 \approx 1.4$ standard deviations below the mean. Using Table 7 for $z = 1.4$ we see that the value 0.9192 means that approximately 92% of the area under the curve is found above 1.4 standard deviations below the mean. So our six run estimate of the probability of obtaining a negative NPV would be $1 - 0.9192$ or approximately 8% which, as we realize, understates the true probability.

The output from a simulation exercise need not be solely in text form. It can be presented graphically – for example as a plot of the distribution of NPV or as a **risk profile** of a form to be described in the following section. In a risk profile, the chance that the net present value will be above (or if preferred, below) given figures is plotted. Here again it should be emphasized that in applied work of this nature far more than six runs of a model would be carried out.

The data to be used in a simulation should be the best available estimates of the distributions of the actual values of variable factors influencing present value. However, it has been argued that the discount rate values to be used in the simulation should be estimates of the risk-free rate, as the discount rate should already include an allowance for risk. This argument carries more force the nearer the company is to operating within a perfect capital market and less force the further away the investor is from this situation.

If a perfect capital market exists, and a project-specific risk-adjusted discount rate has been arrived at which fully reflects the information available about the project to a properly diversified ownership, then a simulation exercise is likely to be of more limited value. But the assumption of such conditions begs all the important questions about the environment in which an investment decision is to be made, the multi-period character of investments and the information used in determining the level of risk adjustment. Within the framework of the capital asset pricing model, one example of the use of simulation would be to give estimates of net returns from simulated sampling of the components of cash flow in any period. In this context, the net return data are then discounted at a rate determined by the model. Another example usage would be to examine the effects of possible management initiatives to improve financial performance as illustrated in section 6.15.

6.12 Single investment risk analysis

This section describes ways in which probability data on a project can be analysed and suitable statistics derived for management decision-making. First consider the case of a known, discrete probability distribution of returns in each year. Suppose that in a typical year t there are three possible returns R_{t1}, R_{t2} and R_{t3} that can occur with probabilities p_{t1}, p_{t2} and p_{t3}. The **expected** return for the year $E(R_t)$ is given by the sum of the returns each weighted by its probability of occurrence:

$$E(R_t) = p_{t1}R_{t1} + p_{t2}R_{t2} + p_{t3}R_{t3}$$

or, in general, if there are m possible values for the return in year t, by:

$$E(R_t) = \sum_{i=1}^{m} p_{ti}R_{ti}$$

If a similar situation exists in each of the n future years of a project and for the outlay in year zero, then the expected net present value, ENPV, is given by:

$$\text{ENPV} = \sum_{t=0}^{n} E(R_t)(1+r)^{-t} \tag{6.21}$$

where $E(R_0)$ is the expected value of the outlay on the project and $100r\%$ is the appropriate discount rate.

Possible decision rules involving expected net present value are discussed later. For the moment let us see how the arithmetic works out. Consider a numerical example. A project runs for three years with the distributions of returns in each year as shown in Table 6.26.

Table 6.26

Year 1		Year 2		Year 3	
Return	Probability	Return	Probability	Return	Probability
10 000	0.1	20 000	0.4	10 000	0.3
12 000	0.6	30 000	0.6	16 000	0.5
16 000	0.3			20 000	0.2

Suppose that the initial outlay for this project is certain to be £42 000 and that the discount rate is 10%. We shall first find the expected return in each year. For year 1 the result is that $E(R_1) = 13\,000$. The workings are:

R_{1i}	p_{1i}	$p_{1i}R_{1i}$
10 000	0.1	1 000
12 000	0.6	7 200
16 000	0.3	4 800
		13 000

Similar calculations for years 2 and 3 give expected returns of 26 000 and 15 000 respectively.

The present value of these expected returns, the expected gross present value, EGPV, is then given by:

$$\begin{aligned} \text{EGPV} &= 13\,000(1.1)^{-1} + 26\,000(1.1)^{-2} + 15\,000(1.1)^{-3} \\ &= 44\,576 \end{aligned}$$

so that:

$$\text{ENPV} = 44\,576 - 42\,000 = 2576$$

This figure of £2576 is expected (in the mathematical sense) and of course there is a range of possible outcomes. Table 6.27 shows the possible combinations of returns in each year in units of £k, and the chance that each particular pattern will arise on the assumption that the returns in any year are independent of the returns in any other year. It should be noted that the ENPV formula (6.21) applies whether or not the returns are independent.

Table 6.27

Cash flow (£k) . . .			Probability	NPV	P*NPV
10	20	10	0.012	−8.867	−0.106
10	20	16	0.020	−4.359	−0.087
10	20	20	0.008	−1.354	−0.011
10	30	10	0.018	−0.603	−0.011
10	30	16	0.030	3.905	0.117
10	30	20	0.012	6.911	0.083
12	20	10	0.072	−7.049	−0.508
12	20	16	0.120	−2.541	−0.305
12	20	20	0.048	0.464	0.022
12	30	10	0.108	1.216	0.131
12	30	16	0.180	5.724	1.030
12	30	20	0.072	8.729	0.628
16	20	10	0.036	−3.412	−0.123
16	20	16	0.060	1.095	0.066
16	20	20	0.024	4.101	0.098
16	30	10	0.054	4.852	0.262
16	30	16	0.090	9.360	0.842
16	30	20	0.036	12.365	0.445
			1.000		2.576

The fifth column in Table 6.27 gives the net present value of each cash flow pattern given the initial outlay of £42 000 and the arithmetic mean, the ENPV, is shown at the foot of the sixth column.

Summing the probabilities associated with positive net present values gives the overall probability of achieving a positive NPV. This is 0.714 which is, of course, also the chance that the yield on the investment will exceed 10%. Conversely, there is a 28.6% chance of making a loss in present value terms or equivalently that the project's yield will be below 10%. The probability that NPV exceeds some value other than zero can be worked out in a similar fashion: for example the probability that NPV exceeds £2000 is 0.498.

As we have seen, it can be useful to have a measure of the spread of NPV about its mean value. The standard deviation of NPV is given by the formula:

$$sd_{NPV} = \sqrt{\Sigma p_i(NPV_i - ENPV)^2} \qquad (6.22)$$

in which the probabilities p_i are the values of column four of Table 6.27 and the NPV_i are the NPV values in column 5 of the table.

The **variance** of net present value is the average **squared** departure of NPV from its mean value and is therefore the square of standard deviation. Standard deviation and variance are the most commonly used measures of dispersion in this context. Table 6.28 extends the workings of Table 6.27 to calculate the standard deviation of NPV using equation (6.22).

The value at the foot of the fourth column in Table 6.28 if multiplied by 1 000 000 is the variance of net present value, with the result that the standard deviation of NPV is:

$$sd_{NPV} = \sqrt{(27\ 202\ 000)} = £5216$$

Table 6.28

Probability	NPV – ENPV	(NPV – ENPV)²	P²(NPV – ENPV)²
0.012	–11.443	130.931	1.571
0.020	–6.935	48.089	0.962
0.008	–3.929	15.440	0.124
0.018	–3.178	10.100	0.182
0.030	1.330	1.768	0.053
0.012	4.335	18.793	0.226
0.072	–9.624	92.628	6.669
0.120	–5.116	26.178	3.141
0.048	–2.111	4.457	0.214
0.108	–1.360	1.849	0.200
0.180	3.148	9.910	1.784
0.072	6.153	37.863	2.726
0.036	–5.988	35.856	1.291
0.060	–1.480	2.191	0.131
0.024	1.525	2.326	0.056
0.054	2.276	5.182	0.280
0.090	6.784	46.028	4.142
0.036	9.790	95.837	3.450
			27.202

The standard deviation of NPV is a proxy measure of the total risk for the investment and takes no account of possible offsetting variations in other projects that might be undertaken by the same investor. It is a **proxy** measure of risk because perceived risk has a psychological component and is not directly measurable. It should be recognized that standard deviation is by no means a perfect measure of risk. For example, it might be argued quite reasonably that only the **downside** variation – the NPV values below the mean – constitutes risk. Such a **semi-standard deviation** measure makes sense but is awkward to handle. Fortunately, it is frequently the case that standard deviation and semi-standard deviation move together and standard deviation is normally used.

To interpret the value of the standard deviation of NPV, it needs to be seen in relation to the mean figure. If NPV is normally distributed then 95% of net present values will lie within 1.96 standard deviations of the mean (ENPV). Using the data from the numerical example, this would mean an approximately 2.5% chance of an NPV of less than –7647. (The true probability is 1.2% in the case of this rather coarse approximation to a normal distribution.)

With the mean and standard deviation values obtained, reference to Table 7 giving areas under the standard normal curve can be used to find the probability that NPV is below (or above) given values. The outcomes will be approximate to an extent depending on the nearness of the distribution of NPV values to normal. Table 7 shows the area under the curve up to z standard deviations away from the mean (above or below). Zero NPV is of particular significance since it represents breakeven. If the data of the present example are used for illustration, zero NPV does not appear to be far from the mean, in fact it is:

$$z = 2576/5216 = 0.494$$

standard deviations below the mean. Reference to Table 7 (using interpolation between $z = 0.49$ and $z = 0.50$) gives the probability of not making a loss as 0.6893, so that the chance of a loss-making NPV is 1 minus this figure or 0.3107. This figure compares well with the true probability of 0.2860 in this particular example. It is a matter of judgement, but an approximately 30% chance of a loss might be considered high. Thus the standard deviation of 5216 might be thought to be high in relation to a mean value of 2576.

Now consider an example in which returns in one year *do* influence returns in another year. Suppose that a project has an initial outlay of 1000 – known with certainty – but after one year could return 700 with probability 0.6 or 500 with probability 0.4. **Provided** that the 700 return materializes, there is then in the second year a 0.3 chance of a return of 500, a 0.35 chance of a return of 600 and a 0.35 chance of a return of 700. On the other hand, if the return of 500 occurred in the first year, then the return in year 2 could be 800 with probability 0.25, 750 with probability 0.4 or 600 with probability 0.35. This information is presented in tree diagram form in Figure 6.4.

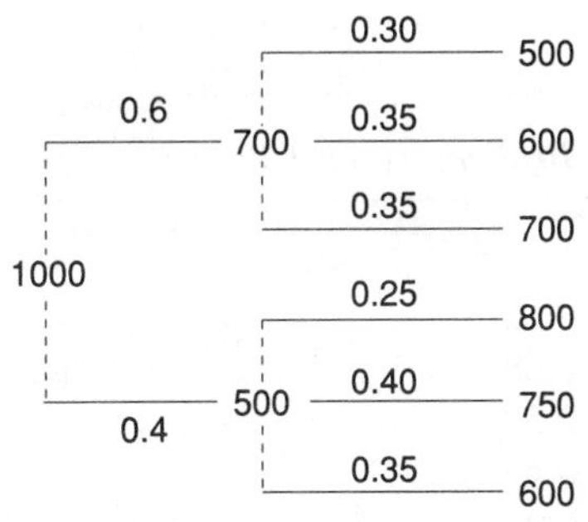

	Probability (p)	NPV	p (NPV)
500	0.18	49.59	8.93
600	0.21	132.23	27.77
700	0.21	214.88	45.12
800	0.10	115.70	11.57
750	0.16	74.38	11.90
600	0.14	−49.59	−6.94
	1.00		98.35

Figure 6.4

From Figure 6.4 it can be seen that there is a 0.18 (= 0.3 × 0.6) chance of the project's giving a return of 700 in the first year and 500 in the second. Therefore, with a 10% rate of discount, there is a 0.18 chance of the net present value being:

$$\frac{700}{(1.1)} + \frac{500}{(1.1)^2} - 1000 = 49.59$$

The other possible values of NPV and their respective probabilities are as shown in Figure 6.4. It will be seen that one combination of outcomes would result in a negative net present value with probability 0.14. The ENPV of the investment emerges as 98.35, which is the sum of products of the possible values of NPV and their chance of arising.

The variability of net present value can also be measured. Workings for the calculation of the standard deviation of NPV in this case are shown in Table 6.29.

Table 6.29

Probability (p)	(NPV – ENPV)	(NPV – ENPV)²	p(NPV – ENPV)²
0.18	−48.76	2 377.57	427.96
0.21	33.88	1 148.15	241.11
0.21	116.53	13 578.99	2851.59
0.1	17.36	301.21	30.12
0.16	−23.97	574.41	91.91
0.14	−147.93	21 884.44	3063.82
			6706.51

Thus the standard deviation of net present value is:

$$sd_{NPV} = \sqrt{(6706.51)} = 81.89$$

Although the assumption of near normality is a little bold in this case, we note that zero NPV is about 1.2 ($\approx 98.35/81.89$) standard deviations below the mean. Using Table 7, the area given above this value is 0.8849, so that the chance of a negative NPV would be deduced from this as 0.1151 which is not too far away from the true value of 0.14.

A **risk profile** for the investment can be constructed from the probability and present value columns of Figure 6.4. The risk profile states the chance of achieving at least any given value of NPV. As we have seen, the chance that NPV will exceed 0 is $p = 0.86$ (= 1 − 0.14) while the chance that NPV will exceed 100 is:

$$p = 0.21 + 0.21 + 0.10 = 0.52$$

Information of this nature is presented in tabular form in Table 6.30 in relation to the actual values of NPV that are possible in this case.

Table 6.30

Values (x)	Probability (NPV > x)
$x < -49.59$	1
$-49.59 \leq x < 49.59$	0.86
$49.59 \leq x < 74.38$	0.68
$74.38 \leq x < 115.70$	0.52
$115.70 \leq x < 132.23$	0.42
$132.23 \leq x < 214.88$	0.21
$214.88 \leq x$	0

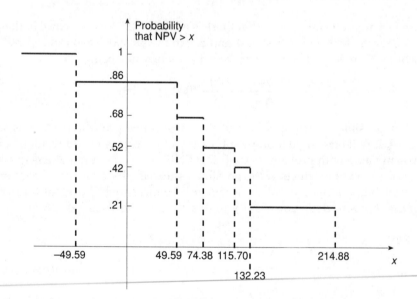

Figure 6.5

So, for example, the probability that NPV is greater than 85 is seen from Table 6.30 to be 0.52 since $x = 85$ is in the range 74.38 to 115.70. The risk profile can also be shown in diagrammatic form. Figure 6.5 shows the cumulated probabilities of Table 6.30.

The step function character arises because the example involves a discrete probability distribution. Figure 6.5 is sometimes called the **optimists' diagram** because it is drawn in terms of the chances that NPV will **exceed** certain values. The cumulated probabilities can also be expressed in terms of the chances that NPV is less than particular values. The results are shown in the **pessimists' diagram** of Figure 6.6.

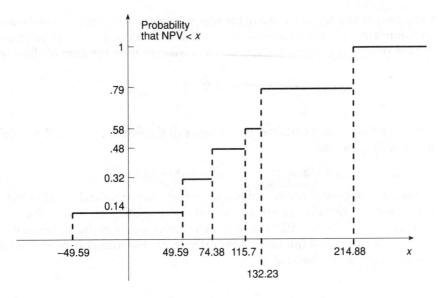

Figure 6.6

Both forms of risk profile diagram are useful ways of highlighting the implications of the probability distribution of net present values.

Now consider the general case where there may or may not be dependence between the returns. Consider an n year project with returns represented as:

$$R_0 \quad R_1 \quad R_2 \quad R_3 \ldots R_{n-1} \quad R_n$$

where the returns R_t are random variables, where R_0 represents the initial outlay and where R_t has a mean value of $E(R_t)$ and variance σ_t^2. The expected net present value, ENPV, is given by:

$$\text{ENPV} = \sum_{t=0}^{n} E(R_t)(1 + r)^{-t} \tag{6.23}$$

so that the expected net present value of the project as a whole is the present value of the expected returns in each year. So in the case of a two-year project, the ENPV is given by:

$$\text{ENPV} = E(R_0) + \frac{E(R_1)}{(1 + r)} + \frac{E(R_2)}{(1 + r)^2} \tag{6.24}$$

We shall work towards an expression for the variance of net present value by finding first the variance of an individual return, then the variance of the present value of a return, then the variance of the undiscounted sum of returns and finally, drawing things together, the variance of the discounted sum of returns, i.e. the variance of NPV itself. The variance of the year t return is written as:

$$\sigma_t^2 = E(R_t - E(R_t))^2 \tag{6.25}$$

where equation (6.25) is read as 'the expectation of the squared departure from the mean is the variance'. In the case of a discrete distribution of returns, the expectation would be found by weighting each squared deviation by its chance of arising and summing. (In the case of a continuous distribution of returns, integration is required.) The variance of the present value of the year t return will be:

$$E\left(\frac{R_t - E(R_t)}{(1+r)^t} \right)^2 = \left(\frac{1}{(1+r)^t} \right)^2 E(R_t - E(R_t))^2 = \frac{\sigma_t^2}{(1+r)^{2t}} \tag{6.26}$$

Thus the variance of the present value of the return in year t is the variance of the return discounted, but using as the exponent of $(1 + r)$ *twice* the value of t. The variance of the undiscounted sum of returns is the sum of the variances plus the sum of the covariances:

$$\text{var}\left(\sum_{t=0}^{n} R_t\right) = \sum_{t=0}^{n} \sigma_t^2 + \sum_{\substack{s=0 \\ s \neq t}}^{n} \sum_{t=0}^{n} \text{cov}(R_s, R_t) \tag{6.27}$$

The covariance between two variables is a measure of the extent to which the variables move in step with each other:

$$\text{cov}[R_s, R_t] = E[(R_s - E(R_s))\,(R_t - E(R_t))] \tag{6.28}$$

Note that the covariance could be positive (if the returns in years s and t tend to increase or decrease together), negative (if returns are inversely related) or zero (if the returns are unrelated). In (6.27) there will usually be many more terms in the covariance summation than in the variance summation. Now bring (6.27) and (6.26) together. The result is the expression for the variance of NPV:

$$\sigma_{\text{NPV}}^2 = \text{var}\left(\sum_{t=0}^{n} \frac{R_t}{(1+r)^t}\right)$$

$$= \sum_{t=0}^{n} \frac{\sigma_t^2}{(1+r)^{2t}} + \sum_{\substack{s=0 \\ s \neq t}}^{n} \sum_{t=0}^{n} \frac{\text{cov}(R_s, R_t)}{(1+r)^{s+t}} \tag{6.29}$$

For the case where $n = 2$, expression (6.29) can be spelt out as:

$$\sigma_{\text{NPV}}^2 = \sigma_0^2 + \frac{\sigma_1^2}{(1+r)^2} + \frac{\sigma_2^2}{(1+r)^4} + \frac{2\,\text{cov}(R_0, R_1)}{(1+r)} + \frac{2\,\text{cov}(R_0, R_2)}{(1+r)^2} + \frac{2\,\text{cov}(R_1, R_2)}{(1+r)^3} \tag{6.30}$$

In expression (6.30) note the powers to which $(1 + r)$ is raised in each denominator. Each covariance term appears twice since $\text{cov}(R_0, R_2)$ is identical to $\text{cov}(R_2, R_0)$. The term $\text{cov}(R_0, R_2)$ is the covariance of the initial outlay and the year 2 return.

Two simplified cases present themselves from (6.29). The first is that of returns which are independently distributed in each year. In this event the covariance terms are all zero and the variance of NPV reduces to:

$$\sigma^2_{\text{NPV}} = \sum \frac{\sigma_t^2}{(1+r)^{2t}} \tag{6.31}$$

which in the two-year case would give:

$$\sigma^2_{\text{NPV}} = \sigma_0^2 + \frac{\sigma_1^2}{(1+r)^2} + \frac{\sigma_2^2}{(1+r)^4}$$

The second special case is that where returns are perfectly correlated between the years. The coefficient of correlation, r, is given by:

$$r = \frac{\text{cov}(R_s, R_t)}{\sigma_s \sigma_t} \tag{6.32}$$

where σ_s is the standard deviation of returns in year s. The value of r must lie in the range $+1$ to -1. A value of $+1$ indicates perfect positive correlation, the returns moving in lockstep with each other. If $r = +1$, then $\text{cov}(R_s, R_t) = \sigma_s \sigma_t$ and it is possible to rewrite expression (6.29) as:

$$\sigma_{\text{NPV}}^2 = \left(\sum_{t=0}^{n} \frac{\sigma_t}{(1+r)^t}\right)^2 \tag{6.33}$$

which in the case of $n = 2$ would produce:

$$\sigma_{NPV}^2 = \left(\sigma_0 + \frac{\sigma_1}{(1+r)} + \frac{\sigma_2}{(1+r)^2} \right)^2$$

So in both of these special cases the calculation of the variance of net present value is greatly simplified.

To illustrate the use of expression (6.30) consider again the first example in this section where returns were independent. The value of $E(R_1)$ was £13 000. The calculation of σ_1^2 is shown in Table 6.31(a) while comparable workings for σ_2^2 and σ_3^2 are shown in Tables 6.31(b) and (c).

Table 6.31 (a)

Probability (p)	R_t	$R_t - E(R_t)$	$(R_t - E(R_t))^2$	$p(R_t - E(R_t))^2$
0.1	10 000	−3000	9 000 000	900 000
0.6	12 000	−1000	1 000 000	600 000
0.3	16 000	3000	9 000 000	2 700 000
				4 200 000

(b)

Probability (p)	R_t	$R_t - E(R_t)$	$(R_t - E(R_t))^2$	$p(R_t - E(R_t))^2$
0.4	20 000	−6000	36 000 000	14 400 000
0.6	30 000	4000	16 000 000	9 600 000
				24 200 000

(c)

Probability (p)	R_t	$R_t - E(R_t)$	$(R_t - E(R_t))^2$	$p(R_t - E(R_t))^2$
0.3	10 000	−5000	25 000 000	7 500 000
0.5	16 000	1000	1 000 000	500 000
0.2	20 000	5000	25 000 000	5 000 000
				13 000 000

The variances of returns in the three years are 4 200 000, 24 000 000 and 13 000 000 respectively. The initial outlay is fixed, so that $\sigma_0^2 = 0$. Recalling that in this example returns in each year are independent of other years, insertion of this data into equation (6.31) gives:

$$\sigma^2_{NPV} = 0 + \frac{4\ 200\ 000}{(1+r)^2} + \frac{24\ 000\ 000}{(1+r)^4} + \frac{13\ 000\ 000}{(1+r)^6}$$

which, with $r = 0.1$ gives:

$$\sigma^2_{NPV} = 27\ 201\ 558$$

so that the standard deviation of net present value, σ_{NPV}, is:

$$\sigma_{NPV} = \sqrt{(27\ 201\ 558)}$$
$$= £5216$$

which confirms the value obtained earlier on.

Now consider the example of Figure 6.4, in which outcomes in the two years were not independent. The first step is to find the mean value of the return in each year. Outlay in this case is certain, so that $E(R_0) = 1000$. In year 1, the expected value of return, $E(R_1)$, is:

$$E(R_1) = 0.6(700) + 0.4(500)$$
$$= 620$$

while for year 2:

$$E(R_2) = 0.18(500) + 0.21(600) + 0.21(700) + 0.1(800)$$
$$+ 0.16(750) + 0.14(600)$$
$$= 647$$

Before proceeding note that:

$$\text{ENPV} = \frac{620}{(1.1)} + \frac{647}{(1.1)^2} - 1000 = 98.35$$

which confirms our earlier result. We next find the variances of return in years 1 and 2 and the covariance of returns between the years. The workings are shown in Table 6.32.

Table 6.32 (a)

Probability (p)	R_t	$R_t - E(R_t)$	$(R_t - E(R_t))^2$	$p(R_t - E(R_t))^2$
0.6	700	80	6 400	3840
0.4	500	−120	14 400	5760
				9600

(b)

Probability (p)	R_t	$R_t - E(R_t)$	$(R_t - E(R_t))^2$	$p(R_t - E(R_t))^2$
0.18	500	−147	21 609	3890
0.21	600	−47	2 209	464
0.21	700	53	2 809	590
0.1	800	153	23 409	2341
0.16	750	103	10 609	1697
0.14	600	−47	2 209	309
				9291

(c)

Probability (p)	$R_1 - E(R_1)$	$R_2 - E(R_2)$	$(R_1 - E(R_1)) \times (R_2 - E(R_2))$	$p(R_1 - E(R_1)) \times (R_2 - E(R_2))$
0.18	80	−147	−11 760	−2117
0.21	80	−47	−3 760	−790
0.21	80	53	4 240	890
0.1	−120	153	−18 360	−1836
0.16	−120	103	−12 360	−1978
0.14	−120	−47	5 640	790
				−5040

Table 6.32(a) gives the variance of return in year 1 as $\sigma_1^2 = 9600$. Similarly, Table 6.32(b) gives the variance of return in year two as $\sigma_2^2 = 9291$ while covariance is found

in Table 6.32(c) to be –5040. Since the initial outlay is fixed in this case, expression (6.30) will simplify to:

$$\sigma^2_{NPV} = \frac{\sigma_1^2}{(1+r)^2} + \frac{\sigma_2^2}{(1+r)^4} + \frac{2\text{cov}(R_1,R_2)}{(1+r)^3}$$

$$= \frac{9600}{(1+r)^2} + \frac{9291}{(1+r)^4} - \frac{10\,080}{(1+r)^3}$$

$$= 6706.51$$

which confirms the result obtained originally. Whichever layout for the workings is used is principally a matter of convenience.

Having obtained the data on ENPV and standard deviation, management must then decide if the combination is acceptable. There are formalized ways in which this can be done, as discussed in section 6.14 for example. These formula-based approaches require the decision-maker to state a function combining the return (here ENPV) and risk (here standard deviation) measures. In the case of two mutually exclusive projects, whichever gave the superior value of the function would then be selected. In the case of an individual project a predetermined threshold value would be used. One of the simplest such formulae is represented by the ratio of standard deviation to expected value; the **coefficient of variation** C, where:

$$C = \frac{\sigma_{NPV}}{ENPV} \qquad (6.34)$$

If the standard deviation of NPV is interpreted as risk, the value of C gives units of risk per unit of return, so the lower the value of C the better. Setting a specific (maximum) threshold value of C to determine the acceptability of an individual project is equivalent to specifying a maximum acceptable probability of making a loss. For example, with normally distributed NPV the requirement that there should not be more than a 10% chance of a negative net present value means (as can be seen from Table 7) that ENPV must be at least 1.28 times the standard deviation, or equivalently the coefficient of variation should not exceed 0.78 (= 1/1.28).

Whether management wishes to use a formula-based approach, such as the coefficient of variation rule, or to weigh the results of the risk analysis in a less formal fashion, is a matter of choice. Either way managerial judgement is involved, with the difference that in a formula approach management is required to crystallize its values into numerical form. The advantages of doing this are consistency of decisions (as long as the formula is adhered to) and knowledge of the rules by all staff involved in the decision process. The main potential disadvantage of a formula approach is spurious quantification. It should always be remembered that the numerical measures are an *aid* to managerial decision-making and not a substitute for it.

6.13 Multiple investment risk analysis

When an investment is not the only source of cash flow for the investor, interactions with existing or other proposed investments must be taken into account. These interactions can be of two kinds. One project may alter the cash flow of another through being complementary to, or in competition with, the other project. In this case it is a matter of identifying the relevant costs of an investment and netting out from the cash flow of a proposed new project the variations in cash flow that it brings about elsewhere. But even when these effects are not present the joint cash flows of two or more risky investments may present a very different picture from that for each project in isolation. The outcome will depend on how the variations in the cash flows of the projects are related to each other, i.e. by their covariance.

We shall not assume here that the company ownership holds fully diversified portfolios, but that the investments under consideration, plus the existing cash flows, represent the assets of the investors. However, if the number of investments is increased in a particular way, full diversification is approached. Consider a firm which already has a limited number of investments which generate, subject to random variation, its existing cash flow. The company is considering taking one of three additional projects. In order to keep the calculations within reasonable bounds, single-period numerical examples are used. However, the analysis is set within a multi-period present value framework.

The firm's first option is one of the most common possibilities in industry – a project that would expand current activities. The firm's existing cash flow (E) is shown in Fig. 6.7.

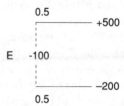

Figure 6.7

The cash flow is an outlay of 100 out with certainty at $t = 0$ followed at $t = 1$ by equally likely outcomes of +500 or −200. The discount rate is 10%. The firm is considering adding an expansion project, A, as detailed in Figure 6.8.

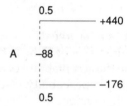

Figure 6.8

The cash flow pattern for A is 88% of the pattern for E, and might represent the establishment of a similar plant on a smaller scale. The two diagrams should be understood in the following fashion. If the +500 materializes for E, then if A has been accepted the +440 return will occur. Similarly, the losses of 200 and 176 would coincide. Consider the data for E by itself.

With the return possibilities for E being represented by R_E and with the expected value of these returns of 150, the variance of return at $t = 1$, σ^2_{1E}, is calculated as follows:

Probability (p)	R_E	$R_E - E(R_E)$	$(R_E - E(R_E))^2$	$p(R_E - E(R_E))^2$
0.5	500	350	122 500	61 250
0.5	−200	−350	122 500	61 250
				$\sigma^2_{1E} = 122\ 500$

With a 10% rate of discount the variance of the net present value for project E is:

$$(\sigma^2_{NPV})_E = \frac{122\ 500}{(1.1)^2} = 101\ 239$$

Thus the standard deviation of the net present value for the existing cash flow is:

$$(\sigma_{NPV})_E = \sqrt{(101\ 239)} = 318.18$$

Using the year 1 expected return of 150, the expected net present value of the existing cash flow is:

$$\text{ENPV}_E = -100 + \frac{150}{1.1} = 36.36$$

The standard deviation and ENPV figures then give a coefficient of variation value of:

$$C_E = \frac{318.18}{36.36} = 8.75$$

Now consider the expansion project A. The expected return $E(R_A)$ at year 1 is 132, and the variance of returns at $t = 1$, σ^2_{1A} is calculated as:

Probability (p)	R_A	$R_A - E(R_A)$	$(R_A - E(R_A))^2$	$p(R_A - E(R_A))^2$
0.5	440	308	94 864	47 432
0.5	-176	-308	94 864	47 432
				$\sigma^2_{1A} = 94\ 864$

With the 10% rate of discount the variance of the net present value for project E is:

$$(\sigma^2_{\text{NPV}})_A = \frac{94\ 864}{(1.1)^2} = 78\ 400$$

Thus the standard deviation of the net present value for A is:

$$(\sigma_{\text{NPV}})_A = \sqrt{(78\ 400)} = 280$$

Using the year 1 expected return of 132, the expected net present value of A is:

$$\text{ENPV}_A = -88 + \frac{132}{1.1} = 32$$

The standard deviation and ENPV figures then give a coefficient of variation value for A of:

$$C_A = \frac{280}{32} = 8.75$$

The two projects are perfectly positively correlated. This being the case, the coefficient of variation will be the same.

Now consider E and A taken together. The cash flow is as shown in Figure 6.9.

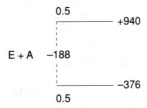

Figure 6.9

The expected return $E(R_{EA})$ at year 1 is 282, being the sum of the separate expected returns. The variance of returns at $t = 1$, σ^2_{1EA} is calculated as:

Probability (p)	R_{EA}	$R - E(R_{EA})$	$(R - E(R_{EA}))^2$	$p(R_{EA} - E(R_{EA}))^2$
0.5	940	658	432 964	216 482
0.5	-376	-658	432 964	216 482
				$\sigma^2_{1EA} = 432\ 964$

With the 10% rate of discount the variance of the net present value for the combined projects is:

$$(\sigma^2_{NPV})_{EA} = \frac{432\ 964}{(1.1)^2} = 357\ 821$$

Thus the standard deviation of the net present value for E and A together is:

$$(\sigma_{NPV})_{EA} = \sqrt{(357\ 821)} = 598.18$$

Using the year 1 expected return of 282, the expected net present value for E + A is:

$$ENPV_{EA} = -188 + \frac{282}{1.1} = 68.36$$

The standard deviation and ENPV figures then give a coefficient of variation for E and A of:

$$C_{EA} = \frac{598.18}{68.36} = 8.75$$

The reader may well have anticipated this outcome, since project A is essentially more of the same. The ENPV and standard deviation are both scaled up in the same proportion.

Now consider an alternative investment B, with details shown in Figure 6.10.

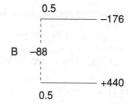

Figure 6.10

Figure 6.10 means that if the return of 500 occurs for E, then at the same time B would lose 176. But if E does badly and loses 200, then B will return 440. Thus E and B are oppositely affected by underlying forces. Investment B would represent an ideal kind of diversification. For B alone, all summary measures (ENPV, variance of return, standard deviation of present value and the coefficient of variation) are identical to those of investment A. But now consider E and B taken together. The result is as shown in Figure 6.11.

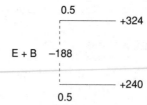

Figure 6.11

It is clear that this combination cannot show a loss at 10% discount. The expected return in year one $E(R_{EB})$ is 282 and the variance of returns at $t = 1$, σ^2_{1EB} is calculated as:

Probability (p)	R	R – E(R)	(R – E(R))²	p(R – E(R))²
0.5	324	42	1764	882
0.5	240	–42	1764	882
				$\sigma^2_{1EB} = 1764$

With the 10% rate of discount the variance of the net present value for E + B is:

$$(\sigma^2_{NPV})_{EB} = \frac{1764}{(1.1)^2} = 1458$$

Thus the standard deviation of the net present value for E + B is:

$$(\sigma_{NPV})_{EB} = \sqrt{(1458)} = 38.18$$

Using the year 1 expected return of 282, the expected net present value of E + B is:

$$ENPV_{EB} = -188 + \frac{282}{1.1} = 68.36$$

The standard deviation and ENPV figures then give a coefficient of variation value for E + B of just:

$$C_{EB} = \frac{38.18}{68.36} = 0.56$$

The ENPV of 68.36 for the combined projects is the sum of the separate ENPVs, but the standard deviation of 38.18 of NPV is dramatically small; in fact since E and B are perfectly **negatively** correlated the standard deviation of the two together is the difference between the individual standard deviations:

$$38.18 = 318.18 - 280$$

The key point is this. A and B are, by themselves, identical as far as cash flows are concerned, but they combine very differently with existing investments. Clearly, given E, B is preferable to A since A and B should not be assessed in isolation from the existing cash flows. If A and B are alternatives, then the investor can choose between three possible cash flow patterns (E, E + A, E + B) which for decision-making purposes could be viewed as three mutually exclusive single projects. As will be seen in a later section, this situation contrasts with that which obtains when complete diversification and other simplifying assumptions are made.

A project which is unattractive in isolation may be acceptable in conjunction with another project with complementary cash flows. For instance, consider project C detailed in Figure 6.12.

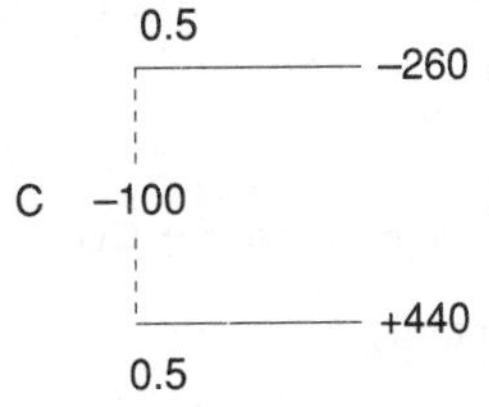

Figure 6.12

This project has negative ENPV even at a zero discount rate and relatively high variance. However, taken in conjunction with E it produces the result shown in Figure 6.13.

Some investors might prefer E + C to E alone because of the guaranteed return. Of course E + C has a lower expected net present value (= +18.18) than E, but also has a zero

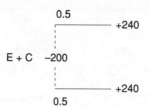

Figure 6.13

coefficient of variation. The yield of E + C at 20% is still comfortably in excess of the discount rate.

In capital rationing, projects should not be assessed independently of the asset set to which they are to be adjoined even under complete certainty. Viewing an asset in conjunction with existing investments is doubly important when returns are risky and where those people on whose behalf the investment decision is to be taken are known to be less than fully diversified.

Perfect negative correlation between the cash flows of investments is unlikely. However, benefit can be obtained as long as covariance is negative. Suppose that the existing project is F as shown in Figure 6.14:

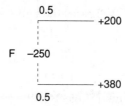

Figure 6.14

and consider a possible additional project, D, as shown in Figure 6.15:

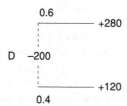

Figure 6.15

Clearly, there is not perfect correlation between F and the D; the return of 280 for D must have some chance of coinciding with 200 or with 380 in F. In a repeated experiment there will be occasions when 280 is bracketed with 200, and others when 380 and 280 occur together.

The variance of return on F and D taken together can be expressed in either of two ways:

Using a covariance term:

$$\text{var}(R_F + R_D) = \sigma_F^2 + \sigma_D^2 + 2\text{cov}(R_F, R_D) \tag{6.35}$$

or using the correlation coefficient, r:

$$\text{var}(R_F + R_D) = \sigma_F^2 + \sigma_D^2 + 2r\sigma_F\sigma_D \tag{6.36}$$

where r is given by

$$r = \frac{\text{cov}(R_F, R_D)}{\sigma_F\sigma_D} \tag{6.37}$$

where σ_F and σ_D are the standard deviations of returns in the two projects individually. Covariance anywhere between –5760 and +5760 is consistent with the cash flow data, with these endpoints corresponding to the extreme possible r values of –0.8165 and +0.8165. To illustrate the negative extreme, this would arise if the association between the projects was as shown in Figure 6.16.

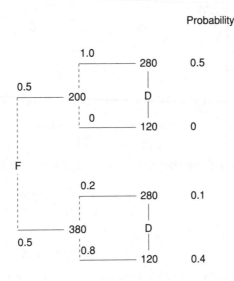

Figure 6.16

In Figure 6.16, the top line indicates that if the 200 return occurred for project F then 280 is certain for project D. Whereas if the 380 return occurred for F then D might produce 280 with probability 0.2 or 120 with probability 0.8. From the column headed probability it will be seen that the probabilities overall for project D outcomes correspond to those given initially.

Let us use (6.35) to examine how the standard deviation of NPV is affected by differing relationships between the returns of F and D. If F and D are as far as is possible, negatively correlated as shown in Figure 6.16, then the covariance is calculated as:

Probability (p)	$R_F - E(R_F)$	$R_D - E(R_D)$	$(R_F - E(R_F)) \times$ $(R_D - E(R_D))$	$p(R_F - E(R_F)) \times$ $(R_D - E(R_D))$
0.5	–90	64	–5760	–2880
0	–90	–96	8640	0
0.1	90	64	5760	576
0.4	90	–96	–8640	–3456
				–5760

the variances of return being, respectively, for F:

Probability (p)	R_F	$R_F - E(R_F)$	$(R_F - E(R_F))^2$	$p(R_F - E(R_F))^2$
0.5	200	–90	8100	4050
0.5	380	90	8100	4050
				8100

and for D:

Probability (p)	R_D	$R_D - E(R_D)$	$(R_D - E(R_D))^2$	$p(R_D - E(R_D))^2$
0.6	280	–64	4096	2458
0.4	120	96	9216	3686
				6144

and for the joint project F + D the variance of return is therefore:

$$\text{var}(R_F + R_D) = 8100 + 6144 - 11\,520$$
$$= 2724$$

Thus in this case, recalling that outlay is fixed, the $n = 1$ case of (6.29) reduces to:

$$(\sigma^2_{NPV})_{FD} = \frac{2724}{(1.1)^2} = 2251$$

So that:

$$(\sigma_{NPV})_{FD} = \sqrt{(2251)} = 47.45$$

Now suppose that the correlation between F and D is zero. In this case with nil covariance:

$$\text{var}(R_F + R_D) = 8100 + 6144 + 0$$
$$= 14\,224$$

In this case, again recalling that outlay is fixed, the $n = 1$ case of (6.29) gives:

$$(\sigma^2_{NPV})_{FD} = \frac{14\,244}{(1.1)^2} = 11\,772$$

So that:

$$(\sigma_{NPV})_{FD} = \sqrt{(11\,772)} = 108.50$$

Now consider the extreme of positive correlation between the returns. In this case the variance of return is:

$$\text{var}(R_F + R_D) = 8100 + 6144 + 11\,520$$
$$= 25\,764$$

Thus in this case, recalling that outlay is fixed, the $n = 1$ case of (6.29) reduces to:

$$(\sigma^2_{NPV})_{FD} = \frac{25\,764}{(1.1)^2} = 21\,293$$

So that:

$$(\sigma_{NPV})_{FD} = \sqrt{(21\,293)} = 145.92$$

These standard deviation figures illustrate the effect of increasing correlation between investments. The calculations could have been expressed in terms of the value of the correlation coefficient. Sometimes this will be more convenient as when data is given in this form. To illustrate, first suppose that $r = -0.8165$. Using formula (6.36):

$$\text{var}(R_F + R_D) = 8100 + 6144 + 2(-0.8165)\,(90)\,(78.38)$$
$$= 2724$$

which confirms the earlier result. Now suppose that $r = +0.6$. Using formula (6.36):

$$\text{var}(R_F + R_D) = 8100 + 6144 + 2(0.6)\,(90)\,(78.38)$$
$$= 22\,709$$

So that:

$$(\sigma^2_{NPV})_{FD} = \frac{22\ 709}{(1.1)^2} = 18\ 768$$

and so in this case:

$$(\sigma_{NPV})_{FD} = \sqrt{(18\ 768)} = 137.00$$

The above examples have concentrated on one period cases. The analysis can be extended to many time periods and any number of projects, although where the number of alternatives is large, simplifying assumptions may be needed to keep information requirements reasonable and the number of combinations within manageable bounds.

We have focused on the variability of NPV induced by variability in returns. There are other sources of uncertainty, principally the discount rate. It is as well to recognize that this is likely to be a volatile parameter. Although some analytical results can be obtained, the relationship between the discount rate and NPV is not very convenient, and simulation is an option for relating the distribution of the discount rate to the variance of present values. Ideally, all sources of variability should be included within the variance of NPV, but there will be many cases where reasonable approximations have to be made.

Having received the information as to the means and variances of present values of the possible combinations of projects the decision-maker must assess these combinations and choose that which best meets their objectives. These approaches provide management information. A managerial judgement that may also involve subjective elements and non-financial considerations must still be made. The following section describes a formal way in which mean and variance combinations can be compared when the decision-maker has a formula reflecting their preferences. In Chapter 9 we consider the case where company ownership is fully diversified.

6.14 Mean-variance analysis

The calculation of ENPV and the variance of NPV is an objective exercise. Making choices between pairs of values of mean and variance is a subjective exercise. Use of any formula for making choices should not disguise the fact that subjectivity is implicit in the formula. Subjectivity means that different investors will have different answers when presented with the same set of choices.

It is reasonable to assume that investors like higher means for net present values but are averse to variance of NPV. So if among undiversified investors, option A offers both higher ENPV and lower variance than does B, all will rank A above B. This only separates wheat from the chaff, eliminating the mean-variance inefficient combinations. This is illustrated in Figure 6.17 where each combination of ENPV and standard deviation gives one point in the diagram.

In Figure 6.17, E + G and E + H are inefficient. For the same return E + G produces more variability than E + A, while E + H has a lower return than E + F for the same variability. E + G and E + H can be eliminated. The remaining possibilities form a frontier

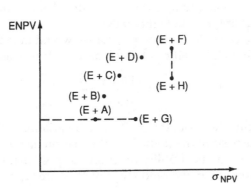

Figure 6.17

of opportunities, with greater return coinciding with greater variability. The investor must choose between these alternatives, although further weeding out may be possible through stochastic dominance.

The choice process can be formalized by assuming that an index of utility given can be constructed:

$$U = f(\text{ENPV}, \sigma_{\text{NPV}}) \qquad (6.38)$$

where U, *ex ante* satisfaction, is the level of expected utility. Things may turn out badly, but the goal is the best *a priori* decision. While approaches making explicit use of utility functions are not usually operational, it is useful to have theoretical support for the techniques. Indifference curves are contours of U, with each curve showing combinations of ENPV and σ_{NPV} which give equal satisfaction. Figure 6.18 introduces indifference curves against the frontier of efficient projects.

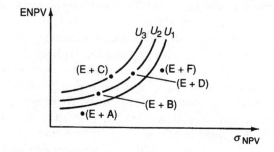

Figure 6.18

The maximum of utility is $U = U_3$ which is obtained from selection of the E + C combination. It is evident that an investor with the indifference curves shown would rank E + B and E + D equally since they both produce $U = U_2$. The other alternatives, E + A and E + F, lie on still lower curves and so are relatively unattractive to the investor.

There are serious difficulties to be overcome in constructing a utility index, particularly in the case of a company shared by many diverse persons. By way of simplification, if the alternatives were grouped fairly close together over a small range of values of σ, then linearity of the indifference curves could reasonably be assumed. We could then write:

$$U = \text{ENPV} - w\sigma_{\text{NPV}} \qquad (6.39)$$

where w is a positive constant to be selected by the investor. The larger is the value of w, the more averse to risk (as measured by σ_{NPV}) is the investor, but unlike the curves of Figure 6.18, this aversion does not rise with increase in σ_{NPV}. Having selected a value for w, and found ENPV and σ_{NPV}, the utility rating for the alternative follows readily.

Another simplified possibility would be to assume that the indifference curves were straight lines from the origin as in Figure 6.19.

In Figure 6.19 $U_3 > U_2 > U_1$. Indifference curves would take this form if utility was inversely proportional to the coefficient of variation, that is where:

$$U = k\frac{\text{ENPV}}{\sigma_{\text{NPV}}} = \frac{k}{C} \qquad (6.40)$$

in which k is a constant. The lower the coefficient of variation in (6.40) the greater is the value of U. This is the basis of the coefficient of variation decision rule.

To illustrate the use of a linear utility function, suppose that the investor's views on the relative magnitudes of variance and mean of NPV are represented by the function:

$$U = \text{ENPV} - 0.001\sigma_{\text{NPV}} \qquad (6.41)$$

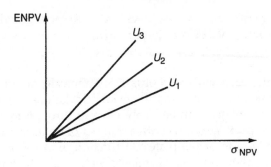

Figure 6.19

Equation (6.41) will be used to rank the investments A, B and C examined in the previous section. The evaluation of the options is shown in Table 6.33 in which U is rounded to the nearest whole number.

Table 6.33

Options	ENPV	σ^2_{NPV}	$0.001\sigma^2_{NPV}$	U
E	36.36	101 239	101.24	−65
E + A	68.36	357 821	357.82	−289
E + B	68.36	1 458	1.46	67
E + C	18.18	0	0.00	18

From Table 6.33, project B emerges as the preferred option giving the highest value of U. Note that E + B would be preferred for any value of w less than 0.0344; beyond this value of w option E + C would be selected. No significance is attached to the absolute values of U nor to the magnitudes of the differences between them. U is used purely as a device for ordering the preferences of the decision-maker. Any order preserving transformation of U would do equally well.

Use of the function (6.40) relating to the coefficient of variation decision rule would reverse the relative ordering between C and B, since the U value for a project with zero variance is infinite. The outcomes in this case are shown in Table 6.34 for a value of $k = 1000$.

Table 6.34

Options	ENPV	σ^2_{NPV}	σ_{NPV}	U
E	36.36	101 239	318.18	114
E + A	68.36	357 821	598.18	114
E + B	68.36	1 458	38.18	1790
E + C	18.18	0	0.00	α

In Table 6.34, note that E and E + A would be rated equally by this measure, since the coefficient of variation is unchanged if both mean and standard deviation are scaled by the same factor.

In considering the variability of NPV we have focused on variance. There is evidence to suggest that **skewness** can also be relevant. Skewness measures asymmetry, and is positive if the longer tail of the distribution is to the right. The desirability of positive skewness for investors is plausible in that it means a relative scarcity of low values on the far left of the distribution. The possible importance of skewness was suggested by Hicks (1939). One measure of skewness involves the third moment about the mean – the average **cubed** deviation from the mean (variance is the second moment). Levy and Sarnat (1982) produced evidence that investors would accept somewhat lower returns in exchange for increased positive skewness. Management could take skewness into account if the reduced chance of very poor returns is of particular value.

6.15 Spreadsheets and what-if analysis

Spreadsheet software, such as Excel, Lotus 123, Supercalc, or equivalent programs, is well suited to present value, yield and financial calculations in general. The effects of changed values of parameters can be easily worked through in a 'what if' (this happened) manner. Most packages come with a number of financial functions, while third-party suppliers provide add-on template constructions that are an alternative to writing your own programs. (For example Gazeley's *Spreadsheet Applications Manual* (1993) Chapman & Hall introduces the techniques and describes a number of investment and management accounting spreadsheet models.) Here we illustrate the use of spreadsheets in the context of a simulation exercise to calculate the net present value of a project under a variety of possible futures.

Table 6.35 shows the initial projected cash flow and net present value for an investment project assuming stable prices, costs and sales and using a discount rate of 15%. The project, which involves the manufacture and sale of a product, runs for 12 years with the net cash flow, R_t, in any year t given by:

$$R_t = (P_t - C_t)Q_t$$

Table 6.35 Simulation: initial solution, stable prices and sales

Time	Price infl 1.00	Cost infl 1.00	Disct rate 1.15	Sales growth 1.00	Outlay 50 000.00		
A	B	C	D	E	F	G	H
t	P_t	C_t	$(1+i)^t$	Q_t	$P_t - C_t$	$F*E$	G/D
0	50.00	30.00	1.00	1000.00	20.00	20 000.00	20 000.00
1	50.00	30.00	1.15	1000.00	20.00	20 000.00	17 391.30
2	50.00	30.00	1.32	1000.00	20.00	20 000.00	15 122.87
3	50.00	30.00	1.52	1000.00	20.00	20 000.00	13 150.33
4	50.00	30.00	1.75	1000.00	20.00	20 000.00	11 435.07
5	50.00	30.00	2.01	1000.00	20.00	20 000.00	9 943.54
6	50.00	30.00	2.31	1000.00	20.00	20 000.00	8 646.55
7	50.00	30.00	2.66	1000.00	20.00	20 000.00	7 518.74
8	50.00	30.00	3.06	1000.00	20.00	20 000.00	6 538.04
9	50.00	30.00	3.52	1000.00	20.00	20 000.00	5 685.25
10	50.00	30.00	4.05	1000.00	20.00	20 000.00	4 943.69
11	50.00	30.00	4.65	1000.00	20.00	20 000.00	4 298.87
12	50.00	30.00	5.35	1000.00	20.00	20 000.00	3 738.14

GPV = 108 412.40
NPV = 58 412.40

where P_t is the sales price of the product, C_t is the unit cost and Q_t is the sales volume, all in year t. The returns R_t are then discounted in the usual way. The initial outlay for the project is £50 000.

In Table 6.35 the numbers at the heads of the P_t and C_t columns (1.00 in both cases) represent the assumed rates of annual increase in prices and costs shown as $1 + r$, where $100r$ is the percentage annual rate of change – zero in this first instance. The next column gives the value of $(1 + i)^t$ where i is the discount rate as a decimal. Q_t is the sales column and the number above it is the annual rate of growth of sales.

Spreadsheets attach a letter to the columns (A to H here) and the column that we have labelled F*E (column G) represents the product of the numbers in column F (the $P_t - C_t$

values) and column E (the values of Q_t). The final column, giving the ratio of column G and column D values, represents the present value of each year's cash flow.

Apart from the initial outlay, the cash flow starts at $t = 1$ (the $t = 0$ row is used to indicate the base values of parameters) and the initial outlay is shown at the head of column F. The gross present value is the sum of the entries in the final column and net present value is GPV less the initial outlay of £50 000. With these initial projections, the investment is therefore worthwhile with NPV = £58 412.

Table 6.36 makes the first of a number of changes to the original scenario. It shows the substantial improvement in net present value that could be achieved if a policy of finding annual cost savings of 2% was implemented successfully.

Table 6.36 Simulation: effects of 2% annual cost reduction

Time	Price infl 1.00	Cost infl 0.98	Disct rate 1.15	Sales growth 1.00	Outlay 50 000.00		
A	B	C	D	E	F	G	H
t	P_t	C_t	$(1+i)^t$	Q_t	$P_t - C_t$	$F*E$	G/D
0	50.00	30.00	1.00	1000.00	20.00	20 000.00	20 000.00
1	50.00	29.40	1.15	1000.00	20.60	20 600.00	17 913.04
2	50.00	28.81	1.32	1000.00	21.19	21 188.00	16 021.17
3	50.00	28.24	1.52	1000.00	21.76	21 764.24	14 310.34
4	50.00	27.67	1.75	1000.00	22.33	22 328.95	12 766.65
5	50.00	27.12	2.01	1000.00	22.88	22 882.37	11 376.58
6	50.00	26.58	2.31	1000.00	23.42	23 424.72	10 127.16
7	50.00	26.04	2.66	1000.00	23.96	23 956.23	9 006.04
8	50.00	25.52	3.06	1000.00	24.48	24 477.11	8 001.61
9	50.00	25.01	3.52	1000.00	24.99	24 987.56	7 103.03
10	50.00	24.51	4.05	1000.00	25.49	25 487.81	6 300.20
11	50.00	24.02	4.65	1000.00	25.98	25 978.05	5 583.81
12	50.00	23.54	5.35	1000.00	26.46	26 458.49	4 945.28

GPV = 123 454.90
NPV = 73 454.90

It will be seen from Table 6.36 that net present value increases substantially to £73 455, this increase being one measure of the maximum present price that it would be worth paying for management to bring the unit cost improvements about. Incidentally, an average personal computer will show the complete revised set of workings in less than a second.

Table 6.37 shows the improvement to the original project that would be brought about by a successful drive to increase annual sales by 2% compound. Note that (in the case of this particular project) the sales growth would bring less of an improvement in net present value than the cost reduction programme. This result would not have been obvious to management *a priori* and may be useful information in drawing up priorities.

The prioritization of management initiatives is fine if competitive circumstances allow. But commercial survival in the 1990s may require management to take parallel action on all fronts. Table 6.38 therefore shows the effects of simultaneous cost reduction and sales increase programmes.

It is interesting to note from Table 6.36 that the combined effects on the net present value of the project (an increase of £28 602) exceeds the sum of the individual effects £26 356. Once again this useful synergy would not have been obvious to all without the benefit of the simulation.

Table 6.39 shows the effect on net present value of a particular inflation scenario in which both sales price and unit costs rise by 5% per annum compound, sales volumes

Table 6.37 Simulation: effects of 2% annual sales growth

Time	Price infl 1.00	Cost infl 1.00	Disct rate 1.15	Sales growth 1.02	Outlay 50 000.00		
A	B	C	D	E	F	G	H
t	P_t	C_t	$(1+i)^t$	Q_t	$P_t - C_t$	$F*E$	G/D
0	50.00	30.00	1.00	1000.00	20.00	20 000.00	20 000.00
1	50.00	30.00	1.15	1020.00	20.00	20 400.00	17 739.13
2	50.00	30.00	1.32	1040.40	20.00	20 808.00	15 733.84
3	50.00	30.00	1.52	1061.21	20.00	21 224.16	13 955.23
4	50.00	30.00	1.75	1082.43	20.00	21 648.64	12 377.68
5	50.00	30.00	2.01	1104.08	20.00	22 081.61	10 978.46
6	50.00	30.00	2.31	1126.16	20.00	22 523.25	9 737.42
7	50.00	30.00	2.66	1148.69	20.00	22 973.71	8 636.67
8	50.00	30.00	3.06	1171.66	20.00	23 433.18	7 660.35
9	50.00	30.00	3.52	1195.09	20.00	23 901.85	6 794.40
10	50.00	30.00	4.05	1218.99	20.00	24 379.88	6 026.34
11	50.00	30.00	4.65	1243.37	20.00	24 867.48	5 345.10
12	50.00	30.00	5.35	1268.24	20.00	25 364.83	4 740.87

GPV = 119 725.49

NPV = 69 725.49

are expected to grow at 2% while the discount rate increases to 20%. As can be seen, the outcome is an NPV figure showing an increase in cash terms.

Table 6.40 shows the effect on net present value of an inflation scenario in which sales price and unit costs are expected to inflate at different rates. Sales price is shown as rising at 6% per annum compound while unit costs are projected to increase at 8% p.a. Sales volumes are expected to grow at 4% while the discount rate remains unchanged from the initial figure of 15%. Table 6.38 shows that the outcome is an NPV figure showing a substantial increase in cash terms.

Many more variations on this theme would be possible. The ease with which such variations on discounted cash flow calculations can be carried out using spreadsheets is hard to exaggerate, and the return in management information from such 'what-if' exercises can be considerable. The initial model does not take long to build (making good use of the spreadsheet's **copy** facility for both data and formulae) and, as stated, each scenario is computed almost instantly.

Table 6.38 Effect of 2% annual cost reduction and 2% sales growth

Time	Price infl 1.00	Cost infl 0.98	Disct rate 1.15	Sales growth 1.02	Outlay 50 000.00		
A	B	C	D	E	F	G	H
t	P_t	C_t	$(1+i)^t$	Q_t	$P_t - C_t$	$F*E$	G/D
0	50.00	30.00	1.00	1000.00	20.00	20 000.00	20 000.00
1	50.00	29.40	1.15	1020.00	20.60	21 012.00	18 271.30
2	50.00	28.81	1.32	1040.40	21.19	22 043.99	16 668.43
3	50.00	28.24	1.52	1061.21	21.76	23 096.38	15 186.25
4	50.00	27.67	1.75	1082.43	22.33	24 169.58	13 819.03
5	50.00	27.12	2.01	1104.08	22.88	25 263.99	12 560.67
6	50.00	26.58	2.31	1126.16	23.42	26 380.04	11 404.82
7	50.00	26.04	2.66	1148.69	23.96	27 518.18	10 345.10
8	50.00	25.52	3.06	1171.66	24.48	28 678.83	9 375.16
9	50.00	25.01	3.52	1195.09	24.99	29 862.45	8 488.77
10	50.00	24.51	4.05	1218.99	25.49	31 069.49	7 679.90
11	50.00	24.02	4.65	1243.37	25.98	32 300.44	6 942.76
12	50.00	23.54	5.35	1268.24	26.46	33 555.76	6 271.81

GPV = 137 014.00

NPV = 87 014.00

Table 6.39 Uniform 5% inflation, 2% sales growth, 20% discount rate

Time	Price infl 1.05	Cost infl 1.05	Disct rate 1.20	Sales growth 1.02	Outlay 50 000.00		
A	B	C	D	E	F	G	H
t	P_t	C_t	$(1+i)^t$	Q_t	$P_t - C_t$	$F*E$	G/D
0	50.00	30.00	1.00	1000.00	20.00	20 000.00	20 000.00
1	52.50	31.50	1.20	1020.00	21.00	21 420.00	17 850.00
2	55.12	33.07	1.44	1040.40	22.05	22 940.81	15 931.12
3	57.88	34.73	1.73	1061.21	23.15	24 569.61	14 218.52
4	60.78	36.47	2.07	1082.43	24.31	26 314.06	12 690.03
5	63.81	38.29	2.49	1104.08	25.53	28 182.35	11 325.85
6	67.00	40.20	2.99	1126.16	26.80	30 183.30	10 108.32
7	70.35	42.21	3.58	1148.69	28.14	32 326.31	9 021.68
8	73.87	44.32	4.30	1171.66	29.55	34 621.47	8 051.85
9	77.57	46.54	5.16	1195.09	31.03	37 079.60	7 186.27
10	81.44	48.87	6.19	1218.99	32.58	39 712.24	6 413.75
11	85.52	51.31	7.43	1243.37	34.21	42 531.81	5 724.27
12	89.79	53.88	8.92	1268.24	35.92	45 551.56	5 108.91

GPV = 123 630.56

NPV = 73 630.56

Table 6.40 Differential price and cost inflation, 4% sales growth

Time	Prince infl 1.06	Cost infl 1.08	Disct rate 1.15	Sales growth 1.04	Outlay 50 000.00		
A	B	C	D	E	F	G	H
t	P_t	C_t	$(1+i)^t$	Q_t	$P_t - C_t$	$F*E$	G/D
0	50.00	30.00	1.00	1000.00	20.00	20 000.00	20 000.00
1	53.00	32.40	1.15	1040.00	20.60	21 424.00	18 629.56
2	56.18	34.99	1.32	1081.60	21.19	22 916.93	17 328.49
3	59.55	37.79	1.52	1124.86	21.76	24 476.39	16 093.63
4	63.12	40.81	1.75	1169.86	22.31	26 098.56	14 921.94
5	66.91	44.08	2.01	1216.65	22.83	27 777.90	13 810.52
6	70.93	47.61	2.31	1265.32	23.32	29 506.84	12 756.62
7	75.18	51.41	2.66	1315.93	23.77	31 275.40	11 757.58
8	79.69	55.53	3.06	1368.57	24.16	33 070.70	10 810.87
9	84.47	59.97	3.52	1423.31	24.50	34 876.46	9 914.07
10	89.54	64.77	4.05	1480.24	24.77	36 672.39	9 064.86
11	94.91	69.95	4.65	1539.45	24.97	38 433.49	8 261.02
12	100.61	75.55	5.35	1601.03	25.06	40 129.25	7 500.44

GPV = 150 849.61
NPV = 100 849.61

6.16 Key concepts

Capital rationing problems involve the selection of an optimal group of investments under financial and other resource constraints. A distinction can be made between hard and soft capital rationing. Hard capital rationing arises when constraints are externally determined. Soft capital rationing corresponds to internal, management-determined limits on resources or investment expenditure.

In single-constraint, Lorie-Savage-type problems, the maximum of net present value is obtained by selecting projects in rank order of the ratio of present value (net or gross) in the initial outlay. This ensures that the projects selected produce the greatest achievement of objective per unit of scarce resource.

Multi-constraint rationing problems require algorithmic methods for solution unless they have particularly simple structures. In the discounted dividend model investments are selected so as to allow dividend payments of maximum present value. Solution by linear programming methods yields marginal valuations for extra funds in each period.

When balance sheet constraints are included in the rationing problem stipulating acceptable ranges of values for financial measures such as return on assets or current ratio, a financial planning model is defined. Financial planning models may include much of the company's main financial activities.

Most investment decisions involve some degree of uncertainty. Investors differ not only in their attitudes towards risk but also in the degree to which they are diversified. Where full diversification can be presumed, there is a strong theoretical case for the methods described in Chapter 9. Otherwise, there are several approaches to the assessment of risk and the way in which the information is taken into account by the decision-maker. In practice management tends to select a narrower range of methods, with payback still being a widely used approach.

The payback period is the time required for the undiscounted cash flow to equal in total the initial outlay. Shorter payback periods are preferred. Disadvantages include the formal exclusion of the cost of capital and post-payback period returns. In practice payback is often used in conjunction with other measures such as yield and it has the advantage of being easily comprehended. The finite horizon method requires a project to show a positive net present value based on returns and costs within a predetermined period. Post-horizon returns are regarded as being insignificant in present value terms if the horizon is long, or a cushion against adversity if the horizon is short.

The accounting rate of return divides annual profit defined as net return less depreciation by the average investment defined as half of the sum of initial outlay and residual value. A project is accepted by the accounting rate of return if its rate of return exceeds a target figure. As between alternative projects that with the greater accounting rate of return is preferred. In practice accounting rate of return may be used as one of a number of measures.

The risk premium method discounts an uncertain cash flow at a rate in excess of that used for secure returns. The additional percentage points are usually judgemental. A variant of the approach divides projects into risk classes with different premia. The cash flow of individual projects can be disaggregated and different premia applied to costs (which are usually more certain) than to externally generated revenues.

Sensitivity analysis calculates ranges of variation (tolerance intervals) for parameters such that the required threshold level of performance is attained. Joint variation of two parameters provides tolerance intervals expressed as a range of relative magnitudes. Multi-parameter analysis calculates the consequences for net present value or yield under different sets of assumptions (scenarios) about parameter changes.

In simulation, samples are taken from the probability distributions believed to describe the range of variation of parameters. Distributions of performance measures such as net present value or yield are then derived. More limited use of simulation is possible within the framework of the capital asset pricing model in which the output may be estimates of net returns. Computer-based simulation in a variety of forms finds increasingly wide usage in practice.

When project returns follow a known probability distribution, the expected net present value and its variance can be calculated. Efficient combinations of variance and expected NPV can then be obtained. These measures, and further measures derived from them, provide an information base for management decision-making in the case of one of more investment opportunities.

6.17 Revision questions

1. Distinguish between hard and soft capital rationing and describe situations in which each may arise.
2. Outline a solution procedure for single constraint rationing problems where investment levels are limited to a maximum of one unit.
3. What solution procedure is likely to be necessary for multi-constraint rationing problems?
4. What is the rationale behind the use of a discounted dividend form of objective function?
5. What are the relative advantages and disadvantages of the following methods: (a) payback period, (b) return on capital and (c) risk premium?
6. Under what circumstances is sensitivity analysis likely to be of value in investment appraisal? Is the use of the method limited to consideration of a single parameter?
7. Explain the ways in which simulation can be used in evaluating capital investment projects. What is meant by a risk profile?
8. What are the properties of points on an efficiency frontier in the context of a limited number of investments? By what means can a point on the frontier be selected?

6.18 References

Bryant, J.W. (ed.) (1987) *Financial Modelling in Corporate Management*, 2nd edn, Wiley.

Gazeley, A. (1993) *Spreadsheet Applications Manual*, Chapman & Hall.

Hicks, J.R. (1939) *Value and Capital*, Oxford University Press.

Levy, H. and Sarnat, M. (1982) *Capital Investment and Financial Decisions*, 2nd edn, Prentice-Hall.

Lorie, J.H. and Savage, C.J. (1955) Three problems in rationing capital. *Journal of Business*, **28** (4).

Myers, S.C. (1976) *Modern Developments in Financial Management*, Praeger, New York.

Pike, R.H. and Neal, C.W. (1993) *Corporate Finance and Investment: Decisions and Strategies*, Prentice-Hall.

Sangster, A. (1993) Capital investment appraisal techniques: a survey of current usage. *Journal of Business Finance and Accountancy*, **20**(3).

Srinivasan, V. (1974) A transhipment model for cash management decisions. *Management Science*, Ser. B, **20**.

Wilkes, F.M. (1983) *Capital Budgeting Techniques*, 2nd edn, Wiley.

Wilkes, F.R., Samuels, J.R. and Greenfield, S.R. (1994) *Investment Decision-Making in UK Manufacturing Industry*, University of Birmingham Research Centre for Industrial Strategy Occasional Paper No. 21, November.

6.19 Further reading

This section includes articles by Bhaskar, Elton, Grinyer, and Trivol and McDaniel on capital rationing. Bhaskar looks at the multi-constraint rationing model in relation to the financing problem; Elton examines the question of discount rates external to the rationing model, while Grinyer's interesting historical review appeared in the first edition of Bryant's collection of articles on large-scale financial modelling. Trivol and McDaniel consider the simultaneous occurrence of restricted finance and uncertainty. The classical articles by Hertz in the *Harvard Business Review* are highly readable and include, for example, discussion of risk profiles.

Hillier's technical book analyses in detail the consequences for present values of correlated cash flows over time and between projects, while Bey includes project life as an additional random factor. Wilkes and Brayshaw's book provides concise reviews of the major topics and numerous worked examples in respect of both rationing and risk. Drury's book covers a number of the topics from a management accounting perspective. Van Horne's text gives a nicely balanced presentation of risk analysis in capital budgeting, while Pike reviews the practical effectiveness of the more technical methods of capital budgeting.

Bey, R.P. (1983) Capital budgeting decisions when cash flows and project lives are stochastic and dependent. *Journal of Financial Research*, **6**, Fall.

Bhaskar, K.N. (1983) Linear programming in capital budgeting: the financing problem. *Journal of Business Finance and Accounting*, **10** (1).

Drury, C. (1992) *Management and Cost Accounting*, 3rd edn, Chapman & Hall.

Elton, E.J. (1970) Capital rationing and external discount rates. *Journal of Finance*, June.

Grinyer, P.H. (1982) The historical development and current practice of corporate modelling in the UK. In J.W. Bryant (ed.), *Financial Modelling in Corporate Management*, Wiley.

Herz, D.B. (1964) Risk Analysis in Capital Investment. *Harvard Business Review*, 42, Jan.–Feb.

Herz, D.B. (1968) Investment policies that pay off. *Harvard Business Review*, **46**, Jan.–Feb.

Hillier, F.S. (1969) *The Evaluation of Risky Interrelated Investments*, North-Holland.

Pike, R.H. (1989) Do sophisticated capital budgeting approaches improve decision making effectiveness? *The Engineering Economist*, **35** (2), Winter.

Trivol, G.W. and McDaniel, W.R. (1987) Uncertainty, capital immobility and capital rationing in investment decisions. *Journal of Business Finance and Accounting*, **14** (2).

Van Horne, J.C. (1992) *Financial Management and Policy*, 9th edn, Prentice-Hall.

Wilkes, F.M. and Brayshaw, R.E. (1986) *Company Finance and Its Management*, Van Nostrand.

1. A company's cost of capital is 10%. It has £4300 available for outlay on the following investments:

			Investment		
year	1	2	3	4	5
0	−2400	−2000	−1800	−1200	−500
1	1500	0	500	350	150
2	1500	0	500	350	150
3	0	1000	500	350	150
4	0	1000	500	350	150
5	0	1000	500	350	150

No investment may be repeated, but a fractional share may be taken in any one.

(a) Which investments should be selected in order to maximize NPV?
(b) What level of NPV could have been achieved had all investments been repeatable?
(c) Estimate the yield on the marginal project taken under the assumptions of (a).
(d) Calculate the overall yield on the total sum invested.
(e) Do you think the cash flow produced by the selected investments is acceptable?

2. A company has the following five investment opportunities:

Investment no:	Profitability index	Initial outlay
1	1.3	500 000
2	1.4	100 000
3	1.1	400 000
4	1.5	200 000
5	1.6	150 000

The company has £750 000 available for investment. Projects 3 and 4 are mutually exclusive. All the projects are continuously divisible. Which projects should be selected to maximize NPV? What is the NPV figure that results?

3. A company has the following seven investments available:

Project no.	1	2	3	4	5	6	7
Outlay							
$t = 0$	4	4	0	6	3	2	2
$t = 1$	4	0	8	4	0	4	2
Return							
$t = 2$	13	7	14	17	6	10	6

Funds already available for outlay are 36 at $t = 0$ and 40 at $t = 1$. All investments are divisible and more than one unit of any investment can be taken. Any surplus funds at $t = 0$ can be transferred to $t = 1$ at a 10% rate of interest. The company's criterion is to select those investments which maximize the present value of its dividend payments (made at $t = 0$, $t = 1$ and $t = 2$). The discount rate for dividends is 25%.

Express the problem in programming terms and show that the problem simplifies to permit easy solution.

4. A small trust company has to decide on the percentage of its total funds to invest in seven possible shares. The shares are classified into three sectors with the following details:

	Agriculture		Manufacturing			Retailing	
Share no.	1	2	3	4	5	6	7
Yield (%)	16	12	8	10	7	15	13

No more than 45% of the total may be in any one sector and no more than 25% can be invested in any one share. At least 20% must be invested in manufacturing. Given these conditions, the objective is to maximize overall yield.

(a) What proportion of the total should be invested in each share?

(b) What is the maximum yield that is achieved?

(c) Suppose that there was no longer a requirement to invest in manufacturing – what effect would the relaxation have on overall yield?

(d) Suppose that (as an alternative to (c)) the maximum that could be invested in any one sector was cut to 40%. How would overall yield be affected?

5. For the following two projects:

	$t=0$	$t=1$	$t=2$	$t=3$	$t=4$	$t=5$	$t=6$	$t=7$
A	−100	5	15	25	55	25	15	5
B	−100	55	25	10	5	10	35	45

(a) Determine which project would be selected on the payback period criterion.

(b) Calculate the net present value for each project at 10% discount and indicate which project would be selected by NPV.

(c) Comment on the results of (a) and (b).

6. Using a discount rate of 10%:

(a) Is the project below acceptable under the finite-horizon method (FHM) with a five-year horizon?

(b) Is the project acceptable under FHM with a seven-year horizon?

(c) Do you think that the FHM method is a suitable criterion in this case?

$t=0$	$t=1$	$t=2$	$t=3$	$t=4$	$t=5$	$t=6$	$t=7$	$t=8$
−3000	1650	750	300	150	300	1050	1350	1250

7. Which of the following projects would be selected on the basis of (a) return on capital and (b) accounting rate of return? Assume zero residual values. Do other criteria lend support for the decision?

Year	A	B
$t=0$	−20 000	−25 000
$t=1$	2 000	10 000
$t=2$	4 000	6 000
$t=3$	10 000	2 000
$t=4$	5 000	10 000
$t=5$	3 000	3 000
$t=6$	5 000	6 000

8. Determine the NPV of the following project at 10%:

$$-500 \quad 200 \quad 250 \quad 300 \quad 350$$

Now find the impact on the net present value of risk premiums of (a) 5 percentage points and (b) 10 percentage points.

9. Initial estimates have been made for an investment as follows:

Initial outlay	£100 000
Sales price	£30
Sales volumes:	
Year 1	4000 units
Year 2	6000 units
Year 3	3000 units
Unit cost	£20
Discount rate	10%
Life	3 years

The £100 000 buys equipment to make a product at the unit cost and sales price above and selling in the volumes shown.

(a) Calculate the maximum tolerable unfavourable change (as a percentage of the original estimate) in: (i) sales price, (ii) unit cost, (iii) sales volume, (iv) initial outlay, (v) project lifetime. Comments on the results. Could the sales volumes be treated separately in the analysis?

(b) Now suppose that sales prices are expected to rise by 10% per annum compound, but unit costs are expected to rise at an annual rate of 20% (both starting at $t = 0$). What initial cash subsidy would now be needed for the project to remain viable?

10. A project requires an initial outlay of £10 000 and runs for three years. The discount rate is 10%. Returns in any year are independent of returns in other years, and in each year have the distribution:

Probability	Return
0.06	1500
0.17	2000
0.22	4500
0.29	6000
0.16	7500
0.10	9400

Given the digit pairs:

27   02   50   35   63   22   29   99   86   25   29   98   15   87
27   84   48   42

(a) carry out a simulation for six runs to estimate ENPV;
(b) use the information obtained in (a) to estimate a value for the coefficient of variation.

11. An investment has the following distribution of returns:

Year 1		Year 2		Year 3	
Return	Probability	Return	Probability	Return	Probability
6000	0.2	8 000	0.5	7 000	0.3
8000	0.4	12 000	0.5	11 000	0.5
9000	0.4			17 000	0.2

Returns in any year are independent of returns in other years. The outlay on the project is fixed at £22 000 and the discount rate is 10%. Find:

(a) the expected NPV;
(b) the variance of return in each year;
(c) the standard deviation of NPV;
(d) the coefficient of variation;
(e) the probability that the project yields less than 10%;
(f) the probability that NPV is negative using the values of (a) and (c) and assuming an approximately normal distribution of NPV. Compare the result with that of (e).

12. A project has an initial outlay fixed at 1500. Return in year 1 could be 1350 with probability 0.4 or 900 with probability 0.6. If the 900 return occurs in year 1, then in year 2 there can be 1200 ($p = 0.2$) or 1050 ($p = 0.8$). If the year 1 return is 1350, then in year 2 there is a 0.7 chance of 600 and a 0.3 chance of 150. The interest rate is 10%. Find the coefficient of variation.

13. With a 10% discount rate, use one of the simplified formulae to find the variance of net present value in the following case:

Probability	R_0	R_1
0.7	−80	+100
0.3	−64	+120

14. Given a 10% discount rate and the following projects:

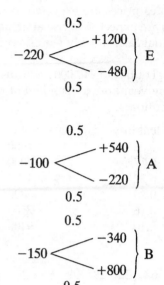

Stating any necessary assumptions, find the coefficient of variation for E, A and B alone and for E + A and E + B. What is the reason for the lower result in the case of E + B?

15. A firm can undertake the following investments:

$$
-250 \Big\langle \begin{matrix} 0.5 & 220 \\ 0.5 & 380 \end{matrix} \Big\rbrace E
$$

$$
-150 \Big\langle \begin{matrix} 0.7 & 140 \\ 0.3 & 340 \end{matrix} \Big\rbrace A
$$

The investments are not mutually exclusive. The coefficient of correlation between E and A is $r = -0.3$. The discount rate is 10%. State the mean-standard deviation combinations for E, A, E + A and the null project. Draw these points on a graph. What do you notice about their arrangement? Suppose now that investor utility is given by: $U = 10(\text{ENPV}) - 0.03\,\sigma^2_{\text{NPV}}$. Which of the alternatives should be selected? What would be implied for the efficiency frontier if fractions of projects were allowed? Where would the optimum now be?

Computer programs written in the Basic language have been used extensively in the preparation of this text. One of the values of this usage is increased accuracy and less chance of typographical error if the program output is sent to a text file rather than to the screen. This is illustrated in the following program used to generate Tables 6.23 and 6.24.

```
REM ch6tabtx.bas generates tables 6.23 and 6.24 as text file

DIM RA(3), RB(2), RC(3), PA(3), PB(2), PC(3)
DIM NPV(3, 2, 3), PROB(3, 2, 3), PNPV(3, 2, 3), deviation (3, 2, 3)

OPEN "c:\ch6table.txt" FOR OUTPUT AS #1

FOR i = 1 TO 3

   READ RA(i)

   READ PA(i)

NEXT i

FOR j = 1 TO 2

   READ RB(j)

   READ PB(j)

NEXT j

FOR h = 1 TO 3

   READ RC(h)

   READ PC(h)

NEXT h

PRINT #1, "Table 6.23"
PRINT #1, "-----------------------------------------------------";
PRINT #1, "---------------------"
PRINT #1, "Cash flow (£k) . . ."; TAB(39); "Probability";
PRINT #1, TAB(57); "NPV"; TAB(70); "P*NPV"
PRINT #1, "-----------------------------------------------------"
PRINT #1 "---------------------"

r = .1

K = 42

sumprob = 0

FOR i = 1 TO 3

  FOR j = 1 TO 2

    FOR h = 1 TO 3

      PROB(i, j, h) = PA(i) * PB(j) * PC(h)

NPV(i,j,h) = (RA(i)/(1+r)) + (RB(j)/(1+r)^2) + (RC(h)/(1+r)^3) – K

      PNPV(i, j, h) = PROB(i, j, h) * NPV(i, j, h)

      sumprob = sumprob + PROB(i, j, h)

    NEXT h

  NEXT j

NEXT i

sum = 0

FOR i = 1 TO 3
```

```
FOR j = 1 TO 2

    FOR h = 1 TO 3

        PRINT #1, RA(i); TAB(14); RB(j); TAB(28); RC(h);

        PRINT #1, TAB(42); USING "#.###"; PROB(i, j, h);

        PRINT #1, TAB(56); USING "##.###"; NPV(i, j, h);

        PRINT #1, TAB(70); USING "#.###"; PNPV(i, j, h)

        sum = sum + PNPV (i, j, h)

    NEXT h

  NEXT j

NEXT i

ENPV = sum

PRINT #1, TAB(42); "-----"; TAB(70); "-----"
PRINT #1, TAB(42); USING "#.###"; sumprob;
PRINT #1, TAB(68); USING "###.###"; ENPV
PRINT #1, "----------------------------------------------------";
PRINT #1, "--------------------"

'table 6.24 follows

PRINT #1,
PRINT #1,

PRINT #1, "Table 6.24"
PRINT #1, "----------------------------------------------------";
PRINT #1, "--------------------"
PRINT #1, "Probability"; TAB(20); "NPV-ENPV";
PRINT #1, TAB(38); "(NPV-ENPV)^2"; TAB(54); "P*(NPV-ENPV)^2"
PRINT #1, "----------------------------------------------------";
PRINT #1, "--------------------"

sumsq = 0

FOR i = 1 TO 3

  FOR j = 1 TO 2

    FOR h = 1 TO 3

        deviation(i, j, h) = NPV(i, j, h) − ENPV

        PRINT #1, USING "#.###"; PROB(i, j, h);

        PRINT #1, TAB(20); USING "###.###"; deviation (i, j, h);

     PRINT #1, TAB(40); USING "###.###"; (deviation(i, j, h)) ^ 2;

PRINT #1, TAB(60); USING "#.###"; PROB(i, j,h) * (deviation(i,j,h))^2

        sumsq = sumsq + PROB(i, j, h) * (deviation(i, j, h)) ^ 2

    NEXT h

  NEXT j

NEXT i
```

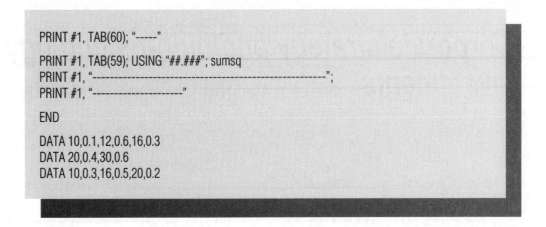

```
PRINT #1, TAB(60); "-----"
PRINT #1, TAB(59); USING "##.###"; sumsq
PRINT #1, "-------------------------------------------------------";
PRINT #1, "--------------------"

END

DATA 10,0.1,12,0.6,16,0.3
DATA 20,0.4,30,0.6
DATA 10,0.3,16,0.5,20,0.2
```

This program is not presented as an exemplary exercise in programming style, but to give some idea of the usefulness of Basic. Both spreadsheets and programming have their place. Spreadsheets give ease of use within limits which are often quite broadly defined. At the price of more time spent in familiarization, the use of a programming language gives virtually unlimited flexibility.

7

Corporate strategy and high-technology investments

7.1	Introduction	212
7.2	Strategic planning	213
7.3	Models of strategic management	214
7.4	Profit impact of market strategy	216
7.5	Investment decisions in advanced manufacturing technology	218
7.6	AMT investment: payback and present values	218
7.7	Discount rates and time horizons	220
7.8	Relevant costs and revenues	223
7.9	An appraisal methodology for strategic investments	226
7.10	The decision environment	227
7.11	Key concepts	230
7.12	Revision questions	231
7.13	References	232
7.14	Further reading	233
7.15	Problems	233

This chapter underlines the importance of clear strategic objectives in corporate decision-making. You will learn how these objectives are formed and how they interact with capital investment decision-making, particularly in the area of advanced manufacturing technology (AMT). You will see how the overall corporate strategic plan disaggregates into financially linked sub-plans allocating the company's scarce resources.

Companies must have an effective strategy to assess watershed investments. Major investments in high-technology manufacturing often have substantial intangible benefits for the organization. Intangibles represent a type of uncertainty which the market may not assess adequately and which need a built-in opportunity for a high-level strategic input to the decision-making procedure. We highlight the importance of the discount rate and time horizon for strategic investments and propose a three-stage methodology.

There is more to investment in industry than the exchange of cash and documents. Investments in industry have to be made to work, so the importance of human factors in major technological investments is also stressed, especially work-force commitment, involvement and skills training. You will see the importance of these and other managerial considerations, pre and post investment in manufacturing industry.

7.1 Introduction

Capital budgeting techniques enable management to make rational decisions based on the cash flows from investments. But for some types of investment the full cash flow impact of the project may be very difficult to establish, and a decision may be made on strategic grounds in the face of a superficially unattractive financial appraisal. Alternatively, a particular investment may appear to be profitable, and yet on strategic grounds a decision will be made not to proceed. To be acceptable, an investment not only has to be profitable, but it has to fit in with the strategic plan of the company.

Much of this chapter deals with a problem that has faced many companies in manufacturing industry for a considerable period: to what extent should investment be made in advanced manufacturing systems and how should such investments properly be assessed? High-technology investment is expensive and the returns are uncertain. But the penalties for error are very great and may threaten the competitiveness and indeed the survival of the enterprise. Decisions need an explicit strategic dimension, taking into account, but not being exclusively driven by, an appropriate quantified financial appraisal.

What do we mean by strategic grounds? What is strategic planning? It is now a key element in MBA programmes and there are many books on the topic. From a corporate point of view is it really a vital exercise, or the current managerial fashion? It is to these questions that we first turn.

7.2 Strategic planning

Strategic planning is concerned with the allocation of resources to achieve a company's objectives. Financial planning is one part of the process. Strategic planning takes into account factors other than those which are directly financial, some of which are non-quantifiable and some of which are judgemental in character. The strategic plan has to be based on more than the access to and control of financial resources. Personnel, supplies, market opportunities and technological change all have to be considered. Indeed, the company may also have broader objectives – social, psychological, regional or national that have to be taken into account.

The plan is based on a careful analysis of the relative strengths and weaknesses of the company, and an assessment of the opportunities in the markets open to it. This means that the strategic plan has to deal with intangibles. We shall give brief details of certain approaches to strategic management, as any capital investment project, to be acceptable, not only has to produce acceptable results in a financial appraisal exercise but also has to fit in with the strategic plan. Strategic management and capital budgeting in fact complement one another as will be seen in later sections of this chapter.

Strategic planning usually starts with determining the **mission** of the business. This grand title is another name for long-range goals and targets. Clearly, in the vast majority of businesses the primary objective is to continue in existence. This can be combined with certain growth targets, some of which can be expressed in financial terms.

The next stage is to analyse the competitive strengths and weaknesses of the company. This involves analysing the structure of the industry or industries in which the company competes and the nature of the competition which it faces. This in turn determines the position of the business with respect to five competitive forces:

1. competition from other businesses in the market place; this depends on factors such as market share and product differentiation;
2. the threat of competition from potential entrants to the market;
3. the power of the buyers;
4. the power of suppliers;
5. threats from substitute products.

In appraising its strengths and weaknesses, the business has now to take into account factors such the following:

1. the global market place – the company might be strong in the home market, but on a global scale it could be weak;
2. the rapid speed of technological change, which means shortening product life-cycles and an emphasis on quality;
3. improvements in information technology.

In undertaking this appraisal of corporate strengths and weaknesses, it is usual to divide the business into what are known as **strategic business units** (SBUs). Each such unit produces a distinct product (or group of products) for an identifiable group of customers. It is, as far as possible within a group, a discrete unit. The strategic planners evaluate each unit and on the basis of this come up with a strategy for the SBUs. It is to these units that the headquarters of the company will allocate investment funds The SBUs are analysed and placed into categories on the basis of their market attractiveness and their competitive strengths in these markets.

On the basis of the analysis of the relative strengths of the SBUs and an analysis of the opportunities in the market in which they operate, a strategy will be formulated for each SBU. A number of alternative strategies will be considered, each will be evaluated and the strategy that best meets the objectives (the mission) of the business will be selected.

If the objectives were seen purely in terms of capital market theory, the goal would be simply to maximize shareholders' wealth. However, as explained in Chapter 1, there are a number of agents with an interest in a company, and so there might be a number of goals to consider, some of which may conflict. So the strategy formulation may be quite complex, with political pressures from different interest groups coming into the evaluation process.

The strategic planning process can be divided into five stages as follows:

- Stage 1: determine corporate objectives;
- Stage 2: evaluate the strengths and weaknesses of the strategic business units;
- Stage 3: determine the potential of each of the markets in which the SBUs operate;
- Stage 4: evaluate the alternative strategies in terms of the objectives, of which one may well be to have a balanced portfolio of products;
- Stage 5: select an appropriate strategy for each strategic business unit.

Once a strategy is decided upon, it is possible to develop an appropriate business plan for each SBU. There will be several interlocking aspects to the business plan including: a marketing plan, a production plan, a human resource plan, a research and development plan, and of course a capital investment plan. Since the overall performance of the business is ultimately measured in financial terms, all these plans need to be brought together in projected financial statements.

Each aspect of the plan needs to be feasible within the total funds available. This means, for example, that in deciding on a human resource plan, finance is ultimately the unit of measurement that has to be used in the analysis. It would be no good meeting agreed staffing targets in terms of numbers of people, if achieving this target resulted in financial distress for the business.

A proposal to invest in any strategic business unit has then to be considered both in terms of the overall strategy to be followed for that SBU and in terms of its financial viability.

7.3 Models of strategic management

The typical strategic plan sets out where it sees the company going over the next ten years or so. In which industries will it expand, and in which will it contract? What growth target has it set itself? Will it rely on internal growth or will it resort to growth through acquisition? Which parts of the company will be sold off? The plan has to satisfy the financial objectives of those making the decisions on behalf of the company.

There are many models that have been designed to assist companies in their strategic planning. One of the earliest of these was developed and marketed by the Boston Consulting Group in 1981. Their approach was to classify each SBU on the basis of its relative market share and its potential growth rate. Relative market share was defined as the sales by the SBU of a particular product divided by the sales of that product by the largest competitor. A colourful nomenclature was developed in which each area of the business – each segment – was classified as a **star**, a **dog**, a **cash cow** or a **problem child** as illustrated in Figure 7.1.

These classifications would be important if it came to making investment decisions. An investment proposal from a division classified as a **dog** would be most unlikely to receive approval, as this would be an area of the business in competitive disadvantage and with little or no market growth possibilities. However, an investment proposed by a division in the **star** category would stand a good chance of being approved. The investment would have satisfied the question: does it fit in with the strategic plan? Of

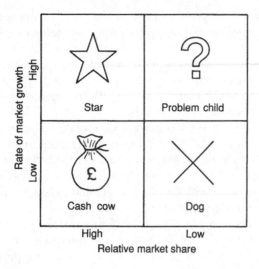

Figure 7.1

course it would still be necessary for the particular investment to satisfy the relevant financial requirements.

In the case of minor schemes, and those in which all major cash flows are well quantified, the relevant financial requirements would be a positive net present value (NPV). However, as we shall detail later, there is a category of high-technology investment where a large proportion of the known (or strongly suspected) benefits cannot be adequately quantified. In such a case, management must make a judgement as to the wider, possibly strategic, value of the investment in the light of any shortfall of the quantified benefits in relation to costs. This theme is developed in later sections of the chapter.

The Boston Consulting Group model, based on developing a product market portfolio, was popular for a number of years, but it was subject to criticism. The matrix relies on just two variables: relative market share and the rate of market growth. These two factors are important, but there are other factors that influence the success (or lack of success) of an SBU and these were ignored. As a result of these criticisms of the product market portfolio approach, other matrices were developed. A more general model referred to as the **directional policy matrix** has the competitive strength of the SBU on the horizontal axis. This would take into account factors other than market share. The matrix display for this model is shown in Figure 7.2.

The strategic policy implications of being located in each square are also shown. The investment implications are easy to deduce. Clearly, with a weak business position and unattractive business prospects, from a strategic point of view there is little reason to

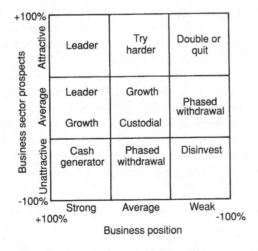

Figure 7.2

invest. With a strong business position in an unattractive business sector, one would be willing to invest minor amounts to maintain the cash generating potential but not to invest large sums as there are no prospects in the market. For the central square representing an average business position with average prospects for the market, careful appraisal would be required before large sums are invested. The product has no particular niche in the market, and it might not be worth trying to obtain one.

A problem with this type of analysis is in achieving consistency when scoring each business unit. Subjective judgement must be an important element in deciding whether a particular unit is in an average or weak business position. In attempting to minimize the differences that would arise if it was left to different individuals to make such judgements, it is usually agreed before the exercise what factors are to be considered when deciding on a unit's business position. Similarly, a list of factors that will be taken into account when deciding business prospects is agreed upon

Not only are the factors agreed upon, but so is the **weighting** to be given to each factor. Weighting is necessary if some factors are considered to be more important than others. For example, when assessing the future prospects in a particular business sector, it might be thought that changes in technology are more important than the prospects for economic growth in the economy. Different weightings would therefore be used. Unfortunately, of course, the appropriate weightings are a matter of judgement, although in principle a sensitivity analysis could be carried out on the values of the weights.

Having decided on the factors influencing the business position, the business sector prospects and the weighting to be assigned to each factor, the next step is to analyse each SBU and give it a score for each of the factors. For example, product quality is an important factor influencing the relative strength or weakness – the business position – of any SBU. We decide that its importance warrants a weighting of 5. In analysing a particular SBU within our company, say a unit manufacturing washing machines, we may give it a score of only 2 for its product quality. We multiply the score by the weighting for each factor to obtain an overall score. With this overall score for the business position and with the overall score for the business sector prospects, we are able to plot the position of the strategic business unit in the matrix.

7.4 Profit impact of market strategy

In plotting a business unit in the directional policy matrix a company takes into account the factors that it believes will influence its business position in the sector in which it operates. These will include its marketing strengths, its technological capability, its human resources, its financial position and its production strengths. The factors and the relevant weightings will vary from one business sector to another.

In the United States one approach to strategic management has been developed which attempts to be less subjective than those described above and which can lead to specific proposals (see The Strategic Planning Institute (1981)). This is the **Profit Impact of Market Strategy** (PIMS) and is the result of a large and continuing study which brings together the experiences of the many businesses taking part in the programme. It is US-based, and over 250 companies operating over 3000 separate business units are involved. They have concluded that there are nine major strategic influences on the profitability of the cash flow position of a business. They estimate that these nine factors account for about 80% of the reasons for business success or failure.

They believe that there are regular and predictable ways in which situations develop, and that business situations are basically alike in obeying the same laws of the market place. Knowledge of these nine major influences therefore assists in formulating a strategy for each business unit. The nine strategic influences in order of importance are given below.

1. **Investment intensity** as measured by investment as a percentage of sales and of value added.

The higher the level of investment intensity the lower is the return on investment.

This may seem surprising, but it is argued that this arises because increased investment can lead to higher wages and lower prices but also to improvements in quality. This last point is important and gives rise to the question: does quality lead to benefits for the business? It might not lead to higher returns in the short run but it can be essential for long-term survival. It must be remembered that the PIMS study is concerned with strategic influences on profitability. This finding is not an argument against increasing the levels of investment in a business; it points to a possible danger. The problem can be overcome by such policies as concentrating the investments in a particular segment of a market, increasing productivity and investing in equipment which is flexible in terms of its purpose.

The other eight main strategic influences are as follows:

2. **Productivity**: an obvious influence on profitability.
3. **Market position**: a high relative market share helps profits and cash flow.
4. **Growth** in the market in which the product is being sold.
5. **Quality** of the product: the PIMS study shows that quality and profitability are strongly linked. A business offering a high level of service and a quality product is more profitable over time than one offering less service with poorer quality. The study finds that quality is important in almost all businesses.
6. **Innovation**: investment in research and development has a positive effect on the profit position of businesses with a strong market position.
7. **Vertical integration**: businesses in stable mature markets benefit from vertical integration.
8. **Cost push**: the influence of increased wages and raw material costs on profitability is complex. Few useful generalizations are possible. (Recall the inflation scenario exercise of Chapter 6.)
9. **Strategic efforts**: attempting to change things can have adverse short-term effects on cash flow. For example, having a high market share is good for cash flow, but the commitment to obtain a higher market share will reduce cash flows while the efforts are being made.

Most of these points have strong intuitive appeal and indeed some are fairly obvious. Each of the points does give some guidance in the strategic planning process, however. The results are based on the position in the United States, but there is no reason to believe that they are not applicable in the UK. The results are also more relevant to larger companies than to small companies.

Although strategic planning is usually implemented as a top-down exercise, it should be a process which takes into account relevant information, feedback and the views of the units being planned. The overall capital budget of a company must be based on strategic considerations; it cannot just be a selection of individual investment proposals that have come forward in an uncoordinated way from the bottom up. The capital investment plan of a company is part of a larger planning exercise.

Strategic planning provides broad indications of the direction in which the business should be moving. In which areas is it worth considering proposals for expansion, and in which areas should the company be divesting? It is against this strategic background that detailed investment proposals are sought and financial appraisals (and any associated judgemental exercises) carried out. As we have suggested, a judgemental element comes in because investment appraisal techniques are not good at dealing with intangibles. Many major decisions have to take into account a number of intangible factors, and hence it is necessary to know the strategic position with regard to the business unit bringing forward the proposal. In summary, strategic management and the capital budgeting process are complementary. We shall now consider a specific type of investment decision in which the intangible factors can be very substantial and where strategic considerations must form an important part of the decision making process.

7.5 Investment decisions in advanced manufacturing technology

During the 1980s mounting criticism was levelled at the largely negative results of applying traditional financial appraisal techniques when certain types of capital investment were being considered. It was claimed that the techniques were holding back UK and US manufacturing industry because they were preventing the introduction of advanced manufacturing technology (AMT) essential to long-term competitiveness. The radical changes in manufacturing processes and systems that have been increasingly implemented in the last 15 years include computer integrated manufacturing (CIM) and the use of flexible manufacturing systems (FMS). FMS can range from single machines to completely integrated factories and can be applied to small-scale batch production or high-volume operations. The argument is that some investment appraisal methods, applied in isolation of the strategic context, can exclude many of the benefits of the new processes. The way in which methods are used can diminish the impact of those benefits which **are** included and some methods fail to pick up the more diffuse benefits altogether. The result is that the new processes are mistakenly not introduced, to the long-term detriment of the business and national performance in manufacturing industry.

Those who wish to see the new technologies introduced to a greater extent have frequently argued that the decision should be a strategic management decision and should be removed from the realm of financial appraisal. If this was so it would be a serious indictment of financial analysis with the implicit conclusion that those concerned with finance and accounting cannot produce techniques that properly take into account the full impact of technology on the manufacturing enterprise.

Thus this issue: the appropriate appraisal of advanced manufacturing technology, although an important matter in itself, also raises the general point that the managerial and market environment in which capital investment decisions are set may constrain and even prevent the use of investment appraisal methods consistent with long-term corporate and national objectives. In the following sections we introduce an appropriate methodology for AMT and other strategic investments with similar cash flow characteristics and address related managerial issues. We argue that:

1. While a suitable methodology for the financial appraisal of high-technology projects **does** exist, inappropriate usage and inadequate data bias selectively against AMT and similar investments.
2. Managerial structures can predispose against certain categories of investment, and the management of the appraisal process may need improvement. A three-stage procedure is indicated.
3. Financial markets may adopt time frames and financial criteria that dispose against advanced technology investments.
4. Macroeconomic policy as transmitted through interest rates has an important bearing on high-technology investment.

First we shall examine appraisal methodologies.

7.6 AMT investment: payback and present values

The first point is simple and fundamental: there is no inherent bias in correctly used methods. Criticisms levelled against financial appraisal *per se* are invalid. Biases against AMT investments fall into two categories:

1. the use of inappropriate techniques of financial appraisal;
2. the misuse of an appropriate technique.

Consider 'type 1' errors first. Heading the list of methods both in terms of frequency of use and in terms of an inherent bias against investments with the financial characteristics of AMT, is *payback*. (Drury (1992) cites a survey by CAM-I showing payback to be one of the two most popular methods of appraising investments in AMT.) In Chapter 6 we saw that the essence of payback is to prefer the option that returns its outlay in the shortest time. By its nature, payback therefore predisposes against long-term investments, and when comparing long-term investments, it will dispose against the option that shows long-term growth in favour of an alternative that has higher initial returns but where the returns are static. Both these characteristics: returns generated over a long-time horizon and long-term growth, are features which characterize AMT investments. The magnitude of these inherent biases is illustrated in the following example.

Consider the choice between the two cash flows below. Investment 'A' shows a cash flow pattern not untypical of an investment in new, flexible manufacturing methods – the kind of investment needed to achieve international competitiveness in manufacturing. Capital outlay is substantial, is required in more than one period, annual returns rise as advantage is taken of the flexibility and quality improvements and a reasonably long-time horizon is involved. Example data (£m) are:

A	$t=0$	$t=1$	$t=2$	$t=3$	$t=4$	$t=5$	$t=6$	$t=7$	$t=8$	$t=9$	$t=10$
	−10	−8	0	3	4	5	6	7	8	9	10

In contrast, option 'B' represents investment in existing process technology; for example cost reduction improvements. Comparable cash flow data to 'A' might be:

B	$t=0$	$t=1$	$t=2$	$t=3$	$t=4$	$t=5$	$t=6$	$t=7$	$t=8$	$t=9$	$t=10$
	−4	1	1	1	1	1	0	0	0	0	0

Investment of this nature typically requires lower capital outlay, displays static returns and has a shorter productive life. Option B pays back its capital in four years while option A takes six years to return the outlay. So, unless moderated by management, financial appraisal using payback would point to the short-term gain selecting the existing process alternative and foregoing the long-term benefits of alternative A.

Most people using judgement would say that the company taking A rather than B had the better long-term prospects. At 10% option A has a net present value of £9 201 198 which represents the increase in shareholders' wealth. In contrast, project B shows a **loss** in present worth terms of £209 213. Alternative B shows a yield of 7.93% while the high-technology project rejected by payback has a yield of 17.75%. Although payback can be modified to lessen the bias, it is preferable to employ more appropriate techniques.

Today's manufacturing technology

In this chapter we consider business strategy and investment in high-technology manufacturing. It has been argued that computer integrated manufacturing **is of itself** a business strategy. This case has made by the Department of Trade and Industry (1989) and the former Advisory Council on Science and Technology (1991).

For the strategy to succeed, the operations of the business must be seen as a unified system rather than as a collection of discrete functions. In addition to manufacture, CIM covers engineering as a whole, production planning, research and development, business planning, sales and marketing, finance and administration. It also implies a developing linkage with related operations at other plants, both those of the company itself and those of suppliers, sub-contractors and customers. The acronym CIM could well be replaced by CIBS: **computer-integrated business strategy**.

Integration is a strategic imperative in many sectors and involves co-ordinated systems in place of 'islands of automation'. Strategic management calls for direct communications between all departments and operations within and, increasingly, between companies. .

A successful strategy for manufacturing technology follows lines similar to that for competitiveness in general: to apply technology effectively to be profitable by being fully responsive to the customer. That is:

technology + strategy = customer satisfaction = profit

A customer-responsive, integrated approach focusing on processes is inherent in business process analysis. (See Hammer and Champy (1993).) The history of the past few decades reveals an interesting picture of the gathering pace of application of high-technology in manufacturing industry. During the late 1960s, the 1970s and the early 1980s manufacturing gained experience from the application of technology. But in the early 1980s the realization grew that technology should be used in a **strategic** way, with the aim of ensuring the competitiveness and profitability of the enterprise. The following list (Department of Trade and Industry, 1989) gives the approximate chronological progression:

1960 Low-cost automation
1970 Automated warehousing
1976 Microprocessors
1978 Microcomputers
1980 Computer-aided design and manufacture (CADCAM)
1982 Computer-aided production management
1983 Flexible manufacturing systems
1984 Computer-integrated manufacturing
1985 Just-in-time/total quality management
1986 World-class manufacturing
1987 Manufacturing automation protocols

Increasingly, CIM is a necessity not simply for competitiveness, but in order to survive in business at all. An appropriate methodology for appraising CIM is therefore very important, with a built-in strategic phase, breadth of view across the organization and the use of realistic and appropriate discount factors.

The correct procedures are discounted cash flow methods, preferably **NPV** but also **yield**, if used appropriately. Although dissatisfaction has been expressed with DCF appraisal methods for high-technology projects, the criticisms apply to the practice rather than the principle. There is no evidence that the NPV-yield approach is inherently inappropriate. It is neutral between technologies and takes into account all available information over the time horizon, making only due allowance for distance from the present and the cost of capital. That is, if it is used correctly. If it is used incorrectly, there is again likely to be an anti-AMT bias.

It is difficult to argue against present value methods in principle, for to reject DCF is to assert that a pound tomorrow is worth the same as a pound today. A rejection of NPV is equivalent to the statement that interest rates are zero. Recent survey evidence (Wilkes, Samuels and Greenfield, 1994; Sangster, 1993; Pike and Neal, 1993; Drury, 1992) shows that firms use several methods in practice, with approximately nine out of ten using payback and about eight out of ten using a DCF method (yield rather more frequently than NPV). In a survey by the CBI (1994) firms said that payback was still their main criterion. Discount rates for capital projects are slow to adjust to reductions in interest rates in general (CBI, 1994; Wilkes, Samuels and Greenfield, 1994) and payback periods are typically short (the CBI survey found an average length of 2.7 years). In 1994 about one firm in three still made no allowance for intangible benefits when appraising AMT investments (Wilkes, Samuels and Greenfield, 1994). The broad pattern of results supports the view that methods have been used in ways predisposing against AMT. This interpretation of the evidence squares with the impressions of managers that the methods have not been giving a true picture of the value of high-technology investments. We now consider the most common sources of error in the use of DCF methods, some legitimate problems that arise in respect of data, and ways in which these problems are best addressed.

7.7 Discount rates and time horizons

A common misuse of discounted cash flow methods is to use a discount rate or target value for yield which is far too high. Values around 30% have not uncommonly been used. A study by New (1994) showed one in five manufacturing units requiring a yield of over 30%. The use of such rates creates a very substantial bias against (a) projects of long duration compared with short-duration alternatives and (b) projects which show a growing rather than static pattern of returns. Since both (a) and (b) tend to be characteristic of projects in advanced manufacturing technology, use of excessive rates will selectively bias against AMT and in favour of the shorter term traditional process investments.

To illustrate, the use of 30% instead of 15% as the discount rate in project appraisal has an enormous effect on present values and investment decisions. At 15% a return ten years hence has a discount factor of 0.2472, and would therefore add 24.72% of its nominal value to NPV. With a discount rate of 30%, the ten-year discount factor is 0.0725 so the contribution to present value is just 7¼% of the nominal amount. And the effects get worse. With discounting at 30%, the present value in 1990 of £1 000 000 received each year for the **whole of the 21st century** was just £242 000! So the use of excessive discount rates is a potent force for short-termism.

With a discount rate of 5%, a return in 2005 adds 61.39% of its face value to NPV in 1995. Thus a country in which manufacturing industry discounts at 5% accords *twice* the significance to tenth-year returns compared to a country where discounting is at 15%. The multiple becomes *eight* when a rate of 30% applies. 'Patient money' reaps long-term rewards of a strategic and international character, but more than this, high discount factors also have substantial effects in the medium term. Table 7.1 contrasts the effects of low, medium and high rates for horizons up to ten years.

Table 7.1

Year of receipt	1	2	3	4	5	6
				% reduction in PV 30% vis-à-vis		% rise in PV 5% vis-à-vis 30%
	PV in 1995 at					
	5%	15%	30%	15%	5%	
1996	95.24	86.96	76.92	11.54	19.23	23.81
1997	90.70	75.61	59.17	21.75	34.76	53.29
1998	86.38	65.75	45.52	30.77	47.31	89.79
1999	82.27	57.18	35.01	38.76	57.44	134.97
2000	78.35	49.72	26.93	45.83	65.63	190.92
2001	74.62	43.23	20.72	52.08	72.24	260.18
2002	71.07	37.59	15.94	57.61	77.58	345.94
2003	67.68	32.69	12.26	62.50	81.89	452.12
2004	64.46	28.43	9.43	66.83	85.37	583.58
2005	61.39	24.72	7.25	70.65	88.18	746.33

Columns 1 to 3 in table 7.1 show the present worth in 1995 of £100 received at 5%, 15% and 30%. Columns 4 and 5 show the percentage reductions between 30% and the lower levels. Column 6 shows, in striking terms, how much more a company using low interest rates will value future returns than a firm applying a higher rate. Thus it is vital to ensure that the interest rate reductions at national level are appropriately reflected in the discount rates applied to capital investment in the UK. Studies by Wilkes, Samuels and Greenfield (1994) and the CBI (1994) suggest that the response of discount rates is at best damped and lagged. Conversely, the long-term damage to the competitiveness of British manufacturing industry of high interest rates at national level must be fully appreciated.

We have seen an illustration of the adverse effects of excessive discount rates on a project as a whole. High interest rates can also have differential effects between the cost and revenue components of an investment because of their different distributions over time. Even over short-term horizons, this effect can bias against projects with cash flows characteristic of high-technology investments. For example, the following cash flow shows two years of net investment followed by sustained growth in net returns.

$$
\begin{array}{cccccc}
t = 0 & t = 1 & t = 2 & t = 3 & t = 4 & t = 5 \\
-15 & -5 & 5 & 10 & 15 & 20
\end{array}
$$

Table 7.2 shows the effects of the three rates of discount on the present values of the years of net benefit (2–5) and the years of net investment (1–2).

Table 7.2

| | Discount rate | | |
	5%	15%	30%
PV net returns	41.18	28.88	18.15
PV net outlays	19.76	19.35	18.85
Net present value	21.42	9.53	–0.70

Clearly, there are disproportionate effects on revenues and costs. A move from 5% to 15% reduces the present value of the years of net return by almost 30%. In contrast, the present value for the years of net outlay falls little more than 2%. If 30% is used in place of 15%, the present value for the years of net return declines by 37%, but that of the net outlays falls only 2.6%. By this time the project has negative present value, probably having already become financially inferior to a conventional process alternative.

The range of discount rates and target values for yield used by UK companies varies over time but in the early years of the 1990s typically ranged from 5% to 32% with an average around 18.5%, though by 1994 the CBI found an average nominal discount rate of 17% (about 3½ percentage points above German levels and almost 7 percentage points above Japanese levels). In the United States the rate was 10% to 40% with an average around 17.1%. While it is impossible to give a benchmark suitable for all periods, in the UK, research suggested that in the late 1980s and early 1990s around 13% would have been a suitable rate of discount or hurdle yield rate for investments of average risk. So there may well have been a tendency to set discount rates some five or six percentage points too high, consistent with Miles' (1992) finding on implied over-discounting by the stock market. We saw earlier on some of the disadvantageous consequences for strategic investment in British manufacturing industry.

As we saw in Chapter 6, one way to allow for risk is to add a risk premium to the discount rate. This principle is an old one, but the capital asset pricing model points out how the premium should be calculated in a more scientific manner. The capital asset pricing model is discussed in detail in the following chapters. Although the model is rarely used in investment decision-making in manufacturing industry, it does have important implications in the context of risk premiums. The theory states that when the ownership of the company holds well diversified portfolios, the risk premium should only reflect that part of a project's risk that cannot be diversified away (the **systematic risk**). Total risk for a project measured by variability of return (yield) adds to the systematic component an **unsystematic risk** which is that idiosyncratic element of variability of return which can be diversified away.

However, as we argue below in terms of managerial reward structures and appraisal, managers' interests may conflict with shareholders' in such a way that they use total risk rather than systematic risk in judging the risk premium. This will be so if the principal measure of a manager's success is the outcome of a major project for which he or she is responsible. This may go some way to account for what appear to be excessive judgemental risk premiums used in the UK for advanced manufacturing technology projects. The risk premium used in assessing such projects may also fail to recognize the ways in which flexible manufacturing systems can reduce variability of return through the capability of producing a wide variety of products.

Scholarly debate about appropriate interest rates for project appraisal risks missing the vital practical point that what is important is to avoid the **gross** bias against high-technology investment implied by really excessive premiums. If, for example, discount rates in the range 13 ± 3% were employed, the gross bias would be removed while still leaving some scope for judgement according to circumstance. The rates can be project specific and the general level of rates should of course be reviewed from time to time as interest rates nationally and internationally show significant shifts.

At present, many companies use a management judgement of target rate of return company wide. This rate also tends to remain unchanged for long periods. Many companies have considerable difficulties in establishing their weighted average cost of capital. In Japan, overt discounted cash flow procedures are infrequently used, but interest costs are included in the assessment. The ways in which this is done are not necessarily at variance with DCF assessments, and there will, as previously mentioned, be an **implied** hurdle yield rate substantially lower than typical UK values.

When an appropriate discount rate has been selected, if advanced technology, strategic investments are to be properly appraised, it is essential than an appropriate time scale is employed. AMT lasts longer, is more adaptable and so can be used for successive generations of products. It is essential that the time scale over which the benefits of the investment are calculated represents the full useful lifetime of the equipment. Such assessments are not easy and can never hope to be precise. The benefits exist, and it is unwise to assume, in effect, that they take the precise value of zero by taking too short a horizon. There is also the problem that the ultimate benefits of AMT may not be fully evident early in a programme of phased modernization. If a chain is as strong as its weakest link, it is only when the last weak link is removed that the full benefit of installing strong links becomes evident. Rather than attempt an arbitrary apportionment of ultimate benefit between the phases (links) assessed in isolation, it is preferable to take a sufficient time scale to enable the move to AMT to be seen in a holistic fashion.

7.8 Relevant costs and revenues

A criticism that is frequently levelled at quantitative methods of investment appraisal in the context of strategic investments in manufacturing is that important benefits are not included in the data for the calculations while some irrelevant costs are loaded in. While evidence suggests that these criticisms have substance and create a significant bias against AMT investments, they are again criticisms of the practice and not the principle of discounted cash flow methods.

A valid quantitative assessment requires all **relevant** cash flows to be included in the analysis. It is the **incremental** cash flows, representing the financial consequences of changes brought about by the investment, that should be considered. Cash flows already fixed before the project under consideration, for example sunk costs or inescapable future commitments, though not unimportant to the company, are irrelevant to the decision and can bias away from the most profitable alternative.

Lost revenues have the same effect on profit as increased costs. So when a project is being evaluated, we should consider whether other revenue earning opportunities would be lost if the project is accepted. These lost revenues are **opportunity costs** and should be included in the cash flow calculations so that all changes caused by the project are taken into account. For example, resources required for the project that would have to be taken from other uses should be costed at their value in the other use. This is the profit the resources would have made, rather than their 'over the counter' costs. Figure 7.3 (Cook (1987)) sets out this economic view of relevant cash flows.

Now consider some examples of what should **not** be included in a project appraisal. As we saw in Chapter 5, allowance for depreciation is not a cash flow item in itself and therefore should not be included in the calculations. But the taxation consequences of writing down allowances represent real changes in cash flow attributable to the investment. These should therefore be included. To this extent depreciation effects are relevant. (The authors have experience of the distortions caused by incorrect use of

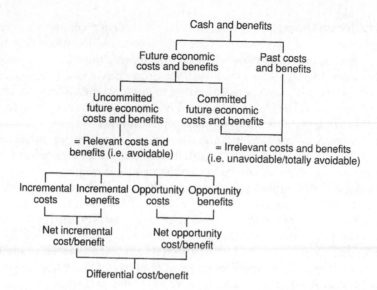

Figure 7.3

depreciation. A paper and box manufacturer always put jobs onto old and inefficient machines while new machines producing high-quality products lay idle! This was because the 'hourly rates' calculated for the machines included depreciation, which was zero for the 'written-off' old machines.)

A similar situation can be created by apportionment of fixed overheads. Depending upon the way that this is done a bias can be created. (In the paper and box example, the error was compounded by allocation of overheads.) That element of overheads which varies as a result of any investment should be included in the financial appraisal. But it is not being claimed that fixed overheads are irrelevant and can be ignored. For long-term viability the excess of revenues over variable costs on all operations must be sufficient to cover fixed overheads. The best way to do this is to maximize the excess of incremental revenues over incremental costs. This said, there is one circumstance where fixed overheads can have a direct relevance. In some sellers' markets, if the price negotiated with the client can be increased by the way in which fixed overheads enter the price calculations this should clearly be done! However, once the price is settled the choice of means by which the service is then delivered to the client should not be distorted by the arbitrary apportionment of overheads.

Having considered relevance, we now turn to the question of measurability. One of the main difficulties in the use of financial appraisal methods is that some of the benefits of high-technology investments are more tangible than others. The tangible benefits include the following:

1. **Inventory savings** in raw materials, work in progress and finished product stocks. A just-in-time (JIT) approach to stock reduction goes hand in hand with CIM and brings substantial savings and reductions in levels of working capital.
2. **Quality improvement cost reductions**: savings identifiable here from standard accounting data include reductions in scrap, the need for fewer quality inspectors and reduced warranty claims. Other cost reductions, for example less production rework, normally have to be estimated separately.
3. **Set-up costs**: the flexibility of AMT systems should lead to identifiable reductions in set-up costs.
4. **Premises costs**: AMT processes usually need less space. One writer described the space management consequence of installation of AMT as 'finding a factory within a factory'. Care is required here, however, as the cash flow consequences may be minimal unless:

(a) there are cost reductions because unused areas can be isolated and savings can be made on heating, lighting, cleaning, maintenance etc., or:

(b) there is a profitable use to which the released space can be put. (This is an opportunity benefit and is less tangible.)

Arbitrary re-apportionment of book costs of floor space that do not relate to cash flow should be excluded from the appraisal on the same grounds as depreciation and fixed overhead.

5. **Training**: the introduction of CIM requires considerable staff retraining, an information campaign and software development the costs of which may exceed the hardware costs by a factor of two. These costs should be budgeted for. Training and education are essential to minimize disruption costs. There is, in effect, an internal research and development component which should be seen as part of the investment. Any residual drain on cash resources due to temporary falls in productivity would have to be estimated and built into the budget.

Now consider the scale of possible savings. A NEDO study showed the areas in which tangible savings in costs had been demonstrated as a result of the introduction of AMT. The study also indicated the extent of the savings, showing total production costs lowered by 14% to 27% across companies. The key areas of savings and the percentage improvements were as follows: labour costs, 30% or more; material costs, 13% to 15%; inventory, 50% or more. In addition floor space savings were typically in excess of 50%, lead times were cut by over 50% and tendering time by 80% or more. However, the savings took time to achieve which would make the investments vulnerable to payback. Kaplan (1986) quotes the case of a Japanese company that installed FMS, and questions whether it would have been installed in the USA (or UK). The system showed very large savings in manpower (from 215 operators to 12), production floor space reduced from 103 000 to 30 000 sq. ft, machines reduced from 68 to 18 and processing time cut from 35 days to 1½. However, with the high cut-off rates used in both the USA and the UK, the project would have appeared unprofitable if the intangible benefits were ignored.

Now let us turn to the most difficult area of all: intangible benefits. There is a school of thought that almost nothing is intangible with suitably rigorous total quality management. While there is a semantic as well as a real area of debate here, few firms at present have the highest levels of TQM. And there is nothing intangible about success. The problem arises in seeing what is necessary to achieve it. The benefits which are hard to measure before AMT is implemented include the following:

1. **Enhanced flexibility**: this is an undoubted benefit which means faster response to changing customer requirements and demand levels, and the opportunity to provide for the needs of individual customers in product specification and order size. An intangible benefit associated with reduced set-up costs is the demand enhancing potential of smaller production runs. A high degree of flexibility presents a challenge to management accounting. A FMS can be switched between tasks on a day-to-day basis and can give possibilities of 'mass customization' combining economies of scale with the meeting of individual customer requirements.

2. **Quality improvements** should increase the relative attraction of the product in the market place and either (a) increase sales or (b) stave off what would otherwise have been a decline in sales as a result of competitors' quality improvements. These effects are unlikely to be quantifiable to an acceptable degree of accuracy in all but the simplest of market situations. A means of treating these and other intangible benefits is discussed below.

3. **Skills improvements**: investment in AMT brings increased awareness of high technology, knowledge and adaptability in the work force at all levels. It is important to capitalize on this by developing more participative managerial approaches that take up and encourage improvements discovered by the work-force. Skills improvements are an example of organization wide benefits that can cut across divisional boundaries. The decision methodology (as suggested below) must allow a systems view to be adopted. This is the internal R & D component again.

4. **Capital decay**: it is a common assumption when considering AMT to assume that the existing level of sales would continue unchanged if the new investment was not undertaken. This view should be challenged as it can lead to substantial underestimation of the benefits of AMT. The manufacturing climate has changed dramatically and there is no sign of the pace of change slowing down. So it cannot be assumed that firms which continue with old methods of production will be able to keep their market position. Continued use of older methods will mean lower levels of sales over time. This leads to the expression **capital decay**. The true revenue benefit of AMT quality improvements is the difference between the new levels of sales with AMT and the declining levels without it.

7.9 An appraisal methodology for strategic investments

In the use of quantitative methods it is good practice to separate out as far as possible the objective and judgemental elements. Judgemental factors can then be given due weight against the background of an agreed data base. The alternative mix of facts and guesswork is unlikely to lead to good decision-making and may result (as has happened in some companies) in the wasteful abandonment of a quantified dimension in decision-making. (An element of judgement remains in the quantified side in deciding what can be measured with sufficient precision.) The approach recommended here and elaborated in Wilkes and Samuels (1991) tries to balance strategic and numerical considerations and has three stages.

The **first stage** is for management to consider the proposed investment in relation to the company's strategic plan. At this stage the proposal may be judged to be inconsistent with the strategic plan and management may rule against the investment on these grounds. So at this stage a proposal may be ruled out, but definite acceptance cannot be given. If the project 'meshes with mission', the proposal moves to the next stage.

The **second stage** consists of the following three steps:

1. **Model construction**: a DCF model of the company's decision problem is constructed. This should not be too complex, but might range from a simple NPV framework to a model with capital constraints. Park and Son (1988) produced an NPV based model with budgetary constraints that breaks down tangible costs in a way relevant to AMT.

2. **Data estimation**: obtaining estimates of cash flow data is the most difficult part of the numerical stage. Estimates are required of all quantifiable cash flow components along with the discount rate to be used in the NPV calculation. While there is no sharp dividing line where intangibility ends and tangibility begins, it should be noted that finance and accounting frequently involve a degree of estimation. Selection of the most appropriate discount rate involves judgement as well as estimation. We have already argued that the discount rate should not be excessive.

3. **Calculation**: this is a straightforward step once the model has been constructed and the data estimated. If net present value is positive, the proposed investment is definitely worthwhile. Recall that the NPV is calculated using estimates of **tangible** benefits only. So if NPV is positive on this basis, the existence of intangible benefits would reinforce the decision and the process terminates.

But if the net present value is negative, the third stage of the process is entered.

The **third stage** is a justification analysis based on the sensitivity approach to uncertainty introduced in Chapter 6. If the tangible benefits do not exceeded tangible costs (which are a good proxy for total costs), in this third stage management must weigh the intangible elements against the shortfall in net present value. The question is: do the benefits from factors such as increased flexibility, greater product attractiveness in the marketplace, and improved employee skills and attitudes justify the cost not covered by the tangible benefits?

In addressing this question each intangible benefit should be analysed in depth. One way of doing this is to assign a points score to each item of benefit. Another approach used by one UK company is to lower the discount rate for the DCF calculations if intangible benefit can be demonstrated. The point scores are not translated directly into cash values, although there is an implied trade-off when a decision is made. The points are generally regarded as ordinal numbers not to be added, so scores of 5 and 5 on each of two attributes of one system do not equal scores of 8 and 2 on the same attributes in another system. The use of scoring systems is often recommended in the strategic management literature. However, in the public sector **additive** points scoring systems are used to prioritize some public works projects for which most benefits, though undeniable, are intangible.

The three-stage procedure is also appropriate to those situations in which there is more than one type of advanced manufacturing system that could be introduced. If the principle of 'going AMT' was strategically acceptable, a decision between the competing alternatives would then be made using the second (quantitative) and third (justification) stages. If the intangible benefits were judged to be the same for each AMT alternative, the decision could then be made, without distortion, according to the outcome of the financial appraisals.

It is not suggested that the three-stage procedure should be a straightjacket. The nature of competitive business is such that there will be situations in which it is at least arguable that the decision should be taken on strategic grounds alone. For example, up to this point we have been assuming that management is assessing a specific AMT proposal. But it is possible that the question of the nature of the company's manufacturing processes may arise not in the form of a relatively detailed proposal but as a general question of policy, and possibly an urgent question at that. In these circumstances, in the absence of cash flow data the second stage of the process could not be carried out, and any early decision would have to be made on purely strategic grounds.

There may also be cases in which the strategic dimension can be seen by management as overwhelming – the 'need to have' argument. If the company's competitors were adopting AMT and if their decision was correct and the company itself did not go ahead along similar lines, it would lose its market position. If the competitors were wrong and the company also adopted AMT, then at least it would still be in business. (This strategic assessment could be formalized in terms of the game theory concept of **minimax regret**.) But it should be noted that when a decision has been taken on purely strategic grounds, where there are tangible costs and benefits involved, any strategic decision implies a bound on the valuation of the intangibles. The issue of evaluating intangible benefits cannot be circumvented altogether. So while there are occasions where a purely strategic judgement is warranted, the three-stage procedure should be 'default mode'.

In section 7.2 attention was drawn to three aspects of the environment for most major financial decisions. In this section we draw out managerial, market and macroeconomic factors that may have a significant bearing on how long-term, large-scale investment decisions are made. In particular, the focus will be upon new and far-reaching systems involving advanced manufacturing technology.

7.10 The decision environment

Consider managerial reward structures. Judgement of performance should be based on measures that are fully in accord with the long-term goals of the enterprise. One way to achieve this would be to award bonuses in relation to the present value of investments undertaken. But current practices can encourage 'short-termism' and can create personal disincentives to invest in projects for which the lifetime exceeds the typical length of time that managers spend in any given post.

A bias against strategic investments in manufacturing can also be created if the practice of using small profit centres is adhered to too rigidly and if there are insufficient mechanisms available to take a company-wide view. Investments in advanced processes are different in character: they are typically larger, with apparently greater uncertainties and more wide-ranging organizational impact. Significant advantages to the enterprise will not be picked up if the only benefits measured are those falling within cost centres or manufacturing cells. Even the best methods of investment appraisal used in this context will be faulty. Ideally, the goods and services flowing between profit centres should be costed and valued at levels designed to achieve corporate objectives. If a cost centre framework is retained for all investment decisions, the issues of transfer pricing must be addressed. It is a mistake to attach the precise value of zero to flows between cost centres, as is implied if they are ignored in financial appraisals.

Much of the gain from investment in AMT-CIM arises from the vigour with which it is implemented. This calls for commitment of staff at all levels who must feel that they own the decision. A high level of information to answer questions and allay anxieties is a minimum requirement. It is preferable in developing commitment if managerial structures are participative. It is clear that 'mere' investment in, and possession of, computer integrated manufacturing processes, is not enough. The investment needs to be carefully selected and made best use of. It is foolish to spend millions on AMT and then skimp on training.

A study on the implementation of just in time methods (Crawford et al, 1988) showed that, while there were substantial gains to be achieved, there are similar kinds of 'cultural resistance' to those found in the introduction of CIM, of which JIT is often a part. The importance of involving people at all levels in the company and persuading them to own the decision was shown by the fact that people problems turn out to be more important than technical problems in determining success. The complexity of implementation means that the full commitment and effort of all employees needs to be drawn upon. Problems included not only lack of union acceptance but also lack of middle-management acceptance. A frequently encountered problem was insufficient training and education. Mixed-management teams with production workers engaged in non-production duties in slack periods proved successful. Indeed this cross training seems essential. A multi-departmental approach to implementation teams is required at all levels. The survey showed average training hours of 13 per worker and 25 per manager. So it may be concluded that either the effectiveness of the training methods needs substantial improvement or, possibly more likely, that the investment of time is simply not enough.

In Japan, first-line supervisors and upwards receive 60–90 days' training and most first-line supervisors in Japan are graduate engineers. International consultants Bain and Company emphasize that 'training should never stop'. The question of scale of investment raises a further point. The use of threshold levels of capital expenditure beyond which senior or board-level managerial approval is required creates a bias towards smaller projects with conventional technology. The ways in which investment decisions are delegated need to be examined. For example, it might be impressed upon branch managers that if there are high-technology ways of meeting a need for which there are low-technology or piecemeal alternatives that fall below the permitted ceiling for delegated powers of decision, it is the manager's duty to draw attention to the high-technology, higher outlay possibilities.

Bias may also be created by psychological factors. Larger investment decisions can often be crucial, and managers can, understandably, be reluctant to depart from methods of appraisal the use of which has coincided with the past survival and success of the company. It helps to overcome these anxieties if decision-making is more broadly based and responsibility is shared. Training can also help to overcome resistances, particularly when newer methods are less user-friendly. UK evidence suggests that the more sophisticated is the investment appraisal methodology, the more confidence management ultimately has in the effectiveness of corporate decision-making.

One of the reasons why strategic investments in manufacturing have sometimes been taken as 'acts of faith' is the often less than adequate quality of financial accounting information. Accounting systems have developed over the years with their own internal rationale which may be at odds with managerial judgement and economic logic. The main focus should be on decisions rather than reports. Established accounting systems may be suitable for audit, though not always for much else. An ideal system should improve measurement to the point where analysis and optimal control of the currently intangible effects of AMT is possible.

This is an ideal of course, and it should be noted that there is probably no single concept of cost that is unambiguous and appropriate for all purposes. So it may be necessary to have more than one set of cost and benefit information: one for matters of report, one for projective sensitivity analysis, one to compute short-term financial measures for the City and one for the assessment of the long-term technological and competitive positions. Such changes are of major significance, and would take time. But it is not necessary to await the development of novel management accounting systems. There is much to be gained from the appropriate use of correct appraisal methods even when the quality of information is less than ideal. Flexible use of existing human resources is important too. Accountants are paid employees and should do as required by senior management.

If the accounting system in a company is not flexible enough, this may reveal a weakness of top management. The accounting system certainly **can** be flexible, and industry is taking the lead here. Groups of companies exchange their ideas and practices on using the accounting system to generate management accounting information. The evidence suggests that firms that have good accounting systems do well – as long as the top management knows what information it is looking for. With AMT it is not simply a question of accountants working in isolation. Leading companies such as Rolls Royce are developing interdisciplinary teams, and other companies are altering structures to bring accountants and engineers together – perhaps under the overall control of a generalist manager.

Breadth of perspective is important in terms of time as well as across the enterprise at any one moment. Where AMT is introduced stage by stage into the manufacturing chain, it is important to take a sufficiently long perspective to look at the changes as a whole. A systems view should be taken in the time dimension as well as across the company as a whole at any instant. The situation must be avoided where only the final stage shows enormous benefit (when the synergies are realized) and the initial stages (which would never be completed) show net losses. This would be equivalent to identifying one of the legs on a stool as the most important simply because it was the last to be added.

The question of time perspective is also important in terms of costs. For example, if life-cycle costing is used as a marketing tool an important edge can be gained and larger and earlier returns to AMT investments can be secured. Consequently the investment itself will be more attractive at the financial stage of the assessment procedure. Japanese companies making products requiring high levels of capital expenditure are more inclined to adopt a life-cycle view of costs and average them out over a longer period. In this way, more favourable pricing is made possible for the AMT made product in the early years of operation. 'Patient' money is not simply patient on the returns side but also in terms of costs. There is an existing methodology for taking the long view in relation to capital costs – the use of annual equivalent annuities as discussed in Chapter 5. This method ensures that the time value of money is properly taken into account in spreading costs over time.

On the expenditure side the evaluation and accounting treatment of R & D expenditure is important. In this context it is worth drawing a distinction between basic fundamental research and R & D expenditures at the development stage. As basic research proceeds, pumping more money in does not necessarily translate into better results. At the development stage, however, additional and specific expenditure can be made the subject of an appraisal. (Here again, a three stage process may be needed.) It is unlikely that fundamental research expenditures can be financially appraised *ex ante*. We could look overall at the correlation between successful companies in a given field and their expenditure levels on fundamental research, although we should be cautious about drawing causative conclusions. For example, one major American corporation consistently spent a great deal on 'research' which had very little obvious connection with its line of business in order to unload excess profits.

It would certainly help if the accounting treatment of R & D in relation to investment in advanced manufacturing methods was amended in ways that improve short-term profitability. Further justification for this is that the decision may well be a watershed decision for the company closely related to its survival and in this sense is one-off. To address this situation, efforts should be made to make the accounting (and fiscal) environment as helpful as possible. Here again a long-term view is necessary. Short-term reductions in exchequer tax take would be more than offset by enhanced performance and revenues in future years.

When deciding on an investment some view of the future must be taken whether or not a formal model is used. While at one extreme the total avoidance of modern methods is a blind alley, at the other pole forecasting techniques should not be used as a substitute for strategic thinking. Technical methods should be used where appropriate, but tempered with judgement. In investments involving AMT the pivotal factor in forecasting is demand for the final product. CIM will involve material requirements planning and manufacturing resource planning in which the demand for items which depend on the demand for the final product can be derived from the demand for the finished product itself.

Longer term trends in product demand can be picked up by regression methods, but there is a vital rôle for managerial judgement of market situation, national and international developments. In this respect we refer again to 'what would happen if' sensitivity analysis – the approach in which the consequences of various scenarios are examined. For example, models that project balance sheets are available. This would commend itself as a worthwhile exercise at the end of which a managerial judgement would still have to be made.

Management's scope for taking the long view is all too often limited by short-term financial pressures. Projected balance sheets may show a situation that would be received badly in the City. While some US studies argue that, in effect, the market looks at cash flow as a whole, the general view is that in the US as well as in the UK the City continues to be preoccupied with short-term considerations. An example is the earnings per share statistic which is regarded as all-important in potential takeovers.

The effect of the pressures to pay back quickly, maintain attractive gearing ratios and generate financial statistics that appeal to impatient money is that management taking an uncompromising longer term strategic view is playing a dangerous game from the company perspective. During a major exercise in introducing new manufacturing methods certain financial statistics can go through a trough leaving the company vulnerable to predation. While some will argue that what matters is that the national manufacturing base is not lost and who owns what is not vital, important points may be overlooked.

Quite apart from the fact that pride in company and nation are important motivating factors for many people, managers in defending the integrity of the company to which they belong may be tempted to avoid AMT investments on the grounds of short-term survival at the expense of competitiveness in the longer term. In this respect a large conglomerate is in a better position to take a longer term full cash flow view and introduce AMT in parts of the organization and to meet the short-term requirements on financial statistics by performance elsewhere in the organization. In contrast, more focused medium-sized firms must look over their shoulders at profit and loss accounts and the balance sheet when AMT-CIM is being introduced throughout the company. The question here is does the company **dare** to take a strategic view? Management may see itself as damned if it does (short-term) and damned if it doesn't (long-term). Clearly the country addressing this dilemma most successfully gains an important strategic advantage.

7.11 Key concepts

Decision-makers in a company need to have clear objectives. They need to consider alternative strategies to achieve those objectives and to decide upon a particular route to follow. This becomes the **strategic plan**. In evaluating the possible alternatives they need to analyse the strengths and weaknesses of the company. This involves considering not just the position of the company in the market place but also the internal organization of the company.

The strategic plan is broken down into a number of subplans for sales, production, human resource management, research and capital investment. The plans involve an allocation of the firm's scarce resources, which are funds and skilled people. These plans are linked in financial terms. To be acceptable, any capital investment proposals have to fit in with the overall strategy of the company and produce reasonable financial returns.

Projects which generate long-term cash flows, particularly those with growing patterns of return, are selectively discriminated against by short-term financial appraisal methods such as payback. Use of excessive discount rates and target yield figures have a similar bias against high-outlay long-running growth projects.

The quantified phase of the appraisal process should be carried out using all relevant cash flows and **only** the relevant cash flows. The **incremental cash flow** – the cash consequences of changes brought about by the investment – should exclusively be considered. Savings on the cost side brought about by high-technology manufacturing relate to inventory, quality, set-up and premises costs. Intangible benefits include enhanced flexibility, mass customization possibilities, product quality and work-force skills improvements and resistance to capital decay.

A three-stage decision methodology is suggested for appraising investment in advanced manufacturing technology. The first stage considers whether the proposed investment fits in with the company's strategic plan. The second stage, the quantified financial appraisal, is an NPV calculation using **measurable** cash flows and an appropriate discount rate. The third stage, where needed, consists of a **justification analysis** where management considers whether the intangible benefits are worth any shortfall in the cash flow revealed in the second stage.

There are possible biases against longer term investments such as AMT in certain management practices. Reward structures may be too closely geared to short-term performance, capital expenditure thresholds above which delegated authority ceases favour smaller traditional process investments and the narrow use of cost centres may obscure benefits produced elsewhere in the organization.

Substantial investment in training and a high level of involvement and participation by staff at all levels are essential in large-scale high-technology strategic investments. An interdisciplinary approach is desirable in which accountants and engineers work together. The accounting system should produce information appropriate for management decision-making.

The shorter term perspectives of financial institutions in the City and vulnerability to takeover may inhibit investment in advanced manufacturing technology in medium-sized firms. Macroeconomic factors such as the reliance on interest rates in macroeconomic regulation and the way that corporate taxation and writing down allowances are structured can affect AMT investments more than traditional process investments.

7.12 Revision questions

1. What are the main factors taken into account in:
   (a) formulating a company strategic plan;
   (b) assessing a company's relative strengths and weaknesses?
2. What are the main stages of the strategic planning process?
3. Outline two models produced as an aid to strategic planning.
4. What are the main strategic influences on corporate profitability?
5. To what extent can CIM be considered as a business strategy in itself?
6. Why are over-high discount rates likely to have a more adverse effect on investments in AMT than on investments in traditional manufacturing processes?
7. Why is the payback method of investment appraisal likely to predispose against AMT investments?
8. Use the present value tables to illustrate the magnitude of the difference in the weight attached to long-term returns at a discount rate of 5% compared with a 30% discount rate.
9. How would you describe the essential characteristic of relevant cash flows for the financial appraisal of investments?

10. Give an illustration of the way in which opportunity costs are relevant to investment appraisal.
11. Give some examples of the tangible benefits of high-technology investment.
12. In what areas are there likely to be intangible gains from investment in AMT?
13. Outline a three-stage methodology appropriate for strategic investments with intangible benefits.
14. What are the managerial structures and practices that may make AMT investments appear less attractive and inhibit their acceptance?
15. Why may large-scale investment in CIM be more difficult and hazardous for the medium-sized company?
16. Explain the importance in investment decision making of the use of:
    (a) a time frame of sufficient length;
    (b) a perspective of sufficient breadth;
    in which to view both the costs and revenues of the competing alternatives.

7.13 References

Boston Consulting Group (1981) *Annual Perspective.*

Computer Aided Manufacturing Incorporated (1988) *Management Accounting in Advanced Manufacturing Environments: A Survey.*

Confederation of British Industry (1994) *Realistic Returns: How Do Manufacturers Assess New Investments?*, CBI.

Cook, C.G. (1987) The commercial impact and control of new manufacturing technology. Unpublished paper, University of Birmingham.

Drury, C. (1992) *Management and Cost Accounting*, 3rd edn, Chapman & Hall.

Drury, C., Braund, S., Osborne, P. and Tayles, M. (1992) *A Survey of Management Accounting Practices in UK Manufacturing Companies*, ACCA Research Occasional Paper, Chartered Institute of Certified Accountants.

Crawford, K.M., Blackstone, J.H. and Cox, J.F. (1988) A study of JIT implementation and operating problems. *International Journal of Production Research*, **26** (9), Sept.

Department of Trade and Industry (1989) *Managing Into the 90's: Manufacturing*, Department of Trade and Industry.

Hammer, M. and Champy, J. (1993) *Re-engineering the Corporation: A Manifesto for Business Revolution*, Harper Collins.

Kaplan, R.S. (1986) Must CIM be justified by faith alone? Harvard Business Review, Mar.–Apr.

Miles, D. (1992) *Testing for Short-Termism in the UK Stock Market*. Bank of England Working Paper Series No. 4, October.

National Economic Development Office (1985) *Advanced Manufacturing Technology*, NEDO.

New, C.C. (1994) *The Internal Investment Requirements of UK Manufacturing Businesses: A Survey of Current Practice in 226 Plants (Management Summary)*, Trade and Industry Committee Second Report Memoranda of Evidence, HMSO.

Park, C.S. and Son, Y.K. (1988) An economic evaluation model for advanced manufacturing systems. *Engineering Economist*, **34** (1), Fall.

Pike, R.H., Sharp, J. and Price, D. (1989) AMT investment in the larger UK firm. *International Journal of Operations and Production Management*, **9** (2).

Sangster, A. (1993) Capital investment appraisal techniques: a survey of current usage. *Journal of Business Finance and Accounting*, **20** (3).

Strategic Planning Institute (1981) *Basic Principles of Business Strategy, The PIMS Program*, Cambridge, MA.

Wilkes, F.M. and Samuels, J.M. (1991) Financial appraisal to support technological investment. *Long Range Planning*, **24** (6), Dec.

Wilkes, F.M., Samuels, J.M. and Greenfield, S.M. (1994) *Investment Decision-Making in UK Manufacturing Industry*, University of Birmingham Research Centre for Industrial Strategy Occasional Paper No. 21, November.

The listing below covers strategic issues in management and investment in advanced manufacturing technology. There are many other books and articles of interest in addition to those listed below. The articles can be found in journals already cited. You are also referred to: the *Strategic Management Journal* (Wiley), *Computer Integrated Manufacturing Systems* (Butterworth), *Project Appraisal* (Beech Tree Publishing) and the *International Review of Strategic Management* (Wiley).

Advisory Council on Science and Technology (1991) *Advanced Manufacturing Technology*, HMSO.

Ansoff, H.I. (1979) *Strategic Management*, Macmillan.

Ashford, R.W., Dyson, R.G. and Hodges, S.D. (1988) The capital investment appraisal of new technology: problems, misconceptions and research directions. *Journal of the Operational Research Society*, **39** (7), July.

Bromwich, M. and Bhimani, A. (1991) Strategic investment appraisal. *Management Accounting*, Mar.

Currie, W. (1990) Strategic management of advanced manufacturing technology. *Management Accounting*, Oct.

Dyson, R. (1989) *Strategic Planning Models and Analytical Techniques*, Wiley.

Finnie, J. (1988) The role of financial appraisal in decisions to acquire advanced manufacturing technology, *Accounting and Business Research*, **18** (70).

Greenley, G.E. (1989) *Strategic Management*, Prentice Hall.

Hundy, B.B. and Hamblin, D.J. (1988) Risk and assessment of investment in new technology, *International Journal of Production Research*, **26** (11).

Institution of Mechanical Engineers (1989) *Innovation, Investment and the Survival of the UK Economy*, London.

Kemper, R.E. (1989) *Experiencing Strategic Management*, Dryden Press.

Kenny, B., Lea, E., Sanderson, S. and Luffman, G. (1987) *Business Policy: An Analytical Introduction*, Blackwell.

McNamee, P.B. (1985) *Tools and Techniques for Strategic Management*, Pergamon.

Pike, R.H. (1989) Do sophisticated capital budgeting approaches improve investment decision making effectiveness? *Engineering Economist*, **34** (2), Winter.

Pike, R.H. and Neale, C.W. (1993) *Corporate Finance and Investment: Decisions and Strategies*, Prentice Hall.

Primrose, P.L. (1991) *Investment in Manufacturing Technology*, Chapman & Hall.

Scott Morton, M.S. (Ed) (1991) *The Corporation of the 1990s*, Oxford University Press.

Thompson, J.L. (1990) *Strategic Management: Awareness and Change*, Chapman & Hall.

Trade and Industry Select Committee (1994) *The Competitiveness of UK Manufacturing Industry, Second Report*, HMSO, April.

Wardlow, A. (1994) Investment appraisal criteria and the impact of low inflation. *Bank of England Quarterly Bulletin*, August.

Wilkes, F.M. (1993) The interest in interest: interest rates and investment appraisal. *Business Studies*, **6** (2), Dec.

1. A manufacturer has a choice between the two projects shown below. The alternatives represent investment in existing process technology (project A) and AMT (project B). Which of the projects would be selected on the basis of the following:
   (a) payback period;
   (b) yield over the full project;
   (c) finite-horizon method with a horizon of
      (i) five years:
      (ii) seven years and using a discount rate of 15%;
   (d) Net present value over the full project lifetimes using a discount rate of:
      (i) 15%
      (ii) 30%
      (iii) 5%

	Cash flow at time:										
	$t=0$	$t=1$	$t=2$	$t=3$	$t=4$	$t=5$	$t=6$	$t=7$	$t=8$	$t=9$	$t=10$
Project A	−10	6	4	3	2.5	2	1.5	1	0.5	0	0
Project B	−25	−20	5	7.5	10	12.5	15	17.5	20	22.5	25

What conclusions would you draw from the results of your calculations?

2. A project consistent with the strategic plan of a company has the following cash flow data:

	Time		
	$t=0$	$t=1$	$t=2$
Costs	15	10	5
Tangible returns	0	20	25
Net cash flow	−15	10	20

Suppose that the data for the tangible elements of return to the investment have been the subject of dispute. The discount rate is 15%.

(a) What percentage reduction in the tangible returns could be sustained without the project having to go to the justification analysis stage?

(b) Suppose that the company is confident that by year 2 the tangible benefits will be achieved in full, but that there are doubts that the full benefits will be achieved in year 2. What is the minimum proportion of year 1 benefit that must be achieved to avoid the justification analysis?

3. Three sets of estimates of cash flow data for a particular high technology project have been prepared on the basis of optimistic, pessimistic and most likely scenarios. A discount rate of 15% is appropriate. The estimates are as follows:

	Time		
	$t=0$	$t=1$	$t=2$
Pessimistic	−20	0	5
Most likely	−15	10	20
Optimistic	−10	20	35

(a) Find the net present values for the most likely scenario and the best and worst case situations.

(b) What is the NPV that would result from a 'learning curve' case in which the worst outcome was taken in year 0, the middling outcome for year 1 and the best outcome for year 2?

(c) Find the net present value that might result from a successful investment emulated by competitors by taking the most likely outlay initially, the optimistic return in year 1 (to reflect the success) and the pessimistic return in year 2 (following the entry of the competitor).

(d) If in each year the pessimistic and optimistic outcomes have a 30% probability of arising while the most likely outcome has a 40% chance of occurrence, find the expected NPV.

(e) (i) Given the probabilities of part (d) draw up a table showing the full range of possible present values.

(ii) Present the information in a risk profile diagram for the investment. In what other diagrammatic form could the NPV information be presented?

Introduction to risk and return

8.1 Introduction   235
8.2 Measurement of investor return
     and risk   236
8.3 Choosing between risky
     alternatives   241
8.4 Return and risk of combining
     investments   243

8.5 Summary and conclusions   247
8.6 Key terms   248
8.7 Revision questions   248
8.8 References   248
8.9 Further reading   249
8.10 Problems   249

This chapter provides an introduction to the concepts and techniques of risk and return which are the foundation necessary for a full understanding of Chapters 9 and 10. Distinction is made between market and non-market risk faced by investors and the significance of portfolio diversification in risk reduction is examined. Methods of calculating both *ex-ante* and *ex-post* security returns are explained as are measures of risk. The significance of covariance and correlation of returns between securities in risk reduction strategies is examined and the computation of expected return and standard deviation of small portfolios is illustrated.

8.1 Introduction

In Chapter 6 we examined a number of methods which sought to allow for risk in project appraisal. The reason that risk exists is that project decision-making is based on expectations about the future. The decision-maker makes forecasts of cash flows likely to arise from a particular course of action. These forecasts are based on what the decision-maker expects to happen given his present state of knowledge. However, in an uncertain world the actual cash flows are almost certain to differ from prior expectations. It is this uncertainty about an investment's actual income that gives rise to risk in business and investment activity generally.

A distinction is often made between the terms 'risk' and 'uncertainty'. Risk is defined as a situation where the parameters of the probability distribution of outcomes are known. For example, although we may not be certain of any given return on an investment in year t, we may know that the possible returns are normally distributed with mean r and variance σ^2. Uncertainty, however, is defined as the situation where various cash flow patterns are possible but probabilistic information is absent or at best incomplete. Although this distinction can be made, in practical decision-making the two terms tend to be used interchangeably.

Everyone would agree that where an investor takes on extra risk then this should be acknowledged and rewarded with extra return; however, before this can be done, risk needs to be defined and measured and agreement reached on what extra return should be given per unit of risk.

In Chapter 6 an intuitive approach was described involving the use of risk premiums where projects were classified according to level of risk with increasing rates of return being demanded as perceived risk increased. However, this approach is very arbitrary and subjective, and in this and the succeeding chapters we shall be seeking to develop a more rigorous and theoretically supportable approach to the rate of return which should be demanded from different types of business activity.

We begin by posing the question: who is it that ultimately bears the risk of projects undertaken by companies? The answer to this is surely the investors in companies. In the case of a company financed entirely by equity, risk will ultimately be borne by the providers of this equity, the ordinary shareholders in the company. This can be simply illustrated by Figure 8.1 where investment funds flow from ordinary shareholders to the company; these funds are then invested in real projects by the managers of the company; these projects in turn earn cash returns which will enable the payment of dividends to shareholders and to the extent that funds are retained will lead to an increase in the underlying value of the shares.

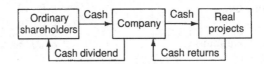

Figure 8.1 Flow of investment funds

This idea can perhaps be more readily appreciated in the context of a company undertaking a single project. In this case the company is merely a convenient device for collecting funds from a number of shareholders to invest in the project. The investors' fortunes are directly related to how well the project performs. If it is highly successful they will benefit accordingly, but if it should turn out to be a disaster they could lose all their investment. For example we could consider investors who have invested in Eurotunnel, the company formed to build and operate the Channel Tunnel. The company's share price performance is directly linked to the cost of building and maintaining the tunnel and net revenues anticipated from traffic using the tunnel. Euro Disney, the company which built and operates the Disney Theme Park just outside Paris, is another company whose future is linked to a single identifiable activity.

If we are to try and relate project risk to the risk investors perceive when investing in the equity of companies, we need to establish how such investors measure both the return and risk from an investment in equity shares. We do this in the next section.

8.2 Measurement of investor return and risk

Research in both the UK and the USA shows that investors in financial securities demand higher returns from risky investments in equities than from comparatively risk-free government securities [1]. This is not surprising and is what we would expect from risk-averse investors. In both countries the average extra return demanded for investing in equities has been between 8% and 9%. This average risk premium over the risk-free rate of interest might be an appropriate premium to demand for an investment having the same average risk as the equity market generally. Historically, then, investors on average have earned a substantial premium for investing in equities rather than government securities. However, this additional return has been accompanied by a higher volatility in earnings, as the average earnings calculation hides the fact that in some years there have been very high positive returns while in others there have also been high negative returns earned by holders of equity investments. Figure 8.2 shows the UK *ex-post* (historic) risk premium from 1919–92. This illustrates the point just made that the long run historic average incorporates both high positive and negative returns. Although it was suggested above that the historic risk premium might be used as a guide to current investor requirements, there are at least two problems associated with this. The first is to assume that returns realized are the same as those expected, and the second is to assume that long-run averages give an indication of what is currently required by investors in the market. Both these factors could bias required returns when historic risk premiums are used to calculate current requirements. We will return to this difficulty in Chapter 10 when we discuss in detail the use of asset pricing models in practical capital budgeting situations.

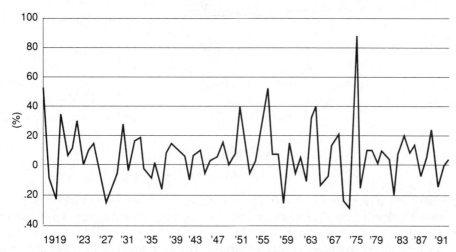

Figure 8.2 The ex-post equity risk premium 1919–92. Equity returns minus long-dated gilt returns

Source: Jenkinson, T. (1993) The cost of equity finance: conventional wisdom reconsidered, *Stock Exchange Quarterly with Quality of Markets Review*, Autumn.

Measurement of single-period return

It is usual to measure the periodic return from an investor's point of view by taking into consideration both dividends received from the share and any change in value over the period concerned. Thus return in period t_1 can be written as

$$R_1 = \frac{D_1 + V_1 - V_0}{V_0}$$

where R_1 is the return in period t_1. D_1 is the dividend(s) received in period, V_1 is the value of the share at end of period and V_0 is the value of the share at start of period. This could also be written as

$$R_1 = \frac{D_1}{V_0} + \frac{V_1 - V_0}{V_0}$$

return = dividend yield + capital gain in percentage terms

This return could be an expected (*ex ante*) return based on a subjective probability distribution drawn up by a financial analyst, or it could be measured historically (*ex post*) to assess the performance of the security concerned.

For example, suppose that a dividend of 10p per share was paid during period t_1 on a share whose value was 100p at the start of the period and 150p at the end:

$$R_1 = \frac{10 + 150 - 100}{100} = 0.60 \ (60\%)$$

or we could say

$$R_1 = \frac{10}{100} + \frac{150 - 100}{100}$$

$$= 0.10 + 0.50$$

$$= 0.60 \; (60\%)$$

i.e. the total return is made up of 10% dividend yield and 50% capital gain. Alternatively, suppose that the dividend paid on another share in t_1 was 5p and that the value was 50p at the start of the period and 40p at the end:

$$R_1 = \frac{5 + 40 - 50}{50}$$

$$= -0.10 \; (-10\%)$$

or

$$R_1 = \frac{5}{50} + \frac{40 - 50}{50}$$

$$= 0.10 - 0.20$$

$$= -0.10 \; (-10\%)$$

i.e. the total return is made up of a dividend yield of 10% less a capital loss of 20%.

Because the capital gain/loss element will often be a significant factor in determining the total return on an equity share there is scope for both high positive and high negative returns given the volatility of stock markets. Thus the crash of 1987 led to average capital losses of 30%, and in some cases losses were very much greater than this figure.

Therefore return is expressed in terms of total return bringing in both dividends and capital gains and losses. In the numerical examples above we have calculated return on the basis that dividend income and both beginning and end-of-period prices are known. This is how historic returns from the ownership of shares are calculated. Calculating estimated returns is a lot more difficult because we shall need to estimate both the dividend expected to be paid during the forthcoming period and also the end-of-period price. In practice, there are a number of different outcomes possible depending upon factors affecting both the individual security and markets generally. Thus the analyst will need to forecast both the range of dividend payments and range of share prices possible during the ensuing period and assign to each value a probability of its occurring.

The risk related to holding an equity share is usually expressed as a measure of the dispersion of expected returns. In the context of expected returns described above, it would be in the form of the variance of expected returns or the square root of the variance, i.e. the standard deviation.

Calculation of expected returns and standard deviation

As described above, if we are trying to estimate the expected returns from holding a security we are likely to consider the possible returns in alternate market conditions and try and assign a probability to each. For example, suppose that we own a share with a current market value of 100p and estimate future possible values and dividends as shown in Table 8.1. We can see that the total return will be 24% if the optimistic version of the market prevails, 12% if normal conditions prevail and 0% if the pessimistic outcome prevails. Before we can make real use of this information we need to estimate the likelihood of each of the different conditions occurring. We do this by using subjective probabilities, i.e. probabilities that are assigned to each possibility by the analyst. They are subjective because they depend upon the decision-maker's opinion rather than being based on a large number of observed similar outcomes which might be the case with objective probabilities. We shall see that in practice historic returns are often used to measure variability of share price returns. Measures of variability and other data relating to risk and return are readily available in various forms on a commercial basis (e.g. Datastream and the London Business School Risk Measurement Service referred to in Chapter 10).

Table 8.1

Possible market conditions	Conditional end-of-period selling price (p)	Conditional end-of-period dividends receivable (p)	Total end-of-period returns (p)
Optimistic	115	9	124
Normal	107	5	112
Pessimistic	97	3	100

Table 8.2

Market conditions	Probability	Return on investment (%)
Optimistic	0.25	24
Normal	0.50	12
Pessimistic	0.25	0

Let us suppose that the decision-maker assigns probabilities as shown in Table 8.2 to the possible returns. This is a simplified version of the probable outcomes and does not allow, for example, for outcomes other than the three stated and lying between the values given. The probabilities sum to unity and, for illustrative purposes, represent the only outcomes considered possible.

The expected return $\bar{R}$ is calculated by multiplying each outcome R_i by the probability P_i that it occurs and summing:

$$\text{expected return} = \bar{R} = \sum_{i=1}^{n} P_i R_i$$

In this case

$$\begin{aligned} R &= 0.25 \times 0.24 + 0.50 \times 0.12 + 0.25 \times 0 \\ &= 0.12\ (12\%) \end{aligned}$$

The expected return (mean) can be regarded as the average outcome or return; in addition we need a measure of how much the individual outcomes differ from the average, i.e. a measure of dispersion. This is usually measured by the variance, or the square root of the variance, i.e. the standard deviation:

$$\text{variance} = \sigma^2 = \sum_{i=1}^{n} P_i (R_i - \bar{R})^2$$

In this case

$$\sigma^2 = 0.25(24 - 12)^2 + 0.50(12 - 12)^2 + 0.25(0 - 12)^2$$

$$= 36 + 0 + 36$$

$$= 72$$

standard deviation $\sigma = (\sigma^2)^{1/2}$

In this case

$$\sigma = \sqrt{72} = 8.49$$

The numerical example used has symmetrical returns, i.e. they are evenly distributed around the most likely outcome. This is termed a normal distribution and is illustrated in Figure 8.3. Normal distributions can be described in terms of their expected return and variance (or standard deviation) alone. Other measures of dispersion could be used. For example, it is sometimes argued that only returns below average trouble investors as above average returns are considered desirable. A measure called the semi-variance which only considers return below the mean is sometimes used; it is calculated by summing the squared deviations below the mean multiplied by the probability of occurrence. In our example the only return below the mean is zero:

$$\text{semi-variance} = 0.25 \, (0 - 12)^2 + 0 + 0$$

$$= 36$$

Although the semi-variance may seem an appropriate measure of risk to adopt it is difficult to use in the context of portfolios, i.e. where more than one asset is held. Empirical evidence suggests that security returns are reasonably normally distributed; in such cases the semi-variance is proportional to the variance. (See the example above where the semi-variance is exactly half the variance.) Therefore we find that for both theoretical and practical purposes it is the variance or standard deviation which is used as the measure of dispersion (risk). The standard deviation has the advantage of being

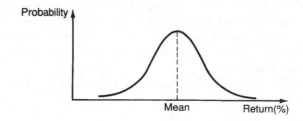

Figure 8.3 A normal distribution

expressed in the same units as the expected return, and it is usual to summarize the return/risk characteristics of a security in terms of its expected return and the standard deviation of the return.

If we assume that investors appraise securities on the basis of expected return and standard deviation of returns, and if we further assume that these investors are risk averse, then they will prefer high expected returns and low standard deviations. This point is emphasized in Figure 8.4 where two investments are shown which both have the same expected return of 10% but where investment B has a greater dispersion of possible returns. This makes investment B riskier than investment A and this greater dispersion or spread is reflected in the standard deviation of B which is 30% compared with that of A which is 15%. Given that the expected return of both the securities is the same, most investors would opt for A over B.

It should be clear from the foregoing discussion that, other things being equal, investors will prefer an investment giving the highest expected return for a given level

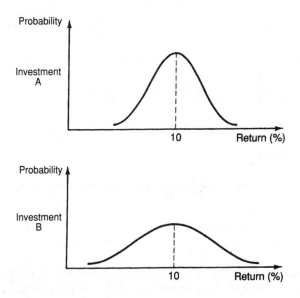

Figure 8.4 The investments have the same expected return but B is riskier

of risk or one that has the lowest risk for a given level of expected return. This is an important point which figures prominently in the discussion on portfolio theory. However, these only relate to specific instances where pairs of investments either have the same expected return or the same standard deviation. What is the position where investments have increasing levels of return accompanied by increasing levels of standard deviation? How do we choose between alternatives in this situation? This is the point discussed in the next section.

Let us suppose that investors agree on possible outcomes of securities and their related probabilities in different states of the world. The calculation of expected return and standard deviation of return becomes a question of mechanics and is agreed by all. However, making choices between alternative investments is subjective. Consider the five securities in Table 8.3.

8.3 Choosing between risky alternatives

Table 8.3

Security	Expected return $\bar{R}$	Standard deviation σ
A	0.05	0
B	0.10	0.08
C	0.22	0.25
D	0.10	0.18
E	0.15	0.25

Given these five securities, which should an investor choose? The available investments are plotted in Figure 8.5 with standard deviation on the horizontal scale and expected return on the vertical scale. We can see that securities D and E can be eliminated from the choice. D is eliminated because security B has the same return but a lower risk than D, while security C offers a higher return at the same risk as E. We are then left with a choice between securities A, B and C. Investors must thus choose

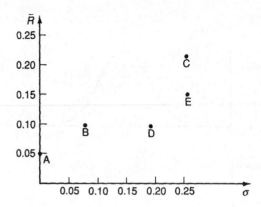

Figure 8.5 Plot of return and standard deviation

between securities A, B and C. This choice is entirely subjective and depends upon each individual's attitude to risk and the extra return that might be required for taking on extra exposure to risk. An investor who is very risk averse might opt for investment A. This has a zero standard deviation and might therefore be a risk-free government security. Securities B and C offer increasing returns for additional risk.

This process of subjective choice was discussed in Chapter 6 when the construction of a utility index to enable choices to be made between risky alternatives was examined. Adapting (6.38) we could say that

$$U = f(\bar{R}, \sigma)$$

i.e. expected utility is a function of expected return and standard deviation, and will be positively related to the former and negatively related to the latter. Utility functions for individuals can be represented by indifference curves, contours of U, with each curve showing combinations of $\bar{R}$ and σ yielding equal satisfaction. Figure 8.6 includes indifference curves imposed on the diagram showing the alternative risky investments. The maximum of utility is $U = U_3$ obtained from selection of security B. The other alternatives lie on even lower curves and would be relatively unattractive to the investor.

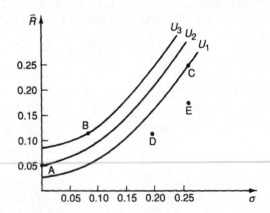

Figure 8.6 Indifference curves

As discussed in Chapter 6 it would be very difficult to construct a meaningful utility index. These problems make the model practically useless as a decision-making tool. It would be both difficult and time-consuming to attempt to derive an individual's utility function and it is questionable whether the resulting function would bear any resemblance to reality. This is because it would be necessary to derive a function by requiring a potential investor to state the certain amounts he would be prepared to accept as an alternative to a series of risky outcomes. It would be necessary to assume that the investor's attitude to risk would not change over time and that his attitude to hypothetical situations would be the same as his attitude to real risk with real money involved. However, the expected utility model does provide a representation of how investors are likely to view risk, and risk-averse investors are likely to have utility functions in the form of a quadratic equation. There will be a trade-off between risk and return, with higher expected return yielding higher utility and higher standard deviations reducing utility. What will differ between individuals, and therefore give rise to different risk preferences and different families of indifference curves, is the rate of trade-off between risk and return. In this analysis all investors are regarded as rational wealth-seeking risk averters, but the extra return required per unit of risk will vary between individuals depending on their own personal attitudes towards risk. Figure 8.7 shows three groups of indifference curves: group A illustrates a cautious risk averter who requires a lot of extra return per unit of risk, group C indicates a risk taker who is prepared to take on extra risk for less increase in return, and group B shows a 'middle of the road' investor somewhere between A and C.

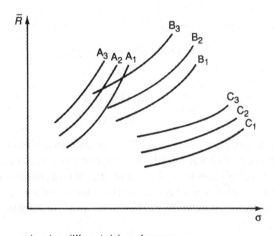

Figure 8.7 Indifference curves showing different risk preferences

In our discussion so far we have examined risk and return in the context of single investments. In the previous section we discussed how an investor might choose between alternative investments, given their measures of expected return and standard deviation. However, the investor has other alternatives as he may choose any combination of the available investments in addition to each investment individually. In this section we examine some of the implications of holding investments together as a preliminary to our fuller discussion on portfolio theory in the next chapter.

In considering risk/return characteristics of individual investments choice was based on expected return and standard deviation. When combining investments we shall once again be considering the expected return of the combination (or portfolio as it is usually called) and its standard deviation. Table 8.4 gives information about three investments: A, B and C. A might be considered more attractive than C as it has the same expected return as C but a lower standard deviation. However, if we compare the projected returns in alternative possible conditions we can see that A and B have their highest and lowest returns in the same conditions, while C gives high returns when A and B are giving low returns, and low returns when A and B are giving high returns. The important point being made here is that when combining investments together it is not sufficient to look at the standard deviations of the individual investments. We also need to look at how the returns of pairs of securities vary with one another. The expected return on a portfolio of two securities is the value-weighted average of their expected returns. In the general case, if a proportion X was invested in security A and the balance of wealth $1 - X$ in security B, the expected portfolio return would be

$$\bar{R}_p = X\bar{R}_A + (1 - X)\bar{R}_B$$

If 0.5 (50%) of wealth was invested in A and $1 - 0.5$ (50%) in B, then

$$\bar{R}_p = 0.5 \times 12 + 0.5 \times 14$$

$$= 13\%$$

However, when we calculate portfolio variance we need to consider not only the individual variances of the investments but also the way in which their returns vary as measured by the covariance. The covariance term for investments A and B is given by

$$\begin{aligned}
\text{cov}(R_A, R_B) &= \Sigma P_R(R_A - \bar{R}_A)(R_B - \bar{R}_B) \\
&= 0.25(24 - 12)(28 - 14) \\
&\quad + 0.50(12 - 12)(12 - 14) \\
&\quad + 0.25(0 - 12)(4 - 14) \\
&= 42 + 0 + 30 \\
&= 72
\end{aligned}$$

The covariance can also be written as

$$\text{cov}(R_A, R_B) = \rho_{AB}\sigma_A\sigma_B$$

It follows that

$$\rho_{AB} = \frac{\text{cov}(R_A, R_B)}{\sigma_A\sigma_B}$$

The term ρ_{AB} is called the correlation coefficient and measures the extent to which the returns of pairs of securities vary with one another. It can take on values between +1 and −1; a correlation coefficient of +1 indicates that the investments move up and down together in perfect positive correlation, while a value of −1 would indicate countermovement of equal and opposite proportions, i.e. perfect negative correlation.

Table 8.4

Market condition		Probability	Return on investments (%) A	B	C
Optimistic		0.25	24	28	4
Normal		0.50	12	12	8
Pessimistic		0.25	0	4	28
	Expected return	$\bar{R}$	12	14	12
	Variance	V	72	76	88
	Standard deviation	σ	8.49	8.72	9.38

In this case the correlation coefficient would be

$$\rho_{AB} = \frac{\text{cov}(R_A, R_B)}{\sigma_A\sigma_B}$$

$$= \frac{72}{8.49 \times 8.72}$$

$$= 0.97$$

Investments A and B therefore have high positive correlation and the scope for risk reduction is limited. Remembering that we have X invested in A and $1 - X$ invested in B, the variance of this two-security portfolio is given by

$$V_p = X^2V_A + (1 - X)^2V_B + 2X(1 - X) \operatorname{cov}(R_A, R_B)$$

or, using the standard deviation symbols

$$\sigma_p^2 = X^2\sigma_A^2 + (1 - X)^2\sigma_B^2 + 2X(1 - X) \operatorname{cov}(R_A, R_B)$$

and substituting $\operatorname{cov}(R_A, R_B) = \rho_{AB}\sigma_A\sigma_B$, we obtain

$$\sigma_p^2 = X^2\sigma_A^2 + (1 - X)^2\sigma_B^2 + 2X(1 - X) \rho_{AB}\sigma_A\sigma_B$$

The first two terms in the equation are the individual variances weighted by the square of the proportion invested in each. The third term is more interesting as it considers the way in which the returns of each pair of securities vary with one another. The term is always twice the product of the proportions invested in each as it considers the covariance of A with B and of B with A. These are always the same, of course.

If we now calculate the variance of our portfolio of A and B we obtain

$$\sigma_p^2 = (0.5)^2 \times (8.49)^2 + (0.5)^2 \times (8.72)^2 + (2 \times 0.5 \times 0.5 \times 72)$$

$$= 73\%$$

$$\sigma_p = \sqrt{73} = 8.54\%$$

The standard deviation of the portfolio, 8.54, is very close to the weighted average of the standard deviations of A and B; this is because the returns are closely related as evidenced by the correlation coefficient of 0.97. Let us now examine what happens when we hold B and C in equal amounts. First of all the expected return is as before:

$$\bar{R}_p = X\bar{R}_B + (1 - X)\bar{R}_C$$

$$= 0.5 \times 14 + 0.5 \times 12$$

$$= 13\%$$

However, we shall find that the covariance and hence the correlation coefficient are both much lower:

$$\operatorname{cov}(R_B, R_C) = 0.25(28 - 14)(4 - 12)$$
$$+ 0.50(12 - 14)(8 - 12)$$
$$+ 0.25(4 - 14)(28 - 12)$$

$$= -28 + 4 - 40$$

$$= -64\%$$

(covariances can be negative as well as positive). We can also calculate the correlation coefficient between B and C:

$$\rho_{BC} = \frac{-64}{8.27 \times 9.38}$$

$$= -0.82$$

B and C have a high negative correlation and the resulting variance of the portfolio reflects this:

$$\sigma_p^2 = (0.5)^2 \times (8.72)^2 + (0.5)^2$$
$$\times (9.38)^2 + (2 \times 0.5 \times 0.5 \times -64)$$

$$= 9\%$$

$$\sigma_p = 3\%$$

When we combine investments B and C together in equal amounts the standard deviation of the portfolio is only 3%; thus while the expected returns of portfolios of A and B and B and C are the same (13%) the risk of a portfolio of B and C is only about one-third of the risk of a portfolio of A and B. This is due to the high negative correlation between the returns of B and C, whereas the returns of A and B have high positive correlation.

In our example we considered only two security portfolios, but the principles remain the same when larger portfolios are considered. As portfolios increase in size so the opportunity for risk reduction also increases. The formulae for N investment portfolios are as follows:

$$\bar{R}_p = \sum_{i=1}^{N} X_i \bar{R}_i$$

$$\sigma_p^2 = \sum_{i=1}^{N} X_i^2 \sigma_i^2 + \sum_{i=1, j \neq i}^{N} \sum_{j=1}^{N} X_i X_j \text{cov}(R_i, R_j)$$

where X_i is the proportion of wealth invested in investment i.

The first term in the variance formula is the sum of the individual investment variances multiplied by the square of the amount invested in each. The second term is the covariance term. Each covariance term is multiplied by twice the product invested in each investment. Although a 2 does not appear in the equation the double summation brings in the covariance between securities 1 and 2 and 2 and 1 which of course are the same. For example with a three-security portfolio the double-summation term would be

$$\sum_{\substack{i=1 \\ j \neq i}}^{3} \sum_{j=1}^{3} X_i X_j \text{cov}(R_i, R_j) = X_1 X_2 \text{cov}(R_1 R_2) + X_1 X_3 \text{cov}(R_1, R_3) + X_2 X_3 \text{cov}(R_2, R_3)$$
$$+ X_2 X_1 \text{cov}(R_2, R_1) + X_3 X_1 \text{cov}(R_3, R_1) + X_3 X_2 \text{cov}(R_3, R_2)$$

As $\text{cov}(R_1, R_2)$ is the same as $\text{cov}(R_2, R_1)$ and so on,

$$\sum_{\substack{i=1 \\ j \neq i}}^{3} \sum_{j=1}^{3} X_i X_j \text{cov}(R_i, R_j) = 2X_1 X_2 \text{cov}(R_1 R_2) + 2X_1 X_3 \text{cov}(R_1, R_3) + 2X_2 X_3 \text{cov}(R_2, R_3)$$

Implications of very large portfolios

Let us consider a case where equal amounts are invested in a large portfolio. Then

$$\sigma_p^2 = \sum_{i=1}^{N} \left(\frac{1}{N}\right)^2 \sigma_i^2 + \sum_{\substack{i=1 \\ j \neq i}}^{N} \sum_{j=1}^{N} \frac{1}{N} \frac{1}{N} \text{cov}(R_i, R_j)$$

First of all suppose that investments are independent and therefore all the covariance terms are zero. In this case the value of the second term in the above equation is zero and

$$\sigma_p^2 = \sum_{i=1}^{N} \left(\frac{1}{N}\right)^2 \sigma_i^2 = \frac{1}{N} \bar{\sigma}_j^2 ,$$

where $\bar{\sigma}_i^2$ is the average variance of the investments. As N becomes larger the variance of the portfolio becomes smaller and with a very large portfolio approaches zero.

Therefore with a very large portfolio of independent investments we could have zero variance. However, we find that in most markets investments have some positive correlation and the covariance term is positive. If we now reconsider the variance calculation including the second term we begin with

$$\sigma_p^2 = \sum_{i=1}^{N} \left(\frac{1}{N}\right)^2 \sigma_i^2 + \sum_{\substack{i=1 \\ j \neq i}}^{N} \sum_{j=1}^{N} \frac{1}{N} \frac{1}{N} \text{cov}(R_i, R_j) = \frac{1}{N} \bar{\sigma}_i^2 + \frac{N-1}{N} \sum_{\substack{i=1 \\ j \neq i}}^{N} \sum_{j=1}^{N} \frac{\text{cov}(R_i, R_j)}{N(N-1)}$$

We have previously seen that the first term is the average variance; the final term is also an average. There are N values of i and $N-1$ values of j; remember that there is one less value of j since it cannot equal i. The final term is therefore the sum of the covariances divided by the number of covariances; it is the average covariance. Rewriting, we have

$$\sigma_P^2 = \frac{1}{N}\,\overline{\sigma}_j^2 + \frac{N-1}{N}\,\overline{\text{cov}}(R_i, R_j)$$

We have previously stated that as N becomes very large the first term tends towards zero while the second term will approach the average covariance. We can see that in a large portfolio the individual risk of investments can be diversified away, but the risk contributed by the covariance terms will remain.

As we have seen, the covariance term reflects the way in which investment returns move together. Most securities will tend to move in the same direction to a greater or lesser degree because of common macroeconomic factors affecting all securities; however, the individual risk of securities can be diversified away by holding a sufficiently large portfolio.

Figure 8.8 illustrates the risk reduction from holding a portfolio of UK securities. The vertical axis measures the risk of the portfolio as a percentage of the risk of an individual security, while the horizontal axis shows the number of securities in the portfolio. We can see that risk can be substantially reduced by holding a comparatively small portfolio of between 10 and 15 securities. However, the diagram shows that the marginal benefit decreases as more securities are added and that there seems to be a limit to the benefits of diversification. This is because, although unique risk relating to individual securities can be diversified away, the risk relating to the common association between securities, which is often called market or systematic risk, remains.

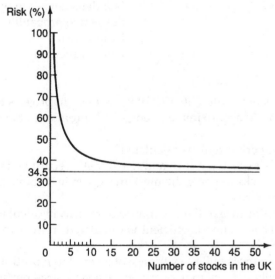

Figure 8.8 Portfolio risk reduction

Investors require extra return for taking on higher levels of perceived risk. In the case of equity investors in companies risk will be related to the business activities being undertaken by the company. Research supports this view as average returns on risky (equity) investments have exceeded returns on risk-free (government) securities by between 8% and 9%.

Investors measure their expected return on the basis of both expected dividend and capital gain/loss. Dividends tend to be more predictable than changes in share prices, and therefore the risk of equity investment is related to the volatility of share prices. This volatility is expressed as a measure of variance or standard deviation of returns. It can be calculated on the basis of a distribution of *ex ante* expected returns or, as is more usual, from historic returns.

8.5 Summary and conclusions

Investors will therefore select investments on the basis of expected return and standard deviation of returns. Where one investment dominates by either having a higher return for a given risk (standard deviation) than any other or a lower risk for a given level of return choice will be easy. However, where securities have increasing levels of risk as return increases the choice is not so obvious. Utility theory could be used to derive individual risk functions but there are serious doubts on the practical use of this theory.

When securities are held in combination, while expected return is simply the weighted average of the expected returns of the two or more securities involved, the standard deviation depends crucially on the covariance or correlation between each pair of securities. By holding securities together it is possible to reduce risk, and this reduction is greater the lower the correlation between securities. When very large portfolios are held it is found that risk unique to individual securities can be eliminated and that the only risk that remains is the covariance risk relating to securities' common association with each other. The ideas that have been introduced in this chapter are very important for an understanding of portfolio theory and the capital asset pricing model which we examine in the next chapter.

8.6 Key terms

Correlation coefficient
Covariance of returns
Expected return and standard deviation
  of large portfolios
Expected returns
Indifference curves
Market risk
Portfolio expected return

Portfolio variance and standard deviation
Risk and uncertainty
Semi-variance
Single-period return
Standard deviation of expected returns
Subjective probabilities
Unique risk
Utility functions

8.7 Revision questions

1. Explain who bears the ultimate risk of investment in projects by companies.
2. What has been the approximate average risk premium obtained for investing in equities?
3. How are single-period returns calculated?
4. Explain how the expected return and risk of risky securities are usually calculated.
5. State any drawbacks to using the measures given in 4 above and suggest an alternative measure of risk.
6. Explain the significance of the covariance of returns in calculating portfolio risk.
7. Show how the correlation coefficient is calculated from covariance and standard deviation terms.
8. In what circumstances will the variance of a very large portfolio diminish to zero?
9. What will usually happen to the variance of a very large portfolio?
10. Can all risk be eliminated if a sufficiently large portfolio is held?

8.8 References

1. Dimson, E. and Brealey, R.A. (1978) The risk premium on UK equities, *Investment Analyst* (52), 14–18, December.
   Allen, D., Day, R., Hirst, I. and Kwiatkowski, J. (1986) Equity, gilts, treasury bills and inflation. *Investment Analyst* (83), 11–18, October.
   Ibbotson, R.G. and Sinquefield, R.A. (1992) *Stocks, Bonds, Bills and Inflation*, Ibbotson Associates, Chicago, IL. (Updated annually.)
2. Solnik, B. (1975) The advantages of domestic and international diversification, in *International Capital Markets* (eds E.J. Elton and M.J. Gruber), North-Holland, Amsterdam.

Brealey, R. (1983) *An Introduction to Risk and Return*, 2nd edn, Blackwell, Oxford.
Elton, E.J. and Gruber, M.J. (1991) *Modern Portfolio Theory and Investment Analysis*, 4th edn, Wiley, (an introduction to risk and return is given in the early chapters).

8.9 Further reading

8.10 Problems

1. A share had a price of 250p at the start of the year, paid a dividend of 12p during the year and had a price of 235p at the end of the year. What is the percentage return on the share for the year?

2. Probus shares currently sell for 520p per share. You intend to buy the shares today and hold for two years. During those two years, you expect to receive dividends at the year-ends that total 55p per share. Finally, you expect to sell the Probus shares for 548p per share. What is your expected holding-period return on Probus shares?

3. The probability that the economy will experience moderate growth next year is 0.4. The probability of a recession is 0.3, and the probability of a rapid expansion is also 0.3. If the economy falls into a recession, you can expect to receive a return on your portfolio of 2%. With moderate growth your return will be 5%. If there is a rapid expansion, your portfolio will return 10%.
   (a) What is your expected return?
   (b) What is the standard deviation of that return?

4. Suppose the expected returns and variances of shares A and B are

$$\bar{R}_A = 0.2, \bar{R}_B = 0.3, \sigma_A^2 = 0.1, \text{ and } \sigma_B^2 = 0.2, \text{ respectively.}$$

   (a) Calculate the expected return and variance of a portfolio that is composed of 60% A and 40% B when the correlation coefficient between the stocks is –0.5.
   (b) Calculate the expected return and variance of a portfolio that is composed of 60% A and 40% B when the correlation coefficient between the shares is –0.6.
   (c) How does the correlation coefficient affect the variance of the portfolio?

5. Shown below are the possible rates of return that you might obtain over the next year from investing in shares V and Z.

State of economy	Probability of state occurring	Share V return if state occurs	Share Z return if state occurs
Recession	0.3	–10%	10%
Normal	0.4	20%	10%
Boom	0.3	50%	10%

   (a) Determine the expected return, variance and standard deviation for share V.
   (b) Determine the expected return, variance and standard deviation for share Z.
   (c) Determine the covariance and correlation between the returns of share V and share Z.
   (d) Determine the expected return and standard deviation of an equally weighted portfolio of share V and share Z.

6. If a portfolio has a positive weight for each asset, can the expected return on the portfolio be greater than the return on the asset in the portfolio that has the highest return? Can the expected return on the portfolio be less than the return on the asset in the portfolio with the lowest return? Explain.

7. You are faced with a choice of shares from among the three detailed below:

Market condition	Probability	Return Share A	Share B	Share C
Optimistic	0.25	16	4	20
Normal	0.50	12	6	14
Pessimistic	0.25	8	8	8

(a) Calculate the expected return and standard deviation for each share.

(b) Calculate the correlation coefficient and covariance between each pair of investments.

(c) Calculate the expected return and standard deviation of the two- and three-share portfolios formed by combining together equal proportions of the shares (i.e. two-security portfolios, half and half; three-security portfolio, one-third, one-third and one-third).

8. Is the variance of a well-diversified portfolio determined by the variance of the individual securities? Explain and discuss.

9. Standard deviation as a measure of risk pays as much attention to upside risk as to downside risk. As investors are more concerned with downside risk and the likelihood of losing their money it follows that standard deviation is not a satisfactory measure of risk. Explain and discuss.

10. The following information relates to the actual price at the end of each month and dividends paid during month of two securities over the past seven months.

Month	Security D Price (p)	Security D Dividend (p)	Security E Price (p)	Security E Dividend (p)
1	123		57	
2	119	1p	62	
3	121		70	1p
4	123		72	
5	125		81	
6	126	3p	86	
7	126		92	

(a) Calculate the rate of return for both securities for each month.

(b) Calculate the average rate of return for both securities and the standard deviation of returns.

(c) Calculate the correlation coefficient between the two securities.

(d) Calculate the average return and standard deviation of an equally weighted portfolio of D and E.

Portfolio theory and capital asset pricing model

9.1 Introduction   251
9.2 Analysis of a two-asset portfolio   252
9.3 Extension to a multi-asset portfolio   256
9.4 Risk-free asset combined with
     risky securities   258
9.5 Capital asset pricing model   261
9.6 Implications of the capital asset
     pricing model   264

9.7 Summary and conclusions   265
9.8 Key terms   265
9.9 Revision questions   265
9.10 References   266
9.11 Further reading   266
9.12 Problems   266
9.13 Appendix: The capital asset
     pricing model   268

Chapter 8 introduced the idea that it is possible to lower risk by holding a number of different securities: a portfolio. This chapter shows how to calculate and manipulate data relating to two- and three-security portfolios and examines the scope of portfolio theory. The implications of introducing a risk-free asset into the analysis is explained and leads into an examination of the capital asset pric- ing model (CAPM). A distinction is drawn between risk as measured in the context of portfolio theory and under the CAPM framework. In particular the capital market line is distinguished from the security market line; the significance of CAPM in risk evaluation is discussed and provides a link to its application in Chapter 10.

9.1 Introduction

In Chapter 8 we saw that the risk return characteristics of financial securities could be expressed in terms of a security's expected return and the variance or standard deviation thereof. Investors would prefer those securities offering higher return and lower standard deviation when faced with a choice between single investments. It was also observed that when two securities were held together, while the expected return of the resulting combination was merely the value-weighted average of the expected returns of each individual security, the risk of the combination as measured by the standard deviation could be less than a simple weighted average if the expected returns on the securities were less than perfectly correlated. In this chapter we continue to develop these ideas with a view to determining how rational risk-averse investors would manage their affairs given these opportunities to reduce the risk of their overall investment holding below the simple average of the risk of the individual investments.

The term 'portfolio' is applied to a situation where an investor invests in two or more different assets. Investors in financial securities will usually, therefore, hold a portfolio of stocks and shares, while a large divisionalized company might hold a portfolio of business assets. In our development of portfolio theory we shall be concentrating on investment in financial securities. The basis of portfolio theory was first developed by Markowitz [1] as long ago as 1952. The basis of the theory accords with intuitive thinking that it is less risky to invest money in a number of securities than a single security; bearing in mind that investment is undertaken on the basis of expectations about the future, it is hoped that unexpected bad news concerning one company will be compensated by unexpected good news about another. Markowitz formalized the analysis and provided the tools for identifying efficient portfolios which, as we shall see, are those offering the highest return for a given level of risk or the lowest risk for a given level of return. We shall use some simple mathematics in illustrating the theory and in addition will support our discussion with diagrams which are often easier to understand. Most of the analysis will be undertaken using the simplest portfolio possible, a two-asset portfolio, but the conclusions are capable of extension to multi-asset portfolios and appropriate formulae will be given. We assume that investors are rational wealth-seeking risk-averters with utility functions as illustrated in Fig. 8.7, and further that the choice between individual investments and portfolios is based on the expected return and the standard deviation of expected returns.

9.2 Analysis of a two-asset portfolio

Let us suppose that we are faced with the opportunity of investing in two securities which we shall call security A and security B. The risk return characteristics of these securities are summarized as follows.

Security	Expected return $\bar{R}$	Standard deviation σ
A	0.10	0.08
B	0.22	0.20

Clearly an investor could put all his money in either security A or security B. But is it possible to improve his position by investing partly in A and partly in B?

Let us suppose that the investor invests a proportion X in security A and the balance of his wealth, i.e. $1 - X$, in security B. The expected return from the resulting portfolio will be

$$\bar{R}_P = X\bar{R}_A + (1 - X)\bar{R}_B$$

Since

$$\bar{R}_A = 0.10 \text{ and } \bar{R}_B = 0.22, \bar{R}_P = 0.22 - 0.12X$$

This simple equation shows that the expected return of a portfolio is solely related to the proportion of wealth invested in each constituent security. The highest expected return from the portfolio could be achieved by investing everything in security B, i.e. $X = 0$, while the lowest return could be obtained by investing everything in security A, i.e. $X = 1$. Between these ranges the expected return changes linearly and is purely dependent upon the amount invested in each security.

We saw in Chapter 8 how the risk of a combination of securities is dependent upon the relationship between the expected returns of the two securities. The formula for the variance σ^2 of a two-security portfolio is given by the following formula:

$$\sigma_P^2 = X^2\sigma_A^2 + (1 - X)^2\sigma_B^2 + 2X(1 - X)\,\text{cov}(R_A, R_B)$$

The covariance term $\text{cov}(R_A, R_B)$ was introduced in the previous chapter and is a measure of the way in which the returns of the two securities vary with one another. A high positive covariance would indicate a positive relationship, while a negative covariance would indicate the reverse. The covariance term can be broken down into its contributory components as follows:

$$\text{cov}(R_A, R_B) = \rho_{AB}\sigma_A\sigma_B$$

The correlation coefficient is a measure of the strength of the relationship between the two distributions of expected returns. The correlation coefficient can take on values between +1 and –1. A value of +1 indicates perfect positive correlation with the returns of the two securities moving with the same proportion and in the same direction for all possible values. A value of –1 indicates perfect negative correlation with movement in one security being mirrored by an equal and opposite movement by the other security. Between these two extremes (+1 and –1) the value of the correlation coefficient will indicate the relationship between the two sets of returns. A value of zero for the correlation coefficient would indicate that there was no relationship between the distribution of returns.

Our next step will be to examine the effect on portfolio risk of different values of the correlation coefficient. We shall begin by examining the two extremes, and first of all we shall consider the effect on portfolio risk where $\rho_{AB} = +1$ (i.e. perfect positive correlation). If we substitute $\rho_{AB} = +1$ into the variance equation it becomes

$$\sigma_p^2 = X^2\sigma_A^2 + (1 - X)^2\sigma_B^2 + 2X(1 - X)\sigma_A\sigma_B$$

This is a perfect square, and if the square root is taken it gives us the formula for the standard deviation of the portfolio:

$$\sigma_p = X\sigma_A + (1 - X)\sigma_B$$

If we substitute the values for σ_A and σ_B given earlier into the above equation we obtain

$$\sigma_p = 0.2 - 0.12X$$

This is a linear equation similar to the one obtained for the expected return on the portfolio, and it says that the risk of the portfolio is a linear function depending upon the proportion invested in each security. Figure 9.1 illustrates the portfolios of combining together securities A and B in different proportions where the correlation coefficient between the two securities is +1. It will be observed that these combinations lie on a straight line between A and B and that there is a linear relationship between expected return and standard deviation.

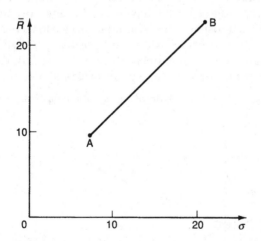

Figure 9.1 *Perfect positive correlation*

We now examine the situation where there is perfect negative correlation between the two securities, i.e. where $\rho_{AB} = -1$. We shall see that in this situation maximum gains can be obtained from diversification. While the calculation of the expected return on the portfolio remains unchanged, if we substitute $\rho_{AB} = -1$ in the basic equation, the calculation of the variance and standard deviation is as follows:

$$\sigma_P^2 = X^2\sigma_A^2 + (1 - X)^2\sigma_B^2 - 2X(1 - X)\sigma_A\sigma_B$$

We find that after substituting for $\rho_{AB} = -1$ we have a perfect square, and if the square root is taken as before we find the standard deviation:

$$\sigma_p = \pm \, [X\sigma_A - (1 - X\sigma_B)]$$

If we substitute the values for σ_A and σ_B given above in the equation we have

$$\sigma_p = 0.28X - 0.2$$

It might appear at first sight that we could obtain a portfolio with 'negative risk', for example if we put X equal to zero. However, variance and standard deviation can never be less than zero and we can observe that the solution for the standard deviation shown above has both positive and negative values. With perfect negative correlation, though, it is possible for our two-security portfolio to have a standard deviation of zero, i.e. to be a fully hedged portfolio. This can be illustrated using the values given for the standard deviation of the two securities comprising our two-security portfolio.

We saw above that the standard deviation of the two-security portfolio with perfect negative correlation could be expressed as

$$\sigma_p = 0.28X - 0.2$$

If we set $\sigma_p = 0$ and solve for X, we can find the proportions we would have to invest in the two securities to obtain a fully hedged portfolio. Setting $\sigma_p = 0$ we have

$$0.28X - 0.2 = 0$$

$$X = 0.715$$

To obtain a fully hedged portfolio we should therefore invest 71.5% of our wealth in security A and 28.5%, i.e. $1 - X$, in security B.

Figure 9.2 illustrates the resulting combinations where two securities are perfectly negatively correlated. The lines AD and BD contain all combinations of security A with security B. At point D we have the zero-risk portfolio, the proportions of which we have just calculated.

Figure 9.3 combines the findings of Figs 9.1 and 9.2. The resulting triangle ADB gives the limits of diversification for all possible levels of correlation between the two securities. Because securities tend to be positively linked in some way through their relationship with the market it is unusual for individual securities to have a negative correlation with other securities. Most securities will have a positive correlation with other securities, lying between 0 and +1. Let us suppose that our two securities have a positive correlation of 0.5; then substituting this value in the basic equation for variance gives

$$\sigma_p^2 = 0.0304X^2 - 0.064X + 0.04$$

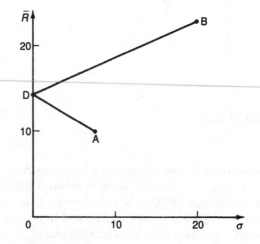

Figure 9.2 *Perfect negative correlation*

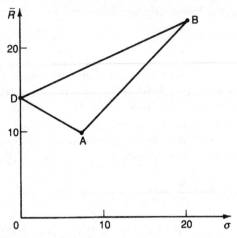

Figure 9.3 *Limits of diversification*

If we formed a portfolio consisting of half our wealth invested in security A and half in security B, then the standard deviation of this portfolio would be

$$\sigma_p = [0.0304(0.5)^2 - 0.064 \times (0.5) + 0.04]^{1/2}$$

Solving we have

$$\sigma_p = 0.125 \ (12.5\%)$$

This figure can be compared with the standard deviation of a similar portfolio where there was perfect positive correlation. In this case the standard deviation would merely be a weighted average of the standard deviations of the constituent securities. In the case of securities A and B a portfolio with half invested in each would have a standard deviation of

$$\sigma_p = 0.5 \times 0.08 + 0.5 \times 0.20$$

$$= 0.14 \ (14\%)$$

We can thus see that as correlation decreases so the scope for risk reduction by diversification increases. Figure 9.4 illustrates the risk–return combinations of investing in two securities with a positive correlation of 0.5. This type of curve, represented by a quadratic function will be the usual case when combining individual securities. We can

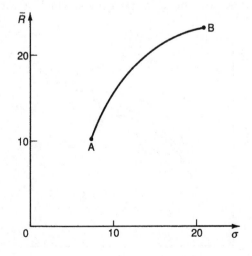

Figure 9.4 *Correlation of +0.5*

therefore conclude that the lower the correlation the greater are the benefits of diversification.

9.3 Extension to a multi-asset portfolio

We have thus far limited ourselves to a two-asset portfolio so that the limits and benefits of diversification could be clearly identified. However, portfolios will normally consist of a larger number of securities, and in fact the benefits of diversification are likely to increase as the size of the portfolio increases.

As stated in the previous chapter, in the general case with N securities rather than two the equations for risk and return become:

$$\overline{R}_p = \sum_{i=1}^{N} X_i \overline{R}_i$$

$$\sigma_P^2 = \sum_{i=1}^{N} X_i^2 \sigma_i^2 + \sum_{i=1}^{N} \sum_{\substack{i=1 \\ j \neq i}}^{N} X_i X_j \, \mathrm{cov}(R_i, R_j)$$

The expected return is merely the weighted average of the returns of the securities comprising the portfolio. The variance of the portfolio consists of two summations. The first is straightforward enough as it is the sum of the square of the proportion invested in each security multiplied by the security variance. The more important of the two summation terms is the second, the covariance summation. In a portfolio consisting of a large number of securities, the variances of returns on individual securities are relatively unimportant contributors to the variance of return on the portfolio as a whole. This point is fully discussed in Chapter 8. The important factor is how the returns on securities vary together. There are just N terms in the variance summation but $N(N-1)$ in the covariance summation. Note that if one more possible security was to be added to a portfolio, then this would add one term to the variance summation but $2N$ further terms would have to be included in the covariance summation. This is because in calculating the portfolio variance we have to consider the relationship between each security and every other security. Figure 9.5 shows the position where four securities are considered. Lines indicating the two-security portfolios have been drawn. The top line joining A and C indicates the four-security portfolio and can be seen to contain the most desirable portfolios, i.e. those offering the highest return for a given level of risk or having the lowest risk for a given level of return. If we then consider Fig. 9.6, this seeks to represent all the portfolios resulting from considering the whole population of securities relating to a particular market. Once again the most desirable portfolios have been emphasized, and these comprise those lying between A and B. Markowitz called them efficient portfolios. These are the only portfolios which a rational person should

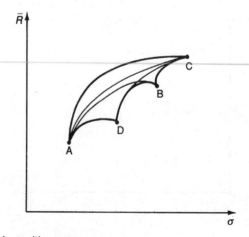

Figure 9.5 *Combining 4 securities*

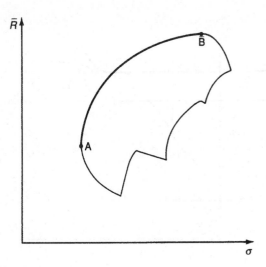

Figure 9.6 *All possible portfolios*

consider investing in as they contain the highest return for a given level of risk or the lowest risk for a given level of return. However, it would not be possible to say which portfolio any individual investor would prefer as this would depend solely on his attitude to risk and return as represented by his utility function. This utility function, as discussed earlier in Chapter 8, could be represented by a set of indifference curves as illustrated in Fig. 9.7 with the individual trying to establish himself on the highest indifference curve possible.

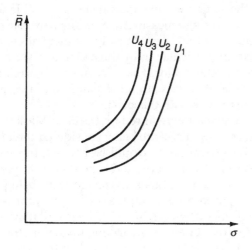

Figure 9.7 *Indifference curves*

Figure 9.8 shows the efficient set of portfolios as illustrated and described earlier with indifference curves relating to two different investors X and Y. Investor X is comparatively risk averse and therefore locates himself at a position on the efficient frontier giving him a lower return and a lower risk than investor Y who clearly is prepared to take on extra risk in order to obtain a higher return. The tangency points of the indifference curve on the efficient frontier indicate the personal optimum portfolio for each individual investor.

An extension to the multi-asset portfolio therefore enables us to identify efficient portfolios, but it is not possible to say that any of the efficient portfolios resulting is any

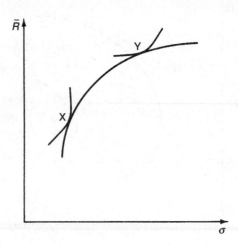

Figure 9.8 *Efficient portfolios with two optimum portfolios*

better than any other efficient portfolio. However, all investors should be choosing from the set of efficient portfolios and it would be useful if this set could be identified.

The practical use of portfolio theory is hampered by the input data required. In order to carry out the necessary calculations we need to compute the expected returns on each share over the next period, the estimate of risk as represented by standard deviation of expected return on each security and the covariance or correlation of returns between each pair of individual securities.

One of the main tasks of security analysts is to estimate the future performance of shares monitored. At the same time the analyst should be able to estimate the uncertainty of the return. However, the measurement of the pairwise covariance or correlation presents a different sort of problem. Most investment advisory firms tend to have analysts who specialize in particular industries. One analyst might specialize in oil shares, and another in the retail sector. The calculation of correlations requires an estimate of how oil shares might move with retail shares and it would be difficult for the organizational structure to cope with this problem.

The sheer volume of information required for the basic Markowitz model can also be a severe disadvantage. If N securities are being considered then N expected returns, N variances and $N(N-1)/2$ covariances would be needed. In total, then $(N/2)(N-3)$ items of data are necessary. Ball and Brown [2] cited the example that if all the 1300 or so stocks traded on the New York Stock Exchange were being considered, then the number of estimates required as data inputs would be approximately 850 000. This would be quite impracticable. Therefore it would be useful if investor optimum portfolios could be identified without necessarily having to identify the efficient set of portfolios first and then find the optimum portfolio based on the individual investor's utility function. In the next section we examine the effect on portfolio selection of introducing the opportunity to invest in a risk-free asset in addition to risky securities.

9.4 Risk-free asset combined with risky securities

We continue our analysis by considering two alternative options which may be open to the investor: investing in a riskless asset (lending) and borrowing to finance investment.

Figure 9.9 illustrates the position where investments in three portfolios A, M and B all located on the efficient frontier are combined with risk-free investment and borrowing. We can see that all investors would wish to locate themselves on the line R_fMX as this line dominates all other investment opportunities and offers the highest return for a given level of risk or the lowest risk for a given level of return. Portfolios lying on the line joining R_f and M are partly invested in the portfolio of risky assets located at point

M and partly in the risk-free asset. Clearly at R_f everything is invested in the risk-free asset and at M everything in the risky portfolio. Beyond M to X the portfolio is geared, and consists of borrowing at the risk-free rate and investing the amount borrowed plus the investor's initial wealth all in the portfolio of risky assets at M. The line R_fMX is termed the capital market line (CML) as it represents the market equilibrium trade-off between risk and return. Under this scenario there is now only one portfolio of risky assets which would be of interest to all investors irrespective of their personal attitude to risk: this is the portfolio at M. This would be the portfolio of risky assets held by all investors in equilibrium and by definition is the market portfolio of all risky assets. The portfolio held by all investors in risky securities will comprise a value-weighted proportion of all risky securities. Figure 9.10 illustrates this point The investor located at P lying between R_f and M is comparatively risk averse and would be investing partly in the market portfolio and lending the balance of his investment at the risk-free rate; the investor located at Q, however, would be borrowing funds at the risk-free rate and investing the borrowed money plus his original investment all in the portfolio of risky assets at M.

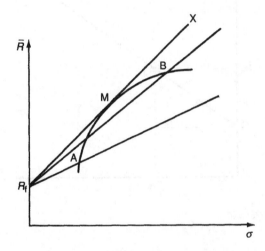

Figure 9.9 *Efficient portfolios and risk-free lending and borrowing*

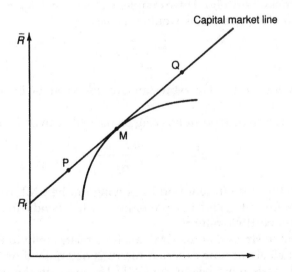

Figure 9.10 *Efficient portfolios on CML*

This leads to the idea of a separation theorem similar to the separation theorem of the single-period investment–consumption model. In this case the portfolio of risky assets which all investors would wish to invest in is the same and does not rely on their individual attitudes towards risk and return. All investors will hold the same risky portfolio with different proportions of borrowing or lending. We shall still need to know individual attitudes towards risk and return in order to identify the proportion invested in each. Figure 9.11 isolates the CML. The expected return of a portfolio lying on the CML is given by

$$\bar{R}_p = X\bar{R}_m + (1 - X)\bar{R}_f$$

where $\bar{R}_p$ is the expected return on the portfolio, $\bar{R}_m$ is the expected market return, R_f is the risk-free rate of return, and X and $1 - X$ are the amounts invested in the market portfolio and the risk-free asset respectively.

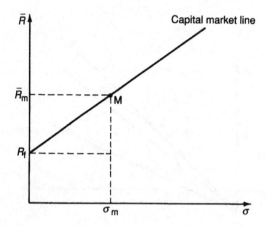

Figure 9.11 *Capital market line*

The standard deviation of the portfolio is simply

$$\sigma_p = X\sigma_m \quad \sigma_f = 0 = \rho_{fm} = cov(R_f, R_m)$$

We can see from Fig. 9.11 that the slope of the CML is $(\bar{R}_m - R_f)/\sigma_m$. This measures the extra return per unit of risk in excess of the risk-free rate that investors can expect for investing in a risky portfolio. For example, suppose that $\bar{R}_m = 20\%$, $\sigma_m = 10\%$ and $R_f = 12\%$. The market price of risk would then be

$$\frac{20 - 12}{10} = 0.8$$

This means that for every 1% of extra standard deviation the investor would expect to receive an additional 0.8% return over the risk-free rate.

The expected return on a portfolio lying on the CML can be written as

$$\bar{R}_p = R_f + \frac{\bar{R}_m - R_f}{\sigma_m} \sigma_p$$

The expected return for efficient portfolios lying on the CML can thus be viewed in terms of the risk-free rate plus a risk premium which depends upon the size of the standard deviation of portfolio returns.

It is important to stress that the CML analysis relates only to efficient portfolios. It says nothing at all about how expected return is determined on inefficient portfolios and individual assets lying below the CML. However, in the next section, building upon the analysis thus far, we turn to the pricing of inefficient portfolios and through the medium of the capital asset pricing model derive an expression for the returns of these inefficient portfolios and individual assets.

In the previous sections of this chapter we have seen how a rational risk-averse investor can maximize his return per unit of risk (measured by standard deviation of expected returns) by investing only in efficient portfolios of risky securities. When the opportunity to lend and borrow at the risk-free rate of interest was introduced, we found that there was only one portfolio of risky securities that would be of interest to all investors – the market portfolio situated at the point where the lending/borrowing line was at a tangent to the efficient frontier. This prescriptive approach is an example of normative economics with investors being advised what they should do. With the development of the capital asset pricing model (CAPM) we are dealing with positive economics where we describe how individual risky assets are priced.

In Chapter 8 we discussed how the total risk of a security could be divided between market and non-market risk. Figure 9.12 stresses this point that as increasing numbers of securities are added to a portfolio the non-market or unsystematic risk decreases while the level of systematic or market risk remains unchanged. The unsystematic risk relates to risk unique to the security (the term specific risk is also sometimes used). This risk will relate to unexpected pieces of good and bad news relating specifically to the company or the industry in which it is engaged. If a portfolio is held, unexpected pieces of bad news pertaining to some companies are cancelled out by unexpected pieces of good news relating to others. However, no matter how many securities are held in the portfolio, market risk remains. This risk reflects market-wide economic factors affecting all securities to some extent. Some securities will be more sensitive to market factors than others and will therefore have a high market or systematic risk, while others will not be so dependent upon mainstream economic activity and will have a lower systematic risk. Examples of market factors would include news on changes in rates of interest, inflation and other macroeconomic factors including expectation of a change in government!

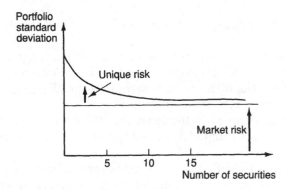

Figure 9.12 *Unique risk eliminated but market risk remains*

If the opportunity to lend and borrow at the risk-free rate of interest exists then all investors will locate themselves on the CML and invest in a combination of the market portfolio coupled with risk-free borrowing or lending. The market portfolio by definition contains all available securities; all unsystematic risk will therefore have been eliminated and the market portfolio will face only market risk. In this situation individual risky assets will be priced by reference to their relationship to the market generally, i.e. on the basis of their market risk alone, since any unsystematic risk will have been diversified away by incorporating them in the market portfolio. In this context a security's standard deviation, which reflects both unsystematic and systematic risk, is no longer the appropriate measure of risk. It is the covariance of the individual securities with the market which is now the appropriate measure of risk. This measure of risk is called beta and is usually represented by the symbol β.

The CAPM was originally developed independently by Sharpe, Mossin and Lintner [3] and is often referred to as the Sharpe–Mossin–Lintner form of the CAPM. The CAPM equation or security market line (SML) is usually written as

$$\bar{R}_i = R_f + \beta_i(\bar{R}_m - R_f)$$

where $\bar{R}_i$ is the expected return on the ith risky asset, R_f is the rate of return on a risk-free asset, $\bar{R}_m$ is the expected return on the market portfolio and

$$\beta_i = \frac{\text{cov}(R_i, R_m)}{\sigma_m^2} = \frac{\rho_{im}\sigma_i\sigma_m}{\sigma_m^2} = \frac{\rho_{im}\sigma_i}{\sigma_m}$$

A derivation of the CAPM is contained in the appendix to this chapter. This derivation builds on the idea that in equilibrium the only portfolio of risky securities of interest to investors is the market portfolio and that risk will therefore be related to each individual asset's relationship with the market. As the assumptions are important for the derivation of the model these are given here while the appendix shows the mathematical derivation.

Assumptions for derivation of the capital asset pricing model

The derivation of the CAPM requires a set of assumptions as is the case with any model which seeks to describe real world phenomena. A fuller discussion of the assumptions is contained in the next chapter, but at this stage the reader is cautioned against immediate dismissal of the CAPM on the basis of 'unrealistic assumptions'. We should not necessarily be concerned with how realistic or reasonable assumptions are but with how well the model helps us to understand, explain and predict what is being modelled. The assumptions are as follows.

1. Investors are risk averse and assess securities on the basis of expected return and standard deviation or variance of return. Higher return for a given standard deviation is preferred.
2. All investors have a single-period planning horizon and this is the same for all investors.
3. Everyone in the market has the same forecast, i.e. everyone agrees on the probability distributions of the rates of return (i.e. homogeneous expectations).
4. Investment opportunities in the market are the same for all participants although the amounts invested differ between participants.
5. A perfect market is assumed in the sense that there are no taxes and transaction costs; also, securities are completely divisible and the market is perfectly competitive.
6. Investors can borrow and lend freely at the riskless rate of interest.
7. The stock of risky securities in the market is given; all securities that were to be issued for the coming period have been issued and all firm financial decisions have been made.

There are clearly many differences between the operation of markets and the activities of investors in the real world and the idealized conditions assumed for derivation of the CAPM. We shall return to this point later but first we discuss the CAPM in more detail.

The SML is plotted in Fig. 9.13. It should be noted that the measure of risk used is beta; by definition the beta of the market portfolio is equal to unity. In equilibrium all securities will be priced so that they plot along the SML. Remember that expected return in the CAPM context depends upon the market risk beta, and that it is quite possible for securities with different levels of total risk to have the same measure of market risk and hence the same required return.

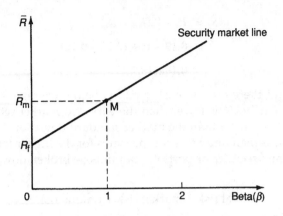

Figure 9.13 *Security market line*

The SML equation can be rewritten using the expanded definition of beta given above:

$$\bar{R}_i = R_f + \beta_i(\bar{R}_m - R_f)$$

$$= R_f + (\bar{R}_m - R_f)\ \frac{\mathrm{cov}(R_i, R_m)}{\sigma_m^{\,2}}$$

Remember that $\mathrm{cov}(R_i, R_m) = \rho_{im}\sigma_i\sigma_m$ where ρ_{im} is the correlation between the return on security i and the market. The equation then becomes

$$\bar{R}_i = R_f + (\bar{R}_m - R_f)\ \frac{\rho_{im}\sigma_i\sigma_m}{\sigma_m^2}$$

$$= R_f + (\bar{R}_m - R_t)\ \frac{\rho_{im}\sigma_i}{\sigma_m}$$

This can also be written as

$$R_i = R_f + \frac{\bar{R}_m - R_f}{\sigma_m}\ \rho_{im}\sigma_i$$

The preceding equation is written in a similar form to and can be compared with the equation for the CML previously discussed. In the CML the risk premium depends upon the standard deviation of the portfolio alone, while in the SML the risk premium depends not only on the standard deviation of the security but also on its relationship with the market as reflected in the value of the correlation coefficient. This explains why it is possible for securities with high total risk measured by their standard deviation to have low market risk when measured by beta. We shall illustrate these points with a numerical example.

Suppose that we are given the following information about security i, the market and the risk-free rate of return: $\bar{R}_m = 20\%$, $R_f = 12\%$, $\sigma_m = 25\%$, $\sigma_i = 30\%$ and $\rho_{im} = +0.75$. First of all we calculate the beta of security i:

$$\beta_i = \frac{\rho_{im}\sigma_i}{\sigma_m}$$

$$= \frac{0.75 \times 0.30}{0.25}$$

$$= 0.90$$

We can then calculate the expected return of security i:

$$\bar{R}_i = R_f + \beta_i(\bar{R}_m - R_f)$$

$$= 0.12 + 0.90(0.20 - 0.12)$$

$$= 0.192(19.2\%)$$

Note that $\beta_i < 1$ and therefore its market risk is below average; because of this the expected return of i at 19.2% is lower than the expected market return. Although the total risk of i at 30% is greater than the market standard deviation, because correlation with the market is less than unity this compensates for the higher total risk.

The total risk of any security or portfolio can thus be broken down into two components as follows:

$$\text{total risk} = \text{market risk} + \text{unique risk}$$

For security i this would be expressed by the following equation:

$$\sigma_i^2 = \beta_i^2 \sigma_m^2 + \sigma_{DI}^2$$

The unique risk can be calculated by substituting the values for total risk, beta and market risk from above:

$$(0.30)^2 = (0.9)^2(0.25)^2 + \sigma_{DI}^2$$

$$\sigma_{DI} = 0.198(19.8\%)$$

It is this unique diversifiable risk that can be eliminated by holding security i in a sufficiently large portfolio, leaving only market risk which depends on i's relationship with the market.

9.6 Implications of the capital asset pricing model

The introduction of beta as a measure of risk simplifies the computational problem emphasized in our discussion on portfolio theory. In order to calculate the variance of a portfolio it was necessary not only to know the standard deviation of each security in the portfolio but also the covariance or correlation of each pair of securities. However, when we use the CAPM the measure of risk used is beta which, if calculated directly for each individual security, greatly reduces the number of computations necessary. Also the beta of a portfolio of securities is merely the value-weighted average of the betas of the individual securities in the portfolio:

$$\beta_p = \Sigma W_i \beta_i$$

In terms of risk of individual securities those with high betas, i.e. greater than unity, will be regarded as high-risk high-return securities. The expectation would be that the securities would show above average gains in a rising market and greater than average falls in a declining market; such securities are sometimes referred to as aggressive securities. However, securities with betas less than unity are referred to as defensive securities as they can be expected to show smaller than average losses in a falling market but will generally experience lower than average gains in a rising market. Investors will thus be able to assess the risk of their portfolios and make any adjustments necessary to bring it to a desired level of risk.

When we began our discussion on risk and return in Chapter 8 the point was made that in assessing the risk of projects managers should be seeking to identify how investors assess the risk of investing in companies specializing in particular lines of business activity. It was initially suggested that risk might be measured in terms of standard deviation of expected returns; in fact the development of our analysis on portfolio theory continued with this assumption and calculated measures of standard deviation for portfolios. However, when we extended our analysis to the CAPM it was found that the measure of risk as far as shareholders was concerned changed from standard deviation to beta. The reason for this is that shareholders are regarded as rational and risk averse and will therefore hold portfolios of securities so that unsystematic risk can be diversified away. The result of this will be that investors face only systematic risk; the required return on individual shares will therefore be based on systematic risk rather than total risk as measured by standard deviation. If we assume an all-equity company producing a single product, then the required return on projects will reflect the required return by investors in the equity of the company. It would therefore be appropriate for managers to use beta as a measure of the project risk in such a situation. Therefore, given the beta of the equity of such a company, all that would be required would be a measure of the risk-free rate of return and the expected market return to enable the manager to calculate a project rate of return. The application of the CAPM to capital budgeting is dealt with in the next chapter. We shall also discuss how betas are measured in practice and examine some of the problems associated with the use of the theoretical CAPM in a practical situation.

9.7 Summary and conclusions

Portfolio theory is concerned with identifying a set of efficient portfolios either offering the highest return for a given level of risk or having the lowest risk for a given level of return. It is assumed that investors use expected return and the standard deviation thereof as their basis of choice between alternative portfolios. Having obtained the efficient set of portfolios, an individual's optimum portfolio can be determined in relation to that individual's utility function which can be represented by a set of indifference curves. The importance of the correlation between pairs of securities in determining portfolio risk was emphasized. The lower is the correlation the greater is the scope for risk reduction. With securities having perfect negative correlation ($\rho = -1$) it would be possible to construct a fully hedged portfolio, i.e. one with zero risk as measured by standard deviation. Problems occur in making practical use of portfolio theory not just because of the volume of data required but also in estimating the covariance or correlation between each pair of securities. When the opportunity to borrow and lend at the risk-free rate of interest is introduced, investors will all invest in portfolios located on the CML; portfolios will comprise the same market portfolio of risky securities with either lending or borrowing at the risk-free rate of interest.

The CAPM divides risk between systematic/market risk and diversifiable/unique risk. The latter can be diversified away in a portfolio but market risk, measured by beta, cannot. In equilibrium conditions return will be priced by reference to market risk alone which relates to an asset's sensitivity to the market generally. This relationship is summarized in the SML equation

$$\bar{R}_i = R_f + \beta_i(\bar{R}_m - R_f)$$

9.8 Key terms

Beta
Capital asset pricing model
Capital market line
Efficient portfolios
Fully hedged portfolio
Market risk
Perfect negative correlation in security returns
Total risk

Perfect positive correlation in security returns
Personal optimum portfolio
Portfolio beta
Portfolio theory
Non-market risk
Security market line
Separation theorem

9.9 Revision questions

1. Draw a diagram showing the risk–return combinations of a two-security portfolio with (a) perfect positive correlation and (b) perfect negative correlation.
2. The greatest reduction in risk occurs in which of the following cases:

(a) there is perfect positive correlation between returns;
(b) there is no correlation between returns;
(c) there is perfect negative correlation between returns.
3. What are efficient portfolios? Illustrate diagrammatically.
4. Are all efficient portfolios optimum portfolios?
5. How does the efficient set of portfolios change when risk-free borrowing and lending are introduced?
6. What is the equation for the capital market line?
7. How does the measure of risk used in the capital asset pricing model differ from that used in portfolio theory analysis?
8. What is the equation for the security market line?
9. What does beta measure?
10. Assets with high total risk measured by standard deviation can have lower than average betas. True or false? Explain why.

9.10 References

1. Markowitz, H.M. (1952) Portfolio Selection, *Journal of Finance*, **7**, 13–37, March.
2. Ball, R. and Brown, P. (1969) Portfolio theory and accounting, *Journal of Accounting Research*, Autumn.
3. Sharpe, W.F. (1964) Capital asset prices: a theory of market equilibrium under conditions of risk, *Journal of Finance*, **19**, 425–42, September.

Mossin, J. (1966) Equilibrium in a capital asset market, *Econometrica*, **34**, 768–83, October.

Lintner, J. (1965) The valuation of risk assets and the selection of risky investments in stock portfolios and capital budgets, *Review of Economics and Statistics*, **47**, 13–37, February.

9.11 Further reading

The serious student is referred to the original articles listed above. There are many textbooks explaining both the original theories and some simplifications of them. Good coverage is contained in the following.

Elton, E.J. and Gruber, M.J. (1991) *Modern Portfolio Theory and Investment Analysis*, 4th edn, Wiley, New York.

Modigliani, F. and Pogue, G.A. (1974) An introduction to risk and return, *Financial Analysts Journal*, **30**, 68–80, March–April 1974; 69–88, May–June.

Wagner, W.H. and Lau, S.C. (1971) The effect of diversification on risk. *Financial Analysts Journal*, **27**, November–December.

9.12 Problems

1. Distinguish between an efficient portfolio and an optimal portfolio.
2. What is the general relationship between the gains from diversification and the correlation among security returns?
3. Define 'systematic' and 'unsystematic' risk.
4. Which of the following statements is true and which is false?

   (a) The expected return on a share with a beta of 2 is twice that of the market portfolio.
   (b) A share plotting above the SML is overvalued.
   (c) A share held as a sole investment and having a beta of 2 is twice as risky as holding the market portfolio.
   (d) The total risk of a share determines its contribution to the risk of a well-diversified portfolio.

5. Comment on the following advice:

   (a) An investor holding a portfolio need only consider the systematic risk of securities.

(b) Only unsystematic risk is relevant to the investor holding just one security.

(c) A cautious investor should always consider total risk.

(d) No one should hold an asset that gives an expected return below the risk-free rate of return.

(e) Never buy an asset if its expected return is less than that on the market as a whole.

6. You have £10 000 to invest in either or both of two securities Wye and Zee with expected returns and standard deviations as follows:

	$\bar{R}$	σ
Wye	10%	20%
Zee	12%	25%

The correlation ρ between the returns of the two securities is 0.5.

(a) Calculate the expected return and standard deviation of the following portfolios:

Wye	Zee
100%	—
—	100%
50%	50%
25%	75%
75%	25%

(b) Use the values calculated in (a) to plot the set of portfolios and identify the efficient set.

7. The expected return on the market portfolio is 12%, with an accompanying standard deviation of 4%. The risk-free rate of interest is 5%. Place each of the portfolios

A	$\bar{R}_A = 19$,	$\sigma_A = 8$
B	$\bar{R}_B = 25$,	$\sigma_B = 12$
C	$\bar{R}_C = 16$,	$\sigma_C = 6$
D	$\bar{R}_D = 32$,	$\sigma_D = 16$
E	$\bar{R}_E = 22.5$,	$\sigma_E = 10$
F	$\bar{R}_F = 8$,	$\sigma_F = 2$

into one of the following categories: efficient, inefficient or super-efficient. In the case of an inefficient portfolio state what the standard deviation should be for efficiency with the given expected return.

8. Two particular assets A and B are known to lie on the SML. A, which has a beta of 0.5, carries a risk premium of 4%. B has an expected return of 20% along with a beta of 1.75. In the light of this information, determine whether the securities below are overpriced or underpriced:

Security	Expected return	Beta
1	20	2.00
2	14	0.75
3	15	1.25
4	5	−0.25
5	31	3.25

9. The following data relate to three quoted securities over the period January 1989–December 1993.

	$\sigma(R)_i$	β_i
A Midland Commodities	0.40	0.7
B Fax International	0.28	0.9
C Green Chemicals	0.32	1.2

The pairwise correlations between the returns of these securities are

$$r_{AB} = 0.14$$
$$r_{AC} = 0.50$$
$$r_{BC} = 0.40$$

(a) Using the Sharpe–Lintner CAPM and assuming that $E(R_m) = 0.18$ per annum and $R_f = 0.10$ per annum , calculate the expected annual return on each stock. Why is $E(R_B) > E(R_A)$ when $\sigma(R_A) > \sigma(R_B)$?

(b) Compute the expected return and variance of equally weighted portfolios of the following stocks: (i) A and B; (ii) A and C.

(c) Given that $\sigma(R_B) = 0.28$, $\sigma(R_C) = 0.32$ and $r_{BC} = -1$, what portfolio weights for B and C would create a perfectly hedged portfolio?

(d) As financial adviser to the Federation of Chemical Company Employees advise on the policy of the Green Chemical pension fund manager not to invest in blue chip chemical companies including ICI, Glaxo and Dow. Further comment on the plan of Green to introduce an equity participation scheme for employees.

10. As an investor in an equilibrium market containing many different assets you currently have 50% of your wealth in a risk-free asset and 50% in the four assets below:

Asset	Expected return	β asset	Invested in asset
A	7.6%	0.2	10%
B	12.4%	0.8	10%
C	15.6%	1.2	10%
D	18.8%	1.6	20%

(a) Calculate the current β and expected return of your portfolio.

(b) Assume that you want an expected return of 12% and intend to obtain it by selling some of the risk-free asset and using the proceeds to buy the market portfolio. Calculate the set of weights in the revised portfolio.

(c) If you hold only the risk-free asset and the market portfolio, what set of weights would give you an expected return of 12%?

(d) Explain the significance, if any, of the beta concept to investors in quoted securities.

9.13 Appendix: The capital asset pricing model – a derivation of the security market line

The CML provides the equilibrium relationship for efficient portfolios but says nothing about inefficient assets. The equilibrium conditions for securities and inefficient portfolios can be determined from the mathematical relationships between the market portfolio M* which lies on the CML and the securities that comprise the portfolio.

Take any asset i with $\bar{R}_i$ and σ_i at point B in Figure 9.A1 and consider the combinations that result from investing a fraction of funds x_i in asset i and $1 - x_i$ in the market portfolio M*. At point B, $x = 1$; at M* the market portfolio is held ($x_i = 0$) but some i will be in market portfolio. At B_1 none of asset i is held ($x_i = -V_i$, where V_i is the proportion of M* represented by asset i), i.e. at B_1 asset i is sold short to make the net holding zero.

The expected return $\bar{R}_p$ and the variance of return σ_p^2 of the portfolios along BM^*B_1 can be expressed as follows:

$$\bar{R}_p = x_i\bar{R}_i + (1 - x)\bar{R}_m \tag{9.A1}$$

$$\sigma_p^2 = x_i^2\sigma_i^2 + (1 - x)\sigma_m^2 + 2x_i(1 - x_i)\, \text{cov}(R_i, R_m) \tag{9.A2}$$

We can deduce that at M* both the CML and BMB_1 are tangential to AM^*A_1. Therefore the slope of the CML must equal the slope of BM^*B_1 at M*. We know that the slope of the CML is $(R_m - R_f)/\sigma_m$. All we need do is find the slope of BMB_1 at M* and set the two equal to determine the equilibrium rate of return on asset i. The slope of BM^*B_1 is the derivative $d\bar{R}_p/d\sigma_p$ of $\bar{R}_p$ with respect to σ_p. By the chain rule of differentiation

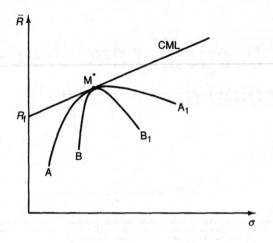

Figure 9.A1

$$\frac{d\bar{R}_p}{d\sigma_p} = \frac{d\bar{R}_p / dx_i}{d\sigma_p / dx_i}$$

From equation (9.A1)

$$\frac{d\bar{R}_p}{dx_i} = \bar{R}_i - \bar{R}_m \tag{9.A3}$$

From equation (9.A2)

$$\frac{d\sigma_p}{dx_i} = \frac{x_i[\sigma_i^2 + \sigma_m^2 - 2\,\mathrm{cov}(\bar{R}_i, \bar{R}_m)] + \mathrm{cov}(\bar{R}_i, \bar{R}_m) - \sigma_m^2}{\sigma_p} \tag{9A.4}$$

At M*, $\sigma_p = \sigma_m$ and $x_i = 0$; therefore,

$$\left(\frac{d\sigma_p}{dx_i}\right)_{x_i = 0} = \frac{\mathrm{cov}(\bar{R}_i, \bar{R}_m) - \sigma_m^2}{\sigma_m} \tag{9.A5}$$

$$\frac{d\bar{R}_p}{d\sigma_p} = \frac{\text{equation (9.A3)}}{\text{equation (9.A5)}} = \frac{(\bar{R}_i - \bar{R}_m)\sigma_m}{\mathrm{cov}(\bar{R}_i, \bar{R}_m) - \sigma_m^2} \tag{9.A6}$$

However at M* the slope of CML equals the slope of BM*B$_1$. Therefore

$$\frac{(\bar{R}_i - \bar{R}_m)\sigma_m}{\mathrm{cov}(\bar{R}_i, \bar{R}_m) - \sigma_m^2} = \frac{\bar{R}_m - \bar{R}_f}{\sigma_m}$$

Simplifying, we obtain

$$\bar{R}_i = R_f + (\bar{R}_m - R_f)\frac{(\mathrm{cov}\,\bar{R}_i, \bar{R}_m)}{\sigma_m^2}$$

We have obtained an equation (the SML) which gives the expected return on an individual security as a function of the risk-free rate of return, the return on the market and the relationship of the individual return with the market return.

10 Capital budgeting and the capital asset pricing model

10.1	Introduction	270	10.7	Realism of the capital asset pricing model	287
10.2	Project risk and return	271			
10.3	Measuring equity betas and beta books	273	10.8	Arbitrage pricing model	289
			10.9	Summary and conclusions	290
10.4	Ungearing equity betas	282	10.10	Key terms	290
10.5	Multi-activity companies	283	10.11	Revision questions	291
10.6	Single-company cost of capital and the capital asset pricing model	285	10.12	References	291
			10.13	Further reading	291
			10.14	Problems	292

In this chapter we apply the principles developed in the previous two chapters in the calculation of project required returns (cost of capital). The problems of adapting CAPM for practical use are examined and particular attention is given to the potential problem of using historic data in computing required returns for new projects. Sources of information and the computation of betas are discussed. The significance of debt in the company capital structure on beta computations is discussed and illustrated. The importance of CAPM for multi-activity companies is discussed and comparisons are made between using a single-company cost of capital and CAPM approach. Potential advantages and drawbacks of using the CAPM approach are discussed and a distinction is drawn between the arbitrage pricing model (APM) and CAPM.

10.1 Introduction

In this chapter we seek to apply the theory of investment developed in the previous two chapters to the evaluation of risk and return of projects by company managers.

We have seen how an investor in financial securities can reduce risk by holding a portfolio of securities. In fact a comparatively small portfolio (12–15 securities) would eliminate most of the specific or non-market risk. Ultimately, by holding a proportion of all available securities (the market portfolio) all non-market (unique) risk would be eliminated and the investor would be left facing only systematic or market risk. Because non-market risk can easily be diversified away securities will be priced according to their market risk only; this market risk will be measured by the beta of the security. Those securities with high market risk (high betas) will have required returns above the market average while those with low betas and low market risk will have lower required rates of return.

The capital asset pricing model (CAPM) approach which is used and developed in this chapter can be summarized as follows:

1. The return managers should require on projects should be related to that required by investors in the company.
2. Investors are assumed to hold diversified portfolios to reduce the risk of their total investment.
3. Rational investors will diversify away all non-market or specific risk.
4. The market will therefore price risk on the basis of systematic or market risk only.
5. The measure of risk used will be beta (β) which measures the covariance of returns with the market as a whole.

In this context the expected return on any asset i can be written as

$$\bar{R}_i = R_f + \beta_i(\bar{R}_m - R_f)$$

where $\bar{R}_i$ is the expected return on asset i, R_f is the risk-free rate of interest, β_i is the beta of asset i and $\bar{R}_m$ is the expected return on the market portfolio of risky assets.

10.2 project risk and return

In the previous section it was stressed that the return on projects which managers should aim at should be related to a return required by investors in the company. If we first of all consider the case of a company financed entirely by equity or ordinary shares, then both the risk and return currently demanded will reflect the perceived risk of the current activities being undertaken by the company. If we further assume that the company is undertaking a single business activity then the beta of the equity share held by the investor should be identical with the beta of the project currently being undertaken by the company. In this context the company can merely be seen as a device for collecting investment funds from different investors and investing the total of such funds in a particular business activity.

Given the basic CAPM equation, then both the return required by an investor in the equity of the company and the return required from the business activity undertaken by the company can be represented by the now familiar basic CAPM equation:

$$\bar{R}_i = R_f + \beta_i(\bar{R}_m - R_f)$$

It is clear that for a financial manager in a company to make use of the theory to calculate a project cost of capital it is necessary to estimate R_f, β_i and $\bar{R}_m$. The CAPM equation is forward looking, i.e. it is seeking to measure the expected return on an asset over the next period of time. This is the return that the manager will require, but whereas the CAPM model deals only with a single period, in most cases the manager will be looking at projects which span a number of years. It is clear then that some assumptions are necessary when adapting the single-period CAPM to multi-period use.

In the context of the CAPM it is usual to represent the risk-free rate R_f by the rate of return currently required on three month treasury bills. These are short-term government securities and are regarded as the nearest thing to a risk-free investment that is possible in an inherently uncertain world. In the context of the model this is fine; however, it has just been pointed out that in most instances projects will extend over several years rather than just a single short period. In these circumstances the risk-free return could be related to a government security having the same maturity as the life of the project. For example, with a five year project the risk-free rate could be related to the yield to maturity on a five-year government security. Many companies use real rates of return in project appraisal. In these circumstances the real risk-free rate of return can be approximated by using the redemption yield on an appropriate index-linked government security.

In theory the beta of the project could be calculated by drawing up a subjective probability distribution for both the project and the market and then calculating the variance and standard deviation of market returns and project returns and the covariance of the market and project returns. This clearly requires forecasting the expected market return and distribution thereof for a number of years where a multi-period project is concerned. It is more usual to base the beta measurement on historic betas calculated using regression analysis. That is, the responsiveness of returns on any particular ordinary share could be obtained by plotting the return on the individual security against the market return.

The final part of the formula, $\bar{R}_m - R_f$, is termed the market risk premium and in theory is the expected excess return on the market portfolio over the risk-free rate of return. However, once again there are forecasting problems in determining this risk premium term, and in applying the theory historical measures are frequently used. The historic average for the UK has been estimated by Dimson and Brealey over a 60-year period at 9% and by Allan *et al.* for 1919–84 at 9.15% [1]. These estimates are comparable with the 8.4% risk premium on US shares estimated on a long-term basis by Ibbotson and Sinquefield [2]. It must be stressed that the figure of around 9% is a long-term historic average rather than the expected risk premium used in the theoretical model. It is necessary in using this figure as a risk premium to assume that long-run historic averages reflect *ex ante* expectations and that these average risk premiums reflect current and future expected risk premiums.

Over the past decade many texts on corporate finance and other books written for practitioners have suggested that a market risk premium of between 8% and 9% based on historic data could be used in determining cost of capital in a CAPM framework. The effect of this can be illustrated for a project of expected life of ten years and average market risk (beta of one) using 1994 yields on government securities. The redemption yield on conventional gilts maturing in 10 years in August 1994 was 8.4% while index linked gilts of the same maturity yielded 3.7%. Assuming a market risk premium of 9% and a beta of one implies costs of capital as follows:

$$\text{market or money rate of return:}$$
$$8.4 + 1 \times 9 = 17.4\%$$
$$\text{real rate of return (allowing for inflation):}$$
$$3.7 + 1 \times 9 = 12.7\%$$

These figures suggest that average projects in late 1994 should have been appraised using a real discount rate of 12.7% or if cash flows had been adjusted for inflation a money rate of return of 17.4%. Although these rates may not be very different from rates being used by UK companies they have been criticized as exaggerating the returns actually expected by investors in the summer of 1994. This is not a trivial point as the use of an excessively high discount rate could lead to the rejection of potentially profitable projects, particularly longer term projects where high discount rates penalize them relative to short-run projects. The reason that long-run average historic risk premia are used is that obtaining estimates of expected future risk premia is very difficult. How do you do it? One way is to ask investors and in fact this approach was taken by the UK Monopolies and Mergers Commission (MMC) in their report on the rate of return that should be applied to the privatized British Gas pipe lines. The MMC surveyed eight fund managers and asked them what real (pre-tax) rate of return they expected on equity investments. The target rates ranged between 6 and 8% except for one fund whose target was 5 or 6%. Assuming a real risk-free return of 3.5% this would imply an equity risk premium from 2 to 4%. This is much lower than the 9% often assumed and would have a huge effect on project hurdle rates implying an increase in UK investment rates if adopted. However it could be argued that a sample of only eight is too small to adopt completely new criteria for assessing risk.

The use of the 9% historic risk premium is justified on the basis that although expected returns should be used expected returns cannot be observed while historic returns can be observed. Additionally by taking long-run returns covering over 80 years it is assumed that investors are unlikely to be systematically mistaken in their expectations. This approach also assumes that risk premium is relatively consistent over time. Table 10.1 shows the real ex-post returns on equities and gilts (UK government securities) from 1919 to 1992. In addition, figures are shown for the periods 1946–92 and 1963–92. The figures in the table reflect a number of interesting points.

First the figure of 9% risk premium is based on arithmetic average returns; annual returns are added and divided by the number of years' returns. This will always produce higher returns than geometric averages; given the volatile nature of equity markets this is an important point. For example, suppose we consider a two-year period; in the first period prices increase by 100% while in the second they decrease by 50%. The arithmetic average is 100 + (–50)/2 = +25%, however, the geometric return is zero as prices will be back where they started. Another significant reason why the *ex-post* estimates of equity risk premium are so large is that there have been significant periods during which gilt returns have, on average, been very low or negative in real terms. This suggests that investors suffer due to unexpected inflation which they systematically under-estimate. However it could be argued that the introduction of index-linked gilts makes this less likely to occur in the future as investors will be using the real returns available on these securities as a yardstick for their required returns on conventional gilts.

The effect of a systematic error in estimating gilt returns will have meant an over-estimation of the risk-premium measured using historic returns. There could even have been a greater exaggeration if equity returns were under-estimated. We can also see that the average risk premia are not consistent over time with the 1963–92 period producing significantly lower figures than the longer run averages.

Table 10.1 Real ex-post returns on equities and gilts 1919–92

	1919–92 %	1946–92 %	1963–92 %
Geometric averages			
Equity returns	7.3	6.3	5.9
Gilt returns	1.5	–0.4	1.3
Ex-post risk premium	5.8	6.7	4.6
Arithmetic averages			
Equity returns	9.7	8.9	9.1
Gilt returns	2.4	0.3	2.0
Ex-post risk premium	7.3	8.6	7.1

Source: Jenkinson, T. (1993) The cost of equity finance: conventional wisdom reconsidered, *Stock Exchange Quarterly with Quality of Markets Review*, Autumn.

Taken together these points suggest that there is quite a strong case for suggesting that the use of long run historical data may not be the most appropriate way of estimating future returns expected by investors. As the use of models incorporating risk premia based on historic data is fairly popular this suggests that the cost of equity may be being overstated in many cases.

In the above example the project beta was assumed to be one; in the next section we examine how project betas can be identified using available information.

10.3 Measuring equity betas and beta books

In this section we discuss how betas can be obtained for use in project evaluation. Let us assume that our company is financed entirely by equity and that we are considering an expansion which has the same average level of risk as the company as a whole. In these circumstances it would be appropriate to use the beta of the equity share capital as a measure of the project risk.

The equity beta could be measured by comparing its price movement with market movements over a period of time. The returns of two hypothetical securities are plotted against the market return in Figs 10.1 and 10.2. A scatter diagram is produced and a line of best fit is drawn through the points. The slope of the line represents the beta of the security. In Fig. 10.1 a low-beta security is represented while in Fig. 10.2 a high-beta security is shown. In fact in most cases calculations of beta are already available. The London Business School (LBS) publishes a quarterly *Risk Measurement Service* containing calculations of betas and other statistical information for most UK companies of any significance. The betas are calculated using a standard least squares regression programme. The monthly returns for each security over the previous five years (i.e. 60 observations) are regressed against the monthly market returns as represented by the FT actuaries all-share index. Other databases also include beta measurements and other useful information; see for instance Datastream. In many instances company managers will therefore have direct access to the beta of their equity shares. Table 10.2 shows a page from the LBS publication which as well as giving the calculated betas also contains other useful information.

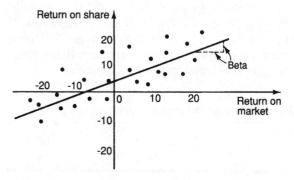

Figure 10.1 *Low beta share*

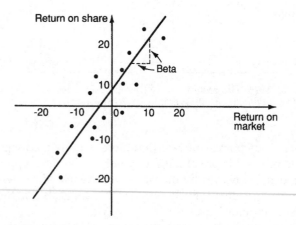

Figure 10.2 *High beta share*

General company information includes the Stock Exchange daily official list number, the company name and the industry to which the company belongs. The market capitalization shown is the market value of the company's ordinary shares in £ million. Trading frequency shows the number of days between transactions; zero would indicate daily trading while 99 would indicate very infrequent trading. The code letter M indicates membership of the mid 250 FT actuaries share index with F indicating

Table 10.2 Sector Leaders (excluding investment trusts)*

SEDOL number	Company name	FTSE-actuaries classification	Market capit'n	Trading freq	Index	Velocity % p.a.	Beta	Variability	Specific risk	Std error of beta	R-sq'rd	Qly abn return	Ann abn return	Ann act return	Gross yield	P/e ratio	Price 31:3
718875	RTZ Corp 'Reg'	Msc Mine	8753	0	F	46	1.15	25	17	.13	56	10	6	22	3.1t	30.4	822
803414	Shell Trnspt&Trd 'Regd'	Oil Int	21843	0	F	18	.74	17	12	.09	51	-3	7	19	4.5t	20.0	659
138495	British Petroleum	Oil Int	19046	0	F	29	.83	23	19	.14	34	3	5	19	3.0t	33.8	349
155405	Burmah Castrol	Oil Int	1597	0	F	46	.94	24	18	.13	42	4	4	18	5.0t	17.7	818
318866	Enterprise Oil	Oil Exp	1959	0	F	60	.92	28	23	.17	30	-4	-34	-19	5.0t	23.4	398
531696	Lasmo	Oil Exp	908	0	M	97	.95	36	33	.22	18	10	-34	-20	1.3t	na	121
971344	Wimpey (George)	BuildCon	674	0	M	123	1.42	39	31	.21	37	11	22	41	3.5t	27.4	187
878230	Taylor Woodrow	BuildCon	665	0	M	86	1.38	46	39	.24	25	19	60	79	1.2t	38.8	159
970073	Wilson Bowden	BuildCon	461	.1	M	15	1.22	33	26	.18	37	5	18	35	2.3t	18.7	495
092104	Beazer Homes	BuildCon	449	na			na	na	na	na	na	na	na	na	3.9	14.0	160
728700	Redland	BuildMat	2783	0	F	57	1.01	28	23	.16	35	-1	15	30	5.8t	22.8	539
976402	Wolseley	BuildMer	2368	0	F	39	1.21	26	17	.13	58	13	36	53	2.0t	27.1	888
105853	Blue Circle Industries	BuildMat	2256	0	F	57	1.16	32	26	.18	35	4	37	54	4.3t	na	326
583299	Caradon	BuildMat	2152	0	F	57	1.32	32	23	.17	47	-4	5	24	3.1t	11.6	363
726641	RMC Group	BuildMat	1843	0	F	51	1.11	28	22	.16	41	8	38	54	2.7t	29.9	936
068707	BPB Industries	BuildMat	1642	0	M	83	1.28	32	24	.17	43	2	44	62	3.3t	44.0	330
874120	Tarmac	BuildMat	1589	0	F	108	1.42	41	34	.22	32	10	36	55	4.0t	na	173
459497	Imperial Chemical Industries	ChemCom	5699	0	F	39	.80	22	18	.13	36	6	29	42	4.3t	38.7	789
108120	BOC Group	ChemCom	3413	0	F	56	.84	20	14	.11	48	14	-12	2	4.0t	16.7	716
228482	Courtaulds	ChemCom	2102	0	F	54	1.08	24	17	.13	53	14	-22	-6	3.3t	14.2	523
408808	Hansons	DivIndrl	13612	0	F	39	.97	21	13	.10	60	8	8	23	5.3t	19.0	269
067889	BTR	DivIndrl	12533	0	F	37	1.14	25	17	.13	56	6	-10	6	4.3t	15.0	360
896265	Tomkins	DivIndrl	2750	0	F	66	1.18	28	20	.15	49	14	-17	0	3.4t	17.6	246
967666	Williams Hldgs	DivIndrl	1914	0	F	66	1.48	30	17	.13	66	14	2	22	4.1t	24.7	388
365334	General Electric	Electrnc	8096	0	F	43	.69	20	16	.12	32	-9	-14	-2	4.4t	15.0	296
096162	BICC	Electrcl	1537	0	M	72	1.13	30	23	.17	40	16	14	31	5.5t	28.3	436
141147	British Steel	Metallgy	2841	0	F	127	1.18	38	33	.22	26	20	52	69	1.3	na	142

Table 10.2 cont.

SEDOL number	Company name	FTSE-actuaries classification	Market capit'n	Trading freq	Index	Velocity % p.a.	Beta	Variability	Specific risk	Std error of beta	R-sq'rd	Qly abn return	Ann abn return	Ann act return	Gross yield	P/e ratio	Price 31.3
807041	Siebe	Eng Div	2532	0	F	83	1.14	31	25	.18	35	12	20	37	2.2t	23.6	592
747761	Rolls Royce	Aero Def	2213	0	F	102	.74	31	28	.20	15	18	39	51	3.4t	30.4	181
868673	TI Group	Eng Div	1835	0	F	52	1.08	27	20	.15	44	8	21	37	3.6t	21.8	394
127158	British Aerospace	Aero Def	1835	0	F	187	.82	46	44	.26	8	24	67	80	2.1t	na	485
818270	Smiths Industries	Aero Def	1419	0	M	69	.99	24	18	.13	45	10	38	53	3.1t	19.4	475
476407	Johnson, Matthey	Metallgy	1148	0	M	49	.99	27	21	.16	37	18	21	36	2.2t	23.4	602
457963	IMI	Eng Div	1105	0	M	52	1.04	25	18	.13	48	13	16	32	3.7t	23.4	340
537575	Lucas Industries	Veh Comp	1444	0	M	70	1.43	33	24	.17	49	12	43	62	4.5t	76.1	194
395182	GKN	Veh Comp	1421	0	M	73	1.08	26	19	.14	45	12	7	23	4.8t	36.6	538
907606	T & N	Veh Comp	1130	0	M	94	1.31	34	26	.18	40	19	20	38	6.0t	25.6	225
965411	Arjo Wiggins Appleton	Pack&Pap	2331	0	F	56	.76	32	29	.22	15	27	48	60	2.8	31.1	286
115971	Bowater	Pack&Pap	2232	0	F	63	1.09	24	17	.13	54	7	-22	-6	3.5t	15.8	447
259471	De La Rue Co	Printing	1805	0	F	60	.99	27	22	.16	36	15	25	40	2.5t	24.9	937
819143	Smurfit (Jefferson) Ir	Pack&Pap	1552	0	I	60	.88	32	29	.20	20	15	9	23	1.5	27.1	319
927057	Coats Viyella	Div Text	1541	0	F	78	1.29	30	22	.16	49	-1	-12	6	4.4t	15.6	228
228794	Courtaulds Textiles	Div Text	527	0	M	81	1.26	32	24	.18	43	24	-25	-7	3.4	17.8	519
094553	Pentland Group	Footware	307	0	M	19	1.49	41	33	.22	36	-7	-49	-29	4.1t	31.0	85
071114	Baird (William)	Clothing	263	0	Mh	94	.91	25	20	.15	35	6	-23	-9	4.8t	17.1	231
083205	Bass	Brewery	4634	0	F	57	1.06	25	18	.13	50	6	-13	2	4.7t	13.9	532
783969	Scottish & Newcastle	Brewery	2761	0	F	59	.78	22	18	.13	33	3	7	20	4.1t	16.6	520
960502	Whitbread	Brewery	2709	0	F	38	1.09	22	13	.10	65	-3	3	19	4.3t	14.4	519
381932	Grand Metropolitan	SprtWine	9403	0	F	42	1.22	25	15	.11	64	5	-9	8	3.6t	18.8	452
396000	Guinness	SprtWine	9395	0	F	37	.83	22	18	.13	37	3	-17	-3	3.4t	20.4	467
018508	Allied Lyons	SprtWine	4828	0	F	34	1.15	24	15	.11	61	-11	-17	-1	5.1t	20.8	543
913216	Unilever	Food Man	8227	0	F	28	.74	19	15	.11	40	-9	-25	-12	3.1t	14.6	1013
161242	Cadbury-Schweppes	Food Man	3862	0	F	42	.85	22	17	.13	40	-1	-12	1	3.9t	15.2	465
056100	Assocd.Brit.Foods	Food Man	2510	0	F	19	.54	18	15	.12	25	4	8	18	3.3t	11.9	559
914123	United Biscuits	Food Man	1744	0	F	58	.92	21	15	.12	50	1	-28	-13	5.8t	25.9	332

727699	Reckitt & Colman	Hshd Req	2293	0	F	38	.92	20	14	.10	55	-8	-9	5	3.6t	13.6	611
816605	Smith & Nephew Assd	HlthCare	1496	0	F	48	.75	20	16	.12	36	-2	-21	-8	4.4t	13.0	138
030041	Amersham Intnl	HlthCare	629	0	M	56	.85	32	29	.20	19	12	42	55	1.6t	35.9	1094
916572	Unichem	HlthCare	413	0	M	32	.85	23	18	.17	34	11	13	26	2.8	16.2	289
371784	Glaxo Holdings	Pharmact	18262	0	F	31	.66	24	21	.15	21	-12	-8	4	5.0t	15.3	600
989529	Zeneca	Pharmact	6855	0	F	33	na	na	na	na	na	-5	na	na	4.7t	14.0	725
819392	Smithkline Beecham 'A'	Pharmact	5100	0	F	58	.73	24	20	.15	26	-3	-19	-7	3.7t	12.2	372
947293	Wellcome	Pharmact	4991	0	F	62	.84	37	34	.22	14	-7	-36	-23	3.8t	12.4	575
819518	Smithkline Bchm/Beckman Corp	Pharmact	4349	0	F	33	na	na	na	na	na	na	na	na	.0t	na	332
068116	B A T Industries	Tobacco	14103	0	F	27	.88	25	21	.15	33	-12	-19	-5	6.3t	11.9	458
460251	Inchcape	VhclDist	2707	0	F	65	1.33	28	18	.13	60	2	-28	-10	3.6t	15.2	515
309644	Electrocomponents	DisIndcp	1082	0	M	31	1.16	25	16	.12	59	5	15	32	2.0t	28.8	515
331841	Farnell Electronics	DisIndcp	769	0	M	62	1.00	25	19	.14	42	8	37	52	1.4t	30.3	572
889403	Thorn EMI	Leisure	4518	0	F	60	1.09	23	14	.11	62	15	9	25	3.8t	21.8	1061
381125	Granada Group	Leisure	3194	0	F	144	1.42	35	27	.19	43	17	24	43	2.0t	21.8	551
724593	Rank Organisation	Leisure	3187	0	F		1.31	27	17	.13	61	7	38	56	4.0t	21.0	387
905804	Forte	Hotl&Cat	2228	0	F	56	1.44	33	23	.16	52	9	22	41	3.6t	na	258
500254	Ladbroke Group	Hotl&Cat	2213	0	F	115	1.55	34	23	.16	55	31	-8	12	3.9t	83.6	194
733782	Reuters Holdings	Publisng	8148	0	F	46	1.00	30	25	.18	30	17	36	51	1.6t	27.2	1960
730879	Reed International	Publisng	4661	0	F	44	1.33	26	14	.11	72	1	8	26	2.8t	23.6	830
677608	Pearson	Publisng	3532	0	F	64	1.07	25	17	.13	51	12	46	61	2.5t	23.7	641
341925	Carlton Communications	Broadcst	1958	0	F	110	1.40	34	24	.17	47	2	-3	16	2.7t	20.2	863
767640	Sainsbury (J)	Food Ret	6696	0	F	39	.66	23	20	.15	23	-12	-31	-19	3.4t	13.1	374
884709	Tesco	Food Ret	4185	0	F	82	.83	24	19	.14	33	5	-19	-6	4.3t	9.9	213
049241	Argyll Group	Food Ret	2844	0	F	89	.60	21	19	.14	22	-5	-32	-21	5.5t	9.3	253
057200	Asda Group	Food Ret	1681	0	F	112	1.10	52	49	.28	12	13	-28	-12	3.5t	17.6	58
565402	Marks & Spencer	Ret Dept	11309	0	F	27	.96	22	16	.12	50	-4	10	24	2.6t	22.4	407
384704	Great Univ Stores	Ret Dept	6105	.3	F	39	.30	18	17	.13	8	-5	60	68	2.4t	34.5	607
384726	Great univ Stores 'Anv'	Ret Dept	5340	0			.94	22	16	.13	48	na	24	38	2.5t	17.5	2210
111441	Boots Co	RetChnSt	5246	0	F	34	.94	22	15	.12	50	-10	-8	7	3.4t	18.6	504
981116	Kingfisher	Ret Dept	3840	0	F	56	1.27	29	20	.15	52	-17	-13	4	3.2t	15.4	577
787002	Sears	Ret Dept	1725	0	F	68	1.11	26	18	.14	49	-3	3	19	3.8t	116.3	114

Table 10.2 cont.

SEDOL number	Company name	FTSE-actuaries classification	Market capit'n	Trading freq	Index	Velocity % p.a.	Beta	Variability	Specific risk	Std error of beta	R-sq'rd	Qly abn return	Ann abn return	Ann act return	Gross yield	P/e ratio	Price 31:3
733038	Rentokil Group	Bus Supp	2223	0	F	24	1.24	27	18	.13	58	4	-12	6	1.6t	23.5	228
133025	BET	Bus Supp	1186	0	M	54	.94	37	233	.22	18	0	28	43	1.6t	na	127
416102	Hays	Bus Supp	1143	0	M	37	.84	21	16	.12	45	3	7	20	2.5	24.7	283
194390	Chubb Security	Security	1020	0	M	77	1.11	23	19	.27	36	7	22	38	1.8	22.3	365
771287	Salvesen (Christian)	Bus Supp	755	0	M	45	.88	24	19	.14	36	-17	-41	-27	3.8t	14.2	261
067340	BAA	Transport	5108	0	F	41	.83	23	19	.14	34	0	14	28	2.1t	27.0	1000
680048	Peninsular & Orient 'Dfd'	Transport	4136	0	F	64	1.30	32	24	.17	45	17	10	28	5.5t	10.1	693
129057	British Airways	Transport	3854	0	F	76	1.24	29	21	.15	49	-2	34	52	3.3t	19.6	404
618715	NFC 'Var Vtg Ord'	Transport	1587	0	F	67	1.25	29	20	.15	51	7	-22	-5	3.8t	32.5	229
941916	Waste Management Intnl	Poll Con	2025	.1		6.8	1.04	33	29	.28	23	-4	-27	-12	na	23.2	540
779098	Scapa Group	Oth Bus	551	0	M	35	1.32	28	18	.13	59	9	-16	3	3.0t	17.1	233
632016	National Power	Electric	5946	0	F	41	.98	25	21	.20	33	2	28	43	3.0	13.7	465
697822	PowerGen	Electric	4217	0	F	40	.93	26	22	.21	28	5	50	65	2.6t	14.0	538
790828	Scottish Power	Electric	3375	0	F	42	.75	19	15	.15	39	-4	20	33	3.5	15.4	414
301338	Eastern Electricity	Electric	1785	0	F	66	.77	20	16	.16	35	6	38	51	3.8	13.5	675
829788	Southern Electric	Electric	1771	0	F	44	.87	25	22	.20	28	-1	27	41	4.0	12.1	653
134330	British Gas	Gas Dist	13048	0	F	33	.95	22	16	.12	50	-6	-14	1	6.0t	na	301
140843	British Telecom	Telecomm	24345	0	F	29	.96	22	15	.12	51	-11	-22	-7	5.1t	17.2	392
162557	Cable & Wireless	Telecomm	9940	0	F	37	1.23	54	50	.28	14	-5	10	27	2.1t	24.0	455
719210	Vodafone Group	Telecomm	5231	0	F	40	1.36	36	28	.19	39	-4	19	38	1.8	23.4	516
886006	Thames Water	Water	2065	0	F	55	.80	22	17	.14	37	-4	-12	1	5.1	9.2	525
798510	Severn Trent	Water	2046	0	F	59	.73	22	18	.14	31	-2	3	16	4.7	8.3	570
646233	North West Water Group	Water	2013	0	M	56	.73	21	17	.13	35	-4	-3	10	5.1	8.8	540
032412	Anglian Water	Water	1558	0	F	53	.69	23	20	.16	24	-7	-9	3	5.1	9.5	526
400495	HSBC Holdings $H10	Banks	12869	0	F	14	1.83	30	19	.28	61	-11	4	27	.0	na	754
078201	Barclays Bank	Banks	8509	0	F	43	1.36	27	15	.11	70	-7	11	30	3.6t	27.0	524
625395	Natnl Westminster Bank	Banks	7632	0	F	49	1.40	29	18	.13	63	-14	-8	11	5.0t	13.1	459
521103	Lloyds Bank	Banks	7181	0	F	51	1.19	26	17	.13	58	-5	-9	8	4.9t	11.8	559

Code	Company	Sector															
004455	Abbey National	Banks	6099	0	F	46	1.07	24	16	.13	54	0	10	26	3.8	15.6	465
400547	HSBC Holdings	Banks	6070	0	F	80	na	na	na	na	na	na	na	na	4.0	10.3	739
870612	TSB Group	Banks	3290	0	F	84	1.05	26	19	.14	44	-2	13	29	4.5t	14.9	215
754783	Royal Bank of Scotland	Banks	3250	0	F	56	1.49	32	20	.15	59	0	40	60	3.4t	18.1	408
838609	Standard Chartered	Banks	2499	0	F	77	1.40	35	27	.19	42	-5	31	50	2.9t	10.8	1041
076454	Bank of Scotland 'Ord Stk'	Banks	2212	0	F	44	1.14	25	16	.12	58	-8	35	52	3.1t	37.8	190
216238	Commercial Union	Ins Comp	3183	0	F	52	1.03	23	16	.12	53	-3	-17	-1	5.4	18.2	572
368537	General Accident	Ins Comp	2798	0	F	52	1.23	28	20	.15	51	-5	-3	14	5.5t	12.4	620
859633	Sun Alliance Group	Ins Comp	2616	0	F	55	1.13	27	19	.14	48	-6	-14	3	5.7t	14.5	324
755214	Royal Insurance Hldgs	Ins Comp	1765	0	F	80	1.39	37	29	.20	38	-9	-25	-6	3.4t	11.8	272
394231	Guardian Royal Exchange	Ins Comp	1571	0	F	50	1.22	33	27	.19	36	-11	-12	5	5.2t	2.4	181
709954	Prudential Corp	Life Ass	5752	0	F	56	1.11	24	16	.12	56	-6	-19	-3	5.4t	14.5	304
004154	Lloyds Abbey Life Group	Life Ass	2716	0		46	1.22	26	16	.12	61	3	-18	0	5.8t	na	391
511524	Legal & Gen Group	Life Ass	2243	0	F	46	1.11	25	17	.13	52	2	-8	9	5.5t	15.0	459
580610	Warburg (S G) Group	Mer Bank	1647	0	F	71	1.52	32	20	.15	61	-8	3	23	3.3t	19.1	757
779407	Schroders	Mer Bank	1198	0	M	20	.96	26	21	.15	36	-6	20	35	1.7t	10.9	1193
786634	Schroders 'NV Ord'	Mer Bank	324	.3	F	28	na	na	na	na	na	na	na	na	1.8t	10.5	1145
939029	Warburg(S G)Grp 'Cnv Dfd'	Mer Bank	30	6	F	12	na	na	na	na	na	na	na	na	nat	na	469
580858	Mercury Asset Management Grp	Misc Fin	1110	0		8.0	1.44	32	21	.15	58	-6	21	40	3.3t	18.7	611
594019	MAI	Misc Fin	872	0	M	126	1.18	28	20	.15	49	10	39	56	3.2t	16.9	268
549763	M & G Group	Misc Fin	725	0	M	17	1.34	29	19	.14	58	4	11	29	3.2t	20.1	963
701433	Provident Financial	Misc Fin	650	0	M	46	.91	24	19	.14	39	16	40	55	4.1t	15.5	486
163992	Caledonia Invs	Misc Fin	551	0	M	12	.68	20	17	.13	31	10	47	59	2.9t	22.9	663
128269	INVESCO	Misc Fin	493	0	M	95	1.69	46	37	.23	36	16	69	91	1.9t	79.2	198
504502	Land Securities	Property	3197	0	F	48	.90	21	15	.11	51	-15	11	25	4.6t	18.6	627
549804	MEPC	Property	1815	0	F	53	1.13	27	19	.14	48	-10	8	25	5.6t	27.3	446
136701	British Land	Property	1200	0	M	65	1.17	34	28	.19	31	0	53	70	2.2t	34.4	399
814104	Slough Estates	Property	939	0	M	62	1.33	34	26	.18	41	-2	27	46	4.1t	34.8	244
406501	Hammerson	Property	876	.1	M	30	1.10	32	27	.19	30	-8	-4	13	3.6t	25.1	349
173418	Capital Shopping Centres	Property	744	na			na	na	na	na	na	na	na	na	3.9	187.3	206

*These shares, grouped by FTSE – Actuaries sector, represent the largest companies within each UK sector.
Source: London Business School, April–June 1994.

membership of the FTSE 100. Trading velocity shows the average value of shares recently traded as an annual percentage of market capitalization.

The risk measures shown include beta, the variability, which is the total risk of the share as measured by its standard deviation, and the specific or unique risk, which is the risk that can be eliminated by holding a fully diversified portfolio. The standard error is a measure of the potential error in the beta estimate; the lower is this figure the more confident we can be in the beta given. The R^2 figure shows in percentage terms the amount of market risk in the total variability of the shares.

The quarterly abnormal return and annual abnormal return show in percentage terms the performance of the share relative to the market as a whole over the last quarter and the last year respectively. These measure the difference between the actual return on the shares and the return available over the same period from an investment in a diversified portfolio with the same beta. This abnormal return, which may be either positive or negative, is often termed the 'alpha' of a security. The annual actual return shows the percentage return over the last year (dividend and capital gain/loss). The gross yield figure gives the prospective dividend yield on the company shares; the price-to-earnings ratio is also given together with the share price of each share at the end of the last quarter.

Managers working within most UK companies of any significance will therefore have access to significant amounts of information for use in project appraisal and other purposes.

To use the betas contained in the LBS risk measurement service or other databases the manager needs to assume that betas calculated on the basis of historic information are reliable indicators of current and future risk. Sharpe and Cooper [3] carried out a study of the stability of betas using US data. They looked at New York Stock Exchange common stocks (ordinary shares) over the years 1931–67. The stocks were divided into ten equal classes according to their risk as measured by beta; the stocks with lowest betas were placed in class 1 with progressively higher betas in succeeding classes and class 10 containing those securities with the highest betas. They then looked at the way in which stocks change class over time. Table 10.3 shows the percentage of stocks which remained in the same risk class after five years and also those which remained within one risk class after five years. The figures seem to indicate that stocks with high or low betas tend to be fairly stable, particularly if stability is taken to be remaining within one risk class. It is quite possible that companies could change their risk class over time, but it must also be recognized that the betas are calculated from a limited number of observations and it is quite possible that some of the changes may be due to measurement errors.

Measurement errors tend to cancel out when betas of portfolios are used. Financial managers may therefore be well advised to use betas relating to industrial sectors rather

Table 10.3

Risk class	Percentage in same risk class after five years	Percentage within one risk class after five years
10	35	69
9	18	54
8	16	45
7	13	41
6	14	39
5	14	42
4	13	40
3	16	45
2	21	61
1	40	62

than individual company betas. Another reason for using industry betas is that the financial manager will wish to relate the measure of risk to the particular type of project being appraised; unless the project is identical with the average risk level of the company, the beta of the company would not be appropriate. Many companies carry out a wide range of different activities; these companies are often split into operating divisions. The beta of the equity of such a company would reflect these different activities, and in an all-equity company the beta of the equity could be written as

$$\beta_e = \Sigma W_a \beta_a$$

where β_e is the beta of equity, W_a is the proportion of value in activity A and β_a is the beta of activity A.

We can see that there are good reasons, therefore, for using industry betas rather than individual company betas. The LBS risk measurement service also publishes industry betas and Table 10.4 shows a listing of some of these. It is interesting to note that the general level of betas is what we would expect. Those activities most sensitive to mainstream economic activities, e.g. capital goods industries, have high betas, while those relating to goods and services likely to be in demand irrespective of the economic cycle, e.g. food manufacture, have lower betas.

Table 10.4 London Business School, Risk Measurement Service, industry betas

Gold mining	0.77
Oil	0.79
Building and construction	1.29
Diversified engineering	1.13
Engineering contractors	1.10
Vehicle components and assembly	1.25
Breweries	0.97
Spirits, wines and ciders	1.03
Food retailers	0.75
Food manufacturers	0.82
Electricity utilities	0.89
Gas distribution	0.94
Tobacco	0.90
Healthcare	0.83
Hotels and caterers	1.24
Textiles	1.17
Banks	1.40
Property	1.06
Leisure	1.18

The financial analyst within a company may well decide that the standard industrial classifications are not appropriate to his project. In these circumstances it may be possible for him to identify a number of individual companies carrying on similar activities and to construct his own industrial classification based upon these selected companies. However although intuitively the idea that portfolio betas might be more stable than individual securities seems appealing, more recent academic research has suggested that this may not necessarily be the case. In a recent piece of empirical research Gregory-Allen et al. [4] concluded that greater confidence in portfolio betas is not justified. It remains to be seen whether the conventional wisdom of portfolio betas having greater stability continues to prevail or whether it will be undermined by further empirical results similar to that of Gregory-Allen et al.

The use of ordinary share or equity betas in this section has usually been prefaced by the assumption that the company is all equity. The reason for this is that when a company is financed partly by debt and partly by equity then the beta of the equity as well as reflecting the business risk of the particular activities undertaken will also reflect the financial risk of the equity shareholders resulting from the existence of debt in the capital structure. This problem is examined in the next section.

10.4 Ungearing equity betas

The point has just been made that the beta of the equity of a geared company will be higher than that of an equivalent ungeared company because of the financial risk involved. In fact this idea can be illustrated in the context of portfolio betas.

Suppose first of all that an all-equity company invests half its funds in a risky project with a beta of 1.2 and the other half in the risk-free asset. We would expect the beta of equity to be calculated as follows:

$$\beta_e = 0.5 \times 1.2 + 0.5 \times 0$$

$$= 0.6$$

In this case the shareholders' funds are invested half in a risky asset and half in a risk-free asset, and the beta of the equity will be the value-weighted average of the two.

Now suppose that a hitherto all-equity company borrows at the risk-free rate so that the amount borrowed is equal to shareholders' funds and invests the amount borrowed plus shareholders' funds in risky projects. The borrowing can be regarded as a negative investment and the beta of the equity could be written as follows:

$$\beta_e = 2 \times 1.2 + (-1 \times 0)$$

$$= 2.4$$

Figure 10.3 illustrates the point just made using the security market line (SML). The actual risky project has a beta of 1.2; if half the equity shareholders' funds are invested in this and half are lent at the risk-free rate, then the equity beta will be 0.6, reflecting a weighted average of the betas of the securities invested in. If, however, the company borrows and invests the original shareholders' funds plus an equal amount borrowed into the risky project, then the shareholders' funds will be riskier and will have a beta of 2.4. The borrowing moves the equity beta further up the SML to the right. Therefore, if we have the equity beta of a company with borrowing in its capital structure and wish to obtain the beta of the risky assets being invested in, we would need to write β_e as follows:

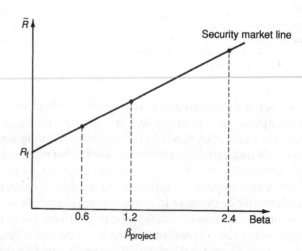

Figure 10.3 *Equity beta and debt*

$$\beta_e = \beta_a \, \frac{E + D}{E} - \beta_d \, \frac{D}{E}$$

where E and D are the market values of equity and debt respectively. Rearranging to express the beta of the asset, we have

$$\beta_a = \beta_e \, \frac{E}{E + D} + \beta_d \, \frac{D}{E + D}$$

For example, if we are told that the equity beta of a company carrying out a single business activity is 1.8 and that the total values of equity and debt are £8 million and £4 million respectively, we could calculate an asset beta as follows:

$$\beta_a = 1.8 \times \frac{8}{8 + 4} + 0 \times \frac{4}{8 + 4}$$

$$= 1.8 \times \frac{8}{12} + 0 \times \frac{4}{12}$$

$$= 1.2$$

In our example we have assumed that the debt in issue is risk free, i.e. $\beta_d = 0$. The example also ignores corporate taxation for the moment. In large well-established companies with moderate levels of debt or in other companies with a low level of debt in the capital structure the assumption that $\beta_d = 0$ is not unreasonable. If the beta of debt is not zero, then it is likely to take on fairly low values, 0.1 or 0.2 perhaps, and these values can then be inserted into the basic equation above to calculate the beta of the asset.

If the interest paid can be deducted for corporation tax purposes then this makes equity safer than would otherwise be the case. If t is the rate of corporation tax, the formula for ungearing beta becomes

$$\beta_a = \beta_e \, \frac{E}{E + D(1 - t)} + \beta_d \, \frac{D(1 - t)}{E + D(1 - t)}$$

If the beta of debt is assumed to be zero then the second term would disappear, leaving

$$\beta_a = \beta_e \, \frac{E}{E + D(1 - t)}$$

$$= \frac{\beta_e}{1 + D(1 - t)/E}$$

10.5 Multi-activity companies

The point has been made a number of times that the beta of a portfolio is the value-weighted average of the betas of the assets comprising the portfolio. If an investor in financial securities wishes to know the systematic risk of his portfolio then he can calculate it in this way. A financial manager in a company looking at the overall risk of company activities should calculate the risk in exactly the same way, using as a basis the beta of each business activity and the proportion which the value of that activity bears to the total value of the organization. The overall asset beta of a multi-activity company will therefore reflect an average of the differing activities undertaken. In addition we have just seen that the equity beta of such a company will also reflect any borrowing undertaken by the company. We can now understand that the equity betas of companies contained in beta books need to be used with some care. Not only will those companies' betas reflect borrowing but the ungeared betas, when obtained, may also reflect a variety of different business activities. When combined with the problem of instability of individual betas compared with portfolio betas there seem to be added reasons for using industry betas where available. However, even industry betas need to be ungeared by using average debt levels for each industry.

A motive sometimes advanced to support a policy of acquiring other businesses is that of diversification. Although this may not always be advanced as the major reason in many instances, it is often put forward as support for such a policy. At first sight it might appear that this is a reasonable motive; it seems to fit in with the ideas discussed under portfolio theory where risk reduction was achieved by holding a greater number of securities. However, in the context of the CAPM it makes no sense for company management to adopt a policy of diversification when shareholders are already assumed to be fully diversified and to be facing only market risk. If companies themselves diversify, then they will be only duplicating what shareholders are already assumed to have done for themselves. If investors are already holding a mixture of the market portfolio combined with the risk-free borrowing and lending, then for individual ownership of companies to change adds no extra value. Of course if value is added in another way by, for example, bringing a better management team to the acquired company or allowing tax losses to be used by the enlarged group, then this will benefit investor wealth, but these items of extra value have nothing to do with diversification. Even where investors are holding a portfolio other than the market portfolio, diversification by companies may not enhance investor diversification. However, it is possible that project/activity diversification by companies might lead to lower variability of overall earnings and therefore make managements' position more secure, but this could be at the expense of equity holders' welfare.

The approach to risk discussed to date is sometimes criticized on the basis that it might be applicable to substantial shareholders of large companies, but is it necessarily applicable to small companies with a handful of shareholders, with such shareholders having a significant part of their wealth invested in the company? There are many smaller companies owned by families and associates where this would be applicable. In these circumstances, for example, the principle of diversification by the company may also appear to be beneficial as far as shareholders are concerned as this will also add to their own personal diversification. In these circumstances is beta still the appropriate measure of risk? The answer would still seem to be yes, although as discussed below this is a more controversial issue. Industrial and commercial activities are predominantly in the hands of large organizations owned by diversified investors. The appropriate measure of risk for these companies and their owners is beta, as has previously been discussed. Risk and return from business activities will be based on this measure of risk. If smaller organizations base their required return on other criteria, say total risk, and this leads to a higher rate of return being demanded by the smaller company, then this could lead to rejection of otherwise viable projects. All companies, be they large or small, will be competing in the same product and service markets and if small companies require a higher return than larger companies this could place them at a competitive disadvantage.

However, as noted earlier other views could be advanced. In Chapter 13 dealing with stock market efficiency the 'size effect' is discussed. This relates to empirical evidence showing that smaller companies have consistently produced positive abnormal stock market returns (the issues and evidence are reviewed and discussed by Dimson and March [5]). This is saying that smaller companies have produced higher returns than they should, given their beta values. The issue is discussed in Chapter 13 where reasons are suggested for this anomaly. We need to consider whether managers in smaller companies should add an additional small company premium when evaluating projects. One view has already been expressed, i.e. risk is project/activity related and required return should be the same irrespective of the company undertaking the activity. However, it could be argued that if the market consistently requires equity investments in smaller companies to give a higher rate of return, then managers in such companies should build this extra risk premium into their cost of capital structure. On average, smaller UK companies have outperformed their larger counterparts by approximately 6% per annum; in more recent years there has been an annualized rate of 12%. These are very substantial premiums and it must be questioned whether they will persist given the competitive nature of capital markets. If a small company premium is to be added then how large should it be? A problem here is that if a substantial premium is added otherwise viable projects might be rejected. It has been suggested that there may be a number of reasons rather than one single factor why smaller companies have produced higher returns than expected. One reason might be due to underestimation of small company betas due to thin trading of shares in smaller companies. It could be that CAPM does not fully explain risk and that investors require higher returns from smaller companies to allow for lower marketability and higher dealing costs. Taken individually, the reasons suggested would not explain the abnormal returns earned; even collectively it is difficult to see them accounting for the high extra returns obtained, particularly in recent years.

Given the continuing uncertainty surrounding the reasons for the existence of a small company premium and the associated difficulty of predicting existing and future expectations of the size of premiums, it is suggested that financial managers in small companies should continue to use market-determined measures of risk relative to the project being appraised. It would then be possible to undertake a sensitivity analysis on the discount rate used to see the effect on project viability of different levels of small company risk premiums.

CAPM assesses risk by expressing the relationship between individual project returns and the market for risky assets as a whole. This approach is forward-looking and related to the risk of the project and its forthcoming returns. It does not necessarily relate required return on projects to be undertaken to the return currently being earned by investors in the company. The latter approach would only be correct where the new project to be undertaken has the same level of risk as the average risk of projects currently being undertaken by the company. Even if the new project is an expansion of an activity already being undertaken, the overall single company cost of capital may not be appropriate because it may reflect the average return currently required from a variety of different activities.

Figure 10.4 compares the use of a single-company cost of capital with the CAPM approach. Use of a single-company cost of capital would require projects to earn a rate of return of R_i or more to be adopted. That is, all projects would face the same hurdle rate irrespective of their level of risk. However, if the CAPM approach is used, then for adoption the project rate of return would have to plot either on or above the SML; in this case the rate of return would be tied to risk as measured by beta. Figure 10.4 contains two shaded areas A and B. Area A contains low-risk projects having an expected rate of return lower than the single-company cost of capital. If the latter was used as the hurdle rate, then these projects would be rejected. However, projects in that area lie above the SML; and therefore have a return equal to or greater than that required for their level

10.6 Single-company cost of capital and the capital asset pricing model

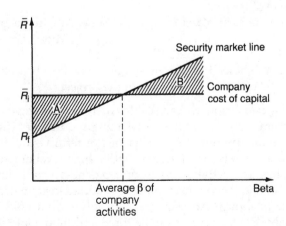

Figure 10.4 *CAPM compared with single cost of capital*

of risk. In contrast, area B will contain projects lying above the single-company cost-of-capital line but below the SML. These projects would be accepted using a single-company cost-of-capital criterion but rejected using the CAPM approach. If single-company cost of capital is used there could be a tendency to accept high-risk projects which, although giving a return greater than an average cost of capital, do not give a high enough return to compensate for their level of risk, while low-risk low-return projects would be rejected.

Although companies not using the CAPM approach might use varying hurdle rates, these are often intuitive and not based on any sound basis. The CAPM provides a rational framework for evaluating individual project risk.

Factors affecting beta

Although the CAPM approach to capital budgeting is not without its critics it does provide a useful way of thinking about risk in project appraisal. First of all the idea that required return should be related to the risk of the project being appraised seems sensible. There does not appear to be much logic in basing required return on, say, the cost of specific borrowing which might be related to the overall strength and assets of an organization rather than to the specific project under consideration. For example, a wealthy individual may be able to borrow money at keen rates of interest because of the security that can be offered to potential lenders; however, when faced with alternative ways of investing the borrowed money the individual will surely base the required return not on what the money has cost but on how he views the risk of the investment being made. If the investment is in the equity of quoted companies the individual should be using the CAPM approach! There is surely no difference as far as the financial manager is concerned, who should be relating required return to the risk of the business activity being undertaken.

There are two factors which are likely to affect the systematic risk of a project more than any others.

1. The relationship between expected project revenues and mainstream economic activity. When discussing industry betas it was pointed out that those activities most closely connected with mainstream economic activities (e.g. capital goods industries) had higher betas. This reflects the sensitivity of these industries to mainstream economic activity. Therefore, if the sales of a project are likely to be buoyant when the economy as a whole is buoyant but to fall sharply when main line economic activity falls, a high beta activity is indicated. However, if demand for the product or service is likely to be unaffected by the level of economic activity, then a low beta project would be indicated. Of course, if an activity can be identified giving higher returns when the economy as a whole is doing badly, then this would be regarded as a very valuable constituent of a portfolio; the activity would have a low beta and a low required rate of return.

2. The second factor which can affect the value of beta relates to the proportion of fixed costs in the project cost structure. The higher the proportion of fixed costs the higher the project beta that can be expected. We discussed in Section 10.4 how fixed finance costs in the form of debt lead to a higher-equity beta. Fixed costs in the project cost structure have the same affect on the beta of the project.

If we combine these two factors we can see that a project with revenues strongly associated with mainstream market activities and a high proportion of fixed costs would be particularly risky and an appropriately higher rate of return should be demanded for such a project. A capital goods manufacturer with a high level of fixed costs would be an example of such business activity. However, a business activity having low correlation with the market and low fixed cost would be expected to have an appropriately low beta and lower rate of return. An example here might be a gold mining company employing casual labour which can easily be hired and fired. Gold is a good example because historically it has been purchased by investors uneasy about market conditions in times of economic and political instability. Typically, gold mining shares have high total risk as measured by standard deviation but low market risk as measured by beta.

A consideration of these two factors gives some indications as to why betas might change over time. For example, activities whose cash flows have a high correlation with mainstream economic activity might include the sale of certain luxury items. If these luxury items over time become regarded as mere necessities, then the beta of the activities might be expected to change. Similarly, if the cost structure of a business changes from one having a high proportion of fixed costs to a low proportion or vice versa, then once again the beta of the particular activity can be expected to change.

Our discussion of the development and use of portfolio theory and the CAPM has been conducted in a rather uncritical manner to date. In Chapter 9 the assumptions necessary to derive the CAPM were listed and briefly commented on. In the next section we shall discuss some aspects relating to the realism of using CAPM as a practical tool in decision-making.

The CAPM is derived under a set of restrictive assumptions relating to the way in which investors are assumed to behave and the perfection of capital markets through which transactions take place. These assumptions were listed in full in Chapter 9.

10.7 Realism of the capital asset pricing model

Investors are assumed to be rational risk averters who assess securities on the basis of expected return and standard deviation. Since they are rational risk averters they prefer a higher return for a given standard deviation. These seem reasonable assumptions. In addition, all investors are assumed to have the same single-period planning horizons and to have the same forecast of returns and risk concerning that period. In other words, investors have homogeneous expectations. These are more tenuous assumptions, but if information is freely available to all then forecasts should not differ too widely and market prices should reflect some sort of consensus view.

The free availability of information is a pre-condition for perfect markets to exist, and the CAPM assumes the existence of perfect markets where there are no taxes or transaction costs, investors can lend and borrow at the risk-free rate of interest and information is freely available to all. It is clear that in practice markets do not exhibit this degree of perfection. The market assumptions are necessary for the theoretical model so that continuous and costless trading can take place, ensuring that in equilibrium all assets lie on the SML; the existence of capital market imperfections might lead to assets failing to reach equilibrium prices and plotting either slightly above or slightly below the SML.

All economic models, of which the CAPM is but one, are simplifications of the real world. We should not expect any model to be exactly replicated in practice, but if we are to try and use a model to make forecasts about the future we need to have some idea of its relevance and robustness to the real world. Casual observation seems supportive of the model; historically, investors have required higher returns for investing in company equities than in relatively risk-free government securities. It also seems that investors are concerned with non-diversifiable risk. For example, shares of gold mining companies have low betas and averaged returns below the market average despite having high total risk as measured by standard deviation of returns. The reason for this is that gold has been seen as a haven during times of economic and political crisis; returns promise to be higher when the market as a whole is uncertain. Another point that could be mentioned is that diversification *per se* does not seem to add value as far as investors are concerned. As investors are assumed to hold fully diversified portfolios, for companies to diversify adds no extra value. Investment trusts, which provide portfolio diversification and often invest in hundreds of different companies, have in recent years sold at below asset value, i.e. the price of investment trust shares has failed to reflect fully the market value of underlying investments. This has in fact made them takeover targets for insurance companies and pension funds. In addition, diversifying mergers do not seem to have always led to increases in value.

It seems that company managers too are beginning to believe that this might be the case. In recent years restructuring has been undertaken by many companies whereby divisions which it is considered do not fit in to the core operation of the business have been sold off, sometimes to the divisional managers in the form of management buy-outs. Other companies have floated off segments of the business as separate companies as ICI did with Zeneca. These are demerging operations implying that extra value might be created by dividing up the company. Instead of the $2 + 2 = 5$ synergy claims for merger and acquisition activity we now have claims that $5 = 3 + 3$! In fact gains may well arise from more focused management of both the core business and the separately managed divisions. Both acquisitions and divisional sell-offs have potential to enhance shareholder wealth; however it is unlikely that value will be added just because of either merger or demerger. Value will be created by increasing revenues or reducing costs of operation. It is important in evaluating any strategy that the sources of potential gain or loss are accurately identified. Value is only created when all the costs of enhancing revenue including the cost of capital are covered leaving a net present value arising from the strategy under consideration.

For some years the CAPM has been regarded as a useful tool for both analysts of financial securities and financial managers in business organizations. However, it is not without its critics and will doubtless be replaced when another model is developed which improves on its theoretical appropriateness and practical usefulness. It is this combination of theory and its practical application which so far have maintained the interest in CAPM. Another model, the arbitrage pricing model, might take over the mantle of CAPM in the future, but there may be a little time to go before this happens.

It is perhaps worth pointing out at this stage that, although the CAPM has been seen by many as a reasonable approximation of reality, there are a number of problems that exist in adapting the theoretical model for practical use. This factor also causes problems when empirical tests of the model are undertaken. The first point to make is that the model is *ex-ante*, i.e. it is based on expectations about the future. We cannot observe expectations but we do have access to actual returns. Hence empirical tests and data for practical use tend to be based almost exclusively on historic returns (*ex-post* information). Another point to make is that in theory the CAPM market portfolio includes all risky investments world-wide, while in practice this is replaced by a surrogate which is usually a market index of ordinary shares relating to a particular national stock market. The use of national surrogates can be questioned as the movement of investment funds increases in the current deregulated international markets.

The latter point is central to a powerful criticism of tests of the CAPM advanced by Roll [6] who argued that tests performed with any portfolio other than the true market portfolio were not tests of the CAPM but merely tests of whether the proxy market portfolio was efficient or not. The conclusion flowing from Roll's work is that the CAPM cannot be tested unless the exact composition of the market is known and used in the tests. In Roll's words: 'Unfortunately it [CAPM] has never been subjected to an unambiguous empirical test. There is considerable doubt, moreover, at least by me, that it ever will'.

Roll's criticism cast a shadow over the vast number of tests of the CAPM that had been carried out up to that time and continue to be carried out. If this makes us cautious in our approach then perhaps it is no bad thing, but it should be stressed that Roll is not saying that the CAPM does not hold but that it has not been possible to test whether it holds or not.

There have in fact been literally hundreds of tests of the CAPM, and the reader will be relieved to learn that it is not intended to review all of them here! In addition to the two major problems mentioned above, there are other statistical problems inherent in all empirical tests of the CAPM which were analysed by Miller and Scholes [7]. These difficulties and criticisms coupled with the vast array of data make firm conclusions difficult to draw.

The hypotheses most commonly tested by researchers are as follows.

1. Return is linearly related to beta with higher values of beta giving proportional increases in return.

2. Beta should be the only factor explaining rate of return and there should be no extra return for bearing unique risk.
3. The SML derived should have an intercept of R_f and a slope of $R_m - R_f$, or if the alternative version of the model applies (see below) an intercept of R_Z and a slope of $R_m - R_Z$. (It should be noted that there is an alternative version of the SML called the two-factor model with R_Z substituted for R_f; R_Z is the expected return on the minimum variance portfolio that is uncorrelated with the market portfolio.)

The studies, most of which have been conducted in the USA, tend to use monthly returns, with dividends reinvested, on listed common stocks (ordinary shares) as their basic data. Betas are calculated, usually using a time series of five years of monthly data in a first-pass regression. The securities are then grouped into portfolios and a cross-sectional regression is run to test the various hypotheses.

With so many tests and so much controversy surrounding the validity of their results it is not easy to draw definite conclusions. There is some encouragement in that return and systematic risk appear to be linearly related for securities and portfolios over long periods of time; in addition, return does not appear to be related to unique risk. These are supportive of the model. However, the tests seem to imply that low-beta securities earn more than the CAPM would predict while high-beta securities earn less.

10.8 Arbitrage pricing model

CAPM provides a simple and intuitively appealing description of risk and return, and the key variables required for operational use are easily obtained. However, as we have seen, there are some problems with the theory and it could be suggested that the relationship between return and risk is far too complex to be described by the relationship with a single market index.

The most likely potential successor to CAPM is the arbitrage pricing model (APM). APM's potential value to company managers lies in its attempt to explain the risk–return relationship using several factors rather than a single index. The APM, first derived by Ross [8], is a more general equilibrium model than CAPM, and the mean–variance framework is replaced by an assumption that each security's return depends on a number of independent factors. APT requires returns to be linearly related to a set of factor indices and the actual return R on any security can be written as

$$R = E + b_1 F_1 + b_2 F_2 \ldots + e$$

where E is the expected return on security, b_1 is the sensitivity of security to changes in factor 1, F_1 is the difference between actual and expected values of factor 1, b_2 is the sensitivity of security to changes in factor 2, F_2 is the difference between actual and expected values of factor 2 and e is a random term unrelated to factors and idiosyncratic to security.

APM requires the use of factor analysis to determine the factors determining security returns. Chen *et al.* [9] concluded that the four important factors were unanticipated inflation, changes in the expected level of industrial production, changes in the default risk premium on bonds and unanticipated changes in the term structure of interest rates.

APM works on the principle that a security's returns are determined by its sensitivity to the factors identified. A market equilibrium is established by assuming that arbitrage activities would take place so that it was not possible for a portfolio to yield better returns than that indicated by its average sensitivity to the various factors. That is, if a certain combination promised better returns than that indicated by its risk sensitivities, traders would take the opportunity to buy or sell short so that additional risk-free returns were generated. This would continue until no arbitrage opportunities existed, when Ross showed that the expected return E could be written as

$$E = R_f + b_1(F_1 - R_f) + b_2(F_2 - R_f) \ldots$$

where R_f is the risk-free rate of return, F_1 is the expected return on a portfolio with unit sensitivity to factor 1 and no sensitivity to any other factor, and F_2 is the expected return on a portfolio with unit sensitivity to factor 2 and no sensitivity to any other factor. The terms in parentheses can be regarded as risk premiums, and what is being said here is that the expected return on a security is a function of the risk-free rate of return plus risk premiums which depend on the security's sensitivity to various factors, of which four are suggested above.

Empirical testing of the APM is still in its early days, and as with CAPM there are no firm results proving or disproving the theory. However, both models are useful in providing a framework for thinking about how risk and return might be determined in a competitive but uncertain environment.

10.9 Summary and conclusions

It was emphasized that risk and return are related to the type of business activity undertaken and will determine the rate of return demanded by investors which should also be used by company managers in project appraisal. Risk should be related to non-diversifiable risk (market risk in a CAPM framework) as unique risk can be diversified away by holding a portfolio of securities.

The use of CAPM involves adaptation of a single-period *ex-ante* model to appraise multi-period future projects. In these circumstances it is necessary to use a surrogate risk-free return, perhaps relating to a yield to maturity on government securities. In addition, betas tend to be measured using past returns and it is necessary to assume some sort of stability if they are to be used as a risk measure for future activities. The market risk premium term $\bar{R}_m - R_f$ is often based on historical averages, and again it is necessary to assume that the actual premiums realized reflect expectations and that long-run average premiums give an indication of current and future premiums.

Commercial beta books, e.g. the LBS publication, are a useful source of information but need to be used with care. Because of potential measurement errors and difficulty of classification, industry betas might be more satisfactory than individual company equity betas. A company's equity beta will reflect all business activities undertaken and also any borrowing in the financial structure. Equity betas of geared companies (i.e. those with borrowing) can be ungeared to give betas which relate solely to the risk of underlying business activities; a project rate of return could be calculated based on the ungeared beta.

The two main factors affecting systematic risk (beta) were identified as firstly the relationship between a particular business activity and mainstream economic activity and secondly the proportion of fixed to variable costs in the project cost structure. CAPM is a single-factor model relating risk to a project's relationship to the market alone. This may be a simplification, but there is some support for risk's being related to systematic rather than unique risk. APM suggests that risk and return are affected by a number of factors, and in time this theory may take over from CAPM when more developments have taken place enabling easier operational adaptation.

10.10 Key terms

Abnormal return
Alpha
Arbitrage pricing model
Beta book
Beta determinants
Beta stability
CAPM and diversification by companies
CAPM criticisms and tests
CAPM and single cost of capital

Historic betas
Industry betas
Market risk premium
Project risk
R^2
Small companies and CAPM (size effect)
Standard error
Ungearing betas
Ungearing betas and taxation

1. What measures of R_f and $\bar{R}_m - R_f$ could be used to determine a project cost of capital where the project has the same risk as the market?
2. Explain how betas are calculated by commercial services.
3. What does a low standard error indicate in beta estimation?
4. What does the R^2 figure show?
5. Explain the term 'abnormal return'.
6. Are betas stable over time?
7. What does ungearing beta mean? How do you do it?
8. Is the ungeared equity beta of a multi-activity company an appropriate measure of risk for a new project? Explain your answer.
9. Is diversification by companies good for shareholders?
10. Is CAPM appropriate for risk measurement in small companies?
11. Explain the circumstances in which CAPM and a single-company hurdle rate would give conflicting advice.
12. What factors might affect the value of company betas?
13. In simple terms how does APM differ from CAPM?

1. Dimson, E. and Brealey, R.A. (1978) The risk premium on UK equities, *Investment Analyst* (52), 14–18, December.
   Allen, D., Day, R., Hirst, I. and Kwiatkowski, J. (1986) Equity, gilts, treasury bills and inflation, *Investment Analyst* (83), 11–18, October.
2. Ibbotson, R.G. and Sinquefield, R.A. (1986) *Stocks, Bonds, Bills and Inflation*, Ibbotson Associates, Chicago, IL, 1982; *Stocks, Bonds, Bills and Inflation: 1986 Yearbook*, Ibbotson Associates, Chicago, Il.
3. Sharpe, W.F. and Cooper, G.M. (1972) Risk–return classes of New York Stock Exchange common stocks, 1931–1967, *Financial Analysts Journal*, **28**, 46–54, 81, March–April.
4. Gregory-Allen, R., Impson, C.M. and Kavafiath, I. (1994) An empirical investigation of beta stability: portfolios vs. individual securities. *Journal of Business Finance and Accounting*, **21** (6), Sept.
5. Dimson, E. and Marsh, P. (1989) The smaller companies puzzle, *Investment Analyst*, **91**, 16–24, January.
6. Roll, R. (1977) A critique of the asset pricing theory's tests; Part I: On past and potential testability of the theory, *Journal of Financial Economics*, **4** (2) 129–76, March.
7. Miller, M. and Scholes, M. (1972) Rates of return in relation to risk: a re-examination of some recent findings, in *Studies in the Theory of Capital Markets* (ed. M.C. Jensen), Praeger, New York, 47–78.
8. Ross, S.A. (1976) The arbitrage theory of capital asset pricing, *Journal of Economic Theory*, **13**, 343–62, December.
9. Chen, N.F., Roll, R.W. and Ross, S.A. (1986) Economic forces and the stock market: testing the APT and alternative pricing theories, *Journal of Business*, **59**, 383–403, July.

Black, F., Jensen, M.C. and Scholes, M. (1972) The capital asset pricing model: some empirical tests. In *Studies in the Theory of Capital Markets*, (ed. M.C. Jensen), Praeger, New York.

Fama, E.F. and MacBeth, J. (1973) Risk return and equilibrium: empirical tests, *Journal of Political Economy*, **71**, 607–36, May–June.

Gibbons, M. (1982) Multivariate tests of financial models: a new approach, *Journal of Financial Economics*, **10**, 3–28 March.

Roll, R. (1977) A critique of the asset pricing theory's tests; Part I: On past and potential testability of the theory, *Journal of Financial Economics*, **4** (2), 129–76, March.

Stambaugh, R.F. (1982) On the exclusion of assets from tests of the two-parameter model: a sensitivity analysis, *Journal of Financial Economics*, **10**, 237–68, November.

Ross, S.A. (1976) Arbitrage theory of capital asset pricing, *Journal of Economic Theory*, **13**, 341–60, December.

1. Ms Dale was given the following securities by her mother a year ago and they are her only quoted investments; the following relates to the risk of the securities and their performance over the past year.

Share	No. of shares	Current share price	Beta	Specific risk	Annual abnormal return
Alpha Oil	2000	450p	1.2	38%	+12%
Gamma Engineering	1000	250p	1.1	45%	−10%
Delta Rental	1000	300p	0.9	28%	+2%

(a) Identify what you understand by the term beta.
(b) Identify what you understand by the term specific risk.
(c) If the market risk is 24% what is the total risk of Alpha Oil?
(d) If the return on the FTSE All Shares Index over the last year was 25% and the risk-free rate 12% what was the actual return on Gamma Engineering?
(e) If the expected risk-free rate over the next 12 months is 10% and the market risk premium expected is 9%, what return should Ms Dale expect from her holdings of securities?
(f) Do you think Ms Dale's portfolio is adequately diversified in equities?

2. Midland Industries has three operating divisions:

Division	Percentage of firm value
Food	50
Chemicals	30
Machine tools	20

The Finance Director wishes to estimate divisional costs of capital and has identified three companies carrying out similar activities:

	Equity beta	Debt/ equity
Amalgamated Foods	0.9	0.40
Sludge Chemicals	1.2	0.25
Chunky Tools	1.4	0.50

(a) Estimate asset betas for each of Midland's divisions on the assumption that debt can be regarded as risk free.
(b) If Midland's debt to equity ratio is 0.25 what is its equity beta?
(c) If the risk-free rate of return is 10% and the expected return on the market is 18%, what is the cost of capital for each of Midland's divisions?
(d) How reliable do you consider the costs of capital calculated in (c)?

3. (a) Describe the CAPM and explain how it may assist in the determination of the discount rate used in the appraisal of capital projects.
(b) Discuss the major difficulties inherent in its **practical** application and use.

(ACCA, Financial Management, June 1982)

4. Until about a year ago Victoria PLC operated only in the light engineering industry but, owing to expansion, now operates three separate divisions – light engineering, food retailing and luxury goods. Victoria has previously utilized the weighted-average cost of capital to appraise the expected cash flows of all investment projects and the use of this discount rate had been considered successful. However, this year the use of the weighted-average cost of capital as the discount rate had produced results whereby all proposals from the fairly risky luxury goods division and a few proposals from the medium-risk light engineering division appear acceptable. Most projects from light engineering and all proposals submitted by the low-risk food retailing division have been rejected. The management of Victoria are wondering whether their project selection procedures are correct and are considering the suggestion that 'investment projects be appraised using a dis-

count rate equal to the after-tax cost of debt finance because this year all projects are being financed either by newly raised debt or by zero-cost retained earnings. The cost of debt is therefore a sufficiently conservative indication of the cost of capital.'

(a) Comment on the suggestion to use the cost of debt as the discount rate for appraisal purposes and on the assertion concerning the cost of retained earnings. Discuss the validity of Victoria's use of a weighted average cost of capital discount rate:
   (i) in the past when only one division was operating;
   (ii) now that three separate divisions are in operation.
(b) Explain how the discount rate for use in the financial aspects of project appraisal should be determined for use in Victoria's three unequally risky divisions. Explain how this approach may be applied in practice and specify what constitutes risk for discount rate determination purposes.

(ACCA, Financial Management, June 1983)

5. The average equity β value for a group of similar companies in the motor industry is 1.32; their average debt to equity ratio is 0.20. The debt-to-equity ratio of Arden Motors is 0.30 while the risk-free rate of return is currently 12%. The market risk premium can be assumed to be 9%.

(a) What is the required return on the assets of Arden Motors?
(b) What is the required return on the equity of Arden Motors?

6. A firm is considering the following projects, and the expected returns calculated by way of IRRs are as follows:

Project	Beta	Expected return
A	0.5	12%
B	0.8	13%
C	1.2	18%
D	1.6	19%

(a) Which projects have a higher expected return than the firm's current 15% single cost of capital?
(b) Which projects should be accepted?
(c) Which projects could be accepted or rejected incorrectly on the basis of the cost of capital as hurdle rate?

You may assume that the risk-free rate is 8% and the market risk premium is 7%.

7. The total market value of the equity of Lucav PLC is £6 million and the total value of its debt is £4 million. The beta value of the equity is estimated to be 1.5 and the expected market risk premium is 10%. The risk-free rate of interest is 8%.

(a) What is the required return on the Lucav equity?
(b) What is the beta of the company's existing portfolio of assets?
(c) Estimate the company's cost of capital.
(d) Estimate the discount rate for an expansion of the company's present business.
(e) Suppose that the company replaces £3 million debt with equity. Does the beta of the equity change?
(f) What would the company cost of capital be now?
(g) If the company wishes to diversify into another industry with a beta value of 1.2, what would be the required rate of return?

8. The management of Nelson PLC wish to estimate their firm's equity beta. Nelson has had a stock market quotation for only two months and the financial manager feels that it would be inappropriate to attempt to estimate beta from the actual share price behaviour of such a short period. Instead it is proposed to ascertain, and where necessary adjust, the observed equity betas of other companies operating in the same industry and with the same operating characteristics as Nelson as these should be based on similar levels of systematic risk and be capable of providing an

accurate estimate of Nelson's β. Three companies have been identified as firms having operations in the same industry as Nelson which utilize identical operating characteristics. However, only one company, Oak PLC, operates exclusively in the same industry as Nelson. The other two companies have some dissimilar activities or opportunities in addition to operating characteristics which are identical with those of Nelson.

Details of the three companies are as follows.

- Oak PLC: observed equity beta, 1.12; capital structure at market values is 60% equity, 40% debt.
- Beech PLC: observed equity beta, 1.11. It is estimated that 30% of the current market value of Beech is caused by risky growth opportunities which have an estimated beta of 1.9. The growth opportunities are reflected in the observed beta. The **current** operating activities of Beech are identical with those of Nelson. Beech is financed entirely by equity.
- Pine PLC: observed equity beta, 1.14. Pine has two divisions – East and West. East's operating characteristics are considered to be identical with those of Nelson. The operating characteristics of West are considered to be 50% more risky than those of East. In terms of financial valuation East is estimated as being twice as valuable as West. Capital structure of Pine at market values is 75% equity, 25% debt. Nelson is financed entirely by equity. The tax rate is 40%.

(a) Assuming all debt is virtually risk free, determine three estimates of the likely equity beta of Nelson PLC. The three estimates should be based separately on the information provided for Oak PLC, Beech PLC and Pine PLC.

(b) Explain why the estimated beta of Nelson, when eventually determined from observed share price movements, may differ from those derived from the approach employed in (a).

(c) Specify the reasons why a company which has a high level of share price volatility and is generally considered to be extremely risky can have a lower beta value, and therefore lower financial risk, than an equally geared firm whose share price is much less volatile.

(ACCA, Financial Management, December 1984)

9. An all-equity company is expected to generate £48.5 million in dividends per annum in perpetuity and has a beta coefficient of 1.85. Another company, also all equity, is expected to generate £37.8 million in perpetuity and has a beta coefficient of 0.68. The risk-free rate of return is 7.5% and the expected return on the market is 13.8%.

(a) If the two firms were to merge, and if no scale economies or managerial synergies were expected from the merger, what would be the value of the combined firm?

(b) If the merger of the two firms were to result in managerial synergies that are expected to increase the annual dividends of the combined firm by £3.85 million but to leave its systematic risk unaltered, what would be the value of the combined firm?

(c) Compare the results obtained in (a) and (b) with the sum of the values of the two companies as separate entities. Explain any differences which arise and comment on the benefits of mergers to investors in the context of the CAPM.

10. Hotalot plc produces domestic electric heaters. The company is considering diversifying into the production of freezers. Data on four listed companies in the freezer industry and for Hotalot are shown below:

	Freezup	Glowcold	Shiverall	Topice	Hotalot
	£000	£000	£000	£000	£000
Fixed assets	14 800	24 600	28 100	12 500	20 600
Working capital	9 600	7 200	11 100	9 600	12 700
	24 400	31 800	39 200	22 100	33 300

Financed by:

Bank loans	5 300	12 600	18 200	4 000	17 400
Ordinary shares[1]	4 000	9 000	3 500	5 300	4 000
Reserves	15 100	10 200	17 500	12 800	11 900
	24 400	31 800	39 200	22 100	33 300
Turnover	35 200	42 700	46 300	28 400	45 000
Earnings per share (in pence)	25	53.3	38.1	32.3	106
Dividend per share (in pence)	11	20	15	14	40
Price/earnings ratio	12:1	10:1	9:1	14:1	8:1
Beta equity	1.1	1.25	1.30	1.05	0.95

[1]The par value per ordinary share is 25p for Freezeup and Shiverall, 50p for Topice and £1 for Glowcold and Hotalot.

Corporate debt may be assumed to be almost risk-free, and is available to Hotalot at 0.5% above the Treasury Bill rate which is currently 9% per year. Corporate taxes are payable at a rate of 35%. The market return is estimated to be 16% per year. Hotalot does not expect its financial gearing to change significantly if the company diversifies into the production of freezers.

Required

(a) The equity beta of Hotalot is 0.95 and the alpha value is 1.5%. Explain the meaning and significance of these values to the company.

(4 marks)

(b) Estimate what discount rate Hotalot should use in the appraisal of its proposed diversification into freezer production.

(11 marks)

(c) Corporate debt is often assumed to be risk free. Explain whether this is a realistic assumption and calculate how important this assumption is likely to be to Hotalot's estimate of a discount rate in (b) above.

(5 marks)

(d) Discuss whether systematic risk is the only risk that Hotalot's shareholders should be concerned with.

(5 marks)

(25 marks)
ACCA, June 1989

11. Amble plc is evaluating the manufacture of a new consumer product. The product can be introduced quickly, and has an expected life of four years before it is replaced by a more efficient model. Costs associated with the product are expected to be:

Direct costs (per unit)
- Labour:
  3.5 skilled labour hours at £5 per hour
  4 unskilled labour hours at £3 per hour
- Materials:
  6 kilos of material Z at £1.46 per kilo
  Three units of component P at £4.80 per unit
  One unit of component Q at £6.40
  Other variable costs: £2.10 per unit

Indirect costs
- Apportionment of management salaries £105 000 per year
- Tax allowable depreciation of machinery £213 000 per year
- Selling expenses (not including any salaries) £166 000 per year

- Apportionment of head office costs £50 000 per year
- Rental of buildings £100 000 per year
- Interest charges £104 000 per year
- Other overheads £70 000 per year (including apportionment of building rates £20 000. N.B. rates are a local tax on property).

If the new product is introduced it will be manufactured in an existing factory, and will have no effect on rates payable. The factory could be rented for £120 000 per year (not including rates), to another company if the product is not introduced.

New machinery costing £864 000 will be required. The machinery is to be depreciated on a straight-line basis over four years, and has an expected salvage value of £12 000 after four years. The machinery will be financed by a four-year fixed rate bank loan, at an interest rate of 12% per year. Additional working capital requirements may be ignored.

The product will require two additional managers to be recruited at an annual gross cost of £25 000 each, and one manager currently costing £20 000 will be moved from another factory where he will be replaced by a deputy manager at a cost of £17 000 per year. 70 000 kilos of material Z are already in stock and are not required for other production. The realizable value of the material is £99 000.

The price per unit of the product in the first year will be £110, and demand is projected at 12 000, 17 500, 18 000 and 18 500 units in years 1 to 4 respectively.

The inflation rate is expected to be approximately 5% per year, and prices will be increased in line with inflation. Wage and salary costs are expected to increase by 7% per year, and all other costs (including rent) by 5% per year. No price or cost increases are expected in the first year of production.

Corporate tax is at the rate of 35% payable in the year the profit occurs. Assume that all sales and costs are on a cash basis and occur at the end of the year, except for the initial purchase of machinery which would take place immediately. No stocks will be held at the end of any year.

Required
(a) Calculate the expected internal rate of return (IRR) associated with the manufacture of the new product. (15 marks)
(b) What is meant by an asset beta?
   If you were told that the company's asset beta is 1.2, the market return is 15% and the risk free rate is 8% discuss whether you would recommend introducing the new product. (5 marks)
(c) Amble is worried that the government might increase corporate tax rates.
   Show by how much the tax rate would have to change before the project is not financially viable. A discount rate of 17% per year may be assumed for part (c).
   (5 marks)
   (25 marks)
   ACCA, June 1989

11 Introduction to derivatives and option theory

11.1	Introduction	297		11.8	Application of option pricing theory to corporate finance	315
11.2	Types of options	300		11.9	Summary and conclusions	316
11.3	Simple option strategies	306		11.10	Key terms	317
11.4	Call options and futures compared	308		11.11	Revision questions	317
11.5	Factors affecting option values	309		11.12	References	317
11.6	Binomial valuation formula	312		11.13	Further reading	318
11.7	Black–Scholes option valuation formula	313		11.14	Problems	318

This chapter introduces the concept of derivative securities in general and then goes on to look at options and option pricing in more detail. The chapter begins by describing and distinguishing between forwards, futures, options and swaps; this chapter confines itself to a detailed examination of options while the other derivatives are dealt with in Chapter 20. The nature of put and call options is fully explained and distinction made between American and European options. The factors determining option values are explained and valuation models incorporating these factors are covered. The calculation of option values using put-call parity, binomial and Black-Scholes option valuation models are illustrated. The chapter concludes with a discussion on the use of options by corporate managers.

11.1 Introduction

Derivatives are securities whose value depends on the value of other more basic variables; these include the value of linked assets, for example, commodities, ordinary shares, bonds, currencies, etc. Derivatives include forward contracts, futures contracts, swaps and options. Although our main concern in this chapter is with options we begin with a review of derivatives in general.

In recent years the volume of trading in some markets in derivatives has increased considerably to the extent where they are more significant than the underlying assets to which they relate. Market volatility has had a lot to do with this growth as asset holders have sought to hedge open positions through the use of derivatives and speculators have seen opportunities for profit in volatile markets.

Derivatives, also known as contingent claims, are not fixed in the volume of supply as normal equity and bond issues. Their existence and creation depends on the existence of counterparties, market participants willing to take alternative views on the outcome of the same event. For example, traders taking different views on the future pricing of a share, a currency, interest rates, a commodity etc. may enter into a transaction which reflects these views without necessarily buying or selling the underlying asset. Most derivative positions are closed off by a cash settlement either way rather than by transfer of the related asset.

Some derivatives are traded on exchanges where contracts are standardized and completion of the contract guaranteed by the exchange; futures and options are examples of derivatives which are traded on specialist exchanges. Some derivative transactions are 'over the counter' (OTC) transactions where a financial intermediary puts together a transaction which is tailored precisely to the needs of the client; futures and swaps are increasingly OTC transactions.

What are derivatives and how do they work?

The simplest derivative security is a forward contract. This is an agreement to buy or sell an asset at a fixed future date at a price agreed now. For example an exporter receiving payment at a future date in a foreign currency may choose to sell the currency forward at a price agreed now thus fixing the amount to be received in terms of the domestic currency. Conversely an importer with a future bill to pay in a foreign currency may choose to buy the currency forward. Both these would be examples of covered positions where gain or loss on the forward would be offset by an equal and opposite loss or gain on the amount to be received or paid. Forward contracts, like any other derivative, can be used for speculation. An investor who considers that sterling will increase in value relative to the US dollar could buy a sterling forward contract. This would be termed a 'long position'; if sterling was sold then the investor would have taken a 'short position'. Forward contracts are also available on interest bearing securities; for example companies may enter into forward rate agreements where interest rates are agreed now for deposits or loans to be made at a future date.

Futures contracts are similar to forward contracts in that there is an agreement between two parties to buy or sell an asset at a future date at a price fixed now. Futures are more liquid in that they are usually traded on a regulated exchange. The exchange guarantees the integrity of the contract in that if one party was to go bankrupt it would not affect the other party.

Although the ability to trade futures provides flexibility they may be less flexible in other aspects as futures contracts are standardized. This means that the amount, quality of asset and delivery date of futures contracts are pre-specified and a hedger may not be able to obtain perfect cover by using futures. Forward contracts, on the other hand, can be agreed precisely to cover the risk faced by the hedger. It is possible that futures may be more readily available to some companies than forwards and where risk exposures are changing rapidly may enable the company to cover these risks more quickly.

Forwards and futures, like other derivatives, enable their purchasers to take levered positions. If a purchase was made in the cash market then cash would have to be paid for the asset. Entering a forward contract for the same amount requires no initial cash payment although in practice financial institutions may require a speculator to deposit funds with them which would earn interest for the speculator while providing a margin for the financial institution.

With a futures contract the broker will require an initial deposit in a margin account. As the futures price changes the margin account will be debited or credited with losses or profits on a daily basis; this is called marking to market. The investor can withdraw any balance exceeding the initial margin but will have to make good the deficit should the margin fall below a pre-set limit.

A more recent derivative development has been the use of swaps. A swap is an agreement between two parties to exchange cash flows at stated future times in accordance with the terms of the agreement. Swaps are typically entered into for currencies and interest rates. The simplest type of swap is an ordinary or plain vanilla interest rate swap whereby one party agrees to pay another party cash flows equal to a fixed rate of interest on a notional sum for a number of years in return for receiving interest at a floating rate on the same notional sum for the same period of time. On each interest payment date one party sends the other the difference between the two interest payments. Note that no exchange of principal is involved.

This type of deal might be used by a borrower who has borrowed on floating rate terms but is concerned that rates might rise. By agreeing to pay a fixed rate and receive a floating rate the borrower effectively ties down future liabilities to a fixed amount. Of course if interest rates fall losses will be made. Swaps can also be used to speculate on currency and interest rate movements and because of the leverage effect big positions can be taken. However any uncovered derivative dealing carries high risk and huge losses have been made by organizations that have got their forecasts wrong.

The use of derivatives in managing risk is covered in Chapter 20 and many worked examples are shown of how they can be used. Unfortunately some companies have suffered losses by going beyond the hedging use of derivatives and trying to boost profits through position taking in commodities, currencies or interest rates. Companies need clear policies on the use of derivatives and internal controls to ensure that these policies are being followed. This is not always easy as many new derivative products are being produced which are difficult for even corporate treasury specialists to understand fully. This can make the monitoring process very difficult. We now turn to the main discussion of this chapter which concerns options and their valuation.

Businessmen, and indeed individuals, often talk about 'keeping their options open'. This is generally understood as providing the opportunity to undertake alternative courses of action at some future date. For example, an individual might pay a building contractor a non-returnable deposit on a house which gives the individual the right to proceed to buy the house at a later date or alternatively to forfeit the deposit and not proceed with the purchase. As we shall see later, essentially the individual would be holding a call option on the purchase of the house. Although there are many examples of options occurring in transactions relating to 'real' assets, much of the writing and analysis has been developed in the context of options in financial markets. Basically an option allows an investor to buy or sell an asset on or before a future date at a price that is settled when the option is taken out.

Option trading in shares has been conducted in the Stock Exchange in London for over 200 years. At various times its popularity has waned and at certain times trading in options on the floor of the Stock Exchange was banned. The volume of option trading in the late 1970s was very low; it was estimated at being less than 1% of total share dealings by volume of shares [1]. Conventional option dealing of this sort required that the parties to the option, i.e. the person taking out the option to buy or sell shares and the second party either agreeing to sell or buy shares at a future date, had to be matched through an intermediary. There was limited interest in this type of option trading both because of the lack of a secondary market where options could be bought and sold and also because of a lack of information on all the option possibilities available to investors.

These limitations and the success of a traded option market in Chicago led to the setting up of the London Traded Options Market (LTOM) in 1978. Initially the shares of only ten companies were listed with trading only in call options. There are now options traded on over 70 individual large companies, and in addition options can be traded on the level of the FTSE index. In the UK it is still possible to enter into conventional options, although most interest tends to be centred on traded options. The LTOM has now merged with the London International Financial Futures Exchange (LIFFE). LIFFE was set up in 1982 and now offers an international portfolio of derivatives, including futures on bonds, interest rates and the FTSE index.

The Chicago option market was started in 1973 and it was also in that year that the paper on option valuation by Black and Scholes [2] was published. Their theoretical model enables the equilibrium value of an option to be determined, and it is the basis for most of the analysis in this field at both the professional and academic level.

Options can therefore have significance both for analysis of projects and for strategies involving financial securities. We shall begin by reviewing and describing the various types of options, concerning ourselves first of all with options on financial securities. The valuation of options will then be discussed, as will the significance of option pricing theory to company managers.

11.2 Types of options

An option is a contract giving the holder a right to buy or sell a stated security at a specified price, called the striking or exercise price, on or before a specified date. The value of any option is directly related to the value of its underlying security. Options represent a claim against the underlying security and thus are often called contingent claim contracts. Although complex option trading strategies are common, all the strategies can be analysed in terms of basic put and call options and the underlying security.

Call options

Call options are the most common form of options. A call option gives the holder the right to buy a fixed number of shares at a specified price, either before or at a fixed future date. American and European options differ in that European options can only be exercised at expiry date whereas American options can be exercised any time up to and including expiry date. A call option with an exercise price below the current market value is referred to as an 'in-the-money option'; however, where the exercise price is above the current market value the option is referred to as an 'out-of-the-money option'.

If a call option is exercised, then the exchange of shares is between two investors. It is thus a secondary market activity and there is no effect whatsoever on the company which has issued the securities. The investor who issues the call is known as the writer of the call, while the other investor purchases the call. Figure 11.1 shows the profit per share arising to the holder of a call option at expiry date. The figure assumes that the call option was purchased originally for £10 with an exercise price of £100.

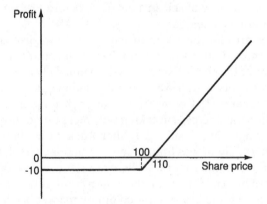

Figure 11.1 *Call option holder*

The holder of the call option will not exercise the option unless the share price is at least £100 at exercise date. At any price below £100 it would be cheaper to buy on the market rather than exercise the option. The holder would just break even if the market price at expiry was £110. The holder would be able to buy the underlying security for £100 and sell on the market for £110, thus just covering the price paid for the option of £10. For the moment we are ignoring both transaction costs and the time value of money. We can see that as the price rises above £100, so the value of the option increases on a pound for pound basis.

Let us now examine the position of the writer of the call option. Figure 11.2 shows the position of the writer of the call option. The writer of the call option receives the purchase price of the option and will be called upon to supply the shares if the price at expiry is £100 or greater. We can see that the position of the writer is a mirror image of the purchaser of the call option. Any profit made by the holder of the call will result in an equal and opposite loss by the writer of the call. Option dealing can therefore be referred to as a zero-sum game.

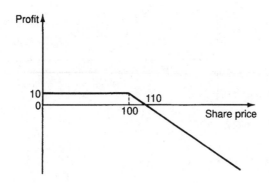

Figure 11.2 *Writer of call option*

If the option is an American option exercisable before expiration date, then if the share price was above £100 then a profit could be made by exercising the option. However, with traded options it is usual for the option to be sold on the market. The sale may be to an individual who wishes to take a position in the option or it could be to an investor who has written an option and wishes to liquidate the position.

Although option transactions are entered into between individuals, because they involve the passage of time it is still possible that decisions taken by companies will affect the value of the underlying shares. For example, both bonus/scrip issues and dividends will affect the share value. A one-for-one bonus issue would normally be expected to result in the share halving in value; cash dividends will normally result in a lower ex-dividend market price. Most options are protected against bonus/scrip issues by an automatic adjustment in the exercise price and the number of shares that can be purchased with one option. It is less usual to make adjustment for cash dividends and no adjustments are made to traded options. The possible impact of dividend payments will have more significance the longer the option has to run to expiry. This would be the case where option valuation models are adapted to value warrants and convertibles.

Put options

A put option gives the holder the right to sell shares at a specified price on or before a specified date. A put, like a call, is a transaction between two investors. Once again it is secondary market activity which has no effect on the value of the firm. Figures 11.3 and 11.4 show the profit at expiry date for a put with an exercise price of £100 that originally cost £10. Figure 11.4 shows the profit to the writer of a put which would never be greater than the premium received for writing the put. However, Figure 11.3 shows that for prices above £100 the owner of the put would be better off selling shares in the market as the price received would be greater. Therefore for prices above £100 the exercise value is zero. However, for prices below £100 the owner of the put would wish to exercise the option instead of selling on the open market. For prices between £100 and £90 a loss would be made because of the £10 premium paid, but below £90 the owner of the put would make money on a pound for pound basis as the price becomes lower. Once again the payoff for the owner and writer of the put are exactly opposite. One makes money as the other loses.

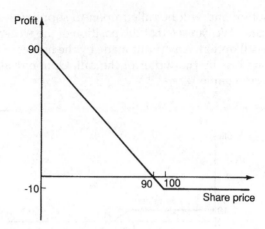

Figure 11.3 *Put option holder*

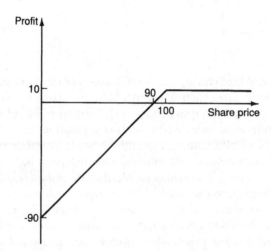

Figure 11.4 *Writer of put option*

Puts, like calls, are rarely exercised before expiration. If the share price declined then the value of the put option would rise, but instead of exercising the option the owner would sell the right on the market.

Options have attracted increasing interest as the opportunities for hedging and speculation have been recognized in increasingly volatile markets. As we shall see later, volatility of price is an important determinant of option prices. The *Financial Times* provides details of option prices both for traditional three month options and those traded on LIFFE. In the latter market nine month option contracts are created every three months, so that at any time there will be three series of options outstanding with a maximum time to expiry of three, six and nine months.

Table 11.1 shows the prices of options on LIFFE on 9 June 1994. The table is taken from the following day's *Financial Times*. We can see that each of the companies quoted has three series of calls and puts outstanding with a range of exercise prices. The current value of the underlying security is shown in parentheses beneath each company name. For example Hanson has two series of puts and calls expiring in August, November and February with one exercise price (240) below the current value of 250 and one above. As the call exercise price increases, so the call option value decreases as the potential opportunity for gain decreases; naturally with puts there is the opposite effect, with higher exercise prices being reflected in higher put option values. With both

Table 11.1 LIFFE equity options

Option		Calls Jul	Calls Oct	Calls Jan	Puts Jul	Puts Oct	Puts Jan
Allied-Lyons	540	36	51	–	9	17½	–
(*564)	589	11	25½	–	33½	42	–
Argyll	240	8½	16½	21½	15	19	24½
(*241)	260	3	9½	14	31	33½	37½
ASDA	50	7	8½	10½	2	4	5
(*55)	60	2	4	6	7	10	11
Brit Airways	390	16½	29	35	16½	25	30
(*396)	420	6	15	23	37½	43½	48½
SmKl Bchm A	390	21	32½	40	12½	22½	30½
(*396)	420	7½	19	27	30½	41	47½
Boots	500	41½	54½	62	5½	13	19½
(*530)	550	11	25½	34½	27½	35½	43½
BP	360	27½	36	42	7½	14	18½
(*376)	420	3½	11½	16	45	50	53
British Steel	130	11½	16	19	4½	8	10
(*137)	140	6	11	14½	9½	13	15
Bass	500	34	47	56	10½	18	31
(*519)	550	10½	22½	31	38½	45	59½
Cable & Wire	425	29½	–	–	10½	–	–
(*447)	450	15	–	–	22	–	–
Courtaulds	500	32	48	56½	9½	19	26½
(*519)	550	8½	23	32	38	47	53½
Comm Union	500	47	51½	59½	7	16	23
(*535)	550	14½	23½	33	27	42½	46½
ICI	800	36	53	67½	18½	37½	48½
(*813)	850	13	30	46	48	67	76
Kingfisher	500	41	52	63½	7½	19	26
(*527)	550	13½	31½	38	33½	42	51½
Land Secur	600	47½	59½	67	4	10½	16
(*636)	650	14	29	36½	23½	30½	37
Marks & S	390	25½	36½	43	5½	11½	15
(*406)	420	9	21	27½	20	25½	29½

Option		Calls Aug	Calls Nov	Calls Feb	Puts Aug	Puts Nov	Puts Feb
Hanson	240	17½	21	25	4½	9½	13
(*250)	260	7	12	15	14½	20	23½
Lasmo	134	14	17½	–	7½	12	–
(*139)	154	6	8½	–	19½	23	–
Lucas Inds	180	15½	22½	24	6½	14	16½
(*186)	200	5½	13	16½	18	26	28½
P & O	650	35	51½	60	23½	44	50
(*658)	700	14	29	38½	53½	76½	81
Pilkington	160	21	27½	29½	4	7½	11
(*176)	180	8½	16½	18½	14	17	20½
Prudential	300	14½	22½	28	12	21	22½
(*300)	330	4	11	15½	33½	40	41
RTZ	850	37½	64	80½	28½	46½	53
(*851)	900	18	41½	57½	60	74½	80½
Redland	500	31	46	53½	15½	29½	34½
(*508)	550	10½	23½	31	47½	60½	65
Royal Insce	240	25½	32½	38	6	14½	15
(*255)	260	13½	22	28	14½	24½	25
Tesco	200	23½	29	32	4	8	11½
(*217)	220	10½	16½	21	12	17½	20½
Vodafone	500	31	50	58	18½	29½	37½
(*514)	550	10½	27	35	50½	59	66½
Williams	325	27	34½	–	5½	12½	–
(*342)	354	10½	19	–	19½	27½	–

Option		Jul	Oct	Jan	Jul	Oct	Jan
BAA	900	38½	61	72½	18½	31	39
(*927)	950	15	36	47½	48	58½	66
Thames Wtr	460	23	30	33	16	25	32
(*476)	500	5	14	17	46½	50½	57½
NatWest	460	19	29	39½	16	28	32½
(*460)	500	5½	14	23½	44	54½	57½

Table 11.1 *cont.*

Option		*Calls* *Jul*	*Oct*	*Jan*	*Puts* *Jul*	*Oct*	*Jan*
Sainsbury	390	17½	30½	37½	14	24	30
(*391)	420	6½	17	24½	35	41½	47½
Shell Trans.	650	56½	66	72½	3½	14½	18½
(*697)	700	19½	32½	41½	19	32½	37½
Storehouse	200	20	25	29	4	8	11½
(*216)	220	7	13½	18	14	17½	21½
Trafalgar	79	11½	–	–	2½	–	–
(*86)	88	6	–	–	6	–	–
Unilever	1000	33	57	72½	23½	34½	43
(*1002)	1050	12½	33	49	55	64	70
Zeneca	700	25½	41	53	19½	36½	43½
(*700)	750	7	20½	32	54½	68½	74½
Option		*Aug*	*Nov*	*Feb*	*Aug*	*Nov*	*Feb*
Grand Met	420	19½	34	40½	16½	24½	30½
(*425)	460	5½	17½	23½	44½	49	55
Ladbroke	140	24	29	31	3	6	7
(*158)	160	11	17½	20½	11	15	16½
Utd Biscuits	300	23½	37½	41½	5	12	15½
(*319)	330	11½	22	26	18½	28½	31
Option		*Jun*	*Sep*	*Dec*	*Jun*	*Sep*	*Dec*
Fisons	140	9	18	21	2	9	14
(*146)	160	1	9	13	16	22	26½
Abbey Natl	420	13	29½	39	3	17	23½

Option		*Calls* *Jun*	*Sep*	*Dec*	*Puts* *Jun*	*Sep*	*Dec*
Amstrad	30	2½	5	6	1	3	4½
(*31)	35	1	3	4	4½	6	7½
Barclays	550	8	31½	45	7½	31	36½
(*550)	600	1	12½	24½	52	64½	68
Blue Circle	280	9	25	31	2½	14	19½
(*285)	300	2	15	22	16½	26	31
British Gas	260	20½	28½	31½	1	6½	12
(*278)	280	5	16½	20	6	14	22
Dixons	180	15½	22	26½	1	9½	13
(*193)	200	2	11½	17	8½	21	23½
Hillsdown	160	13	21	24	1	6	7
(*171)	180	1½	9½	14	11½	16	17½
Lonrho	130	7	15½	19½	2	11	13½
(*135)	140	2	11	15	7	16½	19
Natl Power	420	9½	30½	39	5½	21	26½
(*424)	460	1	13½	22	38	45	50
Scot Power	330	18½	30	35	2	17	21
(*345)	360	2	14½	21	17½	33½	36½
Sears	120	4½	11	13	2	7	8½
(*122)	130	1	6	8½	9	12½	14½
Forte	220	17	27½	30	1	8	12
(*234)	240	3	16	19	8	17½	22
Tarmac	155	5	–	–	3	–	–
(*156)	174	1	–	–	19½	–	–
Thorn EMI	1050	46	75½	97½	3	46½	62
(*1089)	1100	13	49	71½	21	73½	89
TSB	220	6	17½	23	2½	13	16½
(*223)	240	1	8	15½	17½	25	28½

Option		*Aug*	*Nov*	*Feb*	*Aug*	*Nov*	*Feb*
Brit Aero	420	54	70½	82	12	27½	34½
(*457)	460	29½	49½	62½	29	46	54
BAT Inds	420	24½	34	44	18½	26½	29½
(*427)	460	7½	19	26½	46½	52	54½
BTR	360	25½	33	40	8	16	19½
(*374)	390	9½	18	25½	3½	32	35
Brit Telecom	360	23	28	31½	13	17	23½
(*374)	390	7½	14	18	32½	35	41
Cadbury Sch	460	22½	33½	42	14	24	26½
(*464)	500	7½	16½	24½	41	49	50½
Eastern Elec	600	27½	42½	53½	31	44	52
(*605)	650	9½	23	34½	68½	76½	83
Guinness	460	29	39	49½	9	17	21½
(*475)	500	8½	19½	29½	30½	38½	44½
GEC	300	16	22	25½	10½	15	18½
(*309)	330	3	9	13	32	34½	37

Option		*Jun*	*Sep*	*Dec*	*Jun*	*Sep*	*Dec*
Tomkins	220	4½	14½	19½	4	14½	17½
(*221	240	1	6	11½	21	28½	31
Wellcome	550	29	55	67½	3	26	36½
(*573)	600	3	30	44	31½	54	63½
Option		*Jul*	*Oct*	*Jan*	*Jul*	*Oct*	*Jan*
Glaxo	500	60	72½	78	6½	23½	31
(*548)	550	27	42½	51½	24½	49	56
HSBC 75p shs	700	46	72½	89	27½	50½	63½
(*715)	750	24	49	66	56	78½	90
Reuters	487	23½	35½	–	18½	29	–
(*489)	500	16	29½	43	25	35	42½
Option		*Aug*	*Nov*	*Feb*	*Aug*	*Nov*	*Feb*
Rolls-Royce	180	17½	24½	27½	6	12	14½
(*190)	200	7	15	18½	17	23	25½

*Underlying security price. Premiums shown are based on closing offer prices. 9 June, Total contracts: 32 482 Calls: 19 155 Puts: 13 327.
Source: *Financial Times*, 10 June 1994.

types of option the longer to expiry the greater is the value as there is more time in which significant price changes may take place. Information on the traditional options market which predates traded options by centuries is also given in the *Financial Times*. These are available on any security provided counterparties are available for each leg of the option. They are arranged individually through brokers and unlike traded options are not readily transferable.

11.3 Simple option strategies

We shall begin our brief discussion on option strategies with a note of warning. Option dealing is often regarded as a very exciting and profitable activity. It can indeed be both of these, but it can also be nervy and highly expensive! Table 11.2 contrasts the investment of £1000 in call options with a similar amount invested in the underlying security. It is assumed that call options with an exercise price of 105p can be purchased for 10p on a security currently trading at 100p. If the price was to rise to 150p by exercise date then an investment in options would yield a total profit of £3500 and a return of 350%, while an investment in the underlying security would yield a profit of £500 and a return of 50%. However, suppose that the price at exercise date was only 105p. As the exercise price and market price were the same, the option would go unexercised and the option buyer would lose the premium paid of £1000. A loss of 100%! However, the buyer of the security would experience a gain of £50 or 5%. Any gains made by the holder of the call option would of course be reflected in identical losses made by the writer of the option. Holding options on their own can therefore be seen to be a risky investment. Both high returns and large losses are possible, and therefore an investor in options should expect to receive a high rate of return to compensate for the level of risk involved. However, we shall see that when options are held in combination or with the underlying share, then a low-risk strategy can result.

The options literature makes for racy reading because of its colourful terminology involving the use of terms such as strips and straddles. An infinite number of combinations of puts, calls and the underlying security could be considered, but we shall confine ourselves to examining a limited number of potential option strategies. Combining a put and call with the same exercise price and expiry date is called a straddle. Likewise combining two puts and a call is termed a strip, while the combination of two calls and a put is called a strap. Figure 11.5 shows the payoff at expiry for the holder of a straddle, while Figure 11.6 illustrates the payoff from the point of view of the writer. A straddle position would be appropriate for someone who believes that the price of shares will show significant movement either up or down but is unsure of the direction of movement. If there was a single straddle writer, then he would have to believe that the share price was going to trade close to the exercise price. However, it seems more likely that there will be separate writers for the put and call option held by the holder of the straddle position.

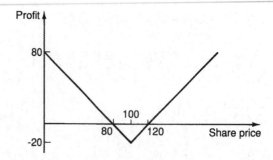

Figure 11.5 *Holder of straddle*

Table 11.2 Option trading compared with purchase of shares

	Options		Shares
Purchase of 10 000 call options at 10p	1 000	Purchase of 1000 shares at £1	1000
Exercise price £1.05	—		—
Assume price at exercise date £1.50			
Cost of options	1 000	Cost of shares	1000
Exercise price, 10 000 at £1.05	10 500		
	11 500		
Sale at market value 10 000 at £1.50	15 000	Sale at market value 1000 at £1.50	1500
Profit	£3 500	Profit	£500
	350%		50%
Assume price at exercise date £1.05			
Cost of options	1 000	Cost of shares	1000
As current price equals exercise price		Sale at market value 1000 at	
price option not exercised	—	£1.05	1050
Loss	£1 000	Profit	£50
	100%		5%

As well as being held in combination, options can also be combined with the share on which they represent a claim. Figure 11.7 shows the payoff resulting from owning a put and also owning the share. An exercise price of £100 is assumed together with a current share price of £100 and a put premium of £10. The figure shows three lines: one for the share (or long position), one for the put purchased and one for the combination. The strategy reduces the return at higher share prices but limits potential losses should the share fall in price.

Another example of this type of strategy involves holding the share and writing a call option on the share. This is referred to as writing a covered call. Figure 11.8 shows the payoff arising from this strategy, and again three separate lines, one for the share, one for the call written and one for the combination, are shown. As can be seen, an investor who follows this strategy, rather than just owning the share, increases the return at low share prices while reducing returns at higher share prices. This strategy might be used by a portfolio investor in slack markets to try and increase portfolio return.

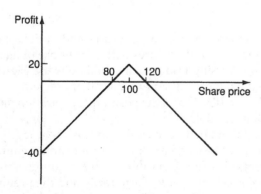

Figure 11.6 *Writer of straddle*

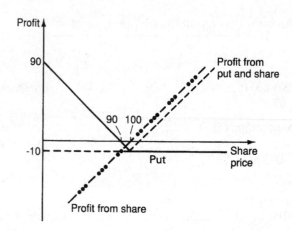

Figure 11.7 *Share and put option*

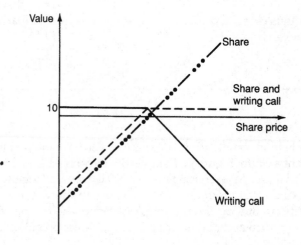

Figure 11.8 *Share and writing call option*

We have examined only a few of the many combinations of options and shares available. One point which did emerge was that on their own options are high-risk investments but when held in combination or with the share it is possible for risk to be reduced. As we shall see this is an important factor in deriving models of option valuation.

11.4 Call options and futures compared

A mistake is sometimes made by regarding futures and options contracts as identical. This is definitely not the case. With futures both parties are obligated to complete the transaction, either by a reversing trade or an actual delivery. Figure 11.9 contrasts the situations faced by (a) the buyer and writer for a call option and (b) the buyer and seller of a futures contract. The option shows the position at expiration date, while the futures position is shown at delivery date.

As shown in Fig. 11.9(a), no matter what the price of the underlying stock, at expiration an option buyer cannot lose and an option writer cannot gain. Option buyers pay writers for putting themselves in this position with a premium at the outset of the contract. The exercise price is set more or less arbitrarily and the premium negotiated. In a broader sense, the premium is the equilibrating factor, bringing quantity demanded and quantity supplied together in the options market.

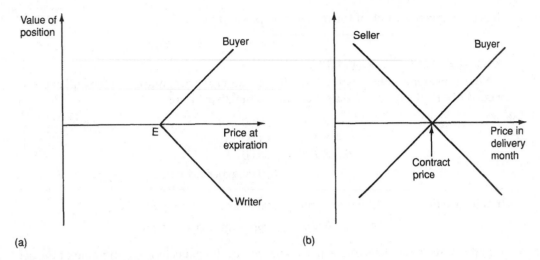

Figure 11.9 *Call option and futures compared*

The situation is quite different with a futures contract. As shown in Fig. 11.9(b), the buyer may gain or lose, depending on the price in the delivery month, and so may the seller. The higher is the original contract price, the greater is the likelihood that the buyer will lose and the seller will gain. The lower is the original contract price, the greater is the likelihood that the seller will lose and the buyer will gain. The contract price is negotiated in the attempt to find a value that will lead both parties to consider the resulting prospects worth their while.

In the futures market, the contract price is the equilibrating factor, bringing together the quantity demanded and the quantity supplied. No money is paid by either party to the other.

We saw in the previous section that the option price or premium is the factor determining equilibrium in the option market. It is therefore important to determine those factors which affect option value so that appropriate valuation models can be derived.

The value of a call option at expiry date can be stated as follows:

$$V_\text{o} = \max(V_\text{s} - E, 0)$$

11.5 Factors affecting option values

where V_o is the value of the option at expiration, V_s is the value of the underlying share at expiration, E is the exercise price and max means the maximum of $V_\text{s} - E$ or zero. Options always have a minimum value of zero as the holder will only enforce the option if it is profitable.

Option values clearly depend on the share price and the exercise price. However, this is only looking at the position at expiration of the option. We are interested in obtaining a value prior to expiration. When we consider the situation one period prior to expiration we do not (cannot) know what the value will be at expiry, but instead will formulate some sort of probabilistic belief about the value one period hence.

Suppose that we hold an option expiring in 90 days time with an exercise price of £10 and that the current market value is also £10. If this position was to hold at expiration the option value would be zero. However, with time to run to expiry as long as a probability exists that the price will exceed £10 before expiry, the option should have a positive value. If the expected value of the share at expiry was £10 represented by the distribution

$$
\begin{array}{llr}
0.3 \times £5 &=& £1.5 \\
0.4 \times £10 &=& £4.0 \\
0.3 \times £15 &=& £4.5 \\
\hline
& & £10.0 \ \text{expected value}
\end{array}
$$

then the expected value of the option at expiry date would be

$$0 \times 0.3 + 0 \times 0.4 + (15 - 10) \times 0.3 = £1.50$$

Remember that $V_o = \max(V_s - E, 0)$.

Now consider another share, also with an exercise price, market value and expected valued of £10 at expiration date, but having the distribution

$$
\begin{aligned}
0.3 \times £0 &= £0.00 \\
0.4 \times £10 &= £4.00 \\
0.3 \times £20 &= \underline{£6.00} \\
&\quad £10.00 \text{ expected value}
\end{aligned}
$$

In this case the expected value of the option at expiry date would be

$$0 \times 0.3 + 0 \times 0.4 + (20 - 10) \times 0.3 = £3.00$$

Both shares have the same expected value but the expected option value of the second security is twice that of the first. Why should this be? If we examine the respective probability distributions, we can see that the second security has a wider dispersion around the mean. This higher volatility makes the option more valuable. It should be noted that although there is the possibility of a lower value in the second share than the first, this does not matter as the option value cannot be less than zero; it is the possibility of a higher value which makes the option more valuable.

The holding of a call option can also be regarded as a deferred purchase of the underlying security as the exercise price does not have to be paid until a later date. This means that the option value will be affected by the level of interest rates. The higher are the interest rates the greater will be the value of the option because the present value of the exercise price will be lower. Clearly the longer the time to expiration the higher will be the option value as again the present value of the exercise price will be reduced. In addition, the longer is the time to expiration the greater will be the opportunity for higher share values to result from share volatility. Our discussion to date suggests that option values are determined by the following:

1. the current price of the share;
2. the exercise price of the option;
3. the volatility (variance) of returns on share;
4. the time to expiration;
5. the short-term interest rate.

Figure 11.10 sets out the limits of the value of a call option and also the more usual pattern of valuation. The highest possible value is shown by line X, indicating a value

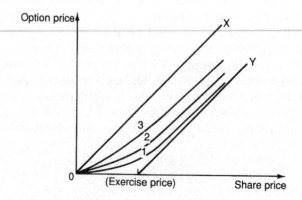

Figure 11.10 *Limits of option valuation*

equal to the underlying share. This value would occur only if there was a very long time to expiration (perhaps a perpetual option) and if exercise was not expected in the near future, i.e. the present value (PV) of the exercise price approaches zero.

The lowest value that the option can have is that represented by line Y; zero up to exercise price and Y for values greater than exercise price. This would be the value at expiry. Most options will lie between these two bands represented by lines 1, 2 and 3, indicating a convex relationship where the value of the option commands the greatest premium over the theoretical value at exercise price and where the premium declines with increases in the value of the share beyond that point.

Put–call parity [3]

In section 11.3 we looked at a limited number of strategies involving the use of options and the underlying share. If we add to these the opportunity to borrow at the risk-free rate of interest, then it is possible to devise alternative strategies with the same value at expiry. This enables certain basic relationships to be derived. For ease of analysis we assume a European option and that no dividend will be paid on the underlying share before expiry of the option.

Figure 11.11 shows the situation at expiration from buying a call and writing a put, both exercisable at £100. Whatever the value of the share at expiry £100 will be paid and the share will be acquired. An alternative strategy giving the identical payoff would be to borrow the PV of the exercise price (i.e. a PV of £100) and buy the share now; at expiry date £100 would be paid in repayment of the loan and you would be left holding the share as in the put–call combination. We can thus say

> value of put – value of call = PV of exercise price – share price

or

$$P - C = \frac{E}{1 + r} - S$$

where P is the value of the put, C is the value of the call, E is the exercise price, r is the risk-free rate of interest and S is the current share price.

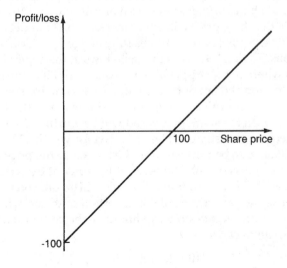

Figure 11.11 *Buy call; write put; position at expiry*

This basic identity can be used to express the value of any of the components in terms of the others. For example,

$$P = C + \frac{E}{1 + r} - S$$

11.6 Binomial valuation formula [4]

We now move on to consider option pricing formulae. The simplest of these is the binomial option pricing formula and we shall present a detailed derivation in this section. The basis of this valuation formula and also the more rigorous Black and Scholes formula [2] is that it is possible to construct a risk-free hedged portfolio by buying shares and writing call options on the shares. As the resulting portfolio is risk free it would be expected that only a risk-free rate of return would be obtained. This then enables us to obtain a value for the call option.

Both models to be discussed are for the European call. As traded options are of the American variety it may seem that there is more academic than practical merit in this approach. However, Merton [5] made a number of observations on the comparison of European and American options. The first point to make is that the American call is a European call with the additional opportunity to exercise before expiry date. It follows that an American call cannot be worth less than a European call having the same expiry date and exercise price. Another conclusion is that it never pays to exercise an American call before expiry date provided that the share does not pay dividends or the exercise price is adjusted for dividend payments. The reason for this is that, although the share price might be trading above the exercise price prior to expiry, there is still the chance that the price will rise further before expiry. Suppose that an investor holds an American call with an exercise price of £10 on a share currently selling for £12. It would seem that the investor should exercise the call immediately rather than holding it and exercising at a later date. However, with a traded option there is the opportunity to sell the call to another investor. The American call will have two sources of value: the value of an immediate call (£2) plus the value of the chance to call from now to expiration date. Therefore provided that an American call will not pay dividends before the expiration date or the exercise price is dividend protected it can be valued as a European call. In addition, when examining put–call parity in the previous section we derived a relationship between the value of puts and calls. Therefore the valuation formula for a call can also be used to value puts. Having established the relevance of European call option valuation models we shall proceed to examine the binomial option pricing formula.

It is required to value a call one period before expiration given the following information: present price of share, £10; exercise price of call option, £10; risk-free interest rate, 25%. Assume that the share price will either increase to £15 or decrease to £5 by the exercise date. It should be possible to construct a fully hedged position by buying shares and writing call options. Table 11.3 shows the cash flows at the beginning of the period and the end of period where one share is purchased and two calls written. It can be seen that at the end of the period the net outcome will be the same irrespective of whether the £15 price or the £5 price prevails. The reason for this is that if the share price at the end of the period is £15 then the share purchased will be worth £15 while the holder of the call written will require two shares to be delivered for which £20 will be paid ($2 \times$ £10). These shares will have to be purchased in the market at the price of £15 each and a total cost of £30 giving a loss of £10. However, if the price at exercise date is £5 then the value of the one share held will be £5, and the calls will go unexercised and will have a value of zero. Because the strategy results in a certain outcome whichever possible share price results, the return on the strategy should be the certain return, i.e. the risk-free rate of return. We can therefore say

$$(10 - 2C)1.25 = 5$$

$$C = £3$$

We can see from the above equation that we have a net investment of £4, i.e. the cost of one share minus the premium received on writing two calls, and as the outcome of this net investment is certain we would expect to earn the risk-free rate of return. In this case we required one share for every two calls written. The shares-to-option ratio is often called the hedge ratio or option delta. In our example the option delta is 0.5. Options will have to be priced in accordance with this model, otherwise opportunities would occur for dealers to earn riskless profits. Arbitrage activity would ensure that all options are priced in accordance with the formula above.

Table 11.3 Cash flows in fully hedged position

		Flows at t_1	
		Possible share prices	
	Flows at t_0	£15	£5
Buy one share	−10	15	5
Write two calls	+2C	−10	—
		5	5

A general formula for the value of a call option with one period to expiry can be written as

$$C_o = H\left(P_o - \frac{P_L}{1+r} \right)$$

where C_o is the value of the call option with one period to expiry, r is the risk-free rate of interest, P_o is the current share price, P_L is the lower value of the share at end of period and $H = (C_u - C_L)/(P_u - P_L)$ is the hedging ratio. C_u is the upper value of the option at the end of the period and C_L is the lower value of the option at the end of the period; P_u is the upper value of the share at the end of the period.

While the foregoing illustrates the principles of option valuation it makes the unrealistic assumption that there are only two possible prices for the share at the end of the period. While it would be possible to make the example slightly more realistic by assuming sub-periods, the calculations would become more complicated without adding greatly to the realism. Fortunately Black and Scholes have devised an option valuation formula which assumes that a share's returns are normally distributed, and this allows for a more realistic assessment of option values.

11.7 Black–Scholes option valuation formula

The Black–Scholes model was developed in 1973 and is the basis for most of the analysis in this field, at both the professional and the academic level. It was based on the principle discussed above that if capital markets are in equilibrium the call option will be priced so that the rate of return on hedged portfolios is equal to the risk-free rate of return.

The model indicates that the equilibrium value of the option does not depend on the expected rate of return on the share, but on the factors intuitively identified in section 11.5. These were the current share price, the exercise price of the option, the volatility (variance) of return on share, the time to expiration and the short-term interest rate. Although four of the five variables are relatively easy to determine, the standard deviation can cause problems. The simplest approach to estimating this variable is to measure the recent past variability of the share price and assume that this variability will continue to apply over the life of the option.

The assumptions for the Black–Scholes model appear to be severe.

1. There are no penalties for or restrictions on short selling.
2. Transaction costs and taxes are zero.

3. The option is European.
4. The share pays no dividend.
5. The share price is continuous.
6. The market operates continuously.
7. The short-term interest rate (risk-free) is known and constant.
8. The share price is 'log normally' distributed.

Although these assumptions are the sufficient conditions for the Black–Scholes model to be correct, if they do not hold a variation sometimes does. It is possible, for example, for the formula to be adjusted to account for dividend payments.

The model states that the current value of a call option is given by the formula

$$P_o = P_s N(d_1) - \frac{E}{e^{rt}} N(d_2)$$

where

$$d_1 = \frac{\ln(P_s/E) + (r + \sigma^2/2)t}{\sigma t^{1/2}}$$

and

$$d_2 = \frac{\ln(P_s/E) + (r - \sigma^2/2)t}{\sigma t^{1/2}}$$

$$= d_1 - \sigma t^{1/2}$$

P_s is the current price of the share, P_o is the current price of the call option, E is the exercise price of the call option, r is the continuously compounded riskless rate of interest, σ is the standard deviation of the continuously compounded annual rate of return on the share, $e = 2.7183$ is the exponential constant, t is the time (in years) remaining before expiration of the option, $\ln(P_s/E)$ is the natural logarithm of P_s/E and $N(d)$ is the probability that a deviation less than d will occur in a normal distribution with a mean of zero and a standard deviation of unity. (Those readers who wish to see the proof of the model should refer to the original paper [2].)

We now use the model to value the call option on a share given the following information: $P_s = 100p$; $E = 90p$; $r -= 0.10$; $t = 0.25$ (90 days, i.e. a quarter of a year); $\sigma = 0.30$. First we need to calculate d_1 and d_2:

$$d_1 = \frac{\ln(100/90) + (0.10 + 0.30^2/2)0.25}{0.30 \times 0.25^{1/2}}$$

$$= 0.944$$

$$d_2 = d_1 - \sigma t^{1/2}$$

$$= 0.944 - 0.30 \times 0.25^{1/2}$$

$$= 0.794$$

(the natural logarithm of 100/90 is 0.10536).

The expression $N(d_1)$ is the probability that a normally distributed random variable will have a value less than or equal to d_1. The value of this cumulative normal distribution can be read from Table 7 at the end of the book. Using this table and interpolating we find the following values:

$$N(d_1) = N(0.944) = 0.827$$

$$N(d_2) = N(0.794) = 0.786$$

We can now complete the calculations:

$$P_o = 100p \times 0.827 - \frac{90p}{\exp(0.10 \times 0.25)} \times 0.786$$

$$= 82.7p \frac{90p}{1.025} \times 0.786$$

$$= 82.7p - 69.0p$$

$$= 13.7p$$

The model indicates that a call option to buy one share of the company being considered has an equilibrium value of 13.7p. If the actual option price is less than 13.7p, it is being undervalued and it is a good buy for an investor. Alternatively the investor could construct a riskless hedge by buying shares and writing calls as shown in the previous section. It can be shown that if we accept the Black-Scholes formula as correct, the appropriate hedge ratio is given by $N(d_1)$ which in our example was 0.827. This means that for every call option written, 0.827 of a share should be purchased.

The above calculations are straightforward but time-consuming without a programmed calculator or microcomputer. The model is used by option dealers, particularly in the USA on the successful Chicago Board Options Exchange. Fortunately the dealers do not need to go through the calculations that have been shown. If they did they might miss the opportunity to deal in the option! If a programmed calculator is not available, then option tables, based on the Black–Scholes model, that allow the appropriate equilibrium values to be read off can be used.

The numerical example in the previous section used the Black–Scholes model to value a call option on a security. It is probably true to say that this will be the most common use of the model in practice, i.e. by investors and traders in share options. However, it has become increasingly recognized that a knowledge of options and their value can be useful for managers in companies. This is because managers encounter options in their day-to-day activities concerning both projects and their financing. It may be that in some circumstances the existence of options is not clearly recognized or that they are not valued correctly. These options could include the following.

The option to expand

A small project or even an apparently unprofitable project can be made more valuable if it gives the company the option to expand when economic prospects improve. That option to expand in the future clearly has a value. When valuing a current activity, perhaps to decide whether to continue, any option of this kind should be included in the value of the activity to the business. For example it may not be immediately profitable to enter a particular field of high technology activity, but if the company does not proceed it will lose its option to expand in what promises to be a growing market. It would be possible, given the necessary estimates for the five factors determining option value, to use the Black–Scholes model to calculate the value of a project's option to expand. This, of course, is a call option. Some care needs to be exercised as the manager will have to incorporate more estimates into his calculation because of the lack of a market for projects.

The option to abandon

The option to abandon represents a put option on the project. This option may be very valuable on some projects where it may be possible to abandon a project and sell off assets rather than continue with a project which is yielding negative net present values (NPVs).

Underwriting costs

When a company arranges for a new issue to be underwritten it is essentially buying a put option from the underwriters. The fee paid in the past has often been based on a percentage of the issue proceeds, whereas in fact the actual value of the option will depend upon the five factors previously discussed. If the issue price is a rights issue at a reasonable discount on current market value and there is only a short time from announcement to issue, underwriting fees based on a fixed percentage of issue proceeds might lead to an overpayment by management for the put option facility. There is clear scope for negotiation based on the use of the Black–Scholes model to value the option.

Equity as a call option on the firm's assets

Whenever a company has debt in its capital structure, then equity shareholders can be regarded as holding a call option on the firm's assets with an exercise price equal to the amount due to debt holders on redemption. When we examined put–call parity we found that

value of put – value of call = PV of exercise price – share price

or, in symbols,

$$P - C = \frac{E}{1 + r} - S$$

In this case the value V of the firm replaces the share S as the risky asset. If, on the maturity date, V exceeds the face value D of the bonds (PV of the exercise price in equation above), the shareholders will exercise their call option by paying off the bonds and keeping the surplus. However, if the value of the firm is less than the face value of the bonds, the shareholders will take advantage of the limited liability and default on the debt by not exercising their option. At maturity the shareholders' wealth W will be the maximum of zero or $V - D$.

Substituting V for S and W for C in the basic equation we obtain

$$W = V - (B - P)$$

This says that the equity W, a call option, is equal to the value V of the firm minus risky debt $B - P$, which itself is equivalent to the PV B of risk-free debt minus the value P of a European put option.

It should be noted that any investments undertaken by a geared firm which lead to an increase in specific or non-market risk will increase the wealth of shareholders at the expense of debt holders, even if the total value of the firm is unaltered. We can see that increasing the risk of the firm will increase the value of the put option written by debt holders. This reduces the value of debt and results in a corresponding increase in equity. These are just a few examples of options which occur in the corporate financial environment. Others will include warrants which are long-run call options but have the added complication of changing the capital structure when exercised and convertibles which can be regarded as a fixed interest security with a call option attached. In fact debt instruments have become increasingly complex. For example during the 1980s many companies issued so called puttable convertibles enabling holders to convert into equity at a later date but also carrying the right to have the company buy back the bonds at a premium on issue price. The holders of the bonds therefore have a call option enabling them to convert into equity and also a put option allowing them to sell the bonds back to the company at a higher value. There are implications with this type of issue not only for the way in which it is valued by the investor and the issuing company alike, but also for the way in which it is treated in the accounts of the company.

11.9 Summary and conclusions

We have seen that options give the holder the right to buy or sell assets at a fixed price on or before a specified date. Share options are the most familiar type of options and the put option gives the holder the right to sell shares while the call option gives the holder the right to buy shares at the exercise price. Options do not have to be exercised, and if the share price is below the exercise price in the case of a call option at expiry the holder will not be forced to exercise his option. This contrasts with futures where there is an obligation by both parties to complete the contract. It was noted that American options can be exercised at any time up to and including the expiry date, while European options can only be exercised on the expiry date. The factors affecting option value were identified as the current price of the share, the exercise price of the option, the volatility (variance) of returns on the share, the time to expiration and the short-term interest rate.

It was noted that, while options held on their own are very risky investments, by holding them either in combination or with the underlying security it was possible to reduce risk. This was an important factor in developing valuation models where it was noted that by holding the underlying share and at the same time writing call options it was possible to produce a fully hedged portfolio. This principle is at the basis of option valuation models; if it is possible to devise a fully hedged risk-free portfolio, then markets will ensure that only the risk-free rate of return can be earned on such a portfolio.

In addition to using option valuation models to value the options on shares it was noted that managers in companies are frequently dealing with options, although they may not necessarily be explicitly recognized as such. Examples given and discussed were the option to expand a project and the option to abandon a project, which are a call option and a put option respectively. It was also noted that the equity of any geared firm could be regarded as a call option on the firm's assets.

The option pricing model is both powerful and useful. It is probably true to say that its use is still in its infancy and is confined mainly to the valuation of traded options and, to a lesser extent, other financial securities. However, the corporate manager should be on the look-out for options when making both investment and financing decisions. The existence of options can add value and justify potential courses of action which might otherwise be ruled out by a more conventional approach.

11.10 Key terms

American and European options	Expiry date
Binomial valuation	Option
Black–Scholes call option valuation formula	Put–call parity
Call option	Put option
Call options and futures	Straddle and strip strategies
Exercise/striking price	Traded options

11.11 Revision questions

1. State the characteristics of put and call options.
2. Distinguish a European from an American option.
3. Illustrate diagrammatically the value of put and call options at exercise date.
4. Why is an uncovered position in call options riskier than holding the underlying security?
5. Give one example of how an option might be used to hedge risk in financial security dealing.
6. What are the fundamental differences between options and futures?
7. List the factors which determine option value.
8. State the basic put–call parity relationship.
9. What is meant by the hedging ratio/option delta?
10. (a) In a geared company debt holders have a call option on the firm's assets.
    (b) In a geared company equity holders have a call option on the firm's assets.
    Which statement is correct? Why?

11.12 References

1. Payne, A.F.T. (1981) The market for options in London, *Investment Analyst*, April.
2. Black, F. and Scholes, M. (1973) The pricing of options and corporate liabilities, *Journal of Political Economy*, **18**, 637–54, May–June.
3. Stoll, H.R. (1969) The relationship between put and call option prices, *Journal of Finance*, 802–24, December.

4. Cox, J.C., Ross, S.A. and Rubinstein, M. (1979) Option pricing: a simplified approach, *Journal of Financial Economics*, **7**, 229–63, September.
5. Merton, R.C. (1973) Theory of rational option pricing, *Bell Journal of Economics and Management Science*, **4**, 141–83, Spring.

11.13 Further reading

Black, R. and Scholes, M. (1973) The pricing of options and corporate liabilities, *Journal of Political Economy*, Vol. 18, pages 637–54, May–June.

Cox, J.C., Ross, S.A. and Rubinstein, M. (1979) Option pricing: a simplified approach, *Journal of Financial Economics*, **7**, 229–263, September.

Hull, J. (1993) *Options, Futures and Other Derivative Securities*, 2nd edn, Prentice Hall, Englewood Cliffs, NJ.

Merton, R.C. (1973) Theory of rational option pricing, *Bell Journal of Economics and Management Science*, **4**, 141–183, Spring.

11.14 Problems

1. Explain what you understand by the option strategy termed a 'straddle'. Use diagrams to illustrate the options involved and the potential profit from such a strategy. Why might an investor use a straddle?

2. Six months ago you purchased a call option on 1000 shares in Frisky PLC at 10p per share. The share price six months ago was £1.10 while the exercise price is £1.20. The current price, just before expiry, is £1.35.

   (a) Should the option be exercised?
   (b) What is the profit/loss on the option dealing?
   (c) Compare the result in (b) with the strategy of investing the same amount of cash in shares six months ago.

3. Analyse the relative risk and payoff of the following strategies:

   (a) buy share;
   (b) buy call;
   (c) buy share and buy put option on the share;
   (d) buy share, buy put and write call;
   (e) buy share and write call option on the share;
   (f) sell put.

4. (a) Critically appraise the factors which determine the theoretical value of options highlighting any problems that might be encountered in incorporating them in a formal valuation model.
   (b) Explain how option theory might be useful in evaluating underwriting fees to be paid in connection with a proposed rights issue.

5. A financial dealer recently advised a client holding a well-diversified portfolio of shares to write calls on all the share holdings he owned or as many as were traded on the LIFFE. He explained that the client could not lose money but would benefit from the premiums received. Evaluate this strategy and the dealer's view that the client could not lose. If only a few options were traded on the portfolio shares, what alternative strategy would you suggest?

6. Using the binomial pricing model calculate the hedging ratio and the value of a call option with one year to expiry from the following data: current share price, £5; exercise price, £6; value expected at expiration, either £8 or £4; risk-free rate of return 10%.

7. Use the value of the call option obtained in problem 6 plus the other data in the question to calculate the value of a put option. What is the principle involved here?

8. Explain how call options differ from futures and evaluate their use in hedging risk.

9. Use the Black–Scholes model to calculate the value of a European call option on a non-dividend paying share from the following data: current share price, £2.80; exercise price, £4.00; expiry date, six months' time; instantaneous standard deviation of return, 0.5; continuously compounded risk-free rate of interest, 6%.

10. You are employed by a company which includes amongst its assets a piece of city centre land. This land is currently in short-term use as a car park with the revenues being sufficient just to cover expenses and taxes in connection with ownership. You have been approached by a developer who wishes to acquire a one year option to purchase the land. The land has just been professionally revalued at £3.5 million and the developer has suggested an option exercise price of £4 million. For the past five years similar sites have increased in value by 20% per year with an annual standard deviation of 15%. The current risk-free rate of interest is 12%. You are required to calculate the value of the call option to enable negotiations to take place.

12 Stock markets and equity share capital

12.1	Introduction	320		12.10	Stock splits	358
12.2	The global equity market	322		12.11	Rights issues	359
12.3	Stock markets around the world	323		12.12	Preference shares	373
12.4	The London Stock Exchange	325		12.13	Venture capital	375
12.5	Types of company	339		12.14	Key terms	376
12.6	Types of equity share	341		12.15	Revision questions	376
12.7	Methods of raising equity capital	345		12.16	References	377
12.8	Financial terminology	349		12.17	Further reading	377
12.9	Scrip dividends and scrip issues	354		12.18	Problems	378

This chapter begins by considering the advantages that follow from a country having an established stock market. It gives an overview of stock markets around the world before examining in detail the workings of the London stock market.

Many different classes of securities are dealt with in stock exchanges. This chapter concentrates on one such security, namely equity shares. The characteristics of equity shares are examined together with the methods of raising equity capital in stock markets.

12.1 Introduction

- Companies, governments and international organizations issue securities. These securities are sold to investors and the money raised is received by the issuer. This is referred to as a **primary market**. The seller of the security is the body issuing the security.
- The first-time buyer of the security may wish to sell the security at some time. This first-time buyer sells to another investor. This is known as a sale in the **secondary market**. The cash that is exchanged does not go to the company, government or other body that issued the security.
- It is an advantage (but not a necessary condition) to have an organization, to help bring into contact the potential buyer and the potential seller of the securities. Such an organization's role is to assist with the exchange of securities. It is commonly called a **stock exchange**. A stock exchange can be a physical place, it can be a system of telephone links, or as is becoming more common it can be a network of computers.
- A **stock market** is a place where securities can be bought and sold. It can be in a building, a grand special-purpose building to impress investors, or somewhere to keep out of the rain. The market can even be in the open air.

- The securities traded in a stock exchange can be conveniently divided into two categories, equity-type securities and debt-type securities. This distinction has, however, become blurred with new types of securities issued that can under certain circumstances be debt and under other circumstances equity. These new types of security are complex capital instruments, sometimes called quasi equity or mezzanine finance.

Advantages of a stock exchange

There are now more stock markets in developing countries and in the newly industrialized countries than in the older developed countries. The term 'emerging stock markets' is an expression used to refer to the markets in the developing countries, although a few of these markets have existed for a long time (the market in Bombay was established in the last century).

The major stimulus to the creation of such emerging markets came in the 1980s. With political opinions moving away from a belief in planning as a means of achieving economic growth to a belief in the advantages of the market place, so stock markets were a natural development. The World Bank encourages the creation of such markets. Developing countries could see the success of the stock markets in such countries as Hong Kong, Singapore, Malaysia and Korea and hoped to be able to repeat the success.

The benefits of having a stock exchange in a country can be looked at from four points of view. First in respect of the economy, there are the benefits to society in general. Then there is the point of view of those directly involved with the exchange of securities, namely the financial intermediaries. Finally there are those who wish to invest funds through the market and those who wish to obtain funds from the market.

The gains to the economy come from:

1. an improved utilization of existing domestic savings and encouraging new savings;
2. channelling these savings to where they can (hopefully) be most efficiently used;
3. attracting foreign savings, namely portfolio investment;
4. assisting in the privatization process;
5. providing a market for corporate control; i.e. an opportunity for inefficient firms to be taken over and run by more efficient managers.

To savers who wish to invest the advantages include:

1. enabling them to spread their risk over a number of investments; the market allows portfolio preferences to be satisfied;
2. an opportunity to earn higher rates of return from equity investment than available on alternative investment opportunities; an opportunity to provide some cover against inflation;
3. providing a liquid investment opportunity, with securities that can easily be traded in the market should cash be urgently needed;
4. for some the opportunity to gamble;
5. an opportunity to invest in imaginative types of financial securities.

For companies and others seeking funds, the advantages of a stock exchange listing include:

1. access to investment capital;
2. an opportunity to expand the size of the business through acquisition without losing control of the business;
3. an opportunity for fast-growing and young companies to obtain finance;
4. an opportunity to improve company financial gearing, and to be less dependent on bank finance;
5. the fact that the market attaches a price to risk and enables risk to be transferred;
6. an opportunity to become known to national and world investors.

The possible problems with a stock market include:

- Is it a fair game – do all buyers and sellers involved in the market have equal opportunities to make profits?
- Is it well regulated?
- Does it benefit larger firms and organizations at the expense of smaller firms and organizations and larger investors at the expense of smaller investors?

12.2 The global equity market

The global market in equity shares was slower to develop than the global market in bonds. It is also less obvious in that one does not hear or read about Euro-equities or an Asian equity market in the same way as a Euro-bond market or an Asian dollar market. It is also different in that the equity shares concerned in cross-border trading are listed on national markets and are subject to the rules and regulations of that national market; they are not free from national market regulation as are Eurobonds. Nevertheless there is a huge and growing market trading equity securities across national frontiers.

The demand for such a market has come from both investors seeking diversification in their portfolios and from companies seeking to raise money in different national equity markets.

The global equity market is such that on the London Stock Exchange the turnover of foreign equity shares as a percentage of the daily total turnover is on average over 50.0%. London is the national market with the highest level of international activity. The second highest market in terms of international activity is the New York Stock Exchange with the turnover of foreign equities representing 8.0% of total activity.

Around 60% of the world's equities that are traded outside their home markets pass through the London international equity market, which accounts for more than 90% of cross-border trading in Europe. London dominates in cross-border equity trading in Europe. To illustrate this point, 1993 was the busiest year, up to that time, for trading in foreign equities on London's international equity market. Turnover reached £671 billion – an increase of 83% on the 1992 record. European companies' equities accounted for £428 billion, almost 64% of the total and a 77% increase on the previous year. Trading in French companies' equities was over £114 billion, and in German companies' equities over £95 billion. London is clearly attractive to foreign companies seeking to raise funds, to foreign investors wishing to sell shares that they own, and to foreign investors wishing to buy shares in non-UK companies.

The USA is also attractive to foreign companies seeking a listing. Equally important for the USA as a global centre is its wealth. One-third of all the equity shares in the world are held by US investors. The US investors, particularly the financial institutions, can either invest in the shares of foreign companies quoted on the stock exchanges in the USA or they can buy shares of non-US companies listed in markets in other countries.

In Chapter 26 we will deal with the reasons why a company may wish to be listed on a stock exchange outside its own country. Here we will consider why investors want a global market and the way in which this is developing.

Investors gain from diversification. It is less risky to hold equity investments in a number of companies than to invest all one's funds in the equity of just one company. This is obvious – it is accepted that one should not put all one's eggs in one basket. It is equally risky to place all one's investments in companies whose success depends on the economy of one country. Although the economics of the world are becoming increasingly linked, it is clear that if some economies are going to perform well some will perform less well.

Therefore a careful investor will diversify his or her portfolio such that its performance is not dependent on the relative success or failure of one economy. It has been shown in the international diversification portfolio literature that up to a point international diversification not only increases the average annual returns that can be earned, but also at the same time reduces the risks associated with those returns.

Investors therefore wish to be able to buy shares quoted in companies outside their own country. It is possible for them to do this at any time of the day or night. There is now 24-hour trading in securities. If an investor in London wakes up in the middle of the night and wishes to buy shares in the Walt Disney Corporation she can do so. If the London market was open she could have bought them there, instead she calls a dealer/broker's office, and they will be able to purchase the shares in the New York market which could still be open. If the New York market is closed the shares can be purchased in Tokyo.

This is the global market in equity shares. We will return to the topic in Chapter 26.

We will return to the topic in Chapter 26.

There are over 80 countries with official stock markets. In some of these countries there are stock markets in more than one city. Each of these markets is a national market in which those issuing securities and those buying securities are required to follow the laws and regulations of the country in which the market is based. Some of these countries encourage foreign companies and foreign governments to issue securities in their national market. Many of these countries encourage foreign investors to buy securities in their national markets. It can be seen from Table 12.1 that the market value of overseas companies listed in London exceeds the market value of listed domestic companies. This does not mean that there are more overseas companies than domestic companies in number listed on the market, just that they are larger.

12.3 Stock markets around the world

Table 12.1 International stock market comparisons: market value of equities as at 31/12/92 (listed on the major (principle) market*)

	Domestic £ billion	Overseas £ billion	Total £ billion
Europe			
Germany	218	N/A	218
Luxembourg	8	132	140
Paris	217	N/A	217
London	634	1553	2187
Vienna	12	244	267
North America			
NASDAQ	411	N/A	411
New York	2508	105	2613
Toronto	160	205	365
Far East			
Hong Kong	114	N/A	114
Tokyo	1583	417	2000
Korea	71	–	71
Australia	88	88	176
Mexico	92	N/A	92

*Not USM.   N/A = not available.

London has for a very long time been open to foreign companies who wished to be listed on the exchange, as had New York and Paris. With deregulation and other changes in the 1980s, stock markets in other countries became open to foreigners. To be listed in a country means satisfying the requirements of the country. Table 12.2 shows the number of companies listed on the major markets. The following points should be noticed.

- London has more overseas companies listed than any other market.
- The overseas companies listed in London are the leading multinationals. Their market values in total exceed the market value of all the domestic companies listed.

Table 12.2 Stock market comparisons: number of companies listed on principle markets at 31/12/92

Exchange	Domestic	Overseas	Total
London	1878	514	2392
Amsterdam	251	246	497
Germany	425	240	665
Paris	515	217	732
Switzerland	180	240	420
New York	1969	120	2089
NASDAQ	3850	261	4111
Tokyo	1651	110	1761

- Although in the USA, NASDAQ has a large number of overseas companies listed, the size of the market in terms of the market value of the companies is relatively small.
- Although London has more companies listed than New York, the total market value of the listed companies is higher in New York.

The USA now wishes its stock exchanges to attract more foreign companies than it has in the past. The regulating body in the USA, namely the Securities and Exchange Commission (SEC), announced in 1993 and 1994 measures to make it easier for foreign companies to be listed in the USA. The measures are designed to reduce disclosure requirements and to reduce the red tape involved in seeking a US listing. The measures included are:

- no longer requiring quarterly accounting information;
- simplified prospectus documents;
- acceptance of certain international accounting standards for accounting purposes, rather than US GAAP;
- simplifying the process of registering share issues with the SEC.

With the US actively seeking to have more foreign companies listed on their national stock markets, and with the countries of the European Union accepting the policy of mutual recognition of companies listed in each other's stock exchanges the growth of the international side of national markets seems assured.

As well as being a market for UK company shares London has also for a long time been a major market for non-UK equity shares. It also holds a central position in the Eurobond market. It has developed as a leading international market, partly because historically Britain's wealth meant its funds could be attracted into investments in foreign stocks and shares and partly because of its minimal regulation.

This chapter is concerned with the market for equity shares. But it has to be appreciated that the London Stock Exchange deals in securities other than equity. Table 12.3 gives a list of the market value of all securities dealt with on the Exchange.

Trading of stocks and shares can take place anywhere. It does not have to be on the floor of an exchange building. One financial institution can trade with another via a telephone. Licensed dealers can create a market for shares. In fact, the capital market is any place where negotiable long-term securities of companies and the public sector are traded. Having said this, it is nevertheless the case that the most important part of the capital market in the UK is the official Stock Exchange in London.

The Stock Exchange in London is an independent association of members whose origins go back to the 17th century. It is the ambition of most companies in the UK to have their shares listed on the Stock Exchange. The Exchange is the oldest in the world and is one of the largest.

Table 12.3 Securities listed on London Stock Exchange (excluding USM and SEAQI) as at 30/9/93

	Number of securities	Nominal value (£m)	Market value (£m)
Companies			
Equities (UK and Irish)	1980	58 812	717 280
Equities (Overseas)	636	69 722	1 850 753
Preference capital (UK and Irish)	961	5 243	16 282
Preference (Overseas)	76	461	1 496
Loan capital (UK and Irish)	673	16 959	21 009
Public sector			
British government	102	184 917	213 604
Irish government	46	13 545	14 606
County stocks, public boards etc.	88	233	198
Overseas	163	4 120	5 217
Eurobonds			
UK companies	1038	72 920	74 855
Irish companies	23	1 570	1 409
Overseas companies	1898	170 630	165 383

As mentioned earlier there are two aspects of stock exchange activity. One is referred to as the primary market, i.e. obtaining new funds for companies and the public sector. Investors buy shares and bonds and the money raised goes directly to the issuer of the securities. The other activity, which is in fact by far the largest, is called the secondary market: it is a market which enables buyers and sellers of securities to trade with each other. They trade in the securities of companies or of the public sector, but no funds move to the issuer of the securities. The buyer, one investor, pays the seller, another investor, and the security changes hands.

Tables 12.4 (a) and (b) give details of the money raised in London by listed UK and Irish companies over recent years. It should be remembered that these are issues by companies, and that in addition to this activity, the public-sector bodies also obtain substantial funds from the stock market.

The figures in the table relate to new money raised in the primary market. It is interesting to observe the variability in the amounts raised from one year to the next.

12.4 The London Stock Exchange

The full title of the market is 'The International Stock Exchange of the UK and the Republic of Ireland'. The Stock Exchange in London goes back over 200 years but the new title came into existence only in 1986. The title resulted from a merger between 'The Stock Exchange' and an 'International Securities Regulatory Organisation' (ISRO). The later body had been set up in 1985 to look after the nearly 200 international security houses that were involved in dealing in London. These securities houses were dealers in Eurobonds and equities quoted on foreign exchanges (including American Depository Receipts (ADRs). They were operating in London independently of the Stock Exchange.

There was a certain amount of tension between the members of the old Stock Exchange and these new international dealers. Members of the Stock Exchange, partly

Table 12.4(a) Money raised by UK and Irish companies

	Total companies listed		New companies		of which Further issues		Eurobonds		USM	
	No.	Money raised (£m)	No.	Money raised (£m)	No.	Money raised (£m)	No.	Money raised (£m)	No.	Money raised (£m)
1983	2519	4 580.2	79	1591.6	2483	2 918.6	n/a	70.0	n/a	252.4
1984	3094	9 001.3	87	5950.2	2951	2 531.1	n/a	520.0	n/a	261.7
1985	3242	13 845.8	80	1462.2	2941	5 144.7	221	7 238.9	n/a	344.6
1986	4111	23 249.0	136	8874.2	3760	267.8	215	7 107.0	n/a	446.1
1987	4883	26 655.7	155	5002.4	4633	16 042.7	95	5 610.5	n/a	935.3
1988	4072	19 857.2	129	3789.9	3872	9 943.5	71	6 123.8	575	1019.0
1989	3956	26 580.7	110	7578.1	3749	9 557.0	97	9 445.6	661	851.9
1990	3205	27 853.7	120	7094.9	2953	6 783.9	132	13 974.9	453	507.1
1991	3319	35 131.1	101	7474.1	2985	14 287.1	233	13 369.9	319	377.5
1992	2876	24 227.6	82	2937.0	2488	7 934.0	306	13 356.6	277	202.7
1993	**2655**	**49 134.8**	**180**	**5966.3**	**1941**	**18 422.8**	**534**	**24 745.7**	**212**	**309.4**

Source: Quality of Markets Review

Table 12.4(b) Money raised by companies, by securities issues (listed Companies – UK & Irish)

	Equities (£m)	Convertibles (£m)	Debs and loans (£m)	Participating redeemable preference (£m)	Preference (£m)	Eurobonds Foreign currency (£m)	Eurobonds Sterling denominated (£m)	Total (£m)	Listed overseas companies (£m)	USM (£m)
1980	1 098	222	45	193	62	27	–	1 647	3 606	14
1981	2 493	253	43	60	60	–	–	2 909	8 338	87
1982	1 776	73	891	231	49	100	–	3 120	10 013	118
1983	2 569	99	461	1274	108	70	–	4 581	8 611	252
1984	6 899	173	490	858	61	520	–	9 001	16 567	262
1985	4 775	795	597	431	9	7239	–	13 846	15 955	344
1986	14 019	320	1243	528	33	7107	–	23 250	24 520	446
1987	18 648	982	1275	30	111	2512	3099	26 657	8 328	940
1988	9 935	2166	1207	20	407	1654	4470	19 859	9 211	1022
1989	12 626	1308	2421	23	758	3318	6126	26 580	12 896	853
1990	12 035	667	814	65	299	6514	7459	27 853	12 636	507
1991	18 312	1502	1023	80	844	4564	8806	35 131	24 082	377
1992	7 113	1828	1151	35	744	4297	9060	24 228	31 051	203

because of restrictive practices such as single capacity and minimum commission charges, were not capturing very much of the growing new international business. If, for example, British investors wished to purchase equity shares in a German company they would go to an ISRO securities dealer. With so many changes taking place in the City of London following the 'Big Bang' and with the question arising of forming a regulatory body to cover the whole of the securities market, the two bodies decided that rather than fight each other they would merge to help strengthen London as a financial centre.

Table 12.5 gives information on the level of turnover in equity shares. This reflects the secondary market activity. The amount of money changing hands in this secondary

Table 12.5 Equity turnover in UK and Irish equities

	Value (£m)	No. of bargains	Shares traded (m)	Average daily value (£000s)	Average bargain value (£)
1985	105 554.3	5 567 798	53 655.0	417 211	18 958
1986	181 211.4	7 638 445	77 901.0	716 251	23 724
1987	520 907.9	13 557 455	133 917.2	2 058 925	38 422
1988	325 589.1	7 099 717	143 208.0	1 286 913	45 859
1989	395 477.3	8 272 536	159 173.1	1 569 354	47 806
1990	315 625.0	6 910 820	134 040.7	1 247 530	45 671
1991	360 460.8	8 279 956	155 412.3	1 424 746	43 534
1992	433 858.9	8 507 598	181 939.9	1 708 106	50 997
1993	**563 967.4**	**10 343.533**	**215 456.4**	**2 229 120**	**54 524**

Source: *Quality of Markets Review*

market is 20 to 30 times greater than the amount of new money raised for companies in the primary market. London has a particularly active secondary market, reflecting a large amount of short-term trading and a considerable amount of merger and takeover activity.

Trading system

In the middle and late 1980s dramatic changes took place in the organization, membership and dealing system of the Stock Exchange. The changes taking place in 1986 were referred to as the Big Bang. Prior to these changes most trading took place on the central market floor of the Stock Exchange. It was face-to-face dealing. Jobbers operating on the floor of the Exchange made markets in the shares of companies. If a broker wished to buy or sell shares on behalf of a client he or she walked around the floor of the exchange to enquire the prices being quoted by different jobbers.

The major changes were as follows.

1. The separation of member firms into brokers and jobbers ended. All firms could act both as brokers, representing clients, and as principals, buying and selling on their own behalf. They became market makers.
2. Ownership of member firms by overseas companies was allowed.

Following the Big Bang, a computerized system was introduced, the Stock Exchange Automated Quotation (SEAQ), with the result that dealing prices were displayed on computer screens, which were located not only on the floor of the exchange but also in brokers' and market-makers' offices. Bargains could be completed by telephone. This meant that it was not necessary for market-makers to be located on the floor of the Exchange. The majority of business soon came to be conducted from purpose-built offices around the City, with many market-makers only keeping a minor presence on the floor of the Exchange to look after the smaller brokerage firms. The face-to-face negotiating is therefore a thing of the past.

SEAQ

SEAQ works in the following way. Market-makers enter into their computer terminals bid and asking prices. These are the prices at which they are willing to deal in the securities in which they make a market. The Stock Exchange has a large central computer which records this information, and passes it on to brokers. A broker wishing to buy shares in a particular company will be able to look at his own computer screen and see all the prices being quoted by the market-makers in that company. In addition the broker will see information on the recent trading in that company's shares, the volume and the prices. If the broker wishes to buy or sell he or she telephones the market-maker offering the best price. When the deal is agreed the market-maker reports the fact to the SEAQ centre, and the deal is then entered into the computer so that all users can be aware of the transaction that has taken place.

In 1994 the system was criticized by the Office of Fair Trading because some of the privileges allowed to market-makers gave them an unfair advantage. Market-makers can in fact delay the reporting of large deals and they do not need to disclose their own shareholdings of more than 3% of a company. These privileges give them valuable information not available to those with whom they deal. The SEAQ allows for trading in over 2100 UK and Irish stocks. Approximately one half of these are classed as 'liquid' stocks, which as is explained below means that there is active trading in the stocks. For each of these stocks there are numerous market-makers, with as many as 18 or more market-makers being willing to trade in the most active stocks.

The other half of the SEAQ UK securities are classed as 'illiquid'. For most of these securities there are only two or three market makers willing to quote prices and to trade.

In addition to SEAQ, there is the SEAQ International market system. Through this market it is possible to buy and sell shares in non-UK or Irish companies. Some of these overseas companies will be listed on the official list, some will not be. The SEAQ International offers quotations on over 1100 overseas companies. As was shown in Table 12.2 there are over 500 overseas companies and 636 overseas securities on the 'official' list. In addition to these there are in the region of 470 further overseas securities being traded in SEAQ International. The largest number of listed and SEAQ International companies are from the USA, followed by Japan, South Africa, Germany and France.

Share classification

In the mid 1980s a new classification system for the equity shares quoted on the market was introduced. Shares of a company were classified as either alpha, beta, gamma or delta.

The alpha shares were the most traded shares, the beta shares being the next most well traded shares, gamma were the third group. Gamma shares needed at least two market-makers. Typically such shares were in companies with low levels of capitalization. Shares which do not meet gamma requirements were classed as delta shares; typically such shares only had one market-maker.

At the end of 1990 there were 168 alpha companies, but as these were the biggest companies the trading in the shares of these accounted for over 60% of the market turnover. There were 579 beta companies, 1406 gammas and 67 deltas.

In 1991 the Stock exchange changed the classification and market-maker system. The equity shares of a company were to be classified into one of 12 bands, based on the average daily turnover of that company's shares. The system introduced a new measure of activity, the Normal Market Size (NMS). This is a figure for each company based on the annual turnover of a company's equity shares.

This calculation for each company, based on the value of the turnover of equity shares in a year, leads to an average (normal) institutional bargain size in terms of number of shares. For example the value of the annual turnover of shares in Abbey National plc in 1992 was £1911 million, and application of the appropriate formula results in an average institutional bargain size in number of shares of 49 018 shares. This fits into the NMS shares band which centres around 50 000 shares. This places Abbey National in the 4th category from the top. The top band centres on 200 000 shares and the lowest band centres around an average bargain size of 500 shares.

One use of the NMS bands is that these sizes become the minimum quote size that market-makers are obliged to use when making a quote. The twelve bands are further divided into what is called liquid stocks and less liquid stocks. The less liquid stock are the two smallest bands (with 500 bargain size and a 1000 bargain size). There are approximately half of the listed companies in these less liquid bands.

The number of market-makers dealing in less liquid stocks is of course small, there being approximately 800 companies with 3 or less market makers in their shares. At the other extreme the shares of the 24 most liquid companies (those in the highest bands) have 18 or more market-makers dealing in their securities. The extreme variation in the range of marketability and interest in the shares quoted on the London market can be seen from these figures.

The smaller NMS companies, the less liquid, are essentially of interest only to small private investors, whereas the large NMS, highly liquid stocks are of interest mainly to the large institutions and other major companies.

During the 1980s and into the 1990s the London Stock Exchange undertook a project with the object of introducing a paperless trading system for stocks and shares. The project was called Taurus, which stands for Transfer and Automated Registration of Uncertified Stock. It was felt necessary to introduce such a system in order to make London fully competitive with other leading international stock markets. Under the system share certificates would no longer be needed. Details of shareholders would be maintained in a network of computers linked to a central control system. Companies would continue to maintain on computer a register of their shareholders, but no document of title would be issued. Unfortunately the project failed. It cost £350 million before being abandoned. After the failure of the project the Bank of England took over responsibility for developing such a system.

European single market

Many steps are being taken to integrate the financial markets and financial services within the European Community. The Community periodically issues directives which seek to eliminate barriers and to harmonize practices. Member states then introduce changes in their own laws to meet the wishes of the directive. As a result of this process changes have been introduced in the UK in Banking, Insurance and the Capital Markets.

The Community directive on the Mutual Recognition of Listing Particulars became operative from 1 January 1990. This brings into line the listing requirements throughout the Community. One of the major effects as far as the UK was concerned was to reduce for an official Stock Exchange listing the requirement for a company to have a minimum of a five year trading record to the minimum of disclosure for the last three years.

A Public Offerings Directive, operative from May 1991, results in similar prospectus requirements for all stock exchanges in the Community. The requirements for a 'Continuation' of a listing will also be made the same for all the stock exchanges in the Community. This again will result in a relaxation of requirements for UK companies. For example they will not need to disclose as much information about acquisitions they have made and the realization of assets following the harmonization of requirements as they did when London had its own unique rules.

Full listing

There are in fact different markets for shares provided by the Stock Exchange in London. This section deals with the main market, with what is known as the 'Official List'. The other markets are dealt with in the following sections.

A company may decide to seek a quotation to satisfy its shareholders who would prefer to hold shares for which a market price has been established and which can easily be sold should the need arise. Major shareholders may wish to sell their shares in the company at some time in order to diversify their portfolios so as to avoid holding the bulk of their wealth in the shares of a single company.

Unquoted companies often find their growth limited by a shortage of funds and so seek a quotation to gain access to additional sources of finance. The quotation may be thought to increase the status of a company; it certainly provides it with increased publicity. To raise fixed-interest capital it is necessary to provide the lender with a certain amount of security. A quotation in the market adds to the reputation of the company and so the security. Large investors, such as insurance companies and pension funds, prefer investing in quoted companies, from the point of view of both equity shares and debentures, because of the increase in the marketability of the securities.

A company has to be over a certain size to obtain a market quotation, and it can be difficult for companies below this size to obtain either loan or equity capital, particularly as more and more of the savings are invested through institutions. One argument in favour of a company obtaining a stock market quotation is that the increased marketability will lead to improvements in the share price.

If a company wishes to obtain a quotation on the stock exchange it needs to submit an application, which will be considered by the Council of the Exchange to see if the applicant qualifies for acceptance. For an admission to the Official List of the Stock Exchange in the UK there are certain procedures and minimum requirements that need to be satisfied. These include the following.

The sponsor

When a company wishes to have its shares listed in the Stock Exchange it requires a sponsor or a listing agent. Sponsors and listing agents will normally be investment banks or corporate brokers. For public sector issuers and issuers of specialist debt securities a sponsor is not required; a listing agent can be used, who can be the lead manager of the security being sold.

The sponsor must, in the case of a new applicant to the exchange, satisfy itself having made due and careful enquiry of the issuer and its advisers, that the issuer has satisfied all relevant conditions for listing and other relevant requirements of the listing rules.

Where a company prepares listing particulars or any circular containing proposals to be put to shareholders in general meeting concerning, for example, a refinancing or reconstruction of the issuer or its group which includes a working capital statement, the sponsor must report to the Exchange in writing that it has obtained written confirmation from the issuer that the working capital available to the group is sufficient for its present requirements.

Where, for example, a profit forecast or estimate appears in listing particulars, or any circular, the sponsor must report that it has satisfied itself that the forecast or estimate has been made after due and careful enquiry by the issuer.

Conditions for listing

A company to be listed must normally have published or filed audited accounts which cover at least three years prior to the listing (12 months in the case of a USM company seeking a listing on the Official List). These accounts must have been prepared in accordance with the applicant's national law and, in all material respects, with United Kingdom Accounting Standards, United States Accounting Standards or International Accounting Standards.

It is possible for a company to have accounts for a period less than three years, but only if the Exchange is satisfied that such acceptance is desirable in the interests of the applicant or of investors and investors have the necessary information available to arrive at an informed judgement concerning the applicant and the securities for which listing is sought.

There are numerous other conditions that must be satisfied, concerning such matters as a need for continuity in management over the period covered by the accounts and the need for the directors of the company to have 'collectively appropriate expertise and experience for the management' of the business.

If a controlling shareholder exists the company applying for admission 'must be capable at all times of operating and making decisions independently of any controlling shareholder'. A controlling shareholder is any person who can exercise or can control the exercise of 30% or more of the votes at general meetings. A further need in this situation is for the composition of the Board of Directors to be such that 'significant decisions are taken by directors of whom the majority are independent of any controlling shareholder'.

These requirements are interesting in view of the very much wider debate on corporate governance, and the wish in large companies not to have the same person as chairman and chief executive. These listing requirements are seeking to avoid family control of listed companies.

Market capitalization

Except where securities of the same class are already listed, the expected aggregate market value of all securities to be listed must be at least:

1. £700 000 for shares; and
2. £200 000 for debt securities.

The Exchange may admit securities of lower value if satisfied that there will be an adequate market for the securities concerned. The exact requirements will of course change over time.

Marketability

To be listed securities must be freely transferable. To be listed at least 25% of the class of security to be listed must be in the hands of the public when trading in the company's shares begins. The shares must be in the hands of the public in one or more of the member states in the European Union. Shares owned by the public in non-member states may be taken into consideration if these shares are listed in the state concerned.

A percentage lower than 25% being made available to the public, at the time when trading in the shares begins, may be acceptable if it is a particularly large company. There will in this case be many shares available for dealing and so a reasonable market in the shares should develop. The public are defined as persons who are not associated with the directors or major shareholders.

If the percentage of a class of shares in the hands of the public falls below 25% or such lower percentage as has been agreed, this may result in suspension or cancellation of listing. The Exchange will allow a reasonable time to restore the percentage, unless this is precluded by the need to maintain the smooth operation of the market or to protect investors.

In the absence of exceptional circumstances the issue of warrants or options to subscribe for equity shares must be limited to not more than 20% of the issued equity share capital of the applicant at the time of issue of the warrants or options. Rights under employees' share schemes will not be included for the purpose of this 20% limit.

Rules of the Stock Exchange

The company must undertake to observe the rules of the Stock Exchange. The listing rules (appearing in what is known as the Yellow Book) are being continually revised. A new edition of the Book was published in December 1993. The Exchange requires certain information to be provided each year and at times of a new issue additional to that required by law. This information is required in order to give investors the greatest possible knowledge about the company's directors or promoters, the business in which it is engaged, its profit record and the prospects for profits and dividends.

In recent years the number of companies listed on the main London Stock Exchange has been falling. One of the reasons, of course, is that a number of companies disappear through takeovers and mergers. However, this does not hide the fact that there has been evidence of a decline in the appeal of a stock market listing. For smaller companies the costs of obtaining a quotation are relatively high and therefore the potential rewards for successful owners of small and medium-sized businesses from the sale of shares were not providing sufficient compensation for the disadvantages of a listing. The listing rules are demanding and the rules tend to be rigorously applied.

Costs of obtaining and maintaining a quotation on a market arise in two ways, the initial costs and the annual costs. Initially, in order to meet the requirements of the market certain costs need to be incurred. Higher reporting standards need to be met which increases annual costs.

However, there are economies of scale in the issuing of shares. There is a large fixed overhead element in the cost: advertising, administration, the printing of the prospectus, commission fees and legal expenses. Because of the fixed element the costs of raising small amounts of finance can absorb a high proportion of the amounts raised. Having obtained a quotation, annual fees need to be paid to the market and the higher costs of meeting reporting requirements continue. In addition, management time has to be spent on satisfying shareholders' needs, in particular the request for information. Once shares have been sold to the public, in particular to institutions, their interests are only ignored at the directors' peril.

During the 1970s there was a dramatic fall in the number of companies seeking new quotations in the listed market. In the five years from 1975 to 1980 an average of only 12 companies each year had 'gone public'. This caused considerable concern and led to wider publicity being given by the Stock Exchange to Rule 163(2) (this became 535.2 and later 4.2) and to the creation in 1980 of the USM. In 1989 the Stock Exchange moved to make it easier for companies to obtain admission to the official list. This included the relaxation of the requirement that a company needed a five year trading record to be admitted; a three year record would be all that was required.

The prospectus

When the public is asked to subscribe for the shares of or debentures in a company, the invitation involves the issue of a document setting out the advantages to accrue from an investment in the company. This document is termed a prospectus and it is in most cases illegal to issue to the public any form of application for shares or debentures in a company unless it is accompanied by a prospectus complying with the Companies Acts. An issue to existing shareholders or debenture holders need not be accompanied by such a prospectus, nor need an issue which is uniform with shares or debentures previously issued and quoted on a stock exchange.

A prospectus is defined as 'any prospectus, notice, circular, advertisement, or other invitation, offering to the public for subscription or purchase any shares or debentures of a company'.

If the prospectus includes a statement by an 'expert', i.e. an engineer, valuer, accountant or any other person whose profession gives authority to a statement made by him, the expert must give his written consent to the inclusion of the statement in the prospectus and the fact that he has done so must appear in the prospectus. Statements by experts are often required. Examples are as follows: valuers, valuing assets of the company; engineers, stating the use of a process or machine; accountants, commenting on the profits of the company and its subsidiaries.

If a business is to be purchased out of the proceeds of the issue, the prospectus must contain a report by named accountants qualified for appointment as auditors on profits or losses of the business for the five preceding years, and assets and liabilities at the last date that accounts were made up.

Fees have to be paid to all these advisers, in particular sponsors, merchant banks, solicitors and accountants. It was estimated that the average fixed costs associated with a listing was, in 1993, £350 000. This is regardless of how much money was being raised.

The unlisted securities market

The USM opened in 1980 and its closure began in 1994. It was a market regulated by the Stock Exchange, but separate and distinct from the market in securities admitted to the 'Official List'. For a number of years it was a success.

When it was launched there were 11 companies making up the market. By the end of 1981, 76 companies were quoted on the market, of which 30 had previously had their shares traded under the 163(2) rule. The new companies included those in the high technology business, property developers, retailers and travel companies. By 1990, over 440 companies were quoted on the market. Table 12.6 shows the number of companies 'listed' and Table 12.7 shows the amount of new funds being raised.

Table 12.6 Historic market values of USM

Date	Companies	No. of securities	Nominal value (£m)	Market value (£m)
31.3.81	31	n/a	n/a	431.6
31.3.82	95	n/a	n/a	996.7
31.3.83	145	n/a	n/a	1424.0
31.3.84	225	n/a	n/a	2961.2
31.3.85	282	n/a	n/a	3333.6
31.3.86	339	n/a	n/a	3890.3
31.3.87	367	n/a	n/a	6392.3
31.3.88	370	422	904.3	6708.1
31.3.89	417	450	1126.1	9153.3
31.3.90	442	453	1111.6	8296.0
31.3.91	412	423	1094.1	6149.1
31.3.92	337	344	885.5	5592.7
31.3.93	291	299	761.2	5523.4
31.6.93	275	283	702.3	5852.1
30.9.93	**263**	**272**	**673.5**	**5625.3**

Source: *Quality of Markets Review*

Table 12.7 New funds raised by USM

	Number of new issues	Funds raised total £m	Method of Issue			3rd market transfers included in the foregoing
			Introduction	Offers	Placings	
1984	101	181	10	11	76	–
1985	98	203	9	13	75	–
1986	91	300	6	13	72	–
1987	72	184	7	4	61	–
1988	87	303	12	3	72	5
1989	67	147	15	1	51	3
1990	47	40	35	1	11	27
1991	10	11	6	1	3	3
1992	6	20	3	0	3	–
1993	10	55	1	–	9	–

Source: KPMG Corporate Finance

Requirements for admission to the USM were less onerous than the requirements of the listed market, with only 10% of a company's issued share capital needing to be made available.

Only a two-year trading record was required (three years prior to 1991) but in certain circumstances the Stock Exchange would accept a company which had no past trading record but which had a fully developed product or project ready to be commercially exploited. The cost of raising finance on the USM was usually between 5% and 10% of the amount of finance raised. However, costs did vary considerably, depending upon the number of shares being issued, the size of the company, the complexity of its operations and the method of issue.

Companies entering the USM were usually smaller than those which would be seeking a full listing. Most of the companies whose shares were traded on the USM had a market capitalization of between £1 million and £5 million; although there was no lower limit to the market capitalization required, it was normally expected that it would be greater than £0.5 million. Profits before tax were normally expected to be in excess of £0.25 million per annum.

Most USM companies had more than one market-maker for their shares, which meant that there was competition and as a result buyers and sellers could obtain a price approaching the 'intrinsic' value of the share. Without competition between market-makers this need not have happened. Over 70% of the companies quoted had four market-makers or more.

When companies first came to the USM many of the shares being offered to the public were those of the founders of the businesses, who were selling their shares to realize the rewards for their entrepreneurial efforts. The USM was alleged to have created over 500 millionaires. Of course some of the shares being sold were newly created shares, designed to raise new money for the companies concerned.

The advantages to a company of having its shares traded in the USM included the following.

1. Founders of companies could realize cash by selling their shares.
2. Medium-sized companies could obtain equity finance for expansion. Being quoted could also result in banks taking a more favourable attitude towards loan funds as the public standing of the company was increased.
3. A medium-sized company could take over another company by offering shares which had a market in which they could be traded.
4. The company could reward and encourage its employees through share option schemes.

The disadvantages included the following.

1. An increased amount of financial disclosure was required.
2. As a result, there was an increased possibility of being the target of a takeover bid, and with a more dispersed share ownership there was less control over the outcome of the bid.
3. There could be pressure from new shareowners for the rate of dividend payments to be increased.

Important changes to the Rules of the USM came into effect in 1994, in order to implement amendments to the European Union's Listing Particulars Directive. Decisions made at the level of the European Community now have a major impact on the rules of the London Stock Exchange. These particular changes were designed to make it easier for a company to move from the USM to a listing on the 'Official List'. A company could make the transfer without being required to offer investors any additional securities.

Unfortunately, as can be seen from Tables 12.6 and 12.7, the USM lost its popularity. By 1993 the number of companies quoted at the exchange had fallen to 275, and the number of new companies admitted to the exchange in 1992 had fallen to 6 (from a peak admission of 101 in 1984).

What had gone wrong for the USM? One of the main reasons for its decline was, as explained above, that it has become easier for companies to obtain a listing on the main exchange than it was when the USM was started. Following the adoption of the European Community listing requirements (including only three-years' trading before being listed on the official market), the relative attraction of the USM declined despite the fact that it was made easier for companies to obtain a listing on the USM.

The London Stock Exchange announced that no new companies were to be admitted to the USM after 1994, and that the market would close at the end of 1996. The hope was expressed that after 1994 medium-sized companies seeking a new listing would apply for a full 'official' listing, and that most companies with a quotation on the USM at that time would transfer to a full listing.

Alternative Investment Market

The Stock Exchange in 1994 announced plans to establish an 'Alternative Investment Market' to replace the USM, the new market being designed to satisfy the capital needs of those companies outside the scope of the Official List. The proposal was that the market would have no minimum listing requirements with respect to the financial or trading records of companies. The market would be designed to appeal to the smaller company and would be open to all investors.

It was argued in 1994 by some critics of the proposals that it might be better if the London Stock Exchange did not look after any new market, and that it would be an advantage to companies and investors if the market was managed by a body in competition with the official market. The London Stock Exchange however acted quickly with the 'Alternative Investment Market' proposal to avoid losing business when the USM closed down.

The AIM, being designed for smaller companies, replaces the USM and Third Market. It is intended to keep regulations in the market as low as possible, not to have a restriction on the minimum amount of shares that need to be in public hands, and the need for a sponsoring body to be optional. The idea is to provide an exit route for entrepreneurs and venture capitalists. The risk for investors will, however, be higher than in the official market.

There are other bodies who from time to time come forward with ideas about setting up markets in competition. One such proposal has come from the European Venture Capital Association. Their idea is that a Pan European Stock Market be established for fast-growing companies. It would seek to attract to this European market entrepreneurial led companies of any size. The market would allow companies to raise equity finance at an earlier stage in their growth than allowed by the official 'national' exchanges. The plan is to call the market EASDAQ and to launch it to coincide with the implementation in 1996 of the EU directive on the free movement of financial services across borders.

The third market

A third market was established by the Stock Exchange in 1987. It was designed to offer an opportunity for listing to companies that might find the entry requirements to the USM too onerous and to provide a market-place for young growing companies. In the early 1990s this market was discontinued. This was because proposals were introduced to reduce the trading record requirement for companies seeking admission to the Official List from five to three years, and to the USM from three to two years. With these proposals accepted new companies could go straight to the USM.

Third Market companies were sponsored and monitored by Stock Exchange members. The market was under the control of the Stock Exchange. The market was a direct competitor of the OTC, and when it was created it was expected that some of the then OTC companies might seek a listing on the Third Market because it was to be better regulated and offered a more liquid secondary market. There were no initial entry fees or annual fees for being quoted on this market and the cost of raising funds was not significantly different from that for the USM (in percentage terms).

As at the beginning of 1989 to be admitted to the market it was necessary to have had a trading record of at least one year with annual accounts unqualified by the auditor. There was no minimum percentage of equity that had to be made available to the public and no minimum size requirement.

Trading in unlisted securities

The London Stock Exchange, unlike most stock exchanges, allows trading by members in securities of companies not listed in either the Official List or any of its other lists. Trading based on what was called Rule 535.2 (and later became 4.2) was allowed in what were seen to be occasional transactions in the securities of unlisted companies. This rule was introduced in the 1950s.

Dealings in the shares of unlisted companies was allowed provided that prior approval had been obtained, despite the fact that the company may not be disclosing the information that would be required had it been a listed company. In principle the shares of any public company can be dealt in by Stock Exchange members. Approval for dealing in shares under this Rule had to be sought but was usually rapidly given and presented no problems to the brokers. However, there were problems in the development of a regular market in a particular company's shares under this Rule as the Stock Exchange reserved the right to object to such continuous trading in the shares of any one company. The Rule was supposed to be used for companies whose shares would be traded infrequently, and up until the 1970s the companies whose shares had been traded under the Rule were mainly football teams and small breweries which had particular regional interests but not national appeal, and where regional brokers would match buyers and sellers.

This market offered many of the benefits of an OTC market, but very few people knew of its existence. In response to pressure from the Wilson Committee the Stock Exchange gave wider publicity to this Rule, resulting in a greater response than had been expected. A number of companies issued securities with a view to having them traded under the Rule.

The Stock Exchange were then concerned that this facility for irregular dealing was growing into an unregulated market. There were no rules with regard to the information that the companies should disclose, and it was difficult to define what volume of trading should be called irregular. One result was that the Stock Exchange, seeing that there was a need for a market place for the shares in medium-sized companies, launched the USM in November 1980.

In 1988 the Exchange relaxed the requirements for dealing under this 535.2. Member firms of the Exchange no longer required further permission to deal in an unquoted security, once permission to deal in that security had been given. The application procedure is quick and simple. Only the latest set of reports and accounts needs to be submitted. Once permission has been given it remains open for a 12-month period.

Table 12.8 shows the number of companies traded under this Rule 535.2. In 1993 an average of 170 trades per day were undertaken. Most companies whose securities are traded under this rule are small in size, with the average market capitalization being between £5 million and £10 million. This market is ideal for companies who only have a few shareholders – for example a family company. It is also a useful market for new companies who do not have a two-year trading record. A number of companies have built up their shareholder base while being traded under this rule, and have then transferred to one of the listed markets.

In 1994 a new Stock Exchange Rule Book was introduced and this rule became number 4.2.

Table 12.9 shows a comparison of the three markets controlled by the London Stock Exchange.

Table 12.8 Companies trading under Rule 535.2 (now Rule 4.2)

	1990	1991	1992	1993
Number of new applications	68	90	73	79
Total no. of companies trading	216	222	222	240

Table 12.9 Comparison of Official List and USM with existing 535.2 dealing facility (as at end 1993)

	Official List	USM	Rule 535.2
Trading record	3 years	2 years	No requirement
Shares in public hands	25%	10%	No requirement
Minimum size	£700 000	No requirement	No requirement
Advertising requirement on flotation	Box advertisement in one national newspaper	As for the Official List	No requirement
Distribution rules for raising money	Placings: up to £25m. Intermediaries offer: £25m–£50m. Offers: 50% if raising over £50m	As for the Official List	None
Estimated minimum cost of joining	Approx. £350 000 minimum	As for the Official List	Nominal cost only if not raising funds. If raising funds, then the cost would relate to the issuing of a prospectus under the Companies Act – cost approx. £20 000–£50 000 minimum
Ongoing obligations of a company	Continuing obligations as set out in the Yellow Book	As for the Official List except for minor differences e.g. class tests and shareholder approval	No ongoing obligations set by the Exchange; companies must comply with UK company law

The future

The London Stock Exchange, although of major importance in terms of company finance, cannot sit back on its laurels. Its position as the major market in Europe is being threatened by Paris and Frankfurt.

The need for a large central market is being questioned. The physical presence of an exchange is no longer important. Brokers can now deal with market makers through screens. The reputation of the London Exchange for its ability to guard investors' interests and to control its members was undermined by such scandals as Blue Arrow, Guinness and Polly Peck. The attempts in London to introduce a modern trading system, Taurus, ended in failure and a huge waste of member firms' money.

Stock markets face the challenge from commercial organizations around the world who can take advantage of new technology to compete with brokers and dealers. Investors will buy shares where they can do so most cheaply. There are trading systems to handle the buying and selling of shares outside the Stock Exchange.

London dominates through SEAQ International equity trading, through which some

60% of the total world foreign share trading is done. The French and German authorities resent this because it deprives their national markets of business. The European Union have introduced an investment services directive that could lead to changes. The Big Bang of 1986 was a shock to the City of London but there is more to come.

The over-the-counter market

It is possible for the shares of any public company to be traded. If a seller can find a buyer, a deal can be arranged. The purpose of a market is to make it easier for a seller to find a buyer. The Stock Exchange, the Alternative Investment Market and Rule 4.2 provide such market-places but there is a good deal of trading of shares outside these markets. An important characteristic of an OTC market is that it is independent of any official Stock Exchange. A small OTC market began to develop in the UK in about 1972. Such a market already existed in the USA.

In fact, the OTC market in the USA is very large, with the shares of over 4400 companies being traded in the market. Of course, the companies tend to be small and medium in terms of size, with the result that the market value of all the shares listed is only in the region of 20% of the market value of the shares listed on the major US market, the New York Stock Exchange. Nevertheless, it is a very important equity market. It is run by the National Association of Securities Dealers, and they operate a sophisticated trading system, the Automated Quotation System (NASDAQ), which was used as the model for the SEAQ system which was introduced into London.

In the UK a firm of investment bankers, MJH Nightingale, began operating an unofficial market in the early 1970s. Although initially not many companies had their shares traded in this OTC, a great deal of interest was shown in this development, and it indicated that there was a need for a market outside the Stock Exchange. This OTC grew and at its peak there were in the region of 230 unquoted companies whose shares were being traded in the market.

The OTC grew during the early 1980s, but died away in the late 1980s. The reasons for its decline included bad publicity resulting from the hard selling techniques used by a few of the dealers and a lack of liquidity in the market, with holders of shares who wished to sell sometimes having to wait for some time before a buyer could be found. Often a company's shares were only dealt with by one dealer, and there were suggestions that on occasions the shares the dealer was recommending to clients were the ones in which they had a large holding. Prices tended to be volatile and there was a high failure rate amongst companies whose shares were being traded.

A final difficulty was that, from 1986, as a result of the Financial Services Act, dealers had to apply annually for a licence to deal. Some dealers found they were not allowed to continue in business. The OTC market in the UK has not been a success.

Licensed dealers

Licensed dealers are companies, other than members of the Stock Exchange, which are licensed to carry on the business of dealing in securities. Much of their activity is dealing in the smaller companies whose shares are traded on the OTC market. However, they are licensed to deal in the shares of companies quoted on one of the other exchanges. In fact, they have been very active in the trading in government privatization issues. They advertised in the press at the time of such issues as British Telecom and British Gas that they were willing to purchase the letters of allotment received by investors. Stockbrokers were reluctant to make a market in letters of allotment.

Such dealers are 'licensed' by the Department of Trade and Industry (DTI). In the 1960s and 1970s licenses were fairly readily granted. The DTI made enquiries about applicants but, as the Wilson Committee pointed out in the 1970s, there were only a few refusals or revocations. The criticism of the ease with which licenses were granted increased and the Gower Report on investor protection recommended changes in the legislation. In the 1980s a few licensed dealers collapsed, losing money for some investors.

Following the reorganization of the City in 1987 licensed dealers needed to obtain authorization from the relevant new regulatory body. Harvard Securities, at the time the largest market-maker in OTC stocks and shares, failed to obtain the authorization. The Securities and Investments Board (SIB) had criticized the practices that Harvard had been pursuing, particularly its hard sell tactics. Following the failure to obtain authorization, Harvard Securities ceased trading in 1988.

Why were the authorized dealers receiving so much criticism? Some dealers would do anything to sell shares to investors. The dealers were often engaged in pushing the shares of small companies. These were high-risk investments, but this was not always made clear to investors. The OTC market in the UK was not well regulated. Little was known about the companies involved. If an investor wanted to sell a share in such a company it was far from certain that a buyer could be found. The initial contact of the dealer with a prospective buyer was often on the telephone, with exaggerated claims being made. The facts given were often out of date, and the salesman was rewarded by commission on the sales made. As a result of several scandals and tighter regulations, the number and activities of licensed dealers has fallen. However, it should be appreciated that some of the licensed dealers have played an important part in the capital market in the UK in recent years. They have shown that there is a demand for unlisted securities, for an OTC market.

If a group of individuals wish to work together with the object of carrying on a trade or business to make a profit or earn a living, the two forms of association open to them are either a partnership or a company limited by shares.

One of the attractive features about being a company limited by shares is that the owners' liability for the debts and actions of the company is limited in amount to a predetermined share – the nominal value of the shares they own.

The Companies Act 1985 divides companies into 'public companies' and 'private companies'. The vast majority of companies are limited by shares. However, there are two special types of company: one which is limited by guarantee and one which is not. The latter is referred to as an unlimited company.

12.5 Types of company

Public companies

A public company can be formed by two persons; it is limited by shares and has a share capital. This means that the owners of the company, the shareholders, have only a limited liability for the debts of the company. The owners, in agreeing to purchase a share, are only committing themselves to place funds in the business up to the par value (the nominal value) of that share. If the company should fail and there are not sufficient funds available to pay the creditors, the tax collector, the employees or those who have made loans available to the company, then these people will just have to take what little is available from the sale of the assets of the company. The owners of the company will not have to pay more money into the business to satisfy debts; the owners' private assets cannot be touched.

The name of the company must end with the words 'public limited company', the authorized abbreviation being PLC. Such a company must state in its memorandum of association that it is a public company. The authorized minimum share capital is currently £50 000, though the Secretary of State may by order specify some other sum. Over time, public companies may well have to increase their share capital to keep pace with an increasing minimum size. Failure to do so will mean that they have to become private companies. A public company cannot restrict the right to transfer its shares.

Private companies

In numerical terms, the majority of companies in the UK are private companies; however, in terms of size, they are usually the smaller companies. There is no minimum amount of share capital for a private company. A private company is defined as one that does not state in its memorandum of association that it is a public company. The name of such a company must end with the word 'limited', with the abbreviation being 'Ltd'. The same meaning of limited liability applies to shareholders of private companies as that explained above for shareholders of public companies.

Prior to the Companies Act 1980, a private company was prohibited from inviting the public to subscribe for its shares or debentures, but this provision has been slightly amended. In order to remain 'private' a company still cannot offer shares to *any* member of the public, but it can, if its articles provide, make an offer to a limited group of people. An offer is possible where only the person receiving the offer may subscribe for the shares or debentures being offered and it is merely a domestic concern of the persons making and receiving the offer. It is of domestic concern if it is made to any existing member of a family, an existing employee or his family, an existing debenture holder, a lineal descendant, trustees of a member of the family or employees under an employees share scheme.

Prior to 1980 a private limited company was limited to 50 members (shareholders). Following the 1980 Act, the number of members is not as constrained. This change was necessary to enable employees to own shares and so become members of the company. A private company is restricted in the right to transfer its shares. Therefore any sale of shares by one shareholder to another must be tightly controlled.

If a private company wishes to issue new shares to raise finance, either existing shareholders have to subscribe or the new shares have to be carefully placed. If an existing shareholder wishes to dispose of the shares he holds, he has to find another buyer and the price must be negotiated. In the past, if a number of shareholders of a private company wished to dispose of their shares, the two most common methods were either to sell the whole of the company or to go public. However, in not every case did all the shareholders of the company wish to sell, and so the first of these two options was not always available. It is the ambition of many private companies to go public one day and float their company on the market, but the timing of this step is very difficult. The company needs a good profit record, which means that one or two bad years, perhaps because of an economic depression, can put back the timing of the issue.

Issuing houses and merchant banks are sometimes willing to place the shares of a private company with a few private individuals or institutions, but shares in private companies are not marketable, cannot easily be transferred and are therefore not very attractive to investors. It might be difficult to find buyers of shares in private companies at prices acceptable to the vendors.

The price that can be obtained from issuing shares in a market place should be higher than can be obtained from a private placing. In a market place there is competition for shares with many buyers. With a placement there is no competition. An institution buying shares in a private company has to be compensated for the lack of liquidity. The institution may not find it easy to dispose of the private company shares when it wishes to do so. The institution is therefore looking for a higher return, to compensate for this risk, than an investor buying a publicly quoted share in a market. The higher return is achieved by paying a lower price for the share when it is issued than would be obtained in a market place for an easily tradable share.

One reason for needing to establish a price for a company's shares, even though there may be no wish at present to sell the shares, arises in connection with estate duty. A market value of shares in a public company will be accepted as the value for tax purposes whereas the value of shares in a private company is subject to negotiation between the Inland Revenue and the executors or their advisers. The uncertainty surrounding the amount of the estate duty may be prolonged if the negotiations are protracted.

On occasions, a shareholder in a private company may prefer a negotiated price rather than a market price. If a shareholder controls a company in which the shares do not have a market value, for tax purposes his financial interest will be assessed mainly on asset values. If he were to sell the shares the value attached to his investment might rise, because market prices are usually based on earnings expectations which for a successful company leads to higher values than those based on assets.

A private company can find itself in a crisis when one of its shareholders dies. The shareholder's estate has to pay taxes: to obtain the funds it may have to sell shares. The other shareholders may not have enough liquid resources to buy the shares. Therefore, either an outside buyer has to be found for the shares or the shareholders have to sell some of their assets to provide funds to buy the shares.

A private company may find growth through both internal investment and external expansion very difficult. With regard to the latter situation, to take over other companies is very much easier if payment can be made in the form of shares. Payment by an issue of shares is common with public companies. It appeals to the bidding company because they may not have the necessary funds to pay in cash. Also, there are reasons why the shareholders of the selling company would in many cases prefer a share-for-share exchange: one is that they have to pay any capital gains tax that arises immediately if payment is in the form of cash. Shares in private companies are not likely to be acceptable because of their limited marketability.

One disadvantage of a private company is that it is limited in the amount of funds it can raise. It might be thought that if the few shareholders of the company are rich enough they could supply all the funds that the company requires. However, in the UK over time there have become fewer and fewer families that can afford to provide the funds required by their fast-growing successful private companies. If the private company is not successful or if the owners do not want it to grow, then it is less likely that the financial needs of the company will exceed the resources of the shareholders.

Finance can usually be provided by the small number of shareholders as the private company grows to a certain size, but if expansion is to continue beyond that point the only possibility could well be to enlarge the number of shareholders, which means going public. The banks will help the private company up to a point, but again they have their ideas of the correct balance between equity capital and borrowed funds and may well put pressure on the private company to enlarge its equity base before more loan finance will be provided.

There are three possibilities open to a private company wishing to go public. One is to change its status but not to invite the public to subscribe for the company's shares. If it does this it has to file with the Registrar of Companies a statement in lieu of a prospectus. This is not a full prospectus but a statement containing similar information. Immediately much of the privacy attached to the affairs of a private company disappears. A second possibility is to invite the public to subscribe for the company's shares, but without seeking a stock exchange quotation. The third possibility is to have the shares of the company quoted and dealt with on a stock exchange.

Ordinary shares

An equity interest in a company can be said to represent a share of the company's assets and a share of any profits earned on those assets after other claims have been met. The equity shareholders are the owners of the business – they purchase shares (commonly called ordinary shares), the money is used by the company to buy assets, the assets are used to earn profits, and the assets and profits belong to the ordinary shareholders. Equity shares entail no agreement on the company's part to return to the shareholders the amount of their investment. The directors are under obligation to maintain the assets intact, i.e. not to allow them to drop in value. Whether the original investment in the business keeps its value depends on how well the company is managed and the use to which the funds are put. An equity interest therefore represents a stake in the assets of the business which the shareholder cannot ask the company to repay plus an income stake, i.e. a share in the company's profits.

If an equity shareholder wishes to regain the money he has invested, he must either find a buyer for his shares or force the company into liquidation. It is possible that the company itself may wish to purchase the shares.

This is possible in certain situations. The ease with which the shareholder will find a buyer depends on the price that he is asking for the shares and on the marketability of the particular company's shares. The shares of companies quoted on a stock exchange are more marketable than those that are not, and existing owners, other things being equal, should be able to find buyers. The alternative method of realizing an equity stake – bringing about the liquidation of the company – is of course a very different matter. It means that all the assets of the company are sold, liabilities and prior claims are met and the funds that are left are paid out to the equity shareholders. These are draconian measures indeed, and would be resorted to only in the most serious circumstances.

The equity shareholders, as an interest group, are the last to have their claims met by the company, all other interests – employees, creditors and holders of debentures – come before them. It is these ordinary shareholders, with their equity stake in the business, that take the greatest risks. If the company does badly, they are the first to lose their investment; if it does well, all the profits belong to them – after the other interests have been settled.

If the company gets into difficulties, the ordinary shareholders are last in the queue of claimants on the assets just as they are the last to benefit from the profits. The claims to income of bankers and debenture holders take precedence, and these obligations must usually be met before the owners can withdraw any profits. If a company has entered into a loan agreement in which it promises to pay interest at certain dates, these payments have to be made whether the company makes a profit or not, and certainly before any profits are distributed.

There are no formal limits on the size of the claims of the equity owners on the company's profits. Once all prior claims have been met, all the profits belong to the owners, whether they are distributed as dividends or retained in the business.

The prior claims themselves are, of course, limited; a fixed rate of interest determines what is paid out on a loan, and the same is true of debentures. It is possible that a debenture deed might insist on having a certain sum of money put aside each year out of the profits to provide for repayment; this is called a sinking fund. Beyond this, holders of debentures have no claim on the profits.

The amount that the ordinary shareholders receive varies from year to year depending on the performance of the company, but because their investment bears the greatest risks they will, on average, expect a higher rate of return than that accruing to the more secure forms of investment.

The rights of an equity shareholder normally include:

- the right to receive a share of dividends distributed;
- the right to receive a share of the net assets of the business should it be liquidated;
- the right to vote on important issues, such as merger bids or takeovers bids for the company;
- the right to attend general meetings of the company;
- the right to vote on elections of members of the board of directors;
- the right to be able to share in any new issue of equity shares by the company – the pre-emptive right.

One way in which an equity interest differs from any other type is that it normally confers on the investor the right to vote on matters concerning the company. The democratically minded will see this as fair; if the equity owners are the owners of the business, they are entitled to a considerable say in the management of the company. Usually the equity shareholder can exercise his voting rights at the company's general meetings, at which directors are appointed to carry out the day-to-day management of the company, the annual accounts are proffered for the critical scrutiny of the owners, any new issues of shares are put forward for approval and other important items of policy may be discussed with a view to ratification. It seems both reasonable and appropriate that the owners of the business should vote on important matters such as these (which is not to deny that the directors will need sufficient freedom to manage the business without consulting the owners on every issue), and the vast majority of ordinary shares do in fact carry voting rights.

However, there are some ordinary equity shares in existence which carry no voting rights. Investors buy these risk-bearing shares on the understanding that they have no voice in the management of the company.

This particular point leads to a general one. Equity shares do not, in fact, constitute a homogeneous class of shares. There are several different types of equity shares carrying varying rights to participate in assets and profits; a certain class may, for example, rank in advance of another for the payment of dividends.

Preferred and deferred ordinary shares

Ordinary shares are sometimes subdivided into preferred ordinary and deferred ordinary. The former rank for payment of an agreed rate of dividend before the latter receive anything, but after the preferred shareholders have received their dividend, the deferred holders participate in the allocation of profits. The rate of dividend that the preferred holders receive before the deferred holders are allowed an allocation depends on the particular terms of the capital issues of the company. In some cases, the agreement may also admit the preferred holders to a share in the profits after they have received their priority percentage.

Founders' shares

As equity shares go, founders' shares are a rarity. Normally issued to the original promoters of the business, they draw from the profits, as a rule, only after all other categories of equity shares have received fixed rates of dividend. If the business prospers, there may be profits left over for the owners of the founders' shares. If the business is extremely successful, these shares may be very valuable, since they usually entitle the holders to all or at least a considerable proportion of any surplus profits, the holders' reward for contributing towards the perhaps unforeseeable success of the business.

Non-voting shares

Such non-voting shares that do still exist were usually issued by companies who at one time were family owned. As the business grew the company needed to increase its equity base, but the family wished to maintain control and one way to do this was to issue non-voting equity shares. With the recognition in recent years of the wider public responsibilities of companies, the idea of ownership without representation has become increasingly unpopular and pressure to discontinue this form of financing has grown. In particular, the large institutional investors do not like this type of share.

Purchase by a company of its own shares

For many years the UK was out of line with the USA and certain other European countries in that a UK company was not permitted to purchase its own shares. The Companies Act 1981 changed the position and gave companies the power to purchase their own shares subject to certain restrictions. It was felt that this change would benefit private companies where the situation has occurred in which certain shareholders become 'locked in', i.e. are unable to find a purchaser for their shares. It also provides a company with an alternative way of rewarding shareholders, the company being able to purchase shares rather than pay dividends. The purchase should force up the price of the remaining shares in shareholders' possession. It reduces the number of shares and increases the earning per share. Following the Act the company itself, subject to certain conditions, became able to buy the shares.

The conditions that must be satisfied before a company can purchase its own shares are as follows.

1. The company must be authorized to do so by its articles of association.

2. The company must, after the purchase, have other shares in issue, at least some of which are not redeemable. This condition is designed to prevent a company's issued share capital from consisting of redeemable shares only. Without this condition, the company could redeem its whole share capital and thus cease to have any members.
3. A **public** company must, after the purchase, satisfy the requirements of the Companies Act 1985 in respect of its allotted share capital, and, in particular, its allotted share capital must not be less than the authorized minimum.

The following conditions that apply to the redemption of shares also apply to a company purchasing its own shares.

4. A company may not purchase unless those shares are fully paid.
5. The terms of purchase must provide for payment at the time that the shares are purchased.
6. All companies may, in general, purchase shares either out of distributable profits or out of the proceeds of a new issue of shares made for the purpose of purchase. In addition, a **private** company may make a payment out of capital to purchase shares, provided that it is authorized to do so by its articles of association.
7. Where the shares that are being purchased were issued at a premium, a proportion of any premium payable on this purchase may be paid out of the proceeds of an issue of shares made for the purpose of the purchase.

A company must treat purchased shares as being cancelled on purchase. Thus the purchase of shares will reduce the issued share capital by the nominal amount of the shares purchased. However, the purchase will not reduce the authorized share capital.

Thus a company cannot purchase its own shares, hold them as 'treasury shares' and then resell them. In contrast, this practice is permitted, subject to certain limitations, in the USA and also by the EEC Second Directive. Buy-backs, as they are called, are much more common in the USA than they are in the UK. One reason is that raising new money causes a lot of trouble, so why give back what you already have? There are, however, large buy-backs by some companies. In 1994 Boots bought back 9% of their own shares, costing £500 million. At the time they had a large amount of cash available as a result of the sale of a subsidiary.

Shares issued under share option schemes

Most companies now offer share option schemes to their executives and certain classes of employees. These options allow those involved to purchase shares of the company at a predetermined price. The options are normally exercisable a number of years after the offer is made. There are tax advantages in not exercising the options within 3 years of issue.

The price at which the offer may be exercised is usually approximately the market price at the time the offer is made. Say Company X makes an offer on 1 January 1994 enabling each of its employees to purchase 100 shares (at the price that day, say £1.50) on 1 January 1997. If in 1997 the share price of Company X has risen to say £3.00, an employee would be keen to exercise the option and could purchase the shares from the company at £1.50 and sell them immediately in the market at £3.00. If, however, the price of the shares had fallen, and on 1 January 1997 was only £1.00, the employee would not exercise the option.

Employee share 'schemes' exist for either encouraging or facilitating the holding of shares in a company by, or for the benefit of, employees or former employees of a company or its subsidiaries. The schemes can also apply to spouses, widows, widowers or children of such employees or former employees. There are various advantages of such schemes. Normally a company cannot provide financial assistance to individuals to enable them to buy the shares of a company. However, this is possible in certain circumstances.

There are numerous methods by which equity shares can be brought to the stock market in order to raise funds for the company. We will differentiate between methods that can be used by companies that already have equity shares listed, and companies bringing equity shares to the market for the first time.

The London Stock Exchange lists in its Yellow Book the following methods for companies already listed

1. an offer for sale;
2. an offer for subscription;
3. a placing;
4. an intermediaries offer;
5. a rights issue;
6. an open offer;
7. an acquisition or merger issue (or vendor consideration issue);
8. a vendor consideration placing;
9. a capitalization issue (or bonus or scrip issue) in lieu or dividend or otherwise;
10. an issue for cash;
11. an exercise of options or warrants to subscribe for securities; and
12. such other method as may be approved by the Exchange either generally or in any particular case.

For companies with equity shares not already listed the methods are either an introduction or one of the methods listed below. It should be appreciated that for a company's first issue in the market, sometimes the money raised from the sale of shares is not to be used in the company, but is to be received by the founding shareholders of the company, who are selling the shares they own.

The methods that can be used by new entrants are dependent on the value at the offer price of the portion of the equity shares being offered or placed in the United Kingdom. The methods are as follows:

Value of equity shares at offer price	*Methods available*
Not more than £25 million	offer for sale
	offer for subscription
	placing (which may be combined with an offer for sale, offer for subscription or intermediaries offer)
	intermediaries offer
More than £25 million but not more than £50 million	offer for sale
	offer for subscription
	placing (which must be combined with an offer for sale, offer for subscription or intermediaries offer)
	intermediaries offer
More than £50 million	offer for sale
	offer for subscription

We will now give brief details of the different methods.

Offer for sale and offer for subscription

The company offers shares to an issuing house, which then offers the shares to the general public by advertising a prospectus in which the issue price is shown. The company may take this action because it wishes to change its status to that of a public company – the commonest reason for making an offer for sale – and will therefore be attempting to alter the character of its ownership by making the shares more widely held. In such a case it is not always an issue of new shares but a sale of existing ones to a different group of investors. With an offer for sale on subscription the shares are sold to the issuing house by the existing shareholders at an agreed price; the issuing house then offers them for sale at a slightly higher price to the public.

New shares in a company can also be sold directly to the public. If a quotation is to be sought in a stock exchange, the issue must be handled by a stockbroker in that stock exchange, but whether or not a quotation is required the whole issuing operation is usually directed by an issuing house. The issuing house will in this case be acting as an agent of the company.

With an offer for sale on subscription, some of the securities may be placed with clients of the sponsor (the issuing house) and any securities house that assists with the offer. The condition is that normally there are at least 100 placees and not more than 50% of the securities being sold are so placed.

It is also possible for existing shareholders, directors, employees and past employees of the issuing company to be placed on a special privileged list. The names on the list receive a preferential allocation of the shares, so long as the allocation does not amount to more than 10% in aggregate of the value of the offer.

Public issue

A public issue is a form of offer for sale. Again the public is being offered shares at an agreed price, only this time the offer is being made direct by the company. The issue is still administered by an issuing house, but this time the public is buying the shares direct from the company, and not from an issuing house. The shares might again either be those belonging to existing shareholders or be new shares, i.e. the vendors of the shares may be either the shareholders or the company.

The issuing house as an agent might advise the company on the issue price, but its influence on this price is obviously not so great as when it owns the shares itself and sells them, as in an offer for sale. This method is normally used only for large issues by well-known companies. The costs can be high; for issues of £10 million, the costs can be in the region of 8% of the money raised. For smaller issues the costs can absorb 14% of the money raised.

Placing

Shares, debentures and other securities are 'placed' when, instead of being offered for sale to the general public, they are sold privately to the clients of the issuing house or broker handling the issue.

Fixed-interest securities tend to be placed mainly with institutions such as insurance companies and pension funds. These institutions, together with investment trusts and unit trusts, are also taking a growing proportion of the offers for sale of ordinary shares. The expenses of an offer for sale are usually higher than for a placing. The Council of the Stock Exchange decides whether permission can be given for a placing or whether the issue has to be made by way of an offer for sale. When the consideration for shares being sold is large, placing permission is unlikely to be given, but this is always subject to the Stock Exchange's discretion.

Because placing is the least expensive method of issue, small issues are usually placed rather than offered for sale. But if there is likely to be substantial public interest in the issue, or if it is difficult to fix a price on the shares because of a lack of established criteria, then even a small issue may be offered for sale, perhaps by tender. The problem of deciding on a price for the transfer of the shares is a real one. A private company, protected from dealing, cannot have the share price determined for it by supply and demand, and in being placed, the shares are again insulated from the market. The selling shareholders therefore have to be careful that they obtain the full value of their investment. Placings are not underwritten. If it should prove impossible to place the whole of an issue, then the price may have to be lowered to such a level that it can be placed, or the issue abandoned.

Small initial public offers (defined in 1994 as those up to £25 million) may be placed by the sponsor with its own clients. However, to ensure a reasonable market, there must be at least 100 placees. These are in addition to directors of the company and their families, and existing shareholders of more than 3% of the issued capital.

There must be at least one market-maker who is independent of the sponsor. At least 5% of the securities being sold should be offered to this independent market-maker.

Stock exchange introduction

A stock exchange introduction may happen when either the shares of the company are already quoted on another stock exchange, or the company already has a wide spread of shareholders and wishes to obtain a quotation. In neither case will new money be raised for the company. The stock exchange only permits an introduction in those cases where it is satisfied that there will be, over time, a free market in the shares. In a case where the shares are not already quoted on another market, the stock market will require advertising as for a placing, though of course no new shares are being sold. On certain occasions it will also require shareholders to make shares available as the basis of a free market.

Intermediaries offer

'Intermediary' includes member firms of the Stock Exchange and authorized security houses. An intermediary may apply to the sponsor of an offer for shares in medium-sized offers. They would do this on behalf of their clients who are not on the sponsor's list.

One result of such 'offers' is a wider distribution of ownership of the new shares. The intermediary must allocate the shares to its clients at the issue price.

Open offer

An open offer is similar to a rights issue except in one aspect. It is an offer to existing shareholders to subscribe to the new issue in proportion to their existing issue. But there is not a negotiable document (a right) which can be sold should the existing shareholder not wish to take up the offer.

Tender

Shares are offered to the public and potential investors are invited to name the price that they are willing to pay. The keen buyer will bid high; the less enthusiastic buyer will offer a lower price. Although the company does not suggest or even know the price at which the shares will ultimately sell to the bidder, it does name a reserve price – the minimum price below which they will not be sold. The investor therefore knows the lowest selling price and can, if he wishes, make an offer above this level.

The price at which the shares are eventually issued is the highest price which will dispose of all the shares. For example, if a company offers 10 000 shares to the public, and 10 000 investors offer £1 or more for the shares, then all the shares will be sold if the price is set at £1. It is possible that, in total, 20 000 investors offered £0.75 or above for the shares, but the 10 000 who offered between £0.75 and £1 will not receive an allocation. The shareholder does not necessarily have to pay the price he offered for the shares: 1000 of the investors may have offered as much as £2 for the shares, but they will only have to pay a price of £1 per share because this was the price which cleared the issue. The Stock Exchange watches this method of issue very carefully to prevent abuse. It will not allow a multi-tiered price structure, i.e. more than one price at which the shares are to be issued. Only one striking price is allowed. The company may wish to ensure that their shares are widely held and to check the tendency for a small group of high bidders to obtain significant proportions of the shares. To do this it may be in the company's interest to strike a selling price slightly below that at which the issue could be cleared, and then allocate to each investor who bid above this price only a proportion of the shares that were asked for. In this way the shares will be more widely distributed.

The pricing of shares of companies that have not previously had a quotation is very difficult, and the advantage of the tender method is that it leaves the fixing of the price to the public. This price is not determined by an issuing house. The company receives the full benefit of the issue, and if the public forces a high settlement price the company receives the entire amount.

Stags

If the issuing house in charge of an offer or placing underestimates the price that the public is prepared to pay for the shares, the company loses potential capital. If the shares in the example quoted in the section on tenders had been offered to the public at a price of, say, £0.75, they would have been oversubscribed. As soon as dealing began, the excess demand for the shares would force their price up to £1 or more, and the margin between that and the asking price would represent lost opportunities for the company. The company would receive only £0.75 per share – the issuing price. The gains when the price rises above this level accrue to the shareholders who were fortunate enough to receive an allotment.

The breed of speculator known as a 'stag' gambles on situations like this. He subscribes for new issues whose price seems to promise an excessive demand. If he is allocated a number of these shares and if the price does rise as anticipated, he sells his allocation at a profit. If an offer is heavily oversubscribed and the price soars, the stag does very well out of it; if he miscalculates the issue and the demand is unexceptional, he is left with shares whose market value approximates to the price he paid for them.

Offers for sale by tender should reduce the margin between issue price and eventual market price and so reduce the opportunities for stags to make quick profits.

Underwriters

The correct pricing of a new issue of shares is extremely difficult. If the price of an offer for sale is set too high, the demand for the shares will be less than the supply and so not all the shares will be taken up by the public. To avoid the possibility that the company will not dispose of all the shares it is issuing, and so receive less funds than it expected, it is usual to have an issue of shares underwritten.

The lead underwriters are normally the issuing houses, who will usually subcontract the risks to sub-underwriters such as insurance companies and pension funds. They receive a fee based on the value of the issue. In return for the fee they agree to purchase all or a proportion of the issue not taken up by the market. The price that they pay the company for any shares that they purchase is often at a discount on the price quoted in the offer for sale. They receive their underwriting fee whether or not they need to take up any shares.

For many years in London the total underwriting fee has been at 2% of the capital raised, of which 1¼% goes to the institutions acting as sub-underwriters. The Office of Fair Trading has criticized this practice. It is claimed these fees are much too high considering the risks involved, and that the fixed fee structure means that financially strong companies subsidize the weak companies. It means a company making an issue cannot shop around for the best price.

The underwriting system is a form of 'put' option. In return for a fee the company has the right to sell shares to underwriters at a prearranged price. If the issue is a failure the underwriter has to purchase the shares at a price which will be above the market price. It has been argued that the lead underwriter receives 0.75% for doing very little and taking a very little risk.

Vendor placings

Two new methods of raising finance first appeared during the mid-1980s: vendor placings and vendor rights. One reason for their introduction was to overcome a problem that could arise in connection with mergers and takeovers. When one company is taking over another a situation often arises where new shares have to be issued to raise cash. The normal procedure to follow in such a situation is for the acquiring company to call an extraordinary general meeting and to seek the approval of the shareholders to suspend their pre-emptive rights. This can be inconvenient and there is the risk that shareholders will say no. An alternative that emerged was vendor placing and vendor rights.

There were other reasons why these new forms of issue were introduced. One was that a queuing system existed when it came to the issue of new shares. The Bank of England controlled the timing of the issues in the stock market. The objective was to avoid too many issues being offered at any one time and so swamping the market. The queuing problem could be inconvenient to companies who wished to raise cash quickly.

A further 'advantage' of these two methods is that they provide a loophole in the conditions that need to be met before merger accounting techniques can be utilized.

Vendor placings can put the small investor – the small shareholder – at a disadvantage. The small shareholder experiences a dilution of his or her holdings. The decision to waive pre-emptive rights taken at the extraordinary general meeting will hardly be influenced by the number of votes of the smaller shareholder. When the vendors eventually place their shares it will most probably be with the large institutional investors. The institutional shareholders therefore need not suffer any dilution in their percentage shareholding. It is the small shareholders who experience this dilution of shareholding power. Vendor placings and vendor rights are discussed further in Chapter 24.

Certain basic financial terms will now be explained. The terms are used many times in the book and their usefulness is discussed; at this point they are being defined.

12.8 Financial terminology

Dividend yield

Dividend yield is a simple enough concept. It is

$$\frac{\text{dividend per share}}{\text{price per share}} \times 100$$

This is a measure of the annual percentage return a shareholder receives from dividends, based on the current share price. It is not the total actual return earned by a shareholder for a company because it ignores the annual capital gains. It is also based on the current price of the share which is not necessarily the price the shareholder paid for the share.

A company pays dividends to shareholders net of a taxation deduction. The amount deducted is remitted to the Inland Revenue. The amount to be deducted has varied from time to time. As from April 1994, the amount is a reduced basic income tax rate of 20%. This means that if the gross dividend to be paid is 100p per share, the tax deduction is 20p (i.e. 20% of gross). This is the same as a rate of 25% on the net dividend (80p × 25%).

The result of this deduction at source is that if an individual shareholder pays income tax at this 20% rate, he will have no further liability to tax in respect of the dividend. If, however, an individual shareholder is liable to income tax at a higher rate (say 40%), he will be liable to the difference between the tax payable on the dividend at the higher rate (40p) and the tax that has been deducted at source (20p).

If a shareholder is not liable to income tax, for example the shareholder is a pension fund, they can reclaim the tax that has been deducted from the dividends.

When calculating dividend yields, should the calculation be based on the net dividend paid or on the gross dividend? An individual can calculate his or her own net dividend. An outsider can determine the gross yield or the yield net of the basic or the reduced rate of tax. The net yield equals

$$\frac{\text{dividend per share net of tax deducted}}{\text{share price}} \times 100$$

If a company pays a net dividend of 5p for the year ended 31 December 1994 and its share price is 100p, the net dividend yield is:

$$\frac{5}{100} \times 100 = 5\%$$

The gross yield to reflect the 20% tax credit is:

$$5\% \times (0.25)\ 5\% = 6.25\%$$

The gross dividend yield is regarded by many as being a more useful measure than the net dividend yield. This is because not all shareholders pay the same rate of income tax and so the net yield is not the net of tax yield to all shareholders. The gross yield, i.e. before any income tax is deducted, is the same for all shareholders. The *Financial Times* quotes the gross dividend yield in its daily share price statistics (see Table 12.10, penultimate columns). In the share price statistics a number of signs and symbols appear, the meaning of which can be extremely complex. The only way to understand these is by reading the explanation given in the newspaper.

The tax payment deducted from dividends and handed over to the Inland Revenue is an advance payment of the company's annual corporation tax bill. This advance corporation tax (ACT) payment can be offset against the total annual tax bill.

If a company happens to be in a loss-making situation in a year it will not be liable to pay corporation tax. However, if it has paid dividends during the year it will have made an advance corporation tax payment. It will not be in a position to offset this payment.

Earnings per share

With the corporation tax system the calculation of earnings per share is somewhat complicated. Depending on what assumption is made concerning dividends and hence the amount of tax which is paid, we can have different earnings per share figures. The two most common methods of calculating earnings per share are the nil method and the net method.

We will illustrate these two methods by means of a simple example. Assume that a company reports in its annual accounts that its total profits are £150 000, but it has profits chargeable to UK corporation tax of only £100 000. This is because the company has high capital allowances and substantial overseas earnings. The rate of corporation tax is 33%, and the rate of advance corporation tax is 20% of gross dividends. The number of shares outstanding is 200 000.

Nil method

This method is based on earnings after tax, on the earnings available for distribution. It ignores the effect of the dividend policy for a company on the level of tax paid. Those who support earnings per share calculations based on the nil method argue it provides the best indication of one company's performance relative to another company.

	[£]
Profits before tax	150 000
Corporation tax (100 000 × 33%)	33 000
	117 000
Number of shares	200 000
Earnings per share	£0.585

Net method

In the net method earnings are effectively the net dividend, plus any retained earnings after allowing for unrelieved advance corporation tax. Assume that the company being used as an example distributed net dividends of £100 000. The total ACT paid on these dividends is therefore £25 000 (either (£100 000 × 25%) or (£125 000 × 20%)). The gross dividend is £125 000.

There is, however, a maximum amount of ACT that can, in any accounting period, be set off against the corporate tax liability. The amount that can be offset cannot exceed the ACT rate (in 1994/95 this equals 20% on gross) times profit subject to corporation tax. In this example this maximum amount is £20 000 (£100 000 × 20%). The difference between this maximum (£20 000) and the amount deducted from dividends (£25 000) is known as surplus (unrelieved) ACT. This can be carried back or carried forward against future corporation tax liabilities.

This surplus ACT effects the earnings per share as measured by the net method. The calculation is:

		[£]	
Profits before tax		150 000	
Corporation tax (100 000 × 33%)		33 000	
		117 000	(nil)
Unrelieved ACT on dividends		(5 000)	
Profits after tax		112 000	(net)
Gross dividend	125 000		
ACT	25 000		
Net dividends		100 000	
Retained earnings		12 000	

$$\frac{\text{net earnings}}{\text{number of shares}} = \frac{112\,000}{200\,000} = £0.560$$

It should be noted that if there is no unrelieved ACT then the net basis gives the same EPS figure as the nil basis. For most companies the two methods give the same result. It is those companies with substantial overseas earnings that show a significant difference.

The danger in using EPS figures when comparing the performance of one company with that of another can be clearly seen. It is essential to ensure that one is comparing figures calculated under similar assumptions.

The total tax charge of a company will contain some elements which do not vary with the proportion of profits being distributed as dividend, and some elements that do vary with dividends. The element that does not vary includes corporation tax on profits, tax attributable to dividends received and overseas tax which is unrelieved because the rate of overseas tax exceeds the rate of UK corporation tax. The variable element includes irrecoverable ACT, which is that part of the tax that has been deducted from dividends which is greater than the total corporation tax payment justifies. The variable element also includes overseas tax unrelieved because dividend payment restricts the double tax credit available.

The statement of Standard Accounting Practice that covers EPS differentiates between the nil distribution basis illustrated above and the net basis. With the net basis of determining EPS, the charge for taxation not only includes the corporation tax payable but also the other fixed and variable elements of taxation referred to above. The nil basis only deducts the constant element of tax from earnings. As the Statement explains:

It can be expected that most companies, in normal circumstances, will not incur either of the variable elements of taxation, so that for them calculations on the net basis and the nil basis will produce the same result. The companies where the two methods are most likely to produce divergent figures are those which have income taxed overseas, a significant proportion of which is distributed.

The Statement, in fact, recommends that:

quoted companies should report in their accounts earnings per share primarily on the net basis. Where, however, there is a material difference between earnings per share calculated on the net basis and on the nil distribution basis, it is most desirable that the latter also be shown.

Adjustments also have to be made to the denominator in this EPS figure. Usually it is based on the weighted average of the number of shares in issue during the year.

Reference is also often made to 'fully diluted earnings per share', which takes into account not just the number of shares that have currently been issued but also the numbers that would need to be issued if all those on offer in the various share option schemes of the company needed to be issued. The options which give an opportunity to purchase equity, as well as options on convertible loan stock issues, include those that have been issued to directors and employers.

Dividend cover

One way of determining whether or not the shares of a particular company are a good investment is to look at the dividend cover. This is one indication of the riskiness of the investment. It is the number of times by which available profits after tax cover the dividend payment. It indicates how far earnings could fall before dividends need to be cut. Because of the alternative measures of EPS the calculation can be complicated. The calculation is basically either

$$\frac{EPS}{\text{dividends per share}}$$

or

$$\frac{\text{total profits available for distribution to ordinary shareholders}}{\text{dividends paid to ordinary shareholders}}$$

We have to decide, however, which earnings figure to use and whether to take dividends gross or net of ACT.

Earnings yield and price-to-earnings ratio

The earnings yield is simply

$$\frac{EPS}{\text{share price}} \times 100$$

This particular yield is not often used. The much more common way of expressing earnings in relation to price is by the price-to-earnings ratio. This is simply the share price expressed as a multiple of EPS. It indicates how many times the current level of earnings investors are paying for a company's shares. Once again, however, we are faced with the problem of deciding which EPS figure to use.

The *Financial Times* in its daily Share Information Service quotes a price-to-earnings ratio for a large number of companies. This ratio is based on the relationship between the daily share price and the net EPS figure. However, where a difference of 10% or more would have arisen in the ratio if the nil basis had been applied, the ratio is shown in parentheses.

The meaning and interpretation of the price-to-earnings ratio will be returned to many times in this book. The above outline will serve as an introduction.

The price-to-earnings ratio is seen by many analysts as being the best single method of comparing the market value of one share with that of other shares in a similar risk class. The higher the price-to-earnings ratio the 'better' the company is thought to be – it indicates the market has growth expectations. The ratio is therefore very important when it comes to determining the price at which new shares should be offered to investors.

Financial Times statistics

The *Financial Times* lists the prices of about 3000 equity based securities, including many which have their primary listing outside the UK. It is not always appreciated that companies pay the newspaper to have their names and share prices published. Companies are listed by industry sectors. With some companies the price of any warrants and 'A' or 'B' class shares are listed.

We show in Table 12.10 the details given for companies classified as being in the chemical sector. This is an extract from the paper for one day in August 1994.

Table 12.10 Extract from *Financial Times*, 12 Aug. 1994

CHEMICALS

				1994		Mkt	Yld	
	Notes	Price	±	high	low	Cap £m	Gt's	P/E
AGA Skr		£5 11/32	–7/32	*£7 25/32	£4 23/32	576.5	12.4	Φ
Akzo Fl		£81 9/16	+1/8	£82 9/32	£62 23/32	3,757	2.9	21.4
Allied Colloids	hN□	147xa	+2	*147	115½	774,4	2.6	23.6
Amber Ind	N	755	....	755	705	29.6	3.3	15.7
BASG DN		£134 5/8	–13/32	£136½	£106 9/16	7,868	7.0	–
BOC	♣N□	714	–31	767	627	3,405	4.1	30.1
BIP	♣N□	322xd	....	*373	287	433.1	3.9	20.4
BAYER DM		£151 1/16	–15/32	£159 21/32	£129 27/32	10,132	6.0	–
Brent	N□	125	....	131	98	84.4	4.0	–
British Vita	□	267	....	309	233	579.1	3.5	22.4
Cambridge Iso $	✠	18	....	25	18	2.35	–	–
Canning (W)	♣N□	196	+1	199	153	55.5	4.6	33.2
Cementone	♣□	65	–4	109	65	14.3	5.3	29.3
Warrants		27	–2	48	27	0.23	–	–
Courtaulds	N□	532	–16	580	467	2,138	3.5	42.9
Croda	N□	377	+2	384	327	497.6	2.8	19.2
Doeflex	♣N	95	....	133	95	10.1	6.1	10.8
Engelhard $		£16 5/16	+3/32	£20 7/8	£14½	1,564	1.8	–
European Colour	♣N□	55½	....	58	35½	16.7	2.6	19.8
Gibbon Lyons	✠N	134xd	....	149	132	12.2	5.1	Φ
Hickson	♣N□	162	–6	223	160	283.0	6.3	15.3
Hoechst DM		£144 9/32	–2 3/32	£148 9/32	£108 21/32	8,531	5.1	–
Holliday Chemical	†qN□	247	–3	*250	153¼	256.7	2.2	20.0
ICI	N□	843xd	–14	868	728	6,094	4.1	68.1
Inspec	Z□	219	–3	232	178	186.7	0.8	–
Kalon	♣N□	164	–½	191½	148½	219.6	3.2	16.6
Laporte	♣N□	798	–7	843	704	1,529	3.2	21.6
MIM	♣□	74	....	76	48	27.5	–	–
Manders	N	346	–2	405	332	137.4	3.6	18.2
McLeod Russel	N□	116	....	127	100	70.2	6.6	18.1
Metrotect Inds	♣N□	103xd	....	128	99	24.8	4.2	Φ
Perstorp SKr		£24 5/8	–2 3/32	£32 3/16	£22¼	120.4	1.6	31.0
Porvair	♣N	310	....	349	265	47.7	1.7	23.3
Scapa	♣N□	217xd	–1	272	186	514.3	3.4	18.5
Sutcliffe Speak	♣N□	49	....	66	44	27.6	1.3	28.8
Wardle Storeys	N□	390	–4	490	361	97.1	5.5	20.4
Wellington	W□	203	....	220	203	48.0	3.2	19.6
Wolstenholme	♣N	238	+15	738	570	54.6	3.0	18.4
Yorkshire	♣†N□	426xd	+2	*483	380	195.1	2.4	20.2
Yule Catto	N□	323	+2	*336	258	321.4	2.4	24.5

It will be seen that in addition to well-known British chemical companies such as ICI and Courtaulds, the main leading foreign companies such as Bayer and BASF from Germany, and Akzo from the Netherlands also appear. By the side of the name of these foreign companies the currencies in which the shares are denominated is given. A number of symbols also appear, perhaps the most important being □ which indicates the shares are relatively actively traded.

The price is the closing price of the previous day. It does not mean shares can be bought at this price. The price is the mid price of the best bid and offer price at the end of the day. If an investor is buying he or she will pay more than this price; if selling they will receive a lower price. For the less liquid shares, those with less trading, the spread between the bid and offer price can be wide and so the price paid or received may be significantly different from the price as listed.

It should also be appreciated that the price given in the newspaper is the one at which a market-maker is ready to deal in small volumes. For a large transaction the prices might well be different.

The high and low price for the year is self-explanatory. The layout shown in the table is the traditional way in which the FT indicates the extremes in price that have occurred over a period of time. The newspaper has plans to move to a 52 week rolling high and low.

The market capitalization is the number of shares in issue times the share prices.

The *Financial Times* quotes the gross dividend yield, which as explained above is the net yield adjusted to reflect 20% tax credit for UK ACT. The yield is based on the most recent twelve month dividend per share, divided by the latest closing share price expressed as a percentage.

The price earnings ratio is the share price divided by the most recent 12 months earnings per share. Unfortunately, as explained, there is more than one way of calculating the EPS of a company. There is a taxation issue that has already been discussed and an accounting issue. We will now deal with the accounting measurement issue. There is a difference in accounting between exceptional items of income and expenditure and extraordinary items of income and expenditure. We will not deal with the technical aspects of deciding when an item is exceptional and when it is extraordinary. It is very much a matter of interpretation, and the practice developed in the 1980s of calling it exceptional if it was revenue and extraordinary if it was cost.

The reason for this was that the accounting standard at the time said that if an item was exceptional it could be taken 'above the line' and so would boost the earnings figure and so EPS, but if it was extraordinary it had to be taken below the line and so would not affect EPS.

The practice developed in some companies of taking an item above the line if it was favourable, but classifying it as an extraordinary item if it was unfavourable so that it would not reduce the earnings per share figure.

In the UK in 1992 the Accounting Standards Board introduced FRS3 in an attempt to overcome this problem. Unfortunately the statement did not receive universal support. The Institute for Investment Management and Research, a body made up of people involved in the investment industry, produced their own statement with an alternative formula for how EPS should be calculated. This attempts to eliminate from the EPS figure 'truly exceptional elements in corporate earnings'. The *Financial Times* is adopting the IIMR definition.

12.9 Scrip dividends and scrip issues

One way of issuing new equity shares to existing shareholders is by the distribution of a scrip dividend. As an alternative to paying out cash dividends during a year, a company may choose to pay a scrip dividend. This is essentially a transfer to the shareholder of a number of additional equity shares without the shareholder having to subscribe additional cash.

Advantages to the company include:

1. retaining cash within the business – no cash is distributed to shareholders;
2. a small increase in the permanent share capital base.

Disadvantages to the company include the fact that the administrative costs of scrip dividends can be relatively high.

Advantages to the shareholder include the fact that he receives a dividend which he can convert into cash whenever he wishes (although of course he gives up the cash he may have received as a dividend). The shareholder does not, of course, have an automatic flow of cash to benefit his bank statement at regular intervals. To realize cash from the scrip dividends entails selling the shares, and fluctuations in price could mean that raising urgently needed cash involves selling at a disadvantageous time, though it could also mean the opposite. The company pursuing a policy of issuing scrip dividends would appeal to a different type of investor from a company paying cash dividends.

The key issue arising with this type of dividend payment is the effect of the new shares on the existing share price. If the new shares, the scrip dividend, are issued at the same percentage rate as would be given with a straightforward cash dividend, say 5% so that five new shares are given for every 100 shares held, this does not guarantee a 5%

return to the shareholder. The size of the issue ought to be determined by a realistic assessment of the extent by which the shareholder's wealth will be increased as a result: if, for example, the company anticipated that the issue would precipitate a fall in share price, it should offer more than a 5% increase in the number of shares. Scrip dividends are taxed as if they were cash distributions; therefore, from the shareholders' point of view, they are taxed at income tax rates rather than at capital gains tax rates.

An individual shareholder who elects to take scrip shares instead of a cash dividend will be treated as having received gross income of an amount which, when reduced by an amount equal to income tax at the lower rate, is equal to the cash equivalent. For example, if the shareholder takes scrip shares in respect of which the cash equivalent is £80, the shareholder will be treated as having received gross income of £100, and as having paid income tax of £20.

Similar to a scrip dividend is a scrip issue of fully paid equity shares, sometimes called a capitalization issue or a bonus issue. A company may decide to capitalize its reserves, using the amount involved to increase the number of its equity shares which are issued to existing shareholders. It is similar to a rights issue where shareholders do not have to pay to take up the additional shares. The company is not using its current year's profit to support the issue, but is using its capital reserves.

Enhanced scrip dividends

This a scrip dividend worth more than the value of the alternative cash dividend. Traditionally if a cash dividend offered to a shareholder was say £1 per share, then the option of a scrip dividend would be worth £1 of shares. With an enhanced scrip dividend the value of the scrip dividend offered as an alternative might be worth say £1.50. In the late 1980s a number of UK companies began to offer their shareholders this alternative version of a scrip dividend, and not surprisingly the take-up of such offers was very high. The take-up of a traditional scrip was only about 5% but the take-up for the enhanced scrip dividends was around 90%.

One trouble with taking up the offer of an enhanced scrip dividend was that traditionally the shareholder was left with a number of shares above a possible planned level. To overcome this problem, the scrip dividend offer was sometimes accompanied by a separate offer of an arrangement to sell the new shares received. The company arranges for a bank or other financial institution to buy these shares off the shareholder without dealing commissions being incurred. The price the bank or other institution will pay for these shares distributed as the scrip dividend is specified.

An example of such an enhanced scrip dividend was an offer by BICC. Holders of 92% of BICC shares took up the offer of the enhanced scrip dividend, and 17% took up the additional offer to be able to sell the shares received. The shares were sold to the Swiss Bank Corporation (SBC).

One advantage of a scrip dividend that is taken up by shareholders include retention of cash by the company, and a thinly disguised form of rights issue. This means existing shareholders can maintain their level of participation in the equity of the company.

Example 12.1

We will answer a typical question on the subject of scrip dividends and stock splits. The question is taken from an examination of the Chartered Association of Certified Accountants.

The managing director of Lavipilon plc wishes to provide an extra return to the company's shareholders and has suggested making either:

1. A 2 for 5 bonus issue (capitalization issue) in addition to the normal dividend.
2. A 1 for 5 scrip dividend instead of the normal cash dividend.
3. A 1 for 1 share (stock) split in addition to the normal dividend.

Summarized balance sheet Lavipilon plc (end of last year)

	£m
Fixed assets	65
Current assets	130
Less: Current liabilities	(55)
	140
Financed by	
Ordinary shares (50 pence par value)	25
Share premium account	50
Revenue reserves	40
Shareholders' funds	115
11% debenture	25
	140

The company's shares are trading at 300 pence cum div. and the company has £50 million of profit from this year's activities available to ordinary shareholders of which £30 million will be paid as a dividend if options (1) or (3) are chosen. None of the £40 million revenue reserves would be distributed. This year's financial accounts have not yet been finalized.

Required:

(a) For each proposal show the likely effect on the company's balance sheet at the end of **this** year, and the likely effect on the company's share price.

(9 marks)

(b) Comment upon how well these suggestions fulfil the managing director's objective of providing an extra return to the company's shareholders.

(3 marks)

(c) Discuss reasons why a company might wish to undertake
(i) a scrip dividend,
(ii) a share (stock) split.

(5 marks)

(d) The managing director has heard that it is possible for the company to purchase its own shares. Explain why the purchase of its own shares might be useful to a company. Assume that the shares do **not** need to be cancelled after purchase.

(8 marks)
(25 marks)
ACCA, Dec 1988

Answer

First we will look at the effect of the proposal on the balance sheet. The 2 for 5 bonus issues requires the issue of 20 million new shares. The company would probably elect to debit the share premium account for this capitalization issue. To debit the revenue reserve account could reduce opportunities in future to pay dividends.

The 1 for 5 scrip dividend requires the issue of 10 million shares. The value of these is £30 million. As the question tells us this £30 million will be deducted from the P & L account. This amount will be credited part to ordinary shares and part to the share premium account.

With the stock split, twice the number of shares will be in issue, but each share will now only have a 25 pence par value.

The net assets of the company will increase by the £50 million profit figure if no dividend is paid. The net assets will only increase by £20 million if a dividend is paid.

Balance sheet

	Bonus issue	Scrip dividend	Stock split
Net assets	160	190	160
Ordinary shares	35	30	25
Share premium account	40	75	50
Revenue reserves	60	60	60
	135	165	135
Debentures	25	25	25
	160	190	160

If the stock market is efficient the price of the shares will fall. This is because the number of shares in existence have increased with each of the three possibilities. The number of shares has increased, and the market has been told nothing about improved profits in the future. No extra cash has been raised. The share price under each of the three alternatives should be:

Bonus issue

$$\text{old value} + \text{new value} = \frac{[50 \text{ million shares} \times £3] + [20 \text{ million} \times £0]}{70 \text{ million shares}}$$

$$= \frac{£150 \text{ million}}{70 \text{ million}} = £2.14 \text{ per share}$$

Scrip issue

$$\frac{£150 \text{ million} + [10 \text{ million} \times £0]}{60 \text{ million}} = £2.50 \text{ per share}$$

Share split

$$\frac{£150 \text{ million} + 50 \text{ million} \times £0]}{100 \text{ million}} = £1.50 \text{ per share}$$

If the market is efficient the shareholder is equally well off under each of the alternatives. Prior to any change a single share is worth £3.

With bonus issue, the shareholder now holds 1.4 shares for every 1 old share: $1.4 \times £2.14 = £3$.

With the scrip dividend the shareholder now holds 1.2 shares: $1.2 \times £2.50 = £3$.
With the stock split the shareholder now holds 2 shares: $2 \times £1.50 = £3$.

The answer to the remainder of this question can be found in either the text of this chapter or in Chapter 17 on dividends.

12.10 Stock splits

A stock split (sometimes called a share split), like a scrip dividend, increases the number of shares in a company without raising any new funds. The procedure is simple: the company reduces the par (nominal) value of each share, and announces that its investors no longer hold, say, one share with a par value of £1; instead, they own two shares with a par value of £0.50 each.

One of the reasons sometimes given for a stock split is to create shares of lower denominations with increased marketability. If the marketability of the company's shares improves, the value of the investor's holding should increase. Suppose, for example, that a shareholder has 100 shares selling at £50 per share; the result of a split (say one additional share for each one held) is that his holding is increased quantitatively to 200 shares. Its total value should remain unchanged, with each share now worth £25 instead of £50, but the effects of increased marketability might mean that the price of the 'split' share only falls to £26, in which case, of course, the shareholders' wealth is increased.

Stock splits have been the subject of much research. It has been observed that stock splits usually occur shortly after there has been an increase in share price and that following the announcement of the split there is a positive share price reaction. The reason for this positive reaction is not fully understood, however. The stock split does not affect the issuing company's future cash flows, and so does not affect its value. One explanation is that the market interprets the announcement of the split as indicating that dividends will increase in the near future.

Fama *et al.* [1] examined the process by which share prices adjust to a stock split. The study is based on information from 940 stock splits in the USA. A stock split is defined as an exchange of shares in which at least five shares are distributed for every four formerly outstanding; it therefore includes a stock dividend of 25% or greater. It is shown that stock splits are usually preceded by a period in which the rate of return on the stock is unusually high. Return includes both dividends and capital gains. The companies are earning above average returns over this pre-split period. However, the stock market is not sure that these above average earnings will be maintained.

The announcement of a proposed split suggests that the high earnings are expected to continue. Most announcements of stock splits are either accompanied or followed soon after by the announcement of proposed dividend increases. It is well known that once a large company increases its dividends, it is extremely reluctant to reduce it. Therefore any dividend increase indicates to the investor that the earnings are expected to be maintained. This means that at the suggestion of a stock split the share price will adjust upwards.

The study suggests that the reason that the share price rises is because investors assume that the information regarding the stock split indicates that dividends will rise. They therefore alter their impression of the value of the share in line with the higher expected stream of dividends. Once 'the information effects of dividend changes are taken into account, the apparent price effects of the split will vanish'. The study finds support for the efficient market hypothesis which implies that the only way to make money out of a stock split is through inside information regarding the proposed split or change in dividends.

The research of Asquith *et al.* [2] indicates that stock splits also convey earnings information. Usually companies who make a stock split show significant earnings increases in the year before the announcement. Research shows that these earnings increases appear to be permanent, with earnings continuing to increase for a number of years after the split. Therefore the announcement of a split indicates to the market that the past increases in earnings are likely to continue into the future and are of a permanent rather than transitory nature.

The impact of stock splits has been examined in the USA, Canada and the UK. Some studies have found that capitalization issues have no influence on share prices, but other studies have found the opposite. However, all the studies showed that no profitable trading rules could be based on the announcement of capitalization issues and that the market adjusted share prices instantaneously and accurately for new information.

12.11 Rights issues

A rights offer is an offer of a company's shares to its existing shareholders. It gives the existing shareholders the first opportunity to purchase a new issue of shares. The terms of the offer are that each existing shareholder has the right to be allotted a certain number of shares upon payment of the asking price. The number of shares he is offered is determined by the percentage of his existing share ownership in relation to the total number of company shares; he is offered a similar percentage of the new shares to be issued. This means that if the shareholder takes up the offer he will maintain his existing percentage ownership of the company. This offer does not have to be accepted personally by the existing shareholders. They may sell the right separately from the share, or sell the share with the rights offer attached. Table 12.11 provides recent historic information on the numbers and size of rights issues in the UK listed and unlisted securities markets.

Table 12.11 Rights issues: historic series

	Listed – UK and Irish			Unlisted securities market	
Year	No.	Proceeds (£ million)	Year	No.	Proceeds (£ million)
1980	95	1 059 785	1980	1	1 456
1981	108	1 971 974	1981	4	9 296
1982	75	901 707	1982	5	12 132
1983	134	2 007 043	1983	24	81 231
1984	113	1 674 182	1984	19	66 394
1985	135	4 054 753	1985	26	127 450
1986	194	5 618 673	1986	32	109 646
1987	215	8 452 950	1987	52	404 114
1988	132	5 745 810	1988	37	277 757
1989	117	4 604 129	1989	53	316 397
1990	101	4 890 901	1990	42	348 833
1991	158	10 133 388	1991	28	139 360
1992	74	4 134 339	1992	21	94 078
1993	**129**	**9 594 661**			

At times of a depressed stock market, equity capital does not have great appeal either to investors or to issuers. However, in such times, raising equity capital by means of a rights issue does have advantages over the alternative ways of appealing to shareholders for more funds. If the terms of the rights offer are correct and if shareholders have the funds available to take up the offer, the fact that the stock market price is low does not mean that the company is selling a stake in the business to outsiders at a bargain price. The existing shareholders are being given the opportunity to continue to maintain the same percentage holding in the business after the issue as they had before the issue.

Rights issues pose a number of controversial questions. What, for example, is the value of the offer to the shareholder? How many shares should the company issue, and what is the capital cost to the company of funds raised from this source? In theory these questions can be answered with confidence, but a number of researchers in the field disagree on the way that the market reacts to rights issues. The problems involved will be examined in this chapter.

The success of a rights issue (where 'success' means selling all the new shares) depends upon the size of the issue, the price asked for the shares and the investors' expectations of the earnings that will result from the use of the funds. The number of shares issued and the priced asked for the shares are functions of the amount of funds to be raised. The earnings that will result depend upon the amount of funds invested as well as the expected rate of return. Thus the first problem is the common factor – the amount of funds to be raised.

Funds to be raised

Two factors jointly determine the number of new shares that a company will need to issue: the amount of new funds that the company wishes to raise and the price it considers reasonable to ask for these new shares. The first of these factors needs to be looked at carefully. As with all capital expansion programmes, the amount of funds to be raised depends upon the earnings that can be obtained from the new investments compared with the cost of the funds. The company must ensure that it can earn on the funds that it obtains a rate at least equal to the opportunity cost of this source of capital; it must ensure that the existing shareholders are at least as well off after the issue as they were before. This means that the earnings from the new funds must be sufficient, when capitalized, to increase the market value of the company by the amount of the new funds.

The amount of funds that should be raised by a new rights issue is therefore dependent on the earnings of the company on these new funds, and the rate at which the market capitalizes earnings for such a company. It is a matter of the company convincing the market of the earnings that will result from the new funds.

Earnings per share

Rights issues present a complication when it comes to calculating earnings per share. Shareholders like to be able to observe how the earnings per share (EPS) of a company have increased over time. Comparative statistics give the EPS for one year and this can be compared with the EPS for the next period. If a rights issue takes place and shares are offered at a price less than the full market price, the shareholders may appear to have received something of a bonus. However, the share in one year, say t, is not the same as the share in the year after the rights issue, say $t + 2$. A share in year t is equal to the sum of the share in the year $t + 2$ plus the bonus element of the rights issue. It is recommended in the appropriate Accounting Standard that, in order to obtain comparable figures over time, the past EPS figures should be multiplied by a factor which is the ratio of the theoretical ex rights price of share to the actual cum rights price on the last day of quotation cum rights.

This means that if the EPS were 25p in 1992 and in 1993 there was a rights issue, where the theoretical ex rights price was £1 and the actual cum rights price on the last day the shares were traded with rights was £1.25, then the adjusted EPS for 1992 would be 20p, i.e. (25p × 1/1.25). This change is necessary because after the rights issue, because of the bonus element, each new share is not claiming quite as much of the earnings as each old share. Following the issue EPS figures produced by the company will be based on the new type of share, and so for comparative purposes, earlier EPS figures need to be scaled down.

Example 12.2

Assume that a company, Stanley Park PLC, contemplating a new issue of capital has the following financial situation. Its balance sheet can be summarized as

Ordinary shares 3000 at £1			
nominal value	£3000	Assets	£9000
Retained earnings	£2000		
Debentures (10%)	£4000		
	£9000		£9000

The net asset value per share is £1.67 (= £5000/3000). The company is earning approximately 17% on its existing total assets, before interest and taxes, made up as follows:

Total earnings	£1508
Interest	£400
	£1108
Tax (35%)	£388
	£720

Earnings per share (£720/3000) = £0.24

The possible capital issues and their resulting returns are as follows:

New funds	Expected net returns (£)	Average rate of return on new investments
2000	300	15%
3000	360	12%
4500	405	9%

The market's rate of capitalization for a company of this type is 12%; this is the market's required earnings yield, and is equivalent to a price-to-earnings ratio for the company of 8.33:1.

If the market behaved rationally, valuing the company on 'the capitalized earnings of the firm at the market's normal rate of capitalization for a firm of this type', the total value of the company before the issue would be

$$720/0.12 = £6000$$

After raising £3000 the value would be

$$£1080/0.12 = £9000$$

Raising this amount of capital satisfies the constraint that the earnings from the new issue must be sufficient, when capitalized, to increase the market value by the amount of the new funds. This would not have been the case if £4500 had been raised:

$$\text{new value} = £1125/0.12 = £9375$$

The new funds raised were £4500 and the increase in market value was only £3375.

If however, the rate of return on the additional funds had been greater than the market's rate of capitalization, the market value of the firm's shares would have moved upwards. This would have happened if only £2000 had been sought by the rights issue.

There is a further problem in the year which the rights issue is made. A different number of shares will have been issued at the end of the year compared with that at the beginning of the year. It is recommended that the weighted-average share capital for the year be calculated. The weighted-average share capital is the average number of shares ranking for dividends during the period weighted on a time basis.

Price of rights issue

Having determined the amount that can be raised from a rights issue, it is necessary to determine the number of shares to be issued and to decide on their price. The firm already used as an example could have raised the chosen £3000 through many combinations of number of shares times share price. It is not usual to issue the new shares at the existing market price. In the UK, rights issues are often priced below the existing market price of the firms' existing shares.

It can be shown that if the market correctly estimates the earnings the company will obtain from investing the new funds, and if the ex rights share price is based on a correct estimate of future earnings, the price at which the new rights shares are issued need not cause anxiety to the existing shareholders. They will be at least as wealthy after the issue as before, whatever the price of the rights issue. This satisfies the requirement that new issues should leave existing shareholders at least as well off as they were before the rights issue, and this remains true even if the shareholders sell their rights instead of subscribing personally. The lower is the share price at which the rights issue is offered, the more valuable of course will be the rights when they are sold separately.

To illustrate this point it is necessary to show how the ex rights price will be arrived at.

Theoretically the ex rights price will be equal to a weighted average of the pre-rights price and the rights price, with any adjustment above or below this value depending on the profitability of the project for which the rights are issued compared with the profitability of the rest of the company's investments.

To begin with it will be assumed that the new funds will earn the same rate of return as the old funds. Then the ex-rights price is

$$P_P \; \frac{N_O}{N} + P_N \; \frac{N_N}{N}$$

where P_P is the pre-issue price, P_N is the new issue price, N_O is the number of old shares, N_N is the number of new shares and N is the total number of shares.

Returning to the earlier example of Stanley Park, if 2000 new shares were issued at £1.50 per share, the ex rights price would be

$$£2 \times \frac{3000}{5000} + £1.50 \times \frac{2000}{5000} = £1.80 \text{ per share}$$

If the existing shareholders are offered a rights issue of two new shares at a price of £1.50 for every three existing shares, the effect for the shareholders exercising the option would be the equivalent of sacrificing their existing investment plus an additional payment of cash (in total £6000 + £3000) in return for a total of 5000 shares valued at £1.80 per share, i.e. £9000. They should be satisfied with this position; the £9000 now in the company is earning 12%, whereas previously £6000 was earning this rate.

If they exercised only half the option and sold the remaining rights, it would be equivalent to surrendering the original investment of £6000 plus the payment for the new shares of £1500, and in return they would own 4000 shares valued at £1.80 per share (£7200) plus the value of the rights on 1000 new shares which could be sold at £0.30 per right (£300). Therefore they would be no worse off after having given up £7500 and received £7500.

The value of the rights on one new share is simply the difference between the ex rights market price and the price at which these shares can be purchased under the option – in this example it is £1.80 – £1.50.

The value of a right on one old share can be expressed as

$$\frac{P_e - P_N}{n}$$

where P_e is the expected market price of the share after the rights issue, P_N is the price of the share offered under the rights issue and n is the number of rights on old shares required to purchase one new share. This simply means that, as the share is offered at a reduced price to existing shareholders, the value of that right is the difference between what they are being asked to pay for it and the price at which they can sell the share when the time in which the rights can be exercised has ended.

To determine the value of a right it is necessary to adjust the difference between the possible buying and selling prices of the new shares to existing shareholders in order to allow for the fact that the ownership of one existing share may not entitle the holder to one complete new share. If the offer is, say, one new share for every four existing shares, the value of one right, attached to each existing share, is only a quarter of the price difference.

The option only remains open for a certain period of time. A date is decided upon by the company after which dealings in the company's shares become ex rights. This means that the shares can then be traded in, free of the rights option. This is the day after the posting of the allotment letters for new shares.

In the Stanley Park example it can be shown that even with a different asking price, say £1 per share, the existing shareholders will still be no worse off, provided that the market appreciates the earnings the company expects to earn on the new funds. Three thousand shares now need to be issued to raise the £3000. A one-for-one offer is being made. The ex rights price will be

$$£2 \times \frac{3000}{6000} + £1 \times \frac{3000}{6000} = £1.50 \text{ per share}$$

Taking up the entire option is equivalent to surrendering the £6000 existing investment plus £3000 cash, again £9000, in return for 6000 shares valued at £1.50 (£9000). If only half the option is taken up by existing shareholders, they will give up the existing £6000 plus the new subscription of £1500. In return they will hold 4500 shares worth in total £6750 and receive from the sale of the options £750 ($= 1500 \times £0.50$).

It can be seen, therefore, that in theory neither the number of shares that is issued nor the price at which they are issued is important in affecting the position of existing shareholders. All that matters is that the correct amount of money is raised and that the market is made aware of the earning power of the new investment.

In practice it is necessary that the asking price under the rights offer should appear acceptable; the discount should not be so small that it fails to attract shareholders, nor so large that it looks ridiculous and can only raise the necessary amount of capital by the issue of a large number of new shares. If, of course, the shares are offered at a zero price they then resemble a scrip issue where new funds are not being sought but retained earnings are being capitalized. The purpose of a rights issue is to raise new funds. A scrip issue usually has the objective of reducing the price of the company's shares on the market which it achieves by increasing the number of shares without increasing the value of the company. The difference between a rights issue and a scrip issue is therefore that the main objective of the former is to raise capital, whereas the main objective of the latter is to alter the terms attached to the shares. It is only if the price of the rights issue is low that the two objectives may be achieved simultaneously. We shall return to this point in the following section.

Ex rights price

In the above example only one situation was considered in arriving at the ex rights price, namely that the yield on new capital is expected to be the same as the yield on the old capital. If the two yields are not expected to be the same, the ex rights price formula needs to be amended to

$$\frac{P_P N_O + P_N N_N (Y_N / Y_O)}{N}$$

where Y_N is the yield on new capital and Y_O is the yield on old capital. If in the example of Stanley Park PLC the company had only raised £2000 worth of new funds by issuing, say, 2000 shares at £1 and invested them to earn extra returns of £300, the new capitalized value of the company would have been £1020/0.12 = £8500, and the price per share would have been £8500/5000 = £1.70. The value of the company would have risen by £2500 as a result of only £2000 of new funds. The ex rights price would be calculated on the basis of the above formula:

$$\left(£2 \times \frac{3000}{5000} \right) + \left(£1 \times \frac{2000}{5000} \times \frac{15\%}{12\%} \right) = £1.70$$

The example illustrates the point that even where the new funds earn a higher return than that earned by existing funds, the existing shareholders are not affected by the price at which the rights shares are issued. Most companies making a rights issue offer the shares at a price lower than the existing market price. In this example, where 2000 shares are issued at a price of £1 per share, those shareholders taking up half the offer give up claims to £6000 plus the new subscription of £1000 in cash. In return they receive 4000 shares worth £1.70 per share, and from the sale of rights they receive £700: total value, £7500. The shareholders taking up all the offer would give up £8000 and receive in return shares worth £8500 (5000 × £1.70). Clearly it makes no difference whether the existing shareholders take up all the options or not; whatever proportion they take up, they will receive the full benefit of the £500 gain in value.

If the £2000 had been raised by the issue of 4000 new shares offered to existing shareholders at a price of £0.50 per share, the existing shareholders would still receive the £500 gain in market value. The ex rights price would be

$$\left(£2 \times \frac{3000}{5000} \right) + \left(£1 \times \frac{2000}{5000} \times \frac{12\%}{12\%} \right) = £1.60$$

The shareholders would again be giving up £8000 and in return hold 7000 shares worth £1.214 each, a total of £8500. If they sold the rights, the rights on each new share would be worth £1.214 − £0.50 = £0.714, and the value of the rights on 4000 shares would be approximately £2858. The 3000 shares are now worth in total £3642. Thus the value of the shares plus the rights shows a £500 gain on the original position, i.e. £3642 + £2858 − £6000.

The crucial factor in this analysis is the expectation of the market about the earnings that will result from the investment of the new funds. In the example it was shown that the existing shareholders could be indifferent to the price of the rights issue. However, the ex rights share prices of £1.70 and £1.214 were both dependent on the market's expecting the new funds to earn 15%. If the market anticipated earnings of anything less than 15%, thereby casting doubt on the company's expectations, the existing shareholders could lose with a rights issue (if they do not exercise their rights). The size of the opportunities lost by existing shareholders would depend upon the percentage of the rights issue they took up.

For example, assume that the market only expects the new funds (£2000) to yield the same return as the capitalization rate, namely 12%. According to the formula the ex rights price would be £1.60. If the shareholders exercise the full option, situation A applies:

Situation A

Value at pre-rights position	3000 shares at £2	£6000
Purchase of rights issue	2000 shares at £1	£2000
		£8000
Value at ex rights position	5000 shares at £1.60	£8000

This £8000 investment is in fact earning £1020, i.e. the £720 old plus £300 new (see the investment schedule on p. 360), a rate of return of 12.75%. If, however, the shareholders exercise only half the option, then situation B occurs:

Situation B

Value at pre-rights position	3000 shares at £2	£6000
Purchase of rights issue	1000 shares at £1	£1000
		£7000
Value at ex rights position	4000 shares at £1.60	£6400
Sale of rights	1000 × £0.60 (= £1.60 − £1)	£600
		£7000

In situation B the shareholder is only earning 12.75% on his £6400 investment, a position inferior to that offered by situation A. On the proceeds of the option sale he would be earning only the equivalent market capitalization rate of 12%. This is not the same situation as that of the earlier examples in which the shareholders did not themselves purchase all the rights. In the earlier examples, the market correctly anticipated the earnings. In the later situation, because the shares of the company are undervalued, the shareholders who do not buy all the rights themselves are missing the opportunity to earn an above average yield, and they do not receive the full benefits on the sale of the rights because the ex rights price is low.

It can be seen that the existing shareholders' financial position is dependent on the valuation that the market places on the company after the rights issue, and if this results in an undervaluation, their position depends upon the proportion of the rights issue for which they subscribe.

Market reaction to a rights issue

From observing actual price behaviour it can be seen that the price of the existing shares of a company often falls slightly when the announcement of a rights issue is made. The price is further adjusted downwards when dealings in the rights start, and again falls when dealings become ex rights. There are of course exceptions to this, particularly in the case of high-performance companies.

The fact that the share price falls should not be a surprise, as it has already been shown that the price would be expected to fall if the rights issue is offered at a price below the initial market price; the size of the fall depends on the size of the discount. The existing shareholders do not necessarily lose because of the fall in price; what is important is that the ex rights price should settle quickly at its true value.

Some financial commentators react strangely to the fall in price after a rights issue. For example, an issue by Shipton Automation of one additional share at a price of £0.25 for each old share, at a time when the existing price was £0.425, caused a comment in the press that the price 'plunged' to £0.3063. Using the formula on page 362 one would have expected the price to fall to £0.3375, i.e.

$$\text{ex rights price} = \frac{£0.425}{2} + \frac{£0.250}{2}$$

The difference between £0.3375 and £0.3063 is really not so dramatic.

The fall in the share price of at the time of the announcement of a rights issue is caused by the following.

1. The price is marked down by jobbers in anticipation of some shareholders being forced to sell their rights through inability to find the money to pay for the new shares.
2. There is an increase in the supply of the shares on the market.
3. Where the price of the new shares is pitched as closely as possible to the pre-announcement share price, it is usually announced that the dividend will be maintained. However, the earnings yield, calculated on the previous year's net profits, will probably be reduced. Of course, this can be remedied by a forecast of increased

profits for the current year. The usefulness of calculating an earnings yield based on a past year's profit when it is known that the investment base has increased could be severely criticized.

A further fall in the share price at the onset of dealings in the rights often happens as a result of the sale of rights by those investors who cannot take them up. However, such a fall may have been anticipated (see 1 above) or may be offset by the following factors:

1. strong demand for the shares – if the company is fast-growing, demand may be such that after adjustment downwards to the ex rights price the share price starts moving up rather than down;
2. certain investors and institutions who specialize in new issues and in acquiring shares depressed by a rights issue.

The earlier analysis was based primarily on earnings yield. It was shown that if the market anticipates the earnings correctly, then, through the use of the relevant market capitalization rate, the value of the company and thus the value of each share can be assessed. The assumption that the rate of earnings on the new investment would be at least the same as that on the existing investment does not mean that the EPS needs to be maintained. The important variable is the new earnings yield – the relationship between the new earnings per share and the new price. It is this that the company will wish at least to maintain. Consequently, as shown below, if the shares are correctly priced ex rights, this relationship is in fact maintained.

In the Stanley Park example earnings before the rights issue were £720, the EPS was £0.24 and the price-to-earnings ratio was 8.33:1. On the issue of the new shares, earnings rose to £1020 giving EPS of £0.204; the new ex rights price was, however, £1.70, which gives a maintained price-to-earnings ratio of 8.33:1 and a maintained earnings yield of 12%.

When making a rights issue, companies often offer forecasts of the expected profits from the new investment. It is possible to translate this into the EPS expected after the investment, and then, given the earnings yield on shares in similar companies, to calculate a share price. It is possible that a rights issue may alter the price-to-earnings ratio of a company because the gearing of the company is being changed. The equity is being increased without an increase in the debt. The effects of gearing will be discussed in Chapter 18.

Earnings are not the only factor that influences share price, however. Dividends also have an important effect and the dividend statement accompanying the rights issue can influence the ex rights price. If the dividend per share can be maintained at the rate in effect before the rights issue, with the expected fall in ex rights price the dividend yield will in fact have risen.

Returning to the Stanley Park example, if the dividends before the rights issue were £300, i.e. £0.10 per share, the dividend yield would be 5% on the £2 share price. After the rights issue it was anticipated that the price would settle at £1.70; if dividends are maintained at £0.10 per share, the dividend yield is now 5.9%. The company would have to distribute £200 of its extra £300 earnings to maintain the same dividend per share, paying a total dividend of £500. To maintain the same dividend yield of 5% on the new price means paying a dividend per share of only £0.085, i.e. a total dividend of £425. To maintain the dividend yield may be all that is needed to satisfy shareholders, and ensure that the market adjusts to a reasonable ex rights price. This policy also helps the company's cash flow position, which may be crucial in the early years of a new project's life.

A company may state that it will maintain its earnings yield with the new investment, but there is no certainty that it will be able to do this in the first year of a new project's life. However, it may be vital to maintain at least its dividend yield. The dividend is something that the company can control with comparative ease, while the earnings will depend on how long it takes for the project to be brought to its full level of profitability.

So far in this chapter we have made rights issues seem a very mechanical and arithmetic affair. But, as has been emphasized, there can be either enthusiasm in connection with new issues of stock through rights or, as is sometimes the case, criticism by stockholders of rights offerings. Opinions vary because the stock market is not mechanical; it does not always have full information on the possible returns from a new investment, and can therefore react with waves of pessimism and optimism.

A rights offer may lead the shareholders of a fast-growing company to believe that the company is confident and that it will continue to expand; it draws attention to the company's good performance in the past. Psychological factors such as these boost the demand for a company's shares, and so cause prices to rise to a level not justified by the real situation. The psychological factors could of course work the other way. One reason for the frequent fall in share price some time after a rights issue arises out of the shareholders' concern with the latest reported figures and disregard of time lags. Few new investments start to realize returns before some time has elapsed, with the exception of a rights issue in which the funds raised are used to finance an acquisition.

This means that a reported fall in the EPS following the issue can cause the share price to fall, despite the fact that in a present value sense the investment is profitable to shareholders. This does not always happen.

The empirical evidence on the adjustment of share prices to rights issues does confirm the proposition that the market has a one way expectation. It is assumed that companies making rights issues will be able to maintain their dividend rates on share capital enlarged by the issue. It has been found that the conventional formula (shown on page 362) for predicting ex rights prices is, in fact, highly accurate.

A rights issue is usually underwritten. The underwriters' commission can be high. If the exercise price is set near the current market price many shareholders will irrationally not feel that they are getting a bargain and so they will not subscribe. The shares will therefore be left with the underwriters. If the exercise price is set well below the existing market price it is more likely that the rights will be taken up by shareholders. There have been 'deep discount' rights issues where the discount on the pre-issue price can be as high as 40–50%. In such situations underwriting cover might not be taken, thus avoiding the cost. With lower levels of discounting, an underwriting contract might be entered into, but the underwriting commission should be reduced. The above behaviour of shareholders may be illogical, knowing as we do that it does not matter what the exercise price is; the important factor is that the rights are exercised by existing shareholders.

One event that should worry the company and the underwriters is if the market price drops below the exercise price. In this situation the underwriter will become crucial. Again, the exercise price set well below the existing market price should avoid this danger.

Cost of rights issue

The cost of capital from rights issues depends upon the proportion of the new issue subscribed for by the existing shareholders. When they subscribe for the whole of the issue the cost of the rights funds is the same as the cost of equity funds. If the shares are undervalued at the ex rights price and the existing shareholders do not take up all the rights, the cost of rights funds will be higher than the cost of other forms of new equity. The cost of equity capital is determined by the required yield at the new issue price plus of course any costs of issue. In the case of a rights issue the existing shareholders have the option of realizing cash on the sale of the rights as an alternative to holding the shares.

Two examples will be considered, the first where the market adjusts the ex rights price to the correct valuation and the second where the shares are undervalued after the rights issue. We shall use the Stanley Park example. First we shall consider the situation where £3000 is raised to finance a new project. We shall assume that the cost of capital before the rights issue was the market's capitalization rate of 12% and that the new project will earn 12%. If the ex rights price settles at the level of the capitalized value of the earnings (the company is giving an earnings yield of 12%), then this remains their cost of capital, excluding the initial issue costs.

In the second example we shall use the situation as described on page 362: 2000 new shares are issued at a price of £1 per share. We shall now assume that the market expects that the new investment will earn only 12%. The ex rights price will be £1.60:

$$\left(£2 \times \frac{3000}{5000} \right) + \left(£1 \times \frac{2000}{5000} \times \frac{12\%}{12\%} \right) = £1.60$$

In fact, the earnings on the new funds are at a rate of 15%. Let us assume that only 50% of the rights are taken up by the existing shareholders. The cost of capital to the company is given by the formula:

$$\frac{Y_N C_N + S(C_O - M_O)}{C}$$

where Y_N is the earnings yield at the new issue price, C_N is the capital subscribed by new shareholders, C_O is the capital subscribed by old shareholders, C is the total new capital subscribed, S is the shareholders' cost of capital and M_O is the funds received by old shareholders from the sale of rights. The earnings yield on the new issue price depends upon the total returns to the business (£720 + £300), the total number of shares (5000) and the price at which the new shares were issued (£1). This in fact gives a yield of

$$\frac{£0.204}{£1} = 20.4\%$$

Half the capital raised is subscribed by new shareholders. The sale of rights will give the existing shareholders total receipts of £600, i.e. (£1.60 – £1) per share with the rights on 1000 shares being sold. Substituting these values into the equation, the cost of capital raised under a rights issue in these circumstances is

$$\left(20.4\% \times £1000 \right) + \left(12\% \times \frac{£1000 - £600}{£2000} \right) = 12.6\%$$

It can therefore be seen that if the rights issue causes an undervaluation of the company's shares, because the market does not appreciate the return that will result from the investment of the new funds, this raises the cost of capital. The cost of capital is crucially dependent upon the proportion of the issue taken up by existing shareholders. The smaller is this proportion, the higher is the cost of capital to the company. When the rights issue is fully taken up, undervaluation by the market is not so important; in the example the cost of capital can be shown in this situation to be the normal market cost of 12%. The company can minimize its cost of capital at the time of a rights issue by ensuring that as much as possible of the issue is taken up by existing shareholders.

The reason that the cost of capital behaves in this way when the market undervalues the shares is that the company is having to compensate the existing shareholders for the unjustified fall in market price, and when the profits start to accrue later the company will be giving a higher return than necessary to the new shareholders who purchased the rights. If there are no new shareholders, and existing shareholders take up the entire offer, the undervaluation is not important in terms of the cost of capital because all the original shareholders will receive the full above normal market yield when the returns flow in from the investment. Provided that the market correctly values the company's shares after a rights issue, the cost of capital, in terms of the required earnings of the company, will be the same as if the funds were raised under a new equity issue. With a new equity issue, however, there is a danger that the asking price will be set too low, which would raise the cost of capital.

One advantage of a rights issue is that more of the funds collected are retained because the issue costs of a rights offer are less than the issue costs of a normal equity issue. The administrative and underwriting costs of the rights issue are lower. The offer is aimed at a smaller investing public, namely the existing shareholders, so that the administrative costs are less. It is cheaper to contact existing shareholders than to advertise for new ones.

With the new issue price set below the market price there is less likelihood of a rights issue not being subscribed. The market price, as it fluctuates, is less likely to fall below the low issue price of a rights issue. If the company obtaining the new capital is reasonably well respected, the risks which account for part of the underwriting costs are likely to be low.

With a typical rights issue of £100 million or more, the costs in 1994 would have taken up between 3% and 4% of the funds raised. These costs would include 1.25% of the amount raised for underwriting, 0.50% for the merchant bank and 0.25% for the broking house handling the issue. Capital duty is also involved. Smaller rights issues, those involving under £3 million, can incur costs amounting to 8% or more of the money raised.

Illustration

To illustrate the principles of a rights issue a question taken from the examinations of the Chartered Association of Certified Accountants will now be considered. (Taxation can be ignored in this question.)

Example 12.3

Harris PLC is about to raise finance by increasing its 12 million ordinary shares with a one for three rights issue. Total debt in the capital structure comprises the following:

	Book value (£million)
16% debentures	10.0
16% bank loan	10.0
Various short-term loans and overdrafts at current interest rates	0.2

The debentures have a further life of nine years and are redeemable at par. The fixed-interest 16% bank loan is guaranteed by the bank to be available for a further nine years. Both the debentures and the bank loan were initially arranged several years ago when interest rates were high. Interest rates have since fallen.

The money raised by the rights issue will be used as follows.

1. To fund a new contract to which Harris is already committed and which requires an initial outlay of £1 million. The contract has a profitability index (ratio of present value (PV) of future net cash inflows to PV of initial capital outlay) of 1.4, and full details of the contract have been public knowledge for several months.
2. To reduce borrowings by buying back, at current market value, and cancelling the £10 million debenture issue. The debentures are currently priced in the market to yield 8% per annum, the current yield on such corporate debt.

Total finance required in 1 and 2 will be rounded up to the next whole £100 000 for the purpose of the rights issue. The excess funds raised will be used to reduce short-term borrowings and overdrafts.

The company intends to announce full details of the rights issue on 1 July when the market price per share prior to the announcement is expected to be £5. The company is confident that the whole issue will be purchased, but the managing director is concerned that the discount at which the issue is made may raise the cost of equity capital and hence the weighted-average cost of capital.

(a) Calculate
   (i) the issue price per share;
   (ii) the theoretical ex rights price per share;
   (iii) the value of the right attached to each Harris share before being traded ex rights.

(8 marks)

(b) Briefly explain whether the concern of the managing director is justified. (2 marks)
(c) Discuss whether this rights issue could be expected to alter the cost of equity and/or the weighted-average cost of capital in any way. (4 marks)
(d) After setting the issue price (calculated in (a)) but before announcing the rights issue, Harris decides to reduce borrowings by redeeming the 16% bank loan at its face value of £10 million rather than buying back the debentures at market value. The possibility of the redemption at face value is now known only to the company and its bankers but will become public knowledge when the rights issue is announced on 1 July. The market had expected the bank loan to run for its full remaining nine years of life.

The excess cash generated by the rights issue, after reducing borrowings and funding the £1 million contract, will be invested in a project which has a profitability index of 1.2. The market is not aware of this project and will remain unaware until its details become public knowledge when the rights issue is announced.

Calculate:

(i) the share price on 1 July immediately after the announcement of the rights issue but before the shares are traded ex rights;
(ii) the theoretical ex rights price per share.

Briefly explain your calculations and also explain whether they assume that the market is displaying the weak, semi-strong or strong level of market efficiency.

(6 marks)

(20 marks)

Suggested solution

Part (a)

The total funds to be raised are to be used to fund a new contract and to buy back the debentures. The market price of the debentures is not known, but can be estimated. It is assumed that the market is rational and is valuing a debenture at the PV of the cash flow that will be received over the debenture's life. Therefore the total funds to be raised are as follows:

	PV factor 8%		(£million)
To fund contract			1.0
Market value of debentures: interest payments,			
£1.6m p.a. for nine years	6.247	9.995	
Redemption, £10m in nine years	0.500	5.000	14.995
Total			15.995

Rounded to £16m.

(i) A one for three rights issue will increase the number of shares by 4 million and £16 million is needed. Hence the issue price per share must be £4.

As details of the contract are already public knowledge any impact on share price will already have taken place. Similarly, as the repurchasing of the debenture is at market value based on current rates of interest, this is unlikely to affect the share price.

(ii) The total value of equity after rights issue is as follows (see formula p. 362):

Existing shares	12 million at £5	= £60 million
New shares	4 million at £4	= £16 million
	16 million	= £76 million

The theoretical ex rights price per share is £76/16 = £4.75.

(iii) Each three shares currently held give the right to purchase, for £4.00, a share which will be worth £4.75. The value of such rights attached to three existing shares is 75p (i.e. £4.75 − £4.00). Hence the value of the right attached to one share is 25p.

Part (b)

The fact that the shares are being offered under the rights issue at a discount on the current price should not affect the cost of equity provided either that the market is efficient in valuing the securities or the existing shareholders take up the entire rights issue. If the market misinterprets the way in which the funds are to be used and some exiting shareholders sell the rights, then there could well be a wealth transfer, with a possible reduction in the wealth of existing shareholders.

Part (c)

At this point in the book we have not considered the cost of capital and capital gearing, and so this part of the question will not be considered in detail. The main point to make is that the weighted-average cost of capital will change as there is a change in the debt-to-equity ratio. The rights issue is increasing the equity base and the funds raised being used to reduce the level of gearing.

Part (d)

(i) In this case the rights issue announcement will provide new information which will cause the market to revise its valuation of the firm and also of the firm's equity. The revision will be caused by the following:

Reduction of debt liability

The market's perceptions of a nine year life for the bank loan will cause its value, as calculated in part (a) (i), to be (approx.)	£15m	
This liability can be cancelled for the sacrifice of its face value of	£10m	
Leaving a benefit to equity of:		£5m

Profitable use of excess cash

The excess cash of £5m is placed in a project with NPV £1m. This NPV accrues to equity:	£1m
Total revision of equity value:	+£6m
Previous equity value:	£60m
Revised equity value:	£66m

The share price after the revision of expectations should move towards £66m/12m = £5.5.

(ii) Total equity value after the rights issue:

Existing shares after revision of expectations	12m at £5.5	£66m
New shares	4m at £4	£16m
	16m	£82m

The theoretical ex rights price per share is £82/16 = £5.125.

It is assumed that the market is efficient in the semi-strong form and reacts to publicly available information, but it not efficient in the strong form and requires information to be made public before it can be incorporated into market valuations. This topic is fully discussed in the next chapter.

Pre-emption rights

For a long time there has been a stock exchange requirement, which became a legal requirement from 1980, that companies wishing to make a further issue of equity shares for cash have to offer them first to existing shareholders. The justification for providing this 'right' is that existing shareholders may wish to maintain a certain percentage holding in the company. By offering them this right they have the chance to do so. If the new issue of shares were offered to all potential investors, existing shareholders could find their percentage holding declining.

The Stock Exchange Yellow Book states:

Issues for cash of securities having an equity element must, in the absence of exceptional circumstances, be offered in the first place to the existing equity shareholders in proportion to their holdings unless the shareholders have approved other specific proposals. Such approval may take the form of either general disapplication of the statutory pre-emption requirements not more than fifteen months prior to the issue, or prior approval for a specific issue. Holders of other securities having an equity element must be permitted to participate if the rights attached thereto so require.

The financial institutions in the UK, who already own in the region of 70% of all shares, attach considerable importance to these pre-emptive rights. They argue that it means that their voting power is not diluted and that the alternative of selling shares to other shareholders often depresses share prices. These rights exist in the UK but not in the USA. However, even in the USA a firm's articles of incorporation sometimes state that shareholders have a pre-emptive right to subscribe to new offerings.

The pre-emptive right provision often has restrictions placed upon it. For example, it would not apply to issues of shares to employees, and to issues under share option schemes.

There is criticism of these restrictions. It is claimed that it is a restrictive practice, and that the stock markets should be opened up to more competition in the demand for shares by offering new shares to all investors. It is claimed that this would reduce the cost of raising money for the company. Companies themselves point out that if they were not tied by the pre-emptive rights clause they could raise money more quickly and cheaply through placements than through rights issues.

These pre-emptive rights only apply to issues for cash; they do not apply to equity shares issued in exchange for assets. Therefore a share-for-share exchange at the time of a takeover does not contravene the pre-emptive rights. But what if the shareholders of the victim firm want cash rather than shares? It is here where 'vendor placings' have provided to be useful. Vendor placings technically do not offend the rights of pre-emption. The company issuing the new shares is not selling them for cash. The shareholder of the victim company is given shares in the acquiring company in exchange for shares in the victim company. The acquirer has arranged for an institution to be willing to buy these new shares immediately for cash from the shareholder of the victim company. The institution could then sell the shares or perhaps place them with clients. It is even possible for the original shareholders of the acquiring company to buy these new shares from the institution.

With the hectic takeover activity following the Big Bang, a number of companies persuaded their investors to waive their pre-emptive rights. But some major UK financial institutions showed that they did not like what was going on by voting against some of the waiver proposals. They did not like a practice that was developing for companies to have the rights of existing UK shareholders waived and then for the new shares to be sold to institutional investors in other countries.

In 1987 Fisons had to abandon a plan to place £110 million of new equity amongst institutional investors. This new issue was equivalent to 5.5% of the authorized capital. However, Barclays Bank obtained permission to issue £210 million of new equity in the US and Japanese markets.

The disagreements between companies and their institutional shareholders were partly resolved by a working party that was set up. New guidelines were issued in 1987.

Any non-rights issues would be limited in any one year to 5% of the company's issued capital. The maximum amount of discount on the pre-issue market price was agreed upon; there would be no deep discounts. Agreement to waive rights for a 12 month period would be obtained from shareholders, and then, provided that the issue was within the guidelines, specific approval would not be required for new issues.

As a source of permanent or long-term finance for a company, preference shares have declined in popularity since the changes embodied in the corporation tax system were introduced. In fact, many firms took steps at the time to convert existing preference shares into debentures.

Preference shares usually entitle their holder to a fixed rate of dividend from the company each year. This dividend ranks for payment before other equity returns, and so the ordinary shareholders receive no dividend until the preference shareholders have been paid their fixed percentage. Preference shares carry part-ownership of the company and allow due participation in the profits of the business. In fact, their dividend is an appropriation of profits and so if a bad year means no profits, it means no dividend for the preference shareholders.

This point constitutes the essential distinction between preference shares and debentures. Debenture holders are not part-owners of the company; their interest claims have to be met whether the company has made a profit or not. Interest payments are not an appropriation of profits. It is for this reason that the tax treatment of each of the two forms of fixed percentage capital is different. Debenture interest, as a charge, is a tax-deductible expense, and like any other form of expenditure it reduces the company's tax bill. Preference dividends, as an appropriation of profits, are not tax deductible. Tax is payable on the profits figure before the preference dividends are deducted. Consequently, a company earning profits and committed to paying out, say, 8% on capital raised, would prefer to be paying it on debentures (for which the interest charge is net of tax) than on preference shares for which the company would have to stand the gross cost.

On cost grounds alone a company would not normally choose to issue preference shares unless the dividend rate is less than or equal to the cost of interest (after tax allowance) on a debenture. At present and in the foreseeable future this is unlikely to be the case with the relative risks of the two securities. If a debenture has a coupon rate of, say, 10%, corporation tax at 35.0% would mean that the cost to the company would be only 6.5%. To offer preference shares with a dividend rate of the order of only 6.5% would be practically out of the question, particularly as debentures are the safer form of investment with prior claims to both interest and capital.

Other factors require consideration, however. The issue of debentures increases leverage, whereas the issue of preference shares increases the equity base: the two forms of capital are not strictly interchangeable. A company might find it impossible to raise more debt capital but still be able to raise preference capital. These points will receive further attention later in this chapter.

Redeemable preference shares

Usually preference shares are irredeemable; they provide permanent capital which does not have to be repaid. If the preference shareholder wishes to dispose of his holding he must sell the share in the stock market.

Companies whose articles authorize them to do so can, however, issue redeemable preference shares that either carry a prearranged redemption date or can be redeemed at the company's option. The redeemable preference share would have a price behaviour similar to that of a debenture; the only difference between the two securities, from the investor's viewpoint, is that the debenture would offer the more secure income stream.

Preference shares issued in this manner can be redeemed only if they are fully paid, and the funds used come out of profits available for dividend or out of a fresh issue of shares made specifically for that purpose. If there is premium payable on redemption, it can only be paid out of profits or out of the company's share premium account.

The specific terms on which the preference shares can be redeemed depend on the company's articles. When redemption is not financed by a fresh issue, the company must create, from the profits which would otherwise have been available for dividend, a 'capital redemption reserve fund' worth the nominal amount of the shares to be redeemed. This fund can only be reduced as if it were paid-up capital of the company, but it can be used for issuing bonus shares to members of the company.

The redemption of preference shares does not constitute a reduction of the authorized capital. Preference shares cannot be converted into redeemable preference shares if they were not sold as such.

Participating redeemable preference shares

Participating redeemable preference shares allow the shareholder to participate in a further share of the profits after they have received a fixed rate of dividend. The fixed rate is usually lower than on an ordinary preference share, because of the added attraction of participation in the general level of profits.

For example, a preference share may carry a dividend rate of 8% and allow the holder to share in additional profits, with the additional profits being divided between equity and preference holders in some specified proportions. Some issues may allow the equity owners to receive a certain dividend before the preference shareholders participate.

Convertible redeemable preference shares

Convertible redeemable preference shares have the added attraction of a right to be converted into ordinary shares at some date. They are in certain aspects similar to convertible debentures.

Cumulative redeemable preference shares

If a cumulative preference share receives no dividends in one year because the company has failed to make a profit, it will receive it in another when the position has improved. The dividends accumulate until the company can afford to pay, and the shareholder then receives the backlog and the current dividend for the year in which payment is made. This does not necessarily apply to all preference shares: it is strictly true only of those that are specified as being cumulative.

The preference shareholder suffers temporary losses by having to wait one or more years for the dividend, although his position is better than that of the equity shareholder who receives nothing back for the dividends lost in years when the company cannot afford to pay.

In their respective claims to dividend, the holders of cumulative preference shares take priority over equity holders, so that only after the cumulative liability for preference dividends has eventually been met can ordinary shareholders again receive any dividend. With non-cumulative preference shares, of course, the dividend rights terminate at the end of each financial year.

Auction market preferred stock (AMPS)

This is one of the complex capital instruments that emerged in the late 1980s. AMPS is a preference share with a floating rate of dividend. From the point of view of the issuing company it is a form of equity. From the point of view of the investor it is similar to debt, except that if the company does not earn sufficient profits no return is received.

Most AMPS are denominated in US dollars, and are traded in the US financial market. They are often issued however by non-US companies.

The idea of the floating rate of dividend is attractive to investors (if interest rates rise) and to the issuing company (if interest rates fall). If certain conditions are met, AMPS are attractive from a tax point of view to US resident investors.

As with many other new financial instruments there are difficulties in deciding whether AMPS should be classified as debt or equity from a financial gearing point of view. The dividends (as opposed to interest) and the non-guarantee of an annual payment suggest it is equity. But the fact that the level of dividend payment floats in line with the level of interest gives it certain debt characteristics.

Because the annual payment to investors depends on whether or not profits are earned, the dividend rate paid has to be higher than the interest rates in the money market. The cost to the company of an AMPS, because of the higher annual payments and the lack of a tax shield, is higher than the cost of short-term debt.

The preference shares are auctioned to investors. Each potential investor states the level of dividend rate they require before they will purchase the AMPS. The auction agent receives these bids from the investors' brokers, and then sets the dividend rate that will be paid. The agent does this on the basis of the lowest possible rate which will clear the entire issue. The AMPS can be redeemed.

Advantages and disadvantages to the company of preference shares

One advantage of preference shares is that when the company earns no profits, no dividend has to be paid on them. The interest on debentures, however, always has to be paid, profit or no profit, and these payments can be an alarming drain on the liquidity of a company already in some degree of financial difficulty.

The non-payment of share dividend is, however, something that a company should aim to avoid. To the financial community it would represent an unmistakable symptom of financial weakness, and as such it would have an adverse effect on the company's share price. On occasions a company might find it expedient to pay the preference share dividend out of accumulated reserves rather than omit payment because of inadequate profits.

A company that does expect to earn profits will find the cost of debentures considerably less than the cost of preference shares. The payment of preference dividend qualifies for none of the tax concessions that ease the payment of interest. Apart from this, preference shares command a higher percentage rate for payment than debentures: since they are riskier than fixed interest loans, in terms of both income and capital repayment, they have to offer an attractively higher rate of return.

The only situation, therefore, in which the company might find the cost of preference shares lower than that of debentures is when it is running at a loss – in which case investors would hardly be enthusiastic about subscribing for preference shares.

Preference shares are, however, cheaper than equity shares – a reflection, again, of the relative risks involved. The preference holders receive their fixed dividend before the ordinary shareholders are allowed any participation in the profits; and in the case of liquidation, they recoup their capital before the ordinary holders. The disadvantage from the investor's viewpoint is that since the preference shares normally receive only a fixed return, they cannot reap added benefits if the business is very successful.

The maximum cost of preference shares is easily computed: it is equal to the dividend rate, so an 8% preference share has an 8% cost to the company. There are none of the uncertainties surrounding the expectations of the shareholder that exist with equity shares.

It is possible for preference shares to be issued at a discount, in which case the cost to the company would be the dividend yield on the issue price. If the shares are issued at a premium the cost is computed in the same way.

12.13 Venture capital

The capital market is good at providing new equity funds for large companies and providing a market for their existing shares. When companies are very small there is a good chance that a few shareholders can provide all the risk capital that is required. However, there is a gap between these two situations which has not really been satisfied. The larger private company or the smaller public company may wish to raise new capital for an investment in which there is a risk. Fixed-interest capital, even if available, is not, therefore, appropriate. The capital required is called 'venture capital'; the providers of this capital are being asked to share in the risks. Merchant banks were once willing to provide such funds but it is doubtful whether they were ever able to provide funds on a sufficient scale to satisfy the total need.

There has been a gap in the UK for a long time in the provision of funds for venture capital needs. One reason is that an increasing proportion of the available funds flows into the hands of institutions who are not likely to use them for venture capital needs. It is not thought appropriate for pension funds and the like to take these sort of risks with their contributors' money.

There are practical reasons why newer small firms find it harder to obtain funds to finance their growth than well-established larger firms. A firm is borrowing funds or obtaining new equity in anticipation of being able to realize a prospective stream of future earnings. The capital markets will normally have more confidence in a firm with a known record than in a new entrant. Even though the new firm and the established firm have the same technology and wish to do exactly the same thing with the money raised, the market will take into account that it has experience of one firm but not of the other. Experience is of importance, and unless the existing firm is known to be inept it will have an advantage. Reputation, which is to say prior experience, is of special importance in establishing the terms of finance for transactions that involve large discrete commitments of funds.

The reason for this is that the capital market has incomplete information about companies. The market cannot always distinguish, from the information provided, between a good company and one that is not quite so good. The market is therefore thrown back on its experience of the companies involved. The less well known applicant will be at a disadvantage: the risks to the provider of funds are high and therefore the costs to the applicant if the funds are obtained will also be high.

There have been numerous attempts to fill this venture capital gap. At one time it was thought that the government should provide such finance. When this happens, it is really taxpayers who are taking the risks.

Another approach is to encourage rich people to invest in venture capital situations. If the investors make losses, however, they would wish to be able to claim these against tax. Such a system to encourage the wealthier members of the community to invest in risk capital is the Business Expansion Scheme.

There have also been many private financial institutions that have been set up to fill the venture capital gap. These will be considered in Chapter 26 when we return to the subject of venture capital.

12.14 Key terms

Dividend cover	Rights issues
Dividend yield	Scrip dividends
Intermediaries offer	SEAQ International
Licensed dealers	Secondary markets
Liquid stocks	Sponsors
NASDAQ	Stags
Offer for sale	Stock split
Over the counter market	Underwriters
Preferred shares	Unlisted securities market
Price-to-earnings ratio	Vendor placings

12.15 Revision questions

1. What is a private company?
2. What was the USM? Why was it created and why was it brought to an end?
3. What is the over-the-counter market? What are the advantages for a company having its shares traded on this market?

4. What are the advantages and disadvantages of the 'tender' method of issuing shares? Why does its popularity change over time?
5. What are the factors that have to be taken into account when pricing a new issue of shares?
6. Examine the reports in the financial press at the time of one of the major 'privatization' issues. What factors seem to have influenced the pricing of the particular issue?
7. It has been claimed that pre-emption rights have put major UK companies at a disadvantage relative to their competitors. Why should this be so? Examine the issues involved.
8. What are scrip dividends?
9. The less informed investor believes that he understands the term 'earnings per share'. Why should he be careful when comparing the EPS of one company with that of another?

12.16 References

1. Fama, E.F., Fisher, L., Jensen, M. and Roll, R. (1969) The adjustment of stock prices to new information, *International Economic Review*, February.
2. Asquith, P., Healy, P. and Palepu, K. (1989) Earnings and stock splits, *Accounting Review*, July.

12.17 Further reading

The *Bank of England Quarterly* regularly publishes articles on special topics concerning equity shares and the capital and money markets. Examples are given below.

Bank of England (1990) New equity issues in the United Kingdom. *Quarterly Bulletin*, May, pp. 243–52.
Bank of England (1987) Change in the Stock Exchange and regulations in the City, *Bank of England Quarterly*, February.
Bank of England (1987) Pre-emption rights, *Bank of England Quarterly*, November.
Bank of England (1988) The equity market crash, *Bank of England Quarterly*, February.

The following books and articles provide further information on the workings of stock markets.

Bannock, G. and Doran, A. (1987) *Going Public, The Markets in Unlisted Securities*, Harper & Row, London.
Bar-Yosef, S. and Brown, L.D. (1977) A reexamination of stock splits using moving betas, *Journal of Finance*, September.
Buckland, R. and Davies, E.W. (1987) *The Unlisted Securities Market*, Harper & Row, London.
Grinblatt, M.S., Masulis, R.W. and Titman, S. (1984) The valuation effects of stock splits and stock dividends, *Journal of Financial Economics*, December.
Marsh, P. (1979) Equity rights issues and the efficiency of the UK stock market, *Journal of Finance*, **34**, September.
Russell, G.R. (1990) *Initial Public Offers: Report of the Review Committee*. The Stock Exchange, London.
Rutterford, J. (1993) *Introduction to Stock Exchange Investment*, 2nd edn, Macmillan, London.
Scott-Quinn, B. (1990) A Strategy for the International Stock Exchange, *National Westminster Quarterly Review*, May, pp. 43–58.
Thomas, W.A. (1989) *The Securities Market*, Philip Allen.
White, R.W. and Luszig, P. (1980) The price effects of rights offerings. *Journal of Financial and Quantitative Analysis*, March.
Wolff, C.C.P. (1986) Pre-emptive rights versus alternative methods of raising equity on the London Stock Exchange. *Investment Analyst*, April, pp. 3–15.

1. The issue to the public of an application for shares or debentures in a company must normally be accompanied by a prospectus. What are the main features of a prospectus?

2. Describe the advantages and disadvantages to a medium-sized company of obtaining a quotation.

3. For what reasons, other than the need to raise outside finance, might a private company take the necessary steps to secure a Stock Exchange quotation?

4. In what circumstances might a company make a 'stock split'? What would be the effect of such a decision on the company, the share price and the shareholders' wealth?

5. Clearly distinguish an offer for sale by tender from other methods of raising equity capital and describe the process by which the price is set and the shares allocated in an offer for sale by tender. Outline the circumstances when the use of an issue by tender would be an appropriate way of raising equity.

6. What are the main advantages and disadvantages to a company of raising finance by issuing the following:
   (a) ordinary shares;
   (b) redeemable convertible preference shares;
   (c) deferred ordinary shares;
   (d) convertible debentures.

7. Outline the features of a rights issue of equity capital, and suggest why this method of issuing fresh equity may be preferred by shareholders.

8. (a) Explain the following terms in relation to equity investment:
      (i) dividend yield;
      (i) price-to-earnings ratio.
   (b) The shares of Company A which owns and develops commercial property show a dividend yield of 1.5% and a price-to-earnings ratio of 40, while those of Company B, a machine tool manufacturer, yield 6% with a price-to-earnings ratio of 13. Suggest circumstances which might account for those divergent stock market ratings.

9. Cashless PLC is quoted on the Unlisted Securities Market. Its share price is £5 and the estimated market capitalization rate applied to its expected earnings is 15%. Cashless announced a rights offer of equity on a one for four basis at £4 per share.

   (a) Assume that the proceeds of the rights issue will be invested by the company to earn a 15% perpetual return. Identify the theoretical ex rights price of the shares, and the value of a right attaching to one 'old' share in these circumstances.

   (b) Assume instead that the rights offer announcement indicated an intention to invest the proceeds in a new product line offering an expected return of 20% in perpetuity, but having the same risk as that of the present firm. The 'market' is widely regarded as semi-strong efficient, and the company projections are generally regarded as reasonable.

      Identify the ex rights value of each share in these circumstances. What is the value of a right attaching to an 'old' share? What will happen to the share price immediately following the rights announcement? Why?

10. (a) Coppice PLC plans to obtain a listing on the UK Stock Exchange. The company wishes to raise approximately £3 million, and the Stock Exchange authorities have informally indicated that either an offer for sale or a placing would be permitted. Coppice's finance director has obtained information about the costs associated with new issues. This information is detailed below:

Issuing house commission (not including underwriting)	0.5%
Underwriting commission*	1.5%
Accounting and legal fees:	
Offer for sale	£40 000
Placing	£15 000

Capital duty payable to the government on the proceeds of the issue	1%

Advertising:

Multiple page advertisement in a national newspaper	£50 000
Small advertisement in a national or regional newspaper	£3 000

Share registration costs: £1000 plus £1 per shareholder

Stock Exchange initial fee:

Offer for sale	£4 000
Placing	£2 000

Other costs:

Offer for sale	£25 000
Placing	£10 000

The company pays tax at a rate of 35%

*In an offer for sale, underwriting commission will effectively be deducted from the issue price in determining the price that the company receives.

(i) Discuss how an offer for sale differs from a placing. (6 marks)

(ii) Estimate the total after-tax issue costs if Coppice PLC uses an offer for sale. (3 marks)

(iii) If Coppice PLC decided to seek a listing on the Unlisted Securities Market what difference would this make to the method of issue and to the costs involved? (3 marks)

(b) Coppice eventually decides to enter the stock market by using an offer for sale. Its merchant bank considers that the issue should comprise 2 million shares at a price of 145p per share. The 2 million shares will form half the company's issued ordinary share capital. As an alternative, the merchant bank suggests an offer for sale by tender. The merchant bank is willing to underwrite a tender issue of 2 million shares with a minimum price of 140p per share. Coppice agrees to the issue by tender and receives the following tenders:

Price tendered (pence)	Number of applicants at the price	Number of shares bid for at the price
175	2	22 000
170	84	74 000
165	127	192 000
160	410	724 000
155	1123	928 000
150	2254	1 324 200
145	3520	4 956 000
140	6410	12 230 000

The company decides to allocate the same percentage of the number of shares that were requested to all successful tenders.

(i) Estimate the amount of funds that the company will raise from the tender, net of issue costs, and the average size of shareholding that will result. (4 marks)

(ii) Suggest reasons why tenders are not the most frequently used method of raising equity finance. (4 marks)

(c) One year later the after-tax earnings of Coppice PLC are £1 million for the year just ended and the company's price to earnings ratio of 9 is relatively high for the industry. Coppice decides to expand, and to raise further funds by means of a rights issue of 500 000 shares at 8 per cent discount on the current market price.

(i) Estimate the value of a right prior to the shares being traded ex rights and the theoretical ex rights price.

(ii) Under what circumstances would the market price be likely to move exactly to the theoretical ex rights price?

(5 marks)

(25 marks)

ACCA, June 1987

11. 'Rights issues are attractive from a company's point of view when the market is climbing, but they are not worth the risks and administrative costs when the stock market is falling.' Discuss.

12. Parbat Ltd has an issued capital of 2 million ordinary shares of 50p each and no fixed-interest securities. It has paid a dividend of 70p per share for several years, and the stock market generally expects that level to continue. The market price is £4.20 per share cum dividend. The firm is now considering the acceptance of a major new investment which would require an outlay of £500 000 and generate net cash receipts of £120 000 per annum for an indefinite period. The additional receipts would be used to increase dividends. Parbat is appraising three alternative sources of finance for the new project.

(a) Retained earnings. The usual annual dividend could be reduced. Parbat currently holds £1.4 million for payment of the dividend which is due in the near future.

(b) A rights issue of ordinary shares. One new share would be offered for every ten shares held at present at a price of £2.50 per share; the new shares would rank for dividend one year after issue, when cash receipts from the new project would first be available.

(c) An issue of ordinary shares to the general public. The new shares would rank for dividend one year after issue.

Assume that, if the project were accepted, the firm's expectations of future results would be discovered and believed by the stock market, and that the market would perceive the risk of the firm to be unaltered.

(a) Estimate the price ex dividend of Parbat's ordinary shares following acceptance of the new project if finance is obtained from (i) retained earnings or (ii) a rights issue.

(b) Calculate the price at which the new shares should be issued under option (c) assuming the objective of maximizing the gain of existing shareholders.

(c) Calculate the gain made by present shareholders under each of the three finance options.

(d) Discuss the advantages and disadvantages of each of the three sources of finance.

Ignore taxation and issue costs of new shares for (a), (b) and (c) but **not** (d).

13. (a) Nonet plc, an unlisted company, has decided to arrange a Stock Exchange main market listing in order to raise £20 million in new share capital. Explain what types of issue are possible and discuss the advantages and disadvantages of each type.

(b) Discuss whether it might be appropriate for Nonet to raise the £20 million by issuing convertible preference shares. (ACCA, June 1990)

14. Distinguish between primary markets and secondary markets.

15. A medium-sized UK company recently made a 1 for 4 rights issue which was underwritten at 140p to finance one of its growth divisions. The share price prior to the announcement was 173p which was just above the bottom of the shares' 1992–93 trading range. The share price after the announcement was 171p.

The rights issue was the final part of a financial reorganization which included a private placement in the US capital markets for a slightly larger amount of equity capital than the rights issue and the switching of short-term debt into medium- and long-term borrowings at fixed rates of interest.

A company spokesperson indicated that the immediate affect of the reorganization will be to reduce gearing from 70% to about 20%. Over the next two years gearing will rise to 40% before falling back again.

Required:
(a) Calculate the theoretical share price expected following the rights issue announcement. Provide economically justifiable reasons for any difference you find between your price and the price reported in the above quote. (5 marks)
(b) Several small investors, who are new to the stock market, have expressed concern that they will lose money if they do not subscribe for the new shares. They have asked you for advice on whether or not they should borrow money to take up their rights. Provide full details of the advice you would give them.
(5 marks)
(c) The great majority of rights issues are underwritten which many academics find puzzling because the fees are thought to be high in relation to the risk to which the company is exposed, particularly if the issue is deeply discounted. These academics view the underwriting agreement as an option which is amenable to valuation using option pricing theory. Explain the underwriting agreement as an option and what information is required for its valuation.
(6 marks)
(d) Discuss briefly the advantages and disadvantages of a rights issue versus a private placement of shares. (5 marks)
(e) Suggest reasons for the switch from short-term debt to fixed interest rate debt given that the UK yield to maturity curve was upward sloping at the time.
(4 marks)

16. National Sand is a public sector company that is about to be privatized. The company's advisors have suggested that a tender issue is used with a minimum price of 120 pence.

The company will issue 400 million shares, with issue costs estimated to be 3% of gross proceeds. A market research survey suggests that the likely pattern of tenders is:

Price (pence)	Number of shares tendered for (million)	Number of applicants
150	5	10
145	20	250
140	80	10 000
135	200	200 000
130	350	410 000
125	1200	1 500 000
120	1500	1 800 000

Required:
(a) Explain the advantages and disadvantages of a tender issue for National Sand.
(5 marks)
(b) Calculate the average share holding that is likely to result from the tender issue. State clearly any assumptions that you make. (3 marks)
(c) Shortly after the issue the government unexpectedly announces that 10% of the net proceeds of this issue may be retained by the company to be invested, the remainder of the proceeds returning to the government. The company's directors have identified four areas for new investment:

	Amount to be invested (£m)	Expected profitability index
(i) Golf	10	1.20
(ii) Other leisure activities	20	1.10
(iii) Construction	10	1.06
(iv) Foreign acquisitions	the balance of the 10%	1.05

Existing investments have a zero net present value.

Required:

(i) Estimate the expected share price of National Sand once the government's action and the company's investment plans become public knowledge.

(ii) State clearly any assumptions that you make.   (4.5 marks)

ACCA, Dec. 1992

17. The directors of Denetter plc wish to make an equity issue to finance an £8 million expansion scheme, which has an expected net present value of £1.1 million, and to refinance an existing £5 million 15% term loan which is due to mature in five years' time. There is a £350 000 penalty charge for early redemption of this loan. Denetter has obtained approval from its shareholders to suspend their pre-emptive rights and for the company to make a £15 million placement of shares which will be at the price of 185 pence per share. Issue costs are estimated to be 4% of gross proceeds. Any surplus from the issue will be invested in commercial paper, which is currently yielding 9% per year. Denetter's current capital structure is as follows:

	£000
Ordinary shares (25 pence par value)	8 000
Share premium	11 200
Revenue reserves	23 100
	42 300
15% term loan	5 000
11% debenture 1998–2001	9 000
	56 300

The company's current share price is 190 pence, and debenture price £102. Denetter can raise debenture or medium-term bank finance at 10% per year. The stock market may be assumed to be semi-strong form efficient, and no information about the proposed uses of funds from the issue has been made available to the public. Taxation may be ignored.

Required:

(a) Discuss the factors that Denetter's directors should have considered before deciding which form of financing to use.   (5 marks)

(b) Explain what is meant by pre-emptive rights, and discuss their advantages and disadvantages.   (6 marks)

(c) Estimate Denetter's expected share price once full details of the placement, and the uses to which the finance is to be put, are announced.   (11 marks)

(d) Suggest reasons why the share price might not move to the price that you estimated in (c) above.   (3 marks)

                     (25 marks)

ACCA, June 1992

18. National Sand is a public-sector company that is about to be privatized. The company's advisors have suggested that a tender issue is used with a minimum price of 120 pence. The company will issue 400 million shares, with issue costs estimated to be 3% of gross proceeds. A market research survey suggests that the likely pattern of tenders is:

Price (pence) tendered for	Number of shares (million)	Number of applicants
150	5	10
145	20	250
140	80	10 000
135	200	200 000
130	350	410 000
125	1200	1 500 000
120	1500	1 800 000

Required:

(a) Explain the advantages and disadvantages of a tender issue for National Sand.

(5 marks)

(b) Calculate the average share holding that is likely to result from the tender issue. State clearly any assumptions that you make.

(3 marks)

(c) Shortly after the issue the government unexpectedly announces that 10% of the net proceeds of this issue may be retained by the company to be invested, the remainder of the proceeds returning to the government. The company's directors have identified four areas for new investment:

	Amount to be invested (£m)	Expected profitability index
(i) Golf	10	1.20
(ii) Other leisure activities	20	1.10
(iii) Construction	10	1.06
(iv) Foreign acquisitions	the balance of the 10%	1.05

Existing investments have a zero net present value.

Required:

(i) Estimate the expected share price of National Sand once the government's action and the company's investment plans become public knowledge.

(ii) State clearly any assumptions that you make.

(4.5 marks)

(25 marks)

19. Netherby plc manufactures a range of camping and leisure equipment, including tents. It is currently experiencing severe quality control problems at its existing fully-depreciated factory in the south of England. These difficulties threaten to undermine its reputation for producing high quality products. It has recently been approached by the European Bank for Reconstruction and Development, on behalf of a tent manufacturer in Hungary, which is seeking a UK-based trading partner which will import and distribute its tents. Such a switch would involve shutting down the existing manufacturing operation in the UK and converting it into a distribution depot. The estimated exceptional restructuring costs of £5m would be tax-allowable, but would exert serious strains on cash flow.

Importing rather than manufacturing tents appears inherently profitable as the buying-in price, when converted into sterling, is less than the present production cost. In addition, Netherby considers that the Hungarian product would result in increased sales, as the existing retail distributors seem impressed with the quality of the samples which they have been shown. It is estimated that for a five-year contract, the annual cash flow benefit would be around £2m p.a. before tax.

However, the financing of the closure and restructuring costs would involve careful consideration of the financing options. Some directors argue that dividends could be reduced as several competing companies have already done a similar thing, while other directors argue for a rights issue. Alternatively, the project could be financed by an issue of long-term loan stock at a fixed rate of 12%.

The most recent balance sheet shows £5m of issued share capital (par value 50p), while the market price per share is currently £3. A leading security analyst has recently described Netherby's gearing ratio as 'adventurous'. Profit-after-tax in the year just ended was £15m and dividends of £10m were paid.

The rate of corporation tax is 33%, payable with a one-year delay. Netherby's reporting year coincides with the calendar year and the factory will be closed at the year end. Closure costs would be incurred shortly before deliveries of the imported product began, and sufficient stocks will be on hand to overcome any initial supply problems. Netherby considers that it should earn a return on new investment projects of 15% p.a. net of all taxes.

Required:

(a) Is the closure of the existing factory financially worthwhile for Netherby?

(5 marks)

(b) Explain what is meant when the capital market is said to be information-efficient in a semi-strong form.

If the stock market is semi-strong efficient and without considering the method of finance, calculate the likely impact of acceptance and announcement of the details of this project to the market on Netherby's share price.

(6 marks)

(c) Advise the Netherby board as to the relative merits of a rights issue rather than a cut in dividends to finance this project. (6 marks)

(d) Explain why a rights issue generally results in a fall in the market price of shares.

If a rights issue is undertaken, calculate the resulting impact on the existing share price of issue prices of £1 per share and £2 per share, respectively. (You may ignore issue costs.) (6 marks)

(e) Assuming the restructuring proposal meets expectations, assess the impact of the project on earnings per share if it is financed by a rights issue at an offer price of £2 per share, and loan stock, respectively. (Again, you may ignore issue costs.) (4 marks)

(f) Briefly consider the main operating risks connected with the investment project, and how Netherby might attempt to allow for these. (8 marks)

(35 marks)

ACCA, Managerial Finance, June 1994

13 *Stock market efficiency*

13.1	Introduction	385
13.2	The efficient market hypothesis	386
13.3	Tests of the efficient market hypothesis	389
13.4	Fads and bubbles	399
13.5	Insider dealing	400
13.6	Doubts about stock market efficiency	404
13.7	Market anomalies	407
13.8	Implications of the efficient market hypothesis	411
13.9	Summary	419
13.10	Key terms	420
13.11	Revision questions	420
13.12	References	420
13.13	Further reading	423
13.14	Problems	424

From an economics point of view the efficiency of a stock exchange is the key to the optimal allocation of available funds. From an investor's point of view it is necessary to have an efficient stock exchange to ensure the investor is involved in a fair game.

The leading stock exchanges in the world have been tested many times in order to determine whether or not they are efficient. In recent years certain anomalies have been detected. These have lent support to those who have doubts about the concept. The efficient market hypothesis has important implications for financial analysts, accountants and for financial managers.

13.1 Introduction

The interface between investors in financial securities and company managers responsible for issuing securities arises in the financial markets. These markets exist to enable this contact to be made and transactions to take place. Equity investors make what is essentially a perpetual investment in that ordinary shares carry no redemption date. As investors rarely have an infinite time horizon, to encourage investment they must be persuaded that they can sell their shares at a fair price some time in the foreseeable future. For this to happen security markets must price shares efficiently by incorporating into the price all information currently available about the company and economy as a whole. If this is the case the investors will be encouraged to buy shares through markets because they know that they are paying a fair price and likewise will be able to sell at a fair price. Similarly, company managers will be able to obtain funds through these financial markets at a cost which reflects the risk of the business activities being undertaken. This notion of efficiency is therefore very important not only from an individual investor's point of view but also for company managers. The efficient allocation of financial resources is an important determinant of economic growth. In many countries it is believed that the market-place provides the best means of allocating resources. There are those who believe (and those who did believe) that planning is a more efficient method of allocation. In fact, in most countries we find a mixture of both methods.

Stock markets are created to bring together those people who have funds to invest and those who need funds to undertake investments. The markets strive to be efficient. Over 70 countries now have stock exchanges, and over half of these are in the developing countries of the world. Clearly, these countries believe that a stock market provides a good way of allocating resources.

The influence of a stock market on resource allocation is both direct and indirect. It is direct in that the market influences whether or not a company quoted on the market will be able to obtain new funds through the market. The ability to raise finance depends upon the stock market's assessment of a company's future prospects. The indirect influence is that a poor past performance with poor future prospects results in a relatively low share price. This can affect the company's borrowing position even outside the market, and can make the company a possible takeover target. The stock market is therefore extremely important in the allocation of funds. To make the best use of the finance available within a country, a stock market should be organized efficiently, the securities traded should be correctly priced, and investors should have confidence and so continue to invest their savings through the stock exchange.

13.2 The efficient market hypothesis

A question which can be asked of any stock market is whether or not it is efficient. In order to answer this question we need to be clear what we mean by efficiency. First it should be realized that it is not the same as that well-loved economic concept of the perfect market. For a stock market to be a perfect market the following conditions would need to be satisfied [1].

1. It would need to be frictionless, i.e. without transaction costs and taxes. There should be no constraining regulations limiting freedom of entry and exit for investors and companies seeking funds. All shares should be perfectly marketable.
2. All services in the market should be provided at the minimum average cost, with all participants price-takers.
3. All buyers and sellers should be rational expected-utility maximizers.
4. There should be many buyers and sellers.
5. The market should be informationally efficient, i.e. information should be costless and received simultaneously by all individuals.

No market, whether a stock exchange or any other market, satisfies all the conditions required for it to be classed as perfect. Fortunately, we can relax some of the perfect market assumptions and still have what is called an efficient market. The assumptions of costless information, a frictionless market place, and many buyers and sellers are not necessary conditions for the existence of an efficient capital market. What therefore is an efficient capital market?

Here we have a problem. There is a wide generally accepted dictionary definition of the word 'efficient', but the word ' "efficient" in connection with the market hypothesis' (EMH) has a narrower meaning which is easier to satisfy. In fact, this hypothesis is one of the most important concepts in the modern literature of finance.

First we shall consider the wider meaning of the word efficiency. The word in common daily usage, can be defined as 'functioning effectively and with the least waste of effort'. What does 'effectively' mean? Turning to a dictionary again, we find the definition, 'capable of producing a result'. With this definition in mind, we can think of at least five results that we would expect from an 'efficient' stock exchange.

1. Funds coming to the exchange are allocated to where they can be most effectively used. This is first-period [2] or allocational efficiency. Over time there is pressure on firms to employ their resources effectively.

2. Those who provide funds to the market are involved in a fair game. This involves all the familiar tests of stock market efficiency. At any point in time, a share price reflects all information concerning events that have occurred and all events that the market expects to take place in the future. This is pricing efficiency.

3. We would not expect the operation of an efficient market, in itself, to lead to predictable changes in wealth distribution in the second period. This is Mossin's second-period efficiency. With a 'fair game' the distribution of wealth amongst investors in the second period should be similar to that in the first period. Some investors will have gained, and some will have lost, but the distribution should remain the same, with no one class of investors being able to maintain a position where they show persistent above average returns. This is an implication of pricing efficiency.

4. The efficient market should satisfy the social and political goals set for it by the society in which it operates. It may be thought that this is not relevant to the stock exchanges of the developed Western countries, but clearly it is. A stock exchange is seen as a part of the private enterprise system, an important part of a property owning democracy.

5. The market itself carries out its operations at as low a cost as possible. This is operational efficiency.

It is appreciated that there is a considerable amount of overlap between these five points. For example, 3 might come within 4 in that the government does not want inequalities in wealth distribution to be increased; 3 and 2 are also somewhat interrelated in that if the 'game' is fair, there should be no need to worry about the effect of the stock exchange on wealth distribution. An important issue is how much deviation from a fair game can a market stand before second-period efficiency becomes important?

Allocational efficiency

Three types of efficiency have been identified above: allocational, pricing and operational. Allocational efficiency means that the market channels funds to those firms and organizations with the most promising real investment opportunities. Allocational efficiency requires both pricing efficiency and operational efficiency. The absence of either can lead to the misallocation of resources.

Operational efficiency

Operational efficiency means that buyers and sellers of securities can purchase transaction services at prices that are as low as possible given the costs associated with having these services provided. This must be distinguished from pricing efficiency in which at any point in time prices are said to 'fully reflect' all available information that is relevant to the determination of values. By definition, then, any new relevant information is quickly and accurately impounded in prices.

Pricing efficiency

When the efficiency of a stock exchange is discussed in the literature of finance, it often just means efficiency with respect to pricing. Virtually all testing of the EMH has been based on testing for pricing efficiency. Unfortunately the data are not readily available for testing for allocational or operational efficiency.

As explained the EMH applies just to pricing efficiency. It does not refer to allocational efficiency and does not explain the relationship between the efficiency of the stock market and the efficiency of the economy in total. The hypothesis states that an efficient capital market is one in which prices of traded securities always fully reflect all publicly available information concerning those securities. Thus, by implication, security prices adjust instantaneously and in an unbiased manner to any piece of new information released to the market.

Sometimes this is referred to as information arbitrage efficiency; it means abnormal profits cannot be achieved systematically by trading on the basis of publicly available information.

There are three sufficient conditions for market pricing efficiency: all available information is costless to all market participants, there are no transaction costs and all investors take similar views on the implications of available information for current prices and distribution of future prices of each security. Samuelson [3] and Mandelbrot [4] have proved that, under these conditions, security prices will move randomly. These sufficient conditions are somewhat unrealistic and restrictive because not only are there transaction costs, but not all information is available to all existing or potential investors, nor is it costless, and of course investors do not always agree upon the implications of the available information. Stockbrokers have research departments which expend funds in generating information in the form of research reports etc. which is not freely available to all investors. These research departments are financed from the charges made to clients for the bargains struck in the market on their behalf. Nevertheless, those conditions are only sufficient ones and despite their not being completely satisfied it is still possible for the market to be classed as efficient, and it is the testing of this hypothesis that has led to numerous empirical research studies.

If the stock market is efficient, share prices would be expected to 'fully reflect' the available information. To test whether it is, we must specify how the process of price formation is expected to operate. It is generally assumed that the share price would adjust to the expected levels of returns, allowing for risk, suggested by the information being considered. This is known as a 'fair game' model.

This means, in its simplest form, that as information which suggests higher profits for a company becomes available, the price of that company's shares is expected to rise up to a point where the expected yield is comparable with that on other shares in a similar risk class. If information which suggests increased risks for a company becomes available, unless there are also expected higher returns, the share price will fall. This will give a higher expected yield on the share, which should be comparable with that of other shares in the same risk class.

The EMH can be tested by comparing the actual price or actual return with the expected price or expected return, where the expected figure is arrived at based on a model of how, given a set of information, the share prices are determined.

The fair game model, which represents the efficient market model, was expressed mathematically by Fama [5] in the following form:

$$Z_{i,t+1} = R_{i,t+1} - E\left(\frac{\overline{R}_{i,t+1}}{\phi_t} \right)$$

where $Z_{i,t+1}$ is the unexpected or excess return for security i in period $t + 1$, $R_{i,t+1}$ is the observed (actual) return for security i at time $t + 1$, $E(\overline{R}_{i,t+1})$ is the expected return at time $t + 1$ and ϕ_t is the information set available at time t.

The model states that the unexpected (excess) return for security i in period $t + 1$ is given by the difference between the observed return in that period and the expected return based on the information set ϕ_t, and that under the fair game model the expected excess return based on the information set ϕ_t is zero.

To test this fair game model some technique for estimating security returns is required. How do we arrive at a figure for Z_i? Models for such estimations do exist. The estimates of the expected return on a particular security are usually based on adjusting the expected return on a market portfolio or a market index for individual security characteristics. The actual returns are then compared with the estimated returns and the residuals are analysed. The models that have been most often used to estimate the expected returns are the capital asset pricing model (CAPM) and the market model [6].

The significance that can be attached to the tests of the fair game model depend on the validity of the forecasting models that have been used to estimate the expected returns. The CAPM and the market model can be criticized, but so can all economic forecasting models. In fact, we do not have an accurate method for estimating expected returns.

Beaver [7] has criticized the fair game model. He pointed out that the term 'information set ϕ' is not well defined, that the meaning of the term 'information' is unclear, and that the phrase 'assumed to be fully reflected in prices' is ambiguous.

Fama was aware of the ambiguity of the term 'fully reflected': 'The definitional statement, that is, efficient market prices "fully reflect" available information, is so general that it has no empirically testable implications. To make the model more testable the process of price formation must be specified in some detail. In essence we must define somewhat more exactly what is meant by the term "fully reflect"'.

The EMH can be tested at three levels. What is known as the weak form test attempts to ascertain whether knowledge and analysis of past price data can be used to advantage. If it can, it means that the fair game model has to be rejected. The semi-strong test examines whether knowledge of all publicly available information can be used to beat the market. The strong test considers whether any knowledge, publicly available or not, can be used to beat the market.

Weak form tests

The weak form of the EMH states that current security prices fully reflect information given the market regarding historical events, and investors, knowing the historical sequence of prices, can neither abnormally enhance their investment return nor improve their ability to select shares. This implies that share price data relating to today and the past contain no information that can be used to earn profits in excess of those produced by a naive buy and hold strategy. It implies that there are no mechanical rules based on historical share price patterns which can be used to earn profits in excess of the average market return.

Numerous statistical studies have shown that the movement of stock market prices over time approximates to a random walk. A random walk is generated by drawing random numbers and plotting these in the order that they are drawn. The random numbers are generated by choosing a mean and standard deviation for the series, so that the dimensions of the simulated series approximate to the dimensions of the actual series.

The random walk hypothesis suggests that the following question should be answered in the negative: given the price at the end of one period, can one predict the price at the end of the next period? The hypothesis relates to short-run periods but specifies no particular length. Weeks or months would be the appropriate units of measure. The very long run is excepted from the predictions of the hypothesis.

The findings when the hypothesis is tested imply that studying the movement in the price of a company's share provides no sure guide for predicting tomorrow's price. The relationship between today's price and tomorrow's price is purely random.

Although the prediction of absolute levels is ruled out, the prediction of relative levels is not. A list of past GEC share prices will not indicate what tomorrow's share price will be, but it may be possible to predict the position of GEC's share price movement relative to all other company share price movements.

Of course, over the long term there has been upward movement in share prices, and it is expected that this will continue in the future. This is because the gross national product of most countries has increased over time, and with the emphasis still on economic growth it is hoped that this trend will continue. However, this upward trend can at times be very slow-moving and there can be periods of two or more years when there is a trend the other way. The gradual upward trend is not fast enough for most investors to be able to use it profitably within their investment horizons. Therefore this predictability of the long-term trend is not very useful to investors.

At first the findings on random walk caused concern to investment analysts. But the results do not mean that analysts cannot usefully make predictions. As noted, the

13.3 Tests of the efficient market hypothesis

findings do not invalidate forecasts of relative levels of prices. Indeed, the results of the weak form test only discredit the use of past prices as a basis for forecasting future prices.

The random walk hypothesis when applied to share prices merely states that future price changes cannot be predicted from past price changes. The new 'Adam Smith' is mistaken in claiming that 'the trouble with the random walk myth centres on the fact that, on the one hand it assumes a highly competitive efficient stock-pricing mechanism and, on the other hand, it denies the rewards to those "capable well-informed" experts who make this market what it is, by operating in it' [8]. The hypothesis does not deny that the 'experts' who play a large, and tenacious, part in 'making the market what it is' can earn returns above average. All that it means is that if the experts had no information other than past price changes they would not be very successful in forecasting absolute prices. They do have other information.

Serial correlation

The random walk hypothesis has been well tested using a variety of statistical techniques. One of the simpler tests, adopted by a number of authors, is to estimate the correlation coefficients between the price changes of a company share at different periods of time. For example, is there any correlation between the most recent price change and the one for the previous period?

Given a series of data on price P_t for different periods $t = 1, 2, 3, \ldots, n$, the price changes

$$X_t = P_t - P_{t-1}$$

are calculated, producing a series of share price changes. The average price change is

$$\overline{X} = \frac{1}{n-1} \sum_{t=1}^{n-1} X_t$$

The difference between an actual change and the average change is

$$X'_t = X_t - \overline{X}$$

Estimates of the serial correlation between the actual change and the series of changes can then be made:

$$r_s = \frac{\Sigma X'_t X'_{t-s}}{\Sigma (X'_t)^2}$$

Kendall [9], in one of the earliest studies to use this technique, analysed the Actuaries Index of Industrial Share Prices for the London market for the years 1928–38. He used weekly series for each of 18 industrial groupings, with one additional aggregate grouping. He did not consider the price changes of individual firms' shares, but used the changes in the index of prices for the various groupings. He tested for serial correlation, using lags from one to 29 weeks, i.e., he tested whether the change in market price this week is related to that of last week, two weeks back and so on up to 29 weeks back. The results support the random walk hypothesis, showing very little connection between the price changes in one week and those in any other week.

Kendall's conclusions are interesting. They are that investors can, perhaps, make money on the stock exchange, but not, apparently, by watching price movements and coming in on what looks like a good thing. Such success as investors have seems to be due to one or more of the following:

1. chance;
2. the fact that at certain times all prices move together so that they cannot go wrong;
3. having inside information about a company or some economic event so that they can anticipate a movement;
4. being able to act very quickly;

5. being able to operate on such a scale that profits are not expended on brokers' fees and stamp duties.

The research by Brealey and by Cunningham based on UK stock market indices does reveal a certain degree of non-randomness in share price movements [10]. However, the non-randomness that they found – the serial dependence of the series of prices – was small and not really sufficient to invalidate the EMH. One criticism that can be made of some of these studies is that they have measured movements in stock market indices rather than the movements of actual company share prices. For a number of reasons, this could lead to spurious relationships. One problem is that the prices that are used to make up an index for a particular day are not necessarily the actual prices at which deals can be made at that time. A number of the share prices that are used to make up an index for a day are prices quoted on previous days. If there is no trading activity in a share on one day, then it is a previous day's price that is used in the index. It is possible that the particular share could not be bought at the price being used in the index.

Kemp and Reid [11], using UK data on actual individual share price movements rather than indices, found that some non-random price changes existed in 80% of their sample. However, the percentage of companies with non-random movements was reduced to 50% once 'no change' data were removed from the price series. This means that if there was no trading in a particular share during a period and so the price did not change, then it was eliminated from the sample.

Run tests and filter tests

A technique which has also been used to test the random walk hypothesis in share price movements examines the runs in the data. It is of interest to know how many successive price changes are positive or how many successive price changes are negative. The analyst might be consoled for not being able to predict absolute price levels on the basis of past prices if he knows that he can predict that the next change will be in a definite direction.

One of the studies of this possibility was that of Fama [12], who considered the daily change in price of 30 US companies. He analysed the length of runs, the number of runs and whether they were pluses or minuses. He concluded that his analysis showed no indication of dependence between price changes. The direction of the price change of one day was independent of the direction of any other day's price change. The distribution of the length of runs is similar to that which would be expected from pure chance.

This result, as with all the others on random walk, suggests that either there is no relationship between one period's price change for a particular share and another period's price change, or that the statistical techniques are not powerful enough to be able to identify any such dependence.

Another approach which has been used to try to identify significant relationships in share price movements is the filter technique. This simply attempts to filter away any short-term price movements and so to isolate the significant long-term movements. Alexander [13] suggests that the use of this technique can provide profits in excess of those that can be obtained using a simple buy and hold policy.

The way in which the filter approach works is as follows. First a decision is made on the filter level that will be adopted – say, for example, that this is 10%. This means that, starting from a certain date, if the daily closing price of a share moves up at least 10%, buy and hold the security until its price moves down at least 10% from a subsequent high. At this time simultaneously sell and go short. Price moves of less than 10% in either direction are ignored. The short position is held until the daily closing price rises by at least 10% above a subsequent low, at which time one covers and buys the share.

Results of a considerable number of empirical tests examining a considerable number of filter rules indicate that the filter technique does not outperform a simple buy and hold policy after transaction costs are accounted for.

The weak form tests deal with two main issues: the extent that successive security price changes are dependent on prior changes, and the profitability of trading systems. The research tries to determine whether there is any statistical relationship between successive daily changes in security prices, because if the change of one day could be related to the change of the next day then an investor could forecast what would occur in the future and, through trading, profit accordingly. Tests have been conducted on stock and commodity prices in the UK and USA, and the results have shown that, in general, the extent of dependence between successive price changes is negligible [14].

One problem with testing for efficient markets relates to the statistical techniques employed. Over time increasingly sophisticated techniques are being utilized. The condition for the markets to be weak form efficient is that the changes (the first differences) in security prices from one period to another are unpredictable, i.e. changes in prices follow a random walk.

The shortest intervals over which the tests of the random walk referred to above were undertaken were daily price changes. The closing price on one day was compared with the closing price on the next day. It has been suggested that this time interval is too long in which to identify the serial correlation in price movements; rather, the price at the end of one hour should be related to the price at the end of the previous hour.

Indeed, research has now been undertaken in which the price is being recorded on a 15 minute basis, and the series of prices obtained is tested to see if the movement is random. Those supporting this idea of non-randomness of price movements over very short periods of time argue that upward and downward trends can be identified within a day. They argue that the price on the hour is not unrelated to the price half an hour earlier. The results of these tests will be discussed in section 13.7.

If it is found that price movements over these very short time intervals are not random, then it would give the opportunity for those investors who are able to follow the movement of prices closely over a day to make above normal gains. It would give an advantage to those who are close to the market and can respond quickly. Technically the share price at any time is publicly available information, but access to this information is not equally available to all. Only those who know the price hour by hour could benefit. It could be, however, that although predictions can be made over short periods of time, the changes are not large enough to compensate for the transaction costs of trading. This is discussed later.

Semi-strong form tests

The semi-strong form test of the EMH is concerned with whether current prices of shares reflect public knowledge about the underlying company, and whether the speed of price adjustment to the public announcement of information is fast enough to eliminate the possibility of abnormal gains. Thus the question of whether it is worth some effort to acquire and analyse this public knowledge with the hope of gaining superior investment results, if answered in the negative, would support the EMH. Generally, the evidence suggests that the share price adjustment is quick and in the appropriate direction, thus confirming the EMH.

The first and most important study adopting the semi-strong approach was that of Fama et al. [15]. They analysed the adjustment of share prices in the USA in response to the publication of new fundamental information. The information they used was that implied by stock splits. Firth [16] carried out similar tests on stock splits in the UK. He found that share prices adjusted to this new information quickly and that it was not possible to profit from the information once it had been released to the public. Marsh [17] found that in the UK share prices also reacted very quickly to the announcement of a rights issue, and the price behaviour following the announcement was entirely consistent with the semi-strong form of the EMH.

The conclusion is that the market seems to adjust efficiently to this publicly available information. As with the weak tests the market is shown not to react to these sets of information in quite the way that might be expected. Information of the semi-strong type is little better than weak information when it comes to prediction. Thus again the EMH cannot be rejected: no group of investors can use this class of information to give them above average gains.

One possible method of prediction that has attracted attention in the literature is concerned with using interim earnings data to predict the annual profit performance. Green and Segal [18] attempted to assess the accuracy of predictions of annual earnings based on first-quarter interim reports. Their conclusions were that such reports were not clearly superior to those using only annual data, and the forecasts based on the interim model were not superior to the forecasts based on the annual models as a group. Brown and Niederhoffer [19] later showed that the best of the interim-based predictions was consistently better than most of the annual-based predictions. Further improvements came with the release of each additional quarterly report. Since the quality of prediction improves with each new interim report, the market must be increasing its anticipatory powers as the announcement date of the annual report approaches.

A number of studies have shown that the market does not immediately, on the day of announcement, assimilate unexpectedly favourable or unfavourable quarterly earnings information [20]. There is a 'post-announcement drift' in response to the unexpected news. The fact that the share price does not respond immediately and fully to the new information in the quarterly announcements has been claimed to be evidence of semi-strong inefficiencies.

Another explanation is, however, that quarterly earnings announcements are only a subset of the information on earnings expectations. Investors are concerned at any one time with a number of indicators of future profitability. The publication of quarterly earnings figures is only one indicator. Therefore the share price should not be expected to move immediately in line with unexpected changes in the quarterly figures. Other factors need to be considered by investors, and consequently there will be a drift of the share price in the direction indicated by the unexpected change but not a total price adjustment in one sudden change.

Usefulness of accounting numbers

Good quality accounting information is necessary to ensure that capital markets remain efficient. Many of the semi-strong tests of the EMH have attempted to determine the link between accounting information and the movement of share prices. How useful are accounting numbers?

In fact, the publication of the annual report has been shown not to be of great significance to the stock market. Nearly all the results are known or have been anticipated before the date of publication. Ball and Brown [21] found that for US companies most of the information contained in the final report had already been anticipated before its release; the anticipation was very accurate, and the drift upwards or downwards in share price had begun 12 months before the report was released. With regard to the value of the information contained in the final report, no more than 10%–15% has not been anticipated by the month of the report. The value of the information conveyed by the report at the time of its release constitutes on average only 20% of the value of all information coming to the market in that month. About 70% of all information appears to be offsetting, which means that it is of no lasting use for decision-making, although it may cause investors to act in the short run. Therefore only 30% of all information coming to the market at the time of the final report has a continuing value.

Investors build up expectations about earnings, and when actual results are announced some portion of these will have been anticipated already. Therefore this expected part should already have been reflected in the share price. If the market is efficient, only the unexpected part of the total information would be relevant to the market and should ensure that the securities price reacts quickly and in the appropriate direction. If the actual change in earnings was greater than that forecast by Ball and Brown from a regression model, this was termed 'good news', while 'bad news' was when the actual unexpected income change was less than that expected from the model. The hypothesis tested by the researchers was that if the released information contained 'good news' the stock price should rise, and if instead it contained 'bad news' the stock price would fall, while 'no news', i.e. actual equalled forecast, should have no effect on the share price.

A 12-month period prior to the announcement date followed by a subsequent six-month period was investigated, and the portion of change which reflected general price movement in a specific security price was removed. The share prices of the 'good news' companies gradually rose throughout the 12 months prior to the announcement date. Conversely, 'bad news' companies found their share price gradually declining prior to the announcement date. In some cases adjustments still continued for approximately two more months after the announcement.

Ball and Brown found that 50% or more of all the information about an individual firm that becomes available during the year is incorporated in the year's earning figure. Since most of this information has already been captured by the market, they found that on average only 10%–15% of the price adjustment took place in the announcement month. These results are not surprising because a substantial part of the accounting information provided on the announcement date has been leaked to the market through formal interim reports, statements by corporate officials or investigations by analysts confirmed by corporate contacts.

Before the reader rushes off to the library to read up carefully the Ball and Brown studies he should be reminded of their underlying assumptions. Firstly they were *ex post* studies, i.e. they were carried out after the event, and secondly the prediction model generated depended on the period under study and was therefore only relevant to that period. Investors' expectations change over time and their prediction models likewise, and so it would be preferable to examine the effect of financial data on investor decisions independently of any specific prediction model.

Information relating to mergers

In a UK study by Franks *et al.* [22] the EMH was tested using information released at the time of mergers. They analysed the mergers in the brewery and distillery industry in the UK and found that, on average, the market began to anticipate a merger at least three months prior to the announcement date. There was movement in the share price over this three month period which could not be explained by past behaviour or publicly available knowledge, and the researchers suggest that some information about the proposed merger must have been released to some people. Over this three month period abnormal share price returns to the shareholders of the acquired firm averaged 26%. Similar results have been found in studies of mergers in the USA. The fact that abnormal gains prior to the public announcement of a takeover or merger could be obtained might suggest that the market was not efficient. But there are certain other facts that need to be taken into account before coming to this conclusion. The sample used in the study contained only mergers which were concluded and it is possible, indeed most likely, that a number of other mergers reached the stage of being discussed by the parties involved, but the fact that they never got to the stage of completion and announcement meant that they were not included in the sample. The same investors who acted on the mergers that were eventually announced and so made gains may also have acted on the mergers that were not announced and made losses. Overall, therefore, they may not have been obtaining above average returns.

The study by Franks *et al.* also showed that once a merger announcement was made, there was only a very limited opportunity for above normal returns and any gains could soon be swallowed up in transaction costs. Therefore the market was efficient in that, once information was made publicly available, it reacted quickly. Firth [23] undertook a similar study, investigating takeovers in the UK. He showed that there was abnormal increases in the share price of companies to be acquired before the merger was announced. This indicates that there are leaks of information before the official announcement of the bid, but the fact that these leaks were confined to a small number of investors meant according to Firth that there was not a major inefficiency in the market.

There have been a number of studies evaluating the informational content of published management forecasts and of investment analysts' published earnings forecasts. They provide strong evidence for the semi-strong form of market efficiency. The market adjusts quickly to the published information, and those who receive it cannot use it to make abnormal gains. However, there is some evidence of price movement before the publication of analysts' forecasts and predictions, and these movements are in the direction that would be expected from knowledge of the predictions. Somebody with knowledge of the analysts' predictions can make and has made abnormal gains.

'Outsiders'?

Investment analysts are regarded as 'outsiders'. Through their work, however, they do have greater knowledge about companies than other outsiders. They are continually monitoring industries and companies and revising their earnings forecasts. Is this informational advantage used to make above normal returns?

We have to consider this question at two levels. First, do the analysts use their information to their own advantage and to the advantage of their closest clients? This is called primary dissemination of the information. Secondary dissemination results from the published recommendations of analysts. The question that arises therefore is can those who read these published tips use this information to make above average gains, or is it just those who benefit from primary dissemination that can do so.

Analysts search for inside information; they can be expected to search up to the point where the expected marginal revenue resulting from the information that they find will equal the marginal cost of the search. The evidence seems to suggest that the analysts and special clients do have an informational advantage that allows them to earn abnormal returns. This means that on this point the stock markets fail the strong form efficiency tests. Abdel-Khalik and Ajinkya [24] have shown that in the USA trading strategies could be formulated to earn abnormal returns on the basis of private knowledge of the revisions of earnings forecasts made by financial analysts. They went on to show that no abnormal returns could be earned after the week of the public disclosure of the revisions. The market could therefore be said to be efficient in a semi-strong sense: it adjusted quickly to the information once it was made public.

Strong form test

Judging the efficiency of the stock market by observing how share prices adjust to all available information, whether publicly available or not, is known as a strong form test. It has been found that certain investors do have access either to privileged information or to significant information before other people, and it is not doubted that they can use this to obtain above average profits. Professional analysts and certain people within companies have access to such information. But there is no evidence that any other class of investor consistently has information which gives them a preferential position in market trading. In the sense that a few people do have information earlier than other investors and so can make an above average gain, the market may be thought to be inefficient. This is not so, however, for it applies only to a very small group. The vast majority of investors are not in such a favourable position.

A number of researchers have provided evidence that 'insiders' do have what is called 'informational advantage' [25]. This means they are able to use this price-sensitive information to earn 'abnormal' returns from their investments. The law attempts to protect the less informed investors in their dealings with those with inside information. A director of a company knows the up-to-date position of his company, and it would clearly be unfair to allow him to use this information when entering into a buy or sell transaction with an investor who had no such up-to-date information. It would be a form of deception. The position of insiders is examined in section 13.5.

Of course, one way of making money on the market is to obtain information before other investors, or to react more quickly to the information than other investors. One further prescription for successful trading is to act in the same way as the expert. Usually, however, the uninformed investor finds out too late the way that the informed investor has acted. But it has been shown that it is possible to make a small gain by acting in the same way as the informed investor, but by doing so only one or two days later. It is like standing on the expert's coat-tail – a small amount of gain is left over for other investors after the experts have taken advantage of their knowledge. This trading technique simply states that some money can be made not only by obtaining the information oneself, but by behaving quickly in the same manner as the informed investors.

Nobody denies that with inside information it is possible to make above average returns. The importance of the findings of the studies on this subject is that they suggest that gains can be made by examining the way in which the people with inside information invest. When insiders build up their holdings of a particular share, that share can be expected to outperform the market during the following months. Insiders also tend to sell a share more than the average investor before that share experiences a large decrease in price. Knowledge of the way that the insiders are trading can therefore be useful in predicting price moves. The problem then becomes one of ascertaining the actions of insiders. This is not as easy in the UK as in the USA, as in the USA knowledge about the dealings of insiders is made publicly available for other investors to see.

In the UK certain categories of insiders are obliged to file a report of their sales and purchases of shares to which they have price-sensitive information.

One interesting research study that indicated that the market was not strong form efficient was that of Levy and Lerman [26]. It is usually believed that shares in companies whose current price-to-earnings ratio is low offer the potential for a higher return than shares in companies with a high price-to-earnings ratio. If winners can be spotted amongst these low price-to-earnings shares the potential return is considerable. An insider with access to information about company earnings long before it is published should be able to select those shares with a low ratio which are going to do better than expected. This is what Levy and Lerman found. The sophisticated investor and the insider could make excess profits by investing in stock with low price-to-earnings ratios.

The balance of evidence does, however, indicate that the US and UK exchanges are strong form inefficient.

One type of investor who may be thought to have superior inside information is the newspaper financial journalist, the tipster. The tipster has at least advance knowledge of information to be given in the newspaper for which he writes. He knows the shares that will be recommended for purchase. He is in a similar position to the investment analyst, whose recommendations can influence the level of a company's share price.

Firth investigated the behaviour of a wide number of tipsters, in particular looking at what happened to the share price of their portfolio recommendations [27]. It is known that the prices of the shares which investors are advised to buy are frequently marked up by market makers the day after the advice is given in the newspapers. This means that either there has been very rapid trading activity or that the market maker has decided to anticipate purchasers' intentions. The result is that by the time most investors have the opportunity to purchase the recommended share, they are buying a correctly priced security and there is little prospect of a further rapid increase in price. The tipster knows that the share price is going to move up after publication of the advice and so the tipster could, if he was so inclined, buy some shares before the article appears and sell them a day or two after it has appeared and so make a gain. City editors tend to ban their tipsters from indulging in such activities. Firth, investigating a number of situations and not one particular case, found no evidence that financial journalists derived profits themselves from trading in the shares that they recommended.

Informed investors

Informed investors are of course different from inside dealers. An efficient market needs informed investors, and one interesting explanation of the random walk phenomenon in share prices distinguishes between two classes of investors, the informed and the uninformed. The informed investors, who have relevant information, anticipate how the trading of the uninformed will be affected by the delays in obtaining the information. They can therefore act on the expected price changes that will eventually result when the uninformed investors obtain the information. The two classes of investors operating in the market could generate the random effect in price movements.

Cootner [28] offers a similar explanation. The experts have their own idea of the direction that prices will follow as a result of information not generally available. They will only enter the market if they think that the actual price varies considerably from what they consider to be the correct price. If they think that a price has risen too high they will start to unload the shares at this high price, which will have the effect of pulling the price down. If they think that a price is too low they will start buying the shares at this cheap price, which will have the effect of pushing the price up. There are therefore upper and lower barriers through which it is difficult for the price to move; instead, it moves in a random walk fashion between the barriers. In the short run the price moves in this way because of the uncertainty of the uninformed investors and their resulting random transactions. Over the medium and long run the experts allow the barriers to change. However, perhaps surprisingly, the findings suggest that, except in the very long run, all price movements are random.

The reason that there are upper and lower barriers is that, while it is difficult for the informed investor to name a specific price for a share as the correct value, he does know a price range within which the share is reasonably priced. He will alter the range, the upper and lower barriers, as he receives relevant information. By obtaining this before the non-expert investor, he can make gains on his trading.

Example 13.1

(a) You are required, using the following information, to predict the share prices of Alpha Plc and Beta Engine Plc on Day 4, 6 and 12 if the market is:

(i) semi-strong efficient;
(ii) strong-form efficient

Day 1: Alpha Plc has 4 million shares with a market price of £4 per share. Beta Engine Plc has 2 million shares with a market price of £2 per share.

Day 4: The management of Alpha, meeting in private, decided to make a cash takeover bid for Beta Engine Plc at a price of £4 per share. Both companies have the same earnings per share (EPS) of 40 pence but Alpha has a P/E ratio of 10 while Beta Engine has a P/E ratio of only 5. The management of Alpha also expect to obtain synergistic benefits from the takeover amounting in present value terms to £6 million.

Day 6: Alpha publicly announces the unconditional offer to purchase all the shares of Beta Engine; details of the expected savings are not announced and therefore are not public knowledge.

Day 12: Alpha announces details of the savings which will be derived from the takeover.

(b) What would your share price predictions have been if the purchase consideration, decided upon on day 4 and publicly announced on day 6, had been financed by one newly issued share of Alpha for each Beta Engine share?

Answer

(a) Cash Offer

Alpha

Day 4

Semi-strong: We are told what happened at a private meeting. This is not publicly available information and so the market does not react.

Strong: Price adjusted to reflect 'privately' available information which includes knowledge about the price and the synergistic gains. If it is assumed the bid will be successful then the price immediately moves to its new 'true' value.

The market value of A before the bid was £16 million and of B £4 million. The combined company is worth £20 million less the cash payment of £8 million. The new company is therefore worth £12 million plus the synergistic gain of £6 million. There are 4 million shares which gives a value per share of £4.50.

Day 6

Semi-strong: The market knows the 'cost' of the bid but not the gains. It believes the value of the combined company to be only £12 million. With 4 million shares the price becomes £3 per share.

Strong: Price remains correctly valued, because all information is reflected in price.

Day 12

Semi-strong: Price moves to its true value of £4.50.

Beta

Day 4

Semi-strong: No change, information of bid not publicly available.

Strong: It is known bid price will be £4, so price moves to this level.

Day 6

Semi-strong: Bid price becomes publicly known, so price adjusts.

Summary

	Semi-strong market		Strong market	
	Alpha	Beta	Alpha	Beta
Day 1	£4	£2	£4	£2
Day 4	£4	£2	£4.5	£4
Day 6	£3	£4	£4.5	£4
Day 12	£4.5	£4	£4.5	£4

(b) Share for share exchange

Alpha

Day 4

Semi-strong: No change, information not publicly available.

Strong: Price adjusts to reflect privately available information. Value of new company is £26 million (£16 + £4 + £6). Number of shares 6 million. Therefore value per share £4.33.

Day 6

Semi-strong: Public information is only about the bid, not the synergistic gains. Therefore total value £20 million, which gives a value per share of £3.33.

Strong: Price remains at 'true' value.

Day 12

Semi-strong: Price moves to its true value.

Beta

Day 4

Semi-strong: No change.

Strong: Price moves to its true value.

Day 6

Semi-strong: Public know of bid, but not of gains. It is known shareholders of Beta will receive one share in Alpha in exchange for one share in Beta. Market believes on day 6 value of Alpha share will be £3.33.

Day 12

Semi-strong: Price moves to true value.

Summary

| | Semi-strong | | Strong | |
	Alpha	Beta	Alpha	Beta
Day 1	£4	£2	£4	£2
Day 4	£4	£2	£4.33	£4.33
Day 6	£3.33	£3.33	£4.33	£4.33
Day 12	£4.33	£4.33	£4.33	£4.33

It has been observed that share price movements are more volatile than would be expected if all trading was based on fundamental information. Roll has shown that most idiosyncratic moves in the price of a particular company's shares cannot be explained by public news [29]. There are significant price moves on days when there is no public news that would be expected to influence the share price. Cutler *et al.* [30] found that the days where there is the largest market movement in price are not the days with the most important fundamental news.

When the movements in share price over time are studied, what are referred to as 'bubbles' can be observed, these being 'explosive' movements in share prices, or deviations from movement based on fundamental information. A number of explanations for such bubbles have been proposed.

One such explanation is noise trading by naive investors. This is called a 'fad'. As mentioned above a number of years ago Cootner [31] referred to informed and uninformed investors. These two classes of investors have been given many names. The uninformed are sometimes called 'noise' traders or liquidity traders. The informed are sometimes called 'arbitrageurs' or 'rational speculators'. As explained above it is this latter group who do the work of bringing the company's share price towards its fundamental value. Some shifts in the demand for a share are completely rational, but some are not. The uninformed investor can be irrational – they can introduce a systematic bias into the market. The change in demand can be based on sentiment or the unjustified expectation of uninformed investors. On what is called a fad.

The uninformed investor may be responding to the advice of a stockbroker or a financial guru. The investor might be just following what is seen to be a trend, to be imitating strategies that they believe will lead to above average returns. One of the strongest tendencies of the less informed investor is to chase the trend. That is to buy shares following their rise, and to sell shares following a fall. The change in demand is not based on fundamental news, but on noise. Technical analysis (which is explained on page 415) can also lead to changes in demand not based on fundamental information.

The informed investor, the arbitrageurs, take advantage of actions of the noise trader. This might not mean to always sell when the uninformed are buying. It might be in the arbitrageur's interest sometimes to jump on the bandwagon for a while. This is called feedback trading. If the uninformed are buying the arbitrageur buys for a while, but has to be careful to sell near the top and take profits. The arbitrageur is for a time therefore helping to feed the 'bubble', it is only when selling that he or she is helping to bring the price down to its fundamental value [32].

13.4 Fads and bubbles

George Soros, a famous successful investor (investing in the foreign exchange market as well as stock market), does not always try to counter the irrational waves of buying and selling a security [33]. He is sometimes prepared to ride the wave, but to get out before the uninformed. This tactic has been described as 'Pumping up the Tulips'.

Booms and crashes in stock market prices are easy to explain if informed investors do on occasions engage in feedback trading – if they do 'Pump up the Tulips'. They are certainly easier to explain in this way, than by assuming that informed investors always trade to bring an actual market price of a share back to its fundamental value. The informed investor only engages in limited arbitrage. On occasion he or she is willing to go along with the trend, the trend being based on fads, sentiment and noise.

13.5 Insider dealing

Insider dealing involves an individual buying or selling shares on the basis of price-sensitive information not yet publicly available. The inside dealer is aiming to exploit the information before it is transmitted to the market. A crucial question is how did the 'insider' obtain the knowledge.

Insider dealing is a very controversial issue. One extreme view is that it is similar to robbery: the insider is taking money away from the person with whom he/she deals who is not aware of certain important facts. Another criticism is that the insider is disturbing the working of a free market: he or she is destroying investors' confidence in the market.

At the other extreme some would argue it is not a crime. Any buyer (and/or seller) of shares in the market should beware. If one trades in any market one takes risks. Why would anybody want to buy a share unless they thought it would lead to gains? It could be argued that the Stock Exchange is all about one person making a gain at someone else's expense. Some economists actually see the practice as beneficial and believe that it should not be prohibited. Insiders can actually be seen as moving the market price in the right direction.

Insider dealing is a way of redistributing wealth. It moves it towards those with inside knowledge and away from those without it.

Why insider dealing is an important issue from the point of view of stock market efficiency is because the strong form test of the market efficiency is concerned with price movements in response to any information. That is information whether publicly available or not. It has been found that within limits share prices in the market reflect all publicly available information. They do not however reflect information not available to the public. People with access to non-public information (insiders) can therefore make above average returns. If 'inside dealing' is known to be taking place in the stock market, it will frighten investors without inside knowledge and keep them out of the stock market. The view is taken therefore in most stock markets that an individual may not deal in securities of a company if he or she has price-sensitive inside information which is held by virtue of being a connected person or having obtained inside information from such a person. Similarly, an insider must not counsel or procure others to act on inside information and must not communicate such information to anyone else.

In 1990 the Secretary of State argued that he believed the number of insider dealing cases in the UK was 'probably on the decline'. However, many believe that the occurrences of insider dealing have not dropped as markedly as would have been expected since it became illegal in 1980. The international aspects of markets and modern telecommunications have made the crime easier to commit and harder to detect, consequently there can be little confidence that insider dealing is on the decline.

The regulations

Insider trading in the UK is subject to both statutory and non-statutory regulation.

It has only been a criminal offence since 1980, prior to that the practice was scarcely frowned upon. The offence now warrants a maximum ten-year jail sentence and a large fine. It has been argued however that the possible deterrents are not being used properly.

The legislation in Britain has concentrated on viewing insider dealing as a criminal offence. The authorities still see criminal law as the 'appropriate way of dealing with the crime'. In 1985 the Company Securities (Insider Dealing) Act was introduced to tighten the existing law. The legislation provided four main definitions of an insider. They are:

- individuals who are connected with a company;
- individuals contemplating takeovers;
- public servants;
- tippees of each of these categories.

In each of these cases to be considered an insider the individual must either possess or obtain unpublished price-sensitive information regarding the securities in question. For an insider there are three main offences that can be committed, the first being the most blatant and obvious, actually directly dealing in the securities.

Secondly, the insider can counsel or procure another individual to deal in the securities. Finally, the insider can communicate information to any other person, knowing that that person or someone else will deal in those securities.

The Criminal Justice Act of 1993 further updated the legislation relating to insider dealing and implemented the EC directive on insider dealing. The London Stock Exchange also made a number of changes in the same year to the aspects of their Rules concerned with insider dealing.

The Criminal Justice Act 1993 made changes to the legislation, the most important being the definition of 'insiders'. It was extended to cover anyone who obtains inside information as a result of his/her employment/position. Prior to this change there had to be a more direct 'connection' between an insider and the company whose shares were dealt in. This change greatly increases the scope for investigations.

The 1993 Act increased the scope of the legislation in certain other respects: namely the securities covered; the markets regulated; and the geographical area of the offence. Dealing now includes any off-market deal made through a professional intermediary as well as those on a recognized stock exchange. Securities was given a wider meaning and will include debt securities, depositary receipts, options and futures. The offences now cover markets in 19 European countries and extend to any investments made through intermediaries, and disclosure or encouragement made to persons in the UK from anywhere in the world.

Inside information is defined as specific price-sensitive information relating to particular securities which have not been made public. The Act provides that it will be judged price-sensitive when, if made public, it would be likely to have 'a significant effect' on the price of any securities.

The efficiency of stock markets relates directly to the speed of and the subsequent reactions to information. The aim of any regulation is to ensure that the market operates freely on a basis of equality between the buyers and the sellers. One problem is that for this to happen there needs to be instantaneous disclosure of information. In practice a few people will always be better informed than the vast majority. The Stock Exchange believes that quicker disclosure may be the best solution; making companies release information more quickly will be more effective than any laws could ever be. This will mean there will be less people better informed for a shorter period.

The 1993 Exchange guidelines were designed to curb the selective leaking of price-sensitive information, which could give rise to insider dealing. The guidance is designed to help companies decide when they need to make a company announcement, and urges them to issue more of them. They should release regular statements regarding current trading conditions.

This move by the Stock Exchange followed the case of London International Group in February 1993. The company was reprimanded by the Exchange for not releasing a profits warning through the correct channels. The profits warning was only released to a selected group of analysts who were present at the company on 1 February. By the end of trading that day the shares had fallen by 8%, wiping £37m off the company's market value. The real message to all companies now is that 'when in doubt put the information out'. It is argued that where a company complies with its obligations under the Stock Exchange's Listing Rules, to release price-sensitive information to the market as a whole rather than selectively, then companies will have nothing to fear from the rules and legislation. Increased formal disclosure will do much to cut down on the opportunity to carry out insider dealing. It would reduce the period available for important information to be misused or leaked, thereby helping to prevent insider dealing from the outset.

One group of individuals who will always be (or should always be) knowledgeable about a company are the directors. The Companies Act (1985) required directors to notify the company of any interests that they have in the company's shares. Dealings in the shares and holdings of shares are recorded and are available for inspection at any time. It is unlikely that directors will deal on specific price-sensitive information, but they will always have an overall informational advantage. They will always have better information as to the company's day-to-day activities. The market is aware of the possible significance of such director dealings and much interest is now taken as to just why the director is dealing. The dealings of directors have now become a vital indicator to the market on how a company is really performing. The directors are often dealing on information that is not widely available.

An unusual example of directors' dealings came to light in the case of Ivor Goodman. Goodman has the status of being the only insider in Britain to be sent to jail. However he was only caught due to the open way in which the insider deal was carried out. Goodman was chairman and major shareholder of Unigroup plc. In 1987 the company's directors became aware that the forthcoming results were likely to show a loss rather than the anticipated profit of £900 000. Goodman then gave his entire holding of 692 000 shares to his girlfriend, in what he claimed was a gift. Almost immediately his girlfriend sold the shares netting nearly £1.2 million. Three days later Goodman resigned as chairman.

The purchasers of the shares were not told of the losses the company was facing which would have made the shares less attractive. Also the fact that as chairman Goodman was resigning was significant information. Goodman was sentenced to 18 months in jail, of which nine months were suspended.

A recent EU proposal on insider dealing states that if a company is buying shares in another with the intention of launching a bid, the company has to say so before buying the shares. This will quite clearly prove highly unpopular with UK companies. Companies need time to build up a stake in the target company in order to obtain a large enough stakeholding in the company to launch a full-scale bid. If the proposal becomes law it will give the target company an extended timespan to prepare defensive actions.

Some action seems necessary in takeover situations. A 1989 study by the London Stock Exchange found that approximately 80% of suspected insider deals actually happen immediately before or after a takeover bid. A prominent financial journalist has stated that it is difficult to recall a takeover bid which did not leak in some way.

Detection of insider dealing

It is difficult to obtain evidence on illegal insider dealing. The culprits often use foreign-based companies, in say Panama or Guernsey, that are nominee vehicles. This allows the people behind the deal to trade through such companies without being identified.

The culprit could be an employee of a bank or an investment analyst in the UK. The person would buy or sell through a nominee name in an offshore financial centre. This has been made a little more difficult by firms now recording all phone calls through the office. Nevertheless an employee of a merchant bank who knows of a takeover bid that is to take place can pass on the information secretly to someone who would deal through a nominee company. A phone call could be made from a phone box in London to one in, say, Gibraltar.

Undoubtedly, unusual and suspicious price movements do take place. For example in 1993, there were dramatic falls in the share price before the announcement of bad news in two British companies, Tiphook and Spring Ram.

In the UK it is very difficult to make an insider trading case stick. In the years between 1980 (when such dealing was made illegal) and 1994 the Stock Exchange referred in the region of 200 cases to the DTI. This has led to only 22 convictions, with only one person jailed. As mentioned above the one person was a company chairman who did not try to cover his tracks. In the UK usually the system only catches small transgressions. The USA is more effective in catching insider dealers. They can subpoena witnesses, and settle cases out of court.

In Britain there is no single enforcement agency. Incidents of insider dealing are detected usually by the Insider Dealing Group at the Stock Exchange. The role of this group is to study share price dealing movements, with particular attention paid to the period prior to price-sensitive announcements. The modernization of trading practices in markets has made it easier to commit insider dealing; it has also made it easier to detect the practice. An advanced surveillance team in the Group rely on an advanced computer system to detect unusual movement. They generally receive between 400 and 2000 alerts per day. An alert is classed as out-of-the-ordinary on the basis of the level of trading volume and price movement. When this happens the details will be checked and the vast majority of cases will be cleared. Spotting movements that are suspicious is the easy part; collecting evidence that will stand up in court is very hard indeed.

If the Stock Exchange believes that there is clear prima facie evidence of insider dealing the case will be passed to the DTI. Upon receiving the case the DTI can follow one of four possible courses of action. They can take no further action if they disagree with the Stock Exchange; they can authorize the Exchange to prosecute; they can also prosecute themselves or (the most common course of action) they can appoint inspectors to undertake further investigation. The inspectors have wide-ranging powers and can interview people beyond those directly under suspicion. One fundamental problem is that the DTI simply do not have the resources to undertake extensive original investigatory work.

The penalties imposed for insider dealing are considered by many to be grossly inadequate. The toughest penalty is imprisonment, with a maximum jail term now of ten years. Fines can also be imposed on insiders and there is also the loss to the insider's reputation and possible livelihood.

The most famous of the recent insider dealing cases in the UK was that of Geoffrey Collier, who at the time was the joint head of Morgan Grenfell Securities. In 1987 Morgan Grenfell were advising a company named Hollis over a takeover bid which was to be launched the following day on a company called AE. Prior to the announcement of the bid, Collier tried to purchase 50 000 shares in AE, via a friend in Los Angeles in the name of a Cayman Island company. The order was split between two brokerage firms at an execution price of 237p. At the end of the day's trading, after the bid was announced, the share price has risen to 267p. One of the brokerage firms was clearly suspicious about the transaction and complained to the other one. It was found that the buyer was a Cayman Island company, Pureve, and because of the lack of jurisdiction the trail could have ended there. However by a stroke of fortune a broker at one of the firms who had previously worked with Collier recognized that Pureve belonged to Collier. Morgan Grenfell was duly informed of what had happened and Collier resigned. In the end Collier was given a suspended prison sentence of 12 months, suspended from work for 2 years and given a £25 000 fine.

The case contrasts with the most famous insider dealing case in the USA. Dennis Levine, formerly managing director of Diexel Burnham Lambert Inc., was charged in May 1986 with supplying inside information to Mr Ivan Boesky. The Securities and Exchange Commission (SEC) alleged that Boesky traded on this information knowing it to have been obtained through either misappropriation or breach of fiduciary duty. Boesky was fined $100 million by the SEC, barred for life from the US securities industry and sentenced to three years' imprisonment. Most of the accusations of insider trading in the USA have concerned information about impending takeover bids.

An important question is what constitutes price-sensitive information. The regular dialogue between analysts, fund managers and companies is a vital link in the market.

Analysts gain specialist knowledge about particular sectors and can advise investors as to the best investments to make. It is claimed the insider dealing rules threaten the very source from which analysts' get much of their information, the company.

Much of the focus on analysts' relations with the companies has arisen due to the conviction of Edinburgh based analyst Thorold Mackie. Mr Mackie had been analysing the shares of Shanks and McEwan for many years and had built up a close relationship with the management of the company. In 1991 after a meeting with the chairman Peter Runciman, Mackie was convinced that he should change his original profit forecast for the year. The original estimate was a profit for the year of £38.5 million; he decided to downgrade this to £35 million and the company was taken off the recommended long-term buy list. Mackie also spoke on a Friday to salesmen in the brokerage firm where they were employed. On the following Monday and Tuesday there was some selling of the shares. Mackie simply believed he had been involved in the kind of chat that an analyst is 'supposed' to have with a company. However, on the Wednesday Runciman contacted Mackie and accused him of breach of confidence. Later Runciman argued that he gave Mackie price-sensitive information, and that Mackie was as a result an insider.

One week later Shanks and McEwan issued a profits warning and it was at this point that Mackie was investigated. In March 1992 he was charged and in March 1993 he was convicted for insider dealing and fined £25 000. Mackie argued that Runciman never explicitly stated that there was to be a profits warning, merely that there would be little by way of earnings growth per share. The doubts in this case are twofold. Firstly, did Mackie receive any unpublished price-sensitive information? If we believe what Mackie claims then what he received was general information and was not 'precise and specific'. The second factor is that Mackie did not use the information for his own private gains. He owned many shares in Shanks and McEwan but did not deal in them. One could argue that the close relationship he had developed with the company was a legitimate one. However, by selling before the company's official profits warning the clients of the brokerage firm received £1.39 million more than if they had sold afterwards. The problem for analysts is that clients increasingly want informational advantages.

In February 1994 the Scottish Court of Criminal Appeal quashed Thorold Mackie's conviction for insider dealing. The court decided that there was insufficient evidence in law for a conviction. In this case this pointed to the lack of evidence as to the conversation between Mackie and Runciman. As mentioned above evidence is the big problem in the vast majority of insider dealing cases.

13.6 Doubts about stock market efficiency

In 1978 Jensen told us that 'the efficient market hypothesis is the best established fact in all of the social sciences' [34]. In 1988 he went further, telling us that 'no proposition, in any of the sciences is better documented' than the efficient market hypothesis. It is true that there is much research evidence indicating that stock market prices (in the USA in particular) appropriately incorporate all currently available public information. Nevertheless there are sweeping statements; particularly as Jensen does admit in the 1988 study that the evidence is 'not literally 100 percent in support' of the hypothesis [35]. What can we say about the evidence on the efficiency of stock markets?

It is important to appreciate the following.

1. The semi-strong test of the EMH, also referred to as information arbitrage efficiency, does not imply rational prices. It does not imply that the share price of a company reflects its fundamental value.

2. At the best the weak form and semi-strong form tests indicate that it is not possible to identify persistent opportunities through stock market trading to achieve excess profits. The tests indicate that the EMH cannot be rejected on the basis of the data being used – this does not mean that the tests prove that the market is efficient. The empirical tests in fact can neither confirm nor disconfirm that stock markets are 'efficient'. The tests do not establish that a stock market is efficient. All they show is that it cannot be proved that it is inefficient.

3. There are important differences between the stock markets in Europe and the US stock markets. In the UK the financial institutions own a much higher percentage of the shares of UK companies than is the case with financial institutions in the USA. As Peacock and Bannock point out this means that in the UK there are not always a large number of buyers or sellers of a company's shares which as every first-year economics student knows is a necessary condition for perfect competition [36]. We should be careful before assuming that findings based on the situation in the USA apply to the UK.
4. Most of the empirical evidence used to support the EMH was published in the 1960s and 1970s. More recent research has explored a number of 'anomalies' with respect to the behaviour of share prices. There are alternative hypotheses that, rather than imply the market is efficient, imply that there are large and persistent valuation errors. These hypotheses refer to 'fads', 'speculative bubbles' and the 'inflation illusion'.

Researchers have been kept busy on both sides of the Atlantic, for over 30 years studying how share prices react to new information. It has almost become heresy for financial economists to suggest that the stock market is less than efficient. But for a share price to reflect publicly available information (which is what has been found) does not mean that the share price reflects the fundamental value of the share (sometimes referred to as the true or intrinsic value of the share).

One basic problem is that we do not know what is the 'fundamental value' of a share. We have to rely on valuation models that of necessity need to be based on certain assumptions. Even having estimated a true value we then have to decide how far away from this true value the actual price of a share has to be before we say the market is underestimating or overestimating and is therefore inefficient. A third problem is what percentage of quoted companies need to have their shares under- or over-priced before we say the market is inefficient.

Black caused a stir when in his presidential address to the American Finance Association, he stated 'I think almost all markets [he was referring to US stock markets] are efficient almost all of the time.' Almost all he explains means at least 90% of the time [37]. In fact if 10% of the time markets are not efficient this gives a lot of opportunity for 'bargain purchases' of undervalued shares. Black pointed out that a certain amount of trading in shares was motivated by 'noise'. He wished to contrast 'noise' with 'information'. From the market's point of view all trading is good as it makes markets liquid, whether or not the trading is based on facts.

Black's views of what at any point of time the relationship between a true (intrinsic) value and the actual share price should be in an efficient market leaves a lot of room for those engaged in investing in equities to exploit price gaps. Black refers to the market being efficient if it results in the actual price of a company's shares being within a factor of two of its true value. This factor of course represents his view of a reasonable price and Black admits it is arbitrary but he states 'intuitively, though, it seems reasonable to me, in the light of sources of uncertainty about value'. The above comments suggest that either the markets are not so efficient at interpreting the information given in company financial statements or that the statements do not give sufficient information for the intrinsic value to be determined.

Valuation problems

As Stiglitz points out the existence of asymmetric information means that 'managers can take actions which affect the returns to those who provide capital' [38]. In the 1980s the 'management of earnings disclosure' became an art and unfortunately became not uncommon both in the US and the UK. The manipulation of reported earnings means that one group of market participants have information and an understanding not available to other participants. On the question of understanding, doubts arose particularly in the late 1980s as to whether financial analysts, who had the necessary information, were able to understand its true importance.

Modigliani, a Nobel economics prize winner, has expressed concern with the efficiency of the stock market. He believes that irrational investors are present in the market [39]. He wrote in 1988, that he had 'become a bit disenchanged with the indiscriminate use of superrationality as the foundation for models of financial behaviour'. Modigliani examines the effects of inflation on market valuation. He believes the market fails to 'understand how to value equities in the presence of significant inflation, which results in systematic, predictable error'. Modigliani and Cohn offer an explanation for some of the unexpected movements in share price, namely the existence of irrationality on the part of a subset of investors [40]. Campbell and Kyle show how the presence of such a subset of irrational investors can result in under- or over-valuation of shares persisting over time [41].

Bhattachara, reviewing the literature on the valuation of equities in the stock market, concludes 'the accumulation of evidence presents, in my view, a murky picture vis-à-vis the prevalence of rational (information efficiency) valuation in the stock market' [42]. Roll and other researchers have found that significant movements in individual share price and stock market indices cannot on many occasions be related to public news, and vice versa [43]. The announcement of fundamental news does not on occasions move prices. It is not just news that leads to movements in share prices; the action of uninformed investors also moves prices.

It is claimed by supporters of the efficient markets that the anomalies that have been identified are not of major importance. The ones that have been found only affect a minor part of stock market activity. There does not seem to be anything systematic about them which would give grounds for concern that the stock market is not on the whole a fair game.

It is accepted that discrepancies do exist between actual share prices at any one time and what are thought to be 'true' (intrinsic) values. The research of Bernard and Thomas suggests that the market only allows small discrepancies to arise, which they estimate to be on average up to a 2% difference for larger firms and up to a 6% difference for smaller firms [44].

The studies mentioned above have all been published in the USA and are primarily based on the situation in that country. There has been a vast amount of empirical research in the USA testing the efficient market hypothesis. Whittington, in his overview of financial accounting theory, asserts that 'the empirical approach has become almost a cult among ambitious young academics, especially in the USA' and refers to 'the age of the computer' which facilitates this type of research [45].

There is a certain amount of evidence relating to the efficiency of the London Stock Exchange, but much less evidence on the efficiency of the other stock exchanges in Europe. In fact the concept of the efficient market hypothesis is of more interest and of more significance in some countries than in others. This is because in some countries stock exchanges are of more importance in the financial system than in others.

The results of the German EMH tests that have been undertaken are consistent with the findings of the studies which were carried out in the USA and the UK. Stock prices not only react to the publication of annual reports, but the German investors also seem to anticipate to some degree the information which is published in the accounts. As far as the anticipation of information is concerned Coenenberg singles out companies which, due to their size, are obliged by the Commercial Code to disclose more data than their smaller counterparts [46]. The stock price reaction after the publication of the annual reports of these big companies is relatively minor, thus reflecting that there are less surprises resulting from the publication of the accounts of large companies than small.

According to Coenenberg the German EMH test seems to indicate that German investors do not simply take reported figures at face value. He points out how difficult it is in Germany to interpret the aims of accounting policies correctly, especially with the trade-off faced by management between a minimization of the company's tax burden and the optimistic profits impression which it may want to convey in its report. Futhermore, he argues that, depending on the amount of published information, it is not always possible to identify the impact of accounting policies clearly.

Choi and Levich 'take it as given that US capital markets are highly efficient' [47]. They refer to 'the conventional notion that European capital markets are more likely to be inefficient in a weak form sense'. It will be remembered that weak form efficiency implies that knowledge of past changes in share price will not be useful in predicting future changes in share price. If stock markets are not weak form efficient then it is possible to predict future price changes on the basis of past price changes.

Choi and Levich point out that contrary to what may be thought the evidence is that many European stock markets are weak form efficient. Hawawini examined the literature on weak form efficiency of the markets in 14 European countries [48]. He concludes that in most of these countries 'when returns are measured over intervals longer than a week, the Random Walk Model cannot be rejected'. This says nothing of course about movement within a week. There is much less literature on the semi-strong efficiency of European markets. Hawawini's review of the literature for France and the UK indicates that these countries are semi-strong efficient but that Germany is not. The studies indicate that for France and the UK the share prices that are set by the market do not leave opportunities for abnormal returns for investors who have publicly available information. The findings are that market prices quickly reflect accounting information and those operating in the market are not misled by changes in accounting rules.

Although most of the evidence produced over the last twenty years indicates that the major stock markets of the world are efficient in a weak form and semi-strong form sense, doubts are now being raised. It is becoming fashionable to critize the idea that stock markets are efficient. The problem is that the theory has perhaps been oversold in the past.

One form of criticism relates to the mathematical analysis that has been used in the past to test the hypothesis. New mathematical analysis of stock market prices show there is often unexpected predictability. This is being explained by the fact that those who trade in the market do not all think the same way [49]. They reason differently about the information they receive, they have different time horizons and different attitudes towards risk. It has been suggested that the more advanced computer models now being developed allow opportunities to outperform the market at least for a while. Such opportunities result from the way in which information is interpreted and used by the participants in the market. The information is efficiently and fairly distributed; it is how it is used that creates opportunities.

The efficient market hypothesis does not say anything about how market participants incorporate news into investment decisions.

13.7 Market anomalies

Statistical studies have shown that there is a tendency for mean share price returns to vary as follows:

1. At different times during the trading day. (It has been found in the USA, dividing a day into 15 minute periods, that the first 45 minutes of trading on Mondays produces negative returns, whilst on other weekdays it is positive. It has also been found that prices rise on all weekdays during the last 15 minutes of trading.)
2. Across the days of the trading week, with below average return on a Monday.
3. Across the months of the year, with high returns in January in the USA and in April in the UK.

Knowledge of these timing and seasonal patterns means that it would appear to be possible to exploit these inefficiencies to make above average returns. Just an understanding of these patterns in *ex post* share price returns and the adoption of an arbitrage strategy could lead to 'beating the system'.

Unless we can explain what causes irregularities, we cannot be confident that they will continue to occur. It could just be that they have occurred for chance reasons, with some people being lucky and benefiting from them. It could be that they are unlikely to occur in the future. Unless we have a satisfactory explanation – a theory that explains why they are happening – we have little reason to expect them to recur.

We shall now consider possible explanations for these anomalies.

Hours of the day

As was mentioned above trading at different times of the day can give above or below average returns. Two examples were mentioned; a third is that prices rise between 12.30 p.m. and 1.30 p.m., followed by a fall after lunch between 2.30 p.m. and 3.15 p.m.

A number of research studies have come up with similar conclusions, but with slight variations. For example the so called 'weekend effect' has been found by one researcher to begin to take effect on Friday afternoon. Few explanations have been offered for these intra-day effects. Most researchers on the subject have first shown the existence of such patterns and then indicated that further research is required before an explanation can be offered.

Day of the week effect

One explanation for this effect is to be found in the fact that the actions of investors are not consistent throughout the trading week. At weekends investors evaluate their own portfolio and initiate their own 'sell' decisions; they sell first thing on a Monday. 'Buy' decisions, in contrast, are usually initiated by brokers, and such actions are constant throughout the week.

The study by Abraham and Ikenberry [50] found that between 1982 and 1991 share prices on the New York Stock Exchange fell on Mondays by an average of 0.11%. They typically rose during the rest of the week. In fact seven of the worst 15 trading days were on a Monday.

It was found that there was disproportionately heavy selling of small amounts of shares on Mondays. Typically the sales were by individual investors, the weekend being the time when individuals consider their investment portfolio.

Months of the year effect

One of the more popular explanations for the patterns that give above average returns in April in the UK is the tax-loss selling hypothesis. The basis of this is that investors who have accrued losses on certain investments during a year have an incentive to engage in fiscal-year-end selling strategies. They sell the shares on which they show losses in order to create a tax shield against capital gains tax liabilities that arise on shares they hold that have made gains [51].

The result of so many investors in the UK selling shares in March (end of tax year) is to depress share price levels. Once into the new financial year the tax reason for selling disappears and the share levels rebound to their price levels before the end of the tax year. This means that buying shares at the beginning of either January (USA) or April (UK) and selling at the end of the respective month produces higher levels of return than can be obtained by adopting a similar strategy in the other months of the year.

Annual effects

Studies covering long time periods illustrate a so-called 'corrective' behaviour of share price returns. This is that the prices of individual shares or portfolios of shares that perform badly in one year are likely to do well in the next. The reverse also happens for shares that perform well in one year, but the process in asymmetric. It is the losing shares in one period that show the greater positive returns during the next.

Short-term overreaction

The more powerful statistical techniques now being employed in statistical analysis are revealing a number of anomalies. One of the most important of these, from the point of view of long-term decision-making, is that the market tends to 'overreact' in the short run.

Experimental and survey evidence indicates that there is a tendency for individuals to overweight recent information and underweight basic data. From a stock market point of view this means investors overreact to new earnings figures, and as a result stock prices can and do depart at least in the short run from their underlying fundamental values. The returns from a company investment in long-term projects such as those in R & D and advanced manufacturing systems are not reflected in the earnings figures for the early years of a project's life. Therefore, although such investments increase the fundamental value of a company, they are not immediately reflected in the market price of a company's shares.

De Bondt and Thaler and other researchers have found evidence that in the USA investors overreact to short-term earnings movements [52]. Investors focus on the immediate past and do not look beyond the immediate future. There is a close correspondence between share price returns and changes in the short-term earnings outlook. Investors, on average, have an excessively short-term orientation. There is no reason to believe that these results, based on the situation in the USA, do not apply to the UK; we have a similar financial system. As explained, the implications are not good for companies that undertake investments that will not show early earnings figures. They also indicate that it is important to management to show 'good' current earnings figures.

These findings are not, of course, what one would expect from an efficient market. But there is now increasing evidence that share prices do take swings away from fundamental values. The evidence is that these 'erroneous' movements away from fundamental values are eventually corrected: there is a mean reversion in share prices.

Poterba and Summers also show that there are transitory components in share prices; that is, there can be a move in the short run away from fundamental values. They found this with UK data as well as US data. These transitory components, this mispricing, are large in relation to what one would expect with stock market efficiency. This overreaction of the market to good and bad short-term earnings figures leads to volatility in investors' returns. The volatility in the market returns for investors is greater than what one would expect if market prices reflected fundamental values.

The implication of the short-term overreaction for those preparing accounts is to encourage them to emphasise short-term performance and to show a 'good' earnings per share figure. Long-term investments are reflected in the share price in the long run; they increase the fundamental value of the company, but the present value of such investments is not necessarily reflected in the price in the short run. This encourages 'the management of earnings disclosure'. It is why financial reports have to be read with care.

Size anomalies

Research has shown that in the long run the returns from investing in smaller companies give a slightly higher return than the average market performance across companies of all sizes. If the market is efficient this should not happen, i.e. unless the market risks from investing in smaller companies is above the average market risk. An investor knowing of this irregularity could devise trading rules to produce consistent above average returns.

Research in the USA found that smaller companies outperformed other companies over time on average by 4% per annum on a compound basis. Research was later conducted on data from many other countries and similar results were obtained. Dimson and March [53] published results for the UK based on the performance of as many as 1200 companies with market capitalizations of £100 million or less. They found that, on average, the small firms outperformed the larger firms by 6% per annum.

Fama and French have shown that it is possible to predict the prices of the shares of small firms [54].

How can this size effect be explained? Among the explanations that have been offered are the following.

Growth prospects

It is a fact that it is easier for small companies to grow more quickly than large, simply because of the lower starting base. Dividends and earnings of smaller companies do grow faster than those of the average size company. But this does not really explain the above average share price performance we are concerned with. If everyone knows that small companies show faster growth, then investors pay more for their shares, based on current earning levels, than they would for companies with slower growth. This is why faster-growth companies of any size have higher price-to-earnings ratios than lower growth companies.

Risk

Do smaller companies have higher non-diversifiable risks (betas) than large companies? If this is the case then investors would want an above average return to compensate for the risk. It has in fact been shown that smaller companies do have above average betas, but it has also been shown that this difference in betas is not sufficient to give a complete explanation of the size effect [55].

Trading costs

It is more expensive to trade in the shares of small companies than in those of large companies. The reason is that, because of infrequent trading in such securities, the commissions asked by dealers and the spread between the bid and offer price are higher than is the case for the more frequently traded larger companies. To compensate for their higher costs, investors require a higher gross profit on any buy/sell transaction in the shares of small companies. The empirical research that highlights the size effect is based on above average gross returns. The impact of high trading costs will bring down the net returns on the buying and selling of shares. This could mean that the net return from trading in small company shares is not very different from the average net return for all companies. If, however, the small company shares are not traded frequently, but are held for, say, a number of years, then the additional trading cost averaged over the years the shares are held will be low, and above average net returns can be obtained.

Seasonality

It has been observed in the USA that much of the size effect occurs in the month of January [56]. This means that the price of company shares falls in the last days of December and rises in the early days of January. This seasonal effect has been observed for all companies, not just small ones. As mentioned above, this so-called fiscal-year-end effect occurs in the UK between the end of March and the beginning of April. Possible explanations for this irregularity include actions taken by investors to reduce their capital gains tax bills. At the end of the tax year they realize their losses to be used to offset against gains. This has been referred to as 'the bed and breakfast' technique.

Seasonal irregularity could therefore be part of the explanation of the size irregularity, with institutional and private investors adjusting their portfolios for tax reasons.

The evidence does not come up with support for any one explanation of the size effect. The shares of small companies have been shown to be able to outperform the market. This has been the case for many years in a number of countries. We have a number of possible explanations for this effect, each contributing something to our understanding of the irregularity.

Lack of information

The market has less information about small companies than about large companies. Analysts spend less time studying the financial position of small companies. It is less likely therefore that the market price of smaller companies represents the fundamental value of the share of such a company, than for a large company. This means that there is an opportunity for the aware investor to make above average returns through investing in smaller companies. For the market to be efficient in the valuation of a company it is necessary to have a number of analysts studying the performance of a company. This is a problem in smaller capital markets, where there may not be enough analysis. It is a problem in the larger markets, because it is not possible for analysts to be knowledgeable about all quoted companies.

Can the market be fooled by creative accounting?

The fact that the major stock markets of the world – London, New York and Tokyo – were efficient was for a long time accepted as an act of faith. To suggest otherwise was to imply that one did not really understand the concept and did not know how to follow the vast empirical evidence on the topic. Recently, however, the evidence is being re-examined. The current position is that there is strong consistent evidence that markets such as London and New York are efficient, but there are some anomalies. These anomalies have shaken the faith of a few.

If the market is efficient, it should not on the whole be fooled by creative accounting techniques. Some investors might be, but not the overall market. Watts [57] concludes that 'manipulating reported earnings through accounting changes to increase the corporation stock prices will in most cases be a futile exercise'. The words 'in most cases' should be noted.

Most studies detect little or no reaction in the share price of a company to new accounting disclosures or to changes in accounting practices. Changes in inventory valuation methods, foreign currency translation methods, moves from the cost method to the equity method in reporting the earnings of related companies and moves from the merger to the acquisition accounting approach have been studied. No consistent evidence has been found that the resulting change in earnings per share affects the market price.

However, the directors of companies do still continue to manipulate earnings per share figures. They know of the existence of the EMH, but they still act as if they believe that the 'adjustment' or 'window dressing' of the financial accounts is worthwhile. Perhaps the fact that it has only been found that manipulation does not mislead the market in most cases encourages them. It has not been found that it does not work in *all* cases. The directors hope that their company accounts might be one of the few that the market does not 'read' properly in the short term.

The management of earnings disclosure

Creative accounting, has now been given a respectable name, 'the management of earnings disclosure'. Production people and sales people feel that it is they who are responsible for earning the profits of a company. Engineers often claim that it is they who are responsible for creating the wealth of a company or a country. This may be true. But it is the accountants who decide when shareholders and other investors will be told about the profits. It is possible to delay the disclosure of profits that have been earned, and to speed up the recognition of profits that will be earned.

Davidson, Stickney and Well, in discussing what they refer to as 'accounting magic', define the managing of earnings disclosure as:

A process of taking deliberate steps within the constraints of generally accepted accounting principles to bring about a desired level of earnings. [58]

Holmes and Sugden writing in 1990 refer to the fact that financial analysts expect some companies to 'try to show continuous growth year after year and to pull out all the stops to avoid reporting a downturn'. [59]

Smith lists 12 possible accounting techniques that can be used as a means of manufacturing profit. [60]

These techniques are:

1. Write down of pre-acquisition costs or potential future costs.
2. Profits on disposal of a business.
3. Deferred purchase consideration.
4. Extraordinary and exceptional items of income and expenditure.
5. Off-balance sheet finance.
6. Contingent liabilities.
7. Capitalization of costs.
8. Brand accounting.

9. Changes in depreciation policy.
10. Convertible securities.
11. Pension fund accounting.
12. Treatment of foreign currency items.

In fact all aware users of accounts know which are the items that allow for earnings manipulation. It is not always easy, however, to ascertain from the information disclosed exactly how a particular item has been treated.

Evidence of manipulation

Lev in his survey article on the usefulness of earnings research, concludes that 'prima facie evidence on manipulation of financial information is widespread' [61]. He quotes from Scholes *et al.* (1988) who found evidence of income smoothing [62]. Even banks have been found to manage their earnings disclosure. Allen and Saunders found 'almost 85% of banks in the sample window dressing their balance sheet upwards' [63].

McNichols and Wilson (1988) found evidence that firms manage their earnings 'by choosing income – decreasing accruals when income is extreme' [64]. This means that they adopt a policy of income smoothing. It is quite easy for banks to do this through varying their policy on bad debt provision. The reason a firm might wish to reveal lower income is of course to avoid criticism from regulatory agencies. The researchers believe however that whereas managers are able to alter some accruals the discretionary component of total accruals is only a small portion. A small portion of the debtors figure can, however, be a large portion of the profits figure.

A question that has worried investors and analysts for some time is what percentage of companies engage in the management of earnings disclosure. There are high profile cases that hit the headlines, such as Asil Nadir and Polly Peck, and Robert Maxwell and his group of companies. But the impression that those who are engaged in finance like to give is that these are just isolated cases, and that 99% of companies do not engage in deliberate manipulation in order to mislead.

It came as somewhat of a shock therefore when in the UK in 1992, Smith wrote his book entitled *Accounting for Growth* [65]. The contents of the book were greeted by many with surprise as was the fact that the author was an insider. The contents should not however have been a surprise to anyone engaged in the actual analysis of company accounts.

The results he reported were based on an analysis of the actual reporting practices of the major UK companies. Smith's research received widespread publicity as at the time of undertaking the research he was a banking analyst for UBS Phillips & Drew, one of the major UK brokers. He examined 12 areas in which dubious accounting methods were possible, and found that one company adopted as many as nine of these manipulation techniques. Two companies used eight, four used seven, 15 used six. To be fair there were a number of companies that only adopted managing disclosure practices in one of the 12 areas, and a few companies that had no dubious practices.

An interesting case study is that prepared by Brink that examines changes over a long period of time; it illustrates the problems. Brink analyses the actual changes in Philips' accounting policies from 1912 to the present time [66]. He also attempted to attach motives for the changes and the choices made by the board of the company. As Brink pointed out his conclusions are subjective as 'no research was conducted into what went on behind closed doors in the managers' boardroom'.

Philips is a particularly interesting company to examine as not only is it one of the largest European companies, it also has a respected reputation in the field of financial reporting. Brink points out the company has with 'increasing frequency changed the principles used in determining its results'. With respect to recent changes Brink believes the reasons given in the financial report to explain the changes have not always been convincing. 'The figures leave the strong suspicion that an improvement in the company result was a motive. Every important change in accounting occurred in a period of decreasing results, and each change led to a higher result.'

There were some occasions, however, where the company appeared to change its own policies in response to changes in accounting standards. For the company to have maintained its own policies and just to respond to the changes being forced upon it by external authorities would have led to a deterioration in the reported results of the company. Brink believes that 'in such situations, a company like Philips has a legitimate right, or even a duty, to change its policies on this point'. This is what the management of earnings disclosure is all about. The analyst has to decide whether the change in a company's accounting policies is a response to a 'genuine' need to change or an attempt to window dress.

It should be pointed out that what can appear to be manipulation can in fact be a genuine reflection of changed circumstances. For example, reducing the depreciation charge by lengthening the useful life of an asset could just be recognizing new knowledge. It would have been difficult for an airline company to appreciate the useful life of a Boeing 747 when it was first introduced.

Problems can arise, not because of any attempt to manipulate the reported figures, but just because of the fact that accounts have to be prepared every 12 months. At the end of an accounting period, many transactions will be incomplete, and in order to estimate profits many assumptions have to be made.

Why earnings management occurs

The reason why the earnings figures that are disclosed might be managed include:

1. Directors' remuneration schemes can create an incentive to manage earnings figures. Directors' bonus schemes are on occasions linked in some way to earnings per share. Directors often have only short-term contracts, sometimes one year or less. Why not speed up the recognition of profit so as to benefit from it as early as possible? The director may not be in office when profits on long-term ventures would normally pass through the accounts.
2. Asymmetry in information – managers have 'private' information that they can use when determining compensation or profit sharing rules among interested parties in the company.
3. Directors or one shareholder group may want to impress a 'prospective' shareholder group with the firm's past performance (inviting/encouraging takeover bid/buy-out).
4. Following a takeover bid, management wishes to impress its existing shareholders with its own performance.
5. Firms will smooth income to create an impression of a low variability in income to give the impression to lenders of low risk, therefore low interest rates.
6. Earnings fixation. In the UK (and in the USA) the users of accounts and consequently the preparers of accounts have become obsessed with the earnings figures – with what is sometimes called the bottom line. Whereas at one time in the UK, and still in some other countries accounts had a stewardship role, now the emphasis has shifted to earnings performance. It is the earnings per share, and the associated price earnings ratio, that dominate analysis of a company's performance and consequently investment prospects.

Tinic refers to the 'functional fixation hypothesis' which in the stock market context means that 'decision makers who are unfamiliar with different methods of producing accounting outputs rely on bottom line accounting numbers without paying attention to the procedures used in generating them [67]. If this hypothesis were proven it would mean that the efficient market hypothesis was incorrect; and that share prices do not reflect all available information. Tinic was not able to resolve the issue as to which hypothesis best explained stock market prices. The hypothesis does however illustrate the danger in users of accounts relying on the 'bottom line'.

The efficient market hypothesis and the investment analyst

Many changes have taken place in recent years in the securities industry. The ending of minimum price commissions on share dealing and the introduction of negotiated commissions has had an effect on the research undertaken by investment analysts and stockbrokers.

With negotiated commissions the buyer of shares has the opportunity to shop around to find a broker – a dealer – who is charging the lowest commission commensurate with the service that is being offered. Those buyers who want the benefit of research advice have to pay for it; those that do not want the advice do not.

As a result of negotiated commissions and the realization of how difficult it is to beat the market, there has been a change in emphasis in investment strategy in the USA and the UK. There has been an increase in interest in the concept of risk in investment. There are now unit trusts that just attempt to give a performance equal to that of the Stock Market Index, and they aim to achieve this with a low level of risk and with a policy of minimizing expenses by as little switching of investments as possible.

The efficient market does not mean that investment research should not be undertaken. In fact, paradoxically for the efficient market hypothesis to hold, it is necessary for many people to analyse and attempt to interpret the information that is made available. It is the action of competing investors that makes the market efficient. Each decision-maker, each investor, is searching for good companies that will make attractive investments. When they identify such companies, they force up the price of the share to one which, in the end, just leads to average returns. It is important that investors continue to seek good companies and then to buy the shares. For them not to do so, for them not to try to benefit from knowledge they obtain, would lead to inefficient markets – to share prices that do not reflect all the available information.

In an efficient market, the returns obtained depend upon a number of factors, one being the level of risk of the investments in a portfolio. If an investor is prepared to take heavy risks he can achieve above average performance for a time. Another factor is luck. A third factor is the level of transaction and management expenses paid for the portfolio management. A large amount of switching of investments increases expenses, and so the gross gains on the share dealings need to be higher to show an average profit net of expenses.

There are two other possible ways in which above average returns can be earned. One is for the investor to obtain inside information. This would give the investor the opportunity to earn exceptional returns, but as regulations on trading by insiders are tightened up, this reduces the opportunity for this type of gain. The second way in which such gains can be made is for a new form of analysis, a new insight into the stock market, to be discovered. The person or firm that discovers such a method would use the approach to make gains for themselves, but would probably not wish to make the technique known to others. This is a good reason for investment research. To try to discover such techniques has a cost, of course, and until the new technique gives above average results the net returns can be quite low.

An advantage of negotiated commissions is that if an investor wishes to encourage the search for such a technique, he can pay for it. If an investor wishes to be satisfied with an average performance from a portfolio at a reasonable level of risk, he can pay a low level of commission. It should be emphasized that it is an unconventional type of research that needs to be carried out. The same research that is being undertaken by all other brokers will not lead to above average returns. It could simply be an exceptional ability at interpreting the information that is available to all that is needed.

There is evidence which suggests that the lower is the level of transaction costs the easier it is to obtain above average returns. Those who do not have to bear heavy transaction costs can make above average profits. A high level of trading with a high level of transaction cost appears to do little for performance. In the USA, Niederhoffer and Osborne [68] have shown that those investors who do not have to pay any commission expenses or who pay very little can and do achieve superior risk-adjusted investment returns.

The evidence seems to suggest that the most profitable strategy for a portfolio manager is on average a buy and hold strategy rather than one with a great deal of switching. The new direction in research is to spend time analysing the risk preferences of the clients and the risks attached to any particular portfolio of securities. A particular portfolio can then be designed to meet the needs of a particular group of investors. The wishes of the clients have to be taken into account more when there are negotiated commissions than when there is a set scale of fees. The client will not have to take all the services which a broker is offering but will be able to shop around to find one offering only what he needs.

One investment philosophy postulates that it is not the decision on which company's share to buy that is of major importance, but the timing of the purchase and sale. The price of even what can be classed as a relatively weak company's share fluctuates over time and so gains can be made by the investor from buying and selling at the 'right' times. The problem then becomes no longer one of deciding which shares are underpriced or overpriced, but a matter of deciding when the turning points in the movement of share prices will occur. It is claimed by the analysts who support this philosophy that it is more rewarding to forecast market turning points than to try to estimate the 'real value' of company shares. The problem with attempting to determine whether a particular share is undervalued at a particular point of time is that even though the analysis may be correct, the investor may have to hold the share for a long period before the share price moves to its correct value and gains can be realized. More immediate gains can be made from reacting to expected turning points in the market.

It is obviously true that finding an undervalued share can lead to considerable gains, but for an institution that has a large amount of funds to invest and wishes to spread these over a number of company shares, it may be more worthwhile to study turning points and invest in shares that will change in line with the expected price movement.

Fundamental analysis versus technical analysis

The 'efficient' market implies that, given the available information, there is an intrinsic value for a share, and that the actual share price will equal that value. This means that a market analyst cannot expect to purchase shares that are underpriced unless he has inside information or responds more quickly to new information than other investors. This does not mean that he does not or should not try.

Analysts who try to determine the intrinsic worth of a share undertake what is referred to as fundamental analysis. There is another group of analysts who do not concern themselves with the factors that influence the worth of a particular share. They analyse charts and look for patterns in the movement over time of a company's share price. These 'chartists' undertake what is referred to as a technical analysis.

If investors expect a certain thing to happen, the action expressing their expectations can make sure the event does come about: it is a self-fulfilling prophecy. For example, if investors for some reason expect share prices to fall, they will start to sell, a bear market will be created, and prices will duly fall. It is on the basis of these psychological factors influencing share prices that a chartist can be successful. The chartist studies the movement of share prices over time, either the aggregate price level or the prices of a particular company. He looks for either recurring patterns of price movements or recurring interrelationships between stock price movements and other market data.

One situation that a chartist would identify, cause by the behaviour of investors, is referred to as a 'resistance zone' or 'supply area'. Suppose for example that a share is sold in considerable volume at a price of £1.25, and many investors acquire it at this price. The volume of business in the share then falls, and the price consequently declines. The shareholders will tend to hold onto the share until the price recovers. As the price slowly moves through £0.80 and £0.90 to £1.10 these former buyers will still be reluctant to sell at a loss; it is when the price approaches £1.25 that it would be expected that many of the former buyers would begin to sell. The price of £1.20 or £1.25 has become a 'supply area'.

Another such situation arises where an investor, thinking of buying a particular share at a price of say £0.40, suddenly finds the price has jumped to £0.60. He hears stories explaining the rise and generally boosting the shares of that particular company. The investor is annoyed that he did not buy the share when it first occurred to him. If the price of that company's shares ever gets back to near £0.40, he will buy. The price of £0.40 has become a support area. Investors may not actually think this way but if they act as if they do, the results will be the same.

One technique of the chartists that has been shown statistically to be useful for prediction purposes is the study of advances and declines. Records are kept on most stock exchanges of the number of shares which advance and decline on a particular trading day. Dividing these numbers by the number of shares traded on the exchange on the particular day gives the proportion of shares advancing and declining, and therefore shows the proportion remaining unchanged. It has been demonstrated that given knowledge of these movements in the shares on the market for one day, it is possible to predict the number of advances and declines for the next day.

This analysis of what is called the breadth of the market 'can be used to determine the major turning points in the market as a whole'. The theory is based on the notion of stock market cycles. It is based on the idea that bull markets are long drawn out affairs, during which time the individual shares gradually reach their peak, with the number of shares reaching their peaks accelerating as the market averages rise towards the turning point. When a share has reached its peak, obviously its next price movement is a decline, so that the number of shares showing a decline in their price accelerates as the market index approaches its turning point.

The breadth of the market is defined as the cumulative net advances or declines, that is the addition of the net advances or declines over a period of time. Obviously if different researchers begin their cumulative calculations on different dates, the series of results they will obtain will differ. This does not matter too much, however, as it is the change in the level that is being studied, not the absolute level.

The breadth of the market needs to be studied in conjunction with an index of stock market prices. Normally the index and the breadth statistics move in line: both are rising or both are falling. It is claimed by the supporters of this theory that when the two series move out of line this indicates an expected turning point in the market. When the breadth line starts to decline, with the index still rising, this indicates that the bull market will shortly be coming to an end.

Many techniques are used by chartists in addition to the two ('the breadth of the market' and 'resistance areas') that have been mentioned. Practically none of the techniques has been found to be statistically valid. But chartists survive, along with other types of analysts. Whatever technique is used it must be correct a sufficient number of times because chartists remain in business. The techniques that the chartist use, such as 'the head and shoulders' and 'downside breaks', might be given colourful names and be hard to justify in theory, but at least they must have kept investors as satisfied as the apparently more sophisticated approaches.

In the short term at least the movement of a company's share price follows a random pattern. However, there are reasons why at certain times there might be a significant change in the direction of movement. The theory of turning points is not concerned with the near impossible task of predicting the changes over the medium and longer term. The long-term trend in share prices is known to be in an upward direction, but this is not a smooth path. The national income of most developed countries is expected to increase over time, but nevertheless there are business cycles in which in certain years or certain periods the total national income may well fall from the level of the previous year or the previous period. The profits of companies fluctuate through these business cycles, and there is thought to be a relationship between the level of stock market prices and overall business activity. If this relationship can be established and it becomes possible to forecast the level of business activity, then a method of predicting at least part of any share price movement will have been established.

Historically the incomes of firms have tended to move together. There is evidence that a certain amount of the change in any company's profits in a year is due to economy-wide effects and to industry effects. One study has found that about one-half of the variability in the level of an average firm's earnings per share from year to year could be associated with effects common to other firms [69]. Of this, 10–15% of the change could be associated with the movement of the industry profits (variance of firms within this industry), and 35–40% could be associated with the variability of earnings data averaged over all firms.

King reached a similar conclusion when studying the factors influencing company share price changes over monthly intervals [70]. Some of the information which became known during these periods was concerned with the overall economy, such as changes in national production or interest rates; other pieces of information were relevant to a particular industry, such as changes in order levels or in technology. King, after examining the effects of these changes, concluded that 'the typical stock has about half of its variance explained by an element of price change that affects the whole market. Note, however, that there is a considerable variation in these figures from industry to industry as well as over time.'

Part of the changes in a company's earnings can therefore be anticipated from economy-wide data. Certain relationships exist between the level of stock market prices and overall business activity; these relationships have been sufficiently stable in the past to expect them to recur in the future.

One way to attempt to predict turning points is simply to forecast the level of the stock market indices. Some companies' prices will have turned before the index changes direction, but others will change after. Attempts have been made to ascertain which companies' share prices lead the market. Coen, Gomme, and Kendall have had some success in forecasting the Financial Times Index and the Standard and Poors Index [71].

The peaks and troughs in the stock market frequently precede turning points in general business activity. It is, therefore, necessary to forecast the economic turning points several months in advance of the event if an investor is to act before the changes occur in the stock market price levels. There are now many agencies and researchers forecasting the movement of the national income and overall company profitability.

Individual companies can, however, perform in a manner not expected from the trend in aggregate levels. The justification for forecasting aggregate profit levels is that the stock market index moves in line with profit levels. It is suggested that forecasting turning points in profit levels and so in the stock market index enables an investor to decide when to buy and sell. It is possible, however, that a particular company's earnings will not behave in the same way as the trend, and so its price will not move in the same direction as the index. This is one difficulty with the approach of forecasting aggregate profits and the share price index, rather than the profits and share price of particular companies.

The Ball and Brown study concentrating on macroeconomic indicators and industry indicators fails to explain about 50% of the variance between the change in profit levels of companies [72]. This variance can be explained by factors internal to a particular firm, and the quality of the management is obviously of key importance in determining this element of the profit. While there are many factors outside the control of management that influence the level of profits, the studies suggest that 50% of the difference in the change in profit levels can be accounted for by individual company differences.

An individual company's past profit levels cannot be relied upon as a guide to its future profits. Past profits may, however, be used to give an indication of above-average management ability. Accordingly, the forecasting of economy and industry factors together with knowledge of the quality of a particular company's management may give some guidance to the future company profit level.

One implication of the finding on the overreaction to short-term news is that a good investment strategy for investors is to invest in shares that have recently declined in value. The decline could well be the result of the market overreacting to bad short-term earnings figures. It is now known that the market will, over time, revert back to fundamental values, resulting in a gain to the investor following the suggested strategy above that which would be expected if the current price accurately reflected the available information.

The overreaction to short-term news (referred to in the section on anomalies) increases the volatility in investors' market returns and thus their risks. Because of the higher risks they concentrate, understandably, on a short-term horizon. In fact if it were realized that stock price movements contain large transitory components, then for long horizon investors the stock market may be less risky than it appears to be when the variance of single period returns is extrapolated.

In other words, if it was appreciated that the stock market was not efficient in all respects, that share prices do not follow a random walk, then investors might take a longer-term approach to equity investment. The market overreacts in the short run but the evidence is that it then corrects itself and moves over time to fundamental values; there is what is referred to as mean reversion. This indicates that early movements are later corrected, and so risks are less than if this mean reversion did not occur.

Implications of the efficient market hypothesis for company financing decisions

The hypothesis has some implications that should concern the company financial manager. We shall consider three of these.

1. Can the timing of the issue of shares affect the cost of capital?
2. Does the sale of new shares affect the price of the existing securities?
3. Are there companies that can be purchased at bargain prices?

What we often find is that the folklore on these topics leads to decisions which are out of line with what we would expect from the existence of an efficient stock market and its resulting implications. The lessons of the EMH and the empirical support found for it are not always learned by company financial managers. Sometimes it is a matter of the implications not being understood; sometimes it is a matter of the EMH not being believed.

Issuing new shares

A company is thinking of issuing new shares. The EMH tells investors that the current price of the company's shares reflects all publicly available information. If the directors have good news about the future that has not yet been made available to the market, to sell new shares at the current price would not be in the interest of the current shareholders. When the market has absorbed the good news the share price will rise. It is at this point that the new shares should be sold. With this policy new shareholders are having to pay a fair price for the shares: they are not obtaining a bargain.

If, however, the directors have inside knowledge of bad news, the release of which will depress the share price, to sell shares at the current price will benefit existing shareholders. It will of course mean that new shareholders lose. In whose interest should directors act? There are of course laws concerned with trading on the basis of inside information.

Clearly the EMH does have implications for the timing of share issues. However, it is only because of inside information that the timing of new issues should matter. It is not because stock market prices are perceived to be 'high' or 'low'. Sometimes it is suggested that managers are reluctant to issue new shares after there has been a general fall in share prices, and that they are keen to issue new shares after a general rise in prices. If this is the case it is illogical according to the EMH. A sequence of past prices, ending in a rise or a fall, tells us nothing about future prices. According to the EMH, to attempt to beat the market is on average a waste of time. Selling equity at a price which is classed as 'high' based on past movements does not mean cheap finance. The price is high because investors expect good returns in the future. They pay this 'high' price, and the company has to deliver these good returns to satisfy them.

In the absence of information not available to the market, to try to time issues to catch the market while it is at a high will on average be a waste of time.

Sale of large blocks of shares

A second area of concern to financial managers is the effect on the share price of a sale of new shares. It might be thought that the new shares increase the total supply, and an increase in supply without an increase in demand will mean that share prices fall. Certain practitioners do believe that new issues depress prices, but if the market is large enough to be able to absorb the issue, is efficient and is convinced that the new funds will earn a return at least as high as the return earned on existing funds, there is no logical reason why the share price should fall.

The share price will reflect the available information. Therefore it is important when making the issue to convince the market that the level of earnings will be maintained. If investors believe that the directors of the company have inside information and that this is affecting the timing of a new issue, then they may require a discount on the pre-issue price. Also, if they believe that an issue is being timed to catch a market high, then the share price might fall following news of the issue.

The empirical evidence on this topic does indicate that the market is efficient and can absorb large issues by a company without depressing prices. A study of the US market by Scholes [73] showed that the average effect of secondary offerings was a slight reduction in share price, but that the size of the fall was independent of the size of the issue.

Acquisitions

One motive for a merger or acquisition is to obtain a bargain. This means that the directors of the acquiring company believe that the shares of the victim company are underpriced. The EMH tells us that the share price should reflect all publicly available information. In general this has been shown to be the case. Therefore, unless the directors of the acquiring company have information not available to the market, they cannot expect to show above average returns from basing an acquisition policy on the 'bargain' motive. On some occasions the shares of a company acquired will have been undervalued and they will win, but on other occasions the shares will have been overvalued and they will lose. On average the market price will reflect the intrinsic value.

Financial rewards

If managers know the market is not efficient, in that there is mispricing in the short run, it could benefit them to make use of this fact. The market will overreact to good short-term earnings figures, thus give the market what it wants. The earnings figures can be manipulated in the short run. Even if the management does not want to resort to manipulation it may still be concerned about investing funds in projects with a long-term horizon which do not give them the opportunity to show early profits. From the managers' point of view, projects that will make them look good in the short run are more attractive than those with long-term horizons. In the short run the 'exaggerated' share price could result in bonuses, promotion, or a share price which could be used as a base for an acquisition strategy. At least the high price is a protection against being taken over by predators. This leads to 'financially aware' management concentrating on short-term performance. We are not saying that in the long run the market price will not move to reflect fundamental values, but the long run is the future! Better for the managers good results now.

13.9 Summary

There are three levels of market efficiency. In most respects the leading stock exchanges appear to be efficient; however, there are anomalies and there is evidence that the markets do not always satisfy the strong form tests.

It is necessary to understand what efficiency means with respect to the pricing of a company's shares. How does new information affect the share price? Do those operating in the market all have access to the same information?

Financial managers in companies need to appreciate the efficient market concept as it has lessons with respect to the timing of new issues, dividend announcements and manipulating accounting numbers.

13.10 Key terms

Allocational efficiency
Anomalies
Creative accounting
Earnings fixation
Efficient market hypothesis
Fads and bubbles
Fair game model
Fundamental analysis

Good news/bad news
Insider dealing
Pricing efficiency
Random walk
Semi-strong test
Technical analysis
Weak form tests

13.11 Revision questions

1. Do all share prices reflect intrinsic values?
2. Is it worth the effort for a particular company to engage in creative accounting techniques?
3. In what respects might stock markets not be efficient in all aspects?
4. It has been suggested in some countries that any investor would be foolish to trade in shares without having access to inside information. Would this, in your opinion, be the situation in the London Stock Exchange?
5. Why are some investors sceptical about the EMH?
6. Is an implication of the EMH that it is never worth one company taking over another company because it believes that it can buy it at a bargain price?
7. Does the EMH mean that there are no abnormal returns available to the well-informed investor?
8. Does the EMH mean that in selecting a portfolio of shares one might just as well rely on sticking pins in the list of companies shown at the back of the *Financial Times*, as on reading and absorbing the information given elsewhere in that paper?
9. What is the semi-strong test of the EMH? Why is it so called? What are its implications?
10. Why do companies spend so much money in producing 'glossy' annual reports, when the evidence suggests that most of the information contained is reflected in the company's share price before the release of the report?

13.12 References

1. Copeland, T.E. and Weston, J.F. (1983) *Financial Theory and Corporate Policy*, 2nd edn, Addison-Wesley, Reading, MA.
2. Mossin, J. (1977) *The Economic Efficiency of Financial Markets*, Prentice Hall, Englewood Cliffs, NJ.
3. Samuelson, P.A. (1965) Proof that properly anticipated prices fluctuate randomly, *Industrial Management Review*, **6**, 41–9, Spring.
4. Mandelbrot, B. (1966) Forecasts of future prices, unbiased markets and martingale models, *Journal of Business (Security Prices), A Supplement*, **39**, 242–55, January.
5. Fama, E.F. (1970) Efficient capital markets: a review of theory and empirical work, *Journal of Finance*, 383–416, May.

6. Markowitz, H.M. (1959) *Portfolio Selection: Efficient Diversification of Investments*, Wiley, New York.

7. Beaver, W. (1981) *Financial Reporting: An Accounting Revolution*, Prentice Hall, Englewood Cliffs, NJ.

8. Smith, A. (1968) *The Money Game*, Random House, New York.

9. Kendall, M.G. (1953) The analysis of economics time series, Part 1 – Prices, *Journal of the Royal Statistical Society*, 11–25.

   Granger, C.W.J. and Morgenstern, O. (1969) *The Predictability of Stock Market Prices*, Princeton University Press.

10. Brealey, R.A. (1970) The distribution and independence of successive rates of return from the British equity market, *Journal of Business Finance*.

    Cunningham, S.W. (1973) The predictability of British stock market pricers, *Applied Statistics*, **22**.

11. Kemp, A.G. and Reid, G.C. (1971) The random walk hypothesis and the recent behaviour of equity prices in Britain, *Economica*, **38**.

12. Fama, E. (1965) The behaviour of stock market prices, *Journal of Business*, 34–106, January.

13. Alexander, S.S. (1961) Price movements in speculative markets: trends of random walks, *Industrial Management Review*, 7–26, May.

14. Fama, E.F. Efficient capital markets: a review of theory and empirical work, *Journal of Finance*, **25**, 287–417 (this paper provides a comprehensive bibliography of studies up to 1970 including work by Bachelier, Roberts, Cootner, Osborne, Kendal, Cowles, Moore, Granger and Morgenstern, as well as by Fama himself).

15. Fama, E.F., Fisher, L., Jensen, M.C. and Roll, R. (1969) The adjustment of stock prices to new information, *International Economic Review*, February.

16. Firth, M.A. (1977) An empirical investigation of the impact of the announcement of capitalization issues on share prices, *Journal of Business Finance and Accounting*, Spring.

17. Marsh, P. (1977) Ph.D Dissertation, London Graduate School of Business Studies.

18. Green, D., Jr and Segal, J. (1967) The predictive power of first-quarter earnings reports, *Journal of Business*, 44–45, January.

19. Brown, P. and Niederhoffer, V. (1968) The predictive content of quarterly earnings, *Journal of Business*, 488–98, October.

20. Ball, R. (1978) Anomalies in relationship between securities, yields and yield-surrogates, *Journal of Financial Economics*, June–September.

    Joy, O.M. and Jones, C.P. (1978) Earnings reports and market efficiencies: an analysis of the contrary evidence, *Journal of Financial Research*, Spring.

    Rendleman, R.J., Jones, C.P. and Latane, H.A. (1982) Empirical anomalies based on unexpected earnings and the importance of risk adjustments, *Journal of Financial Economics*, November.

    Foster, G., Olsen, C. and Shelvin, T. (1984) Earnings releases, anomalies and the behaviour of security returns, *Accounting Review*, October.

21. Ball, R. and Brown, P. (1968) An empirical evaluation of accounting income numbers, *Journal of Accounting Research*, 159–78, Autumn.

22. Franks, J.R., Broyles, J.E. and Hecht, M.J. (1978) An industry study of the profitability of mergers in the United Kingdom, *Journal of Finance*.

23. Firth, M. (1976) *Share Prices and Mergers*, Saxon House.

24. Abdel-Khalik, A.R. and Ajinkya, B.B. (1980) Accounting information and efficient markets. In *Handbook of Accounting and Auditing* (eds J.C. Burton, R.E. Palmer and R.S. Kay), Warren, Gareham, and Lamont, Boston, MA.

25. Finnerty, J.E. (1976) Insiders and market efficiency, *Journal of Finance*, September.

    Jaffe, J.J. (1974) Special information and insider trading, *Journal of Business*, July.

    Lorie, J. and Niederhoffer, V. (1978) Predictive and statistical properties of insider trading, *Journal of Law and Economics*, April.

26. Levy, H. and Lerman, Z. (1985) Testing p/e ratio filters by stochastic dominance rules, *Journal of Portfolio Management*.

27. Firth, M.A. (1972) The performance of share recommendations made by investment analysts and the effects on market efficiency, *Journal of Business Finance*, **4**.
28. Cootner, P. (1962) Stock prices: random vs. systematic changes, *Industrial Management Review*, 231–52, Spring.
29. Roll, Richard R. (1988) R-squared. *Journal of Finance*, **43**, July, 541–66.
30. Cutler, David M., James M. Porterba, and Lawrence H. Summers (1989) What moves stock prices? *Journal of Portfolio Management*, **15**, Spring, 4–12.
31. Cootner, P. op. cit.
32. De Long, J. Bradford, Andrei Shleifer, Lawrence H. Summers, and Robert J. Waldemann (1989) The size and incidence of the losses from noise trading. *Journal of Finance*, **44**, July, 681–96.
33. Soros, George (1987) *The Alchemy of Finance*, New York: Simon & Schuster.
34. Jensen, M.C. (1978) Some anomalies evidence regarding market efficiency. *Journal of Financial Economics*, **6**, June/Sept., 95–102.
35. Jensen, M.C. (1988) Takeovers: their causes and consequences. *Journal of Economic Perspectives*, **2**(1).
36. Peacock, A. and Bannock, G. (1991) *Corporate Takeovers and the Public Interest*, Aberdeen University Press.
37. Black, F. (1986) Noise, *Journal of Finance*, **41**, 529–34.
38. Stiglitz, J.E. (1988) Why financial structure matters, *Journal of Economic Perspectives*, **2**(4), 121–6.
39. Modigliani, F. (1988) MM – past, present, future, *Journal of Economic Perspectives*, **2**(4), 149–58.
40. Modigliani, F. and Cohn, R.A. (1979) Inflation, rational expectation, and the market, *Financial Analysts Journal*, **35**(2), 24–44.
41. Campbell, J.Y. and Kyle, A.S. (1988) *Smart Money, Noise Trading and Stock Prices Behaviour*, Princeton University, mimeo.
42. Bhattachara, S. (1988) Corporate finance and the legacy of Miller and Modigliani, *Journal of Economic Perspectives*, **2**(4), 135–47.
43. Roll, R. op. cit.
44. Bernard, V.L. and Thomas, J. (1990) Evidence that stock prices do not fully reflect the implications of current earnings. *Journal of Accounting and Economics*, **13**, 305–40.
45. Whittington, G. (1986) Financial accounting theory: an overview, *British Accounting Review*, **18**(2), Autumn, 4–41.
46. Coenenberg, A.G. (1988) *Jahresabschluß und Jahresabschlußanalyse*, Verlag Moderne Industrie, Landsberg am Lech, 10th edn.
47. Choi, F.D.S. and Levich, R.M. (1990) *The Capital Market Effects and International Accounting Diversity*, New York University, Irwin.
48. Hawawini, G. (1984) *European Equity Markets: Price Behaviour and Efficiency*, New York University Monograph Series in Finance and Economics.
49. *The Economist* (1993) (Supplement) Frontiers of Finance, 9–15, Oct.
50. Abraham, A. and D. Ikenberry (1994) The individual investor and the weekend effect. *Journal of Financial and Quantitative Analysis*, June.
51. Gultekin, M. and Gultekin N. (1983) Stock market seasonality: international evidence. *Journal of Financial Economics*, December.
    Haugen, R.A. and Lakonishok, K. (1988) *The Incredible January Effect*, Dow Jones, Irwin, IL.
52. De Bondt, W.F. and Thaler, R.H. (1987) Further evidence on investment overreaction and stock market seasonality. *Journal of Finance*, July.
    Poterba, J.M. and Summers, L.H. (1988) Mean reversion in stock prices: evidence and implications. *Journal of Financial Economics*, **22**, 27–59.
53. Dimson, E. and March, P. (1986) Event study methodologies and the size effect. *Journal of Financial Economics*, **17**(1), 113–42.
54. Fama, E.F. and French, K.R. (1988) Permanent and temporary components of stock prices, *Journal of Political Economy*, **96**, 246–73.

55. Roll, R. (1981) A possible explanation for the small firm effect, *Journal of Finance*, September.

Reinganum, M. (1982) A direct test of Roll's conjecture on the firm size effect, *Journal of Finance*, March.

Chan, K.C., Chen, N. and Hsieh, D. (1985) An exploratory investigation of the firm size effect. *Journal of Financial Economics*, September.

56. Keim, D. (1983) Size related anomalies and stock return reasonability: further empirical evidence, *Journal of Financial Economics*, June.

Keim, D. and Stambaugh, R. (1984) A further investigation of the week-end effect in stock returns, *Journal of Finance*, July.

57. Watts, R. (1986) Does it pay to manipulate E.P.S., in *The Revolution in Corporate Finance* (eds. J.M. Stern and D.M. Chen), Blackwell, Oxford.

58. Davidson, S., Stickney, C. and Weil, R. (1987) *Accounting: The Language of Business*, 7th edn, Horton, Arizona.

59. Holmes, G. and Sugden, A. (1990) *Interpreting Company Reports and Accounts*, 4th edn, Woodhead Faulkner, Cambridge.

60. Smith, T. (1992) *Accounting for Growth*, Century Business, London.

61. Lev, B. (1989) On the usefulness of earnings and earnings research: lessons and directions from two decades of empirical research. *Journal of Accounting Research*.

62. Scholes, M.S., Wilson, P. and Wolfson, M.A. (1990) Tax planning, regulatory capital planning and financial reporting strategy for commercial banks. *Review of Financial Studies*, **3**(4), 625–50.

63. Allen, L. and Saunders, A. (1988) Incentives to engage in bank window dressing: manager vs stockholder conflicts, working paper, Hofstra University.

64. McNichols, M. and Wilson, P. (1988) Evidence of earnings management from the provision for bad debts. *Journal of Accounting Research*, **26**, Supplement, 1–31.

65. Smith, T. *op. cit.*

66. Brink, H.L. (1992) A history of Philips' accounting policies on the basis of its annual reports. *European Accounting Review*, **1**, 255–75.

67. Tinic, S.H. (1990) A perspective on the market's fixation on accounting numbers, *Accounting Review*, **65**(4), 781–96, Oct.

68. Niederhoffer, V. and Osborne, H. (1986) Market making and reversal on the stock exchange. *Journal of the American Statistical Association*, Dec.

69. Ball, R. and Brown, P. (1968) An empirical evaluation of accounting income numbers. *Journal of Accounting Research*, Autumn, 159–78.

70. King, B.F. (1966) Market and industry factors in stock price behaviour. *Journal of Business*, Jan., 139–90.

71. Coen, P.J. Gomme, E.D. and Kendall, M.G. (1969) Lagged relationships in economic forecasting. *Journal of the Royal Statistical Society*, A, 132.

72. Ball, R. and Brown, P. *op. cit.*

73. Scholes, M. (1972) The market for securities: Substitution versus price pressure and the effects of information on share prices. *Journal of Business*, April.

You will notice from the extensive list of references for this chapter that there is a lot of material available. Some interesting further reading is listed below.

13.13 Further reading

Atkins, A.B. and Dyl, E.A. (1993) Reports of the death of the efficient markets hypothesis are greatly exaggerated! *Applied Financial Economics*, **3**, 95–100.

Bromwich, M. (1992) *Financial Reporting, Information and Capital Markets*, Pitman, London.

Demski, J. and Feltham, G. (1994) Market response to financial reports. *Journal of Accounting and Economics*, **17**.

Dimson, E. (ed.) (1988) *Stock Market Anomalies*, Cambridge, Cambridge University Press.

Fama, E.F. (1991) Efficient Capital Markets II. *Journal of Finance*, **46**, Dec. 1575–1617.

Manne, H. (1966) *Insider Trading and the Stock Market*, Free Press, New York.

Rosenberg, B., Reid, K., and Lanstein, R. (1985) Persuasive evidence of market inefficiency. *Journal of Portfolio Management*, **12**, 9–16.

Shleifer, A. and Summers, L.H. (1990) The novice trader approach to finance. *Journal of Economic Perspectives*, **4**(2), 19–33.

The Economist (1993) Frontiers of Finance (Supplement), 9–15 Oct.

West, K.D. (1988) Bubbles, fads and stock price volatility tests: A partial evaluation. *Journal of Finance*, **43**(3).

Zarowin, P. (1990) Size, seasonality and stock market overreaction. *Journal of Financial and Quantitative Analysis*, **25**, 113–25.

13.14 Problems

1. Explain why new equity issues are more common when share prices are high than when the share price index is low. To what extent can the reasons given be considered inconsistent with the efficient markets hypothesis?

2. Describe the efficient market hypothesis and distinguish between its three forms. Discuss the relevance of the hypothesis for the internal financial management of publicly quoted companies.

3. It has not been possible to disprove the efficient market hypothesis in the advanced capital markets of the USA and the UK. Describe the types of empirical research undertaken to test the validity of the hypothesis. Pay attention to the manner in which efficiency is interpreted in the tests you describe.

4. (a) Explain what you understand by the term 'efficient markets model' and compare efficiency in this context with the economist's idealized perfect market model.

   (b) Outline and appraise the types of empirical research undertaken to test the validity of the efficient markets hypothesis.

5. 'The results of this paper have indicated that on average managers of unit trusts in the UK have not been able to forecast share prices accurately enough to outperform a simple buy-and-hold policy.' (Firth)

   Firth's work seems to confirm Jensen's earlier research on US mutual funds. Discuss the validity of their findings and the implications of their conclusions for unit trust managers and investors if they are correct.

6. (a) Explain the differences between the three forms of the efficient market hypothesis. How does the existence of an efficient capital market assist corporate financial management and planning?

   (b) Company A has two million shares in issue and Company B has five million.

   On day 1 the market value per share is £1 for A and £2 for B.

   On day 2 the management of B decide, at a private meeting, to make a cash takeover bid for A at a price of £1.50 per share. The takeover will produce large operating savings with a present value of £1.6 millions.

   On day 4 B publicly announces an unconditional offer to purchase all shares of A at a price of £1.50 per share with settlement on day 15. Details of the large savings are not announced and are not public knowledge.

   On day 10 B announces details of the savings which will be derived from the takeover.

   Ignoring tax and the time value of money between day 1 and 15, and assuming that the details given are the only factors having an impact on the share prices of A and B, determine the day 2, day 4 and day 10 share prices of A and B if the market is

(i) semi-strong form efficient and

(ii) strong form efficient.   (15 marks)

ACCA, Financial Management,
December 1984

7. 'Among the investment lessons that the efficient market hypothesis teaches us are the following:

   • Randon selection of securities is as good as any other. Therefore, practise your dart throwing skill.
   • A buy-and-hold policy is as good as any other. Therefore, it is not necessary to follow and keep up with the fundamentals of the companies in which you own securities.' (Bernstein, 1975).

   (a) Explain what you understand by the term 'efficient market hypothesis' and describe the categories of test relating to the model and their significance for the validity of the model.
   (b) Examine the validity of the above statements for (i) the investment manager of a large pension fund and (ii) a small private investor.

8. 'Recent evidence suggests either that the market is inefficient or that the capital asset pricing model is inadequate.' Discuss.

9. Discuss the relative merits of an index fund and an actively managed portfolio of quoted investments and comment on the basis on which the manager of an investment portfolio might seek to justify the employment of an investment analyst.

10. Discuss the scope for management action to minimize the cost of capital in an efficient market. In relation to this objective comment specifically on the significance of pre-emptive rights for existing shareholders to subscribe to new issues of equity, the discount to market price at which such new issues are made and the timing of such issues in relation to market 'highs'.

11. The ABC Pharmaceutical Company announces that it is to produce a new drug. It was not known before the announcement that the company had been successful in its research programme into the effects of this drug. The price of an equity share in ABC before the announcement was £2.30.

    Consider the following scenarios:

    1. Following the announcement the price of an equity share in ABC jumps to £3, and then over the next week falls back to £2.70.
    2. Following the announcement the price of an equity share jumps to £2.70 and stays there.
    3. Following the announcement the price slowly climbs to £2.70.

    Question
    Which scenario indicates an efficient market? Which do not? Why?

12. 'The evidence on the Capital Asset Pricing Model is mixed. The theory fits the data fairly well but there are some anomalies.' Comment on the above statement.

13. Discuss the recent attempts to curb insider dealing in the context of a general view that history has demonstrated that it cannot be policed.

14. The 70-year-old chairman, chief executive and founder of a computer company dies. The price of that company's shares falls from £3 to £2. Is this fall in price evidence of an inefficient stock market? Why?

15. The following statement contains several errors. Explain what these errors are.

    According to the efficient market hypothesis all share prices are correct at all times. This is achieved by prices moving randomly when new information is publicly announced. New information from published accounts is the only determinant of the random movements in share price.

    Fundamental and technical analysts of the stock market serve no function in making the market efficient and cannot predict future share prices. Corporate financial managers are also unable to predict future share prices.

16. Discuss the implications of the Efficient Markets Hypothesis for managerial decisions in each of the following areas:

(a) the choice of accounting policies;
(b) dividend policy;
(c) the timing of new share issues.

(10 marks)
ICAEW, July 1993

14 Long-term debt finance

14.1	Introduction	427
14.2	Debentures and bonds	428
14.3	Medium-term notes	430
14.4	Long-term bank and institutional borrowing	432
14.5	Register of charges	433
14.6	Corporate bond market	434
14.7	Mezzanine finance and junk bonds	436
14.8	The value of fixed-interest securities	438
14.9	The cost of debt capital	443
14.10	Bonds: a variety of features	445
14.11	Securitzation	447
14.12	Redemption of bonds	448
14.13	Call provision	449
14.14	Special-purpose transactions	452
14.15	Long-term versus short-term borrowing	455
14.16	Interest-rate swaps	461
14.17	Debt–equity swaps	464
14.18	Repayment of loans	464
14.19	Convertible loan stock	468
14.20	Warrants	477
14.21	Revision questions	483
14.22	References	483
14.23	Further reading	483
14.24	Problems	484

The early parts of this chapter are descriptive. There are then sections on the valuation of fixed-interest securities, on the call provision and on convertible loan stocks and warrants.

The reader should appreciate the different types of loan finance and the guarantees and covenants involved. There are changes taking place in the bond market and in the type of securities being traded: these should be understood. There are well-developed techniques for valuing bonds, which can be utilized to value convertibles and warrants.

The chapter considers the methods for valuing the cost of debt capital.

It is often difficult in the accounting and finance area to draw demarcation lines. One problem arises in drawing a line between long-term and medium-term funds. The distinction is bound to be to some extent arbitrary. This chapter covering long-term debt finance will consider debentures, loan stock, bonds, long-term loans from banks and other financial institutions, and convertibles and warrants.

14.1 Introduction

Finance provided by mortgages, leasing, commercial bills and certificates of deposit will be considered in the chapter on medium-term finance. It is accepted that this classification is not always perfect; for example some mortgages may be for a longer time period than some long-term bank loans.

The distinguishing features of debt finance are as follows.

1. From an investor's point of view it is less risky than equity finance. Interest is paid out before dividends, and in the event that the company goes into liquidation the providers of debt finance are paid back before the shareholders receive anything.
2. From the point of view of the borrowing company it is less expensive than equity finance. Because the risks are less, the investor is satisfied with a lower expected rate of return. Further, because interest is an expense, which has to be met whether or not profits are earned, it is tax-deductible.

14.2 Debentures and bonds

A debenture is a document issued by a company containing an acknowledgment of indebtedness which need not give, although it usually does, a charge on the assets of the company. The Companies Acts define 'debenture' as including debenture stock and bonds. It is quite common for the expressions debenture and bond to be used interchangeably. Company debentures can also be referred to as 'loan stock'.

Usually a debenture is a bond given in exchange for money lent to the company. Debentures can be offered to the public only if the application form is accompanied by a prospectus. The company agrees to repay the principal to the lender by some future date, and in each year up to repayment it will pay a stated rate of interest in return for the use of the funds. The debenture holder is a creditor of the company, and the interest has to be paid each year before a dividend is paid to any class of shareholder.

Debentures and debenture stock can be secured or unsecured. It is usual, however, to use the expression 'debenture' when referring to the more secure form of issue, and loan stock for less secure issues. When secured this is by means of a trust deed, the objects of which are to provide for the security of the money advanced by the debenture holders, to set out the terms of the contract between the company and the debenture holders and to make provision for such things as the holding of meetings of debenture holders. The deed usually charges in favour of the trustees the whole or part of the property of the company. The advantages of a trust deed are that a prior charge cannot be obtained on the property without the consent of the debenture holders, the events on which the principal is to be repaid are specified, and power is given for the trustees to appoint a receiver and in certain events to carry on the business and enforce contracts. An alternative to receivership is for restructuring or rescheduling to occur, with the terms or the dates for repayment being altered to help the borrower.

The debentures can be secured by a charge upon the whole or a specific part of a company's assets, or they can be secured by a floating charge upon the assets of the company. The latter case is known as a general lien, whereas the debenture issued on the security of a specific asset is a mortgage debenture or mortgage bond. With a floating charge, when the company makes a default in observing the terms of the debentures, a receiver may be appointed and the charge becomes fixed, with the power to deal in the assets passing into the hands of the receiver.

The loan agreement signed by the borrower should contain the following provisions:

- the repayment schedule;
- the arrangements for a possible 'prepayment' of the debt (not all lenders are keen to allow this to happen and so it is as well to make clear at the outset whether it is allowed and if so what penalty will be charged for early repayment);
- the interest charges;
- whether a 'commitment fee' is payable by the borrower, even if all the credit allowed has not been drawn;
- the information that the borrower will be expected to provide to the lender over the period of the loan;
- the borrower's negative covenants.

Covenants

Almost all bond and debenture deeds and an increasing percentage of bank loan agreements contain restrictive 'negative' covenants. These covenants restrict the borrower's right to take certain actions until the debt has been repaid in full. The items covered could include the following:

- the incurring of any further debt unless this is already agreed to in the borrowing agreement;
- the disposal of any assets;
- the payment of cash dividends, redemption of shares, the issue of options etc. unless already agreed to in the agreement;
- the maintenance of certain levels of working capital;
- the maintenance of a 'loan collateral value' (referred to in Chapter 3), which is the relationship between expected future cash flows and the total level of debt;
- the maintenance of a certain 'debt service ratio', i.e. annual cash flow to annual interest and repayment charges.

These covenants are designed to protect the lenders. They do not protect the lender in the event of default, but they do influence some of the factors that could lead to defaults.

The lender's risk can be significantly reduced by what are known as credit enhancements. These include credit insurance, third party guarantees and collateral. These are all techniques designed to control the damage after a company has defaulted on a loan agreement.

In public as well as private companies, one limit on the size of a company's borrowing will be imposed by those who operate in the capital and money markets, i.e. the investors. They have an idea of the acceptable level of debt a company should raise, based on their opinions of a safe level of gearing. In addition to this, the articles of association of a company usually place a limit on the level of borrowing of the company, based on some relationship with the equity, i.e. the shareholders' funds invested in the company.

The articles of association usually restrict the power of directors to borrow. The typical wording of a paragraph in the articles is as follows:

The Director shall restrict the borrowings . . . so as to ensure that the aggregate amount of all monies borrowed by the company and/or any of its subsidiaries shall not, at any time, without the previous sanction of an ordinary resolution of the company, exceed the share capital and consolidated reserves.

This is stating that the borrowing shall not be greater than the capital plus reserves. The expression 'share capital and consolidated reserves' would include both capital and revenue reserves, including any share premium accounts or capital redemption reserve funds that had been set up. The goodwill and other intangibles might well have to be deducted from the reserves in working out the base for the borrowing level, the justification being that these are not assets of the company that could easily be realized. Whether or not these assets are excluded depends, of course, on the wishes of those who draw up the articles.

Repayment

A company that issues debentures or loan stock will have to repay the principal at some known date in the future, or in certain circumstances at some earlier date if it so chooses. To provide the funds for repayment the company can either place so much of its profits aside each year (into a sinking fund) which at the time for redemption will be sufficient with interest to repay the amount borrowed, or it can rely on having enough funds on hand at the time of redemption either from the profits of that year or from the proceeds of a new issue of capital. Often a company allows itself a number of years in which to repay; for example the redemption date may be given as 2000–2003, which means the company can repay part of the borrowing in each of the three years. This obviously gives the company a greater choice in planning the necessary repayment.

There is no statutory formality, as in the case of shares, in respect of the issue of debentures at a discount. In negotiating a loan, the company is entitled to make whatever arrangements are available and suitable in the circumstances. Provision may be made for the redemption of the debentures at par or at a premium at the end of a specified period; or the company may take power to redeem, at its option, even before the expiration of that period, on certain stated terms. The Act even allows for the debentures to run indefinitely.

During the life of a debenture, in order to secure an early discharge, a company can offer the holders an immediate consideration higher than or equal to the amount originally paid on the debenture. The consideration can either be in the form of cash or fully paid-up shares equal to the value of the consideration.

Debentures issued at a discount cannot be exchanged during their life for fully paid-up shares worth the par value of the debenture, as this would be equivalent to the issue of shares at a discount. The debentures issued at a discount can, however, be exchanged for paid-up shares of a value equal to the amount paid on the issue of the debentures. This is, however, likely to be less attractive to the debenture holders as no premium is being offered for early redemption. As explained for debentures issued at par, a consideration higher than the amount originally paid can be offered during their life, and the issue of paid-up shares is a valid method of paying that consideration.

There is a class of debenture that can be issued that is called 'irredeemable'. This term is, however, confusing for the company does have an option to redeem. As with ordinary debentures there is nothing to stop the company from purchasing the irredeemable debentures from the holders either with their agreement, or by simply purchasing the debentures as they become available on the market. The holder of an irredeemable debenture does not, however, have a date specified by which redemption must take place – he cannot demand repayment. Consequently, not being very attractive to investors this is a rare method of raising finance. With this class of debenture the holder is precluded from demanding payment, but the company can redeem at its option. It is perhaps more meaningful to refer to this type of debenture as 'perpetual' rather than irredeemable.

Reference was made above to the fact that debentures and bonds do not have to be redeemed at par, or even at the 'final' redemption date. As an alternative to varying the interest rate, it is possible to vary the amount paid on redemption and the timing of the redemption. One example of this is a £69 million Eurosterling 4.5% subordinated bond redeemable in 2001, which was issued by Storehouse in 1987. Holders were given the option to redeem the bonds on 2 April 1992 at 129.17%, rather than to wait until 2001 and redeem at 100%. Whether they would wish to do so depended of course on what they thought would happen to interest rates between 1992 and 2001 and on their own liquidity situation.

Another type of security is the medium-term note (MTN). A note is a promise to pay a certain sum at a named date. A company wishing to obtain funds writes such a note and sells it in the market-place. Company treasurers want as many options as possible. They want to be able to borrow anything from overnight money to long-term debt. The MTN, which is an alternative to a bond, is one option. The MTN can have a maturity of anything from nine months to 15 years. Notes can be issued with floating interest rates, so that the interest charges move in line with market rates. The MTN helps the company treasurer to control the portfolio of his debts.

14.3 Medium-term notes (MTNs)

The basic 'plain vanilla' MTN is an unsecured promissory note. A company promises to pay holders of the notes a certain sum at a certain maturity date, or maturity band, a maturity band being a period, say between nine months and a year, within which repayment will take place.

Companies can sell these MTNs in the financial markets. MTNs can be issued at fixed rates of interest, floating rates or zero coupon rates. They can be priced at a premium or a discount. The major currency of issue is the US $. There is a large market in such notes, particularly the floating rate version (FRNs) in the Euromarkets. The subject is discussed more fully in Chapter 26 on international finance.

The MTN comes between short-term commercial paper and longer term unsecured debt securities. Their principle features are:

- the most popular period for maturity is five years, although maturities do range between nine months and over 20 years;
- issues are priced by reference to the spread on the government bonds of the currency in which they are issued;
- there is flexibility in issue arrangements;
- issuers come to the market on a continuous offer basis, with each tranche of debt being designed to satisfy the medium-term needs of the company; a tranche can be quite small;
- issuers are usually companies with a good credit rating; this is necessary for the investor, as the notes are unsecured;
- issue costs are generally lower than for similar types of debt instruments; the issue need not be underwritten;
- there is a secondary market for such notes.

The MTNs can be listed on stock exchanges, with London and Luxembourg being particularly popular.

The particular advantages to the companies issuing such securities are that they are a convenient and not expensive way of meeting working capital needs. If a company is in an industry that takes a long time to develop new products, for example the motor car industry, then MTNs can help satisfy working capital needs between the time when the investment in a new model begins and when the car is launched in the market.

Floating rate notes (FRNs)

As the name implies these are promissory notes with a floating interest rate. The coupon rate is linked to a floating reference rate, for example LIBOR. In the 1990s these notes have become increasingly popular in the Euromarkets, one reason being uncertainty about US interest rates. With the most popular currency of issue for the notes being dollars, investors became concerned in the 1980s about fixed rate notes. This resulted in a move in borrowing patterns away from straight Eurobonds to ordinary FRNs and then to structured FRNs (which are explained below).

Ordinary FRNs share many of the features of MTNs. They are attractive to investors if interest rates are expected to rise, but less attractive to the issuers as they commit the issuer to possible higher funding costs. In fact FRN issuers have mainly been banks and other financial institutions. They have issued such notes in order to attempt to match their floating rate assets (deposits) with floating rate liabilities.

In the 1990s variations on the simple FRN began to appear, termed structured FRNs. The principal types are as follows.

Reverse FRNs

These are structured to produce rising coupons as a floating reference rate falls. The coupon is calculated as a fixed rate less a floating reference rate (e.g. 12% less DM six month LIBOR). The notes contain an implicit interest rate cap with a strike price equal to the fixed rate element, as well as non-negativity clauses to prevent rates falling below zero.

Collared FRNs

These contain caps and floors, thereby generating maximum and minimum returns (e.g. minimum coupon of 5% and maximum of 8% for dollar FRN).

Step-up recovery FRNs (SURFs)

These pay interest linked to yields on comparable longer-maturity bonds. With a positive yield curve they provide higher yields for the longer maturity.

14.4 Long-term bank and institutional borrowing

As well as raising debt finance by the sale of securities in the capital market or by the placement of securities by financial institutions with their clients, it is also possible for a company to borrow directly from a bank or other financial institution. No tradable security is issued. The bank makes the loan and normally carries it on its own books for the life of the loan. The borrower repays the bank. The word 'normally' is introduced because on occasions the bank might try to sell the debt to other investors.

Traditionally the clearing banks in the UK have been willing to provide short- and medium-term funds for business. From the late 1970s, they moved into the longer-term loan business. This partly reflected changes in the demand side, but also changes in the supply side. As the funds raised in the capital market from debenture and bond issues declined, companies turned to the banks.

Term lending by banks, largely at variable rates of interest, has proved to be attractive to companies. Long-term loans are usually considered to be those for periods of more than ten years. All the clearing banks now offer such loans.

The three factors to be considered by a company with any loan are the interest charge, the security required and the repayment schedule.

Costs

The interest rate on term loans can be fixed or it can be floating. The floating rate is usually in the range of 2%–6% above base rate. The exact percentage above base that is charged depends on the creditworthiness of the borrower. On occasions, in addition to the interest charge, an initial arrangement fee or negotiation fee has to be paid. This is usually in the region of 1% of the loan.

Security

Usually the bank will want the loan secured, either on the guarantees of the directors or by a charge over the assets of the business. Under the terms of the government's Loan Guarantee Scheme (discussed in Chapter 27), it may be possible for a business to obtain a loan without security. The bank may also require the company to sign covenants that restrict the company's rights to issue other debt, to sell assets or perhaps to pay dividends.

In the chapter on mergers and acquisitions leveraged takeovers will be discussed. The dangers of high levels of leverage (gearing) are illustrated in that chapter with two cases which involve companies that suffered downturns in sales shortly following taking on high levels of borrowing to finance acquisitions. One thing that proved to be necessary in the financial restructuring arrangements was for the covenants to be renegotiated.

A case where banks needed to refinance a company during a downturn in its economic performance was that of Wang Laboratories in the USA. In 1988–9 the company lost $424 million. The company had debts of more than $900 million comprised of bank debt, bonds and short term Euromarket paper. Under the refinancing arrangement a consortium of banks agreed to provide an additional $100 million of debt. Certain debts that were due for repayment prior to the rescheduling were rolled over for nine months. In order to secure the original loans Wang had pledged assets to a number of banks. Under the restructuring arrangement the banks allowed Wang to raise money from the sale of some of these assets and plough this back into the business as working capital, rather than use it to repay the debts.

When companies get into financial difficulties, banks very often have a difficult choice to make: should they keep to the covenants and possibly force the company out of business or should they relax the terms of the covenants?

Repayments

It is sometimes possible to negotiate a rest period during which time repayment of the loan is not required. Such periods are sometimes referred to as grace periods or holiday periods. Usually such repayment holidays are for no longer than two years. Such periods are intended to allow the borrowing business time to become established or re-established and to start to generate sufficient cash flow before it has to begin to repay the loan.

As mentioned above long-term loans can be obtained from financial institutions other than the main high street banks. Insurance companies occasionally make loans to businesses for periods up to 20 years. There are also specialist financial institutions who make loans to companies. One of the most well known in the UK is Investors in Industry (3Is). There is also the European Investment Bank, which is one of the European Union institutions. These specialist financial institutions will be considered later in the book.

14.5 Register of charges

In the UK mortgages, debentures and other charges have to be registered both in the company's own register of charges and with the Registrar of Companies. This is of the utmost importance – failure to register leads to the imposition of fines on the company.

In order for any interested party to discover what charges are held against the assets of a company, it is necessary to examine the register held by the Registrar of Companies. Particulars of certain charges, together with the instrument creating them, must be registered. The register is open to public inspection. The following list shows the type of charges which can be found by inspection:

- a charge to secure an issue of debentures;
- a charge on uncalled share capital;
- a charge evidenced by an instrument which, if executed by an individual, would require registration as a bill of sale;
- a charge on land or an interest therein;
- a charge on the book debts of the company;
- a floating charge on the undertaking or property of the company.

Bearer versus registered securities

In the UK not only does the existence of a debenture need to be registered, but also a register of who owns the debenture, bond or loan stock needs to be maintained. This is a record of who has a claim against the company. The claims are referred to as registered securities.

In many countries a company has a choice whether to issue what is known as a bearer security or a registered security. As explained above, in the case of a registered security the name of the purchaser is recorded in a register at the company. This means that for tax purposes it is known who is the holder and who will be receiving the dividend or interest payments. In contrast bearer securities are unregistered. This makes it possible for investors to collect the interest or dividends and for the tax authorities not to know who is receiving this sum of money. A bearer bond has interest coupons attached to it and these are sent to the company or handed to a bank when the holder wishes to obtain interest due. The production of the coupon means that the holder receives interest.

Not surprisingly perhaps investors are willing to accept lower interest rates on bearer bonds than on registered bonds of comparable risk. The secrecy is of value. However, there is one important danger with bearer securities: if they are lost or stolen it is difficult to prove ownership. Therefore they need to be stored in a safe place. Loss of a registered security is not so crucial; ownership can be proved and a replacement certificate received.

In many countries it is possible for equity shares to be either in a registered form or a bearer form. Again, it is not unusual for bearer equity securities to trade at a higher price than the registered securities.

14.6 Corporate bond market

The amount of money raised each year on the London Stock Exchange through the issue of debentures and bonds is shown in Table 12.4(b). As can be seen the amount raised each year is extremely variable. In the early 1980s the corporate bond market was nearly dead. In 1980 only £45 million was raised. This increased through the decade to £2421 million in 1989, but interest in the market fell away again in the early 1990s.

The Wilson Committee's Report on the Functioning of Financial Institutions drew attention to the problems of the long-term fixed-interest industrial debenture market. The supply of debentures and unsecured loan stock issued by industrial companies had almost completely 'dried up' at the time of the report, i.e. 1980.

One of the reasons for the reluctance of companies to issue such securities was the volatile nature of interest rates. Governments have tended to use interest rates as a way by which to attempt to control inflation and/or exchange rates. It is dangerous for a company to commit itself to pay a particular interest rate which is the current rate at the time of issue when in a short period of time the level in the market-place might fall. The company is then committed to service a relatively expensive debt issue.

One solution to the problem of volatile interest rates was to issue index-linked loan stock. The indexing could apply either to the amount that is paid on redemption or to the amount of the annual interest payment. The government had issued a number of index-linked securities, but this solution did not prove popular with the corporate borrower. The issue of loan stock (bonds) with options attached to convert into equity, or with warrants attached enabling the holder to purchase equity, turned out to be much more popular.

In fact, in the 1980s companies produced a number of imaginative securities with which to appeal to the investor interested in purchasing debentures and loan stock. These will be referred to in the next few pages. One way around the fixed-interest problem from the point of view of the borrower has been the interest rate swap. This is a way in which the corporate treasurer can adjust a company's borrowing portfolio to obtain the required balance of fixed-rate versus floating-rate borrowing (see Chapter 20).

A second problem with the bond market was that for many years the government were big borrowers. They tended to crowd out corporate borrowers in the domestic market. Government-fixed interest stock dominated the market.

To the investor, the choice between government gilt edged stocks, local authority bonds and company debentures rests mainly upon the relative yields being offered. The risks clearly differ and the investor would expect the company securities to offer higher yields than the issues by central and local government. This means that government borrowing forces up the cost of this form of capital for companies. When governments borrow, they do not have to be as interest conscious as do companies. A company has to be sure that it can earn returns on the funds borrowed that are greater than the cost. The government is not subject to such market discipline. It need not be, for the returns it obtains from using borrowed funds cannot usually be measured in financial terms. If interest rates rise, it does not cut off government borrowing, but it can cut off company borrowing.

It should be appreciated that there are now two aspects to the sterling bond market, a domestic market and an international market. The domestic market is for sterling denominated debentures and bonds issued in London on the Stock Exchange. The international sterling bond market is again a market for securities denominated in sterling but they can be bought and sold not only through dealers in London but also in centres in other countries dealing in international securities. They can be bought by anyone with pounds and sold by anyone who wants pounds.

The international market began with the issue of what were known as bulldog bonds.

These are bonds denominated in pounds sterling issued outside the UK. The issuers included industrial companies, banks and building societies. The market was boosted by the arrival of interest rate swaps. Of course, it is only the larger internationally known firms that issue in this international market. Medium-sized firms can usually only issue in the domestic sterling bond market.

The Bank of England issued guidelines for capital market issues in sterling. The guidelines relate to such matters as the structure of the instruments and the methods of issue. For a number of years the Bank of England operated a system where issuers in sterling bond and equity markets needed to obtain consent for the timing of an issue in the domestic market before it proceeded. The objective was to ensure that there was not a clash in timing between rival issues which would have made it difficult for the market to absorb. The requirement to obtain Bank of England approval was ended in 1989, but the Bank still monitors the flow of issues and keeps track of developments in the market.

The government have helped boost the bond market by a decision to exempt qualifying corporate bonds from capital gains tax. They also made it possible for UK companies to pay interest on Eurobonds on a gross basis. This means that foreign purchasers are not put off by the deduction of UK tax. New arrangements were introduced to facilitate the issue of zero-coupon and other deep discounted bonds.

The sterling bond market is usually thought of as being a long-term market. However, there is a short-term aspect to it. In 1985 a provision was made to enable companies to issue short-term corporate bonds, i.e. bonds with a maturity of between one and five years. Provision was also made for the issue of commercial paper, i.e. paper with a maturity of between seven days and one year. The Euro commercial paper market proved to be particularly attractive to borrowers. Initially, those issuing commercial paper were companies with net assets of at least £50 million whose shares were listed on the Stock Exchange in London. The paper had to be issued and transferred in minimum denominations of £0.5 million and there were requirements for disclosure of information about the issue. The rules regarding who could issue such commercial paper were later relaxed and now companies with assets of at least £25 million are allowed to issue such debt. Issues are also now permitted by unlisted companies as long as they meet certain minimum requirements. The minimum denomination for the paper was reduced to £100 000.

There is now a reasonably healthy sterling bond market based in London with both domestic and international dealing. It is particularly helpful to companies as it enables them to obtain debt finance in a form other than bank borrowing. It enables companies to have access to a fixed-interest capital market and so increase their range of financing opportunities.

Bond dealers

From the point of view of investors, bonds might not seem to be such an exciting security as equity. With equity prices depending on forecasts of profits, and with prices changing when new information reaches the market, equity prices are volatile. Bond prices do move but move slowly. Bond dealers can, however, make large sums of money. If one is dealing in very large sums of money, a small movement in the price of a bond can mean profits which are considerable. Bond dealers have become quite glamorous figures in the financial community. (A successful popular book by Lewis (1990) dealing with the life of a bond dealer was entitled *Liar's Poker*.)

Unfortunately for some, all investment involves risk, and some dealers make losses. Glaxo announced in July 1994 that it had closed its Bermuda-based treasury operation. It did this after the bond dealers in its treasury department made losses of £100 million on the company's bond portfolio.

The company's treasury department managed the firm's cash portfolio which consisted at times of £2 billion. These funds were invested in a number of financial instruments. The company emphasized that its losses were the result of falling bond prices and not the result of speculation by its treasury department. Nevertheless the company decided to hand over responsibility for the investment of its cash balances to external fund managers.

<table>
<tr><td>

14.7 Mezzanine finance and junk bonds

</td><td>

Mezzanine finance is the name attached to a form of finance that combines features of both debt and equity. It is a form of finance that is popular in the following situations:

1. management buy-outs (MBO);
2. leveraged acquisitions;
3. financing capital-intensive projects;
4. the recapitalization of companies; and
5. when public companies go private.

</td></tr>
</table>

Mezzanine finance tends to be used when a company has used all the bank borrowing that it can obtain and it does not have access to further equity. It is a form of borrowing that often enables a company to move beyond what is normally considered to be acceptable levels of gearing. It is therefore of higher risk than more traditional forms of borrowing. The features of mezzanine finance are:

- it is often unsecured debt, ranking below senior debt;
- typically the interest rate charged is a floating rate, costing between 2% and 4.5% above LIBOR;
- frequently the return on this high-risk investment includes an 'equity kicker'. This offers equity participation in the company that is borrowing the funds, either through warrants or share options. If the venture being financed turns out to be successful the lender can obtain an equity stake in the company.

One situation in which it is possible to issue such securities is if the company is seen to have a safe and positive future cash flow. This could be the position with an MBO, in which an established business is moving into new hands. With an above normal level of gearing, a high positive cash flow is normally required in order to pay the high levels of interest payments. Most forms of mezzanine finance result from private placements of debt with investors and direct borrowings from an institution with no secondary market in the debt.

There are investors who may be prepared to lend to companies in a not normal situation if there is the possibility of very high returns. Such high-risk investors are prepared to buy 'junk bonds'. Junk bonds are a form of mezzanine finance. If events turn out well they pay very high rates of interest. They are bonds which like other bonds can be traded in the market place.

Although a junk bond market has not developed in the UK, there is considerable interest in other forms of mezzanine finance. It has been estimated that in the region of 40% of MBO's use mezzanine finance, and in the average MBO deal £20 million of funds is provided from this source. The use of mezzanine finance in company restructuring situations will be discussed further in Chapter 25.

As with many new forms of finance, very descriptive names are introduced. With mezzanine finance these include the following.

Strip financing This is a financial arrangement for a company consisting of providing a variety of different types of mezzanine finance, each with different costs and risk characteristics.

Stepped interest This is borrowing with lower levels of interest being charged in the early years of the loan than in the later years. The repayment by instalments of the sum borrowed may also be delayed so that it does not start until the second half of the loan period.

Junior mezzanine This as the name implies ranks for repayment below senior mezzanine, which itself ranks for repayment below senior debt. With junior mezzanine there may be little or no interest payments. The return hopefully comes in the form of a possible future equity stake in the company.

Junk bonds Junk bonds are considered to be high-risk, but they do offer the possibility of high interest rates. They are usually issued by companies with a low credit rating. In the USA, where such bonds were created, Standard & Poor give a credit rating to bonds issued by companies. Bonds issued by top-class companies are given an AAA rating; junk bonds usually have a B rating which is the next to lowest rating, i.e. CC. In return for this level of risk the interest offered on junk bonds can be 5% or more above that on AAA bonds.

Such bonds proved very popular in the USA in the 1980s, with issues increasing ninefold between 1980 and 1986. They were particularly popular as a means of raising finance to fund leveraged buyouts and they financed a large number of corporate raiders. The bonds were popular with some investors and an active secondary market developed in the USA.

In the 1980s there was talk of a market for junk bonds developing in the UK. It was argued that it would help build up a corporate debt market and there are many who would benefit from the development of such a market. It is a source of finance for companies, and investment bankers benefit with underwriting fees, trading commissions and advisory income.

There have been attempts in the UK to finance an acquisition by the issue of high-risk bonds. One such attempt was the proposals contained in the initial bid by Hoylake to buy British American Tobacco. However, with no market-place for trading in such bonds, they would be left in the hands of either the financial institutions who purchase them to provide cash for the bidder or the shareholders of the acquired company who accept them in exchange for their shares.

The junk bond market is technically referred to as the 'high-yield bond market'. It has grown in the USA from a small unimportant market in the early 1970s to a 'dynamic continually increasing force in corporate finance'. In 1991 the size of the market was over $209 billion. Its significance can be judged from the fact that in that year this high yield debt market accounted for 25% of the total corporate debt market.

The average annual return to investors from these high-yield, high-risk securities, over the period 1978 to 1988, was 12.1%. These are high returns, but what about the risks? The market was in disarray in 1990 as defaults on interest and capital repayments mounted. Returns for a small period of time were, on average, negative. There was much bad publicity after the market's leading underwriter and trader in junk bonds went bankrupt, namely Drexel Burnham Lambert. But the market survived. It offers high returns in some years and low returns in others, and high defaults in some years and low in others. This is what one would expect from a high-risk market. There is some confusion on the overall default rate in this market.

Despite the adjective 'junk' being used, the failure rate on such securities is not that bad. Altman found that for B-rated bonds (which is the dominant junk-bond category) the annual mortality rate over the period from 1970 to 1991 was an average 5% per year.

How can this be interpreted? Say a junk bond is issued with a ten-year life. That means that interest should be paid each year and the bond redeemed at the end of the period. There is a chance each year that the bond will default (that it will cease to be of value). The longer the life of the bond the greater the cumulative default rate will increase. The probability of default on any bond increases with the age of the bond. Altman finds that, over the period from 1970 to 1991 for B-rated bonds, 5 years after issue 19% of the bonds had defaulted, compared with only 7% for BB-rated bonds, and 1.5% for BBB-rated bonds [1]. For the extremely high-risk category CCC, the percentage was 31% and for the AAA category there is 0% default.

These figures have to be interpreted with caution because they are often based on a small population size. They do indicate, however, what the high-yield bond market is all about.

Terminology

The valuation of annuities and perpetuities, and the yield to maturity, has been introduced in sections 5.1, 5.2 and 5.3 of the book.

Perhaps the most confusing aspect of valuing bonds for the reader new to the subject is the terminology. A number of expressions are used to mean the same thing. There is basically one equation used to value bonds.

$$V_t = \frac{I_1}{(1 + r)} + \frac{I_2}{(1 + r)^2} + \frac{I_3}{(1 + r)^3} + \frac{R_n}{(1 + r)^n}$$

This is the familiar present value equation. Five variables are involved. A student can be given values for any four of the variables and be asked to calculate the fifth. For example the student can be given I, r, n and R and be asked to calculate V. Or the student can be given n, V, I and R and asked to calculate r.

The meaning of the variables (with alternative expressions that can be encountered) are

V_t = value of the bond at time t (sometimes called the price at time t);
I = annual amount of interest paid to the holder of a bond (which is equal to the coupon rate (C) on the bond times nominal value of the bond (P));
R = redemption value of the bond;
n = period of time from now to redemption;
r = market capitalization rate/discount rate/annual required rate of return on similar bonds/redemption yield;
C = coupon rate (the rate of interest paid by the company to holders of the bond);
P = par (nominal) value of a bond (sometimes called face value).

The following points need to be appreciated by a student new to the subject:

1. It is possible to value a bond at any date after issue. The value (the price) will vary over time.
2. I is the annual interest paid on the bond. It is fixed (or the formula that will be used to ascertain the amount to be paid is fixed) at the time the bond is first issued.

   The coupon rate is not the same as r which is the market capitalization rate at the time the bond is being valued. r will vary over time, depending on such factors as government policy. With a fixed interest rate bond neither I nor C will vary over time.
3. All bonds will have a par (nominal/face) value. In the simplest case a bond will be sold (issued) by the company at its par value. In the simplest case this par value (issue price) will equal the redemption value. It is, however, possible to issue bonds at a discount (issue price less than par value). It is also possible to redeem a bond at a premium (redemption value higher than par value).
4. The coupon rate (C) is the rate of interest being offered on the face value of the bond. For example, debenture stock might be issued at a price of say £90 or £110, but be issued in units of £100 nominal value. The interest rate being offered on the £100 unit is referred to as the coupon rate.

   The issue price is the price at which the bonds are initially sold by the company to the investors. Debenture stock can be issued at a premium or a discount, so that the £100 units referred to above can be issued at say £90 or £105 a unit.
5. The market price is the price at which the bond is being traded in the market on a particular day; it is the price which one investor pays another investor. This is a function of the coupon rate which is announced at the time of issue together with the risk class of the particular company issuing the debenture and the current market rate of interest.

Irredeemable bonds (interest in perpetuity)

The vast majority of bonds are referred to as 'dated', which means that a date is given when they will be redeemed. There are however some bonds trading in the market that are 'undated'. A well-known example of this is the UK government 3.5% War Loan. This was a bond issued during the Second World War to raise finance to help with the war effort. It was undated and 50 years after the war it has still not been redeemed. It is still however traded. The British government continue to pay 3.5% interest per annum to the current holders of the bond. When interest rates in the economy fall (the market capitalization rate) the price of this 3.5% War Loan rises, as do the price of dated securities. No doubt the original purchasers of this bond gave up waiting for the British government to repay and sold to other investors.

One form of undated bond issued by the British government is called a **'consol'**. This is a bond that provides interest in perpetuity. It is never redeemed.

Let us assume that in 1990 a company issued a number of £100 par 8% irredeemable debentures. Investors buying such a security would be acquiring a right to receive an annuity of £8 forever. The amount that they would be willing to pay for such a debenture in 1994 would approximate to

$$P = \frac{100 \times 8.0}{r}$$

where r is the rate of interest being offered in 1994 on securities in the same risk class as this particular company's debentures. If in 1994 r equals 11.0% then the price of the debenture in the market at that time would be approximately equal to $100 \times 8.0/11.0 = £72.72$.

If in 1995 interest rates were to rise to a level where $r = 14.0\%$, then the price of the debenture would fall to approximately

$$p = \frac{100 \times 8.0}{14.0} = £57.14$$

or, to put it another way, the price would fall to a level where the interest yield equalled 14% (i.e. $14\% = 8\% \times 100/57.14$).

The interest yield is simply the annual interest received expressed as a percentage of the current market price of the security.

With our security above at the time it was issued in 1990 the interest yield was

$$\frac{8 \times 100}{100} = 8\%$$

In 1994 it was

$$\frac{8}{72.72} \times 100 = 11\%$$

In 1995 it was

$$\frac{8}{57.14} \times 100 = 14\%$$

With an irredeemable bond the interest yield equal the market capitalization rate, that is the rate currently being offered in the market. This is not the case with a redeemable bond.

Redeemable bonds

For a redeemable security there is a factor other than the interest payment that has to be taken into account. This is the capital repayment. As the date of redemption comes near, an investor will be willing to pay a price for the security higher than that which would give an interest yield equivalent to the existing market rates. This is because the time when the investor is to receive the repayment of the investment is approaching.

As an example let us suppose a government bond with a coupon rate of 5% is redeemable in one year's time. What would be the price of that bond today if the market rate of interest on bonds in a similar risk class is 10%? The holder of the bond will receive in 12 months' time interest plus the redemption value of the bond (£100).

At the beginning of this section we showed an equation; if we substitute the above values in the equation we obtain:

$$V = \frac{5}{(1.10)} + \frac{100}{(1.10)} = 95.46$$

The bond would be selling for £95.46. This only gives an interest yield of

$$\frac{5}{95.46} \times 100 = 5.24\%$$

We might ask why anybody would pay £95.46 for a security giving an interest yield of only just over 5%, when they could obtain a higher yield on other investments. In the example we have assumed the yield on other securities is 10%. The answer is that they are not buying the bond for the £5 interest, but for the £100 that they will receive when the bond is redeemed in 12 months' time. The *Financial Times* quotes two yields for fixed interest securities, the interest yield and the redemption yield.

The redemption yield (yield to maturity) is the total return (taking into account capital repayment as well as interest payments) that will be obtained from holding on to the security until its redemption. The redemption yield is sometimes above the interest yield and sometimes below it. The relationship depends on the coupon rate on the bond and the current interest yields in the market.

If the coupon rate on a particular bond is above the current interest yields in the market the redemption yield will be lower than the interest yield. If the coupon rate is lower than the current interest yields the redemption yield will be higher than the interest yield. (The reader can check the accuracy of this statement by observing yields quoted in the *Financial Times* for different bonds.)

Let us say that we are now at 1 January 1993 and we are considering purchasing a £100 debenture in Company S which is repayable at par on 31 December 1994. The coupon rate is 12%, payable annually on 31 December. The market price of the debenture is currently £90. We wish to know the redemption yield.

The formula for redemption yield is

$$V_t = \frac{I}{1 + r} + \frac{I}{(1 + r)^2} + \ldots + \frac{I}{(1 + r)^n} + \frac{R}{(1 + r)^n}$$

where V_t is the market price of security today, R is the redeemable value, I is the annual interest payment, r is the redemption yield and n is the number of years to redemption. Substituting the values in our example into the above equation gives

$$90 = \frac{12}{1 + r} + \frac{112}{(1 + r)^2}$$

Solving this equation gives r equal to approximately 18%. The redemption yield on the debenture stock is therefore in the region of 18%.

Semi-annual interest

In fact, the interest on company debentures and government stocks is usually paid in six-monthly instalments. The redemption yield in such cases is found by solving the following equation:

$$P_t = \frac{I/2}{1+r/2} + \frac{I/2}{(1+r/2)^2} + \frac{I/2}{(1+r/2)^3} \cdots \frac{I/2+R}{(1+r/2)^n}$$

Illustrating with the same example as above, except that this time the interest is payable semi-annually, gives

$$90 = \frac{6}{1+r/2} + \frac{6}{(1+r/2)^2} + \frac{6}{(1+r/2)^3} + \frac{106}{(1+r/2)^4}$$

We can solve this equation using a present value (PV) of annuity table (Table 3 at the end of the book) and a table to give the PV of a single sum (Table 2 at the end of the book). The PV of £6 to be received at the end of each of four periods, with a 9% interest rate, is £19.44, and the PV of £100 to be received at the end of the fourth period with an interest rate of 9% is £70.84. Summing these two gives £90.28, which is close to the current market price of £90. Therefore $r/2$ is 9%, which means that the redemption yield r is close to 18%.

There is in fact always a difference between redemption yields calculated with interest paid on an annual basis and with interest paid on a semi-annual basis. It is always preferable to receive interest payments earlier rather than later. But in this example, with the debenture being near to its date of redemption, the effect of the difference is very small.

Financial Times statistics

Although the prices listed in Table 14.1 relate to UK government gilt-edged securities, they are indicative of the statistics that are available in connection with company bonds. In the table by the side of the name of the issue is given the coupon interest rate (interest rate paid as percentage of the face value of the bond). The year when the bond will be redeemed is also shown.

The interest yield column is the interest payment as a percentage of the closing price. The redemption yield as explained shows the total return received (as a percentage) if the security is held to maturity.

Table 14.1 UK gilts prices

Notes	Yield Int.	Red.	Price £	+ or −	1994 High	Low
Shorts" (lives up to five years)						
Treas 9pc 1994	8.91	5.52	$100^{31}\!/\!_{32}$		$103^{13}\!/\!_{32}$	$100\tfrac{7}{8}$
12pc 1995	11.67	5.72	$102^{13}\!/\!_{16}$	$-^{1}\!/\!_{16}$	$107^{5}\!/\!_{32}$	$102^{13}\!/\!_{16}$
Exch 3pc Gas 90–95	3.05	5.33	$98^{5}\!/\!_{32}$		$98^{9}\!/\!_{16}$	$97\tfrac{3}{4}$
10¼pc 1995	9.89	6.34	$103\tfrac{5}{8}$		$107^{25}\!/\!_{32}$	$103\tfrac{5}{8}$
Treas 12¾pc 1995	11.89	6.70	$107^{7}\!/\!_{32}$	$-^{1}\!/\!_{16}$	$113\tfrac{5}{8}$	$107^{7}\!/\!_{32}$
14pc 1996	12.77	6.95	$109^{21}\!/\!_{32}$	$-^{1}\!/\!_{16}$	$117^{3}\!/\!_{16}$	$109^{21}\!/\!_{32}$
15¼pc 1996	13.50	7.20	113	$-^{1}\!/\!_{16}$	$121^{15}\!/\!_{16}$	113
Exch 13¼pc 1996	12.06	7.23	$109^{29}\!/\!_{32}$		$117^{25}\!/\!_{32}$	$109^{13}\!/\!_{16}$
Conversion 10pc 1996	9.52	7.60	$105\tfrac{1}{2}$	$-^{7}\!/\!_{32}$	$112\tfrac{7}{8}$	$104^{11}\!/\!_{16}$
Treas Cnv 7pc 1997	7.12	7.76	$98^{11}\!/\!_{32}$xd	$-\tfrac{3}{8}$	$100\tfrac{5}{8}$	$98^{1}\!/\!_{16}$
Treas 13¼pc 1997	11.85	7.76	$111^{27}\!/\!_{32}$	$-^{9}\!/\!_{16}$	$121^{11}\!/\!_{16}$	$111^{27}\!/\!_{32}$
Exch 10½pc 1997	9.90	7.88	$106^{1}\!/\!_{16}$xd	$-^{5}\!/\!_{16}$	$114^{7}\!/\!_{32}$	$105^{27}\!/\!_{32}$
Treas 8¾pc 1997	8.58	8.06	$102^{1}\!/\!_{32}$xd	$-^{9}\!/\!_{32}$	$110^{7}\!/\!_{16}$	$101^{11}\!/\!_{16}$
Exch 15pc 1997	12.60	8.19	$119\tfrac{1}{2}$	$-^{11}\!/\!_{32}$	$131^{19}\!/\!_{32}$	$118^{27}\!/\!_{32}$
9¾pc 1998	9.33	8.33	$104^{15}\!/\!_{32}$	$-\tfrac{1}{4}$	$114^{21}\!/\!_{32}$	$104^{5}\!/\!_{32}$
Treas 7¼pc 1998	7.47	8.32	$97^{7}\!/\!_{16}$	$-^{3}\!/\!_{16}$	$106^{7}\!/\!_{32}$	$96\tfrac{5}{8}$

Table 14.1 *cont.*

Notes	*Yield* *Int.*	*Red.*	*Price £*	*+ or –*	*1994* *High*	*Low*
Treas 6¾pc 1995–98	7.08	8.33	95 5/16	–5/16	102	94 27/32
14pc '98–1	11.92	8.57	117 15/32	–½	131 7/32	117¼
Treas 15½pc '98	12.44	8.41	124⅝	–7/16	140 3/16	124 13/32
Exch 12pc 1998	10.68	8.57	112 5/16	–13/32	125 31/32	112⅛
Treas 9½pc 1999	9.15	8.54	103 13/16	–½	116 5/32	103 9/32
Five to fifteen years						
Exch 12¼pc 1999	10.77	8.67	113¾	–½	128 7/32	113⅜
Treas 10½pc 1999	9.76	8.65	107 17/32	–15/32	121 5/16	106⅞
Treas 6pc 1999	6.62	8.42	90⅝xd	–½	101 21/32	89 25/32
Conversion 10¼pc 1999	9.61	8.73	106 21/32	–17/32	121 13/32	105⅞
Treas Fltg Rate '99	–	–	99 25/32xd		100 3/32	99 25/32
9pc 2000	8.84	8.67	101 27/32xd	–21/32	116 3/16	101⅛
Treas 13pc 2000	10.91	8.86	119 5/32	–25/32	136 25/32	118 3/32
10pc 2001	9.44	8.87	105 15/16xd	–¾	122 1/16	104 9/16
7pc '01	7.66	8.70	91⅜	–	106 5/16	90 3/32
7pc '01 A	7.67	8.72	91 5/16	–¾	101 7/32	89 29/32
9¾pc 2002	9.25	8.90	105 13/32xd	–¾	123 9/32	103⅝
8pc 2003	8.36	8.80	95 23/32	–¾	113 15/32	94 1/32
10pc 2003	9.31	8.90	107⅜xd	–27/32	127 1/16	105 15/32
Treas 11½pc 2001–4	10.25	9.09	112 5/32	–27/32	129 17/32	110⅞
Funding 3½pc '99–4	4.78	7.51	73 9/32	+3/16	86 5/32	71 1/16
Conversion 9½pc 2004	9.05	8.85	105	–1 1/16	125 3/16	103
Treas 6¾pc 2004	7.70	8.66	87⅝	–1	105⅛	85 25/32
Conv 9½pc 2005	9.00	8.81	105 17/32	–15/16	125½	103⅜
Treas 12½pc 2003–5	10.31	9.16	121 7/32	–15/16	143 7/16	119 1/32
7¾pc 2006	8.31	8.75	93 9/32xd	–1 1/16	112 17/32	91½
8pc 2002–6	8.42	8.84	94 31/32	–15/32	111⅝	93 1/16
Treas 11¾pc 2003–7	10.17	9.17	115½	–⅞	136 1/32	113⅝
Treas 8½pc 2007	8.60	8.75	98 25/32	–1	119 9/32	96 15/16
13½pc '04–8	10.55	9.15	128	–3/16	151 9/16	125¾
Treas 9pc 2008	8.74	8.71	103	–1 1/16	124 11/16	101
Over fifteen years						
Treas 8pc 2009	8.44	8.71	94¾	–1	115 9/16	93
Treas 6¼pc 2010	7.77	8.57	80 7/16	–1	98 3/32	78 9/16
Conv 9pc Ln 2011	8.69	8.69	103 17/32	–1 3/16	126 11/16	101 1/32
Treas 9pc 2012	8.69	8.67	103⅝	–1 11/32	127⅝	101 3/16
Treas 5½pc 2008–12	7.39	8.42	74⅜xd	+¼	93⅞	72 1/16
Treas 8pc 2013	8.43	8.63	94 27/32	–1 9/32	117 23/32	92 5/16
7¾pc 2012–15	8.29	8.60	93½	+1/16	114¾	91 1/16
Treas 8¾pc 2017	8.55	8.58	102⅜xd	–1 15/32	128¾	99 23/32
Exch 12pc '13–'17	9.23	8.83	130	–1 21/32	159½	127⅛
Undated						
Consols 4pc	8.57	–	46 11/16	+1/32	59¾	44 15/32
War Loan 3½pc	8.54	–	41	–1/16	54 13/32	39 13/16
Conv 3½pc '61 Aft.	6.16	–	56 25/32		71	55¾
Treas 3pc '66 Aft.	8.35	–	35 15/16		44⅝	33⅝
Consols 2½pc	8.67	–	28 27/32	–31/32	38½	28 5/16
Treas 2½pc	8.60	–	29 1/16		37⅝	27 15/32

In Chapter 15 we deal with the cost of equity funds, both new equity and funds provided from retained earnings. The cost of fixed-interest capital is much lower than that for these two sources of equity funds. If the coupon rate of interest on a long-term loan is 15.0%, the lender will receive this amount which will be subject to income tax. The net figure received by the investor need not concern the company, as the company's duty is finished once it has provided the agreed gross rate of interest. The cost to the company of a 15% coupon rate of interest is reduced, because such interest is an expense deductible in the corporate tax assessment.

Table 14.2 Tax-shield effect of interest payments

	Company A 'All equity capital' £	Company B 'All loan capital' (if possible!) £
Profits before interest and tax	250	250
Interest expense	0	150
	250	100
Corporation tax at 33%	83.3	33.3
Profits after tax	166.7	66.7

Interest is deducted from profits in calculating the tax for the year. Taking 33% as the corporation tax rate, that proportion of the interest payment is borne by the tax authority. In the example being used this brings the after-tax monetary cost for the company down to 10%.

This tax shield effect of interest payments is illustrated in Table 14.2. Two companies invest in the same type of project: one company (B) is entirely financed by loan capital (coupon rate 15%); the other (A) is entirely financed by equity capital. The investment costs £1000. Company A, because it has no loan capital, has to pay £50 more tax than Company B, even though their profits before-tax and interest are the same.

The equity investors of Company A have to be satisfied out of the £166.7 available for distribution. The investors in Company B have been satisfied and there is still £66.7 left over. The result is that if Company A paid its shareholders £150 of dividends (the same as received by investors in Company B) its retained profits would only be £16.70.

It should be appreciated, however, that the tax-shield effect only works for profitable companies. An unprofitable company obviously does not have any profits which are subject to tax, and so its interest charges cannot be used to reduce its tax bill. Therefore the unprofitable company has to meet the full cost of its interest payments itself.

The tax-shield effect does not work if a company is not paying tax for whatever reason. Such companies can accumulate the unused relief until they do have taxable profits, but the benefits will have been reduced from a present value point of view.

Inflation

The cost of debt capital is reduced still further when allowance is made for inflation. Suppose in the example above that £1000 is borrowed by Company B at the beginning of the year, and that the interest is paid at the end of the year. Suppose also that the capital is to be repaid at the end of the year so that £1150 cash will actually be leaving the company at the end of the year. The company will, however, have saved £50 on its tax payment. This £50 would have needed to be paid in an additional tax on profits if the company had not used borrowed finance. The outflow is therefore £1100 after taking account of the tax saving. If the annual rate of inflation is 5% then in real terms (at the beginning of the year prices) only £1048 is the net outflow. (£1100/1.05). This means that the £1000 has been obtained at a cost in real terms, after tax, of 4.8%.

The relevant equation for calculating the after tax cost in real terms is:

$$\frac{1 + i(1 - t)}{1 + P} - 1$$

where i = coupon rate
t = corporation tax rate
P = annual inflation rate

Substituting the above values

$$\frac{1 + 0.15 (1 - 0.33)}{(1 + 0.05)} - 1 = 0.048 = 4.8\%$$

Cost of bonds

The above description of the way to approach the cost of borrowed funds can be formalized. The monetary cost of debt is the return required by investors in the market place on securities of a similar risk class, adjusted for the tax shield effect.

The appropriate formula for a bond (ignoring inflation) is:

$$K_D = \frac{I(1 - t)}{V_D}$$

where K_D = cost of debt
I = annual interest to be paid (coupon rate $\times$ nominal value of bond)
t = company's effective corporation tax rate
V_D = current value of the bond

Let us suppose that a company issues either 1000 irredeemable bonds (or very long-term bonds) each of £100 nominal value. The bond has a 10% coupon rate. At the time the bond is issued the coupon rate equals the current interest rate in the market for bonds in a similar risk class. The company's effective tax rate is 30%. The cost of the debt finance at the time the money is raised is therefore:

$$K_D = \frac{10\ 000\ (1 - 0.30)}{100\ 000} = 7\%$$

This cost of capital can be used as the hurdle rate for capital investment appraisal decisions. As shown above the cost at the time of issue is 7%. Does this cost of 7% mean that a proposed project should automatically be undertaken if it offers returns of above this hurdle rate? The answer is not necessarily. We will illustrate the dilemma. Suppose the £100 000 is raised at time $t = 0$. At that time a proposal to purchase a new machine is being considered. The forecasted cash flows are:

Year	0	1	2	3
	−100 000	+38 803	+38 803	+38 803

The yield on this project is 8%. This suggests that ignoring other factors the project should be undertaken, as the yield is higher than the cost of debt capital. We are assuming it is an all debt financed company.

Let us say that the finance was raised at the time $t = 0$, but that instead of undertaking the project at $t = 0$, the project is delayed a year, and it is now proposed to start the project at $t = 1$. In the time between when the money was raised and the new proposed starting date for the project the interest rate on securities such as our company's debenture has risen to 9%. Should the project still be undertaken? The answer is no.

If the 7.0% cost is compared with the expected yield on the project of 8% the project looks attractive. But a new opportunity has arisen: the money which has been raised at 7.0% could now be invested in the money market to earn 9%. This is better than investing in the project at 8%.

It is the current interest yield at the time an investment is being considered that determines the cost of debt. It is not the actual net cash that is leaving the company to service the debt (which might be based on what is being paid for funds raised some time ago) that matters but the current interest yields in the market.

The cost of debt for a company at any time will be equal to the risk-free rate of interest at that time plus a risk premium which depends on the market's view of the relative riskiness of the debt. As interest rates in the market place rise and fall so will the cost of debt of a company.

If a company has bonds which are quoted on the stock market the yield earned by investors can be observed. If a company does not have its bonds listed it can estimate their cost by observing the yields on bonds of companies in a similar risk class.

The above example was based on an irredeemable bond. For a redeemable bond it is the redemption yield that determines the cost of capital. Let us assume a bond is paying 8% interest per annum, the redemption value is £100 and the bond is due to be redeemed in three years' time. Its current market price is £75. The corporation tax rate is 30%. Then the cost of capital (K_D) can be estimated using the following equation:

$$75 = \frac{8(1 - 0.3)}{1 + K_D} + \frac{8(1 - 0.3)}{(1 + K_D)^2} + \frac{8(1 - 0.3)}{(1 + K_D)^3} + \frac{100}{(1 + K_D)^3}$$

$$K_D = 0.17 = 17\%$$

Floating interest rates

Debentures are normally issued in fixed units of £100 nominal value and as explained can be sold at a premium or discount. They can in fact be redeemed at a value which is different from the £100. The interest rate offered is normally set in relation to the current market rates being offered on debentures in the same risk class. It is now becoming not unusual to issue debentures with a floating rate of interest which is tied to a market rate, for example the six months interbank rate. The level of interest paid on the loan can vary over the life of the debenture in line with movements in the rates in the market.

The use of floating rates has become necessary because of the large fluctuations in interest rates over comparatively short periods of time. It is in the interests of investors who may not wish to buy a security with a rate of interest which is fixed for a long period of time and which may therefore become out of line with other rates being offered in the market. It can also be in the issuing company's interest, as it would be reluctant to pay a fixed interest rate over a longer period of time if that rate rose above current market rates.

To make the debentures attractive to investors a number of other features are often linked to the security.

Deep discounted bonds

Deep discounted bonds are those where the coupon rate being offered is well below the market rate at the time of issue. There might even be no annual interest being offered, in which case they are referred to as zero coupon bonds. Such bonds, to be attractive, have to be offered to investors at a price which is at a discount compared with the value at which they will be redeemed.

The attraction of these bonds to the investor is that, although low or zero interest yield is being offered, the redemption yield can be high. For example, suppose that in 1980 a company made a debenture stock issue, offering zero interest, redeemable in ten years' time; in 1980 the stock was being offered at £50 to be redeemable at £100. The redemption yield can be calculated using the formula

$$P_t = \frac{I}{1 + r} + \frac{I}{(1 + r)^2} \cdots \frac{R}{(1 + r)^n}$$

With the annual interest being equal to zero this becomes

$$50 = \frac{100}{(1 + r)^{10}}$$

Solving the equation gives $r = 7\%$. This means that the annual interest yield is zero, but at the time of issue the annual redemption yield is 7%. Whether this is attractive to an investor depends on whether or not he needs an annual cash flow, and how at the time of issue a 7% annual return compares with current market rates of return on investments with similar risk characteristics.

The attraction of this form of issue to a company is that, if it has current cash flow problems, it is a way of immediately raising funds that does not result in any short-term cash outflow. It is also attractive to a business that is wishing to raise funds for a long-term project but does not expect to generate cash inflows for a number of years.

Until 1983 zero coupon and deep discounted bonds were not allowed to be issued in the UK. At that time the government, in its attempts to revive the corporate bond market, removed the embargo, but taxation problems were still a deterrent on the issue of such securities, with the difficulty arising over the taxation treatment of the increase in value of the bond as it approached redemption. Certain of the problems were resolved, however, for bonds issued after March 1984.

The bonds are issued at a discount which is defined as the difference between the issue price of the security and the amount payable on redemption, excluding any interest. A deep discounted bond is one in which this discount is more than 15% of the amount payable on redemption, or more than 0.5% per annum over the life of the security to the redemption date. The discount is regarded as income accruing over the lifetime of the security. When the holder makes a disposal he is charged income tax on the discount accrued up to the date of the disposal less the discount accrued up to the date of acquisition. There is also a capital gains tax adjustment.

The legislation treats the deep discount as accruing over the life of the security on a compound interest basis. The amount of the discount which is deemed to accrue in a period for income tax purposes is called the income element.

When a deep discounted security is issued, a calculation is made of the rate of interest at which the issue price would need to be invested (applying that rate on a compounding basis at the end of each income period) to provide the redemption consideration and to pay any periodic interest on the security. This rate is called the 'yield to maturity'. The income element for the first income period is $A \times B/100 - C$ where A is the issue price, B is the yield to maturity and C is the interest attributable to the income period. The income element for subsequent periods is calculated using the same formula, except that A is the issue price plus the income elements of earlier periods (the 'adjusted issue price'). The yield to maturity and the income elements for all income periods making up the life of the security can be calculated at the outset. An example should help to clarify the position.

Z Ltd issues stock on 1.7.89 in units of £200 for redemption on 30 June 1996 at £400. Interest at 2% per annum on the redemption price is payable half-yearly on 31 December and 30 June. There will be 14 income periods each of six months, the first of which will end on 31 December 1989. The yield to maturity can be calculated and is equal to 6.57% per income period. The income element for the first income period is

$$\frac{200 \times 6.57}{100} - 4 = £9.14$$

where the 4 equals the interest paid for six months (1% × £400). For the next income period to June 30, 1990 the issue price is increased by £9.14 and the income element is

$$\frac{209.14 \times 6.57}{100} - 4 = £9.74$$

As at 1 July 1990, the market price would become £218.88, i.e. £209.14 + £9.74. If an investor purchased stock on 1 July 1990, he would pay £218.88. The income element over the next six months is £10.40 leading to a price at the end of that six month period of £229.28. If the investor sells at 31 December 1990, he will be charged income tax on the gain of £10.40 and on the interest he received (1% on £400).

Convertible deep discounted bonds

A variation on the deep discounted bond is a bond issued at a low coupon rate which is convertible into equity shares from a date in the future. Such convertible bonds have been issued by such well-known companies as Burtons, ASDA and Lonrho.

The attraction of such securities depends on the terms of the conversion. If the shares to be received are worth much more than the price paid for the bond, the investor is receiving for a number of years the below-market rates of interest in exchange for a gain at the time of the conversion, similar to a deep discount. Alternatively, the terms of the bond may be such that they pay interest rates just below market rates during the life of the bond, with the prospect of a small capital gain when the bond is exchanged for equity shares. A variation offered with some convertible bonds is that, if the holder opts not to convert, it is possible to receive instead an increase in interest rates paid on the bond backdated to the time of issue.

14.11 Securitization

Asset-backed security issues started in the USA, and were first introduced in the UK in 1985. They in total still only account for a small proportion of UK company debt finance. At the end of 1993 there had been 94 such issues, with a total value of £16 billion.

Securitization involves putting together a claim on an asset or assets of a company and for this claim to be sold in the market place. Prior to this type of arrangement a company would pledge a particular asset or assets to a bank and the bank would advance money on the security of these assets. The disadvantage of this was that the company was having to deal directly with one bank and the bank itself was not in a position to pass on this debt to another party. By putting the assets into a claim and selling the claim in the market-place, the seller should be able to obtain a more competitive price. One reason for this is that the claim is offered to a number of buyers and the initial buyer knows that he should be able to sell the claim to another investor should the need arise. The claim on the company is represented by a security. It is this security that is sold in the market-place. The vast majority of the companies selling such securities are financial institutions. However, some are engaged in industry.

The assets of the organization seeking funds are removed from its balance sheet. Instead, the borrowing institution receives new funds from investors who have purchased the negotiable financial instrument transferring ownership of this asset. The borrowing institution is selling off an asset (a claim) and receiving cash. The investor is giving up cash and in return receiving a security, which is an asset. The security is a claim to an asset or it can be a claim to a future cash flow stream. The investor buys the security without recourse, or in some cases with limited recourse, to the seller of the security. The assets being sold by the financial institutions include commercial paper, mortgages, car loans, credit card receivables, and export credit.

An obvious benefit to the financial institution selling the security is to remove an asset with possibly a long maturity from its balance sheet and to receive cash. This clearly improves its liquidity – it can lend again. It also improves its gearing. A market has developed for the exchange of these securities.

If a company, say a financial institution, is able to sell some of its debtors to another company, then clearly the transaction is a sale; the debtors figure in the balance sheet will be reduced and the cash figure increased. The trouble arises in respect of a sale with a right of recourse. If the purchaser of the debts can come back to the seller in the case where the debts sold cannot be collected, then the seller of the debts has a contingent liability and has to be concerned about possible bad debts.

For example, suppose that a building society sells to a third party £50 million of mortgages it has issued. It would have received the repayment of the mortgages over time, but by selling them now it turns the future receivables into cash. With the increase in securitization in financial markets, building societies have been doing just that. The building society continues to manage the mortgages and to handle the collections, but it passes on the amounts received plus possibly an agreed rate of interest to the buyer of the mortgages. The building society sometimes continues to carry the risk of non-payment on the mortgages; the buyer of the mortgages has recourse. How is the sale of the mortgages to be accounted for? How is the outstanding risk accounted for? Can the mortgages be removed from the balance sheet, with recognition of relevant gain or loss in the accounts? What happens if there is recourse in the case of bad debts to the seller – in the above example, to the building society making the transfer?

An example of such an arrangement in the UK occurred in the case of the National Home Loans Corporation (NHLC). In 1987 they had sold a £50 million bundle of mortgages as marketable securities. A good business reason for such an action was to enable the financial institution to increase its funds available for future lending purposes. In this case the corporation argued that to show these securities as a liability in its accounts would be misleading, as the new holders of the securities had no right of recourse against the NHLC if the mortgages turned out to be bad debts. One problem that did arise was that often the assets, in this case the mortgages, were sold to a controlled non-subsidiary company, which in turn sold the bundle of mortgages as marketable security. The right of recourse was against the non-subsidiary, not against the 'parent' company. In the UK in the past such subsidiaries did not need to be consolidated in group accounts; now they do (see page 453).

Securitization can arise with a manufacturing company. In the USA, General Motors' finance subsidiary put together a package of $4 billion of loans it had made to customers to enable them to purchase cars, and sold these in the market; it created a security out of its loans receivable. The purchaser of the security passed cash to General Motors' finance subsidiary, and in return received a stream of payments over time from those who obtained their cars by borrowing from the finance subsidiary.

The key question in these situations is whether the benefits and related risks remain with the seller of the receivables or are transferred to the purchaser. If significant risks remain with the seller – the company that packaged the receivables to sell – then the receivables should remain as an asset in that company's balance sheet. The funds received result in a debit to cash and a credit to a liability account. The resulting presentation shows both the receivables due and the liability resulting from the cash received from the sale.

14.12 Redemption of bonds

It is usual to date debentures and bonds, that is to give the particular year or years in which the bonds will be redeemed. The cash to repay the debenture holders can be obtained either by (a) making a new debenture issue, (b) from funds available as a result of the trading activities in the year of redemption, or (c) funds placed into a sinking fund.

Many debenture issues have a provision in the deed which requires the issuing company to create a sinking fund as a means of discharging the debt. This means that the company creates a separate fund (usually administered by a trustee) into which it makes equal periodic payments over the life of the debenture. The amounts deposited in the fund earn interest, and this amount plus the fund itself could be used either to repay all the debentures at a particular redemption date or to repay a proportion of the debentures in one year, a proportion in the next year and so on.

In the latter situation the debenture would have been dated for a period, e.g. 1995–8. In such instances individual debentures holders do not know if their debentures will be selected for retirement in a particular year or whether they will even have to wait until the final redemption date. The number of debentures that are to be retired in a particular year depends upon the rate at which the company pays into the sinking fund. With some such issues the company wishes to retire a certain percentage, say 75%, of the securities before the final maturity date. In other cases the annual contribution to the sinking fund may be a fixed percentage of the company's earnings in each year, or sufficient to retire a fixed percentage of the securities outstanding in each year.

Usually such sinking fund arrangements contain a provision that if the debentures are being sold in the market below their par value then the company is allowed to purchase those debentures available in the market and to regard such purchases as part of the annual contribution to the sinking fund. With all retirements, as opposed to market purchases, the company pays the holder the par value of the debenture. If the debenture is selling in the market at above par value at the time when it is to be retired (which should not happen), then the debenture holder suffers a loss, for all that he will receive from the company is the par value.

With the sinking fund approach the amounts deposited in the fund plus the interest earned mean that when the time for repaying the debenture arises, there is just sufficient in the fund to meet the debt. All the debentures are retired at the same date.

To illustrate this approach, let us assume that a company issues a £100 000 debenture on 1 January 1990, to be redeemed on 31 December 1999. The debt is to be discharged by the sinking fund method. Twenty equal semi-annual deposits will be made, the first due six months after the debenture is issued. The fund receiving the deposits pays 6% interest compounded semi-annually. The interest earned on the sinking fund is not necessarily at the same rate as the coupon rate paid on the debenture. In order to determine the amount deposited in the fund every six months, we make use of a 'terminal value for an annuity' table, as we are not interested in present values but in terminal values. We need to know what amounts deposited regularly, earning a certain rate of interest, will accumulate to £100 000 in 10 years' time. The terminal value we are seeking is £100 000, and we are to make 20 payments with interest accumulating at 6%. Table 4 at the end of the book shows that the relevant factor is 36.7856. Dividing the £100 000 by 36.7856 gives £2718.

The semi-annual deposit required into the sinking fund is therefore £2718. Twenty such payments, plus interest, will accumulate over 20 periods to the £100 000. This is one method that can be adopted to ensure that sufficient funds are available to repay a debt on a fixed date in the future.

14.13 Call provision

A company does have some choice over the date at which it will redeem its debentures. With the perpetual debenture the company can choose to redeem the debt whenever it so wishes, and the debenture holder is forced to settle. With a redeemable debenture, even after having named a date for redemption in the deed, the company can try to induce a holder to settle at an earlier date by making him an offer.

This is not the same as the option open to US companies. A US company can 'call' in its debenture stock; it can enforce holders to redeem at any time it so chooses up to and obviously including redemption date. A UK company can merely make an offer to its debenture holder; if the investor does not want to accept the offer, he can continue to hold the debenture and only be forced to exchange at the date set for redemption.

This call provision is a tool of financial management that is not open to UK companies. It is worth considering the value of this right. It has received considerable attention in US literature, and although UK companies do not have exactly the same opportunities with all debentures, they do with perpetual debentures, and if they can make the offer sufficiently attractive they have some choice with redeemable debentures. Another limited option available to UK companies is the actual date of redemption. Usually an issue does not give a single date for redemption; rather, a period of time is mentioned during which they will redeem.

This call privilege is also important to borrowers and lenders in mortgage arrangements, lease agreements and many long-term loans. The conditions and terms under which the issuer of the debenture may repay all or part of his obligations before the date of maturity are usually included in the loan agreement. At one extreme the call privilege is not allowed; at the other extreme there is complete freedom to call whenever the borrower wishes. There are several intermediate positions. One may be not to allow redemption until a certain number of years have passed, or to allow the call only a certain number of years before maturity. On occasions the borrower may have to pay a premium if he exercises his call privilege.

The reasons why the borrower may wish to call in the debt early include the following:

1. to take advantage of falls in interest rates by refunding;
2. the borrower's repayment ability may be better than anticipated;
3. business changes may necessitate a change in capital structure;
4. tax changes may encourage refunding;
5. the terms of the debenture may place restrictions on the firm which make refunding desirable or necessary.

The major reason advanced for early repayment is because the opportunity arises to borrow at lower interest rates.

However, any debt is two-sided. The investor must be considered as well as the borrower. The reasons for the investor resisting an early repayment are as follows:

1. the investor's plans for the future are based on a steady constant yield;
2. repayment may affect the investor's ability to service his own long-term obligations;
3. there may not be suitable reinvestment opportunities available.

It is apparent that the borrower's gain could be the investor's loss. Thus there is a conflict of interest which must be resolved at the time of the contract. A reduction in interest rates makes it financially worthwhile for the borrower to refund an issue. Thus it is apparent that the right to call a debt can have a value to the borrower. Similarly the lack of the right to call is valuable to the investor, in that it protects his investment. If the right to call is exercised then this will benefit the borrower at the expense of the lender. This has been recognized by the market and attempts have been made to either compensate or protect the lender.

One method of compensating the investor is by requiring the borrower to pay a call premium if he refunds the issue; in other words, the lender will be paid more than the face value of the debt. Alternatively, the borrower may be able to call the debt at par but may perhaps be required to pay a higher rate of interest on the issue for this privilege. Another method by which the investor is protected is through call deferment – the borrower must wait a certain length of time before he has the right to call the debt. If the period of deferment is small in relation to the length of the debt, then this aids the borrower. If it is long in relation to the debt period it aids the lender.

Consider the situation where the borrower, the company, wishes to repay the debt prior to the date set for its redemption. When interest rates are expected to fall in the future, the value of this privilege is high, for the borrower can refund the loan by borrowing at the new lower rates and using the proceeds to pay off the debt bearing the high interest rates. Even if the present period is one of rising interest rates, but there is an expectation of a fall in the future, the privilege has a value.

There is a value in the call privilege to the borrower. How much should the company borrowing be willing to pay for the option to call before maturity? The greater is the fall in interest rates, the greater is the possible interest saving. The three factors determining the borrower's interest saving are the size, the timing and the probability of a decline in interest rates. The borrower has to estimate these three variables in order to determine the value of the call option. For example, suppose that a company is currently paying 10% interest on a £100 000 debenture, although the current interest rate has dropped to 5%. The debenture still has ten years to run. If the company recalls the debenture and repays the capital from the proceeds of an issue of a new 5% debenture redeemable in ten years' time, it will save itself an interest bill of £5000 per year. If the costs of refinancing are equal to 1% of the value of the new issue, £1000, the present value (PV) of the call privilege can be calculated. The fact that interest is a tax-deductible expense would have to be taken into account.

At times of falling interest rates the lender does not benefit from receiving this call. The interest loss to the lender, if he can reinvest at the same new rate as the borrower will have to pay, is equal to the borrower's interest gain. However, the investor has to incur costs in finding a new use for his funds. Consequently, the value that has been calculated above can only be referred to as the minimum call premium. The lender would need to be offered a premium of at least this amount if he has to be induced to surrender the debenture. This simple approach ignores the subjective factors that are important in the company's reasons for making a call. However, it does offer an analytical approach to the call problem.

An example follows that shows how a debenture can be valued and also shows one method of valuing a call provision. Assume that an 8% debenture has three years of its life left to run. It was issued at a time when 8% was the appropriate interest rate, but since that date interest rates have been rising although this is not expected to continue. The interest rates in the market over the next three years are expected to be $r_1 = 0.10$, $r_2 = 0.11$ and $r_3 = 0.08$. As a return for owning one £100 debenture the holder will receive interest payments of £8 per annum for three years, and then £100 on redemption at the end of the third year. It is a simple matter to determine the PV of the debenture; all that is required is that this cash inflow be discounted at the appropriate rate of interest.

If, instead of a variable future interest rate, it is assumed that the rate will remain at 10% over the next three years, the PV of the debenture is given by

$$V(0) = \frac{8}{1.10} + \frac{8}{(1.10)^2} + \frac{108}{(1.10)^3} = £95.08$$

An investor would be willing to pay less than £95.08 for the debenture, as it would then be a profitable investment. He would not be willing to pay more than £95.08, as then the PV of his cash outlay would exceed the PV of his cash inflow.

We now return to the case where interest rates are expected to change over time. If there is no call provision, the expected values of the debenture at the beginning of each of the three years are respectively

$$V(0) = \frac{8}{1.10} + \frac{8}{1.10 \times 1.11} + \frac{108}{1.10 \times 1.11 \times 1.08} = £95.73$$

$$V(1) = \frac{8}{1.11} + \frac{108}{1.11 \times 1.08} = £97.30$$

$$V(2) = \frac{108}{1.08} = £100.00$$

At the beginning of the first of the three years an investor would value the debenture at £95.73. Now let us assume that the company can call the debenture at a price of £96 from the end of the first of these last three years. If it called at the end of the first year the company would have to pay debenture holders £96, but it could immediately issue new bonds with exactly the same terms as the old, without a call provision and with two years to run, at a price of £97.30. This is the value of the bond at the beginning of the second year. The company would make a profit of £1.30 per bond by calling and reissuing.

This is not quite realistic, however, as the bond has been valued at the beginning of the first year, ignoring the call provision. If the market allows for the fact that the bond may be called at the end of the first year, the maximum price it would pay per bond at the beginning of the period would be £(8 + 96)/1.10.

With the call provision therefore, the bond is worth £94.55 at the beginning of the three years, whereas without the call it would have been worth £95.73. The PV of the bond has been reduced by £1.18 as a result of the call provision. In this case of certainty, this is equal to the profit that the company could make from calling the bond at the end of the first year and reissuing a similar non-callable bond. It would cost the company £96 to call the bond, and the price to be obtained from selling a new bond at the end of the first year would be £97.30. This is a profit of £1.30 per bond, which has a PV of £1.18 = 1.30/1.10.

The value of the call provision to the company, and the cost of the provision to the investor, are equal under the above conditions of certainty. In conditions where expectations about future interest rates differ this need not be the case. It is possible to develop models that show the optimum time to refund and show the gains that can be made under conditions of uncertainty, but as these are less relevant to the UK situation than the US situation they will not be dealt with further.

14.14 Special-purpose transactions

What became known as special-purpose financial transactions began to appear in the UK in the mid-1980s. Indeed, it is claimed that some companies were willing to pay large sums of money to those who could come up with new financing techniques that were good enough to satisfy the auditors. Special-purpose financial transactions are financial arrangements, the object of which is to provide finance for a company but not to disclose the true nature of the transaction in the financial accounts. They differ from normal transactions in that they are designed either so that their existence is not revealed or their true position is hidden. It is what is called creative accounting.

The concept is now new. A number of 'off the balance sheet' techniques have been known about for some time. The legal form of such transactions does not reveal the true commercial effects. For example, with a financing lease, the lessee never owns the asset but uses it to obtain the same rewards and risks as go with ownership. What changed in the 1980s was the number of schemes being devised. The better known ones are described below.

Sale of stock/inventory

We shall illustrate the sale of stock technique using the case of a company that operates a distillery, a business in which it is normal to carry high levels of stock in the form of maturing whisky. It is usual practice for the company to borrow to finance the stock, but let us assume it is approaching its borrowing limits set by its Articles of Association. A scheme can be devised whereby a merchant bank purchases the unmatured whisky, giving the distiller the option to purchase it back when it reaches maturity at a price that represents the original sale price plus interest over the period that the merchant bank 'owns' the whisky. Of course, the whisky never leaves the distiller's premises, even though for a time it is legally owned by the bank.

It can be argued that this is a genuine transaction. The distillery company has sold the whisky, and may or may not buy it back. The appropriate accounting treatment depends on the particular circumstances of the case. In many such deals the repurchase price to the distiller is predetermined. It represents the original sale price plus an interest charge and is expected by both parties to be below the value of the whisky at the time of repurchase, so that the distiller is almost certain to wish to buy it back. In form, the whisky has been sold and so, following normal accounting rules, it need not appear as stock in the accounts of the distiller. The profit on the sale can be immediately shown in the profit and loss account. No interest charge need appear in the distiller's accounts during the period that the whisky is maturing, and certainly no loan has been received from the merchant bank. When the whisky has matured and is bought back from the bank and sold, the profit margin to the distiller will have been reduced by the finance charge paid to the merchant bank. Although in form the distillers have not received a loan, it can be argued that in substance they have. The 'loan' has been secured by the whisky stock. It is off the balance sheet financing. The distiller has the free use of the funds obtained from the merchant bank during the period of the deal, and has been able to show a profit much earlier than if it had been necessary to wait until the mature whisky is sold.

In contrast, the sale of stock at the current spot market price, with an agreement to repurchase in the future at the then spot market price, is not a special financial arrangement. This is because the distiller, with the sale, has relinquished control over the amount of the net future cash flows. The amount to be received will depend on future market conditions. The distiller does not control the rewards. In these circumstances the transaction should be treated initially as a sale and later as a repurchase.

Assignment of work in progress

A similar situation to the artificial sale described above is the 'assignment of work in progress'. A construction company may be engaged in a large contract that will take many years to complete. As with the distillers, there is the danger that large amounts of money can be tied up in stocks, in this case in work in progress. In this situation the company can agree to assign irrevocably all the amounts that it will receive during the period of the construction contract to a bank. In return, the bank will agree to make period payments to the construction company. The construction company now knows with certainty what cash it will receive from the bank and when, rather than being faced with an uncertain cash flow stream to be received from the purchaser which depends on stages of completion, with possible payment delays through disputes and time lags. With this arrangement the construction company can receive cash in advance of payments it will have to make, whereas payments from the purchaser for work in progress produce cash only when the costs have been incurred. Again, this is in substance a company receiving a loan, but in form it is the sale of stock. At the completion of the contract the construction company receives final payment and repays the bank for the advances it has received plus, of course, a financing charge. It has in the past in the UK been treated by many companies as off the balance sheet financing, but could be seen as a special financial arrangement.

In this situation some reference to the transaction will need to appear in the accounts. The bank could well require a performance bond from the construction company, guaranteeing that the work will be completed. This is in a way the security for the 'loan'. The existence of such a bond means that a contingent liability has been created, and this will at least need to be disclosed by way of a note in the accounts of the construction company.

Redeemable preference shares

One way in which it was possible for a group of companies to raise finance without its true nature being disclosed in the consolidated accounts of a group is by means of a subsidiary company issuing redeemable preference shares. It is the subsidiary that issues such shares, which can carry a dividend equal to the current market rates of interest. A bank purchases the shares, receiving a level of dividend similar to the interest it would receive on a loan.

These preference shares will be shown as such in the subsidiary's own accounts, but not in the consolidated accounts. If the subsidiary is consolidated in the group accounts, the preference shares will appear as part of minority interest – as equity shares issued by the group but not held by the holding company. Few people analysing accounts bother to look at the individual accounts of subsidiaries, relying instead on the group accounts. The subsidiary can pass the funds thus raised around the group to provide finance wherever it is needed. The transaction is in reality closer to a loan than an issue of risk-bearing equity capital. The funds will be repaid to the bank at an agreed date, and the finance charge is similar in amount to the appropriate interest payments. If, however, the funds had been raised by the subsidiary as a loan, then it would have needed to have appeared as such on the face of the consolidated accounts. For window-dressing purposes, there can be advantages in having funds tucked away as a 'minority interest' in the group accounts. Changes in accounting standards have made such transactions more difficult to hide.

Non-subsidiaries

In the 1980s a number of companies set up what are known as controlled non-subsidiary companies. Because the wording of the Companies Acts before 1989 was based on legal control rather than economic control, it was possible to be able to have effective control over the decision-making of another business but not to have to consolidate its accounts in the group accounts. An advantage of this is that the non-subsidiary can be used to raise finance through borrowing which does not have to be disclosed in the group accounts. The non-subsidiary is treated in the holding (parent) company accounts as an associate company. The borrowings of an associate company are not shown as part of the total borrowings of a group of companies – unlike the borrowings of a subsidiary company that are included in the total. This 'associate company' can raise cash and distribute it through the group. The parent company can 'sell' assets to the invisible 'subsidiary' which can be used as security for the loans. All these transactions will misrepresent the true gearing position of the group.

Steps have been taken to prevent this happening in future. The new definition of a subsidiary means that economic rather than legal control is the key factor in deciding whether consolidation is required. The Companies Act 1989 introduced these changes. From 1 January 1990 all undertakings actually **controlled** by the parent company needed to be consolidated in the group accounts. This had the effect of bringing onto the balance sheet certain 'off balance sheet' special purpose vehicles. The main changes to the definitions were as follows.

1. All subsidiary **undertakings** are to be consolidated, including partnerships and unincorporated associations carrying on a trade or business.
2. The test of a subsidiary based on equity share capital was replaced by one based on voting rights; a parent company is one which holds a majority of the rights to vote at general meetings. Any rights held by a nominee on behalf of the parent are treated as held by the parent.
3. Subsidiaries also include undertakings where the parent
    (a) is a member and has the right to appoint or remove directors holding a majority of the voting rights, or
    (b) is a member and controls, on its own, a majority of the voting rights pursuant to an agreement with other shareholders, or
    (c) has the right to exercise a dominant influence (including at least a right to direct the undertaking's operating and financial policies) by virtue of either provisions in the memorandum or articles, or a written contract (a 'control contract'), or
    (d) actually exercises a dominant influence over the undertaking or is managed on a unified basis with it.

In this last subsection the parent must also have a 'participating interest', i.e. an interest in shares of the subsidiary held on a long-term basis to secure a contribution to its activities by the exercise of control or influence arising from those shares. A holding of 20% or more is presumed to be a participating interest unless the contrary can be demonstrated.

The effect of these changes was to extend the meaning of 'subsidiary undertaking' to a number of arrangements where judgement was required to determine whether the parent actually controls the subsidiary. One test is whether the parent company is in a position to ensure that dividends would always be paid in accordance with its instructions. The terms 'dominant influence' and 'managed on a unified basis' are not defined in the Act because the government wished 'the ordinary spirit of the language of the legislation' to be followed. Many factors have to be considered in interpreting these requirements, including the distribution of other shareholdings and any special rights of particular shareholders.

The question of whether a company, when seeking funds, should at a particular time raise debt or equity is discussed in Chapters 15 and 18, where the cost of finance and the appropriate levels of capital gearing are considered. If a company has decided to borrow, then a further question needs to be settled, namely the maturity of the borrowing. Should the company raise short-term, medium-term or long-term debt? To answer this question we need to know the following:

1. the existing maturity structure of the company's borrowing;
2. how much finance is needed;
3. the use to which the funds are to be put, in particular the likely returns, the risk and the expected time period over which the funds will be needed;
4. the existing level of interest rates on loans of different time periods;
5. the expected future direction of interest rates.

In this section we shall concentrate on points 4 and 5, the interest rate aspects of the decision. With regard to point 1, a company will not want all its debts maturing at or near the same date. If all the loans of a company can be phased so that their repayments are spread over a number of years it will make cash flow management somewhat easier. The problem of the total amount of debt that can be raised in relation to equity is discussed in the chapter on capital gearing.

The significance of the way in which the funds are to be used is to some extent controversial. There are those that argue the way in which the funds are used is not important. The company raises funds so that its overall cost of capital is at a minimum. The funds raised are then used as and when required. The supporters of this view would argue that in general there is no link between the source of funds used to finance a project and the decision whether to go ahead with the project; the financing and the investment decisions are in general independent. It is of course accepted that there are a few projects, for example those in overseas countries, where the project would not be undertaken at all if it were not for some local form of finance. This point is returned to in the chapter on cost of capital and the chapters covering the use of funds.

To return to the discussion of interest rates, the difference between the interest rate on long-term loans and the interest rate on short-term loans can vary over time. It might be thought that the financial manager should base his decision on whether to borrow long-term or short-term money on where the cheapest money is to be found. This is not necessarily so.

The term structure of interest rates

It is important to understand why the differences between long- and short-term interest rates occur. As a starting point it is reasonable to assume that, the further into the future the lender has to wait before the loan is repaid, the greater will be the risks of default and so therefore the greater the return the lender would normally expect to compensate him for his risk. It is, in fact, the case that on most occasions the further into the future is the maturity date on the loan, the greater is the interest that has to be offered by the borrower in order to persuade the lender to part with his money.

The relationship between the differing periods to maturity of loans and their respective interest yields is referred to as the term structure of interest rate. For an accurate comparison of the variation by maturity it is necessary to compare the yields on securities with different dates of repayment but broadly the same risk class.

The relationship between maturity and interest rates can be plotted to show a 'yield curve' (see Fig. 14.1). The yield curve is more meaningful if the securities being considered are of comparable quality. The yield curve can be upward sloping (A), level (B) or downward sloping (C), although the first of these three is the most common.

The term structure of interest rates at any time is a function of investors' expectations regarding the movement in interest rates over time and their attitudes towards risk. On occasion the interest rates on long-term loans are lower than the interest rates on short-term loans, and the yield curve is falling. This can be accounted for by the fact that the

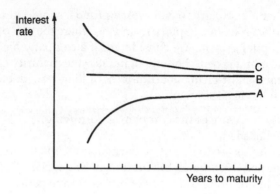

Figure 14.1

expected future course of short-term interest rates is downwards. Investors expecting short-term rates to fall in the future would be willing to lend long-term money at lower interest rates than the current short-term rates. This would be because they expect that in the future, in say one year, the then short-term interest rates would be lower than the current long-term interest rates. Conversely, one factor that can explain why long-term interest rates are above short-term interest rates today is that short-term interest rates are expected to rise and so investors will not take the risk of lending long now at the relatively low rates being currently offered. Another factor explaining the upwards yield curve is, of course, risk. There is risk attached not only to the movement in the future rates of interest but also to the solvency of the borrower.

Investors are not able to forecast the future movement in interest rates with any accuracy. They will have ideas of what they consider to be normal rates of interest, and if current short-term rates are below their ideas of normal rates, they will expect short-term interest rates to rise over time and so will charge higher interest rates on long-term loans than the current short-term rates. If, alternatively, the actual current short-term rates are far above their ideas of the normal range then the gap between short- and long-term rates will not be great for they will expect the short-term rates to fall in the future. If the current short-term interest rates are near the lower bound of expectations, then the yield curve will be upward sloping. If current short-term rates are near the upper bound of interest expectations, the yield curve could well be downward sloping. Uncertainty about the future, the state of the economy and the levels of inflation has to be taken into account and could well alter conclusions based merely on expected movements in interest rates.

Another factor affecting interest rates is the attitude of the financial institutions, the big lenders, who wish to maximize their returns subject to risk. When interest rates are high the investors will wish to lengthen the average maturity of the loans that they advance. This is so that they can obtain high interest rates for a long period of time. The opposite attitude to the length of the loan is taken by companies when interest rates are high: they will want to borrow short-term debt and not tie themselves to high interest rates for many years. The borrowers hope that interest rates will fall and they will be able to take advantage of the lower rates in the future.

Factors influencing a company's decision

The interest rate that a company has to pay when borrowing is not the only cost to be taken into account when deciding on the maturity date. The cost of issue has to be taken into account. Although the actual cost of short- and medium-term interest rates may be less than the long-term interest rates, the fact that short- and medium-term finance has to be raised more often than long-term finance increases the total issue costs.

Usually the interest rate differential and the flexibility of short-term debt make this form of borrowing attractive when compared with long-term borrowing. If a company finds that it is in the position where it no longer has need of the funds that it has obtained through short-term borrowing, then the debt will soon be due for repayment. In some cases a company may require finance to meet seasonal needs, and short-term finance is clearly much more convenient. The funds can be raised at the times when the company needs the cash and then repaid when the money is not needed. When the period of need arises again the funds can be borrowed short-term and then later paid back. This can be contrasted with funds obtained from long-term financing where the money is needed to meet short-term needs. The money would then be in the company's hands through different stages of the economic cycle and when, on occasion, more money was available than was needed, this would have to be invested in short-term assets.

Clearly the rate of return that the company can obtain from investing in the money market is less than the cost of borrowing in that market. However, although flexibility and interest costs may favour short-term debt there are disadvantages. These disadvantages can be classified under three headings.

1. the uncertainty connected with obtaining future finance;
2. the future level of interest rates;
3. the risk of insolvency.

To finance the purchase of long-term assets with short-term funds is bad strategy. There can be no certainty about the amount of short-term finance available in the future, and if an asset intended for use over a number of time periods is purchased with funds obtained from a short-term source, difficulties could arise when repayments of the loan have to be made. If the company fails to generate enough funds from its own operations to repay the debt, the asset may have to be sold to raise the cash. Therefore, while short-term loans may be available at certain times and are a relatively cheap source of funds, it is not always in the company's long-term interests to raise as much as possible from this source.

A company financed with short-term funds runs the risk of being unable to refund its loan, i.e. of being unable to obtain a new loan to pay off the maturing loan. Of course, if interest rates fall, the company that borrowed long-term money is left paying higher interest charges in each year. Another danger of funding an operation from short-term rather than long-term debt arises when interest rates are expected to rise.

The type of asset that the company wishes to acquire does, to some extent, affect the type of borrowing it should go for. If a company is heavily invested in highly liquid assets, then it is not surprising if a high proportion of its borrowing is in a short-term form. Typical of this type of company would be a commodity dealer. It is liquidity of assets more than earnings stability that permits a firm to borrow a large proportion of its funds on the short-term basis. Earning stability affects the net capacity of a company to borrow, i.e. how much debt it can obtain in relation to its equity. The borrowing capacity of a company will be discussed in the chapter on capital gearing; here we are only interested in the debt structure of a company, the time to maturity of its debts.

A company can benefit from fluctuations in interest rates if it acts wisely. If a company knows that it needs a certain amount of long-term debt financing and long-term interest rates are expected to fall, the company could well postpone its borrowing until the long-term interest rates are cheaper. This, of course, may mean that the investment requiring finance has to be postponed. Alternatively, the company can finance the asset through short-term borrowing and take the next opportunity to borrow long-term and repay the short-term loans. The short-term borrowing may be a way of deferring entry into long-term commitments.

It has been observed that businesses have frequently relied heavily on short-term debt during the early phases of a business recovery. This is because the businesses need to build up working capital assets and they wish to take advantage of the lower short-term rates. The companies typically delay long-term borrowing until the short-term rates overtake the long-term. This may be a less than optimal policy. The company takes advantage of the short-term rates to borrow short-term, but at the time they borrow they should remember that the long-term rates are also lower than they will be in the future. Companies should be aware that it can be advantageous to borrow long at low points in the interest rate cycle. In the same way, just because long-term borrowing costs are lower than short-term costs at a particular point of time, this does not mean that a company should borrow long-term. It could be that both the long- and short-term rates are due for a fall and the company should have waited to borrow long-term finance in the future even though at this future date the longer-term rates are higher than the short-term rates.

Even if long-term rates are far above short-term rates, we would still expect some companies to borrow long-term funds. The reason is that short-term financing can affect a firm's chance of finding itself insolvent. The more frequently a company has to borrow to obtain funds the more danger it is in that it cannot meet its debts on the due dates. The maturity structure of debt affects the risk of insolvency primarily through the frequency of refunding.

As indicated, there are many factors to be taken into account when a company is deciding on the maturity structure of its borrowing. A certain amount of short-term borrowing and a certain amount of long-term borrowing is usually desirable. One of the most important factors to take into account when deciding on the balance is the relevant cost. The information required on cost is the cash outflow associated with the different borrowing alternatives. This involves forecasting interest rates into the future and so, as with most decisions, there is a great amount of uncertainty involved. Nevertheless, if the decision is to be made just on the basis of cost, the most desirable form of borrowing is that which has the cost stream with the lowest expected PV, with the costs covering not just interest but all those associated with the issuing process. Other factors that have to be considered include availability of funds and alternative uses of funds.

Example 14.1

Question

The managers of a small company, Capit Ltd, plan to borrow £200 000 to invest in buildings, equipment, and working capital. It will take more than 18 months before significant cash inflows are generated from the investment. The managers are worried about servicing the interest on the borrowed funds for an 18 month period as interest rates have recently been volatile.

The company's advisors believe that there is an equal chance of interest rates rising or falling by 2% during the first six months. After the first six months there is a 60% chance of rates continuing to move by a further 2% in the same direction as in the first six months in each future six month period and a 40% chance of a 2% movement in the opposite direction. Interest is payable at the end of each six month period.

The managers are undecided whether to borrow the £200 000 in either:

1. £150 000 short-term floating rate loan at an initial interest rate of 15% per year and renewable every six months, plus a £50 000 five year fixed rate loan at 17% per year.
2. £50 000 short-term loan, £150 000 five year loan, both on the same terms as (1) above.

All loans are secured. Interest rate reviews for floating rate loans are every six months.

Issue costs/renewal costs are 1% of the loan size for each short-term loan, and £800 for the five-year loan. Issue costs are payable at the end of the previous loan period except for the initial loans where issue costs are payable at the start of the loan period. Tax relief is available on interest payments 12 months after the interest has been paid. No tax relief is available on issue costs. Corporate tax is at the rate of 25%. It is expected that £19 500, £18 500 and £15 500 will be available to service the loans in the first, second and third six-month periods respectively. Any unused surplus may be carried forward to the next six monthly period.

Required:

(a) Discuss which form of financing Capit Ltd should use.

(b)Estimate which form of financing is expected to be cheapest for Capit Ltd during the 128-month period. For each financing method calculate the probability of the company being unable to service its interest payments during the 18 month period. Assume that financing will continue to be required after the 18-month period. The time value of money, and any possible income from investing surplus cash between six month periods may be ignored.

ACCA, June 1990

Answer

(a) One of the 'rules' of finance is to try to match the maturity of a loan with the life of the asset the funds are being used to finance. It is clearly dangerous to purchase buildings and equipment with a life of say ten years with a short-term loan. When the short-term loan has to be repaid there is no guarantee that the loan can be rolled over or that a further source of borrowing can be found. It is also not certain that sufficient cash flows will have been generated from the investment at the end of the 18 months referred to in the problem. It could be a tragedy for the company if the assets had to be sold in order to repay the loan.

In this case, therefore, although the short-term borrowing is cheaper it is also riskier.

(b) There are four possible outcomes for the short-term loan as can be seen from the following decision tree.

Interest rate for first six months	Probability	Interest rate for second six months	Probability	Interest rate for third six months	Probability	Outcome
				19%	(0.6)	A
		17%	(0.5)			
				15%	(0.4)	B
15%	(1)			15%	(0.4)	C
		13%	(0.5)			
				11%	(0.6)	D

Alternative 1 (£150 000 short + £50 000 medium)
We will now calculate the expected interest cost for each six month period

1st 6 months

£150 000 × 15% × 1/2	=	11 250
50 000 × 17% × 1/2	=	4 250
Estimated cost		15 500

2nd 6 months

50% chance of £150 k × 17% × 1/2	=	12 750
£50 k × 17% × 1/2	=	4 250
		17 000

50% chance of £150 k × 13% × 1/2	=	9 750
£50 k × 17% × 1/2	=	4 250
		14 000

Expected cost [0.50 × 17 000] +

        [0.50 × 14 000]   =   15 500

3rd 6 months

0.50 × 0.60 = 0.30 chance of

£150k × 19% × 1/2	=	14 250	
£50k × 17% × 1/2	=	4 250	18 500

0.50 × 0.40 = 0.20 chance

£150k × 15% × 1/2	=	11 250	
£50k × 17% × 1/2	=	4 250	15 500

0.50 × 0.40 = 0.20 chance

£150k × 15% × 1/2	=	11 250	
£50k × 17% × 1/2	=	4 250	15 500

0.50 × 0.60 = 0.30 chance

£150k × 11% × 1/2	=	4 250	
£50k × 17% × 1/2	=	4 250	12 500

Expected cost [0.30 × 18 500]

        + (0.40 × 15 500)

        + (0.30 × 12 500)   =   £15 500

- As can be seen the expected interest cost for each period is £15 500, giving a total expected cost for the 18 months of £46 500.
- The total issue costs are:

5 year loan	£800
plus issue costs + 3 renewals	£6000

- Tax relief of (£15 500 × 25%) = £3875 will be available in 18 months' time.

This gives a net cost of £49 425 over the 18-month period (46 500 + 6800 – 3875).

Alternative 2

Using a similar approach it can be shown the net cost over the 18 months of alternative 2 is £48 175.

Alternative 2 is the cheapest.

Risks

The management is worried about being unable to service the interest on the borrowed funds. We will now consider which alternative seems to be the safest.

Alternative 1

- First 6 months: we are told £19 500 will be available which is sufficient to service interest.
- Second 6 months: £18 500 available – sufficient.
- Third 6 months: £15 500 available. There is only one outcome where the interest cost will be greater than this amount. The probability of it occurring is 0.30.

There is a 30% chance.

Alternative 2

It will be found that there is no chance of the cash inflow not being sufficient to service the debt. Under the worst scenario at the end of the third six-month period the cash flows are as below.

Interest	£17 500
Issue cost	500
Tax relief	(4 125)
	£13 875

The cash available is £15 500 plus the surpluses carried forward from the two earlier periods.

Alternative 2 is the cheaper and less risky.

Interest-rate swaps have increased dramatically in popularity over recent years. There are two principal reasons why a company may wish to engage in such swaps. One is to alter the balance of its portfolio of loans. If a company feels that too many of its loans are at fixed interest rates, and it finds another company that feels that too many of its loans are at variable interest rates, the two companies may be happy to conduct an interest-rate swap.

14.16 Interest-rate swaps

The second reason is that the situation often occurs where an interest-rate swap results in both companies making savings on their borrowing costs. At first it can seem hard to accept that both companies can gain and nobody loses. It is true however and it occurs because of market imperfections. An example below will demonstrate the point.

The subject is discussed more fully in Chapter 20 on treasury management where further examples are to be found.

In its simplest form one party, say Company C, which has borrowed funds at a fixed interest rate, gets together with another party, say Company D, which has borrowed at a floating rate, and the two agree to service each other's loan. In effect, Company C finishes up paying a floating rate of interest and Company D a fixed rate.

In its simplest form the transaction is conducted in just one currency. Both companies, referred to as 'counterparties', will show their own loans in their balance sheets. Some companies disclose their actual interest rate commitments (resulting from swap agreements) in notes in their annual accounts.

The arrangement becomes slightly more complicated when a bank becomes involved. A bank may act as a broker bringing the two companies together or as one of the principals. The motive behind the swap arrangement is that the company that has borrowed at a fixed rate wishes to service a floating rate loan. With the other company the position is reversed. We will illustrate an interest rate swap with an example.

Example 14.2

A company XYZ has borrowed on a line of credit from a UK bank at a floating rate of interest, say the London interbank offered rate (LIBOR) plus a premium. The rate at the time of the swap is 5.5% + 2.5%. Another company, Gresham, has borrowed in the Euro market at a fixed rate of 8.19%. The directors of XYZ want to transfer from a floating-rate commitment to a fixed-rate loan. This wish could be based on expectations that interest rates will rise dramatically in the future or because it wants a better balance of debts in its portfolio.

The directors of Gresham wish to transfer its debts from fixed interest to a floating rate. For the purpose of a swap, an intermediary bank will bring the parties together. The bank will of course charge for its services. XYZ will finish up servicing the fixed-rate debt of Gresham, and Gresham will service the floating rate debt of XYZ.

The Intermediary bank could arrange for XYZ to pay 8.22%, and keep 0.03% for itself, passing on the 8.19% to Gresham to pay the Eurobankers. The counter-arrangement is that with the current interest rates Gresham pay 9.52% to the bank, who pass on 9.50% to XYZ (LIBOR + 4.0%). Of course, with the latter transaction the rate paid by Gresham could change from one period to another as the market interest rates change. XYZ has reduced its risks, as it knows that the maximum amount it will have to pay is 8.22%. In diagrammatic form the transaction appears as in Fig. 14.2.

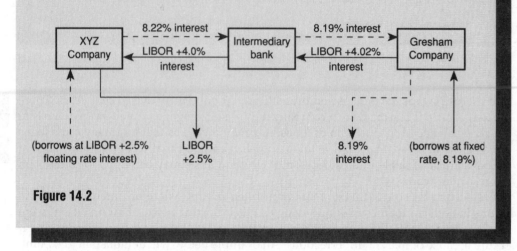

Figure 14.2

We will now use the same example to demonstrate the second reason for an interest rate swap, namely to save on borrowing costs.

Example 14.3

Let us assume that the XYZ company is larger and has a better reputation than the Gresham company – it can borrow more cheaply (whether fixed or floating rate debt). If XYZ wished to borrow in the Euromarket it would have to pay 7.19%. If Gresham wished to borrow at a floating rate from a UK bank it would pay LIBOR + 4.5%.

As can be seen in Table 14.3, XYZ has a comparative advantage of 1% in fixed rate borrowing and of 2% in floating rate borrowing. The difference of 1% is the possible gain from a swap transaction.

The rule in a swap is (a) for each company to borrow under the terms with which the company has the greater comparative advantage or the least comparative disadvantage. This means XYZ borrows floating and Gresham borrows fixed; (b) the companies service each other's debts.

Table 14.3 Potential gain

	XYZ	Gresham	XYZ's comparative advantage
Fixed	7.19%	8.19%	1.0%
Floating	LIBOR + 2.5%	LIBOR + 4.5%	2.0%
Possible net gain			1.0%

We illustrate the gains each company (and the intermediary bank) makes from the swap in Table 14.4. We keep the same arrangements as in the example above: i.e.

XYZ borrows at floating rate (LIBOR + 2.5%)
Gresham borrows at fixed rate (8.19%)

All we now take into account is the opportunity gain or loss from entering into the swap transaction compared with borrowing in the market directly.

Table 14.4 Potential gains from swap

XYZ

On floating	Pays to UK bank	LIBOR + 2.5%	
	Net receipt from intermediary bank	LIBOR + 4.0%	+ 1.50%
On fixed	Pays to intermediary bank	8.22%	
	Opportunity cost in market	7.19%	
		Loss	− 1.03%
		Net gain	+ 0.47%

Gresham

On floating	Pays intermediary bank	LIBOR + 4.02%	
	Opportunity cost in market	LIBOR + 4.5%	
		Gain	+ 0.48%
On fixed	Pays in Euromarket	8.19%	
	Receives from intermediary bank	8.19%	0
		Net gain	+ 0.48%
Intermediary bank	0.03% From XYZ		
	0.02% From Gresham	Gain	+ 0.05%

In Table 14.4 it can be seen that XYZ make a gain on the floating rate side of the deal, but lose on the fixed rate side. They are paying Gresham 8.22% fixed rate, whereas if they had gone directly to the market they could have borrowed for 7.19%. On balance however they gain.

Gresham break even on the fixed rate side of the deal, but gain on the floating rate side. If they had borrowed at floating rates in the market they would have had to pay more than they are paying XYZ.

Of course there are many ways in which the 1% total gain from the transaction can be divided. Who gains most is a matter for negotiation between the two counterparties. Also for any agreed split of the gains there are many different combinations of interest rate transfer payments that give the desired net outcome.

The accounting treatment of an interest rate swap is relatively straightforward. Each swap party should report on its balance sheet its original underlying borrowing from its lenders and any accrued interest payable thereon, since it continues to be obligated to pay these amounts. In the usual swap arrangement, the parties do **not** assume responsibility for paying the other party's borrowing: rather, the principal amount of the borrowing serves as a memorandum or notional amount upon which the interest rate swap payments are based. Thus, one party's balance sheet does not include the other party's principal amount, and vice versa. In the profit and loss account, the net settlement amount under the swap agreement (resulting in a net interest receivable or payable from/to the other swap party) should be accrued each period and reported as a net adjustment to the interest expense for the underlying borrowing. Assuming that the transaction is material, the existence of the swap and its terms (including its impact on the interest cost of the underlying borrowing and the period of the agreement) should be disclosed in the footnotes to the financial statements (usually in the note dealing with debt).

14.17 Debt—equity swaps

In the USA one type of financial restructuring that has proved to be very popular at certain times is the debt–equity swap. With this the holders of a company's debentures and loan stock are invited to exchange that security for equity in the company.

From the company's point of view there are number of advantages.

1. There is a reduction in the level of gearing, with equity replacing debt.
2. When market interest rates are significantly higher than the coupon rate on outstanding debt, it is possible to have an even more favourable effect on the gearing ratios. This is illustrated below.

A 5% bond maturing in 20 years is clearly not worth its par value when current interest rates are, say, at 10%. An approximate indication of the market price would be £50 for a £100 bond. This means that the company can offer the holders of such a bond equity shares worth just over £50 and it should prove to be attractive. This adjustment has the effect of reducing the level of gearing if the gearing is based on the market values of debt and equity: £50 of debt is replaced with just over £50 worth of equity.

If the debt-to-equity ratio is based on book values, the effect of the re-capitalization is exaggerated. The book value of the debt (£100) is higher than the market value. On book value calculations therefore, £100 worth of debt is eliminated from the balance sheet, i.e. the par value of the debt, and replaced with £50 worth of equity.

Another form of financial restructing is a debt-for-debt swap. This again would occur when current interest rates are very much higher than interest rates at the time that the debt was issued.

14.18 Repayment of loans

There are a number of different types of loan, all of which require different methods of repayment. These will be illustrated with examples. Let us assume that a company borrows £100 000 from a bank on 1 January 1994 and the nominal interest rate payable per annum is fixed at 10%. Tax will be ignored.

Term loan

This is the simplest type of loan. The £100 000 is borrowed for a fixed term, in this case four years. The interest is payable on 31 December each year and the capital sum is repayable as a single payment on 31 December 1997. The cash outflow, what is called the 'annual debt service' of the company, is therefore

End of:

1994	1995	1996	1997
–£10 000	–£10 000	–£10 000	–£110 000

The borrowing company has to consider how it will repay £100 000 at the end of 1997. As mentioned above it has at least three options: it could place money aside each year as with a sinking fund; it could hope to be able to repay the amount out of the net cash inflows in the year 1997; it could 'refund' the £100 000 by borrowing again in 1997 and using this cash inflow to repay the 1994 loan.

Mortgage style loan with equal payment each period

With this method, the annual debt service (the interest and capital repayments combined) is the same each year. This type of loan is similar to those used for purchasing a home by means of a mortgage loan, and is also the usual type of loan arranged for countries when borrowing in the Euromarkets or when borrowing from commercial banks.

Using the same example as above, with the repayment over four years and the first repayment being made a the end of the first year, the annual cash outflow would be as follows:

End of:

1994	1995	1996	1997
–31 547	–£31 547	–£31 547	–£31 547

The way in which this annual service charge was arrived at was to calculate the annuity that would be received in each of four years, if a payment of £100 000 was now made with interest at 10% per annum.

The PV of an annuity table (Table 3 at the end of this book) gives the discount factor for four periods, with 10% interest per annum, as 3.1699. Dividing the capital sum of £100 000 by this gives £31 547.

In this problem we were given the PV, the number of years and the interest rate; we then calculated the annual flow. The more usual way in which Table 3 is used is to know the annual flow, the number of years and the interest rate, and then to calculate the present value.

The debt service charge in each year is a mixture of capital repayment and interest. Table 14.5 shows the details of the repayments.

Table 14.5

	Total repayment	Interest	Capital	Capital balance at start of year
1994	£31 547	£10 000	£21 547	£100 000
1995	£31 547	£7845	£23 702	£78 453
1996	£31 547	£5475	£26 072	£54 750
1997	£31 547	£2867	£28 680	£28 680

Payments more frequent than annually

The examples in this section are all based on interest paid on an annual basis. There are of course many loans where interest needs to be paid at more frequent intervals, say six monthly. The same techniques and the same tables can be used with monthly quarterly and half yearly payments as well as with annual payments.

Let us assume in the above mortgage style loan example that the interest rate is now quoted as 5% semi-annually, with interest and capital repayments over four years at six-monthly intervals. The repayments would now be:

$$\begin{array}{ccccc} 30.6.94 & 31.12.94 & \dots & 30.6.97 & 31.12.97 \\ -\text{£15 472} & -\text{£15 472} & \dots & -\text{£15 472} & -\text{£15 472} \end{array}$$

This service charge has been calculated using Table 3. This time we observe the factor for eight periods at 5% interest per period, which is 6.4632. The £100 000 loan is divided by this factor to give eight payments of £15 472.

Annual equivalent interest rates

It will be noted that this service charge is not one half of that for the four year loan with annual repayments. This is because the capital repayments are being made earlier than in the annual repayment case and the effective interest charge is different. It should be appreciated that a 5% interest half yearly is equivalent to an annual rate of 10.215%, i.e. $(1.05)^2$.

The way that the equivalent annual interest charge can be estimated in the case where interest rates are quoted at intervals shorter than one year is to substitute the quoted rate of interest r and the frequency n of payments in the following equation:

$$\text{equivalent annual interest rate} = (1 + r)^n$$

Therefore a loan with interest quoted at 2% per month compounded is equivalent to an annual rate of 26.82%, i.e. $(1.02)^{12} = 1.2682$. The compounding means that interest is being charged on the interest that has not been paid as well as on the capital. Table 1 at the end of the book gives the amount of 1 at compound interest rates.

The other way in which interest rates might be quoted in loans where equal repayments are required is to quote the annual interest rate but to require payments at intervals more frequently than once a year. Let us say in our above example that the £100 000 is borrowed at an annual interest rate of 10%, but repayments are required quarterly.

Using the equation above we can calculate the quarterly interest rate that is equivalent to an annual rate of 10%:

$$1.10 = (1 + r)^4$$

Table 1 indicates that over four periods, a factor of 1.10 arises somewhere between the 2% and 3% interest rates. In fact, the quarterly compound interest rate is approximately 2.4%. The company is required to repay the £100 000 with 16 equal quarterly payments at an interest rate of 10% per annum. Each payment will be approximately £7600. This can be estimated using Table 3. The relevant factor for an interest rate of 2% is 13.5777 and for an interest rate of 3% is 12.5611. The factor for an interest rate of 2.4% is in the region of 13.16.

Certain loans require the first repayments to be made at the date the contract is signed, i.e. at the beginning of the term of the loan. All subsequent payments are also at the beginning of the payment interval. This is sometimes referred to as an 'annuity due'. The annuity where no payment is needed at the beginning of the term of the loan is an 'ordinary annuity'.

Returning to the example above where the £100 000 was repayable in eight semi-annual instalments with an interest rate of 5% half yearly, we shall now assume that the first payout is due at 1 January 1994, and then every quarter.

We are now faced with an annuity of eight payments, the first being immediate. PV of annuity tables (such as Table 3) are based on ordinary annuities and do not allow for a payment at the beginning of the term. In fact what we are faced with is an immediate payout of cash, with the remaining seven payments in the form of an ordinary annuity.

We look up the PV factor for the seven payments, which with interest at 5% is 5.7864; the factor for the first immediate payment is 1.0000. These two factors are added together and divided into the £100 000 to give

$$\frac{\text{£100 000}}{6.7864} = \text{£14 735}$$

The eight repayments under this type of loan arrangement would each be of £14 735.

Grace periods

Some loans do not require capital repayments during their early years of the term. Loans with grace periods (also called rest periods or holiday periods) can sometimes be negotiated when a new business or a small business is borrowing from a bank. Such a grace period could be particularly important when the funds raised are to be used to finance a major project which will take time to develop before it starts to generate cash inflow. Grace periods are also often found in loans by commercial banks to governments. Again, the idea is to allow time for a project to be completed and start to generate returns before needing to worry about capital repayments.

There are at least three variations on loans with grace periods. In one, interest is charged and payable during the grace period but capital repayments do not have to be made during this period. In another, interest is charged but is not payable until the grace period finishes. The interest is accumulated during the grace period and added to the capital repayment, and the total is repaid over the remaining period of the loan. With this latter approach the borrower is in fact borrowing both the capital sum and the interest charge arising during the grace period. The third possibility is for no interest to be charged during the grace period.

We shall illustrate the first and second approach. Suppose, as in our earlier example, the borrower obtains £100 000. The life of the loan is four years and interest is 10% per annum. The grace period is two years.

Interest charged during grace period

It is being assumed that after the grace period the debt service charge is to be the same in each of the remaining two years of the period of the loan. The cash outflows would be:

31.12.94	31.12.95	31.12.96	31.12.97
−£10 000	−£10 000	−£57 620	−£57 620

The first two years' outflows are simply the interest on the capital sum. The outflows in the last two years are arrived at by obtaining the PV factor for an annuity for two years with interest at 10%. The factor of 1.7355 is divided into the £100 000.

Interest charged but not payable during the grace period

In this situation the interest is accumulated during the grace period and added to the capital sum for eventual repayment. The unpaid interest over the two years accumulates to £21 000 as at January 1996, i.e. $[(1.10)^2 - 1.00] \times £100 000$. The total debt at 1 January 1996 is therefore £121 000. The cash outflows for 1996 and 1997 are again calculated using the PV of an annuity table. The outflows in this case would be:

31.12.94	31.12.95	3.12.96	31.12.97
0	0	−£69 721	−£69 721

Clearly grace periods are a valuable concession to the borrower. In the two examples used as illustrations, they are providing a repayment schedule which should benefit the borrower. It should be appreciated, however, that they are not lowering the interest rate being charged. In both cases illustrated the full nominal rate of 10% per annum is effectively being paid. Grace periods only reduce the effective rate of interest below the nominal rate if no interest is charged during the grace period.

Loans with equal capital repayments each year

This type of loan is somewhat unusual, but can arise particularly in instances where the interest rate charged varies over the life of the loan. The mathematics are relatively simple, with the interest payments each year being based on the balance of the capital remaining to be paid at the beginning of that year.

In the example being used in this section, the annual cash outflow would be:

	31.12.94	31.12.95	31.12.96	31.12.97
Capital repayment	–£25 000	–£25 000	–£25 000	–£25 000
Interest payable	–£10 000	–£7 500	–£5 000	–£2 500
	–£35 000	–£32 500	–£30 000	–£27 500

As can be seen with this method the early years have higher debt service charges than the later years. This could be a disadvantage to the borrower.

To compare the relative advantages of the different types of loan it is necessary to know the expected returns and the timing of the returns from the project to be financed. One approach would be to select the loan with the cash outflows that most closely matched the timing of the cash inflows of the project.

Another approach would be simply to compare the PV of the returns from the project with the PV of the loan costs using conventional discounting methods. The alternative debt service charge schedules could be deducted from the cash inflow figures, and the resulting net figures discounted at the equity cost of the company. This would show the net PV obtained on the shareholders' funds.

In this section we have shown seven different repayment schedules for the same £100 000 loan over a four year repayment period. A borrower, of course, is most unlikely to be given a choice between the seven alternatives. The borrower, particularly if a small company, could well be offered a loan and given no choice as to how it will be repaid. The situation can arise, however, when a company with some bargaining power does have the opportunity to make a choice between two or three alternative types of loan.

14.19 Convertible loan stock

The characteristics of convertible loan stock issues are that, while they are sold initially as loan stock receiving an appropriate rate of interest, the holder is given the option of converting this loan stock within a given time period into equity shares at a specified price. The advantage to the company of this form of capital is that initially the loan stock assists the capital gearing, and, of course, the interest, with the advantage of the tax shield, reduces the cost of the capital in the years when it remains loan capital. The advantage to the shareholder is that he can wait to see how the share price of the company moves before deciding whether to invest in the equity. If the company is successful and the share price rises, the investor will be keen to exercise the option; if not, he is free to retain the loan investment. The holder is usually given the opportunity to convert on at least two dates in each year, dates on which the option is exercisable.

An example of a convertible loan stock issue is the ICI issue in September 1984 of £100 million of convertible Eurosterling bonds. At the time this was the largest issue that had been made in the Eurosterling market. (The Eurosterling market, as explained in Chapter 26, consists of Eurobonds issued in sterling.) The annual coupon rate on the ICI bond is 8.5%, which at the time of issue was below the market rate on non-convertible issues which was in the region of 11.5%.

The conversion option allows holders to convert the bonds into shares during the 15 year life of the bond. The conversion price was set at a level which was between 20% and 25% above the market price of the shares at the time that the convertible was issued. The ICI share price in September 1984 was in the region of £6 per share, and the conversion price was set at £7.50.

If the holder of the convertible bond does not wish to convert, one option available was selling the bond back to ICI after five years at 112% of the issue price. This was a safety net for bond holders which could be taken if the share performance of ICI up to 1989 was not good enough to make conversion into equity shares attractive.

Value of convertible security to an investor

The value of a convertible security depends upon what happens to the share price of the issuing company over the life of the security. If the share price rises above the conversion price and the investor expects it to remain above this level, he will exercise his option to convert when he is able to. If it does not rise above this level, or he expects any increase above the level to be only temporary, the investor will not wish to exercise the option.

The value of the convertible security depends on expectations regarding the future share price. The *ex ante* yield on the convertible is probabilistic; it depends upon a number of factors. If assumptions are made, for example if it is assumed that the share price grows at a certain rate per annum, then the value of the conversion privilege can be calculated as at any date in the future.

For an investor considering converting the debenture at some time in the future, the yield he can expect to receive can only be determined by forecasting the expected share price. The value of the shares to be received at the time of conversion can be expressed as in the following formula (it is emphasized that this is the total value to be received):

$$C_t = P_0(1 + g)^n R \tag{14.1}$$

where C_t is the conversion value of the debenture at time t, P_0 is the share price today, g is the estimated annual percentage rate of growth of share price, R is the number of shares to be received on conversion of one debenture and n is the number of years to conversion.

In addition to receiving the shares at a date in the future if and when the conversion is exercised, the holder also receives in the intervening period the interest on the debenture. This means that the total receipts due to the holder can be expressed as

$$V = I_1 + I_2 + I_3 + \ldots + I_n + P_0(1 + g)^n R \tag{14.2}$$

where I_n is the interest paid on the debenture in year n and V is the total receipts due to the holder. The current price at which the convertible debenture is being sold is known, and so the expected yield to be received from holding such a security can be determined using the following formula:

$$M = \sum_{t=1}^{n} \frac{I}{(1+r)^t} + \frac{P_0(1+g)^n R}{(1+r)^n} \tag{14.3}$$

where M is the price paid for convertible debenture and r is the internal rate of return (yield).

This approach utilizes Brigham's valuation model [2] and can be used to estimate the yield that an investor can expect, given assumptions about the date that he will convert and the change in share price over time. The same formula can of course be used to determine the growth in share price that must take place to give a required rate of return to the holder of the convertible debenture. This point is of special interest, because whatever else it may be worth the security has a straight debt value – the price which investors would be willing to pay just to receive the stream of future interest payments plus the redemption of the loan at the end of the period. A useful comparison can therefore be made between the value of the security as loan stock and its value as equity.

Two premiums will be referred to in the analysis:

$$\text{conversion premium} = \frac{\text{market value of convertible loan stock}}{\text{number of shares at conversion date}} - \text{current share price} \tag{14.4}$$

$$\text{rights premium} = \frac{\text{market value of convertible} - \text{value as loan stock}}{\text{number of shares at conversion date}} \tag{14.5}$$

These equations show the premiums per share. To ascertain the premium per unit of convertible loan stock, it is necessary to multiply the premium per share by the number of ordinary shares that can be obtained by converting one unit of loan stock.

To illustrate the use of the above formula, let us assume that a company (Barston PLC) issued a 10% convertible debenture (£100 par) on 1 January 1989. It could be converted into 80 equity shares of Barston at any time between 1 January 1994 and 31 November 1998. The convertible security was being sold for £95 on 1 January 1990. The price of the equity shares on 1 January 1990 was £0.90 and was expected to rise by 10% per annum. The gross yield on the security for an investor purchasing at the 1 January 1990 price can be estimated by using equation (14.3). We shall assume that the convertible debenture is held until the first conversion date, namely 1 January 1994. Then

$$95 = \frac{10}{1+r} + \frac{10}{(1+r)^2} + \frac{10}{(1+r)^3} + \frac{10}{(1+r)^4} + \frac{0.90(1.10)^4}{(1+r)^4} \times 80$$

Solving the equation gives r equal to approximately 11%. The expected yield for the investor buying the convertible at 1 January 1990 at £95 was therefore 11%.

The conversion premium on each Barston convertible debenture as at 1 January 1990 was equal to £0.2875 per share, given by £95/80 – £0.90.

To calculate the rights premium at 1 January 1990, we need to know the value of the convertible as simple loan stock. This depends upon the current interest yields in the market place on loan stock in a similar risk category to that of Barston. We shall assume that such an interest yield is 12%, which means that the value of the simple loan is £83.33. (At this price an interest payment of £10 gives a yield of 12%.)

The rights premium per share is therefore £0.1458, i.e.

$$\frac{£95 - £83.33}{80}$$

The rights premium represents the excess value of the convertible security over an equivalent loan stock with the same rate of interest. The situation is illustrated in Fig. 14.3 which depicts the situation in which the increase over time in the price of the company's shares is satisfactory and is expected to continue; consequently, a rights premium exists, since the rights option has a value. The line CM'' represents the conversion value of the convertible security at the various points in time. The market value is higher than the conversion value because investors expect the share price in the future to rise above its present level and so expect the rights to be worth even more.

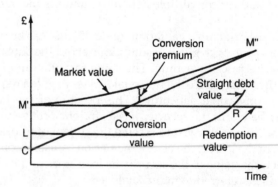

Figure 14.3

With the Barston example, the value of conversion to the holders of the security at 1 January 1990 was £72 (80 shares of £0.90 per share). The market value of the convertible is £95. This difference, represented in Fig. 14.3 as the gap between the $M'M''$ line and the CM'' line, reflects the required increase in ordinary share value to make conversion worth while. As the diagram shows, the two lines move closer together until they meet. At this point, conversion should start to take place.

The rights premium is the difference between the *LR* line and the *M'M"* line, i.e. the difference between the convertible security valued as a convertible and as a straight loan stock. In the early years of the security's life, the floor of the conversion value can be determined by its value as a loan stock, but as the share price rises its minimum value will eventually be determined by its worth as a convertible security. While it is still valued as loan stock the conversion premium will exceed the rights premium. However, if the share price rises as expected, as the time for conversion approaches the conversion premium will be lower than the rights premium.

As the conversion value of the security increases, its market value (which begins by being higher) also rises but at a slower rate, and the two values eventually become identical. There are at least two reasons for this. First, with the arrival of the conversion period the holder will be able to exercise the option and receive the conversion value; the market price should be kept from rising too far above this value otherwise the potential holder will be in danger of a loss. This prevents wide spreads arising between the market value and the conversion value. Convertible debentures can be purchased on the stock market on any trading day. On the date that they are first issued by a company, they sell for a premium (the rights premium) above the price which would be paid for a simple debenture that merely secured a stream of interest payments. This is because the investors, at that time of issue, expect benefits to accrue to them through the share conversion option, and for the same reason the interest yield will be lower on a convertible than on a straight debenture. If, however, the company's share price does not perform well over time, the price of the convertible debenture could well fall to a level giving the same yield as a straight debenture with no options.

Value as a debenture

If the price of the equity shares that are being offered in exchange for the convertible debt should fall or should not rise as much as is necessary to make conversion worthwhile, the value of the convertible security is that of a straight debt issue. The rights premium would be zero, with the value of the convertible equalling the value of loan stock.

The conversion premium in this case represents the recovery required in the ordinary share before conversion becomes an attractive proposition. This situation is illustrated in Fig. 14.4 where the market value of the convertible loan stock falls to the value of a straight debenture. This would happen if the share price of the company slumped and the investors considered the value of the right to convert as zero. The rights premium would consequently be zero. There would still be a conversion premium, however, because when the company decided at the time of issue on the number of ordinary shares to be exchanged for the loan stock, the expectations regarding future share price were higher than could later be justified.

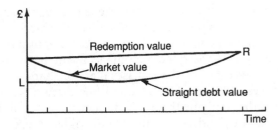

Figure 14.4

The redemption value is simply the amount of debt that will be redeemed at some time in the future. The convertible loan stock can be issued at par value, or at some value below this; in Fig. 14.4 it is shown as being issued at par. The market value of the stock falls as expectations change regarding the value of the rights until it becomes valued simply as loan stock. The reason that the value of the convertible as a debenture is shown to rise over time is that convertible securities usually carry a lower interest rate than a pure debt issue. Consequently, as the yield on the convertible is below that on a normal loan, its value as loan stock is initially below par, but as the maturity date approaches, with maturity at par, the two lines move towards each other.

The price of the ordinary shares on the market may rise above the equivalent ordinary share price under the option, but the holder still might not convert. He may wish to hold the convertible loan stock, receiving a yield on the loans perhaps greater than the dividend yield on the equity, and convert only on the final date at which the option can be exercised. As the ordinary share price increases above the equivalent share value, the market value for the convertible will still be equal to the conversion value. The two values will be equal because investors would only be prepared to purchase the convertible in the market at a price equal to the conversion value.

This brings out the second important factor causing the market value and the conversion value to converge, namely the relationship between the yield on the convertible loan stock and the yield on the share for which it can be exchanged. The interest on a convertible is fixed at a certain rate; however, the dividends paid on a share normally rise. This means that the dividend yield on the equivalent share price rises to meet the yield on the fixed-interest loan stock, so that as the time for conversion approaches, the gap between the market value and the conversion value closes, as shown in Fig. 14.3.

The exact value L_t of convertible loan stock as a normal debenture can be determined from the following equation:

$$L_t = \sum_{k=1}^{T-t} \frac{I}{(1+i)^k} + \frac{M}{(1+i)^{T-t}}$$

where T is the year of redemption, t is the present year, $T - t$ is the number of years to maturity of the debenture, i is the market interest yield on an equivalent risk debt issue, I is the interest paid each year and M is the redemption value at maturity.

Conversion premium

As explained, the difference between the market price of the convertible security and its conversion parity is called the conversion premium. Weil *et al.* [3], as a result of examining the literature on the subject, summarize the explanations given for the premium under seven headings, some of which are more appropriate to the situation in the USA than in the UK.

1. **Transaction costs:** brokers' commissions are lower on debentures than on shares, and therefore the convertible debenture deserves a premium to reflect the saving in costs over obtaining the company shares directly.
2. **Income difference:** if the stream of future interest receipts exceeds the stream of expected future dividends, a premium should arise. The income stream is of course safer than the dividend stream, which also leads to a premium.
3. **Financing costs:** in the USA margin requirements mean that a greater percentage of the costs can be borrowed for bond purchases than for share purchases.
4. **Anti-dilution clauses:** often convertible securities carry a clause prohibiting any action on the part of the company that might reduce the value of the security such as the payment of stock dividends, or the use of new rights issues.
5. **Price floors:** there is a floor to the price of a convertible. It has a certain rate of interest and a certain maturity value, which together with the market rate of interest will determine the lowest price of the security. There is no such guarantee with equity shares.
6. **Volatility of price:** the larger the fluctuations in share price over time, the greater is the potential gain and consequently the more valuable the option to convert.

7. **Duration:** the longer the life of an option the more valuable it must be; thus the longer the time to conversion the greater the premium will be.

These seven variables were examined by Weil *et al.* in an attempt to explain the premium on convertibles. Although most of the results were not conclusive, the main finding of their paper was surprisingly that the floor is of negligible importance in explaining the premium. This is contrary to the emphasis of opinion in the literature, which focuses squarely on the price floor as the main factor causing the premium.

One of the reasons for the non-significance of the floor variable in the study is that the value of the convertible as a bond does generally move with changes in the rate of interest. In so far as rising interest rates means the value of fixed interest securities fall as do share prices, then the 'floor' will not provide much of a safeguard. If interest rates rise, interest yields rise and for dividend yields to rise in line, share prices will fall. Therefore the 'floor' will not work if there is a general downturn in the economy; it can work if it is only the price of the issuing company's share that is falling and the rest of the market is stable.

Convertible securities obviously become less attractive to a purchaser at times when the stock market is expected to decline. A purchaser would not wish to convert when share prices are falling, and so in fact he is left holding a simple debenture.

In an empirical study of UK convertible loans Skerratt [4] concluded that such securities were attractive to certain investors because 'the coupon exceeded the dividend yield on equity and there was an opportunity to reap advantages of equity growth, although since the conversion premium was, in most cases, positive, the growth possible from convertibles was less than from equity. Thus, the likely holder would be a cautious optimist, expecting share prices to rise. There are few optimists about once the stock market starts to decline. Convertibles are therefore a security for issue in 'bull' markets.

The Skerratt study, based on the position in the UK of a number of convertible loan issues, found that the influences determining a substantial proportion of the variation in convertible prices were as follows:

1. the market price of the equity;
2. the income difference;
3. the number of opportunities available for conversion;
4. the relative safety of the convertible compared with the equity;
5. the length of time to elapse before the first opportunity for conversion.

These features of convertible evaluation are similar to those found in the US study by Weil *et al.*

Advantages of convertibles to the company

If the rate of conversion is correctly determined, this method of finance may offer the company two advantages over other forms of finance. First, as earnings grow the debt is self-liquidating. The ordinary share price will reflect the increasing earnings. When the share price reaches the price at which conversion is worth while, debentures will be exchanged for ordinary shares. Therefore the company does not have to find new finance to pay off a debenture when the time for redemption is approaching. By converting, the bond-holders are saving the company from having to fund the debt.

It could, of course, be argued that the existing shareholders are being made to suffer by having the debt reduced in this way. It may be in the existing shareholders' interest not to have new equity created but to have a new loan floated to provide the finance to pay off the old loan. This would certainly be the case if the conversion of the debentures, by increasing the number of the shares, lowered their price. A fall in earnings per share, as explained earlier, could well have this effect. However, the empirical studies on this point do not find that the share prices fall after conversion.

The second attractive feature of convertible debentures that offer advantages to the company is that the conversion does not harm the company's capital structure; if anything it helps it. The company has to pay the interest bill on the convertible, but does not have to repay the capital. It is in effect a convenient method of avoiding the need to raise a second round of funds for repayment purposes.

The conversion of debt into equity does not increase the total capital employed of the company. Should the company wish to expand it can now make another issue of debt capital as its gearing will have fallen as a result of the conversion. The use of convertibles became for a time part of a cycle: debt – conversion into equity – new debt – conversion into equity and so on. To continue such a financial exercise, however, the company needed to produce the earnings performance that enabled the share price to continue to rise.

The type of convertible stock issued by companies has changed over time. Convertibles were once regarded as a special type of borrowing, designed to meet a short-term situation, but they then became looked upon as deferred equity. Early conversion dates gave way to possible conversion over long periods of time. The tax relief available on interest, but not on dividends, undoubtedly contributed to this lengthening in the time in which the conversion option was being offered. A typical convertible stock offers conversion at a price about 10%–15% above the market price of the ordinary shares at the time of issue.

Example 14.4

Question

Groso plc has decided to invest in a major new product. The investment involves considerable risk, and will have a large effect on the company's earnings.

Depending on the success of the new product the company's total earnings before interest and tax (EBIT) might change as follows in the second year of the product's life.

Success of new product	Probability	Growth in EBIT in year 2
Excellent	0.1	40%
Good	0.4	25%
Average	0.3	15%
Poor	0.1	5%
Failure	0.1	–10%

Earnings before interest and tax are expected to increase by 5% in the first year of the project, before the full effect of the new product is known.

The new product will be financed by either:

1. A 1 for 5 rights issue at a 15% discount on the current market price plus a £30 million debenture issue at a fixed interest rate of 13% per year.
2. A £50 million 9% convertible debenture issue plus a reduction in the company's dividend of £20 million for next year only. The convertible debenture may be converted into 32 ordinary shares anytime between 4 and 5 years in the future.

Except for the possible reduction in dividend, no internally generated funds are available.

The company's most recent balance sheet and profit and loss account are summarized below:

Balance sheet

	£000	£000
Land and buildings (at cost)		53 450
Plant and machinery		68 900
Investments		8 500
		130 850
Stock	66 270	
Debtors	61 400	
Marketable securities	3 500	
Bank	1 800	
		132 970
Creditors	41 450	
Proposed dividend	14 000	
Taxation	12 000	
Overdraft	28 500	
		(95 950)
		167 870
Financed by:		
Ordinary shares (25p par value)		25 000
Reserves		91 870
10% preference shares (£1 par value)		18 000
10% debenture 1998		18 000
Floating rate term loan (maturing in five years)		15 000
		167 870

Profit and loss account

	£000
Turnover	302 400
Earnings before interest and tax	84 000
Interest	7 110
Taxable income	76 890
Taxation	26 912
	49 978
Preference dividend	1 800
Ordinary dividend	28 500
Retained earnings	19 678

The market price of the company's ordinary shares is 234 pence. The preference shares are quoted at 200 pence and the debentures are trading at £85 (per £100 par).

Required:

Discuss the advantages and disadvantages of the two financing packages. Support your discussion with calculations where relevant and state clearly any assumptions that you make.

ACCA, Dec. 1988

Answer

We will first consider the effects on earnings per share of each of the two financing packages. Currently EPS is:

$$\frac{\text{Earnings available}}{\text{Number of shares}} = \frac{£48\ 978}{100\ 000} = 49\text{p}$$

First alternative

- Rights issue plus debentures;
- A one-for-five rights issue means the issue of 20 million new shares. The price of the new shares being sold to holders of the rights will be 199p (i.e. $0.85 \times £2.34$).

Assuming that there is no significant change in interest payments on the floating rate term loan and the overdraft, estimates of earnings per share in the next two years are:

	Year 1	£000 Year 2				
		Excellent	Good	Average	Poor	Failure
EBIT	88 200	123 480	110 250	101 430	92 610	79 380
Interest	11 010	11 010	11 010	11 010	11 010	11 010
Taxable profit	77 190	112 470	99 240	90 420	81 600	68 370
Taxation[1]	27 017	39 365	34 734	31 647	28 560	23 930
	50 173	73 105	64 506	58 773	53 040	44 440
Preference dividend	1 800	1 800	1 800	1 800	1 800	1 800
	48 373	71 305	62 706	56 973	51 240	42 640
Earnings per share	40.3p	59.4p	52.3p	47.5p	42.7p	35.5p

[1]Assumed to be 35%.

Dilution in EPS is expected in year 1 before the full effect of the new product is known. In year 2 substantial dilution is expected if the product is 'poor' or a 'failure' and slight dilution if 'average' success is achieved. Good or excellent results, of which there is a 50% probability, produce increases in EPS. The interest charge is £7.11 million plus the additional interest of £3.9 million.

Second alternative

£50 million convertible debenture and dividend reduction. The convertible debenture will require additional annual interest payments of £4.5 million.

The reduction in dividend, assuming that the next dividend would increase by 5% to £29.925m, would mean a fall in dividend per share from 29.925 pence to 9.925 pence, but this is a one-off event.

The estimated earnings per share are:

		£000				
	Year 1	Year 2				
		Excellent	Good	Average	Poor	Failure
EBIT	88 200	123 480	110 250	101 430	92 610	79 380
Interest	11 610	11 610	11 610	11 610	11 610	11 610
Taxable	76 590	111 870	98 640	89 820	81 000	67 770
Taxation	26 807	39 155	34 524	31 437	28 350	23 720
	49 783	72 715	64 116	58 383	52 650	44 050
Preference dividend	1800	1800	1800	1800	1800	1800
	47 983	70 915	62 316	56 583	50 850	42 250
Earnings per share	48p	70.9p	62.3p	56.6p	50.9p	42.3p

Earnings per share are significantly higher in both years with this financing strategy.

Gearing

An important issue in the question in Example 14.4 is the effect of the financing packages on Groso's level of gearing. Gearing will be considered in detail in Chapter 18. Using market values the loans plus preference shares as a percentage of shareholders' equity is:

$$= \frac{28\ 500 + 15\ 000 + (18\ 000 \times 2) + (18\ 000 \times 0.85)}{100\ 000 \times 2.34}$$

$$= 0.405$$

$$= 40.5\%$$

This is a low level of gearing, even after including preference shares as non-equity. If the gearing is calculated based on book values it is found to be 68%. The effect of the first financing alternative will be to increase the numerator by £30 000, and to increase the denominator by (20 000 × £1.99). This is not changing the level of gearing by very much.

With the second alternative the effect on gearing depends on if and when the debentures are converted into equity. When the convertible debentures are issued the gearing level will rise. However, if they are converted the gearing level will fall substantially.

Other issues

A crucial factor affecting share price will be the market's reaction to the dividend reduction in the second alternative. Although this reduction is only for one year, investors would need to be persuaded that this is the case. Usually a cut in dividends is not well received by the market. Dividends are discussed in more detail in Chapter 17.

A further type of capital issue is loan stock which cannot in itself be converted into equity but which gives the holder the right to subscribe at fixed future dates for ordinary shares at a predetermined price. Many issues have been offered with these terms. The subscription rights, called 'warrants', entitle the bond-holder to obtain a certain

14.20 Warrants

number of the company's ordinary shares at an agreed price. This is different from a convertible issue of loan stock, where the loan stock is given up if the conversion right is exercised. With a warrant the bond-holder keeps the original loan stock, and has the choice of using the warrant to obtain ordinary shares in addition.

The advantage to the company of this form of issue is that the loan stock is maintained until the date of redemption. The warrants also enable the company to raise new equity capital: there is no need to substitute one form of capital for another, as there is with a convertible loan. The company retains both forms of capital up to the date of the redemption. The new equity can be used as a base to raise further loan capital in the future. In contrast, convertible loan stock may only help the short-term situation for a company; the loan raises the level of gearing, but when the loan is converted the gearing falls again. If convertible stocks allow early conversion, the assistance to the level of gearing could be very short-term in nature. Some long-term gearing benefits are obtainable from convertible loan stock that carries an interest rate similar to the yield on debentures, and which is intended for conversion later in its life. But it is still true that when the conversion is exercised the gearing is lowered. Late conversion is obviously preferable from the company's viewpoint, but riskier for the investor – unless the company makes the coupon sufficiently attractive, by making it similar to one on debt capital, so that the investor is less likely to think of the convertible stock as deferred equity.

Loan stock with warrants maintains the character of a loan stock throughout its life and will therefore require the usual security of loan capital. As long as the company is sure that it will need a new inflow of external capital in the future when the warrants are exercised, this type of issue will have advantages both to the company and to the investor.

As with a convertible issue, the price at which equity can be purchased, on the predetermined dates when the rights are to be exercised, is above the market price at the date of issue. If, however, the market price moves as the company hopes, the market price at the time for exercising the rights should be above the rights price. This form of loan stock with the warrants attached has become more attractive than the straight type of debenture because of the opportunity offered by the equity option of sharing in the future profits of the company. It is a capital instrument which provides an equity kicker.

Valuation of warrants

The theoretical value of a warrant is $(M - O)N$, where M is the market price of the ordinary share today, O is the exercise price of the warrant and N is the number of shares that each warrant allows the owner to buy [5].

For example, suppose that a warrant entitles a holder to buy one share at a price of £1. He may exercise this warrant at any time over the next three years. The present price of the shares is £2. The value of the warrant appears to be simply £1 = (£2 – £1) × 1. The price of the warrant should not fall below £1, for that is the value of the warrant if it is exercised on the market today.

The price of the warrant can rise above £1 if the prospects for the company are good. If the price of the warrant on the market is £1.50, it means that it is being sold at a premium of £0.50. Is it a good or bad buy at this price? It depends on the present value gained or lost by incurring this expenditure. The holder may not wish to exercise the option to convert into shares with these prices.

If the warrant is to be exercised this has to be completed before an expiry date. If we assume that the holder waits to the end of the period before exercising the option – and a study in the USA [6] showed that almost all warrants remained unexercised until shortly before expiry date – then the PV of exercising the option on expiry date can be calculated. In the above example, £1 has to be paid by the holder of the warrant in three years time. With a cost of money of 10%, the PV of this outlay is £0.75 = £1/(1.10)³.

The market price of the warrant is £1.50; the PV of the payment on exercising the option at the expiry date is £0.75. The PV of the share is only £2. Someone who purchases the warrant today has a present cost of £2.25 (= £1.50 + £0.75) if he wishes to obtain the share at the expiry date.

This is not a good investment with a PV cost of £2.25 to obtain a share with a present value of £2.00.

If the price of the warrant was only £1.20, it would be a good buy, however. Buying an option at £1.20, and paying £1 to the company at the end of year 3, which has a present cost of £0.75, means that for an outlay of £1.95 the investor has access to a share worth £2. The holder of the warrant has to decide whether to exercise the option now or to delay until nearer the expiry date. The choice is between a PV cost of £1.95 and receiving the share in three years' time, or paying £2 and receiving dividends over the three years. He would be indifferent to whether to exercise the option now or later, when the following equation holds:

$$M_0 - P_W = V_D + V_W$$

where M_0 is the price of a share today for which warrant can be exchanged, P_W is the price of the warrant, V_D is the PV of after-tax dividends over the remaining years of the warrant's life and V_W is the PV of the cost of exercising the warrant at the end of its life.

With the above example, this equation gives

$$£2 - £1.20 = x + £0.75$$
$$£0.05 = x$$

Therefore the break-even PV of the dividends over three years is £0.05, which, with money costing 10%, is a dividend of approximately £0.02 per year. If the company is paying a higher dividend than this per share, it would be in the warrant holder's interest to exercise his option now. If the company is paying a lower dividend rate he should hold the warrant and realize nearer the expiry date.

In the first example, where the warrant had a price of £1.50, there was obviously no question of whether it was worth exercising the option now in order to receive the dividend. It was in the interests of the existing warrant holders if they wanted dividends to sell the warrants and buy shares, for it was only costing them £0.50 to obtain a share this way, whereas with the exercise of the option it would have cost them £1 to obtain a share.

In the case where a warrant appears to be clearly overpriced, it would seem attractive to sell the warrant short and buy the shares. Short selling means selling shares (or warrants) you do not own at the moment and borrowing the same number of shares from somebody else to deliver to your purchaser. You hope that the share price will fall, so that when you buy the shares at a later date to return to the person who lent them to you for the first transaction you will be able to buy at a lower price than the one you received on your selling deal. To carry out this transaction it is necessary either to be able now to borrow the shares you have to deliver or to agree to deliver the shares at a future date.

In the UK this form of trading is not as attractive as in the USA. It is less profitable because in the UK sale proceeds are not received until they are covered by securities or by cash. The securities therefore either have to be borrowed with a possible interest charge or purchased on the market. Alternatively, 70% of the value of the securities sold short has to be deposited with the broker. Therefore this form of trading is not so profitable in Britain. However, it is an interesting example of financial trading in securities.

At the beginning of this section it was stated that one approach to valuing a warrant is to take the difference between the market price of the share and the exercise price of the warrant. However, it has been pointed out that this approach is too simplistic. The value of a warrant can rise above this difference. It is partly because of this simple approach to valuing warrants that they are seen as a financial instrument that can lead to very high percentage capital gains.

To be in line with other valuation techniques in finance, the current price of a warrant should equal the PV of the difference between the future price of the share and the exercise price of the warrant. This relationship can be expressed as

$$P_W = \frac{M_0(1 + g)^n - 0}{(1 + k)^n}$$

where g is the expected growth rate in share price, k is the cost of capital appropriate to the warrant's risk class and n is the number of time periods expiring before the warrant is exercised.

It can be shown that the potential gains from buying a warrant are greater than the potential gains from buying the share to which the warrant relates. Similarly it is possible to make a greater loss. Assume that the price of the warrant at time t_1 equals the current price of the share less the price that would have to be paid when the warrant is exercised plus the premium on the warrant. Assume that the following situation develops:

	t_1	t_2	Change
Share price	£20	£40	+100%
Warrant price	£10	£28	+180%

The exercise price is £12, so that at time t_1 there was a premium of £2 on a warrant, i.e. £22 would have to be paid to obtain a share valued at £20. Time t_2 is the last date for exercise of the warrant, and so at that date the difference between the warrant price and the share price is exactly equal to the subscription price, the cost of exercising the warrant. As can be seen a greater gain can be made from holding the warrant over the period than from holding the share. With any increase in the price of the share this will be the case.

If, however, the share had fallen in price, a greater loss would have been incurred from holding the warrant rather than holding the share:

	t_1	t_2	Change
Share price	£20	£15	−25%
Warrant price	£10	£3	−66%

This is the gearing effect of warrants.

Certain criticisms can be applied to this approach. It can be argued that if there is an efficient capital market, why in the first situation would the seller of the warrant be prepared to give up such large expected gains? If the buyer and seller have similar knowledge of the affairs of the company, why would the present holder of the warrant sell it for £10 when he has expectations that the warrant will rise in price? We have in the example introduced a premium into the valuation of the warrant, £2. Clearly, with an efficient capital market this premium would not be enough. The situation used in the example could only hold if the buyer and seller had different expectations about the company concerned, i.e. they have different expectations with regard to the growth rate of the company's share price. Given an efficient market, it is unlikely that the holder of the warrant would show a gain of 180% and the holder of the share a gain of 100%.

Equity derivatives

One type of equity derivative is a 'covered warrant'. This is an option on a company's shares sold by a third party (sometimes with the company's permission). The seller of the warrant does have available the necessary quantity of the underlying shares in case the buyer of the option decides to exercise the option. This is why it is referred to as a covered warrant.

It can be contrasted with a 'synthetic warrant', with which the seller of the warrant does not hold the full complement of the underlying shares. The seller of the warrant might have to purchase the shares if the buyer exercises the option, or the seller might at the time of writing the option hedge using existing options or shares.

As mentioned above, it is not the company whose shares are the subject of the option that is involved in writing the warrant, it is a third party. At the end of the 1980s such options were available on the shares of a wide range of European companies. The attraction of an option is that if the share price rises with a bull market the buyer of the option can make considerable gains, whilst if the share price falls, the loss is limited to the cost of the option premium.

One particular innovation in the market is referred to as the 'basket warrant'. This is an option on a basket of shares, usually in a specific sector of an individual stock market. For example, Salomon Brothers, a merchant bank, issues warrants in London on US food, oil and pharmaceutical baskets.

It should be appreciated that such 'equity derivatives' in no way raise finance for the companies involved, although the speculation in the warrants could affect the price of their shares.

Illustration

A worked example will illustrate the valuation techniques that have been described above with respect to both convertible debentures and warrants. The question used is taken from a Financial Management paper of the Chartered Association of Certified Accountants (Example 14.5).

Example 14.5

Conver PLC and Warran PLC each have in issue two million ordinary shares each of £1 nominal value. The only other securities each company has current in issue are as follows.

Conver PLC: 25 000 units of convertible debentures each with a nominal value of £100 and a coupon interest rate of 12% payable yearly. Each £100 unit may be converted into 20 ordinary shares at any time until the date of expiry and any debentures remaining unconverted will be redeemed that day at 105.

Warran PLC: 500 000 warrants each of which provides the holder with an option to subscribe for one ordinary share at a price of £5.00 per share. The warrants can be exercised at any time until the date of expiry.

The ordinary shares of both companies, the convertible debentures and the warrants are all actively traded in the stock market.

(a) Determine the value of each £100 unit of convertible debentures and of each warrant **on the date of expiry** if the share price for each company immediately prior to the latest time for conversion or exercise were to be (i) £4.40, (ii) £5.20, (iii) £6 and (iv) £6.80. Ignoring any possible taxation consequences, advise holders of the convertibles and warrants whether they should exercise their conversion and option rights in each of the four cases (i)–(iv). (5 marks)

(b) Indicate the likely current market price, or likely range of current market prices, of each £100 unit of convertible debentures if they have a further 5 years before expiry and the current share price is (i) £4.40, (ii) £5.20, (ii) £6 and (iv) £6.80. The appropriate pre-tax rate of interest on a five year debt security is 8% per annum. (5 marks)

(c) Explain the reasons for any differences between the valuation for the convertible debentures derived in (a) and (b). Outline the major factors which determine the market price of warrants and convertibles. (6 marks)

(d) Show the basic earnings per share for each company:
   (i) in a year when all convertibles and warrants remained outstanding for the whole period;
   (ii) for the first full year following conversion of all convertibles and exercise of all warrants.
   Profits for each company can be taken as £1.2 million per year before considering interest payments, taxation and earnings from the investment of any newly raised funds. The corporation tax rate is 50%. Any additional funds will be reinvested within the firm to earn 10% before tax.
   (4 marks)
   (20 marks)

Suggested solution

Part (a)
The value of the convertible debenture on the date of expiry, namely the final conversion date, depends on whether it is converted into equity or retained as a debenture. If converted its worth is 20 equity shares. If retained as a debenture it is worth £105. The worth of the convertible at the different possible share prices is therefore

	With share price			
	£4.40	£5.20	£6.00	£6.80
As equity	£ 88	£104	£120	£136
As debt	£105	£105	£105	£105

With the share price at either £4.40 or £5.20 it is not worth converting. With the share price at either £6 or £6.80 it is worth converting.

The warrant entitles the holder to purchase an ordinary share at a price of £5 per share. If the actual share price in the market on the date of expiry is £4.40, the holder of the warrant would not wish to exercise his option. If he wants further equity shares in the company it will be cheaper for him to purchase the share in the market than to exercise his option. In the other three situations given in the question he will wish to exercise the option. The value of the warrant in the three situations in £0.20, £1.00 and £1.80, respectively.

Part (b)

In the question the convertible security still has five years left before expiring. Its value as debt is £119.42, obtained by solving the following equation:

$$V = \frac{12}{1.08} + \frac{12}{(1.08)^2} + \frac{12}{(1.08)^3} + \frac{12}{(1.08)^4} + \frac{12}{(1.08)^5} + \frac{105}{(1.08)^5}$$

(i) If the current share price is £4.40, the value of the security if converted is £88 (i.e. $20 \times$ £4.40). The question asks for the likely current market price, which in the circumstances given would be somewhere in the region of £119.42, its value as a debt issue. There might be a modest premium on this price, but as the equity share price is so far below that at which conversion is just worth while, it would at best be a low premium.

(ii) With the share price at £5.20, the value of the equity obtained upon conversion becomes £104, still below the debenture value. The likely current market price depends upon expectations about the future share price. As Fig. 14.3 shows, the market value will be above the straight debt value where the share price is increasing at a 'satisfactory' level. In the situation referred to in this part of the question a larger premium above the £119.42 price might be expected than with the former £4.40 share price.

(iii) In this case the conversion into equity would result in a holding of shares worth £120. Therefore this is the likely minimum market price of the convertible.

(iv) In this case conversion would give £136 worth of equity. Therefore £136 is the likely minimum price of the convertible.

Part (c)

The answer to this part of the question is well covered in the above text.

Part (d)

	Basic earnings per share	
	Before conversion/ exercise	After conversion/ exercise
Convertible	(£000)	(£000)
Earnings	1200	1200
Interest payments	300	–
	900	1200
Tax at 50%	450	600
	450	600
	(000)	(000)
Number of shares	2000	2500
Earnings per share	22.5p	24p

Warrant	(£000)	(£000)
Basic earnings	1200	1200
Return on additional funds £2 500 000 at 10%		250
	1200	1450
Tax at 50%	600	725
	600	725
Number of shares (thousand)	2000	2500
Earnings per share	30p	29p

14.21 Revision questions

1. What is a debenture?
2. Give details of the type of conditions one would expect to see in a 'restrictive covenant'. What are covenants designed to achieve?
3. What is the main difference between a mortgage and an unsecured bond?
4. What is securitization?
5. In relation to a bond, what does the term 'callable' mean? A convertible debenture has been referred to as a straight bond with a call option. What does this mean?
6. What is a floating rate bond?
7. What is a deep discounted bond?
8. Explain how interest rate swaps work.
9. What is the main difference between a convertible bond and a bond with a warrant attached?
10. Is a warrant like a call option? Why?
11. What effect do warrants and convertibles have on the position of existing shareholders?

14.22 References

1. Altman, E.I. (1992) Revisiting the high yield bond market. *Financial Management*, Summer.
2. Brigham, E.F. (1966) An analysis of convertible debentures; theory and some empirical evidence, *Journal of Finance*, March pp 35–54.
3. Weil, R.L. Jr., Segall, J.E. and Green, D. (1968) Premiums on convertible bonds, *Journal of Finance*, June, pp 445–63.
4. Skerratt, L.C.L. (1974) The price determination of convertible loan stock, *Journal of Business Finance and Accounting*, Spring.
   Skerratt, L.C.L. (1971) Convertible loan stocks, *Journal of Business Finance*, 3, (3).
5. Samuelson, P.A. (1965) Rational theory of warrant pricing, *Industrial Management Review*, Spring.
   Whittaker, J. (1967) The evaluation of warrants, *The Investment Analyst*, October.
6. Kassouf, S.T. (1966) *A Theory and an Econometric Model for Common Stock Purchase Warrants*, Analytical Publishers Co., New York.

14.23 Further reading

For a general introduction to the financial markets see:

Peasnell, K.V. and Ward, C.W.R. (1985) *British Financial Markets and Institutions*, Prentice Hall.

Rutterford, J. (1993) *Introduction to Stock Exchange Investments*, Macmillan.

An up-to-date account of the sterling bond market is given in *Bank of England Quarterly Bulletins*.

Other relevant reading material includes:

Altman, E.I. (1990) Setting the record straight on junk bonds: a review of the research on default rates and returns. *Journal of Applied Corporate Finance*, Summer, 82–95.

Cordes, J. and Sheffin, S. (1983) Estimating the tax advantages of corporate debt. *Journal of Finance*, March.

Henderson, J. and Scott, J.P. (1988) *Securitization*, Woodhead-Faulkner, Cambridge.

Lewis, M. (1980) *Liar's Poker*, Penguin.

McDonald, R.L. (1984) How big is the tax advantage of debt. *Journal of Finance*, July.

Myers, S.C. (1984) The capital structure puzzle. *Journal of Finance*, July.

Rutterford, J. (1985) An international perspective on the capital structure puzzle. *Midland Corporate Finance Journal*, Autumn.

14.24 Problems

1. An irredeemable £100 bond was issued in 1990, offering a 10% coupon rate. In 1994 the market rate of interest on securities in a similar risk class is 8%. What will be the value of the bond in 1994?

2. A zero coupon bond was issued on 1 January 1990. It is redeemable on 1 January 2000 for £1000. The bond was sold for £463.20 in 1990.

   Required:
   (a) What was the market rate of interest on such securities in 1990?
   (b) It is now 1 January 1996, and the market rate of interest on such securities is 12%. What will be the value of the bond?

3. A 12% debenture has three years of its life remaining. The market rate of interest on such securities is now 15%. What will be the value of the bond in the market?

4. A company issued an 8% debenture ten years ago. It is due to be redeemed at par in four years' time. The debenture has a current market price of £100 cum interest. What is the cost of debt capital to the company (ignore tax)?

5. In the above question (4) assume the interest is to be paid semi-annually. What is the annual cost of debt capital to the company?

6. A company has a £100 million bank loan repayable in five years' time. The interest rate payable on the loan is 12% per annum. The company pays corporation tax at 30%. What is the after tax cost of the bank loan to the company?

7. A company has issued a 15% bond redeemable at par in four years' time. The bond currently sells in the market for £120 ex interest. The corporation tax rate is 30%. What is the after-tax cost of this bond to the company?

8. Suppose that British Telecom sold an issue of bonds with a 10 year maturity, at £100 par value, a 12% coupon rate and annual interest payments.

   (a) What would the market price of bonds be if the going rate of interest on bonds such as these fell to 8% two years after they were issued?
   (b) What would the market price of bonds be if the going rate had risen to 14% two years after the initial offering?

9. A company has a loan of £50 000 due to mature in four years time. The company wishes to put aside equal amounts of money each year to enable it to meet the liability when it should fall due. Interest rates are 6% per annum.

   Say how much money should be set aside at the end of each of the next four years to be able to discharge the debt.

10. The Nevel Co. Ltd, which is still effectively controlled by the Nevel family although they now own only a minority of shares, is to undertake a substantial new project which requires external finance of about £4 million, a 40% increase in gross assets. The project is to develop and market a new product and is fairly risky. About 70% of the funds required will be spent on land and buildings. The resale value of the land and buildings is expected to remain about, or above, the initial purchase price. Expenditure during the development period of four to seven years will be financed

from Nevel's other revenues with a consequent strain on the firm's overall liquidity. If, after the development stage, the project proves unsuccessful, then the project will be terminated and its assets sold. If, as is hoped, the development is successful, the project's assets will be utilized in production and Nevel's profits will rise considerably. However, if the project proves to be extremely successful, then additional finance may be required to expand production facilities further. At present Nevel is all-equity financed. The financial manager is uncertain whether he should seek funds from a financial institution in the form of an equity interest, a loan (long or short term) or convertible debentures.

Describe the major factors to be considered by Nevel in deciding on the method of financing the proposed expansion project. Briefly discuss the suitability of equity, loans and convertible debentures for the purposes of financing the project from the viewpoint of (a) Nevel and (b) the provider of finance. Clearly state and justify the type of finance recommended for Nevel.

11. 'In recent years it has been rare for medium- or long-term debt to be issued at a fixed interest rate; a floating (or variable) rate of interest, usually a few percentage points different from some variable base interest rate, has become much more common.'

Briefly outline, from the viewpoint of corporate financial management, the main merits and disadvantages of issuing floating rate debt. Indicate how a firm which has medium- or long-term floating rate debt should incorporate the cost of the debt in its weighted-average cost of capital.

12. Your firm has several different issues of long-term debt as well as a portfolio of short- and medium-term loans at a variety of interest rates, including some variable rates. One issue of debt, the £3 million 9.5% debenture 1993–8 could be redeemed now or at any time up to 1998. The financial director is concerned about the choice of timing for the redemption of this debenture.

(a) Briefly discuss the main advantages and disadvantages of including **fixed-interest** debt finance in the firm's financial structure.

(b) Outline, and describe the impact of, the main factors to be considered when deciding on the timing of debenture redemption. Consider both the case where the redemption must be financed from the issue of further funds and the case where no further funds need be issued.

(c) Discuss the extent to which it is rational for a firm to obtain, at any one time, debt finance from a variety of sources with various durations and at different interest rates rather than utilizing only the source which offers the lowest effective interest charge.

13. Your client is considering the investment of a substantial sum in one of three interest yielding securities. Some details relating to each **unit** of the three securities are as follows.

	Security		
	A	B	C
	£	£	£
Annual interest:			(Note 2)
years 1–3	30	0	5
Redemption value:			
year 3	(Note 1)	100	100
Expected annual yield over three years	13%	12%	

Note 1: Security A has a life of ten years and will be redeemed for £100. If your client chooses this security then it would be sold immediately after the year 3 interest payment is received at a price sufficient to provide a yield to the purchaser of 14% per annum over its remaining 7 years of life.

Note 2: The interest and redemption values given for security C are quoted in today's money values whereas the actual payments will be directly linked to the level of the retail prices index. This index stands at 100 and expected future levels are as follows:

	Level	Movement in year
End of year 1	110	+10.0%
2	118	+ 7.3%
3	123	+ 4.2%

Each unit of Security C is currently priced at £99.00.

It is thought that interest rates for short-term investment will be as follows: for a two year investment made at end of year 1, gross annual yield 10%; for a one year investment made at end of year 2, gross annual yield 9%. Both these yields refer to investments which pay all accumulated interest and repay principal only at time 3.

(a) Calculate the current market prices of securities A and B. Determine the equivalent annual yield on security C expressed in money, rather than real, terms. Advise your client in which of the three securities he should invest if the objective is to maximize wealth at time 3. Ignore taxation.

(b) Indicate the main factors to which you would draw your client's attention if the decision were being carried out as a practical exercise.

ACCA, Financial Management, June 1984

14. In recent years your company has made substantial use of debt financing and it is now generally agreed to be overgeared both in book value and market value terms. Further use of debt will probably lead to a drop in the firm's bond rating. You would like to advise that the next major capital investment be financed with a new equity issue but unfortunately both the firm's securities and the market have been performing poorly. In fact, the rate of return on investment has been just equal to the cost of capital. As shown in the financial statement below the market value of the firm's equity is less than its book value. This means that even a profitable project may decrease earnings per share if it is financed by new equity. The firm is considering a project which costs £400 000 but has a present value of £500 000 (i.e. a net present value of £100 000) and which will increase total earnings by £60 000 per year.

The chairman of the firm argues that the project should be delayed for three reasons.

(a) It is too expensive for the firm to issue new debt.

(b) Financing the project with new equity will reduce earnings per share because the market value of equity is less than book value.

(c) Equity markets are currently depressed. If the firm waits until the market index improves the market value of equity will exceed the book value and equity financing will no longer reduce earnings per share.

Balance Sheet as of 31 December 1991 (£000)

Equity	4 000	Fixed assets	8 000
Debt	6 000	Working capital	2 000
	10 000		10 000

Number of shares in issue	1 000 000
Current price per share	£2.00
Total earnings for the year ended 31 December 1991	£600 000

You are required to appraise critically the chairman's reasons for delaying the project Your answer should contain comparative numerical calculations on the effects on earnings per share of adoption of the project and issue of new shares.

15. Your company wishes to raise new debt capital on the stock market. Your managing director has heard of warrants and traded options and suggests that an issue of debt, accompanied by either attached warrants or traded options might be attractive to investors and have benefits for your company.

Discuss whether you consider your managing director's suggestion to be useful.

16. Several years ago Nopen PLC issued 15% 15 year loan stock with warrants attached. The warrants may be exercised at any time during the next four years and each warrant allows the purchase of one ordinary share at a price of 400p. The company has also issued a 9% convertible debenture which is due for redemption at the par value of £100 in five years' time. Conversion rights, which are available at any time up to the redemption date, allow the conversion of one debenture into 25 ordinary shares. The current market yield on straight debentures for a company of Nopen's risk class is 12% per year.

Estimate the minimum market price of a warrant and of a £100 convertible debenture if the current share price of Nopen is 300p, 420p and 500p.

Explain why the market price of a warrant or convertible debenture is likely to be more than the price that you have estimated. Taxation may be ignored.

ACCA, Dec. 1987

17. Bestlodge PLC is planning to build production facilities to introduce a major new product at a cost of £12 million. The board of directors has already approved the project. The investment is expected to increase profit before interest and tax by approximately 25%. No internally generated funds are available.

The finance director has suggested three possible sources of finance:

(a) a five year £12 million floating-rate term loan from a clearing bank, at an initial interest rate of 10%;
(b) a ten year 46 million deutschmark fixed rate loan from the Eurocurrency market at an interest rate of 7%;
(c) a rights issue at a discount of 10% on the current market price.

The company's share price is 170p and the debenture price is £108. The current summarized financial statements are shown below.

Summarized balance sheet

	£000	£000
Fixed assets at cost less depreciation		38 857
Current assets	18 286	
Current liabilities	(16 914)	
Net current assets		1 372
		40 229
Financed by:		
Share capital		
Ordinary shares of 25p each		7 200
Reserves		19 863
Loan capital		
11% debenture stock 1994–7		13 166
		40 229

Summarized profit and loss account for the year

	£000
Sales	57 922
Profit before interest and taxation	7 744
Debenture interest	1 448
	6 296
Taxation	3 148
Profit available for ordinary shareholders	3 148
Ordinary dividend	2 250
Retained profits	898

Corporation tax is at 50%

Exchange rates

	DM/£
Spot	3.7010–3.7028
1 Year forward	3.4760–3.4785

(a) Acting as a consultant to Bestlodge prepare a report discussing the advantages and disadvantages of each of the three suggested sources of finance. Illustrate how the utilization of each source might affect the various providers of finance. (Relevant calculations are an essential part of your report.) (16 marks)

(b) Suggest other sources of finance that might be suitable for this investment.

(4 marks)

ACCA, Dec. 1985

18. Securitization is a term that refers to at least two distinct innovations in financial markets that became notable in the 1980s. In its first usage, the term refers to the transformation of non assets, like loans, into marketable assets, securities. In its second variant, securitization refers to the way firms borrow funds; firms that had traditionally borrowed from banks increasingly have sold securities in financial markets.

Discuss the above statement including in your answer an examination of the factors which have stimulated developments.

19. On page 468 reference is made to an ICI issue of convertible Eurosterling bonds. Ascertain what has happened to the price of this security in relation to the price of the equity share.

20. The senior management of Allodge is reviewing the company's capital structure.

Balance sheet as at 31 December 1988

	£m
Tangible assets	318
Investments	3
Total fixed assets	321
Current assets	
Stocks	20
Debtors	280
Investments	10
Cash at the bank and in hand	1
	311
Creditors: amounts falling due within one year	
Bank loans and overdrafts	43
Unsecured loan stock	5
Taxes	56
Trade creditors	254
Accrued expenses	1
Other creditors	24
Dividends	13
	396
Net current liabilities	(85)
Total assets less current liabilities	236
Financed by	
Creditors: amounts falling due after more than one year	
13.5% Debenture 1995	30
US dollar 8% bonds 1996[1]	25
7.5% Convertible debenture 1998	15

Capital and reserves	
Called up share capital	
Preference shares (£1 par value)	20
Ordinary shares (50 pence par value)	35
Share premium account	4
Profit and loss account	107
	236

---

[1]The principal of the fixed interest rate US dollar bond has been swapped into floating rate sterling.

The company requires £30 million in usable new finance to expand its existing operations. The suggested sources of this finance are:

 (i) An underwritten rights issue at a price of 348 pence per share.
 (ii) A rights issue which is not underwritten at a price of 302 pence per share.
 (iii) A placing at the current market price with the company receiving a price of 368 pence per share.
 (iv) Early redemption of the 13.5% debenture which is to be replaced by a new £60 million debenture at an interest rate of 12% per year maturing at the same date as the existing debenture. Corporate tax is at the rate of 35%.

The market price of the company's ordinary shares is 375 pence, of the preference shares 305 pence, of the 13.5% debenture £104, the convertible debenture £97, and the total market value of the US Bond is £41.25 million. The current spot rate is $1.7106–$1.7140/£. Issue costs are expected to be 1.5% of gross proceeds for the underwritten rights issue, and 0.5% for the non-underwritten rights issue. Redemption of the debenture would incur administrative costs of £50 000 and issue of a new debenture a further £25 000.

Required:

(a) One manager states that suggestion (ii) will be unfair to existing shareholders as it will lead to a fall in share price of approximately six pence greater than suggestion (i).

   If the ex-rights market price moves to its theoretical value demonstrate numerically whether a shareholder with 5000 shares who purchased 60% of his allocated new shares would suffer with suggestion (ii) relative to suggestion (i).
   (7 marks)
(b) Briefly discuss the relative advantages and disadvantages of each of these suggested forms of equity finance. (5 marks)
(c) If suggestion (iv) is adopted there would be a premium of £1 500 000 payable for early redemption of the existing 13.5% debenture.

   The existing debenture may be assumed to have six years to maturity.

   Calculate whether early redemption of the debenture would be beneficial to Allodge.

   Recommend whether the company should make a new £60 million debenture issue. (9 marks)
(d) Suggest why the company has swapped the principal of the US fixed interest rate dollar bond into floating rate sterling. (4 marks)
ACCA, Dec. 1989

21. Toces Ltd is a small, specialist retail company that has traded for five years. Summaries of the company's latest financial accounts are shown below:

Profit and loss accounts for the years ending 31 March

	1991 £000	1990 £000
Turnover	2420	1920
Cost of sales	856	650
Gross profit	1564	1270
Other expenses	1296	1041
Profit before taxation	268	229
Taxation	67	57
	201	172
Dividends	50	50
	151	122

Balance sheets as at 31 March

		1991 £000	1990 £000
Tangible fixed assets (net)		2728	2460
Stock		873	829
Debtors		12	10
Cash		6	10
		3619	3309
Less:	Trade creditors	(740)	(682)
	Overdraft	(386)	(290)
	Taxation	(45)	(40)
	Term loan[1] (1995)	(1250)	(1250)
		1198	1047

[1]Interest payable 1991 £212 500, 1990 £175 000.

Share capital and reserves	1991 £000	1990 £000
Ordinary shares (10 pence par value)	100	100
'B' shares (10 pence par value)[2]	100	100
Share premium account	491	491
Other reserves	507	356
	1198	1047

[2] 'B' shares are 'family' held and have one tenth of the voting rights of ordinary shares.

The company wishes to expand and hopes to raise £2 million. £500 000 would be used to establish new shops, £250 000 for increased working capital, and £1 250 000 to repay the existing floating rate term loan.

Toces' directors have contacted several institutions and have been offered a £2 million 14.5% per year fixed rate secured loan from an insurance company and a 4.8 million Swiss franc loan at a fixed interest rate of 10% per year by a Swiss bank. The insurance company requires the option to purchase 500 000 new ordinary shares at 10 pence per share as part of the deal.

A third offer has been made by a venture capital company which would provide a £1 million five year loan at the fixed interest rate of 15% per year, and £1 million in equity finance (1 000 000 new ordinary shares at a price of £1 per share).

All loans are repayable at the end of five years and interest is payable annually at the end of the year.

Inflation in Switzerland is expected to be at 8% per year less than in the United Kingdom for the next few years. The current exchange rate is SF2.40/£1.

Required:
(a) What factors should Toces' directors consider before deciding how to finance the proposed expansion? (6 marks)
(b) Appraise Toces' plans for using the £2 million. (4 marks)
(c) Discuss the advantages and disadvantages to Toces of each of the three financing offers.

Relevant calculations must be shown. State clearly any assumptions that you make. (10 marks)
(d) If none of these three offers were accepted by Toces suggest alternative sources of finance that might be available to the company. (5 marks)

(25 marks)

ACCA, Dec. 1991

Share price valuation and the cost of capital

15.1	Share valuation	492
15.2	Dividends and share values	494
15.3	Valuation based on earnings?	504
15.4	The capital asset pricing model and share values	507
15.5	Valuation based on free cash flow	512
15.6	Country differences in valuation methods	513
15.7	Does it pay to manipulate earnings?	513
15.8	Pricing new issues	517
15.9	The valuation of a company	521
15.10	The cost of equity capital	540
15.11	Key terms	549
15.12	Revision questions	549
15.13	References	549
15.14	Further reading	550
15.15	Problems	551

In this chapter we are concerned with questions of valuation. For example:

1. What price does a company ask for its shares when they are first sold to the public?
2. How does the market value a company's shares when they are traded on a day-to-day basis?
3. How does one company value another company?

We are also concerned with the complementary problem of what the cost of capital is to the company.

The question of the valuation that an investor places on an equity share and the cost to the company of equity finance are related. The valuation depends on what the investor expects to earn from the investment in the future, and the cost to the company of equity finance is based on satisfying the shareholders' expectations. The cost of equity is not based on a contractual obligation to pay a certain rate of return whatever the profit level as in debt finance. The equity owners' return depends on the level of earnings of the company. The managers of the company have to keep the equity owners satisfied, and so the cost of equity is based on meeting shareholders' expectations. It is these same expectations that influence how much an investor will pay for a share, i.e. the value that is placed on it.

15.1 Share valuation

We begin by considering how equity shares can be valued. In theory the valuation should be based on the present value of dividends to be received. However, there is a controversy: there are arguments indicating that the dividend decision of the company is irrelevant to the share value. It can be shown that under certain situations the value of a share should be the same whether a company's earnings are paid out as dividends or retained within the company. This irrelevancy proposition will be briefly mentioned here but discussed more fully in Chapter 17.

In theory we know what the intrinsic value of a share should be. We can examine whether or not the actual share price quoted on the stock exchange equals the intrinsic value (true value) of a share.

If shares can be valued on an earnings as well as a dividend basis the question again arises as to whether creative accounting techniques can mislead the market. The earnings figure for any year is an estimate which is produced according to accounting conventions. Can the directors of a company create a situation in which the actual share price differs from its true value by manipulating the numbers in the annual financial statements?

Considering how important the share price of a company is to many of its decisions and to the future of the management, it is disappointing to most that the process of share price determination appears to be so subjective. The cost of capital, the potential for growth through external acquisition and the very survival of the company as a separate entity depend on the price of the company's shares. Yet what lies behind one of the key factors by which management is judged, and consequently a factor that determines their survival – namely the share price – is often only vaguely understood.

This chapter is designed to give some idea of the relationship between share prices and variables such as earnings, the profit distribution policies of companies and accounting reporting principles. It is not possible to discuss all aspects of the relationship between the capital market and a company's share price, for this would require a complete book. However, the various theories relating to share prices will be examined together with the empirical evidence on the subject.

The price of a share, like the price of anything else, depends upon supply and demand and the company has an influence over part of the supply, namely the new shares that it issues. However, of the shares being sold on the market at any one time a large proportion are 'old' shares, i.e. those which have previously been issued and are being traded again, a source of supply over which the company has only limited influence. The demand for the shares is again not under the control of the company. However, the company by its performance, and by the information it makes available to the market, can influence the demand for its shares and the willingness of existing holders to sell. It is therefore necessary for the management to understand the workings of the stock market, to know about the behaviour of share prices and to know the methods being used by those who make a living from buying and selling shares. Only then will managers be in a position to act in the best interests of their shareholders.

Is it possible to calculate what a share is worth? There are numerous differences of opinion, but they can all be characterized within two limiting cases.

At one extreme is the belief that price is determined by a rational process, that there is some true value for a company share and that this is based on the economic value of the company. This is the intrinsic value. The price of the share depends on the value of the company, which in the case of a going concern is based on the present value of the cash flow (earnings) to be received by the company. After prior claims have been met, the cash flow belongs to the shareholders; the number of shareholders is known, and so the value per share can be determined. The other extreme is the view that it makes no sense to talk about a 'true value' for a company share, that there is no such thing as an intrinsic value. Share prices are what they are only because of what purchasers and sellers expect them to be. The prices are determined by anticipatory and speculative factors, and the expected earnings of a company are only one among a number of factors which influence investors. Price is the outcome of demand and supply pressures, and demand is in turn affected by hunches and speculation.

Such pressures will undoubtedly cause the share price to rise and fall, and the day-to-day price movements may well follow a random path, both because hunches may be irrational and because information which gives rise to speculation comes to the market at irregular intervals. However, this does not mean that with a given set of knowledge there is not a 'true value' for a share.

While the price on any one day may not be the same as the intrinsic value, daily prices would be expected either to fluctuate about this true value or to move towards this true value over time. Baumol [1], after considering the evidence, believes that 'earnings do ultimately and solely determine the value to be derived by shareholding and that if shareholders do learn at all well from their experience, their purchasing patterns will, in the long run, force stock prices to conform rather closely to these prospective earnings opportunities of the firms whose shares they buy. We have strong reasons to suspect that in a rough and ready way, security prices do follow closely the developments in company prospects.'

This merely says that in the long run the actual share price will move towards its value as based on expected earnings – 'its true value'. The share price may be there now, but if it is not the movement of the actual price to meet the true value need not happen in the short run. The long run might be a considerable period of time, and this is one of the problems.

For instance it is a problem with one popular type of investment policy, namely one which attempts to identify and then to purchase shares that are undervalued. Undervaluation means that the true value of a share based on earnings expectations is above the actual market price. The theory suggests that in the long run the actual price will move towards the true value, and so the investor will make a gain. This seems a sound investment policy. But how long does the investor have to wait for the actual price to rise to the true value? If this is a matter of two or more years the investor might not be interested.

Both theories of share price determination given above may provide a useful insight. The intrinsic value approach may not explain the share price on a particular day, but it indicates the direction in which the share price will move in the long run. The price on any particular day can be explained by the other theory, which merely states that price is determined by demand and supply on that particular day and the demand on the day in turn can depend on uninformed investors, perhaps acting on a hunch. It could also be due to the random nature of the timing of new information coming to the market. This would help to explain the phenomenon of 'random walk' movements in share prices which has been observed by so many researchers on the subject. The idea of two different groups of investors – the informed and the uninformed – will be considered later.

It is because of this uncertainty about when the actual price will approach the true value that analysts have become slightly less enthusiastic about the undervalued shares approach to investment. Many of them have changed the emphasis of their research either towards forecasting the turning points in share price movement or to selecting a balanced portfolio of investments and holding on to them. There has been a growth in the number of index-matching funds being sold to investors. The turning point idea is that all share prices will change direction more or less at the same time, and so the important factor to determine is when the turn will come. In a market fall some shares will fall less than others, and in a market rise some shares rise faster than others; therefore it is also important to be able to identify these shares.

15.2 Dividends and share values

There is no single generally accepted method for determining the correct true valuation of a company share. It is possible to approach the problem in different ways. A share entitles the owner to a stream of future dividends. Therefore one approach is to take the value of the share as corresponding to the present value of this stream of dividend payments. Obviously there is considerable uncertainty surrounding the size of the future dividends; indeed it is partly as a result of changing expectations about future dividends that share prices fluctuate.

Of course the owner of a share at any one point of time will usually consider his returns as accruing not just from dividend payments but from the additional gains resulting from any capital appreciation on the share. Normally, the owner does not intend to hold the share in perpetuity; he wishes to sell it and obtain capital gains. But when the share is sold, the buyer is also simply purchasing a stream of future dividend payments and so, once again, the price is determined by future dividend expectations. The reason that the capital gain arises is because expectations about the future dividend stream rise between the time when the investor purchases the shares and when he sells them.

This theory can be demonstrated [2]. Suppose that an investor buys a share expecting to hold it for two years: the value of the share to him is the present value of the two dividend payments plus the discounted value of the price he expects to receive on selling the share. If P_0 is the price of the share today, P_2 is the price of the share at the end of the second year, D_1 is the dividend per share to be received at the end of the first year and i is the discount rate, which is the market capitalization rate which is the required rate of return on shares in the risk class being considered, then

$$P_0 = \frac{D_1}{1+i} + \frac{D_2}{(1+i)^2} + \frac{P_2}{(1+i)^2}$$

The investor who buys the share at the end of the second year pays P_2 for it, and expects to hold it for two further years. Therefore, looked at from time zero,

$$\frac{P_2}{(1+i)^2} = \frac{D_3}{(1+i)^3} + \frac{D_4}{(1+i)^4} + \frac{P_4}{(1+i)^4}$$

The price at the end of the fourth year and all future prices are determined in a similar manner. Therefore the equation for the price of the share at the present time can be rewritten as

$$P_0 = \frac{D_1}{1+i} + \frac{D_2}{(1+i)^2} + \frac{D_3}{(1+i)^3} + \frac{D_4}{(1+i)^4} + \cdots = \sum_{t=1}^{\infty} \frac{D_t}{(1+i)^t}$$

The dividend received will be net of tax under the imputation system.

Growth in dividends

The dividends of most companies are expected to grow. Evaluation of the share price must allow for this, and indeed it is possible to incorporate these growth expectations explicitly in the valuation model. In the model just described the dividends had to be forecast for each year separately. If g is the expected percentage annual rate of growth, the formula becomes

$$P_0 = \frac{D_0(1+g)}{1+i} + \frac{D_0(1+g)^2}{(1+i)^2} + \frac{D_0(1+g)^3}{(1+i)^3} \cdots = \sum_{t=1}^{\infty} \frac{D_0(1+g)^t}{(1+i)^t}$$

This can be rewritten as

$$P_0 = \frac{D_1}{i-g}$$

It is being assumed that growth is at a constant rate per annum or that there are only slight deviations each year about a long-term trend.

The above equation can only be used if the growth rate g is lower than the discount rate i. As the formula is written, price is determined at time zero, that is before the dividend for year one has been declared.

The following illustrates a practical application of the equation. Suppose that a company has a growth rate in dividends of 4% per annum, and that the market's capitalization rate for a company in this risk category is 8%. If the dividend at the end of the first year is expected to be £0.50 per share, the expected share price today would be

$$P_0 = \frac{£0.5}{0.08-0.04} = £12.50$$

The dividend yield based on the expected dividend of this company is 4% (0.5/12.50 × 100%) which may be below the market level, but the investor can expect the share price to grow by 4% per annum to give him a return similar to those he can expect elsewhere in the market. The price in one year's time would be

$$P_1 = \frac{D_0(1+g)^2}{(1+i)^2} + \frac{D_0(1+g)^3}{(1+i)^3} + \dots$$

$$P_1 = \frac{0.5408}{(1.08)^2} + \frac{0.5624}{(1.08)^3} + \dots$$

which is £13.

The discount rate applicable to a company is a function of the interest rates in effect at the time and the degree of risk associated with that company. In the context of the capital asset pricing model (CAPM), the risk premium would be related to systematic risk (see Chapters 9 and 10).

In fact some companies, although earning profits, elect not to pay dividends. This is a matter of deliberate financial policy, and not a measure forced upon them by financial difficulties. The above theory of share valuation can still be applied to these companies, since one day presumably they will start paying dividends. This is the only basis on which shareholders can obtain any returns from the company; in the final analysis dividends must be paid or assets realized, otherwise there is no logic in anybody holding the shares. The reason that the price of the shares rises is that with the retention policies of the company, the rapid growth alters investors' expectations about the future size of dividends. At some time in the future, large dividends can be paid. Therefore once again it can be said that dividends determine the company's share price.

It is, of course, a difficult matter to forecast the stream of future dividends payments. Some companies go through periods when their earnings grow at an above normal rate, and their dividends then, if allowed to, also tend to grow at an above normal rate. It cannot be assumed, however, that a period of above average growth will continue into the future. To estimate a level for the share price of a company that is presently enjoying above average performance it is usual to assume that the above average growth will continue for a number of years and that the dividend will then revert to a near normal rate of growth.

Example 15.1

The way in which the share price can be calculated for a company with an above average growth rate in dividends is as follows. Let us assume that the appropriate market rate of discount is 8%, and that the company is expected to enjoy an above average performance for eight years, with dividends growing at say 10% per annum. After that time, because of competition and the company losing its present technological or marketing lead, the growth in dividends will revert to the average for all companies – say 4%. The present dividend is £0.1 per share. Three sets of calculations need to be completed before the appropriate share price can be determined.

1. The present value (PV) of dividends over the next eight years is as follows:

Year	Dividend	Discount factor	PV
1	0.110	0.926	0.102
2	0.121	0.857	0.104
3	0.133	0.794	0.106
4	0.146	0.735	0.107
5	0.161	0.681	0.110
6	0.177	0.630	0.112
7	0.195	0.583	0.114
8	0.214	0.540	0.116
			0.871

2. Value of share at end of year 8:

$$P_8 = \frac{D_9}{0.08 - 0.04} = \frac{0.2226}{0.04} = 5.56$$

3. Value today of price at end of year 8:

$$\frac{5.56}{(1.08)^8} = 3.006$$

4. Value of share today = £(0.871 + 3.006) = £3.877.

The growth formula can be used to estimate the market's capitalization rate, i.e. the expected return for companies within a risk class. The formula can be rewritten as

$$i = \frac{D_1}{P_0} + g$$

which indicates that the market capitalization rate equals the expected dividend yield D_1/P_0 plus the expected rate of growth of dividends. This version of the formula is in fact one approach to estimating the cost of capital.

If we consider the shares of Guinness PLC during the first six months of 1989, the highest share price was 533p and the lowest 329p, with the gross dividend for the year ending 31 December 1988 being 11.50p. If we take the mid-share price between the high and low of 431p, this gives us a gross dividend yield of 2.67%.

It is difficult to know what the expectation of investors was with respect to the annual growth rate of dividends. However, if we analyse the growth rate of the company dividends over the few years prior to 1989 we see that it averages out at approximately 12% per annum (from 6.44p in 1984 to 11.50p in 1988). This would give a net dividend D_1 (for year ending 31 December 1989) of 12.88p. The market capitalization rate, i.e. the cost of equity capital to the company after corporation tax, would therefore be

$$i = \frac{12.88}{431.00} + 0.12 = 0.15 = 15\%$$

This would be the annual rate of return that shareholders would have expected to earn in 1989 from holding shares in the same risk class as that of Guinness PLC. They would be receiving this return in the form of capital gain plus dividends.

Eurotunnel PLC, in their offer for sale of equity shares in November 1987, made use of this present value of dividend theory. They produced financial projections for the period from when they forecast dividends would first be paid in 1994 to when their concession ends in 2041. They pointed out that the present value of projected dividends over this period, discounted at an annual rate of 12%, would be £24 inclusive of tax credits and £17 excluding tax credits. This, it implied in its offer documents, would be (or should be) the value of the equity shares in mid-1994. It would have been if the projections had proven to be correct and if the market had believed the projections, if the market had adopted a 12% discount rate and if the dividend valuation model was used to value shares.

Unfortunately for Eurotunnel the projections proved to be wildly optimistic. The Tunnel was not even open to the public by mid-1994, the project cost over double the estimates, and the financing of the project had to be renegotiated with many acrimonious discussions taking place. The share price of Eurotunnel showed a high in 1994 of £5.92, and in mid-1994 was £3.07.

It may be thought that the above equation for valuing shares is naive, based as it is only on the PV of expected future dividends. Theoretically, however, it is correct. It is only through distributions that the shareholders obtain a return from the company. Unfortunately it is not possible to test the theory as we do not know what future dividends will be. Investors have expectations about future dividends, but we do not know what they expect and different investors may well have different expectations. There are many approaches to valuing shares; the approach based on dividend expectations is only one possibility.

Estimating g

As the Eurotunnel case shows it is difficult to forecast future dividends. In a way however it is unfair to quote this one company, as its only investment project was always recognised as extremely high-risk. Most companies have a track record and it is possible to analyse their past performance to obtain, it is hoped, some guidance on their future growth prospects. Of course industry and economy wide factors would also need to be taken into account.

One way to estimate g is by use of the following formula

$$g = \text{retention ratio} \times \% \text{ return on retained earnings in the past}$$

The retention ratio (sometimes called plough back ratio) = profits retained in business divided by profits available for distribution to shareholders. It is the inverse of the payout ratio i.e. $(1 - \text{payout ratio})$

A fast-growing new company typically retains a larger proportion of the profits it earns than would a more established company. The rate at which the dividends paid by a company will grow depends not only on the policy with regard to retention but also on the profitability of the projects in which the funds are invested.

A financial analyst can observe a company's past policy with regard to retentions, but would find it difficult to ascertain the rate of return being earned by the company on new investments. An assumption usually made is that the new investments will earn the same rate of return as the present return on equity.

Example 15.2

Brixton plc has earnings per share for the year just completed equal to £1. It has a policy of retaining 70% of its earnings. The rate of return it earns on its equity is currently 16%, and it is expected to be able to maintain this level. Therefore

$$g = 0.70 \times 0.16 = 0.112 \text{ or } 11.2\%$$

If the market capitalization rate on such shares is equal to 13%, we can estimate the price of Brixton's shares

$$P_0 = \frac{D_i}{i - g}$$

$$P_0 = \frac{£0.30(1.112)}{0.13 - 0.112} = £18.53$$

The price earnings ratio of the company would be

Price per share/earnings per share

£18.53/£1

18.53:1

Example 15.3

Fast-growing companies have higher PE ratios than slower growing companies. We can illustrate this by comparing Brixton plc with a less dynamic company. Let us suppose Streatham plc, a company in the same risk class as Brixton, also has earnings per share of £1. Streatham have a retention rate of only 50%, and earn 14% on their equity funds. For Streatham

$$g = 0.50 \times 0.14 = 0.07 \text{ or } 7\%$$

The price of Streatham's shares will be

$$P = \frac{£0.50 \, (1.07)}{0.13 - 0.07} = £8.92$$

The price earnings ratio of Streatham will be 8.92:1. The two companies have identical earnings per share, but investors would be willing to pay a price for the shares which is a higher multiple of the one company's earnings than that of the other company.

The reader may think that the above examples ignore growth financed by funds other than retained earnings. This is true, but the ability of companies to attract debt finance is influenced by the amount of equity finance in a business. A company that ploughs back a high proportion of its profits is likely to be able to attract a larger amount of borrowed funds than a company that ploughs back lower levels of its profits. What has been demonstrated above is not the complete picture, but it is indicative of the overall position.

How much of the price paid for a share is for future growth?

In the example above with the two companies Brixton and Streatham we demonstrated why the PE ratio of companies can vary. The PE ratios we calculated were based on estimates of the future rate of growth of the companies. It was suggested that even though the current earnings of the two companies was the same, investors would be willing to pay more for the shares of the one company than of the other company because of the future growth prospects. The investor are buying growth. The estimate of the rate of growth of a company will of course vary from one analyst to another. It has to be appreciated that the actual PE ratio to be found in the market place associated with any company's shares is very subjective. It is based only on expectations of growth.

The growth results from investing the retained earnings of the company and investing any new funds obtained. If we assume the company decided not to grow it could payout as dividends all its earnings. The company would still have enough funds to replace assets as they became worn out because the company will have provided for depreciation before arriving at the figure for earnings available for distribution. The value of a company with a no-growth policy can be estimated by calculating the present level of earnings continuing in perpetuity.

One approach to deciding whether or not a share is over- or under-priced is therefore to break down the share price into two component parts. An investor when buying a share could be seen as buying a stream of earnings at their present level plus a growth element. On one day in June 1994, the PE ratio of Bodyshop plc was 23.1 : 1 (it had in the past been as high as 50 to 1) and the PE ratio of Clinton Cards plc was 12.3 : 1. The price of Bodyshop on that day was £2.46 and of Clinton Cards £1.43. Both companies are quoted in London and are classified in the *Financial Times* as being in the 'Retailing: General' sector. How can this difference in PE ratios be explained?

We will estimate how much of the price on that one day can be explained as the purchase of a continuing stream of earnings at their present level and how much can be explained as purchasing growth. Bodyshop's most recent earnings per share had been 10.7 pence per share (based on the PE ratio). Let us assume the market capitalization rate for such retailing shares is 10%. Then the value of a Bodyshop share based on a stream of earnings in perpetuity equals:

$$\frac{£0.107}{0.10} = £1.07$$

The actual share price on the day was £2.46. Therefore investors were paying £1.39 for growth. Only 43.5% of the price they paid can be explained as buying earnings at their present level in perpetuity. 56.5% of the price was based on growth expectations.

In contrast the most recent earnings per share for Clinton plc had been 11.6p per share. This gives a value for dividends received in perpetuity of:

$$\frac{£0.116}{0.10} = £1.16$$

The market price on the day was £1.43. Therefore only £0.27 was being paid to purchase growth. This gives a division of the price for Clinton of 81% being for a purchase of the current levels of earnings in perpetuity and only 19% for growth. Bodyshop sell health and beauty products and had been seen for some time as a glamour stock with the company growing very quickly. It was a high-profile company receiving much publicity. In contrast Clinton sell greeting cards; they had grown over time, but in a less well-publicized manner.

Example 15.4

We shall now illustrate the relationship between dividends and share price by means of a worked example. The following is a Financial Management question of the Chartered Association of Certified Accounts.

Zed PLC is considering the purchase of some, or all, of the share capital of one of two firms – Red Ltd and Yellow Ltd. Both Red and Yellow have 1 million ordinary shares issued and neither company has any debt outstanding.

   Both firms are expected to pay a dividend in one year's time – Red's expected dividend amounting to 45p per share and Yellow's being 27p per share. Dividends will be paid at yearly intervals and will increase each year. Red's dividends are expected to display perpetual growth at a compound rate of 6% per annum. Yellow's dividend will grow at the high annual compound rate of 33⅓% until a dividend of 64p per share is reached in year 4. Thereafter growth will be 5% per annum indefinitely.

   If Zed is able to purchase all the equity capital of either firm then the reduced competition would enable Zed to save some advertising and administrative costs which would amount to £225 000 per annum indefinitely and, in year 2, to sell some office space for £800 000. These benefits and savings will only occur if a complete takeover were to be carried out.

   Zed would change some policies of any company taken over – the details are as follows.

1. Red: no dividend would be paid until year 3. Year 3 dividend would be 40p per share and dividends would then grow at 10% per annum indefinitely.
2. Yellow: no change in total dividends in years 1–4, but after year 4 dividend growth would be 25% per annum compound until year 7. Thereafter annual dividends would remain constant at the year 7 amount per share.

   The expected rate of return for the risk inherent in each company is 15%.

(a) Calculate
   (i)   the valuation per share for a minority investment in each of the firms Red and Yellow which would provide the investor with a 15% rate of return:
   (ii)   the maximum amount per share which Zed should consider paying for each company in the event of a complete takeover.
   (Taxation may be ignored for the purposes of part (a).)

(b) Comment on any limitations of the approach used in part (a) and specify the other major factors which would be important to consider if the proposed valuations were being undertaken as a practical exercise.

Answer

The question can in fact only be answered properly by using the share valuation model based on the PV of future dividends. It is in fact inviting the student to use the reduced-form version of the model, which is applicable when the growth in dividends is expected to be at a constant rate:

$$P_0 = \frac{D_1}{i - g}$$

Part (a)

(i) We are told that the required rate of return by an investor is 15% This means that for Red Ltd the present share price equals £5. The formula is

$$P_0 = \frac{£0.45}{0.15 - 0.06}$$

For Yellow Ltd the share price is £5.033, calculated as follows. Expected dividends and their PV for years 1–4 are

Year	Dividend	PV factor	Present value
1	27p	0.870	£0.235
2	36p	0.756	£0.272
3	48p	0.658	£0.316
4	64p	0.572	£0.366
			£1.189

The value, at the end of year 4, of future dividends is

$$\frac{£0.64 \times 1.05}{0.15 - 0.05} = £6.72$$

The value at present of this sum is

$$£6.72 \times 0.572 = £3.844$$
$$\text{Total value} = £5.033$$

(ii) To value the savings we need to know how to calculate the value of an item to be received in perpetuity. Table 3 at the end of the book gives us the PVs of an annuity. The longest period for an annuity shown in the table is, however, only 50 years. The way to calculate an annuity is perpetuity is to multiply the figure to be received by $1/i$ or, to use the nomenclature in Table 3, $1/r$. With this problem we multiply by 1/0.15, which equals 6.6667. It can be seen that this is close to the PV factor for an annuity at 15% over 50 years.

Value of savings and benefits achieved by Zed PLC if takeover is achieved:

	PV (£000)
Annual savings	
£225 000 × 6.6667	1500.0
Sale of property	
£800 000 × 0.756	604.8
Total value	£2104.8

Value of Red Ltd to Zed PLC following changes in dividend policy:

Total dividend = £400 000 commencing in year 3, with growth rate 10% per annum
Value at end of year 2 = £400 000/(0.15 − 0.10) = £8 million
Present value (£000) = £8000 × 0.756 = £6048

Value of Yellow Ltd to Zed PLC following changes in dividend policy:

Dividends, and their present value, for years 1–7 are

Year	Total dividend (£000)	PV factor	PV (£000)
1	270	0.870	234.90
2	360	0.756	272.16
3	480	0.658	315.84
4	640	0.572	366.08
5	800	0.497	397.60
6	1000	0.432	432.00
7	1250	0.376	470.00
			2488.58

Value, at the end of year 7, of future dividends:
£1 250 000/0.15 = £8 333 333

Value at present of year 8 and future dividends:
£8 333 333 × 0.376   3133.33
                                  £5621.91

Total increment effect of a takeover of:
(i) Red Ltd:

	(£000)
Value of Red Ltd	6048
Incremental value to Zed PLC	2104.8
Total value	8152.8

Maximum value that can be offered per share   £8.15

(ii) Yellow Ltd:

	(£000)
Value of Yellow Ltd	5621.91
Incremental value to Zed PLC	2104.80
Total value	7726.71

Maximum value that can be offered per share   £7.73

Part (b)

The approach used in part (a) was to base equity valuation only on future dividends with no consideration being given to underlying asset values which may be of importance in a take-over.

Limitations of dividend growth model

1. smooth dividend growth – in reality dividends may display some volatility from year to year:
2. perpetual growth and infinite life – it is unrealistic to expect infinite life of the firm, but due to discounting this assumption may produce a good working approximation to valuation;
3. constant discount rate or expected rate of return;
4. the possibly differing tax treatment of dividends and capital gains is ignored.

Other factors which should be considered include risk, the quality of the management of Red Ltd and Yellow Ltd, and the method of financing the take-over.

Example 15.5

The management of Fame Electronics, a rapidly growing and profitable private company, is considering applying for a stock market listing. This will provide existing shareholders with an opportunity to sell their shares while allowing the firm to raise the additional funds which will be necessary to finance its planned capital expenditure programme. The earnings of the firm over the next financial year are expected to be about £8 million, dividends will be limited to £2 million and £6 million will be reinvested. As it is intended to spend £10 million on new investments next year it is planned to raise £4 million from a new issue of shares. Over the next three years dividends will be limited to 25% of earnings as opportunities to earn above normal rates of return from new investments are anticipated. No further new issues are planned and it is expected that all investment after next year will be financed from retentions. While the expected rate of return on similar risk shares is about 10%, the management of Fame Electronics anticipate an average rate of return on new investments planned for the next three years of 20%. As competition intensifies it is expected that the return on new projects will fall to the rate of return required by shareholders. From year four onwards it is expected that the firm will continue to grow at above the average rate but new investments are not expected to yield more than 10% per annum and the company plans to revert to 50% payout ratio.

Required:

Ignore taxation.

1. Estimate what the market value of the company should be at the end of year three.
2. What do you consider to be an appropriate market value for the firm today?
3. What proportion of the market value today is due to growth opportunities?
4. Calculate the price earnings ratio and explain its usefulness and main drawbacks as a valuation model.

Answer
1. We are given sufficient information to be able to estimate the market value of the company using the dividend growth model. We can estimate g for year four and onwards and we are given the market's expected rate of return (10%). We need to calculate the dividend for year four.

| | | Year | | |
	1	2	3	4
Earnings	8	10	11.5	13.225
Dividends	2	2.5	2.875	6.6125
Retained earnings	6	7.5	8.625	
New equity	4			
Funds invested	10	7.5	8.625	
Return on new investment (20%)	2	1.5	1.725	

g = retention rate $\times$ expected returns (in future)

$\quad$ = 0.50 $\times$ 0.10

$\quad$ = 0.05

$$V = \frac{D4}{i-g} = \frac{6.6125}{0.10-0.05} = £132.25 \text{ million}$$

2. The value today is the discounted sum of the dividends for the next three years and the value at the beginning of year 4 (end year 3)

$$V = \frac{2}{(1.10)} + \frac{2.5}{(1.10)^2} + \frac{2.875}{(1.10)^3} + \frac{132.25}{(1.10)^3}$$

$$= £105.41 \text{ million}$$

3. Without growth opportunities the company is worth the present value of its current earnings continuing in perpetuity.

$$V = \frac{8}{0.10} = £80 \text{ million}$$

This is 75.90% of the value with growth. 24.1% of the price today is due to growth opportunity.

4. The price earnings ratio is approximately 13 to 1 $\left(\text{i.e. } \frac{105.41}{8}\right)$. Its usefulness and drawbacks have been discussed above.

15.3 Valuation based on earnings?

Graham *et al.* [3] wrote in 1962 that the 'predominant role of dividends has found full reflection in a generally accepted theory of investment value which states that a common stock is worth the sum of all the dividends to be paid on it in the future, each discounted to its present worth'.

Not all would agree with the view that dividends have a predominant role in influencing share price. A great deal of theoretical and empirical work over the last 50 years has been concerned with the precise effect of a company's dividend policy on its share price. The research that has been undertaken has not found one single factor that explains the level of share price across all companies for all periods of time. In some time periods dividends seem to dominate the market's thinking; in other periods the market seems to be absorbed with earning figures. In some companies the shareholders are more interested in dividends than retained earnings; in other companies the position is reversed. Dividend policy will be discussed in Chapter 17. There is a considerable controversy on the subject. An important proposition, put forward by Modigliani and Miller [4], is that if certain assumptions are made, the dividends decision is irrelevant in determining the share price. This will be considered in Chapter 17.

At this point all that need be said is that shares are sometimes valued on the basis of the earnings per share. We shall now consider this approach. Probably the most popular approach to valuing a share is by use of the price-to-earnings ratio. This is the earnings multiplier approach, where today's earnings per share are multiplied by a factor which takes into account growth expectations. Investors will be willing to pay a price which is a higher multiple of today's earnings per share for a fast-growing company than for a slow-growth company. Consequently a high price-to-earnings ratio indicates that the market thinks that the company has good growth prospects. The popularity of this approach can be seen from the fact that many daily newspapers publish the price-to-earnings ratios of the leading companies on their financial pages. The price-to-earnings ratio is now part of the language of investment.

When valuing the share of a particular company the investor has to begin by making an assessment of what he considers to be the appropriate price-to-earnings ratio . It is not always satisfactory to take the average ratio for the appropriate category. It is often difficult to place a company into a particular category of shares. For instance, if the average price-to-earnings ratio for an industry is taken as the yardstick, we have to be careful to allow for any individual company differences due to such factors as diversification.

The ratio can be used to decide whether a share is undervalued or overvalued. For example, if the appropriate price-to-earnings ratio for a company is assessed as 15:1 and the actual market ratio for the company at the current price is 12:1, then the share is being undervalued. The share would have to rise in price by 25% before what is considered the appropriate price-to-earnings level would be reached.

One question that arises is whether the earnings which are used in the calculation should be the last actual earnings figures recorded or some 'normalized' earnings.

If reported annual earnings are used, the ratio can vary according to the stage of the trade cycle for which the earnings figures are being given. Price-to-earnings ratios based on normalized earnings can be said to be more meaningful as a basis of calculation only if we are interested in a long-term assessment of the share value. If we are interested in valuing a particular share's price for short-term price movement, the actual earnings figures may prove a better base.

The analyst who is interested in long-term share price movements not only has to forecast the future earnings of the company, but also the expected movement in the overall market price-to-earnings ratios – in other words, in the degree of confidence the market is placing on expected future growth. The analyst assessing a share price by this method has to forecast the expected earnings of the company in the next period, the relevant price-to-earnings ratio for the category of shares to which the company belongs and the expected change in overall price-to-earnings levels. The calculation of prices through the use of the now popular price-to-earnings ratio still involves many unknowns.

The apparent simplicity of the price/earnings ratio approach should not lead to false confidence in its accuracy. It is undoubtedly an easy approach and so less expensive in terms of time and effort, but this says nothing about its accuracy. The method is computationally easier than the PV of dividends approach, but it involves just as many assumptions. Its simplicity merely hides the complexity of the problem.

The dividend valuation model can be reconciled with the price-to-earnings approach. If

$$P_0 = \frac{D_1}{i - g}$$

if K is the payout ratio and E_1 is the expected earnings per share for the current year, then

$$P_0 = \frac{KE_1}{i - g}$$

and so

$$\frac{P_0}{E_1} = \frac{K}{i - g}$$

P_0/E_1 is the price-to-earnings ratio based on the expected earnings per share for the current year. The formula emphasizes that expected growth is a key factor in determining the ratio: the higher is g, the greater is the price-to-earnings ratio. To illustrate the use of the equation, let $D_1 = £1$, $K = 0.4$, $i = 15\%$ and $g = 10\%$. Then

$$P_0 = \frac{1}{0.15 - 0.10} = 20$$

$$\frac{P_0}{E_1} = \frac{0.40}{0.15 - 0.10} = 8$$

and

$$E_1 = 2.5$$

If the expected growth rate of the company is 13% then

$$\frac{P_0}{E_1} = \frac{0.40}{0.15 - 0.13} = 20$$

and the price of the share is

$$P_o = \frac{1}{0.15 - 0.13} = 50$$

Unfortunately the formula cannot be used if $g > i$.

Using the above it is possible to work out what earnings growth assumptions are built into the current price of any share. A similar exercise can be carried out to estimate the dividend growth assumption built into the share price. However, in both methods it is assumed that the price is basically determined by a single variable, either dividends or earnings growth. But other variables do influence the ratio.

Earnings growth rate

We shall illustrate the technique with an example, in which we assume that after seven years all companies are expected to be giving the same yield to shareholders who purchased at time zero on the price they paid at time zero. Of course, when seven years have elapsed, not all companies will in fact be in this position: there will still be a range of yields to investors just as there is today.

However, it is not possible to say what the distribution of these yields between industries will be like, since it is impossible to identify the industries that will have above average earnings yields or vice versa. Companies and industries will probably not maintain the relative positions that they have today; all the empirical evidence works against any such idea, and in any case it would make nonsense economically. If one industry or one company could continue to show above average rates of return for its shareholders, capital resources would continue to move into that industry or company until eventually its rates were brought back to the average. In the absence of knowledge about the specific companies and industries likely to have above and below average returns in the future, it is reasonable to assume that investors, when buying shares at time zero, expect all companies to be giving at some time in the future the same earnings yield on that money invested.

If the average earnings yield on all companies' shares at the present time is 5%, which is a price-to-earnings ratio of 20:1, it can be shown that with an average annual growth in earnings of 4% on the price paid for shares today, there will be an earnings yield of 6.6% in seven years' time

present earnings yield $\times 1.04^7$ = earnings yield after seven years
$$5\% \times 1.04^7 = 6.6\%$$

As previously mentioned, it is assumed that all companies will be showing a 6.6% earnings yield in seven years' time on the money invested at the beginning of the period (at time zero). The existing earnings yield for a company is known, and so it is a simple matter to calculate what has been assumed explicitly or implicitly by investors as the rate of growth in the earnings of the company in arriving at the share price at time zero.

Let us take as an example a company that has an earnings yield at present of 3% (that is a price-to-earnings ratio of 33:1); for the share price to be correct the earnings of the company will have to grow at approximately 12% per annum, i.e.

$$3\% \ (1.12\%)^7 = 6.6\%$$

It is a 12% growth assumption that is built into the share price at the beginning of the period. This is at a time when the average annual growth in earnings is 4%.

15.4 The capital asset pricing model and share values

The share valuation model described above is based on a discount rate, which we refer to as the market capitalization rate on shares in the risk class being considered. It is here that we can make use of the CAPM which should assist us in obtaining the correct discount rate. The CAPM gives insights not only into problems of calculating the cost of capital, but also into problems of valuing securities.

The dividend model so far described has not explicitly considered risk. Risk is the possibility that the actual returns, say the actual dividends, will deviate from the expected dividends. In the real world there is uncertainty, and this has to be allowed for in any analysis. With some companies there is a greater risk, a greater possibility that actual outcomes will differ from expectations, than there is with other companies. The CAPM shows one way in which risk can be accommodated in financial analysis. Its particular contribution is that it shows that in market equilibrium a share will be expected to provide a return which is commensurate with its unavoidable risk.

The model explains that risk can be broken down into two components, namely systematic risk and unsystematic risk. The former type of risk represents that which arises because of underlying movements in the economy, in the overall level of share prices. This risk cannot be diversified away by an investor holding the securities of more and more companies. This is the unavoidable risk and is measured by what is known as the beta factor. It is the risk that has to be taken into account when valuing shares.

Unsystematic risk, however, arises from movements in a particular company's returns not associated with general market movements. This arises because of individual company characteristics, and an investor can avoid this type of risk by diversifying his shareholdings over a large number of companies.

The impact of this model on investment theory – and so on share price evaluation – has been considerable. Although the model has been fully discussed in Chapters 9 and 10, we shall use a simple example to show how it can be applied in share price evaluation.

If we assume that unsystematic risk is diversified away by the investor, the model states that the expected return on an asset j is

$$\bar{R}_j = R_f + \beta_j(\bar{R}_m - R_f)$$

where R_f is the risk-free rate of return, β_j is the sensitivity of the asset's return to that of a market portfolio, $\bar{R}_m$ is the expected return from holding the market portfolio and $\bar{R}_j$ is the expected return on asset j.

The way in which this model can be used in share evaluation is that it enables us to determine the relevant discount rate to use in discounting expected returns to arrive at the PV. In section 15.2 we dealt with the model that relates the market value of a share to the discounted sum of future dividends. The dividends were discounted at a rate i which we described as the market capitalization rate of shares of the class being considered. In fact i equals $\bar{R}_j$. The CAPM enables us to calculate this capitalization rate.

We will illustrate the technique with two examples.

Example 15.6

The managing director of Wemere, a medium-sized private company, wishes to improve the company's investment decision-making process by using discounted cash-flow techniques. He is disappointed to learn that estimates of a company's cost of equity usually require information on share prices which, for a private company, are not available. His deputy suggests that the cost of equity can be estimated by using data for Folten plc, a similar sized company in the same industry whose shares are listed on the USM, and he has produced two suggested discount rates for use in Wemere's future investment appraisal. Both of these estimates are in excess of 17% per year which the managing director believes to be very high, especially as the company has just agreed a fixed rate bank loan at 13% per year to finance a small expansion of existing operations. He has checked the calculations, which are numerically correct, but wonders if there are any errors of principle.

Estimate 1: *Capital asset pricing model*

Data have been purchased from a leading business school

    Equity beta of Folten: 1.4
    Market return: 18%
    Treasury bill yield: 12%

The cost of capital is $18\% \times (18\% - 12\%)\ 1.4 = 26.4\%$

This rate must be adjusted to include inflation at the current level of 6%. The recommended discount rate is 32.4%.

Estimate 2: *Dividend valuation model*

Year	Folten plc Average share price (pence)	Dividend per share (pence)
1990	193	9.23
1991	109	10.06
1992	96	10.97
1993	116	11.95
1994	130	13.03

The cost of capital is: $\dfrac{D_1}{P-g}$ Where: D_1 is the expected dividend

                                        P is the market price
                                        g is the growth rate of dividends (%)

$$= \frac{14.20}{138-9} = 11.01\%$$

When inflation is included the discount rate is 17.01%

Other financial information on the two companies is presented below:

	Wemere £000	Folten £000
Fixed assets	7 200	7 600
Current assets	7 600	7 800
Less: Current liabilities	3 900	3 700
	10 900	11 700

Financed by		
Ordinary shares (25 pence)	2 000	1 800
Reserves	6 500	5 500
Term loans	2 400	4 400
	10 900	11 700

Notes

1. The current ex-div share price of Folten plc is 138 pence.
2. Wemere's board of directors has recently rejected a take-over bid of £10.6 million.
3. Corporate tax is at the rate of 35%.

Required

(a) Explain any errors of principle that have been made in the two estimates of the cost of capital and produce revised estimates using both of the methods.

State clearly any assumptions that you make. (14 marks)

(b) Discuss which of your revised estimates Wemere should use as the discount rate for capital investment appraisal. (4 marks)

ACCA, June 1990

Answer

The errors of principle include:

Estimate 1

1. Use of R_m rather than R_f in the CAPM equation.
2. No adjustment is necessary to the estimate obtained from the CAPM equation, as the estimate of R_m, R_f and β all incorporate the effects of inflation. For example R_m is the monetary rate of return, and includes the increase above real rates that shareholders expect to allow for losses due to inflation.
3. It is suggested by the deputy managing director that the CAPM estimate can be used for investment appraisal. It is only the cost of equity funds and not the WACC.
4. The equity β used is that of Folten which is based on that company's level of gearing. Wemere have a different level of gearing.

Estimate 2

5. The dividend valuation model formula is incorrect.
6. No inflation adjustment necessary.
7. WACC required.

The reader should attempt to calculate the cost of capital of Wemere based on the CAPM approach. The market weighting of gearing based on the takeover bid values for Wemere is 81.5% equity and 18.5% debt. To estimate Wemere equity beta it is first necessary to 'ungear' Folten's equity beta and then to adjust this to allow for the different levels of Wemere.

The company has been offered £10.6 million for 8 million shares. This values each share at £1.325.

Using the dividend valuation for Wemere, the cost of equity

$$= \frac{D_1}{P} + g$$

$$= \frac{14.20}{132.5} + 0.09$$

$$= 0.107 + 0.09$$

$$= 0.197 = 19.7\%$$

The weighted average cost of capital is

$$= \left(19.7\% \times \frac{81.5}{100}\right) + \left(13\% (1 - 0.35) \times \frac{18.5}{100}\right)$$

$$= 17.62\%$$

Example 15.7

Summarized financial data for Univo plc is shown below:

Profit and loss accounts

£000

	1992	1993	1994[1]
Turnover	76 270	89 410	102 300
Taxable income	10 140	12 260	14 190
Taxation	3 549	4 291	4 966
	6 591	7 969	9 224
Dividend	2 335	2 557	2 800
Retained earnings	4 256	5 412	6 424

Balance sheet (£000)	1994[1]
Fixed assets	54 200
Current assets	39 500
Current liabilities	(26 200)
	67 500
Ordinary shares (50 pence par value)	20 000
Reserves	32 500
10% debenture 1999 (£100 par value)	15 000
	67 500

[1]1994 figures are unaudited estimates.

As a result of recent capital investment stock market analysts expect post tax earnings and dividends to increase by 25% for two years and then to revert to the company's existing growth rates.

Univo's asset (overall) beta is 0.763 and beta of debt is 0.20. The risk free rate is 12% and the market return 17%. The current market price of Univo's ordinary shares is 217 pence, cum 1994 dividend, and the debenture price is £89.50 ex. interest. Corporate tax is at the rate of 35%.

Required

1. Using the dividend growth model estimate what a fundamental analyst might consider to be the intrinsic (or realistic) value of the company's shares. Comment upon the significance of your estimate for the fundamental analyst.

   Assume, for this part of the question only, that the cost of equity is not expected to change. The cost of equity may be estimated by using the CAPM. (10 marks)

2. If interest rates were to increase by 2% and expected dividend growth to remain unchanged, estimate what affect this would be likely to have on the intrinsic value of the company's shares.

   (3 marks)
   ACCA, Dec. 1991

Answer

Equity β:

$$\beta_{asset} = \beta_e \frac{E}{E + D(1-t)} + \beta_d \frac{D(1-t)}{E + D(1-t)}$$

E is the ex div market value of equity 40 million $\times$ 210 pence = £84 million.
D is the ex interest market value of debt £15m $\times$ 0.895 = £13.425 million.
Therefore

$$0.763 = \beta_e \frac{84}{84 + 13.425(0.65)} + 0.20 \frac{13.425(0.65)}{84 + 13.425(0.65)}$$

$$\beta_e = 0.82$$

1. Dividends are expected to grow by 25% per annum for two years and then to revert to the past growth rate. The past growth rate is equal to 9.5% i.e. (2335 $\times$ 1.095) = 2557

$$(2557 \times 1.095) = 2800$$

The dividend per share for 1994 $= \dfrac{2800}{40\ 000} = £0.07$

To use the dividend growth model we need to know the market's required rate of return on equity in Univo plc. The question tells us that the market's return is 17%. It is tempting to use this figure but to do so is incorrect. This is the market's average return on equity. It is the figure used in the CAPM formula. We need to estimate the required return for Univo, that is the cost of equity.
   The CAPM equation is:

$$K_e = R_f + \beta_e (R_m - R_f)$$

We know that R_f equals 0.12, and that R_m equals 0.17 (the value referred to above). Therefore the cost of equity equals approximately 16% i.e. (0.12 + 0.82 (0.17 − 0.12).

We can now calculate the value of the share.

	Dividend		Discount factor (16%)		Present value
Year 1	7.0p (1.25)	$\times$	0.862	=	7.54p
Year 2	7.0p (1.25)^2	$\times$	0.743	=	8.13p
					15.67p

The value at the beginning of year 3 (end of year 2) will be:

$$\frac{10.94\,(1.095)}{(0.16 - 0.095)} = 184.31\text{p}$$

This has present value of 136.94p, giving the value of the share today as £1.53 (i.e. £1.37 + £0.16).

2. If interest rates were to increase by 2%, the required return on equity shares would also increase. We will assume the required rate of return on equities would also increase by 2%. This gives a cost of equity for Univo plc of 18%. We need therefore to discount the dividends by 18% rather than 16%. The resulting estimate of the share price following the change in interest rates is £1.16.

15.5 Valuation based on free cash flow

One form of share price evaluation model is based on cash flow. This approach takes into account the fact that retained earnings, depreciation and new funds are invested each year in the business, and this total increased investment earns a certain rate of return which benefits the investors. If the cash flow per share that is free to be invested is determined, then the present value of the expected returns from investing that amount can be determined. The earnings per share (EPS) approach only considers part of the cash that the company has to invest each year. Both the EPS and the cash flow approaches are based on expectations of the rate of return that management can earn on funds.

A study in the USA by Kaplan and Roll [5] has indicated that companies are valued more on the basis of their cash flows than on their reported earnings. They found that a change in accounting reporting practice which affected reported earnings of companies but did not affect their cash flow did not have a lasting effect on their share prices. The accounting change initially affected prices, but the change did not fool the market for long, and the temporary alteration in value of the shares soon disappeared. This is similar to the earnings drift referred to in the previous section.

Lee and Lawson [6] are strong advocates in the UK of cash flow accounting. They believe that it is much more relevant to investors than profits based on historic cost figures.

In an examination of the relationship between equity cash flows and equity market values, Lee [7] concludes that 'cash flow data re-expressed in terms of a base-year price level constitute highly relevant information for stock market investors'. This point will be returned to in the chapter on cash flow management. In the UK it is now a requirement that companies publish a cash flow statement in their annual reports. Some investment analysts produce statistics for each company showing the current price as a multiple of free cash flow per share as opposed to earnings per share.

It is possible to criticize valuations based on accounting earnings figures because earnings are based on many conventions and assumptions. Also it is possible for the management of a company to smooth earnings figures over time and to create a good impression for at least a short period of time. Those problems were considered in the chapter on stock market efficiency. To base valuations on earnings can therefore be worrying.

Cash flow figures provide an alternative basis for valuation purposes. There are crude measures of free cash flow (available cash) that can easily be obtained. For example:

revenue − operating cost − investment expenditure = available cash

Such figures can however be dangerous if they are based on profit and loss account and balance sheet figures. The user of the accounts must be sure that creative accounting techniques have not been employed. Also it must be appreciated that the figures taken from the balance sheet and profit and loss account are based on accruals concepts and can only be used as approximations of cash flow. For example revenue needs to be adjusted for opening and closing debtors' figures to obtain true cash flow.

UK companies now have to publish a cash flow statement with their annual financial statements and so it is possible to determine more accurately the free cash flow.

We have explained the alternative techniques for valuing a company. The popularity of each of the techniques varies from country to country. The valuation process can be based on estimates of either the future profits, the future dividends, the net asset values or the cash flow of the company. In the UK it is possible to accumulate a large amount of information, financial and otherwise, on such matters. In many other countries it is not always so easy to obtain such information. If the valuation method is based on earnings it is necessary to select the basis by which the earnings estimates will be converted into a valuation figure. This earnings valuation method (PE ratio) is the most popular method used in the UK, one reason for this being that with a well-developed stock market in the UK it is possible to obtain information on share values of comparable companies that can be used as a benchmark. As explained the simplest way of doing this is by observing the price earnings ratio that is being used in the stock market to value the shares of an approximately similar company. This ratio is then used, with knowledge of the current earnings per share, to estimate an appropriate price per share.

15.6 Country differences in valuation methods

In France a similar approach is commonly adopted: namely, an estimate of maintainable earnings per share is multiplied by an appropriate price earnings ratio. In the USA there has also traditionally been an attraction to the price earnings multiple approach, but lately there has been a move towards valuations based on free cash flows.

In Germany a different approach is more popular, particularly for smaller firms. There are far fewer companies listed on the stock exchanges in Germany than in the UK. Therefore it is not so easy to find suitable stock market data for comparative analysis. When financial accounts are available in Germany, they need to be adjusted if the wish is to use them to estimate future maintainable profits.

The accounts will have been prepared on a basis to satisfy taxation rules. There could also be secret reserves that need to be estimated. An additional practical problem is that many German companies fail to file their accounts at the local company registry office.

As a result of the lack of suitable price earnings multiplier information from the stock market in Germany, when maintainable profits have been estimated they are often valued by reference to the current medium-term interest rate plus a percentage to allow for risk. The profits are capitalized at this estimated required rate of return. It is similar to capitalizing at a risk-free rate plus a risk premium.

In Italy there is even less data available from the capital market about suitable rates of return. Often a hybrid basis of valuation is used, this being the estimated net asset value of the company plus a premium based on the earning power of the company above the industry average. This method is explained more fully later in this chapter.

If equity shares are valued on the basis of dividends per share, then there is no problem of interpreting data. Dividends are a precise figure – an actual sum of money that changes hands. However, if shares can be valued on the basis of the earnings per share then we have a potential problem. Because of the measurement problems, the earnings per share figure reported in a company's accounts must be an 'estimate'. An auditor signs a statement to say that this earnings per share figure is 'true and fair'. But there is more than one 'true and fair' figure that could be reported, and some are possibly truer and fairer than others.

15.7 Does it pay to manipulate earnings?

There is no such thing as a (true) correct profit or loss (earnings) figure to reflect a year's activities. There is a range of possible profit or loss figures that can be produced based on the assumptions that are made. At one end of the range is what some would regard as the 'exaggerated' profit figure, and at the other end is what others would regard as the excessively cautious profit figure. The fact that there is a possible range of profit figures (even with increasingly demanding accounting standards), and not a unique figure, should not come as a surprise to anybody who knows something about accounting. The profit and loss account reports the performance over a period of time, but the business does not usually come to an end at the close of that period: contracts may be only half completed; goods may have been produced but not sold; equipment that has been purchased is still usable; not all customers have paid for goods and services received. Accounting reporting does not just involve measuring what has happened in the past; it also, of necessity, involves making assumptions about certain aspects of what will happen in the future.

The accounting profession is of course very concerned at the range of earnings figures that a company can or could report to its shareholders. In the 1960s what was known as a 'credibility' gap developed. This later became known as an expectations gap.

Any credibility gap is important, because one of the factors that influence investors, bankers and others in their decision-making is how they interpret the financial statements presented to them. The investors' decisions are important, for not only do they affect the demand for a company's shares, but at times of mergers and takeovers they can affect the survival of a company in its existing form. In the UK the reputations of some businessmen were built up on the basis of their use of creative accounting. Even conservative executives sometimes had to abandon their more prudent assumptions when preparing accounts, or run the risk of seeing their companies taken over because they were not producing the performance of what were thought to be the more dynamic companies. There was clearly a need for accountants to tidy up reporting practices.

The accounting profession in the UK has in the 1990s changed its accounting standard setting procedures to try to reduce the opportunities for the management of earnings disclosure. Accounting standards-setting is one attempt to improve the reporting system. It is, however, not the end of the story, and within five to ten years it is reasonable to assume that we will be trying other methods to improve communication between businesses, shareholders, potential investors, employees, the government and all other users of accounts.

In the 1970s the business world, the financial community and the accounting profession had high expectations from accounting standards. By the mid-1980s, considerable disillusionment had set in. In the UK, the level of non-compliance was increasing. The position has improved in the 1990s. A Financial Reporting Review Panel was established, to examine the annual reports and accounts of companies to ensure that the practices followed complied with accounting standards and statutory requirements. The Panel has the power to take action which can lead to a company being required to prepare revised accounts.

The Panel have been successful in that a number of companies have as a result of criticism made changes and adjustments to their published accounts. One of the Panel's spectacular successes was in 1992 with Trafalgar House where criticism of the reclassification by the company of certain properties from current assets to fixed assets and of the treatment of a number of other items led to revised accounts needing to be presented. The criticism also led to other changes which resulted in the removal of the Chairman and of the Managing Director of the company.

There was one other area of major concern with accounting standards. The accounting standard-setting bodies either could not agree on the appropriate treatments or else took too long to come to a recommendation. Accounting at the time of changing prices is an example of the first problem; off-balance-sheet financing is an example of delay.

In the USA there was concern that, on many of the major issues that were emerging in the fields of finance and accounting, there were no standards or recommendations with regard to the appropriate accounting treatment. It was taking a considerable time for the FASB to produce a standard, and during this period the preparers of accounts could do as they liked, to the confusion of the users. The FASB, in an attempt to overcome this problem, set up an 'Emerging Issues Task Force'. In the UK there is also a considerable lag between the time when an accounting issue emerges and the time when, if at all, a standard or statement is produced. A similar task force has been set up in the UK entitled the 'Urgent Issues Task Force'.

Market reaction to earnings information

A number of studies have examined the use made by investment analysts of annual financial reports [8]. Studies based on the situation in the UK show that the annual reports and communications with management are the two most important sources of information for analysts. These are followed in the order of perceived importance by interim reports, offer prospectuses, press releases and with advisory services of least importance.

It must be remembered that information is coming to analysts continuously over time. They react to such information on a continuous basis. The share price is continually changing to reflect the information. Annual reports are only produced once a year. In theory the price of a share in the market place reflects the true value of a share, the true value being based on what information is available at any time.

Within such a free market system what impact does the disclosure of the financial results of a company have on investors? A number of studies have shown that at the individual company level the share price does react to the announcement of earnings, but in general the movement at the time of the announcement is not as great as might be expected [9]. The reason for this is that the market has anticipated much of the year-on-year news content of annual financial reports. Earnings announcements and the subsequent publication of the annual report allow the revision of expectations to be made. Investors and bankers form expectations of all future variables that they consider to be significant in the valuation of bonds and shares. There is uncertainty attached to these valuations. The announcement of earnings figures resolves one source of this uncertainty.

In an early pioneering study, Ball and Brown found that for US companies most of the information contained in the final report had already been anticipated before its release; the anticipation was very accurate, and the drift upwards or downwards in share price had begun 12 months before the report was released [10]. With regard to the value of the information contained in the final report, no more than 10–15% has not been anticipated by the month of the report. The value of the information conveyed by the report at the time of its release constitutes on average only 20% of the value of all information coming to the market in that month. About 70% of all information appears to be offsetting, which means that it is of no lasting use for decision-making, although it may cause investors to act in the short run. Therefore only 30% of all information coming to the market at the time of the final report has a continuing value.

Investors build up expectations about earnings, and when actual results are announced some proportion of any movement will have already been anticipated. Therefore this expected part of any movement should already have been reflected in the share price. If the market is efficient, only the unexpected part should not already have been reflected in the share price. If the market is efficient, only the unexpected part of the total information would be new to the market and the efficient market should ensure that the security's price reacts quickly and in the appropriate direction.

The early work of Ball and Brown was based on quite simple analysis. Since then there have been hundreds of other studies into the relationship between a company's earnings and its stock market returns. The more recent studies have refined the analysis but have not enhanced our understanding of the extent to which earnings figures are utilized by investors. The evidence over the past 20 years shows a consistent picture with earnings and earnings-related information explaining between 2% and 5% of the times series variability of share price returns over short periods of time, and up to 7% for longer periods of time. The statistical results are not really so surprising because a substantial part of the accounting information provided on the announcement date has been made available to the market through interim reports, statements by corporate officials or investigations by analysts confirmed by corporate contacts.

Similar results have been found in other studies. Beaver *et al.* [11] showed that typically it is share price movements that lead the announcements of earnings movements. To repeat, however, these results only apply to the larger companies on which much information is available. Even so, these earnings announcements do convey useful information.

Evidence is now beginning to appear which suggests that the market should take more notice of the information contained in financial statements. Ou and Penman [12] find that the market under-utilizes financial statement information in predicting whether current earnings changes are transitory or permanent. Bernard and Thomas [13] interpret the way in which share prices move following the earnings announcements (what is referred to as drift) as reflecting the fact that those who operate in the market give incomplete recognition to the implications of the current earnings figures for future earnings. They are slow to appreciate the messages that the current figures give with respect to the future.

This apparently minor role of accounting earnings numbers in security valuation might seem worrying, particularly as the justification for the expensive accounting reporting system is to provide useful information for decision-making. What is the explanation for it? Lev offers three explanations, of which the third is of the most significance for our purposes [14]. The first explanation is that earnings figures might be very useful to investors but that the statistical techniques used by academic researchers are not good enough to detect this fact. A second possible explanation is that investors are irrational and that stock markets are less efficient than is sometimes assumed.

The third explanation is that because published earnings are based on many assumptions and strategic management choices as to which accounting policies to adopt, the actual figures published are not the ones used by analysts. In other words it is the information content of the actual reported profit figure that is low and not useful in predicting future profits. If analysts carry out their own adjustments to the published figures, it could be that these adjusted figures do show a very good relationship with security returns.

It is in fact strange that nearly all researchers take the published earnings figures at face value and use these in their statistical analysis. We know that adjustments are required in order to be able to compare the published earnings of one company with those of another. This is necessary, even without allowing for 'creative' techniques, just to make the assumptions comparable. Much of the research on the usefulness of earnings figures has been wasted effort because it ignores the quality of the published earnings figures and the adjustments needed to make figures comparable. Recent research in the USA into the market reaction to earnings announcements emphasizes the significance to the results of the 'quality' of the earnings figures. If the figures are distorted, different investors will interpret them in different ways, leading to a confused market reaction [15].

The point has been made that not all people who analyse accounts or who undertake research in the earnings/share price area actually look at the published accounts. Often they make use of the on-stream data supplied by many agencies. As Brennan points out 'the careful consideration given by practising accountants to the manner in which earnings are reported, and to which items are included in earnings, stands in marked contrast to the casual attitude of most researchers towards the definition of the variable under investigation [16].

Much of the research into the information content of accounting reports is undertaken by non-accountants, who have access to the large computerized databases. It is easy to regress one set of numbers (readily available) on another set (equally readily available). It is not easy to go through a set of financial accounts considering every footnote and trying to assess its implications. It is time-consuming and requires more than a basic knowledge of accounting. It requires the researcher to read between the lines.

Perhaps therefore we should not be too worried that a large amount of academic finance research finds it difficult to discover a relationship between unadjusted published earning figures and share price movements. Accountants know it is not possible to compare the earnings figures of one company with another without making adjustments.

One object of the process of harmonization of accounting standards in the EU has been to assist in bringing about an effective and efficient European capital market. It is argued that if analysts in one country are unable to correctly interpret the financial accounts of a company in another country, this will not lead to efficient portfolio investment decisions. Misunderstandings and indeed uncertainty will limit the gains that could be achieved from a single market in finance. Choi and Levich in an empirical study conclude that 'a major implication of our findings is that accounting differences are important and affect capital market decisions of a significant number of market participants we surveyed regardless of nationality, size, experience, scope of international activity and organisational structure' [17].

Accounting information is therefore found to be important in valuing shares. Even for companies about which much is known, the publication of the annual accounts confirms or denies expectations that have been built up.

15.8 Pricing new issues

The price at which a new issue of shares is offered to the market is based mainly on the price and yields on comparable issues already being traded. It is usually settled in negotiations between the company, the issuing house and the broker. The price in an offer for sale must appear attractive to the underwriters and also, of course, to the public. In a placing, the price must seem attractive to the clients of the brokers and issuing house who are subscribing for the shares. Usually the issuing house would like to see the development of a small premium on the issue price which occurs when the market price settles a little above the issue price. This would give them and their clients a small profit in return for taking up the issue.

In order to make a new issue attractive to investors, the yields offered are usually a little above that of similar traded securities. Investors must be attracted to purchase the new shares in preference to existing securities. If, in a placing, the shares cannot be sold at the decided price, the vendors (the selling shareholders) must accept a lower price or the issue must be abandoned. Either way, it will be embarrassing, since part of the costs will already have been incurred.

Before an issue is made to the public, it is usual to insure against the risk of inadequate subscription by having the issue underwritten. Underwriters agree to take the number of shares specified in the underwriting letter if the public do not subscribe for them. They do not guarantee that the public will take up the shares; they simply agree to subscribe for the shares themselves in the event of an inadequate public response to the offer. The purpose of having an issue of capital underwritten is to ensure that the company obtains the necessary capital.

Although the underwriting or placing of the shares assures the company or the share owners of the proceeds of the issue, this is no guarantee that the issue will be a success. To set the price so high that the issue is left with the underwriters is not necessarily of benefit to the company or the share owners. The latter may obtain the benefit of a high price for their shares in the short run, but the price of the shares is likely to remain weak for a considerable time after the issue. This will, of course, affect the value of any shares still held by the original shareholders and may adversely affect the company's ability to raise money even after the underwriters have succeeded in disposing of their own holdings.

In determining the asking price the company's broker will consider first the market rating of similar companies already quoted, taking into account their relative financial strength, profit record and the future prospects as far as it is possible to judge them. A company may have a magnificent profit record, but if the profit figures or reports recently issued by similar companies indicate a general downturn in profits, this will be an important consideration.

Perhaps the most important factor in determining the flotation price for a company's shares is the forecast of its level of maintainable profits. Such profits are a function of the level of profits on existing assets and the profits expected on any new investment to be financed with the proceeds or part of the proceeds of the new issue. If the shares being sold to the market are those belonging to the existing shareholders of the company, then the company will not receive any increase in its funds; if the shares are new, then the receipts from the sale of these will add to the funds of the company. The profit forecast therefore depends on the use to which the proceeds of the share flotation are to be assigned, with any proceeds intended for new investment adding to the level of maintainable profits.

A simple example will illustrate the issues to be considered when deciding upon a price. Assume a company coming to the market for the first time wishes to raise £50 000. It will be able to maintain profits of £5000 per annum. (The scale of the amount to be raised does not matter.)

Assume that the forecast net profits of a company are £5000, after financing a new investment. The company can comfortably rely on maintaining profits at this level and providing a normal rate of profit growth. The policy-makers agree that a certain amount of money, in this case say £50 000, is needed, part of which would be used to finance the investment. A crucial decision will involve two variables: the number of shares to be issued, and their price. In theory the desired sum could be raised by many combinations of numbers of shares and share price. In practice, however, there are tacit limits to the range of prices considered appropriate for the shares. There is a feeling, which has only limited logical basis, that below a certain price a new share is too cheap, and above a certain price a new share is too dear. This is of necessity extremely arbitrary.

This ideal price range only applies to new shares coming on to the market. A company that is already traded in the market will issue its shares at or near its existing market price, and so, knowing both the share price and the amount of capital that it wishes to raise, it merely needs to divide the one into the other to determine the number of shares it should issue.

We continue with the example of a company coming to the market for the first time. As a result of the investment, total net profits are expected to be £5000. If 100 000 shares are issued, this will give an EPS of £0.05. If companies in the same risk class have shares with a price-to-earnings ratio of 10:1, the asking price for the new issue could be set at about £0.50 per share. An issue at this price might be feasible, but let us assume that it only just qualifies for the 'ideal' price range. An issue of 50 000 shares would give net EPS of £0.10; with the required price-to-earnings ratio of 10:1, the asking price would be £1.

In both the above circumstances the company would obtain the required amount of funds – £50 000. If, however, a suitable price-to-earnings ratio was only 8:1, the share price would be only £0.40 and the issue of 100 000 shares would realize only £40 000. By issuing more shares the company could still not obtain the £50 000. If 125 000 were issued, the net EPS would be £0.04, the share price would be £0.32 and only about £40 000 would be raised. The total amount of funds that can be raised is simply the expected total earnings multiplied by the price-to-earnings ratio. The only way in which the company could hope to raise £50 000 of equity finance, with expected earnings of £5000 and a price-to-earnings ratio of 8:1, is by disguising its future earnings expectations or by attempting to justify a higher price-to-earnings ratio. The effect on existing shareholders of the price at which new shares are issued is discussed in the sections on rights issues and capital gearing.

The denomination of the shares needs to be considered further. Dividend rates were once expressed in terms of a percentage of the nominal value of a share, and it was considered bad public relations, and certainly embarrassing in trade union negotiations, to declare a dividend of, say, 100% of nominal value. If in the above example 50 000 shares are issued, EPS will be £0.10. If a gross dividend of approximately £0.06 could be paid for a share selling at the price of £1, this gives a gross dividend yield of 6%, which has to be compared with the current level of dividend yields. If the par (nominal) value of the share were set at, say, £0.75, this would give a dividend of 8% of par.

If par were set at £0.10, the dividend rate would be 60% which might give cause for alarm. In fact the practice has grown of declaring dividends as simply a sum of money per share.

In summary, management has to ascertain

1. the maintainable level of profits;
2. the desired price-to-earnings ratio;
3. the desired dividend cover;
4. the desired dividend yield.

Given all the relevant information on these matters and knowledge of share prices of similar types of company, an asking price for the new shares can be determined. One of the difficulties, here as elsewhere in finance, is the selection of comparable companies that can be used as a guide.

We shall now illustrate an approach to answering questions on the pricing of new issues. The question that follows is taken from a Financial Management paper of the Chartered Association of Certified Accountants.

Example 15.8

At a meeting of the directors of the Alpha Co Ltd, a privately owned company, in May 19X5 the recurrent question is raised as to how the company is going to finance its future growth and at the same time enable the founders of the company to withdraw a substantial part of their investment. A public quotation was discussed in 19X4 but because of the depressed nature of the stock market at that time consideration was deferred. Although the matter is not of immediate urgency the chairman of the company, one of the founders, produces the following information which he has recently obtained from a firm of financial analysts in respect of two publicly quoted companies Beta Ltd and Gamma Ltd which are similar to Alpha Ltd in respect of size, asset composition, financial structure and product mix:

		Beta Ltd	Gamma Ltd
19X4	Earnings per share	£1.50	£2.50
19X0–4	Average earnings per share	£1.00	£2.00
19X4	Average market price per share	£9.00	£20.00
19X4	Dividends per share	£0.75	£1.25
19X0–4	Average dividends per share	£0.60	£1.20
19X4	Average book value per share	£9.00	£18.00

On the basis of this information the chairman asks what you think Alpha Ltd was worth in 19X4. The only information you have available at the meeting in respect of Alpha Ltd is the final accounts for 19X4 which disclose the following:

	Alpha Ltd
Share capital (no variation for 8 years)	100 000 ordinary £1 shares
Post-tax earnings	£400 000
Gross dividends	£100 000
Book value	£3 500 000

From memory you think that the post-tax earnings and gross dividends for 19X4 were at least one-third higher than the average of the previous five years.

Making **full** use of the information above: answer the managing director's question.

Suggested solution

There are three sets of ratios that can be used to give guidance on the appropriate price to ask for the Alpha shares. One is EPS, the second is dividends per share and the third is the asset value per share. We begin with earnings. The EPS of Alpha in 19X4 was £4.00 (i.e. £400 000/100 000). The post-tax earnings in 19X4 were one-third higher than the average of the previous five years. Therefore the average net EPS over the previous five years was £3.00.

The price-to-earnings ratio in 19X4 was 6:1 (i.e. £9:£1.50) for Beta and 8:1 (i.e. £20:£2.50) for Gamma. If one takes the mid-point of these two price-to-earnings ratios, i.e. 7:1, then such a multiple applied to the EPS of £4.00 for Alpha in 19X4 would give a market price of £28. The EPS of Alpha has increased over the last few years, as has been the case for the other two companies.

The gross dividend per share of Alpha in 19X4, was £1 (i.e. £100 000/100 000) and the average for the previous five years was £0.75 (i.e. £75 000/100 000). The dividend yield of Beta in 19X4 was 8.3% (i.e. (£0.75/£9.00) × 100) and the dividend yield of Gamma was 6.3% (i.e. (£1.25/£20.00) × 100). Taking a figure in the middle of these two as one acceptable to the market gives a suggested price for Alpha shares of approximately £13.70, i.e.

$$\frac{£1}{\text{share price}} \times 100 = 7.3\%$$

This is a much lower value than that obtained based on the price-to-earnings ratio. One reason is that Alpha has appeared to pursue a low-payout policy. In 19X4 they only distributed a quarter of their post-tax earnings to shareholders, whereas both Gamma and Beta distributed half of their available earnings to shareholders. If Alpha announced when going public that they planned to increase their payout ratio it may reduce the fears on dividends of certain investors. Of course, not all investors are interested in high dividends; those investors who have high marginal tax rates may prefer the company to retain the profits and, as a result, for the share price to appreciate. Such shareholders, upon selling their shares, would only be taxed on the increase in their wealth at the capital gains tax rate. Many institutional shareholders like dividends as they have tax advantages, and so it would be as well for Alpha to make some announcement about future dividends if it wished to appeal to the institutional shareholder.

The final set of comparative figures relates to the book values per share. These are £35 for Alpha, £9 for Beta and £18 for Gamma. The ratio of the share price to the book value is 1.00 for Beta and 1.10 for Gamma. The same multiple for Alpha would give a price of approximately £35. This measure is, however, the least important and the least reliable of the three being considered.

On balance it seems that a price in the region of £28 per share would seem the most appropriate, i.e. with the information given in the question. Price-to-earnings ratios move about over time and the issue has to be priced to have appeal at the time of issue. In the stock market conditions of 19X5 and 19X6 a different price-to-earnings multiple might be appropriate.

The pricing of new issues is undoubtedly difficult, and is made no easier by the fact that companies naturally want the best of all worlds: the highest possible price, but one that they can maintain in the market. Issuing houses are supposed to be experts at fixing the appropriate price, and one would expect the price fixed for an issue to be close to the equilibrium price, i.e. the level about which the market price will eventually fluctuate. Sometimes, however, they make mistakes. An example was the sale by the UK Government of £100 million of shares in Cable and Wireless. This was an offer for sale by tender, with a minimum price set at £2.75. It was expected that the issue would be oversubscribed, with the resulting striking price (the price at which the shares are sold) well above the minimum price. In fact the issue was undersubscribed; the striking price was the minimum price, and nearly 30% of the issue was left with underwriters.

When a company issues shares which are underpriced they are in fact adding to the cost of the issue. If they offer shares at £2.00 and they are oversubscribed, the market price could well settle at say £2.50. This £0.50 difference does not benefit the company; it benefits those who were lucky enough to be allocated shares at a price that turns out to be below the price at which the market settles. This is an opportunity loss to the company; they could have received the extra £0.50 if the issue had been correctly priced.

The adjustment and eventual stabilization of the market price can create a gap between the price at which the shares were offered to the public and the market equilibrium price. This gap is called the market discount. In calculating the discount the market price has to be adjusted to allow for any changes in the general market level, i.e. to ensure that the measured gap is the result only of factors concerned with the particular share being considered. The difference can be expressed as a percentage of the net size of the issue, defined as the total capital raised less administrative costs. As mentioned, this market discount is part of the cost of the new issue.

Underpricing of new issues

There is a theory and much empirical evidence that indicates that initial public offerings are underpriced. The theory is referred to as the 'Winners' Curse' [18].

The theory is based on the well-accepted assumption that there are two groups of investors, the informed and the uninformed. The former group have information about the companies who are making their first public offering that is not available to the latter group. This informed group only subscribe to an 'initial public offering' when they expect the market price after the issue to exceed the offer price.

In contrast, the uninformed investor initially subscribes to all initial public offers. This means that if the actual offer price is above its intrinsic value only the uninformed investors will subscribe. They will finish up holding all the shares. This is referred to as the 'Winners' Curse'. Over time the uninformed investors when they subscribe to new issues will learn what is happening to them and adjust their investment policies. If companies continue to overprice the new issues, the uninformed investor will have learned to stay out of the new issues market. The new issues therefore become undersubscribed. Over time new issuers and those that advise them learn that to overprice does not benefit them.

In contrast, if the new issue is underpriced, both groups of investors subscribe. Therefore the issue is fully subscribed or over-subscribed. This is one explanation of why most initial public offerings are underpriced.

The model makes a number of assumptions. If an issue is underpriced it is the company or rather the existing shareholders of the company who lose. An important question is whether or not the winners' curse model which is applicable to the new issues market in general should worry an individual company? Why should an individual company underprice its initial public offering and therefore lose funds it could have raised, just for the benefit of the new issues market in general? One answer to this question is that it is investment bankers that advise companies on the price of new issues and it is in the bankers' interests to consider the new issues market in general. Each investment banker will be involved with many new issues. It will be in the bankers' interest therefore to advise on an initial offer price for a particular company which is below the intrinsic value of that share. This underpricing is in the interest of an active new issues market in general, even though not in the interests of individual companies.

There is much evidence that initial public offerings are underpriced. The above theory offers an explanation as to why this underpricing occurs. Not all writers on the subject of finance accept the theory.

The above analysis has been concerned with valuing a single share. When an investor is buying a single share he or she is buying a stream of future dividends. As a minority shareholder the investor has no influence over the dividend decision. When an investor or another company buys all or, in fact, anything over 50% of the total shares of a company, again it is a stream of future cash flows that is being purchased. However,

15.9 The valuation of a company

this time the investor is in a position to influence the level of these future cash flows. The theory of valuation is the same, namely the present value of future cash flows, but in the latter case the investor may be willing to pay more for each share purchased because with the purchase comes control.

The valuation of a company can be described as 'sophisticated guesswork': it is inevitably an inexact exercise. It is based largely on estimates. There are a number of recognized techniques for arriving at a valuation, all of which can lead to different answers. The final price agreed for the purchase is of course the result of negotiation and bargaining; all the techniques can do is provide a framework for discussion. The techniques supply the upper and lower valuations within which the price will eventually be fixed.

An essential preliminary to any purchase or merger negotiation is the valuation of the company to be acquired. This valuation can be based on cash flow, earnings or assets, or on some combination of the three. It is obviously desirable to value the intended purchase by a number of different methods to obtain a range of possible values which will be important in the negotiations. There are a number of standard approaches to the valuation problem, some of which will be explained here.

The value which a company may initially attach to another company is not always the final price at which the purchase is made. If the directors of the company to be purchased resist the initial offer, they can usually obtain better terms for shareholders. In a takeover situation, once a bid is made the directors of the bidding company often seem to feel committed to continue with the attempted purchase by submitting higher bids. To some extent their prestige is felt to suffer if they are successfully fought off by the intended victim company. This can mean that they pay a higher price for the company than can be justified on economic grounds.

It must not be thought that valuation problems only arise at the time that a business is to be purchased. It may be that a private company needs to be valued for tax purposes. It should also be appreciated that, although valuation disagreements do arise in connection with mergers and takeovers, particularly the well-publicized contested mergers and takeovers, not all acquisitions involve major valuation problems. It is possible to purchase a private company or a small public company simply as a result of amicable negotiations. The one company approaches the other company with the object of a straight purchase. This is very common where private companies wish to sell their businesses. They can either approach a buyer or wait to be approached. There are merger brokers in existence that try to bring together companies that wish to buy with those that wish to be sold. Banks, investment banks and merchant banks also provide meeting places for potential buyers and sellers. If two companies come together this way, then it can simply be a matter of the two managements meeting and negotiating a satisfactory price.

The buying company needs to examine the accounts of the selling company to ensure that they are prepared on an understood and acceptable basis. The real meaning of the disclosed profit figure needs to be determined. Very often the accounting practices of the buying and selling companies can differ, and the buyer needs to standardize the accounts of the seller in order to determine the impact of the acquisition on its own financial performance. The buyer would also need to know the present and future tax liabilities of the seller. If it is a private company that is being sold, there is no need to appeal to large numbers of shareholders. It is often the case that once the major shareholder of the business is satisfied, this will ensure that the purchase goes through. The seller usually has a minimum price in mind when deciding to seek a buyer and it is then a matter of the acquiring company trying to buy as near that minimum price as possible. An important factor in the decision might well be the attitude of the acquirer to the management of the selling company. It could well be that some managers of the company to be sold wish to continue in post and some buyers might be willing to allow this to happen whereas others may not be prepared to offer any sort of guarantee. Service contracts and the like can clearly be important factors influencing the recommendation to be made on whether the purchase should go through. It is only if the major shareholders of the company are not happy with the price that is being offered and are therefore reluctant to sell that a takeover situation may arise. An analysis of the distribution of shareholdings in the company it is hoped to purchase can quickly give the intended buyer guidance as to whether there is any point in continuing to negotiate or in making a bid. If the majority shareholders are not satisfied with the terms, there may be little point in continuing with the case.

Present value of future receipts

Theoretically the valuation procedure is straightforward. The purchasing company is buying a stream of future returns. The purchaser is buying the difference between its own cash flow before the acquisition and the combined companies' cash flow after the acquisition. The difference needs to be estimated, discounted and summed up to give its PV. The PV of the receipts from the purchase which can be expressed mathematically as

$$PVR = \frac{C}{i}\left[1 - \frac{1}{(1+i)^n}\right]$$

where PVR is the PV of returns, C is the increase in the annual cash flow of the purchasing company as a result of the acquisition, i is the discount factor and n is the number of years.

As an example, assume that the result of purchasing a company will be to increase the annual cash flow by £1000, the appropriate discount rate is 10% and the number of years over which the returns will be taken into account is 50. The value of the acquisition is therefore

$$\frac{1000}{0.10}\left[1 - \frac{1}{(1.10)^{50}}\right] = £9915$$

The purchasing company should be willing to pay up to £9915 for this acquisition, but given the forecasts no higher price can be justified.

The approach can be made more realistic by allowing for an annual growth in the cash flow. As a second example, assume that the initial increase in cash flow is £1000 and that this is expected to increase by 4% per annum; the value then is £15 658. The formula that should be used in this situation where the cash flow is growing at a compound rate of g% per annum is

$$PVR = \frac{Can}{(1+g)i_0}$$

where

$$i_0 = \frac{i-g}{1+g}$$

and the notation an/i_0 represents the PV of an annuity of £1 per year, discounted at a rate i_0. Table 3 at the end of this book gives the PV of annuities.

As a third example, assume that detailed forecasts of cash flows are made for the five years following acquisition, but for the years after that it is assumed that they will grow at a similar rate to that of the rest of industry. The cash flows for the next five years are estimated as £1000, £1200, £1500, £1900 and £2600; they will then grow at 4% per annum. Again, the horizon is taken as 50 years and cash flows beyond that point are ignored. The value of the company to be purchased is therefore

$$\frac{1000}{(1.10)} + \frac{1200}{(1.10)^2} + \frac{1500}{(1.10)^3} + \frac{1900}{(1.10)^4} + \frac{2600}{(1.10)^5} + \frac{2600(1.04)}{(1.10)^6} + \cdots$$

$$+ \frac{2600(1.04)^{45}}{(1.10)^{50}} = £21\ 250$$

The difficulties in the practical application of the approach are as follows:

1. forecasting future annual cash flows;
2. the number of years' cash flows on which the calculation will be based;
3. the appropriate discount rate.

It is not necessary to provide a detailed forecast for many years into the future; either the terminal value can be estimated for some future date, or the cash flows beyond a certain date can be assumed to grow at a constant rate. However, five year forecasts should not be beyond any company. The budgeting and planning processes of companies are often expressed, at least in part, over five year periods. If a company is not thinking of its position in the future, one might well question its ability to manage the combined operation.

On occasion, even though the purchase has been made, the acquiring company still has to incur additional outgoing: loans, for instance, may have to be provided for the new subsidiary. The estimated cash flows from the purchase may be dependent on this additional outlay, which must obviously be taken into account when the benefits of the possible acquisition are assessed. The cash flows have to justify the purchase price plus any additional investment that may be required. Unfortunately the purchasing firm does not always know of this need for further finance in advance of actual acquisition.

An interesting question arises in connection with the future returns. Undoubtedly past earnings will give some indication of the future earnings, but allowance must be made for the fact that the new management may wish to use the assets in a different way, even perhaps for a different purpose. It is the maximum additional cash flow that will result from the use of the new assets that should be used in determining the value. When gains from an acquisition are calculated they are usually taken to be the difference between the present, namely the actual, returns and the possible future returns after the acquisition; it needs to be emphasized, however, that the base should not be present actual returns but the optimum returns that could be achieved in the present situation. The gains from the acquisition should be thought of as the increment above that which could be achieved in the status quo, assuming that the company has not reached its optimum position.

Other problems

The discount rate that should be used in the calculation is based on the cost of capital of the purchasing company. The object is to purchase the company as cheaply as possible. The alternative forms of security that can be offered have different costs to different companies at different points of time. The company will wish to choose the method that has the lowest cost and yet will be sufficiently attractive to induce the shareholders of the victim company to sell.

One way in which the cost of capital to the acquiring company can be estimated is to take the opportunity cost of the securities being exchanged. If a company is purchased by a share-for-share exchange, the opportunity cost of these shares is the price at which they could have been sold in the stock market. The price paid is therefore the number of shares given up times the price at which they could have been sold in the market. The same type of calculation can be made to determine the value of any debentures or convertible debentures issued in exchange for a company.

An alternative approach to calculating the cost would be to determine the performance in terms of earnings, dividends or interest that has to be achieved over time to keep the holders of these new securities satisfied. This is similar to calculating the cost to a company of the different types of securities. These costs are in terms of shareholders' expectations. With an acquisition, the effect of the new issue of securities on the existing capital structure of the purchasing company would need to be considered.

With a perfect capital market, the cost of the acquisition as calculated under the first method (the price at which the securities could be sold on the market) would be equal to the cost calculated under the second method (the performance the company must achieve to satisfy the holders of the security).

This does not necessarily mean that the cost of capital should be based on the particular source of capital that is being used to pay for the acquisition. It is the average cost of the next round of capital that is raised by the purchasing company that is relevant, and the particular securities issued in payment may be only one part of this. For example, debt capital may be issued in payment for the acquisition, but this does not mean that the appropriate cost to be covered is that of debt. The debt could only be issued because of the security provided by the equity base. The next time that capital is required it will probably have to be from a source which is more expensive than debt. The discount rate to be used is therefore the average cost of the next package of capital, which could consist of retained earnings, new equity, a rights issue and debt.

Risk

Risk is an important factor to be taken into account when valuing a company. This does not mean the uncertainty surrounding the expected profits of the company to be acquired. Rather, it means the effect of the cash flow of the purchased company on the cash flow of the acquiring company. A motive for many acquisitions is the wish to reduce the risk of the acquiring company. One way in which this can work is simply that the larger a company, the safer it is. Large companies are less likely to be the victims of takeovers and they are more likely to have the financial resources to see them through difficult economic conditions. Buying up other companies clearly makes one larger and therefore, on the face of it, it makes one safer – it reduces risk. That is not to say that buying up bad companies, i.e. companies in difficulty or with little future, will reduce risks; rather it will add to them because of the impact on profits. But buying up reasonable companies can help to reduce the risks associated with company size.

A more thoughtful analysis of the impact of the cash flow of the acquired company on the cash flow of the purchasing company is desirable than that above. Clearly one motive for an acquisition is diversification. If two companies are seasonal, and one has its peak profit periods in the winter and the other in the summer, by coming together they will overcome certain peak season problems, for example those associated with finance. If one company relies on wet weather for good sales and another on sunny weather, by coming together they would be better able to withstand a run of years with either good or bad weather. A company that makes lawnmowers is safer if it is in a group where its dependence on the weather for a few months of the year is not so critical to the shareholders.

Acquisitions can clearly reduce risk. This means that the shareholders of the acquiring company have their risks reduced. So do the providers of loan capital.

The CAPM has already been discussed at various points in the book and will not now be covered again. The point that is being made is that when valuing a company the effect of the acquisition on the risks of the acquirer needs to be taken into account. The effect can be quantified. A reduction in risk means that the cost of capital is reduced. Investors and bankers may be willing to provide funds at a lower cost after the acquisition than before. The way in which this can be allowed for in calculating the value of the company to be purchased is, with the PV approach, to discount the future cash flow at a lower cost of capital than that being used by the acquiring company before the attempted acquisition. With the price-to-earnings approach the way in which it would be allowed for would be to use a higher multiple to allow for the fact that the market will reassess the company after the acquisition.

Myers [19] has pointed out that perhaps a different discount rate should be used for the different elements of the cash flow resulting from an acquisition. More is known about existing operations than about anticipated growth opportunities. The risks of the cash flows associated with the latter type of development is greater and so should be discounted with higher rates. A number of writers have criticized the idea that mergers are advantageous to shareholders simply because they reduce the probability of bankruptcy. It is pointed out that this ignores the disadvantageous effect for shareholders of the removal of the limited liability of the separate firms. When there are two firms, one can go bankrupt and the other can continue. When they combine, the one can possibly bring the other down.

The point being made is that it is not obvious, nor should it be taken for granted, that, because mergers reduce the probability of bankruptcy, they are advantageous. They could lead to a much more serious business collapse than if just one of the firms goes under.

Values based on share prices

It has been found in practice that not all firms actually use the discounted cash flow (DCF) approach when it comes to valuing a company for takeover or merger purposes. This could be because the acquisition decision is a particularly complicated form of investment decision or because the PV techniques themselves have inherent weaknesses. An alternative explanation is that the use of EPS calculations and price-to-earnings ratios for determining the value of a particular acquisition or merger fits in well with the fact that the financing decision is an integral part of the merger or acquisition proposal. For an acquisition which is to be paid for by cash, the DCF technique is appropriate, but, the argument goes, for a decision which is to be paid for by a combination of debt and equity capital, the effect on the earnings per share is revealing and important.

If a company to be taken over has an existing market value, i.e. it is a quoted company, then the acquirer will have to pay a price somewhere in the region of this market figure. If only a few changes in the future policy of the acquired company are to be expected, then shareholders and investors would have little reason to expect a much higher valuation than that based on the existing price. If, however, substantial changes are expected to occur in the cash flow or in the financial policies of the acquired company, or if synergy will affect the cash flow, then a considerable premium may well have to be paid above the existing market price.

There are a number of reasons why the market may wish to increase its valuation of the company to be acquired above the level existing before the suitor appeared on the scene. These reasons include economies of scale, monopoly strength, changes in investment policies, better management, sale of surplus assets, lower taxes and better information. Equally important is the fact that the merger may reduce the systematic risk of the cash flows of the two companies. There may also be changes in financial policies such as borrowing or dividend policies.

The valuation exercise from the acquiring company's point of view is to estimate the maximum purchase price that they would be willing to pay in order to obtain the company. This is the price that they would pay which would leave their shareholders no worse off after the acquisition than they were before.

Franks *et al.* [20] make the important point that if we assume efficient capital markets, then the payment of a premium above the market price in order to purchase a company can be justified only if the acquirer is going to change the growth expectations of the acquired company or alter the risk profile of the combined operations. However, it is possible that the market is not perfect and the purchasing company's management has information that leads it to believe that the existing share price of the company to be acquired is too low. One is saying in this case that the market is not perfect – that one person has better information than another or interprets the known information in a different way to another. Therefore the justification for paying above market value is either the ability of the bidder to increase growth rates, or the ability of the bidder to lower the discount rate by reducing the risk or the fact that the company to be acquired is undervalued.

There is a further point to consider, namely that at certain times the bidding company's shares may be overvalued. If this is appreciated by the directors of the bidding company, it can use this high market price to purchase companies cheaply. The bidder would, of course, need to use shares to pay for the acquisition. It would be justified from the point of view of the acquiring company's shareholders if the bidder had reason to believe that the company's share price would drop in the future and so would be taking advantage of a short-term distortion in market prices.

Of course, many companies do not have their shares traded on an exchange, and so in valuing such companies there is not the starting point of a market price. In valuing such a company, the price-to-earnings ratio for similar companies that are traded on a market can be used as a base. The fact that the shares of unlisted companies lack marketability will normally mean that a slightly lower price-to-earnings ratio should be applied than that for listed companies. This lower price-to-earnings ratio would be multiplied by the EPS of the company being valued in order to arrive at a price.

The discount to be applied in reducing either the price-to-earnings ratio or, alternatively, the premium to be applied in increasing the required earnings yield would depend on any restraints placed on the transfer to shares and the number of shares being purchased. The acquisition of a small minority holding would mean a larger discount. The acquisition of 100% of the shares would mean that no discount was necessary.

Valuation by capitalizing earnings

One of the simplest methods of assessing the value of a company is to use some predetermined notion of the rate of return that an investor would expect on this particular type of investment, and then, having decided on the earnings of the company, to calculate the capital sum that would result in such a rate of return. The steps used in this approach are as follows.

1. Select a past period for investigation.
2. Estimate the maintainable profits of the company to be acquired, after making any necessary adjustments for such factors as existing levels of directors' remuneration, depreciation or bad debts. It is important to allow for any increased profit potential which may develop with improved management or the possible synergy from the combined operations.
3. Establish the acceptable normal rate of return on capital invested in a similar type of company, allowing for the industry effect, the size of company and the level of capital gearing.
4. Capitalize maintainable profits at a rate established as the acceptable rate of return. If, for example, £10 000 is the maintainable earnings after corporation tax and the normal rate of return in such companies is 8%, then a purchase price of £125 000 would be justified because £10 000/0.08 = £125 000.

The problem with this type of approach is that the estimate of earnings is usually based on historical earnings. Whether this is a straight average of the past five years' earnings or some weighted average attaching greater importance to earnings in more recent years, it is still based on past performance.

Although the estimates are based on established figures, which is important in negotiation, the extent to which the past can assist in determining maintainable future profits is still a debated point.

Price-to-earnings ratio

The capitalized earnings approach is sometimes expressed in a slightly different way. To capitalize earnings at 8% is in fact to multiply the earnings by 12.5. The popular stock market ratio of price to earnings does exactly this – multiplies earnings by some factor. Capitalizing earnings at 8% is exactly the same as adopting a price-to-earnings ratio for the purchase of a company of 12.5.

The price-to-earnings ratio is normally thought of as the multiple of the earnings that an investor would pay for a small number of shares in a company. If the total shares of a company are being purchased, the market price-to-earnings ratio may have to be adjusted. A new management now has control of the assets, and so the earnings and growth potential could well change. Nevertheless, it is not uncommon to hear managers talking in terms of being willing to purchase a company for ten to twelve times its earnings. This is identical with looking for an initial earnings yield of 10%–8.33%.

Asset value

As an alternative to the earnings approach, it could be argued that the purchaser is acquiring a set of assets. It is not the future earnings that the purchasing company is buying, but a collection of assets which have to be managed to achieve the earnings. If the existing managers were to leave the acquired company, there is no guarantee that the previous earnings level could be maintained. The purchaser cannot 'buy' the managers as there is no guarantee that they will not leave after the merger. The earnings basis of valuation, it can be argued, is based on the assumption that the old managers will stay on, or that any new managers put in to run the business will be able to maintain the profit level. If this assumption is not completely justified, then the asset value of the company should at least be considered.

This once again emphasizes the importance of management in an acquisition. It also indicates how vital to the earnings basis of valuation can be the assumption of an unchanged management team. Of course, the management is interchangeable between some companies in which case these considerations are less significant, but it cannot always be taken for granted that past profit levels will be maintained.

Normally it must remain true that if the purchased company is to continue with its existing type of business, the earnings basis would seem more relevant for valuation than the assets basis. If, however, the whole of the purchased company is to be sold, or parts of the purchased company are to be sold, then the realizable value of the assets is important. Earlier it was stated that the existing price of the company's shares should provide a minimum level for valuation purposes. However, it is possible that the price of a share of the company is lower than the net asset value per share. In this case the asset value per share could set the lowest valuation level.

A company is in a bad way if the share price is below the net asset value per share. If the net assets per share, based on balance sheet values, are close to the values that could be realized on the liquidation of the assets, the directors, in the best interests of the shareholders, should liquidate the company and sell off the assets. One of the constraints imposed on management is to ensure that their share price is above the asset value per share. This is the q ratio referred to in the chapter on mergers and acquisitions.

Realizable values

The value of the assets as they appear in a balance sheet are not necessarily their liquidation value or realizable value; this would have to be determined by a separate assessment of each asset. The saleable value of property, for example, may be higher with vacant possession than when the property is occupied; once free for some other use, its value might well have increased above that assigned to it on the balance sheet.

Assets are not necessarily shown in balance sheets at their current market values. In fact they very rarely are. They are shown at a mixture of values, with some at the original cost of purchase and others revalued but possibly at different dates. In the UK the reality is that we have a system of selective revaluation, with the assets to be revalued and the dates when this will take place being at the discretion of the directors of the company. Information about significant differences between the values shown in the balance sheet and current market values should be shown in the notes to the financial accounts.

A company should be consistent. This means it should treat all assets within a certain class in a similar way. All assets within a class should be either at historical cost or be revalued at a similar date. Assets which should be revalued at regular intervals include the following classification:

- property (excluding fixed assets specific to the business);
- quoted investments;
- inventory of a commodity nature.

When assets are revalued they should be valued by a qualified valuer.

Unfortunately with the vast majority of companies it is not possible to rely on the asset values shown in the balance sheet to obtain a current value of the business. The net assets and the capital employed figures of a company are often quoted and are used in numerous financial ratios, but because of the mixture of valuation methods employed the resulting figures can be suspect.

This, then, is an alternative method of valuing a company: the determination of the value to the purchaser of all the assets. If a price has to be paid for the company above the value of the sum of assets, then an amount has been paid for goodwill. This is where the selling company receives a reward for any above average performance, for the above average ability of its managers or for its advantageous market position. Only if a company is to be purchased and its assets liquidated would this asset valuation be the sole criterion for determining valuation. Normally a potential purchaser would consider both the earnings possibilities and the underlying asset values.

Berliner method

The Berliner method is a technique for valuing a company which takes into account both the earnings and the assets of the company to be purchased. The steps involved are as follows.

1. Select a past period for investigation.
2. Estimate the maintainable profits.
3. Determine the acceptable rate of return to an investor on a similar investment.
4. Capitalize the maintainable profits at the rate established in 3. It will be noticed that the procedure so far is exactly similar to that used under a capitalization of earnings.
5. Value the net tangible assets on a going concern basis.
6. Take the average of the value established at 4 and the value at 5 – the mean of the earnings valuation and the asset valuation.

Clearly, this approach attempts to combine both bases of valuation; not surprisingly, all the difficulties that apply to the two methods separately apply in conjunction here. The averaging of the two methods is not inspired by any particular theory; it is simply a compromise which may provide a practical solution if the bargaining parties cannot agree on the basis of valuation.

Dual capitalization of profits

Dual capitalization of profits is a compromise approach similar to the Berliner technique. The steps are as follows.

1. Select a past period for investigation.
2. Estimate maintainable profits.
3. Determine the acceptable yield for an investor on capital invested in
   (a) tangible assets, in a similar risk class,
   (b) intangible assets.

This third step recognizes that there are two types of asset: those which have greater security because they have an inherent and recognizable value, and those, such as goodwill and brands, that are less tangible, not marketable and so risky by their very nature.

4. Value tangible assets.
5. Calculate the amount of the profits in 2 that are attributable to tangible assets. To do this simply calculate the amount that will give the acceptable return at the rate in 3(a) on the value of tangible assets in 4.
6. Deduct the profits attributable to tangible assets from the estimate of maintainable profits to arrive at profits applicable to intangible assets.

7. Capitalize the profits applicable to intangible assets at the appropriate rate 3(b).
8. Add the value in 7 to the value in 4 to arrive at the total value of the business, i.e. the capitalized value of the profits on the intangible assets plus the value of the tangible assets.

As an example, assume that the estimate of maintainable profits for a business is £1100 per year. The expected yield on tangible assets is 10% and that on intangible assets is 15%. The value of tangible assets is £8000. Then the calculations from step 5 are as follows:

5. Tangible assets of £8000 with an expected rate of return of 10% means that £800 of the profits are attributable to the tangible assets.
6. £1100 − £800 = £300: profits attributable to intangible assets.
7. £300/0.15 = £2000: the value of the intangible assets.
8. £8000 + £2000 = £10 000: the value of the business.

This technique, despite its apparent sophistication, gives a valuation which is no better and no worse than (with the exception of the discounted PV) that produced by other techniques. While it is possible to distinguish between tangible and intangible assets, it is not easy to identify the rates of return that would be required on the two separate types.

Super-profit approach

The final method to be described is similar to the last, but is more widely known and used. The idea behind it is that there is a normal rate of return that can be earned on assets of a certain type, but over a certain number of years it may be possible to earn profits in excess of this normal level. The purchaser will buy in addition to the normalized value of the assets a number of years' super-profits.

The procedure is as follows.

1. Value the net assets of the business on a going concern basis.
2. Establish an acceptable rate of return on assets of this type.
3. Find the annual profits that would be assumed to result from the use of the assets so as to earn the rate established in 2.
4. Estimate the profits that can be expected to be earned by the business over the next few years.
5. Deduct the acceptable profit figure in 3 from the estimated profits in 4. If the estimate is higher the difference can be regarded as super-profit.
6. Multiply the super-profits by a factor to be agreed – say 3 or 5 to represent the number of years' super-profits being purchased.
7. The value of the business is 1 plus 6, i.e. the value of the net assets plus, say, five years' purchase of super-profits.

As an example, assume that the net assets of the business are valued at £8000 and the normal rate of return on such an investment is 10%. From step 3 the procedure would be as follows.

3. A 10% return on £8000 results in profits of £800.
4. The profits are estimated as being £1100 for the next few years.
5. The difference between the estimate and the acceptable level is £300.
6. It is agreed to purchase five years' super-profits.
7. The value of the company is £9500 comprising net assets valued at £8000 plus £1500 super-profits (5 × £300).

The value of the super-profits, ultimately the difference between the purchase price and the value of the assets acquired, would be entered in the accounts as goodwill.

The number of years' super-profits to be purchased would, of course, depend on negotiation and the number of years that the purchaser thought the company could maintain the advantageous position. This acknowledges the fact that the above average level of performance cannot be continued indefinitely – an important point which the earlier simple capitalization of earnings techniques did not explicitly take into account. This is another simple mechanical process that can be employed once the difficult task of estimating profits and deciding on a capitalization rate has been settled. Clearly, the technique would not be greatly complicated if super-profits were also discounted.

Tax consequences

In addition to the asset values and earnings power, which supply the basis for the standard valuation techniques, there are certain other factors to be considered which can increase or reduce the value arrived at by the use of a formula. One such factor is the taxation position of the company to be purchased. It can be worth while purchasing a company that has been operating at a loss. The accumulated losses can be offset against the future profits to reduce tax commitments. As a simple example, assume that a company has accumulated tax losses of £50 000. Under certain circumstances it would be worth paying up to £16 500 for this company, if the effective corporation tax rate is 33%. This £50 000 can be offset against future taxable profits and the effect will be to reduce the liability of the purchaser for tax by approximately £16 500. The purchased company may also have capital allowances that can be carried forward and used.

However, the losses and capital allowances carried over can only be used by the purchaser against future profits earned from the transferred business. They cannot be used to reduce tax payable on the profits earned in the main business in which the purchasing company is engaged: the business in which it is engaged before and after the acquisition. Where the purchased business is absorbed into the existing business of the successor company, it may be necessary to apportion the total profits, to ascertain the profits against which the losses can be offset. The transfer is not automatic, however; there are certain conditions that have to be satisfied in order that the unused trading losses and capital allowances can be transferred.

The transferor (purchased company) has to cease to carry on the trade. The successor (purchasing company) has to begin to carry on that trade. The company must carry on with the trade of the purchased company; it cannot sell the assets and use the resources for some other purpose. Losses cannot be regularly traded. The company that is being purchased must belong at the time of the purchase to principally the same group of shareholders who owned the company one year earlier. A further condition is that the purchasing company must itself have a tax charge either one year before the transfer or within two years after.

The situation described is where it is desired to set off losses on the transfer of a business – setting off past losses incurred under one ownership against the future profits earned with a new ownership. The rules are different when dealing with current losses incurred by companies already part of a group. Generally it is possible to set off the trading losses of one company against the profits of another company if they are members of the same group or consortium and the results relate to the same period.

Debt position of company to be purchased

The debt position can work in two ways, either adding to the earnings valuation of the purchase or reducing its value.

The liabilities of the company will have to be taken over, and as these will have to be met either immediately or at the time specified for redemption in the future, allowance must be made for this repayment. The liability is the present value of the future interest or dividend payments plus the present value of the future capital repayment. Assume that the purchasing company will have to pay 8% interest on £10 000 of outstanding debentures, which will have to be redeemed in five years' time; with a cost of capital of 10% the liability has a PV of £9242. The interest payments have a PV of £3033 and the capital repayment has a PV of £6209.

The benefit of preference shares can vary. If such shares are redeemable at some date in the future, the liability will be calculated in a similar way to that of debentures. If, however, they are irredeemable, the liability will be equal to the PV of the future dividend of the preference shares.

The offer for the purchase of the company can include an offer for the preference shares. Such a purchase offering loan stock for preference shares is desirable at certain times because the interest on loan stock (unlike the dividend on preference shares) is a tax-deductible expense, and so the exchange of loan stock for preference shares lowers the cost of capital for the company.

The existing debt position of the company to be acquired may add to its purchase value if it is at present undergeared. The acquisition of new assets, paid for by the issue of new shares, will alter the capital gearing of the purchasing company. If the newly acquired assets have not already been used to raise loans, the purchasing company can use them as security for a loan. This will enable the purchasing company to obtain cheaper funds than would have been possible without the purchase. The extent of the opportunity for gearing made available by the new acquisition will depend on the method of payment, the existing borrowing of the purchased company and the financial position of the acquired company.

Suppose, for example, that company X is purchased for £1 million. This is the value of its assets. Its debt capital, which has been purchased, is £100 000. It is thought possible to raise debt capital to the extent of 30% of the value of the assets, and the necessary cover on the extra interest payments will be available. Then an additional £200 000 of borrowing potential is made available by the purchase. The interest charge on such debt is assumed to be 5% net of tax, and it would have to be repaid within 20 years. To the purchaser the net outflow of funds is interest of £10 000 for 20 years and then the repayment of £200 000 in 20 years' time, which with a discount rate of 10% has a total PV of £114 700. The PV of the inflow of funds is £200 000 from raising the debenture. Therefore the purchasing company has made a gain with a PV of £85 300 which could be added to the value of the potential acquisition. These calculations depend on the opportunity to earn a rate of return of 10% on investments.

Examples

We shall now illustrate the use of certain of the valuation methods by answering three questions that have been set in recent professional accounting examinations. These questions are typical of those that involve valuation problems. The first two questions (Examples 15.9 and 15.10) are from Financial Management Papers of the Chartered Association of Certified Accountants. The third illustration (Example 15.11) is based on an examination question of the Institute of Chartered Accountants in England and Wales.

Example 15.9

You are the financial manager of a medium-sized engineering firm XYZ Ltd which has just reported record profits of £250 000, after tax and interest and preference dividends, and has declared an ordinary dividend of 15%. Despite the record profits, which maintain the previous pattern of overall growth but with cyclical fluctuations, the company has been faced with liquidity problems which have restricted its operational flexibility.

XYZ has received a suggestion from ABC Ltd that the two companies should consider merging. ABC Ltd is a relatively new company – formed six years previously – which has had a spectacular and consistent growth in profit and whose products complement those of XYZ Ltd. The most recent profits of ABC Ltd were £375 000 after tax and interest with an ordinary dividend of 10%. The reason for suggesting the merger given by ABC Ltd is that they have also been having liquidity problems and that an enlarged size could help overcome these. ABC's initial approach did not go into any detail but simply suggests that exploratory talks should be opened and that to make these talks purposeful they should assume that both company's profits will increase by 10% in the next period and that for amalgamation purposes a fair prices-to-earnings ratio would be 15 for ABC and 10 for XYZ.

The executive directors have called a meeting to discuss the matter and have asked you to analyse the implications of ABC's suggestion and to list the factors which should be considered at this stage in respect of this analysis.

The summary of the most recent balance sheets of ABC Ltd and XYZ Ltd are as follows.

Summary balance sheets for year ended . . .

	ABC Ltd	XYZ Ltd
Net assets	£3 000 000	£2 500 000
Share capital		
Ordinary £1 Share	£750 000	£400 000
6% Preference Shares	—	100 000
Reserves	1 500 000	2 000 000
10% loan stock	750 000	—
	£3 000 000	£2 500 000

Suggested solution

First we shall calculate the earnings per share for the two companies based on the most recent profits:

$$ABC \; Ltd \quad EPS = \frac{£375\,000}{750\,000} = £0.50$$

$$XYZ \; Ltd \quad EPS = \frac{£250\,000}{400\,000} = £0.625$$

It is suggested by ABC that fair prices-to-earning ratios would be 15 for ABC and 10 for XYZ. That would result in share prices at present of £7.50 for ABC and £6.25 for XYZ. A valuation for the companies based on share price times the number of shares would give £5 625 000 for ABC and £2 500 000 for XYZ. This is interesting as the value we have reached on an earnings basis for XYZ is almost equal to its adjusted net asset value of £2 400 000, i.e. £2 500 000 less £100 000 preference shares. The adjusted net assets of ABC are £2 250 000, i.e. £3 000 000 less the £750 000 loan stock, and the suggested earnings valuation is exactly 2.5 times that figure.

The proposal from ABC places a value on itself of over twice its apparent asset value and values XYZ at approximately its book value. This difference could possibly be justified if either the growth prospects for earnings of ABC are much better than those of XYZ, or if the assets of ABC are much in excess of their book value.

We are told that ABC has had a spectacular and consistent growth in its profits over the last six years, but bygones are bygones and even ABC is talking about a similar increase in profits next year to that of XYZ, i.e. 10%. The suggested prices-to-earnings ratios of 15 for ABC and 10 for XYZ are presumably based on the difference in past growth performance. But is this difference expected to continue into the future? Unless the directors of XYZ believe that it is the ABC part of the new company that will continue to provide the faster growth in the future, then their own company is being undervalued in relation to ABC. They should enter into negotiations with the directors of ABC to improve the terms of the merger. One point that XYZ can make, in addition to the above, is that they have the lower level of capital gearing and so it is mainly their assets that will be used in future as a base to raise more loan capital.

XYZ need to make a counter-proposal. They should be able to negotiate an improvement in the terms being offered by ABC, which are really only an introductory offer, an initial asking price, which appears to be very favourable to ABC. There are a number of ways of arriving at an alternative valuation. The initial offer by ABC was valuing ABC at £5.6 million and XYZ at £2.5 million, being roughly a 70% to ABC and 30% to XYZ division of the shares of the new company. XYZ might base their counter-proposal on asset values, on the basis of the respective contribution of the companies to the assets of the new business. The assets may need to be revalued, but on the basis of the adjusted net assets shown above the shares of the new company should be divided roughly 50:50 (£2.25 million to £2.40 million). This may not have appeal to ABC because of their superior past growth record, but by way of reply the directors of XYZ could point out that ABC do now have a liquidity problem. It may be that it is not intended to form a new company, in which case it would be possible for one company to take over the other, and the negotiations are then to determine how many shares of the one company are to be issued to acquire the assets of the other company.

Clearly there is a wide gap between the ABC proposal and the suggested counter-proposal of XYZ. There is plenty of room for manoeuvre by both companies. Let us assume that the directors are considering meeting mid way, i.e. a 60:40 split and it is to be arranged by ABC taking over XYZ and issuing shares in exchange for the assets. In fact, on the basis of the most recent figures, the profit contribution by the two companies to the new business is divided 60:40.

We shall analyse the EPS before and after the merger for the two sets of shareholders on the basis of the 60:40 split. There are at present 750 000 shares of ABC, and so to obtain a 60:40 division they would need to issue 500 000 shares to XYZ shareholders. There would then be 1 250 000 shares of ABC and next year's combined profits, allowing for the 10% growth, are expected to be £687 500. That gives an EPS of £0.55, i.e. £687 500/1 250 000, which for the shareholders of ABC is a neutral position, because their present EPS is £0.50 which, with the 10% growth next year, would have given them £0.55.

The shareholders of XYZ would receive 500 000 shares, which is five shares in ABC for every four of their existing shares. Their position next year if XYZ did not merge would be that on four shares (4 × £0.625 × 1.10) they would earn £2.75. With the merger going ahead they would earn on the five shares received in exchange the same amount (5 × £0.55) £2.75. Clearly, the 60:40 division is the neutral position. The companies would need to bargain to see which company, if either, could receive improved terms at the expense of the other. The financial factors that would be taken into account in the negotiations would include a detailed analysis of ABC's past profit performance, the likelihood of the separate companies obtaining the 10% growth in profits, the liquidity position of ABC, what effect the merger will have on future profits and the quality of the assets.

Example 15.10

Alpha Co. Ltd is small private manufacturing company. The directors (who own 90% of the shares) have jointly decided to sell the business as a going concern and have set a price of £200 000 on it. The latest balance sheet of the Alpha Co. Ltd is as shown below and its profits before taxation have always been of the order of £10 000 per annum. Beta Ltd is a quoted company with characteristics similar to Alpha. Currently its 100p ordinary shares are trading at 333p, and the last dividend of 10% was covered 1.5 times.

Summarized balance sheet of Alpha Ltd
Capital

10 000 ordinary shares of £1 each full paid		£10 000
Reserves		£30 000
		£40 000
Current liabilities		
Creditors	£76 000	
Accruals	£6 400	
		£82 400
		£122 400
Fixed assets (net)		£84 000
Current assets		
Stocks	£16 000	
Debtors	20 000	
Prepayments	2 000	
Cash	400	
		38 400
		£122 400

Using the above information and assuming that a corporation tax rate of 50% is applicable to both buyer and seller, assess the reasonableness or otherwise of the value of £200 000 which the directors have put on Alpha.

Suggested solution

There are a number of ways of approaching this problem of valuing the Alpha Co. Ltd. They do not all lead to the same solution and it is not possible to say that one valuation is correct and another wrong. If ten accountants were asked to value the company and they were given no more information about the company than contained in the question, it is possible that we would have ten different answers. It is to be hoped that the answers would not vary greatly and that a figure would emerge which could be the starting point for the purchase negotiations. The question asks whether £200 000 is reasonable figure, and so we shall see where this lies in the range of possible valuations.

First we shall calculate the price-to-earnings ratios. The after-tax earnings of Alpha are £5000. The price being discussed is £200 000. This gives a price-to-earnings ratio of 40:1. This is high even taking into account the fact that levels of price-to-earnings ratios vary from one year to another. This ratio can be compared with that of Beta. The last dividend per share for Beta was £0.10 (10% of 100p). This was covered 1.5 times, which means the earnings per share were £0.15. The ordinary shares are trading at £3.33, which gives a price-to-earnings ratio of 22.2 (3.33/0.15). Even this is high, but it is only in the region of half the ratio being asked for by Alpha.

We shall now consider the asset position of Alpha. The assets less liabilities are £40 000 (£122 400 − £82 400). This means that Alpha is asking for five times its asset value. One balance sheet ratio stands out, namely the current ratio. Current assets equal £38 400 and current liabilities equal £82 400; the difference between the two figures is in the opposite direction to that which is normal. The company is clearly illiquid.

On the basis of both the earnings and the assets the price that Alpha is seeking seems too high. The price could only be justified if there were some facts about the company not revealed in the question, such as assets worth far more than their book value or future earnings possibilities based on new products or new markets, which mean that past earnings are not good indicators of future earnings.

Example 15.11

The board of directors of Oxclose PLC is considering making an offer to purchase Satac Ltd, a private limited company in the same industry. If Satac is purchased it is proposed to continue operating the company as a going concern in the same line of business.

Summarized details from the most recent financial accounts of Oxclose and Satac are shown below:

	Oxclose PLC Balance sheet as at 31 March (£ million)		Satac Ltd Balance sheet as at 31 March (£000)	
Freehold property		33		460
Plant and equipment (net)		58		1310
Stock	29		330	
Debtors	24		290	
Cash	3		20	
Less: Current liabilities	(31)	25	(518)	122
		116		1892
Financed by				
Ordinary shares[a]		35		160
Reserves		43		964
Shareholders' equity		78		1124
Medium-term bank loans		38		768
		116		1892

[a]Oxclose PLC, 50p ordinary shares; Satac Ltd, 25p ordinary shares.

	Oxclose PLC (£ million)		Satac Ltd (£000)	
	Profit after		Profit after	
Year[b]	tax	Dividend	tax	Dividend
t − 5	14.30	9.01	143	85
t − 4	15.56	9.80	162	93.5
t − 3	16.93	10.67	151	93.5
t − 2	18.42	11.60	175	102.8
t − 1	20.04	12.62	183	113.1

[b]t−5 is five years ago, t−1 is the most recent year etc.

Satac's shares are owned by a small number of private individuals. The company is dominated by its managing director who receives an annual salary of £80 000, double the average salary received by managing directors of similar companies. The managing director would be replaced if the company were purchased by Oxclose.

The freehold property of Satac has not been revalued for several years and is believed to have a market value of £800 000.

The balance sheet value of plant and equipment is thought to be a fair reflection of its replacement cost, but its value if sold is not likely to exceed £800 000. Approximately £55 000 of stock is obsolete and could only be sold as scrap for £5000.

The ordinary shares of Oxclose are currently trading at 430p ex dividend. It is estimated that because of difference in size, risk and other factors the required return on equity by shareholders of Satac is approximately 15% higher than the required return on equity of Oxclose's shareholders (i.e. 115% of Oxclose's required return). Both companies are subject to corporate taxation at a rate of 40%.

(a) Prepare estimates of the value of Satac using three different methods of valuation, and advise the board of Oxclose PLC as to the price, or possible range of prices, that it should be prepared to offer to purchase Satac's shares.   (12 marks)

(b) Briefly discuss the theoretical and practical problems of the valuation methods that you have chosen.   (6 marks)

(c) Discuss the advantages and disadvantages of the various terms that might be offered to the shareholders of a potential 'victim' company in a takeover situation.

(7 marks)
(25 marks)
ACCA, Dec. 1986

Suggested solution

There are a number of approaches to the problem of valuing a company that does not have a share price determined in the market place. These include the following:

1. PV of expected future cash flows;
2. dividend valuation model;
3. relevant price to earnings ratio;
4. earnings growth basis/super-profits;
5. value of net assets.

Theoretically the first of these is superior. Unfortunately in this question (and in many such examination questions) we do not have sufficient information to be able to adopt this approach.

First, we shall estimate using the dividend valuation model. To do this we need to estimate the appropriate cost of equity K_e per Satac. We know the share price of Oxclose and so we can establish K_e for that company:

$$K_e = \frac{D_1}{P} + g$$

We need to estimate the expected next dividend. The current is 18.03p per share (£12.62 million divided by 70 million shares). The growth in dividends is approximately 8.8% per annum, which gives a D_1 of 19.62p. Therefore for Oxclose

$$K_e = \frac{19.62}{430} + 0.088 = 0.1336$$

We are told that the K_e for Satac should be 15% higher than that for Oxclose. This gives a K_e of 15.36%. Therefore for Satac the total value of equity is

$$P = \frac{D_1}{K_e - g}$$

$$= \frac{124\,410}{0.1536 - 0.10} = £2\,321\,000$$

This estimate is based on a growth rate in dividends of 10% per annum. This growth was achieved except in the year $t - 3$, which we shall assume was an extraordinary year.

We now use the price-to-earnings ratio approach. We need to multiply the current earnings of Satac by an appropriate price-to-earnings factor. The only information we are given on price-to-earnings ratios is that for Oxclose. This gives a multiple of

$$\frac{430\text{p}}{28.63\text{p}} = 15.02$$

This is higher than we would expect for Satac because Satac is smaller, it is not a quoted company and the past earnings growth of Satac has been less. Let us say that a price-to-earnings ratio of 12.1 is appropriate. Then the price of a Satac share would be given by

$$\frac{P}{28.59p} = 12.00$$

$$P = 343p$$

15.42

This gives a total price of £2 195 200

Net assets basis

	Taking replacement cost (£000)
Plant and equipment	1310
Property	800
Stock	280
Debtors	290
Cash	20
Less: Current liabilities	(518)
Bank loan	(768)
	1414

This assets basis makes no allowance for possible goodwill. As can be seen from the examples above the valuation of a business is far from being an accurate exercise. It depends on many estimates, growth in dividends, appropriate price-to-earnings ratios, future cash flows etc. In the end the price agreed depends on negotiations. The techniques give a base figure from which to negotiate. In this case a price of between £2 200 000 and £2 500 000 would appear reasonable. The asset basis is more appropriate if the acquired company is to be asset stripped.

'A good buy' – past losses or future profits?

On 12 August 1988, the British Government sold the Rover Group to British Aerospace (BAe) for £150 million. It was part of the Government's privatization programme, they were anxious to sell, and agreed to certain conditions that BAe attached to the purchase. These included a delay in the actual payment for 12 months without any interest accruing. The value of this interest saving was estimated to be £22 million. The government also agreed to pay all BAe's acquisition costs, which were estimated at £15 million.

Prior to the sale the government had injected at least £469 million cash into the group to write off all but £100 million of the company's debt. This was done to restructure the balance sheet to make it easier to sell. It injected a further £78 million of regional selective assistance. Tax allowances granted to BAe as part of the deal were worth about £35 million.

There were a number of aspects of the deal which later turned out to be controversial. One was associated with the fact that it was necessary to obtain approval for the deal from the European Commission at the time of the sale. This was to ensure that the sale did not contravene the competition laws of the EU. At the time the Commission approved the sale but limited the amount of financial assistance that the Government could give to assist the purchaser. It was later revealed that the Commission were not told about all aspects of the 'sweeteners' involved. Was the Rover Group's £150 million valuation based on its expected future cash flows or on its past record? When challenged on this point in the House of Commons on 28 November 1989, the Prime Minister said that 'Apart from the year it sold Jaguar, Rover had not made a profit since 1976. . . . The company was only able to carry on at all because of the government guarantee to trade creditors and a government guarantee to the banks. . . . The liability building up on the British taxpayer was enormous. It was a very good thing to be able to privatize Rover under those circumstances.' When the Leader of the Opposition stated that the taxpayers had been 'ripped off' with the sale, the Prime Minister replied 'If there was a rip-off it was the £3000 million of taxpayers' money that had been pumped into British Leyland – Rover since 1975 to keep the company going.' Clearly, therefore, the past record of the company was a major factor in determining the sales price.

What of the expected future cash flows? The corporate plan of the Rover Group before the sale forecast profits before interest and tax of £52 million in 1989, £103 million in 1990, £91 million in 1991 and £142 million in 1992. If these profits could be achieved the purchase price of £150 million (less sweeteners) made the acquisition a bargain.

As more information came to light about the purchase it came to be seen as even more of a bargain. In 1989 the National Audit Office investigated the controversial sale and concluded that the company was worth at least £206 million at the date of the sale. It commented that the price paid fell 'significantly short of the real value of the company'.

It came to light that the Rover Group had a large amount of land and buildings that were superfluous to needs. It was estimated that out of their total sites valued at £514 million, redundant sites were worth at least £34 million. The Audit Office concluded that in future 'taxpayers' interests would be better served by providing for the public purse to share in the benefits arising from any subsequent sale of surplus assets, rather than seeking a fixed price in which the new owner takes all of any subsequent benefits which materialise'.

Another interesting asset that BAe took over was a 40% equity stake in Daf-Leyland. At the time of the privatization this was valued at £50 million. In May 1989 BAe sold 60% of its shareholding in Daf for £89 million. At the end of 1989 the value of BAe's remaining stake in the company was worth £60 million.

With regard to future profits, BAe forecast that before tax and interest it would earn between £52 million and £61 million in 1989, between £104 million and £131 million in 1990, between £91 million and £153 million in 1991 and between £142 million and £252 million in 1992. These predictions give the range depending on what assumptions are made. Not bad results for a purchase price of less than £150 million! However, we must not forget the problem that emerged, namely that the EEC were not told of all of the conditions (the sweeteners) that went with the sale. It could be that all that this case indicates is that it is easy to be wise after the event. It could be that there is an important point of financial principle, namely that it should be the future cash flows that are being sold (or bought) that should determine the price. It does indicate that political considerations can override economic considerations (in the short run?).

What was the outcome? In 1993 the motor vehicles activities of British Aerospace made a profit of £56 million, before interest charges. In their 1992 financial accounts, British Aerospace announced that 'Rover completed a major investment programme'. They also reported that 1992 'saw a continuation of the very low demand levels experienced in 1991'. The accounts show losses before interest on the company's motor vehicles activities of £49 million in 1992, and £52 million in 1991. The three earlier years had shown profits before interest on motor vehicle activities of £65 million, £73 million and £71 million.

British Aerospace caused a surprise and generated much criticism by announcing on 31 January 1994 that they had reached agreement for the sale to the German car manufacturer BMW of their interests in Rover for £800 million cash. In fact BMW would also take over responsibility for Rover's debt which meant that BMW were paying £1700 million in total for British Aerospace interests in Rover.

In the 1993 accounts the chief executive commenting on the sale of Rover stated that the sale was a clear example 'of our determination to carry forward on plans to concentrate our efforts on those enterprises which are strong in international markets and offer very positive cash flows'. With such a policy, one wonders why British Aerospace took over Rover in the first place, and then undertook a major investment programme. Rover were not strong in international markets and to make them so would have required even larger investments. Rover did not even appear to give British Aerospace a positive cash flow, with losses to be covered in addition to the investment programme.

> Nevertheless, Rover was not a bad buy. It cost British Aerospace £150 million and they sold it for £800 million. This is of course only part of the picture. We do not know how much was invested by British Aerospace in Rover, and how it was financed. And we do not know if any tax allowances were received by the British Aerospace group resulting from past losses of Rover.

15.10 The cost of equity capital

We shall now consider how the theory of share valuation can be utilized to obtain an estimate of the cost of capital. The capitalization rate which we use in the dividend valuation model to obtain the PV of a share is in fact the cost of equity finance. As explained in the introduction to this chapter, this capitalization rate is the annual rate of return that the investor expects to earn on a share in the relevant risk class. Those making decisions within the company have to ensure that the performance of the company meets the shareholders' expectations; therefore this capitalization rate is the minimum return that must be earned on equity finance.

The cost of capital is the rate of return that a company must earn on an investment which is just sufficient to maintain the value of the business. An investment that earns a return above the cost of capital will increase the value of the business. An investment that earns a return below the cost of capital will reduce the value of a business. Unfortunately, it is not possible to arrive at a unique figure for such a cost for any business.

The literature offers more than one technique for arriving at a cost of capital. One is referred to as the traditional approach, another is based on the CAPM. The CAPM approach has been discussed in Chapter 10. In this chapter we shall consider the traditional approach. In most situations the alternative methods should give answers which fall within a reasonably narrow range and so provide the businessman with a reasonable cost estimate.

A shareholder investing in the equity of a company has in mind a minimum rate of return that he (she) expects to earn. He buys the shares at a price which he considers makes the shares a worthwhile investment, having compared the cost with the returns that he expects to earn from the shares over time and with the risks associated with the investment. He expects a specific after-tax return from his investment in the company, and it is this return that the company has to earn in order to satisfy the shareholder's expectations.

Given a management objective of maximization of the value to existing shareholders of their equity holdings in the company, the cost of equity capital is the shareholders' personal investment opportunity cost. The shareholders are legally the owners of the business, and the management should run the company, with their interest in mind. To maximize profits does not necessarily maximize the wealth of the ordinary shareholders. Business risks and financial risks can affect the share price. A necessary condition for a maximization of shareholders' wealth would be that net revenues (profits) over time are in some sense maximized. But the maximization of profits is not a **sufficient** condition for the maximization of shareholders' wealth.

The maximization of profits over time generally implies growth of the business. As the company grows, with the investment of the retained earnings, the question of gearing the capital structure has to be considered. At first it will benefit the owners to have loan capital introduced into the business, but as this fixed-interest capital increases, and with it the interest that has to be paid whether or not profits are made, the risks to the owners of the business also increase. These increased risks may reduce the ordinary share price, and consequently the wealth of the holders. Therefore, although an investment may be financed by an issue of debentures costing, say, 10% after tax, and earns after tax, say, 12%, thereby increasing total profits, the wealth of the equity owners may actually be reduced because of the added risks.

The concept of opportunity cost suggests that a shareholder with his investment in one company expects to earn at least the same return from that company as he would from an investment in another company in a similar risk class. If the company cannot provide this return it will find difficulty in attracting new funds. If the company is in this position and if it is acting in the shareholders' interests, it should distribute any profits it earns rather than investing them in the company.

In the economic paradise of perfect competition which assumes equal knowledge by all buying and selling in the market, the long-term discounted expected return of the shareholders will be adjusted through the market price to the same level for each company in the same risk class. Of course the stock market is not perfect; different information is available to different people. It is not possible, however, for one company to reward its shareholders continually with returns – dividends plus capital gains – lower than the average level of returns in the same risk class. If such a below average company did function and the future returns were not expected to increase, the shareholders would sell their holdings if a buyer could be found.

Before showing certain formulae that can be used to estimate the cost of equity capital for a particular company, we shall consider the cost of equity for an average company. This will provide an indication of the range of costs within which a particular company's cost will lie. We can do this either by examining the actual returns that equity shareholders have received over time or by looking at the range of returns earned on different classes of investment at one point in time. That is, we can either adopt a 'time series' or a 'cross-section' approach.

Equity returns over time

It has been shown that figures for historical rates of return vary dramatically from one period to another. [21] Over the period 1966–80 the annual real rates of return before tax on equity investment in the UK varied from a maximum of 44.6% in 1967–8 to a minimum of −50.2% in 1973–4. These figures were based on changes in the FT Actuaries All Share Index, plus the gross dividends paid in a year. They are based on changes from one mid-year to the next mid-year, and are before tax. The actual changes in the index were adjusted by the Retail Price Index to obtain real changes. In the 15 year period, there were positive returns over nine of the years and negative returns over six of the years.

The London Stock Exchange witnessed a prolonged rise from 1981 to mid-1987, with the FTSE index climbing from a level of 600 point to 1600. On 19 October 1987 came a dramatic collapse, with the index falling by 21.7% in two days. Such extreme changes in a short period of time make it infeasible to think of investors' expectations over a particular 12 month period.

What is necessary is to measure the average annual return over a long period of time. Even the task of measuring historic rates of return on equity invested is not simple; it involves a number of problems. For example should geometric means or arithmetic means be used? What time period should be chosen? In particular, what are the starting and closing dates? Historical rates of return differ between industries and between companies of different size, and so in order to estimate the cost of capital, different figures need to be obtained for the various sub-groups. Estimates based on what has happened over the last 20 to 25 years can be distorted by the market collapses of 1973–4 and 1987. The researcher has to be careful what start and end dates are used.

The major US research on annual returns is that undertaken by Ibbotson and Sinquefield [22]. In their study of the average annual returns on equities over the period from 1926 to 1991 they show an arithmetic mean of 12.4%. This is the monetary return before allowing for taxation. It is based on a buy and hold strategy with annual dividends being reinvested in more equity. The annualized average return on long-term corporate bonds over the same period was 5.7%, and the annualized annual return on US treasury bills was 3.9%. If the latter figure is taken as the risk-free rate, this shows a risk premium of 8.5% per annum on corporate equity and of 1.8% on corporate bonds.

The average annual rate of inflation over the period was in the region of 3%, giving a real gross rate of return on equity of approximately 9.4%.

The above equity returns relate to all equities, including large and small companies. The resulting figure is heavily influenced by the large companies. When the average annual return on equities in the small-company sector is calculated it is shown to be 17.5%. This is well above the return on all equities.

This of course reflects the higher risks associated with investing in smaller companies. The investor expects and receives a higher average rate of return from investing in small companies than from investing in larger companies. Some idea of the risk can be seen from the returns in the US in just a single year. In 1990 stock market prices fell. The average return from investing in all common shares in that year was minus 3.2%, the average return from investing in small company shares was minus 21.6%. Small companies show greater volatility in year-on-year returns.

Studies for the UK have come up with roughly comparable figures. A study for the period 1956–66 showed an average of 6.4% in real terms, but this was net of taxes [23]. When it is grossed up it comes close to the 9%.

Another study for the period 1962–81 produced a much lower figure in real terms, but this was heavily influenced by the inflation rates of over 20% per annum that occurred during some years in the 1970s [24].

A comprehensive study by the stock brokers BZW shows that over the 75 years to the end of 1993 the real inflation adjusted rate of return from UK equities was 7.9% a year before tax [25]. This is a little below the return in the USA.

BZW estimate that historically the real cost of equity capital for a company has been between 7% and 10%. They recommended in 1994 that the average UK company should use 8% per annum in real terms after tax as the estimate of the cost of equity.

The Bank of England however estimated that in 1994, seven out of ten British companies were setting excessive hurdle rates for new capital projects [26]. This they believe is not only holding back the growth of the individual companies concerned, but also jeopardizing the UK's economic performance.

The Bank approached the question of determining the cost of capital in two ways. One was by way of a survey, the other by a study of past returns on investments. The survey results were based on the practices of 250 large and medium-sized companies. The inquiry revealed significant differences in the rates of return that companies seek as investment criteria. The companies using required real rates of returns reported targets in the range of 7% to 20% after tax, with an average of around 15%. Nominal targets averaged around 20%.

It should be appreciated that this was the target based on projects being financed with a mixture of debt and equity. It is not the target return on equity. Because debt is cheaper than equity, the target the firms would be seeking on equity would on average be above the 15%.

The Bank of England were critical of these target return figures actually being used and they pointed out the target is significantly above the true cost of capital. They base their estimate on the cost of equity on the idea of a risk-free rate of return plus a premium for risk. The risk-free rate is based on the real yield on index-linked government debt. This in the early 1990s was usually between 3% and 4%. They add to this a risk premium of about 6%, which is based on the average excess return on equities over debt, and is in line with the figures mentioned above.

This 'suggests a required real return on a typical project financed by equity of around 10%'. This is the cost to the company after tax. It is little better than the BZW estimate, but considerably lower than the rate used in practice

Relative returns at any one time

The estimates above are of the absolute returns earned on equity investments. An alternative approach is to consider the relative returns. Much of what determines any shareholder's real rate of return on an investment is beyond the control of the company in which the investment is made. For example, the rate of inflation, government policies, currency exchange rates and the international trading situation all affect a shareholder's return. A company is operating in a financial and economic environment which, to a large extent, determines the returns that the shareholders of that company will receive.

The company is attracting risk finance. Perhaps the way in which a company should be judged is to consider the returns that they provide to their shareholders in relation to the return that can be earned on alternative investments. This is the relative return to that which can be earned elsewhere in the capital and money markets. This is the basis of the CAPM. The required return from holding any capital asset, physical as well as financial, is a function of the risk-free rate of return in the economy plus a premium for the level of the risk of that asset.

If a deposit in a building society offers an interest rate, free of tax, of say 9%, what rate of return must an investor expect on an equity share in order to be induced to purchase the equity share? Shareholders have to bear in mind the risks associated with a company's operations. The interest rate of 9% net of tax on a building society deposit is equivalent to a gross rate of approximately 12% for an investor paying income tax at the 25% rate. If the rate of inflation in the economy is at a rate of, say, 13% per annum, then the depositor in the building society is receiving a negative gross real rate of return of 1%. Such was the situation in much of the 1970s. The gross interest earned each year was not compensating for the loss in the capital value of the deposits. In the 1980s and 1990s, however, with inflation rates at much lower levels, the returns on deposit accounts were positive. If the building societies offer 9% net of tax with the inflation rate in the region of 5%, then the investors are being offered a positive real rate of return of 4% after tax and 7% before tax.

Because of the higher risks, investors in equity have a right to expect a return above the rate received on, say, a building society deposit. The amount of premium that a shareholder should receive to compensate for the level of risk can be estimated. There is a considerable volume of literature on the structure of interest rates and on investment returns which can give some guidance as to the premiums for risk. The difference at any one point of time between interest yields on fixed interest corporate securities, treasury bills, building society shares and dividend yields plus capital gains on equities can give help in arriving at the appropriate risk premium.

In the US study by Ibbotson and Sinquefield [27] the premium on equities over corporate bonds was on average 6.7%. Building society deposits are probably a little safer than the average corporate bond, but against that the returns over time on equity investment in the UK seem to be a little lower than in the USA. Therefore we can take 6% as an appropriate premium. Of course, many problems are encountered in estimating these premiums.

The CAPM considers the question of the appropriate risk premium more deeply. However, in the situation being discussed, if this 6% premium was added to the 9% net rate of return offered to investors by building societies on deposit accounts, the real cost of equity capital for the average company is in the region of 15% in these circumstances. This is the return needing to be earned after corporation tax, and is the return that the shareholder expects.

The discussion in this section and in the previous section relates to the cost of equity finance only. Debt finance is less expensive. It is the long-term expectation of the shareholder that needs to be met. The point made in this section is that the cost of equity capital should depend upon the relative returns available elsewhere to investors. It is the basis of the CAPM. The required return from holding any asset, physical as well as financial, is a function of risk. However, shareholders' attitudes and uncertainty could still make an absolute return the relevant figure.

The return to the shareholder

It will be useful at this stage to illustrate how a return earned by a company benefits a shareholder. We shall illustrate with the 15% return in monetary terms, before tax, that has been arrived at above as the shareholder's required return. It will be shown that, under the assumptions made, the shareholder will be satisfied if the company earns a 20.1% return on the investment before corporation tax.

In the example illustrated in Fig. 15.1 it is assumed that the company, in calculating its 20.1% return on an investment, is doing so in monetary terms. It is also assumed that in earning the 20.1% it is not maintaining the value of the newly acquired assets intact in real terms, but is depreciating the assets on a historic cost basis. The relevant data used in the illustration is:

- The opening value of the company (10 000 shares each with a market value of £1) is £10 000. The company is all-equity financed.
- New investment is financed by the issue of 1000 new shares each with an issue price of £1.
- Ignore issue costs.
- New investment earns 20.1% before corporation tax.
- Assume that the company wishes to pay a gross dividend such that the dividend yield is 7.5%.
- Assume that the rate of ACT is 20% and corporation tax is 33%.

The cost of equity capital for a company in this situation is 15% after corporation tax. It is this return that will satisfy the shareholders. As demonstrated above, this 15% is what the investor could expect to earn on an alternative investment in the same risk class.

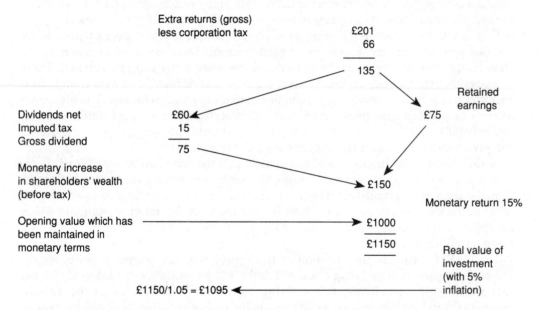

Therefore the real rate of return to shareholders is 9.5% on the £1000 of equity invested.

Figure 15.1

The cost of which funds?

We have for illustrative purposes developed an example in which the cost of equity finance after corporation tax is 15%. The question can be asked: 15% on what? Is it on par value, or on market value? How do retained earnings come into the picture?

It is fairly clear that if new finance is being raised in order to fund an investment, say £1 million of new equity to fund a new factory, 15% on the £1 million needs to be earned in order to justify the investment and satisfy the providers of the funds. The par value of the shares being issued is irrelevant; it is the price that the investor is having to pay that has to be justified. If the par value of the share is £1.00 and they are being sold for £2, it means issuing 500 000 shares to raise the £1 million; it is not 15% on each share that has to be earned. The company needs to earn in total 15% on the market value of the shares (£1 000 000 × 15% = £150 000), rather than 15% per share (500 000 × £1.00 × 15% = £75 000).

The same principle applies when we move to measuring the cost of equity of a business that has been in existence for some time. Let us continue with the above example. Three years after the investment referred to above, the market value of the shares is £3 and no new shares have been issued. The market value of the equity of the company is now £1 500 000 (i.e. 500 000 × £3). It is a total of 15% on the £1 500 000 (i.e. £225 000) that has to be earned to satisfy shareholders. When we move to measuring the weighted average cost of capital for a company, we take into account not only equity funds, but also any debt and preference shares. Therefore the weighting for the equity element should be based on the number of shares multiplied by their market value. There is an alternative approach which is sometimes adopted where the weighting is based on book value, but this is second best.

In the illustration above, the return required from the cash flow is obtained after allowing for corporation tax. However, it is not always correct to take the corporation tax rate of 33% and to deduce that the company needs to earn in the region of 20.1% before corporation tax to give an after-tax return of 15%. The effective tax rate for companies can be less than 33% because of capital allowances and other deductions. The fact that the tax payments do not have to be made immediately at the end of an accounting year also reduces the real cost of such payments.

The illustrations given above include at least one important assumption, i.e. the effect of retained earnings on share prices. It is assumed that the value of a shareholder's investment in the company increases with the value of the funds in the business. A number of factors affect the level of the share price of a company, and assets per share is only one of these. However, if it is thought that the retained earnings can be used in the business as profitably as the other assets, then the share price should move in line with the funds invested per share. This direct relationship should hold in the long run if the new investments are expected to earn the same rate of return as the old investments.

Factors other than earnings and dividends influences share price. The fact that actual share price movements are not always upwards can be a result of these other factors outweighing the earnings considerations. The inflationary effect on asset values tends to increase share price. Before parting with money, the potential shareholder has an expected real rate of return in mind and the company, in the medium and long term, must ensure that its cash flow is such that this expectation is realized. Projects that cannot (in terms of expectations) provide such a return should be rejected.

The traditional approach

The above sections on equity returns and relative returns have been concerned with the returns that a shareholder might expect on an average investment. But of course companies vary: some are in industries that are considered more risky than others; large concerns are generally considered less risky than small ones; some companies have a better image in the minds of the investing public than others. This means that not all companies have the same cost of equity capital. If a small lesser-known company that manufactures or trades in an industry subject to uncertainty or long sales cycles goes to the stock market to obtain equity, it finds that it has to offer its investors the prospects of higher rates of return than would a large well-established company trading in a basic product.

A company can calculate its own cost of capital, although again there is no single agreed method of doing this. As has been explained, there are two approaches a company can adopt to measure its cost of capital, the CAPM and the so-called traditional approach. We will now consider the traditional approach. This basis of the calculation is to determine the performance that the shareholder expects of the company – or rather, the minimum (standard) that the company must achieve to keep the shareholder satisfied and retain his investment. It is the future dividend and share price movements that are relevant here, but of course attempts to forecast share price and dividend movements are both problematical and unreliable. Consequently, as with the calculations for an average company, it is necessary to ascertain the rates that were earned in the past and use these as the basis of the calculations. The market places very heavy weight on current and recent past earnings in forming impressions about future returns.

The earnings of a company in the past are used to indicate the expected earnings in the future. It can be argued that if the shareholders of a particular company were satisfied with their past returns relative to other opportunities, to keep them satisfied the company will need to earn at least this rate in the future.

This might appear to mean that a company which had given a high return to its shareholders in the past would be penalized in that its calculated cost of capital, and so the cut-off rate for future investments, would be high, thus reducing its profitable investment opportunities. Two points can be made in reply to this apparent paradox. First, the estimates of cost of capital will be based partly on current yields, so that once the returns that the shareholders have been receiving are known, the share price of the company should rise, and so bring down the yield.

Secondly, the discredited notion that past growth rates indicate something about future growth rates cannot be ignored, because some investors believe it. A company expected to have a high performance would disappoint its shareholders if its performance proved to be only average, and so its cost of capital might well be higher in terms of the expectations of those providing the funds.

The situation just outlined should only be able to exist in the short run. In the long run the stock market should adjust share prices to eliminate any major differences in capital costs within companies in a similar risk category. A company in which the expected future returns for shareholders are higher than the average for companies in the same risk category would find an increase in the demand for its shares; the price would be bid up, and so the dividend yield and earnings yield of new shareholders would be brought in line with the average.

Several alternative factors or financial indicators have been suggested as the base for calculating the cost of a company's equity capital. Four will now be considered.

If K_e is the cost of equity capital, E_a is the anticipated earnings per share, E_t is the current earnings per share, P_n is the market price per share, D_1 is the cash dividend per share at end of first period, g_D is the expected average annual rate of growth in dividends and g_p is the expected average annual rate of growth of share price, then K_e can be measured using the formulae given below.

1. The dividend yield basis, namely, the dividend yield per share based on the expected current year's dividend divided by the current market price per share and expressed as a percentage:

$$K_e = \frac{D_1}{P_n}$$

The company would have to earn at least this yield to keep the shareholders content.

This is a poor measure of cost, as it does not allow for any growth. Normally a shareholder expects the returns from his equity investment to grow over time with respect to either the value of his capital or the income he receives. The company should allow for this expected growth when calculating the cost of its capital.

2. The dividend yield plus an allowance for future growth:

$$K_e = \frac{D_1}{P_n} + g_D$$

or

$$K_e = \frac{D_1}{P_n} + g_P$$

Here it is recognized that the current market price of a share either reflects expected future dividends, or the expected increase in share price. The company must meet these expectations.

To illustrate this approach, let us assume that a company has its shares quoted on the Stock Exchange and the current price per share in £1.50. The gross dividends per share over the last four years have been 7p, 7.7p, 8.5p and 9.3p. The dividends are expected to continue to grow at this rate of 10% per annum. The appropriate gross dividend yield is therefore 6.8%, i.e.

$$\frac{D_1}{P_n} = \frac{10.2}{150} \times 100 = 6.8\%$$

Therefore, the cost of the equity capital to the company is 16.8%:

$$K_e = \frac{D_1}{P_n} + g_D = \frac{10.2}{150} + 0.10 = 0.168$$

This is the cost to the company after corporation tax. One point should be noted: this cost relates to the existing equity shares of a company. It is assumed that the shares are quoted on a market and a price exists. If new equity shares were to be issued, then the P_n that would be used in the calculation to determine the cost of the new equity capital would be the price per share received by the company net of underwriting and flotation costs. It would be the actual amount received by the company for each share it issues.

3. The earnings yield basis, namely the last reported earnings per share divided by the current market price per share:

$$K_e = \frac{E_t}{P_n}$$

This is not a very sound method of calculating the cost of capital. It claims that because the current dividend yield of a particular company is, say, 4% and the dividend is covered 1.5 times, the cost of capital to the company is 6% (i.e. 4% × 1.5). This takes for granted the shareholders' continued satisfaction with this present rate of dividend, and the earnings cover of dividends – a fallacious assumption because, although the shareholder may be satisfied with this return for one year, he will expect a growth in his earnings in the future. He may be prepared to accept a lower rate of return than he can obtain elsewhere for one year or in the short run, but only because he expects improvements in the future. He will not accept this below average return indefinitely.

4. The future earnings yield basis. Some writers argue that the price-to-earnings ratio should be used as the basis for calculating the cost of equity capital. The price-to-earnings ratio is, of course, a measure which behaves in a similar manner to the earnings yield. An alternative would be to base the calculation on expected future earnings. Hence

$$K_e = \frac{E_a}{P_n}$$

There is no generally accepted model, although most of the theoretical work that uses the traditional approach is based on the second type of approach. The technique used earlier in this section, where an attempt was made to calculate the cost for an average company, was based on this second model. The cost equalled the dividend yield plus the expected increase in share price. The rate of growth of either dividends or share price depends on the earnings in each period and the rate of retention.

To determine its cost of capital using the traditional approach, a company would select whichever of the above financial models it thought appropriate and then substitute its own values in the equation.

Cost of retained earnings

It has sometimes been suggested that the retained earnings of a company provide a free source of funds. This can easily be shown to be untrue. The company must consider the income that the shareholders could obtain if the earnings had been distributed instead of being retained, and if it cannot earn at least an equivalent amount of income on these funds, it should return them to the shareholders.

Some would argue that under a pure capital market theory companies should distribute all their profits to their shareholders. The shareholders would then have the opportunity to reinvest these funds where they could earn the highest returns, and this process, once widespread, would help to develop a more efficient distribution of capital. Companies with profitable investment opportunities, which under the present system might find themselves in a position of capital shortage, would be able to attract the increased funds available. One of the reasons why this free-market system does not work is that it is not in the interests of those who manage the company. Another is that it would be a costly process to distribute all profits and then invite equity holders to subscribe for new issues. However, the company must bear in mind that it should only retain earnings if it can justify doing so after taking into account the cost differences.

There are two ways of considering the cost of retained earnings. The first follows the line of reasoning that we adopted for new equity finance, namely the shareholders' opportunity cost. It is the return that the shareholder can earn outside the company that it is the criterion that should be adopted for ascertaining the cost of retained earnings.

The second approach is referred to as the 'rights issue' approach. In this approach retained earnings are seen as equivalent to a fully subscribed rights offer with certain tax advantages. Retaining the funds within the business increases the value of the shares. The existing shareholders obtain the sole advantage of this policy. If all earnings were paid as dividends and a simultaneous rights offer was made, shareholders might be liable to tax on the dividends and would only be able to subscribe to an amount equal to the net receipt from dividends.

Clientele effect

One problem with all these approaches to measuring the cost of capital is similar to the difficulty that arises when considering the effect of dividend policy on the valuation of a company, i.e. not all shareholders are the same. The shareholders of a company have a variety of taxation positions, a variety of expectations and a variety of preferences. A company cannot expect to satisfy all its shareholders when it makes financial decisions.

However, it has been suggested that the characteristics of a company, including perhaps its dividend policy, attract a particular class of shareholder. This is known as the clientele effect, the hypothesis being that each company attracts its own clientele. The management of a company chooses its dividend policy, and therefore its retained earnings policy, to satisfy the preferences of its clientele.

The management could of course change its dividend policy, but if it does so it accepts that some of its present shareholders will sell and it will attract a new group of shareholders. Its clientele will change. The impact of the clientele approach to the measurement of the cost of capital is that a company can think of the tax position of its particular 'clientele', and of the investment opportunities available in the market-place to its 'clientele'. Its shareholders at any one time are a 'sub-group' of all investors, and members of the sub-group have somewhat similar characteristics.

Depreciation

If one looks at the sources and application of funds statement for a company, one source of finance is shown as being depreciation. However, it is not necessary for depreciation to be brought into the calculations to determine the company's cost of capital. It is money that is to be used to maintain the value of the business, to replace worn-out assets. It is maintaining the value of capital already invested in the business. As the asset is being used up, money is being put aside to maintain the total value of the investment.

Depreciation is neither equity finance nor debt finance. It arises because an investment has already been made, and it is necessary to record in some manner the expiration of the original cost of the investment. Revenue is being earned and not paid out to suppliers, employees or shareholders, but is being put aside to replace the structure of the business. Depreciation should not enter into the cost of capital calculation.

15.11 Key terms

Capital asset pricing model
Clientele effect
Credibility gap
Dividend growth model
Intrinsic value
Off balance sheet finance

Price–earnings ratio
Realizable values
Super-profits
True value
Weighted average cost of capital
Winners' curse

15.12 Revision questions

1. What is the PV formula for the valuation of a share based on dividend growing at a constant amount per annum?
2. What is the relationship between the reported earnings per share of a company, the dividend per share and the share price?
3. What is the relationship between the expected rate of return of shareholders and the cost of equity capital of a company?
4. What is the risk premium on equity investment over gilt edged bonds? How can it be calculated?
5. The returns to shareholders vary from one year to the next. Does this mean we cannot use past returns to help us predict next year's returns?
6. What are the criticisms of the weighted average cost of capital approach?
7. There are many ways of valuing a company. List these ways, commenting on the strengths and weaknesses of each.

15.13 References

1. Baumol, W.J. (1965) *The Stock Market and Economic Efficiency*, Fordham University Press, New York.
2. Gordon, M. (1959) Dividends, earnings, and financial policy, *Review of Economics and Statistics*, May.
3. Graham, B., Dodd, D.L. and Cottle, S. (1962) *Security Analysis* (3rd edn), McGraw-Hill, New York.
4. Modigliani, F. and Miller, M.H. (1958) The cost of capital, corporation finance and the theory of investment, *American Economic Review*, June, pp 261–97.
   Modigliani, F. and Miller, M.H. (1958) The cost of capital, corporation finance and the theory of investment – reply, *American Economic Review*, September, pp 655–69.
   Modigliani, F. and Miller, M.H. (1963) Corporate income taxes and the cost of capital: a correction, *American Economic Review*, **53**, (3), pp 433–43.
   Modigliani, F. and Miller, M.H. (1966) Some estimates of the cost of capital to the electric utility industry, *American Economic Review*, **56**, pp 333–91.
5. Kaplan, R.S. and Roll, R. (1972) Investors' evaluation of accounting information: some empirical evidence, *Journal of Business*, April.
6. Lawson, G.H. (1978) The rationale of cash flow accounting, in *Trends in Managerial and Financial Accounting* ed. Van Dem, C. Martinus Nijhoff.
   Lee T. (1984) *Cash Flow Accounting*, Chapman & Hall, London.
7. Dewing, A.S. (1953) *The Financial Policy of Corporations*, p 287, Ronald Press Co., New York.

8. See Arnold, J. and Moizer, P. (1984) A survey of the methods used by UK investment analysis to appraise investments in ordinary shares, *Accounting and Business Research*, Summer.

Vergoossen, R.G.A. (1993) The use and perceived importance of annual reports by investment analysts in the Netherlands, *European Accounting Review*, Sept., **2**(2) 219–43.

9. A good survey article is that of Lev, B. (1989) On the usefulness of earnings and earnings research: lessons and directions from two decades of empirical research', *Journal of Accounting Research*.

10. Ball, R. and Brown, P. (1968) An empirical evaluation of accounting income numbers, *Journal of Accounting Research*, Autumn, 159–78.

11. Beaver, W.R., Lambert, R. and Morse, D. (1980) The information content of security prices, *Journal of Accounting and Economics*, **2**, pp 3–28.

12. Ou, J.A. and Penman, S.H. (1989) Financial statement analysis and the prediction of stock returns, *Journal of Accounting and Economics*, Nov.

13. Bernard, V.L. and Thomas, J.K. (1989) Post earnings announcement drift: delayed price response or risk premium, *Journal of Accounting Research*.

14. See Lev (1989) *op. cit.*

15. Brennan, M.J. (1991) A perspective on accounting and stock prices, *Accounting Review*, January, pp 000–00.

16. Brennan (1991), *op. cit.*

17. Choi, F.D.S. and Levich, R.M. (1990) *The Capital Market Effects and International Accounting Diversity*, New York University, Irwin.

18. See Rock, K. (1986) Why are new issues underpriced, *Journal of Financial Economics*, **15**, 187–212.

Tinic, S.M. (1988) Anatomy of initial public offerings of common stock, *Journal of Finance*, **43**, 789–822.

19. Myers, S. (1977) Determinants of corporate borrowing, *Journal of Financial Economics*, November.

20. Franks, J.R., Miles, R. and Bagwell, J. (1974) A critique of merger valuation models, *Journal of Business Finance and Accounting*, **1**(1), Spring.

21. Jones, P.D. (1982) The real return in UK equities, 1962–1981, *The Investment Analyst*, 63, pp 15–20.

Merrett, A.J. and Sykes, A. (1966) Return on equities and fixed interest securities: 1919–1966, *District Bank Review*, June; Rates of return standards: the cost of capital, *Accountancy*, January, 1966.

Brigham, E.F. and Pappas, J.L. (1969) Rates of return on common stock, *The Journal of Business*, July.

De Zoete and Bevan (1974) *Equity and Fixed Interest Investment, 1914–1974*, London.

22. Ibbotson, R.G., and Sinquefield, R.A. (1993) *Stocks, bonds, bills and inflation*: SBBI Yearbook, Ibbotson Associates, Chicago.

23. See De Zoete and Bevan, *op. cit.*

24. See Jones, *op. cit.*

25. BZW (1994) *Equity/Gilt Study – Investment in the London Stock Market since 1918*, 39th issue, London.

26. Wardlow, A. (1994) Investment appraisal criteria and the impact of low inflation, *Bank of England Quarterly Bulletin*, Aug. **34**(3), 250–4.

27. Ibbotson, R.G. and Sinquefield, R.A. (1993), *op. cit.*

15.14 Further reading

Measuring the cost of capital is a very complex issue. The articles listed below give an indication of the issues involved.

Arditti, F.D. (1973) The weighted average cost of capital: some questions on its definition, interpretation and use, *Journal of Finance*, Sept.

Brennan, M.J. (1973) A new look at the weighted average cost of capital, *Journal of Business Finance*, Summer.

Frankel, J.A. (1991) The Japanese cost of finance: a survey, *Financial Management*, Winter.

Gordon, M.J. and Gould, L.I. (1978) The cost of equity capital: a reconsideration, *Journal of Finance*, June.

Harris, R. (1986) Using analysts' forecasts to estimate shareholders' required returns, *Financial Management*, Spring.

Keane, S.M. (1978) The cost of capital as a financial decision tool, *Journal of Business Finance and Accounting*, Autumn.

Marsh, P. (1982) The choice between equity and debt: an empirical study, *Journal of Finance*, March.

Mayer, C.P. (1986) Corporation tax, finance and the cost of capital. *Review of Economic Studies*, **53**, 93–112.

Scott, D.F. and Petty, J.W. (1980) Determining the cost of common equity capital: the direct method, *Journal of Business Research*, March.

Weston, J.F. (1991) Some financial perspectives on comparative costs of capital, *Business Economics*, April, 33–7.

15.15 Problems

1. A company's last dividend was £0.50 per share. Dividends are expected to increase by 10% per annum. The expected rate of return on shares in the same risk class is 20%. What is the market value (market price) of an equity share in this company?

2. A company has recently paid a dividend per share of £0.20. The price of the share in the stock market is £4.00. The par value of the share is £1.00, and it had been initially sold to shareholders for £2.00. The company's policy is to increase dividends by 8% per annum.

   What is the cost of equity capital to the company?

3. A company has issued 1 000 000 equity shares each with a nominal value of 25 pence. The dividend of the company over recent years has been

$$
\begin{aligned}
t - 5 &= 5 \text{ pence} \\
t - 4 &= 5.5 \text{ pence} \\
t - 3 &= 6.3 \text{ pence} \\
t - 2 &= 6.3 \text{ pence} \\
t - 1 &= 7.2 \text{ pence} \\
t &= 8.0 \text{ pence}
\end{aligned}
$$

   The current market price of the share is £1.00 ex dividend.

   Calculate the cost of equity capital for the company.

4. 'A share can be perceived as the present value of a future stream of dividends. However, this does not imply that dividend policy affects the value of the share.'

   Discuss.

5. Allote PLC is proposing to obtain a quotation on the Stock Exchange. The company wishes to raise £4 million of usable funds through an offer for sale of new ordinary shares. The £4 million will be invested in new projects. Administration and issue costs are expected to be 7.5% of the gross receipts from the offer for sale.

   Allote PLC wishes to estimate the number of shares it should issue and the price at which the shares should be issued. For the issue to be successful the company has been advised that it should make the issue at a discount of 15% on whatever share price is estimated as appropriate by means of comparisons with a similar quoted company (or companies) in the same industry. Summarized financial details of four quoted companies in the same industry are shown below:

	Benate	Cebate	Delate	Effate
Share price	195p	278p	46p	526p
Earnings available to ordinary shareholders	£3.00m	£1.01m	£1.09m	£6.17m
Dividend paid	£1.43m	£0.66m	£0.57m	£2.86m
Net book value	£31.00m	£9.00m	£8.6m	£58.5m
Market capitalization	£39.00m	£12.51m	£12.604m	£75.218m

	Benate	Cebate	Delate	Effate
Gearing (total debt to total equity)	46%	36%	53%	31%
Equity beta	1.14	1.16	1.22	1.18
Growth rate, average over five years	7%	7%	5.5%	5.5%

The summarized accounts of Allote PLC for the latest financial year are as follows:

Profit and loss account	£000
Turnover	31 894
Operating costs	28 284
Net interest payable	902
Profit before taxation	2 708
Taxation	948
Profit attributable to ordinary shareholders	1 760
Ordinary dividends	792
Retained profit	968

Balance sheet	£000
Fixed assets	7 430
Current assets	7 302
Less current liabilities	(3 112)
	11 620
Financed by	
Ordinary shares (10p)	1 800
Reserves	6 620
Bank term loan	3 200
	11 620

Allote believes that the new investment will produce an annual post-tax return of 14.5% which will allow the company to achieve an overall growth rate of 6% for the foreseeable future. The company's proposed dividend policy is to maintain a pay-out ratio of 45% as long as this does not lead to a reduction in dividends per share. The company can borrow at 2% above the treasury bill yield of 6%. This rate has not changed significantly for several years and is not expected to change in the near future. The return on the market is estimated to be 10%.

(a) Using the dividend valuation model and one other valuation technique advise Allote PLC of the number of shares that the company might issue and the price at which the shares might be issued. (A range of values may be included if you consider this to be appropriate.) (14 marks)

(b) Give possible explanations of why the share price of Delate and Effate differ by 480p although the companies have experienced similar growth rates during the last five years. Discuss how important this difference in share price is likely to be to investors. (6 marks)

ACCA, June 1987

6. A private company which has an existing share capital of 500 000 shares of £0.50 par value is contemplating seeking a public quotation. It estimates that it needs to raise about £500 000. The earnings have been growing at about 10% per annum and for the last year were £100 000. The price-to-earnings ratios of companies in the same industry vary between 8:1 and 12:1. The company estimates that it could pay a dividend out of last year's earnings of £60 000.

How many shares would you advise the company to issue and at what price? What information additional to that given in the question would you like to have available?

7. The directors of New Products Ltd are giving preliminary consideration to the making of an offer for sale of shares of the company. The summarized accounts for the last five years show the following (in £000):

Capital employed	1994	1993	1992	1991	1990
Share capital	340	340	340	340	340
Reserves	1840	1620	1470	1270	1050
Loans	300	370	350	350	370
Deferred taxation	1040	810	550	220	190
	3520	3140	2710	2180	1950
Employment of capital					
Fixed assets	2520	2320	2100	1790	1660
Associated companies	130	120	290	130	120
Net current assets	870	700	320	260	170
	3520	3140	2710	2180	1950
Results					
Turnover	9560	8070	7390	5980	4730
Trading profit	1560	1440	1510	1320	950
Profit before tax	670	530	590	580	510
Tax	368	298	320	300	280
Dividend	82	82	70	60	50
Retention	220	150	200	220	180

The share capital consists of fully paid ordinary shares of 250 000 and the current dividend represents a net amount of 6p per share.

Two companies which are considered to be competitors in the major markets are already quoted and the most recent data from the *Financial Times* relating to them are shown below:

1994				+ or	Div		Yield	
High	Low	Stock	Price	−	net	Cover	Gross	P/E
277	201	Company A 50p	202	−4	6.23	3.5	4.7	9.3
168	132	Company B 25p	132	−3	3.27	5.6	3.8	7.2

(a) Advise the directors on the possible price range that might be obtained, showing clearly the alternative methods of calculation you have used.

(b) State the further information you would require to prepare the accountant's report to be included in the offer for sale documentation.

8. Bell PLC is not subject to taxation and has calculated its cost of equity and debt capital as follows.

	Total amounts		
	Book values (£ million)	Market values (£ million)	Cost (%)
Equity:			
10 million shares issued	50	80	15
Debt:			
irredeemable debentures	20	20	10

Bell wishes to invest in a new project which will provide expected annual cash flows in perpetuity. Investment in the project can be at several different levels. The project will be financed entirely from the net proceeds of the issue of 3 million shares (issue costs £600 000) and £6 million 10% debentures issued at par (issue costs £400 000). Issue costs will be borne by Bell at the time the issue of securities is carried out.

The price and method of issuing shares are still not determined. Three specific possibilities are under consideration:

(a) shares issued at their current market value:
(b) shares issued to existing shareholders at a discount of 25% from current market value;
(c) shares issued to entirely new shareholders at a discount of 25% from current market value.

The financial director estimates that, because of the additional risks involved, undertaking the project will increase the cost of all issued equity to 16%, but will not alter the cost of the debt.

For each of the three possibilities concerning the issue price method for Bell's new equity determine:

(a) the net amount available for investment in the proposed project;
(b) the minimum expected internal rate of return required from the net investment in the proposed project if the wealth of the existing shareholders is not to be reduced.

ACCA, Financial Management,
Dec. 1983

9. Stock market analysts sometimes use fundamental analysis and sometimes technical analysis to forecast future share prices. What are fundamental analysis and technical analysis?

10. Crestlee plc is evaluating two projects. The first involves a £4.725 million expenditure on new machinery to expand the company's existing operations in the textile industry. The second is a diversification into the packaging industry, and will cost £9.275 million.

Crestlee's summarized balance sheet, and those of Canall plc and Sealalot plc two quoted companies in the packaging industry, are shown below:

	Crestlee plc £m	Canall plc £m	Sealalot plc £m
Fixed assets	96	42	76
Current assets	95	82	65
Less current liabilities	(70)	(72)	(48)
	121	52	93
Financed by:			
Ordinary shares[1]	15	10	30
Reserves	50	27	50
Medium and long-term loans[2]	56	15	13
	121	52	93
Ordinary share price (pence)	380	180	230
Debenture price (£)	104	112	—
Equity beta	1.2	1.3	1.2

[1]Crestlee and Sealalot 50 pence par value, Canall 25 pence par value.
[2]Crestlee 12% debentures 1998–2000, Canall 14% debentures 2003, Sealalot medium-term bank loan.

Crestlee proposes to finance the expansion of textile operations with a £4.725 million 11% loan stock issue, and the packaging investment with a £9.275 million rights issue at a discount of 10% on the current market price. Issue costs may be ignored.

Crestlee's managers are proposing to use a discount rate of 15% per year to evaluate each of these projects.

The risk-free rate of interest is estimated to be 6% per year and the market return 14% per year. Corporate tax is at a rate of 33% per year.

Required:
(a) Determine whether 15% per year is an appropriate discount rate to use for each of these projects. Explain your answer and state clearly any assumptions that you make. (19 marks)
(b) Crestlee's marketing director suggests that it is incorrect to use the same discount rate each year for the investment in packaging as the early stages of the investment are more risky, and should be discounted at a higher rate. Another board member disagrees saying that more distant cash flows are riskier and should be discounted at a higher rate. Discuss the validity of the views of each of the directors. (6 marks)

ACCA, Dec. 1992

11. Manu plc, a quoted company, is considering making an offer for the shares of the privately owned Europa plc. Relevant financial information on the two companies is as follows:

	£000	
	Manu	*Europa*
Land and buildings	7 600	1200
Plant and machinery	8 400	2420
Current assets	7 420	2100
Current liabilities	4 920	1600
Financed by:		
Ordinary shares*	2 000	540
Share premium	6 500	1600
Revenue reserves	5 300	1980
Long-term debt	4 700	—
*Manu 50 pence shares, Europa 25 pence shares		
Turnover	11 000	2400
Profit after taxation	1 400	500
Dividend	600	200
Retained earnings	800	300
Expected growth in dividends	8%	10%
Market price	350 pence	—

Additional information:
Some £200 000 of Europa's inventory is in poor condition and could be sold only for an estimated £20 000. £55 000 of debtors have been outstanding for more than six months and it is expected that only 20% will be recovered. Land and buildings have an estimated market value of £2.0 million. Plant and machinery could be sold for £1.2 million although their replacement cost is £2.8 million.

Required:
(a) Use **three** valuation techniques to estimate a value or range of values for the shares of Europa. Europa's cost of equity is estimated to be 20% higher than Manu's cost of equity.
(b) Comment on the different valuations produced by the three methods.
(c) Assess the extent to which the three methods of valuation you have used provide reliable estimates of economic value.

12. The British Industrial Group plc (BIG), a large conglomerate, is considering acquiring an interest in Bertram Ltd, a private company. You have been asked by the directors of BIG to advice them on the value of Bertram Ltd's shares.

Bertram Ltd has manufactured domestic appliances since its incorporation in the 1940s. In recent years its management has adopted a policy of maintaining dividend growth at approximately 10% p.a. Bertram Ltd's summarized accounts for the years ended 31 December 1989, 1990 and 1991 are as follows:

Profit and loss account for the year ended 31 December

	1989 £m	1990 £m	1991 £m
Profit on ordinary activities after tax	14.60	18.72	20.30
Extraordinary items	(2.60)	(4.80)	(5.00)
	12.00	13.92	15.30
Dividends	4.00	4.40	5.00
Profit retained	8.00	9.52	10.30

Balance sheet as at 31 December

	1989 £m	1990 £m	1991 £m
Fixed assets	46.39	48.83	50.67
Net Current Assets	77.21	84.29	92.75
	123.60	133.12	143.42
Issues share capital (share of 5p)	2.00	2.00	2.00
Share premium account	6.00	6.00	6.00
Reserves	85.60	95.12	105.42
14% Debentures (1995)	30.00	30.00	30.00
	123.60	133.12	143.42

At 31 December 1991, fixed assets were as follows:

	Net book value £m	Estimated market value £m
Freehold land and buildings	19.67	25.00
Plant and equipment	31.00	31.00
Total	50.67	56.00

Freehold land and buildings include a warehouse with a net book value of £3 million and an estimated market value of £5 million which has remained unused since 1987.

The debenture stock of Bertram Ltd, on which interest is payable annually on 31 December, is redeemable at par on 31 December 1995. Debentures of a similar risk-class to those of Bertram Ltd are currently offering a yield of 10%.

The cost of equity of listed companies in the same industry as Bertram Ltd and which are similarly geared is estimated at 16%. The average price earnings ratio of such companies is 8.0.

Corporation Tax at the rate of 33% is payable at the end of the accounting period to which it relates and all ACT can be offset against such tax. The directors of BIG have not yet decided what proportion of the share capital of Bertram Ltd they wish BIG to acquire and you have been asked to consider the possibility of acquiring either a minority or a majority stake.

Required:
Produce a report for the directors of BIG which uses three different techniques to value the shares in Bertram Ltd which are to be acquired. In each case, describe the circumstances in which the technique is appropriate and state any additional information that you would require.　　　　　　　　　　　　　(25 marks)
ICAEW, July 1992

Short- and medium-term sources of finance

16.1	Short-term bank borrowing	558	
16.2	Bank overdrafts	559	
16.3	Revolving underwriting facility	566	
16.4	Medium-term bank borrowing	566	
16.5	Bills of exchange	567	
16.6	Acceptance credits	567	
16.7	Trade credit	570	
16.8	Factoring	572	
16.9	Invoice discounting and credit insurance	573	
16.10	Deferred tax payments	574	
16.11	Government guaranteed loans	574	
16.12	Merchant banks	574	
16.13	Export finance	576	
16.14	Project finance	581	
16.15	Hire purchase	582	
16.16	Sale and lease-back	584	
16.17	Mortgaging property	585	
16.18	Leasing	585	
16.19	British government sources	597	
16.20	European sources	599	
16.21	Revision questions	601	
16.22	References	601	
16.23	Further reading	602	
16.24	Problems	602	

This is mainly a descriptive chapter. It gives details of the sources of finance available to businesses over the short to medium term.

Short-term borrowing can be defined as funds made available for short periods of time. Clearly, three month borrowing is short-term and, although there is no agreed definition, it is probably fair to say that money borrowed for periods of up to one year is short-term borrowing. Short-term financial needs, e.g. funds normally required to buy materials or pay wages, should be financed with short-term borrowing.

One year to five year borrowing is medium-term. Not all would agree on where the dividing line comes between short-term and medium-term finance, or between medium term and long term.

One analytical technique that is dealt with in the chapter is the lease versus buy decision.

16.1 Short-term bank borrowing

Companies in the UK rely more on short-term financing than do companies in other European countries. A survey in 1994 indicated that 70% of UK business relies heavily on overdrafts, compared with 37% in Germany relying on short-term funds. The trouble with short-term finance is that it is inflexible and unreliable. This is a particular problem for the medium to smaller sized company which can be dependent on this form of finance.

In contrast only 42% of UK companies had loans of over two years duration compared with 74% in Germany. Such percentages do vary over time but they are indicative of the financing pattern of UK companies.

Companies in the UK can borrow short-term funds from a number of different categories of banks and institutions. These include in the UK the London, Scotland and Northern Ireland clearing banks, the acceptance houses and other British banks, foreign-owned banks operating in the UK and the consortium banks. With deregulation they can also borrow in international finance markets and in domestic markets in foreign countries. In fact the London clearing banks are the main providers of short-term funds to UK business. These banks provide over 50% of the total of short-term loans taken out by the business sector.

There are many foreign-owned banks operating in London. One of the main reasons for their presence in the UK is to participate in the Eurobond and Eurocurrency markets. However, some of them are interested in lending sterling to UK companies.

Accepting houses

Accepting houses are a number of merchant banks who have a special role in the money market. They, in common with all other merchant banks, take deposits which are mainly short-term in character and make loans with a longer average maturity. They deal predominantly with the corporate and financial sectors and are mainly engaged in wholesale banking. Their chief banking role is as procurers of funds. They attract deposits, including certificates of deposit, in sterling and other currencies. Most of their advances are term loans, often for periods of five years or more. Their lending tends to be in the financial sector, but they also lend direct to companies in the manufacturing and service industries.

The select group of merchant banks known as accepting houses are all members of the Accepting Houses Committee. The largest and best known are Kleinwort Benson, Schroder Wagg, Hambros, Hill Samuel, Samuel Montague and Morgan Grenfell. Accepting houses, as the name suggests, take on acceptance business, which means guaranteeing bills of exchange. They charge a commission for accepting responsibility for payment. They in turn are able to discount the bills at the Bank of England or in the discount market.

Discount houses

The discount market is the market in which a variety of short-term financial instruments can be bought and sold. The market deals in UK treasury bills, local authority bills, commercial bills, certificates of deposit and other British government and local authority securities. The dealers make a market in these short-term financial instruments. They quote prices at which they are ready to deal, in a similar way to market makers in the Stock Exchange. The dealers include the discount houses, who make up the London Discount Market Association and the money trading departments of the major banks.

The discount houses play an important part in the UK monetary system. They accept an obligation to bid for all the treasury bills on offer each week, and to be able to finance these purchases they borrow at call or short notice from banks. They have access to the Bank of England as a lender of last resort.

The discount houses have been important in fostering the use of commercial bills as a means of providing short-term finance for industry. They also act as market-makers in the certificate of deposit market, holding a portfolio of such certificates for this purpose. Their role in this market is very important. A company and investor or bank who accepts a certificate of deposit knows that, should it be necessary, it is possible to sell the certificate to or through the market created by the discount houses.

16.2 Bank overdrafts

Short-term borrowing of the kind made available principally by the clearing banks in the form of overdrafts is very flexible. When the borrowed funds are no longer required they can quickly and easily be repaid. It is also comparatively cheap because the risks to the lender are less than on long-term loans, and loan interest is a tax deductible expense. The banks issue overdrafts with the right to call them in at short notice. Such advances are, in fact, legally repayable on demand, although enforcing the letter of the law on this point is often impractical since it would hardly be in the bank's interest to drive its client into a dangerous financial position if that looked likely. Normally the bank assures the borrower that he can rely on the overdraft not being recalled for a certain period of time, say one year or six months.

However, the borrower must be careful of what he does with the money he has obtained on these terms. If it is recalled, the company has to be able to repay, which would be awkward if the funds had been used to purchase fixed assets. In such a case the company might have to sell assets it had obtained for long-term use, or at least dispose of inventory in an unpalatable hurry. Any plans that involve an overdraft or other form of short-term loan should therefore refer closely to the company's cash flow analysis so that it is quite clear how long the funds will be needed and when they can be repaid.

When credit conditions are normal, the clearing banks are generally prepared to lend to a client whose business shows a healthy state of profitability and liquidity. Usually the bank will require fixed or floating charges on assets as security for advances, or, in the case of private companies, obtain a personal guarantee from the owners. The bank must be satisfied that the price of the goods or commodities offered as a guarantee is not so volatile that the security might easily lose its value. The banks often also want the right to appoint a receiver in the event that the company defaults on the repayment terms of the overdraft or exceeds the overdraft limit.

Banks prefer self-liquidating loans – those likely to be repaid automatically and reasonably quickly. These might include, for example, cash to finance a specified contract that will eventually result in a cash inflow for the company, or a loan to a trading company for the purchase of goods or commodities which could be offered as security. Firms which carry large stocks of materials may obtain a loan or an overdraft secured by pledging the stocks: the stocks are held in bond and all movements in and out are reported to the bank.

Another purpose for which short-term bank borrowing might typically be used is to iron out seasonal fluctuations in trade. The banks assist in providing temporary funds to finance production on the assumption that the goods or products will be sold in a later season. Agriculture is the obvious example of an industry where this type of borrowing is needed.

The cost to a company of bank borrowing depends on the creditworthiness of the borrower and upon the general level of interest rates in the market. The annual cost is usually between 2% and 5% above the bank's 'base rate', although 'blue chip' companies can borrow at a 'finer' rate.

The cost of borrowing should be calculated in real terms rather than money terms, i.e. after adjusting for inflation. All students of finance will appreciate through their private transactions that periods of high inflation make borrowing less painful; however, they make lending less profitable. The borrower obtains money that he can immediately use to make a purchase at today's prices. Later he pays back the monetary sum that he borrowed. The lender will receive the money back, but at the time that he receives it, as a result of the rise in the price of goods, he will not have enough money repaid to him to purchase the same good that the borrower acquired a few months earlier.

The real cost of borrowing was negative for a number of years in the 1970s. In 1971 the base rate plus the 'blue chip' lending margin was 6.86% and the annual rate of inflation was 9.42%, giving a real cost of −2.56%.

However, the 1980s saw a change with the 'real' cost of borrowing becoming positive and comparatively expensive. The annual rate of inflation fell, but a change in Government macro-economic policy to one of high interest rates pushed up the real cost. In mid-1988 the base rate of the London Clearing Banks was 9%, which meant that the interest charged on an overdraft to an average company was in the region of 12%. With the annual inflation rate at 5%, this gave a real cost of borrowing of +7.0%. By 1989 the base rate had almost doubled to 15%. This increase was the result of government policy which believed that high interest rates would lead to reduced consumer demand, which would in turn lead to reduced inflation. It was also thought that high interest rates would protect the value of the pound. One result, however, was a fall in the level of investment by companies. With inflation at 6%, the real cost of borrowing was 9% at base rate and 12% at the rate at which most companies had to borrow in the UK, which was considered to be very expensive.

In the 1980s the UK banks became somewhat careless in their approach to lending. Each bank was seeking growth; they were each endeavouring to increase their share of the lending market at the expense of other banks; and they were ignoring lessons from the past. The level of competition meant that their traditional cautious approach was sometimes forgotten. Bank credit officers were urged to lend funds and they were not always well trained in the latest techniques that the management of a company could use to window-dress their accounts. They ignored what would happen when (as there always is at some time) there was a recession.

The result was that the Third World country debt problems combined with a downturn in the economic performance of the industrialized countries (a recession) led to massive bad debts. Table 16.1 shows the total provisions for bad debts that three large UK banks needed to make. These results meant that the banks changed their attitude towards lending to companies.

Table 16.1 *Provision for bad debts from major banks*

	Operating profit before bad and doubtful debts		Charge for bad debts in developed economies	
	1991	*1990*	*1991*	*1990*
Barclays	2033	1964	1679	1072
Midland	948	743	903	703
Nat. West.	2027	1686	1986	1119

Source: Collett, N. and Schell, C. (1992) *Corporate Credit Analysis*.

Companies also changed their attitude towards banks. Research carried out in 1992 estimated that US, Japanese and Continental European banks had obtained a 25% share of the accounts of UK companies. Another finding of research at this time was that there was widespread dissatisfaction with banks over the level of fees and poor quality of service. We can assume that this perception of UK banks helped further the penetration of the foreign banks in the UK.

As a result of their bad debt experiences of the late 1980s and early 1990s the banks have changed a number of their policies.

Banks from the early 1990s tried to encourage borrowers to switch from the very popular short-term overdraft facility to term loans. They tried to do this by charging very high interest rates on unauthorized overdrawing on overdraft facilities. Other incentives used included relaxed collateral arrangements on term loans, and interest holidays on term loans.

The banks have been very successful with this policy of reducing the use of overdrafts. One bank reduced the total amount advanced on overdrafts in a year by 43%. The switch was to term loans, with some loans being of a medium- to long-term duration.

Bank borrowing is usually the cheapest form of finance for a company, the only exception being that under certain conditions finance may be available for export purposes at a cheaper rate. Interest on bank borrowing is charged only on the outstanding balance. Alternative sources of finance are usually for a fixed term, and interest has to be paid on the borrowed funds over the full term of the loan. With a bank overdraft any cash that flows into the company can easily be used to reduce the balance of the advance and so reduce the interest that has to be paid.

The normal type of bank advance made on short notice may be renewable through negotiation; much will depend of course, on the other demands for bank funds and on the continued security of the loan. If the overdraft is continually renewed, that is turned over from period to period, then the bank is in effect providing medium- or even long-term finance. Judging from the accounts of certain companies, the use of bank borrowing as a continuing source of finance is not an uncommon phenomenon; however, the risk attached to this policy is always that the bank may decide to recall, which would force the company to seek new finance at what may well be an inconvenient time.

To illustrate the factors to be taken into account when a loan application is being considered, we shall show one approach to answering an examination question on this subject. The question is adopted from one set for the examinations of the Chartered Association of Certified Accountants.

Example 16.1

The summarized balance sheet of MacSuit and Coat Ltd, together with extracts from its revenue account for the year ended 31 March 1993 are given below.

This small company manufactures clothing and is managed by two young capable energetic directors with a good knowledge and experience of the trade. They have made loans to the company to the full extent of their personal resources and currently require funds to finance a large contract worth £60 000 from reputable first-class buyers for a quantity of suits. They have applied to their banks for an unsecured overdraft limit of £15 000 to finance the contract. They have offered the bank manager their personal guarantees and postponement of their own loans. They do not wish to offer a secured debenture as they feel that this would precipitate action from the company's creditors.

You are employed by the bank in its regional office as the accountant advisor to bank managers in the region in respect of requests such as this. Write a report to the bank manager analysing the information available to you, in the context of the request made, and advising him of the risk to the bank in granting the overdraft.

MacSuit and Coat Limited

Balance sheet as at 31 March 1993

Share capital – ordinary shares of £1 fully paid		£3 000
Profit and loss account		£500
		£3 500
Loans by directors		£5 500
Current liabilities		
Accrued expenses	£5 000	
Trade creditors	£55 000	
		£60 000
		£69 000
Fixed assets		
Plant and machinery (cost *less* depreciation)		£10 500
Motor vehicles (cost *less* depreciation)		£1 500
Goodwill		£1 800
		£13 800
Current assets		
Cash at bank	£11 800	
Trade debtors	£17 000	
Stocks and work in progress	£23 500	
Prepayments	£2 000	
Preliminary expenses	£900	
		£55 200
		£69 000

Extracts from the profit and loss account for the year ended 31 March 1993

Sales £230 000	Purchases of stock	£140 000

Profit for the year (after all expenses including those below)	£4 550
Provision for corporation tax	Nil
Provision for depreciation of fixed assets	£1 800
Provision for directors' remuneration	£6 400

Suggested solution

The points that might be brought out in the answer include the fact that the current ratio and the liquidity ratio show dangerous signs of overtrading. The trade creditors figure is high, particularly in relation to the debtors figure; the company is clearly giving very much more credit than it is taking. The owners' capital is very small, particularly if the intangible assets, goodwill and preliminary expenses are taken out of the balance sheet. The argument for doing this is that these assets could not be realized.

The amount that the company owes shows that it has overextended its resources. The loans by the directors and their equity stake finance only a small proportion of the assets. The fact that the company has a cash balance at the bank is largely due to the credit that is being taken from suppliers. The company is vulnerable and would have to come to an end if the creditors asked to be paid quickly.

The profit for the year is good in relation to the money invested in the business. However, the fact that no corporation tax was payable last year indicates that the company was then unprofitable. The profit and loss account balance brought forward also suggests lack of profitability in earlier years.

If the bank were to grant an overdraft it would be taking a considerable risk. The company has few resources of its own and its survival depends on the actions of its creditors. The risk might be thought worth taking if the proposed contract is very profitable. The reputation of the buyer gives strength to the overdraft application. The value of the personal guarantees would need to be examined.

The lending decision

Following on from Example 16.1 we will now look in a little more detail at the factors a bank takes into account when deciding whether or not to make a loan available to a company. There are qualitative factors the banker will take into account as well as quantitative. First there are some general issues to be considered:

1. How much is to be borrowed, and for how long?
2. What is the purpose of the advance?
3. **Source of repayment**   This depends on the bank's approach to lending, which may be, on the one hand, based on so-called 'liquidation analysis' and on the other hand on 'going concern analysis'. The former, in its simplest form, values a company on what it would be worth in liquidation whereas the latter is trying to establish the long-term financial strength of the firm.
4. **Creditworthiness**   This is the critical point of the whole procedure. The bank's lending officers will, in order to form a picture of clients' creditworthiness, rely on several sources of information and will attach varying degrees of importance to them.
5. **Borrower's own contribution**   Normally the borrower is expected to put some money in the project or the venture. This is an indicator of the borrower's confidence in the future success of the plan.
6. **What security is being offered?**   In most cases bank advances are not totally secured. Many loans approved are based purely on the creditworthiness of the borrower. The purpose of asking for some sort of security is of course to provide the

bank with an asset which can produce the funds with which to repay the advance should the customer fail to do so. A problem is that in the last resort the value of any security can be massively discounted when liquidation arises. An example is in the late 1980s recession in the UK where the values of property dropped between 25% and 50%.

Some bankers like to employ a check-list approach to lending. One form of classification which has been advocated is the four Cs of credit which later became seven Cs [1]. These include:

- character
- capacity
- capital
- conditions
- customer relationships
- competition
- collateral

These are proposed as the factors to be looked at by a lending officer. However many bankers have commented that they are not in favour of these kinds of mnemonics. They tend to consider them as 'unwieldy tick-lists which would lead to a superficial approach to their job'. A list which was produced in the 1930s had temperance as a key factor to consider!

A more financial statement orientated approach is urged by many. The Committee of London Clearing Bankers [2] suggested that the financial analysis should be conducted following two different approaches: the liquidation approach and the going-concern approach. According to the former, the accounting value of the company's assets is expected to exceed by a decent margin the value of the liabilities. This is sometimes known as asset-based lending. The going-concern approach, on the other hand, focuses on the analysis of the company's future viability, which is reflected ultimately in the ability to generate profits and cash. If this is the case, the financial statements (in particular the cash-flow statement) are used as a guide in order to form views about a company's future performance.

The Committee of London Clearing Bankers expressed the view that both approaches must be used when assessing creditworthiness but that the going concern should take precedence over the liquidation approach. However, the evidence suggests that UK bankers are much closer to the pure liquidation approach.

One explanation for such a preference may lie in the historical role that banks have played in the development of the UK economy and its centralized structure. In UK, we do not find the German-style in-house bank involvement at board level which can provide better control and monitoring for the banks. Thus, secured lending has seemed to be the only safe way to proceed, especially lending to small businesses. In such cases the question 'will the profits generated be sufficient to meet the repayments?' is not always the major question considered.

A key factor in lending decisions is the cash-flow position. A company's projected statements and the historical pattern of its cash flows should be analysed. The cash-flow statement became a requirement in financial statement reporting in 1988 in the US and replaced the sources and applications of funds statement in the UK in January 1992. Such cash statements are perceived to be one of the most useful tools in corporate credit analysis used not only by banks but by various types of analysts. As Terry Smith wrote, 'profits are someone's opinion whereas cash is a fact . . . the lack of sufficient cash is what makes businesses fail not lack of profits' [3].

The underlying principle behind the cash-flow analysis is the perception of the company as a going concern. Cash-flow lending not only recognizes the fact that a company's ability to repay the loans is based on its cash inflows but also that the worth of a business's assets is ultimately based on their future ability to produce cash.

Credit rating systems

Increasingly banks are using credit scoring systems in deciding on business loans. It is argued that it reduces the human factor which involves subjectivity. The supporters of the new technology claim that it can help not only with the pure lending decisions but also offers administrative advantages and portfolio control over loan officers. As far as the administrative advantages are concerned it means banks can use and allocate their human resources more efficiently. For example, the use of on-line expert systems can be used as substitutes for senior officers' involvement in the preliminary stages of credit decisions which may be done by less experienced officers. Credit assessment systems may help in getting rid of the paperwork involved in such decisions and in setting credit authorization criteria.

The latest feature of these systems is their interactive ability as well as the fact that they try to capture the qualitative dimension of the lending decision. Much of the time they are designed to engage in a question-and-answer session with the user. The system may ask crucial questions like: is the company in a growth industry? To this question the loan officer can answer with various degrees of certainty; even vagueness and uncertainty are accepted. The most recent developments in the field of artificial intelligence are the so-called neural networks. These are systems with built-in logic that is capable of learning new things and thus rebuilding score cards as conditions change.

An expert system developed by NEC for Sumitomo Bank uses probability theory and provides business diagnostics. It analyses companies' performance in terms of composition of finance, sales ability, administrative skills and results obtained by management [4].

These expert systems look at patterns by taking into consideration the most frequent mistakes discovered by the analysis of the previous lending decisions and as a result it may express the degree of certainty to be attached to loans.

The way in which artificial intelligence could look at a profit and loss account, for example, would be to examine up to three years of financial statements and look at items like interest pay-out and profit before taxes as well as a number of ratios. A Japanese bank (Mitsui) has built a scoring system in order to analyse balance sheets using a public database as well as the bank's own database. This system examines the following areas:

- safety, focusing on the company's own capital ratio, fixed assets and acid test;
- profitability, gross capital profit and sales/profitability ratio;
- company's size, yearly business and number of employees;
- liquidity, reflecting cash-flow collection period and cash deposit ratio;
- future prospectives, looking at the average growth in the last five years, and average capital growth over the same period; and
- productivity, calculating sales per employee and similar criteria.

Similar systems have been adopted by UK banks. Midland Bank uses a credit assessment system (CAS) in its 50 corporate banking centres. This system analyses the customer's balance sheet, works out ratios and gives the customer a credit score ranging from 0 to 100.

The role of the new technology may be questionable on a number of counts. All these models mainly base their 'judgement' upon financial ratios or combinations of financial ratios and the 'quantifiable' elements of qualitative information. This approach may turn out to be extremely dangerous for the small and medium business sector.

The recent recession in the UK showed that little reliance could be placed on the figures published by a number of big corporations. The underpinning theories behind these expert systems are the numerous failure prediction models which have not proved their value yet and many think never will. The problems with this mechanistic approach are more acute with small businesses, because of the weakness of the financial reports and because of the nature of the relationships between the lending bankers and the small businesses.

16.3 Revolving underwriting facility

With the revolving underwriting facility (RUF), rather than offer a borrower a loan over a set period of years, a bank will underwrite the borrower's access to funds at a specified rate in the short-term commercial paper market throughout an agreed period. This type of arrangement is only likely to be available to large companies. Although the borrower may be well known to its lead bank (the underwriter) and even to the first purchaser of the notes, the notes will be sold in the secondary market and further purchasers may not be familiar with the corporate name or its rating. It is the name of the underwriting bank that helps sell the security.

During the period of the arrangement the borrower will issue a successive series of short-dated promissory notes up to the total of the facility. These notes will bear interest at a rate agreed at the outset, probably linked to the London interbank offer rate (LIBOR). At each new issue the interest rate is likely to be different, depending on movements in LIBOR. However, the spread, again agreed at the outset, will remain constant. The bank undertakes to sell the notes in the market at a price fixed by the RUF agreement and underwrites the issues by agreeing to purchase the instruments themselves should the market fail to take them up. In many respects this is similar to the acceptance credit tender panels which are gaining popularity among borrowers. What the banks are doing under a RUF is not giving an undertaking to lend funds themselves but merely guaranteeing the borrower's credit rating and in doing so ensuring that the company will be able to sell the notes and so obtain finance.

The bank offering the RUF is paid an underwriting fee and commission on the sale of the notes. In theory both the bank and the borrower benefit from this arrangement: the borrower is provided with direct access to finance, and the bank is supporting a customer without necessarily reducing its own liquidity. It is part of the move to securitization.

16.4 Medium-term bank borrowing

Traditionally, most bank advances to companies have been of a short-term nature, usually overdraft arrangements. This tradition in the UK goes back many decades. Banks saw themselves supporting companies in their trading transactions, but not as providers of long-term capital.

In the 1970s the position changed. The clearing banks started to make contractual medium-term loans. Now all the major banks offer medium-term loans. The loans are usually secured by a fixed or floating charge on the company. In addition, borrowers often have to covenant to maintain a prescribed level of interest cover and possibly current assets cover.

The interest charge is usually variable at between 2% and 5% above the bank's base rate. Some of the schemes offer fixed interest rates, but because in such circumstances the risks to the banks are greater, the rate charged is higher, in the region of 4%–6% above the bank's base rate. An arrangement fee often has to be paid to the bank, which can be as high as 1.5% of the amount borrowed.

Many of the bank loan schemes that are offered can be taken out not just for medium periods of time but also for long periods. For example, the National Westminster Business Development Loan scheme can be for terms of from one to twenty years. The scheme covers working capital loans which would be for medium periods of time and fixed asset loans which would be for longer periods. The other British banks and the foreign-owned banks also provide medium-term loans.

In addition, the banks offer a range of business start-up loans and venture loans. These will be dealt with in Chapter 27.

Fixed-term lending by the clearing banks has grown in importance both to borrowers and as a proportion of the banks' total advances. It is now a welcomed source of finance to companies. These term loans can either be repayable in a lump sum at the end of the loan period or repayable in periodic instalments. The borrower can negotiate with the bank to obtain the terms best suited to the expected future cash flow. It is possible to arrange 'rest' periods during which time only the interest on the loan is payable. The capital repayments by instalments do not begin until the rest period ends. This type of rest period followed by repayment by instalments is more common than the method of repayment by a single lump sum at the end of the term.

16.5 Bills of exchange

A post-dated cheque is a simple example of a bill of exchange. When a cheque signed on 1 January is dated 1 April or 1 July, the signatory is asking his bank to pay the prescribed amount in three or six months' time. The signatory, a buying company, can send this cheque to a supplier who will dispatch goods; the supplier is in fact giving three or six months' credit, and can choose either to retain the cheque and present it himself for payment on the due date, or to sell it to a bank or discount house. With a commercial bill of exchange, however, the supplier prepares the bill. A bill is defined as 'an unconditional order in writing, addressed by one person to another, signed by the person giving it, requiring the person to whom it is addressed to pay on demand, or at a fixed or determinable future time, a sum certain in money to or to the order of a specified person, or to bearer' (Bills of Exchange Act 1882, section 3).

Bills of exchange are now used mainly in connection with overseas shipments. The seller of the goods can obtain cash immediately after the goods are dispatched, either because the bill has an early maturity date or because he discounts the bill. The buyer of the goods can delay payment of the bill, which is particularly important with overseas orders because he may have to wait some time before receiving the goods. The bill of exchange therefore helps both buyer and seller with their finance, which is valuable for all transactions but is of added importance if the goods are a long time in transit and neither party has possession of them.

The cost of funds provided by a bill of exchange depends upon the rate at which the bill is discounted. If the seller of the goods presents the bill to a bank, which buys it at a discount rate of 2%, a £100 bill payable in three months' time would have a cost of 2/98 = 2.04%. The seller has had to surrender £2 to receive £98. This is equivalent to an annual interest rate of $(1.0204)^4 - 1 = 8.4\%$.

Bills cover periods ranging from 60 to 180 days, but are usually for 90 days. They are usually for over £75 000 in value. The discounts charged on a 90 day bill would be based on the three month interbank rate, and usually are at a rate somewhere between 1.5% and 4% above this interbank rate. The actual discount rate would depend upon the risks involved, mainly the creditworthiness of the seller and buyer. If credit insurance is arranged, it results in a 'finer' discount rate.

16.6 Acceptance credits

An acceptance credit has much in common with a bill of exchange. To obtain finance under this type of arrangement a company draws a bill of exchange on a bank. The bank accepts the bill, thereby promising to pay out the amount of the bill at some specified future date. The bill itself is then worth something as the holder is to receive a sum of money at a future date. This bill can then be sold either at once or when the funds are needed. It is sold in the money market to, say, the discount houses. It is similar to an ordinary bill of exchange between two companies, but now one of the parties is a bank. A bill bearing a reputable bank's name can be sold in the money markets at a lower discount rate than a bill bearing the name of a medium- or small-sized company because of the reduced risk.

Merchant banks were the first to offer this sort of finance. They would sign bills promising to pay a sum of money to the holder of the bill at some future date. These credits (bills) were then sold in the market so that the money could be made available at once to the company who was the other party to the bill. When the date mentioned in the bill arrived, say one year after issue, the company would pay the issuing bank the value of the bill and the bank would pay the current holder of the bill its face value. The leading merchant banks still dominate this field, but other banks, including the clearing banks, now also offer acceptance credits. Sometimes a syndicate of banks issues the credit.

Of course, the company drawing the bill has to be able to satisfy the bank providing the credit that their money is safe both from the point of view of capital repayment and interest payments. It is unlikely, therefore, that a company that has been unable to satisfy its own bankers that it is safe for a loan will be able to satisfy another bank or a syndicate of bankers that it is safe to make available a certain level of credit. The point about acceptance credits that is particularly interesting is that the company can be sure that the credit will be made available for a longer period than the usual bank overdraft. This type of syndicated credit is quite common in Germany.

The company does not have to discount the bill immediately it is issued; it can retain it and use it as part of its credit facilities. From the company's point of view these acceptance credits are similar in nature to a medium-term overdraft with either a fixed or a variable rate of interest. The bank signing the bill is helping to make available to the company a certain level of credit. The company can then use these funds as it requires them, up to the agreed maximum. The length of period over which the credit is made available depends on negotiations, but can be as long as five years. From the company's point of view it represents an alternative source of finance; money is being obtained from a source other than the company's banker.

Acceptance credits can be cheaper than overdrafts. The acceptance rate moves in the same direction as the base interest rate. The rate is fixed on the acceptance credit for three months or longer, and so a company can find this form of finance cheaper than an overdraft when interest rates are rising. The overdraft rates will adjust more quickly to changes in base rates.

Acceptance credits are usually for relatively large values, in excess of £250 000. Of course, banks will be careful to set an upper limit for acceptance credits from a company and will wish to be sure that the company will have adequate funds available for immediate repayment on the maturity of the credit. Some banks will charge a commitment fee if they have agreed to allow a company to draw credits up to a certain limit. This applies if the company has not obtained credits up to the agreed limit and is chargeable on the undrawn balance.

Acceptance credit facilities have proved to be very popular. Companies have found that they can often borrow more cheaply in the money market, for periods of from one month to six months, through using acceptance credits than through a traditional bank overdraft. Of course, the company is locked into a fixed interest rate for the period of the credit rather than the variable interest rate applying to overdrafts.

Certain of the banks have offered their favoured clients the possibility of using acceptance credits on a roll-over basis as an alternative to taking out a term loan. The bank would agree to sign a bill to make, say, £1 million available to Company X in six months' time. Company X could then take this bill to a discount house who would immediately provide the money. The company would receive the face value of the credit less the discount charged. At the end of the period the company would repay the face value via the bank. The roll-over element means that the bank would guarantee that when the first bill had been repaid they would accept another bill for the same amount for a further period.

Bank borrowing versus capital markets borrowing

Large companies have direct access to borrowing in the capital market. They have become less dependent on borrowing direct from a bank. Medium-term notes and floating-rate notes have already been discussed in the chapter on debt. The banks have responded to the competition by offering very competitively priced loans to the large businesses. This has been to some extent at the cost of smaller and medium sized firms. As will be discussed in the chapter on the smaller business, the cost of bank borrowing to this sector has been relatively high, particularly in the 1980s. Due to fierce competition between the banks, the large firms have faced very competitive loan supply conditions. The rates of interest charged on large firms' loans have been very close to base rates. In some cases competition was so intense that rates as fine as one-16th over LIBOR were negotiated with an average under 1% above base rate. Studies carried out in different areas of England found evidence of this. For example, in the North of England 'the rate charged for the well capitalised or blue chip companies was around 1 per cent above national base rates namely a cost of finance which is competitive with the central capital markets' [5]. However, firms which were relatively less well capitalized were charged at approximately 3% and in some cases 4% above the base rate. Moreover, companies with relatively low capital base and a fluctuating track record would be charged in excess of 4%.

A report prepared for the Chancellor of the Exchequer by the Bank of England into bank lending policies to the small business illustrated the difficulties faced by the smaller business [6].

The data provided to the Bank of England by the seven banks that participated in the survey showed an interesting shift over two years. The distribution of loans in a series of margin bands are presented in Tables 16.2 and 16.3. We can clearly see that the vast majority of the small firms lay within the 2% to 4% margin band. However, between 1991 and 1992 there is a noticeable shift in the higher turnover group (£1–10 million). It is clear that 21% of the high turnover group were moved by the banks from the 0–2% cost band to the 2–4% band in 1992. This evidence could justify to some extent the allegations made by the small and medium size firms that the cuts in the interest rates that were taking place at the time were not passed on to them and that they were being asked to pay for the banks' worsening profit margins.

Table 16.2 *Average margins charged over base rate* (%)

	Turnover <£1 million	Turnover £1–10 millions
November 1992	3.0 to 4.7	2.3 to 2.9

Source: Bank of England 1993.

Table 16.3 *Proportion of lending in cost margin bands* (per cent)

	Turnover <£1 million		Turnover £1–10 million	
	June 1991	Nov. 1992	June 1991	Nov. 1992
Margin bands (%)				
0–2	21	20	56	35
2–4	59	61	40	61
4–6	16	16	3	3
6–8	4	3	1	1
>8	—	—	—	—

Source: Bank of England 1993.

Disintermediation

This clumsy word means cutting out the role of financial intermediaries. The word refers to the process of companies lending to and borrowing from other companies. A company with surplus cash will lend to another company. This cuts out the bank or other financial intermediary. Clearly it means the borrowing rates will be less than if a bank was involved because the costs of the intermediary have been avoided.

Rather than a simple loan, it is often a financial security that is traded. The one company (usually a well-known company) that wishes to obtain finance now will issue a promissory note, in which it promises to pay a certain sum of money at a specified future date. This note is then sold at a discount in the market place. It could be purchased by another (non-financial) company. This is known as 'commercial paper'. The paper might be resold a number of times during its life. It is usually used for short-term borrowing. At the maturity of the note the issuing company pays its face value to whoever is the holder at that moment.

16.7 Trade credit

One of the most important forms of short-term finance in the economy is the trade credit extended by one company to another on the purchase and sale of goods and equipment.

To receive goods and delay payment of the account is a recognized form of short-term financing: the goods can be used to provide returns or benefits throughout the period that elapses before the bill has to be settled. For the receiving company this is similar to buying goods with a bank overdraft, except that an overdraft carries the obvious interest charge. When the finance is provided by another company, the cost is not so obvious.

If, however, a cash discount is offered to encourage early payment and the receiving company does not take advantage of this, then there is a clear cost. Assume that a 1% cash discount is offered for payment within 30 days. The cost of capital for credit taken for these 30 days is

$$\frac{1\%}{100\% - 1\%} = \frac{1}{99} = 1.01\%$$

Taking such credit for 30 days is the equivalent to an annual interest rate of $(1.01)^{12} - 1 = 12.7\%$.

Trade credit is not necessarily a cheap source of finance. On occasions, trade credit is used because the buyer is not aware of the real costs involved – if he were, he might turn to alternative sources to finance trade. However, other forms of finance are not always available, and for a company that has borrowed as much as possible trade credit may be the only choice left. This is an important source of funds for many small companies.

It would be pardonable to assume that if no cash discount is offered for prompt payment, the cost of finance from this source is zero. For better or worse, a *carte blanche* for abusing the system is a rare commodity: if a buyer persists in delaying to pay his accounts, the supplier may in the end prefer not to deal with them. The subject of credit management is dealt with in Chapter 22.

At one time large companies often played an important role as informal benefactors by allowing small companies periods of credit. This has changed. Certain large companies now have a notorious reputation among small firms for taking a long time to pay as creditors but demanding ruthlessly prompt payment when the position is reversed.

A company which provides credit to another is in fact putting itself in the position of a banker whose advance takes the form not of cash but of goods for which payment will be deferred. This use of trade credit between companies is extremely important from both an industrial and a national point of view.

Advantages of trade credit

When the customer's creditworthiness is well established, trade credit becomes a convenient informal affair, and is indeed a normal part of business in most industries. The offer of trade credit by a seller is part of the terms of sale – a sales promotion device by which he hopes to attract business. The amount of credit offered will depend on the risks associated with the customer. In certain cases, the seller may agree to sell only a 'safe' quantity of goods.

Trade credit is, however, double-edged. It is both a selling device used to attract customers and a desirable source of funds, and as such could conceivably cause a company both profit and loss simultaneously. In the role of buyer, a company would want to obtain as much credit as possible without losing too much discount or goodwill; as seller, it would prefer its customers not to take too long over paying their accounts.

For example, if a company purchases £120 000 of goods during a year and takes on average 45 days to pay, its creditors figure will average approximately £15 000; if it sells £240 000 of goods during a year and collects, on average, in 90 days, its debtors figures will be £60 000. The company is extending net credit of £45 000. The company would find it desirable to minimize its debtors and maximize its creditors (as long as the costs do not exceed those attached to other forms of capital). Seen in terms of industry as a whole, this is a paradoxical situation. Usually it is the smaller and fast-growing firms that have the greatest need for trade credit.

It is possible for an outsider to calculate the collection period of a company and so find out how quickly the company is collecting its debts. However, it is not possible to calculate the period of credit that the company is taking on its purchases. Neither the purchases figure nor the amount of the creditors figure that relates to goods purchased is shown in the accounts. If the cost of goods sold is not shown as a separate figure it can be obtained by deducting trading profit from the sales, but how much of this relates to purchases cannot be ascertained. Often the creditors figure includes accrued expenses – wages that still have to be paid, for example. The financial management, if it is worth its salt, will know the importance of controlling the level of net credit, but an outsider – such as one of the owners of the company – will not find proof of that fact in the annual accounts.

Terms of credit

Terms of credit vary considerably from industry to industry. Theoretically, four main factors determine the length of credit allowed.

1. **The economic nature of the product**: products with a high sales turnover are sold on short credit terms. If the seller is relying on a low profit margin and a high sales turnover, he cannot afford to offer customers a long time to pay.
2. **The financial circumstances of the seller**: if the seller's liquidity position is weak he will find it difficult to allow very much credit and will prefer an early cash settlement. (If credit terms are being used as a sales promotion device by the seller's competitors, he may have to allow credit, and try to improve his liquidity by some other method.)
3. **The financial position of buyer**: if the buyer is in a weak liquidity position he may have to take a long period in which to pay. The seller may not wish to deal with customers of this kind, but if he is prepared to take the risk so as to obtain the sale, he will have to grant credit.
4. **Cash discounts**: when cash discounts are taken into account, the cost of trade credit can be surprisingly high. The higher the cash discount being offered the smaller is the period of trade credit likely to be taken.

In many industries, credit terms are recommended by trade associations. In others, established custom defines the normally accepted conditions. In some industries where there is a long time lag between the purchase of materials or commodities and the sale of the finished product, the suppliers may be prepared to give long-term credit. Firms in the engineering industries have developed ways of assisting each other. One common method is the 'free issue of materials' system, whereby the manufacturer is provided with free materials that have already been bought by the eventual purchaser of the finished product. When the product is completed the eventual purchaser then has to pay the additional value-added costs of the manufacturer.

Another system permits small engineering firms to obtain assistance from a customer towards the costs of tooling for special contracts. Arrangements similar to this are often part of government contracts. An important issue always likely to arise in agreements of this kind concerns the ownership of the tools; if they belong to the customer, he is in a position to exert considerable pressure over the manufacturer.

Certain large manufacturers which sell through authorized agents might well offer long credit or loan terms to the agents. This enables the agent to purchase the materials or products from the manufacturer who is advancing the credit or loan. The manufacturer benefits from this arrangement in that his products are made more readily available to the public, for if an agent is in liquidity difficulties the manufacturer also has to suffer through his products not being well displayed or stocked. This type of financial assistance is common in certain sectors of the motor trade, in particular petrol stations, and in the sale of spare parts and accessories.

The motor trade also furnishes plenty of examples of trade credit in reverse, with car manufacturers insisting on early payment or even payment in advance from their distributors. This means that the distributors have to command large financial resources in order to pay promptly for the cars, which must then be displayed, sold and eventually paid for before the cash cycle is complete.

16.8 Factoring

Factoring involves raising funds on the security of the company's debts, so that cash is received earlier than if the company waited for the debtors to pay. Basically most factors offer three services:

1. sales ledger accounting, dispatching invoices and making sure the bills are paid;
2. credit management, including guarantees against bad debts;
3. the provision of finance, advancing clients up to 80% of the value of the debts that they are collecting.

The client need not use all these services; it can choose whichever it requires.

Sales ledger administration

The factor providing sales ledger administration will take on responsibility for the sales accounting records, credit control and the collection of the debts. It is claimed that, with his experience, the factor will be able to obtain payment from customers more quickly than if the company were to be responsible for the collection.

The cost of this administrative service is a fee based on the total value of debts assigned to the factor. The fee is usually between 1% and 3%. It is based on the amount of work that needs to be carried out.

Credit management/insurance

For a fee the factor can provide up to 100% protection against non-payment on approved sales. Of course, the factor has to decide whether the debt is worth covering. The credit standing of the company's individual customers will be analysed carefully before a guarantee can be obtained.

Provision of finance

Provision of finance is the main reason why companies use the service of factors. For a small fast-growing company a factor provides a good means of releasing funds tied up in debtors. It provides a good source of working capital.

Factors will provide finance if required, thus improving a company's liquidity position, but this finance is not cheap, and since bank borrowing is both flexible and less expensive, any company in liquidity difficulties should approach a bank first. However, factoring can be particularly useful when a company has exhausted its overdraft and is not yet in a position to raise new equity.

Factors assess every client and, in fact, turn down many applicants. They do not see themselves as the last financial resort for companies in difficulties; they are not interested in bad companies. The implications for a company when it obtains funds through factoring are not similar in all respects to the implications of normal borrowing. The charges do not have to be registered, and the client's borrowing ratios are not affected.

The factor usually allows 80% of the value of debts to be borrowed when the invoice is despatched to the customer. The remaining 20%, less charges, will be paid either after a specified period or when the invoice is paid by the customer. The charge is based on the amounts borrowed at a particular time, with the interest rate 2%–5% above base rate.

Confidential invoice factoring

In the conventional factoring procedure the factor sends a statement to the customer who purchased goods from the factor's client, and the customer repays the factor. With **confidential** invoice factoring, the customer is unaware that a factor has intervened in the transaction. No third party is introduced into the buyer–seller relationship. The client receives an advance on the copy invoices he sends to the factor, but he is still responsible for collecting the debt. He is now acting as an agent for the factor; he sends the invoice to the purchaser, collects the debt and then forwards the receipts, to the extent of the advance, to the factor.

The maximum amount which can be raised by a company through factoring depends on its annual turnover and its average collection period for debts. If it takes on average 90 days to collect a debt, then on any one day approximately a quarter of the annual turnover will be debtors. A factor will normally advance up to 80% of this debtors figure, or, to put it another way, as much as 20% of the annual turnover of the company could be made available in the form of cash.

The cost of this confidential invoicing depends, of course, on the cost of money at the time and on the standing of both the borrower and the borrower's customers. It is usually based on a percentage per month charged on the money used for as long as the debt remains outstanding. Of course, the factor has to cover the cost of his borrowing and administrative costs, and to earn a suitable profit for the risks he is taking.

16.9 Invoice discounting and credit insurance

Invoice discounting is purely a financial arrangement which benefits the liquidity position of the user. Again, it is designed to overcome the problem of tying up working capital in book debts.

A company can convert an invoice into cash through specialized finance companies. Either separate invoices or a proportion of a company's book debts can be discounted, although the full face value of the invoice is not usually advanced. The company makes an offer to the finance house by sending it the respective invoices and agreeing to guarantee payment of any debts that are purchased. If the finance house accepts the offer, it makes an immediate first payment of about 75% of the value of the invoices. The company then accepts as collateral security a bill of exchange for this 75%, which means that at a specified future date, say after 90 days, the loan must be repaid. The company is responsible for collecting the debt and for returning the amount advanced, whether the debt is collected or not.

The cost of this service depends upon the risks and administrative costs involved; it includes an interest charge on the amount advanced plus a service charge. The cost is not cheap. For invoice discounting, the cost of funds advanced can be between 3% and 6% above the base rate. A potential borrower offering a book debt as security will find that any lending institution – bank, factor or finance house – will be more willing to make the advance if the debt is insured. The procedure is familiar enough: the client pays a premium to the insurance company in return for the amount of the invoice . The cost of the insurance will depend on the amounts involved and the risks attached to the debt.

16.10 Deferred tax payments

Another source of short-term funds similar in character to trade credit is the credit supplied by the tax authorities. This is created by the interval that elapses between the earning of the profits by the company and the payment of the taxes due on them.

As long as the company continues to earn stable or expanding profits, tax payment deferred in this way comprises a virtually permanent source of finance. The tax bill for one year is paid out of next year's profits. Consequently, although a part of any year's profits will be reserved for tax payment purposes, these funds do not have to be relinquished to the tax authorities immediately and so can be used by the company to earn profits. The company must ensure, however, that when the time for payment arises it has liquid resources available.

16.11 Government guaranteed loans

The government guaranteed loans scheme was established by the UK Government in 1981 to encourage bankers to lend money to small- to medium-sized businesses which had exhausted all the normal channels for obtaining finance, and to which the banker might have been prepared to lend but for the lack of security and/or track record.

Under this scheme, the Government guarantees the banker that in the event that the customer is unable to repay the loan, the Government will pay the banker 70% of the money outstanding. For his part, the banker may not take any personal security from the borrower. However, the borrower is expected to pledge business assets as security for the loan.

Loans may be for a period up to seven years with the possibility of a capital repayment holiday. Interest rates are arranged by the lending banker and the Government makes a 3% charge for the guarantee, which is a percentage of the amount of the loan outstanding. There is a maximum amount which can be borrowed under this scheme.

There have been a number of criticisms of the scheme. The percentage of bad debts has been high because, it is said, the banks only take the riskier projects to the Government scheme. Safer borrowing proposals are carried by the bank.

The scheme is also criticized by borrowers because the interest rate charges are high. In addition to the bank's normal charge above base rate there is the high guarantee charge. Similar schemes have existed for many years in other leading industrial countries. The scheme helps new and small businesses to obtain finance. It is discussed further in Chapter 27 on small business finance.

16.12 Merchant banks

Merchant banks (which include acceptance houses) have historically been more associated with the provision of risk 'venture' capital than have the clearing banks. However, the amount of money that the merchant banks have available to invest compared with the resources of the clearing banks is comparatively small. It is often commented in the UK that there has not been sufficient finance available in the venture capital market.

The merchant banks are selective when it comes to making investments. Their lending policies vary enormously from one bank to another. Many of the large merchant banks take the view that the provision of finance of less than £250 000 is not worth bothering with. It is reported that, of the total number of loans of the largest merchant banks, only about 25% are to small firms. However, there are smaller merchant banks that are willing to invest smaller amounts of money. There are those who would be willing to invest in the region of £50 000. In order to make large sums of money, say £3 million or more, available to a company, merchant banks sometimes combine together to form a syndicate.

It is hard to define the typical investment that they will undertake. At one time they would only provide loans if they could obtain a minority equity stake, and the package was usually composed of equity funds and loan money. Now, the bank is not usually looking for a permanent stake in the company but rather a profitable investment, and it is likely that it will attempt to dispose of its equity investment in a company five or so years after making the investment. The bank hopes to obtain its return through capital appreciation over this period. If a suitable return within this period is not possible, the bank may not be interested in longer-term investment. When the bank thinks that it is time to dispose of the shares, the existing owners of the company will, in most cases, be given the chance to buy them before they are offered to outsiders. This is referred to as the exit route.

The factors that the banks take into account when deciding on whether or not to invest in a company are the management of the company, the business it is in and the case that is being made for finance. It is difficult to judge the quality of management, and one important guide is past achievement. The bank will want to see the financial accounts for the last few years. Of course, this makes it more difficult for new businesses to attract funds than for those with a proven record. The banker will also be concerned with the already existing financial commitment of the owners of the business. If they have backed their ideas with their own money, it will give a good impression. As a general rule, the banks will consider lending an amount equal to the amount of the existing shareholders' funds already invested or retained in the business. Therefore it is easier for those with financial resources to obtain backing for their ideas than for those with only limited funds. Experience is another important factor, which unfortunately works against start up situations.

The financial case must be well presented, showing, amongst other things, the expected future profits and cash flow of the business in the medium- and long-term plans. It is now accepted that the chance of any one set of forecasts being accurate is very remote, and so it is often worth while preparing more than one set of estimates, based for example on more optimistic or pessimistic assumptions than the most likely outcome. It can be impressive to present profit and cash flow forecasts based on pessimistic assumptions about, say, competition and inflation, and still be able to show the investor that there is little risk attached to his future income and capital repayment. It must be remembered that bankers are financial people and although the most impressive engineering plans and proposals may be presented, at some stage the banker will wish to see the proposals expressed in the type of financial terms with which he is familiar.

A complaint sometimes made about merchant banks is that they are more interested in the security offered on their investment than on the strength of the argument for future profitability. They will look for guarantees and assets that can be pledged as security for the loans. They will naturally be interested in the details of any other borrowing of the company and of its existing banking arrangements.

The 3Is

The Industrial and Commercial Finance Corporation (ICFC) was set up in the UK in 1945 specifically to assist the smaller company seeking loan and equity capital. Undoubtedly ICFC was successful. In 1983 a company Investors in Industry (3Is) was formed to take over ICFC and another merchant bank, Finance for Industry (FFI). The 3Is was 85% owned by the English and Scottish clearing banks and 15% owned by the Bank of England.

In the summer of 1994, the 3Is company was floated on the London Stock Exchange as an investment trust. The company floated 45% of its equity. It was the shares of the original shareholders that were being sold but they adopted different attitudes towards the float. The Royal Bank of Scotland decided to sell it entire stake, whereas the National Westminster Bank retained most of its original shares.

3Is is the largest investor in unquoted companies in Europe. Since its formation in 1945, it has invested more than £6bn in some 12 000 businesses. Between 1989 and 1994 it has invested £2.3bn in over 4000 companies. It invests some £400 million annually, and at mid-1994 held a portfolio of investments in about 3500 companies. 3Is is very active in the financing of management buy-outs. It estimates it finances in the region of 40% of all MBOs.

Almost a quarter of the value of its portfolio is in companies with sales of less than £5 million. It makes investments in some companies without insisting on a timetable for flotation. It claims that it is able to put such investments in its 'bottom drawer' and to pull them out only when they begin to perform well. It is able to do this because of its wide investments base: it is much bigger than the traditional venture capital company.

Because it has a network of 18 regional offices it is in a better position to be able to identify and work with companies at a local level. But as with all venture capital companies it has its failures.

The 3Is and its subsidiaries have shown themselves willing to provide various types of loans, often unsecured, and to invest for periods from 10 to 20 years. This is a lending period which has sometimes been thought to have been neglected by the other financial institutions. They advance medium-term loans in amounts between £1 million and £25 million and sometimes even above this. The interest rates charged are either fixed or variable or a combination of both. Finance is provided only if a proposal is commercially justifiable.

It is not 3Is policy to obtain control of a business or to interfere in the management. If 3Is purchase equity in a company, only a minority stake is sought. Under normal circumstances a seat on the board of directors is not required, and a nominee director will be sought only with the mutual agreement of the rest of the board.

Typical 3Is customers have assets of less than £1 million. They first approach 3Is for a variety of reasons. Most of them have gone beyond the point where development can simply be financed from retained funds, personal sources, and bank borrowing, while still being nowhere near the stage of possible access to the new issue market. They are keen to expand, but without wishing to yield majority control or damage their position as independently owned and managed concerns.

An analysis of customers has shown that they receive a mixture of finance from the bank: secured loans and debentures, sometimes the purchase of preference shares of convertible loans and sometimes subscription to a proportion of ordinary shares.

16.13 Export finance

It is possible for a company to obtain loans from a number of sources to assist with exporting. There are the normal ways of raising finance which apply whether the money is needed to fund domestic sales or export sales, and there are special ways only available to assist with exporting.

The normal sources include the following.

1. Overdrafts, at floating rates, payable on the amount borrowed.
2. Short-term fixed-interest loans.
3. Discounted bills of exchange, with documentary letters of credit: the purchaser's bank undertakes to pay at the maturity of the bill, and the exporter's bank discounts the bill; in the event of non-payment by the importer there is no recourse to the exporter.
4. Acceptance credits: an exporter can often arrange a revolving acceptance facility with his bank, up to an agreed amount. Each bill is discounted by the bank. As that bill is paid by the purchaser, the exporter can arrange for new bills to be discounted. If the purchaser, the importer, fails to pay, the bank has recourse against the exporter.

The above methods of raising finance can usually be used to obtain pounds sterling or foreign currency. The advantage of borrowing in a foreign currency is that if the export is to be paid for in a foreign currency, it is possible to match the debt against the currency to be received. This avoids foreign exchange risk.

One way in which it is possible to increase the probability that a bank will lend money to finance a company during the period between the production and despatch of goods for export and the receipt of cash from the foreign buyer is through the use of an export credit guarantee.

In fact in the region of 85% of UK exports are financed by traditional bank overdrafts. Most banks seek security for such loans. They like credit insurance on the debts of the overseas buyer as security. Without such insurance on the amount to be received they are reluctant to lend to support exports.

The government and exporting

How is such export insurance obtained? It can be obtained from either the public or private sector.

There was much talk in the 1980s of the government's withdrawing entirely from this field and leaving all such insurance in the hands of the private sector. It should be pointed out that in most competitor countries the government does provide such insurance. The UK Government in fact backed down from its plan to close down its export credit insurance activity carried out by the Export Credit Guarantee Department (ECGD).

The ECGD or private sector is a government department that has the role of assisting companies with their exporting. It issues guarantees appropriate to the terms of sale, and with these guarantees the exporting company is able to borrow from a bank.

With an ECGD guarantee behind a company's exports, the banks may be willing to advance up to 100% of the value of an individual invoice and to advance up to 90% of the value of an invoice for trading on open account. The amount actually advanced will depend upon the type of goods exported, the length of the credit period being made available to the purchaser, and the country to which the goods are being shipped.

The central government of a country has a role to play in encouraging and helping its companies export. In fact some governments do more to help their companies than do other governments. British companies complain that they are at a competitive disadvantage to their continental competitors in that the British government does not do enough. It is often claimed for example that French companies receive greater export credit insurance support, with greater availability at lower cost, from their government, than do British companies from the UK Government.

The argument for the government to become involved is that exporting is not only important to the company involved but also to the country. The balance of payments position of a country is crucial to the economic well-being of a country. It helps determine what policies a government can afford to pursue. Exporting is not just for private benefit, but also for the public's benefit.

It is for this reason that governments support their companies in export markets. It becomes a competition for business not just between a company in one country and a company in another country, but also between one government and another government.

The ways in which the government can help, include:

- trade counsellors in embassies in a country helping businessmen when they visit that country;
- giving advice to companies on how to export, and on the conditions and requirements in a particular country;
- assistance with finance, in particular export guarantee cover.

In the late 1980s the UK Government divided the export credit insurance business into two. ECGD withdrew from the short-term insurance business, leaving this to the private sector. The short-term insurance division of the ECGD was sold off to the Dutch insurance company NCM. In fact, however, the UK Government have found it necessary to continue to support, indirectly, the short-term business. They do this by providing reinsurance support to NCM to underpin its operations. It has been thought necessary to do this because of a lack of capacity in the private reinsurance market.

The UK Government in response to criticism that it does not do enough to help British exporters, doubled, in the five years between 1991/92 and 1996/97 the amount of money available for ECGD cover. The total level of ECGD cover (for medium- to longer-term insurance needs) was in 1993/94 £2.7 billion. A large proportion of this cover is however targeted for use only in certain overseas markets.

Another way in which government helps exporters is through making credit available to purchasers. Governments in developed countries provide financial aid to developing countries. Financial aid is not the same as a grant; the funds are not necessarily free. Aid is defined as finance made available at favourable terms, where 'favourable' means at an effective cost which is 25% or more less than commercial rates.

Such aid is usually tied. This means it can only be used to purchase goods or services from companies from the country providing aid. The UK government will make a loan available to a country at favourable terms. The money borrowed is to be used to purchase UK-made goods. One source of finance therefore for UK companies is through obtaining contracts in developing countries in which the UK government has provided aid finance.

Usually it is a UK bank that is responsible for the distribution of this aid finance. The bank has the funds available that can be borrowed by companies in the country receiving the aid. For example, in 1994, Lloyds Bank had 'credit lines' in place in Brazil worth over $1 billion. This is medium-term to long-term finance that can be used to buy British goods. If a UK company sold goods to a Brazilian company, the Brazilian company could obtain credit from Lloyds out of this $1 billion. The UK exporting company would be paid for the goods, and at the end of the credit period the Brazilian company would pay Lloyds according to the agreed terms.

Barclays de Zoete Wedd had in 1994 a credit facility worth $38.25 million to enable the Brazilian Navy to finance goods supplied by UK defence contractors.

In addition to bilateral arrangements in the form of tied aid, the multilateral development agencies also provide considerable amounts of finance to developing countries. The World Bank, the IBRD, and organizations such as the European Union fund projects and technical assistance programmes. Companies from around the world compete to obtain this work. The funds flow into a developing country as financial assistance and then move out of the country as foreign companies obtain the contracts.

Governments of exporting companies on occasions provide finance directly to companies to assist them obtain valuable export work. However the rates of interest which national governments charge their companies is carefully monitored and regulated by the OECD. The intention is to avoid unfair competition with some governments providing very soft loans. There are OECD agreed 'minimum rates of interest for officially backed export credits'.

Supplier credits

The ECGD and NCM are not themselves a source of finance for companies. They do not offer loans but make it easier for companies to obtain loans from the banks. When exporting, a company has to be able to offer an attractive deal to the overseas buyer. The factors influencing whether or not the exporting company obtains the business include the quality of the product, the price, the delivery date and possibly the credit terms attached to the sale. Does the UK supplier wish to be paid by the buyer immediately on the goods and documents being delivered or one month after delivery, or is he offering a period of credit? If a period of credit is being offered to the foreign buyer, say six months, then the exporter will need sufficient working capital to be able to finance the production of goods and to be able to pay interest or sacrifice earnings on the funds tied up in the sale. This credit may be carried by the exporter through his normal overdraft arrangement with a bank, or possibly the bank will discount the invoice. An alternative approach is for the exporter to obtain from the ECGD or NCM a guarantee that the bank will have any loan it advances repaid even if the overseas buyer does not pay for the goods or contract work at the end of the period of credit. It is the bank that makes the loan to the company and the insurer that provides the guarantee. On shorter-term business the buyer gives a promissory note or accepts a bill of exchange; the insurer is then prepared to give an unconditional guarantee to the exporter's bank that it will pay 90% of the value of the invoice when it becomes six months overdue.

Most of the credit insurance provided is what is described as 'comprehensive short term'. Short term refers to goods sold on credit of up to six months. Comprehensive means that the exporter does not have to inform the insurer of each individual sale. There is an agreed upper credit limit for a 12month period. It is only when a large amount of credit is being advanced to a new customer that the insurer will need to be informed.

Where an exporter wishes to give credit for more than six months it is possible to obtain an extended policy. However, credit will not be given for more than five years. Each extended contract needs special approval, and a special premium is paid. The cost for this credit insurance has two elements: an annual payment on the issue of a policy, and a premium paid monthly which is based on the value of the business receiving cover. The rate of premium payable has varied over time. In addition to this insurance cost, the company will, of course, have to pay interest to the bank on the supplier credit advanced.

Buyer credits

For larger business deals an alternative way for companies to finance their export sales is by means of buyer credit financing. This is possible on major projects and on capital goods business where the contract value is over £250 000. Under this arrangement the exporter is paid by the buyer in cash immediately upon delivery of the goods or satisfactory completion of the contract. To enable this to happen the exporter, the exporter's bank and the ECGD or private insurer will arrange for a loan to be made to the overseas buyer. Instead of the buyer's being offered deferred payment terms, he is now offered a loan to enable him to pay the exporter as soon as he is satisfied with the goods or the contract work. Buyer credit guarantees are available to banks making such loans to the foreign purchaser.

Under this buyer credit arrangement, the overseas buyer is normally required to pay the supplier 15%–20% of the contract price out of his own resources. The remainder is to be paid to the exporter from funds made available from a loan either to the overseas buyer or to a bank in the buyer's country. The funds have been lent by a UK bank and guaranteed. The loan is normally for less than the value of the goods and services supplied by the UK exporter.

Under this buyer credit arrangement, the UK supplier is able to export free from risk. The borrowing relationship is between the UK banker and the overseas borrower, with the insurer acting as a guarantor. The companies who would be attracted to this method of financing overseas sales include those who are highly capitalized in relation to the value of their overseas sales. In such situations large borrowings to finance exports, even though guaranteed, would result in balance sheets giving the impression of a high-risk company with heavy borrowing relative to equity.

Insurers can also assist in providing lines of credit to overseas borrowers if the money is to be used to assist them to place orders for UK capital goods. This is similar to the buyers' credit facilities just described, except that it is available on smaller contracts. The exporter is again to be paid in cash, with the cash coming from the loans made available to overseas borrowers by UK banks. On some occasions the borrowers are, in fact, foreign governments. The overseas borrower, whether a government, a bank or a company, can draw on the credit up to an agreed amount.

There are various other more specialized financing arrangements in which the ECGD and other insurers will become involved. It may be thought the ECGD services are generous, but it must be remembered they are in line with services offered by similar government departments in other countries, and without these services being available, UK exporters would be at a considerable disadvantage in the highly competitive export markets of the world. To avoid unfair competition there are international bodies that monitor and attempt to control and set acceptable standards for such export credit agencies. For example, the EU and the OECD are concerned with arrangements being offered within their respective member countries and they try to agree on the best terms that they will allow to be offered in any country.

A large proportion of the advances by banks to companies consist of this guaranteed finance. The banks, although guaranteed, have to find the finance required. The loans are not refinanced through the Bank of England or through a government department.

Credit insurance and letters of credit

Although ECGD is the main UK provider of credit insurance on exports, it is not the only one. There are a number of commercial credit insurance companies. Cover can be negotiated to fit the needs of the exporter. A bank will be willing to advance all or a proportion of the value of an invoice backed by commercial insurance, just as it would with ECGD insurance.

An irrevocable letter of credit is another way of financing exports. With this the buyer in a foreign country arranges with his own bank in that country to give instructions to a bank in the UK to pay the exporter when certain conditions are met. The exporter would have to present certain documents at the specified time to the bank in the UK, and would then receive the value of the order. With these letters of credit, bad debt risks are reduced. With this method it is the buyer that has to make arrangements for obtaining the credit with a bank in his own country. It is good for the exporter, but not so good for the buyer.

Support for exporters

The Department of Trade and Industry provides assistance and some financial support to companies who wish to export. There are a number of schemes designed to help the exporter, ranging from providing assistance in researching the export market, through help in making contacts with potential buyers, to providing financial help with selling the goods.

Smaller firms can obtain a grant towards buying market research information or undertaking inhouse studies. In addition the Department of Trade and Industry fund an 'Export Market Information Centre'. Financial support is available for companies who wish to take part in trade missions, for those who take part in trade fairs, and to assist potential buyers with inward missions.

An overseas project fund is available to assist companies seeking large overseas contracts (outside the European Union). The fund can be used to cover the costs of feasibility studies and consultancy fees. If the contract is won the assistance is repayable plus a premium.

A network of Export Development Counsellors is available to assist smaller companies seeking information, and they have some financial support they can make available.

Performance bonds

Performance bonds are guarantees usually given by the banks or by insurers to a buyer, guaranteeing that a particular contract will be honoured. They have arisen because the sizes of some of the contracts awarded were so large that they dwarfed the financial resources of the company that was to undertake the work. Many of the construction projects awarded, typically from the Middle East for construction of harbours, roads and airports, were for a higher value than the worth of the company undertaking the work. Often the customer, the buyer, would be asked to make an advance payment on the value of the contract and understandably wanted some guarantees that, if paying in advance, the work would one day be completed or he could recover any losses suffered.

The way that the bond scheme works is that the company engaged in the construction, heavy engineering or the supply of capital goods will ask a bank to provide a guarantee. The bank will issue a performance bond to a foreign buyer. The buyer will only ask the bank to meet the bond if the company undertaking the work defaults. The performance bond has a cost to the construction companies or the supplier of capital goods, and this has to be met in addition to any overdraft arrangements that it has with the bank. The bank has a contingent liability in that, if the company defaults on the contract, it will have to meet the value of the bond. Some of the contracts that have to be covered are very large, and to reduce the risk if only one bank issues the bond, a syndicate of banks may be involved in the issue.

Countertrade

Countertrade is a method of financing trade, but goods rather than money are used to fund the transaction. It is a form of barter. Goods are exchanged for other goods. This was particularly fashionable in the 1980s, when many deals exchanging petroleum for manufactured goods took place. These deals were outside the OPEC export quotas set for the countries concerned. It was a way of avoiding the quotas on sales. Countertrade was also popular in deals with developing countries and East European countries as both groups were short of foreign exchange and so keen to resort to barter. They wished to import and had goods that they wished to export. Negotiation determined how much of one good was exchanged for the other.

The spectacular growth period of this form of trade has now passed. A number of companies engaged in this business as intermediaries lost money and found themselves with goods they could not move. Countertrade is now a normal part of international trade, accounting for some 10%–15% of the total. There are many forms of countertrade, one of which is a triangular management, with A shipping goods to B, who ships goods to C. Then C ships goods back to A in return for the original transaction.

Forfeiting

With forfeiting a bank purchases a number of sales invoices or promissory notes from a company. The selling company obtains immediate cash, and the purchasing bank has a claim to a stream of income to be received in the future. Usually the bank purchasing the debts would only do so if the banks of the companies purchasing the goods guaranteed payment of the invoices. The invoices involved are often concerned with export transactions. The bank which has purchased the invoices can in fact sell them to another party. They become a security to be traded in the market place.

Factoring

An alternative form of financing is through a factor. The factor will buy the overseas debt and in return make an immediate cash payment to the exporter of part of the value of the receivable. They will of course also, if required, take over the record-keeping, the credit control and the debt collection. Factoring has the reputation of being expensive.

A typical exporting situation and the choice faced by a company will be explained. A company exports 90% of its £2 million turnover to large multinational companies. The company receives payment on average within 90 days from the time when the goods are dispatched. This means on average its level of debtors is £500 000 ($^{90}/_{360}$ × £2 million). The company can fund this either by taking time to pay its suppliers, by short-term borrowing, or by using the services of a factor.

The first of these alternatives is risky. Let us say the company has an overdraft facility of only £100 000. It could ask the bank for a larger overdraft arrangement, but there is the possibility that the bank would be reluctant because of the large proportion of overseas debts. The exporter could turn to other short-term borrowing arrangements or to a factor. The company could expect the factor to grant a facility covering up to 85% of the value of its debtors, with an agreed upper limit. The factor would provide finance and a debt collection service in the buyer's country.

Project finance is a form of medium-term borrowing that has been developed for a particular purpose. The underlying idea behind this type of finance is that the security against which the funds are advanced is a project rather than the standing or potential of the borrower, or an asset of the business. With most loan applications, it is the credit standing of the borrower that is the factor that decides whether the money will be advanced, but with project finance, although the credit standing of the borrower is of some importance, the key consideration is the financial viability of the project.

16.14 Project finance

This type of finance grew in importance during the 1970s, particularly in international business. One reason for its growth was the increasing size of many investment projects that required funding. Many of the North Sea oil developments were funded with this type of finance. Many small companies participated in North Sea oil investment and they were of such a size that it would not have been possible for them to raise the finance required against the security of their own balance sheets. However, such companies were able to generate the necessary borrowings against the security of the oil that they were seeking to extract. The banks making the loans were taking certain risks: first whether or not the exploration work would lead to the discovery of oil, and second that the future price levels for oil would justify the expenditure. Because the investments were long-term ventures, there was uncertainty with regard to the cost of the exploration work. With this type of loan the banks do not have the usual recourse to the assets of the borrower if the project fails. They are taking risks above those which they are normally willing to incur. The banks have traditionally been reluctant to enter into long-term lending and even when venturing into medium-term lending have not usually been interested in projects maturing beyond seven years. This traditional time horizon was not long enough for oil and other natural resource projects.

The largest single source of project finance is said to be the World Bank. However, some of their loans are not strictly project finance, as they are funding of larger-scale operations. Project finance is limited to those cases where it is possible to identify a particular project and to be able to identify an income stream that results from it. The banks need to be able to identify the various risks associated with the particular project. This is different from the usual type of financial risk analysis that the lender normally undertakes, which is assessing the creditworthiness of a company. To compensate for the higher levels of risk in project finance over their traditional means of providing finance, the banks frequently require higher returns on their loans than is normal, and on occasion seek returns in the form of royalties over and above the interest payments. Banking syndicates are formed in order to provide the finance for very large projects.

Often energy developments are funded with this type of finance, for example nuclear power stations and hydroelectric schemes. The development of project finance has enabled small companies to bid for very large contracts and it has also become possible for small countries to engage in the development of their natural resources. An alternative name for this method of financing is 'natural resource financing'.

It is possible to identify alternative forms of project financing depending on who takes the risks. At one extreme there is the situation where the borrower takes no risks at all. If the project is not a success, it is the lender that loses the money. The lender takes all the commercial and political risks. A second type of loan involves the borrower in taking a certain amount of the risk. The borrower may be at risk until the project comes on stream. Once the commercial operations begin, it is the lender that takes on the risk. This type of financing is often arranged for complex industrial projects which involve new or untried technological methods. It is reasonable in such cases for the constructor, the borrowing company, to cover the risk as to whether or not the project will work. It was this division of risk that was accepted in financing many of the North Sea pipeline projects. The third type of situation arises where the borrower takes the commercial risks while the lender assumes the political risks. This would be particularly important in projects in developing countries where there is always the threat of nationalization. Finally, there is the project where the lender takes no risk at all, but advances the money on the guarantee of some third party that the loan will be repaid if there is default. The guarantee may be provided by governments or by some state agency in the country where the work is taking place.

16.15 Hire purchase

Hire purchase is a source of medium-term credit sometimes used for the purchase of plant and equipment. Initially a hire purchase company purchases the required equipment, but it can immediately be used by the hiree, who after a series of regular payments, which includes an interest charge, becomes the owner of the equipment. The hiree has the advantage of the use of the equipment over the period that he is making the payments, and so obtains the benefits from using the equipment without having to incur a large capital outlay.

The legal framework of the hire purchase agreement is that the hire purchase company hires out the equipment to the intended purchaser, who is given an option to purchase the equipment for a nominal sum when the hiring rents have been paid. The legal title to the equipment does not rest in the hiree until the completion of the agreement.

In terms of cash flow the hiree has to make an initial payment and a series of instalments, rather than one large cash outlay at the time of first using the equipment. The funds that can be saved by only having to make a small initial payment at the beginning of the period rather than the full purchase price are available for investment elsewhere. However, hire purchase tends to be an expensive form of finance. The eventual purchasing company (the hiree) is entitled to claim taxation relief in respect of any investment allowances. It can also obtain tax relief on the interest element in the payments it makes.

The significance of hire purchase in the financial structure of the economy is that it is a convenient source of medium-term credit on fixed terms for the purchase of equipment, where the equipment itself can provide adequate security for the loan and the loan can be paid off by regular instalments.

The security on any loan is important. For the equipment itself to provide the security, the life of the asset must be greater than the period of the agreement, so that if the agreement is broken there is still an asset in existence which has a value. It is desirable that the value of the asset is at all times greater than the amount of the outstanding indebtedness. However, this requirement is not always enforced.

Effective rates of interest

With an overdraft and many types of loan, the interest charge is based on the outstanding balance of the debt at particular points of time. As a company reduces its overdraft at the bank, so its interest charge falls. Providers of instalment credit calculate interest in a way which differs from that on overdrafts and term loans. Interest is charged on the amount of the full loan for the whole period of the agreement, even though the borrower is, in fact, repaying the capital at intervals throughout the period of the agreement. Each payment is a mixture of capital and interest. Interest is being charged as though the amount of the loan was not repaid until the end of the period, even though in fact the amount of the loan is being reduced throughout the period.

An example will illustrate this point. Assume that a company enters a hire purchase agreement to acquire a piece of equipment and the equipment cost is £1000. The period of the hire purchase agreement is three years. If the finance company is quoting a rate of 12% interest on the agreement, it means that the total interest charge will be £360, i.e. £1000 $\times$ 0.12 $\times$ 3. The company will have to repay £1360 over the three years, i.e. 36 monthly payments of £37.77.

If L is the initial value of the equipment, i is the 'add on' interest rate, t is the length of the agreement and n is the number of payments each year, then

total interest charged = Lit
total value being advanced = $L(1 + it)$
size of each payment = $L(1 + it)/tn$

In each monthly payment the company is repaying part loan and part interest and yet the interest is still being calculated on the full value of the capital sum advanced.

The 'true' rate of interest can be determined by calculating the discount rate that equates the present value of the series of payments with the initial loan. The discount tables at the end of this book provide figures for returns and payments for different time periods. They can be used for monthly periods as well as annual. With the hire purchase example it can be seen that with this method of payment, the 36 monthly approach, they give a true rate of interest well above the 'add on' rate. The true rate for the 36 month case is 23.8%.

We can obtain an approximate answer using an annuity table. The £1000 capital sum divided by the monthly payment of £37.77 gives a factor of 26.48. Table 3 shows 35 periods but not 36. The factor of 26.48 approximates to the factor for 35 periods with a 2% rate of interest. Each payment is for a monthly period. This rate of just under 2% per month gives 23.8% per annum. In this example the true rate is approximately twice the add on rate.

16.16 Sale and lease-back

It is possible to convert certain assets which a company owns into funds, and yet for the company to still continue to use the assets. For example, if a building is sold to an insurance company or some other financial intermediary and then leased back from the purchaser, the company has secured an immediate cash inflow. The only cash outflow is the rental payments that it now has to make. These rental payments are allowed as a tax-deductible expense. However, the company may be subject to capital gains tax, which will arise if the sale price is in excess of the written down value as agreed by the tax authorities.

This financing possibility is particularly applicable to assets which appreciate in value, such as land, buildings or some other form of property. It is particularly appropriate to companies owning the properties freehold, and to institutions such as insurance companies or pension funds which are interested in holding long-term secure assets. The property is leased back at a negotiated annual rental, although with long lease-backs there will need to be a provision for the revision of the rental at certain intervals of time. Clearly the sale and lease-back releases funds which can be used for some other investment. A number of takeovers have been financed by this means. Assets were sold and leased back: the cash obtained from the sale was used to finance the purchase of another company. If the acquired company had substantial property so much the better, for this property could then be sold to an insurance company and leased back.

With sale and lease-back, funds are released for use elsewhere in the business, and in the short run the assets used by the company do not change. It must be remembered, however, that the leased asset no longer belongs to the company; the lease may one day come to an end and then alternative assets will have to be obtained. Also, the company is no longer obtaining the possible capital appreciation on the asset. Therefore there are costs to this process in addition to the lease payments that have to be made. The costs have to be compared with the increase in profits that can be obtained by having more working capital available.

As an example of a sale and lease-back arrangement, assume that a trading company owning a commercial property is offered £150 000 for the sale of the premises by an insurance company. The company is then to be allowed to rent the property from the insurance company, with the rental being fixed at a level of £13 000 per annum for the next five years and then being subject to review. This rental is giving the insurance company a 'yield' of 8.7% on its investment, which at the time is considered reasonable. This yield figure, which is often quoted in such transactions, is a crude yield; it is not discounted, and it is based simply on the first year's rent against initial investment.

From the trading company's point of view, it has to decide whether the profits it could make each year from investing the £150 000 cash it would obtain would be greater than the amount of the annual rental it had to pay. The amount of the rental payments after the fifth year are not known with certainty, but then neither are the profits. Taxation has to be taken into account, the rental payment being a tax-deductible expense, and the profits earned being subject to tax. Terms offered can be quite favourable to companies wishing to enter into such agreements. For example, if the owner occupier of a property sold that property to an institution for £1 million and then leased it back, the initial rent could probably be arranged to be comparatively low. A number of companies have used such arrangements to help their short-term profit performance. Had the occupier wished to raise the £1 million by borrowing, the annual interest charge would be higher. Sale and leaseback can therefore be a profitable way for the occupier and owner of property to raise funds when rents, interest rates and the value of property are right. One problem with the sale and lease-back arrangement, however, is that there are rent reviews to be taken into account. Although in the above example the owner–occupier may initially be able to obtain a rent at only 5% of the sum realized, it is possible that at the first rent review after, say, five years, the rent charge could double.

An alternative way of raising money on a property is through a mortgage. There are disadvantages to mortgages. One is that a mortgage has an adverse effect on the debt-to-equity ratio of a company. The mortgage obligation appears as a debt in the company's balance sheet and so increases the total debt in relation to the shareholders' fund. Under a sale or lease-back arrangement, no debt arises. One asset disappears from the balance sheet and is replaced by cash. Sale and lease-back arrangements convert the fixed assets of a company into liquid assets.

One variation on the conventional sale and lease-back arrangement is for the occupier to retain the freehold title of the property. The institution merely buys a long leasehold and then rents the property back. This does not always appeal to institutions but, if it can be arranged, the occupier does retain the long-term reversion of the property.

An alternative to sale and lease-back is, as mentioned above, mortgaging. It may be possible for a company to arrange to borrow money by means of a mortgage on freehold property. The most likely institutions prepared to lend on such a basis are insurance companies, investment companies and pension funds. Building societies are reluctant to lend to companies, and in any case there are limitations on the amount that they can lend in any year to corporate borrowers; they may be more willing to grant mortgages to the proprietors of small unincorporated businesses. Repayments of principal plus interest may be spread over a long period of time. The rate charged is somewhat in excess of the base interest rate.

The main advantage of a mortgage is that ownership of the property remains with the mortgagor and therefore the benefits that come from the ownership of a rapidly appreciating capital asset are not lost. In addition, as with any other long-term borrowing, the real cost of making repayments of principal will be reduced over time by inflation, and the cost of paying interest will be reduced by both inflation and tax relief. However, since capital repayment is involved, instalments together with interest will represent a considerably higher annual cost than the initial rentals payable under a sale and lease-back arrangement, especially if the mortgage is for a relatively short period.

This means that less money will be available for investment within the business in the early years under a mortgaging arrangement than with a sale and lease-back. However, over time the advantages may well swing back in favour of mortgaging. Under a sale and lease-back transaction the company becomes a tenant paying a rental. The company receives the sale price of the property but has to finance rental payments which may be expected to increase in line with movements in market rents at each review. With inflation reducing the real costs of repayment, and with rental payments increasing over time and continuing indefinitely, the cash outflow under a sale and lease-back arrangement could be higher in the later years than under a mortgage arrangement.

16.17 Mortgaging property

Leasing is a popular form of medium- or short-term finance. The distinguishing feature of a lease agreement is that one party (the lessee) obtains the use of an asset for a period of time, whereas the legal ownership of that asset remains with the other party (the lessor). The leasing agreement, unlike a hire purchase arrangement, does not give the lessee the right to final ownership. If a manufacturing company is satisfied to be able to use a particular asset without owning that asset, then leasing is a possibility.

Leasing accounts for between 20% and 25% of all new assets acquired. The reasons for leasing will be considered below, but first we define some terminology.

The lessee is the company making use of the equipment, and in return paying a rental to the lessor. The lessor, typically a finance company, initially purchases the equipment and then leases it out for a period of time. It is up to the two parties to agree on the terms

16.18 Leasing

of the agreement. A leasing agreement can be for a period running from only a few months to the entire expected economic life of the asset.

At the end of the period of the lease the ownership of the assets still remains with the lessor. Therefore normally any residual value of the underlying leased asset belongs to the lessor. For legal and tax reasons it is necessary to ensure that leasing arrangements appear as proper arm's length rental transactions. With long-term leases it is quite common for the lessee to be given an option to enter into a 'secondary lease' when the period of the 'primary' lease has expired. This means that the lessee can continue to use the equipment, even though still not the legal owner. The rental payments required during the period of the secondary lease are usually very low, and are often referred to as 'peppercorn' rents. This effectively means that although the lessee has not been given the option to purchase the asset at the end of the first agreement, he is given the opportunity to continue to use the asset at almost negligible cost, which, as far as use of the asset is concerned, is not so different from ownership.

Any attempt to classify leases into categories must, to some extent be arbitrary, but two broad classifications can be identified, namely 'finance leases' and 'operating leases'. A finance lease can usually be identified by the fact that the lessor is assured by the initial agreement of the full recovery of his capital outlay plus a suitable return on the funds he has invested. Sometimes it is referred to as a 'full payout' lease. The risks and rewards of ownership have effectively passed to the lessee. The risks and rewards from the use of the asset are, of course, also with the lessee. The lessee has signed an agreement covering more or less the full economic life of the asset and has agreed to pay fixed annual amounts. The lessor knows the return that will be obtained.

The second type of lease, known as an 'operating lease', is usually for a shorter period of time than a finance lease: certainly it is for less than the estimated economic life of the asset. During the period of the lease agreement the net cost of the equipment to the lessor is not fully recovered. It is the lessor that retains the usual risks and rewards that come from the ownership of the asset as distinct from the use of the asset. If the life of the asset turns out to be less than expected, perhaps because of obsolescence or damage, it is the lessor that loses. Consequently it is usually the lessor that assumes responsibility for repairs, maintenance and insurance under an operating lease. If the second-hand value of the asset turns out to be less than expected, it is the lessor who loses.

The life of an operating lease agreement is not always known at the outset, for the lease may be cancelled or cover only a short period with the options open for a succession of short periods, each being less than the economic life of the asset. Where rental periods are extended, these will be on a negotiated economic basis. The rental payments, together with the tax and any other benefits received by the lessor over the period of a particular lease, will not necessarily cover the cost of the asset. The lessor may sell the asset at the end of any of the short periods of a lease. When the operating lease agreement is signed the lessor does not know whether he will recover his capital and earn a return. There are future agreements to be negotiated and a sale to be arranged.

Reasons for leasing

There are at least four reasons why leasing has grown in popularity.

1. A company may not actually have the funds available to purchase the asset. It may not have any other alternative sources of funds. The purchase of large pieces of equipment such as Boeing 747 aircraft and large oil tankers can be very expensive. The purchase of a large mainframe computer can be beyond the means of small companies. Leasing is therefore a source of finance, a way of being able to obtain the use of an asset upon payment of the first rental. Even if a company has funds available, it may prefer to use these funds for some other purpose, either where they can be more profitably used or where the acquisition of the other asset cannot be linked to a particular form of finance such as leasing.

2. There can be considerable tax advantages in leasing. If a company has not been showing taxable profits in the years prior to its decision to acquire an asset, it will not be able to obtain the immediate advantages of any investment allowances. Up until 1984 a company was allowed free depreciation on many investments, which meant that it could write off 100% of the cost of the asset against its taxable profits at any time it chose. If the company had to pay tax in the year it wished to acquire the asset, the allowances could offer an immediate cash benefit. If the company was not paying taxes it could not obtain an immediate benefit. These companies could only obtain the early advantage of the investment allowances through leasing. The lessor company had profits: it purchased the asset, obtained the tax allowances, and passed the advantages of the lower net cost on to the lessee in lower rental payments. Subsequent examples will illustrate the way in which this works.
3. A company may not wish to own a certain type of asset, for example a computer. These machines can quickly become out of date, and the company may wish always to have available the most up-to-date equipment. There are always some companies who are willing to use second-hand computers. Therefore it is convenient to lease a new computer for, say, four years and then to replace it by leasing another new machine. The lessor takes the machine back at the end of the four years and leases or sells it to another customer. This takes the risks and trouble out of the hands of the lessee.
4. It is often suggested that leasing does not interfere with other possible borrowing or credit facilities. Traditionally leasing was seen as 'off the balance sheet' financing. A company did not need to record the asset with its other fixed assets in its annual balance sheet. The company has use of the equipment, just as much as if it owned the equipment itself – the equipment is used to earn the profits that appear in the accounts, but because the company does not have a legal title, the equipment was traditionally not shown as one of the assets of the company. This can affect the profit-to-asset ratio of a company. A company that leases its equipment can show in its accounts a higher return on its assets than a company that purchases the equipment. If the earnings from using the asset exceed the rental, a profit will be shown and the assets in the balance sheet will not reflect the use of the leased asset.

The traditional accounting entries accompanying leasing make a company appear to be in a better borrowing position than a company that purchases equipment outright. If debt ratios are considered of importance, then leasing rather than financing a purchase by borrowing could improve the future borrowing capacity of a company. For example, consider two companies *A* and *B* who initially have an identical financial position. Their initial balance sheets appear as follows:

Equity capital	£1000	Total assets £2000
Debt capital	£1000	

If the companies wish to obtain an asset costing £1000 and company *A* purchases the equipment with finance provided by a new issue of debt capital, whereas company *B* leases the equipment, then the resulting balance sheets of the two companies would, with the traditional accounting approach, appear as follows:

Company A

Equity	£1000	Total assets £3000
Debt	£2000	

Company B

Equity	£1000	Total assets £2000
Debt	£1000	

The debt ratio in company *A* is now 66.67%. The debt ratio in company *B*, the company leasing the equipment, is only 50.0%. This could suggest to possible new lenders that company *B* is in the better position to receive new debt capital. The obligations under the leasing agreements are not shown in the annual accounts. Company *B* appears to be in the better borrowing position, despite the fact that the lease payments are a fixed charge that the company will have to meet for a number of years.

Accounting treatment

This 'off the balance sheet' aspect of leasing has now to some extent disappeared in the UK. Finance leases have to be capitalized. The leased asset appears in the balance sheet as do the obligations arising under the leasing deal. The asset appears on one side of the balance sheet, and the liability on the other.

It is emphasized that the capitalization of the leased assets only applies to finance leases and not to operating leases. There are major companies who as a result of this requirement structured their new leasing deals so that they could be classed as operating leases and so kept off the balance sheet. The decision to capitalize leased assets was controversial. The major issue or principle that had to be decided was whether a lease is in essence the transfer of a right to use property. If it is, then it can be argued that the lessee should recognize in his accounts that he has the use of an asset and also that there is a liability to meet. In legal terms the lessee company does not own the asset, but in substance the company has a legal right to use the asset. The controversy revolves around whether one believes that a balance sheet should only list items which are legally owned.

The way in which the accounting entries will be handled with capitalization is shown in the following example. The leased asset has a purchase price of £1000 and is being leased for five years for a rental of £300 per annum payable in advance: the first payment is on 1 January 1990. The lessee decides to depreciate the asset on a straight-line basis over a five year period. The leased asset would appear in the balance sheet as follows.

Balance sheet as at	Cost	Accumulated depreciation	Written down value
31.12.90	£1000	£200	£800
31.12.91	£1000	£400	£600
31.12.92	£1000	£600	£400
31.12.93	£1000	£800	£200
31.12.94	£1000	£1000	0

The total rentals payable under the lease will be £1500 (i.e. 5 × £300). This is made up of the repayment of the capital element of £1000 and £500 interest. As will be familiar to those readers repaying a building society mortgage, the early payments will have a large interest element, whereas the latter payments will be mostly repaying capital. The accounting treatment for leases in the books of lessees is that the outstanding capital element of the debt should be shown as a liability in the balance sheet. The annual interest element in the rentals should be charged to the respective year's profit and loss account and the capital element of the rental debited to the liability account. More than one method is allowed for dividing payments between the capital and interest elements. One convenient method for allocating the rental payments over the period of the lease is by the sum of digits method. It provides a good approximation to the more precise approaches. It works in the following way. There are five payments. Sum the number of payments: 5 + 4 + 3 + 2 + 1 = 15. The first payment therefore contains 5/15 of the total £500 interest, the second payment 4/15 and so on.

The annual charge to the profit and loss account, with the interest element allocated according to the above rule, is therefore as follows:

Year to	Interest	Depreciation	Total
31.12.90	£167	£200	£367
31.12.91	£133	£200	£333
31.12.92	£100	£200	£300
31.12.93	£67	£200	£267
31.12.94	£33	£200	£233

If the asset was to be purchased the depreciation charge in the profit and loss account could be the same as above. If the acquisition was financed through borrowing there would also be an interest charge. It is emphasized that there are alternative methods of allocating the interest charge over time, as there are alternative methods of depreciating.

The liabilities for future rental payments appear in the balance sheet but only in respect of the capital element. At the beginning of 1990 the capital element of the payments is £1000 but the first rental of £300 consists of an interest charge of £167 and a capital repayment of £133. Therefore the balance sheet liability as at 31 December 1990 appears as £867. The second year payment is £133 interest and £167 capital, the third year £100 interest and £200 capital and so on.

Therefore the liability side of the balance sheet appears as follows.

Balance sheet as at	Leasing obligations
31.12.90	£867
31.12.91	£700
31.12.92	£500
31.12.93	£267
31.12.94	0

With this accounting method the capitalized liabilities arising from this transaction do not necessarily equal the capitalized value of the asset in each year. However, it would be possible using a different depreciation method and different methods for allocating interest to ensure that in each year the two items appearing in the balance sheet equalled each other.

Anybody wishing to lend money to a company that has leased assets should be in a position to know what payments the company is already committed to. The accounting standard requires the lease obligations to be shown. The lease payments are a regular commitment similar to interest payments on loans. It is a legal obligation to pay a certain sum of money each year. It is normal for a prospective lender to calculate the interest cover of the borrowing company, i.e. the excess of profits over interest payments. If a borrower has lease payments to make, it is important that the prospective lender should know this so that he has the information to enable him to determine the risks involved.

In the example shown, it has been assumed that the cost of the asset is not in doubt. In some cases, however, it may not be obvious what cost figure should be used. The asset may be available at different prices to different buyers. The practice to be followed is to take a 'fair value', i.e. the selling price that would have been obtained if the lessor had sold the asset to an unrelated purchaser at the inception of the lease.

Ordinarily, this would be the normal selling price of the asset. However, in the market conditions prevailing at the date of the leasing agreement, the fair value may be less than the normal selling price. The situation can arise where the lessee does not know the cost of the asset: he does not know what it cost the lessor or what is a fair market price.

In such cases, to obtain a cost figure that can be used for balance sheet purposes, the future stream of rental payments can be discounted and summed to obtain the present value. The discount rate that is to be used by the lessee to obtain the present value is normally the company's incremental borrowing rate. The incremental borrowing rate is defined as 'the rate that, at the inception of the lease, the lessee would have incurred to borrow the funds necessary to buy the leased asset on a secured loan with repayment terms similar to the payment schedule called for in the lease'.

However, if the lessee knows the lessor's implicit interest rate used to calculate rental payments, and the implicit rate of the lessor is less than the lessee's incremental borrowing rate, then the lessee will use the implicit rate for discounting purposes. The interest rate implicit in the lease is defined as the discount rate that, when applied to the minimum lease payments, causes the aggregate present value to be equal to the fair value of the leased property to the lessor minus any investment tax credit obtained by the lessor.

Leasing versus buying

We shall illustrate the financial decision-making technique required at the time when purchasing or leasing is being considered with an example.

Example

At 1 January 1992 a new machine cost £50 000 to buy. The machine would also require an input of £10 000 working capital throughout its life. It is estimated that if acquired it would earn the following pre-tax operating net cash flows:

Year	
1	£20 500
2	£22 860
3	£24 210
4	£23 410

The company is considering whether to lease or buy the machine. A lease could be arranged in which the company, the lessee, would pay an annual rental of £15 000 per annum for four years, with each payment being at the beginning of the respective year. If the company were to purchase the machine it would obtain the finance through a term loan at a fixed rate of interest of 11% per annum. The company believes that the appropriate after-tax cost of capital for a machine with the risk characteristics of the one being considered is 12%. Corporation tax is payable at the rate of 35% one year in arrears, and capital allowances are available at 25% on a reducing balance basis. It is not anticipated that the machine will have any value at the end of the lease period, but if it does still have a useful life the lessee would be able to enter into a secondary leasing agreement. Both the lessor and the lessee can ignore the financial consequences of a secondary leasing agreement. If the machine is in a satisfactory condition, it can be used during a secondary lease period, but the rental will only be a small nominal amount. The leasing company has to budget to recover its cash outlay and earn a reasonable profit during the period of the primary lease; any rental receipts beyond that are just a bonus. This is a typical situation in a finance lease.

There are a number of approaches to solving a lease versus purchase problem. We shall illustrate the more popular approach. In this leasing is regarded as a source of finance. This requires two decisions to be made. First we shall decide whether, if we do wish to obtain the use of the machine under consideration, we should purchase it or lease it. Which is the least expensive: purchasing or leasing? Having decided on the lease expensive method of financing the use of the machine, we can then compare the costs with the returns expected to be earned for the use of the machine. The second question is: do the returns justify the cost?

There are a number of cash flow streams to consider:

1. the net cash flow stream resulting from the financing method being adopted:
2. the net cash flow resulting from operating the asset:
3. the investment of working capital:
4. any residual value.

These cash flow streams (with the exception of working capital) can have taxation implications.

We shall begin by calculating the cash flow streams associated with the methods of financing. The PV of the cash flow associated with leasing is to be compared with the PV of the cash flow associated with purchasing. This can be expressed as

$$\text{NPV} = \left[\sum_{i=0}^{t} \frac{P_i}{(1+m)^i} + \sum_{i=0}^{t+1} \frac{T(P_i)}{(1+q)^i} \right] - \left[\sum_{i=0}^{t} \frac{L_i}{(1+n)^i} + \sum_{i=0}^{t+1} \frac{T(L_i)}{(1+q)^i} \right]$$

where P_i is the cash flow in year i resulting from a decision to purchase the equipment, $T(P)_i$ is the cash flow in year i resulting from investment allowances, L_i is the cash flow in year i resulting from a decision to lease the equipment, $T(L)_i$ is the cash flow in year i resulting from a tax saving on lease payments, m is the discount rate appropriate to cash flow with the properties of the purchasing cash flow stream, n is the discount rate appropriate to cash flow with the risk properties of the leasing cash flow stream and q is the discount rate appropriate to tax savings. There are two parts to this equation: the after-tax cost of purchase and the after-tax cost of leasing. We shall calculate them separately.

First we shall determine the appropriate discount rates. The lessee's borrowing cost is 11%, which gives an after-tax cost of 7.15%, i.e. $11\%(1 - 0.35) = 7.15\%$. We shall take this as m. For practical purposes q will be taken as equal to n or m. It will be argued in the next section that leasing is usually a direct replacement for borrowing. Therefore m can be taken as equal to n. As will be explained below, this assumption is only valid if investors regard the lease and the loans as being perfect substitutes for each other from the point of view of capital structure and the riskiness of the cash flows. Table 16.4 shows the net cost of purchase and Table 16.5 the net cost of leasing. As can be seen the NPV of the costs of leasing are slightly greater (by £104) than the NPV of the costs of purchase. If the company wishes to use the machine, on financial grounds it should purchase it.

Table 16.4

Year	1 Investment	2 Capital allowance	3 Tax shield on allowance (35%)	(1) + (3) Net cash flow	PV × factor =	PV of cash flow
0	−50 000			−50 000	1.000	−50 000
1		12 500			0.933	
2		9 375	+4375	+4 375	0.871	+3 811
3		7 031	+3281	+3 281	0.813	+2 667
4		21 094[a]	+2461	+2 461	0.759	+1 868
5			+7383	+7 383	0.708	+5 227
						−36 427

(a) with balancing allowance.

Table 16.5

Year	Lease payment	Tax shield	Net cash flow	PV × factor =	PV of cash flow
0	−15 000		−15 000	1.000	−15 000
1	−15 000	+5250	−9 750	0.933	−9 097
2	−15 000	+5250	−9 750	0.871	−8 492
3	−15 000	+5250	−9 750	0.813	−7 927
4		+5250	+5 250	0.759	+3 985
					−36 531

We now move to the second stage of the decision-making process (Table 16.6). We shall decide whether or not the machine is a good investment. The NPV of the after-tax operating cash flow needs to be calculated. This cash flow stream will need to be discounted at the rate appropriate to the business operating risks. These will be different from the risk associated with leasing or purchase cash flows.

Table 16.6

Year	Operating cash flow	Tax payable	Net	PV factor 12%	PV
1	+20 500		+20 500	0.893	+18 307
2	+22 860	−7175	+15 685	0.797	+12 501
3	+24 210	−8001	+16 209	0.712	+11 541
4	+23 410	−8474	+14 936	0.636	+9 499
5		−8194	−8 194	0.567	−4 646
					+47 202

The risk associated with the annual tax payments has two elements. One is risk associated with changes in the rate of corporation tax, and the other is associated with the operating cash flow on which the tax calculation is based. The tax payment figure is the corporation tax rate multiplied by the taxable profits. Although it can be argued that the tax-rate risks may be low and therefore an interest-rate based discount rate would be appropriate, it can also be argued that the level of taxable profits is higher risk and therefore the operating cash flow stream discount rate is more appropriate. We shall use the same discount rate for the operating cash flow stream and the tax payable on that stream.

The discount rate to use to obtain the PV of this cost-saving stream is not the one that is to be used for discounting the payments associated with leasing or purchasing the machine. The reason that a different rate is used is that whereas the lease payments and the interest payments are known with certainty, the costs that can be saved by operating the new machine are very much estimates. The predictability of the two streams are very different. Whereas the discount rate for the more certain stream can be taken as the cost of borrowing, we will take as the discount rate for anticipated revenues or cost saving the firm's cost of capital. We are told in this example that the after-tax cost is 12%. The PV of the returns clearly exceeds the PV of the costs of finance.

There is one more cash flow stream to take into account, and that is the working capital. This money was invested at the commencement of the project and it is assumed that it will be returned at the end of the project's life. This involves a cost to the company. The PV of the outflow is £10 000, and the PV of the inflow, discounted at the same rate as the operating cash flow, is

$$10\ 000 \times 0.636 = £6360$$

This is an NPV of −£3640.

We can combine the three PVs that we have obtained to evaluate whether or not the investment in the machine is profitable:

NPV of net operating cash flows	+47 202
NPV of purchasing the machine	−36 427
NPV of working capital investment	−3 640
Overall NPV	+£7 135

The investment is clearly profitable, and should be financed by borrowing.

Leasing versus borrowing

In the above example the discount rate applied to the cash flow stream resulting from purchase is the same rate that has been applied to the cash flow stream resulting from leasing. This is assuming that the cost of capital in both cases is the same, which is assuming that leasing is a direct replacement for debt finance. It is assuming that the risks attached to both cash flows are the same. In most cases this assumption is correct.

When a company enters into a finance leasing arrangement, it is required to record on the liabilities side of the balance sheet the obligations under leasing contracts. To the user of the accounts this is clearly seen as a form of borrowing. Companies have target gearing ratios. The precise level of the target ratio might depend on ideas regarding an optimal level, it might depend on institutional constraints in that banks are not prepared to lend more than a certain percentage of the shareholders' funds, or it might depend on restrictions written into a company's articles of association.

If an amount of, say, £50 000 is shown in the balance sheet as an obligation under leasing contracts, the banks will add this amount to the amount of other forms of borrowing to determine the total debt of the company. It is this latter figure that will be measured against the shareholders' funds when the actual level of gearing is calculated. If the actual level of gearing equals the target level, no more borrowing will be possible. If the company had not entered into the £50 000 leasing deal, it would have been able to borrow another £50 000. Leasing is therefore replacing debt finance.

As mentioned above, leasing was once referred to as 'off the balance sheet' finance. This was before Accounting Standards required the capitalization of finance leases. It was possible that when leasing was off the balance sheet lease finance was not replacing debt finance. It was possible that banks did not take into account obligations under leasing arrangements when considering whether companies were at their target gearing levels. In such a situation, when one form of finance was not a replacement for the other, the opportunity cost of obtaining finance was not necessarily the cost of borrowing. But when leasing is a substitute for borrowing and when the level of risks of both cash flow streams is the same, then the opportunity cost of leasing is the cost of borrowing.

Discount rate

The discount rate that should be used in all investment decisions is the opportunity cost. If the firm is not in a capital rationing situation and if it can obtain additional funds should it need them, then we have argued above that leasing is a direct substitute for borrowing and so the opportunity cost of leasing is the cost of borrowing. There can be a complication when, say, £100 worth of leasing is not replacing £100 worth of borrowing. It could be that the debt capacity of the kind of equipment being leased is different from that of the existing assets of the company. The leased equipment could then either increase or decrease the gearing possibilities of the lessee. If £100 of lease liability is a substitute for less than £100 of debt, then a cost of capital other than the borrowing rate will need to be used.

The point being made is that the borrowing rate is only justified if the leasing deal on a particular project does not have financial side-effects, i.e. if it does not disturb the normal gearing and cost of capital of the lessee. If the leasing deal does have financial side-effects then the appropriate discount rate is the borrowing rate adjusted for these side-effects.

One formula which can be used for estimating the appropriate discount rate for such a leasing deal is:

$$r^* = r(1 - T_C L_j)$$

where r^* is the adjusted after-tax discount rate, r is the opportunity cost of capital for a similar deal with no side-effects, T_C is the marginal corporation tax rate and L_j is the particular leasing deal's proportional contribution to the company's borrowing power. L represents the effect of leasing on the borrowing power of the company. If £100 of leasing only replaces £80 of debt capacity, $L = 1/0.80$. It is sometimes suggested that £100 of leasing does not have as much impact on future borrowing possibilities as £100 of borrowing. Alternatively, perhaps because of risk considerations, the £100 of leasing might replace £120 of debt, in which case $L = 1/1.20$. It should be emphasized that this formula is only one technique for making some allowance for the possible financial side-effects of leasing. In most cases, in practice it is assumed that $L = 1$, in which case the appropriate discount rate in a leasing decision is the after-tax cost of borrowing.

If a company believes that lease finance is not a substitute for loan finance, then the appropriate discount rate would either be the company's weighted average cost of capital or, using the capital asset pricing model approach, the risk-adjusted cost appropriate to the type of asset being leased.

If a company is in a capital rationing situation and is still able to lease, then clearly leasing is not a substitute for debt. To the company leasing is the only possible way of funding the use of the asset, in which case the discount rate should, as just explained, be either the weighted average cost of capital or the risk-adjusted cost appropriate to the asset. Technically such a company is not in a capital rationing situation, as it is still able to obtain the use of assets through leasing arrangements. In a true capital rationing situation, where financing the use of an asset through a leasing deal means that some other investment cannot be undertaken, the discount rate to use is the return that would have been earned on the investment that is not to be undertaken. This is the clear opportunity cost of obtaining the use of one asset by leasing, rather than the use of some other asset by other financing means.

It has been argued in this section that in the vast majority of cases the discount rate that should be used in leasing decisions is the after-tax cost of borrowing. This is certainly the most straightforward approach, but the assumptions that are being made should be remembered when adopting this approach.

The following is a short question taken from the Financial Management paper of the ACCA. It merely involves making certain calculations. The only question of principle is what discount rate should be used.

Example 16.2

Your firm intends to obtain the use of an asset but is uncertain of the best financing method to be employed. The financing methods under consideration are as follows.

(a) To borrow and purchase the asset. Borrowing would cost 12% before tax, the current competitive market rate for debt. The asset would cost £90 000 to purchase and will have a guaranteed salvage value of £10 000 after five years. Expenditure on the asset qualifies for a 25% writing-down allowance.

(b) To lease the asset. Two financial leases are being considered and the details are as follows:

| | Payments to be made | |
| Year | Lease A | Lease B |
	(£000)	(£000)
0	20	4
1	20	8
2	20	16
3	20	30
4	20	50

If the asset is leased, the salvage value will accrue to the lessee. The firm's weighted-average cost of capital is 15%. Lease payments are made at the beginning of each year.

Advise on the best method of financing the use of the asset if the firm is

(a) subject to corporation tax at 50% with a one year delay and has large taxable profits;
(b) permanently in a non-taxable position.

Suggested solution

Two possible discount rates are mentioned in the question: the borrowing cost of 12%, and the weighted average cost of capital of 15%. The first point to note is that all the cash flows that will be discounted in the answer can be taken to be riskless streams. If we borrow we know the interest charge, we know the tax position and we have guaranteed salvage value. If we lease we know what the lease payments will be.

The second point to note is that leasing is being considered as an alternative to borrowing. We shall assume that there are no financial side-effects from leasing, and therefore we can consider leasing as a substitute for borrowing. The 12% cost mentioned in the question is the before-tax cost. It is this 12% that will be used as the discount rate for part (b) of the question where, because the firm is in a permanent non-taxable position, there is no tax shield. For part (a) of the question we shall discount at 6%, the after-tax cost of borrowing (allowing for the 50% tax shield).

(a) Taxable position: the figures for purchase and leasing are shown in Tables 16.7–16.9.

Table 16.7 Purchase

Year	Investment (£000)	Tax saving (£000)	Salvage value (£000)	Net cash flow (£000)	Discount factor at 6%	PV (£000)
0	90			90.00	1.000	90.00
1		−11.25		11.25	0.943	−10.61
2		−8.45		8.45	0.890	−7.52
3		−6.35		6.35	0.840	−5.33
4		−4.75		4.75	0.792	−3.76
5		−3.05	−10.00	13.05	0.747	−9.75
6		−5.65[a]		5.65	0.705	−3.98
				PV of costs		−49.05

[a] Balancing allowance.

Table 16.8 *Lease A*

Year	Lease payment (£000)	Tax (£000)	Cash flow (£000)	Discount factor at 6%	PV (£000)
0	20		20	1.0	20.00
1	20	−10	10		
2	20	−10	10		
3	20	−10	10	3.465	34.65
4	20	−10	10		
5		−10	−10	0.747	−7.47
			PV of costs		47.18

Table 16.9 *Lease B*

Year	Lease payment (£000)	Tax (£000)	Cash flow (£000)	Discount factor at 6%	PV (£000)
0	4		4	1.0	4.00
1	8	−2	6	0.943	5.65
2	16	−4	12	0.890	10.68
3	30	−8	22	0.840	18.48
4	50	−15	35	0.792	27.72
5		−25	−25	0.747	−18.67
			PV of costs		47.86

(b) Non-taxable position: the figures for purchase and leasing are shown in Tables 16.10–16.12.

Table 16.10 *Purchase*

Year	Cash flow (£000)	Discount factor at 12%	PV (£000)
0	90	1.0	90
5	−10	0.567	−5.67
		PV of costs	84.33

Table 16.11 *Lease A*

Year	Cash flow (£000)	Discount factor at 12%	PV (£000)
0	20	1.0	20
1	20		
2	20	3.037	60.74
3	20		
4	20		
		PV of costs	80.74

Table 16.12 *Lease B*

Year	Cash flow (£000)	Discount factor at 12%	PV (£000)
0	4	1.0	4.0
1	8	0.893	7.144
2	16	0.797	12.752
3	30	0.712	21.36
4	50	0.636	31.8
		PV of costs	77.056

If the firm is paying tax at 50%, it should lease the asset under option A. The PV of the costs of purchase is more than the PV of the costs of the leasing possibilities.

If the firm is in a permanent non-taxable position as can be seen from Tables 16.10, 16.11 and 16.12 the cheapest way of financing the use of the asset is to lease through option B.

Lessor's decisions

In the example on p. 590, the lessor's cash flow ignoring tax is

$$-50\,000 + 15\,000 + \frac{15\,000}{1+i} + \frac{15\,000}{(1+i)^2} + \frac{15\,000}{(1+i)^3}$$

The lessor invests £50 000 at time zero and immediately receives the first lease payment of £15 000. The next three lease payments are received in each of the next years. What is the lessor's cost of capital and tax position?

If the lessee can claim the same capital allowances as the lessor, both have the same cost of capital, and if the leasing company does not add on a profit percentage or if the cost of capital to the lessee plus the add-on percentage is the same as the cost of capital to the lessor, then the lessee will be indifferent whether to lease or buy. Leasing can be attractive to a lessee when he is faced with different cash flows from those of the lessor.

A number of factors in practice mean that a difference usually arises. These include:

1. Different costs of capital for lessor and lessee. It is often assumed that because many leasing companies are subsidiaries of banks, and so are able to obtain funds at a lower cost than the lessee, the discount rate they use should be lower than the lessee's. In fact, the lessor does face risks when purchasing an asset and leasing it out. They are risks associated with non-payment and with the probable residual value of the asset. If the lessor is using a risk-adjusted cost of capital to calculate the required lease payments the difference between the discount rate of the lessor and lessee may not be very great.
2. Differences in tax rates between the lessor and lessee. If the lessor pays at a higher marginal tax rate than the lessee, then both lessors and lessees can benefit from a leasing deal. It is the Inland Revenue that loses in that it collects less tax than it would have done if the desired user of the asset had made a purchase.
3. Utilization of capital allowances was once one of the most popular reasons for leasing as opposed to purchasing. If the lessee had insufficient taxable profits to be able to take advantage of the 100% depreciation possibility in the year of purchase or shortly afterwards, it was usually beneficial to lease the asset rather than purchase it. Leasing companies usually had the taxable capacity and could pass on the benefits of the early tax allowances in lower lease payments. This has now become less important with lower levels of allowances.
4. Residual values at end of the primary leasing contract. If a company buys an asset, at any point in time the value of that asset belongs to the company. The value of the asset depends on obsolescence, maintenance and the market conditions at the time. The owner of an asset is unsure of the future value of the asset. In a leasing deal the asset belongs to the lessor during the period of the lease period. However, who obtains any residual value of the asset at the end of the leasing agreement is a matter of agreement between the lessor and lessee. It is not possible to generalize on this matter, but on occasions, the lessee can negotiate for a generous residual value to be paid over by the lessor at the end of the leasing period. Agreements with regard to residual value can help to determine whether leasing is preferable to purchase.

16.19 British government sources

Central government and local government attempt to encourage industry to invest. Central government wishes to encourage the 'right' kind of investment, for example investment in new technology, and also wishes to encourage companies to set up factories in depressed areas of the country. It can encourage companies by making finance available, by reducing taxation or by direct controls.

Local government wishes to create wealth and employment in the area for which it is responsible; again, it can offer financial incentives.

We shall examine government involvement in the finance of industry, although it should be appreciated that some of the schemes for making funds available to industry have a comparatively short life. Different governments have different views on the necessity of helping industry and on the best way of achieving this, and in addition the need for government finance varies with the health of the economy.

The government, through taxation, has an influence on the extent to which a company can finance itself. Investment grants and allowances, permissible depreciation deductions are matters of government policy that influence the level of retained profits.

The government can vary the level of corporate taxation and it can also vary the investment allowances to affect the profits left over after taxation. A government's policy on investment incentives and depreciation allowances affects the flow of funds between the two sectors.

When operating through the tax system, with say investment allowances, assistance is being provided on a national scale. Often governments wish to be more selective and support will depend upon the location of a project, upon the sector of industry or type of business activity.

We shall begin by considering the general support schemes and then move on to look at the more selective schemes.

General support

1. Research and technology: there are a number of ways in which the Government encourages industry to undertake research and development. The tax allowances on investment in research and development are more generous than on items of capital expenditure. The Government encourages collaboration between industrial firms' universities, and research agencies.
2. Export support has been discussed elsewhere in this chapter. Assistance is provided in many ways, including providing an information service, undertaking market research and providing financial support for trade missions.
3. The Guaranteed Loan Scheme assists smaller companies to obtain finance.

Regional enterprise grants

The Government through the DTI makes grants available for investment projects in most manufacturing and some service sectors that are undertaken in certain regions. The grant in 1994 was at the level of 15% of expenditure on fixed assets in the project up to a maximum of £15 000. Eligible costs include plant and machinery, buildings, and purchase of land and vehicles used solely on site. Unfortunately firms are only eligible for such grants if they employ less than 25 people.

The assistance is therefore very limited in amount provided, and in firms that are eligible. It is designed to support specific types of investment in the areas of the country that need special assistance.

Projects are eligible if they take place in a development area or in certain intermediate areas. Development areas are areas of high unemployment, and include regions around Glasgow, Newcastle and Liverpool, and parts of South Wales and South West England. Intermediate areas are to be found in Derbyshire and South Yorkshire.

Regional grants for innovation projects

These are available to firms embarking on projects which lead to new or improved projects and processes. To be eligible a firm must again be either new or be small. 'Small', for the purposes of this grant, is defined as employing less than 50 persons.

Grants are available for up to 50% of agreed project costs up to a maximum of £25 000 for a particular project.

Other enterprise initiatives

The two forms of regional grant described above are part of what is called 'Enterprise Initiatives'. From time to time there are other types of support offered under this government programme. One is 'Support for Products Under Research' (SPUR).

Under this programme a grant can be made available to help smaller firms develop new products and processes which involve a significant technological advance. Smaller firms are defined for this purpose as those employing 500 or less people. The level in 1994 was a grant of up to 30% of eligible project costs can be made available, up to a maximum of £150 000.

Local/regional authority funding schemes

Many local and regional authorities provide financial support for firms operating in their own locality. The schemes are usually designed to help smaller companies. Most of these schemes have been designed to complement finance provided through the market, or to fill a gap in the market. They are clearly aimed at encouraging firms to invest in a city, town or region.

In comparison to lending by conventional banks this form of lending has higher levels of risk. Security in the form of assets, cash flow, and personal guarantees is usually taken first by the banks and mainstream investors in the project who are seeking profit. The local authority's objective is primarily to create employment in the region. The more social the objectives of the providers of finance, the less the emphasis on the security of the investment.

Most of the specialized local funding agencies have a public-sector financial base, and are therefore subject to Treasury scrutiny. In Treasury terms 'additionality' is what is sought from public expenditure, i.e. something that would not otherwise happen. This is relatively easy to prove for major investment projects but very difficult for a locally based project.

One scheme which operates in the City of Birmingham adopts the following criteria in deciding on the eligibility of an application for support.

- **Location:**   Must be based within the City boundary.
- **Trade:**   Will be in manufacturing or related services to industry (for example, plating, heat treatment and packaging, but not distribution, warehousing, consumer services or retailing). The trade will be expected to provide a net benefit to the City's economy.
- **Viability:**   Project and business must be viable.
- **Main finance:**   All other sources of finance must have been explored. Typically the fund will invest alongside other sources of finance such as banks, and government grants.
- **Need:**   The fund is not intended to substitute for other sources. Short- to medium-term finance can be provided.
- **Project:**   The project will normally be expansion, relocation, consolidation or re-financing of business, or exceptionally start-ups, where at least five jobs will be created or preserved over two years.
- **Application:**   A business plan, must be produced which demonstrates the principal's understanding of the market.
- **Monitoring:**   Monthly management accounts and annual audited accounts are required to be seen.
- **Board policy:**   The Funding Agency must be satisfied that the board of the company will be progressive in relation to being good employers, in its policies for ploughing back surplus profits into the business and in attempting to recruit from within the City boundary.

In one City of Birmingham scheme, entitled the 'Business Investment Scheme', the scale of the possible support in 1994 was that grants in the range of £5000 to £30 000 could be provided. To be eligible over five jobs needed to be credited. In another scheme 'Small Business Assistance Scheme' grants of up to £5000 could be made available again for creating up to five jobs.

The European Investment Bank

The European Investment Bank (EIB) was created in 1958 with the object of making loans available to public and private borrowers. The EIB does not seek to attract deposits from the public. Its finance is derived from two sources: first that subscribed by member states of the EU, and second that borrowed on the international capital markets. Member states each agree to subscribe a certain amount of money; Germany, France and the UK subscribe the largest amounts of capital and each agrees to put in an equal amount. In addition to the subscribed funds the EIB has borrowed extensively in international capital markets.

The bank is non-profit-making and seeks only to cover its expenses and to set aside sufficient reserves to deal with any possible loss from defaults on loans. It finances projects for developing the less developed regions of the EU, for modernizing or converting existing undertakings, for developing fresh activities within the EU and for supporting projects of common interest to several member states.

It is a source of long- to medium-term loans with money being advanced for periods of between seven and twelve years. The interest rates charged on loans are reasonable since the EIB is non-profit-making. EIB loans are about 2% cheaper than borrowing from comparable UK sources. The EIB does not charge higher rates for riskier projects or for borrowers with a low credit rating. However, it does require guarantees either from the Government of the country that is receiving the loan or from a suitable financial institution.

The EIB, in common with other activities in the EU, expresses money values in terms of the European Currency Unit (ECU). In fact, EIB loans are made in a range of currencies (including ECUs) depending on the borrower's preference. However, the EIB measures the volume of its lending plans in terms of ECUs and in fact some of its borrowing is in ECUs.

The ECU is a currency basket formed of fixed quantities of the currencies of the EU countries. These quantities, together with the ECU exchange rates of the currencies involved, determine the weight of each currency in the basket. The conversion rate of any individual currency, say the pound sterling, against the ECU can vary day by day depending on the movement of the pound against the other currencies within the ECU. There is an official ECU conversion rate which is published daily.

It should be appreciated that there are no ECU notes or coins in circulation. However, it is possible to borrow and lend in ECUs. The borrower, a company or a government, can then convert these ECUs into whatever currency is needed. The repayment would be in ECUs, again involving a conversion. The ECU is convenient for bookkeeping and political purposes. The EU needs a single unit of measurement for purposes of its budgets and planning, and would like a unit which was reasonably independent of the US dollar. Rather than select one of the currencies such as the French franc or the German mark, which would be politically sensitive, it is easier to use as a measure a currency which is not linked to any one country and which does not depend upon the actions of any one national government.

One problem with the EIB's loans is that they have to be repaid in the currency in which they are borrowed. Therefore a borrower has to take into account not only the interest charge but the possible exchange loss from movements in the value of currencies.

At one time the EIB was criticized for only providing large sums of money to very large creditworthy customers. It was useless for small companies to apply to the EIB for money as it preferred to make loans of not less than one million units of account. The only way in which smaller borrowers could take advantage of this fund was through financial institutions such as 3Is which borrowed from the EIB and then lent the money received in small amounts to a number of borrowers.

In 1978 a change took place when the EIB announced that, in future, it would make a large sum of money available to finance small- and medium-scale industrial ventures. The sum would be specially earmarked for smaller and medium-sized firms. The EIB operates this scheme through agency arrangements. Barclays and the 3Is act as UK agents. A customer who wants a smaller EIB-funded loan applies to one of these agency banks.

The EIB can provide loans for capital investment projects in industry or related services mainly in areas of high unemployment and for projects involving advanced technology, environmental protection, transport, telecommunications and energy. The loans can be up to one half of the project's cost, and can be for periods up to 12 years in duration.

As mentioned above loans can be made available to all size companies. If a company is seeking £7 million or more, it usually negotiates directly with the EIB. Smaller loans are managed through EIB intermediary banks.

Research and development support

The EU supports R&D into new technologies, in order to 'meet the challenge of aggressive markets like Japan and the United States'.

The Community's programmes aim to assist industry to improve Europe's technology base and to assist firms in exploiting the internal market. In practical terms this largely amounts to international collaboration on R&D projects partly funded by industry and involving industries, universities and other organizations working together across Europe. The emphasis is on pre-competitive research, which usually lies beyond basic research but does not specifically involve near-to-the-market developments.

European Coal and Steel Community (ECSC) conversion loans

The ECSC provides fixed interest rate, medium-term loans for projects which create new jobs in regions suffering job losses because of the decline of the coal and steel industries.

The loans can be to any industry, and can be for up to 50% of the fixed asset cost. The loans are usually for up to eight years, with a few years' grace period on the repayment of capital. If they can be obtained they are therefore attractive.

The loans are usually in foreign currencies, and must be repaid in those currencies. There is therefore a considerable exchange risk. The UK government has at times however been prepared to offer exchange risk guarantees, for industrial projects costing not more than £500 000.

If the company pays an annual service charge it obtains the guarantee, which means it takes on only a sterling liability, with the government covering any foreign exchange risks.

16.21 Revision questions

1. For what reasons are small companies likely to find raising term finance more difficult than larger companies?
2. What is an acceptance credit?
3. What is the difference between a finance lease and an operating lease?
4. What are the advantages of leasing? Are the reasons compatible in the light of the Modigliani and Miller insight about the relevance of the financing decision to the value of the firm?
5. What are the advantages and disadvantages of financing a company's working capital requirements using (a) normal bank advances and (b) other types of short-term borrowing?
6. What are the advantages and disadvantages of using a factor?
7. List the ways of financing exports?
8. What is the main role of the ECGD?

16.22 References

1. White, L.R. (1990) Credit analysis: two more C's of credit, *Journal of Commercial Bank Lending*, Oct.
2. National Economic Development Council (1986) *Lending to Smaller Firms*, NEDC, London.
3. Smith, T. (1992) *Accounting for Growth*, Century Press, London.
4. Chorafas, D. and Steinmann, N. (1991) *Expert Systems in Banking*, Macmillan.
5. McKillop, D.G. and Hutchinson (1990) *Regional Financial Centres in the British Isles*, Gower, London.
6. Bank of England (1993) Bank lending to small businesses, *Bank of England Quarterly Bulletin*, Feb.

7. Accounting Standards Committee (1984) *Accounting for Leases and Hire Purchase Contracts*, SSAP 21.

16.23 Further reading

To keep up to date with changes that are taking place in the methods of financing companies it is necessary to read current journals. These include the *Bank of England Quarterly*, the quarterly publications of the leading banks and *Business Weekly*, the publication of the Department of Trade and Industry. A selection of interesting books and articles is given below.

Look what credit scoring can do now, *ABA Banking Journal*, May 1994.
Bank of England (1990) Venture capital in the United Kingdom, *Bank of England Quarterly Bulletin*, Feb. 78–83.
Collet, N. and Schell, C. (1992) *Corporate Credit Analysts*, Euromoney Books.
Donaldson, T.H. (1983) *The Medium-Term Loan Market*, Macmillan.
Economist Newspaper (1989) How banks lend, *Economist*, 4 Feb.
National Westminster Bank (1992) Banks and small to medium sized business financing in the UK, *National Westminster Bank Quarterly Review*, Feb.

For discussion on the leasing issue, see:

James, A.N.G. and Peterson, P.P. (1984) The leasing puzzle, *Journal of Finance*, 39.
Hochman, S. and Rabinovitch, R. (1984) Financial leasing under inflation, *Financial Management*, Spring.
McConnell, J.J. and Schalheim, J.S. (1983) Valuation of asset leasing contracts, *Journal of Financial Economics*, Aug.

16.24 Problems

1. Beaver PLC is considering entering into an agreement with a factoring company. The main details of the proposed factoring agreement are:

   (a) The agreement will be for a minimum period of 2 years, thereafter cancellable at three months' notice.
   (b) Basic factoring services will be provided for a charge of 1½% of Beaver's annual turnover, the charge payable annually in arrears. Entering into the factoring agreement will enable Beaver to save £60 000 per year in office and other expenses – the savings being effected in a lump sum each year end.
   (c) The factor is willing to advance Beaver up to 80% of the invoice value of factored debts immediately a sale is invoiced. A commission of 2½% will be deducted from the gross amount of any funds advanced (i.e. up to 80% of invoice value). The factor will also charge interest at 15% per annum, applied on a simple monthly basis, on the gross funds advanced, i.e. before deduction of the 2½% commission. Both interest charge and commission will be deducted from the funds advanced to Beaver.
   (d) The factor is confident that the average collection period will be reduced from the current figure of 90 days to 70 days, or perhaps to only 60 days, although a transition period of up to 6 months will be required before the reduction is fully effected. On receipt of cash from Beaver's invoiced debtors the factor will immediately pay to Beaver all sums outstanding concerning that invoice.

Beaver's annual credit sales amount to £7.2 million which are spread evenly throughout the year.

Required:

   (a) Calculate the effective annual factoring cost, as a percentage of the funds improvement caused by factoring, for a full year after any transition period under each of the following separate conditions:

(i) Beaver will not take advantage of the factor's willingness to advance funds but the factor will reduce the average collection period to 70 days. (3 marks)
(ii) Beaver will take full advantage of the factor's willingness to advance funds and the average collection period:
(a) remains at 90 days, and (4 marks)
(b) is reduced to 60 days. (4 marks)

(b) Beaver can borrow at 16% per annum and could, by spending £30 000 per annum payable at the end of each year, reduce the average collection period to 80 days without factoring whereas the factor would reduce the collection period to 70 days. Advise Beaver whether it should enter into the factoring agreement and, if so, whether funds should be obtained from the factor rather than by borrowing. (9 marks)

(You may assume a 360 day year split into 12 equal months. Taxation may be ignored.) *(ACCA, Financial Management, June 1983)*

2. Corcoran Ltd is a small manufacturing company which is experiencing a short-term liquidity crisis during 1994. The company accountant has estimated that by the end of October 1994 a further £200 000 of extra funds will be required. Since the company already has a large overdraft, its banker will not advance any more funds. Three solutions to the problem have been put forward:

(a) Option 1. A short term loan of £200 000 could be raised for 6 months from 1 September 1994 at an annual interest rate of 18%. This would be obtained through a finance company, but there would be no costs involved in raising the funds.

(b) Option 2. The company could forego cash discounts of 2% which are obtained from suppliers of raw materials for payment within 30 days. The maximum credit which could safely be taken is 90 days. Monthly purchases of raw materials amount to £102 041 before discounts. Corcoran Ltd would forego the discount for 6 months before reviewing the position again.

(c) Option 3. The company could factor its trade debtors. A factor has been found who would be prepared, for a period of 6 months from 1 September, to advance Corcoran Ltd 75% of the value of its invoices less the deduction of factoring charges, immediately on receipt of the invoices. (You may assume that all invoices are sent out at the end of the month of sale.) The factoring charges would consist of:
(i) an interest charge of 15% p.a. on the amount of money advanced, calculated on a day-to-day basis, and deducted in advance;
(ii) a fee for taking on the task of collecting debts, amounting to 2% of the total invoices and deducted in advance. Monthly sales are expected to be £300 000. The factor would pay the balance owing on the invoices on receipt of the money from the debtors. On average, debtors pay at the end of the month following the month of sale. As a result of using the factor, Corcoran Ltd estimates that there would be savings in administration costs of £4 000 per month. Any surplus funds in excess of the £200 000 required would be used to reduce the bank overdraft, which costs 1% per month.

Required:

(a) Show which of the three options is cheapest. (15 marks)
(b) If the factoring arrangement is the option preferred, what would be the cash flow position for receipts for the period September 1994–April 1995? (5 marks)
(c) Briefly explain the other considerations which should be taken into account when choosing between the three options. (5 marks)
Ignore taxation. (25 marks)

3. Newlean Ltd has experienced difficulty with the collection of debts from export customers. At present the company makes no special arrangements for export sales.
As a result the company is considering either:

(a) employing the services of a non-recourse export factoring company;

(b) insuring its exports against non-payment through a government agency.

The two alternatives also provide new possible ways of financing export sales. An export factor will, if required, provide immediate finance of 80% of export credit sales at an interest rate of 2% above bank base rate. The service fee for the debt collection is 2½% of credit sales. If the factor is used administrative savings of £12 500 per year should be possible. The government agency short term comprehensive insurance policy costs 35 pence per £100 insured and covers 90% of the risk of non-payment for exports. For a further payment of 25 pence per £100 insured the agency will provide its guarantee which enables bank finance for the insured exports to be raised at ⅝% above bank base rate. The finance is only available in conjunction with the government agency comprehensive insurance policy. Newlean normally has to pay 2½% above base rate for its overdraft finance.

Newlean's annual exports total £650 000. All export orders are subject to a 15% initial deposit.

Export sales are on open account terms of 45 days credit, but on average payment has been 30 days late. Approximately ½%, by value, of credit sales result in bad debts which have to be written off.

Clearing bank base rate is 10%.

Required:

(a) Determine which combination of export administration and financing Newlean Ltd should use.   (15 marks)

(b) Outline the main debt collection techniques with respect to sales in the home market that are available to financial managers.   (5 marks)

(c) Discuss how a manufacturing company might devise an effective debt collection system.   (5 marks)

(25 marks)

ACCA, Dec. 1985

4. (a) Worral Ltd is a wholly owned subsidiary of Grandus PLC. Grandus traditionally allowed its subsidiaries considerable freedom of action, but the board of directors of Grandus are concerned about Worral's recent performance and working capital management. As a result Grandus's board of directors has given the managers of Worral one year in which to increase the company's current ratio to at least the industry average, without adversely affecting other aspects of the company's performance.

Summarized financial details of Worral Ltd (£000)

	1991	1992	1993	1994	Industry Ave 1994
Turnover	8234	8782	8646	9182	—
Profit after tax	486	492	448	465	—
Current ratio	1.84	1.61	1.52	1.48	1.60
Acid test	0.97	0.93	0.90	0.84	0.95
Gearing	75.4%	74.6%	79.2%	85.8%	75%
Bad debts/sales	0.5%	0.9%	1.2%	1.5%	0.5%
Collection period (days)	60	73	92	107	60

Worral's managers are considering three possible courses of action:

(i) Increase long-term loans by £300 000 and use the proceeds to reduce the company's overdraft.

(ii) Offer a cash discount of 3% for payment in 14 days. The normal terms of sale allow 60 days credit. All sales are on a credit basis. If the cash discount is offered 50% of customers are expected to take it, and bad debts are expected to be halved. The annual cost of administering the cash discount scheme would be £30 000.

(iii) Use the services of a non-recourse factoring company at a commission of 2.5% of turnover and finance charges of 4% over bank base rate on funds advanced immediately. Worral would take the full finance facility available on all credit sales, and would use the proceeds to reduce current liabilities. The use of a factor is expected to result in credit management cost savings of £135 000 per year.

Bank base rate is 11%. Worral pays 2% above bank base rate for its overdraft.

Summarized balance sheet year ending 31 December 1994

		£000
Fixed assets		3200
Current assets:		
Stock	2100	
Debtors	2684	
Cash	90	4874
Less current liabilities:		
Overdraft	1650	
Other	1643	3293
		4781
Financed by:		
Shareholders' funds		3461
11% long-term loan 2015–19		1320
		4781

The long-term loan is from Grandus PLC. Long-term loans to subsidiaries are charged at their cost to Grandus. Grandus 11% £100 Debentures are currently trading at £82.74.

Required

(a) Critically evaluate the three suggestions and recommend which alternative should be selected. All relevant calculations must be shown.

(19 marks)

(b) Briefly describe three ways, in addition to factoring, that a company might obtain finance by using debtors as security.

(6 marks)

(25 marks)

5. The directors of Expos PLC are currently deciding whether to lease or buy a new machine. The machine, which would attract a 100% first year allowance (i.e. can be fully depreciated in the year of purchase), costs £70 000 and has a life of five years, after which time it will have zero scrap and resale values. If the machine were to be leased, the lease agreement would specify five annual payments of £16 300, payable annually in advance. Lease payments would start on 1 January 1984, the same day on which purchase of the machine would take place. The company's accounting reference date is 31 December.

The company's tax advisers are unsure whether or not the company will have to pay any corporation tax on the profits of the next five years, as they are currently awaiting judgement on a tax reduction scheme that they have devised. Consequently, the directors of Expos PLC would like to know whether to lease or buy the machine, both if the company has to pay corporation tax on the profits of the next five years, and if the company has no corporation tax liability over that period. Expos PLC pays tax twelve months following the end of its accounting year. If the company has a corporation tax liability, the effective corporation tax rate will be 52%.

You may assume for simplicity that the company's effective cost of capital will be 10% per annum if no corporation tax liability arises during the next five years and 5% per annum if the company is liable to pay corporation tax.

You are required to:

(a) prepare calculations showing whether the machine should be bought or leased, assuming that

    (i) Expos PLC will have no corporation tax liability during the next five years and   (4 marks)

    (ii) Expos PLC will have to pay corporation tax on its profits for the next five years and   (9 marks)

(b) explain the difference between a finance lease and an operating lease, and discuss the importance of the distinction for corporate financing.   (12 marks)

Note: Ignore advance corporation tax.

ICAEW, Financial Management, Dec. 1983

6. (a) Describe and discuss the arguments advanced in favour of equipment leasing. Do all these arguments stand up to rigorous scrutiny?

(b) Selly Oak University needs a new computer. It can either buy it for £520 000 or lease it from Compulease. The lease terms require Selly Oak to make five annual payments (first instalment payable immediately) of £140 000. Selly Oak has charitable status and pays no tax. Compulease pays corporation tax at 50% with a 12 month lag and can claim 100% capital allowances for tax purposes. The computer will have no residual value at the end of year 4. The bank has quoted an interest rate of 20% for loan facilities.

    (i) Should Selly Oak University lease or buy the equipment?

    (ii) How much money is the lessor making from the lease?

7. The West Midland Company is considering a proposal to acquire a new machine. Because of the shortage in cash available to purchase the machine, the lease financing alternative will have to be considered as well. The finance department has been able to provide the following estimates:

Expected useful life	5 years
Purchase price	£230 000
Lease payments (per annum)	£72 000
Annual operating costs (if purchased)	£26 000 (fixed for the five years)
Annual operating costs (if leased)	£6 000
Scrap value	NIL

In addition you are given the following information:

    (i) The cashflows tale place at the end of each year, except the initial capital expenditure and the lease payments being required at the beginning of the year.

    (ii) The machine, if purchased, would qualify for a 100% first year capital allowance.

    (iii) The corporation tax rate is 50%.

    (iv) There is a 12-month lag in the payment of taxes and in the receipt of tax allowances.

    (v) The company's cost of capital is 20%, and its current net of tax long-term borrowing rate is 8%.

You are required to advise the company whether it should purchase or lease the machine.

Show calculations in arriving at your recommendation identifying any important assumptions.

8. Colin, a workshop proprietor, has discovered an investment opportunity, a new welding machine. He obtains the following estimates in connection with the installation of this machine:

Annual net revenue	£30 000
(received in cash at the end of each year of operation)	
Initial outlay – purchasing	£120 000
leasing	£12 000

	£	£
Lease payments		24 000
(payable at the end of each of the next 5 years)		
Useful life of the machine		5 years

Colin is not sure if he should go ahead. He knows he could raise finance to buy the machine by selling either some of the debentures he owns (presently earning only 4%), or some of the shares he holds in a publicly quoted company earning 10% and considered to be of the same risk as the welding machine opportunity. The salesman of the welding machines offers to summarize the problem and carries out the calculations given below:

	£	£
Annual revenue	30 000	
Annual lease payments	24 000	
Annual net revenue	6 000	
Initial outlay for lease		12 000
10% on above initial outlay	1 200	
Annual benefits from leasing welding machine	4 800	

You are required to:

Recommend to Colin whether he should have the machine installed or not. Show calculations in arriving at your recommendation **identifying any important assumptions.**

9. Edgbaston Biotech PLC, a young but expanding company quoted on the London Stock Exchange, is considering a further expansion opportunity.

   The expansion requires the purchase of capital equipment costing £2 million on which first year allowances of 100% are available. It is anticipated that cash revenues will just cover cash costs for the two years following the purchase of the equipment but that in the next eight years cash revenues will exceed cash costs by £600 000 p.a., by which time it is anticipated the equipment will have zero economic value having been superseded by new technology.

   Up to now Biotech has been financed entirely by equity and the after-tax cost of equity has been estimated at 16% p.a. However, ICFC have agreed to provide a loan of £1 million with interest at 12% p.a. to fund this project; the terms of the loan provide for interest-only payment for the first three years followed by interest and repayments of capital of £200 000 p.a. over the next five years. As an alternative ICFC have offered leasing terms for the equipment requiring 10 annual instalments of £290 000, the first payable on acquisition of the equipment.

   Required:

   (a) Advise the company on the value of alternative courses of action available on the assumption that it will be in a substantial tax-paying position throughout the life of the project. (Assume rate of corporation tax of 50%.) Explain and justify any quantitative methods used.

   (b) On the assumption that past and projected expansion make the payment of mainstream corporation tax unlikely in the forseeable future make whatever adjustments you consider to be necessary in your advice offered in (a) above. Explain and justify any quantitative models used.

   (c) Examine the financial implications of leasing and discuss the problem of identifying a suitable evaluative model.

10. Offshore Ltd operate internationally, specializing in the survey of sea-beds for possible mineral deposits. They are currently evaluating the investment potential of a deep-sea gas field that has been recently discovered off the English coast.

    The company estimates that there is a 70% probability that the field will have a five-year production life and a 30% probability that it will have an eight-year life. The estimated annual extraction tonnages are given below:

	5 Year Life		8 Year Life	
Million ton/year	Probability		Million ton/year	Probability
40	0.45		35	0.84
60	0.55		60	0.15

The United Kingdom government insists that it shall have sole purchasing rights of the gas and the expected price is £40 per ton. However, there is a 20% probability that world demand will make the government offer a price of £65 per ton. The price finally agreed with the government is expected to remain constant throughout the life of the field. It is estimated that the extraction costs of a five year field would be £34 per ton while an eight year field would have costs of £32 per ton. The fixed cost of operating the extraction platform and pipeline are estimated at £140 million per year.

Offshore Ltd has already spent £10.5 million on preliminary drilling but an additional outlay of £1000 million will be required before production can start. Two years after this payment the first production costs and revenue will arise and can then be assumed to arise at each following year end.

Offshore Ltd is based in a tax-haven and pays no taxes of any nature. The risk-adjusted discount rate appropriate to the project has been estimated at 16%, although Offshore Ltd intends to borrow substantial funds at 14% from South Bank, City of London.

You have been approached as a financial consultant by the company who wish to be advised on:

(a) The desirability of the investment based on your calculation of the expected net present value.

(b) Assuming that South Bank can utilize 100% capital allowances, calculate the range of annual lease payments acceptable to both lessor and lessee for an 8 year financial lease covering the £1000 million outlay, the first payment to be made immediately.

(State clearly any assumptions you make.)

11. Ceder Ltd has details of two machines which could fulfil the company's future production plans. Only one of these machines will be purchased.

The 'standard' model costs £50 000, and the 'de-luxe' £88 000, payable immediately. Both machines would require the input of £10 000 working capital throughout their working lives, and both machines have no expected scrap value at the end of their expected working lives of 4 years for the standard machine and 6 years for the deluxe machine.

The forecast pre-tax operating net cash flows associated with the two machines are:

	Years hence (£)					
	1	2	3	4	5	6
Standard	20 500	22 860	24 210	23 410		
De-luxe	32 030	26 110	25 380	25 940	38 560	35 100

The deluxe machine has only recently been introduced to the market and has not been fully tested in operating conditions. Because of the higher risk involved the appropriate discount rate for the deluxe machine is believed to be 14% per year, 2% higher than the discount rate for the standard machine.

The company is proposing to finance the purchase of either machine with a term loan at a fixed interest rate of 11% per year.

Taxation at 35% is payable on operating cash flows one year in arrears, and capital allowances are available at 25% per year on a reducing balance basis.

Required:

(a) For both the standard and the de-luxe machine calculate:
   (i) payback period;
   (ii) net present value.

Recommend, with reasons, which of the two machines Ceder Ltd should purchase.

(Relevant calculations must be shown.) (13 marks)

(b) If Ceder Ltd was offered the opportunity to lease the standard model machine over a 4 year period at a rental of £15 000 per year, not including maintenance costs, evaluate whether the company should lease or purchase the machine.

(6 marks)

(c) Surveys have shown that the accounting rate of return and payback period are widely used by companies in the capital investment decision process. Suggest reasons for the widespread use of these investment appraisal techniques.

(6 marks)

(25 marks)

ACCA, Dec. 1986

The dividend decision

17.1	Introduction	610
17.2	Dividend irrelevancy in perfect capital markets	612
17.3	Dividend payments may increase shareholder wealth	614
17.4	Dividend payments may reduce shareholder wealth	617
17.5	Dividend payments and taxation	617
17.6	Practical issues in dividend policy	619

17.7	Share repurchase and scrip dividends	622
17.8	Empirical evidence on dividend payments	624
17.9	Summary and conclusions	627
17.10	Key terms	627
17.11	Revision questions	628
17.12	References	628
17.13	Further reading	629
17.14	Problems	629

This chapter examines the theory and practices of corporate dividend policy. Alternative views on the effect of dividend policy on share valuation are discussed and the significance of dividend policy in imperfect markets is considered. Informational aspects of dividend payments are discussed as are the potential formation of clienteles attracted by particular policies. The impact of both corporate and personal taxes on the dividend decision are examined including problems relating to unrelieved advance corporation tax (ACT). The payment of foreign income dividends is also covered. The growing use of share repurchase by companies as an alternative to dividend payments is discussed. Finally, evidence relative to the significance of dividend policy both from shareholder and managerial perspectives is reviewed.

17.1 Introduction

Dividends are periodic cash payments made by companies to their shareholders. Preference share dividends are usually fixed by the terms of issue and are therefore not subject to policy decisions of company managers. However, payment of dividends to ordinary shareholders is a matter of company policy to be decided by the board of directors. It is an observable fact that the proportion of earnings paid out as dividend to ordinary shareholders can vary quite considerably from company to company.

The ability of a company to pay dividends will be related both to profitability and liquidity. There must be distributable profits from which to pay dividends and cash available to make the actual payment. Within these constraints dividend policy will be determined by the directors of the company who may decide to recommend distribution of either a high or low proportion of profits. The policy adopted should be aimed at maximizing shareholder wealth in line with corporate objectives, and we need to examine whether there is any particular dividend policy which maximizes shareholder wealth. Is a high dividend payout policy better than a low payout policy?

At first sight it might seem that the answer to the question is obvious. General dividend valuation models tell us that the value of a share is equal to the present value of the dividend stream; therefore would not high dividends mean a high share value? The answer to this is, it depends! If it were possible to increase the current dividend payment without affecting future payments in any way, then share value would be increased. But a moment's thought should tell us that because dividends are a cash payment they reduce the resources of the company and unless replaced by new capital issues could affect the short- and long-term investment prospects and hence the dividend-paying ability of the company. This is what makes the dividend decision difficult to analyse in a real world situation because it can impact on both the investment and financing decisions. It is therefore frequently analysed by assuming that investment and borrowing are given and that changes in dividend payments are accommodated by identical changes in issue of new equity. This was the approach adopted by Miller and Modigliani (MM) [1] which we shall examine in detail later.

Porterfield [2] suggested a simple model for analysing the dividend payment which is useful in identifying factors which might affect shareholder wealth and suggesting a framework for future discussion. Porterfield suggested that it would be worthwhile paying a dividend if

$$d_1 + P_1 > P_0$$

where d_1 is the cash value of the dividend to the shareholder, P_1 is the forecast ex dividend market price of the share immediately after the dividend announcement and P_0 is the market price before the dividend announcement. The equation is saying that if the sum of the dividend payment plus the share value after payment of the dividend is greater than the share value before the dividend announcement then a dividend should be paid. This is because shareholder wealth will be greater with the dividend payment than without it.

It is worth considering factors which could affect the values of d_1, P_1 and P_0 in the equation above. Before the dividend announcement P_0 will be reflecting the company's prospects in terms of future profitability and related dividend payments. This will be some sort of investor consensus based on all available information relating to the company, the industry it operates in and current market conditions. The information will include forecasts of future dividend payments to be made.

When announced, the dividend d_1 may be about the same, higher or lower than market anticipation. The actual cash value of the dividend to shareholders will vary between shareholders depending on their respective marginal income tax rates. Tax-exempt shareholders, e.g. pension funds, particularly under an imputation system of corporation tax, will enjoy a higher cash benefit than a shareholder paying tax at the highest marginal tax rate (40% at the time of writing). The ex dividend share price P_1 will be affected by the dividend payment itself which causes a decline in company resources but may also be affected by the change in dividend payment, if any, compared with what the market expected. This change, commonly referred to as an informational effect, may arise because of revised expectations about the future prospects of the company.

The discussion so far suggests that the value of dividend payments to shareholders depends on a number of factors relating to the value of d_1 and P_1. It has been suggested that d_1 varies with shareholder marginal tax rate while P_1 depends on how much share prices decline because of the cash dividend paid and how much share prices change because of revised expectations on announcement of the dividend payment. In fact the equation can be adapted to summarize three views advanced on dividend policy.

If $d_1 + P_1 > P_0$, then dividends enhance shareholder wealth and higher dividends would be preferred. This was the accepted wisdom advocated by a number of writers prior to MM's irrelevancy theorem which can be summarized as $d_1 + P_1 = P_0$, i.e.

shareholder wealth is not changed by dividend payments as the share value declines by the amount of dividend paid. A third view, based on shareholder taxes, claimed that because dividends have in the past been taxed more highly than capital gains, then $d_1 + P_1 < P_0$.

These three main views will now be discussed, beginning with the MM approach. As their analysis is conducted on the assumption of perfect capital markets it provides a good starting point and a basis for discussing alternative views where market imperfections are considered.

17.2 Dividend irrelevancy in perfect capital markets

MM began by examining the effects of differences in dividend policy on the current price of shares in an ideal economy characterized by perfect capital markets, rational behaviour and perfect certainty. Under such a set of restrictive conditions they concluded that dividend policy was irrelevant in that the share price was independent of the particular policy followed. As the assumptions are important, particularly when the applicability of the MM theorem to the 'real' world is considered, it is useful to set out their precise meaning in detail.

In 'perfect capital markets' no transactor is large enough to have an appreciable impact on the then ruling price. All traders have equal and costless access to information about the ruling price and about all other relevant characteristics. There are no transaction costs and no tax differentials either between distributed and undistributed profits or between dividends and capital gains.

'Rational behaviour' means that investors always prefer more wealth to less and are indifferent as to whether a given increment to their wealth takes the form of cash payments or an increase in the market value of their holdings of shares.

'Perfect certainty' implies complete assurance on the part of every investor as to the future investment programme and the future profits of every corporation. Because of this assurance, there is, among other things, no need to distinguish between stocks and bonds as sources of funds. Because of this the analysis assumes an all-equity firm.

Under these assumptions if dividend policy is to be irrelevant the price of each share must be such that the rate of return (dividends plus capital gains per pound invested) on every share will be the same throughout the market over any given interval of time. This rate of return is defined as the discount rate that equates the present value (PV) of the dividends received during the period plus the end-of-period selling price to the current share price:

$$P_0 = \frac{d_1 + P_1}{1 + K_e} \tag{17.1}$$

where P_0 is the current share price, d_1 is the dividend per share during the period, P_1 is the end-of-period share price and K_e is the internal rate of return or, in equilibrium, the cost of equity capital. Equivalently

$$K_e = \frac{d_1}{P_0} + \frac{P_1 - P_0}{P_0} \tag{17.2}$$

If we assume an all-equity firm and multiply equation (17.1) by the current number N_0 of shares outstanding, the total market value V_0 of the firm can be written as

$$V_0 = N_0 P_0 = \frac{d_1 N_0 + P_1 N_0}{1 + K_e} \tag{17.3}$$

However, as dividend policy affects the amount of new equity financing required, P_1 in the above equation depends on d_1. To overcome this apparent dependence it is necessary to equate sources of corporate cash to uses during period 1:

$$Y_1 + P_1(N_1 - N_0) = d_1 N_0 + I_1 \tag{17.4}$$

where Y_1 and I_1 are earnings and investment in period 1 and N_1 is the total number of shares outstanding at time 1. As before, this identity states that for an all-equity firm earnings plus receipts from the sale of new shares must equal dividends plus investment. From (17.4) above we can observe that:

$$d_1 N_0 = Y_1 - I_1 + P_1(N_1 - N_0)$$

Substituting this value in equation (17.3) gives:

$$V_0 = \frac{Y_1 - I_1 + P_1(N_1 - N_0) + P_1 N_0}{1 + K_e} = \frac{Y_1 - I_1 + N_1 P_1}{1 + K_e}$$

As $V_1 = N_1 P_1$

$$V_0 = \frac{Y_1 - I_1}{1 + K_e} + \frac{V_1}{1 + K_e} \qquad (17.5)$$

Since d_1 does not appear in equation (17.5) directly, the only way that current dividends can influence share price is if they affect one of the variables which does appear. Y_1 depends on the profitability of past investments and hence is independent of dividends in any period; similarly K_e depends only on the risk borne by equity shareholders and not on the firm's dividend policy. V_1 might depend on dividends, but if so the dependence will be on future not current dividends. In fact V_1 can be expressed as a function of V_2 and so on to give

$$V_0 = \sum_{t=1}^{\infty} \frac{Y_t - I_t}{(1 + K_e)^t} \qquad (17.6)$$

It can therefore be concluded that, given a firm's investment policy, the dividend pay-out it chooses to follow will affect neither the current price of its shares nor the total return to its shareholders.

In addition to the irrelevance of dividends, the earnings-investment model also illustrates a number of interesting facts about ordinary share values. Firstly it characterizes the firm as a giant capital expenditure project with Y_t representing cash inflows and I_t cash outflows; the value of the firm is the PV of these inflows minus the PV of the outflows discounted at an appropriate risk-adjusted discount rate. This ties in with our previous valuation analysis. In fact an appropriate rate for the whole firm might represent an average rate where a number of activities of different risk are undertaken. If the firm were broken down into sub-units, then its total value would be the sum of the PVs of these sub-units.

We could say that the market value of an all-equity firm equals the difference between the PVs of its earnings and its investment discounted at the cost of equity capital. Secondly, the model stresses the fact that the value of a share is not simply the PV of future earnings per share. This would only be true in the extreme case where the firm made no new investments and issued no new shares.

Because of the need for the sources and uses of cash to be equal as summarized in equation (17.4) any change in dividend payment will lead to an equal and opposite change in the amount of money raised from new issues. Suppose that a company is currently valued at £1 million and has in issue 1 million shares valued at £1 each. Further suppose that the company's current income exactly covers its investment requirement. Any dividend to be paid by the company will have to be met by a new issue of equity.

Let us examine the implications of the company's paying a dividend of 20p per share:

	Company	Individual share
Current value	1 000 000	1.00
Less: Dividend payment	200 000	20
	800 000	80p
	200 000	
New issue	£1 000 000	

Simultaneously with the payment of the dividend a new issue will be made of 200 000/0.80 = 250 000 shares, i.e. to raise £200 000 the company will have to issue 250 000 shares priced at 80p per share, which is the value of shares after allowing for the dividend payment to 'old' shareholders. The value of the company after dividend payment and new issue remains at £1 million; there are now 1 250 000 shares in issue valued at 80p per share. 'Old' shareholders have received a cash dividend of 20p per share and their shares have declined in value from £1 to 80p; their total wealth is unaltered. 'New' shareholders have purchased shares at a price which reflects the true value of the company.

If the company did not pay a dividend, existing shareholders could 'manufacture' their own dividend by selling some of their shares on the market to new shareholders (Table 17.1). A holder of 100 shares would need to sell 20 shares at £1 each to obtain the cash equivalent of a dividend of 20p per share. The shareholder would be left with 80 shares valued at £1 plus £20 cash. This would be the same position as if a dividend had been paid, except that in that case the residual holding would be 100 shares at 80p. This result relies entirely on the assumptions set out in detail at the beginning of this section. Perfect capital markets are necessary so that costless transactions can be undertaken at correct prices; the prices in turn reflect the perfect certainty enjoyed by all participants in the market with investors indifferent between dividends and capital gains.

Table 17.1

	Holder of 100 shares, cash dividend	'Homemade' dividend by selling through market
Value prior to dividend/sale	100	100
Cash dividend at 20p per share	20	Sale of 20 shares at £1 20
Residual value	80	80

Given the assumptions there is now almost complete agreement that MM are correct, and in recent years the dividend issue has concentrated on imperfections in their assumptions. In particular, the existence of taxes, both corporate and personal, needs to be considered as does the absence of certainty about the future. Both these factors are discussed in later sections, beginning with the traditional view of dividends which regarded them as more valuable than the equivalent retention partly because they were regarded as less risky and resolved, to some extent, uncertainty about the future.

17.3 Dividend payments may increase shareholder wealth

The irrelevancy conclusions of MM challenged the conventional wisdom of the time. Up to that point there had been almost complete agreement by both finance theorists and corporate managers that investors preferred dividends to capital gains and that companies could increase or at least maintain the market value of their shares by choosing a generous dividend payout policy. The popular view was that dividends represented a more certain form of income than equivalent capital gains and that therefore they would be valued more highly than the equivalent amount of uncertain and riskier capital gains.

This view was summarized by Graham and Dodd [3] in their now classic text on security analysis when they wrote:

the considered and continuous verdict of the stock market is overwhelmingly in favor of liberal dividends as opposed to niggardly ones. The common stock investor must take this judgement into account in the valuation of stock for purchase. It is now becoming a standard practice to evaluate common stock by applying one multiplier to that proportion of the earnings paid out in dividends and a much smaller multiplier to the undistributed balance.

Support for the 'bird-in-hand' argument came from Myron Gordon [4] who argued that investors will apply a lower rate of discount to the expected stream of future dividends than the more distant capital gains. This view is encapsulated in the Gordon valuation model which places higher values on securities offering higher dividend growth.

The belief in the importance of dividend policy seems to be reinforced by the actions of business-people, investors and government. Company directors, as we shall see later, seem to regard dividend payments as important. Shareholders and their advisers frequently seek to persuade directors to increase dividend payments. In the late 1960s and mid-1970s, when the UK government was seeking to contain inflation by a statutory wages and prices policy, it was also felt necessary to introduce a dividend policy which limited the percentage increase companies could make in their dividend payments [5]. This was an indication to wage-earners that as their annual increases were restricted then it was only fair that shareholders should likewise have their returns restricted by a similar amount. Of course, if MM are right then any dividend restrictions imposed could be regarded as purely cosmetic.

It might appear initially that Gordon's argument demands support and that MM chose to ignore the differential risks of dividends and capital gains. However, the MM analysis stressed that provided that the investment policy could be taken as given, then any change in dividend policy had to be reflected by an equal change in the amount of fresh equity raised by the company. Thus any increase in dividend payment would be reflected by an equal additional issue of equity. If existing shareholders were to gain by an increase in dividend payment, then new shareholders would have to be persuaded to take on additional risk without receiving full recompense for it. There would thus be a transfer of risk from existing to new shareholders. We now consider the case of an existing shareholder who receives a cash dividend. This shareholder could either place the money on deposit in a bank or reinvest the dividend in new shares in the company. If the investment is made in a bank then a return near to the risk-free rate of return will be earned, while if the investor reinvests in the company in new shares he will expect to receive a risk-adjusted rate of return relative to the business risk of the company. This business risk will be determined by the type of business activity that is being undertaken. This intuitive approach suggests that risk is not related to whether return is received in the form of dividend or capital gain but depends crucially on the type of activity being undertaken by the company, i.e. the rate of return which shareholders expect depends not on the form in which increases in wealth accrue but on the risk of the investment activities undertaken by companies. This approach was stressed in the earlier chapters on risk in project appraisal.

Confusion may have arisen because the shares of companies with high dividend payouts have a tendency to figure amongst the lower-risk securities, and other things being equal low-risk securities sell at premiums compared with high-risk securities. However, the question to be addressed is whether higher dividends cause a reduction in risk or whether the high dividends are a consequence of the companies' activities being conducted at a lower level of risk. There is support for the view that companies carrying out riskier activities choose a low payout policy [6]. It does not seem unreasonable that when management views future earnings as highly uncertain then they keep dividends low to avoid the possibility of a reduction if the investment turns out badly. The argument being made here is that it is not the level of dividend payments which causes companies to be rated as high or low risk, but that the level of business risk of a company as predicated by its investment policy will have a significant effect on the dividend policy adopted by the company's management.

There is wide acceptance for MM's conclusion of dividend irrelevancy given their assumption of perfect and efficient capital markets. However, there would again be agreement that in the real world their model would be deficient. In fact the extent of this deficiency would vary according to the country examined. In the UK and USA markets are widely accepted as efficient if not perfect, but in other countries around the world the degree of efficiency has often been considered to be at a lower level than in the more sophisticated markets of the UK and USA. The dividend debate can therefore be considered in terms of both market imperfections and inefficiencies or, as has been suggested by at least one author, in terms of whether shareholders are fully rational.

There may be natural clienteles for both high and low payout stocks. For example, pension funds, for tax reasons, trust funds, because of the way in which income is defined, and retired investors looking for income to live on all prefer companies with high payout policies. It could be argued that if investors require cash then this could be obtained by selling securities in line with the MM argument. However, it is both more convenient and less costly (because of transaction costs) for companies to pay higher dividends to those shareholders requiring them. It has also been argued in the past that a clientele exists for low payout shares and that younger investors paying higher marginal rates of income tax might prefer to have lower dividends and higher capital gains. The existence of clienteles was acknowledged by MM who suggested that shareholders would be attracted to the policy which best suited them and that there would be sufficient companies with different policies to satisfy all clienteles. In the circumstances no company could increase its value by changing its policy.

The role of dividends in conveying information has been noted by a number of writers [7]. In this context a change in the level of dividend payment is regarded as conveying information on how company directors view future prospects. An increase in dividend would be regarded as conveying optimism about future profitability, while a decline in dividend would signify pessimism about the future. The value of such an information channel is probably best considered in the environment of a country where both the quality and reliability of information may not be as great as in the UK or USA. An example might be a developing country with a less sophisticated legal and regulatory framework. Miller [8] has made the important point that it is not necessarily the direction of the dividend change which matters but how the level of dividend payment compares with what was expected generally by the market. He discusses this view in the context of rational expectations. A simplistic view would be that if there is a dividend increase then prices should rise not necessarily because of the dividend increase but because of the information that this conveys about future company profitability, i.e. directors may be using dividend increases as a method of signalling future prosperity to the shareholders. A reverse effect might be expected from a decrease in dividend payment. However, before any dividend payment the market will already have a view on what dividend it expects the company to pay. In a world of rational expectations it is only unexpected dividend changes which provide the market with clues about unexpected future changes in earnings. It is these unexpected changes which will trigger off price movements that may appear to be reactions to the dividend change. This discussion can be taken a stage further in that if company directors believe that markets respond to unexpected changes in dividend payments then perhaps an increase in share price could be brought about, at least in the short term, by paying a higher dividend than anticipated even if it means losing investment opportunities. This approach should not work in a world of rational expectations. The market itself will realize that this option is open to directors, that they may be tempted to increase dividends as described and therefore expect an even larger dividend than before at any given level of earnings. To raise the dividend further in the hopes of generating a surprise would be too costly in terms of foregone future earnings. Also, a reduction in dividend would be counter-productive because the market will be expecting a larger dividend as a means of increasing share price. The market would interpret a disappointingly low dividend as a sign of bad news. The line of argument would seem to suggest that company directors have little leeway in deciding upon changes in their level of dividend payments. If the dividend is not up to expectations, then the share price is likely to fall. However, if an excessive payment is made, then there may be both lost investment opportunities and unnecessary extra financing expenses.

This line of argument was developed mainly in the USA [9] and was related to the differential tax treatment of cash dividend payments and capital gains. In both the UK and the USA dividend payments are regarded as income and are therefore subject to income tax at the taxpayer's top marginal rate. However, until fairly recently capital gains have been treated differently and subject to tax on realization at a lower single proportional rate. In the UK it would have been possible at one time to pay a tax rate of 98% on dividends while capital gains were being taxed at a maximum rate of 30%. It can be seen that in this type of tax regime arguments could be put forward for shareholders to receive additions of wealth in the form of capital gains rather than dividends. Although in the USA this tax differential was not so marked, the corporate tax system (for a fuller discussion of which see Section 17.5) when combined with the personal system of taxation meant that in almost every case capital gains were to be preferred to dividends.

The supporters of this view claimed that the market valued firms with low payout policies more highly than firms with high payout policies. It was claimed that where companies paid dividends and consequently had to make new issues to finance their activities shareholders' interests were not best served. It was pointed out that such companies could finance their requirements by cutting dividends and making fewer new issues. This would have the dual benefit of saving shareholders from paying income tax and also reducing transaction costs on new issues. In order to evaluate this point of view it is necessary to undertake a fuller examination of the consequences of taxation for dividend policy and this we now do in the next section.

17.4 Dividend payments may reduce shareholder wealth

A proper analysis of the effects of taxation on dividend decisions should include not only the impact of the corporate and personal tax systems but also any interaction between the two taxes. It is important to consider the type of tax regime operating, particularly as the UK system of company taxation is different from the US system where much of the literature on dividend policy originates.

In the UK companies are taxed under an imputation system of corporation tax. A progressive system of personal income tax is in force with the first £3000 of taxable income being assessed at 20%, the next £20 700 at 25% and the balance at 40%. This is in fact much less progressive than at times in the past when it was possible for very rich people to pay over 90% on marginal income. Capital gains are now taxed at the taxpayer's marginal income tax rate, whereas prior to the Finance Act 1988 they were taxed at a proportional rate which was often lower than the taxpayer's marginal income tax rate. One advantage of capital gains which still continues is that they are taxed only on realization, i.e. sale of the security. Thus deferring taking a profit defers the payment of capital gains tax and additionally capital losses can be offset against gains; there is also an exemption limit of the first £5800 realized in any year. The major difference in the USA is that there is a classical system of corporate taxation which was in fact the system operative in the UK up until 1973. The development of personal taxation in the USA has followed similar lines to that in the UK, so that the distinction between the taxation of dividends and capital gains is much less pronounced.

The main difference between the two systems of corporation tax can be illustrated using a numerical example:

17.5 Dividend payments and taxation

	Classical system £000	Imputation system £000
Profit before corporation tax	5000	5000
Less: corporation tax at 33%	1650	1650
	3350	3350
Less: dividend	1000	800
	2350	2550

(assuming ACT of ²⁄₉ under imputation system)

Under the classical system there is no connection between the corporate and personal systems. The payment of the dividend would be regarded as gross income for tax purposes and subject to income tax at the shareholder's marginal tax rates. However, under the imputation system the dividend paid has a tax credit attaching to it of ²⁰⁄₈₀ (¼) of the cash payment. If the receiving shareholder does not pay tax in the 40% tax band no further tax will be payable. However if tax is payable at this higher rate a further 20% becomes payable; for example a higher rate taxpayer receiving cash dividends of £800 would be assessed on £1000 dividend income, £800 plus tax credit of £200 (¼ × £800). The tax liability would be:

£1000 at 40%	400
Less: imputed tax credit	200
Additional tax payable	£200

If the shareholder does not pay tax a refund equivalent to the tax credit can be reclaimed from the Inland Revenue. Thus if a tax-exempt pension fund received cash dividends of £800 the tax credit of £200 would be refunded giving a total benefit of £1000.

When making the distribution the company has to pay advance corporation tax (ACT) to the Inland Revenue which the company can offset against its next payment of mainstream corporation tax. The imputation system thus links together the corporate and personal systems. For ease of illustration a rate of corporation tax of 33% has been used for both systems, but in practice it is likely that the rate of corporation tax under a classical system would be lower than the rate under an imputation system.

We shall now examine the implications of the different tax systems for dividend policy. If an amount D was available for distribution under a classical system of corporation tax then the after-tax value to the shareholders would be

$$(1 - m)D$$

where m is the shareholders' marginal income tax rate, while under an imputation system the after tax benefit would be

$$\frac{1-m}{1-s}D$$

where s is the rate of imputation or basic rate tax. However, if no dividend was paid but the benefit was reflected in the share price and the shares sold, the net shareholder benefit would be

$$(1 - z)D$$

where z is the shareholders' rate of capital gains tax. The decision on whether or not to pay a dividend, other things being equal, could be formalized as follows.

Under a classical system of corporation tax pay dividend where

$$1 - m > 1 - z$$
$$m < z$$

That is, a dividend would only be optimal where the marginal rate of income tax is less than the rate of capital gains tax. This is unlikely ever to be the case and is reflected in the US writings on this topic. However, following the US 1986 Tax Reform Act theoretically m should equal z.

Under an imputation system of corporation tax pay dividend where

$$\frac{1-m}{1-s} > 1 - z$$
$$m < z + s(1 - z)$$

Although under a classical system dividends would never be optimal, under the imputation system shareholders with low marginal rates of tax might prefer dividends to capital gains. If we consider pension funds which pay no taxes on their income, for them $m = z = 0$ and a dividend payment is more valuable than the equivalent retention by the company. In fact, under an imputation system where dividends and capital gains are subject to the same rate of personal tax (as currently in the UK) dividends should always be preferred to capital gains irrespective of the shareholders' marginal rate of income tax.

There are, however, a number of reasons why this should not necessarily be the case in practice. First for a number of reasons the effective rate of capital gains tax is likely to be lower than the shareholders' marginal tax rate. The cost of a security for computing gains is increased in line with inflation, thus the taxable gain will be lower than the monetary gain. In addition capital gains can be deferred by not selling securities or setting off gains against losses on shares sold. There is also an annual exemption (currently £5800) given on capital gains. Secondly, the payment of higher dividends may mean that some companies are unable to offset fully ACT payments against their mainstream liabilities; this may arise because of excess capital allowances, losses brought forward or overseas income attracting double tax relief. The latter problem arises where a UK company earns a significant proportion of profits overseas and pays tax in the country where profits are earned. The UK has double tax agreements with many countries whereby tax paid in one country can be offset against potential liability in another country. In many cases this means that no UK tax is payable on the overseas profits and therefore, until recently, ACT paid on dividends from overseas profits increased unrelieved ACT. However the Chancellor of the Exchequer, Kenneth Clarke, announced in his budget speech on 30 November 1993 an optional foreign income dividend scheme to enable companies to obtain repayment of surplus advance corporation tax when dividends are paid out of foreign source profits. This scheme, which commenced on 1 July 1994, has the following features.

- It is optional.
- Companies can pay dividends out of foreign income and receive special tax treatment.
- Although ACT is payable in the normal way any surplus ACT arising from the foreign income dividend is repayable.
- Shareholders receiving a foreign income dividend are treated as if the dividend has borne tax at 20% at source but no refunds of tax will be made to taxpayers should they not be liable to income tax.

These new arrangements create another sort of distribution with special tax provisions relating to both companies and shareholders. They are part of a government strategy designed to reduce the £5 billion surplus ACT which includes the phased reduction of the rate of ACT from its former 25% to its current 20%.

Taken together these actions should benefit company cashflows by first of all reducing conventional ACT payments and then allowing unrelieved ACT to be reclaimed in respect of foreign income dividends. However, there will be some losers; pension funds and other tax-exempt shareholders will have their tax refunds reduced. Companies could find that, although they are better off, the value of employee pension funds decreases thus increasing the liability of the company to the pension fund! What remains to be seen is whether dividend payments increase so that some of the cash benefit derived by companies is passed on to shareholders. Another strategy adopted by companies has been to offer shareholders a scrip dividend instead of a cash dividend and this is discussed in 17.7 below.

Dividend payments

UK companies have normally declared and paid two dividends in respect of each financial year. The first payment, known as an interim dividend, is paid during the financial year and is normally the smaller of the two. At the end of the financial year it is usual for a final dividend to be recommended which will be included in the annual accounts

17.6 Practical issues in dividend policy

as a provision. While a board of directors is empowered to declare and pay interim dividends, shareholders' approval must be obtained at the annual general meeting before payment of the final dividend. Of necessity, the meeting will be held some time after the end of the company's financial year, and therefore payment of the final dividend will not be made until well into the company's subsequent financial year. With the growing international nature of financial markets some large UK companies are now moving to the US system of quarterly dividend payments, but this is likely to affect only a comparatively small number of companies.

Distributable profits

The Companies Act 1985 requires that dividends only be paid out of accumulated net realized profits. This includes the realized profits for both the current year and previous years. Because there is no precise definition of realized profit in the Act the Consultative Committee of Accountancy Bodies issued guidance statements on the determination of realized and distributable profits. Essentially, the statements are of the view that profits normally identified by Accounting Standards and calculated in accordance with generally accepted accounting principles will be regarded as realized profits. Profits available for distribution are calculated after deducting any accumulated realized losses from previous years. In addition, for public companies a distribution may only be made to the extent that accumulated distributable profits exceed net unrealized losses.

Other legal constraints

There have been occasions in the past when the UK Government has restricted dividend payments made by companies. Dividend controls were first introduced in the UK in the late 1960s and then reintroduced in 1973. With controls, the annual percentage increase in the dividend per share that companies were allowed to make was limited. The controls were part of the Government's anti-inflation policy and were seen as a *quid pro quo* for restrictions in price and wage increases. However, with a change to a Government having a different policy, dividend restriction ended in 1979.

Companies must therefore be aware of any legal rules relating to dividend payments when formulating dividend policies.

Liquidity

The distinction between profits and cash has been stressed in an earlier chapter. Because a company is showing a high level of profitability it does not necessarily mean that the company will have large amounts of cash at its disposal. It is frequently the most profitable rapidly expanding companies which are most pressed for liquid funds. In order to pay a dividend a company clearly requires cash, and therefore the availability of cash resources within the company will be a factor in determining dividend payments. It could be argued from a theoretical point of view that provided that the company is profitable it will be able to borrow in capital markets to enable it to pay whatever rate of dividend it wishes. However, for a variety of reasons the directors may not wish to adopt such a strategy and prefer to meet any dividend payments from the company's current resources.

Current debt obligations

The company may already have debt obligations which require repayment. It may intend to replace current debt with another security issue on maturity or alternatively may be setting aside amounts to a sinking fund to fund repayment on maturity. If the company's policy is to repay the debt by transferring amounts to a sinking fund this will usually require a higher level of earnings to be retained.

When making existing borrowings the company may have had to make covenants with regard to the level of cash dividends paid to ordinary shareholders. A covenant of this kind is designed to protect the lender and may limit the level of payments, define the earnings from which dividend payments can be made or require certain liquidity ratios to be maintained at certain minimum levels.

Investment opportunities

Growth companies faced with many investment opportunities may prefer to finance their expansion by retaining a large proportion of profits. The alternative would be higher levels of dividend payments followed by rights issues to shareholders; although it could be argued that under the present tax regime such a policy would not necessarily be against shareholders' interests, there is also the matter of issue costs to consider. There is a high element of fixed costs in new issue expenses, making a smaller issue of securities proportionally more costly than a larger issue. As an expanding company is likely to require a regular flow of new money for projects, it is likely that a low dividend payout policy will be adopted by smaller rapidly expanding companies. There is the additional point that smaller companies are likely to find it costly and difficult to raise funds from outside the company either in the form of debt or equity, while larger well-established companies with a longer track record are likely to find it easier to gain access to capital markets.

Volatility

Shareholders do not like unpleasant surprises. (Of course like every one else they just love pleasant surprises!) Company directors are therefore wary about setting a level of dividend payment which they think may in some circumstances be unsustainable. A company with relatively stable earnings will therefore be more likely to adopt a higher payout policy than a company with a volatile pattern of earnings.

Control

The control of a company is determined by the ownership of the ordinary share capital. The way in which a company chooses to finance its activities may have an impact on the control of the company. If shares have to be sold to new shareholders outside the present group of shareholders then this could lead to dilution of control within the company. It is also possible that high levels of debt may also restrict the freedom of activity of the owners of the company with regard to certain policies. These may be additional reasons to encourage particularly smaller companies to adopt a lower payout policy.

Taxation

The potential effect of taxation on dividend payments has been analysed in a previous section. The current UK position has been complicated by the reduction in the rate of ACT, the possibility that it could be reduced further and the introduction of foreign income dividends. Reduction in the tax imputed to dividends reduces their value to all categories of taxpayer. Besides, as the effective rate of capital gains tax is likely to be below (perhaps substantially in some cases) the shareholders' marginal tax rate, some shareholders may prefer capital gains to dividends. With regard to conventional dividends there is still likely to be a continuum of shareholders with some preferring high dividends and some preferring no dividends at all. Exempt shareholders such as pension funds would prefer a high payout policy, basic rate taxpayers would be indifferent between dividends and retentions while higher rate taxpayers would prefer retentions to dividends. It is possible that there will be some conflict of interest between shareholders in a company, and it will be the directors who will have to resolve this conflict by adopting a policy which is satisfactory to all the groups outlined above. To some extent there may be a 'clientele effect' whereby shareholders with low tax rates are attracted to high payout companies and shareholders with high tax rates are attracted to low payout companies. However the effectiveness of a clientele policy will to some extent be determined by portfolio considerations.

The directors of a company will also consider any ACT implications. Should a company be in a position where there is a limit to the amount of ACT which can be offset against mainstream tax liability the directors may well seek to set the level of distribution so that maximum relief can be obtained. If this action is not taken and ACT is paid which cannot in the short or medium term be offset against mainstream corporation tax liabilities, then effectively the company will be making an interest-free loan to the government. If the ACT proves irrecoverable then the company will have paid additional corporation tax purely because of the level of its distribution. Companies with foreign earnings can now pay foreign income dividends and reclaim any surplus ACT arising. This saves the company money but tax exempt shareholders cannot reclaim any imputed tax, thus reducing the value of the dividend to important groups such as pension fund investors.

17.7 Share repurchase and scrip dividends

In addition to the payment of cash dividends to shareholders other strategies available include scrip dividends and share repurchase. Both of these were introduced in Chapter 12 on equity capital. A scrip dividend is a small scrip or bonus issue which capitalizes distributable profits in the form of extra shares, leaving it to the shareholder to decide on whether to keep the extra shares or sell on the market for cash. Prior to 1965 scrip dividends were not treated as income and thus there were tax advantages for shareholders in this form of issue. However scrip dividends still offer advantages to investors and companies; they are particularly useful to companies with surplus ACT but no foreign income to pay foreign income dividends. From the company perspective scrip dividends mean that cash does not leave the company and no ACT has to be paid. Some companies have offered enhanced scrip dividends instead of cash dividends where the value of shares is set above the cash dividend. These companies include RTZ, Ladbroke, BAT and Forte. Shareholders accepting extra shares instead of a cash dividend are normally treated as receiving a dividend equal to the cash that could have been taken. Tax is deemed to have been paid at the basic rate. If the value of the shares taken as stock dividend differs from the cash dividend by 15% or more the shareholder is deemed to have received a dividend equal to the value of the shares at the date of issue. Therefore enhanced scrip dividends, provided the enhancement is below 15% of the cash dividend, will not give rise to any additional income tax liabilities. This will be most beneficial and therefore attractive to higher rate taxpayers. Table 17.2 is an extract from the 1993 accounts of BAT Industries. The note shows that the enhancement offered was 50% with a take up by shareholders of 92%. This strategy reduced the group's ACT liability by £107 million. Figure 17.1 distils comments on BAT's dividend policy covering both enhanced scrip dividends and foreign income dividends.

Another possible strategy arises from the ability of companies to repurchase their own shares following the provisions included in the 1981 Companies Act. This option has long been permissible and widely practised in the USA and it is becoming more popular in the UK as company managements recognize its potential in an integrated financial strategy. The discussion which follows concentrates on share repurchase by quoted companies.

A number of reasons have been suggested for share repurchases, including the following:

1. return of surplus cash to shareholders;
2. increase of earnings per share (EPS) and hence share price;
3. buyout of large holdings of unwelcome shareholders;
4. achievement of desired capital structure.

Table 17.2 *Extract from 1993 accounts of BAT Industries*

	Pence per share	1993 £m	Pence per share	1992 £m
Interim 1993 paid 14 October 1993	7.9	243	7.3	216
Final 1993 payable 1 June 1994	12.2	375	11.3	335
	20.1	618	18.6	551

The number of shares in issue has been adjusted for the 1 for 1 capitalization issue approved by shareholders at the Annual General Meeting held on 18 May 1993, and the prior year comparative figure for pence per share has been adjusted accordingly.

At the AGM, approval was given for an Enhanced Share Alternative to the 1992 final dividend, whereby shareholders could elect to receive shares worth 50% more than the cash equivalent of the final dividend. Valid elections totalled 92% of the shares then in issue. In accordance with FRS4 'Capital Instruments' the total amount of the cash dividend that would otherwise have been paid is included in the table above and an adjustment made to share capital and reserves during the current year.

The interim dividend paid was reduced by **£9 million** 1992 £12 million as a consequence of shareholders electing for shares as an alternative to cash, and the comparatives have been restated to comply with FRS4 under which dividends are shown at their cash equivalent. The benefit of the share alternative is taken directly to reserves.

Elections during the year, including the Enhanced Share Alternative, enabled the Group's liability for ACT to be reduced by **£107 million** 1992 £7 million.

In the first case share repurchase can be seen as an alternative to a higher dividend payment or leaving the cash on deposit. Share repurchase may involve higher transaction costs than dividend payments but may be more flexible in that there are different methods of repurchase which may not involve all shareholders and which allow choice to be influenced by tax implications which may be significant.

Share price could be improved over time if company management had access to positive information unknown to the market. However, this would effectively be insider trading and could benefit remaining shareholders at the expense of those bought out. The EPS advantage is debatable in that it is an accounting measure and not necessarily related to any increase in the value of the company. It has been suggested that 'the EPS benefits of share repurchases are minimal for most companies' [10].

Share repurchase of large holdings has taken place in the USA to ward off unwanted takeover threats (so-called greenmail). However, this type of activity is to be discouraged rather than encouraged as it tends to promote speculative activity by arbitrageurs taking positions in companies in the hope of being bought out by management at an enhanced price. A UK example of a large share repurchase was the 1989 purchase by BP

The company was one of the first to use the controversial enhanced scrip dividend in 1993 and in 1994 was one of the leaders in using the foreign income dividend. Both have the express purpose of saving unrelieved advance corporation tax, but there may be fewer companies who choose to pay FIDs. In part that is because the FID regulations are onerous. Although earning almost three-quarters of its income abroad, BAT only decided that it should issue a FID after extensive work. Other companies may not pay enough overseas tax on their earnings to qualify. In addition FIDs have the same cash-flow advantages as enhanced scrips, which were often used by companies with as much of a cash flow as a tax problem.

Institutional reaction may also be mixed. BAT has structured its FID so that tax-exempt funds such as pension funds do not suffer, but the main gain goes to tax paying shareholders. There may be some reaction to this, despite the fact that FIDs put taxpaying and tax-exempt shareholders on an equal footing. However, taxpayers will have to accept that if the company does not pay a FID in future years, their payment may fall.

Unless companies are allowed to stream foreign income to taxpaying shareholders and UK income to tax-exempt shareholders, FIDs will have limited appeal. However this policy would make it difficult to distinguish between those companies which earn substantial income abroad, and for whom the FID regulations were devised, and those companies who pay excessive dividends from inadequate UK profits.

Figure 17.1 BAT dividend policy

of 790 million shares built up by the Kuwait Investment Office, a move forced on BP by the UK Government.

In 1994 many of the Electricity Distribution Companies took powers to buy back substantial amounts of shares. These companies generate substantial cash flows from their trading activities but a contributory factor may have been the large cash mountain caused by consumers prepaying electricity bills in March 1994 to avoid value added tax levied on payments from 1 April 1994 onwards. The companies therefore had substantial cash resources surplus to immediate requirements and likely to increase from normal trading activities. With short-term interest rates low and managers confident about the future of their companies, share repurchase could be argued to be the best use for these surplus funds

The ability to adjust capital structure through share repurchase gives management an additional way of increasing the proportion of debt in the capital structure (gearing). The alternative would be to take on extra borrowing. However, it might be argued that the risk of existing debt holders and remaining equity holders will be increased by equity repurchases.

Of great importance to listed companies contemplating share repurchases are the regulation and tax consequences of such transactions. Regulations are necessary to ensure that creditors and remaining shareholders are not disadvantaged by share repurchases with which they may not be directly involved. Tax laws have sought to maintain treatment consistent with cash dividend payments. UK quoted companies can repurchase shares in three ways:

1. purchase in the stock market;
2. arrangements with individual shareholders;
3. tender offers to all shareholders.

Prior permission must be obtained for any repurchase from shareholders and holders of any warrants, options or convertibles. Prior clearance is also necessary from the Takeover Panel. Payments for repurchased shares must be made from distributable profits and all repurchased shares must be cancelled.

A listed company repurchasing its own shares must treat the excess of cash paid out over capital subscribed as a dividend payment. ACT must be paid on this excess and is available for offset against mainstream liability in the normal way. There would clearly be difficulties in some cases with unrelieved ACT. The tax position of selling shareholders will depend on whether the repurchase is direct or through the market.

With a direct repurchase there is symmetry of treatment with the company. The repayment of the capital element is dealt with under capital gains tax rules while the excess is treated as if it was a net dividend. For example, any tax-exempt holders would effectively be able to reclaim the ACT paid by the company, as was the case with the Kuwait Investment Office referred to above. This treatment is not possible with market repurchases; in this case all proceeds received by shareholders are regarded as capital and the transaction is dealt with under capital gains tax rules. We can see from this brief examination that the type of repurchase could be very important for taxpayers in different categories. Given an MM world of perfect capital markets, shareholders would be indifferent between cash dividends and share repurchases. However, with real world imperfections both companies and their shareholders will need to consider the impact of taxes on share repurchase strategies.

17.8 Empirical evidence on dividend payments

MM's conclusion on the irrelevance of dividend policy presented a strong challenge to the conventional wisdom of the time. Up to that point it was almost universally accepted by both theorists and corporate managers that investors preferred dividends to capital gains and that companies would enhance their market value by choosing a generous dividend policy. The empirical work undertaken prior to the production of the MM paper seems to support the pro-dividend school of thought. Many studies had demonstrated a strong positive correlation between dividend payout ratios and price earnings ratios. That is, on average, companies with higher dividend payout ratios tended to have higher price-to-earnings ratios and vice versa. However this early work received strong criticism to the extent that it has been thoroughly discredited [11].

The main problem with this type of study is that dividend payout ratios and price-to-earnings ratios tend to move together whether companies are doing well or poorly. This point may be appreciated if it is considered how each ratio is calculated:

$$\text{payout ratio} = \frac{\text{dividends per share}}{\text{earnings per share}}$$

$$\text{price-to-earnings ratio} = \frac{\text{current market price}}{\text{earnings per share}}$$

As companies seek to maintain a stable dividend policy a temporary decline in earnings per share may not affect the level of dividend payments. Therefore a decline in earnings per share with a maintained dividend would lead to a high payout ratio. As share prices reflect the discounted value of benefits to be received from share ownership for the foreseeable future a decline in earnings for one year may not lead to a sharp fall in price; indeed, the price reaction will depend upon what the market had been expecting. In these circumstances because of the way in which the price-to-earnings ratio is calculated a fall in earning which is not accompanied by a proportionate fall in price would lead to a higher price-to-earnings ratio. We therefore have a situation where a decline in earnings leads to both an increase in the payout ratio and an increase in the price-to-earnings ratio. Consider what now happens if an unexpected increase in earnings takes place. Again, because of the stability in dividends which company directors seek any increase in dividend payments is likely to be small. Therefore the payout ratio would fall with substantially higher earnings but little or no increase in dividends. Again, it is likely because of market expectations that the price increase would not be proportional with the increase in earnings. Therefore the price-to-earnings ratio would decline.

We can see that where a company experiences fluctuations in the level of its earnings, dividend payouts and price-to-earnings ratios will tend to move together. Another factor which ties in with volatility of earnings discussed in section 17.6 was the problem that early studies experienced in coping with different risk levels of securities. It was pointed out that higher-risk companies with high volatility of earnings tend to pay low dividends and lower-risk companies pay high dividends. Risk is a factor determining price-to-earnings ratios: high-risk companies will tend to have lower price-to-earnings ratios than low-risk companies. As high-risk companies will also tend to pay lower dividends and low-risk companies higher dividends, there will be a natural correlation between low payout and low price-to-earnings ratios and high payout and high price-to-earnings ratios.

The next challenge to MM came not from researchers seeking to show that dividends increase shareholder wealth but from the emerging group claiming that, for tax reasons, dividends decreased shareholder wealth. This arose from the differential tax treatment of dividends and capital gains under a classical system of corporation tax as discussed in section 17.5. By introducing corporate and personal taxes into the MM model Brennan [12] proved that shareholders' wealth decreases when dividends are paid out. A number of studies based on various versions of Brennan's model were undertaken with a view to testing whether investors required high rates of return on ordinary shares with high dividend yields. This would be the expectation if Brennan's model was correct. Black and Scholes [13] tested for the relationship between security returns and dividend yield by forming well-diversified portfolios and ranking them on the basis of their systematic risk (beta) and then by dividend yields within each risk class. Their conclusion was that dividend yield had no effect on security returns. A contrary conclusion was reached by Litzenberger and Ramaswamy [14], who also tested the relationship between dividends and security returns. Using the Brennan model they concluded that risk-adjusted returns are higher for securities with higher dividend yields. The implication is that dividends are undesirable; hence higher returns are necessary to compensate investors in order to induce them to hold high dividend yield securities. A number of similar studies undertaken at around the same time give support for Litzenberger and Ramaswamy. However, there are a number of problems connected with testing for the dividend effect in this way. The tests tend to use portfolios of securities, whereas individual security returns are needed to obtain statistically powerful results. In addition the use of beta as a measure of systematic risk is subject to a great deal of error. Finally, investors use dividend announcements to estimate expected returns. That is, it is not necessarily the level of dividend payments *per se* which might influence returns but the change in dividend payment from what was expected; in other words, the information affect. As Litzenberger and Ramaswamy used monthly data for individual securities the criticism concerning use of portfolios was overcome. Long [15] undertook a detailed analysis of two classes of shares issued by a US company. The types of share were virtually identical in all respects except for dividend payouts. The conclusion of this study was in fact that dividends are desirable to shareholders and that they will require a lower rate of return on shares which pay a high dividend yield. This, of course, is contrary to the Litzenberger and Ramaswamy studies.

We can therefore see that there is conflicting evidence on the value of dividends to shareholders, and the issue remains unresolved. A number of studies have been undertaken on the effect of dividend announcements on the value of the firm. This effect is often referred to as the information effect, i.e. the announcement of a change in dividend leads to revised expectations and a change in the value of the firm. A number of studies have been undertaken by Pettit [16], Watts [17], Kwan [18] and Aharony and Swary [19]. The empirical evidence (with the exception of Watts's study) indicated that dividend changes do convey some unanticipated information to the market. Although Watts did find a positive dividend announcement effect, he concluded that the information content was not of economic significance as it would not enable a trader with monopolistic access to the information to earn abnormal returns after transaction costs.

The research discussed to date has examined how shareholders respond to dividend announcements and payments. It would also be useful to ask management how they view dividend payments and the factors that they take into account in making such payments. Lintner [20] conducted interviews with 28 companies to investigate how they determined dividend policy. The work carried out by him suggested the following.

1. Managers concern themselves with change in the existing dividend payout rate rather than the amount of the newly established payout as such.
2. Most management sought to avoid making changes in dividend rates that might have to be reversed within a year or two.
3. Major changes in earnings were the most important determinants of the companies' dividend decisions.
4. Investment requirements generally had little effect on changing the pattern of dividend behaviour.

Lintner's findings suggest that the US company management interviewed at the time regarded dividends as an important decision, that dividends were paid irrespective of forecast levels of investment and that management were reluctant to increase dividends unless they were reasonably sure that they would be able to maintain the higher level of payment permanently. Lintner developed a simple explanatory model consistent with the findings outlined above:

$$D_t - D_{t-1} = C(BE_1 - D_{t-1})$$

where D_t and D_{t-1} are the dividends payable in the years signified by the subscripts, C is the rate of adjustment adopted by the company, B is the target payout ratio and E_1 is the earnings per share for that year. The equation states that companies will adjust their dividend payout gradually as earnings change rather than by immediately increasing their dividend by the percentage increase in earnings. The more conservative the company, the more slowly would the adjustment take place and therefore the lower would be the adjustment rate C. Fama and Babiak [21] investigated a number of different models for explaining dividend behaviour. Of the many models used, Lintner's proved to be one of the two best.

The conclusion is that the US corporations examined increased dividends only after they were reasonably sure that they would be able to maintain them permanently at the new level. The research suggests that not only do company directors think that dividends are important but they recognize that market participants also regard them as being important and are therefore anxious not to convey bad information by having to alter the trend of dividends once they have been established.

More recent work undertaken by Farrelly *et al.* [22] has expanded and updated Lintner's study. A questionnaire mailed to 562 firms listed on the New York Stock Exchange yielded 318 responses. The views obtained were supportive of Lintner's earlier findings and indicated that managers believe that dividend policy is relevant and influences the value of share prices.

17.9 Summary and conclusions

Research and behaviour indicate that market participants consider dividends to be important. Lintner's study suggested that company managers considered decisions on dividends to be important and there seems no reason to change this view. Managers seek to smooth dividend payments from year to year by only adjusting gradually to changes in earnings. Unexpected fluctuations are avoided wherever possible because of the potentially adverse information that might be conveyed, leading to uncertainty and a volatile share price.

MM demonstrated that in perfect capital markets dividend payments were irrelevant to shareholder wealth; however, when imperfections are considered the position is less clear cut. Taxation, corporate and personal, can make a difference. In the UK the imputation system of corporation tax makes dividends particularly attractive to tax-exempt shareholders; these will include pension funds which are an important group of shareholders with influential managers. Attempts to change dividend policy drastically may lead to pressure from institutional investors, as has been the case from time to time.

A consistent dividend policy does not mean that all companies will have similar payout ratios. Expanding companies with many investment opportunities are likely to pay out a lower proportion of earnings than companies with few or perhaps no investment opportunities. Retentions are a favoured source of finance for new investment, and company directors will try and adopt a dividend policy which satisfies shareholders yet at the same time leaves sufficient retentions for investment purposes.

Investors in small high-growth companies will usually expect a low dividend policy and be prepared to sacrifice current income for the prospect of higher capital gains in the future. In time, growth will tend to level off, perhaps because of competition, and a higher payout policy might then be adopted. Investors are unlikely to complain if a previous high-growth low-payout company subsequently increases its dividend payout; however, if a previous high-payout company changed policy and decided to cut dividends, perhaps to reduce borrowing or to obviate the need for an equity rights issue, shareholders might not necessarily agree. Any change of this sort would need careful preparation and explanation to major shareholders to avoid potential adverse effects on share price.

17.10 Key terms

Adjustment rate (per Lintner)
Bird-in-hand argument
Clientele effect
Effective tax rate
Imputation and classical tax systems
Informational effect

Marginal tax rate
Rational expectations
Scrip dividend
Share repurchase
Signalling

17.11 Revision questions

1. It has been suggested that dividends may increase/decrease/not affect shareholder wealth. Delete as appropriate.
2. What are the assumptions necessary to sustain MM's dividend theorem?
3. How could a shareholder 'manufacture' dividends? Why might a shareholder not choose to do this?
4. What is meant by the 'information content' of dividends?
5. What is the 'clientele effect'? What is its significance for company dividend policy?
6. What were the principal reasons for Gordon *et al.* and others suggesting that high dividends would increase shareholders' wealth?
7. Why are personal taxes considered important in the dividend policy debate?
8. Would the system of company taxation be important in evaluating dividend policy? Why?
9. Why is the effective rate of capital gains tax often lower than the shareholder's marginal tax rate?
10. List the factors that management might consider in determining dividend policy.
11. List the three ways in which UK companies can repurchase shares.
12. If a company was to double its profits would it also be likely to double its dividend payment?

17.12 References

1. Miller, M.H. and Modigliani, F. (1961) Dividend policy, growth and the valuation of shares, *Journal of Business*, **34**, 411–33, October.
2. Porterfield, J.T.S. (1965) *Investment Decisions and Capital Costs*, Prentice-Hall, Englewood Cliffs, NJ.
3. Graham, B. and Dodd, D.L. (1951) *Security Analysis: Principles and Techniques*, 3rd edn, McGraw-Hill, New York.
4. Gordon, M.J. (1959) Dividends, earnings and stock prices, *Review of Economics and Statistics*, **41**, 99–105, May.
5. Counter Inflation (Dividends) Order 1973.
6. Rozeff, M. (1986) How companies set their dividend payout ratios. Reprinted in *The Revolution in Corporate Finance* (eds J.M. Stern and D.H. Chew Jr), Basil Blackwell.
7. Hakansson, N. (1982) To pay or not to pay dividends, *Journal of Finance*, 415–28, May.
8. Miller, M.H. (1986) Behavioural rationality in finance: the case of dividends, *Journal of Business*, **59**, 451–68, October.
9. Miller, M. and Scholes, M. (1978) Dividends and taxes, *Journal of Financial Economics*, 333–64, December.
10. Dodd, J. (1989) Does share repurchase boost EPS? *Professional Investor*, November.
11. Friend, I. and Puckett, M. (1964) Dividends and stock prices, *American Economic Review*, 656–82, September.
12. Brennan, M.J. (1970) Taxes, market valuation and corporate financial policy, *National Tax Journal*, **23**, 417–27, December.
13. Black, F. and Scholes, M. (1974) The effects of dividend yield and dividend policy on common stock prices and returns, *Journal of Financial Economics*, 1–22, May.
14. Litzenberger, R.H. and Ramaswamy, K. (1979) The effect of personal taxes and dividends on capital asset prices: theory and empirical evidence, *Journal of Financial Economics*, 163–95, June.
    Litzenberger, R.H. and Ramaswamy, K. (1980) Dividends, short selling restrictions, tax-induced investor clienteles and market equilibrium, *Journal of Finance*, 469–82, May.
    Litzenberger, R.H. and Ramaswamy, K. (1982) The effects of dividends on common stock prices: tax effects or information effects? *Journal of Finance*, 429–44, May.
15. Long, J.B., Jr. (1978) The market valuation of cash dividends: a case to consider, *Journal of Financial Economics*, 235–64, June–September.
16. Pettit, R.R. (1972) Dividend announcements, security performance and capital market efficiency, *Journal of Finance*, 993–1007, December.

17. Watts, R. (1973) The information content of dividends, *Journal of Business*, 191–211, April.
18. Kwan, C. (1981) Efficient market tests of the information content of dividend announcements; critique and extension, *Journal of Financial and Quantitative Analysis*, 193–206, June.
19. Aharony, J. and Swary, I. (1980) Quarterly dividend and earnings announcements and stockholders' returns: an empirical analysis, *Journal of Finance*, 1–12, March.
20. Lintner, J. (1956) Distribution of incomes of corporations among dividends, retained earnings and taxes, *American Economic Review*, 97–113, May.
21. Fama, E.F. and Babiak, H. (1968) Dividend policy: an empirical analysis, *Journal of the American Statistical Association*, 1132–61, December.
22. Farrelly, G.E., Baker, H.K. and Edelman, R.B. (1986) Corporate dividends: views of the policy-makers. *Akron Business and Economic Review*, 62–74, Winter.

17.13 Further reading

An analysis of the effects of corporate and personal taxes on dividends (and financing) is given by King. A number of readable and up-to-date articles, particularly those by Miller and Brealey, are contained in Stern and Chew. The rationale for share repurchases and the legal and taxation framework are discussed in a Bank of England publication.

The original analysis of dividend policy in a perfect capital market is contained in:

Miller, M.H. and Modigliani, F. (1961) Dividend policy, growth and the valuation of shares, *Journal of Business*, **34**, 411–433, October.

While the traditional view on the value of dividends is put in:

Gordon, M.J. (1959) Dividends, earnings and stock prices, *Review of Economics and Statistics*, **41**, 99–105, May.

Bank of England (1988) Share repurchase by quoted companies, *Bank of England Quarterly Bulletin*, August.

Brealey, R.H. (1986) Does dividend policy matter? in *The Revolution in Corporate Finance* (eds J.M. Stern and D.H. Chew Jr), Basil Blackwell.

King, M. (1977) *Public Policy and the Corporation*, Chapman and Hall.

Miller, M.H. (1986) Can management use dividends to influence the value of the firm? In *The Revolution in Corporate Finance* (eds J.M. Stern and D.H. Chew Jr), Basil Blackwell.

Stern, J.M. and Chew, D.H., Jr. (eds) (1986) *The Revolution in Corporate Finance*, Basil Blackwell.

For an analysis of how companies set dividend payments see:

Lintner, J. (1956) Distribution of incomes of corporations among dividends, retained earnings and taxes, *American Economic Review*, **46**, pp. 97–113. May.

17.14 Problems

1. Over the past decade Radnor PLC has achieved an average annual growth in dividends of approximately 7% and is about to declare a dividend 8% higher than that paid last year. This level is consistent with expectations contained in recent press comment. However, Radnor is offered an opportunity to invest in a project which promises a discounted cash flow return considerably above the weighted-average cost of capital but which will produce no significant cash flows for about three years. The only funds available are those which would otherwise be used for the dividend, and undertaking the project would entail not paying a dividend at all this year. The managing director is of the opinion that shareholders deserve some reward and suggests that if the dividend is passed (i.e. not paid this year) the company should make a bonus issue of shares to give shareholders 'a dividend of a capital nature'.

Advise Radnor on the major theoretical and practical factors to be considered before arriving at a decision concerning undertaking the project or paying a dividend. Comment on the managing director's suggestion for rewarding shareholders. (20 marks)

(*Chartered Association of Certified Accountants, Dec. 1982*)

2. The chairman of the board of Oak Tree Ltd has announced that the company will change its dividend policy from paying a target proportion of 'normalized' earnings per share. Instead, dividends will be paid out as a residual, i.e. any cash flows left over after the firm has undertaken all profitable investments will be paid out to shareholders. In view of the increased variability of dividends to be paid in future years analyse the possible effects of the change in policy on the value of the firm. Your analysis should contain reference to both the certainty and uncertainty cases.

3. 'Dividend policy is irrelevant.' Discuss this statement, paying particular attention to the assumptions required to support it.

4. XYZ Ltd have just paid a dividend of £0.20 per share. The market expects this dividend to grow constantly in each future year at the rate of 6% per annum. The cost of capital for XYZ Ltd is currently 8%. As soon as the dividend was paid, however, the Board of XYZ Ltd decided to finance a new project by retaining the next three annual dividend payments. The project is seen by the market to be of the same risk quality as the existing projects and it is expected that the dividend declared at the end of the fourth year from now will be £0.25 per share and will grow at the rate of 7% per annum from then on. You hold 1000 shares in XYZ Ltd and your personal circumstances require that you receive at least £200 each year from this investment.

   (a) Assuming that there is a perfect market in XYZ Ltd's shares and that the market uses a dividend valuation model, show how the market value of its shares has been affected by the board's decision.

   (b) Show how you can still achieve your desired consumption pattern in the first three years while improving your expected dividend stream from then on.

5. About nine years ago Haaste PLC, a large and old-established firm, ceased paying dividends because of its poor financial performance and mounting losses. Following considerable reorganization and investment the firm is now an efficient, profitable and soundly managed organization. Consideration is being given to recommencing the payment of dividends, but when initially discussed at board level there was no agreement on the merits of this step. Three main views were expressed:

   • a stable dividend policy should be introduced as soon as possible;
   • dividends are irrelevant to shareholders;
   • dividends should be paid only when the firm has no investment opportunities which promise a return equal to or greater than that required by shareholders; this situation is unlikely to arise for several years.

   (a) Outline, and explain the importance of, the main points which should be considered when deciding upon corporate dividend policy. Comment on the three main views expressed by Haaste's Board. (15 marks)

   (b) It is proposed that there be a change in taxation to a system which penalizes corporate retained earnings and favours distribution of profits, thereby effectively forcing all companies to distribute all earnings. Examine the implications of such a change from the viewpoint of (i) corporate financial management, (ii) shareholders and (iii) the workings of the financial system and financial institutions. (10 marks)

(Total 25 marks)

(*Chartered Association of Certified Accountants, Financial Management, June 1984*)

6. In the past when governments have enacted incomes policies they have invariably also restricted the level of dividend increases that companies can make. The argument has been that it is only fair that the 'wages of investors' (dividends) should be under the same restraint as wages paid to work people. Discuss the reasoning behind the dividend restraint policy and comment on its scope for providing equity with an incomes policy.

7. Supporters of dividends as enhancers of shareholder wealth have supported their view by pointing out that shares with high dividend yields tend to have above average price-to-earnings ratios. Discuss the validity of this evidence.

8. Many quoted companies with small capitalization value either pay no dividends at all or have very low payout policies. Discuss why this might be and whether this policy could be expected to continue.

9. UK companies, like their US counterparts, can now use share repurchase as part of their financial strategy. One motivation suggested for share repurchase is to increase earnings per share. Consider the following information relating to a company:

Profit after tax	£5 million
Number of shares in issue	10 million
Earnings per share	50p
Share price	£6
Price-to-earnings ratio	12

Suppose that the company repurchases 2 million shares at £6 per share. The number of shares in issue will now be 8 million and the earnings per share will increase to 62.5p; if the price-to-earnings ratio remains at 12, the share price will rise to £7.50. Discuss this analysis and the general view expressed that share repurchase can boost earnings per share.

10. (a) How does the tax treatment of open-market share repurchases differ from direct repurchase?

   (b) Discuss the tax implications of both types of repurchase from the point of view of the company, a pension fund investor and a wealthy private investor.

11. The board of directors of Deerwood plc are arguing about the company's dividend policy.

   Director A is in favour of financing all investment by retained earnings and other internally generated funds. He argues that a high level of retentions will save issue costs, and that declaring dividends always results in a fall in share price when the shares are traded ex div.

   Director B believes that the dividend policy depends upon the type of shareholders that the company has, and that dividends should be paid according to shareholders' needs. She presents data to the board relating to studies of dividend policy in the USA in 1983, and a breakdown of the company's current shareholders.

Company group (10 companies per group)	USA dividend research Mean dividend yield (%)	Average marginal tax rate of shareholders (%)
1	7.02	16
2	5.18	22
3	4.17	25
4	3.52	33
5	1.26	45

Deerwood plc: analysis of shareholding

	Number of shareholders	Shares held (million)	% of total shares held
Pension funds	203	38.4	25.1
Insurance companies	41	7.8	5.1
Unit and investment trusts	53	18.6	12.1
Nominees	490	32.4	21.2
Individuals	44 620	55.9	36.5
	45 407	153.1	100.0

She argues that the company's shareholder 'clientele' must be identified, and dividends fixed according to their marginal tax brackets.

Director C agrees that shareholders are important, but points out that many institutional shareholders and private individuals rely on dividends to satisfy their current income requirements, and prefer a known dividend now to an uncertain capital gain in the future.

Director D considers the discussion to be a waste of time. He believes that one dividend policy is as good as any other, and that dividend policy has no effect on the company's share price. In support of his case he cites the equation by Modigliani and Miller

$$nP_0 = \frac{1}{1+p}\left[(n+m)P_1 - I + X\right]$$

Where P_0 = market price at time 0
P_1 = market price at time 1
n = number of shares at time 0
m = number of new shares sold at time 1
p = capitalization rate for the company
I = total new investments during period 1
X = total profit of the company during period 1.

Required:
Critically discuss the arguments of each of the four directors using both the information provided and other evidence on the effect of dividend policy on share price that you consider to be relevant.

(25 marks)

ACCA, Dec. 1989

12. (a) Pavlon PLC has recently obtained a listing on the Stock Exchange. 90% of the company's shares were previously owned by members of one family but, since the listing, approximately 60% of the issued shares have been owned by other investors. Pavlon's earnings and dividends for the five years prior to the listing are detailed below.

Years prior to listing	Profit after tax (£)	Dividend per share (£)
5	1 800 000	3.6
4	2 400 000	4.8
3	3 850 000	6.16
2	4 100 000	6.56
1	4 450 000	7.12
Current year	5 500 000 (estimate)	

The number of issued ordinary shares was increased by 25% three years prior to the listing and by 50% at the time of the listing. The company's authorized capital is currently £25 million in 25p ordinary shares, of which 40 million shares have been issued. The market value of the company's equity is £78 million. The board of directors is discussing future dividend policy. An interim dividend of 3.16p per share was paid immediately prior to the listing and the finance director has suggested a final dividend of 2.34p per share. The company's declared objective is to maximize shareholder wealth.

    (i) Comment upon the nature of the company's dividend policy prior to the listing and discuss whether such a policy is likely to be suitable for a company listed on the Stock Exchange. (6 marks)

   (ii) Discuss whether the proposed final dividend of 2.34p is likely to be an appropriate dividend:

if the majority of shares are owned by wealthy private individuals;

if the majority of shares are owned by institutional investors.

(10 marks)

(b) The company's profit after tax is generally expected to increase by 15% per annum for three years, and by 8% per annum after that. Pavlon's cost of equity capital is estimated to be 12% per annum. Dividends may be assumed to grow at the same rate as profits.

    (i) Using the dividend valuation model give calculations to indicate whether Pavlon's shares are currently undervalued or overvalued. (6 marks)

   (ii) Briefly outline the weaknesses of the dividend valuation model.

(3 marks)

(25 marks)

ACCA, June 1986

18 Gearing and company cost of capital

18.1	Introduction	634
18.2	Capital structure implications	635
18.3	Overall cost of capital: weighted-average cost approach	639
18.4	Adjusted present value method	645
18.5	Traditional view of capital structure	648
18.6	Capital structure in perfect capital markets	649
18.7	Capital structure and corporate and personal taxes	653
18.8	Capital structure and financial distress	658
18.9	A target debt/equity ratio?	660
18.10	Summary and conclusions	663
18.11	Key terms	664
18.12	Revision questions	664
18.13	References	664
18.14	Further reading	665
18.15	Problems	665

The chapter begins by reviewing how and why debt affects risk and return from the viewpoint of both the company and its investors. The effect of different debt levels on gearing ratios and earnings per share illustrate this point. The calculation of overall cost of company finance using a weighted average cost of capital (WACC) is discussed and illustrated. The use of WACC in project appraisal is critically evaluated as in the use of adjusted present value (APV) as an alternative to WACC. Alternative views on the significance of debt policy on firm value are examined, including those of Modigliani and Miller (MM) and the traditional approach. The significance of taxation both corporate and personal on the debt policy problem is investigated and the trade-off between the tax advantages of debt and increasing risk of insolvency discussed. Agency problems and the pecking order theory relating to choice of financing are also covered in this chapter.

18.1 Introduction

In the previous chapter we examined dividend policy and in particular whether any pattern of dividend payments would maximize shareholder wealth. In this chapter we turn our attention to another decision that corporate managers must make concerning shareholders' wealth namely the way in which the long-term capital requirements of the company should be financed. In Chapter 12 the nature of equity capital was examined and its cost discussed. Chapter 14 examined the differing types of debt and their cost. It was noted that typically the cost of debt is lower than that of equity because from the investor's point of view debt carries less risk. Our earlier discussion on risk and return stressed that there will be a constant trade-off between these factors with investors demanding higher levels of expected return for higher levels of perceived risk. It was also observed in the examination of debt that debt interest payments are tax deductible. If we couple together lower cost and tax deductibility it would appear that debt finance would in most cases be preferable. However, we also need to consider the effect on risk and hence return demanded by equity shareholders as the level of debt increases in the capital structure.

The terms gearing and leverage are both used to refer to the level of debt in a company's capital structure. We shall tend to use the word gearing as this has been the accepted usage in the UK whereas leverage is the term used in the USA. However, with the increasing internationalization of capital markets the term leverage is coming into more popular use in the UK. A highly geared or levered company would be regarded as one having a high proportion of debt in its capital structure, while a low geared or levered company would be one having a low proportion of debt in its capital structure.

In Chapter 10 we found that the beta of equity in geared companies was higher than that in ungeared companies, indicating that debt in the capital structure increases risk from the point of view of equity shareholders. Because of extra risk rational equity holders will demand a higher level of return and the capital structure debate is partly concerned with the trade-off between the higher return demanded by equity shareholders against the benefits derived by the company from lower-cost and tax-deductible debt.

We begin the chapter by looking at different measures of gearing, and by considering the accounting implication of different levels. We consider how the level of gearing affects the very important earnings per share measure. We then move on to consider how the level of gearing affects the cost of capital of a company. We look at the traditional weighted cost of capital approach, and the adjusted present value method which incorporates financing side effects directly into the present value calculations.

18.2 Capital structure implications

It is usual to use ratios to indicate levels of gearing as was fully discussed and illustrated in Chapter 3. In this chapter a number of points and issues covered in Chapter 3 are related to the debate covering corporate borrowing and its risk and reward implications for equity investors. Although there may be a little duplication with Chapter 3 the development enables a rounded approach to the debate to be adopted. If a fuller discussion of ratio analysis is required the readers are referred back to Chapter 3. The gearing ratio is regarded as an indicator of risk as high levels of debt create a high fixed-interest commitment which must be paid by the company irrespective of whether profits are made or not. It is usual for financial analysts to measure gearing by reference to balance sheet figures expressing debt as a ratio of total assets or alternatively equity; however, we need to recognize that debt and equity relationships can also be expressed in terms of market value which in many cases may bear little resemblance to balance sheet values. In Chapter 10 when equity betas were ungeared it was market values that were used rather than book values. However, both approaches have their benefits. A balance sheet approach might enable a distinction to be made between tangible and non-tangible assets. In the past lenders have been more willing to advance loans on the basis of tangible, i.e. physical, assets which are usually saleable, rather than intangible assets which, although having value in a continuing business, may have little or no value if the business is discontinued. The use of market values can be more realistic where balance sheet values bear little resemblance to current values and where valuable assets, e.g. brand names and trademarks, are not included on the balance sheet. A further approach to gearing is to relate interest payments to the profits available to pay them. Here interest cover is calculated, i.e. the number of times that interest payments could be made from current earnings. The higher is this multiple the lower is the perceived risk arising from the debt in the capital structure. The interest cover approach has assumed greater importance as the drawbacks of using balance sheet values has been increasingly recognized by analysts. Both the balance sheet gearing ratio and the interest cover ratio suffer from being static measures relating to a point in time and do not take into consideration potential risk over the life of a loan. It must be recognized that, although textbook analysis tends to make the simplifying assumption that there is only one kind of debt and also in many cases assumes that this debt is perpetual, in the real world there are many different types of debt with many differing interest rates and repayment dates.

Table 18.1 is an extract from the 1993 Annual Report of United Biscuits (Holdings) plc. This shows a variety of borrowings both in loans of different terms and currencies and also substantial lease obligations. The note also indicates in the analysis by currency that it is after allowing for related swaps. The diversity of borrowing opportunities and subsequent derivative activity in both currency and interest rate swaps make the calculation of cost of capital for large companies much more problematic than is often assumed in text book or examination examples. However, the principles of calculation remain unchanged; analysts and consultants will draw on basic theory and coupled with their knowledge of financial markets produce realistic estimates (and that is all anyone can produce) of the company's cost of capital.

Gearing levels also vary from country to country. There are many reasons for this. They include different systems of corporate governance, different historical developments and different tax structures.

The OECD in 1989 reported the following average levels of debt as a percentage of total capital for companies in the respective countries:

Japan	81%
France	63%
Germany	61%
UK	56%
USA	45%

These figures have to be interpreted with caution. Different accounting standards and practices distort the figures. It is, however, correct that such differences do exist and the rankings of the countries in terms of gearing is in line with the above listing.

The fact that debt usually has to be repaid either at a specified date or over a specified period means that managers must consider not only periodic interest payments but also repayments of principal as well. In addition to the balance sheet and income statement ratios mentioned above, managers will also need to construct cash budgets covering the life of the loan so that any potential shortfalls arising from loan repayments can be identified and planned for.

We shall now illustrate a number of the issues raised so far with the help of the example shown in Table 18.2. The example considers three alternative levels of gearing and examines the effect of these on profits and earnings per share. Capital structure A involves no debt, while B and C use increasing amounts of debt.

The gearing ratios could be expressed by either expressing debt as a ratio of total assets or equity. The respective ratios for each alternative are shown in the table. It should be noted that in practice there are likely to be other items which make the calculation of either debt to total assets or debt to equity more problematic. It is usual for debt in the ratio to be stated as total debt which includes all current and income tax liabilities in addition to long- and medium-term loans. Total assets usually include all fixed and current assets, although some analysts might include only tangible assets, excluding such items as goodwill, patents, trade-marks etc.

An alternative way of expressing the borrowing position is to use the borrowing ratio:

$$\frac{\text{long-term borrowing} + \text{overdrafts and acceptances}}{\text{capital employed}}$$

It is often a matter for debate whether bank overdraft should be included in debt or borrowing ratios. This is because bank overdrafts are repayable on demand and have therefore been included as current liabilities in the balance sheet. However, in practice a number of companies, particularly smaller companies, have used overdrafts as if they were a continuing source of finance. The realistic level of total borrowing therefore

Table 18.1 *United Biscuits Annual Report 1993: Loans, overdrafts and finance lease obligations*

	1993 £m	1992 £m
Group		
Bank loans and overdrafts		
Bank loans	43.2	60.0
Overdrafts	37.6	57.6
	80.8	117.6
Debenture and other loans		
8% debenture stock 1993/98 (secured)	—	9.0
11.55% European Investment Bank 1999	10.0	10.0
10.35% European Investment Bank 2001	13.0	13.0
9.6% NLG150m private placement 2000	52.1	54.4
9% US$125m guaranteed notes 2001	84.4	82.6
6.5% US$75m guaranteed bonds 1996	50.6	49.5
US$330m revolving credit facility 1997	20.9	99.1
US$ Commercial Paper	49.4	—
A$ Commercial Paper	76.2	—
8.7%–11.54% US$37.5m senior notes 1999/2002	20.3	28.1
2%–8.45% US$ Equipment purchase obligations 1994/2013	13.2	12.3
US$ mortgages 2004	0.3	1.3
	390.4	359.3
Finance lease obligations	7.6	7.9
	478.8	484.8
Repayable as follows:		
After more than five years – by instalment	23.2	32.6
– other	153.6	151.1
Between two and five years	94.4	177.8
Between one and two years	8.7	10.1
	279.9	371.6
Under one year – cash equivalents	123.3	63.8
– other	75.6	49.4
	198.9	113.2
	478.8	484.8
Analysis by currency (after related currency swaps)		
Sterling	32.9	36.7
US dollars	196.0	240.5
Dutch guilders	105.1	110.4
Australian dollars	100.2	—
Other European currencies	42.3	97.2
Other	2.3	—
	478.8	484.8

Company At 2 January 1993, the company had £9m of 8% debenture stock 1993/98 outstanding which was redeemed on 15 June 1993. The company had no loans, overdrafts or finance lease obligations outstanding at 1 January 1994.

Table 18.2

A new company is considering three alternative ways of financing its activities involving different combinations of debt and equity. The three alternatives, A, B and C, would produce the following balance sheet and income statement figures.

Alternative balance sheet projections

	A	B	C
Ordinary shares of £1 each	100 000	80 000	50 000
12% debt	—	20 000	50 000
	£100 000	£100 000	£100 000
debt-to-total assets	—	0.20	0.50
debt-to-equity	—	0.25	1.00

Effect on income and earnings per share of different levels of gearing and earnings

	A			B			C		
	(i)	(ii)	(iii)	(i)	(ii)	(iii)	(i)	(ii)	(iii)
1 Earnings	8000	12 000	16 000	8000	12 000	16 000	8000	12 000	16 000
2 Interest at 12%	—	—	—	2400	2 400	2 400	6000	6 000	6 000
3	8000	12 000	16 000	5600	9 600	13 600	2000	6 000	10 000
4 Taxation 33%	2640	3 960	5 280	1848	3 168	4 488	660	1 980	3 300
5	5360	8 040	10 720	3752	6 432	9 112	1340	4 020	6 700
EPS	5.4p	8.0p	10.7p	4.7p	8.0p	11.4p	2.7p	8.0p	13.4p
Interest cover	—	—	—	3.3	5	6.7	1.3	2	2.7

includes overdrafts as well as longer-term loans. The figure of capital employed is a little more contentious. Traditionally capital employed (total net assets) was taken to be total assets minus current liabilities where, as explained, current liabilities included overdrafts. However, to obtain comparable statistics for capital employed in different companies it is necessary not to deduct the assets financed by overdrafts. Capital employed in the borrowing ratio therefore includes the bank overdraft.

Where the debt ratio is expressed in the form of a debt-to-equity ratio it is emphasized that shareholders' funds (equity) are the sum of ordinary capital, preference capital and all reserves. Whichever approach to measuring a company's level of gearing is adopted, it is likely that comparisons will be made either in a time series to track the level of gearing from year to year or by comparing with similar companies or an industry average. Therefore it is vital that all relevant ratios are calculated on a consistent basis either from year to year or between companies where cross-sectional comparisons are being made. As with all ratio analysis more will be gained by comparisons from year to year or between companies than trying to specify absolute standards to adhere to. This may be so because absolute standards or norms may be flexible as methods of business and their financing change. In the example we can see that the gearing ratios increase from A through to C.

The table illustrates the effect on earnings per share (EPS) under each capital structure assuming three possible levels of profits. These are shown for each of the three structures under the three columns. A charge for taxation has also been included in the illustration. If we assume that the range of earnings shown represents lowest outcome, expected outcome and highest outcome respectively we can examine the effect on returns to ordinary shareholders as represented by EPS.

We can see that with structure A the EPS ranges from 5.4p to 10.7p. With increasing levels of debt in the capital structure, as in B and C, EPS at the lowest level of profitability declines while EPS at higher levels of profitability increases. One argument advanced for high levels of gearing is that it leads to an increase in EPS for ordinary shareholders. The example shows that this is the case only when the rate of return earned on assets is higher than the level of interest paid on debt. The second column for all three structures shows the same EPS at 8.0p; this is where total profits are £12 000, a return of 12% on assets employed and the return required on debt. Where the company earns less than this, higher levels of gearing will lead to a decrease in EPS; where the company earns more higher gearing will indeed increase EPS. It may be thought that if the company is optimistic about future profitability, then higher levels of gearing should be taken on. However, the example illustrates another factor related to gearing in that increasing levels of gearing also increase the risk as far as ordinary shareholders are concerned. This is illustrated by the way in which the range of EPS values increases with the level of gearing. It would seem that rational investors should require an increase in return on equity as the risk increases. Increasing levels of risk are also reflected in the declining interest cover ratios shown for different levels of gearing. External analysts, whether representing potential shareholders or suppliers, would regard this as an indication of higher risk.

Another interesting point which we can also gain from the illustration is the effect of different levels of gearing on the total return paid to providers of capital, both debt and equity. Let us consider the second column for A, B and C. In A the total payment to providers of capital will be the £8040 paid to ordinary shareholders shown in row 5. In capital structures B and C rows 2 and 5 will show the amounts earned by providers of debt and equity respectively. In structure B this is £8832, and in C it is £10 020. The reason that the total earnings to providers of capital increases in this case is entirely due to the tax shield provided on interest payments.

A number of factors have been determined relating to the effect of debt in the capital structure; among these are the lower return required on debt because of lower perceived risk, that debt interest is deductible against corporation tax, that debt in the capital structure increases the risk of equity shareholders and that debt increases EPS provided that the return on assets is greater than the coupon rate on debt.

We shall proceed to review and analyse the alternative views on the effect of debt in the capital structure, beginning with the traditional view that it is possible to identify an optimum level of debt for each company. In the analysis which follows the value of equity and debt will be related to market value and to balance sheet values. While ratio analysis tends to use accounting numbers, financial theory is concerned with the value of companies as indicated by markets which gives a direct measure of investor wealth.

18.3 Overall cost of capital: weighted-average cost approach

Companies obtain their funds from a mixture of equity and debt sources. It is these funds that are channelled into investments, and so the return that the investments earn must be sufficient to cover the cost of the debt and of equity capital. There are many factors that affect the relative levels of debt and equity that a company utilizes. All that will be considered at this point is how the cost of debt and equity are combined to obtain an overall cost of capital for a company.

First it should be appreciated that it is usually wrong to regard the required rate of return for a particular investment as the cost of the actual source of funds that financed that investment. It may be possible to trace the funds that support one investment directly to borrowing and the funds for another investment to retained earnings. To argue that the cost of borrowing is less than the cost of retained earnings and that the required rate of return on one investment is less than the required return on the other is wrong. Debt is cheaper than equity, but only because there is an equity base for the company that takes the risk. If the company did not have the equity funds it could not borrow. Hopefully, each year profits are retained and this increase in the equity base enables more borrowing to take place. The borrowing is not independent of the equity funds. The costs of the two need to be combined in some way.

The traditional approach is to determine the weighted-average cost of capital. The weighting is usually based on market values but sometimes on book values. Theoretically market values are best.

The cost of each source of capital is calculated separately and then weighted by the proportion of the total capital coming from that source. For example, suppose that 60% of a company's capital is equity, and 40% debt. If the cost of equity were 16% and the cost of debt 6% then the weighted average cost of capital would be 12%, i.e. (60% × 16%) + (40% × 6%). It has been argued that the existing capital structure can be used to calculate the cost of capital. This is because the capital structure of a company changes only slowly over time. Therefore the present level of gearing is indicative of the next period's level.

There is considerable discussion in the literature as to whether the cost of capital is independent of the level of gearing. In the above example we took the cost of equity and debt as 16% and 6% respectively; the point at issue is whether these respective costs only apply at the 60:40 level of gearing. If the company were to change its equity-to-debt ratio to, say, 80:20 or 40:60, would the cost of the individual sources of finance themselves change? If the cost of equity and/or the cost of debt changes, does this alter the overall cost of capital? These points will be considered later in this chapter.

At this point we shall assume that gearing only affects the cost of capital of a firm via the taxation implications of debt interest. We shall also assume that the costs of the individual sources of finance are not affected by the level of gearing.

The weighted-average cost can be based on book values or market values. To illustrate the approach when the weightings are based on book values, assume that the total capital of Tanworth PLC based on book values appearing in its balance sheet is made up as follows:

Ordinary shares	40%
Retained earnings	25%
Long-term debt	20% (with coupon rate of 15%)
Short-term debt	15% (bearing interest at 9%)

The long-term debt was issued a number of years ago and the yield in the market-place at present on long-term debt is 12%. The yield in the market on short-term debt is 9%. The rate of corporation tax is 33%.

The after-tax cost of the long-term debt is therefore 8% (i.e. 0.12 (1 − 0.33)) and of the short-term debt 6% (i.e. 0.09 (1 − 0.33)). The cost of equity is 16%.

The weighted average cost of capital (based on book values) is therefore 12.90%. The full computations are shown in Table 18.3.

Table 18.3

	Weighting (%)	Cost in money terms, after corporation tax (%)	Weighted monetary cost (%)
Ordinary shares	40	16	6.40
Retained earnings	25	16	4.00
Long-term debt	20	8	1.60
Short-term debt	15	6	0.90
			12.90

This is the cost in monetary terms. It does not take into account the point that was made earlier, namely that the real cost of borrowing at times of high inflation can be negative because the company is repaying the debt in a deflated currency. The reader can if he wishes rework the examples in this section using the real cost of capital rather than the monetary cost.

The approach adopted above involves making use of the values taken from the balance sheet. The value of reserves depends on financial accounting decisions such as when to revalue assets. The weightings used to calculate the cost of capital are therefore dependent on accounting valuation decisions. This approach is therefore often criticized.

In the alternative approach to estimating the cost of capital the current market values of the different elements of the capital structure are used as the weighting factors. If in the above example the company had 15 000 000 shares outstanding with a market value, allowing for possible short-term fluctuations in price, of £2.50, the long-term debt capital consisted of 5 000 000 debentures each with a market value of £1.05, and the short term debt was £4 000 000, then the cost of capital would be calculated as shown in Table 18.4. The average cost of capital after corporation tax weighted by market values is therefore 14.25%.

Table 18.4 (*in 000s*)

	1	2	3	4	5
			Market value	*Cost in money terms after corporation tax (%)*	*(3) × (4)*
	Shares	*Price*			
Ordinary shares	15 000	£2.5	37 500	16	6000
Long-term debt	5 000	£1.05	5 250	8	420
Short-term debt			4 000	6	240
			46 750		6660

$$\text{Weighted-average monetary cost of capital} = \frac{6660}{46\,750} \times 100 = 14.25\%$$

A company, it is sometimes argued, will be interested in the current cost of capital, as calculated, for at least two reasons: first for assessing the profitability of individual investments, and second for measuring the performance of the company in the past. Calculating the cost of capital with the existing capital structure may give some standard against which past performance can be measured. However, as a base for determining the advisability of future investment proposals it can be severely criticized. It is the anticipated future cost of capital that should be used as a base; the capital that will be invested in the particular project may change the average cost of capital to the company and it is this incremental cost that has to be covered by returns. The historical level of gearing is not necessarily the correct weighting factor; if the company plans to change its gearing levels, it is the incremental weighting of the next package of finance that is appropriate.

We shall now show how the weighted-average cost-of-capital concept can be used to answer a typical examination question on the subject of cost of capital.

Example 18.1

Calculate the cost of capital of the companies shown in Table 18.5 and comment on your answer.

Suggested solution

We begin with some observations on the relative risks of the two companies. The net earnings per share of Packer is 30p, i.e. £0.6/2. The net earnings per share of Gregg is 25p, i.e. £0.25/1. The price-

Table 18.5

	Packer and Co.	Gregg Ltd
Number of ordinary shares (£1)	2 million	1 million
Net profits attributable to ordinary shareholders	£0.6 million	£0.25 million
Gross dividends	£0.5 million	£0.2 million
Market value per share	£3	£2
Market value of debt	£3 million	£1.5 million
Market value of equity	£6 million	£2 million
Gross interest yield on debt	10%	11%
Annual growth rate of dividends over last five years	12%	10%

to-earnings ratio of Packer is equal to 10:1, i.e. £3.0/£0.3. The price-to-earnings ratio of Gregg equals 8:1, i.e. £2.0/£0.25.

The difference in the price-to-earnings ratio can be explained in terms of the greater financial risk of Gregg. It has a higher level of gearing and this increases the risks of the equity shareholder. We do not know about the comparative operating risks of the two companies. Packer is a larger company which again means that it can be considered lower risk, a safer business with more reserves and financial muscle. We know that Packer has a higher growth rate in its dividends over the last five years which would, of course, have an effect on the respective price-to-earnings ratios.

We shall now calculate the cost of equity capital using the dividend yield plus the growth rate in dividends approach. The gross dividend per share for Packer is 0.25p, i.e. £0.5m/2m. We shall assume that this is the expected gross dividend for the current year. The gross dividend yield is therefore equal to 8.3%, i.e. £0.25/£3.00 × 100. The gross cost of equity capital is therefore 20.3%. The gross dividend per share for Gregg is 20p, i.e. £0.2m/1m. The gross dividend yield is equal to 10%, i.e. £0.20/£2.00 × 100. The gross cost of equity capital for Gregg is therefore 20%. The shareholders of Packer are prepared to accept a lower dividend yield than the shareholders of Gregg, but have higher growth expectations.

We shall now use market values to find the weighted-average cost (Table 18.6).

Table 18.6

	Percentage of value of company	Cost of specific capital source	Weighted cost
Packer			
Equity	66.6%	20.3%	13.52
Debt	33.3%	6.7%	2.22
			15.74%
Gregg			
Equity	57%	20.0%	11.40
Debt	43%	7.3%	3.14
			14.54%

The cost of debt capital used in the calculation needs some explanation. It has been assumed that the rate of corporation tax is 33% and the cost to the company of the debt is shown after taking into account the tax-shield effect. The companies are both earning profits, and so they will be able to use their interest payments as a tax-deductible expense. The interest rate on debt is higher for Gregg than for Packer because of the higher level of gearing. The overall cost of capital for Packer is higher than for Gregg, perhaps because Gregg has a higher level of capital gearing, presumably nearer the optimal level.

Marginal cost of capital

The theory of capital budgeting leads to the conclusion that projects should be accepted if they have a positive net present value calculated after discounting the revenue and cost streams at the marginal cost of capital to the firm. If the alternative internal rate of return criterion is used, all projects that have an internal rate of return greater than the marginal cost of capital would be accepted. Emphasis is being placed on the marginal cost of capital, for it is only returns above this cost that add to the total value of the firm. This raises two important points concerning the cut-off points for new investments. First, it is the marginal cost of capital that should be considered. Second, it is implied that it is the cost of the sources of capital being used to finance the particular project under consideration that is appropriate. These points will be examined.

Weston [1] has proposed that the incremental cost should be used, i.e. the marginal cost reflecting the changes in the total cost of the capital structure before and after the introduction of the new capital. Lindsay and Sametz [2] propose a similar concept, that of 'sequential marginal costing'. They suggest that as companies expand, their marginal cost of capital rises sharply. Therefore it is not appropriate to use the weighted-average cost; this is lower than the marginal cost.

In theory it is easy enough to calculate such a marginal cost – it is simply the difference between the total cost with the existing capital structure and the total cost with the structure that will exist once the investment has been undertaken. This is the marginal cost of new capital in the business, that which is introduced to finance the proposed project.

For example, continuing with Tanworth PLC (p. 641), suppose that a large new investment is under consideration for which finance is to be raised. The total cost is £10 000 000, which will be obtained from a new issue of 2 000 000 ordinary shares at £2.50 per share and a further issue of long-term debt to raise £5 000 000. Because of the change in the capital structure, with a new level of risk for the holders of debt, and because of the change in the risk category of the equity shares resulting from this new investment, the cost of capital from each specific source will change. It is estimated that the cost of ordinary shares in money terms will now be 17.0%, the net cost of long-term debt will be 8.5% and the net cost of short-term debt will be 6.5%. The total cost of capital has risen by £1696 as a result of raising £10 000 000 of funds. The cost of this new capital is therefore 16.96%, and it is this cost that has to be covered by returns. Table 18.7 shows the computations.

There is a temptation to think that, with £5 000 000 being raised by debt capital with a cost of 8.5% and £5 000 000 raised by equity with a cost of 17%, the marginal cost

Table 18.7 *Tanworth PLC: revised cost of capital (in 000s)*

	1	2	3	4	5
				Cost in money terms after corporation tax	
	Shares	*Price*	*Market value*	*(%)*	*(3) × (4)*
Ordinary shares	17 000	£2.5	42 500	17	7225
Long-term debt	9 762	£1.05	10 250	8.5	871
Short-term debt			4 000	6.5	260
			56 750		8356

$$\text{Weighted-average monetary cost of capital} = \frac{8356}{56\,750} \times 100 = 14.72\%$$

$$\text{Marginal cost of capital} = \frac{8356 - 6660}{10\,000} \times 100 = 16.96\%$$

would be 12.75%, which is $(0.5 \times 8.5\%) + (0.5 \times 17\%)$. However, the change in the cost of the original capital needs to be taken into account. It is not possible to calculate the relevant cost of capital for a new project by merely looking at the cost of the individual sources being employed; the effect on all capital, old and new, needs to be considered.

Another approach to the problem of estimating the cost for a particular project takes into account the imputed borrowing power of the project in question. Whether the project is in fact financed by as much debt as it enables the company to raise is immaterial. The project has added to the borrowing base for the company, and it should receive the credit for this. Either the actual debt charges or the imputed debt charges with the project's borrowing power would be deducted from the cash flow from the project to give a rate of return on the actual equity component of the investment or an imputed equity component. The equity requirement will be determined by the projects included in the budget, and the debt requirements by the borrowing power. A disadvantage of this method is that it brings together and possibly confuses the analysis of the project and the financing decision. Also there are practical problems in estimating borrowing potential.

When a project is large and fundamentally affects the capital structure of a company, as has been shown, it is possible to approximate to a marginal (for the project) cost by calculating the cost before and after undertaking the project. This approach is satisfactory only if the project is large relative to the size of the company and the position of the business can be identified as different after the investment to what it was before the investment. It is also only valid if the decision about the source of capital that is being used to finance the investment is made by the market. If the decision about the source of capital that is to be used is merely a question of management's deciding arbitrarily that out of a pool of funds so much from one source is going to one project and so much from another source to another project, then it is not possible to identify separately the capital costs of one project.

On many occasions it is not possible to identify the source of funds that are used on a particular project. In such cases, and where a project is a relatively small part of total investment, the overall cost of capital needs to be used. This cost should be the increase in costs that result from the next increment of capital the company will obtain. That is not the cost of just the next increase from one source, say loan funds, but the entire next round of capital – the equity, the retained earnings and the loan capital. The project is being financed out of this next increment of funds, and it is the marginal cost resulting from this balanced increment that is appropriate.

A firm does not usually float issues of equity capital and debt capital simultaneously; usually one follows the other. Each issue of debt is dependent upon some equity base. Consequently an investment financed with funds from a debt issue needs to earn more than the interest rate attached to the debt. The equity holders need to receive some additional return to compensate for their higher risks. Similarly, a new issue of equity increases the borrowing base, and so access to cheaper capital. It is the cost of the next package of capital and the effect on the costs of the existing capital of this new increment that is the appropriate cost. This new capital will be invested in a number of projects which in total must cover the marginal cost of the capital.

Two major problems that emerge using the WACC approach to calculate the cost of capital for a project appraisal exercise are whether or not the actual debt equity ratio of a firm equals the target ratio, and whether or not the debt/equity ratio being used to finance a particular project equals the target ratio for the firm.

The WACC is based on the overall financial structure of a company. If the actual level of the debt/equity ratio is equal to the target ratio then this is the average cost of capital to the firm and there is no problem. Because the raising of both new debt and new equity tends to be lumpy, the actual ratio at any one time might be a little different from the target ratio.

It is the target ratio that should be used in determining the WACC. To use the actual ratio would distort the future investment projects and financial structure just because at a particular time the debt/equity was not at the target level.

The second problem arises if the target debt/equity ratio for the firm is not the same as the balance of finance being used to fund a particular project. Let us suppose the target ratio for the firm is 50% debt and 50% equity. A particular project, however, will be financed by 75% debt and 25% equity. One reason for this could be that the project is in a particular country where the government is making subsidized loans available in order to provide an incentive for the project to go ahead. In this case the adjusted present value (APV) approach should be used.

The project would be discounted at the firm's overall cost of capital with an added credit being taken into account for the savings arising from employing above normal levels of debt. This approach is explained and discussed in the next section.

In Chapter 10 the use of risk-adjusted discount rates that related specifically to projects under review was emphasized; in many multi-activity companies the use of a single discount rate could give misleading advice. As well as risk, discount rates may also reflect current financing policies of the company. The use of the after-tax weighted average cost of capital K_0 can be written as

18.4 Adjusted present value method

$$K_0 = K_e \frac{V_e}{V_e + V_d} + K_d(1 - t_c)\frac{V_d}{V_e + V_d}$$

where K_e and K_d are the cost of equity and debt respectively, t_c is the corporate tax rate and V_e and V_d are the market values of equity and debt respectively. This calculation reflects the current cost of both equity and debt; these costs will be reflecting current risk and current projects. In addition the tax rate will be the current tax rate rather than any anticipated rate. The use of this formula as the hurdle rate in project appraisal requires a number of assumptions.

1. The project under appraisal has the same systematic risk as the average systematic risk of projects currently undertaken.
2. The company is at its target level of gearing and the new project will be financed by the same mix of debt and equity.
3. All cash flows are perpetuities; this relates both to project cash flows and to debt which is assumed to be also perpetual.

Implicit in the use of the weighted-average cost of capital, therefore, are a number of assumptions which in practice may be violated. With small-scale projects these violations may not be significant (although if repeated for a number of small projects they might be), but as projects grow in size large errors are possible. Clearly the question of risk is very important, but financing and other side effects could also be significant. Will the new project support a higher or lower proportion of debt than at present? Will this debt be repaid or can it be regarded as perpetual? Are there any special costs or benefits associated with the project that make it different from current activities? Having pointed out the problems how can they be incorporated in the project analysis?

The approach suggested is appealingly simple. First of all determine the NPV of the project assuming it is an all-equity financed mini-firm, i.e. assume that the project is the only activity and use a risk-adjusted discount rate appropriate to the project's level of systematic risk. This gives us the base case NPV. We then calculate the present value of any side-effects associated with the project; examples of such side-effects might be tax shield on loan interest payments, subsidized loans, issue costs etc. The PV of side-effects calculated are then added/subtracted to the base case NPV to give an adjusted net present value (APV). In summary

APV = base case NPV ± PV of side-effects

An added advantage of this approach is that side-effects can be calculated separately and PVs calculated using the discount rate appropriate to the cash stream being valued. For example, with the tax shield on debt interest the tax shield should be discounted at the before-tax interest rate (to use after tax would involve double counting the benefit). The tax shield itself could be calculated using whatever effective rate of taxation was appropriate; in this chapter the effects of both corporate and personal taxes on the benefits of debt interest tax shields are discussed. Finally, and importantly, the actual debt interest payable will form the basis of the calculation rather than incorporating the effect through the use of weighted-average cost of capital which assumes perpetual debt.

To illustrate the equivalence of the different approaches under the restrictive assumptions we now set out a simple illustration (see Example 18.2).

Example 18.2 Adjusted present value, weighted-average cost of capital and project appraisal

In certain circumstances APV and weighted-average cost of capital can be shown to give equivalent results. Consider a company i with a capital structure at market value comprising 40% debt and 60% equity. The expected return on the market R_m is 14%; the company borrows at the prime rate of 9% K_d which is also the risk-free rate R_f; the beta of the company's equity is 1.2.

Using CAPM to calculate the expected return on equity we have

$$R_i = R_f + B_i(R_m - R_f)$$
$$= 0.09 + 1.2(0.14 - 0.09)$$
$$= 0.15(15\%) - \text{expected return on equity}$$

To find an asset beta we need to ungear the equity beta. Assuming for the moment that tax can be ignored:

$$\beta_a = \beta_d \frac{D}{D+E} + \beta_e \frac{E}{D+E} = 0 + 1.2\left(\frac{6}{10}\right) = 0.72$$

$$K_a = 0.09 + 0.72(0.14 - 0.09)$$
$$= 0.126 \text{ or } 12.6\%$$

where K_a is the required return on an asset of that risk class.

Using the weighted-average cost of capital, we obtain

$$K_0 = 0.09\left(\frac{4}{10}\right) + 0.15\left(\frac{6}{10}\right) = 0.126 \text{ or } 12.6\%$$

If we now assume that the rate of corporation tax is 33% and that debt interest is tax deductible, the weighted-average cost of capital becomes

$$K_0 = 0.06\left(\frac{4}{10}\right) + 0.15\left(\frac{6}{10}\right) = 0.114 \text{ or } 11.4\%$$

Ungearing beta, we obtain

$$\beta_a = \frac{\beta_e}{1 + (1 - t_c)(D/E)} = \frac{1.2}{1 + 0.67(4/6)} = \frac{1.2}{1.44} = 0.83$$

$$K_u = 0.09 + 0.83(0.14 - 0.09)$$
$$= 0.1315 \text{ or } 13.15\%$$

In this case K_u is the pure return required from an asset without considering any advantage of tax shield on debt interest payable. We now use the rates of return calculated to evaluate a simple project.

Consider an investment requiring £100 outlay which will yield £11.40 per annum after tax in perpetuity and having the same systematic risk as the company's existing business. Using weighted-average cost of capital, we obtain

$$\text{NPV} = -100 + \frac{11.40}{0.114} = -100 + 100 = 0$$

This shows that the NPV of the project *after* taking financing benefits into account is zero. Using K_u, we obtain

$$\text{NPV} = -100 + \frac{11.40}{0.1315} + \text{PV of tax shield}$$

The first two terms on the right-hand side of the equation give the value of the project as a project, while the final term concerns the financing side-effect. The equation gives the APV of the project.

The value of the project is £100 and is assumed to support 40% debt, i.e. £40. The annual interest payment is £3.6 which with tax of 33% gives a tax shield of £1.20 per annum:

$$\text{APV} = -100 + \frac{11.40}{0.1315} + \frac{1.2}{0.09} = -100 + 86.7 + 13.3 = 0$$

The two approaches give the same result but note that perpetuities have been used for illustrative purposes as they are implicit in the weighted-average cost of capital model. If we did not use perpetuities we would obtain different results from each approach. The APV approach also shows that the project value is negative ($-100 + 86.7$) and that it is only the tax shield on the debt interest which makes the overall project and financing package marginally acceptable.

An adjusted discount rate could also be obtained using the MM formula (see section 18.6 below):

$$K_g = K_u(1 - t_c L)$$

where K_u is the expected return on a pure equity stream (i.e. ungeared), t_c is the rate of corporation tax and L is the project's marginal contribution to the firm's debt capacity as a proportion of the firm's present value. Therefore

$$K_g = 0.1315(1 - 0.33 \times 0.4)$$

$$= 0.1315 \times 0.868$$

$$= 0.114 \text{ or } 11.4\%$$

This is the same as the weighted-average cost of capital figure obtained previously. Use of the MM formula on a historic basis, i.e. using existing risk and debt levels, requires the same assumptions as the weighted-average cost of capital approach. However, a specific project return could be used rather than existing returns, and a project level of gearing could also be used if this was different from the existing gearing ratio.

It should be stressed that identical results were obtained in Example 18.2 only because perpetuities were used. In addition, the gearing level was assumed to remain the same, 40% debt and 60% equity. For this to happen it was assumed that £40 was borrowed; this represents 40% of the PV of the project, i.e. 40% of the PV of cash flows to be received. In this case because the project just broke even (NPV = 0) this was also 40% of the initial outlay. But generally in order to maintain the level of gearing it would be necessary to borrow 40% of the PV of future flows. The problem is that in order to calculate a forward-looking adjusted discount rate, one using proposed new gearing levels, we need to know the value of the project but to do this we need to discount future cash flows. But to do this we need an adjusted discount rate! There is a circularity here which needs to be broken, and the APV approach avoids the problem by disentangling the project appraisal and valuation from financing and other side-effects.

When discounting project cash flows it is common to use a single discount rate, usually a risk-adjusted rate, for all relevant incremental cash flows. However, use of an APV approach indicates that it is quite possible, in fact necessary, to use discount rates appropriate to the cash stream being discounted.

In our illustration the tax shield on debt interest was discounted using the debt interest rate (before tax for the reasons explained). It may therefore be appropriate to consider and question the risk characteristics of other cash inflows or outflows to see whether they are entirely dependent on the success or failure of the project, and therefore merit the use of the project rate, or if they are more certain than this then a lower discount rate, perhaps the after-tax cost of debt, might be appropriate. The reason for the use of the after-tax borrowing rate for such flows to be received is that, if they were reasonably certain, the company would be able to borrow against the receipt of the flows and the cost of borrowing would be the appropriate discount rate.

An example of this type of inflow would be an agreed government subsidy payable over a number of years conditional on setting up the project. Once the project is set up the receipt is more or less certain. Care needs to be exercised particularly where tax shields are concerned. They may appear reasonably certain but to benefit from tax shields the company must be in a tax-paying position. Also the valuation of future tax shields is dependent on the levels of future tax rates. Tax shields are most valuable when tax rates are at their highest! When taxes are reduced the value of tax shields is reduced as leasing companies have found in recent years.

<table>
<tr><td>**18.5 Traditional view of capital structure**</td><td>The traditional view of company capital structure suggests that the average cost of capital does depend on the level of gearing. The implication is that there is an individual company optimum level of gearing at which cost of capital will be minimized and the value of the firm maximized. When a company has both equity and debt in its capital structure, then the cost of capital can be expressed as a weighted-average cost of capital where the cost of each type of capital in the company is weighted by its proportional value in the total value of the company. This is normally expressed as follows:</td></tr>
</table>

$$\text{weighted-average cost of capital} = K_0$$

$$K_0 = K_e \frac{V_e}{V_e + V_d} + K_d \frac{V_d}{V_e + V_d}$$

where K_e is the cost of equity capital, K_d is the cost of debt capital, V_e is the market value of equity and V_d is the market value of debt.

The above formula does not consider taxation, and if this is to be taken into account then the after-tax cost of debt should be used in the calculation. This would be $K_d(1 - t)$ where t is the rate of corporation tax. The formula becomes:

$$K_0 = K_e \frac{V_e}{V_e + V_d} + K_d(1-t)\frac{V_d}{V_e + V_d}$$

We will use these formulae in the analysis which follows.

The traditional view of capital structure was that as the level of gearing increased over moderate debt ranges the average cost of capital fell because of the lower cost of debt capital compared with equity capital. It was assumed that moderate amounts of debt did not add significantly to the risks attached to holding equity, so that initially the company would not have to offer higher returns to its equity shareholders. This would cause the weighted-average cost of capital to decline, thus increasing the value of the company. As the proportion of debt in the capital structure rises, two things happen: first, the equity shareholders realize that their investment is becoming riskier and therefore demand a higher rate of return from the company; second, lenders advancing money to an already geared company will also recognize increasing risk on their investment as the level of gearing rises and expect a higher rate of return on succeeding tranches of debt advanced. The result of this on the cost of capital is that the increasing cost of both debt and equity will tend to cancel out the advantage gained by substituting lower-cost debt for equity. Thus, although traditionalists claim that overall cost of capital is initially reduced by introducing debt into the capital structure, it is recognized that as the level of debt increases the total cost of capital no longer decreases and eventually starts to rise again at higher levels of debt. This view is summarized in Fig. 18.1 which shows a U-shaped cost-of-capital curve; the optimal level of gearing is where the average cost of capital is at its lowest point, at the trough of the U. Figure 18.2 illustrates the effect of the traditional approach on the value of the firm at different levels of gearing. If the traditional approach is accepted, then there is a level of gearing for each firm at which the cost per unit of capital is at its lowest point. Managers would therefore have to identify this optimum level of gearing and ensure that their company maintained its capital structure at this level. There does seem to be an element of irrationality in the traditional view in that equity shareholders are expected to ignore an element of risk. It is questionable whether investors would be prepared to accept the same rate of return from companies in similar industries with different levels of gearing. In fact, this lies at the heart of the MM analysis which is considered in the next section.

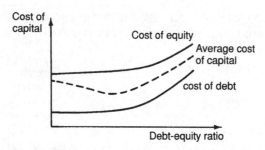

Figure 18.1 *Traditional view of debt and cost of capital*

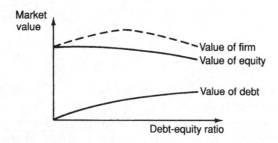

Figure 18.2 *Traditional view of debt and value of firm*

Modigliani and Miller [3] were the first to carry out a rigorous analysis of the effect of gearing on cost of capital and firm value. MM criticized the traditional view which was the accepted wisdom of the time and questioned whether it was possible for firms to reduce the cost of capital in the way that was described in the previous section.

MM argued that, under a restrictive set of assumptions, gearing would have no affect on either cost of capital or firm value. Once again the assumptions on which they base their arguments are important and they are as follows.

1. Perfect capital markets exist where individuals and companies can borrow unlimited amounts at the same rate of interest.
2. There are no taxes or transaction costs.

18.6 Capital structure in perfect capital markets

3. Personal borrowing is a perfect substitute for corporate borrowing.
4. Firms exist with the same business or systematic risk but different levels of gearing.
5. All projects and cash flows relating thereto are perpetuities, and any debt borrowed is also perpetual.

Under such assumptions MM demonstrated that it was the income generated by the firm from its business activities which determined value, rather than the way in which this income was split between providers of capital. If two firms with the same level of business risk but different levels of gearing sold for different values, then shareholders would move from the overvalued to the undervalued firm and adjust their level of borrowing through the market to maintain financial risk at the same level. In this way shareholders would increase their income while maintaining their net investment and risk at the same level. This process of arbitrage would drive the price of the two firms to a common equilibrium total value. The example below illustrates the MM arbitrage process. In the illustration both companies generate the same level of income and have the same business risk, but Thompson, the geared company, is valued in total at £1 million more than Lilley.

Example 18.3 Illustration of MM arbitrage in perfect capital markets

Lilley and Thompson are companies in the same class of business risk. Both companies have annual earnings before interest of £1 million but different capital structures. The companies are currently valued on the market as follows:

	Lilley	Thompson
Equity	5 000 000	4 000 000
8% debt	—	2 000 000
	£5 000 000	£6 000 000

Let us suppose that Chappell owns 5% of Thompson's equity. His income will be

Total Thompson earnings	1 000 000
Less: debt interest at 8%	160 000
	£ 840 000

$$\times \frac{5}{100} = £42\ 000$$

MM would say that Lilley and Thompson should both have the same total market value because they have identical levels of earnings and risk.

Chappell could sell his equity in Thompson for £200 000 (5% of £4 million), borrow £100 000 at 8% from the market to maintain his total risk (business and financial) at the same level and invest the whole £300 000 in Lilley's equity. He will then own 6% of Lilley (6% × £5 million = £300 000).

Chappell's income would then be

Total Lilley income	£1 000 000

$$\times \frac{6}{100} \qquad 60\ 000$$

Less: interest on personal loan 8% × £100 000	8 000
	£ 52 000

Chappell could increase his income by £10 000 while maintaining total risk at the same level. MM said that this arbitrage would result in the total values of Lilley and Thompson moving to the same equilibrium value.

MM would say that under their assumptions it would be possible for an equity holder in Thompson to sell his holding, borrow on the market to maintain his total risk at the same level, i.e. business and financial risk, and invest the total in Lilley. The shareholder will then be able to increase his total income after paying interest on the personal loan while maintaining his overall risk at the same level. The result of this arbitrage process would be that the equity value of the overvalued company, in this case Thompson, would decrease while the equity value of the undervalued company, Lilley, would increase until a point was reached where the total value of both companies was the same. For ease of illustration it has been assumed that the companies are of the same size. This is not necessary. All that is required is that there exist companies in the same risk class. For example, if Lilley's cash flows had been twice those of Thompson the expectation would be that Lilley's value should be twice that of Thompson.

Let us assume that in this example Thompson's debt and Lilley's equity are trading at equilibrium prices and the selling arbitrage results in Thompson's equity declining in value to £3 million. The resulting values and cost of capital will be as follows:

	Lilley	Thompson
Equity	5 000 000	3 000 000
8% debt	—	2 000 000
	£5 000 000	£5 000 000
Cost of equity	1 M/5 M = 0.2 (20%)	(1 M − 0.16 M)/3 M = 0.28 (28%)
Cost of debt		0.16/2 M = 0.08 (8%)

As Lilley is financed solely by equity its weighted-average cost of capital (WACC) will be the cost of equity, i.e. 20%. In Thompson's case

$$WACC = 0.28 \times \frac{3}{5} + 0.08 \times \frac{2}{5} = 0.2 (20\%)$$

Thus MM say that the weighted-average cost of capital is the same irrespective of the level of gearing and is equal to the equity rate of return in an ungeared firm. Also, the value of a firm in a particular risk class is equal to the annual cash flow income discounted at the rate of return required from an ungeared firm. In the case of Lilley and Thompson

$$total\ market\ value = \frac{1000\ 000}{0.2} = £5\,000\,000$$

MM express their conclusions on gearing, cost of capital and the value of the firm in the form of three propositions as follows.

Proposition 1

The market value of any firm is independent of its capital structure. Further, the market value of any firm is given by capitalizing its expected total earnings at the capitalization rate appropriate to an all-equity company of that risk class. This result is ensured by the operation of the arbitrage process previously described.

Proposition 2

The expected rate of return on equity increases linearly with the gearing ratio. This can be illustrated using the weighted-average cost-of-capital formula previously examined. If K_u is the return required on the equity of an ungeared firm, then we know that this is equal to the weighted-average cost of capital of all geared firms in the same risk class. We can write

$$K_0 = K_u = K_e \frac{V_e}{V_e + V_d} + K_d \frac{V_d}{V_e + V_d}$$

Multiplying throughout by $V_e + V_d$ we obtain

$$K_u V_e + K_u V_d = V_e K_e + V_d K_d$$

Dividing by V_e gives

$$K_u + \frac{K_u V_d}{V_e} = K_e \frac{V_d K_d}{V_e}$$

$$K_e = K_u + \frac{V_d}{V_e}(K_u - K_d)$$

This expression shows that the expected return on the equity of a geared company is equal to the expected return on a pure equity stream plus a risk premium dependent on the level of debt in the capital structure. The effect on the cost of equity of introducing debt into the capital structure is that the cost of equity rises linearly to offset the lower-cost debt directly, giving a constant weighted-average cost of capital irrespective of the level of gearing.

Proposition 3

The cut-off rate to be used in investment appraisal is the rate of return appropriate to an all-equity firm. This is the case because in an MM world the weighted-average cost of capital is constant and equal to the cost of equity in an all-equity firm. This follows from proposition 2 where the cost of equity increases linearly to offset exactly the advantage of lower-cost debt financing. The three propositions are therefore entirely consistent and tie in with the arbitrage idea previously discussed. Figure 18.3 illustrates the effect of gearing on cost of capital while Figure 18.4 shows the effect on the value of the firms. The figures stress that in the MM framework both overall cost of capital and firm value are constant irrespective of the level of gearing.

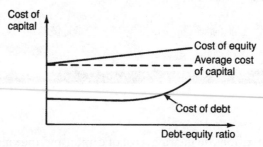

Figure 18.3 *MM (no taxation) and cost of capital*

This is another illustration of the point made when discussing dividend policy that it is the business activities undertaken by the firm which determine value rather than the way in which the fruits of these activities are packaged between the providers of capital. Managers will make more money for their shareholders by concentrating on identifying profitable projects rather than trying to increase wealth through dividend and

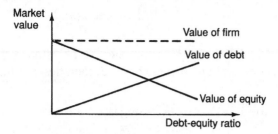

Figure 18.4 *MM (no taxation) and value of firm*

financing decisions. Of course, it must be admitted that MM theory was derived by making simplified assumptions which could be criticized as follows.

1. It could be questioned whether personal borrowing is a substitute for corporate borrowing given the corporate sector's limited liability and its ability to borrow at keener rates of interest than the personal sector.
2. Is it possible to identify companies in the same risk class? Is there such a thing as two identical companies?
3. In the real world taxes and transaction costs exist and these need to be considered.

Despite the criticisms which can be levelled at the unrealistic assumptions made by MM there is almost universal acceptance of their conclusions, given the assumptions made. If different levels of capital structure are to affect both cost of capital and the value of the firm, then we must identify the imperfections in the world assumed by MM. We begin this in the next section where we examine the impact of both corporate and personal taxes on the capital structure decision.

Corporation taxation

The original MM model discussed in section 18.6 did not consider the influence of taxation. When this was pointed out they simply corrected their earlier analysis to allow for corporate taxation [4]. What are the effects of corporate taxation on debt in the capital structure? If we return to the example of the ungeared Lilley and the geared Thompson we can examine the effects of introducing corporation tax of 33% into our analysis.

	Lilley	*Thompson*
Earnings	1 000 000	1 000 000
Less: debt interest	—	160 000
	1 000 000	840 000
Corporate Tax at 33%	330 000	277 200
Available for equity holders	£670 000	£562 800
Total amount for providers of capital	£670 000	£722 800

$$(160\ 000 + 562\ 800)$$

With corporate taxation there is an increase of £52 800 in cash flows to providers of capital in Thompson, the geared company. This increase arises from the tax shield on debt interest paid (160 000 × 33% = £52 800) and increases the amount available to ordinary shareholders. MM suggested that, with corporation tax, as much debt as possible (99.9%) should be included in the capital structure as value was added to the equity shareholders' interest with each £1 of extra debt issued. We shall return to this point later.

If we assume that the return required by equity investors in Lilley remains at 20%, then the market value of equity becomes

$$V_u = \frac{670\,000}{0.2} = \text{£3.35 million}$$

where V_u is the value of the ungeared company. If the value of debt in Thompson and the required return on debt are also unchanged, then designating V_g as the value of a geared company:

value of Thompson = V_g = value of ungeared company + PV of tax shield on debt interest

$$= 3\,350\,000 + \frac{52\,800}{0.08}$$

$$= 3\,350\,000 + 660\,000$$

$$= \text{£4.01 million}$$

This assumes that debt is perpetual and that the tax shield has the same risk as debt.

value of Thompson = value of equity
+ value of debt

and

value of debt = £2 million

Therefore

value of equity = £4 010 000 − £2 000 000

$$= \text{£2.01 million}$$

The present value (PV) of the tax shield above is given by

$$PV = \frac{0.08 \times 2\,000\,000 \times 0.33}{0.08}$$

The 0.08 terms in the numerator and the denominator cancel out, leaving,

$$PV = 2\,000\,000 \times 0.33$$
$$= \text{£660 000}$$

Thus generally,

$$V_g = V_u + V_d t_c$$

where t_c is the rate of corporation tax.

How do these findings affect the three MM propositions outlined in the previous section?

MM Proposition 1 with corporate taxes

The market value of a firm is no longer independent of its capital structure. Value is increased as debt is added to the capital structure because of the PV of the tax shield on interest payments. The market value of a firm is now given by summing its value if all equity and the value of tax shield on interest payments.

MM Proposition 2 with corporate taxes

Although the expected return on equity increases as debt is added to the capital structure the rate of increase is lower because of the existence of corporate taxes:

$$K_e = K_u + (1 - t_c)(K_u - K_d)\frac{V_d}{V_e}$$

The average cost of capital K_g in a geared company also declines with debt financing as follows:

$$K_g = K_u(1 - t_c L)$$

where

$$L = \frac{V_d}{V_e + V_d}$$

Alternatively, the weighted-average cost of capital of a geared firm can be written as

$$K_g = K_e \frac{V_d}{V_e + V_d} + K_d(1 - t_c)\frac{V_d}{V_e + V_d}$$

Using the data for Lilley and Thompson we can calculate the cost of equity and the average cost of capital of Thompson as follows:

$$K_u = 0.2 \text{ (given)}$$
$$K_d = 0.08 \text{ (given)}$$
$$K_e = 0.2 + (1 - 0.33)(0.2 - 0.08)\frac{2.0}{2.01}$$
$$= 0.28 \text{ or } 28\%$$
$$K_g = 0.2\left(1 - 0.33 \times \frac{2.00}{4.01}\right)$$
$$= 0.167 \text{ or } 16.7\%$$

or

$$K_g = 0.28 \times \frac{2.01}{4.01} + 0.08(1 - 0.33)\frac{2.00}{4.01}$$
$$= 0.1403 + 0.0267$$
$$= 0.167 \text{ or } 16.7\%$$

MM Proposition 3 with corporate taxes

The implications of proposition 3 without taxes was that the weighted-average cost of capital was constant irrespective of gearing and that the appropriate cost of capital was that rate appropriate to an all-equity firm. We have just seen in the discussion above that tax deductibility of debt interest leads to a progressive reduction in overall cost of capital. What rate of return should be used in project appraisal?

The use of either formula for K_g given above would result in the mingling of benefits and risks relating to both the project and the means of financing. In addition it would reflect the average risk of existing projects and their financing mix. In Chapter 10 the need for discount rates to reflect project risk was emphasized through the use of an appropriate project beta to calculate required return.

MM developed their ideas well before the capital asset pricing model (CAPM) was available for use. The original tendency was to use the weighted-average cost of capital to calculate K_g to obtain a project discount rate, and assume that the project and its financing were identical in terms of risk and gearing to the existing firm. However, it is suggested that the more appropriate approach is to split the project and financing; the project should still be evaluated as though all equity using an appropriate cost of capital, with separate and explicit adjustment being made for any financing involved. This approach is the adjusted present value (APV), which was discussed in section 18.4 earlier in the chapter.

The result of introducing tax deductibility of debt interest seems to suggest that as much debt as possible should be included in the capital structure. However, debt ratios in the UK are fairly modest and vary considerably between companies. In their analysis

MM assumed that it was certain that firms would be able to obtain benefit for the tax shields in each and every succeeding financial period and that no additional disadvantages accrued with higher levels of gearing. In the past it has not been unusual for UK companies, particularly manufacturing companies, to pay little or no UK tax because of the availability of high allowances for capital expenditure or the existence of double tax relief on overseas income. Tax shields only have value if the company is in a tax-paying position; thus the higher are the levels of gearing the higher is the probability that in at least some periods in the future the company will not be able to benefit from the interest tax shields. Another factor which needs to be considered is that from an investor's point of view debt interest and equity income might be taxed differently, thus leading to investor preferences when personal as well as corporate taxes are considered. A further point we need to consider is that as more debt is added to the capital structure the possibility of potential bankruptcy or financial distress increases. This will be discussed in the next section after we have reviewed the potential effects of personal taxes.

Personal taxation

Investors will evaluate their returns on the basis of what they receive after payment of all taxes both corporate and personal. With personal taxes the after-tax return (both corporate and personal) to an equity holder in an ungeared firm of one unit of income could be written as

$$(1 - t_c)(1 - t_{ps})$$

where t_c is the corporation tax rate and t_{ps} is the personal income tax on equity income. If this sort of income were received as debt interest, the after-tax return would be

$$1 - t_{pd}$$

where t_{pd} is the personal income tax on debt income (i.e. no corporation tax payable because debt interest is tax deductible). Then the gain arising would be

$$(1 - t_{pd}) - (1 - t_c)(1 - t_{ps})$$

If the amount of total income involved was the debt interest being paid, which amounts to $V_d i$ where V_d is the value of debt and i is the rate of interest, then the annual saving would be

$$V_d i[(1 - t_{pd}) - (1 - t_c)(1 - t_{ps})]$$

and the capitalized value of the saving would be

$$\frac{V_d i[(1 - t_{pd}) - (1 - t_c)(1 - t_{ps})]}{i(1 - t_{pd})} = \frac{V_d[(1 - t_{pd}) - (1 - t_c)(1 - t_{ps})]}{1 - t_{pd}}$$

The perpetual discount rate used is the after-tax debt interest rate, i.e. personal taxes. Simplifying the above equation, we obtain

$$\text{value of saving} = V_d \left[1 - \frac{(1 - t_c)(1 - t_{ps})}{1 - t_{pd}} \right]$$

Now if both debt and equity are taxed in the same way at the same rates (i.e. $t_{ps} = t_{pd}$), the gain simplifies to

$$\text{value of saving} = V_d(1 - (1 - t_c))$$

$$= V_d t_c$$

This is the same result as we obtained when only corporate taxes were considered. However the effective tax rate on equity is likely to differ from the effective tax rate on debt. The latter can be characterized by the investor marginal tax rate. In the UK this would range from 0% to 40%. This is realistic as return on debt comes in the form of interest payments. However equity returns come partly as dividends and partly as capital gains. Dividends are themselves complicated in the UK by the existence of an imputation system of corporation tax whereby tax credits attach to dividends paid. As regards capital gains, although taxpayers pay capital gains tax at their marginal rate of income tax on chargeable gains their effective rate is likely to be a lot lower. Tax is only paid when gains in excess of the annual exemption limit are realized. In addition in computing chargeable gains the original purchase price is index linked for inflation and any capital losses can be offset against gains. These factors will mean then that the effective tax rate on equity will be lower than the effective tax rate on debt. Suppose that a shareholder paid tax at 40% on debt interest, but an effective rate of only 16% on equity income, then substituting these values in our basic equation above we obtain

$$\text{value of saving} = V_d \left[1 - \frac{(1-t_c)(1-0.16)}{1-0.40} \right]$$
$$= V_d (1.4t_c - 0.4)$$

With a corporation tax of 33% and debt valued at £100 000, where $t_{ps} = t_{pd}$

$$\text{saving} = 100\,000 \times 0.33$$
$$= £33\,000$$

However, where $t_{ps} = 16\%$ and $t_{pd} = 40\%$

$$\text{saving} = 100\,000(1.4 \times 0.33 - 0.4)$$
$$= 100\,000(0.462 - 0.4)$$
$$= £6200$$

We can see that where the rate of tax payable on equity income is less than that payable on debt income the tax saving on debt in the capital structure is reduced.

In 1977 Miller [5] pointed out that when considering gearing levels the personal tax position should be considered as well as the corporate tax position. He began his analysis by assuming a world in which all equity income came in the form of unrealized capital gains, i.e. $t_{ps} = 0$. In this world the value of saving would be given by

$$V_d \left(1 - \frac{1-t_c}{1-t_{pd}} \right)$$

It can be seen that the maximum saving would occur when t_{pd} was equal to zero and would decrease as this value increased. At the point were $t_c = t_{pd}$ the value of saving would be zero and where t_{pd} was greater than t_c gearing would lead to a lower value of the firm.

In this context Miller began by assuming that companies are financed entirely by equity. Because of the existence of tax shields on debt interest managers would seek to issue some debt to increase the value of the firm. Remember that the initial assumption was that no tax was paid on equity income; therefore initially any shareholders who also paid no tax on debt interest would be prepared to take up the debt. These shareholders would largely be tax-exempt institutions like pension funds. However, as the demand for debt from zero-tax payers was met it would be necessary to offer higher rates of interest to compensate holders for the extra tax being paid on debt interest compared with equity income. The next group of shareholders to take up debt would be those paying comparatively low marginal rates of income tax; however, the rate of interest would have to continue to be increased as each group's demand for debt was satisfied. Companies would continue to issue debt until the rate of interest being paid was equal to

$$\frac{i}{1-t_c}$$

At this point the extra interest being paid by the lender would be exactly equal to the tax shield on the interest paid. At this point also the rate of corporate tax would be equal to the marginal rate of personal tax payable on debt interest.

Miller thus analysed the aggregate supply and demand for corporate debt and this is illustrated in Figure 18.5. The corporate sector as a whole would be prepared to issue debt up to the point where the extra interest paid is exactly compensated for by the tax shield on the debt interest. Investors, however, would be prepared to take up debt provided that they were compensated by a high return so that the after tax return on debt was at least equal to the after (zero) tax return on equity. It is stressed that the optimal level of gearing arising from this analysis is for corporations as a whole. Miller argues that it is not obvious that an optimal level of gearing exists for a single firm. Miller's model, developed in the context of the US tax system, shows the importance of considering personal as well as corporate taxes in analysing the financing decision. However, the model assumes that equity income is taxed at a significantly lower rate than interest income. This was more plausible at the time that the model was developed, but since then tax laws in both the USA and the UK have changed so that realized capital gains are now taxed at the shareholder's marginal income tax rate. Even before these changes the initial argument would seem to suggest that low tax payers like pension funds should be concentrating their investment in debt rather than equities, while highly taxed investors would have the opposite preference, investing only in equities. This type of preference does not seem to be obvious from an examination of appropriate portfolios. The introduction of corporate as well as personal taxes into our analysis suggests that basing the value of saving on corporate taxes alone may overstate tax savings as far as debt is concerned. Again, as was emphasized at the outset of our discussion on personal taxes, the saving depends not just on corporate taxes but on personal taxes as well. Another factor which might limit the amount of debt companies seek to take into their capital structure relates to the increasing risk of bankruptcy and financial distress generally, and this is considered in the next section.

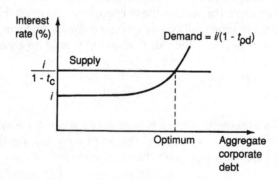

Figure 18.5 *Aggregate supply and demand for corporate debt*

18.8 Capital structure and financial distress

In their 1963 paper MM [4] agreed that when there is corporation tax relief on interest payments then the cost of capital is not independent of the debt-to-equity ratio. The existence of this tax relief provides advantages which favour borrowing. However, as the proportion of debt in the capital structure increases, then not only do the risks of equity owners increase but also those of succeeding providers of debt. With increasing proportions of debt the likelihood of incurring costs of financial distress increase as does the cost of the ultimate financial distress, bankruptcy. Potential financial distress has a cost, and as companies take on higher and higher levels of debt this cost will have a negative affect on firm value offsetting the value of the tax shield from extra interest payments made. In these circumstances the value of a geared firm can be written as

value of a geared firm = Value if firm is all equity financed + PV of tax shield on borrowing − PV of costs of financial distress

The chances of financial distress increase as gearing increases because with debt capital a fixed-interest payment has to be made annually whatever the profit or cash flow position of the company, whereas it is possible to postpone a dividend payment.

The costs of financial distress can be divided into direct and indirect costs. The direct costs include fees for lawyers and accountants, other professional fees and the managerial time used in administration. The indirect costs are less tangible and arise because of uncertainties in the minds of suppliers and customers. They include lost sales, lost profits and lost goodwill. The presence of these possible distress costs is likely to increase the cost of capital because the shareholders will want a greater return for what they see as additional risk. This means that whether bankruptcy costs are a threat or not, the shareholders perceive them as a threat as the level of gearing increases, and it is likely to lead to an increase in the cost of capital.

As can be seen from the equation above, the threat of financial distress costs reduces the benefits of tax relief on debt achieved by higher levels of gearing. Proponents of the importance of distress and bankruptcy costs argue that there is an optimal level of gearing at which the bankruptcy costs, the cost of capital and the tax relief are balanced. Therefore the cost of capital is not independent of the capital structure.

An important issue is whether the tax advantages of debt are outweighed by the financial distress cost of debt. At what level of gearing does the worry of possible financial distress or even bankruptcy so increase the cost of debt that it outweighs the tax shield on debt? Unfortunately there are only a few studies that have attempted to measure the costs of financial distress. Warner [6] studied the evidence of a number of US railroad companies that became bankrupt. He found that bankruptcy costs were greater for firms with higher market value but that firms with lower market value had greater proportional costs. This appears to indicate high fixed costs in bankruptcy and would be particularly significant to a small company deciding upon a gearing level. For example, if a firm is going to pay only slightly greater bankruptcy costs with 80% gearing as opposed to 30%, the firm may well be advised to have an 80% gearing level and take full advantage of any possible tax relief.

However, a crucial point in the discussion is that there is a considerable disagreement as to the 'real' size of bankruptcy costs and hence their importance compared with tax relief. Baxter [7] estimated bankruptcy costs at 20% which, although not as high as the present corporation tax rate of 33%, have to be taken very seriously indeed as a possible counterweight. However, the figure refers mainly to bankruptcies of individuals and some small businesses. Warner's study, however, dealt with large publicly owned companies. He found that the average bankruptcy costs as a percentage of the market value of the firm as at the end of the month in which the petition was filed was 5.3%. These were *ex ante* direct costs, whereas the most important would be expected bankruptcy costs as these would be the figure studied when initially deciding upon a level of gearing. Hence he used the final figures and took them as a proportion of the market value of the firm seven years prior to the petition's being filed. The costs were then as little as 1%. Hence Warner concluded that 'the expected direct costs of bankruptcy are unambiguously lower than the tax savings on debt to be expected at present tax rates in standard valuation models'.

In the previous section we were concerned with the effect of taxation on the optimal capital structure; in this section we have been concerned with the effect of financial distress. The joint effect of taxation and financial distress is illustrated in Figure 18.6. This illustration shows the trade-off between the increase in value arising as a result of the tax-shield effect on debt interest paid and the increase in costs of financial distress as the proportion of debt in the capital structure increases. An optimal level of capital gearing is shown at point B. In practice an optimal level of capital gearing for a firm does appear to exist. However, Miller [5] raised some interesting problems and indicated that calculating an optimal level is extremely complex. One reason why optimal levels of capital gearing do exist is because of institutional restrictions; these are discussed below.

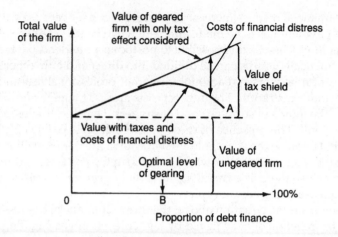

Figure 18.6 *Value of firm with taxes and financial distress*

Students of company finance for over twenty years have had to answer questions on the intricate theories of capital structure. Students whether at university or studying for professional examinations have been expected to understand the ideas of Modigliani and Miller.

There has, however, been disagreement among researchers as to whether firms actually behave as if there is an optimal level of gearing. It is accepted that the MM model does not predict the actual level of gearing of the typical firm, but this is not really surprising. Individual firms have to make allowances for their own potential level of bankruptcy costs (both the legal and administrative costs and the effect on their ability to do business) and of the tax shield effects of debt. Nevertheless there are those who argue that firms behave as if there is a target debt/equity ratio.

One explanation for a target gearing level is provided by the trade-off theory. Financial managers can think of the firm's debt/equity decision as a trade-off – the tax advantages of debt balanced against the risks of distress. There is some controversy as to how valuable are tax shields and what are the costs of financial distress but these disagreements are only variations on a theme. This trade-off theory of capital structure recognizes that target debt ratios may vary from firm to firm. Companies with safe, tangible assets and plenty of taxable income to shield ought to have high target gearing ratios. Unprofitable companies with risky, intangible assets ought to rely primarily on equity financing.

If there were no costs of adjusting capital structure, then each firm should always be at its target debt ratio. However, there are costs, and therefore delays in adjusting to the optimum. Firms cannot immediately offset the random events that move them away from their capital structure targets, so we should see random differences in actual debt ratios even among firms having the same target debt ratios. Because of this adjustment process it is not easy for researchers to identify target ratios.

There is some evidence that companies appear to make their choice of financing instruments as if they have target levels of debt in mind. If this is the case, then in principle companies needing new finance should issue equity if they are above their target debt level and debt if they are below. With no flotation costs, such adjustments could be made instantaneously and continuously. In practice, however, the existence of significant flotation costs gives rise to infrequent 'lumpy' issues, with the consequence that debt ratios fluctuate over time around their target level.

There are those who argue that companies do not have a target debt/equity ratio. Jensen [8] observes that in the USA in recent years organizations have been using public and private debt, rather than public equity, as their major source of capital. The primary providers of such debt are large institutions who designate the agents to manage on their behalf and bind those agents with covenants and contracts governing the use and distribution of cash and profits. This trend, Jensen believes, helps resolve a weakness of the large public corporation, i.e. the conflict between owners and managers over the control and use of corporate resources.

It is also argued by those who do not believe in a target ratio that managers have few incentives to distribute funds. Managers seem to prefer to retain any 'free' cash and engage in such policies as growth through diversification, rather than to return the cash to shareholders to allow them to undertake diversification of their own. If managers have cash to retain this increases their own autonomy and increases their independence from the capital markets. This wish to use internally generated funds fits in with the ideas expressed in the Pecking Order Theory.

Pecking Order Theory

The Pecking Order Theory was first proposed by Donaldson in 1961 [9]. The Pecking Order Theory argues against a target debt/equity ratio. The theory suggests that firms rely for finance as much as they can on internally generated funds. If not enough internally generated funds are available then they will move to additional debt finance. It is only when these two sources cannot provide enough funds to satisfy needs that the company will seek to obtain new equity finance. This theory of course contrasts sharply with the theories which indicate that there is an optimal capital structure for a firm.

One explanation of this 'pecking order' for the supply of finance is issue costs. Internally generated funds have the lowest issue cost and new equity the highest. Firms obtain as much as they can of the easiest and least expensive finance, mainly retained earnings, before moving to the next least expensive debt.

The issue cost explanation of the Pecking Order Theory is somewhat discredited. It assumes companies ignore the full cost of equity capital. It assumes managers are somewhat naive. There are no issue costs associated with retained earnings, but this does not mean that the funds have zero costs. Retained earnings belong to shareholders, if the funds were returned to shareholders they could earn a return on them from investing in the market. The managers of the company need to be aware that they need to earn at least an equivalent amount on the retained earnings, if they are to satisfy the shareholders.

Myers [10] has suggested that firms follow a 'modified pecking order' in their approach to financing. Although Donaldson [11] originally argued that reliance on internal finance enables professional managers to avoid subjecting themselves to the discipline of the capital market, Myers has suggested asymmetric information as an explanation for heavy reliance on retentions. There may be a situation where managers, because of their access to more information about the firm, know that the value of the shares is greater than the current market value based on semi-strong market information. In the case of a new project, for example, managers' forecasts may be higher and more realistic than that of the market. If new shares were issued in this situation there is the possibility that they would be issued at too low a price, thus transferring wealth from existing shareholders to new shareholders. In these circumstances there might be a natural preference for internally generated funds over new issues. The use of internal funds also ensures that there is a regular source of funds which might be in line with a particular company's expansion or renewal programme. If additional funds are required over and above internally generated funds, then borrowing would be the next alternative under this pecking order approach. If management is averse to making equity issues when in possession of favourable inside information, market participants might assume that management will be more likely to favour new issues when they are in possession of unfavourable inside information which leads to the suggestion that new issues might be regarded as a signal of bad news! Managers may therefore wish to rely primarily on internally generated funds supplemented by borrowing, with issues of new equity as a last resort.

Myers and Majluf [12] demonstrate that with asymmetric information, equity issues are interpreted by the market as bad news, since managers are only motivated to make equity issues when shares are undervalued. Asquith and Mullins [13] empirically observed that announcements of new equity issues are greeted by sharp declines in stock prices. Thus, equity issues are comparatively rare among large established companies.

Agency costs

A further explanation that has been offered for the pecking order is agency costs. These are costs either direct or indirect of ensuring that company management act in the best interests of the providers of finance. These costs cover the costs of reporting and being accountable to shareholders, and the costs of the providers of debt monitoring and restricting (bonding) the managers through covenants.

There is however disagreement as to whether the agency costs associated with debt are greater or less than those associated with equity.

Jenson and Meckling [14] drew attention to a number of ways in which agency problems may restrict the level of debt taken on by companies. Agency costs are additional expenses, either direct or indirect, which are incurred in ensuring that agents, in this case company management, act in the best interests of principals, in this case the suppliers of debt. The reason for the existence of these costs is that it would be possible for company management to undertake policies detrimental to providers of debt if constraints of some sort were not placed upon them. For example, it would be possible for the position of debt holders to be adversely affected *vis-à-vis* equity holders by entering into a riskier investment programme. Table 18.8 helps illustrate this point. It shows two possible projects; both have an expected value of £40 000 but project 2's higher risk is indicated by the wider distribution of potential returns. If the required investment in each project is £30 000, to be financed by borrowing, we can see that both the projects have positive net present values (NPVs). However, in the case of project 1 lenders are sure of repayment whichever outcome occurs; with project 2 there is only a 0.5 chance of there being sufficient funds to repay the lenders. We can see that equity holders might prefer project 2 because, if the higher outcome occurs, they will receive £40 000 after paying off debt holders while in project 1 they would receive only £10 000. If the lower outcome occurs in project 2 they would be protected by limited liability from having to contribute to the shortfall due to debt holders while with project 1 the smaller outcome would go totally to the debt holders. It would be particularly difficult if debt holders provided funds in the expectation that project 1 was to be adopted but the firm then undertook project 2 instead. This change would result in a transfer of wealth from debt holders to shareholders. This type of risk shifting, and there are others, explains why debt holders require certain kinds of covenants in debt contracts to protect their position. Agency costs are the cost of writing and enforcing such agreements. An example might be the requirement that dividend payments are limited so that companies cannot pay out excessive dividends, thus diminishing the capital base and increasing the risk of debt holders. Restrictions on the issue of further debt might also be imposed.

Table 18.8

Probability	Project 1	Project 2
0.5	30 000	10 000
0.5	50 000	70 000

Baskin [15] undertook an empirical study in which he regressed the level of gearing against profits. He found that as profits increased the level of gearing declined. The debt to equity ratio was inversely related to profits. This is not the finding one would expect if firms had a target debt/equity ratio. If there was a target, as retained profits increased (i.e. equity) one would expect the level of borrowing to increase. Baskin concluded that the empirical evidence is entirely consistent with the prediction of the pecking order hypothesis.

18.10 Summary and conclusions

In this chapter we have examined the effect of gearing on company profitability, cost of capital and value. We began by illustrating the effects of gearing on profit and earnings per share calculations, noting that as gearing increased so did volatility of earnings per share. We then showed how weighted-average cost of capital could be computed using share and bond costs and the proportions of each in the capital structure. The significance of marginal cost of capital in project appraisal was illustrated and contrasted with weighted average cost before and after raising new finance. The advantages of the adjusted present value approach to incorporate financing and other side effects were examined and illustrated. We then moved on to discuss the alternative views on the effect of debt on company value and cost of capital.

The original traditional view seems to be based upon the idea that higher earnings per share could be generated by the use of debt, but this approach seems to ignore risk as the increasing levels of debt add to the variability of earnings.

MM's papers [3, 4] provided an analytical framework for examining the effect of debt on the value of the firm. Their paper on debt and taxes probably overstates the value of the tax shield to most companies. In suggesting that the value of the firm increased by $V_d t$ it was assumed that the benefit of debt was perpetual and that there were no constraints on being able to use the debt tax shield in each and every succeeding future period. In addition, it was assumed that the rate of corporate taxation would remain unchanged. In fact it is almost certain that the rate of taxation used should be lower than the current rate of corporate taxation, but the estimation of an effective rate of tax to use in the calculation is very difficult.

First of all Miller [5] suggests that the existence of personal taxes reduces the tax-shield benefit below the corporation tax level. In addition, the tax shield will only have value if there are taxable profits to offset interest payments against. An established firm may feel reasonably confident that it will be able to cover reasonable levels of debt interest; however, smaller firms and firms with a high variability of earnings may find that in some years their taxable profit may not be sufficient to cover debt interest. Clearly, another factor here will be the number of other opportunities available to companies to shield income.

We saw that a further factor limiting the amount of debt taken into the capital structure would be the potential costs of financial distress. The higher these potential costs, the lower the level of debt a firm would be encouraged to take on. The level of these costs could be affected by the type of asset involved, being lower for tangible saleable assets than for intangible unsaleable assets.

The foregoing suggests that large companies using tangible saleable assets and having a low earnings volatility might be expected to have a higher level of debt than a smaller company with intangible assets and a high earnings volatility. These are broad categories, and the main purpose of the examples is to highlight the factors which one would expect to affect debt policy.

A final suggestion was that there might be some pecking order which indicated preferred ways in which directors might seek to finance the companies they manage. Retentions are the favoured form of finance followed by debt and as a last resort new equity issues. Retentions are a convenient form of finance as they allow for planned expansion at a pace with which directors feel comfortable. Use of retentions minimizes issue costs and also allows scope for an emergency issue should one be needed. The pecking order approach avoids potential issues of undervalued shares caused by asymmetric information between directors and shareholders.

18.11 Key terms

Adjusted present value
Agency costs
Capital structure
Debt ratio
Financial distress
Gearing and leverage
Gearing and personal taxes
(Miller analysis)

Interest cover
Marginal cost of capital
MM and arbitrage
MM with taxes
Pecking order
Target ratio
Traditional view
Weighted-average cost of capital

18.12 Revision questions

1. Investors in debt require a higher/lower return than equity holders. This is because debt carries a higher/lower risk, while debt makes equity more/less risky and therefore equity holders will require a higher/lower return than in the equivalent ungeared company. Delete, as appropriate.
2. The traditional view of cost of capital regards overall cost of capital as constant. True or false? Explain.
3. Illustrate graphically the traditional view of cost of capital and the value of the firm.
4. List the assumptions that MM made in their initial analysis of capital structure.
5. Explain the meaning of 'risk class' and 'arbitrage' in the MM analysis.
6. What were MM's original conclusions on cost of capital and value of the firm under different levels of gearing?
7. How did the introduction of corporate taxes alter (if at all) the conclusions in question 6?
8. Why might personal taxes affect the capital structure debate?
9. Distinguish between direct and indirect costs of financial distress.
10. How do costs of financial distress affect desired levels of debt?
11. Why might a firm's asset mix affect its ability to borrow?

18.13 References

1. Weston, J.F. and Woods, D.H. (1967) *Theory of Business Finance: Advanced Readings*, Wadsworth, California, p. 18.
2. Lindsay, R. and Sametz, A.W. (1963) *Financial Management: An Analytical Approach*, Irwin, Homewood.
3. Modigliani, F. and Miller, M.H. (1958) The cost of capital, corporation finance and the theory of investment, *American Economic Review*, **48**, 261–96.
4. Modigliani, F. and Miller, M.H. (1963) Taxes and the cost of capital: a correction, *American Economic Review*, **53**, 433–43.
5. Miller, M.H. (1977) Debt and taxes, *Journal of Finance*, **32**, 261–76.
6. Warner, J.B. (1977) Bankruptcy costs: some evidence, *Journal of Finance*, **26**, 337–48.
7. Baxter, N. (1967) Leverage, risk of ruin and the cost of capital, *Journal of Finance*, 395–403.
8. Jensen, M.C. (1989) Eclipse of the public Corporation, *Harvard Business Review*, **5**, 61–74.
9. Donaldson, G. (1961) *Corporate Debt Capacity*, Harvard University Press, Cambridge, MA.
10. Myers, S.C. (1984) The capital structure puzzle, *Journal of Finance*, **39**, 575–92.
11. Donaldson, G. (1971) *Strategy for Financial Mobility*, Irwin.
12. Myers, S. and Majluf, N. (1984) Corporate financing and investment decisions when firms have information investors do not have, *Journal of Financial Economics*, June, 187–221.
13. Asquith, P. and Mullins, D.W. (1983) The impact of initiating dividend payments on shareholder wealth, *Journal of Business*, **56**, 77–96.
14. Jensen, J. and Meckling, W. (1976) Theory of the firm: managerial behaviour, agency costs and ownership structure, *Journal of Financial Economics*, 305–60.

15. Baskin, J.B. (1989) An empirical investigation of the pecking order hypothesis, *Financial Management*, **18**, 26–35.

A suitable starting point is the two MM papers:

Modigliani, F. and Miller, M.H. (1958) The cost of capital, corporation finance and the theory of investment, *American Economic Review*, **48**, 261–96; and (1963) Taxes and the cost of capital: a correction, *American Economic Review*, **53**, 433–43.

Personal as well as corporate taxes are considered in:

Miller, M.H. (1977) Debt and Taxes, *Journal of Finance*, **32**, 261–76.

A number of readable papers on contemporary financial issues are contained in Stern and Chew.

Stern, J.M. and Chew, D.H., Jr. (1986) *The Revolution in Corporate Finance*, Basil Blackwell.

Including:

Myers, S.C. (1984) The capital structure puzzle, *Journal of Finance*, **39**, 575–92.

18.14 Further reading

18.15 Problems

1. ABC PLC and XYZ PLC are two firms which operate in the same industry and are both considered to be in the same risk class. Both companies have gross operating profit of £100 000 per annum. ABC PLC relies on equity sources in its finance while XYZ PLC uses both loan and equity sources. Their capital structure is as follows

ABC PLC: equity	£700 000 (market value)
XYZ PLC: equity	£400 000 (market value)
8% debenture	£400 000 (nominal value – currently traded at par)
	£800 000

At the present time you hold 4% of XYZ's share capital. Assume that both companies pay out all their profit after interest in dividends.

(a) Determine the weighted-average cost of capital of both companies; then comment whether these two companies' ordinary shares are in equilibrium or not.
(b) Show how you may gain from arbitrage whilst keeping your current level of finance risk constant. Assume that you can borrow money at an annual interest rate of 8%.
(Ignore taxation.)

2. ABC PLC and XYZ PLC are two companies with identical levels of business risk. The two companies have different capital structures as ABC has an all-equity capital structure while XYZ is very highly geared. You are given the following information about earnings, dividends, interest payments and market values of both companies:

	ABC PLC Years 1–∞	XYZ PLC Years 1–∞
Annual dividends	£360 000	£200 000
Annual interest	—	£160 000
Total annual cash earnings	£360 000	£360 000
Total market value of equity	£3 600 000	£1 200 000
Total market value of debt	—	£2 000 000
	£3 600 000	£3 200 000

Assume that the capital market is perfect (no taxation, no transaction costs). Assume also that markets for the ordinary shares of ABC PLC and the debentures of XYZ PLC are in equilibrium.

(a) What do you think is the best decision for shareholders in both the companies to make?

(b) Assume that Mr Money holds shares having a market value of £4000 in both of the above companies. Show Mr Money how he can improve his financial position whilst keeping his current level of financial risk unchanged.

(c) Explain how the above is used to confirm the proposal that a company's cost of equity capital in equilibrium can be estimated by the expression

$$K_e = K_0 + (K_0 - K_d)\frac{D}{E}$$

3. 'The optimal financial policy of a firm depends upon the marginal income tax rates of its shareholders' (King). Analyse this statement and discuss its significance for the financial policies of UK companies.

4. You own 6% of the equity in an unlevered company called A Ltd. The total market value of A's shares is £1 000 000 and the expected annual operating earnings are £90 000 into perpetuity. It comes to your attention that there is another firm (B Ltd) which is identical in every way to A Ltd except that it has a mixed capital structure with a debt-to-equity ratio of 1:2. The expected annual operating earnings are of course £90 000 (before the deduction of interest on debt) and the current market value of B Ltd's equity is £600 000. B Ltd's outstanding debt takes the form of £300 000 of 6% debentures, currently being traded at par. Assume that both A Ltd and B Ltd pay out all available earnings in dividends.

(a) Show how you could increase your current dividend expectation, without changing its risk and indicating any assumptions that you would need to make.

(b) What are the implications of the transactions that all rational investors would make in this situation and why are they important for capital budgeting?

5. Alpha Ltd and Beta Ltd are two companies with identical levels of business risk. Both companies have gross operating profits of £90 000 per annum which are expected to be constant indefinitely. The two companies have different capital structures as Alpha relies entirely on equity sources while Beta uses both loan and equity sources. Their capital structures are as follows:

Alpha Ltd	
Equity (market value)	£600 000
Beta Ltd	
Equity (market value)	£340 000
8% irredeemable debentures	
(value in the market at par)	£340 000
	£680 000

At present, Mr Jones holds 3% of Alpha's share capital. In order to increase his income, he is considering switching to an investment in Beta Ltd. A proposal is being considered in this respect by Mr Jones which involves the purchase of 3% of the equity of Beta and the purchase of some of its debentures with the balance of the sum obtained from the sale of his holdings in Alpha Ltd. It has been further suggested to Mr Jones that this proposal will maintain the risk of his portfolio at a constant level assuming that the debentures of Beta Ltd are free of risk. Assuming that corporation tax is charged at the rate of 50% on net profit and that it is payable at the end of the year in which the income arises, and ignoring personal taxation, answer the following.

(a) Find the effect of the proposal on Jones's financial position.

(b) Calculate the equilibrium value of Beta's equity assuming that
 (i) the arbitrage process will be carried out by many investors,
 (ii) the values of Alpha's equity and Beta's debentures would remain unchanged.

(c) Discuss the implications of your calculations for the determination of the optimal financial structure of a firm from a practical point of view.

6. The Board of Directors of Rickery PLC is discussing whether to alter the company's capital structure. Corporate legislation permits Rickery PLC to repurchase its own shares and it is proposed to issue £5 million of new debentures at par, and to use the funds to repurchase ordinary shares.

A summary of Rickery's current balance sheet is shown below:

	£000
Fixed assets (net)	24 500
Current assets	12 300
Current liabilities	(8 600)
	28 200
Financed by:	
25p Ordinary shares	4 500
Reserves	14 325
	18 825
5% Debentures 1997	9 375
	28 200

The company's current ordinary share price is 167p and the debenture price is £80. Rickery's finance director does not expect the market price of the existing ordinary shares or debentures to change as a result of the proposed issue of new debentures. The company expects to pay a premium of 2.5% over the risk-free rate of interest for its new debentures. Rickery's equity beta is estimated by a leading firm of stockbrokers to be 1.24, and the estimated market return is 15%. Debenture interest is payable annually. Issue costs and transactions costs can be ignored.

(a) Evaluate the probable effect on the cost of capital of Rickery PLC if the company restructures its capital:
 (i) if the company pays tax at a rate of 35%;
 (ii) if the company does not expect to pay corporate taxes for the foreseeable future.
All the relevant calculations must be shown. State clearly any assumptions that you make. (12 marks)
(b) Rickery's Finance Director believes that the market price of the company's existing ordinary shares and debentures will not change. Explain why he might be wrong in his belief and suggest what changes might occur.

(8 marks)
(c) What are the arguments for and against the use of book values and market values in establishing a company's target capital structure? (5 marks)
(Total 25 marks)
ACCA, Dec. 1987
7. (a) A colleague has been taken ill. Your managing director has asked you to take over from the colleague and to provide urgently needed estimates of the discount rate to be used in appraising a large new capital investment. You have been given your colleague's working notes, which you believe to be numerically accurate.

Estimates for the next five years (annual averages)

Stock market total return on equity	16%
Own company dividend yield	7%
Own company share price rise	14%
Standard deviation of total stock market return on equity	10%
Standard deviation of own company total return on equity	20%
Correlation coefficient between total own company return on equity and total stock market return on equity	0.7

Correlation coefficient between total return on the new capital
investment and total market return on equity | 0.5
Growth rate of own company earnings | 12%
Growth rate of own company dividends | 11%
Growth rate of own company sales | 13%
Treasury bill yield | 12%

The company's gearing level (by market values) is 1:2 debt to equity, and after-tax earnings available to ordinary shareholders in the most recent year were £5 400 000 of which £2 140 000 was distributed as ordinary dividends. The company has ten million issued ordinary shares which are currently trading on the Stock Exchange at 321p. Corporate debt can be assumed to be risk free. The company pays tax at 35% and personal taxation can be ignored.

Estimate the company's weighted average cost of capital using

(a) the dividend valuation model
(b) the capital asset pricing model.

State clearly any assumptions that you make.

Under what circumstances would these models be expected to produce similar values for the weighted average cost of capital? (1 0 marks)

ACCA, Dec. 1986

8. It has been suggested that in a world with only corporate taxation

value of a firm = value if all equity financed + PV of the tax shield on debt finance

(a) If the above equation applied, what would be the most appropriate capital structure for a company? How far do existing capital structures of companies compare with the most appropriate structure according to the equation?
(3 marks)

(b) Discuss how and why the existence of personal taxation might alter the choice of capital structure suggested in part (a). (7 marks)

(c) If a financial manager agrees with the implications for the choice of capital structure that you have suggested in part (b), what problems might he face in applying them within his company? (3 marks)

(d) (i) Give examples of the possible costs associated with a high level of gearing.
(7 marks)

(ii) Discuss how such costs might influence the capital structure of
(1) a medium-sized electronics company entering the home computer market
(2) an established company owning and managing a chain of hotels.
State clearly any assumptions that you make. (5 marks)
(25 marks)

ACCA, Dec. 1985

9. (a) Identify the limitations of the weighted-average cost of company capital as a discount rate for use in project evaluation. (8 marks)

(b) Harvey Ltd is considering developing a new line of business. Its present financial structure is 40% debt and 60% equity, and its cost of equity is 19%. Corporate taxes are at an effective rate of 30%. The pre-tax cost of debt to Harvey Ltd is 8%, while the risk-free interest rate is 7% and the expected market return is 15%. Charles Ltd is a company engaged solely in the proposed line of business. Its share price performance indicates an estimated equity beta of 1.368. Charles Ltd finances in debt-to-equity proportions of 0.2, and its cost of debt is 7% before tax. Again, the effective corporate tax rate is 30%. Assume that the project requires an initial investment of £1 000 000 and promises perpetual after-tax cash flows, before financing effects, of £150 000 per year. Harvey will finance the project in its existing (market-value) capital structure proportions.

(i) Estimate an appropriate discount rate for use in the evaluation of this project. Comment on the limitations of the estimate you have arrived at.

(8 marks)

(ii) Using this project and the previous data as an example, demonstrate the equivalence of the adjusted present value method, the weighted-average cost of capital approach and the Modigliani-Miller adjusted cost of capital approach to project evaluation by showing that each results in the *same* estimate of project value.

(9 marks)

(25 marks)

10. (a) **Required:**

Explain why financial gearing might be important to a company. (3 marks)

(b) **Required:**

Discuss what factors might limit the amount of debt finance that a company uses.

(5 marks)

(c) Three senior managers of Engot plc are discussing the company's financial gearing. Mr R believes that the financial gearing is 55%, Mr Y believes that it is 89% and Mr Z 134%.

Summarized consolidated profit and loss account for the year ended 31 December 1988

	£000
Turnover	56 300
Cost of sales	45 100
Gross profit	11 200
Administrative and other expenses	6 450
Operating profit	4 750
Interest payable	1 154
Profit before taxation	3 596
Taxation	1 259
	2 337
Extraordinary items	580
Profit for the financial year	2 917
Dividends paid and proposed	970
Retained profit for the year	1 947

Summarized consolidated balance sheet as at 31 December 1988

	£000
Fixed assets	16 700
Current assets	
Stocks	7 040
Debtors	4 800
Cash at the bank and in hand	2 700
	14 540
Creditors: Amounts falling due within one year	
8% loan stock 1989	(1 000)
Bank loans and overdrafts	(2 800)
Trade creditors	(7 200)
Corporation tax	(1 140)
Proposed dividends	(510)

Accruals and deferred income	(2 860)
	(15 510)
Net current liabilities	(970)
Total assets less current liabilities	15 730

Creditors: Amounts falling due after more than one year

Bank loans	(5 600)
12% Debentures 2002	(1 800)
Net assets	8 330

Capital and reserves

Called-up share capital (10p par value)	2 200
Share premium account	1 940
Profit and loss account	4 190
	8 330

Current market data for Engot plc
Ordinary share price 94p
8% loan stock 1989 price £98
12% debenture 2002 price £108

Required:
Explain how each manager has estimated the financial gearing and suggest how each manager might argue that his is the most appropriate measure of financial gearing. State, with reasons which measure of gearing you prefer.

(7 marks)

(d) Engot is in an industry where annual sales might fluctuate widely according to the state of the economy. The company is planning a £5 million expansion which will be financed by either a rights issue at 15% below the current market price, or a debenture at a fixed interest rate of 10% per year.

The probability distribution of sales in each of the next two years is estimated to be:

Probability	Sales
	£000
0.15	56 000
0.20	72 000
0.35	90 000
0.15	108 000
0.15	120 000

Variable costs are approximately 75% of sales, and fixed costs are estimated at £8 000 000. The figures may be assumed to be relevant for all levels of sales. Interest is not included in these costs.

Required:
Prepare a brief report discussing which means of financing Engot should use. Include in your report an estimate, based upon EPS, of the level of sales at which the shareholders of Engot might be indifferent between the use of equity and debt to finance the expansion. Corporate tax is at the rate of 35%.

(10 marks)
(25 marks)
ACCA, *June 1989*

11. C plc and D plc are two companies in the printing industry. The companies have the same business risk and are almost identical in all respects except for their capital

structures and total market values. The companies' capital structures are summarized below:

C plc	£000
Ordinary shares (25 pence par value)	20 000
Share premium account	45 000
Profit and loss account	36 500
Shareholders' funds	101 500

C's ordinary shares are trading at 140 pence.

D plc	£000
Ordinary shares (£1 par value)	25 000
Share premium account	8 000
Profit and loss account	44 000
Shareholders' funds	77 000
12% debentures (newly issued)	25 000
	102 000

D's ordinary shares are trading at 400 pence, and debentures at £100.
Annual earnings before interest and tax for both companies are £25 million.
Corporate tax is at the rate of 35%.

Required:

(a) If you owned 4% of the ordinary shares of company D, and you agreed with the arguments of Modigliani and Miller explain what action you would take to improve your financial position. (4 marks)

(b) Estimate by how much your financial position is expected to improve. Personal taxes may be ignored and the assumptions made by Modigliani and Miller may be used. (7 marks)

(c) If company C was to borrow £20 million calculate what effect this would have on the company's cost of capital according to Modigliani and Miller. What implications would this suggest for the company's choice of capital structure? (6 marks)

(d) Modigliani and Miller's theory of capital structure is sometimes considered to be unrealistic. Discuss the problems with this theory that might concern a financial manager who wishes to ascertain the appropriate capital structure for his company. (8 marks)

(25 marks)

ACCA, Dec. 1988

12. Slohill plc plans to raise finance some time within the next few months. Slohill's managing director remembers the stock market crash of October 1987 when share prices fell approximately 30% during one week, and is worried about the possible effects of a further crash on the cost of capital.

Slohill plc
Summarized balance sheet as at 31 March 1989

	£ million	£ million
Fixed assets at cost less depreciation		262.20
Current assets		
Stock	69.00	
Debtors	82.80	
Bank	27.60	
	179.40	

Less: Current liabilities			
Creditors		75.31	
Dividend		8.99	
Taxation		26.10	
		110.40	69.00
Less: 11% debenture 2004			138.00
Net assets			193.20
Shareholders' funds			
Ordinary shares (£1 par value)			69.00
Reserves			124.20
			193.20

5 year summarized profit and loss account

Year ended March 31	Turnover £m	Profit before tax £m	Tax £m	Profit after tax £m	Dividend £m
1985	583.7	49.63	19.85	29.78	9.86
1986	644.6	58.42	20.45	37.97	10.94
1987	639.5	59.61	20.86	38.75	12.17
1988	742.3	62.43	21.85	40.58	13.48
1989	810.6	74.57	26.10	48.47	14.98

The company's current share price is 546 pence ex div, and debenture price £93. No new share or debenture capital has been issued during the last five years. Corporate tax is at the rate of 35%.

If another crash were to occur it would lead to increased demand for gilts and other fixed interest stocks and a change of approximately 2% in all interest rates.

Required:

(a) Estimate what effect a second stock market crash of the same magnitude as in 1987 might have on Slohill's current weighted-average cost of capital if:
  (i) the crash has negligible effect on the earnings expectations of the company and on the growth rate of the company's earnings;
  (ii) the annual pre-tax growth rate of the company's earnings is expected to fall by 20%.
  State clearly any assumptions that you make. (16 marks)

(b) If a second stock market crash were to occur, advise the managing director of the likely effect on the cost of capital of raising a substantial amount of new capital:
  (i) if the capital raised is all equity;
  (ii) if the capital raised is all debt. (4 marks)

(c) If the capital asset pricing model were to be used to estimate the cost of equity in scenarios (a) (i) and (a) (ii) above explain in which direction the main variables in the model would be likely to move. (5 marks)
(25 marks)
ACCA, Dec. 1989

13. (a) Berlan plc has annual earnings before interest and tax of £15 million. These earnings are expected to remain constant. The market price of the company's ordinary shares is 86 pence per share cum. div. and of debentures £105.50 per debenture ex. interest. An interim dividend of six pence per share has been declared. Corporate tax is at the rate of 35% and all available earnings are distributed as dividends.

Berlan's long-term, capital structure is shown below:

	£000
Ordinary shares (25 pence par value)	12 500
Reserves	24 300
	36 800
16% debenture 31.12.94 (£100 par value)	23 697
	60 497

Required:

Calculate the cost of capital of Berlan plc according to the traditional theory of capital structure. Assume that it is now 31 December 1991. (8 marks)

(b) Canalot plc is an all equity company with an equilibrium market value of £32.5 million and a cost of capital of 18% per year.

  The company proposes to repurchase £5 million of equity and to replace it with 13% irredeemable loan stock.

  Canalot's earnings before interest and tax are expected to be constant for the foreseeable future. Corporate tax is at the rate of 35%. All profits are paid out as dividends.

Required:

Using the assumptions of Modigliani and Miller explain and demonstrate how this change in capital structure will affect:

- the market value
- the cost of equity
- the cost of capital

of Canalot plc. (7 marks)

(c) Explain any weaknesses of both the traditional and Modigliani and Miller theories and discuss how useful they might be in the determination of the appropriate capital structure for a company. (10 marks)
  (25 marks)
  ACCA, Dec. 1991

14. The government has just announced that corporation tax is being reduced from 33% per year to 30% per year and the directors of Varis plc wish to know the likely effect of this change on the company's share price and cost of capital.

The company's current capital structure is

	£m
Ordinary shares (50 pence par value)	30
Share premium	48
Other reserves	62
Shareholders' equity	140
10% debenture (irredeemable)	40
	180

The company's shares are trading at 320 pence ex-div, and the debentures at £125 ex interest.

  Prior to the tax change Varis's beta equity was 1.2. The market return is 13% per year. The tax cut itself is expected to increase the net present value of Varis's operating cash flows by £15 million.

Assume that the cost of debt and market price of debt do not change as a result of this tax change. Ignore advance corporation tax.

Varis's debt may be assumed to be risk free.

Required:

(a) Estimate the company's current cost of capital. (5 marks)

(b) Using Modigliani and Miller's theory of capital structure (with tax) estimate:
   (i) the expected share price after the tax change; (3 marks)
   (ii) the company's expected cost of capital after the tax change. (6 marks)

(c) Explain the reasons for the difference between the old and new cost of capital. (3 marks)

(d) Briefly discuss
   (i) the main limitations of this analysis; (5 marks)
   (ii) the importance in investment decisions of accurate estimates of the cost of capital. (3 marks)

(25 marks)

ACCA, Dec. 1993

15. On 1 January the total market value of the Beranek Company was £60 million. During the year the company plans to raise and invest £30 million in new projects. The firm's present market value capital structure, shown below, is considered to be optimal. Assume that there is no short-term debt.

Debt	£30 000 000
Equity	30 000 000
Total capital	£60 000 000

New bonds will have an 8% coupon rate, and they will be sold at par. Equity shares, currently selling at £30 a share, can be sold to net the company £27 a share. The next expected dividend is £1.20, and dividends are expected to grow at a constant rate of 8% per annum. Retained earnings for the year are estimated to be £3 million. The marginal corporate tax rate is 40%.

(a) How much of the new investment must be financed by new equity shares in order to maintain the present capital structure?

(b) Calculate the cost of capital of both debt and equity.

(c) Explain to an 'uninformed' manager the logic behind the calculation of the cost of new equity funds. He cannot even understand why dividends are a cost. He argues that they are an appropriation of profits, and therefore if the company does not earn profits it does not have to pay dividends – thus how can they be a cost? He is even more bemused by the idea of adding on to the present cost an expected percentage increase in future dividends. Use the Beranek Company to illustrate the points you make.

16. (a) Explain why the adjusted present value technique (APV) is sometimes advocated as being a more appropriate way of evaluating a project than net present value. (4 marks)

(b) Bigoyte Inc is developing a new personal computer with an expected life of three years. The investment has a total initial cost of $283 million, of which $106 million will be provided from internally generated funds, $90 million from a rights issue and the remainder from a fixed rate term loan at 12% per annum. The proportion represented by the term loan reflects the optimum debt capacity of the company.

   Issue costs are estimated at 3.5% for the rights issue and 1% for the term loan. Corporate taxes are payable at a rate of 40% on net operating cash flows in the year that the cash flows occur. The treasury bill yield is 9%, the market return is 14% and an appropriate asset beta for the investment is believed to be 1.5. The project net operating cash flows (after tax) are as follows:

	Year 1	Year 2	Year 3
	$89 million	$198 million	$59 million

Additionally, a residual value of $28 million (after all taxes) is expected at the end of year three.

Estimate the adjusted present value of the investment and recommend whether the investment should be undertaken. (8 marks)

17. Bell PLC is not subject to taxation and has calculated its cost of equity and debt capital as follows:

| | Total amounts | | Cost |
	Book values (£million)	Market values (£million)	%
Equity – 10 million shares issued	50	80	15
Debt – irredeemable debentures	20	20	10

Bell wishes to invest in a new project which will provide equal expected annual cash flows in perpetuity. Investment in the project can be at several different levels. The project will be financed entirely from the net proceeds of the issue of 3 million shares (issue costs, £600 000) and £6 million 10% debentures issued at par (issue costs, £400 000). Issue costs will be borne by Bell at the time that the issue of securities is carried out. The price and method of issuing shares are still not determined. Three specific possibilities are under consideration:

(a) shares issued at their current market value;
(b) shares issued to existing shareholders at a discount of 25% from current market value;
(c) shares issued to entirely new shareholders at a discount of 25% from current market value.

The financial director estimates that, because of the additional risks involved, undertaking the project will increase the cost of all issued equity to 16% but will not alter the cost of debt.

For each of the three possibilities concerning the issue price and method for Bell's new equity, determine the minimum expected internal rate of return required from the *net* investment in the proposed project if the wealth of the existing shareholders is not to be reduced.

19 *Financial planning*

19.1	Strategic planning	676
19.2	Long-term and medium-term financial planning	678
19.3	Financial modelling	680
19.4	Short-term financial planning	684
19.5	Working capital requirements	687
19.6	From rule of thumb to planning models	689
19.7	The operating cycle	694
19.8	Funds flow and cash flow statements	696
19.9	Key terms	700
19.10	Revision questions	701
19.11	References	701
19.12	Further reading	701
19.13	Problems	701

This chapter provides a general introduction to the subject of strategic planning. This is a subject which has taken on increased significance in recent years and the literature has expanded accordingly.

The major issues examined in this chapter are long-term financial planning and medium-term financial planning. It should be appreciated however that many people believe that there is more to a planning exercise than the purely financial aspects.

Short-term financial planning, which covers cash management, is dealt with in the next chapter.

19.1 Strategic planning

It is now quite common for companies and other organizations to produce mission statements, which they often publish. A mission statement shows a company's objectives.

Long-term strategic planning attempts to ensure that the company meets these objectives. There is a vast and growing literature on the subject of strategic planning, which basically involves studying the strengths and weaknesses of the company and ascertaining the company's position within a particular market and industry. When the opportunities and dangers have been explicitly identified strategies are developed to achieve the objectives.

There are three inputs required in the planning exercise:

- the objectives of the company;
- the characteristics of the industry and markets in which the company is engaged;
- the strengths and weaknesses of the company.

Objectives

The company's objectives can be expressed in financial terms or in 'grander terms'. The mission statement of ICI shown in Figure 19.1, is quite socially minded. If a company wishes to publish a mission statement it is for a purpose and these grand objectives are presumably to show the company in a good light – to show that the company is not just there to make profits. Figure 19.2 shows the corporate objectives of De La Rue.

For many companies the main objective is simply to survive, although it would not be written in such terms in a published mission statement. Most businesses give as key objectives the wish to achieve a certain rate of return on investments and to grow at a certain rate. Smaller companies may have objectives such as to achieve a stock market listing. There can of course be all sorts of sub-objectives, such as to achieve a certain market share or to introduce new products or to improve the levels of service offered to customers, or to improve the management of the company.

The chemical industry is a major force for the improvement of the quality of life across the world. ICI aims to be the world's leading chemical company, serving customers internationally through the innovative and responsible application of chemistry and related sciences.

Through achievement of our aim, we will enhance the wealth and well-being of our shareholders, our employees, our customers and the communities which we serve and in which we operate.

We will do this by:

- Seeking consistent profitable growth;
- Providing challenge and opportunity for our employees, releasing their skills and creativity;
- Achieving a standard of quality and service internationally which our customers recognise as being consistently better than any of our competitors;
- Operating safely and in harmony with the global environment.

Figure 19.1 *Mission statement of ICI, 1991*

Corporate Objectives

To retain and build our our position as the world's leading security printing and payment systems group by consistently striving for the best possible performance in quality, innovation, value and service for our customers.

Through continuing enhanced performance, to attain for our shareholders consistent growth in earnings and dividends per share and to communicate effectively to them our objectives and achievements.

To train, motivate, support and reward our staff worldwide, focusing on their vital contribution to the success of the Company and also their involvement in the communities local to their business.

Figure 19.2 *De La Rue's corporate objectives*

Industry and market analysis

The planning exercise involves studying the strength and weaknesses of the company relative to competitor companies engaged in the same industry or industries. The position of suppliers has to be considered. What changes are taking place in supplier businesses? What is the relative bargaining strength of the supplier companies in relation to one's own company?

The requirements of customers in terms of quality requirements, service and price need to be researched. Any changes in customer tastes has to be carefully monitored, as do technological developments and possible new products.

It would not hurt a planning department to study the literature on company failure. There are certain reasons why companies fail, which are discussed later in this book. Failure after failure can be blamed on the same few causes. It is possible for companies to avoid some of these pitfalls if they plan ahead. Obvious problems arise if companies ignore changes in technology in their industry and ignore changes in taste and needs in the markets in which they sell.

Company analysis

When researching what is happening in the industry and markets around the company it is also important to analyse the strengths and weaknesses of one's own company. It is the opportunity for competitive advantage that the planner wishes to identify. Of course, equally important, as mentioned above, is competitive disadvantage. The issues to be considered would include:

- technology;
- distribution channels;
- access to raw materials;
- management structure and succession.

Strategy

Having determined the company's objectives, and analysed its strengths and weaknesses, the next step is to develop strategies to achieve these objectives. Broad strategies could include:

- reducing the range of products or markets in which the company operates;
- expanding into new markets;
- reducing costs so as to achieve a price advantage over competitors;
- a marketing campaign to differentiate the company's products from competitors;
- increasing research and development expenditure to obtain a technological advantage;
- trying to improve market share through acquisition.

Planning

Once a strategy has been agreed it will be written into a plan. This will involve forecasting the company's performance over the medium and long term (Figure 19.3).

Strategies are written into plans and an important element of any plan will be the financial plan. There will be sales plans and production plans, but in this book we are concerned only with the financial plans.

19.2 Long-term and medium-term financial planning

Management consists of three types of operations: planning, decision-making and control. Planning is concerned with exploring alternative future situations or outcomes and the course of action or sequence of management actions necessary to attain the outcomes. Decision-making refers to the selection of one course of action from the candidate set of conceivable courses of action. Such a decision can only be taken rationally if there is an explicitly stated objective on the basis of which the outcomes can be compared. The complexity of decision-making in the financial area is such that a planning model will often prove useful in appraising the relative merits of different outcomes.

Broadly speaking the role of financial management in a firm concerns the prudent administration of the flow of funds through the firm. This includes the determination of what constitutes desirable present and future utilization of funds and determining the most advantageous present and future sources of funding. Fund utilization is conveniently classified into investment in fixed assets (capital budgeting) and in working capital. Fund generation can of course be achieved either by internal means through revenues raised or by external means. The capital structure decision of externally raised

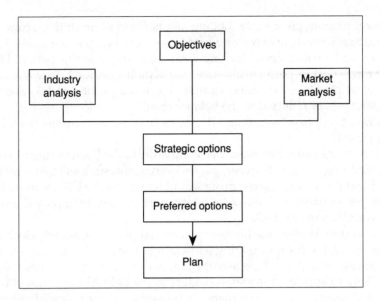

Figure 19.3 *The strategic planning process*

finance, i.e. the optimal proportions of equity and debt components, constitutes the principal financing decision of the firm. Allied closely to that decision is the determination of dividend policy – assessing the required dividend for distribution to equity shareholders.

But the financing and investment decisions need to be taken in accordance with the firm's financial objective. Thus a policy statement on financial objectives is of paramount importance.

Financial planning involves the following:

1. determining the company's financial goals;
2. forecasting certain key variables;
3. analysing the choices open to the company in terms of investment opportunities and finance available;
4. comparing the projected outcomes under the different opportunities available;
5. deciding what action needs to be taken;
6. comparing subsequent performance against the plan.

Financial planning can be divided into the following:

1. medium- to long-term planning;
2. short-term planning including cash budgets.

In the early part of this chapter we shall concentrate on the medium- to longer-term aspects of financial planning which involve answering questions such as the following.

1. When should a new issue of equity shares be made?
2. What should the dividend policy of the company be?
3. What should the level of borrowing for the company be, and should it be short-dated or long-dated?
4. Should the interest paid be fixed or floating?

In earlier chapters we have considered each of these questions. Financial planning brings them all together.

Many decisions have a long lead time. For example, if a car assembly company wants to construct a plant in a new country, the search process, the negotiating process and the construction period can well take up to five years. The company has to have plans as to how it will finance the project over that period.

Long-term planning is usually looking at a horizon of up to five years, although in some industries because of extra long lead times it can be up to ten years. The company has to consider how it can meet its long-term objectives over this period. How will this long lead time affect its performance over the planning period? How will major investment affect its profit performance, as reflected in the profit and loss account, and its financial strength, as reflected in the balance sheet?

What impact will new investment decisions have upon earnings per share over the planning period?

It has been suggested many times that companies in the UK have been forced to adopt a shorter planning horizon than companies in countries such as Japan and Germany. It is claimed that this is because the providers of finance in the UK are more interested in short-term performance and less in long-term performance than providers of finance in the other countries mentioned.

In fact, it is the so-called medium-term financial planning model which is the major instrument in the UK for formulating a financing decision. The medium-term financial planning model essentially forecasts the content of the firm's financial statements as they are likely to appear to the shareholders in the light of the planned trading cycle activities and capital investment plans. Movements in key financial control ratios, of which the debt-to-equity ratio is one, can be seen from the forecasts. The effects of various alternative financing strategies, including dividend payout policy, on the significant financial ratios is ascertained from the model. The feasible set of strategies is reduced by eliminating those which lead to financial ratios that transgress the norms that shareholders are presumed to tolerate.

19.3 Financial modelling

The planning process can be supported by a financial model. We shall work through a small case study to produce a projected profit and loss account and balance sheet. The directors of the company concerned could use these projections to see if they are happy with the decisions that they propose to take. If not, then alternative policies can be fed into the model in an attempt to produce an outcome which meets the goals of the company.

We begin with the position at the end of 1994 showing the latest profit and loss account, balance sheet and funds flow statement of the company, Regis PLC. At that point in time the company has to make a number of decisions with regard to the direction in which it wishes to move.

Those responsible in the company have undertaken a strategic planning exercise. One of the objectives it has set itself is a growth rate of 25% per annum in sales. They wish to examine the financial implications of achieving this goal. They are now at the stage of deciding between a number of alternative ways of achieving this objective. It has been ascertained which of the company's products have strength, and the relationship between various financial variables. They wish to see a projected balance sheet and profit and loss account based on following a certain course of action.

Table 19.1 shows the current financial position of Regis PLC. The Earnings before Interest and Tax (EBIT) as a percentage of sales currently equals 18%. During 1994 the company increased its long-term borrowing and issued new equity shares. At the beginning of the year debt comprised 31% of its long-term finance; at the end of the year it comprised 38% of the total. The increase of £500 000 in fixed assets was made up of the new investment of £750 000 less the year's depreciation. The increase in equity of £280 000 was made up of the retained earnings for the year plus the new issue of shares.

As mentioned, as part of a medium-term financial plan the directors of the company have set themselves a goal of increasing sales by 25%. This is a dramatic increase and will have a number of financial implications. The directors wish to develop a plan and to produce a pro forma balance sheet and profit and loss account showing the impact if this goal is achieved.

There are two techniques that can be adopted to obtain the pro forma statements. One

Table 19.1 *Financial statements of Regis PLC for 1994 (£000)*

Profit and loss account for year ending 31 December 1994

Net sales (S)		3000
Cost of goods sold excluding depreciation (CGS)	2300	
Depreciation (DP)	250	2550
Earnings before interest and tax (EBIT)		450
Interest paid (INT)		50
		400
Corporation tax (TAX)		120
Net profit (NET)		280
Dividends paid (DIV)		100
Retained earnings (RE)		180

Sources and application of funds statement for year ending 31 December 1994

Sources	
Net profit	280
Depreciation	250
New borrowing (ΔD)	320
New issue of shares (NSI)	100
	950
Application	
Increase in working capital (ΔWC)	100
Purchase fixed assets (INV)	750
Dividends paid	100
	950

Balance sheet as at 31 December 1994 (with comparative figures)

	1993	*1994*
Equity (E)	1180	900
Long-term debt (D)	720	400
	1900	1300
Net fixed assets	1500	1000
Net working capital (NWC)	400	300
	1900	1300

is through the use of a computer program. A set of simultaneous equations, which form the basis of the model, are fed into a computer together with certain financial information and the required pro forma statements result. In order to enable the reader to follow the relationships between the variables we shall adopt the second technique and solve the problem manually.

Forecasting the values of variables is the essence of modelling. Two types of variable should be distinguished: exogenous variables, whose values are put directly into the model by the planner, and endogenous variables, whose values are calculated within the model. In order for the model to work we need the following:

1. policy decisions;
2. forecasts of certain key exogenous variables;
3. equations to enable us to calculate the value of certain endogenous variables.

In the model being used for illustrative purposes the policy decisions relate to debt and equity funding.

We shall assume that the directors of the company have adopted the following policies.

1. Dividends paid in a year to be 40% of earnings after tax (NET).
2. Long-term debt to fund 50% of the fixed assets. Any additional funds are required to come from equity issues.

In addition we need a sales forecast and information on the following exogenous variables:

1. the planned or forecast level of sales S_1;
2. the relationship between the cost of goods sold and sales a_1;
3. the interest rate a_2;
4. the corporation tax rate a_3;
5. the depreciation rate a_4;
6. the dividend payout rate a_5;
7. the relationship between the change in the level of sales and the new investment level a_7;
8. the relationship between the level of sales and the level of the net working capital a_6.

We have already been told to plan for a 25% increase in sales. We make the following assumptions on the seven coefficients ($a_a, \ldots, a_7$) and the equations expressing the relationships between the variables are shown below:

$$S = £3\ 750\ 000 \tag{19.1}$$

$$\begin{aligned} \text{CGS (excluding depreciation)} &= a_1 S_1 \\ &= 0.75 S_1 \end{aligned} \tag{19.2}$$

$$\begin{aligned} \text{INT} &= a_2 D_1 \\ &= 0.10 D_1 \end{aligned} \tag{19.3}$$

$$\begin{aligned} \text{TAX} &= a_3\ (S - \text{INT} - \text{DP} - \text{CGS}) \\ &= 0.30\ (S - \text{INT} - \text{DP} - \text{CGS}) \end{aligned} \tag{19.4}$$

$$\begin{aligned} \text{DP} &= a_4 \text{FA}_0 \\ &= 0.10 \text{FA}_0 \end{aligned} \tag{19.5}$$

$$\begin{aligned} \text{DIV} &= a_5 \text{NET} \\ &= 0.40 \text{NET} \end{aligned} \tag{19.6}$$

$$\begin{aligned} \text{INV} &= a_7 S_1 \\ &= 0.05 S_1 \end{aligned} \tag{19.7}$$

$$\begin{aligned} \text{NWC}_1 &= a_6 S_1 \\ &= 0.173 S_1 \end{aligned} \tag{19.8}$$

We are now almost in a position to be able to produce the pro forma statements. We shall just clarify the calculations that will be made by listing the four accounting identity equations that are used to calculate the size of the endogenous variables:

$$\text{FA}_1 = \text{FA}_0 + \text{INV} - \text{DEP} \tag{19.9}$$

$$\text{NWC}_1 = \text{NWC}_0 + \Delta \text{NWC} \tag{19.10}$$

$$\text{NET} = S - \text{CGS} - \text{INT} - \text{DP} \tag{19.11}$$

$$E = E_0 + \text{NSI} + \text{RE} \tag{19.12}$$

We have been given the planned level of sales, and so we can solve the equations where the financial variable is linked to the level of sales. By solving equations (19.1)–(19.8) it is found that CGS (in £000) = £2812, DP = £150, ΔNWC = £250 and INV = £188. Substituting these values in the identity equations gives

$$FA = £1500 + £188 - £150 = £1538$$

As a result of a policy decision, this means that debt $D = 0.5 \times 1538 = £769$. This allows us to determine the interest charge of £77, which enables the pro forma profit and loss account to be constructed:

Net sales S		£3 750 000
Cost of goods sold CGS	£2 812 000	
Depn DP	£ 150 000	£2 962 000
		£ 788 000
Interest INT		£ 77 000
		£ 711 000
TAX		£ 213 000
Net profits NET		£ 498 000
Dividends DIV		£ 199 000
Retained earnings RE		£ 299 000

The policy decision was to tie the level of debt to the level of fixed assets and to obtain any additional funds from a new equity issue. In order to determine whether the level of activities planned for 1995 has produced sufficient funds to finance the planned level of investment or whether there is a need for further external funds, we need to produce the projected flow of funds statement.

Sources

Retained earnings	£299 000
Depreciation	£150 000
Increase in long-term debt (769–720)	£ 49 000
	£498 000

Applications

Planned increase in working capital	£250 000
New investment in fixed assets	£188 000
	£438 000
Balance	£ 60 000
	£498 000

As can be seen the expected source of funds is in excess of the planned application to the extent of £60 000. This results in an increase in working capital above the level planned. We can now produce the pro forma balance sheet.

Equity	
(1 180 000 + 299 000)	1 479 000
Long-term debt	769 000
	2 248 000
Fixed assets	
(1 500 000 − 150 000 + 188 000)	1 538 000
Net working capital	
(400 000 + 250 000 + 60 000)	710 000
	2 248 000

It is not very difficult to produce such pro forma statements for a one year plan, but it is tedious to extend it into longer periods. Fortunately, there are many computer programs that enable such projections to be made. The computer models also allow many different assumptions to be made and the impact of the assumptions on the financial statements to be observed. The computer model also allows us to alter the inputs and so undertake sensitivity analysis.

The aim of planning is to ensure that a given objective is attained with as much certainty as is possible. In almost all financial models the uncertainty with regard to future period sales represents the single most potent problem. Therefore it is customary in even the most simple model to relate variables explicitly to sales wherever possible so that sensitivity analysis can be tested on the model with respect to the uncertain sales variable.

Sensitivity analysis would be prohibitively difficult if the model user had to perform manual adjustments on the values of several variables which are jointly determined. However, a computer program allows us to solve a set of simultaneous equations. Why this is necessary can be illustrated using the above example. In the manual model we have related the level of debt to the level of fixed assets. Let us say instead that the company wished to maintain a ratio of long-term debt to equity of 1:1, i.e. it wishes to relate the level of debt to the level of equity. In order to be able to see the effect of this policy on the projected statements, we need to know the amount of equity at the end of each planning period; to know the amount of equity we need to know the level of profits; to know the level of profits we need to know the amount of interest paid during the period; and to know the amount of interest we need to know the level of debt on which the interest is to be paid, but we do not know the level of debt until we know the level of equity at the end of the period. We are going round in circles: we need simultaneous equations and a computer.

In the manual solution shown above where debt was related to fixed assets, four identifying equations were listed together with seven equations in which the coefficients were introduced. In order to obtain a computer solution to the amended example, with debt a function of equity, we need another three identifying equations:

$$\Delta D = \Delta NWC + INV + DIV - RE - DEP - NSI \tag{19.13}$$

where NSI is the new share issue, which is a value based on policy decisions,

$$NWC_1 = NWC_0 + \Delta NWC \tag{19.14}$$

$$D_1 = \Delta D + D_0 \tag{19.15}$$

Of course, the model can be made much more complicated, with different variables introduced and different financing possibilities considered.

19.4 Short-term financial planning

Short-term financial planning involves considering and answering questions such as the following:

1. What level of cash needs to be on call at various dates during the next planning period?
2. What level of inventory do we need to maintain?
3. How quickly can we pay off the bank overdraft?
4. What period of credit do we grant to our debtors?
5. Should we pay our suppliers quickly and take advantage of the cash discount being offered?
6. What proportion of current assets should be financed by short-term funds?
7. What is working capital and what influences its level?

Short-term financial planning is concerned with what is referred to as working capital. Working capital can be defined as the excess of current assets over current liabilities. It is the same as net current assets. It represents the investment of a company's funds in assets which are expected to be realized within a relatively short period of time. It is not an investment in an asset with a long life but, as the name implies, represents funds which are continually in use and are turned over many times in a year. It is capital used to finance production, to support levels of stock and to provide credit for customers.

The three main current assets are stock, debtors and cash. They can be funded by short-term finance, i.e. current liabilities, or by medium- and long-term finance. The working capital cycle is illustrated in Figure 19.4.

$$\text{working capital} = \text{cash} + \text{debtors} + \text{stock} - \text{short-term liabilities}$$

It can also be defined as

$$\text{working capital} = \text{equity} + \text{long- and medium-term debt} - \text{fixed assets}$$

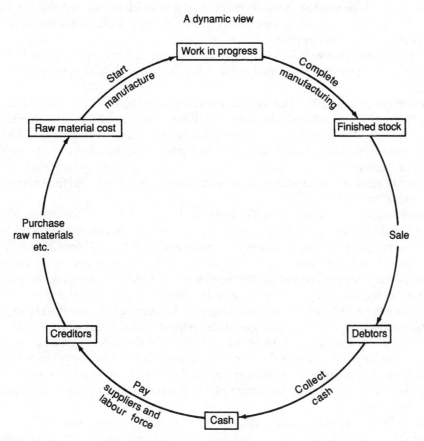

Figure 19.4

As can be seen from the above equations, the more of a business's finance is invested in working capital, the less is available for investing in long-term assets such as buildings, plant and machinery. At most times it is believed that the profits to be earned from investing in long-term assets are greater than the profits to be earned from investing in working capital. At such times, therefore, a business wishes to minimize its own investment in working capital and to concentrate its resources on investments with a longer life than current assets, with as much as is safe of the current assets being financed by current liabilities.

However, in some economic conditions the wisdom of the day suggests that it is better for a business to keep its resources liquid and to invest its long-term finance in current assets. It is argued that at certain times the returns from longer-term investments, in plant and machinery say, are less than those from short-term financial investments. It can be argued that at such times being liquid enables business to take immediate advantage of any financial opportunity that may arise, e.g. opportunities available in the stock market or money market.

Certainly at times the returns from investing in the plant and machinery required in the manufacturing industry have appeared unattractive relative to the returns on short-term investments. However, from the point of view of the overall economy, somebody needs to manufacture so that others can trade.

The problems of short-term financial management are as complex as those which beset long-term financial management.

The manager's objective is to maintain sufficient cash on hand or on short call to meet any normally predictable expense without resorting to costly emergency measures. Ideally, the manager will gauge matters so finely that there is never actually more cash on hand than will be needed, because surplus cash is an idle asset and as such it incurs an opportunity cost – the cost to the company of what it could earn if invested elsewhere in securities or long-term deposits.

There is a danger that with inflation, any money invested in monetary assets is losing value; normally the higher is the rate of inflation, the lower should be the cash balances of the firm.

The extent to which cash is put to effective use within the business will reflect agreeably on the profit levels. However, there are limits. The loss of liquidity due to maintaining very low cash balances and not having overdraft arrangements could lead the company into difficulties. Slowness in paying debts may mean that cash discounts are forfeited or, perhaps more seriously, that suppliers are lost. The key to the management of cash and of all working capital is therefore a matter of striking a balance between risk and profitability.

This can be a complex procedure. For instance, it is possible for a company to become insolvent while it is still recording profits, because profits are calculated on the accrual system of accounting whereas liquidity is a matter of cash flow. Therefore, while a sale may be 'made' and recorded in the year-end accounts, the actual liquidity position of the company is unimproved unless the purchaser has paid by the end of the year.

The traditional accounting statements – the balance sheet and the profit and loss account – are the results of the accrual system of accounting. As previously explained with this method, expenses are charged to the period in which the goods' usage or services are received, which is not necessarily the period in which expenses are paid. For example, wages are normally paid in arrears, and if accounts are to be prepared at a date which is in the middle of a week, the services of the employees will have been received and the expense will therefore be recognized in the accounts although the wages have not yet been paid.

Similarly income is recognized with accrual accounting when a sale has been made, or when interests or dividends are due, which is not necessarily when the income is received. It has been said that any fool can sell an item, but the good salesman is identified by the fact that the customers pay up at the right time. A number of companies still operate the bonus system whereby the salesman is rewarded for making the sale. It might be more prudent in some situations to distribute the bonuses as and when the cash has been collected. It depends whether responsibility for the cash flow lies as much with the salesman as with the finance department. The accrual system of accounting and the treatment of items such as capital expenditures and long-term contracts can cause a problem in the interpretation of company accounts.

However, the fact that there are difficulties in identifying the profit of a company for a period of time, and that this profit figure must depend upon certain assumptions, need not interfere with cash management. When cash comes into a business and when it leaves the business is not a matter of interpretation but a matter of fact. Successful management of working capital or cash depends upon knowledge of the cash flow position of the company.

Table 19.2 lists the factors that influence working capital items. When considering the control of debtors and stocks it is possible to calculate ratios which can be used to monitor movements in these items. For example, the average length of credit being allowed on debtors can be seen from the ratio of debtors to sales. Unfortunately it is not possible to introduce meaningful monitoring ratios for the control of creditors.

Table 19.2 *Controllability of working capital*

Element	Influence
Debtors	Volume of sales
	Length of credit given
	Effective credit control and cash collection
Stocks	Lead time
	Variability of demand
	Production cycle
	No. of product lines
	Volume of – planned output
	– actual output
	– sales
Payables	Volume of purchases
	Length of credit allowed
	Length of credit taken
Short-term finance	All the above
	Other payments/receipts
	Availability of credit
	Interest rates

Purchases, and consequently the creditors' figure, are made up of a mixture of items: materials for stock; materials for consumption; wages and salaries; payment for services, energy, rent; purchase of capital equipment etc.

It is not possible to find an effective measure of volume for purchases, and so control ratios for payables cannot easily be calculated. However, it is possible to observe the movements in the creditors' figure on a week-by-week basis or a month-by-month basis. Any unusual changes can be examined on an item-by-item basis. Relevant questions can then be asked.

Of course the type of working capital required can vary from one industry to another. These industry differences have to be allowed for in any comparisons across companies. What is an acceptable working capital position in, say, the retailing industry would not be acceptable in a manufacturing industry.

A retailing company usually has high levels of finished goods stock and very low levels of debtors. Most of the retailer's sales will be for cash, and even sales on credit are usually handled by an independent credit card company or a financial subsidiary of the retail business (which on occasions is not consolidated in the group accounts). The retailing company, however, usually has high levels of creditors. It pays its suppliers after an agreed period of credit. The levels of working capital required are therefore low: in fact they can be very low, with some retailers having high levels of short-term borrowing.

In contrast, a manufacturing company will require relatively high levels of working capital with investments in raw materials, work in progress and finished goods stocks, and with high levels of debtors. The credit terms offered on sales and taken on purchases will be influenced by the normal contractual arrangements in the industry.

To determine the level of cash that a company requires, it is necessary to prepare a cash budget where the minimum balances needed from month to month will be defined. If expenditures are lumpy or business is seasonal, cash shortages may arise in certain periods. Generally it is thought better to keep only sufficient cash to satisfy short-term needs, and to borrow if longer-term requirements occur. Maintaining a very large cash balance to meet every eventuality likely to arise throughout the planning period is thus discouraged in favour of *ad hoc* borrowing. The problem, of course, is to balance the cost of this borrowing against any income that might be obtained from investing the cash balances. Since cash needs can hardly ever be predicted with absolute certainty, some firms will no doubt opt for a safety stock of cash with which to meet the unexpected. Like any other insurance premium this particular brand of peace of mind involves an opportunity cost.

The difficulty of pinpointing the 'right' level for cash is a theme with variations. Many attempts have been made to develop a model for the control of cash. The famous square-root inventory model has been applied in theory to the problem of an optimal level of cash. This model and others are dealt with in Chapter 20.

The size of the cash balance that a company might need depends on the availability of other sources of funds at short notice, the credit standing of the company and the control of debtors and creditors – a crucial factor for short-term financial planning. The flow of cash in and out of the business can, to some extent, be controlled by such tactics as speeding up the collection of debts (perhaps by offering an attractive discount to buyers), factoring debts, or delaying disbursements of cash to creditors.

The debtors problem again revolves around the choice between profitability and liquidity. It might, for instance, be possible to increase sales by allowing customers more time to pay, but since this policy would reduce the company's liquid resources it would not necessarily result in higher profits. Often the terms of sale are dictated by common practice within the industry; if not, the company can design its own terms with a view to regulating the level of debtors. A company free to exercise some judgement in the matter of its customers can control the total risks attached to its sales, assuming, of course, that it is possible through historical analysis or the use of established credit ratings to classify groups of customers in terms of credit risk. As output changes in relation to capacity the company may choose to change its credit policy. In some industries certain firms devote generous sums to the machinery of debt collection, sometimes with significant results.

If a company has a short-term liquidity problem it can resort to invoice discounting or factoring. These measures, once regarded unfavourably by UK companies, have now become accepted particularly among rapidly expanding small- or medium-sized firms whose growth would normally be hampered if large amounts of capital were tied up in book debts. A proportion of the company's book debts can be converted into cash by discounting through the services of a specialized finance company. Three-quarters of the value of sales invoices can be advanced in return for a bill of exchange for future payment of the advance plus interest. Factors provide added services, such as purchase of all the client's invoiced debts and the arrangement of all debtor control, debt collection and sales ledger accounting. It is even possible to have an undisclosed factor, of whose operations as a third party the buyer is quite unaware since the purchaser pays the debts to the seller in the conventional manner. In this situation, in fact, the seller collects the debts on behalf of the factor. All these services have a cost, but for companies short of working capital the cost may justify itself. The management of debtors is discussed in Chapter 22.

The management of inventories is as important for the company's short-term financial situation as the management of cash, and again a balance has to be found: this time between tying up money which is not earning anything and losing sales, and profits, through not being able to meet an order when it comes in. This problem is discussed in Chapter 23.

The other side of the working capital problem concerns obtaining short-term funds. Every source of finance, including taking credit from suppliers, has a cost; the point is to keep this cost to the minimum. The cost involved in using trade credit might include forfeiting the discount normally given for prompt payment, or loss of goodwill through relying on this strategy to the point of abuse. Some other sources of short-term funds are bank credit, overdrafts and loans from other institutions. These can be unsecured or secured, with charges made against inventories, specific assets or general assets.

The short-term financial problem is one of balancing the options. Cash requirements with seasonal patterns involve deciding whether to use short-term funds, take credit, offer varying discounts, employ factors or maintain large balances. Given the forecasting requirements and the alternative costs, it is theoretically possible to make an optimal decision.

In fact there are a wide variety of approaches to working capital planning and control that management can adopt. These range from simple rule of thumb methods to sophisticated mathematical and computer models.

19.6 From rule of thumb to planning models

The simple approach relies on keeping working capital levels within certain limits, determined by ratio analysis. A number of the commonly used ratios were discussed in Chapter 3. This approach is based on the idea that working capital should be funded in one way and long-term assets in another way. To fund long-term assets with current liabilities would be seen as dangerous, and to fund non-permanent working capital with long-term funds would be seen as a waste. This approach is often found in practice: the disadvantage is that the ratios used as guides are to some extent rules of thumb. However, at any time there are a set of generally accepted levels for certain ratios which can be useful as a guide for planning and control purposes.

The financial manager must always be assessing the long- and short-term problems in terms of the company's capital structure as a whole. Others will certainly be doing so: the investment analysts who can affect the cost of capital for a company by their interpretation of the company's financial strength and growth possibilities make use of financial ratios, as do other companies, banks and credit agencies when deciding whether to advance a company credit and short-term loans. The criticisms of theorists who regard financial ratios as arbitrary rules of thumb have fallen largely on deaf ears among the practitioners. It is true that other factors are considered, but ratios cannot be ignored.

One other way to approach the problem of calculating working capital needs, is to ascertain the funds required to support an extra pound's worth of sales. This has already been referred to in the section on longer-term financial planning. A company may be profitable, it may be growing and it may not have a capacity constraint and will not need any new fixed investment for some time, but it can still have a financing problem.

One fairly accurate way of estimating working capital needs is first to determine the relationships between debtors and sales, creditors and sales, and inventory and sales. The company has a budget or a plan which will show the expected increase in sales over the next period, and by using the relationship determined between sales and the relevant items of current assets and current liabilities, it is possible to estimate the extra working capital needed to finance the expected increase in sales.

It must not be thought that over time this relationship between sales and the funds required as working capital remains static even in the short run. The relationship can vary at different stages of a company's sales cycle and the economic cycle. The funds required for working capital need to be planned in advance of knowledge of actual sales. The level of working capital at any time is based on estimated sales. For example, raw material stocks are partly based on estimates of production levels and work in progress, and finished goods are based on expected sales. Therefore, at times of downturns in economic activity there could well be overstocking.

This is not desirable and the successful company adjusts its stock levels as quickly as possible to the new level of activity. The point being made is that at such times the working capital to sales relationship could well be out of line with the planned level.

One other word of warning is needed when using this practical approach, and that is concerned with the fact that the company may not be satisfied with its existing position.

The fact that last year £0.19 of working capital was needed to finance £1 worth of sales does not mean that the company will be happy with this level in the future. The company may be attempting to reduce the level of its inventories, and so consequently it would be expecting to need a lower level of working capital in the future. Another question which should be considered by those wishing to use this approach is whether the average figures, which are those obtained by simply using balance sheet figures, apply to the marginal needs of, say, the next £1000 worth of sales. It is possible, although in practice not usually likely, that the marginal working capital needs are less than the average needs. This means that although the last £1 million of sales needed £200 000 of working capital, the next £1 million of sales will need a lower figure. It is possible that there are economies of scale with the holding of inventories, but not with debtors and creditors.

With this approach we have in fact only considered part of the working capital requirements, for in addition to inventory and debtors, cash will be needed for the day-to-day operation of the business. As the level of sales increases, so will the need for cash or the availability of cash. The cash-to-sales ratio is, however, not constant over time, and it is not worth adapting the simplified approach of this section to cash holdings. The answer is that although an extra £1 worth of sales needs an extra 20p invested in working capital for debtors and stocks, possibly more pence need to be added cover the cash needs.

This does not represent all of a growing company's needs for additional finance. In addition to increases in working capital to meet higher levels of sales, it may also be necessary to increase fixed capital to satisfy higher levels of sales. The increases required in fixed investment, i.e. in buildings, plant and equipment, are, of course, lumpy – they do not increase in direct proportion with sales. Certain equipment is purchased which will be able to produce x units of goods. It is not necessary to purchase an additional piece of this equipment until sales have increased by x units. At certain times businesses need to increase their production capacity and this requires quite large expenditures on capital equipment. When this new investment has been undertaken the company then has capacity greater than its present needs and it will not have to invest in additional capital equipment until some time has elapsed. The need for funds to satisfy working capital requirements increases in a more direct relationship with sales than does the need for funds for fixed investment.

However, it can be helpful to analyse the relationship between fixed investment and sales in order to see what growth it implies in financial terms. It must be recognized, however, that the cash outflow for fixed investment will not necessarily coincide with the cash inflow from sales.

It can, however, be helpful in financial planning to know that, for example, for every £100 increase in sales, an extra £25 of new funds needs to be provided in order to sustain the rate of growth, i.e. £20 working capital and £5 new fixed investment.

A more sophisticated approach to working capital management – and one that is not new – is the cost balancing technique. Such techniques have been well used in inventory control for a long time. The most well known is the economic order quantity model, which attempts to balance the costs that the business would incur from running out of inventory with the cost of holding inventory. The latter costs include ordering costs, storage costs, obsolescence costs and the opportunity cost from investing funds in an asset that does not earn interest. The inventory model is discussed in Chapter 23.

The same model can be applied to the management of cash and debtors. The same idea is employed, trying to balance the costs of holding too much of the asset with the costs of running out of the asset. The greater the cash on hand or on short call the less is the risk of liquidity problems, but also the greater is the loss of interest from investing short-term rather than long-term. The less the cash on hand or on short call, the greater is the risk of liquidity problems but the less is the loss of interest. One well-known cost-balancing model for the control of cash is described in the appendix to Chapter 20.

The next step up on the ladder of sophistication, but not necessarily in usefulness, is to introduce mathematical programming techniques. This enables us to build constraints into the model. We can say, for example, that we need to maximize profits subject to maintaining a minimum level of cash on hand or on short call. We can make the model dynamic and say that in one period cash at short call should be at least £x, and in another period, because of greater market opportunities, it should be £x + £y. The objective function can also be adjusted to include multiple goals. The models can also take into account the probabilities of different outcomes.

The avoidance of insolvency by the provision of liquidity to meet those creditors requiring payment is the principal short-term aim or constraint on financial management. The optimal deployment of cash surpluses, and more generally the management of working capital, represent secondary goals of short-term financial management.

The aim of insolvency avoidance implies the need to monitor the firm's liabilities continuously. In addition, it is necessary to segregate liabilities according to their status. Liabilities to statutory creditors (Customs and Excise, Inland Revenue, Department of Social Security) are worth distinguishing from liabilities to loan investors and these in turn from trade creditors. Information on discount eligibility on trade creditors' liabilities must also be acted upon.

A computer-based information retrieval system is well suited to this task as the computer data base of liabilities can readily be segregated. It is a straightforward matter to rearrange the list of liabilities according to planned repayment dates. Segregation into different classes will facilitate the optimal funding by allowing consideration of postponement of certain non-statutory creditors.

The capital asset pricing model normally relates to risk and return on long-term assets. It is most often used of course to determine the expected value of a company. In theory the model applies to all assets, and so there is no reason why in theory it cannot be utilized in the management of current assets. One approach that has been adopted in the literature is to attempt to integrate working capital into the total valuation process of the company.

The risk category in which a firm is placed depends not just upon where it invests its long-term assets but also on its working capital position. Cohn and Pringle [1] suggest that, because of the adjustable nature of working capital, the current assets could be used as an adjusted mechanism to offset changes in the real asset value of the firm. This approach, whereby an attempt is made to integrate the short-term, medium-term and long-term objectives of a company in its financial plans, is an important step forward, and is a point now being made by many writers on the subject. One should not see some decisions as long-term investment decisions and others as decisions as to optimum levels of cash, inventory or debtors. There is a need to integrate working capital policies into the capital investment process.

Traditionally, in the discounted cash flow approach to investment appraisal, a single line of figures was included showing the working capital requirements of the project under consideration. The point now being made is that the decision on the level of the working capital and its financing can be crucial to the overall decision on the project. The two decisions should be integrated. The policy on working capital should be integrated with the policy on capital investments. Gentry [2] has designed a model that integrates working capital components into capital investment planning.

Gentry's model is a simulation model. This takes us to yet another level of sophistication. Simulation models are deterministic: they enable a company to calculate what the consequences will be if a particular decision is taken; they enable a company to see what the results are likely to be if certain events happen in the market-place; they enable a company to estimate what will happen if certain assumptions that have been made by the company are not realized. The effect of changes can be analysed using sensitivity analysis.

To conclude, the corporate treasurer has a number of tools to assist in the management of working capital, ranging from simple ratio analysis to simulation models.

Example 19.1

Donac Ltd is a small manufacturing company. Summarized accounts for the last two years are presented below:

Balance sheets as at 31 March

	1991 £000		1992 £000	
Fixed assets		820		1000
Current assets				
Stock	340		420	
Debtors	360		570	
Cash	10		—	
	——	710	——	990
Current liabilities				
Overdraft	140		250	
Trade creditors	280		510	
Other creditors	60		100	
	——	480	——	860
		——		——
		1050		1130
		——		——
Ordinary shares (25 pence)		400		400
Profit and loss account		450		530
		——		——
		850		930
Medium-term bank loan		200		200
		——		——
		1050		1130
		——		——

Profit and loss accounts for the years ending 31 March

	1991 £000	1992 £000
Sales	1800	2900
Gross profit	210	260
Profit before tax	120	160
Taxation	30	40
	——	——
	90	120
Dividend	40	40
	——	——
Retained profit	50	80

Inflation during the last year was at the rate of 10%.

Required:

1. Explain what is meant by overtrading, and discuss how it might be recognized in a company.

(7 marks)

2. Evaluate whether Donac Ltd is overtrading. (9 marks)
3. One of Donac's managers has suggested that the company would be more efficient if it reduced its operating cycle to the minimum possible period of time.

(a) Explain what is meant by the operating cycle of a company and how it might be determined.
  (4 marks)
(b) Discuss whether a company should always try to reduce the operating cycle to the minimum possible period.

(5 marks)
(25 marks)

Answer

1. Overtrading occurs when a company grows at a rate which means its need for funds exceeds the supply of funds. It is partly the result of bad financial planning. It is sometimes referred to as 'under-capitalization', and good planning should be able to avoid such a situation.

   Overtrading occurs most frequently when the company finds itself in a fast growth market, sales grow each month, the company keeps producing to meet higher levels of future sales. The collection of the cash in from sales lags behind the cash outflow and there is not sufficient medium-term finance to meet needs. The company can be profitable during such a process, sales price per unit being well above cost price per unit. The problem is that the costs have to be paid out before the sales revenue comes in.

2. We will now look for symptoms of overtrading in Donac Ltd. The following are the points that should be considered when looking for evidence of overtrading.
   (a) Sales have increased by 61% over the year.
   (b) Debtors have increased by 58%. This is not bad, the debtors rising in line with sales. The average credit period (debtors/sales) is similar at the end of the year to that at the beginning. The company seems therefore to be successful in its debt collection.
   (c) Trade credit at the beginning of the year was 57 days (Trade plus other creditors/turnover × 365). At the end of the year it was 64 days. This is good from Donac's point of view, the company is taking credit which helps to finance growth.
   (d) Short-term borrowing has increased by 79%. This is a faster rate of increase than the rate of growth in sales. Not a good sign.
   (e) The current ratio and the liquidity ratio have declined. Not a good sign: it indicates that the company is operating with lower levels of liquidity.
   (f) The gross profit to sales ratio and the profit before tax ratio to sales have declined – not a good sign.
   (g) The sales to assets ratio has increased, assets being both fixed and current. This means that sales are being supported with lower levels of assets per unit sold. This indication is confusing: it could be interpreted as operating at higher levels of efficiency, but could also indicate overtrading. In view of the other signals it probably means that the latter interpretation is the more correct.
   (h) In an analysis of how the fixed and current assets are being financed, it will be found that the percentage supported by borrowed money has increased. In 1992, shareholders' funds financed only 47% of the gross assets, compared with 56% a year earlier. Although this 1992 level of a gearing (debt/total assets: 53%) is not particularly out of line with what is regarded as normal, the trend is worrying.
   (i) Number of day stock on hand at the end of 1992 equalled 58 days. This was less than the 78 days at the end of 1991. This is not a worrying sign: the company is keeping its stock levels low and is avoiding wasting money on financing costs.

   Having looked at various indicators of overtrading, it is possible to conclude that although the level of debtors, creditors and stock seem as if they are being managed sensibly, all the other signs are worrying. There is an increasing reliance on borrowing, and declining profitability. This could indicate trouble in the future.

   The answers to part (3) of the question can be found in the following section dealing with operating cycles.

The operating cycle is the length of time that elapses between the company's outlay on raw materials, wages and other expenditures and the inflow of cash from the sale of the goods. In a manufacturing business this is the average time that raw materials remain in stock less the period of credit taken from suppliers plus the time taken for producing the goods plus the time the goods remain in finished inventory plus the time taken by customers to pay for the goods. On some occasions this cycle is referred to as the cash cycle.

This is an important concept for the management of cash or working capital because the longer the operating cycle the more financial resources the company needs. Management needs to watch that this cycle does not become too long.

The operating cycle can be calculated approximately as shown in Table 19.3. Allowances should be made for any significant changes in the level of stocks taking place over the period. If, for example, the company is deliberately building up its level of stocks, this will lengthen the operating cycle.

Some writers advocate computation of an annual operating cycle and of a cycle for each quarter, since with a seasonal business the cycle would vary over different periods. The numerators in the equations can be found by taking the arithmetic mean of the opening and closing balances for stocks, creditors and debtors. If a quarterly statement is being prepared, the opening and closing balances for the quarter would be used.

It is difficult to calculate the operating cycle from the annual accounts of a company, as in the UK the inventory figure is not often broken down into its different elements and the purchases figure is not given. Take as an example a company with the figures shown in Table 19.4 where the necessary inventory and purchasing figures have been given. The operating cycle for the year is as follows:

$$\text{Turnover of raw materials} = \frac{19\,200}{240} = 80 \text{ days}$$

$$less \text{ credit granted by suppliers} = \frac{12\,000}{240} = \mathbf{50 \text{ days}}$$

$$\overline{30 \text{ days}}$$

$$\text{Period of production} = \frac{13\,500}{363} = 37 \text{ days}$$

$$\text{Turnover of finished goods} = \frac{12\,500}{363} = 34 \text{ days}$$

$$\text{Credit taken by customers} = \frac{28\,000}{400} = 70 \text{ days}$$

$$\overline{171 \text{ days}}$$

A number of steps could be taken to shorten this operating cycle. The amount of debtors could be cut by a quicker collection of accounts, finished goods could be turned over more rapidly, the level of raw material inventory could be reduced or the production period could be shortened.

The operating cycle is only the **time-span** between production costs and cash returns; it says nothing in itself of the amount of working capital that will be needed over this period. In fact less will be required at the beginning than at the end. Initially, the only expenditure is on materials, but as wages and other expenses are incurred the amount of working capital required increases over the cycle.

It is not necessary to have as available cash at the beginning of the period a sum equal to the estimated cash costs of the production, although over the cycle as a whole it must be possible for the company to have access to such an amount. Short-term working capital is required to support a given level of turnover, i.e. to pay for the goods and services before the cash is received from sales to customers. To determine the amount required it is necessary to know the estimated sales for the period, and the characteristics and scale of the operating cycle.

Table 19.3 *Calculating the operating cycle for a period*

1. Raw materials
period of turnover of raw $= \dfrac{\text{average value of raw material stock}}{\text{purchase of raw materials per day}} =$ *Days*
material stock

Less:

period of credit granted by $= \dfrac{\text{average level of creditors}}{\text{purchase of raw materials per day}} =$
suppliers

2. Period of production $= \dfrac{\text{average value of work in progress}}{\text{average cost of goods sold per day}} =$

3. Period of turnover of finished $= \dfrac{\text{average value of stock of finished goods}}{\text{average cost of goods sold per day}} =$
goods stock

4. Period of credit taken by $= \dfrac{\text{average value of debtors}}{\text{average value of sales per day}} =$
customers

Total operating cycle $\qquad\qquad\qquad\qquad\qquad\qquad\qquad =$

The successful control of working capital or cash depends on detailed budgets which must be as accurate as possible. These are needed for planning balance sheet and profit and loss accounts, and consequently it is common practice for the conventional budgetary system to include estimates of the component parts of working capital. All that is needed for the management of working capital as a whole is that the parts should be put together.

Sources of medium-term working capital include retained profits and funds put aside as depreciation provisions. These are funds which are retained in the business not specifically to be used for short-term expenditures. The funds are reduced by expenditures on capital replacements, and dividend and tax payments. The required levels of medium-term working capital at different points in time can again be ascertained by preparing budgets.

The total working capital required is compared with the net current assets plus overdraft limit to show the required borrowing, or, alternatively, the funds that can be lent and for what period. If the difference between needs and funds available is not large when expressed as a percentage of the budgeted amounts, then no action need be taken. The difference can be assumed to lie within the normal range of forecasting error. If the surplus is large and continuous, however, it would suggest that working capital is in excess of needs.

A company therefore needs to forecast its short-term and long-term working capital needs. The cash budget is obviously a key part of this planning exercise. To prepare

Table 19.4 *Figures from which an operating cycle can be calculated*

	1993	1994	Mean
Raw material inventory	18 000	20 400	19 200
Work-in-progress inventory	12 500	14 500	13 500
Finished goods inventory	10 000	15 000	12 500
Debtors	26 500	29 500	28 000
Creditors	11 000	13 000	12 000
Sales	136 000	156 000	146 000
Purchase of raw material	85 000	90 200	87 600
Costs of goods sold	125 000	140 000	132 500

such a budget it is first necessary to estimate the future level of sales, and so determine the amount and timing of the funds flowing into the business. It is next necessary to forecast the future expenditures. Certain costs will vary directly with the level of sales, perhaps with a linear relationship, other costs vary but in a less than linear relationship because of economies, and yet other costs remain fixed, at least over certain ranges of output. The future cash budget can be developed in this way after allowing for capital expenditure and irregular payments such as dividends and taxation. Cash budgets are discussed further in Chapter 20.

To estimate a funds-flow statement for a future period it is necessary to forecast the expected changes in the balance sheet items. The level of future sales and production activity will be known from the sales and production budgets. Decisions then have to be made on how each balance sheet item will vary with the sales activity. For example, the level of cash that needs to be maintained will increase as sales increase, but there is reason to believe that the relationship should not be linear. Numerous models for the control of cash suggest that cash and near cash should increase at a less than proportional rate to sales. The cash flow analysis together with a decision on safety balances will show the level of cash. Similarly, inventories should increase at a rate less than proportional to the increase in activity. Debtors and creditors, however, may well remain as the same proportion of sales and purchases. Plant and machinery will probably need to increase as sales increase, although the relationship will not be smooth as the assets will be purchased in large units. In projecting the funds-flow statement it is necessary to determine at what levels of production the new equipment needs to be obtained.

The change that will take place in retained earnings will probably not be a constant direct relationship with the change in sales. Increases in dividends do not usually occur every year, and so the retained proportion of profits will vary from year to year.

The changes in the balance sheet items can be tabulated: some items such as debtors will just be a percentage of sales, while others will require analysis to ascertain the new levels that should be expected. It will then be known if shortages of funds are likely to occur and steps can be taken to obtain the funds through borrowing, equity issues or some other form of adjustment.

19.8 Funds flow and cash flow statements

A funds flow statement can take one or two forms. One is a historical document showing what has happened in the past, where the funds have come from and where they have been used. The second type of funds statement is as a tool for financial management, for financial planning. One type of statement relates to the past, the other relates to the future. The statements will disclose the extent to which long-term funds have been used or are to be used to finance working capital needs or vice-versa. It will show whether the purchase of long-term assets has been or will be financed with short-term funds. It will show the movement of funds within the working capital items and whether working capital in total is being increased or decreased.

A funds flow statement differs from a cash flow statement. There are, however, two types of cash flow statement: one relates to the past, and the other to the future. The one concerned with the future is called a cash budget. A cash budget, which will be discussed in the next chapter, is essentially a document for assisting management in planning short-term financial needs and opportunities. For longer-term financial planning, management needs to produce a funds flow statement to cover the needs of the next few years. A funds flow statement does not go into detail concerning the movement of cash: it is more interested in where the funds are coming from over the next few years and how they are to be used. It is necessary to estimate the funds that will be retained in the business each year, which are a function of profitability, depreciation policy and, where appropriate, dividend policies. The need for funds will depend upon capital investment plans and working capital needs, which are both a function of the planned rate of growth, and with longer-term investments, which are a function of the replacement cycle of the capital equipment. Funds may also be needed to redeem debentures.

Any gap between the anticipated use of funds and internally generated finance has to be met from external finance. It is in order to obtain an indication of the amount of external finance required and when it will be needed that companies need to undertake funds flow projections. They can take the necessary steps to ensure that when they will need to raise new equity or issue new loan stock or borrow from their bankers, they are not rushing about at the last minute. Funds flow projections are concerned with these longer-term capital-type items, whereas cash budgets are more involved with short-term cash management.

Cash budgets and projected funds flow statements are essential for financial planning. Historic cash flow and funds flow statements can also be useful. They may indicate something to management that they may have missed if they had concentrated their analysis on just the balance sheet and profit and loss account. Historical cash flow and funds flow statements can also be useful ways of presenting information to shareholders.

In 1975 in the UK the Accounting Standards setting body of the time issued a statement requiring all companies to publish a 'Statement of sources and application of Funds' [3]. In 1991 the Accounting Standards Board issued a Standard (FRS 1) on the subject of cash flow statements [4]. These were to replace the funds flow statements in the published annual report and accounts of companies. Cash flow statements were to be the third published statement. For a long time there had been pressure for such a change from funds flow statements to take place. Funds flow statements are an important planning tool, but the usefulness of historical funds flow statements is limited.

In the USA the change from the requirement to publish funds flow statements to the requirement to produce cash flow statements took place in 1987.

The cash flow statement of Glaxo Holdings plc for 1993 is shown in Table 19.5. This is a good example of the cash flow statements produced by companies. In order to provide a consistent format, companies are required to classify cash flows under five standard headings, these being:

- net cash flow from operating activities;
- returns on investments and servicing of finance;
- taxation;
- investment activities;
- financing activities.

Companies were given the choice of producing either a 'direct method' cash flow statement or an 'indirect method' statement. The former is the more revealing.

A funds flow statement shows the sources of funds of the company, and the way in which these funds have been used. Funds are not cash. It is possible to take over another company and to pay for this by issuing shares or debentures to the selling shareholders. There is no cash involved, and so this transaction would not appear in a cash flow statement, but it would appear in a funds flow statement. The sale of goods on credit would not at the time of sale affect a cash flow statement. No cash has changed hands. All that has happened is that inventories have fallen and debtors risen. This would appear in a funds flow statement. It is necessary in a funds flow statement to distinguish between the movement in long-term and short-term assets and liabilities. It is necessary to distinguish between the use of funds for the purchase of fixed assets and the use of funds to finance increases in working capital.

To illustrate a funds flow statement we shall take as an example the accounts of the XL company which are shown in Tables 19.6 and 19.7. The resulting 'statement of source and applications of funds' is given in Table 19.8. Although the example shows a historic funds flow statement, the items listed are exactly those that would be required to be considered when preparing a projected funds flow statement.

Certain figures in the statement require an explanation, one being the first item, namely profits before tax, £42 000. This is the profit figure shown in the profit and loss account after depreciation and directors' remuneration. The depreciation figure is added back later in the statement as it does not involve the movement of funds out of the business. If the depreciation charge in the accounts were doubled or were equal to

Table 19.5 *Glaxo Holdings plc 1993 Annual Report and Accounts: consolidated cash flow statement for the year ended 30 June*

	Notes	1993 £m	1992 £m
Net cash inflow from operating activities	24	1746	1409
Returns on investments and servicing of finance			
Interest received		186	193
Interest paid		(56)	(74)
Losses on investment activities		(1)	(1)
Dividends paid to ordinary shareholders		(533)	(458)
Dividends paid to minority shareholders		(10)	(10)
Net cash outflow from returns on investments and servicing of finance		(414)	(350)
Taxation paid		(405)	(403)
Investing activities			
Purchase of tangible fixed assets		(608)	(593)
Sale of tangible fixed assets		84	10
Purchase of fixed asset investments		(25)	(6)
Purchase of subsidiary undertaking (net of cash and cash equivalents acquired)		(3)	—
Other movements		3	(1)
Net cash outflow on fixed assets		(549)	(590)
Purchase of non-cash equivalent current asset investments		(9012)	(6838)
Sale of non-cash equivalent current asset investments		8703	7057
Net cash outflow from investing activities		(858)	(371)
Net cash inflow before financing		69	285
Financing			
Issue of ordinary share capital		69	24
New short term loans		1902	1071
Repayment of short term loans		(1875)	(1561)
Net cash inflow/(outflow) from financing	25	96	(466)
Increase/(decrease) in cash and cash equivalents	26/27	165	(181)
Increase in net liquid funds	23/27	483	120

zero, the business would still have the same total amount of funds available for use. There is obviously a tax saving resulting from depreciation, but the tax authorities have their own rules on the level of depreciation that can be deducted in arriving at taxable profits. There is no reason why the depreciation for tax purposes need be the same as that appearing in the published accounts. The purchase of fixed assets is shown as £40 000. This is the difference between the opening value of fixed assets (£42 000) less the year's depreciation charge (£12 000) and the closing balance £70 000. A further adjustment would have been required if there had been an asset revaluation during the year. The amount of the revaluation would have to be taken away from the closing balance of fixed assets. It is necessary to distinguish between the increase in fixed assets

Table 19.6 *Profit and loss account of the XL Company Ltd*

Year ending 31 December 1993 (£)			Year ending 31 December 1994 (£)
220 000	Sales		250 000
170 000	Costs of goods sold		178 000
50 000	Profits		72 000
	Less		
11 000	Depreciation	12 000	
18 000	Directors' remuneration	18 000	
3 000	Interest	3 000	
9 000	Corporation tax	14 000	47 000
9 000	Profit after taxation and interest		25 000
9 000	Proposed dividend		10 000
0	Retained profit for year		15 000

Table 19.7 *Balance sheet of the XL Company Ltd*

Year ending 31 December 1993 (£)		Year ending 31 December 1994 (£)
	Fixed assets	
20 000	Freehold premises	25 000
22 000	Plant and machinery	45 000
42 000		70 000
	Current assets	
58 000	Stock	66 000
29 500	Debtors	42 000
10 000	Cash	12 000
97 500		120 000
	Less current liabilities	
25 000	Creditors and accruals	32 000
11 000	Taxation	17 000
7 500	Dividend	10 000
43 500		59 000
54 000	Net current assets	61 000
96 000	Total net assets	131 000
	Financed by:	
60 000	Share capital	60 000
25 000	Reserves	40 000
11 000	Loans	31 000
96 000		131 000

Table 19.8 *Sources and application of funds statement, 1993–94 of the XL Company Ltd*

	£(000)
Source of funds	
Profit before tax and extraordinary items (72 000 − 30 000)	42
Adjustment for items not involving the movement of funds:	
Depreciation	12
Total generated from operations	54
Funds from other sources	
Loans issued	20
	74
Applications of funds	
Interest paid	(3.0)
Dividends paid	(7.5)
Tax paid	(8.0)
Purchase of fixed assets	(40)
	(58.5)
Net movement	15.5
Increase/decrease in working capital	
Increase in stocks	8
Increase in debtors	12.5
Increase in creditors	(7)
Movement in net liquid funds:	
Increase (decrease) in cash balance	2
	15.5

due to purchase and that due to revaluations. The changes in the working capital items are just the differences between the opening and closing balance sheet values.

The dividends paid figure is shown as £7500. This is the opening liability (£7500) plus the proposed dividend for the year (£10 000) less the closing liability (£10 000). The tax paid figure is arrived at in a similar way: the opening liability (£11 000) plus the charge in the profit and loss account (£14 000) less the closing liability (£17 000).

The above statement is a funds flow statement. This is not a cash flow statement. A cash flow statement for XL will be shown in Chapter 20. The 'bottom line' in a funds statement is changes in working capital. For the purposes of such a statement it does not matter if the sales that have been made have resulted in the receipt of cash at the balance sheet date; whether the cash has been received or is yet to be received, it is still a source of working capital. The 'bottom line' in a cash flow statement is changes in cash.

Not all sources and applications of funds statements can be calculated as easily as in this example. There are many difficult adjustments that can be introduced, e.g. changes in bad debt provisions, but basically the idea is straightforward. All that is required is to interpret the changes in the balance sheet items. A source of funds is any item that has the effect of either increasing an item on the liability side of the balance sheet (i.e. a new issue of shares or retained profits) or decreasing an asset (i.e. the sale of machinery). An application of funds is any item that has the effect of either decreasing an item on the liability side of the balance sheet (i.e. repaying a loan) or increasing an asset (i.e. purchase of land).

19.9 Key terms

Cash flow statements
Funds flow statements
Gearing ratios
Liquidity ratios
Mission statements
Objectives

Operating cycle
Overtrading
Plans
Strategy
Working capital

1. What are the links between corporate strategy and a financial planning model?
2. Are the goals of maximum growth and maximizing shareholders' wealth in conflict?
3. If you were appointed as finance director of a new company, how would you set about constructing a corporate financial model?
4. What are pro forma financial statements?
5. What are the differences between the operating cycle of a company and its cash cycle?
6. What is the purpose of a cash budget?
7. What are the differences between funds flow and cash flow statements?
8. What are the costs that need to be balanced in managing short-term finance?
9. Will net working capital always increase when cash increases? Why?

1. Cohn, R.A. and Pringle, J.J. (1980) Step toward an integration of corporate financial theory, in *Readings on the Management of Working Capital*, K.V. Smith (ed.) West Publishing.
2. Gentry, J.A. (1988) State of the Art of Short Run Financial Management, *Financial Management*, Summer.
3. Accounting Standards Committee (1975) *Statements of Sources and Applications of Funds*, SSAP 10.
4. Accounting Standards Board (1991) *Cash Flow Statements* (FRS 1), London.

A selection of articles and books on corporate strategy and financial planning is given below.

Barwise, P., Marsh, P.R. and Wensely, R. (1989) Must finance and strategy clash? *Harvard Business Review*, Sept.–Oct.

Bhaskhar, K., Pope, P. and Morris, R. (1982) *Financial Modelling with Computers*, Economist Intelligence Unit.

Davidson, K. (1985) Strategic Investment Theories, *Journal of Business Strategy*, Summer.

Gentry, J.R. (1988) The state of the art of short run financial management, *Financial Management*, Summer.

Johnson, G. and Scholes, K. (1993) *Exploring Corporate Strategy*, Prentice Hill.

Lee, C.F. (1985) *Financial Analysis and Planning: Theory and Applications*, Addison-Wesley.

Myers, S.C. (1987) Finance theory and financial strategy. *Midland Corporate Finance Journal*, Spring, pp. 6–13.

Porter, M.E. (1985) *Competitive Advantage*, Free Press.

Smith, K.V. (1979) *Guide to Working Capital Management*, McGraw Hill.

Smith, K.V. and Callinger, C.W. (1988) *Readings on Short term Financial Management*, 3rd edn, West Publishing.

Thompson, J. (1993) *Strategic Management: Awareness and Chance*, Chapman & Hall.

1. (a) Outline the factors that a company should consider when developing a long-term financial plan of duration three years or more.
   Briefly describe the major types of financial model that might be used to assist in the preparation of such plans, and discuss the problems that companies face in long-term planning. (15 marks)

(b) Oxold Ltd uses linear programming to assist in its financial planning. The company wishes to estimate its investment and borrowing levels for the next year. Divisible investment opportunities exist that would require funds of up to £2 million. These investment opportunities are all expected to produce perpetual annual cash flows (after tax) with an internal rate of return of 15% per year. The stock market is expected to capitalize these project cash flows at a rate of 17% per year. Oxold has £1 500 000 cash available. Any surplus cash, after investments have been undertaken, will be paid out as dividends. The company does not wish to issue new equity capital, but is prepared to finance up to 40% of any investment with new long-term debt which can be assumed to result in a permanent increase in the company's capital. The company pays tax at 35%. Oxold Ltd wishes to maximize the total value of the company.

(i) Formulate a linear programming model which could be used to estimate the optimum levels of investment and borrowing for the next year. (Modigliani and Miller's formula for the valuation of a company in a world with taxation might be helpful in this process.) Do not calculate the optimal solution.

(7 marks)

(ii) Discuss briefly whether Oxold Ltd is likely to undertake any investment during the next year:
(1) if no new funds are borrowed;
(2) if the company borrows funds through new long term loans.   (3 marks)
(25 marks)
ACCA, Dec. 1986

2.

	Supermarket chain	Heavy manufacturing	Hotel	Bank
Fixed assets				
Land and buildings	299	132	562	1 329
Plant and machinery	207	312	212	520
	506	444	774	1 849
Associated companies	—	6	117	—
Current assets				
Stocks	180	59	26	
Debtors	10	68	148	132 806
	190	127	174	132 806
Current liabilities	339	76	195	116 663
Net current assets	(149)	51	(21)	16 143
	357	501	870	17 992
Share capital and retained reserves				
Loan capital				
Short-term borrowing				
	357	501	870	17 992

For each company complete what you think would be an appropriate amount of equity (i.e. share capital and retained reserves), loan capital and short-term borrowings.

3. (a) What is meant by business risk? Outline the major factors that determine a company's business risk and comment upon how controllable these factors are by a company.   (8 marks)

(b) Discuss to what extent business risk is of relevance to an investor owning a well diversified portfolio.   (3 marks)

(c) Huckbul Ltd plans to purchase a new machine in the near future which will reduce the company's direct labour costs, but will increase fixed costs by £85 000 per annum. Direct labour costs are expected to fall by 20% per unit of production. The new machine will cost £820 000 and will be financed by a five year fixed-rate loan at an interest cost of 15% per year, with the principal repayable at the maturity of the loan. The company normally pays half of after-tax earnings as dividends, subject to the constraint that if after-tax earnings fall the dividend per share is kept constant. Huckbul expects its volume of sales to increase by 15% during the current financial year. Summarized extracts from the company's most recent financial accounts are detailed below.

Profit and loss account

	£000	£000
Turnover		3381
Operating expenses		
Wages and salaries	1220	
Raw materials	873	
Direct selling expenses	100	
General administration (all fixed)	346	
Other costs (all fixed)	380	
		2919
Profit before interest and tax		462
Interest		84
Profit before tax		378
Corporation tax		151
Profit available to ordinary shareholders		227

Balance sheet

	£000	£000
Fixed assets (net)		1480
Current assets	1720	
Less current liabilities	1120	
		600
		2080
Long-term debt		570
Net assets		1510
Capital and reserves		
Ordinary shares (25p)		800
Share premium account		320
Other reserves		390
		1510

The company is subject to taxation at a rate of 40%.

(i) Evaluate the effect of the purchase of the machine on both the degree of operating gearing and the financial gearing of Huckbul Ltd, comparing the position at the start of the current financial year with the expected position at the end of the current financial year.   (9 marks)

(ii) What are the implications for the ordinary shareholders of Huckbul as a result of the purchase of the machine:
(1) if turnover increases by the expected 15%?
(2) if turnover falls by 10%? (5 marks)
State clearly any assumptions that you make. (25 marks)

ACCA, June 1987

4. The managing director of an iron and steel stockist expects its sales of £1 million to increase by 25% over the whole of the next financial year and he seeks your advice on the most appropriate method of financing the increase. He provides the following information.

Estimated balance sheet position at 31 December 1988:

Fixed assets

Freehold property at valuation		£75 000
Other fixed assets		£25 000
		£100 000

Current assets

Stocks	£252 000	
Debtors	£208 000	
Other	£12 000	
		£472 000

Current liabilities

Bank overdraft (unsecured)	£148 000	
Creditors	£180 000	
Taxation	£46 000	
Other	£22 000	
		£396 000
		£76 000
		£176 000

	Year ending 31 December	Net profit before tax
	1984	£38 000
	1985	£41 000
	1986	£52 000
	1987	£68 000
Estimate	1988	£96 000
Estimate	1989	£120 000

You further ascertain that the bank overdraft limit is £150 000 and has been agreed at that level for the next two years. The company has no plans for capital expenditure in 1989 and it is expected that 50% of the profits after tax will be paid in dividends. Draft a note to your client, making such assumptions as you consider necessary, setting out clearly:

(a) your estimate of the additional finance required, taking into account a very approximate estimate (derived from the information above) of the company's cash flow for 1989;

(b) your practical suggestions for raising the additional finance required.

For business reasons it is not possible to reduce stocks for the existing turnover or lengthen the credit taken.

5. The directors of Adsum Ltd are working on a three-year financial plan. Sales during the period will depend upon the state of the economy.

Economic state:	Probability	Sales (£000 in current prices)		
		Year 1	Year 2	Year 3
Slow growth	0.6	5300	5500	5800
Rapid growth	0.4	6000	7100	8200

If slow growth occurs inflation is expected to be 12% per year and if rapid growth occurs 5% per year. Return on sales (profit before tax to sales) is estimated to be 12% per year in both economic states.

In year 1 assets to the value of £200 000 (after all tax effects) will be disposed of, and in years 2 and 3 new fixed assets costing £1.7 million and £800 000 respectively will be purchased. Disposal and purchase values have been estimated at current prices.

Stock is expected to increase by 80% of the percentage increase in sales, debtors by 90% and creditors by 95%. For example, if sales in year 1 increase by 16% from current financial accounts values, stock at the end of year 1 is expected to increase by 16% × 80% = 12.8% of the current balance sheet value. Sales prices and dividends will be increased in line with inflation, except if this would lead to dividends being less than 22% or greater than 35% of before tax profits, in which case a minimum of 22% or a maximum of 35% respectively would be payable.

Corporate tax is at the rate of 35% and is payable at the end of the year in which profit arises. Capital allowances are expected to be £450 000, £530 000 and £620 000 for years 1, 2 and 3 respectively.

Adsum is not planning to raise external funds by equity or long-term debt issues. A £600 000 overdraft facility exists, which is expected to be available for the three year period, but cannot be increased due to the company's level of gearing.

Summarized current financial accounts of Adsum are shown below:

Balance sheet

	£000
Fixed assets	4400
Stock	2130
Debtors	2920
Cash	80
	9530
Creditors	(3210)
Overdraft	(420)
	5900

Financed by:	
Ordinary shares (25 pence par)	500
Reserves	2400
12% seven year term loan	3000
	5900

Profit and loss account

	£000
Sales	5000
Profit before tax	600
Tax	210
	390
Dividend	150
Retained earnings	240

Required:

(a) Acting as a consultant to Adsum Limited advise the company on the financial implications of its forecasts as presented. Relevant calculations must be shown. Interest on cash balances or on additional overdraft may be ignored. State clearly any assumptions that you make. (11 marks)

(b) Discuss possible remedies for any problems that you identify. (5 marks)

(c) Advise Adsum Ltd on other techniques that might be useful in the company's medium-term financial planning process and comment upon the assumptions that Adsum has used in its plans. (9 marks)

(25 marks)

ACCA, Dec. 1991

6. Why is the management of working capital important?

7. You have been asked to advise on how to develop the planning process for a company. Discuss what stages the company is likely to go through in its corporate planning.

8. The relevant figures for a company are:

From profit & loss account:	(000s)	(000s)
Sales	8000	
Cost of goods sold	5000	
Materials purchased	3000	

From balance sheet:		
Stock – finished goods	1200	
WIP	600	
Raw materials	1000	2800
Debtors		2000
Creditors		600

(a) Determine the operating cycle of the company and comment on its importance.

(b) Target figures are:

	Days
Raw materials in stock	20
WIP materials in stock	12
Finished goods in stock	45
Credit granted to customers	40
Credit taken from suppliers	60

If the targets are achieved what will be the impact on the level of working capital? What will it cost, or save, per year if interest rates are 7%?

9. The directors of CDX plc are examining the company's estimated financial position for the next year.

	£000	
	Current year	Next year
Sales	3500	4400
Cost of goods sold	2980	3300
Purchases	1900	2200
Debtors	680	890
Creditors	450	580
Raw material stock	510	630
Work in progress	200	270
Finished goods stock	380	450

Required:

(a) The company's board of directors considers that the estimate is very favourable as operating profit is expected to increase significantly.

Explain whether you agree with the board of directors, and highlight any factors that you would draw to the board's attention, with recommendations for any action to be taken. Relevant calculations should support your analysis.

(b) The directors are also considering an operational plan for the short-term investment of surplus funds. Prepare a brief report for the directors, discussing the major influences on the selection of short-term investments.

20 Cash and interest-rate management

20.1	Introduction	708
20.2	The management of cash	711
20.3	The collection and payment cycles	712
20.4	Cash transmission techniques	713
20.5	Cash budget	714
20.6	Cash cycle	720
20.7	Cash flow statements	722
20.8	Planning the cash balance	725
20.9	Interest-rate risk management	729
20.10	Interest-rate futures contracts	733
20.11	Interest-rate swaps	742
20.12	Treasury organization and control	748
20.13	Key terms	750
20.14	Revision questions	750
20.15	Further reading	751
20.16	Problems	751
20.17	Appendix: Cash management models	758
20.18	References	765

The growth in treasury specialization over the last twenty years can be linked to the increasing complexity and volatility of financial markets. Treasury management is responsible for:

1. management of cash while obtaining the optimum return from any surplus funds;
2. management of exchange rate risks in accordance with group policy;
3. providing both long- and short-term funds for the business at minimum cost;
4. maintaining good relationships with banks and other providers of finance including shareholders;
5. advising on aspects of corporate finance including capital structure, mergers and acquisitions.

It is the objective of this chapter to explain the various aspects of treasury management activity. Exchange rate risk is dealt with in more detail in Chapter 21; capital structure and the role of mergers and acquisitions will be considered in Chapter 24.

20.1 Introduction

In most large companies it is now quite normal to find one person with the title of treasurer and another person with the title of controller, with both reporting to the director of finance. The treasurer manages the liquid resources which at one time would have been a comparatively routine job in the chief accountant's office. During the 1960s and 1970s the treasury role became more and more specialized.

The reasons bringing about this change include:

1. The adoption of floating rather than fixed exchange rates brought increased risks when trading, borrowing and investing in foreign currencies.

2. An increasingly uncertain financial environment during the 1970s with volatile foreign exchange and interest rates. More reliance on short-term floating rate bank borrowing as long-term corporate debt became difficult to raise, thus increasing the importance of managing interest rate exposure.
3. Financial innovations affected both long- and short-term financing and their management. The growth in eurocurrency markets, and the increasing availability of markets in derivative securities such as options and futures, provided financial managers with new ways of hedging risks. More sophisticated types of new finance were marketed and this increasing complexity demanded greater specialization and knowledge of new markets and financial instruments.
4. Improvements in information technology have provided round-the-clock information relating to world financial markets increasing the scope for more sophisticated financial strategies.
5. Volatile markets and the recognition of the importance of a company's stock market value led to a growth in financial public relations. The need to conduct a dialogue with providers of funds and financial analysts is widely recognized and has become an important role of the finance function.

The management of money became seen as something different from the financial accounting and control function. From an educational and training point of view professional accountants cover some aspects of treasury management in their studies. Company treasurers would argue, however, that there is much more to treasury management than is covered in the training of professional accountants. Hence in the UK in 1979 the Association of Corporate Treasurers was formed with its own examination system. The Association describes the role of treasury management as follows:

> Treasury management concerns the corporate handling of all financial markets, the generation of external and internal funds for business, the management of currencies and cash flows and the complex strategies, policies and procedures of corporate finance. Treasury managers are playing increasingly important roles in business management teams and most large companies now have separate treasury departments. The treasury function is, however, an essential function in all companies, whether it is carried out by a separate department or not. [1]

The main responsibilities of the treasury department are as follows.

Cash management

The efficient collection and payment of cash both inside the group and to third parties will concern the treasury department. The involvement of the department with the detail of receivables and payables will be a matter of policy. There may be complete centralization within a group treasury or the treasury may simply advise subsidiaries and divisions on policy (collection/payment periods, discounts etc.). Any position between these two extremes would be possible. Treasury will normally manage surplus funds in an investment portfolio. Investment policy will consider future need for liquid funds and acceptable levels of risk as determined by company policy.

Currency management

The treasury will manage the foreign currency risk exposure of the company. In a large MNC the first step will usually be to set off intra-group indebtedness. The use of matching receipts and payments in the same currency will save transaction costs. Treasury might advise on the currency to be used when invoicing overseas sales. Possibilities include home company currency, customer country currency or common currency (e.g. US$ as in oil prices). Competition and accepted trade practices are likely to influence the method adopted.

The treasury will manage any net exchange exposures in accordance with company policy. If risks are to be minimized then forward contracts can be used either to buy or sell currency forward. Forward contracts are available in most major currencies but not in less traded or very volatile currencies. An alternative strategy to forward contracts is an immediate purchase of currency or loan of currency, either of which would be self-liquidating when an account is paid or received. These issues are dealt with in the next chapter on foreign exchange markets.

Treasury may also use options and futures in their currency management strategies. As was explained in Chapter 11, options give the right, but not the obligation, to buy or sell currency at an agreed rate over a stated time period. Unlike both forward contracts and futures they give the opportunity for profit while limiting loss to the cost of the option. Futures enable the holder to buy or sell currency at a future date at an exchange rate fixed at the outset of the contract. Futures have low commission charges and require a low initial outlay. However margin payments are required over the life of the contract and with changes in the value of the contract extra payments may be required.

Parallel loans and swaps can also be used to hedge risk. The more traditional parallel loan involves two companies in different countries with a requirement to raise similar amounts in each other's currency. Each makes arrangements to provide the other with an equivalent value loan in the respective company's own currency. Swaps occur when companies agree to exchange funds directly. These transactions which are currently more used than parallel loans involve companies in different countries agreeing to sell each other their own home currencies at current spot rates while simultaneously agreeing to buy back the currencies at an agreed future date and rate. These exchange agreements provide a long-term hedge with low transaction costs. These issues are considered in more detail in Chapter 26.

Funding management

Treasury will be responsible for planning and sourcing the company's short-, medium- and long-term cash needs. Treasury will also participate in the decision on capital structure and forecast future interest and foreign currency rates. The last decade has seen the introduction of more complex capital issues requiring careful analysis. Debt finance with equity warrants attached, zero-coupon bonds and high-risk so called 'junk' bonds have all been issued to provide funds. Equity issues now include convertible preference shares which may be converted into equity or repaid at the holders' option, hence the term 'convertible puttables'. In making these issues some companies may have been too optimistic in their analyses, paying too little attention to the potential leverage and the liquidity position should conversion into equity not take place and repayment be required.

The growth of the Euromarkets also led to a growth in the methods of raising finance. As well as the conventional Eurobonds and Euronotes, securities such as convertible capital bonds appeared. These are bonds issued by a subsidiary, convertible at first into preference shares of the subsidiary then equity shares of the parent.

The treasury will also monitor and manage interest rates and interest rate risk. Should the company invest or borrow at fixed or floating rates of interest? If project finance is required for a number of years then a fixed-rate loan might be preferred as this crystallizes the cost from the company's viewpoint. Even if borrowing is only available at floating rates markets now exist in interest rate swaps whereby the company can swap its floating-rate liability for a fixed-rate liability.

Banking

It is important that a company maintains a good relationship with its bankers. Treasury will carry out negotiations with bankers and act as the initial point of contact with them. Short-term finance can come in the form of bank loans or through the sale of commercial paper in the money market. Companies usually pay a 'commitment fee' to the bank to have short-term facilities available. Companies can also arrange with a bank or group of banks a multiple option facility (MOF) which gives them a choice of interest rates and loans of different duration.

Corporate finance

Treasury will be involved with both acquisition and divestment activities within the group. In addition it will often have responsibility for investor relations. The latter activity has assumed increased importance in markets where share price performance is regarded as crucial and may affect the company's ability to undertake acquisition activity or, if the price falls drastically, render it vulnerable to a hostile bid.

There are three basic reasons why a company would wish to hold some of its assets in the form of cash or cash equivalent. These reasons, according to economic theory, are the transaction motive, the precaution motive and the speculative motive.

The firm must be able to conduct its purchases and sales, and the management of this process involves an analysis of flow of cash in and out of the firm. Any firm needs working capital whatever its form of trading or manufacture. It is not just sufficient to acquire plant and machinery; a sum of working capital initially in the form of cash must be put aside to pay the wages, to buy materials and to meet any other expenses. A product, is manufactured. The product might need to be placed in inventory before it is eventually sold. If the sale is for credit the company may have to wait some time before the cash is received. The cash cycle, the time that elapses between when the company pays its costs and when it receives the cash from sales, indicates the need for cash for transaction purposes. We shall return to this subject when cash budgets are considered.

It is impossible to forecast accurately cash inflow and cash outflow, and the less certain the predictions the greater is the balance that needs to be maintained as a precaution. The nearness of cash on short call will affect the amount that needs to be held for this purpose. If a large amount of securities or other assets can be converted into cash within a day or two, the amount that needs to be held as a cash balance will be less. Some companies rely heavily on bank overdrafts as a source of finance. These companies can often offer as security assets which are easily convertible into cash at short notice. Some types of inventory are very illiquid and take time to convert into cash. Other inventories, such as raw materials and commodities, can quickly be converted into cash and so can act as ideal security for short-term loans. There are sometimes institutional reasons why a company may have to maintain certain cash balances. It may be to satisfy the bank by retaining the amount required as a float to keep the bank's goodwill. It may be written into certain credit arrangements or loan agreements that a balance should be maintained. The company may be expected to maintain agreed financial ratios to satisfy creditors or the bank, and this can necessitate adjusting the cash figure.

One explanation often given for holding cash is that any profitable opportunities that arise can be met immediately. This motive may be strong in the case of a company that exists primarily for speculative purposes. To hold cash or near cash has a cost, which is the earnings that could have been obtained through using the funds elsewhere. The company has to ensure that the gains from the possible speculative opportunities are greater than the earnings from normal investment opportunities. Undoubtedly companies do hold large cash balances at certain times, and on some occasions this could be due to possible speculative opportunities such as a takeover bid. Often, however, a company can arrange to have other sources of funds near at hand should an opportunity arise. Only if there is no possibility of arranging any other form of finance need a firm decide whether the loss of earnings through holding cash is less than the probability that an opportunity will arise and its resulting return.

The corporate treasurer will attempt to control the flow of cash in and out of the business. He or she will wish to delay payments for as long as it is an advantage to do so, and to collect cash as quickly as possible.

20.2 The management of cash

20.3 The collection and payment cycles

The collection cycle

The collection cycle consists of the following:

- receipt of the order;
- credit approval – acceptance of customer, and agreement on discount and price;
- dispatch of goods and documentation;
- posting of invoices stating credit terms and method of payment;
- debtor control;
- enforcement procedures;
- collection and the banking of cash.

As the collection cycle can take 100 days or more, any steps that can be taken to reduce its length are important. Many aspects of the problem will be dealt with in the chapter on the management of debtors, and at this point we shall concentrate on the movement of the cash.

'Float' is a term used to describe the money tied up in the process of collecting debts. It can arise because of the time interval that elapses between the day a customer, a purchaser, posts the cheque to the supplier and the day when the supplier can use the funds for his own purposes. First there can be the time required for postal delivery, which in the UK is between one and three days in most cases. When the supplier receives the cheque and banks it, he will have to wait for the bank to clear the cheque before he can draw on the funds he has deposited. In the UK the total time delay can be expected to vary between four and nine days depending on the postal service, the speed at which the cheque is deposited and delays due to weekends.

Let us say that a customer sends a cheque for £10 000 to his supplier. If the cheque can be cleared within four days rather than nine days, this is earning profits for the receiving company. If interest rates are 10%, then the saving of five days is worth approximately £14:

$$£10\,000 \times \frac{5}{365} \times 0.10 = £14$$

With a large sale to a particular customer, it is clearly important to reduce the size of the float as much as is possible. In the USA, where the problem is potentially of greater significance than in the UK because of the possible longer distance between companies' finance offices and so greater postal delays, many firms have reduced the size of the float by means of decentralized collection and regional banking. This avoids unnecessary cross-country transfer of funds. When large single payments are involved firms have been known to use messengers travelling by air to avoid possible postal delays.

One way in which a company can improve its cash position is through the system of collecting and depositing receipts from its divisional offices. Some small companies only deposit funds at the bank once or twice a week. If the company has an overdraft, the effect of rapidly depositing receipts is obvious: the overdraft is reduced, and so is the interest payment that the company has to make. If the company has a positive cash balance the effect of early deposits is just as important. The early deposit can earn interest on deposit account, enable the company to take advantage of cash discounts by payment of accounts on time or enable the company to carry out further investment of its own.

The implications are important for both large and small companies, for with interest rates as high as those of the last few years the results from early depositing can be quite dramatic. Suppose that a company has annual sales of £2 000 000, which approximates to average receipts on each working day of £8000, and an annual interest rate of, say, 8% (approximately 0.022% per day) has to be paid by the company on an overdraft – or can be earned by the company on the investment of its funds. If the company deposits is collections for the five days of the week on the last day of the week it pays £40 000 into the bank. For this week it has earned no interest. If it deposited its collections in the bank each day it would earn interest of £25–£40 over the five days. The management would have to decide whether the additional depositing of funds was worthwhile. In the above case the earnings or avoided costs resulting from the rapid depositing of funds would provide enough to pay £1000 a year towards the salary of an employee, which may well be considered a worthwhile incentive.

Payments cycle

The payments cycle consists of the following:

- placing the order
- credit control – deciding on priority invoices to be paid quickly and calculating the benefit of discounts
- method of payment – cheque, direct debit or standing order
- payment frequency and timing – policy and past experiences with the creditor

The time taken to pay is referred to as the reverse float. It should be the result of a policy decision, taking into account the available funds, the discounts on offer and the relationship with the supplier. The time taken to pay can be a function of the efficiency of the administration handling payment. The administration is a cost to the business, but savings should not be made to the extent that unintentional delays in payment harm relationships with suppliers.

The final stage of the collection of debts and the payment of suppliers is the movement of cash. In large companies the treasury management function is usually well aware of the opportunities for earning returns through the movement of cash. This can be a neglected subject in smaller businesses. It must be remembered that cheques received and deposited in the bank are not available until they have been cleared. The company receiving the cheque has first to deposit it at its own bank. This receiving bank then needs to present the cheque to the bank that is named on the cheque, i.e. the bank on which it is drawn. Only when the drawing bank transfers the funds to the bank at which the cheque was deposited does the company who received the cheque technically benefit from the receipt of the funds. This clearing process takes time. Of course, if the cheque is deposited in the same bank as that on which it is drawn it can be cleared quickly.

Through the London Clearing Banks system a cheque normally takes about three working days to be cleared. This is the time taken to clear cheques drawn or paid into what are referred to as 'out of town' banks. There is a faster system for cheques paid into and drawn on branches of banks situated within the City of London. This is called 'town' same day clearing, but it cannot be used for cheques for small amounts.

UK domestic bank transfers and direct debits are cleared and have the value transferred on the day of the instruction. Standing orders are cleared on the pre-arranged date. Cash is cleared on the same day at the customer's own branch. With international transfers there is normally at least a two day delay between debiting the paying account and crediting the payee's account.

There are a number of cash transmission techniques. These include netting, cash pooling and direct debiting.

Netting involves netting the flow of funds between units within the same company, and only settling the net amount. It reduces the costs that the company has to pay. Bank charges for fund transfers and foreign exchange transactions involve a fixed charge per transaction and a variable charge based on the size of the transaction. Netting will reduce the variable charge.

Cash pooling operates within a group. All the units in the group transfer their net funds to a central account. This enables surplus funds to be invested to their best advantage and means that one part of the group is not paying interest on an overdraft, whilst another part is earning interest on a cash balance.

Financial secrecy

Companies and other organizations need at times to use 'secret money'. Many financial centres (including West Indian islands, Switzerland and Liechtenstein) provide homes for secret money. Even respectable financial centres provide the opportunity for funds to be 'laundered' or moved to safe homes, although by resorting to proper legal procedures it is sometimes possible to trace the movement of the funds and therefore the homes are not always so secret.

Many companies may need secrecy at certain times with certain types of transactions, for example with mergers and acquisitions when the intention is to catch an opponent off guard. Also sometimes payments are made to individuals in order to secure contracts and the less that is known about these payments the better it is for the parties concerned. Again sometimes trading with a country takes place which is in violation of the home country's trading laws; secrecy is necessary. In 1984 a number of UK trade unions tried to benefit from the 'secret money' channels. They wanted to keep union funds out of reach of UK courts. New trade union laws were being introduced and the unions knew that certain types of strike action would be breaking the law and the unions concerned would be fined. The National Union of Mine Workers sold about £7 million of government bonds and passed the proceeds through banks in the Isle of Man, Ireland and the USA to bearer accounts in Switzerland and Luxembourg.

As is now apparent at some supermarkets and large stores the developments in computer applications have been applied to cash management. It is now possible to have electronic fund transfers. At the time of purchasing goods, the purchaser's account at a bank can be instantly debited through the use of computers. At the moment this system is in its early days, but there are moves to increase its use. It is a natural extension of the use of credit cards.

The management of cash in the USA presents many opportunities not available in the UK. The size of the country and the variety of banking institutions and services offered create different opportunities from those in the UK. For example, if a treasurer in the USA wished to delay payment of a debt to a supplier, he could draw a cheque on a bank situated far from the creditor, thus increasing the delay in clearing the cheque. To overcome this problem US companies have introduced a number of measures. Many companies charge interest on overdue accounts. Banks offer locked-box facilities. This means that a debtor is given the address of a bank or post office located much nearer to them than is the supplier. The cheque is to be sent to the locked box. The box is opened regularly by a bank official who will quickly credit the supplying company's bank account with cheques received. The locked-box arrangement is offered by the bank on a regional basis and helps overcome delays in the postal service brought about by the distances involved.

20.5 Cash budget

The following decisions have to be made.

1. How much cash should be held on hand or at short call?
2. How much should be invested in money market securities?
3. What portfolio of securities should be held? What should the balance be between securities with different maturity dates?

Determining the amount of cash that a firm needs at a particular time is a difficult matter. As already explained, if a firm has too little cash it can be in liquidity difficulties; if it has too much cash it is missing opportunities to earn profits. The problem is to determine how much cash is too much cash. There are many opportunities for lending funds, even for short periods of time, which can all earn interest and so profits for the company.

The key to successful cash management is planning. Money can be earned not only through the manufacture or distribution of products but also through the management of all the assets that it employs. Through its cash budgets, a company can decide on the funds that it will have available for short-term investment. If the business is seasonal or trade is cyclical, cash budgets will show when the surplus funds are available, and what length of time will elapse before they are required. Some companies borrow to satisfy their seasonal or cyclical needs – to finance the buildup in inventories and debtors. They manufacture during the slack sales period and have to wait for the high sales period to arrive before the cash starts to flow back into the business. Other companies accumulate cash during the selling period, invest it and realize these investments to meet the need for cash during the slack sales period.

A simplified example will be shown. A company decides on a policy of maintaining the outflow of cash constant throughout the year, which means that production is to be even throughout the year. The inflow of cash is seasonal because sales are seasonal. The net cash flow is illustrated in Fig. 20.1.

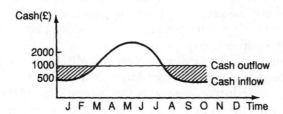

Figure 20.1

The company will not have enough cash flowing in during the period from August to March to meet current needs for outgoings. It can either borrow funds during this period and pay back in April–July, or it can accumulate funds during April–July, putting them into short-term investments and realizing these investments to meets its need for cash in August–March. Cash budgets revealing the demand and supply of cash will show the quantity of funds free for investment and the periods when they are likely to be available.

The same type of decision situation arises when the fluctuations are of longer duration – a cyclical not a seasonal demand. Of course, the choice of policy depends on investment and borrowing opportunities. Some firms, particularly in the capital goods industries where there is a tendency towards fluctuations, attempt to follow a policy of accumulating cash or near cash during a downturn to be ready to finance an upturn in business volume.

It is difficult to make general statements about the size of the cash balance that a company requires. It depends on the particular company and on the economic conditions. Some companies maintain a good relationship with their bankers and have overdraft arrangements which enable them to draw up to an agreed amount. Such companies may never have a positive cash balance. The company clearly has to be careful that it does not let its overdraft rise above the agreed level, otherwise it could endanger its relationship with the bank. The financial manager has to ensure that there is a comfortable difference between the level of the overdraft facility and the actual overdraft level. The size of the permitted overdraft is not known to an outsider. The actual overdraft will, of course, be shown in the balance sheet, but how this has varied over the year or how close it is to its agreed upper level is not known to the outsider. Some companies do not have a good relationship with a banker and so they could well have a relatively small permitted overdraft limit, and to allow for necessary fluctuations over time in the cash flows they may at times have a positive cash balance figure.

The size of the cash balance or the size of the overdraft can also depend on economic conditions. At times banks have plenty of cash available, and in fact encourage companies to borrow. At other times, banks can be in a credit squeeze position; they are short of cash to lend, and so are keen to reduce the size of company overdrafts.

Any company would like to use precise tools in the management of its cash. None of the liquidity ratios referred to earlier in this book make specific mention of cash. The ratios that refer to levels of current assets do not give any specific guidance on how much of this should be cash. One measure that might assist in the management of cash is the ratio of the cash balance to the level of current assets, i.e.

$$\text{Proportion of cash held } = \frac{\text{cash balance}}{\text{current assets}}$$

This is the ratio at one moment of time – is it useful as a tool of financial management? It may give a rough guide to the minimum cash balance a firm should hold. When the ratio is high, explanations can be sought. The situations that call for large cash balances should be indicated in the cash budgets, and so sound financial management would mean that the large balances would arise only when they were needed. Something is certainly wrong if high balances are maintained for a long period.

Ratios can be used by a company to make comparisons with the average for the industry. It is obviously necessary to draw comparisons only with firms in the same industry, as each industry has its own transaction needs and particular methods of financing. However, such comparisons are of limited use. Companies may prepare their accounts at different dates, and the time of year will affect the cash being held. Certain companies might be in exceptional circumstances affecting their cash holding, and this in turn would affect the industry average. Without knowledge of these circumstances it would be dangerous to attach importance to the industry averages.

The key statements by which management can be kept informed about the cash position of the company are the cash budget and the cash flow statement. It is necessary to have these information statements as quickly as possible and as up to date as possible, so that action can be taken on the figures. The cash budget involves estimating what the inflow and outflow of cash will be at fixed intervals over the next planning period. Budgeting over short intervals – weekly or monthly – gives management a better chance to control any surplus of cash or to arrange to meet any expected shortages. A quarterly analysis may be satisfactory. Although within a quarter there may be times when the company has surplus funds, the uncertainty about when these funds will be needed within the business will make it difficult to take advantage of any short-term lending possibilities. Similarly, although the balance estimated for a quarter may indicate cash surplus to needs, within that quarter there could be times when the business is short of cash.

It appears that, in practice, company financial managers rely heavily on the possible sale of short-term investments to replenish the firm's cash balance. The availability of near cash fundamentally affects cash balance management. The company policy becomes oriented towards forecasting heavy future cash needs and purchasing securities of a maturity to match these requirements over time. Such a policy is very dependent on the accuracy of cash flow budgets. To the extent that cash flows are predictable in timing and in size, this reliance on the trading of securities to meet cash needs may be economic. If cash flows can be predicted with a reasonable degree of accuracy, the company can be more dependent on its short-term deposits and securities and needs to maintain smaller cash balances over time. The greater the uncertainty of the cash flow, the larger is the cash balance that needs to be maintained and so the greater the opportunity cost.

Table 20.1 shows a typical cash budget, analysed by monthly periods. The business is seasonal, with the vast majority of the sales taking place in the third and fourth quarters of the year. The row indicating the collection of cash from debtors shows how the receipts from sales were spread out over time, after allowing for the expected delays in payment by customers. Production was planned to be more or less constant throughout the year. The actual balance sheet at the commencement of the period is shown in Table 20.2, as are the estimated balance sheets at the end of each of the four quarters. The

Table 20.1 *M Company cash budget*

	First quarter			Second quarter			Third quarter			Fourth quarter		
	Jan.	Feb.	Mar.	Apr.	May	June	July	Aug.	Sept.	Oct.	Nov.	Dec.
Cash sources												
Collections from debtors	226	122	22	21	12	13	20	15	15	210	210	815
Dividends received	—	—	100	—	—	—	—	—	100	—	—	—
Sale of plant	—	—	—	—	100	—	—	—	—	—	—	—
Total sources	226	122	122	21	112	13	20	15	115	210	210	815
Cash uses												
Cash expenses (labour and other)	76	92	92	71	84	51	50	55	55	40	40	55
Payment to creditors	—	—	—	—	—	—	80	150	150	150	100	100
Taxes	100	—	—	—	—	—	—	—	—	—	—	—
Equipment	—	—	—	—	—	250	—	—	—	—	—	—
Total uses	176	92	92	71	84	301	130	205	205	190	140	155
Beginning balance	200	150	150	150	150	150	150	150	150	150	150	150
+ Source of cash	226	122	122	21	112	13	20	15	115	210	210	815
− Use of cash	(176)	(92)	(92)	(71)	(84)	(301)	(130)	(205)	(205)	(190)	(140)	(155)
Cash balance before loans or repayments	250	180	180	100	178	(138)	40	(40)	60	170	220	810
Desired cash balance	(150)	(150)	(150)	(150)	(150)	(150)	(150)	(150)	(150)	(150)	(150)	(150)
Cash borrowed	—	—	—	50	—	288	110	190	90	—	—	—
Loans repaid	100	30	30	—	28	—	—	—	—	20	70	610
Cash in excess at 31 December												50

budgeted profit and loss accounts are given in Table 20.3. The differences in the values of the balance sheet items from one date to another highlight the difficulty of analysing the accounts of a seasonal business. The impression to be drawn depends so much on the day in the year when the balance sheet is constructed.

Table 20.2 *M Company budgeted balance sheet*

	Opening 1 Jan.	First quarter	Second quarter	Third quarter	Fourth quarter
Fixed assets	800	750	850	800	750
Stock	200	550	650	800	300
Debtors	310	90	300	700	500
Dividends due	50	—	50	—	50
Cash	200	150	150	150	200
	1560	1540	2000	2450	1800
Capital and reserves	1250	1315	1340	1375	1650
Bank loans	160	0	310	700	0
Provision for tax	100	25	50	75	100
Creditors	50	200	300	300	50
	1560	1540	2000	2450	1800

Table 20.3 *M Company budgeted profit and loss account*

	First quarter	Second quarter	Third quarter	Fourth quarter
Opening stock	200	550	650	800
Purchases	150	100	380	100
Depreciation	50	50	50	50
Expenses	260	206	160	135
	660	906	1240	1085
Sales	150	256	450	1035
Closing stock	550	650	800	300
Dividends received	50	50	50	50
	750	956	1300	1385
Profit before tax	90	50	60	300
Tax	25	25	25	25
Profit after tax	65	25	35	275

To estimate the inflow of cash, the firm has to project its sales forecasts over the next 12 months. The fact that sales do not result in an immediate cash flow is of fundamental importance to the distinction between the accrual system of accounting, which is used as the basis for the annual accounts, and the cash flow system of recording, which is necessary for company planning. A sale is made, goods are delivered and the cash flows back into the firm in anything from, say, six to 12 weeks' time. It is the estimate of the cash inflow from the sales that is needed in the cash budget. Allowance also has to be made for delayed payments and possible bad debts.

It is necessary in the cash budgeting exercise to estimate expenditures. The cost of raw materials, wages and other items will have been paid, possibly long before the product is sold. The finished goods may well have to wait in inventory before their sale. The cash budget will need to consider the production schedules to estimate the cash outflow: it is not possible to link the expenses directly with the sales. All other items affecting the cash flow have to be allowed for and shown in the budget. These include dividends and interest (both paid and received), tax payments and any items of a capital nature such as purchase of new equipment or sale of old equipment.

In the example the company has an opening cash balance of £200. After balancing the needs of liquidity and profitability, and discussing with the bank the overdraft facilities available, the management decides that a cash balance of £150 should be maintained. Sales for the year are estimated to be £1891, and so the budgeted cash turnover ratio is given by £1891/£150 which is 12.6. The percentage of cash in current assets varies very much according to which balance sheet is examined: over the four quarters it is 19.0%, 13.0%, 9.1% and 19.0%. On consideration of these figures the management may decide that the cash balance is being maintained at too high a level, particularly during the first and fourth quarters; a short-term loan is being repaid during both of these quarters, and it may make sense to repay the loans as quickly as possible by lowering the chosen cash balance. Another possibility that may be considered is to repay the loans by the instalments proposed in the budget, but to invest some of the £150 balance in short-term securities. The possibilities could be considered and the budget balances altered accordingly.

Once the required cash balance is decided on, the forecast of the cash inflow and outflow will enable the company to see how much money it needs to borrow and how much it has to invest. As can be seen, the company commenced the year with a short-term bank loan of £160. The selling season is over, but the cash still has to come into the business from many of the sales; when this flows in during the first quarter, the company is able to repay the loan. In the second quarter little cash is coming into the business, and the constant level of production, together with the acquisition of new capital equipment, means that cash borrowings need to be made.

In June a capital asset was purchased with funds provided by a short-term bank loan. This might have been unwise: more than one company has been driven into liquidation by financing long-term projects out of short-term funds. Here, however, the practice seems reasonable. It can be seen, as a result of the cash-budgeting exercise, that the build-up in short-term loans is only a temporary phenomenon; later in the year, not only can the bank loan be repaid but also working capital will increase and therefore, because of the growth and profitability of the business, the purchase of the asset with short-term funds seems justified. Without a cash budget, of course, it would not have been possible to say this, since it would not be known that the short-term needs were only a temporary state of affairs and not the start of a liquidity problem which the acquisition of a long-term asset would aggravate. However, it can be seen that it was not necessary to finance the long-term asset with long-term funds, and the addition of long-term funds for the purpose of purchasing the asset, and perhaps paying off the overdraft, would have been unnecessary and wasteful.

In the third quarter the sales period for the product has started, but because cash has not yet started to flow into the business the overdraft continues to increase. It stands at its highest level, £700, at the end of the third quarter. The company benefits from knowing well in advance the amount of funds that will need to be acquired: it can then negotiate with the bank knowing the maximum amount that will be necessary and the time when it will be able to repay.

If the company is unable to obtain the necessary funds from overdraft facilities, despite the fact that it has stock and debtors to offer as security, alternative means of finance will have to be sought. It may be able to sell off some short-term investments, come to arrangements with its creditors or even sell long-term assets. Finally, if all else fails, it may have to go back to its plans for the year, with a view to changing them, perhaps slowing down expansion so that its liquidity position is not threatened. In the fourth quarter, as shown, sufficient cash flows into the business to enable the overdraft to be paid off, and in fact to generate cash in excess of needs. This surplus cash of £50 can now be invested. By the end of this financial year, a cash budget will have been prepared for the next, and so it will be possible to see whether this surplus cash will be needed for next year's working capital. If this year's trend is repeated, that cash is generated during the first three months and, if this is adequate for next year's needs, the £50 can be invested in long-term assets.

Financing working capital requirements can be seen from this exercise to be a short-term problem and should be met as far as possible from short-term borrowing. The company has grown during the year and a decision has to be made on whether a higher level of working capital is required to finance next year's level of operation. As can be seen, net current assets started the year at £450 (current assets of £760 less current liabilities of £310). At the end of the year it had risen to £900 (current assets of £1050 and current liabilities of £150). It is most probable that this level is now in excess of requirements and something should be done to reduce it. This could be achieved through the reduction of current assets, i.e. the investment of surplus cash (when realized through the sale of inventory and the collection of debts) in long-term assets. Undoubtedly the company in this example has borrowing opportunities, and should now try to take advantage of them.

The difference between a cash budget and a funds flow budget can be clearly seen from a comparison of Tables 20.1 and 20.4. The cash budget shows the detailed movement of cash receipts and cash payments each month and how this has resulted in a cash surplus at times and a deficit in the cash balance at other times. Good financial management requires that this is known in advance so that the necessary action can be taken.

The funds flow statement shows that on the basis of the budgets there will be an increase in funds of £450 000, i.e. an increase of nearly 30% of the total assets or 100% of the working capital. Management would review these figures and consider whether

Table 20.4 *M Company budgeted funds flow statement (£000)*

Operating profit before tax		300
Add Dividend receivable		200
Adjustment for return not involving the flow of funds:		
Depreciation		200
		700
Funds from other sources:		
Sale of plant		100
		800
Application of funds		
Purchase of equipment	250	
Tax paid	100	350
Increase in funds		450
Increase (decrease) in working capital		
Increase in stock	100	
Increase in debtors	190	
	290	
Movements in net liquid funds		
Cash	0	
Bank loan decrease	160	450

any action is required. It is possible that the bank loan should be repaid. The increases in stock and debtors appear to be high. An increase in turnover is predicted, and so there will be a rise in the amount required to finance additional assets.

It is important to be aware of weaknesses in the normal approach to cash budgeting. One-figure forecasting is generally out of date. It is advisable to look at a range of possible outcomes, at the situation that may develop under a number of sets of assumptions. Unexpected events can occur, good or bad, which can affect the firm's cash flow. For most companies, the key area of uncertainty affecting the cash budget is the volume of sales. Cash flow is particularly sensitive to changes in sales volume. Not all cash dispersements are proportional to the volume of sales. If the volume of sales falls, certain items of expenses will still have to be met and cannot be reduced proportionately. There are fixed payments that have to be made. Wages are increasingly becoming a fixed element. A company is not able to reduce its labour force in the short run and so reduce its costs. Other fixed items of expenditure include rents and rates.

In handling uncertainty in cash budgets, one can vary the assumptions about sales volume and produce a range of possible cash flow figures. There are many computer simulation approaches to this problem. The sales figures are varied by a certain percentage and the effect on cash flows can be measured. However, this may not be sufficient by itself. It may be important to have a probability estimate attached to the different sales figures and so to the different cash forecasts.

20.6 Cash cycle

The five balance sheets shown in Table 20.2 demonstrate very clearly how dramatically the financial structure of a company can change during a cash cycle. The cash cycle is shaped by seasonal demand, cyclical demand over time and the stages of a product's development. The cash cycle in the above example was created by seasonal demand.

The motor industry traditionally had a cycle of five to six years between one peak of high demand and the next. The cash cycle, which is geared to the stages of a product's development, springs from prolonged initial outlays. Cash has to be available in the early years to finance research and development, and again later to meet promotional expenditures when the product is launched. Only after these stages does cash start to flow back.

The phrases of the cash cycle can be described, in very general terms, as follows. Orders are placed with the firm, which by this early stage has already had to meet the considerable cost of capital equipment. (It is not always necessary to pay for this in cash – other methods, such as leasing, are available – but at least part of the equipment will involve outright settlement.) The orders require the purchase of raw materials. This purchase generates creditors. Labour is employed and paid for, and the work-in-progress inventory increases. The goods are completed, having entailed further cash outlays for direct and indirect overheads, and then move into finished inventories. Many of the manufacturing costs will already have been paid. If the goods are produced to order they will be shipped out of the factory, debtors will increase and perhaps 90 days hence the cash from the sale will be received.

In a firm catering for a seasonal or cyclical demand rather than for purchase by order, production of goods for inventory will often continue during the slack sales period. When the expected high demand comes, much of it will be supplied from the inventory level, so perhaps smoothing out production. This policy rules out the need for high machine capacity to cope with peak demand phases; however, it does entail storage facilities. The firm must also pay out cash during its inventory build-up instead of earning interest, and it must wait for the next stage of the business cycle before the cash starts to flow into the business.

The influence of sales on the level of current assets is illustrated in Fig. 20.2. Over time sales increase but there are fluctuations around a rising long-term trend. There should be a parallel increase in fixed assets, which should eventually be financed by long-term funds. As sales increase, so will the level of current assets. Some of this increase in the permanent current assets will have to be financed out of long-term capital, equity or loan. There is a constraint on the relationship between current assets and current liabilities, for a ratio of 1:1 would certainly be considered dangerous by creditors and bondholders. Only a proportion of the increase in permanent current assets will be financed by current liabilities through the increase in creditors, accrued tax and wages. The temporary increase in current assets, fluctuating through the cash cycle, should certainly be financed by short-term liabilities. It can be dangerous to finance long-term needs out of short-term finance; it is expensive, and so uneconomical, to finance short-term needs out of long-term finance.

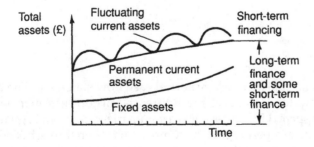

Figure 20.2

Product life cycle

A company's capital budgeting decision normally involves choosing the batch of projects that will produce the highest net present value within the limits of the amount of capital available. Each of the projects will normally need a certain amount of working capital to be set aside for their use; this is in addition to the initial capital cost of the project. Thinking in cash flow terms is an important aspect of managing the company's finances so as to ensure the availability not only of sufficient long-term capital to finance the selected projects but also of adequate working capital to span each project's life. A new product, whether it is accepted for production or abandoned in the development stage, results in a cash outflow for the company, and some products demand heavy cash commitments, especially during the development stage.

This leads to the concept of threshold development cost, which implies that there is a minimum size of firm that can afford certain types of research and development activity. The relevant size depends of course on the speed of technological advance and the industry being considered. The size of the firm needs to be sufficient to be able to spend large quantities on research: it is difficult for a firm below a certain size to undertake successful research activity.

At various stages of a product's development decisions have to be made on whether the expected future returns justify the commitment of any more cash or capital resources. Even when the product has been developed, there is still a period when the net cash flows will be negative, and this applies even to products of a fairly uncomplicated character requiring little development expenditure. When manufacturing begins, work in progress builds up and finished goods are produced. Sales are made, debtors accumulate and eventually the cash flows into the firm.

The cash flows over a product's life cycle are illustrated in Fig. 20.3. The investment decision on whether to go ahead with the product will involve forecasting the cash inflows and outflows over the entire life of the project, and discounting at an appropriate rate to obtain their present worth. In the illustration, the flows are shown as their estimated value for each year of the product's life, which is not, of course, the same as their present value at the time that the decision is made to go ahead.

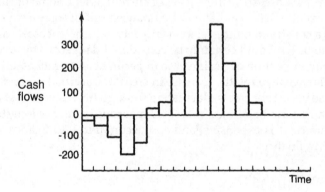

Figure 20.3

20.7 Cash flow statements

One type of financial statement is a historical cash flow statement. The cash budget is useful for planning, for looking at the future; the historical statement is useful for analysing what happened in the past. It is a summarized cash book, giving a picture of the cash transactions in a period that the company has been through. The balance sheet and profit and loss account of the XL Co. Ltd were shown in the last chapter in Tables 19.6 and 19.7 (see p. 699). These relate to the period just completed. A cash flow statement is shown in Table 20.5. It can be contrasted with the funds flow statement based on the same set of accounts shown in Table 19.8.

The accrual system of accounting recognizes income and expenditures in the period in which the benefits were received or the costs recognized. The cash flow system is only interested in the dates when the cash came in and went out of the company.

Table 20.5 *Cash flow statement XL Ltd*

		£
(a) Net cash inflow from operating activities		40 500
(b) Returns on investments and servicing of finance		
Interest paid	3000	
Dividends paid	7500	(10 500)
(c) Taxation paid		(8 000)
(d) Investing activities		
Purchase of assets		(40 000)
(e) Financing activities		
Issue of debt		20 000
Increase in cash		2 000

This Cash Flow statement is in the format required by FRS 1, for the indirect method of presentation. The appropriate workings are:

(a) *Reconciliation of operating profit to net cash inflow from operating activities*

Operating profit	72 000	
Less directors' remuneration	(18 000)	54 000
Adjustments		
Increase in stocks	(8 000)	
Increase in debtors*	(12 500)	
Increase in creditors*	7 000	13 500
Net inflow		40 500

(b) *Return on investments and servicing of finance*

Interest paid		3 000	
Dividends paid			
Opening balance	7 500		
Annual dividends	10 000		
	17 500		
Less closing balance	10 000		
		7 500	10 500

(c) *Taxation paid*

Opening balance	11 000	
Annual charge	14 000	
	25 000	
Less closing balance	17 000	8 000

(d) *Investing activities*

Opening fixed assets	42 000	
Less depreciation	12 000	
	30 000	
Closing balance	70 000	
Additional assets		40 000

* These are debtors and creditors relating to operating activities.

The cash flow figures in such statements give an indication of the funds being generated by the company for future operations. In this particular example, the actual net cash flow figure is only £2000. However, this is after the payment of £40 000 for new assets. Only £20 000 of cash is raised from outside sources through the issue of new debenture stock.

If the net cash flow for a company figure is low it may be the result of heavy capital expenditure during the period and it could indicate that the company will have to seek additional funds by equity issues, debenture issues or a bank overdraft during the next period. If it does not do this, the company may not be able to finance future expansion. A high net cash flow figure would indicate that the company is generating and obtaining funds, perhaps for some future purchase or expansion policy. If it is generating funds without any specific long-term objective in mind and it cannot use them profitably within the company or through investment, it could reward shareholders through future increases in dividends. If the company generates funds without any planned purpose or profitable investment outlets, it may find itself the subject of a takeover bid. There are companies with good ideas held back by a lack of financial resources that find companies with a high net cash flow very attractive.

In 1991 FRS 1 was issued which required UK companies to publish in their annual report and accounts a cash flow statement instead of a funds flow statement. The format of the cash flow statement is prescribed in the Standard. Inflows and outflows of cash and cash equivalents are classified under five headings. These five headings can be seen in the cash flow statement of XL Co. Ltd shown in Table 20.5.

The ASB defined carefully what it means by cash equivalents. These are short-term highly liquid investments that are readily convertible to known amounts of cash. Generally, only investments with maturities of less than three months would qualify.

Companies were given the choice of whether to adopt the direct or indirect method (gross or net method) of presentation. The direct method is the most revealing method. It is essentially a summary of the cash book, showing separate amounts for such items as cash received from sales and for cash paid to suppliers. The ASB encourage the use of this method but it is not the method adopted by most companies.

Table 20.5 presents the information in the format of the indirect method. The indirect method nets certain of the inflow and outflow figures. FRS1 requires certain notes to be provided to support the cash flow statements. These notes are required whether the direct or indirect format is followed. The notes cover

- the reconciliation of the operating profit to the net cash inflow from operating activities;
- an analysis of changes in cash and cash equivalents during the year;
- an analysis of the items within the 'financing' section of the cash flow statements showing the movement between the opening and closing balance sheet.

The first of these required notes for XL Co. Ltd is shown in note (a) to the cash flow statement. The other required notes for XL would be:

Analysis of changes in cash and cash equivalents during the year

Opening balance	10 000
Net cash inflow	2 000
Closing balance	12 000

Analysis of changes in 'finance' items during the year

	Share capital	Loans
Opening balance	60 000	11 000
Cash inflows/outflows	0	20 000
Closing balance	60 000	31 000

The ASB require these reconciliations in order to facilitate the use of both the cash flow statement and the balance sheet in assessing the short-term liquidity, and the longer-term financial viability of a company. The XL example is of course very basic.

The cash flow statement for Wolseley plc is shown in Table 20.6. The cash flow for Glaxo plc was shown on p. 698. These statements illustrate the amount of detail provided to users of accounts.

Although the statement of cash flows being referred to relates to the past, it indicates the type of statement needing to be produced for planning purposes. It is being produced by companies for shareholders and potential investors because it is the cash flow statement that shows most clearly how a company has been using its financial resources. It is needed for shareholder accountability and management purposes.

The investment analyst's cash flow

One other way in which the term 'cash flow' is used is as employed by investment analysts. In this sense it has an entirely different meaning to the accountant's terminology. By 'cash flow' the analyst simply means a company's retained profits plus depreciation. The retained profits are the profits of the year after deduction of taxation, interest and dividends but before any allocation of the profits to different reserve accounts. The depreciation obviously has to be added back to the retained profit figure as it is not an outflow of the cash resources of the business. It should be noticed that it is not the same term as net cash flow as shown in Table 20.5. The analyst's cash flow in the example of the XL Co. would total £27 000, which is the profit after tax less dividends plus depreciation (£25 000 − £10 000 + £12 000).

The analyst's cash flow shows the amount of funds generated by the business that are available to finance the company's investment. It is the total available over the period, and it is arrived at before deducting any capital investments that may have taken place during the year. It is not strictly a cash flow, because the profits may not yet have been realized in cash. The sales may not yet have resulted in cash for the business, but at the end of the year merely be represented by an increase in debtors. Similarly, the expenses deducted in arriving at profits may not yet have resulted in an outflow of the cash from the business; they may be included in the current liabilities of the company.

Cash budgets reveal, among other things, the quantity of funds available to the company for short-term investment. Opportunities in this direction should certainly be taken; to the company, £1 is £1 whether acquired as straight trading profit or as interest on an investment.

Surplus cash will therefore call for an investment decision. This should be based on the necessary facts:

1. the size of the amounts available;
2. the period for which the cash is available;
3. whether there is any possibility that the cash may be required prematurely to make unexpected payments.

The funds should be placed with creditworthy borrowers. The aim should be to secure the maximum interest possible consistent with a satisfactory level of risk and the required degree of liquidity or negotiability. The higher the degree of risk in the short-term investment, the greater should be the interest being offered. The investing company will have to balance the expected interest with the risks.

The fact that a certain investment can easily be realized is important; it is similar to cash at short call and provides a company with a reserve, a safety margin in its cash planning. For example, funds placed on a fixed deposit for three months with a local authority or merchant bank will not normally be repaid before the expiry of the three

Table 20.6 *Extract from Annual Report 1994 of Wolseley Plc*

	1994 £000	1994 £000	1993 £000	1993 £000
Net cash inflow from operating activities				
(Note a)		164 417		156 103
Returns on investments and servicing of finance				
Interest received	14 632		17 210	
Interest paid	(19 877)		(26 466)	
Interest element of finance lease rental payments	(506)		(454)	
Dividends paid	(38 970)		(30 818)	
Net cash outflow from returns on investments and servicing of finance		(44 721)		(40 528)
Taxation				
UK corporation tax including ACT	(11 688)		(23 042)	
Overseas tax	(29 393)		(27 608)	
Certificates of tax deposit	18		(373)	
Tax paid		(41 063)		(51 023)
Investing activities				
Purchase of tangible fixed assets	(48 284)		(33 546)	
Purchase of businesses (net of cash and cash equivalents acquired) (Note f)	(108 679)		(30 837)	
Sale of tangible fixed assets	9 854		8 480	
Minority interest	162		—	
Net cash outflow from investing activities		(146 947)		(55 903)
Net cash (outflow)/inflow before financing		(68 314)		8 649
Financing				
Issues of ordinary share capital	86 200		19 324	
Share issue expenses	(1 782)		(225)	
Net repayment of multi option facility	—		(78 125)	
Repayment of debentures	—		(329)	
(Repayment)/increase of amounts borrowed	(42 965)		170 156	
Capital element of finance lease rental payments	(636)		(1 900)	
Net cash inflow from financing (Note d)		40 817		108 901
(Decrease)/increase in cash and cash equivalents (Note b)		(27 497)		117 550

months. Treasury bills also usually run for three months but they are easily negotiable. This also applies, as their title suggests, to negotiable certificates of deposit issued by the clearing banks.

Call money placed with the clearing banks is liquid, but the interest offered is low. Time deposits with banks offer more attractive interest rates. Whereas deposits in current accounts earn little or no interest, money placed in a deposit account earns higher interest. This form of investment is easy to undertake. It is extremely liquid (only a short period of notice is required before the withdrawal of funds) and any amount can be deposited; there is no upper or lower limit.

Brief details will now be given of the other forms of liquid assets in which UK companies invest.

Certificates of deposit

A certificate of deposit is an acknowledgement of a deposit issued by a bank. This certificate is negotiable. The period of issue is usually for a minimum of three months and a maximum of five years. The rates of interest payable are higher than those on bank bills, and higher than, or at least equal to, those payable on local authority loans and interbank deposits. Therefore they offer reasonably attractive rates of interest to companies with money available for known periods of time.

It may be thought surprising that this form of investment instrument is necessary. Money can always be deposited with banks and a rate of interest earned. If a negotiable security is required, then a local authority bond, or a bank bill, may be thought suitable. However, banks are always keen to attract deposits of large sums of money for a fixed period of time and will also now acknowledge receipt of funds by issuing a negotiable certificate.

A secondary market exists involving the discount houses, who find the certificates an attractive security to hold, particularly those with three months or less to run.

The discount houses as traders in short-term negotiable instruments see this as a natural extension of their activities. The certificate requires an effective and efficient secondary market if it is to be a liquid asset. The company holding the certificate needs to know that a buyer can be found at short notice should it need to convert the certificate into cash before its maturity. The holder wishes to be able to telephone a secondary market dealer, agree a rate of discount and then arrange to deliver the certificate and receive the cash. This is in fact the position in the London market.

There is no need to register the certificate, neither is there any stamp duty or transfer deed. It is the ease of dealing that makes the certificate of deposit particularly attractive to companies with unpredictable cash flows that may at times need cash for unexpected purposes.

British Government securities

Government securities include treasury bills and treasury stock. They are issued on behalf of the central government when they need cash. They can be purchased and sold through the money market, as can the certificates of deposit and local authority securities. In London the discount houses have an important role to play in this liquid asset market. They are able to sell the securities to companies when companies have cash available to buy and are able to purchase the securities immediately when the companies are short of cash and wish to sell.

Local authority debt

Local authority bonds can be purchased with a period to maturity of anything from two days to five years. The investing company, accordingly, would buy a security with a life-span correlated as closely as possible to that of its surplus funds. The interest rate would of course be higher for a bond which had a longer period to run to redemption. Local authority bonds have a lower level of liquidity than most of the other investment options, and the market for them is small.

The financial manager of a company has to maintain a balance between liquidity and profitability. A certain amount of cash or near cash needs to be available. Liquid assets are near cash. A portfolio of liquid assets is required, some of which can be realized within a few days and some within a few months. The shorter the period for which the funds are deposited or the shorter the maturity of the liquid assets purchased, the lower is the rate of return being earned. The funds have to be there when required and yet not be wasted by being placed on call. This involves detailed cash budgeting and awareness of the opportunities available in the monetary market.

Example 20.1

You are the treasurer of a company. It is Monday morning and you have been presented with the next two weeks' estimated cash flows as follows:

Cash flow forecast for two weeks ending 1 April 1994

	Opening balance	−3000

Day	Daily Net Flow
Mon.	−2000
Tues.	−2500
Wed.	+1000
Thurs.	+ 500
Fri.	+1000
Mon.	−2000
Tues.	+1000
Wed.	+ 500
Thurs.	− 500
Fri.	+1000

You are trying to decide how best to cover your borrowing needs. Given the information below:

1. What is the cheapest method of funding?
2. How will you fund the deficits, and give your reasoning (give broad ranges only), given the answer to (1)?

Interest rate information

			per annum
Borrowing pounds via overdraft	(base + 1%)	=	6.5%
Borrowing pounds for 2 weeks	(LIBOR + ⅜)	=	
	(6¹⁄₁₆ + ⅜)	=	6.4375%
Borrowing pounds overnight	(9% + ⅜)	=	9.375%
Borrowing pounds with 7-day notice of repayment	(6⅜ + ⅜)	=	6.5625%
Borrowing short-term US$s		=	3.000%

It will be noticed that all UK advances are based on a ⅜ mark up in interest rates. The minimum issue of US$ is £5 million. Rates include all commissions.

Answer

1. *Borrowing dollars*
If dollars are borrowed they will be exchanged at spot and repaid in two weeks' time. With the rates in the market, there will be a loss on the currency exchange. Let us say:

$$\text{Spot } £1 = \$1.5140$$

and 2 week

$$\text{Forward } £1 = \$1.5159$$

The company will borrow dollars and will have to give up $1.5140 now to obtain £1. When it repays it will receive $1.5159 for every £1. This is a loss of 0.19 of a cent on each £1 over a two week period. This is equivalent to an annual cost of

$$\frac{0.0019}{1.5159} \times \frac{360}{14} = 3.22\%$$

The cost of foreign borrowing equals the interest rate plus (or minus) the loss (or gain) on foreign exchange. In this case this gives a cost of approximately 6.22%. The 'approximately' is introduced because technically there is a very small extra cost of interest on the foreign exchange loss. In this case this equals 0.00375 of 1%.

$$\text{i.e. } \left(0.03 \times 0.0322 \times \frac{14}{360} \right)$$

The cost of $ borrowing is the cheapest of the alternatives despite the foreign exchange loss.

2. *Forecast Cash flows (£000s)*

Daily surplus/deficits		Cumulative
Opening balance		−3000
Mon.	−2000	−5000
Tues.	−2500	−7500
Wed.	+1000	−6500
Thur.	+ 500	−6000
Fri.	+1000	−5000
Sat.		
Sun.		
Mon.	−2000	−7000
Tues.	+1000	−6000
Wed.	+ 500	−5500
Thurs.	− 500	−6000
Fri.	+1000	−5000
Sat.		

As can be seen from the above table the highest level of borrowing required is £7.5 million and the level required does not drop below £5.0 million. This later amount is referred to as the 'core' level of borrowing. This can be funded with the US$ loan (cost 6.22%).

Any excess can be funded from overdrafts at 6.5%.

20.9 Interest-rate risk management

Interest rates in the future are uncertain. A company could be heavily dependent on floating rate debt; if interest rates rise in the future the company has a higher interest cost than it need have done. Alternatively a company could now borrow large amounts of money at fixed interest rates, only to find that interest rates in the market begin to fall. Again the company is faced with higher interest costs than are necessary.

There are now a number of arrangements and financial techniques available to the treasury manager, to enable him or her to reduce the impact of movements in interest rates. These techniques can be used to hedge against losses, or to speculate in the hope of making gains.

The techniques include:
- forward forward loans;
- forward rate agreements;
- interest rate guarantees;
- caps, collars and floors;
- interest rate futures;
- interest rate swaps.

We will now examine each of these techniques.

Forward forward loans

A company may know that it will need to borrow in future. Let us say its cash flow forecasts indicate that in three months' time it will need to borrow £1 million for a six-month period. The treasurer is worried that interest rates will rise over the next three months. The company is faced with an interest rate risk. It can avoid this by borrowing the £1 million now at today's interest rates for a nine-month period.

It does not need the funds for the first three months so it can invest these. If interest rates rise, as expected, it will gain from the higher interest rates through the interest earned for three months. It will not have to pay the higher interest rates on its borrowed funds because it has agreed now the terms of a fixed interest rate loan.

Such a forward forward agreement means the company knows the interest rates it will have to pay in the future. It takes away the uncertainty. It does not mean that it takes away the risk of an opportunity loss. If interest rates fall in future, against the company's expectations, it will finish up paying higher interest charges than it need have done. If it had waited the three months until it needed the money, before it borrowed, it would have borrowed at lower interest rates.

Forward rate agreements (FRA)

This is an arrangement whereby a company can lock itself into borrowing at a future date at an interest rate that is agreed now. It differs from the forward forward agreement, in that the funds are not obtained now, but when they are needed. It is the rate of interest to be charged in the future that is agreed now. Clearly this takes away the uncertainty.

Similarly FRAs can be arranged for investing money. For example a company may know now that it will have £10 million available in one year's time. It is worried that interest rates will fall over the next 12 months. The FRA will fix now the rate of interest that it will earn in the future when the company invests the money.

FRAs are usually supplied by banks. It has to be appreciated that the FRA is a different transaction to the actual borrowing (or the lending) of the funds. The borrowing or lending can be with one bank and the FRA with another bank.

The way in which the FRA works is that it is only the difference between the agreed interest that would be paid at the forward rate and the interest actually paid on the borrowing that is transferred between the company and the bank who enter into the FR arrangement. The FRA does not involve the lending of the principle sum or the actual interest paid on this sum.

Let's say a company enters into an FRA agreement with Bank A. That means it can borrow £1 million at say 12% in six months' time. The period of the loan will be 12 months. In six months' time if the market rate of interest is 14%, the company will borrow from Bank B at 14%, and have to pay Bank B £140 000 interest over the year. It will receive 'compensation' however from Bank A of £20 000 (the difference between interest at 14% and the agreed 12%).

If on the other hand the market rate of interest falls to 9%, the company will borrow from Bank B at 9% and pay Bank B £90 000 interest over the year. It will also however have to pay 'compensation' to Bank A of £30 000.

As can be seen the FRA agreement between the company and Bank A means that the company eliminates the uncertainty. It knows precisely what the cost of its borrowing will be in six months' time. An FRA does not mean the company necessarily gains financially over what it could have achieved without the agreement.

In fact the FRA market is mainly an inter-bank market. Non-bank businesses can often get their banker to quote a 'forward' loan interest rate. This means that not only will a bank tell a customer how much it will cost to borrow today, but also how much it will charge if the customer wishes to borrow in six months' time. In the example therefore the company should be able to get Bank B to agree that it will lend in six months' time at a predetermined interest rate. This eliminates uncertainly, making an FRA unnecessary.

Interest-rate guarantees

Interest-rate guarantees (IRGs) are short-term options, usually with a maximum maturity of one year. If a company wants longer term guarantees it can use caps, collars or floors.

Interest-rate guarantees (IRGs) or interest-rate options (IROs) allow a borrowing company to hedge against upward movements in interest rates. The company can do this without losing (other than the cost of the guarantee or option) if there is a downward movement in interest rate. They are similar in this respect to other forms of options.

Similarly if a company plans to invest funds in the future an IRG or IRO will allow the company to hedge against downward movements in interest rates. If interest rates should rise, the company just invests in the market, earns higher interest and pays the cost of the option.

The IRG involves the payment of a premium to the seller of the guarantee, which has to be paid whether or not the option element of the guarantee is exercised.

A major difference between IRGs and FRAs is that although both protect against downside risk, only the IRG allows the holder the opportunity to gain from a favourable movement in interest rates. If a borrower is worried about interest rates rising by the time the company needs to borrow, both the IRG and FRA will 'lock' the company into the maximum amount of interest that will need to be paid.

If, however, having entered into an FRA or IRG the interest rates fall by the time the company wishes to borrow, only the IRG will allow the company to benefit.

Caps, collars and floors

These are hedging techniques that can be used to cover risk on longer-term borrowing. As the name implies a 'cap' is an upper-level interest rate, and a 'floor' a lower-level interest rate. With a collar a company enters into an arrangement such that it will borrow for a period of time with a floating interest rate, but it knows it will not have to pay more than the 'cap' rate, but on the other hand it will not be able to pay less than the 'floor' rate.

A cap

Let us assume Booker plc wishes to borrow £10 million for five years. The company's bank will only lend the money at a floating rate, of say LIBOR + 2½%. The company's treasurer is worried that interest rates will rise in future.

One solution for the treasurer is to take the loan on the bank's terms, but also to buy an interest rate 'cap' agreement. The cap is for a rate of let us say 14%. At the present time LIBOR is 10%, so the company is paying 12½% interest per annum. Let us say interest rates rise in future and in year 3 of the loan LIBOR rises to 12%. In this situation the cap agreement will become operative.

Booker plc will only have to pay 14%, not the 14½% which is the level of the floating rate.

A 'cap' sets an upper limit on the interest to be paid, but allows the company to benefit from falling interest rates. The company has to pay to enter a 'cap' agreement. How much it will pay depends on how close the level of interest agreed as a cap is to the level of interest rates in the market at the date the agreement is signed.

A collar

It is possible for a company to reduce the cost of hedging with a 'cap' agreement, by simultaneously entering into a floor agreement. The bank's risk in an interest rate cap agreement is that it will lose if interest rates rise in the market but will not gain if interest rates fall. If interest rates fall over time all the bank receives is the premium paid when the agreement is signed.

If the company wishing to borrow enters into an interest-rate floor agreement with a bank at the same time that it enters into an interest rate 'cap' agreement with the bank, it will reduce the premium paid for entering into the hedge. It will be improving the bank's expected financial outcome.

In the example above let us say Booker plc enters into a 'floor' agreement with the bank at say a level of 9.5%, it will improve the bank's position and therefore reduce the premium that the company has to pay. We have described above what happens if interest rates rise. Now with this floor agreement, let us say interest rates begin to fall. Assume LIBOR drops to 6%. Without the floor agreement Booker will only be paying the bank 8½% on its borrowings. It has however entered into a floor agreement. Booker therefore has to pay the 9.5% agreed lower level.

This arrangement whereby a company enters simultaneously into both a 'cap' agreement and a 'floor' agreement is known as a collar.

20.10 Interest-rate futures contracts

The nature and purpose of futures contracts were outlined in Chapter 11. In this chapter the use of one form of futures contract will be considered. An interest rate futures contract has, in common with all contracts, a buyer and a seller. The buyer agrees to receive the interest on a particular sum of money on an agreed future date. The seller of the contract agrees to pay the interest on the sum of money on the agreed future date. The rate of interest is specified in the contract.

Futures contracts are legally binding agreements. Unlike options it is not possible for one of the parties to decide not to exercise the futures contract. The buyer and seller will make profits or losses depending on how interest rates move in the money market between the time when the contract is taken out and when it is time for delivery.

The interest rate futures (IRF) contract is not concerned with the borrowing or lending of the capital sum. As with an FRA the futures deal involves a separate contract, additional to the agreement to borrow or lend a sum of money. An IRF offers the opportunity to hedge against interest-rate risk.

When hedging by means of futures two separate sets of transactions take place, one in the money market (the borrowing or lending of the principle sum) and the other in the futures market. The futures market deal is approximately equal in size to the money market transaction, but is designed to be in the opposite direction. This means that if the company loses in the money market it gains in the futures market. But if it gains in the money market it loses in the futures market.

There are a number of futures markets around the world. The London Financial Futures Exchange (LIFFE) was established in 1982. It is the futures exchange in Europe offering the widest range of futures contracts. The Exchange offers six types of short-term interest-rate contracts, six types of bond futures contracts, and one type of stock market index-linked futures contract.

The contract

Table 20.7 shows an extract from the *Financial Times* of 5 October 1994. The heading shows the name of the contract and the market in which the contract is listed. The first six futures contracts referred to are listed on LIFFE, the last two are listed on the

International Money Market (IMM). The IMM is located in Chicago and is the most important futures market in the world.

The currencies to which the interest-rate futures refer is shown in the headings. The statistics shown include the opening prices of a contract, the change in the day in the price of the contract, intra-day highs and lows, and the estimated volume of trading in the contract on the previous day.

All short-term futures contracts are based on borrowing or lending for a three-month period. This means that the interest rate for borrowing or lending is fixed for a three-month period starting from an agreed future date. Let us say a company enters into such a contract in October 1994. It will be determining the rate of interest at which it will borrow for a three-month period starting at a future date, either December 1994, or March or June 1995.

In the LIFFE the dates for all futures contracts follow a March/June/September/December cycle. The buyer of such a contract on 1 October 1994 could choose a contract with a December starting date. This is the earliest futures contract it could enter into. They would be fixing the interest rate for the first three months of 1995. The contract with a starting date the furthest into the future would be one for 18 months ahead of the next starting date. This means that in October 1994 the borrower could be locking into an interest rate it will pay for three months from the end of June 1996.

It should be appreciated that LIFFE (as are all future exchanges) is a market-place. There is a primary market in which buyers and sellers agree on new contracts. There is also a secondary market in which futures contracts already in existence can be bought and sold before their expiry date. A company that enters into the initial contact to sell a futures at an agreed future date could therefore pass on this commitment to another party, by selling the contract before the expiry date.

It is important to remember that an interest rate futures contract is in fact buying and selling only the cash flow associated with the interest-rate payments. The actual loan has to be obtained from another source. A fully hedged position involves two separate sets of transactions, (1) borrowing *or* lending in the money markets, (2) buying *and* selling in the futures market.

The company entering into futures contracts is seeking to ensure that they will only have to pay interest on a loan at a rate of say 10%. If interest rates in the money market rise to say 12% by the time the company needs the funds the company obtaining the loan will have to pay the lender the 12%, but will make a profit of 2% on the futures contracts. LIFFE and other futures exchanges guarantee this position, so if the counterparty in the futures contracts goes out of business, the exchange authorities will pay the 2% difference.

The tick

The prices of the contracts are not quoted in terms of interest rates. The convention is that they are priced at 100 minus the annual interest rate to be paid. So a contract shown as being priced at 90 is effectively quoting a forward interest rate of 10% per annum (i.e. $100 - 90$). This 10% is the borrowing rate. The normal spread in this market is ⅛th of 1%, which means the interest paid on an investment for the same period would be 9.875% (i.e. $10\% - 0.125\%$).

In Table 20.7 the three-months eurodollar is quoted for December on LIFFE as 93.97 and on IMM as 93.96. This means a borrowing rate of 6.03% or 6.04%.

The movement allowed in these futures prices is in units of one basis point – of one hundredth of 1% (i.e. 0.01%) of the base of 100. This means that the smallest movement in a contract with a price of 90 is to 89.99 or 90.01. This smallest movement is known as the 'tick size' (0.01).

The profit or loss with such movements in futures contracts prices needs to be converted into money. The three-month sterling interest futures market is based on a contract size of £500 000 (see Table 20.7). A movement of one basis point therefore means £50. A further complication is that the price is based on annual interest rates, whereas

Table 20.7 *Extract from* Financial Times *listing futures contracts*

	Open	Sett price	Change	High	Low	Est. vol.	Open int.
Three month sterling futures (LIFFE) £500 000 points of 100%							
Dec.	93.14	93.20	+0.04	93.21	93.12	23 038	165 596
Mar.	92.22	92.28	+0.04	92.29	92.18	18 016	83 085
June	91.61	91.64	+0.02	91.65	91.56	6 655	51 048
Sept.	91.15	91.20	+0.01	91.22	91.14	3 497	52 350
Three month Euromark futures (LIFFE)* DM1m points of 100%							
Dec.	94.63	94.63	−0.01	94.65	94.62	23 978	186 476
Mar.	94.22	94.21	−0.02	94.23	94.19	26 147	169 785
June	93.77	93.79	—	93.80	93.74	13 691	108 340
Sept.	93.41	93.42	—	93.44	93.37	13 417	72 005
Three month Eurolira int. rate futures (LIFFE) L1000m points of 100%							
Dec.	90.64	90.59	−0.10	90.66	90.50	6 755	33 281
Mar.	89.87	89.90	−0.06	89.94	89.85	2 417	16 064
June	89.34	89.37	−0.05	89.42	89.30	1 293	15 517
Sept.	88.90	88.99	−0.04	89.02	88.90	269	15 162
Three month Euro Swiss franc futures (LIFFE) SFr1m—points of 100%							
Dec.	95.62	95.62	—	95.63	95.58	2 799	23 454
Mar.	95.23	95.23	−0.01	95.23	95.20	675	12 077
June	94.86	94.87	−0.01	94.89	94.85	216	6 979
Sept.		94.58	+0.01			0	996
Three month ECU futures (LIFFE) Ecu1m points of 100%							
Dec.	93.59	93.60	−0.02	93.62	93.56	893	7 895
Mar.	93.03	93.01	−0.03	93.05	92.98	1 135	5 561
June	92.50	92.50	−0.02	92.51	92.47	482	2 898
Sept.	92.09	92.10	−0.01	92.10	92.06	85	1 052
Three month Eurodollar (LIFFE)* $1m points of 100%							
Dec.	93.97	93.97	−0.02	93.97	93.97	30	2 123
Mar.	93.57	93.59	−0.02	93.57	93.57	23	1 435
June	93.17	93.18	−0.02	93.17	93.17	28	274
Sept.		92.88	−0.02			0	52
Three month Eurodollar (IMM) $1m points of 100%							
Dec.	93.96	93.95	−0.01	93.99	93.94	135 921	497 081
Mar.	93.58	93.59	—	93.62	93.58	134 624	410 189
June	93.18	93.16	−0.02	93.22	93.15	61 428	298 633
US Treasury bill futures (IMM) $1m per 100%							
Dec.	94.54	94.54	−0.01	94.56	94.52	3 166	20 897
Mar.	94.14	94.14	−0.01	94.16	94.14	1 315	9 394
June	—	93.75	—	93.76	93.73	289	2459

* LIFFE futures traded on APT

the contracts are only for three months. This gives a value per tick (per basis point) on a three-month contract of £12.50.

Example

If interest rates fall by 0.5%, that is by 50 ticks (0.5% ÷ 0.01), an investor who has bought 20 such contracts will therefore gain by 20 × 50 × £12.50 = £12 500 (i.e. the number of contracts × number of ticks × value per tick).

A futures contract will rise in value as interest rates fall in value, the price being 100 less the interest rate. Buying a futures contract does not mean that a sum of money, such as £500 000 × 90, ever has to be paid. The only cash that ever has to transfer between the buyer and seller is the amount covering interest payments.

The hedge

For a company wishing to hedge a loan it will initially sell futures if it expects interest rates to rise. If a company wishes to hedge funds deposited against falling interest rates they will initially buy futures contracts.

The price of a contract (i.e. 90) represents the interest to be paid on a sum of money (i.e. 10%). It is being quoted on an index basis. What a company is buying or selling is the interest over a period of time on a sum of money. The purchaser of the contract will receive that sum of money. The seller will deliver that sum of money. The sum of money is due for delivery in the middle of the agreed month. Very few contracts are in fact left to mature. Offsetting transactions are usually entered into and only the balance of money transferred. This offsetting is illustrated in Example 20.2.

Example 20.2

We will demonstrate how a short-term interest-rate futures contract can be used to hedge against interest-rate risk. The treasurer of Atkinson plc plans to borrow £1 million in two months' time for a period of three months. It is now 1 March. She believes that interest rates will rise in future and wishes to take out a future contract on LIFFE to minimize the company's risk.

The following prices are being quoted on 1 March.

3 month £ sterling futures contract (£500 000)

Mar.	92.00
June	91.00
Sept.	90.00

The current interest rate (in March) is 8%. The market clearly expects interest rates to rise in value. In March the market expects interest rates in June to be 9%. (That is why it is quoting a price of 91.00.) In May interest rates in fact rise to 10%. This will mean the price of June futures contracts being quoted in May will fall to 90.0. Interest rates have risen more quickly than the market expects.

Required

Show how an interest rate futures contract can be used as a hedge by Atkinson plc.

Necessary steps to answer questions

The first step is to calculate the target interest cost. The second step is to decide on the number of futures contracts that need to be bought or sold, to complete a hedge. The third step is to decide the appropriate date for the contracts. The fourth step, and perhaps the most difficult, is to decide whether the company needs to be a buyer or seller of a futures contract.

The rule with regard to buying or selling is that if the company wishes to hedge against rising interest rates it will initially sell futures contracts. (This is called a short hedge.) If the company wishes to hedge against falling interest rates it will initially buy futures contracts (called a long hedge). Why this rule?

If interest rates rise over time, the price of futures contracts fall (100 − interest rate) over time. We initially agree to sell at a future date (something at present we do not own). As the date for delivery gets nearer (the expiry date of the contract), the price of the futures contracts will have fallen. We will then be able to buy in the market a contract with the same expiry date at a cheaper price than we agreed to sell it for. We settle for the difference, a profit. This profit compensates for the higher interest rates we are paying on the actual borrowing.

Let us say that Atkinson plc expects interest rates to rise. It is now 1 March. The company wishes to borrow on 1 May and repay on 1 August.

The treasurer will sell June futures contracts now at a price of 91. In May the treasurer will buy futures contracts at a price of 90. The gain on futures helps offset the higher interest charge paid on the borrowings.

Answer

Step 1

The interest target is 8% × £1 000 000 × ¼ = £20 000. This is based on interest rates at 1 March.

Step 2

Two contracts need to be entered into to cover the £1 million.

Step 3

The company as at 1 March could choose contracts dated March, June or September. The March date is no use as the contracts will have expired by the time the company needs to borrow. Any interest rate movement affecting borrowing in May will affect futures prices only after the March contracts have expired. It would be normal to choose the June contract, the contract with the next expiry date following the date the loan is required.

Step 4

The treasurer wishes to hedge against rising interest rates and so will initially agree to sell futures contracts. Futures contracts will fall in value if as expected interest rates rise. The treasurer will then enter into an offsetting futures transaction by buying futures.

Transactions

Money market   On 1 May the company borrows £1 000 000 at 10% for a three-month period. Interest cost £100 000 × ¼ = £25 000. Loss against target £5000.

Futures market
- *On 1 March*   Sell 2 sterling contracts at £91
  to be delivered in June.   £91
- *In May*   Buy two contracts at £90 for
  delivery in June.   £90
                                                                           ____
- *In June*   Close contracts.   1 = 100 ticks

Total profit 2 (Contracts) × 100 × £12.50 = £2500

This gain of £2500 provides some compensation for the target loss of £5000.

Efficiency of hedge

It should be noted that a futures hedge is not always a perfect hedge. It does not always fully compensate for the changes in interest costs resulting from changes in interest rates in the money market.

The efficiency of the hedge depends on two factors:

1. How close is the movement in the price of future contracts to the movement in actual interest rates? In the Atkinson example, we assumed that the movement in interest rates between March and May was from 8% to 10%. However we only allowed for

movement in the June futures price from 91.0 to 90.0, a much smaller movement. In fact in the market the movement in futures prices is approximately in line with changes in interest rates in the money market.

If we had allowed the interest rates and the futures price to move at the same rate we would have had a perfect hedge, the June futures price moving from 91.0 in March to 89.0 in May:

1 March: Sell two contracts at   £91
    May: Buy two contracts at   £89
                              £2 = 200 ticks

    June: Close the contracts
            Profit = 2 (contracts) $\times$ 200 (ticks) $\times$ 12.50 = £5000

It should be appreciated the movement in futures prices is not always exactly in line with the movement in interest rates. It is not usual therefore to obtain a perfect hedge.

2. The second factor on which the efficiency of the hedge depends is how close is the amount of money covered in the hedge (number of contracts $\times$ size of contract) to the amount of money borrowed or deposited. In our example we had an exact match. The £1 000 000 borrowed equalled two contracts each for £500 000. This is unusual. In futures markets contracts are for standard sizes and so it is not always possible to match the amount to be hedged with an exact number of contracts. It may be necessary to enter into contracts for a greater or lesser amount than the sum at risk.

It might be possible to obtain an exact match in the over the counter market.

Over the counter

There is nothing new about futures and options contracts. They have long existed in the commodities market with deals made between farmers and food processors. The first futures exchange that offered deals in other derivatives, that is in currencies, interest rates and stock market indices, was established in Chicago in 1973.

What is relatively new is what is called the 'over the counter' (OTC) market. This is a market, not based around a specific exchange, in which trades are arranged in any size between a bank and its customer, or between two banks. Such deals are not subject to the regulation of an exchange.

In the OTC market, prices are negotiated between the parties and the terms are 'customized' to suit the needs of the parties. This is in contrast to deals in established exchanges, where prices are quoted, and the terms are standardized.

Example 20.3

The corporate treasurer of Cradley plc plans to borrow 10 million Italian lire in three months' time for a period of three months. There is a possibility of a change in government in Italy and interest rates have recently been volatile. The treasurer has received a number of suggestions as to how to protect against interest rate risk. These include:

1. an FRA in Italian lire;
2. futures contracts in Italian lire;
3. an interest-rate guarantee in Italy;
4. a collar OTC interest rate option in Italy.

The following prices are available. It is now 1 April.

FRA in three months for periods of up to six months at 86.25

Futures
Italian 3 months futures (Lire 1 000 000 contract)
June   88.00
September   87.75

Interest rate guarantee
A guarantee at 13.75% is available at a premium of 0.25% of the amount to be borrowed.

Collar
A collar, with a ceiling exercise price of 13.9% and a floor of 12%, is available at a premium of 0.1% of the amount to be borrowed.

The current base rate in Italy is 12%. Cradley can borrow in Italy at base plus ½%.

Required:

Evaluate with hindsight the effects of the four alternative hedging strategies that have been suggested to the treasurer, if:

1. interest rates in Italy increase in three months' time to a base rate of 14%;
2. interest rates in Italy decrease in three months' time to a base rate of 11%.

Comment on your findings. State any assumptions you make.

Answer

1. *Forward rate agreement in Italian lire*

Effective cost $100 - 86.25 = 13.75\%$
Cost of 3 months loan = L10 million $\times$ 13.75% $\times$ ³⁄₁₂ = 343 750 lire

This is the cost whatever happens to the level of interest rates in the future.
If interest rates rise to 14%, Cradley will borrow in the market at 14.5% and receive compensation from the bank with whom it has an FRA – for the difference of 0.75%. If interest rates fall to 11%, Cradley will borrow in the market at 11.5% and pay compensation of 2.25% to the bank with whom it has the agreement.

2. *Futures contracts in Italian lire*

(a)   Target outcome
      $10\,000\,000 \times 12\frac{1}{2}\% \times$ ³⁄₁₂   = L312 500

With 14% rates in future:
(b)   Expect interest rates to rise, so sell futures now for September delivery.
      Need 10 contacts (loan 10 million lire, each contract for 1 million lire).
      At beginning of July, at the time of borrowing in the money market, undertake reverse futures agreement. That is to buy futures for September date.

(c)   *Transactions*
      Money Market
      Borrow L10 million on 1 July
      Cost
         $10\,000\,000 \times 14\frac{1}{2}\% \times$ ³⁄₁₂   = L362 500
      Loss against target   = L50 000
                        Futures market
      1 April
      Sell 10 futures at 87.75 for September
      1 July
      Buy 10 futures at 85.75 for September

Note: It is assumed the futures contract moves by the same amount (2%) as the move in the interest rates in the money market.

30 September
Close transactions:
- Move of 200 ticks (i.e. 2%)
- Tick size
  L1 000 000 × (100 of 1%) × ³⁄₁₂

  $$= \text{Lire } 25$$

- 10 contracts

Outcome: profit on futures of:

10 × 200 × 25 lire	= Lire 50 000

(d) *Overall cost*

L10 million × 14.5% × ³⁄₁₂	= L362 500
Less profit on futures	50 000
	L312 500

With 11% base rate in future

(b) Sell futures now for September delivery. On 1 July buy futures for September delivery.
(c) Transactions

Money market

Cost of borrowing on 1 July	
L10 million × 11½% × ³⁄₁₂	= L287 500
Gain against target	= L25 000

Futures Market
1 April
Sell 10 futures at 87.75 for September
1 July
Buy 10 futures at 88.75 for September
(Assume futures contract price moves by same percentage points as move in interest rates, i.e. 1%)
30 September
Close transaction:

Move of 100 ticks
Outcome: loss of:

10 × 100 × 25	= L25 000

(d) Overall cost

L10 million × 11.5% × ³⁄₁₂	= 287 500
Plus loss on futures	25 000
	312 500

3. *Interest rate guarantee*

Market rates rise to 14%.
The company has the choice of either borrowing in the market at 14.5% and paying the cost of the option, or to borrow under the terms of the guarantee at 13.75% and paying the cost of the option. Clearly the latter is preferable. The option will be exercised. The cost will be:

L10 million × 13.75 × ³⁄₁₂	= 343 750
plus	
cost of guarantee L10 million × 0.25%	= 25 000
	368 750

Market rates fall to 11%
The option will not be exercised. The cost of the finance will be

L10 million × 11.5% × 3/12   =287 500
plus
cost of guarantee   = 25 000
                                          312 500

4. *Collar*

Interest rates rise to 14%
The option will be exercised. Choice is between borrowing in the market at 14.5% plus premium, or borrowing at 13.9% plus premium.
Cost:

Lire 10 million × 13.9% × 3/12   = 347 500
plus
10 million × 0.1%   = 10 000
                                          357 500

Interest rates fall to 11%
Collar will be effective. It guaranteed that the most Cradley would have to pay was 13.9% (plus premium) and the least Cradley would have to pay would be 12% (plus premium). Cradley having entered into a 'collar' contract cannot take advantage of the opportunity to borrow in market at 11.5%.
Cost with 'floor'

Lire 10 million × 12% × 3/12   = 300 000
plus
Premium   = 10 000
                                          310 000

Summary of costs

	Base rate 14%	Base Rate 11%
FRA	343 750	343 750
Futures	312 500	312 500
Interest rate guarantee	368 750	312 500
Collar	357 500	310 000

With the rates given in the question, clearly the FRA is unattractive. The interest rate guarantee is inferior to the futures contract, because although they have the same cost with interest rates at 11%, the futures contracts have the lower cost at the higher interest rates. The choice is between the collar and the futures. Futures give a lower cost at higher interest rates (the difference between borrowing at 12.5% and 13.9%, plus premium). The collar gives a lower cost at lower interest rates (the difference between 12% plus premium and 12.5%).

Duration

We have seen that firms can hedge interest-rate risk by using interest-rate futures contracts. It is also possible to hedge interest-rate risk by matching the duration of liabilities with the duration of assets. Interest-rate risk is affected both by the maturity date and coupon rate of debt instruments. A risk measure that takes both these factors into consideration is called duration. Duration measures the weighted average maturity of an asset's or liability's cash flows. The weights are determined by present value factors and expressed in years and fractions of years.

The greater the duration the greater the risk; zero coupon bonds will have a duration equal to the time to maturity while the duration of an interest paying bond will be less than the time to maturity with higher coupon bonds having lower durations. Overall risk can be established by calculating the duration of a group of assets or liabilities. This can be done by calculating an average of the duration of the individual items weighted by the market value of each item.

The concept of duration is particularly useful for financial institutions who receive deposits and invest these in a portfolio of securities. They will seek to immunize themselves from interest-rate risk. Immunization occurs when:

$$\begin{matrix} \text{duration of} \\ \text{assets} \end{matrix} \times \begin{matrix} \text{market value} \\ \text{of assets} \end{matrix} = \begin{matrix} \text{duration of} \\ \text{liabilities} \end{matrix} \times \begin{matrix} \text{market value} \\ \text{of liabilities} \end{matrix}$$

The maturity of a bond is clearly a factor to take into account when making an investment decision. It does, however, only indicate when the final cash flow (the redemption) is to be made. It ignores all the interim cash flows resulting from the payment of interest. Duration measures the weighted average time of the cash flow payments. The weights are the present value of the cash flows themselves.

The formula for duration is

$$\sum_{t=1}^{n} \frac{t \times \text{PVCF}t}{K \times \text{TPVCF}}$$

Where

K = Number of periods per annum (i.e. number of interest payments per annum)
n = Number of periods, until maturity ($K \times$ number of years to maturity)
t = period when cash flow to be received
PVCFt = Present value of cash flow in period t (discounted at yield to maturity)
TPVCF = Total PV of all the cash flows.

This looks complicated but is not. The numerator is simply the sum of the time until the receipt (t) of each cash flow multiplied by the present value of the cash flow for the period (t). The denominator is the sum of the PV of the cash flows times K, which is equal to the price of the bond.

We will illustrate the concept of duration with an example. Let us assume we are considering a 9% debenture with 5 years to go before maturity. Interest is paid semi-annually. The price of the bond today is £100. The interest yield and the yield to maturity equal 9%. We are asked to calculate the 'duration' of the debenture.

(1) Periods each of six months	(2) Cash flow per debenture (£)	(3) PV factor at interest rate of 4.5%	(4) PV (column 3 × column 2)	(5) (t × PV) = (column 4 × column 1)
1	4.50	0.957	4.31	4.31
2	4.50	0.916	4.12	8.24
3	4.50	0.876	3.94	11.83
4	4.50	0.839	3.78	15.12
5	4.50	0.802	3.61	18.50
6	4.50	0.768	3.46	20.76
7	4.50	0.735	3.31	23.17
8	4.50	0.703	3.16	25.28
9	4.50	0.673	3.03	27.27
10	104.50	0.644	67.30	673.00
Total			100.00	826.88

$$\text{Duration} = \frac{826.8}{2 \times 100} = 4.13 \text{ years}$$

This is the weighed average time of the cash flow payments. The big payment is of course the redemption. As can be seen this so called 'Macauley' duration is less than its maturity (5 years). For a zero coupon bond the duration is equal to its maturity, this being the only cash payment. If other factors are held constant the lower the coupon rate, the greater the duration of the bond, and the closer it is to its time to maturity.

This measure of duration is used by analysts to measure the volatility of a fixed interest security, the relationship being

$$\frac{-1}{\left(1 + \dfrac{\text{yield}}{K}\right)} \times \text{Macauley duration} \times \text{yield change} \times 100$$

$$= \text{percentage change in price of bond}$$

We will illustrate the use of this formula by continuing with the above example. Let us say there is a change in the market's required yield to maturity from 9% to 10%. Substituting in the equation:

$$\frac{-1}{\left(\dfrac{1 + 0.09}{2}\right)} \times 4.13 \times (+0.010) \times 100$$

The estimate is very accurate for small changes in yields, but is less accurate for large changes.

20.11 Interest-rate swaps

The size of the market for interest rate swaps is huge and yet when they are first explained to those new to the subject few believe such arrangements can work. Here is a situation in which everyone gains and nobody loses. Two companies can come to an arrangement such that both companies reduce their costs of borrowing. The fact that such opportunities exist is due to imperfection in the money market. Basically it is because the risk premiums charged to a company in the fixed rate borrowing market are not necessarily the same as the risk premiums charged in the floating rate market.

Example 20.4

You are the new Finance Director of Douglas plc. The company wishes to borrow £100 million for five years. At a fixed rate of interest this will cost 14% per annum and at a floating rate of LIBOR + 1¼%. A bank has offered to arrange an interest-rate swap for two years with a smaller company Wight plc which can borrow floating rate debt at LIBOR + 2%, and fixed rate borrowing at 15¾%. The bank charges will be ignored.

Because of the existing balance of their debt portfolios Douglas wishes to service a floating rate loan. Wight wishes to service a fixed-rate loan.

Required

Do you think there is an opportunity for an interest rate swap contract? Assume any savings would need to be shared equally between the companies.

Answer

	Douglas	Wight	Difference
Fixed	14%	15.75%	1.75%
Floating	LIBOR + 1.25%	LIBOR + 2%	0.75%
Potential saving			1.00%

Douglas can borrow more cheaply than Wight both fixed and floating rate loans, but its comparative advantage is in fixed-rate borrowing. For both companies to gain from a swap it is necessary for Douglas plc to borrow at fixed rates and to service the floating rate debt.

One solution, which will divide the gains equally, is for Wight to pay Douglas 15¼% fixed, and for Douglas to pay Wight LIBOR + 2%. It should be appreciated, however, that there are many alternative solutions which will result in the gains being shared equally.

Solution

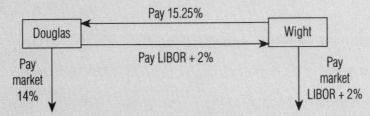

It should be noted that Douglas borrows a fixed-rate loan, even though it services (as is the wish of the company) the floating-rate loan. Douglas's cash outflow now varies over time according to the movement in interest rates.

The fact that these particular inter-company payments result in an equal share of the gain can be proven as follows:

Douglas	*Fixed rate borrowing*		
	Pay the lender	14%	
	Receive from Wight	15.25%	
	Gain		1.25%
Floating			
	Pay Wight	Libor + 2%	
	Opportunity cost	Libor + 1.25%	
	Opportunity loss		0.75%
	Net gain		0.50%
Wight	*Fixed rate*		
	Pay Douglas	15.25%	
	Opportunity cost	15.75%	
	Gain		0.50%
	Floating rate		
	Pay lender	Libor + 2.0%	
	Receive from Douglas	Libor + 2.0%	0
	Net gain		0.50%

Two things need explaining. First, the opportunity cost represents the cost to the company if it had gone to the market and borrowed that form of finance. For example, if Wight had gone to the market for fixed rate finance it would have cost 15.75%, whereas Wight is only paying Douglas 15.25%. This is giving it a saving in servicing fixed rate borrowing of 0.5%.

The second issue is a practical one. A simple approach to working out the rates of interest paid by one company to the other is to hold the rate on the one form of borrowing at the market rate. For example, in this problem the payment from Douglas to Wight to service the floating rate debt (LIBOR + 2%) is the same as the rate paid by Wight to the market. The gains are then all based on the rates for the other form of borrowing.

Remember Douglas actually borrows the fixed rate funds from the market because it can obtain fixed rate borrowing more cheaply than Wight. The issue to be settled is the swap arrangement – how much will Wight transfer to Douglas to service this fixed-rate borrowing.

Solution (based on monetary amounts)

The above was based on interest rates. We will now substitute monetary amounts to prove to the doubters that interest-rate swaps work. The question told us that £100 million was to be borrowed (and the interest-rate streams swapped). Let us assume LIBOR is 12%. It should be appreciated that the capital sums borrowed do not need to be swapped as both companies borrow the same amount (in the same currency).

The cash flows are:

Douglas		*£ million*
Fixed		
Pay lender	—	14.00
Receive from Wight	+	15.25
Floating		
Pay Wight	—	14.00
Net cost		12.75

New cost of floating rate capital 12.75%

This results in a saving of £0.50 million on the cost of floating rate borrowing without a swap (13.25%).

Wight		*£ million*
Pay lender	—	14.00
Receive from Douglas	+	14.00
Pay Douglas	—	15.25
Net cost	—	15.25

This results in a saving of £0.50 million on the cost of fixed-rate borrowing without a swap. It reduces Wight's cost of fixed-rate borrowed capital from 15.75% to 15.25%.

Let us now assume LIBOR equals 15%.

Douglas		*£ million*
Pay lender	—	14.00
Receive from Wight	+	15.25
Pay Wight	—	17.00
The cost of capital is now 15.75%	—	15.75

This again gives a saving of £0.50 million on floating rate debt without a swap (16.5%). It is however more expensive than if Douglas had borrowed at fixed rates.

The company is paying 15.75% for floating rate debt whereas it could have borrowed fixed at 14%. But the company decided before the swap was agreed that it wished to service floating-rate debt. If the market rates of interest rise the cost of floating-rate debt could well be above the cost of fixed-rate debt. The point about the swap arrangement is that for Douglas it has reduced the cost of its floating rate debt – the issue is not whether fixed costs more or less than floating.

For Wight with LIBOR at 15%		*£ million*
Pay lender	—	17.00
Receive from Douglas	+	17.00
Pay Douglas	—	15.25
Net cost	—	15.25

This again gives a saving of £0.50 million over the cost of fixed rate borrowing without a swap.

The market for swaps and other derivatives

The growth in the markets for interest-rate swaps and for currency swaps is dramatic.

The markets grew from almost nothing in the early 1980s to $1000 billion markets ten years later. It should be appreciated that the interest-rate swap market is four times the size of the currency swap market.

The growth reflects not only the use of the market by industrial and commercial companies, but also by financial institutions and public-sector entities. All use these instruments for funding and risk-management purposes.

In the interest-rate swap market approximately half of the deals are inter-bank and half what are termed 'end-users' (that is one non-financial company with another non-financial company). Of course in the 'end-user' market banks often act as an intermediary, charging an arrangement fee.

Approximately half the interest-rate swaps are in US dollars with the other half being in other currencies with the yen, deutschmark and pound sterling being the most popular.

Table 20.8 reveals some interesting aspects of the currency swap market. The currencies involved in the swap are shown, with yen/US dollar swaps being the most common. The value of the swap involving end-users is shown, as is the value that combine an interest-rate swap with a currency swap. An example of this combined swap would be a UK company borrowing a fixed-rate pounds sterling loan, a Germany company borrowing a floating rate DM loan, and each company servicing the other company's debt.

Table 20.8 *Composition of new currency swaps in the first half of 1992*

Currencies	Total notional amount[1,2]	*Of which* Against US dollar[2]	Against other currencies	*Of which* End-user	Fixed/ floating[2]
		in billions of US dollars			
Japanese yen	38.0	26.0	12.1	26.6	16.2
Swiss franc	26.3	8.8	17.5	21.5	7.0
Deutschmark	24.4	10.7	13.7	19.7	9.0
ECU	19.8	11.4	8.4	17.1	9.7
Canadian dollar	16.4	13.8	2.6	15.2	7.3
Pound sterling	15.5	8.2	7.3	13.5	5.2
Italian lira	15.3	8.5	6.8	11.8	8.7
Sub-total	155.7	87.4	68.3	125.4	63.0
Other	49.9	19.2	30.7	35.6	22.3
Minus: double-counting of non-dollar swaps	−49.5		−49.5	−39.1	−16.1
Total	156.1	106.6	49.5	121.9	69.2

[1] Hypothetical underlying amount on which swap payments are based.
[2] Adjusted for double-counting of positions reported by ISDA members.
Source: ISDA.

Worries about derivatives!

There are in fact many other types of derivative, with names such as:

- corridors;
- range-forwards;
- cylinders;
- barrier options;
- compound options.

New, more 'exotic' versions are being created all the time. They are all variations on the themes described in this and other chapters in the book.

A swap is a financial derivative. Financial regulators are concerned with certain aspects of the derivative markets, in particular the swap futures and options markets. They appreciate the value of derivatives to the parties involved, but are concerned about the following issues.

1. The adequacy of risk management practices in the firms involved, and the level of disclosure of the firms' involvement.
2. The pricing models used to value derivative products, with the assumptions made including that of liquidity in the market. The option models become less valid the greater the volatility in the price of the underlying asset. Not all option writers cover their position. With volatility some can face substantial losses. Who will meet these losses if the writers cannot?
3. The deepening linkages across markets that result from derivatives.
4. The lack of transparency (of disclosure) in the derivative markets.
5. They are concerned that, although there is competition for business between option and swap markets and between countries, there is also an increasing level of co-operation. For example in 1993 the International Swap Dealers Association reached agreement which clarified the rights and obligations of swap counterparties in the event of default. This issue resulted from a dispute in the USA in which one counterparty defaulted. The legal issue was whether or not a swap should be considered a futures contract. In the end it was decided that a swap contract was not a form of futures contract.

Many economists and politicians are concerned about the impact of derivatives on the international financial system. The flexibility and linkages between markets mean that they can distort underlying price movements, and limit an individual national government's ability to manage its own economy. This is a general problem as financial markets become global. What derivatives can do is add to volatility in foreign exchange rates, and reduce the effect of government attempts to manage interest rates within a country.

It is also possible for those who play in the derivatives market to lose money. In the USA in 1994 several large mutual funds (unit trusts) lost money through trading in financial derivatives. They had been investing in increasingly complex illiquid derivatives. They had invested in these 'exotic derivatives', in an attempt to outperform their competitors. Unfortunately derivatives are risky and it is possible to lose as well as gain.

Companies have also lost money from trading in derivatives. One such company was Proctor & Gamble, who blamed outside derivative dealers for selling the company risky financial instruments!

A failure that attracted a great deal of attention in 1994 was the case of Metallgesellschaft, a German metals, mining and industrial group. The company lost DM 2.3 billion through trading in oil derivatives. The size of the losses was so great that it nearly led to the financial collapse of the company. The company in 1992 began negotiating long-term fixed-price contracts to sell fuel to petrol stations and small businesses. The selling price was higher than the market price for fuel at the time of the contract. In order to lock into the profit the company hedged by buying futures on the New York Mercantile exchange.

Oil prices began to fall sharply in the market in 1993, reducing the value of the futures contracts. There is disagreement as to why the company lost. Some argue that there was a mismatch between the short-term hedge and the long-term liability. Others argue that the company became concerned about the losses too early. If it had continued to invest in futures, and to pay the margins required by the counterparties the end result would have been satisfactory. One outcome was that the company sacked its treasury managers.

Accounting for financial derivatives

Some forms of derivatives are classed as off balance sheet instruments. They only result in transactions affecting the balance sheet upon reaching maturity. There is a great deal of uncertainty surrounding the amounts involved. For example when a company signs, say, an options contract it is entering into a financial commitment, but the outcome is unclear. Will the company exercise the option and if it does what cash flows will result? Should it report to shareholders that it has entered into such a financial deal? It is now an accounting requirement that although the derivative does not appear on the face of the balance sheet certain details should be given by way of notes to the accounts.

But what details? The US Accounting Standards Board first looked at this problem in 1986, and as at 1994 it was still not satisfied with the disclosure by companies. The UK Standards Board set up a committee to look at the problem in 1994.

There are two major problems: (1) should the derivatives appear on the face of a balance sheet or in notes, and (2) how can a value be placed on such derivatives?

The value of a listed traded option can be ascertained from the price on the exchange, but the value of an OTC option cannot. There are models to value options but they can be unreliable. Users of financial accounts, whether they be investors or regulators (of banks and other financial institutions) wish to know not only the value but also the risks. The value of an option today might be say £2, but what is the maximum amount of loss the writer of the option may have to carry if the value of the underlying asset moves by more than a certain amount?

With interest rate and currency swaps it is becoming increasingly common for companies to provide some information as to the arrangements they have entered into.

Forte plc give details of their borrowing with a note explaining that the interest rate being paid on a number of loans has been changed as a result of swaps (Table 20.9).

Table 20.9 *Extract from Forte Group plc 1993 accounts: interest rate exchange agreements*

The interest rates on loans shown above have been varied by the use of interest exchange agreements which alter interest rates as follows:

	Interest rate shown above	Varied interest rate	Expiry date
† Sterling £180m	Variable	11.9%	Between six and seven years
† Sterling £69m	Variable	10.9%	Between three and four years
US Dollar US$50m	Variable	8.7%	Between one and two years
Sterling £100m	8.375%	Libor + 1.0%	Between four and five years
Sterling £19m	10.6%	Libor + 3.9%	Between three and four years

† These interest exchange agreements were reversed with effect from the end of January 1993. Payments will be made at the rate of £8m and £3m per annum respectively until the agreements expire.

Hanson plc also provide some details of interest rate protection agreements they have entered into (Figure 20.4). They also give details of a specific currency/interest rate swap they have entered into, and of the impact of their interest-rate swap policy. The company had issued $1.25 billion of notes in a US debt offering, comprising $500 million nominal 5½% notes due 1996 and $750 million nominal 7⅞% notes due 2003. The group entered into currency swap agreements to swap the fixed rate $1.25bn into floating rate sterling with six month LIBOR-based rollovers.

Hanson plc also explain in their 1993 accounts that interest rate protection agreements have been entered into which effectively fix interest payments at an average of 3.73% on $1450 million of floating-rate debt due within one year. They mention that they are exposed to loss in the event of non-performance by banks under such agreements, but they do not anticipate any such non-performance.

Debenture loans include £2,658mn relating to amounts borrowed under a US dollar commercial paper programme and £428mn under a sterling commercial paper programme.
Bank loans, overdrafts and debenture loans bear interest at rates ranging from 3.13% to 7% per annum. Interest rate protection agreements have been entered into which effectively fix interest payments at an average 3.73% on $1,450mn of floating rate debt due within one year. Hanson is exposed to loss in the event of non-performance by banks under such agreements. No single bank is party to more than $150mn nominal value of such agreements. Hanson does not anticipate non-performance by any of its counterparties. These agreements expire at various dates to April 1994. Hanson has unused lines of credit for short term borrowing of approximately £2.0 billion at September 30, 1993.

Figure 20.4 *Extract from Hanson plc 1993 accounts*

20.12 Treasury organization and control

Separate treasury departments tend normally to exist within large companies. Although the treasury section may be staffed by a comparatively small number of people these staff are usually well qualified and costly to employ. The decision on whether to operate a separate treasury function and the scope of this function should be taken by comparing the incremental costs of establishing the section with the benefits to be obtained.

The structure of treasury departments can vary quite considerably. Responsibility may be retained by operating units with central treasury merely providing advice, while there may be a fully centralized treasury department with operating units reporting positions to treasury and acting on their instructions.

The tendency is for increasing centralization of corporate treasuries offering potential for greater gains given that most of the treasury costs are likely to be fixed. Centralization itself can take a number of forms two of which are the central agent and central banker model.

Where treasury acts as central agent it transacts business on behalf of operating units rather than these units dealing direct. This approach requires the treasury to transact all the operating units' business with banks or other appropriate organizations. Where the central banker model is adopted then effectively the treasury acts as the group's central banker. All dealing needs are channelled through the central treasury which will only deal externally where needs cannot be satisfied internally. The central banker approach enables treasury to undertake matching and netting off of opposing balances and currency risks leaving only the reduced net balance or exposure to be transacted with outside banks.

The model adopted may determine the status of treasury within the organization. Where an agency role is adopted then treasury might be regarded as a service cost centre. However as the model becomes like that of a central banker the status may change to that of profit centre with treasury covering its costs of operation by charging operating units for services undertaken and profiting from netting off procedures (which are discussed in Chapter 26). Care must be exercised and clear guidelines laid down as more autonomy is given to the treasury department. If company philosophy is for risks (e.g. foreign currency, interest rate etc.) to be minimized with business results not affected by movements in financial markets, this must be clearly stated and treasury act accordingly. A potential danger of treasury being a profit centre is that managers may be judged on results and have an element of profit-related pay, thus providing temptation to engage in speculation by, for example, taking on exposure in foreign exchange which goes well beyond any hedging requirements of the business. This strategy could make big profits but on the other hand can lead to spectacular losses should the exchange rate move in the wrong direction. Large and well-publicized losses made by treasury functions in both public- and private-sector organizations highlight the need for knowledgeable and highly trained staff operating within clear guidelines established at the highest level of the organization.

Treasury information systems

As treasury activities become more centralized and sophisticated they develop into 'mini' banks with computer terminals linked to sources of information both within and outside the group. Treasuries need to obtain information from within the group on cash available/needed, foreign exchange commitments etc. as well as information on markets and rates of exchange, interest etc. In addition they need the capability to transact business speedily with outside banks and brokers. Documentation and reports need to be generated on at least a daily basis and, importantly, the whole operation needs to be conducted under the tightest possible security given that substantial sums are usually involved. A key feature of treasury centralization will be the provision of an information system capable of providing the necessary decision support.

Many companies now prefer to purchase a treasury system from a bank or software house. There is a good supply of these 'ready-made' systems and it will usually be easier to purchase such a system rather than develop in-house systems.

Measuring treasury performance

This is a controversial issue. Management needs to be able to judge the effectiveness of its treasury function. This of course depends on the objectives set for the function. If it is seen as just another profit centre within the group the company has to be very careful to define the levels of risk in which the treasury can operate. Reward has to be traded off against risk. A treasury can hedge, become involved in arbitrage opportunities, spread its trading (this involves taking limited risks – for example, betting on a rise in interest rates by borrowing now for one year, and then investing the funds for short periods as the interest rates rise) and even become involved in speculation. The treasury can take high levels of risk; for a time it can beat the market and show profits; the danger is that it will then lose to the market and show losses.

Where the treasury is centralized and is seen as acting as a banker to the group it should not be seeking to maximize profits. The treasury should charge companies within the group a rate for the services offered that is similar to the scale of a bank's charges. This gives confidence to the managers of companies in the group in that they are not being exploited. The treasury can make a profit, as does a bank by netting transactions, dealing with the outside markets in bulk, and undertaking a certain amount of investment with the short-term funds it has available; but it should not make a profit from high charges to group companies.

If the company wishes to take low risks, the treasury (as a banker) might be instructed to hedge whenever appropriate. The performance yardstick (the benchmarks) for hedging say foreign exchange receivables might be the equivalent of selling all receivables forward three months.

The benchmark (against which the performance of the treasury will be judged) for investing surplus funds could be the rate of return offered in the three months interbank market. This is the target the treasury is expected to achieve. It will not with such a target be encouraged to engage in 'spread trading' for example if they believe interest rates are going to fall lending the surplus funds long term at today's rates.

Control of treasury function

The responsibility for controlling the treasury function rests with the board of directors. A few cases occur each year in which a company reports that its treasury department has made large losses on its activities. The board usually claims surprise at the size of the losses. In order to avoid such surprises the board should ensure internal controls have been established and the actual performance is constantly monitored.

One area where controls are necessary is in the dealing function (in foreign currencies, the money markets and commodities). Many large treasury losses have resulted from unauthorized dealing. Dealing is difficult to control if it is permitted at subsidiary level. This is one argument for a centralized function.

The names of the personnel authorized to deal, and the limits of their authority, should be established. These individuals should be given dealing mandates. Counterparties must be made aware of who in the company is authorized to deal and of the limit on the amount of dealing permitted with that counterparty. The dealers should need to report regularly to superiors on their activities.

Limits may need to be divided between those for immediate settlement, and those for different forward periods. The limits should be based on the level of loss the company is prepared to accept.

A dealer makes a deal. Behind him or her is what is called a 'back office' which is responsible for the settlement of the transactions. This office sends out the confirmation to the counterparties. The work of this office needs to be kept separate from the dealer. If it is not it is relatively easy for a dealer to breach approved limits without other staff being aware of it. The 1995 example of losses by one dealer employed by Barings illustrates the problem of control.

20.13 Key terms

Caps and collars
Cash flow statement
Cash management
Collection cycle
Disintermediation
Financial derivatives
Floors
Forward forward loans
Forward rate agreements
Funding management

Futures contracts
Interest rate guarantees
Interest rate futures
Interest rate swaps
Over-the-counter market
Payment cycle
Ticks
Treasury management
Treasury performance

20.14 Revision questions

1. What are the reasons why a firm might choose to hold cash or near cash?
2. Why do firms sometimes find themselves with idle cash balances (cash surpluses)?
3. What is the money market? What opportunities does it offer to firms with cash available for short periods of time?
4. What is float?
5. How might a firm go about determining its target cash balance?
6. What factor does a firm have to take into account in determining its optimal cash balance?
7. How can a firm speed up its collection and depositing of cash?
8. What are the strengths and weaknesses of cash management models?

The corporate treasury function has assumed greater prominence with the increased volatility of foreign exchange rates and interest rates. A selection of books and articles dealing with the issues and techniques is shown below.

Block, S.B. and Gallagher, T.J. (1986) The use of interest rate futures and options by corporate financial management. *Financial Management*, Autumn.

Collier, P.A., Cooke, T.E. and Glynn, J.J. (1988) *Financial and Treasury Management*, Heinemann Professional Publishing.

Davis, E.W. and Collier, P.A. (1982) *Treasury Management in the U.K.*, Association of Corporate Treasurers.

Donaldson, J.A. (1988) *The Corporate Treasury Function*, ICAS.

Galitz, L. (1993) *Financial Engineering: Tools and Techniques to Manage Financial Risk*, Pitman/Financial Times, London.

Hartley, W.C.F. and Meltzer, Y. (1987) *Cash Management*, Prentice Hall.

Hull, J. (1989) *Options, Futures and Other Derivative Securities*, Prentice-Hall Inc.

Kallberg, J.G. and Parkinson, K. (1984) *Current Asset Management*, Wiley.

Ross, D. (1987) *International Treasury Management*, Woodhead-Faulkner Ltd.

Smith, J.E. *Cash Flow Management*, Woodhead-Faulkner, Cambridge.

Smith, K.V. (1988) *Readings on Short-Term Financial Management*, West Publishing Company.

Watson, A. and Altringham, R. (1986) *Treasury Management, International Banking Operations*, The Institute of Bankers.

Wall, L.D. and Pringle, J.J. (1989) Alternative explanations of interest rate swaps: a theoretical and empirical analysis. *Financial Management*, Summer.

20.15 Further reading

20.16 Problems

1. Why does the rate of interest have a strong influence upon the demand for liquidity and an apparently weak influence upon business investment?
2. The summarized balance sheets of a company for two successive years are as follows:

	Year 1 (£000)	Year 2 (£000)
Source of funds		
Ordinary share capital	1760	1760
Share premium account	207	207
Other capital reserves	440	440
Revenue reserves	2192	2434
	4599	4841
Taxation equilization account	618	622
	£5217	£5463
Employment of funds		
Land and buildings	1388	1354
Plant, equipment and vehicles	1243	1161
	2631	2515
Goodwill and patents	314	341
	2945	2856
Net current assets		
Stocks	2294	2287
Debtors	1879	1974
Cash and bank balances	46	186
	4219	4447

Less:		
Creditors	1069	1118
Current taxation	394	358
Bank overdraft	282	109
Proposed dividend (gross)	202	255
	1947	1840
	2272	2607
	£5217	£5463

Notes on the accounts show the following:

(a) Depreciation has been charged for year 2 as follows:

Land and buildings	£35 000
Plant, machinery and vehicles	£240 000
Goodwill and patents	£9 000

(b) Plant sold during year 2 realized £16 000. It was included at cost in the balance sheet for year 1 at £61 000 with depreciation accumulated of £53 000. The difference between realization and written value was credited to the profit and loss account.

(c) The balance of profit for year 2 after taxation charge and dividend appropriation has been transferred to revenue reserve.

Further enquiries reveal that during year 2 the company made cash payments for total dividends, including tax thereon, amounting to £371 000 and other taxation amounting to £452 000.

Prepare a statement which explains the improvement in the net cash and bank balances during year 2.

3. During the next three months the ABC Co. Ltd will require to find £60 000 for the financing of some new equipment. It had been anticipated that the company would have been able to find the funds for this from internal sources but by the end of June the bank overdraft will have reached the overdraft limit of £25 000. The company does not operate a detailed budgetary planning system but you have been able to obtain the following sales estimates.

	Cash sales	*Credit sales*	*Total sales*
July	£40 000	£200 000	£240 000
August	£45 000	£220 000	£265 000
September	£50 000	£220 000	£270 000

The sales mark-up is estimated to give a gross profit margin of 33.33% on gross cost and £240 000 of goods at sales value will be needed as stock to enable the above sales forecasts to be met. All company purchases are paid for on receipt in order to get the benefit of a 5% discount, and likewise a cash discount of 3% is offered to customers who pay within 15 days. Only 50% of customers pay in time to take the benefit of the cash discount – unlike in the previous year when about 90% did so – 20% pay at the end of 30 days and the remainder at the end of 60 days. On average 25% of the credit sales in any one month to customers who take the benefit of the cash discount will be in debtors at the end of the month. The estimated other expenses payable monthly are as follows:

Fixed	£50 000
Variable	12.5% of gross sales

Cash sales for June – a high sales month – were £20 000 and credit sales were £285 000, of which £185 000 were still outstanding. The opening balances for the beginning of July are as follows:

Stock	£220 000
Debtors	£275 000

Prepare a cash budget for the months of July, August and September along with a report commenting on any other matters that you would wish the directors of the company to consider.

4. The £14 million annual sales receipts of Millack PLC are spread evenly over each of the 50 weeks of the working year. However, the pattern within each week is that the daily rate of receipts on Mondays and Tuesdays is twice that experienced on Wednesdays, Thursdays and Fridays. Receipts for the whole week are usually banked on the Friday of each week, but this practice is being reconsidered. It is suggested that banking should be carried out either daily or twice a week, on Tuesday and Friday. The incremental cash cost to Millack of each banking is £40. Millack always operates on bank overdraft and the current overdraft rate is 14% per annum – this interest charge is applied by the bank on a simple daily basis.

Advise Millack on the best policy amongst the three alternatives for banking receipts. Indicate the annual amount by which Millack will be worse off if it pursued the worst, rather than the best, of the three policies for banking receipts. *Ignore taxation.*

5. (a) Discuss the factors that are likely to influence the desired level of cash balance of a company. (5 marks)

   (b) Mollet Ltd prepares a weekly cash budget. Based upon the experience of previous cash inflows and outflows it has estimated cash flows for the next week, some of which are considered to be definite and some of which have been assigned probabilities of occurrence.

Expected cash outflows		*Probability*
Wages and salaries:		
Basic	£50 000	1
Overtime	0	0.5
	£10 000	0.5
Materials	£70 000	1
Overheads	£10 000	1
Expected cash inflows		
Cash from debtors	£100 000	0.4
	£120 000	0.6

Any surplus cash is invested in six month deposits in the money market and shortfalls of cash are funded by withdrawing cash from these money market investments. Mollet currently has £100 000 invested in the money market. Transactions costs are estimated to be a fixed cost of £10 for each money market deposit and £8 for each money market withdrawal, with a variable cost of 0.05% of the transaction value on both deposits and withdrawals. All money market transactions must be of at least £10 000 in size and in multiples of £10 000. If withdrawals are made from the six month money market deposits prior to the maturity of the deposits, a penalty equivalent to one week's interest on the amount withdrawn is payable. No deposits are due to mature during the next week. The interest rate on six month money market deposits is currently 12% per annum. Mollet's directors have decided that the company must maintain a minimum cash balance of £20 000. The cash balance at the start of the next week is expected to be £40 000.

Determine the level of investment in money market deposits at the start of the next week that will maximize the expected net return from the money market for the week. (12 marks)

   (c) Outline the advantages and disadvantages of using short-term debt, as opposed to long-term debt, in the financing of working capital. (8 marks)

(25 marks)

ACCA, June 1986

6. The finance director of Pondwood Ltd wishes to prepare an estimate of next year's working capital requirements. Sales for the next year are expected to be 85 500

units at a basic unit price of £50. Direct materials, direct wages and direct energy costs are expected to be £15.51 per unit, £17.35 per unit and £4.95 per unit respectively. Administrative salaries are forecast to be £264 000, and distribution and other overheads a total of £92 000. Corporate taxation is at a rate of 35%, payable one year in arrears. The current year's profit before taxation, after deducting interest payments of £118 000 for the company's overdraft, is £311 000. Pondwood offers its customers a 2.5% cash discount for payment within 14 days. On average 40% of customers take this discount, and the remainder take an average of 10 weeks to pay for their goods.

Stocks of raw materials equivalent to four weeks usage are held, and finished goods equivalent to eight weeks demand. The production process takes an average of four weeks. Work in progress is valued at the cost of materials for the full period of the production process and the cost of wages and energy for half the period of the production process. Pondwood is allowed eight weeks credit from its suppliers of raw materials and six weeks credit for distribution and other fixed costs. Energy bills are payable quarterly in arrears. The company pays wages one week in arrears and salaries one month in arrears (one month may be assumed to be four weeks).

Pondwood's existing overdraft facility has recently been extended to cover the next financial year. The interest rate payable on the company's overdraft has remained at 11% per annum during the past year, and is not expected to change during the foreseeable future. The company has utilized its full overdraft facility during the past year.

(a) Evaluate whether, on the basis of the above information, the company's overdraft facility is likely to be large enough to finance the company's working capital needs for the next year. State clearly any assumptions that you make. A monthly cash budget is not required as part of your evaluation.   (15 marks)
(b) What other information would be helpful in the assessment of the company's overdraft requirements?   (3 marks)
(c) Discuss what is meant by (i) an overdraft and (ii) an acceptance credit. What are the advantages and disadvantages of these forms of short-term finance?
     (7 marks)
     ACCA, Dec. 1987

7. Your firm's annual cash budget indicates that surplus funds will be available for periods of between one and five months.

Outline the main factors to be considered before deciding on the investment of the above funds. Specify three potentially suitable investments, or uses, for the above funds and indicate the relative merits, disadvantages and risks of each.

8. MBX is a holding company with two subsidiaries. It is late June and the finance director of MBX is worried about the cash flow position for the next six months commencing July. The group uses a centralized cash management system.

Subsidiary 1 is a manufacturing subsidiary. Sales in June are 82 418 units at a price of £10.60 per unit. Sales have recently been increasing at the rate of 1.5% per month and this trend is expected to continue. Two months' credit is given to all customers, and one month's credit is received on all purchases. Materials, with a unit variable cost of £3.71 are purchased in order to meet expected sales in two months' time. Direct labour costs £3.18 per unit and wages are payable one month in arrears. Production levels are based upon expected sales in one month's time. Overheads, payable one month in arrears, are expected to be £95 000 per month (invoice value) for the next three months, and £101 000 per month for the following six months. Sales price, material and labour costs are expected to rise by 5% in early September. No other changes in price or costs are expected. Other forecast cash flows are: Purchase of fixed assets:

(a) September – Replace 15 salesmen's cars at a net cost of £90 000.
(b) November – Purchase new machinery for planned expansion at a cost of £310 000.

November – Disposal of a small plot of land for the sum of £130 000 (receivable immediately).

Subsidiary 2 acts as an investment company for the group, and has investments in shares and gilts.

Holdings:	Number held	Market price	Dividend or interest due	PE ratio	Expected annual payout ratio
Alpha plc	812 000	152p	October	8	40%
Beta plc	326 000	346p	September	12	50%
Gamma plc	568 000	104p	December	8	50%
2.5% consols (£100 nominal value)	14 300	£33	November	—	—
12% Exchequer 1998 (£100 nominal value)	10 000	£104	November	—	—

Dividends and interest are payable twice a year in equal amounts. Assume that there are no tax adjustments on dividends and interest payments.

The subsidiary has a £400 000 loan over one year ending next March, with a nominal rate of interest of 12%, with repayment by equal monthly instalments which include both interest and principal.

Administrative and other costs of this subsidiary are estimated to be £40 000 per month, payable one month in arrears.

The holding company has administrative and other costs of £60 000 per month also payable one month in arrears and expects to pay a dividend of £400 000 in December and taxation of £470 000 in November. There will be an opening cash balance of £80 000 at the beginning of July.

Required:

(a) Evaluate whether MBX is likely to experience any cash flow problems during the next six months. Cash flows may be rounded to the nearest £1000.

  Discuss how any possible cash flow problems might be overcome.

  The chairman of the company does not wish to dispose of any of its investments except as a last resort, and a maximum of £400 000 overdraft facility is available. The company does not wish to raise any external finance other than possible use of the overdraft.

  State clearly any assumptions that you make. (19 marks)

(b) Explain how computerized cash balance management services offered by major banks and other organizations might assist a financial manager. (6 marks)

ACCA, June 1989

9. (a) Explain and illustrate what is meant by disintermediation and securitization. How can disintermediation and securitization help the financial manager?
(8 marks)

(b) Manling plc has £14 million of fixed rate loans at an interest rate of 12% per year which are due to mature in one year. The company's treasurer believes that interest rates are going to fall, but does not wish to redeem the loans because large penalties exist for early redemption. Manling's bank has offered to arrange an interest rate swap for one year with a company that has obtained floating rate finance at London Interbank Offered Rate (LIBOR) plus 1⅛%. The bank will charge each of the companies an arrangement fee of £20 000 and the proposed terms of the swap are that Manling will pay LIBOR plus 1½% to the other company and receive from the company 11⅝%.

  Corporate tax is 35% per year and the arrangement fee is a tax allowable expense. Manling could issue floating rate debt at LIBOR plus 2% and the other company could issue fixed rate debt at 11¾%. Assume that any tax relief is immediately available.

Required:

(i) Evaluate whether Manling plc would benefit from the interest rate swap
 (1) if LIBOR remains at 10% for the whole year;
 (2) if LIBOR falls to 9% after six months. (6 marks)

(ii) If LIBOR remains at 10% evaluate whether both companies could benefit from the interest rate swap if the terms of the swap were altered. Any benefit would be equally shared. (6 marks)

(c) Manling expects to have £1 million surplus funds for three months prior to making a tax payment. Discuss possible short-term investments for these funds. (5 marks)

ACCA, June 1990

10. (a) Discuss the possible advantages and disadvantages of centralizing the finance functions of a group of companies. (11 marks)

(b) If you were the managing director of a group of companies suggest, giving reasons for your suggestions, what financial ratios (or combinations of financial ratios) you might find useful in order to monitor, evaluate and control the activities of the group. (8 marks)

What problems might exist with the use of financial ratios as a financial control system within a group of companies? (6 marks)

ACCA, Dec. 1988

11. (a) In three months' time your company will need to borrow £5 million for a six-month period. Current interest rates are around 9% p.a. and this annual rate currently applies to all spot and forward rates for up to 18 months.

Your firm is concerned that interest rates may rise from the level of 9% per annum before the loan is obtained.

Advise the treasurer on the financial instruments/securities which may be useful to him in managing this potential interest-rate risk and explain the characteristics of each of them. (15 marks)

(b) Explain an interest rate swap and indicate the conditions under which it may be useful. (10 marks)

12. Assume that you have just taken a job in one of the major British multinational companies. On your first day of work you were given some information from the finance department. The information suggests that the company is considering raising £15 million for a five-year period to finance one of its new medium-term projects. The company is well regarded in the financial markets, and because of this it can borrow at a fixed rate of interest of 9% per annum, and at a floating rate of (LIBOR + ⅜%).

The company's bank has offered to arrange an interest-rate swap for a period of five years with a company which has a lower credit rating and subsequently can borrow at a fixed rate of interest of 10.5% and a floating rate of (LIBOR + 1%). If the company does agree to the swap contract an agreement fee of £50 000 is payable by each company.

Required:

(a) As a financial manager's assistant, evaluate, showing relevant calculations, whether your company should proceed with the swap contract on loans of £15 million.

(b) Let us postulate that your head of department has decided to borrow at the fixed rate of interest and invest the funds in a project which promises a rate of return equal to (LIBOR + 1⅛%), while the second company is to borrow at the floating rate and invest in a project promising a fixed annual return of 11¼%. Given these facts demonstrate how the two companies can eliminate the adverse effects of interest-rate movements on their profitability. Show all your workings.

13. Discuss how interest rate swaps and currency swaps might be of value to the corporate financial manager.

14. (a) It is now 31 December 1991 and the corporate treasurer of Omniown plc is concerned about the volatility of interest rates. His company needs in three months' time to borrow £5 million for a six-month period. Current interest rates are 14% per year for the type of loan Omniown would use, and the treasurer does not wish to pay more than this.

    He is considering using either:
    (i) a forward rate agreement (FRA)), or
    (ii) interest rate futures, or
    (iii) an interest rate guarantee (short-term cap).

    Required:

    Explain briefly how each of these three alternatives might be useful to Omniown plc. (10 marks)

    (b) The corporate treasurer of Omniown plc expects interest rates to increase by 2% during the next three months and has decided to hedge the interest rate risk using interest-rate futures.

    March sterling three months time deposit futures are currently priced at 86.25. The standard contract size is £500 000 and the minimum price movement is one tick (the value of one tick is 0.01% per year of the contract size).

    Required:

    Show the effect of using the futures market to hedge against interest-rate movements:

    (i) If interest rates increase by 2% and the futures market price also moves by 2%;
    (ii) if interest rates increase by 2% and the futures market moves by 1.5%.
    (iii) if interest rates fall by 1% and the futures market moves by 0.75%.

    In each case estimate the hedge efficiency.
    Taxation, margin requirements, and the time value of money are to be ignored. (10 marks)

    (c) If, as an alternative to interest rate futures, the corporate treasurer had been able to purchase interest-rate guarantees at 14% for a premium of 0.2% of the size of the loan to be guaranteed, calculate whether the total cost of the loan after hedging in each of situations (i) to (iii) in (b) above would have been less with the futures hedge or with the guarantee. The guarantee would be effective for the entire six-month period of the loan.

    Taxation, margin requirements and the time value of money are to be ignored. (5 marks)

    ACCA, Dec. 1991

15. Elmdon Heath Ltd. run a chain of golf supply shops. Their business is seasonal in nature. Their forecast sales for 1995 are as follows:

	£000s		£000s
January	20	July	160
February	12	Aug	100
March	12	Sept	48
April	20	Oct	12
May	32	Nov	12
June	100	Dec	48

50% of the company sales are on cash terms, and 50% on credit terms. Of the sales on credit 50% pay during the first month following sale and 50% during the second month.

The company purchases goods 3 months prior to when they are expected to be sold, and pays for them 2 months after purchase. The cost of purchases amounts to 60% of the sales price. Wages and administrative costs amount to £10,000 per month. Deprecation costs are £5,000 per month. A tax payment of £20,000 needs to be made in April.

Required

(a) Prepare a cash budget for 1995. The opening cash balance is £20,000. Assume sales in the last few months of 1994 were similar to those forecast for the final month of 1995.

(b) What are the maximum and minimum monthly cash balances for the year? What policy would you advise with respect to these balances?

(c) How should deprecation costs be treated in a cash budget?

(d) The cash budget is a forecast. If sales in the early months of the year show signs of falling below forecasts how might the company act to protect its liquidity position? How would you allow for uncertainty in preparing a cash budget?

20.17 Appendix: Cash management models

A number of banks in the USA offer their customers access to cash management models. The advent of the personal computer means that the analysis for cash management can range from spreadsheet analysis of the Lotus 1, 2, 3 variety through sophisticated programming models to the world-wide computer network system provided for multinational companies by the Chemical Bank. The object of the models is to set minimum and maximum levels of cash that the firm should carry so as to minimize the cost of holding idle funds and maximize the interest earned on surplus funds. Some models have very restrictive assumptions. All models are dependent for their usefulness on the accuracy of the inputs. Models can be adapted to allow for a range of investment opportunities. Many models can allow for uncertainty, either through sensitivity analysis or through optimistic, pessimistic and most likely forecasts.

The workings of some of the basic cash flow models are explained in this appendix.

The Chemical Bank model seeks to maximize the value of the short-term portfolio of investments subject to the following constraints.

1. Sources of cash and the uses of these funds must be equal in each period. Therefore positive net cash flows are invested and net shortfalls are covered by disinvestment.
2. Limitations are imposed by the user on the amount of funds which can be invested in any one investment; this reflects the risk preference of each user.

The user has to provide the following information:

1. number and duration of investment periods;
2. cash flow projections;
3. borrowing constraints;
4. descriptions of the types of investments;
5. interest rate projections.

Data can be stored from previous runs encouraging the user to manipulate variables to observe their effect on the short-term plan. Restrictions are imposed on the model to prevent it from always preferring long-term over short-term investments. The model has the following specifications.

1. It will accept up to 25 planning periods, and the user is able to specify the length of each period.

2. Up to 45 different investments can be specified.
3. Yields on the investments can be modified over time via specified interest rate projections. A special feature controls investments which extend beyond the planning period. They can either be disallowed or have an interest penalty imposed.
4. The output from the model gives three sets of information for each time period:

   (a) those securities which are not maturing;
   (b) new securities purchased;
   (c) current security holdings.

   In addition the output also contains a marginal short-term investment rate analysis. This shows the value to the firm of any additional funds that the firm can make available during the planning period, or conversely, when the firm is projecting a net cash outflow during a period, the value of reducing this outflow.

Users of the model become aware of the variables that affect the day-to-day management decisions and of the trade-off between liquidity and profits. The model enables a comparison to be made of the impact of investing in instruments with different yields and maturities.

We will now consider the costs and benefits of holding cash and presents two models of cash management: cash as inventory and the Miller–Orr model.

The costs and benefits of holding cash

First consider costs. There can be said to be two types of cost involved in obtaining cash. The first is a fixed cost, which does not vary with the amount held; it comprises the issue cost of the security or the negotiating cost or standard charge attached to obtaining a bank loan or overdraft. The second cost varies with the amount of cash being held; it covers the interest that may have to be paid on borrowings, or alternatively, the interest that could be earned on investing funds in short-term securities. This second cost represents the **opportunity** cost of keeping resources in a cash form.

Before an attempt can be made to determine the amount of cash or near cash that should be held by a company, the costs associated with holding cash must be known. This cost depends on the alternative uses to which the cash can be put and, if it is raised externally, the interest charged.

It is necessary to distinguish between two situations: in the first the company is holding cash to meet future needs and intends to maintain its reserves in this form; in the second the company has obtained funds to meet its short-term needs, but has invested in short-term securities that can be converted into cash at short notice. The cost of holding liquid resources differs between these two situations.

First, if it is cash actually being held in the business that is being considered and if the possible investment rate is $100j\%$, and the borrowing rate is $100i\%$, then one of the following situations will apply:

1. If $j > i$, any funds borrowed at $100i\%$ could have been invested at $100j\%$ so that if, instead of investing them they are held as cash, there is an opportunity cost of $100j\%$ and this will be the appropriate interest cost figure to use;
2. If $j < i$, the firm presumably would not borrow in order to invest at a lower or equal rate and so the interest cost is the interest charge that the firm could have escaped had less been raised or more repaid. This is $100i\%$.

We now turn to the second situation. In practice UK companies do not normally hold cash in very large amounts. UK banks do not require them to do so. If liquid reserves are required to meet unexpected demands for cash, money has usually been invested in short-term securities that can be converted into cash either at call or at one or two days' notice.[1]

---

[1] In this section, when referring to required cash balances, this is meant to include investments at short notice.

The reason that the funds are not being invested in long-term assets is that the company wishes to maintain a certain level of liquidity. It is the optimum amount of liquid assets that we now consider. Although there is no formula for computing the interest cost of holding cash or cash-like assets that applies to all situations, some writers have expressed the interest cost as the cost of capital minus the rate of return on short-term securities. This is often a good enough approximation. For example, if funds are raised at 10% and invested in short-term securities at 6%, there is an interest cost of 4%. The securities, being near cash, can be realized to deal with contingencies requiring cash. However, as soon as any securities are realized they cease to earn the 6% return. Thus, if securities are realized from time to time over a period the true interest cost will be something more than 4%. However, in the cash inventory model to follow later, we shall take the difference indicated above to be an adequate reflection of interest cost, as it is this type of situation which is most often encountered in practice.

The above consideration of costs is not the complete story; there are benefits too. To return to the first situation, even if liquid assets are entirely cash, there is an implied rate of return on the cash if it is at all necessary for profitable activities. We can illustrate this point with two capital budgeting examples.

Suppose that a firm can invest in a project giving the cash flow:

$t = 0$	$t = 1$	$t = 2$
$-30\,000$	$20\,000$	$20\,000$

but to achieve this cash flow, various transactions will be necessary around $t = 1$ and $t = 2$. The firm could pay an agency 10% of its net revenues at these times to handle the transactions. The resulting cash flow for the company is then:

$t = 0$	$t = 1$	$t = 2$
$-30\,000$	$18\,000$	$18\,000$

An alternative for the company would be to set aside working capital of £5000 at $t = 0$ and return this into the cash flow at $t = 2$.[2] If the company took this option, the project's cash flow would be:

$t = 0$	$t = 1$	$t = 2$
$-35\,000$	$20\,000$	$25\,000$

This 'investment' in working capital at $t = 0$ can be thought of as an incremental project giving rise to the improved cash flow at $t = 1$ and $t = 2$. This incremental project is:

$t = 0$	$t = 1$	$t = 2$
-5000	2000	7000

which shows a yield of 40%. This is the implied rate of return on the working capital.

A similar example is provided by self-insurance. In such circumstances, if no contingencies arise it might appear that cash set aside to cover contingencies has been idle and brought no return. This of course would be a false picture, and there is an implied expected return on the cash. To illustrate, suppose that the firm has £10 000. Assume that the firm can invest at 10%. There is a 50–50 chance that a liability of £5000 will arise at $t = 1$. The firm can take out an insurance policy for £3000 at $t = 0$ or hold £5000 in cash. Under the insurance policy option, at $t = 1$ the firm would have:

$$(10\,000 - 3000)\,(1.1) = 7700$$

Under the self-insurance option, the expected value at $t = 1$ is:

$$5000\,(1.1) + 0.5\,(5000) = 8000$$

since there is a 50% chance that the firm still has its 5000 cash at $t = 1$.[3] On an expected value basis it is as if the holding of £5000 cash earns £300 at $t = 1$, which is an implied rate of return of 6%.

[2] In a similar fashion to that of the dcf and tax payments example in Chapter 5.
[3] There is of course a range of outcomes in this case, from 10 500 to 5500.

These examples are intended to show how the implied yield from holding what might be termed 'active cash' can be found. Other illustrations could be constructed. All this is not to suggest that merely holding idle balances is to be encouraged as a rewarding activity. But where the money serves a purpose (which may not always be obvious to casual inspection) the benefits should be properly taken into account.

Inventory model

It has been suggested that a decision on the optimum amount of cash that a company should hold is a similar question to the decision of the optimum amount of inventory [2]. An inventory of cash is being held to meet future demands for cash. Consequently, a similar type of analysis could in principle be used in the control of this financial asset. As an example, the simple square root inventory model discussed in Chapter 23 can be used to determine the optimum amount of cash and cash-like assets that need to be obtained in a given time period and the balance that should be maintained.

Let Q be the optimum amount of cash-like assets to be obtained from outside sources, D be the amount of cash to be used in the next year. The value of D is the maximum excess of outgoings over receipts. Let K be the fixed cost of the financial transactions involved in obtaining new funds and let k be the interest cost of holding cash. We now consider these two types of cost in more detail. The first, the procurement cost, has an average that falls as the amount of money raised in each tranche increases. D is the amount of cash needed in the year and Q is the size of the tranche in which the cash is to be raised. The number of tranches involved, T, will therefore be:

$$T = \frac{D}{Q}$$

so that the average procurement cost per annum will be:

$$KT = K\frac{D}{Q}$$

This average annual procurement cost of raising the cash is shown in Figure 20.A1.

The second cost, representing the interest lost through holding cash-like assets, has

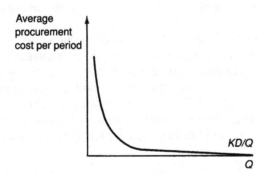

Figure 20.A1

an average cost that increases as the amount of money raised at each tranche increases. If, as is assumed, the demand for cash is spread evenly throughout a period, the cash on hand will fall at a steady rate from the time when it is obtained to when it is used up. The cash on hand at the beginning of the period is the amount raised, Q. At the time the next amount of cash is raised, the stock of cash will have fallen to zero, and so the average level of cash is:

$$\frac{(Q+0)}{2} = \frac{Q}{2}$$

so the average annual cost of carrying cash is:

$$k\frac{Q}{2}$$

which is shown in Figure 20.A2.

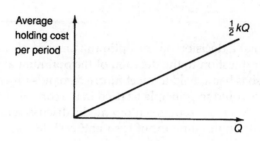

Figure 20.A2

The average **total** cost per annum, C, in maintaining the average level of cash $Q/2$ is therefore the sum of the procurement and holding components:

$$C = k\frac{Q}{2} + K\frac{D}{Q}$$

As shown in Chapter 23, Q^*, the optimum value of Q, is given by the 'square root' formula as:

$$Q^* = \left[\frac{2KD}{k}\right]^{\frac{1}{2}}$$

To illustrate the use of the formula suppose that a firm's annual net outlay of cash exclusive of new financing is £500 000. The firm faces a fixed charge of £500 each time that it raises a tranche of cash of any size. The interest cost of holding cash is 5%.[4] The optimum size of tranche is then:

$$Q^* = \left[\frac{2(500)(500\,000)}{0.05}\right]^{\frac{1}{2}}$$
$$= 100\,000$$

so that money would be raised five times per year, and the average holding of cash would be £50 000.

Of course, different values of the parameters used in the model or different assumptions altogether would have led to different results. In this analysis it has been assumed that the amount of cash required during a period is a known quantity. It has been assumed that, perhaps as the result of accurate cash budgeting, it is possible to forecast the amount that will be required. In reality it may not be possible to predict these amounts with certainty, and there may well be a cost attached to running out of cash. There are also the normal costs of holding cash, which of course increase with the average amount held.

In a situation of uncertainty, formulation of an optimum policy usually involves weighing the costs of carrying funds against the costs of running out of cash. More precisely, where uncertainty exists a plausible objective is to minimize the overall **expected** costs per annum, EC. If we include the procurement cost and holding costs as before, but now add a shortage cost, this can be written as:

EC = expected procurement cost per period
+ expected holding cost per period
+ expected shortage cost per period

---

[4] This may be the difference between the cost of obtaining the funds, say 12% p.a., and the return on short-term securities, say 7%.

Chapter 23 shows ways in which a model of this nature can be solved when sufficient information is available. Here we simply draw attention to the possibility of more sophisticated cash management models based on the inventory approach.

The Miller–Orr model

Miller and Orr [3] suggest that cash balances held by firms should depend upon the following:

1. the opportunity cost of holding cash;
2. the cost of making transfers between cash and security holdings;
3. the exogenously determined and uncontrollable variability in the firm's cash flow.

This last factor, the unpredictable element in the flow of the firm's receipts and payments, is the difficulty in the way of constructing simple rules for cash holding. In the simple inventory type of model such as the one outlined above, it is assumed that the amount of cash to be used in the next period can be determined with some accuracy; it is assumed that cash flows are regular, with infrequent large receipts and frequent small payments. In many cases this is an unrealistic assumption. Miller and Orr develop a model of the demand for money by firms that allows for this uncertainty.

The model has four sets of assumptions. The first set are as follows.

1. The firm has two types of asset – cash and a separately managed portfolio of liquid assets whose marginal and average yield is v per pound per day.
2. Transfers between the two asset accounts can take place at a marginal cost of γ per transfer.
3. Such a transfer takes place instantaneously; there is no lead time.

The second set of assumptions is more relevant to the situation in the USA than in the UK. In the USA it is often the practice that the arrangement between a bank and a customer calls for the maintenance of a minimum cash balance. It is a method of compensating the bank for any services it provides. The size of the balance varies considerably. It is therefore assumed in the model that there is a minimum level below which a firm's bank balance is not permitted to fall.

The third set of assumptions is concerned with the distribution of the possible demands for money. Net cash flows are assumed to be completely stochastic and they behave as if they were generated by a stationary random walk. Let $1/t$ be some small fraction of a working day – thus $1/8 = 1$ hour. During this time the cash balance will either increase by $£m$ with probability p, or decrease by $£m$ with probability $q = 1 - p$.

The fourth set of assumptions is concerned with the firm's objective function. It is assumed that the firm wishes to minimize the long-run average cost of managing its cash balance. The cash balance will be allowed to move freely between an upper and a lower limit. As long as the balance is within these limits no action will be taken, but when the balance reaches the upper limit h above the safety level or the lower limit, i.e. the safety margin itself, a portfolio transfer will take place between the two asset accounts to restore the balance to a required level z above the safety level.

Let $E(M)$ be the average daily cash balance, $E(N)$ be the expected number of portfolio transfers (in either direction), γ be the cost per transfer, v be the daily rate of interest earned on a portfolio and σ^2 be the variance of the daily demand for cash. Then the cost per day of managing the firm's cash balance over a finite planning horizon of T is

$$E(c) = \gamma \frac{E(N)}{T} + vE(M)$$

The objective is to minimize this function, i.e. the cost per day. The result is (asterisks indicate optimum values)

$$z^* = \left(\frac{3\gamma\sigma^2 t}{4\nu}\right)^{\frac{1}{3}}$$

$$h^* = 3z^*$$

The model obtains a relationship between the average cash holding of the firm and the three explanatory variables of the form

$$\overline{M} = \frac{4}{3}\left(\frac{3\gamma\sigma^2}{4\nu}\right)^{\frac{1}{3}}$$

where $\overline{M}$ is the average cash balance that the firm wishes to maintain for transaction purposes, ignoring any minimum cash balances that the bank may wish the firm to hold or any safety level that the firm itself may wish to hold.

The control actions are as follows:

1. when the balance held for transaction purposes falls to the safety level, sell securities of amount £z^*;
2. when the balance held for transaction purposes rises to h^* above the safety level, buy securities of amount £2z.

Therefore the pattern of cash flows appears as in Fig. 20.A3.

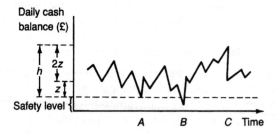

Figure 20.A3

At time A the transaction balance reached zero, and so securities to the value of £z were sold. At time B the transaction balance reached zero, and so again securities to the amount of £z were sold. In addition, cash had left the business and the balance went below the safety level and so sufficient cash had to be realized by the sale of securities to replenish this balance. At time C the balance held for transaction purposes had exceeded the safety level by £h, and so cash was used to buy securities to the value of £2z, thereby reducing the transaction balance to £z above the safety level.

The predictions of this model are said to be extremely robust:

> To the extent that beliefs may be based on *a priori* analysis one should be confident that (a) the variance of cash flows in the firm is the relevant transactions measure, (b) the long-term interest rate is the relevant opportunity cost of holding cash, and (c) the transaction and interest elasticity of money demand in a maximizing firm are, subject to qualifications, respectively plus and minus 1/3. [3]

The most important qualification of the results centres in the representation of the spread in the daily cash balances of the firm by the variance of the cash flow. If a particular firm's transactions produce a diffusion rate that is extremely rapid, i.e. if the daily balances fluctuate over a large range during short periods of time, then the decision rules suggested by the model may not be relevant. However, the model is an interesting example of the way in which a scientific approach is being adopted in financial management. If a company does not have an extremely unpredictable and uneven cash flow, then such a model can be used as a tool of financial control.

1. Association of Corporate Treasurers (1988) *Treasury Management in the UK*, London.
2. Baumol, W.J. (1952) The transactions demand for cash: an inventory theoretic approach, *Quarterly Journal of Economics*, November.
3. Miller, M.N. and Orr, D. (1966) A model of the demand for money by firms, *Quarterly Journal of Economics*, August.

20.18 References

21 Foreign exchange markets

21.1	Introduction	766		21.6	Foreign exchange risk	788
21.2	Meaning of quotations	767		21.7	Key terms	789
21.3	Factors influencing exchange			21.8	Revision questions	790
	rates	770		21.9	Reference	790
21.4	Managing transaction risk	777		21.10	Further reading	790
21.5	Currency futures contracts	784		21.11	Problems	790

In this chapter the workings of the foreign exchange markets are described. The risks faced by companies as a result of international trade and international investment are discussed and the techniques treasury managers can use to reduce foreign exchange risk are examined.

21.1 Introduction

The size and level of activity in the foreign exchange markets (FOREX) grew dramatically during the 1980s. Until the early 1970s many countries had currencies that were fixed by their governments or linked to the US dollar, so there was little volatility in exchange rates. The 1980s saw (a) floating exchange rates with the rate of exchange determined by the market, (b) increasing levels of international business, and (c) the ending of restrictions in many countries on the outflow and inflow of direct and portfolio investment.

In 1992 the daily volume of FOREX dealings worldwide was around $1000 billion. Of this the daily trading values in London were in the region of $300 billion, in New York, $192 billion and in Tokyo $126 billion. In 1986 the daily volume in London had only been $90 billion, in New York $60 billion and in Tokyo $50 billion.

The players

It has been estimated that somewhere between 10% and 20% of FOREX transactions arise from commercial transactions. This does not mean that the remaining 80% to 90% are speculative. Most of this balance are interbank transactions with one bank laying off their foreign exchange exposure with another bank. Let us say Barclays Bank may find at the end of the day that as a result of normal exchange activity it is holding more US dollars than is its wish. It will therefore attempt to sell these dollars (at the best price) to other banks who may feel they are short of dollars in their currency portfolio. A very large commercial transaction in one currency through one bank, say Barclays, can lead to a number of interbank transactions as Barclays spread the currency through other banks. It is rather like one bookmaker laying off a very large bet with other bookmakers!

Speculators

Every time a major currency is forced to devalue articles appear in the press blaming speculators. What is the reality of the situation? Undoubtedly there are speculators, individuals who if they believe a currency will fall in value will sell the currency short.

Let us say Mr S has £1 million in liquid assets. He thinks the pound will fall against the DM. The current spot rate is DM 3.0 = £1. Mr S will sell the £s now and receive DM 3 million. When the pound falls against the DM to say DM 2.5 = £1, he will buy the £1 million back. The cost will only be DM 2.5 million. Mr S has made a profit of DM 0.5 million on the deal.

George Soros, who manages investment funds in the USA, is known as 'the man who broke the bank'. When the pound sterling was forced to devalue on so-called 'Black Monday' in 1993 he is alleged to have made $2 billion from his foreign exchange dealing. He has at times also speculated against the French Franc and other European currencies. He is a speculator.

But it should be appreciated that the amount of funds in the hands of speculators is very small compared with the huge amounts of company and bank money that is traded in the FOREX markets every day. If it was just speculators who tried to anticipate what was happening and acted accordingly they could not move by very much the rates of exchange of the major currencies.

Banks, insurance companies and pension funds hold liquid assets in different currencies. What are they supposed to do if they think a currency is to be devalued? Are they supposed to keep the liquid assets in say pounds and see them fall in value relative to other currencies?

If a UK-based pension fund that is looking after pensioners' assets happens to have £1 million liquid, and it sees the UK government struggling to protect the value of the pound, are they supposed to keep the pounds and be patriotic, or are they supposed to protect the value of the pensioners' assets? In the example at the beginning of this section let us say it is a pension's fund rather than Mr X that has the £1 million. Fund managers who are accused of speculation can clearly say, 'We are just doing our job.'

21.2 Meaning of quotations

The price of foreign currency is usually expressed in terms of local currency. Table 21.1 shows the exchange rate between pounds sterling and a number of the major foreign currencies as at 11 August 1994. The closing spot rate between the pound and the US dollar is shown as £1 = $1.5328. (This is known as an **indirect quote**.) The change in the rate of exchange during the previous day's trading is also shown. As can be seen the £ fell in value against the $ by 0.76 cents on that day.

A bid/offer spread is also given in the extract (namely 324–331). This means that the bid price is £1 equals $1.5324, and the offer price $1.5331. (The last three digits in the mid price are adjusted.) The lower price is the one at which the foreign exchange dealer is willing to sell dollars in exchange for pounds. The higher price is the one in which the dealer is willing to buy dollars in exchange for pounds (the customer will have to give $1.5331 dollars to receive £1).

The size of the spread between the two quoted prices will depend on the exchange dealer and the type of market in which he is operating.

The reciprocal rate is expressing the exchange rate in reverse terms. In the above example we have expressed the pound in terms of a number of dollars. This is referred to as an indirect quote. Taking the mid-point of £1 = $1.5328 we could express the dollar in terms of a number of pounds sterling. The reciprocal $1.5328 = $1/x$ gives $x = 0.6524$. In other words $1 = £0.6524. (This is known as a **direct quote**.)

The UK usually expresses **forex** rates in the indirect form. This is sometimes known as European terms. The USA usually quote using the direct form. This is known as American terms.

Table 21.1 *Extract from the* Financial Times

Aug 11	Closing mid-point	Change on day	Bid/offer spread	Day's Mid high	Day's Mid low	One month Rate	One month %PA	Three months Rate	Three months %PA	One year Rate	One year %PA	Bank of Eng. Index
Europe												
Austria (Sch)	17.1201	+0.043	123–278	17.1481	17.0371	17.1157	0.3	17.1039	0.4	—	—	115.1
Belgium (BFr)	50.1163	+0.1319	972–354	50.1910	50.0870	50.1163	0.0	50.1413	−0.2	49.7913	0.6	116.5
Denmark (DKr)	9.6161	+0.0487	097–225	9.6316	9.5956	9.6206	−0.6	9.6302	−0.6	9.6831	−0.7	116.3
Finland (FM)	8.0358	+0.0505	253–462	8.0510	7.9750	—	—	—	—	—	—	82.3
France (FFr)	8.3307	+0.0212	263–350	8.3472	8.3248	8.3336	−0.4	8.3319	−0.1	8.2921	0.5	109.7
Germany (DM)	2.4328	+0.0075	318–338	2.4384	2.4282	2.4328	0.0	2.4299	0.5	2.4035	1.2	125.8
Greece (Dr)	367.860	+1.256	623–097	368.265	367.238	—	—	—	—	—	—	—
Ireland (I£)	1.0138	+0.0024	130–146	1.0164	1.0120	1.0139	−0.1	1.014	−0.1	1.0144	−0.1	104.3
Italy (L)	2446.27	+2.5	418–836	2457.25	2444.18	2453.07	−3.3	2464.82	−3.0	2510.27	−2.6	75.5
Luxembourg (LFr)	50.1163	+0.1319	972–354	50.1910	50.0870	50.1163	0.0	50.1413	−0.2	49.7913	0.6	116.5
Netherlands (Fl)	2.7337	+0.0084	323–351	2.7420	2.7276	2.7335	0.1	2.7303	0.5	2.7025	1.1	120.3
Norway (NKr)	10.6692	+0.0594	652–731	10.6761	10.5885	10.6662	0.3	10.6767	−0.3	10.6627	0.1	86.3
Portugal (Es)	247.386	+0.606	176–596	248.232	247.176	249.116	−8.4	252.296	−7.9	—	—	—
Spain (Pta)	200.714	+0.761	591–836	201.047	200.390	201.224	−3.0	201.904	−2.4	203.799	−1.5	86.2
Sweden (SKr)	12.0864	+0.1076	765–963	12.1269	11.9518	12.1079	−2.1	12.1584	−2.4	12.3789	−2.4	73.2
Switzerland (SFr)	2.0495	+0.0066	484–505	2.0562	2.0476	2.048	0.9	2.0435	1.2	2.0124	1.8	120.8
UK (£)	—	—	—	—	—	—	—	—	—	—	—	79.4
Ecu	1.2751	+0.0047	743–758	1.2766	1.2735	1.2759	−0.8	1.2765	−0.4	1.2775	−0.2	—
SDR†	0.940325	—	—	—	—	—	—	—	—	—	—	—
Americas												
Argentina (Peso)	1.5319	−0.0076	315–323	1.5377	1.5300	—	—	—	—	—	—	—
Brazil (Rl)	1.3741	+0.0001	730–752	1.3796	1.3694	—	—	—	—	—	—	—
Canada (C$)	2.1115	−0.0051	106–123	2.1203	2.1082	2.1121	−0.3	2.1125	−0.2	2.1213	−0.5	86.4
Mexico (New Peso)	5.2091	−0.0096	048–133	5.2225	5.2037	—	—	—	—	—	—	—
USA ($)	1.5328	−0.0076	324–331	1.5383	1.5305	1.5321	0.5	1.5303	0.6	1.5213	0.8	63.8
Pacific/Middle East/Africa												
Australia (A$)	2.0532	−0.0268	520–543	2.0663	2.0511	2.0531	0.0	2.0545	−0.3	2.0727	−0.9	—
Hong Kong (HK$)	11.8431	−0.0569	396–466	11.8854	11.8265	11.8392	0.4	11.8381	0.2	11.8451	0.0	—
India (Rs)	48.0785	−0.2443	637–983	48.2490	48.0120	—	—	—	—	—	—	—
Japan (Y)	154.984	−0.83	910–058	155.880	154.580	154.594	3.0	153.699	3.3	149.234	3.7	187.7
Malaysia (M$)	3.9262	−0.049	245–278	3.9665	3.9211	—	—	—	—	—	—	—
New Zealand (NZ$)	2.5536	−0.0231	519–552	2.5631	2.5506	2.5575	−1.8	2.5653	−1.8	2.5876	−1.3	—
Philippines (Peso)	40.1965	−0.2763	424–505	40.5505	39.8424	—	—	—	—	—	—	—
Saudi Arabia (SR)	5.7484	−0.0285	468–499	5.7689	5.7401	—	—	—	—	—	—	—
Singapore (S$)	2.3091	−0.0114	078–104	2.3159	2.3060	—	—	—	—	—	—	—
S. Africa (Com.) (R)	5.5352	−0.0278	327–376	5.5616	5.5179	—	—	—	—	—	—	—
S. Africa (Fin.) (R)	7.1227	−0.0246	057–396	7.1457	7.1057	—	—	—	—	—	—	—
South Korea (Won)	1236.16	−2.82	511–721	1239.87	1234.35	—	—	—	—	—	—	—
Taiwan (T$)	40.5665	−0.2004	534–796	40.7096	40.5108	—	—	—	—	—	—	—
Thailand (Bt)	38.4260	−0.1752	019–501	38.5500	38.3770	—	—	—	—	—	—	—

† SDR rate for Aug. 10. Bid/offer spreads in the Pound Spot table show only the last three decimal places. Forward rates are not directly quoted to the market but are implied by current interest rates. Sterling index calculated by the Bank of England. Base average 1985 = 100. Bid, Offer and Mid-rates in both this and the Dollar Spot tables derived from THE WM/REUTERS CLOSING SPOT RATES. Some values are rounded by the F.T.

These differences can confuse those not familiar with the subject. Technically:

- **direct quote** = number of units of home currency to deal in one unit of away currency;
- **indirect quote** = number of units of away currency to deal in one unit of home currency.

The spot rate is the exchange price for transactions to be settled quickly. This normally means that (in the example we are using) the dollar and the pound are to be exchanged within two business days, although in practice deals to be settled within a week are often still called spot transactions.

The alternative to the spot price is the forward price. The forward price applies to a deal which is agreed upon now, but where the actual exchange of the currency is not to take place until an agreed time period has elapsed. The exchange at the date in the future will be at the price agreed upon now. Table 21.1 shows that one month forward price is $1.5321 = £1. There is very little difference between this rate and the spot rate but there is a difference with the dollar becoming stronger. This means that the dollar was trading at a forward premium on the pound. This means that if an agreement was made now to exchange pounds for dollars in one month's time, less dollars would be paid per pound than if the pounds were to be bought at the spot price.

The rate of exchange of the US dollar against the pound at the mid-point was:

Spot rate	1.5328
One month forward	1.5321
Three-month forward	1.5303
One-year forward	1.5213

The premium between the spot and one month forward rate is 0.07 of 1 cent, and between the spot and the one year forward is 1.15 cents. This is sometimes known as the swap rate. We either add the swap rate to, or deduct it from, the spot rate to arrive at the appropriate forward rate.

On occasions two forward rates are quoted (for say three months), one being the bid price for the forward deal, the other the offer price. The forward prices referred to above are based on the mid-point between bid and offer; it is the practice of the FT daily listings to list such mid-points.

As at August 1994 the pound was expected to rise against the Canadian dollar over the next few months. The Canadian dollar was trading at a forward discount against the pound. The relationship between the spot rate, the forward rate and the swap rates for the Canadian dollar was:

Spot rate £1	2.1115
One-month forward rate	2.1121
Three-month forward rate	2.1125
One-year forward rate	2.1213
One-month swap rate	0.0006
Three-month swap rate	0.0010
One-year swap rate	0.0098

With a forward exchange deal it is possible to make an opportunity gain or loss. Suppose that a UK businessman has purchased goods from the USA which he will have to pay for in dollars in three months' time. The value of the goods is $10 000. He has three choices: he could buy the dollars now at the spot rate, which would cost £6524 = $10 000/1.5328; he could enter into a deal now for dollars to be delivered in three months' time, buying at the appropriate forward exchange rate, which would cost him £6530 = $10 000/1.5303 in three months or he could wait three months and buy dollars at whatever the spot rate is at that time. If he follows the first option he could earn interest on the dollars for three months at the interest rate on the dollar. If he follows the second or third option, he should take into account the interest he can earn on pounds sterling over this period. These alternatives will be discussed in a later section.

Cross rates

Exchange rates between currencies are quoted in many markets around the world. These exchange rates have to be in line with each other to prevent dealers making easy gains. One opportunity to exploit differences arises in relation to what are known as cross rates. This can be illustrated with three currencies and let us say three different markets.

In London	£1 = $1.5
In New York	$1 = DM 2
In Frankfurt	1 DM = £0.30

In this situation the market is not in equilibrium. The opportunity exists for what is known as cross-rate arbitrage.

A dealer in Frankfurt with pounds would sell £0.30 and buy 1 DM. They could take the 1 DM to New York and buy $0.50. They could then take the $0.50 to London and buy £0.33. They would have made a gain of £0.03 on the cross-market dealings.

The problem is that the pound is overvalued against the DM. The equilibrium rate of exchange is 1 DM = £0.33. This disequilibrium situation should not arise; if it did it would only be for a brief moment of time. The arbitrage dealers in selling pounds and buying DMs would depress the price of the pound and increase the price of the DM.

21.3 Factors influencing exchange rates

We shall begin with a brief description of the individual factors that influence exchange rates and then explain how they interact.

The balance of payments position

A country may have a balance of payments deficit with its imports exceeding its exports. It has to pay for its imports in foreign currencies and its exports do not earn sufficient foreign exchange to pay for the imports. Therefore it has a shortage of foreign currency. The demand for foreign currency increases. In the absence of other factors, this will tend to put upward pressures on the price of foreign currency against the domestic currency. The country's own currency will fall in value.

Purchasing power parity

This is a complicated theory. However, it basically means that if the rate of inflation in country A is greater than the rate of inflation in country B, the rate of exchange of the currency of country A will fall against the currency of country B.

In its simplest version it is based on the idea that in terms of an international price a product should cost the same wherever it is produced. Let us suppose, for example, that a washing machine was initially priced the same whether it was produced in Germany or the UK (the same price at the then rate of exchange). Let us assume that in the next year inflation was higher in the UK than in Germany, and so the monetary cost of the product became higher in the UK than in Germany and the monetary price became higher. Then, if the exchange rates remain constant, consumers will buy the less expensive product from Germany rather than the more expensive UK product. This means that sales of the UK product will fall. The demand from foreigners for deutschmarks to buy the German product will rise and the demand for sterling by foreigners to buy the UK product will fall. This will mean that, in consequence, the price of the deutschmark will rise against the pound.

The above example refers to the effect of inflation on one product. Of course we would not expect the price of one product to affect the exchange rate. However, the general level of inflation would be expected to have an effect. The purchasing power parity idea is obviously not based on equalling the price of individual goods through exchange rate movements, but on the idea that, where possible, exchange rates move to bring about some sort of general parity in the real price of goods from one country to another.

One implication of this theory is that differences in inflation rates between countries will affect the movements in the exchange rate. The expected difference in the inflation rate would be expected to approximate to the expected change in the exchange rates. In fact it has been found that the estimate of the differential between the inflation rates of two countries is a good estimate of the change in the exchange rate.

Market expectations

It can be argued that the price of one currency relative to another depends upon what is expected to happen in the future. For example, an election to be held in the near future in country X introduces a note of uncertainty, which could affect the exchange rate. A government could be elected which would change policies with respect to such things as inflation, foreign trade and public sector deficits. Those buying and selling the currency of country X will have their own expectations of the future economic position of the country. This will affect the supply and demand for the currency and the relationship between the spot rate and the forward rate.

Some market traders will be willing to accept more risk than others. Some have different expectations to others. It is the interaction of the different traders' expectations that will determine the rates of exchange. Because of the differing expectations, and the consequent problems of forecasting, the best forecast of the future spot rate is the current forward exchange rate. In other words, so many factors can influence the spot rate that will apply in, say, three months' time, with many of the factors counterbalancing each other, that if one wants a forecast of the spot rate that will exist in three months' time one may as well use today's three month forward rate. Why this is so will be demonstrated on pages 775–6.

Interest rate

The interest rates within a country are determined in the money market. The price of money, like anything else, is determined by supply and demand, although in many countries governments do try to manage the interest rate. The demand for money depends on such factors as levels of investment, inflation and public sector borrowing. The supply depends on such factors as the government's policy on money supply, the efficiency of the financial institutions, and the customs and habits within a country.

Relationship between exchange rates and interest rates

There is a strong relationship between the FOREX market and the money market. The relationship between the interest rates in two countries affects the rate of exchange, and in particular the relationship between the spot rate of exchange and the forward rate of exchange.

There are of course many factors other than interest rates that affect the movements in exchange rates over time. However, other things being equal, the currency with the higher interest rate will sell at a discount in the forward market against the currency with the lower interest rate or, to put it the other way, the currency with the lower interest rate will sell at a premium in the forward market against the currency with the higher interest rate. It should be emphasized that what is being discussed is the relationship at a point in time between the spot rate and the forward rate, the premium or discount. In the quotations shown in Table 21.1 the dollar was trading at a premium against the pound. At that date interest rates in the USA were lower than those in the UK.

The reason that these relationships hold is because operators in the money market are free to invest or borrow in the currency that offers them the most favourable interest rates. This will affect the forward exchange rates, as will be illustrated in the following example in which it is assumed that only interest rate differentials affect forward exchange rates.

Suppose that on 1 January the spot rate is £1 = $1.50. The interest rates on money deposited is 13% per annum for pounds sterling and 10% for US dollars. What would we expect the three month forward rate to be that is being quoted on 1 January, if we were only taking this interest rate differential into account and what is known as the interest rate parity theory applies? The forward rate equals the spot rate plus or minus the swap rate, where the swap rate reflects the interest rate differential.

The swap rate can be determined using the following formula:

spot rate × % difference in interest rates × effective time fraction of one year
= swap rate

In the example being used

$$\$1.5 \times \frac{0.10 - 0.13}{1.13} \times \frac{3}{12} = -\$0.009956$$

The way in which the difference in interest rates is calculated should be noted. It can be approximated by taking the simple difference of 3%, but the above method gives a more precise measure. The US interest rate is 2.65% below that for the UK (i.e.: (0.13 − 0.10)/1.13).

In this case the forward pound would be selling at a discount against the dollar, with the fall in the value of the pound over the three month period balancing the interest rate differential. To determine the forward rate we deduct the swap rate from the spot rate:

Spot rate £1	$1.500000
Swap rate	−$0.009956
Three month forward rate	$1.490044

which we shall round off to $1.49.

To prove that this approach works, we shall show that, with the exchange rates adjusted in line with interest rate differentials, it is not possible for gains to be made:

1 January
Step 1.	Sell	$1500	
Step 2.	Receive and deposit		£1000

1 April
Step 3.	Interest received		£32.5
Step 4.	Sell		£1032.5
Step 5.	Receive		
	(at $1.49 = £1)	$1538	

The investor would have been just as well off if he had invested his dollars for three months in the USA at the lower interest rates of 10%. The difference between the spot rate and the forward rate on 1 January allows for the differences in interest rates.

This is known as the interest rate parity theory: it states that in equilibrium the difference in interest rates between two countries is equal to the difference between the forward and spot rates of exchange. It can be expressed mathematically as

$$\frac{i_A - i_B}{1 + i_B} = \frac{F_0 - S_0}{S_0}$$

where i_A is the current interest rate on the currency of country A, i_B is the current interest rate on the currency of country B, F_0 is the current forward rate of exchange between the two currencies and S_0 is the current spot rate of exchange between the two currencies. Two other variables relevant to exchange rate determination that we shall use are the expected inflation rate P_A in country A and the expected inflation rate P_B in country B. We also need one other variable: the expected spot rate of exchange $\bar{S}_T$ between the two currencies at time T.

One detail over which we have to be careful is what time T we are considering. The equations we shall introduce will work for any time period ahead: three months, six months or 12 months. However, we must be careful to use the interest rates (adjusted if necessary) for the same time period as the period for the forward rates.

Substituting the values in the above example into the interest rate equation, and taking the USA as country A and the UK as country B, gives

$$\frac{0.10 - 0.13}{1.13} \times \frac{3}{12} = \frac{1.49 - 1.50}{1.50}$$

$$-0.00664 \approx -0.00667$$

There is a small difference due to rounding-off errors in the above figures. It should be noted that the difference between the annual interest rates has in this case been adjusted to give the difference over a three months period. The forward rate being used was for three months.

The relationship between interest rates and exchange rates can be tested to see if equilibrium exists using either the direct or the indirect method of expressing exchange rates. The formula to be used varies slightly however from one method to the other. We will illustrate with a simple example.

Example 21.1

Let us suppose the spot rate of exchange between the pound and the French franc is £1 = 10FF, and the one-year forward rate £1 = 9.17FF. The interest rate in the UK is 20% per annum, and in France is 10% per annum. Is the market in equilibrium?

Using first the indirect exchange rates and the equations shown above, the forward premium/discount on the exchange rates equals

$$= \frac{f_0 - s_0}{s_0} = \frac{9.17 - 10.0}{10.0} = -0.083$$

The interest rate differential (expressed in a form appropriate for the indirect method) equals

$$= \frac{i_A - i_B}{1 + i_B} = \frac{0.10 - 0.20}{1.20} = -0.083$$

The market is in equilibrium.

If the relationship is to be tested using the direct method:

the spot rate =   £0.10   = 1FF
the one-year forward rate   £1.0905   = 1FF

The forward premium/discount in the exchange rate equals

$$\frac{1.0905 - 1.000}{1.000} = +0.091$$

The interest rate differential is expressed as:

$$\left[\frac{(1 + i_B)}{(1 + i_A)} - 1 \right] = \frac{1.20}{1.10} - 1 = +0.091$$

Interest-rate arbitrage

The relationships in Example 21.1 are based on the equilibrium existing between the money markets and the foreign exchange markets. If equilibrium does not exist, the exact relationships will not hold. Arbitrage is then possible. We shall illustrate this by changing the example on page 771 to one in which interest rate parity theory does not hold

Example 21.2

Let us assume that the UK three month interest rate is again 3% per annum above the comparable US rates. If the market was in equilibrium we would expect the three month forward exchange rate of the pound against the dollar to be below the spot rate by approximately 3%. We shall now assume that this is not the case, and that the spot rate is £1 = $1.50 and the forward rate is £1 = $1.52.

An investor in the US can take advantage of this situation, by taking the following steps:

1 January	Step 1.	Borrow $1500
	Step 2.	Convert the dollars to pounds at the spot rate
	Step 3.	Invest the £1000 in the UK
	Step 4.	Agree to sell pounds against dollars in three months time at the forward rate of $1.52 = £1
1 April	Step 5.	Cash in the UK investment and receive £1000 + £32.5 interest
	Step 6.	Convert the £1032.5 into dollars to give $1569.4
	Step 7.	Pay off the US loan plus interest, $1500 + $37.5. Result profit $31.9

If all those involved in the foreign exchange market had the same expectations and the same attitudes towards risk, and the other factors affecting exchange rates were neutral, then the difference on any day between the forward and spot rates would reflect the differences in interest rates over the forward period. A dealer could gain on the interest earned by exchanging his own currency for one offering higher interest but would lose on the currency side of the deal by receiving a lower rate of exchange at the end of the period than he had paid at the beginning. The interest rate differential is called the interest agio, and the exchange rate differential the exchange agio.

Tests of the interest rate parity theory show that this relationship is usually found to hold in exchange rate markets. When it does not this can usually be explained by government restrictions, transaction costs and tax policies which often mean that it is not easy for investors to exchange currencies and transmit interest and profits to take advantage of opportunities created by interest and exchange rate differences. In the Eurocurrency markets, which are free from government interference, the interest rate parity concept is almost always found to hold.

Interrelationship between variables affecting exchange rates

There is a relationship not only between exchange rates and interest rates, but between exchange rates and inflation rates and between interest rates and inflation rates. These interconnecting relationships are illustrated in Fig. 21.1.

It should be noted that the way in which the exchange rate variables (F_0, S_0, $\bar{S}_T$) have been written in the figure is correct if we are writing the rate of exchange as the number of dollars to be received per pound (i.e. £1 = $1.50). If we were to write the rate the other way around, i.e. how many pounds can we buy with one dollar ($1 = £0.667), we would need to alter the equations in which the exchange rate appears. They would become

$$\frac{S_0 - F_0}{F_0} \quad \text{and} \quad \frac{S_0 - \bar{S}_T}{\bar{S}_T}$$

We shall now examine each of these individual interrelationships.

Relationship between interest rates and inflation rates

Why do nominal interest rates vary between one country and another? One school of economic thought attributes such variations to different expectations with regard to the rates of inflation within countries. If investors could move their funds freely from one country to another, they would move towards countries where they could expect to obtain the highest real rate of interest (nominal rate of interest less the inflation rate). With competition to attract funds, that would mean that the real rates of interest would move so that they were equal in all countries. An investor would not leave money in a country that was paying lower real returns than could be obtained elsewhere.

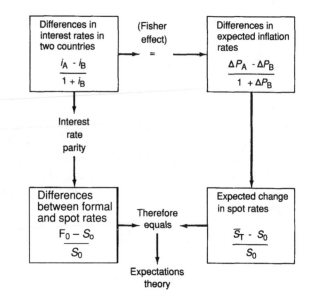

Figure 21.1

Let us say that France and the UK are offering interest rates of 15% and 10% respectively, and the inflation rate is the same in both countries. Investors will move their money to France where they can earn more on their money. However, if the inflation rate in France is expected to be 10% and that in the UK is only 4%, the investors can earn a greater real return in the UK. France would need to raise its nominal interest rates to 16% in order to prevent investors taking their funds out of the country.

The difference in interest rates between two countries is equal in equilibrium to the expected difference in inflation rates between these countries. The equation representing the Fisher effect is

$$\frac{i_A - i_B}{1 + i_B} = \frac{\Delta P_A - \Delta P_F}{1 - P_B}$$

The effect of this is that, with the free movement of capital, the interest rates in a country should be equal to the international real rate of interest adjusted for the difference in the expected rate of inflation in that country compared with the inflation rate world-wide.

Given information on interest rates we are in a position to forecast differences between expected inflation rates, which leads to our being able to forecast differences between forward and spot rates. If we were given information on expected inflation rates we could forecast both differences in interest rates and expected changes in spot rates.

In the example on page 771 we have been given the interest rates, and so we can forecast differences in expected inflation rates. Let us assume that the expected annual rate of inflation in the UK is 8%; then we can calculate that in equilibrium the expected rate of inflation in the USA must be in the region of 5.1%. It should be noted that both the interest rates and the expected inflation rates are annual rates.

Substituting these values in the Fisher equation gives

$$\frac{0.10 - 0.13}{1.13} = \frac{0.051 - 0.080}{1.080}$$
$$-0.027 = -0.027$$

Relationship between exchange rates and inflation rates

This relationship is expressed in the purchasing power parity theory which has already been referred to.

The hypothesis is that the expected difference in inflation rates between two countries equals, in equilibrium, the expected movement in spot rates. It can be expressed in an equation as

$$\frac{\Delta P_A - \Delta P_B}{1 + \Delta P_B} = \frac{S_T - S_0}{S_0}$$

We shall now substitute the values used in our example into the equation to obtain an estimate of S_T the expected spot rate of exchange at time T. It should be noted that the inflation rate figures we are using are annual rates. Therefore we shall obtain an estimate of the expected spot rate in 12 months time. We shall then adjust this expected spot rate in order to reconcile the estimate with the three month figures that we have used elsewhere in the example:

$$\frac{0.051 - 0.08}{1.08} = \frac{\overline{S}_T - 1.5}{1.5}$$

$$0.02685 = \frac{\overline{S}_T - 1.5}{1.5}$$

$$1.46 = S_T$$

We therefore expect that, in equilibrium, the spot rate of exchange in 12 months time will be £1 = $1.46. The three month spot rate should therefore be in the region of £1 = $1.49, i.e. a quarter of the movement over the year.

Relationship between the forward rate of exchange and the expected change in spot rates

We know from the theoretical relationships that we have developed that the difference at any time between the forward and spot rates is equal to the expected change in spot rates. If the three other relationships hold, these two variables must be equal. Indeed it is *a priori* what we would expect. If we knew with certainty what the pound–dollar spot rate would be in, say, six months, that would be the forward rate today. If we know we can buy $1.70 for £1 in six months, we would only be willing to enter into a six month forward deal today at that price. We would certainly not want to enter into a deal if we were offered less than $1.70, and the dealer would not want to offer us more. Of course, this is ignoring risk: the forward deal hedges against risk, from the buyer's point of view; waiting for the future spot price does not.

The basic equation representing this expectations theory is that in equilibrium:

$$\frac{F_0 - S_0}{S_0} = \frac{S_T - S_0}{S_0}$$

Substituting the values that we have been given and have derived in our example gives

$$\frac{1.49 - 1.50}{1.50} = \frac{1.49 - 1.50}{1.50}$$

which is clearly correct. Thus the three month forward rate of exchange is the best estimate of the expected spot rate of exchange in three months' time.

The expectations theory indicates that the percentage difference today between the forward rate and the spot rate is the change expected in the spot rate. The forward rate of exchange for, say, six months is what collective opinions in the market expect the spot rate to be in six months. In fact in six months' time the actual spot rate can turn out to be different from this expectation.

The financial manager of a UK company that has sold goods to the USA, and is to receive payment of $100 000 in three months' time, could wait until the money arrives and then convert the dollars into pounds sterling at the spot rate at the time, or he could sell the dollars forward. He could promise now to deliver the $100 000 in three months' time and to receive in exchange pounds sterling at the rate of exchange currently being quoted as the three months' forward rate. There are many events that could happen between now and three months hence which would result in the spot rate in three months time not being the forward rate now. Dealers are not perfect forecasters. The financial manager of a company might not agree with the market's opinion of what the spot rate will be. The manager might be tempted to gamble on his opinion being better than that of the market.

To conclude this section, exchange rate movements over time are influenced by differences between countries in purchasing power, inflation rate and interest rates. Interest rates themselves are of course influenced by inflation rates and sometimes government moves to influence exchange rates. Sometimes domestic interest rates move to influence exchange rates. We therefore have a circular relationship.

Transaction exposure occurs when there is a time delay between the sale of goods and the receipt of the payments, and it will occur in all foreign trading. The question is: who carries the risk? If an importer agrees to pay in the currency of the supplier then it is the importer who is taking the risk. Alternatively, if a supplier agrees to be paid in the buyer's own currency, then the exporter is taking the risk. Which currency is used for invoicing depends on the bargaining strength of the two parties to the transaction. Usually, in order to sell a product, the exporter quotes a price in the currency of the purchaser. For example, a UK company ships goods to a French purchaser on 1 January and the terms of the sale, which is invoiced in French francs, mean that the French buyer will not transmit the funds until 1 April. The UK company is exposed to an exchange risk during the three month period. If the franc becomes weaker against the pound, the UK company will lose. If the franc becomes stronger against the pound the UK company will gain. Means of hedging against this type of exposure will be discussed.

Transaction exposure can occur within multinational companies with intercompany trading, and with the payment of dividends from subsidiaries to the parent company. In the latter case hedging can again be used. The date of dividend payments will be known in advance, as will the approximate amounts. Arrangements can be made in advance of the date, so that the parent company will not make a monetary loss as a result of any movements in the exchange rates.

The businessman exposed to transaction risk can either run the risk of exchange rate movements or he can take steps to protect his future cash flows from exchange rate fluctuations. If he has sold goods abroad and is prepared to gamble he could, in addition to the profit on the sale of the goods, find that he had made a currency gain. This would happen if the rate of exchange had moved in his favour between the time that he delivered the goods and the time when he is paid. However, it could be that the rate of exchange moves the other way, giving him a currency loss and perhaps meaning that the payment he receives when converted into his own currency does not cover his costs. It is to avoid this possibility that many businessmen seek to avoid the risks of currency movements by adopting one of a number of possible hedging techniques.

Covering in the forward exchange market

Covering in the forward exchange market is the procedure for balancing either sales and the receipt of foreign currency or purchases and the payment of foreign currency, so that there is no net open position with regard to the movement of exchange rates.

Suppose that on 1 January 19X0 a UK exporter sells goods to a US customer, invoiced at $150 000, payment to be made in dollars on 1 April 19X0. The spot rate of exchange on 1 January 19X0 is, say, $1.50 = £1. The exporter, in deciding to sell the goods, has in mind a sales price of £100 000, and he bases his decision on the profitability of the deal on this amount. The rate of exchange will most probably vary between 1 January and 1 April, with the size and direction of the move being uncertain. If the pound strengthens against the dollar, the UK exporter makes a currency loss on the deal. If on 1 April £1 = $1.60, the purchaser receives dollars worth only £93 750. However, if the dollar strengthens against the pound and the spot rate on 1 April is £1 = £1.40, he will make a profit, as the $150 000 will be worth £107 143. He has made a profit on the foreign exchange transaction of £7143.

Rather than run the risk of a possible loss on the currency side of the deal, the exporter may decide to cover the deal. Let us assume that at the time of making the sale on 1 January, he enters into a forward currency deal. He promises to sell $150 000 against pounds to be delivered on 1 April. On 1 January the three month forward rate is £1 = $1.45. The dollar is expected to become stronger against the pound. This forward contract will mean that he receives £103 448. On 1 April the exporter receives a cheque for $150 000 from the purchaser. The exporter delivers $150 000 against the forward contract, and receives in exchange £103 448.

From the beginning of the transaction the exporter knew that he would receive £103 448. It could be that he makes an opportunity gain on the deal, as during the three months that he was waiting for payment the dollar became weaker against the pound. In fact, he may have made an opportunity loss. He sold the dollar in the forward market at a price of $1.45. He was uncertain what the spot price would be on 1 April; if it had turned out that the £1 equalled only £1.40 as a result of hedging, he would have made an opportunity loss. If he had waited and sold the $150 000 in the spot market, he would have received £107 143. Hedging by selling in the forward market has resulted in an opportunity loss of £3695.

However, the exporter was uncertain about the movement of the two currencies, and covering the sale in the market was a form of insurance. He could not know what the future spot rates would be. If the company had not hedged and the pound had strengthened against the dollar, with say a spot rate on 1 April of £1 = $1.55, they would only have received £96 774. A hedge through a forward deal would have resulted in an opportunity gain of £6674 (i.e. £103 448 – £96 774).

Opportunity gains and losses can only be calculated when the eventual spot price is known; it is just looking at the transaction with hindsight. By dealing in the forward market, the exporter is avoiding the risk of losing as a result of movements in the exchange rate. He is also, of course, giving up the chance of gaining as a result of a favourable movement. He is taking a neutral position.

It is the exchange dealer who is taking the risk. He enters a transaction on 1 January agreeing to accept in three months' time a certain number of US dollars, not knowing what the exchange rate will be in April when he has to hand over an agreed number of pounds to a businessman. It is the commercial banks that help make the foreign exchange markets work. They are willing to deal in foreign exchange; sometimes they are willing to speculate. Often, however, it is individual dealers who are the speculators.

Covering in the money markets

An exporter is to receive dollars. He does not know what the dollars will be worth in three months' time. He could borrow dollars on 1 January and convert these to pounds at the spot rate on that day. He will have incurred a dollar debt, but that does not matter because he can repay this borrowing when he receives the dollars from the debtor. He will have hedged by converting the dollars to pounds at the 1 January rate; he need not worry about future exchange rate movements.

To illustrate the technique, we shall continue with the example on the previous page. The spot and forward rates are as above, the borrowing rate on US dollars is 8% and the rate paid on investments in pounds is 12%. The following steps will need to be taken:

1 January	Step 1. Borrow $147 056 for three months
	Step 2. Convert these dollars at the spot rate of £1 = $1.50 to give £98 037
	Step 3. Invest the £98 037 in the UK for three months
1 April	Step 4. Receive $150 000 from US customer
	Step 5. Repay the dollar loan of $147 056 plus three months interest $2944
	Step 6. Realize the investment in the UK and receive £98 037 plus interest of £2941, a total of £100 978

Again, the exporter has taken out a form of insurance. Having borrowed in dollars he does not need to bother what happens to the exchange rate between dollars and pounds as his net exposure in the foreign currency during the three month period is zero. He is owed dollars by his customer and owes in turn a similar amount of dollars to a US bank. He can match his cash flows. Depending on the movement in exchange rates, however, he might make an opportunity gain or loss.

Covering in the options market

There are markets in options for many assets, commodities, shares and foreign currencies. In Chapter 11 both the theoretical aspects of options and details of trading in the options market for shares were described in considerable detail. The theory described applies to options in currencies as well as in shares. The trading techniques are similar. A company engaged in international trade, which is exposed to possible losses, can take out an option as an alternative to hedging in the forward or money market.

In the example above, the UK exporter would have the opportunity to buy an option to be able to sell dollars in three months' time. This is just an option; the writer of the option agrees that he will be willing to purchase dollars in three months time at a price agreed now. The exporter's worry is that the dollar will fall in value. Therefore he buys the option to be able to sell the dollars at an agreed rate. This will limit his loss if the dollar were to fall. He will have to pay a commission to the writer of the option.

If, in fact, the dollar becomes stronger rather than weaker against the pound, the exporter would not need to exercise the option. The cost to the exporter for his peace of mind during the three months he is waiting for payment is the option writer's commission.

Hedging examples

Two problems will now be considered to show how the alternative hedging techniques work.

Example 21.3

Albion Ltd is expanding its operations in France and has ordered the construction of a new factory near Lille. The final payment of 5 000 000 French francs is due in three months time. Albion currently only possesses sufficient liquid funds to finance normal working capital requirements, although £0.5 million, the proceeds from a sale and leaseback deal, should be received in approximately three months' time.

Current foreign exchange market rates applicable to Albion Ltd and money market rates are detailed below:

Foreign exchange market

	French francs/£1
Spot	11.121–11.150
One month forward	11.198–11.224
Two months forward	11.035–11.065
Three months forward	10.948–10.976

Money market	Borrowing	Lending
UK clearing bank	16%	11%
French banque de depôts	11%	8%
Eurofranc	11%	9%
Eurosterling	15.5%	12%
UK treasury bill	—	12%
1 year French bond	—	9.5%

Prepare a report discussing the advantages and disadvantages of the alternatives that are available to Albion Ltd for making payment. Recommend which alternative Albion Ltd should choose.

Suggested solution

There are at least four alternatives open to Albion Ltd.

1. The company could do nothing now. It could wait until the three months had elapsed and then buy French francs at the spot rate at that time. This policy involves taking a considerable risk, as the company does not know if the French franc will become stronger over time against the pound, which could involve them in needing to pay more than if they were to hedge. However, if the French franc were to become weaker against the pound, it would be in Albion's interests to delay payment as long as possible (referred to as a lag in payment).
2. The company could take cover in the forward foreign exchange market. This means agreeing now to buy francs in three months' time at a rate of FF10.948 = £1. This could cost £456 704. At the current spot rate the debt is £449 600. The forward exchange cover therefore has a cost of £7104 above the current spot rate.
3. If the company expects the French franc to appreciate in value, then Albion might decide to accelerate payment of the FF5 million. This is referred to as a 'lead payment'. Albion would need to borrow £449 600 now. It would convert these pounds into French francs and pay off the debt, but it would not be able to repay the borrowing until three months had elapsed. With the cost of borrowing in the Eurosterling market at 15.5%, the cost of this policy would be the interest payment of £17 422. This would appear to be an expensive policy.
4. A further possibility is for Albion Ltd to obtain money market cover. It could borrow pounds now in the UK and immediately convert these into French francs. This is the same as in alternative 3. The money market variation is to invest these French francs in the Eurofranc market rather than to pay the French company. The company needs FF 5 million in three months time. If it exchanges £ for FF now, it eliminates uncertainty about exchange rate movements. It can invest these FF to earn interest. It can earn 2.25% over three months in the Eurofranc market. This means it only needs FF 4.890 million now ($\times$ (1.0225) = 5m). To obtain FF 4.890 million now the company needs £439 700 (converted at spot). It borrows this amount now and pays interest. The steps in the money market hedge are:

Step			
	1.	Now	Borrow £439 700 at 3.875% interest
	2.	Now	Convert to FF 4.890 million
	3.	Now	Invest in Eurofranc market
	4.		In 3 months: cash in Eurofranc investment (4.890 million + 0.110 million)
	5.		Pay for factory
	6.		Repay £ loan plus interest = £456 738

I(Note the above steps are shown in the time sequence but this is not the sequence in which the calculations are made. As shown above the first calculation involves determining how much needs to be invested in FF now to be able to pay the debt on the due date.)

The company does not know what is going to happen to the exchange rate over the next three months. It is only after the elapse of the three months that the opportunity costs of the alternative policies could be worked out, and so the real least expensive alternative determined. At the time of making the decision, the company can either take a risk with alternative 1 or take some cover with either 2 or 4. Alternatives 2 and 4 cost more or less the same because the money market and the FOREX market are in equilibrium.

Example 21.4

Caswell Ltd is due to receive the sum of 5 million Alvanian dollars in three months time and wishes to be able to rely on the sum being sufficient to meet its commitment to an outflow of £2 million sterling at that time. The exchange rate between the two currencies is not fixed and small fluctuations are likely, whereas larger fluctuations are considered less likely but possible.

In an attempt to reduce its foreign exchange exposure and to ensure that the receipt will be sufficient to meet its sterling obligation, Caswell is to undertake a transaction utilizing the financial futures market in order to hedge the **total** amount at risk. The settlement price for a three month future is 2.5 Alvanian dollars to each £1 sterling. Initial margin requirements amount to 3% of the initial gross sterling value of the transaction. Commission costs and taxation may be ignored.

Advise Caswell whether it should attempt to become a 'buyer' or 'seller' of Alvanian dollars in the financial futures market.

On the assumption that, after the cash flows required on entering the transaction, no further cash flows occur until settlement, show the cash flow consequences of the above transaction, for each of the following separate spot exchange rates effective in three months:

(a) $2.00 = £1
(b) $2.50 = £1
(c) $3.00 = £1

Explain how a practical transaction in the financial futures market might not be as effective as the above transaction in keeping Caswell unaffected by exchange rate fluctuations.

Suggested solution

Caswell is to receive Alvanian dollars in three months' time, and so could become a seller of this currency in the future market. The company could enter a futures contract and agree to sell the 5 million dollars and receive in return £2 million in three months' time.

The initial margin requirement is the deposit Caswell needs to make when entering into the future contract. The margin, in this case 3% of the £2 million (i.e. £60 000), protects the foreign exchange dealer against Caswell's inability to meet the call for 5 million Alvanian dollars in three months' time. If in three months' time the dollars cannot be delivered, then the £60 000 is sacrificed. If, however, the dollars are delivered, the £60 000 is returned and all that Caswell has lost is the interest they could have earned on the £60 000 deposit.

The second part of the question provides three different effective spot rates for three months' time. If Caswell entered into the futures transaction, the results of its hedging policy, under the different outcomes, would be as follows.

(a) With $2.00 = £1
   Sale in spot market $5 million   = £2.5 million
   Inflow resulting from futures deal   = £2.0 million
   Opportunity loss   = £0.5 million

   Plus loss of interest on £60 000
(b) With $2.50 = £1
   Break even, except for loss of interest
(c) With $3.00 = £1
   Sale in spot market   = £1.67 million
   Inflow from futures deal   = £2.00 million
   Opportunity gain   = £0.33 million
   Less loss of interest on £60 000

These gains and losses are the resulting opportunity gains and losses if the company has entered into the futures contracts. In all three situations the achieved cash inflow to Caswell in three months is £2 000 000.

In practice the position might be a little more complicated than is indicated above. If the value of the future position falls over the life of the contract, the participants may be required to make some interim payments towards the amount eventually to be delivered. For example, in the first situation shown above, the pound is declining against the dollar; the dealer may require Caswell to make cash payments over the three months equivalent in total to the fall in value of the future contract, i.e. at most £0.5 million. The total payment by Caswell of $5 million will not be affected. The company will not have to pay more; it is just the timing of the company's cash outflow that may change.

Example 21.5

Fidden is a medium-sized UK company with export and import trade with the USA. The following transactions are due within the next six months. Transactions are in the currency specified.

Purchase of finished goods for resale, cash payment due in six months: $447 000.
Sale of finished goods, cash receipt due in six months: $154 000.

Exchange rates (London market)

	$/£
Spot	1.7106 − 1.7140
Three months forward	0.82 − 0.77 cents premium
Six months forward	1.39 − 1.34 cents premium

Interest rates per annum

	Borrowing	Lending
Sterling	12.5%	9.5%
Dollars	9%	6%

Foreign currency option prices (New York market)
Prices are cents per £, contract size £12 500

Exercise price ($)	Calls March	Calls June	Calls Sept.	Puts March	Puts June	Puts Sept.
1.60	—	15.20	—	—	—	2.75
1.70	5.65	7.75	—	—	3.45	6.40
1.80	1.70	3.60	7.90	—	9.32	15.35

Assume that it is now December with six months to expiry of the June contract and that the option price is not payable until the end of the option period, or when the option is exercised.

Required:

(i) Calculate the net sterling receipts/payments that Fidden might expect for its six month transactions if the company hedges foreign exchange risk on
   (1) the forward foreign exchange market;
   (2) the money market.
(ii) If the actual spot rate in six months time was with hindsight exactly the present six months forward rate, calculate whether Fidden would have been better to hedge through foreign currency options rather than the forward market or money market.

ACCA, Dec. 1989

Answer

The net position of Fidden is that a cash payment of $293 000 must be made in six months' time.

(i)(1) Forward market
   Buy $293 000 at $1.6967   =   £172 688

(2) Money market

    Step 1. Borrow £166 296 at 12.5% p.a. (now)

2. Convert to dollars at $1.7106	=	$284 466
3. Invest dollars at 6% p.a.		
4. Cash in dollar investment (in June)	=	$293 000
5. Pay US supplier		
6. Repay UK loan + interest	=	£176 690

Conclusion

The forward market is less expensive than the money market.

(ii) Options

Need to buy $ and sell £. Therefore a put option on £ sterling for exercise in June. Prices available $1.70 and $1.80.

Step 1 At $1.70 we need 14 contracts i.e.

$$\$293\,000 \text{ at } \$1.70 = £172\,353$$

$$\frac{£172\,353}{£12\,500} = 14 \text{ (to nearest higher number)}$$

Step 2 Cost of option

$$(14 \times £12\,500 \times 3.45 \text{ cents}) = \$6037.5$$
$$= £3550$$

Step 3 The 14 contracts will give us 4500 more dollars than we need (297 500 − 293 000). These will be worth £2646 at the spot rate in six months' time.

Step 4 Total cost

$$(£175\,000 + £3550 − £2646) = £175\,904$$

Conclusion

Options at $1.70 are more expensive than the forward market.
Option at $1.80 = £1:

Step 1 Number of contacts

$$\frac{\$293\,000}{\$1.80} = £162\,778$$

$$\frac{£162\,778}{£12\,500} = 13.02$$

This is so close to 13 that it should be possible to take out 13 contracts and deal with the balance in the forward market.

Step 2 Cost of option

$$(13 \times £12\,500 \times 9.32 \text{ cents}) = \$16\,310$$
$$= £9590$$

Step 3 The contacts will give approximately the number of dollars we need

i.e. $$(13 \times £12\,500 \times \$1.80) = \$292\,500$$

Step 4 The total cost equals

$$(£162\,500 + £9590) = £172\,090$$

Conclusion

This is the least expensive. With hindsight the company should have hedged with a $1.80 option.

The first point to make is that this form of foreign exchange hedging is not often used. The London International Financial Futures Exchange (LIFFE) closed down its futures currency market in 1990 because of a lack of business. In London the forward currency market dominates. However, there are futures markets in other countries that offer the opportunity to trade in currencies, for example the markets in Philadelphia and Chicago. It is also possible to arrange an over-the-counter currency futures contract in London and many other cities.

A second point to make is that technically there is much in common between a currency futures hedge and an interest rate futures hedge.

When hedging in the futures market two separate activities will be taking place. One will be a transaction at a future date in the cash market at the spot rate at the time of the transaction. The other activity will be two transactions taking an equal and opposite position in the futures market. Equal means the transactions are of an approximately similar size. Opposite means that if the exchange rate moves so that the person hedging makes a loss on spot rates in the cash market, then the person hedging gains on the transactions in the futures market. Of course if the person hedging gains on the movements in spot rates in the cash market they lose in the futures market. For example if a gain is made from a stronger pound in the cash market, then a loss will result from the hedging transactions in the futures market.

The hedge does not usually result in a perfect match of gains and losses. The price for a currency in the cash market and the price in the futures markets tend to move in roughly parallel fashion, but not always at precisely the same rate. There can also be a mismatch resulting from the fact that in the traded futures market contracts are for a standard amount of currency and this amount might not equal the amount to be hedged.

To repeat with a forward hedge, basically two sets of transactions are taking place. One is a transaction to exchange currency at the spot rate. Let us say a UK manufacturing company makes a sale and will receive US$ in three months' time. These dollars will be exchanged into pounds at the spot rate in three months' time. The second transaction, or rather transactions, is in the futures market with a purchase and a sale of futures contracts, one at one date, one at the other, the intention being that any loss on the spot deal is balanced by a net gain on the two futures contracts. We will illustrate a currency futures hedge with an example in which a company is to receive a foreign currency.

The steps we need to take to arrive at the exact details of the futures contracts are:

1. Ascertain the target outcome.
2. Decide for the first contract which currency we will be buying and which we will be selling.
3. Determine the appropriate date for closing the two contracts.
4. Ascertain the number of contracts we need to buy and sell.

Example 21.6

Fry plc sells goods to the USA on 1 January. It invoices the US purchaser for $150 000 with payment to be received on 1 May. The management of Fry is worried that the dollar will fall in value against the pound over the next few months. They decide to hedge in the futures market.

On 1 January the relevant foreign exchange cash and futures rates were:

Forex (cash market)	
Spot	$1.59–$1.60
3 month forward	$1.60–$1.61
6 month forward	$1.61–$1.62

Sterling futures

Mar.	1.585
June	1.602
Sept.	1.612

It should be appreciated that the price of futures contracts moves in line with prices in the cash market, but that they are not usually exactly the same. For example the six-month forward rate of exchange will only approximate to the rate of exchange quoted for a futures contract expiring at the same date.

On 1 May the actual spot rate turns out to be $1.615–1.625 and the price of June futures contracts $1.620. On 30 June the actual spot rate is $1.620–$1.630.

The first thing to calculate to determine the result of the hedge is the target outcome.

This is based on the spot exchange rate on the day of the sale. As at 1 January the company could expect to receive from the sale $150 000/1.60 = £93 750. Subsequent outcomes will be measured against this target.

On 1 May the company will be buying pounds and selling dollars in the spot market. We wish to hedge against loss against the target outcome. We have to decide upon the details of two futures contracts. One futures contract will be taken out now, the other at (or near) the date of the spot transaction. Both deals will be closed at a date beyond the spot deal.

There are two possible alternatives. One is to agree now to (a) enter a forward contract to buy sterling and sell dollars at some future date (say 30 June) and (b) to carry out the opposite futures deal for the same sterling amount on 1 May also for settlement at 30 June. If the dollar becomes weaker over time against the pound we will receive a better price quoted in January for selling dollars in June than will be quoted to us in May when we wish to enter the second of the forward contracts to buy dollars on 30 June. We will make a gain when we close the forward deal on 30 June which will balance the loss we make in the spot market on 1 May.

The reader should be able to work out that the alternative possibility agreeing now (1 January) to buy dollars in June and on 1 May agreeing to sell dollars in June has exactly the opposite effect to that required. It leads to a loss on the futures deals which will add to the loss on the spot deal.

The rule is that if in the cash market you will be selling a currency at a future date, then the initial futures contracts is also to sell that currency. If on the spot market one is to buy a currency, then the first futures contract is to buy that currency.

In this example our first futures deal is therefore to buy sterling and sell dollars with a June futures contract. Why June? It is usual to fix the date to close out our two opposite futures deals as the first available date after the invoiced amount is received (or has been paid).

To ascertain the number of contracts we need to buy we convert the dollars to be received into sterling, and we usually use the futures price to do this.

$$\frac{\$150\,000}{1.602} = £93\,632$$

Each futures contract is for £25 000 therefore we need to buy four contracts.

Transactions

In futures market

1 January: Enter four sterling futures June contracts, to purchase pounds at a price of $1.602 to £1

1 May: Enter four sterling futures June contracts to sell pounds and buy dollars at a price of $1.620 to £1.

30 June: Close out the two futures contracts.

In spot market

1 May: Sell $150 000 at $1.625 (equals £92 593).

Results

Futures market

January contract:	Buy	4 × £25 000 × $1.602	
Cost			= $160 200
May contract:	Sell	4 × £25 000 × $1.620	
Receive			= $162 000
	Gain	$1800	

Value in pounds in June with spot rate of $1.630 = £1

$$= £1104$$

Spot market

Receive	£92 593
Target	£93 750
Loss against target	£ 1 157

The gain on the futures contract cancels out the loss on the spot deal.

Example 21.7

On 1 July, Douglas plc purchased goods from the USA. The cost of the goods was $320 000, and payment is to be made in four months' time (at the end of October).

The company is considering hedging the transaction in the futures market. Various foreign exchange rates and futures rates are given below:

FOREX rates (as at 1 July)

	£/$
Spot	1.4480–1.4510
3 month forward	1.4842–1.4872
6 month forward	1.5204–1.5235

Futures rates (as at 1 July) for £/$ contracts of £25 000

Sept.	$1.4820 = £1
Dec.	$1.5170 = £1

Required:

Evaluate a futures hedging policy for Douglas.
The spot rate at the end of October turned out to be £1 = $1.48–$1.49.
The futures price (for a December delivery) as at the end of October turned out to be £1 = $1.53.

Answer

1. Target outcome

$$\text{To pay } \frac{\$320\,000}{1.448} = £220\,994$$

2. Futures contracts:
On 1 July enter contracts to buy dollars and sell pounds, for December delivery (first available date following spot transaction).
On 31 October enter contracts to sell dollars and buy pounds for December delivery.

3. Number of contracts

$$\frac{\$320\ 000}{1.5170} = £210\ 942$$

Each contract is for £25 000. Therefore nine contracts are required to fully cover the amount involved.

Transactions

(a) 1 July   Purchase 9 Dec. futures contracts to buy $ (sell £) at a price of $1.5170 (note the $ is expected to get weaker against the £, so payment of a $ debt is expected to become cheaper in sterling terms).

(b) 31 Oct. (i) Buy $'s in cash market.
    (Note: the $ has not weakened against the £ as much as was expected.)
    Cash paid:

$$\frac{\$320\ 000}{1.48} = £216\ 216$$

Gain in cash market against target £4778.
(ii) Sell 9 Dec. futures contracts to sell $ and buy £s at $1.53 equals £1.

(c) 31 Dec. (close out futures contracts)
    (i) July contracts to buy $

Receive $9 \times £25\ 000 \times \$1.517$ $= \$341\ 325$

    (ii) October contracts to sell $

Cost $9 \times £25\ 000 \times \$1.53$ $= \$344\ 250$
Loss in futures market $\$\ \ \ 2\ 925$
which at spot rate in December of £1 = $1.53
Equals loss of $= £1912$

The loss on the futures market is less than the gain on the spot market. This difference is due to a greater difference between the spot rates to that between the futures rates, and the size mismatch.

In retrospect it would have been better not to hedge with futures contracts.

But if the exchange rates had moved in the other direction the company would have lost without a hedge. This will be illustrated. Say $ gets stronger against £ from August.

Assume at 1 Oct.
Spot   £1 = $1.42 – $1.43
and Dec. futures price   £1 = $1.41

Then cost of cash transaction

$$\frac{\$320\ 000}{1.42} = £225\ 352$$

Loss against target   £4 358

Futures transactions at 31 Dec.

1. July contracts

   To receive $9 \times £25\,000 \times 1.517$ = $341 325

2. Oct. contracts

   To pay $9 \times £25\,000 \times 1.41$ = $317 250

   Gain $ 24 075

which at spot rate in December of say $1.4 = £1 equals   £ 17 074

Without a hedge this shows a loss of £4358 (in cash market). With a hedge it shows a net gain.

21.6 Foreign exchange risk

There are three types of FOREX exposure, each of which results in risks for a company. Transaction risk has already been referred to. The other types of exposure and risk are as follows.

Accounting (translation) exposure

Accounting exposure arises not as a result of conversion of currencies but as a result of financial data denominated in one currency needing to be expressed in terms of another currency. Such translation of currencies occurs at the end of each accounting year when the accounts of all subsidiaries have to be expressed in the currency of the parent company in order to present the consolidated accounts of the group. The important question that arises is at what rate of exchange the accounts should be translated.

Economic exposure

The economic value of an asset, or collection of assets, is based on the present value (PV) of the future cash flows that such assets will generate. This approach was discussed in Chapter 4. A company is an asset; therefore in theory its value as a going concern is the PV of its future cash flows. However for a multinational the question arises of the appropriate currency in which to measure the cash flows. The owner of an overseas subsidiary will wish at some time to be able to convert the cash flows generated in the host country currency into another currency. If a subsidiary company is sold locally to another company, taking the cash out of the country will involve a conversion. Therefore the value of the future cash flows is not just influenced by business risks, but also by exchange rate risks. The value of any business at any time depends upon the future cash flows and the expected future exchange rates. We will return to translation (accounting) risk and economic risk in Chapter 26 which is concerned with international financial management. Companies vary in the way they deal with translation and economic risk.

A company faces transaction exposure in a number of situations. These include:

1. normal trade with countries with different currencies;
2. repaying foreign currency loans;
3. sale of fixed assets of subsidiaries in foreign countries;
4. repatriation of profits, and payment of royalties and management charges by foreign subsidiary to parent company.

Most companies have a policy towards hedging against such risks. A few companies tell their shareholders about this policy. As explained above there are a variety of hedging techniques a company can employ, ranging from forward contracts to currency swaps. A few companies provide information on the hedging techniques they have used.

Glaxo in their 1993 accounts state that 'trading transactions in foreign currencies are not normally hedged, except in specific circumstances'. In contrast Coats Viyella explain that 'net trading cash flows in subsidiaries, non-base currency are hedged to 100% of their value in the base currency wherever possible'. De La Rue's policy is generally to protect transaction risk by matching sales or purchases in a currency by equal and opposite commitments in the foreign exchange markets. As at the company's 1993 year end they had sold forward US $63 million.

Most companies hedge against transaction risk. They wish to make their profits from manufacturing and trading not foreign exchange dealing. There are however a few companies that speculate in the foreign exchange markets. Undoubtedly some make gains in some years. However when they make losses and the losses are disclosed they are very heavily criticized.

In 1987 Volkswagen made FOREX losses of DM 473 million. In 1991 Allied Lyons disclosed FOREX losses of £150 million. Allied Lyons lost as a result of aggressive profit seeking and an inadequate system of internal controls. It was estimated that their exposure against the US dollar was at one time in the region of £1.5 billion.

Allied Lyons had sold call options against the dollar. This meant that the buyer of the option had the right to buy dollars from Allied Lyons at a predetermined price. If the value of the dollar in the market rose above the exercise price, the buyer would wish to exercise the option. Allied Lyons were not covered in these deals. The company chairman was forced to resign over this matter. He admitted that the company's treasury team had been 'dealing in foreign currency instruments which were inappropriate, and in which it lacked the requisite trading skills'.

As mentioned earlier financial derivatives can be useful for hedging purposes. But they can also be dangerous. It is not just lack of skills that can lead to losses, it is also judgement. Bankers also make mistakes.

In 1994 the Governor of the Bank of Malaysia resigned. This was because the bank had lost £1.3 billion on foreign exchange deals in 1993, and this followed even larger losses in the previous year. It appeared that the central bank was a speculator in foreign exchange markets.

The 1993 losses were the result of the bank purchasing pounds sterling. The pound was in the European exchange rate mechanism (ERM) at the time and was falling in value. There were attempts being made to protect the value of the pound in order to enable it to stay within the ERM. Obviously the foreign exchange dealers at the Bank of Malaysia believed the attempts to protect the pound would be successful. They were not. The pound sterling fell in value and the bank suffered large losses in the value of its pound sterling holdings.

Accounting exposure	Hedging
Arbitrage	Interest-rate parity
Bid price	Money market hedge
Calls	Options
Cross rates	Puts
Direct quote	Purchasing power parity
Economic exposure	Spot market
Forward market	Transaction exposure
Futures market	Translation exposure

21.7 Key terms

1. What is the purchasing power parity theory?
2. What is interest rate parity theory?
3. What is the relationship between the difference between the forward and spot rates of exchange and the expected change in spot rates?
4. What is the foreign exchange market? Who are the buyers and sellers? Who are the market makers?
5. What are currency swaps?
6. Explain how a company can hedge in the options market.

1. 'An unenviable record', *Financial Times* (1991) 4 May.

There are excellent textbooks on the subject of international finance and the finance of multinational business that have sections dealing with foreign exchange markets. These books include:

Buckley, A. (1992) *Multinational Finance*, 2nd edn, Prentice Hall.
Chalmin, P. and Gombeaud, J.L. (1988) *The Global Market*, Prentice Hall.
Clark, E., Levasseur, M. and Rousseau, P. (1993) *International Finance*, 1, Chapman & Hall.
Demirag, I. and Goddard, S. (1994) *Financial Management for International Business*, McGraw-Hill.
Eiteman, D., Stonehill, A.I. and Moffett, M.H. (1992) *Multinational Business Finance*, 6th edn, Addison-Wesley.
Hamilton, A. (1986) *The Financial Revolution*, Penguin Books.
Holland, J.B. (1986) *International Financial Management*, Blackwell.
Rodriguez, R.M. and Carter, E.E. (1984) *International Financial Management*, 3rd edn, Prentice Hall.
Shapiro, A.C. (1992) *Multinational Financial Management*, 4th edn, Allyn and Bacon.
Tucker, A.L., Madura, J. and Chiang, T.C. (1991) *International Financial Markets*, West.

1. The finance director of Plottit Inc., a large New York based company, has been studying exchange rates and interest rates relevant to the UK and the USA. Plottit Inc. has purchased goods from the UK at a cost of £2 350 000 payable in pounds in three months' time. In order to maintain profit margins the finance director wishes to adopt, if possible, a risk-free strategy that will ensure that the cost of the goods to Plottit is no more than $3 555 000.

Exchange rates (New York)

	$/£
Spot	1.4735–1.4755
1 month forward	1.4896–1.4933
3 months forward	1.5163–1.5181

Interest rates (available to Plottit Inc.)

	New York		London	
	Deposit rate (%)	Borrowing (%)	Deposit rate (%)	Borrowing rate (%)
1 month	13.25	16.5	6.5	10.5
3 months	13.25	17.0	6.75	10.75

(a) Calculate whether it is possible for Plottit Inc. to achieve a cost directly associated with this transaction of no more than $3 555 000 by means of a forward market hedge, money market hedge, or a lead payment. Transactions costs may be ignored.

(b) If, after one month, the UK supplier was to suffer a fire which destroyed all stock and meant that the contract could not be fulfilled, and Plottit had bought pounds three months forward to pay for the goods, what action would you suggest that Plottit should take on the foreign exchange markets? Assume that there is no insurance protection for Plottit Inc.

(c) What is an option forward contract? Would such a contract be of value to Plottit Inc. in this situation?

(Two-thirds of the marks of this question are allocated to part (a).)

ACCA, June 1987

2. (a) Explain what is meant by the terms foreign exchange translation exposure, transactions exposure and economic exposure. What is the significance of these different types of exposure to the financial manager? (8 marks)

(b) Runswick Ltd is an importer of clock mechanisms from Switzerland. The company has contracted to purchase 3000 mechanisms at a unit price of 18 Swiss francs. Three months' credit is allowed before payment is due. Runswick currently has no surplus cash, but can borrow short-term at 2% above bank base rate or invest short-term at 2% below bank base rate in either the UK or Switzerland.

Current exchange rates
Swiss franc/£

Spot	2.97–2.99
1 month forward	2½–1½ premium
3 months forward	4½–3½ premium

(The premium relates to the Swiss franc)

Current bank base rates

Switzerland	6% per year
United Kingdom	10% per year

(i) Explain and illustrate three policies that Runswick Ltd might adopt with respect to the foreign exchange exposure of this transaction. Recommend which policy the company should adopt. Calculations should be included wherever relevant. Assume that interest rates will not change during the next three months. (9 marks)

(ii) If the Swiss supplier were to offer 2.5% discount on the purchase price for payment within one month evaluate whether you would alter your recommendation in (i). (5 marks)

(c) If annual inflation levels are currently at 2% in Switzerland and 6% in the UK, and the levels move during the next year to 3% in Switzerland and 9% in the UK, what effect are these changes in inflation likely to have on the relative value of the Swiss franc and the pound? (3 marks)

(25 marks)

ACCA, June 1986

3. Oxlake PLC has export orders from a company in Singapore for 250 000 china cups, and from a company in Indonesia for 100 000 china cups. The unit variable cost to Oxlake of producing china cups is 55p, and the unit sales price is Singapore $2.862 to Singapore and 2246 rupiahs to Indonesia. Both orders are subject to credit terms of 60 days and are payable in the currency of the importers. Past experience suggests that there is 50% chance of the customer in Singapore paying 30 days late. The Indonesian customer has offered Oxlake the alternative of being paid US$125 000 in three months time instead of payment in the Indonesian currency. The Indonesian

currency is forecast by Oxlake's bank to depreciate in value during the next year by 30% (from an Indonesian viewpoint) relative to the US dollar. Whenever appropriate Oxlake uses option forward foreign exchange contracts.

Foreign exchange rates
(mid rates)

	$Singapore/$US	$US/£	Rupiahs/£
Spot	2.1378	1.4875	2481
1 month forward	2.1132	1.4963	No
2 months forward	2.0964	1.5047	forward
3 months forward	2.0915	1.5105	market exists

Assume that in the UK any foreign currency holding must be immediately converted into pounds sterling.

	Money market rates	(% per annum)
	Deposit	Borrowing
UK clearing bank	6	11
Singapore bank	4	7
Eurodollars	7.5	12
Indonesian bank	15	Not available
Eurosterling	6.5	10.5
US domestic bank	8	12.5

These interest rates are fixed rates for either immediate deposits or borrowing over a period of two or three months, but the rates are subject to future movement according to economic pressures.

(a) Using what you consider to be the most suitable way of protecting against foreign exchange risk evaluate the sterling receipts that Oxlake can expect from its sales to Singapore and to Indonesia, without taking any risks. All contracts, including foreign exchange and money market contracts, can be assumed to be free from the risk of default. Transaction costs may be ignored. (13 marks)

(b) If the Indonesian customer offered another form of payment to Oxlake, immediate payment in US dollars of the full amount owed in return for a 5% discount on the rupiah unit sales price, calculate whether Oxlake is likely to benefit from this form of payment. (7 marks)

(c) Discuss the advantages and disadvantages to a company of invoicing an export sale in a foreign currency. (5 marks)

(25 marks)

ACCA, Dec. 1987

4. As a result of participating in a local Chamber of Commerce trade mission to several European and African countries, Wonderdorm Ltd, a bed manufacturer, has obtained its first export orders. The orders are estimated to total £500 000 from Europe and £300 000 from Africa during the coming financial year. All orders are subject to a 20% initial deposit. Wonderdorm is considering how to administer and finance its exports. The choice of administration is either to establish a small export department responsible for the invoicing and collection of export debts at a cost of £25 000 per year, £15 000 of which is the expected cost of administering debt collection (i.e. excluding any financing or bad debts costs), or to use the services of a non-recourse export factoring company for the debt collection process. The factor charges a service fee of 2.5% of credit sales and offers optional finance facilities at 2.5% above bank base rate on up to 80% of export credit sales. Export sales are to be made on open account terms of 60 days and are payable in pounds sterling. Wonderdorm's bank has offered overdraft finance at 15%. Expert Credit Guarantee Department (ECGD) comprehensive insurance is available at a cost of 32p per £100 insured, and offers 90% cover of the risk of non-payment. ECGD will also offer its guarantee at a cost of 32p per £100 insured which gives access to bank finance at ⅝%

above base rate. The guarantee is only available to companies in conjunction with the ECGD comprehensive insurance.

Experience by other companies in Wonderdorm's industry suggests that the African customers will, on average, be 60 days overdue on their payments, and that 0.75% of African credit sales (by value) and 0.5% of European credit sales (by value) will result in bad debts. Bank base rate is currently 13%.

Exchange rates for selected currencies are detailed below:

	Naira/£	Rand/Naira	Naira/$
Spot	1.2646	1.4077	0.5577
1 month forward	1.2710	1.3985	0.5460
3 months forward	1.2695	1.3880	0.5325
1 year forward	1.2670	1.3760	0.5110

(a) Prepare a report advising Wonderdorm Ltd which method of export adminis-tration and finance to use.

(b) Wonderdorm's prospective African customers, principally in Nigeria and South Africa, suggest that payment should be made in either their own currency or US dollars rather than pounds sterling. Assess whether this proposal is likely to be beneficial to Wonderdorm Ltd during the coming financial year.

5. 'As foreign exchange markets are efficient, it is not possible for a company to accu-rately predict future spot rates'.
   Discuss.

6. 'The equilibrium theories linking exchange rate changes, interest rates, and infla-tion rates provide a valuable conceptual framework for managers of internationally involved enterprises.'
   Discuss these theories, outlining the circumstances under which they are valid.

7.

Currency	Spot	1 month		3 month	
£/$	1.5015–25	3	6	13	17
$/DKr	9.3600–25	90	130	320	360
$/Yen	231.87–97	63	59	185	180

(a) Explain the terms 'spot' and '3 months'.

(b) Determine the outright forward rates for all three currencies.

(c) Assume your firm is dealing in the foreign exchange markets with a dealer who has given the above quotations. At what rate would you deal?

   (i) You buy Yen for $ spot.
   (ii) You buy DKr for $ 1 month forward.
   (iii) You sell $ for £3 month forward.
   (iv) You buy Yen for $ 1 month forward, option over the first month.
   (v) You sell $ for DKr 3 months forward, option over the whole period.

(d) (i) Calculate the spot £/Yen exchange rate.
   (ii) Calculate the £/DKr 1 month forward rate.

(e) UK interest rates are 12% per annum. Using the data given above, determine the annual rate of interest to be expected on a three month US deposit. Explain.
   If the actual rate was 3% per annum higher than you have calculated what would be your best course of action?

8. A UK company has £8 000 000 excess cash available for a period of six months. It is uncertain whether to invest the capital in the UK or to invest it in the USA in order to take advantage of higher interest rates. The rates available are:

£/$ spot	1.7800–1.8000
£/$ 6 months forward rate	10–20 Dis
Sterling 6 months interest rate	8–8¼%
US$ 6 months interest rate	9¼–9½%

Advise the company on whether it should invest its excess cash in the USA or within the UK.

9. Assume that on your first week at work in one of the UK major banks, you were assigned to the Foreign Exchange department. A couple of weeks later the head of the research department was suggesting that he is convinced that the German mark is presently overvalued relative to the US dollar. Your boss wants you to take action on the basis of the following expectations and facts.

Exchange market	
Spot rate	DM 1.7483/$
Three month – forward rate	DM 1.7593/$
Expected spot rate in three months' time	DM 1.8095/$

Money market	
German rates	
Three months	5.8%
Six months	5.6%
Twelve months	5.3%

US rates	
Three months	3.0
Six months	3%₁₆
Twelve months	3⅜

Required:

(a) Are the exchange and money markets in equilibrium? Why? (4 marks)

(b) (i) Is there any way to take advantage of the situation? If so, how? (Without speculating, you can assume any amount to trade with.) (8 marks)

   (ii) What exchange and interest rate trends would appear in the market if a large number of investors took similar action? (5 marks)

(c) How can the bank profit from its forecast of the future spot rate? (4 marks)

(d) Assuming that the real rates of return on the German and US Government bonds (with the same characteristics) are equal, prove analytically that there is consistency between the Fisher Effect, the Interest Rate Parity Theorem, and the Purchasing Power Parity Theorem. (4 marks)

10. Handcomp plc is a British company which imports sophisticated computer based measuring equipment from abroad and re-sells the equipment in the United Kingdom.

   Handcomp has contracted to buy equipment worth 200 million yen (£865 800) from a Japanese multinational company. The equipment will be delivered in six months' time. The 200 million yen is due to be paid on that date.

   The Treasurer of Handcomp is rather worried about this contract since he suspects that the yen may rise in value to 219 yen to the pound from the current 231 yen to the pound, over this period, despite the fact that the forward market suggests only a 2% rise. Such an increase in buying cost would reduce the profit on the sale of the equipment from around £240 000 to £190 000, a significant reduction in profit.

   The Treasurer decided to work out the cost of three methods of hedging this currency risk.

   (i) Take out a six-month forward contract in yen.
   (ii) Buy a yen bond worth 200 million yen on the Tokyo market repayable in six months' time.
   (iii) Do nothing and assume that the forward market prediction of a mere 2% rise in the value of the yen is a correct forecast.

Required:

(a) Calculate the cost of these three methods assuming that the spot and forward market rates and the interest rates on short-term borrowing in Japan and the UK are as follows (ignore tax):

Spot rate now   231 yen per pound
Forward rate: six months forward   226 yen per pound

Current annual interest rates on six month loans:

Japan   6%
United Kingdom   12%

Evaluate each alternative and indicate Handcomp's best course of action.

(b) If the actual spot rate in six months' time is 221 yen to the pound, which option should you have chosen?

11. (a) Explain briefly what is meant by foreign currency options and give examples of the advantages and disadvantages of exchange traded foreign currency options to the financial manager. (5 marks)

(b) Exchange traded foreign currency option prices in Philadelphia for dollar/sterling contracts are shown below:

Sterling (£12 500) contracts

	Calls		Puts	
Exercise price ($)	*September*	*December*	*September*	*December*
1.90	5.55	7.95	0.42	1.95
1.95	2.75	3.85	4.15	3.80
2.00	0.25	1.00	9.40	—
2.05	—	0.20	—	—

Option prices are in cents per £. The current spot exchange rate is $1.9405–$1.9425/£.

Required:

Assume that you work for a US company that has exported goods to the UK and is due to receive a payment of £1 625 000 in three months' time. It is now the end of June.

Calculate and explain whether your company should hedge its sterling exposure on the foreign currency option market if the company's treasurer believes the spot rate in three months' time will be:

(i) $1.8950–$1.8970/£
(ii) $2.0240–$2.0260/£   (7.5 marks)
ACCA, June 1992

12. Tentalot plc, a manufacturer of camping equipment, has just received export orders from France and Portugal. The French order is for 2000 'Designatents' at a unit price of 4250 francs, and the Portuguese order is for 2500 'Reflectatents' at a unit price of 65 000 escudos. Both deals are on credit terms of 90 days.
Assume that it is 1 June.

Foreign exchange rates

	FF/£	Esc/£	$/£
Spot (1 June 1994)	8.36–8.40	262–265	1.465–1.470
1 month forward	8.29–8.34	270–273	1.453–1.460
3 months forward	8.22–8.26	282–286	1.436–1.441

Interest rates available to Tentalot (%)

	UK		France		Portugal	
	Lending	*Borrowing*	*Lending*	*Borrowing*	*Lending*	*Borrowing*
1 month	4.5	8.5	5.5	9	9	not available
3 months	5	8.5	6	9.5	9.5	not available

Currency options (Philadelphia)
$/FF contract size 500 000 Francs

Exercise price (FF/$)	Calls		Puts	
	Sept.	Dec.	Sept.	Dec.
5.80	12.6	16.2	—	0.94
5.70	5.4	8.3	3.8	5.70
5.60	2.3	4.2	14.7	18.30
5.50	0.4	1.3	22.4	25.60

Option premia are US cents per 100 French francs.

Required:

Assuming Tentalot plc is risk averse with respect to foreign exchange risk, evaluate how the company might hedge against the risk of these export sales using the forward market, money market and currency options. Discuss what other hedging alternatives might be available to Tentalot. (25 marks)

13. You are the treasurer of a UK-based company, exporting to Germany. You are currently expecting a receipt of Deutschmarks in 90 days' time. You have decided to cover this exposure. Given the rates below:

(a) Which is the best way to cover the exposure from a financial standpoint, assuming you have sufficient funds for the period but that your customer does not have excess funds?

(b) If you know that your customer has excess liquidity, how might this change your calculations?

(c) If you need to fund yourself for this period how might this change your decision?

(d) What other issues might affect your decision as to how and whether to cover?

Spot	£/DM	2.5700–2.5750
	3 Mo Points	63–88

3 Mo Domestic £		6 1/16–5 15/16
Euro £		6 1/16–6
Domestic DM		7.05–7.15
Euro DM		7 1/8–7

Borrowing spread for both companies 0.5%.

22 *Management of debtors*

22.1	The problem	797
22.2	Deciding an acceptable level of risk	799
22.3	Investigating the credit applicant	802
22.4	Terms of sale	803
22.5	Policy on the collection of debts	809
22.6	Credit insurance	811

22.7	A technical approach	811
22.8	Concluding remarks	814
22.9	Key terms	814
22.10	Revision questions	814
22.11	References	814
22.12	Further reading	814
22.13	Problems	815

An important part of the control of working capital is credit management. The components of a credit policy are

- terms of sale;
- credit analysis;
- collection policy.

Each of these will be examined in this chapter. A certain amount of technical analysis is possible; it is a question of balancing the cost of driving a customer away because of unattractive terms and the cost of delay in receiving payment or even a bad debt.

22.1 The problem

The typical company in the UK has a ratio of debtors to total assets in the region of 20%–25%. This represents a considerable investment of funds, and so the management of this asset can have a significant effect on the profit performance of a company.

By international standards, the UK does not have a good record for the collection of debts. In the UK manufacturing sector it takes on average about 60 days for a company to collect the funds due from a debtor. In contrast, in the USA the average collection period for manufacturing industry is in the region of 40 days.

In the USA there seems to be a more professional approach towards credit management than in the UK. However, it might not be just a matter of more effective chasing up of creditors. It could be that in the UK there are different standards when it comes to paying debts. In the UK attitudes have developed such that the debtor often feels that it is acceptable to delay settlement beyond an agreed period. On occasion, the agreed credit terms are ignored. This is not so much the attitude in the USA, not necessarily because of different ethical standards but perhaps because there is a better information system available to suppliers.

In the USA there is a greater fear amongst companies that if they are late payers, this information will be fed into a credit agency and this will have an unfavourable effect when they next wish to buy goods on credit from any supplier. Credit management is a problem of balancing profitability and liquidity. Credit terms are a sales attraction, and so the longer the time a company allows its customers to pay, the greater are the sales and the possible profits. However, the longer the credit terms the greater is the amount of debtors (accounts receivable) and the greater the possible strain on the company's liquidity.

The credit-issuing policy of a company should answer several questions. For instance, to whom should credit be extended? How much credit should be allowed (at an individual level and in total)? How long should the credit be for? What is to be done about defaulting debtors? The objective of the company is assumed to be to choose the credit policy that, taken in conjunction with its other policy decisions, maximizes its expected profits. It may well be that the credit policy cannot be formulated without reference to constraints. The liquidity position of the company presents an obvious constraint, and production capacity, management capacity and risk may define others.

The problem is thus a programming problem in form, but, even in principle, it is so involved that a complete, rigorous and general formalization would not be useful from the operational point of view. Some of the data that would be required for such a model illustrate the difficulty. The company would need to know the probability of sale to each potential customer as a function of the credit terms offered and the expected timing of the payments received. That is, what is the probability of $x\%$ payment within n days of invoicing given one particular credit term?

The objective function, expected profit, would include as variables the length of credit to be offered, the amount (as a percentage of cash price), any discounts for early payment, the cost of capital for the vendor and each potential customer, production and selling costs, and a variable (say expenditure) reflecting the bad debt collection policy. Therefore, although theoretically it leads to non-optimum results, it may in practice be better to adopt the following approach:

1. have some simplifying assumptions (e.g. divide customers into risk classes) and restrict the problem to that of deciding whether or not to offer an appropriate credit package to each risk class;
2. separate the objective function into parts (e.g. consider the credit-giving and bad debt collection policies separately).

By setting the 'terms of sale' the company can to some extent control its level of debtors (accounts receivable). If it only allows seven days to pay, it rules out customers who want 30 days to pay. By offering only 30 days' credit, it rules out customers who require 60 days to pay. An example of this process is a supermarket, which usually does not offer credit at all and so has few or no debtors. A trading company may even adopt the policy with a particular company or class of companies that it will only supply goods if payment is received in advance.

The relative bargaining strengths of the credit giver and credit receiver are important. If a customer with alternative sources of supply takes a large proportion of the output of a manufacturer geared to producing for him, the customer may be able to dictate the terms of credit between them.

It is always possible that the buyer will ignore the terms of sale and the credit terms offered. It is not unknown for some companies to deduct a cash discount when making a payment, even though the period of time over which the discount was offered has elapsed. The administrative costs to the seller in challenging such a practice can exceed the amount of the discount being contested. Whether such practices can be repeated in future dealings depends on the relative bargaining strength of the buyer and the seller. Unfortunately a seller who is heavily dependent on one large buyer cannot do very much when the buyer continually takes 120 days to pay his bills and deducts a cash discount offered for payment within 30 days!

Recent years have seen attempts at an international level to avoid this kind of dependence, and a policy of diversification at the firm level in terms of both number of outlets and types of products can be attractive to firms in weak bargaining positions.

A company has at least four factors under its control that can influence the number of its debtors and the level of debt:

1. the customers to whom it is prepared to sell;
2. the terms of credit offered on the sale;
3. the cash discount offered to prompt payment;
4. the follow-up procedure on slow payment.

These decision variables will now be considered.

22.2 Deciding an acceptable level of risk

The choice of which customers to sell to is really a question of the level of risk of non-payment that is considered acceptable. With every sale there is some risk that the customer will not be able to pay, but with most large companies the risk is so small that it is not even considered. With certain small illiquid companies the risk of non-payment might be so high that there is no question of selling to them. At some point between these two extremes the company is faced with a difficult choice of whether to sell or not. A £50 order cannot be viewed as simply a £50 cash inflow. The company must consider the present value (PV) of the future volume of sales from the customer. If they accept this order, goodwill is created and future sales may result. However, there is also the chance that the £50 may not be received or may be received late and so, with a PV approach, the order may not be worth as much as £50.

A method of estimating the probability that a particular company will turn out to be a bad payer, perhaps even a bad debt, is required. If a credit risk can be attached to the customer, then a rational decision can be made about whether to trade with them. For example, suppose that a group of customers can be associated with a 10% credit risk, i.e. there is a 1 in 10 chance that they will not pay; then a decision can be made about whether to trade with this group.

Added sales by trading with this 10% risk group	£2000
Amounts on average uncollected (by definition 10%)	£200
Additional revenue	£1800
Marginal production and selling costs associated with the orders (60% of sales)	£1200
Added collection costs	£300
	£1500
Net annual incremental profit	£300

In this situation it would be worth trading with the 10% risk class of customers. As the level of production changes, a different decision may be made. If sales increase and production rises, then, because the company is working nearer the level of full capacity, the additional production costs may also increase; this could mean that it is no longer worth trading with this group. In the reverse situation, as soon as there is a danger that total sales will fall, the company may be willing to sell to a riskier class of customer in order to keep up its production level and so be able to keep down its costs per unit.

The following question is taken from an examination paper of the Chartered Association of Certified Accountants. The solution that follows the question illustrates one way of tackling the problem.

Example 22.1

The summary forecast profit statement and balance sheet of the AB Co. Ltd for the next 12 months is as follows.

Summary profit forecast for next 12 months

	£	£
Sales income (100 000 units)		1 200 000
Less: Variable costs	900 000	
Fixed costs	150 000	1 050 000
Profit		£150 000

Summary balance sheet

	£	£
Investment in fixed assets		1 500 000
Investment in working capital		
Debtors	200 000	
Stock	80 000	
Cash	24 000	
	304 000	
Less: Creditors	60 000	
		244 000
Total investment		£1 744 000

Profit as return on investment = 8.6%.

The directors are concerned about the low return on investment, particularly because of the under-utilization of the investment in fixed assets. There is little likelihood of significant alterations to selling prices and costs, and the only apparent way of improving the situation is increased sales. All sales are on credit and the company operates a very strict credit control procedure which has virtually eliminated bad debts. Because of this a number of potential customers have had to be refused and some existing customers have taken their business elsewhere. The suggestion has been made that a relaxation of the credit control policy could increase sales substantially. Specificially, if the company were to introduce a scheme whereby a 2% discount were given on accounts paid within ten days – at present no discount is given – and if the company were willing to accept 'riskier' customers, the sales would increase by 40%. Probably 65% of the customers would avail themselves of the discount and the average collection period of the remainder would be half of what it is at present. Bad debts would be of the order of 2%–6% of total sales.

   Comment on the above situation making full use of the information given and highlighting any matters that should be brought to the attention of the directors.

Suggested solution

We shall begin by calculating the profit that will result if the new policy is accepted. Sales will increase by 40%.

	£	£
Sales income (140 000 units)		1 680 000
Less: Variable costs	1 260 000	
Fixed costs	150 000	
		1 410 000
		270 000
Less: Cash discount (0.02 × 0.65 × £1 680 000)		21 840
Profit		£248 160

This £248 160 is the profit before allowing for bad debts. It is estimated that bad debts will vary between 2% and 6% of sales. If bad debts equal 2% of sales that will amount to £33 600 and will reduce profits to approximately £214 560. If bad debts equal 6% of sales, that will amount to £100 800 and reduce profits to approximately £147 360. Some adjustment would be required to the estimated profits to allow for the fact that the percentage of companies taking advantage of cash discounts is an estimate, and the estimate of 65% of customers would probably need to be reduced a little if a percentage of the customers turn out to be bad debts. The amounts involved in this adjustment would be small and so will be ignored. It is assumed that fixed costs will not increase even though there has been a 40% increase in sales.

The present rate of return of profit on investments is 8.6% (i.e. £150 000/£1 744 000). One way of determining whether the new sales policy is in the company's interests is to compare the old rate of profits on investment with the new rate. First we shall estimate the level of investment with the new level of sales. The summarized balance sheet will be as follows:

Fixed assets		£1 500 000
Working capital:		
Debtors	79 000	
Stock	112 000	
Cash	33 600	
	224 600	
Less: Creditors	84 000	
		140 600
Total investment		£1 640 600

The debtors figure needs explaining. The present average collection period is two months (i.e. 200 000/1 200 000). For the customers not taking advantage of the cash discount this period is expected to be halved, and so if no customers take advantage of discounts, the debtors figure would be equal to one month's sales which are £140 000. It is thought, however, that 65% of customers will pay within ten days, and therefore the debtors at any date would be expected to be the sum of

$$35\% \times £140\,000 = £49\,000$$

and

$$65\% \times \left(£1\,680\,000 \times \frac{10}{365}\right) = £29\,918$$

$$\overline{£78\,918}$$

For the purpose of projecting a balance sheet, this has been rounded up to £79 000. The fact that some of the debtors are expected to be bad will not influence the level of investment of the company. The company still has to be able to fund this level of trading.

The stock, cash and creditors figures in the above balance sheet are each based on their ratio to sales as with the present level of activity. The return on investment with a 2% level of bad debts is 13.1%, i.e. (214 560/1 640 600). The return on investment with a 6% level of bad debts is 9.0%, i.e. (147 360/1 640 600).

The position is therefore that with a bad debts figure equal to 2% of sales, the new policy is clearly worthwhile, showing a higher absolute profit figure and a higher return on net assets than with the present policy. With bad debts as 6% of sales, the policy may just be worthwhile; the return on net assets has marginally increased, but the absolute profit figure has fallen. If bad debts are expected to be below 5%, it can be shown that the new policy is worthwhile from both a return and an absolute profit point of view.

The company would need to consider the probabilities of the different levels of bad debts arising. It would also need to consider carefully whether its assumption with regard to the future level of debtors is justified. One reason why the new policy appears advantageous is that the total level of investment is reduced because of the reduction in the level of debtors. Is it realistic to believe that all customers, other than bad debtors, will pay within one month, and that 65% will wish to take advantage of the cash discount?

The problem of placing a potential customer in a particular risk category is not easy. However, there are a number of sources of information which may be useful.

Trade references

A new customer can be asked to supply one or two references from other companies with whom they have had business. The wording of the references and the standing of the companies who supplied them will give a guide to the creditworthiness of the customer.

Bank references or banker's opinion

A bank may be asked to comment on the financial standing of its customer. This is of limited use, however, because it only reflects on the behaviour of the company with one particular bank, and the manager of a bank may be reluctant to report unfavourably on one of its own customers. The situation could be very difficult for the bank manager, particularly if the bank itself had funds tied up in the company. In fact banks have a number of standard letters that they send in response to enquiries on their customers' financial standing. The letters are very carefully worded, but the particular letter that is sent in reply reflects the banker's view of the relative creditworthiness of the company. The bank can also say whether a company has pledged its inventory or debtors to secure a loan.

Credit bureau reports or registers

A number of credit bureaux operate in the UK. The selling company can make use of one of these bureaux (one is Dun and Bradstreet) who publish lists showing relevant financial details of many companies, including a credit rating. This is a service that is continually updated and covers many companies. Should the enquiring company require additional information, it can ask for a special credit report on any company. The information given is based upon the record of transactions of creditors of the company, on special enquiries and on published financial information.

Salespeople's opinions

The opinions and impressions formed by salespeople when visiting a customer can be useful additional information.

Published information

The annual accounts can of course be analysed to determine the liquidity position of the customer. The interpretation of such information is discussed elsewhere in this book. The Registrar of Companies keeps records of charges on the assets of a company and details of the directors, as well as the annual reports; these records can be examined. The records provide a useful insight into the financial position of any company. In fact, when an agency is asked to provide a special credit report it often relies heavily on the information in Companies House.

Company's own sales ledger

An examination of how well the customer has paid in the past might give some guide to how well they will pay in the future. It should show at least his willingness to pay. The financial situation of the customer may have changed, however, and so the ability to pay may have altered. A computer is sometimes used within a company to control debts. The computer can store up-to-date information on a customer's creditworthiness: it can store the latest information on the financial position of the customers, and report when a customer's liquidity position becomes dangerous. By keeping a record of the previous experience with the customer, the time it takes to pay and the highest amount of credit previously allowed, information can quickly be provided when any new decisions have to be made on the sales terms for a particular customer. This information could save the company a loss on a possible bad debt.

Traditionally in the UK firms have asked to be supplied with the names of two traders and one banker when deciding on the suitability of a customer for credit. The supplier can perhaps obtain additional information from a credit agency. Discussions with managers of other companies or perhaps divisions within the same company that trade with the same customer can provide useful information. So can visits to the buyer by credit personnel and sales representatives. If a large amount of trade credit is likely to be required over a period of time, then a detailed investigation is obviously necessary. Financial statements of the company may be helpful. The larger the credit investigation the greater is the cost, but if a company placing an order is unknown or has a record of bad debts, then an investigation could well be worthwhile. If the supplying company has many investigations that need to be carried out in a year, it may set up its own investigation unit.

When it comes to credit information, the type of statements that can be obtained in the UK compare unfavourably with those available in the USA. In the USA very much more data can be obtained on the suitability of a buyer for credit; there is great pressure on the credit agencies to provide relevant information and there is strong competition between agencies.

The difference in the quality of the information available can also be seen from the typical bank reference statement. In the UK the banks have traditionally been conservative in providing information on companies. They do not wish to upset the customers and they have a fear of legal action being taken against them as the result of an unfavourable report. Opinions in the UK differ on the usefulness of bank references. There are those who argue that they are of no use whatever, and others who argue that, if you read between the lines, the statements can be useful. In the USA, in contrast, many banks will provide information regarding their customer's approximate cash balance together with an indication of the amount of activity in the account and any known loan commitments that the customer has already entered into. Therefore the seller of goods on credit in the USA has a considerable amount of information when it comes to deciding on the period of credit that it is worth offering to any customer.

Having obtained as much relevant information as possible, the company must decide whether the customer falls within an acceptable risk class. In recent years a good deal of effort has been expended on the problem of devising numerical credit scoring systems for evaluating creditworthiness at the consumer level. Biographical data as well as credit history are employed. Success with these systems has been mixed. There is no reason in principle why a numerical credit scoring system should not be developed to assess business loans. It might prove especially valuable to a company with a large number of small debtor companies. It is amusing to speculate what would be relevant 'biographical' data at company level! For the time being, however, the creditworthiness decision has to be largely a matter of judgement.

Having decided to sell to a customer, the company has next to decide on the credit terms that will be offered and the level of cash discount. First we shall look at credit terms, i.e. the length of time the buyer is given in which to pay. Often credit terms and conditions of sale are settled by the usual terms of trade of the particular industry. A company just adopts the normal standards. Traditionally the majority of trade credit granted in the UK is on monthly terms. This usually means payment on or before the last day of the month following the date of the invoice. For example, if goods were despatched during March, which on average means the fifteenth or sixteenth day of the month, and invoices are sent out at the end of that month, then payment should be expected by the

22.4 Terms of sale

end of April. This unusually fast processing would lead on average to 45 days' credit. If, however, invoices for goods despatched on 15 March cannot be prepared by the end of that month and are not sent out until some date in April, it could well be that payment is not received until the end of May, which is 75 days' credit. The purchasing company needs time to process the invoice, and usually this takes a few weeks.

The time taken to collect a debt clearly depends to a large extent on the credit terms being offered by the supplier. Here again from a seller's point of view the UK compares unfavourably with the USA. In the vast majority of cases in the USA, the stipulated terms are net 30 days. This means that the account should be paid 30 days after delivery or invoice. If cash discounts are offered, they are usually restricted to payment within 10 days and the rate offered is usually in the range of 0.5%–2%. If an account in the USA is overdue, which usually means that it has not been paid 30 days after the receipt of the goods or the invoice, it is very frequent for an interest charge to be levied on the overdue amount. In the UK, although monthly terms are the most usual, as explained above, the purchasers tend to regard this as meaning the end of the month following delivery. This is not the same as 30 days after delivery, for if goods are delivered on, say, 15 March, the UK interpretation would be that the payment is expected at the end of April, i.e. 30 days after the end of the month following delivery. A few large suppliers have tried to improve their cash position by informing purchasers that they are expecting to be paid on the twentieth of the month following delivery, and a few are trying to move to the tenth day of the month following delivery.

With most transactions in the UK the method of payment required is not specified on the invoice. It is generally assumed that the payment will be by cheque, but there is increasing use of direct bank transfer methods. With the bank transfer, the purchaser agrees that the supplier should send the invoice directly to his bank and that the bank will settle within a specified number of days. This is a credit transfer system. The buying company receives a copy of the invoice that has been sent to the bank so that it can be verified. The disadvantage of this approach from the buyer's point of view is that they are no longer in control of the payment date. It would be difficult and perhaps embarrassing for the buyer to tell a bank to delay payment unless there was a very good reason. If payment is to be by direct bank transfer, it is much more likely that the supplier will be paid by the end of the period of credit than if payment is left to the buyer's own administrative machinery.

Of course, the ability of the supplier to encourage customers to use this form of payment depends strongly on the supply situation. If the supplier is in a powerful position, they can insist on this method of payment. Petrol suppliers can do this with small garages.

Cash discount

Traditionally, cash discounts have been offered by the seller to the buyer to encourage early payment. This is to encourage payment before the end of the period of credit. Cash discounts have a cost to the seller and are of value to the buyer. Whether the buyer decides to pay early and take advantage of the cash discount being offered, or to wait until the end of the credit period before paying, depends to some extent on the size of the discount. We shall use an examination question to illustrate how the value of a cash discount can be determined. The question is taken from a Financial Management paper of the Chartered Association of Certified Accountants.

Example 22.2

A supplier who had previously been supplying your firm on the basis that all accounts had to be paid within 30 days of receipt of goods with a 3% cash discount for goods paid within 10 days has notified you that as from the beginning of the next trading period it is extending the period of payment to 90 days with a reduced cash discount of 1% if paid within 20 days. What are the implications for this as far as your organization is concerned?

Suggested solution

First we shall consider the original terms of sale. The cash discount is being offered for early payment; if the buyer decides to take advantage of the discount he is altering his cash flow position. To pay the debt on the tenth day means a cash outflow on that day of, say, £97, and to pay early means avoiding having to pay £100 20 days later. A cash outflow of £97 on the tenth day results in a cash saving of £100 on the thirtieth day. The rate of return on this investment of £97 can be determined by solving the following equation:

$$97 = \frac{100}{1+r}$$

where r is the rate of return we are looking for. In this example it is equal to 3.09%. This is the rate of return earned over only 20 days. We can convert this into an annual rate:

$$3.09\% \times \frac{365}{20} \approx 56\%$$

The way in which this rate of return can be used in the decision-making process is, as with all investment decisions, to compare it with the cost of capital. We shall first assume that the buyer had to borrow money in order to be able to pay the debt on the tenth day.

The calculations show that under the old terms of sale it would have been advantageous for him to borrow the money (assumed to be £97) for 20 days at any annual interest rate below 56%, and to use the money borrowed to pay the supplier and take advantage of the cash discount. The buyer would borrow £97 on the tenth day and repay the debt (the £97) on the thirtieth day with the interest due. If the interest charged over the 20 days is less than £3, the buyer has benefited. If the buyer did not have to borrow, but could use his own financial resources to pay on the tenth day rather than the thirtieth, he is earning a return for 20 days equivalent to an annual return of 56%.

Now we shall consider the new terms of sale, i.e. a 1% cash discount for payment with 20 days with the period of credit extended to 90 days. The value of taking the discount is now equal to an annual rate of 5.3%, i.e. 1/99 × 365/70. The buyer would probably now decide not to take advantage of the cash discount but instead to obtain the extra days' credit being offered. The cost of not taking advantage of the discount is now only 5.3%. It would most likely not be worthwhile for the buyer to use borrowing facilities in order to obtain a 5.3% return, as the interest costs on borrowing could well be above this return. The buyer would also probably not wish to use any of his own resources to take advantage of the cash discount as he should be able to earn a higher rate of return using the resources elsewhere in the business.

The implication of the change in the terms of credit are therefore that before the change it would be worth the purchaser paying early and so obtaining the cash discount, as the cost of not doing so was equivalent to an annual interest charge of 56%. After the change the purchaser will probably adopt a policy of taking the 90 days' credit and then paying the full amount of the debt, and in doing so give up the cash discount.

In fact, the use of cash discounts in the UK has declined in recent years. This is largely because of the practice of some purchasers of taking discounts, whether or not they have paid within the specified time. If this happens it is very difficult for the supplier to try to obtain the amount which has incorrectly been taken as a discount. Buyers have taken the full credit period to pay, say in the above example, after the change, the full 90 days, and have then only paid the amount of the debt less the value of the discount. As a result many suppliers have abandoned cash discounts. Quantity discounts have become fashionable; buyers of large quanities are able to obtain large reductions in the unit price of the goods they buy.

To illustrate one particular approach to the decision whether to offer cash discounts or not we shall consider a problem taken from the examinations of the Chartered Association of Certified Accountants.

Example 22.3

At present the customers of the 'main' division of Jerome PLC take, on average, 90 days credit before paying. New credit terms are being considered which would allow a 5% cash discount for payment within 30 days with the alternative of full payment due after 60 days.

It is expected that 60% of all customers will take advantage of the discount terms. Customers not taking the discount would be equally split between those paying after 60 days and those taking 90 days' credit. The new policy would increase sales by 20% from the current level of £100 000 per annum, but bad debts would rise from 1% to 2% of total sales. The main division's products have variable costs amounting to 80% of sales value.

Jerome's other division, the 'special orders' division, has received an order from Green Ltd, a private company. Green insists that the £50 000 of machinery ordered be supplied on 60 days' credit. The variable costs of production and delivery which would be incurred by Jerome in meeting the order amount to £40 000. Green's creditworthiness is in doubt and the following estimates have been made:

Probability of Green paying in full in 60 days	0.6
Probability of Green completely defaulting	0.4

However, if the order is accepted by Jerome *and* if Green does not default then there is felt to be a probability of about 0.7 that a further eight identical orders will be placed by Green in exactly one year's time and further orders in later years may also be forthcoming. Experience has shown that once a firm meets the credit terms on an initial order the probability of default in the next year reduces to 0.1. Any work carried out on Green's order would take place in otherwise idle time and will not encroach upon Jerome's other activities. Should Green default, the legal and other costs of debt collection will equal any money obtained.

Jerome finances all trade credit with readily available overdrafts at a cost of 12% per annum. An appropriate discount rate for longer-term decisions is 15% per annum.

(a) In the absence of any changes in sales levels and bad debts etc. advise Jerome on the merits of offering the cash discount to main division customers who would otherwise have paid in
  (i) 60 days,
  (ii) 90 days.
  Calculate the annualized implied interest cost of the cash discount terms. (4 marks)
(b) Advise Jerome on the merits of the new main division credit terms after considering their effect on sales levels and bad debts. (8 marks)
(c) Provide information which will assist the special orders division in deciding whether to accept Green's order and to offer 60 days' credit if the order is expected
  (i) to be the only order from Green,
  (ii) to lead to the possibility of further orders from Green.
  Explain the reasons for any differences in your conclusions and comment on any deficiencies inherent in your analysis. (8 marks)
  (20 marks)

(For ease of working, a 360 day year can be assumed.)

Suggested solution

Part (a)

At present the customers of the main division of Jerome take on average 90 days to pay. However, some of the customers do pay after 60 days. If the 5% cash discount is introduced, it is estimated that 60% of customers will pay within 30 days.

The cost of offering this discount can be estimated. We shall estimate a true compound rate and the alternative simple rate. For those customers who previously took 90 days but now pay in 30 days, the effective annual compound rate of interest of the discount being offered is 36.0%, i.e.

$$(1 + r)^n$$

and the effective annual simple rate of interest is

$$\left[100 \times \frac{5}{95} \right] \times \frac{360}{60} = 31.6\%$$

This means that the discounts being offered by Jerome are very expensive. In order to encourage customers to pay 60 days earlier than present, the company is paying a cost equivalent to 36% compound interest. This is much more expensive than the 12% cost per annum of the bank overdrafts at present being used to fund trade credit.

The cost is even higher when a 5% discount is offered to encourage customers to pay 30 days earlier than at present. This applies to those customers at present paying in 60 days, and the effective annual compound rate of interest in this case is

$$\left(1 + \frac{5}{95} \right)^n = 85\%$$

Part (b)

Increased sales		£20 000	
Increased contribution			£4 000
Less:			
Discount taken 60% × £120 000 × 5%		£3 600	
Increase in bad debts			
New level 2% × £120 000	£2400		
Old level 1% × £100 000	£1000	£1 400	£5 000
			(£1 000)
Interest savings on reduced debtors			
Old level £100 000 × $\frac{90}{360}$		£25 000	
New level			
Payment after 30 days			
£120 000 × 60% × $\frac{30}{360}$	£6000		
Payment after 60 days			
£120 000 × 20% × $\frac{60}{360}$	£4000		
Payment after 90 days			
£120 000 × 20% × $\frac{90}{360}$	£6000	£16 000	
Saving in average debtors		£9 000	
Saving at 12% per annum			1 080
Net benefit of new terms			80

The new credit terms appear to be only marginally profitable. The net benefit of £80 does not seem to be very much, after taking into account the trouble of introducing the new scheme and the uncertainties attached to all the estimates. The trouble seems to be that the discounts offered are too high.

Part (c)

(i)

		Probability	Expected value
Benefit if Green does not default			
Contribution	£10 000		
Less: 2 months' credit			
$£50\,000 \times \dfrac{60}{360} \times 12\%$	£1 000		
	£9 000	0.6	£5 400
Outcome if Green defaults	(£40 000)	0.4	(£16 000)
Expected value of outcome			(£10 600)

If the current order is expected to be the only order from Green it should be rejected as its value is negative.

(ii) If further orders are expected then the analysis should consider their expected value. The expected value of the order which is likely to be received in one year is as follows.

		Probability	Expected value
Benefit if Green does not default			
Contribution	£80 000		
Less: 2 months credit			
$£400\,000 \times \dfrac{60}{360} \times 12\%$	£8 000		
	£72 000	0.9	£64 800
Outcome if Green defaults	(£320 000)	0.1	(£32 000)
Expected value of outcome			£32 800

Discounting this for one year at 15% gives a present value now of £28 522. The expected value of the benefits of acceptance of the initial order is now as follows.

		Probability	Expected value
Benefit if Green does not default			
Net contribution of initial order	£9 000		
Present value of expected benefit of subsequent order			
£28 522 × 0.7	£19 965		
Total benefit	£28 965	0.6	£17 379
Outcome if Green defaults on initial order	(£40 000)	0.4	(£16 000)
Expected value of outcome			£1 379

The expected value of the acceptance of the initial order is positive and it therefore appears to be just worthwhile accepting the order. It is only worthwhile offering the credit if future orders are expected.

One of the main problems with this type of analysis arises over the probabilities. Of course, these are very difficult to estimate. It is also difficult to determine whether accepting one order will lead to repeat orders.

Once the sale has been made and the terms offered, the company will wish to ensure that the cash is received as quickly as possible. This sometimes means sending reminders to customers. Chasing bad debts can be an expensive process. The company must ensure that the selling price is adequate to cover all expenses and credit losses. A certain proportion of debts will turn out to be bad, and these losses must be adequately covered by gains elsewhere. In fixing a selling price, allowance should therefore be made for the fact that on average only a proportion, say only 97%, of sales revenue is collected. This means that the company should show a profit on 97% of the sales price. This is assuming that an averaging system is being used by the company with regard to bad debts; in other words a system of cross-subsidization is being employed.

If it is thought bad policy to charge a higher price than is reasonable to customers who pay promptly, i.e. making them pay a proportion of the bad debt expense, then different prices or at least different discounts may have to be offered to different risk categories of customers. For example, the 10% risk class of customers will have to cover the bad debts of this group between them. If, on average, only 90% of the revenue from this group is collected, then the company must ensure that profits on sales to this group are obtained when 90% of the sales revenue is received. This could be achieved by either charging a higher sales price to risky customers than to less risky customers, or by offering lower discounts and poorer credit terms.

One obvious management tool in the control of receivables is a record of the age of the outstanding debts. Each month the debtors figures should be broken down to show the proportion of debts that have received various periods of credit, as for example in Tables 22.1 and 22.2.

Table 22.1 *Analysis of age of debts*

Number of days account has been outstanding	Percentage of total debtors figure (%)	Number of accounts
→ 29	58	1000
30–59	20	400
60–89	15	200
90 →	7	40

Table 22.2 *Collection rate – 'outstandings'*

Month	Sales (£000)	Still outstanding (£000)	Proportion (%)
Current	300	295	98.3
–1	280	220	78.6
–2	290	105	36.2
–3	300	50	16.7
–4	270	25	9.3
–5	275	15	5.5
–6	310	15	4.8
		725	

Steps would then be taken to collect the accounts that are considered to have been outstanding for longer than an acceptable length of time. The first attempt to collect payment would be a simple reminder; later, more serious attempts would include threatening legal action and finally court action itself. It is possible to carry out an exercise to show after what period of time attempts should be made to collect the outstanding accounts. The costs at each stage in the follow-up process should be balanced with the expected returns from the action, i.e. the probability of successfully obtaining payment as a result of the action multiplied by the interest that can be earned from obtaining money now rather than as a result of the next in the order of actions in the follow-up process. If we ignore deterrent effects, which may, however, be quite significant although difficult to evaluate, it is not worth spending more in seeking to obtain payment than the expected returns from chasing the debt. The question of a default policy will be returned to later.

One way to encourage customers to pay on time, i.e. by the end of the agreed credit period, is to charge interest on overdue accounts. If the credit period is for 60 days, say, then at the end of that time, if the invoice has not been paid, the supplier will charge interest at some agreed rate on the amount of the debt. This condition would have to be agreed by the buyer at the time of sale.

This practice of charging interest on overdue accounts has never been very common in the UK. However, the practice is used extensively in the EU and the USA. In fact, in the UK the Law Commission recommended in 1976 that a scheme of statutory interest on contract debts should be introduced. The recommendation was to the effect that interest would start to be paid from a date agreed between the buyer and seller. The recommendation has not been acted upon.

Although this practice is not common in the UK, in recent years a number of companies have been introducing such terms into sale agreements. The extent to which it is possible to introduce such interest charges depends, of course, on the relative strength of the buyer and seller.

One decision that a company has to make is concerned with how much trouble it should go to in chasing up debtors. When should reminders be sent out? When, if at all, should a debt collecting agency be used? At what stage should legal action be taken to recover an outstanding debt?

The decision on more effective chasing of overdue accounts involves balancing the returns from receiving a payment earlier than one would have done otherwise against the costs of the action taken. The benefit from receiving a payment one day earlier can be calculated as follows:

$$(1 + x)^{365} = 1 + r$$

where x is the interest rate for one day (expressed as a fraction), r is the company's annual time preference for money. Then

$$1 + x = (1 + r)^{1/365}$$
$$x = (1 + r)^{1/365} - 1$$

The benefit from receiving a payment of £p n days earlier is

$$[(x + 1)^n - 1] \times £p$$

For example, the benefit from receiving a £5000 debt three days earlier where the company's time preference for money is 15% is

$$x = (1 + r)^{1/365} - 1$$
$$= (1 + 0.15)^{1/365} - 1$$
$$= 0.000383$$

Hence the benefit is $[(0.000383 + 1)^3 - 1] \times £5000 = £5.75$.

We could use the simpler less accurate method

$$x = \frac{r}{365}$$

In the above example this would lead to an estimate of savings of £6.17. These savings would be compared with the cost incurred of obtaining the cash one day early. The costs could be administrative, involving telephone calls or sending letters.

If a company is worried about non-payments it can always take out credit insurance. There are a number of specialist companies that offers such insurance. The service is not cheap, and the actual costs depend upon the type of policy taken out. The credit insurance company does not want to take all the high-risk business and will want the option to be able to refuse insurance or invoices sent to particular customers. There are two types of policy.

Credit insurance on export sales is discussed in Chapter 16. The most important insurer of export sales is the Export Credit Guarantee Department (ECGD) which is a government department. They are merely concerned with insurance of medium-term and long-term credits. It is private-sector insurers that cover short-term export credit sales and domestic credit sales.

Private-sector credit insurers not only provide guarantees, they also provide advice. They will evaluate potential customers in any country. They will comment on the strengths and weaknesses of the exporter's distribution chain. They will provide both political and commercial risk cover for sales to most countries of the world. They of course charge for all the services they provide.

Whole-turnover policy

In this type of policy the premium is a percentage of the insured company's whole turnover. The insured is given a limit of discretion on the value of an invoice. Any account below this amount will be automatically insured as long as the company taking out the insurance uses approved sources of information to assess the buyer's creditworthiness. This may slightly increase costs to the insured as it may mean obtaining more expensive information. For accounts with a value which is above the limit of discretion the insured company must apply to the insurance company for approval for this particular buyer.

Specific account

In this type of policy the insured company can select those buyers' debts which it wishes to insure. The credit underwriter can of course refuse to take the policy. If the debt is insured the premium charged is a percentage of the sales to the particular buyer. Usually the rate of premium charged is higher than for a whole-turnover policy as it is usually the riskier debts that are insured.

The credit problem could be looked at as a capital budgeting problem. The extension of credit represents an investment, the returns to which are increased profits resulting from greater sales. The investment is not normally risk free, and different policies costing the same amount could generate differing patterns of expected returns. The preferred policy would, of course, be that which gave the greatest return on the sum invested. This type of approach will be illustrated by an example. It is assumed that there is a probability p_t that payment will be received during period t. The actions of the creditor company may influence this probability distribution. Such actions would not as a rule be costless. There might be a scheme of progressively diminishing discounts followed by penalty payments. The problem of what action to take or whether to introduce any scheme to speed payment is viewed as a capital budgeting problem in the following numerical example.

A company is owned £1000 by a customer and previous experience leads it to believe that the probability of receiving this payment immediately or in one or other of the succeeding six quarterly periods if no action is taken is as given by column p_n in Table 22.3. It is assumed that payment will be made in one lump sum rather than in instalments.

If the company introduces a discount/penalty scheme of a 3% discount for immediate payment, a 2% discount if payment is made after one quarter and so on, it is believed that the estimated probabilities of payment are as given in column p_d (the amounts that

Table 22.3 *Expected net present value of debts*

Probability of receiving payment and net amount to be received   Expected net present value

Quarter	With no action p_n	With a discount scheme p_d	After legal action p_l	Discount factor	With no action (£)	With a discount scheme (£)	With legal action (£)
0	0	0.2(970)	0 (–10)		0	194	–10
1	0.1(1000)	0.2(980)	0	0.9708	97.09	190.29	0
2	0.2(1000)	0.2(990)	0.2(1000)	0.9429	188.59	186.71	188.59
3	0.3(1000)	0.2(1000)	0.3(990)	0.9151	274.54	183.03	271.80
4	0.2(1000)	0.2(1010)	0.4(980)	0.8884	177.70	179.47	348.29
5	0.1(1000)	0	0.1(1040)	0.8626	86.26	0	89.71
6	0.1(1000)	0	0	0.8374	83.75	0	
Total					907.93	933.50	898.39

would be received are shown in parentheses). Alternatively it can threaten legal action if payment is not made within a year, and column p_l gives the probabilities in this case. The column also shows the net money that would result if payment were received in the particular quarter. Costs are deducted from returns; for instance, in column p_l, quarter 0, there is a cost of £10 for a threatening letter sent at the commencement of this policy. The law suit, it is assumed, would be successful and costs incurred would be recouped in quarter 5. The next column gives the discount factor for each quarter (3% cost of capital per quarter assumed). The remainder of the table gives the expected net present value for each quarter under each scheme. Clearly, the discount scheme is preferred to no action, and the least desirable scheme is legal action.

Example for multi-period horizon

The above analysis is based on an analysis of a single debtor. If a decision is made not to offer credit, then sales will be lost for future periods. The conditions may well differ if the company's horizon extends over several trading periods and if its original estimates of the probabilities of collection from a customer change as more data become available on the paying record of the client.

Consider an example. A company (the vendor) is thinking of extending credit to a potential customer. To simplify the calculations assume that 'credit' means that the purchaser takes delivery of the product and is supposed to pay within a predetermined (short) period. In the event of a default no further credit will be extended. The vendor believes that the probability that the customer will pay is ⅔, but should the sale be made and the customer pay, the vendor revises his estimate of the probability that the customer will pay for future sales. We shall assume that the vendor revises his estimate of the probability as follows. If a sale is made and payment occurs then $p = (2 + 1)/(3 + 1) = ¾$. If subsequently a further sale is made and payment once again occurs, then $p = (3 + 1)/(4 + 1) = ⅘$ and so on.

Revenue on a sale is £900 if payment is received, but a loss of £650 equal to production plus selling costs occurs in the case of default. If payment occurs, it is made after 90 days which marks the start of a new trading period. For discounting purposes we shall assume that a 3% rate of interest is appropriate for the 90 day period. The vendor plans for five periods ahead. Should he offer credit to the customer? The answer to this question will be decided by whether or not the expected net present value (NPV) over the five period horizon, resulting from an offer of credit, is positive or negative.

Column 1 of Table 22.4 gives the vendor's estimate of the probability that the customer will pay for a sale at the end of each period, given that payment has been made in all preceding periods. Column 2 is the vendor's estimate of the probability of reaching a period and receiving payment for a sale (a period would not be 'reached' in the sense that the process stops once a default occurs). Thus, for instance, the probability of reaching period 2 and receiving payment for a sale there is $\frac{2}{3} \times \frac{3}{4} = \frac{1}{2}$.

Table 22.4 *Expected net present value of debts (£) for a multi-period horizon*

Trading period	*1*	*2*	*3*	*4*	*5*	*6*	*7*
				(Columns)			
1	$\frac{2}{3}$	$\frac{2}{3}$	$\frac{1}{3}$	149.191	216.667	−67.476	−67.476
2	$\frac{3}{4}$	$\frac{1}{2}$	$\frac{1}{6}$	108.634	105.178	+3.456	−64.020
3	$\frac{4}{5}$	$\frac{2}{5}$	$\frac{1}{10}$	84.376	61.269	+23.107	−40.913
4	$\frac{5}{6}$	$\frac{1}{3}$	$\frac{1}{15}$	68.265	39.656	+28.609	−12.304
5	$\frac{6}{7}$	$\frac{2}{7}$	$\frac{1}{21}$	56.809	27.501	+29.308	+17.004

Column 3 is the probability of reaching a period and not receiving payment for a sale. Thus the probability of reaching period 2 and no payment being received for a sale is $\frac{2}{3} \times (1 - \frac{3}{4}) = \frac{1}{6}$. Column 4 is the expected gain, which is the probability of receiving payment for a sale in a given period multiplied by the profit that would result discounted back to the present. For example,

$$£149.191 = \frac{2}{3}\left(\frac{£900}{1.03} - £650\right)$$

and

$$£84.376 = \frac{2}{5}\left(\frac{£900}{1.03} - £650\right) \times (1.03)^{-2}$$

Column 5 shows the expected loss, which is the probability of not receiving payment for a sale made in a period multiplied by £650 and discounted. Thus $£105.178 = \frac{1}{6} \times £650 \times (1.03)^{-1}$, where it is assumed that the costs of £650 are incurred at the beginning of each period. Column 6 is the expected NPV of offering credit in a period, where payment has been received in previous periods, and is column 4 minus column 5. Column 7 is the cumulative expected NPV showing expected NPV for one-, two-, three-, four, or five-period horizons. As can be seen from column 7, if the vendor has only a one-period horizon, or in fact any horizon up to four periods in length, then they cannot expect to gain from extending credit facilities. However, if the vendor's horizon is five or more periods, then the expected NPV over such a horizon would be positive.

Bierman [1] gives an extended discussion of the above approach to the credit decision and formulates the problem in terms of dynamic programming, including the possibility of further issues of credit even after a default has occurred. Although generality is gained by the introduction of this possibility it would seem unrealistic in practice. In any case the technique depends heavily on the estimated probability of payment in the various trading periods as given in Table 22.4, column 1, and it should be emphasized that these may not be the real probabilities of payment.

Friedland [2] considers an alternative riskless situation where the problem is to decide upon the length of credit (cash, one month, three months, six months) to offer across the board to all customers. The probability distributions of demand will be different in each case and it is necessary to estimate these, but once obtained the implied optimum length of credit can be derived along with the consequent optimum production and/or inventory levels.

A number of models now exist to help with the problem of credit management.

22.8 Concluding remarks

The management of credit is an important part of financial management. Companies, particularly fast-growing companies, can find their liquidity position under considerable strain if the level of their debtors is not kept in hand. A fast-growing company has to produce for a higher level of future sales than past sales; therefore it invests in equipment and building up inventories to meet these future demands. The company has to pay for these purchases and other manufacturing costs, and if it does not collect receipts from the past lower level of sales in a reasonable time it can find itself with a liquidity crisis.

The management of debtors is essentially a practical problem. Consequently a considerable amount of this chapter has been concerned with the normal routine process of credit management, i.e. investigating customers, deciding on the credit terms to be offered and keeping records of outstanding accounts. Only a small part of the chapter has been devoted to theoretical ideas on debt management. The subject has not been one in which many advanced analytical ideas have been proposed or even developed. This is because of the facts of life of debt management. Whatever credit terms a company may like to offer it can be limited by the practice of the industry. Whatever a company may feel about a certain debtor's always taking a long time to pay, if that customer is an important purchaser, the selling company's bargaining position is very weak.

22.9 Key terms

Cash discounts
Credit analysis
Credit control
Credit insurance
Collection policy

Factors
Terms of sale
Trade discounts
Trade references

22.10 Revision questions

1. What are the major components of a firm's credit policy?
2. What factors should be taken into account when determining the terms of sale?
3. What analysis is it possible to undertake prior to deciding whether or not to grant credit?
4. Is it meaningful to calculate the probability of a customer's defaulting on a debt?
5. What actions can be taken to pursue a purchaser who has not paid within the credit period?
6. What analysis should a good credit management office undertake in order to maintain the number of debtors at a satisfactory level?
7. What is an optimal credit policy? What are the costs that an optimal policy seeks to balance?
8. What is the difference between a cash discount and a trade discount?
9. What is a factor? In what situations could the use of a factor help a company with the control of its working capital situation?

22.11 References

1. Bierman, H., Jr. (1970) *Financial Policy Decisions*, pp. 36–58, Macmillan, New York.
2. Friedland, S. (1966) *The Economics of Corporate Finance*, Chapter 4, Prentice-Hall, Englewood Cliffs, NJ.

22.12 Further reading

The further reading given for Chapters 19 and 20 is relevant. In addition the following four books cover the material of this chapter.

Bass, R.M.V. (1979) *Credit Management*, Business Books Ltd.

Hudson, T.G. and Butterworth, J. (1974) *Management of Trade Credit*, Gower, Epping.

Kirkman, P.R.A. (1977) *Modern Credit Management under Inflation*, Allen & Unwin: Chartered Association of Certified Accountants, London.

Clarke, B.W. (Ed.) (1989) *Handbook of International Credit Management*, Gower Publishing.

22.13 Problems

1. P. Dose Ltd has had a very poor bad debt record and, for this reason, has devised a method of credit control based on analyses of its debt experience and of the personal characteristics of its customers. It ascertained its good and bad debt experience from a sample of actual orders executed. It ranked its customers using a points system from 0 to 100, where 0 denoted a class of customers with the highest percentage of bad debts and 100 denoted a class with the highest percentage of good debts. These analyses led to the preparation of the following statistical table for credit control purposes.

Customers with points rating in the following classes	Cumulative total number of orders received	Cumulative numbers of orders received which turn out Good debts	Bad debts
0–10	1 150	200	950
0–20	2 100	450	1650
0–30	2 850	750	2100
0–40	3 950	1500	2450
0–50	6 600	4000	2600
0–60	8 150	5400	2750
0–70	9 100	6250	2850
0–80	9 500	6600	2900
0–90	9 750	6800	2950
0–100	10 000	7000	3000

This table shows, cumulatively, an analysis of the customers by class and an analysis of good and bad debts within each class per 10 000 orders received; in other words, out of every 10 000 orders received, 8150 will be for customers with a credit rating of 60 and below, of whom 5400 will be good debts and 2750 will turn out bad debts.

During 19X7, the company rejected all orders from customers with a credit rating of 50 and below with the result that a sample profit and loss account, based on the table of 10 000 orders received, appeared as follows:

Sales: 3400 orders executed at average price of £14 each £47 600

Variable costs:		
Purchases		
3400 at £3 average cost	£10 200	
Distribution		
3400 at £2 average cost	6 800	17 000
Contribution to overheads and profit		30 600
Overheads:		
Administration and selling expenses	18 200	
Bad debts 400 at £14	5 600	23 800
Net profit before charging taxation		£6 800

Assume that administration and selling expenses remain constant.

(a) Apply the 19X7 prices and costs to the statistical table to show cumulatively for the first five classes of customers the effect on profits of declining to accept orders in each class. Present your answer in columnar form in terms of contributions to overheads and profit lost, costs saved and the total gain or loss.

(b) Prepare a sample profit and loss account, similar to that shown and based on 10 000 orders received, assuming that all orders from customers with a credit rating of 20 and below are rejected.

2. (a) Discuss the factors to be considered in deciding whether or not to offer a cash discount to debtors for prompt payment of their accounts. (10 marks)

(b) Softtouch Ltd buys products from manufacturers and sells on credit to customers at an average rate of gross profit at 30%. The company is considering relaxing its credit standards and its collection policies and asks for your advice. At present, sales amount to £1 200 000 per year and debtors pay on average 60 days after the date of invoice, exept for 1% of sales representing bad debts. The proposed relaxation of credit and collection policies should increase sales by 10%, but debtors are expected to pay 90 days after invoice, and an estimated 2% of sales should prove to be bad debts. The relevant capital cost for this decision is 12% per year. Softouch pays its creditors 30 days after receiving delivery, and has a policy of holding inventory equal to 50 days of projected sales requirements.

(i) Identify the cash flows relating to one day's sales for the existing policy and for the new policy, assuming that the purchasing and stockholding policies have adapted completely to the new sales level. (8 marks)

(ii) Advise Softouch Ltd. (7 marks)

3. Blue Jays Ltd manufactures several types of knitwear which it sells to a variety of retail outlets. The company expects to suffer a temporary shortage of funds during the first three months of 1984 and its directors are considering three alternative means of meeting the shortfall.

(a) Delay payments to trade creditors in respect of purchases of wool. At present, Blue Jays Ltd receives a cash discount of 2.5% in return for settlement of creditors' invoices within one month of the invoice date. It takes advantage of this discount in respect of all invoices received. The proposed policy would involve payment of 50% of invoices (by value) at the end of two months and 50% at the end of three months.

(b) Offer discounts to trade debtors. At present, Blue Jays Ltd offers no cash discount for early settlement of invoices. On average, 10% of debtors pay one month after invoice date, 36% two months after invoice date and 50% three months after invoice date. 4% of trade debts are bad. The proposed policy would be to offer a discount of 3% for payment within one month of the invoice date. If the policy were implemented, the directors expect that 50% of debtors would pay one month after invoice date, 22% two months after invoice date and 25% three months after invoice date. 3% of trade debts would be bad.

(c) Undertake short-term borrowing. Overdraft facilities are available from the company's bankers at an interest cost of 1% per month. Short-term borrowing could be undertaken to meet all the expected shortfall or just the shortfall remaining after the implementation of either or both of the two alternatives described above.

If either of the first two alternatives were adopted, it would be applied only to invoices received or issued in January, February and March 1984. Thereafter, Blue Jays Ltd would revert to its existing policies. The actual and expected sales of Blue Jays Ltd for the nine months from October 1983 to June 1984 are as follows.

Actual sales:	October	1983	250 000
	November	1983	250 000
Expected sales:	December	1983	200 000
	January	1984	200 000
	February	1984	160 000
	March	1984	140 000
	April	1984	140 000
	May	1984	140 000
	June	1984	160 000

Wool is purchased, and the manufacture of knitwear takes place, in the month before sale. For all types of knitwear, the cost of wool is equal to 30% of selling price. All invoices for sales or purchases are issued or received by Blue Jays Ltd on the last day of the month to which they relate.

(a) Prepare calculations showing the effect on the cash flows of Blue Jays Ltd on a month by month basis if the company
   (i) delays payments to creditors in respect of January, February and March wool purchases, (5 marks)
   (ii) offers discounts to trade debtors in respect of January, February and March sales. (5 marks)
(b) Prepare calculations showing whether either delaying payments to creditors or offering discounts to debtors is worthwhile. (5 marks)
(c) Draft a note for the directors of Blue Jays Ltd advising them on any matters not included in your calculations in (a) and (b) which they should consider in arriving at their decision on whether to change temporarily their existing policies relating to trade creditors and trade debtors. (10 marks)

ICAEW, Financial Management, Dec. 1983

4. Bewcastle Ltd has received an order from a potential new customer in an overseas country for 5000 staplers at a unit price of £1.75, payable in sterling. Bewcastle's terms of sale for export orders are a 10% initial deposit, payable with order, with the balance payable in 180 days. The 10% deposit has been received with the order.

In the past customers from the overseas country have usually taken approximately one year's credit before making payment, and several have defaulted on payment. On the basis of past experience Bewcastle's management estimates that there is a 35% chance of the new customer defaulting on payment if the order is accepted, and only a 50% chance of payment within one year.

Incremental costs associated with the production and delivery of staplers would be £1.25 per unit and, in addition, there is an estimated cost of £500 for special attempts to collect an overdue debt; this cost is incurred one year after the sale is made. When this extra cost is incurred there is a 30% chance of obtaining quick payment of the debt. If, after this action, payment is not received, the debt is written off.

Bewcastle currently has some surplus funds which could be used to finance the trade credit. Prices, costs and interest rates are not expected to change significantly in the foreseeable future. Bewcastle's stapler production facilities have a large amount of spare capacity.

The company considers the granting of export credit to be a form of investment decision, with 14% per year as the appropriate dicount rate.

(a) Evaluate whether Bewcastle should accept the order from the new customer:
   (i) On the basis of the above information.
   (ii) If there is a 50% chance that the order will be repeated at the same time next year. Following payment for a first order the probability of default for repeat orders is 15%. No special attempts to collect an overdue debt would be made at the end of year 2.
   (iii) If the overseas company has stated that it will definitely repeat the order in the second year.
State clearly any assumptions that you make. (14 marks)
(b) What other factors might influence the decision of whether or not to grant credit to this potential customer? (5 marks)
(c) Discuss briefly other methods which might be used to evaluate the creditworthiness of this potential customer. (6 marks)

(25 marks)

ACCA, Dec. 1986

5. Newlean Ltd has experienced difficulty with the collection of debts from export customers. At present the company makes no special arrangements for export sales. As

a result the company is considering either employing the services of a non-recourse export factoring company or insuring its exports against non-payment through a government agency. The two alternatives also provide new possible ways of financing export sales. An export factor will, if required, provide immediate finance of 80% of export credit sales at an interest rate of 2% above bank base rate. The service fee for the debt collection is 2.5% of credit sales. If the factor is used, administrative savings of £12 500 per year should be possible.

The government agency short-term comprehensive insurance policy costs 35p per £100 insured and covers 90% of the risk of non-payment for exports. For a further payment of 25p per £100 insured the agency will provide its guarantee which enables bank finance for the insured exports to be raised at ⅝% above bank base rate. This finance is only available in conjunction with the government agency comprehensive insurance policy. Newlean normally has to pay 2.5% above base rate for its overdraft finance.

Newlean's annual exports total £650 000. All export orders are subject to a 15% initial deposit. Export sales are on open account terms of 45 days credit, but on average payment has been 30 days late. Approximately 0.5% by value of credit sales result in bad debts which have to be written off. The clearing bank base rate is 10%.

(a) Determine which combination of export administration and financing Newlean Ltd should use.   (15 marks)

(b) Outline the main debt collection techniques with respect to sales in the home market that are available to financial managers   (5 marks)

(c) Discuss how a manufacturing company might devise an effective debt collection system.   (5 marks)

                                                                        (25 marks)

                                                                        ACCA, Dec. 1985

6. Quansit Pty is reviewing its credit policy. Currently it extends credit terms of 30 days from invoice date and is considering extending this to 60 days. Current sales are 10 000 units a month, priced at £12. Direct costs are 90% of sales price. The marketing director believes that if the credit period is extended sales will increase by 12%. If the current cost of funds to the company is 11%, should the company extend the credit period:

(a) (i) if the extended credit is only applied to new sales?

   (ii) if the extended credit is applied to existing sales as well?

(b) What other issues should be brought into the discussion, and which other departments in the company should have an input?

7. Tolate Ltd sells goods on credit terms direct to the public. The company has a policy of accepting all orders, without any evaluation of a customer's creditworthiness. However, recent bad debts have caused the company to consider using a credit scoring system of customer evaluation.

Based upon a representative random sample of past customers Tolate has identified the most significant factors associated with 'good' and 'bad' customers and has statistically estimated a points score to be allocated if a potential customer has the specified factor. These are shown below:

Factor	Points score
Married	10
Owns home	15
Car	10
Age 35 or over	15
Lived 3 years at the same address	15
At least two years at the same occupation	15
Less than 3 children	20
	100

Past customers with total scores of 40 or less were split between 'good' and 'bad' customers as follows:

Cumulative number of customers		
Total score	Good	Bad
0	1	20
10	10	300
15	40	700
20	75	1000
25	140	1300
30	200	1400
35	500	1500
40	1000	100

Each 'good' customer rejected below the cut-off credit score is estimated to cost Tolate Ltd £100 in lost profit. Each bad account rejected below the cut-off credit score represents a £50 increase in profit.

Required:

(i) Calculate the cut-off credit score that should be applied by Tolate Ltd.

(ii) A second stage credit evaluation is available for all rejected applications at a cost of £5 per application, and is believed to be 95% accurate. It is much cheaper for Tolate to use the credit score, plus possibly this second stage, than to incur a cost of £5 for all applicants.

Evaluate whether this second stage should be used and, if so, for which credit applicants.

(iii) Suggest alternative forms of customer credit evaluation that might be useful to Tolate Ltd.

ACCA, Dec. 1988

8. Comfylot plc produces garden seats which are sold in both domestic and export markets. Sales during the next year are forecast to be £16 million, 70% to the UK domestic market and 30% to the export market, and are expected to occur steadily throughout the year. 80% of UK sales are on credit terms, with payment due in 30 days. On average UK domestic customers take 57 days to make payment. An initial deposit of 15% of the sales price is paid by all export customers. All export sales are on 60 days credit with an average collection period for credit sales of 75 days. Bad debts are currently 0.75% of UK credit sales, and 1.25% of export sales (net of the deposit).

Comfylot wishes to investigate the effects of each of three possible operational changes:

(a) Domestic credit management could be undertaken by a non-recourse factoring company. The factor would charge a service fee of 1.5% and would provide finance on 80% of the debts factored at a cost of base rate + 2.5%. The finance element must be taken as part of the agreeent with the factor. Using a factor would save an initial £85 000 per year in administration costs, but would lead to immediate redundancy payments of £15 000.

(b) As an alternative to using the factor a cash discount of 1.5% for payment in seven days could be offered on UK domestic sales. It is expected that 40% of domestic credit customers would use the cash discount. The discount would cost an additional £25 000 per year to administer, and would reduce bad debts to 0.50% of UK credit sales.

(c) Extra advertising could be undertaken to stimulate export sales. Comfylot has been approached by a European satellite TV company which believes that £300 000 of advertising could increase export sales in the coming year by up to 30%. There is a 0.2 chance of a 20% increase in export sales, a 0.5 chance of a 25% increase and a 0.3 chance of a 30% increase. Direct costs of production are 65% of the sales price. Administration costs would increase by £30 000, £40 000 and £50 000 for the 20%, 25% and 30% increases in export sales respectively. Increased export sales are likely to result in the average collection period of the credit element of all exports lengthening by five days, and bad debts increasing to 1.5% of all export credit sales.

Bank base rate is currently 13% per year, and Comfylot can borrow overdraft finance at 15% per year. These rates are not expected to change in the near future. Taxation may be ignored.

Required:

(a) Discuss whether any of the three suggested changes should be adopted by Comfylot plc. All relevant calculations must be shown.   (19 marks)

(b) Explain what is meant by forfaiting and comment upon whether it could be of value to Comfylot plc.   (6 marks)

           (25 marks)

ACCA, June 1992

23 *Management of inventory*

23.1	Introduction	821
23.2	The classical model	823
23.3	Variable re-order costs	826
23.4	Cash management model	827
23.5	Lead time	828
23.6	Production for stock	829
23.7	Buffer stocks	830
23.8	Random demand	831
23.9	Random lead time	836
23.10	A service level approach	839
23.11	Periodic review models	842

23.12	The ABC classification scheme	844
23.13	Lot size inventory management	845
23.14	Material requirements planning and just-in-time management	846
23.15	Basic program	848
23.16	Conclusions	849
23.17	Key concepts	849
23.18	Revision questions	850
23.19	References	851
23.20	Further reading	851
23.21	Problems	851

Successful management of manufacturing and distribution requires efficient stock control. Inventory can represent up to 20% or 25% of the total assets of manufacturing companies. This proportion can rise to 40% in retail distribution. Efficiency gains in inventory management can bring significant improvements to overall company financial performance.

We review a selection of stock control models, each of which fits specific circumstances. You will see how the most efficient size of stock re-order or production run might be found, and a computer program in Basic is provided. You will also see examples of how unpredictability in the demand for inventory could be handled.

Approaches to multi-item inventory management are also considered. We argue that just-in-time management provides a complementary range of methods to those based upon the concept of economic order quantity.

23.1 Introduction

Inventory can be classified into three main types depending on the stage of the manufacturing process at which it is held. We can distinguish *pre-production inventory, in-process inventory* and *finished goods inventory*.

Pre-production inventory consists of raw materials and bought-in components or other inputs secured from outside the firm. In-process inventory is **work in progress** and may be held at several points in the production process. Finished goods inventory consists of the firm's products from which sales are drawn.

In general, **any** temporarily idle resource could be thought of as inventory. Stocks have been described as 'money in disguise' – indeed the stock may be of money itself as in the holding of cash. Some cash management problems can, in principle, fit a classical stock-control framework.

The main purpose of inventory is to allow each stage of the production and sales process to operate economically by insulating it from different or varying rates of activity at other stages. But the stocks should not be a cover up for poorly co-ordinated processes. One of the benefits of the just-in-time approach was to bring new thinking to the levels of stock necessary in well-managed production. Finished goods inventory, for example, acts as a cushion between production and sales. Even when demand is at a constant rate it may be uneconomical to produce continually at that rate. For example, if a manufacturer makes 50 different sizes of wheel, economies of scale can be gained by making a year's supply of each in 50 separate production runs averaging one week.

Apart from situations where flexible manufacturing systems (FMSs) are used in the production of durable goods in a demand-led environment, erratic or periodic sales will mean that it is unduly expensive to keep production in lockstep with demand. Inventory gives the ability to satisfy demand promptly without unrealistic variations in rates of production.

Similar considerations apply within the production process itself. If a product must be processed on several machines which operate at different rates or at different times, in-process inventory is desirable. Even if the different stages of production operate at the same rates and the same times, mechanical failures will not be simultaneous so that in-process inventory still has a useful function to perform.

The entire production process may need insulating from irregularities in the arrival of supplies. The price of this security is the cost of holding pre-production inventory. Where security of supply is not considered to be a problem, as when components are sourced from well-integrated suppliers or other parts of the same organization, a just-in-time (JIT) approach may save considerable sums. Raw materials may also be held for speculative reasons if there are expectations of rising commodity prices. The role of inventories as buffers is shown schematically in Figure 23.1 in which manufacturing takes place on two machines in sequence.

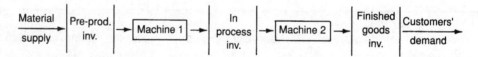

Figure 23.1

There are valid and invalid reasons for holding stock. It has rightly been said that 'stocks buy organization' to the extent that inefficient production and distribution can be masked and sustained by excessive stock levels. But it is not possible to operate efficiently at zero stock levels in all cases. The stock control problem is to find the ideal balance between the costs and benefits of inventory. We shall be looking for the best obtainable stock control policies in a variety of situations. A stock control policy is a rule or collection of rules which determine:

1. the size of stock replenishments;
2. the timing of replenishments;
3. the consequences of out of stock situations.

In the main, the models that follow are expressed in terms of finished goods inventory for a single product. Similar principles apply to in-process or pre-production inventory although materials requirement planning (MRP) methods (section 23.14) may be particularly relevant here.

This fundamental stock control model forms the basis of a number of more advanced models. The assumptions employed by the classical static model are as follows:

1. a single item of stock;
2. all parameters known and constant;
3. instantaneous replenishment of stock;
4. no variable re-order costs.

The parameters of assumption (2) are data for costs and for the rate of demand (or in general the rate of depletion) of stock. Figure 23.2 shows the graph of inventory level against time and has the characteristic sawtooth shape.

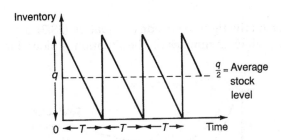

Figure 23.2

The problem is to determine the best value of the replenishment size q. Figure 23.2 starts with inventory at its maximum level and which declines at a uniform rate. When stocks have fallen to zero, it is assumed that they are immediately replenished in full. The length of time required for stocks to go from peak to peak (or equivalently from trough to trough) is one inventory **cycle**. We do not aim to minimize costs per cycle, however. This would be achieved by setting $q = 0$ and keeping no inventory at all. Rather, the objective is to minimize costs per annum (or some other suitable length of time).

Now consider costs in more detail. The costs fall into two categories: holding costs and replenishment costs. Holding costs include storage, insurance, deterioration and interest charges. The second category relates to replacement of stock. There will normally be a fixed and a variable component here. The fixed component will include administrative costs of placing an order if supplies are brought in from outside or the set up costs of machinery if the goods are produced by the firm itself. Variable costs depend on the amount re-ordered. The following notation will be employed:

C_m is the cost of procuring one unit of the item;
iC_m is the cost of holding one item of stock for one year;
C_o is the fixed cost of a replenishment order of **any** size;
A is the annual rate of demand.

The use of the notation iC_m for the holding cost reflects the view that it is frequently the case that annual holding costs are proportional to the value (cost) of an item stocked. The factor of proportionality, i, might typically take values of around 0.2 or 0.3.

Now consider the annual holding costs in more detail. From the holding cost point of view, it is as if half the maximum level of inventory was being constantly held throughout the year. If this is so, we can write:

$$\text{Total holding costs per annum} = \frac{q}{2}iCm \qquad (23.1)$$

Assumption (4) of the basic model means that, for the moment, procurement costs will be ignored. They will be brought into the model in section 23.3. Costs arising from replenishment will be C_o times the number of stock refills needed. If annual demand is for A units of stock and replenishment size is q units, then n replenishments will be needed per annum where:

$$n = \frac{A}{q}$$

n is the number of inventory cycles per annum. We can now write:

$$\text{Total replenishment costs per annum} = \frac{C_o A}{q} \qquad (23.2)$$

so that, overall, total costs per annum, C, are given by:

$$C = \frac{q}{2} i C_m + \frac{C_o A}{q} \qquad (23.3)$$

The only unknown on the right hand side of equation (23.3) is q, and we wish to determine the value of q which minimizes C. The situation is plotted in Figure 23.3.

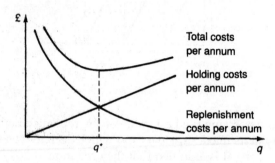

Figure 23.3

Total costs and each component of costs are plotted against replenishment size q. The ideal value of q is that corresponding to the lowest point of the total cost curve; this is marked as q^*. Although it so happens that with this model the minimum of the total cost curve is above the intersection point of the holding and replenishment cost curves, it is **rates of change** that are important. What is being sought is an optimal balance or trade-off between those costs which rise with q (holding costs) and those which fall with q (replenishment costs). The optimal balance is struck where the rate at which holding costs are going up is equal to the rate at which replenishment costs are coming down. Minimizing C with respect to q in equation (23.3) requires that the first derivative be set equal to zero:

$$\frac{dC}{dq} = i C_m - \frac{C_o A}{q^2} = 0 \qquad (23.4)$$

The second derivative requires that, for C to be a minimum;

$$\frac{d^2 C}{dq^2} = 2 \frac{C_o A}{q^3} \geq 0 \qquad (23.5)$$

Since C_o and A are positive numbers this condition is fulfilled for any positive value of q. From the first order condition (23.4) the slope of the holding costs line is $i C_m / 2$ and the slope of the replenishment costs curve is $-C_o A / q^2$, that is, replenishment costs are coming down at the rate of $C_o A / q^2$. Therefore to find the best value of q we set:

$$i C_m = \frac{C_o A}{q^2}$$

Hence

$$q^2 = \frac{2AC_o}{iC_m}$$

and

$$q^* = \left[\frac{2AC_o}{iC_m}\right]^{\frac{1}{2}} \tag{23.6}$$

Equation (23.6) is most important. It is known as the **square root rule**. The best value of q, q^*, is called the **economic order quantity** (EOQ), economic lot size (ELS) or the economic batch size (EBS). We shall use the term EOQ here. Putting the EOQ value of q given by (23.6) into the cost expression (23.3) gives:

$$C = \left(\frac{AC_o iC_m}{2}\right) + \frac{C_o A(iC_m)^{\frac{1}{2}}}{(2C_o A)^{\frac{1}{2}}} \tag{23.7}$$

$$= (2AC_o iC_m)^{\frac{1}{2}} \tag{23.8}$$

The two parts of (23.7) are equal as shown by Figure 23.3, while (23.8) shows the minimum achievable level of inventory costs. Note from (23.6) and (23.8) that the optimal level of inventory varies inversely with iC_m while the level of costs varies directly with the holding cost figure. In both cases the effects of changing iC_m are damped by the square root.

Consider an example. A company faces a demand for 2000 items per annum. Stock replenishment costs are fixed at £100 irrespective of the scale of replenishment. It costs £2.50 to hold one item in stock for one year. What is the EOQ? In this case:

$$C_o = 100 \quad A = 2000 \quad iCm = 2.5$$

So substituting in the EOQ formula gives:

$$q^* = \left(\frac{2(100)(2000)}{2.5}\right)^{\frac{1}{2}} = 400$$

Therefore the EOQ is 400 units, five replenishments (= 2000/400) will be needed each year and the minimum level of annual costs is £1000. Note that if annual sales double to 4000 units per annum with other parameters unchanged the optimal level of inventory will increase by a factor of √2 to 565.69. The square root rule confutes a commonsense rule of thumb stating that if sales double so should stocks. Thus if demand did double to 4000, optimal costs given by (23.8) would be £1414.21. If an EOQ of 800 had been used corresponding annual inventory costs given by (23.3) would be £1500.

Now consider a further example. A company's stock is depleted at a constant rate of 10 units per day. Storage costs per unit per calendar month are 40p and the cost per re-order is £150. At what intervals should replenishments be made and what would be the minimum level of annual costs achievable?

On an annual basis:

$$A = 3650 \quad iC_m = 4.8 \quad \text{and} \quad C_o = 150$$

First find the EOQ. This will be:

$$q^* = \left(\frac{2(150)(3650)}{4.8}\right)^{\frac{1}{2}} = 477.62$$

If we again ignore the problem of fractions for the moment, a replenishment size of 477.62 with an annual demand of 3650 means that the number of stock replenishments per annum, n, will be:

$$n = \frac{3650}{477.62} = 7.64$$

This produces a cycle length or interval between replenishments (as we should expect from the daily demand figure) of 47.76 days. The minimum level of annual costs is found by putting the EOQ value of 477.62 into (23.8). The result is £2292.60.

There would be no dramatic rise in costs if these figures were rounded off to $q = 480$ ordered every 48 days, as substitution in (23.3) will confirm. Annual costs C are not sensitive to small variations in q. The damping effect given by the square root means that the EOQ rule is robust with respect to minor errors or uncertainties in parameter values.

We shall now consider the effects of dropping the apparently restrictive assumptions of the classical static model, beginning with re-order costs.

<table>
<tr><td>23.3 Variable re-order costs</td></tr>
</table>

When re-order costs vary with the size of the re-order because of the unit cost of the commodity, in addition to the costs so far considered the firm now pays C_m per unit to acquire the item for stock. If the firm is manufacturing the good itself, then C_m is the unit variable costs of production. If the firm is a wholesaler or retailer then C_m is the supplier's per unit ordered. It is assumed that C_m is a known constant. In this case, costs for a re-order of size q will now be:

$$C_o + qC_m$$

Note that A/q re-orders per annum will still be necessary. Total costs per annum are now:

$$C = \frac{q}{2}iC_m + (C_o + qC_m)\frac{A}{q}$$

$$= \frac{q}{2}iC_m + \frac{C_o A}{q} + C_m A \qquad (23.9)$$

Since in (23.9) $C_m A$ is a constant term, the EOQ is unchanged and formula (23.6) still applies. Annual costs are increased but it still pays to replenish stock in the same quantities as before. This assumes that the firm intends to satisfy the total annual demand. This does not mean that the unit cost figure can be ignored, but what it does illustrate is that the usefulness of a model cannot always be measured by the plausibility of its assumptions.

Consider as an example a builders' supply merchant which holds stocks of a certain type of tap. Demand for the taps is at the rate of 250 units per quarter. It costs £2 to hold one tap for a year and the merchant's administrative costs of placing a re-order with the manufacturer are £10. At present the manufacturer charges £3 per tap supplied plus a charge of £30 per re-order irrespective of re-order size. The product manufacturer has recently offered an alternative scheme of charges. The price per tap would come down to £2.50 but the charge per re-order would be increased by £120. Is this new arrangement desirable?

To answer the question, the EOQ and corresponding annual cost figures must be worked out under each arrangement to find the one which produces the lower cost. In the first instance:

$$iC_m = £2 \quad C_o = £40 \quad C_m = £3 \quad \text{and} \quad A = 1000$$

Note that the C_o value includes the manufacturer's charge. The resulting EOQ is:

$$q^* = \left(\frac{2(40)(1000)}{2}\right)^{\frac{1}{2}} = 2000$$

and the resulting annual costs are:

$$C = \frac{200}{2}2 + \frac{40(1000)}{200} + 3(1000)$$

$$= 3300$$

Under the alternative scheme the EOQ would be:

$$q^* = \left(\frac{2(160)(1000)}{2} \right)^{\frac{1}{2}} = 400$$

and the resulting annual costs are:

$$C = \frac{400}{2} 2 + \frac{160(1000)}{400} + 2.5(1000)$$

$$= 3300$$

So the new arrangement produces a saving of £100 per annum for the merchant. Although both holding costs and re-order costs have increased, this has been more than compensated by the reduced unit cost C_m.

Cash management has similarities to stock control as we saw in section 20.17, and the framework of the classical model can give useful insight and order of magnitude results. The following example continues the theme of variable re-order costs, and shows how the basic model can deal with inflows as well as outflows.

A company receives inflows of cash at a steady rate amounting to £350 000 per annum. The cash can be invested in securities to earn 12% per annum. Each time an investment is made there is a brokerage charge of £50 + 1% of the sum invested. How many investments of cash should the company make annually? An alternative scheme of brokerage charges is £100 + 0.8% of the sum invested. Which scheme would the company prefer?

The cash is not placed in securities immediately because of the fixed part of the brokerage charges. The company needs to know the ideal size of investment and hence, with the given annual inflow, the number of investments to make each year. The situation is plotted in Figure 23.4 with q being the size of investment.

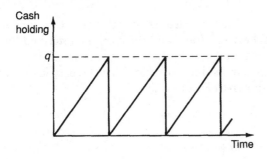

Figure 23.4

The average holding of cash is $q/2$ and the cost of holding £1 in cash for one year is the lost interest, £0.12. Note that to invest each pound costs £0.01. In the original scheme therefore:

$$C_m = 0.01 \quad A = 350\,000 \quad C_o = 50 \quad iC_m = 0.12$$

the square root formula produces:

$$q^* = \left(\frac{2(50)(350\,000)}{0.12} \right)^{\frac{1}{2}} = 17\,078$$

So the optimum number of investments per annum will be:

$$\frac{350\,000}{17\,078} \approx 20.49$$

or about 41 in two years. The total cost works out at:

$$C = \frac{17\,078}{2}0.12 + \frac{50(350\,000)}{17\,078} + 0.01(350\,000)$$

$$\approx £5549$$

For the alternative scheme of charges:

$$C_m = 0.008 \quad A = 350\,000 \quad C_o = 100 \quad iC_m = 0.12$$

the square root formula produces:

$$q^* = \left(\frac{2(100)(350\,000)}{0.12}\right)^{\frac{1}{2}} = 24\,152$$

So the optimum number of investments per annum under this scheme would be:

$$\frac{350\,000}{24\,152} \approx 14.49$$

or about 29 in two years. The total cost works out at:

$$C = \frac{24\,152}{2}0.12 + \frac{100(350\,000)}{24\,152} + 0.008(350\,000)$$

$$\approx £5698$$

So while there is relatively little in it, the company should stay with the original scheme.

23.5 Lead time

We now turn to the instantaneous stock replenishment assumption of the classical model and consider the consequences of its relaxation. **Lead time** is the delay between the placement of an order and the arrival of the goods in stock. Instantaneous replenishment means zero lead time. Let us now suppose that lead time is a known and fixed number of weeks, L.

The presence of a fixed lead time leaves re-order quantity unchanged. Frequency of re-orders, the intervals between them and the costs as described by equation (23.9) are also the same. But the order for replenishment must now be placed when the amount of inventory falls to the level of lead time demand. The level of lead time demand is the **re-order level** R. This is shown in Figure 23.5.

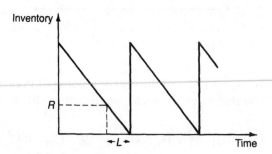

Figure 23.5

By way of example suppose that for the data of the builders' merchant example that there is a lead time of three weeks ($L = 3$). If a 50-week working year is assumed, the weekly demand is for 20 units so that demand during lead time, the re-order level, would be 60 units. The EOQ remains at 400. All the above assumes a fixed lead time. In practice this may be variable, and we return to this matter in later sections.

Many firms that produce a range of several similar products do not keep all items in continuous production. Rather, they have production runs on each item lasting days, weeks or months. Sometimes the anticipated annual demand is produced in one run; on other occasions there may be a number of shorter periods of production each year. This model has features in common with the cash management application of section 23.4 and the non-instantaneous replenishment model introduced in section 23.5.

Consider one item produced by a firm. It will be assumed that there are no effective limitations on storage. The decision required is how much to produce at each run. Alternatively, given a steady rate of production, the problem could be re-expressed in terms of the **length of time** that each run should last. The graph of inventory level versus time in this case is shown in Figure 23.6.

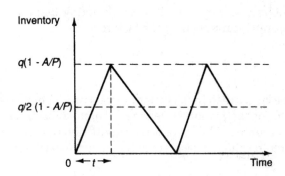

Figure 23.6

Starting from zero, inventory steadily rises while there is production which lasts for a proportion, t, of the year. The rate of stock build-up is the excess of the production rate over the demand rate. When the run is completed inventory declines at the demand rate. Let the amount produced in t be q. With the production rate at P units per annum then:

$$t = \frac{q}{P}$$

Demand during the production run is a proportion of the annual demand, and to satisfy this demand:

$$tA = A\frac{q}{P}$$

Maximum inventory level can be an important measure – for example in terms of storage space requirements. This will be given by the total amount produced less the demand during the production run. That is:

$$\text{Maximum inventory} = q\left(1 - \frac{A}{P}\right)$$

Average inventory is half this level. Maximum and average inventory are as shown in Figure 23.6. Annual holding costs will be given by:

$$\text{Holding costs} = \frac{q}{2}iC_m\left(1 - \frac{A}{P}\right)$$

Replenishment costs **per cycle** (that is, per production run) as before will be given by:

$$C_o + qC_m$$

where C_m in this context represents the unit variable production cost and C_o will give the cost of setting up the equipment for the run. Total replenishment costs per annum will then be given by:

$$\text{Replenishment costs} = (C_o + qC_m)\frac{A}{q}$$

so the total costs to be minimized are:

$$C = \frac{q}{2}iC_m\left(1 - \frac{A}{P}\right) + (C_o + qC_m)\frac{A}{q}$$

and minimization produces the formula:

$$q^* = \left(\frac{2AC_oP}{iC_m(P-A)}\right)$$

This formula can be used as it stands but it is worth noting that the value of q^* in this case is the old EOQ formula multiplied by the factor:

$$\left(\frac{P}{(P-A)}\right)^{\frac{1}{2}}$$

so that the EOQ will be larger than in the instantaneous production rate case. The alternative acronyms for the 'order quantity' referring to batch or lot size, EBS or ELS, might be used in a production context. The faster is the production rate the nearer is the result to the instantaneous replenishment case, since the factor $\sqrt{[P/(P-A)]}$ approaches one as P approaches infinity.

Consider an example. Each time that a firm starts a production run for a product there are set up costs of £400. Production is at the rate of 12 000 units per annum and annual demand is 8000 units. Unit variable cost of production is £30. It costs £7.50 to hold one item for one year. How much should be produced at a time, how many production runs should there be each year, what would the maximum stock level be, how long would each production run last and what are total annual costs? Substitution into the formula for q^* gives output per run as:

$$q^* = \left(\frac{2(12\,000)(400)(8000)}{7.5(12\,000-8000)}\right)^{\frac{1}{2}} = 1600$$

So that five production runs would be needed each year. Maximum inventory is 533.33 (534 in reality). Each production run would last for $t = 1600/12\,000$ of a year (about 49 days). Total annual costs are £244 000.

23.7 Buffer stocks

In the classical model all parameters are assumed to be known and constant. It is a deterministic model. We begin consideration of the relaxation of this assumption with the concept of buffer stocks. Buffer or safety stocks are additional inventory held against unforeseen events such as a surge in demand or a delay in the arrival of stock. In the deterministic world of the classical model, buffer stocks are not needed, but if they **were** added in, inventory would never fall below the level of buffer stock. Both the average level of stock and the re-order level are shifted up by the amount of buffer stock, B. The situation is illustrated in Figure 23.7.

The EOQ is unaffected. Lead time demand is $R - B$, the minimum level of stock is B and the maximum level is now $B + q$. Holding costs per annum and total costs rise by £$B(iC_m)$.

The reason that buffer stocks are held is that demand is often uncertain, as may be the length of lead time. Demand in any period is usually a random variable, although the average rate of demand may be known. So instead of the sharp sides of the sawtooth diagrams we have the rather ragged edges of Figure 23.8.

If re-order level is now set at **average** lead time demand and there is no buffer stock, then if demand during lead time happens to be brisk, all orders during this period cannot be filled at once – a **stock-out** occurs. Figure 23.8 has been drawn on the assumption

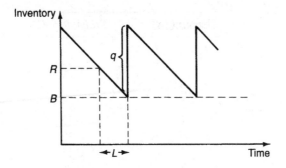

Figure 23.7

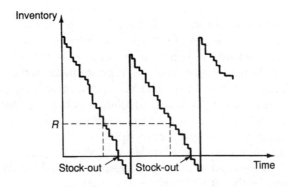

Figure 23.8

that orders during the out-of-stock period can be filled as soon as supplies arrive. This is sometimes called **backlogged demand**. This will not always be the case – some orders may be lost and there will usually be costs associated with stock-outs. These costs relate to lost custom in the future, possible failure to meet contractual liabilities, compensation for delay etc. Any estimate of stock-out costs is subject to question and account must be taken of this fact. But it would be unwise to ignore these costs and so implicitly assume that they are zero. If buffer stocks are kept, then the chance that a stock-out will occur is reduced. The larger the buffer stock the lower is the probability of a stock-out each cycle. As buffer stock is increased, expected stock-out costs are reduced but, of course, holding costs increase. Once again the problem is one of finding the best balance – the level of buffer stock which minimizes:

Buffer stock holding cost + expected stock-out costs

in which both the buffer stock holding costs (BSHC) and expected stock-out costs (SOC) are expressed on an annual basis. These are costs which are **additional** to the holding and re-order costs already determined and which could be thought of as **uncertainty costs**, which we shall call U and write as:

$$U = \text{BSHC} + \text{SOC} \qquad (23.10)$$

In the following sections we examine two ways in which these uncertainty costs could be taken into account.

First consider the search for a minimum of uncertainty costs where there is a known discrete probability distribution of demand in any period. Suppose that a company stocks a single product and has a 50 week working year. Demand for the product in any week is described by the distribution:

23.8 Random demand

Demand (X)	Probability (P)
0	0.07
1	0.10
2	0.11
3	0.13
4	0.15
5	0.17
6	0.13
7	0.08
8	0.04
9	0.02

Demand can only be satisfied from stock. Stockholding costs are £2 per item per year. Fixed costs per re-order are £8 and the variable re-order costs are £15 per unit. The lead time is one week. The penalty for being out of stock is £6 for each unit of demand that cannot be satisfied until new stocks arrive. A more sophisticated approach would make allowance for the length of time for which each unit of unsatisfied demand stands. This could be done in a manner similar to the calculation of holding costs.

We shall need to find the best value of the economic order quantity to find the best balance between holding and re-order costs in the usual way. We then need to go on to find the values for buffer stock and re-order level that keep the uncertainty costs to a minimum. First of all we need to know the average level of annual demand. We shall then use this figure in the EOQ formula. We start by finding the average **weekly** demand and the average level of annual demand that this implies. Multiplying each level of demand by its probability of occurrence and summing the results gives the average (arithmetic mean) weekly demand. A PX column is formed as follows:

$$PX$$

$$0.00$$
$$0.10$$
$$0.22$$
$$0.39$$
$$0.60$$
$$0.85$$
$$0.78$$
$$0.56$$
$$0.32$$
$$0.18$$
$$\overline{}$$
$$\Sigma PX = 4.00$$

So the mean weekly demand is four units and the mean annual demand, A, over 50 weeks is therefore:

$$A = 50(4) = 200$$

Using this value for A to find the EOQ from the square root formula produces:

$$q^* = \left(\frac{2(8)(200)}{2} \right)^{\frac{1}{2}} = 40$$

So the economic order quantity is 40 units. This corresponds to an average of five inventory cycles per annum. This minimizes the inventory costs given by (23.9) (that is, replenishment costs and the costs of holding non-buffer stock) and completes the first stage of the workings. We shall need the number of cycles, n, in the next stage.

In the second stage, the best value for buffer stock, B, is that which minimizes BSHC + SOC. The optimal re-order level then follows as $B + 4$, since average lead time demand is four units. Either the re-order level R or the buffer stock B can be taken as the decision variable in this step. The relationship is:

re-order level = mean lead time demand + buffer stock

that is:

$$R = LW + B \qquad (23.11)$$

where in (23.11) L is the number of weeks lead time, W is the mean weekly demand and B is the buffer stock. We shall express the workings in terms of B. Since in this case there is only a small number of possible levels of demand during any week, *complete enumeration* is possible, and we shall determine BSHC + SOC for the likely practical levels of buffer stock.

To obtain the expected annual costs of stock-outs, SOC, the first step is to find the expected shortage at the end of each cycle. We can then multiply this by the number of cycles per annum (already found) and the cost per unit short (a given datum). This gives the expected annual cost of stock-outs. The expected shortage per cycle depends on the buffer stock level. Suppose that buffer stock was zero. The corresponding re-order level would then be just the mean lead time demand of four units, so shortage would occur if demand during lead time was for five or more units. Although unlikely in practice buffer stock could, conceivably, be negative. For example, if the re-order level was set at 3 units, this would imply a 'buffer' stock of –1. This would mean an increased probability of stock-out, but lower holding costs. However, we shall draw the line here at zero buffer stock, $B = 0$, for which level the workings are shown in Table 23.1.

Table 23.1

Buffer stock level $B = 0$

Demand	Shortage	Probability	$P \times S$
5	1	0.17	0.17
6	2	0.13	0.26
7	3	0.08	0.24
8	4	0.04	0.16
9	5	0.02	0.10
Expected shortage, reorder level 4 =			0.93

In Table 23.1 recall that the buffer stock level of zero corresponds to a re-order level of four. Consequently any level of demand above four units in the one period of lead time produces a shortage four units less than the level of demand. The average of the shortages weighted by the probability of occurrence (the probabilities of the corresponding levels of demand) is the expected shortage per cycle for this level of buffer stock.

Table 23.2 shows the workings for a buffer stock of one unit, which corresponds to a re-order level of five units. Tables 23.3 to 23.5 show the expected shortage calculations for levels of buffer stock from two to four units, with the associated re-order levels being four units higher in each case. Finally, note that the maximum buffer stock is five, for which the expected shortage is zero.

Table 23.2

Buffer stock level $B = 1$

Demand	Shortage	Probability	$P \times S$
6	1	0.13	0.13
7	2	0.08	0.16
8	3	0.04	0.12
9	4	0.02	0.08
Expected shortage, reorder level 5 =			0.49

Table 23.3

Buffer stock level $B = 2$

Demand	Shortage	Probability	$P \times S$
7	1	0.08	0.08
8	2	0.04	0.08
9	3	0.02	0.06
Expected shortage, reorder level 6 =			0.22

Table 23.4

Buffer stock level $B = 3$

Demand	Shortage	Probability	$P \times S$
8	1	0.04	0.04
9	2	0.02	0.04
Expected shortage, reorder level 7 =			0.08

Table 23.5

Buffer stock level $B = 4$

Demand	Shortage	Probability	$P \times S$
9	1	0.02	0.02
Expected shortage, reorder level 8 =			0.02

The next step is to build a table showing the costs associated with each level of buffer stock. Suppose that the buffer stock is one. The expected shortage per cycle is 0.49, but since there are on average five cycles per annum the expected annual shortage is:

$$5(0.49) = 2.45$$

and with a shortage cost of £6 per unit short, the expected shortage cost per annum will be:

$$6(2.45) = 14.7$$

Since the buffer stock is 1, BSHC = 2 and so overall:

$$U = \text{BSHC} + \text{SOC} = 2 + 14.7 = 16.7$$

for $B = 1$ and $R = 5$. Similar calculations are performed for each value of B, and the results are detailed in Table 23.6. (We are taking a short cut here in not working with expected **surpluses** when demand is low. The method can be modified but the effects on the final cost figures are negligible, in no case exceeding 0.1% of the original value.)

Table 23.6

(1)	(2)	(3)	(4)	(5)	(6)
B	ESPC	ESPA	SOC	BSHC	Total
0	0.93	4.65	27.90	0.00	27.90
1	0.49	2.45	14.70	2.00	16.70
2	0.22	1.10	6.60	4.00	10.60
3	0.08	0.40	2.40	6.00	8.40
4	0.02	0.10	0.60	8.00	8.60
5	0.00	0.00	0.00	10.00	10.00

In Table 23.6, entries in column (6) show that the optimal value of B is 3 units so that the re-order level should be $R = 7$. But there is little to choose between buffer stocks of 3 or 4 units, and this raises the question as to how sensitive are the results to changes in the problem parameters. In particular the shortage cost figure may be questionable, and it would be desirable to know the range of values of the shortage cost figure for which the original solution remains optimal. If the shortage cost figure is T, then entries in column (6) can be expressed in terms of T. The results are shown in Table 23.7.

Table 23.7

Buffer stock	BSHC + SOC
0	$4.65T$
1	$2.45T + 2$
2	$1.1T + 4$
3	$0.4T + 6$
4	$0.1T + 8$
5	10

For the original solution to remain optimal, T must be such that the $B = 3$ cost figure of $0.4T + 6$ must not exceed any of the other values. As the value of T rises, the higher levels of buffer stock may become attractive and so the $B = 4$ and $B = 5$ cost figures will set **upper** bounds on T. Whichever sets the **least upper bound** (LUB) will determine the maximum value to which T can rise. Conversely, the lower values of buffer stock may become attractive as T falls. Each entry in the cost column of Table 23.7 for $B = 0$ to $B = 2$ will set a **lower** bound for S and the **greatest lower bound** (GLB) is the relevant one. The workings are as follows:

$$0.4T + 6 \le 0.1T + 8 \qquad \text{so } T \le 6.67 \qquad \text{*LUB}$$
$$0.4T + 6 \le 10 \qquad \text{so } T \le 10$$

$$0.4T + 6 \leq 1.1T + 4 \qquad \text{so } T \geq 2.86 \qquad \text{*GLB}$$
$$0.4T + 6 \leq 2.45T + 2 \qquad \text{so } T \geq 1.95$$
$$0.4T + 6 \leq 4.65T \qquad \text{so } T \geq 1.41$$

So provided the true value of T lies in the range:

$$2.86 \leq T \leq 6.67$$

none of the alternative values of B produces a lower cost figure than $B = 3$. Sensitivity analysis on other problem parameters can also be carried out, although the workings in these cases are complicated by the fact that the EOQ value, and hence the number of cycles per annum, is affected by variations in C_o, A or iC_m.

23.9 Random lead time

The delay between placing a stock re-order and the receipt of the new stock may also be a random variable. Consider an example in which lead time follows a discrete probability distribution but where weekly demand is constant at the level $W = 60$. Suppose that lead time, L, follows the distribution shown in Table 23.8.

Table 23.8

L (weeks)	Probability (P)	PL
1	0.15	0.15
2	0.20	0.40
3	0.30	0.90
4	0.20	0.80
5	0.15	0.75
	Mean length of lead time =	3.00

so that $L = 3$ weeks. The mean lead time demand will then be:

$$LW = 3(60) = 180$$

The analysis would then proceed as in section 23.8 for fixed lead time and random demand, buffer stock being chosen by enumeration to minimize the uncertainty costs. Values of buffer stock considered here might be 0, 60 and 120 corresponding to re-order levels of 180, 240 and 300.

When both lead time and demand are random variables, the problem again centres on the distribution of demand during the lead time. Consider a simple case. Suppose that there are just two values, independently determined, which the length of lead time in weeks and weekly demand may take. For lead time, let the alternatives be as shown in Table 23.9(a) and for demand per week suppose that the alternatives are as shown in Table 23.9(b).

Table 23.9(a)

Lead time (L)	Probability
1	0.3
2	0.7

Table 23.9(b)

Demand (W)	Probability
20	0.6
30	0.4

Note (for later use in the calculation of annual demand) that the mean weekly demand will be:

$$20(0.6) + 30(0.4) = 24$$

The possible combinations of lead time and demand levels are set out in Table 23.10 and the mean lead time demand is calculated.

The arithmetic mean lead time demand is thus 40.8 units. To complete the example let:

$$C_o = 120 \quad iC_m = 5 \quad \text{and} \quad T = 7$$

Also assuming a 50 week year, the mean annual demand is:

$$A = 50W = 50(24) = 1200$$

so that:

Table 23.10

L	Prob	W	Prob	LTD	P	P(LTD)
1	0.3	20	0.60	20	0.180	3.60
1	0.3	30	0.40	30	0.120	3.60
2	0.7	20,20	0.36	40	0.252	10.08
2	0.7	20,30	0.24	50	0.168	8.40
2	0.7	30,20	0.24	50	0.168	8.40
2	0.7	30,30	0.16	60	0.112	6.72

Mean lead time demand = 40.80

$$q^* = \left(\frac{2(1200)(120)}{5} \right)^{\frac{1}{2}} = 240$$

which gives the number of cycles per annum as:

$$n = \frac{A}{q^*} = \frac{1200}{240} = 5$$

Re-order level possibilities would correspond to the distinct values of lead time demand:

$$R = 20 \ 30 \ 40 \ 50 \ \text{or} \ 60$$

Re-order levels **could** be lower – for example zero – but with a mean lead time demand of 40.8, we will draw the line at 20.

Note for later use in calculating the buffer stock holding costs that the corresponding buffer stock levels would be:

$$B = -20.8 \ -10.8 \ -0.8 \ 9.2 \ \text{and} \ 19.2$$

We shall first determine the expected shortage per cycle at each value of R. (As before, we shall not consider expected surpluses.) The results for $R = 20$, 30, 40 and 50 are shown in Table 23.11.

At a re-order level of $R = 60$ there is zero possible shortage. Now bringing in the cost data, we obtain the results shown in Table 23.12, where ESPA is the expected shortage per annum (ESPC × 5 cycles), SOC is the stock-out cost per annum (ESPA × £7) and

Table 23.11

Lead time demand LTD	Shortage S	Probability P	PS
R = 20			
30	10	0.120	1.200
40	20	0.252	5.040
50	30	0.336	10.080
60	40	0.112	4.480
Expected shortage, reorder level 20 =			20.800
R = 30			
40	10	0.252	2.520
50	20	0.336	6.720
60	30	0.112	3.360
Expected shortage, reorder level 30 =			12.600
R = 40			
50	10	0.336	3.360
60	20	0.112	2.240
Expected shortage, reorder level 40 =			5.600
R = 50			
60	10	0.112	1.120
Expected shortage, reorder level 50 =			1.120

Table 23.12

(1) R	(2) ESPC	(3) ESPA	(4) SOC	(5) BSHC	(6) Total
20.00	20.80	104.00	728.00	−99.49	628.51
30.00	12.60	63.00	441.00	−52.79	388.21
40.00	5.60	28.00	196.00	−3.99	192.01
50.00	1.12	5.60	39.20	46.00	85.20
60.00	0.00	0.00	0.00	96.00	96.00

BSHC is the buffer stock holding cost per annum. (This is negative for $B < 0$ due to the saving in holding costs. For negative B the BSHC is given by: $BiC_m + (B^2/2q)iC_m$ in which the second term is the adjustment needed to reflect a triangular area produced when the end of cycle is below the axis.)

So it is optimal to set $R = 50$, corresponding to a buffer stock of 9.2 units, and achieve uncertainty costs of 85.2. As may be confirmed by sensitivity analysis, it is optimal to set the re-order level at 50 so long as the stock-out cost per unit short, T, is in the range:

$$2.23 \leq T \leq 8.93$$

A practical stock control objective is to provide a specified **service level**. This can be defined in a number of ways; here we shall mean the probability, expressed as a percentage, of being able to fulfil an order from stock during lead time. (This has been called the vendor service level. See Lewis (1981).) A 99% service level corresponds to the buffer stock and re-order level being set to achieve a 1% lead time stock-out probability. The level of service chosen may be selected from a range of options to minimize uncertainty costs for the vendor. Alternatively the choice may be driven by competitive considerations.

Suppose that a firm experiences demand averaging W units per week for its single item of stock. Demand in each week is independent of other weeks and is closely approximated by a normal distribution with variance σ^2. Lead time is L weeks. So during the lead time the average demand will be LW units with variance $L\sigma^2$ and standard deviation $\sigma\sqrt{L}$. The distribution of lead time demand is plotted in Figure 23.9.

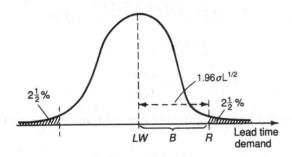

Figure 23.9

There is a 95% chance that demand will be within 1.96 standard deviations of the mean, so that 95% of the area under the curve will be within the range:

$$LW \pm 1.96\sigma\sqrt{L}$$

and just 2.5% of the area under the curve corresponds to extremely high demand or extremely low demand outside this interval. Since it is only the occurrence of **high** demand that can lead to a stock-out, if at the beginning of lead time the re-order level R is set at:

$$R = LW + 1.96\sigma\sqrt{L} \tag{23.12}$$

this produces a 97.5% service level as defined. In (23.12), the term $1.96\sigma\sqrt{L}$ is the buffer stock B. High service levels correspond to a greater buffer stock. Table 7 shows the service level (as a decimal) achieved if buffer stock is set at x standard deviations above the mean (i.e. $x\sigma\sqrt{L}$). For example, with $x = 1.81$ the probability that lead time demand will not be more than 1.81 lead time standard deviations greater than the mean is 0.9649. This is a 96.49% level of service. A 98.3% level of service is achieved if buffer stock is set at $2.12\sigma\sqrt{L}$. If **no** buffer stock is held, Table 7 and Figure 23.9 confirm that just 50% of customers will have orders fulfilled from stock during the lead time period. This also follows from the fact that LW is the average lead time demand.

Consider an example. A company has an average annual demand for stock of 7500 units. The cost of holding one item of stock for one year is £3. Fixed costs per re-order are £200. The lead time is four weeks and there is a 50 week working/sales year. The standard deviation, σ, of demand in any week is 25 units. Demand in any week is normally distributed about the mean and is independent of demand in other weeks. Each stock-out (regardless of extent) is costed at £400. The company wishes to decide between 97.5% and 90% levels of service.

Annual demand of 7500 corresponds to a weekly demand of $w = 150$ with a 50 week year. With $L = 4$ and $\sigma = 25$ the re-order level to give a 97.5% service level is obtained by substitution in (23.12). Therefore:

$$R = 4(150) + 1.96(25)\sqrt{4}$$
$$= 600 + 98$$
$$= 698$$

Now consider the uncertainty costs for this policy. This is the label we are giving to the sum of BSHC and SOC. Since a buffer stock of 98 is kept, the annual buffer stock holding costs will be:

$$BSHC = 98(3) = 294$$

To find the annual stock-out costs, the expected number of stock-outs is needed. This is the probability of stock-out per cycle multiplied by the number, n, of cycles per annum. The probability of a stock-out in any cycle is 0.025 since a 97.5% service level is specified. For the number of cycles per annum we first find the EOQ since $n = A/EOQ$, where A is the annual demand. EOQ is given by the square root rule as:

$$EOQ = \left(\frac{2(200)(7500)}{3} \right)^{\frac{1}{2}} = 1000$$

So that:

$$n = \frac{7500}{1000} = 7.5$$

With 7.5 inventory cycles per annum the expected number of stock-outs will therefore be:

$$0.025(7.5) = 0.1875$$

and the expected stock-out costs per annum will be:

$$SOC = 0.1875(400) = 75$$

Therefore the uncertainty costs, U, with a 97.5% service level will be:

$$U = BSHC + SOC$$
$$= 294 + 75$$
$$= 369$$

Now consider the alternative of a 90% service level. First note that the 'regular' holding and replenishment costs do not change with service level. The only difference is found in the uncertainty costs. With a 90% level of service the buffer stock will be 1.28 standard deviations of lead time demand above the average (from Table 7). Therefore:

$$B = 1.28\sigma\sqrt{L}$$
$$= 1.28(25)(2)$$
$$= 64$$

and buffer stock holding costs will therefore be:

$$BSHC = 64(3) = 192$$

A 90% service level means a 0.1 probability of stock-out per cycle, so that the expected number of stock-outs per annum will be $7.5(0.1) = 0.75$ with a corresponding level of expected cost of:

$$SOC = 0.75(400) = 300$$

Therefore uncertainty costs overall are:

$$U = BSHC + SOC$$
$$= 192 + 300$$
$$= 492$$

So the 97.5% level of service will be preferred by the vendor as well as the customer. The comparison is plotted in Figure 23.10.

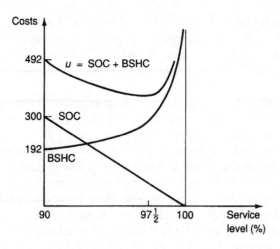

Figure 23.10

An optimal tradeoff is sought between stock-out costs which decline with service level and BSHC which increases. On balance, in this case 97.5% is superior to 90%. A finer gradation of choices is possible by calculating U for, say, intervals of half a percentage point change in service level. By this means it can be confirmed that the overall lowest level is around 98%.

Sensitivity analysis in this context would centre around the stock-out cost figure, T. With a cost of £5 per stock-out the costs as a function of T are as given in Table 23.13.

Table 23.13

Service level (%)	BSHC	SOC	Total (U)
97.5	294	0.1875T	294 + 0.1875T
90	192	0.75T	192 + 0.75T

In order that the 97.5% service level be preferred to 90% it is required that

$$294 + 0.1875T \leq 192 + 0.75T$$

from which the tolerance interval is found as:

$$T \geq 181.33$$

Figure 23.11 plots the uncertainty costs, U, against the stock-out cost figure.

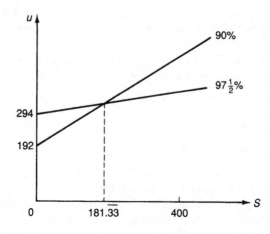

Figure 23.11

There are other definitions of service level that could be employed. For example, the **service function** allows consideration of the average amount by which lead time demand would exceed the re-order level when it did exceed it (see Lewis, 1981).

23.11 Periodic review models

The classical model with random demand is an example of a **re-order level** model. The policy is to place a replenishment order when the stock falls to or below the re-order level. The size of the order is given by the square root rule and is the same each time a stock re-order is made. Re-order level policies require continuous monitoring of stock level. This could be implemented as a simple **two-bin system** where two containers or 'bins' full of the item are used. When one bin becomes empty an order for stock is placed. This should arrive before the second bin is emptied. In this system, while monitoring costs are low, average stock levels are probably higher than necessary.

The **periodic review** policy retains the concept of a re-order level but the stock level is not constantly known; there are periodic **stocktakings**. If at the time of stocktaking inventory is at or below the re-order level, a replenishment order of fixed size is placed. Otherwise there is no re-ordering. The operation of the policy is shown in Figure 23.12.

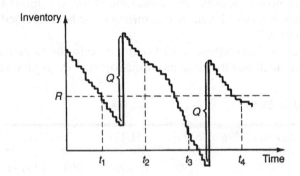

Figure 23.12

At time t_1 there is a stocktaking which reveals inventory level below R so that a replenishment order of size Q is placed. This arrives after a random period of lead time. At the next review at time t_2, stock is above the re-order level so that there is no replenishment order placed at this time. The next review is at t_3 and an order is placed but a lead time stock-out arises. The next review is at t_4. The interval between reviews is fixed in this model and has to be determined, as do both Q and the re-order level R. In comparison with the re-order level policy information costs are reduced but this is at the expense of holding more stock on average and/or increased stock-out costs.

The **re-order cycle** policy dispenses with the re-order level and replenishment orders are placed at every review, but the size of the replenishment order is now variable. The amount of stock ordered is the difference between a maximum inventory level, S, and the level of stock at review. The situation is illustrated in Figure 23.13.

In Figure 23.13, the amount of stock ordered at time t_1 is shown as Q_1 where:

$$Q_1 = S - I_1$$

and at time t_2 it is Q_2 where:

$$Q_2 = S - I_2$$

In comparison with the periodic review policy there is less chance of a stock-out. If the interval between reviews is similar in the two models (it may tend to be longer in the re-order cycle case) the average level of stocks and hence stockholding costs would tend to be higher, although this depends on the value of S. If the interval between reviews is similar then re-order costs will be higher.

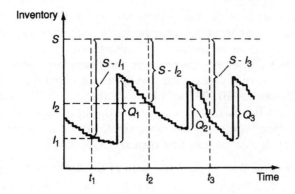

Figure 23.13

The s, S policy combines features of the periodic review and re-order cycle policies. In this case inventory is again reviewed at regular intervals but an order for replenishment is only placed if the stock level at review is at or below the level s. The amount re-ordered, if there is a re-order, is calculated as in the re-order cycle policy – an amount sufficient to bring the stock on hand at review up to the level S. Therefore the amount re-ordered, Q, is given by:

$$Q = \begin{cases} S-I & \text{if } I < s \\ 0 & \text{if } I > s \end{cases}$$

The s, S model is illustrated in Figure 23.14.

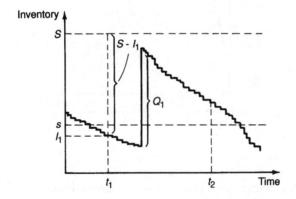

Figure 23.14

In Figure 23.14 it will be seen that no order for stock is placed at time t_2. The classical static model is a special case of the s, S model with $s = 0$ and $S = $ EOQ. While s would normally be positive in the s, S model, if backlogged demand is allowed, a decision is required as to what **negative** level s should take. Again, a balance has to be struck between holding costs which will diminish as s falls and shortage costs which will rise as s falls.

The choice between these and other stock control models depends on the particular company or system under investigation. Although the s, S approach is often appropriate, the other models, or variants of them, may on occasion better exploit the peculiarities of an individual system.

Where more than one item is stocked, optimization can proceed individually if the items do not compete for a common scarce resource such as storage space. If there is competition for a scarce resource, methods of constrained optimization may be usable if only a few products are involved. (See Wilkes and Brayshaw, 1986.)

Where many products are stored, a different approach may be needed. Some chemical companies may have over 20 000 items in stock and in such cases detailed analysis of all products may not be warranted. One method that has gained popularity is the **ABC classification** method originally developed by the General Electric Corporation. In this approach items of stock are ranked by turnover as follows:

- **Category A:** those items that account for most of the turnover (in value terms). It is often the case that just 10% of the product range accounts for 70% of total turnover.
- **Category B:** this is the intermediate section of the product range with, say, 30% of the total number of items stocked accounting for around 20% of total turnover.
- **Category C:** a large part of the product range by number, perhaps 60%, may account for only a small proportion of turnover, say 10%. These are the category C items.

The ABC classification scheme is shown in Figure 23.15. The curve is called the **Pareto curve** and the ABC method sometimes goes by the name of **Pareto Analysis** or **grouping methods**.

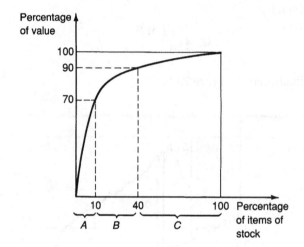

Figure 23.15

The precise shape of the Pareto curve and the break-points between categories will vary between firms but the general point that a small percentage of items make up most of the value is generally true. The measure of value itself may be turnover, profits, capital invested or another measure that the company may decide.

The purpose of the classification method is to direct management effort to where the best results will be obtained. Category A items should receive the greatest amount of control effort with sophisticated forecasting and recording systems and detailed analysis of order quantities and buffer stocks. Category B items would receive less detailed treatment with simpler forecasting methods and rougher estimates of EOQs. Only simple treatment would be warranted for the category C items. A possibility here is the **two-bin system** where the re-order level is $q/2$. This produces fairly large, infrequent orders with minimal cost consequences. No forecasting methods need be used, just an approximate estimate of annual demand. For category C there may not even be a formal system of recording stocks, with sample-based estimates sufficing for audit purposes.

If many products compete for scarce resources, then the approach described in the next section may help. Computer-based systems will be used for at least part of the stock range. Category A and possibly category B items would be included, but the nuts, bolts and slow-moving items of category C might not, but as computing costs decline, the range of items worth recording in detail continues to expand.

A difficulty in implementing EOQ based systems is getting hold of the financial parameters of the model, the re-order and holding costs. It may be that the normal accounting practices of the company do not throw up the required figures. Where many items are stored it may be too difficult or costly to identify the cost components with sufficient accuracy for every item in stock. This would often be the case for category C stock. So a simplification and recasting of the square-root rule which takes these problems into account would be valuable. This is achieved by the **lot size inventory management technique** (LIMIT).

The notation we have been using shows holding cost as a proportion i of the unit cost of the stock, with a typical value of i being around 0.25. In terms of the re-order costs it is likely that C_o, the fixed component of costs per re-order, also tends to have company-wide stability. This would be so in the case where the firm produced its own stock and C_o represented the **set-up costs** of a common type of machinery.

With this in mind the data problems are tackled in the LIMIT approach by re-expressing the square root formula. We had:

$$q^* = \left(\frac{2AC_o}{iC_m} \right)^{\frac{1}{2}}$$

Now define the parameter k as:

$$k = \left(\frac{2C_o}{i} \right)^{\frac{1}{2}}$$

so that optimal lot size is:

$$q^* = k \left(\frac{A}{C_m} \right)^{\frac{1}{2}} \tag{23.13}$$

Therefore, if the value of k is known for the company, or is set by it, all that are needed to use (23.13) are the values of demand and unit cost. These data are more readily accessible over a wider range of items than the original holding cost and replenishment cost data. In fact, the whole approach can be recast with k as a **decision variable** rather than a parameter. This is usually done in the following way. We are familiar with the relationship

$$n = \frac{A}{q^*}$$

where n is the number of re-orders per annum. Substitution into (23.13) with rearrangement gives:

$$k = \frac{1}{n} (AC_m)^{\frac{1}{2}} \tag{23.14}$$

In using this approach, management is presented with a range of values of k averaged over many items of stock. The corresponding total inventory costs are also produced. Management can then select the best, usually the cost-minimizing, value of k which will be used to determine lot sizes from (23.13). The same value of k is used across items. Equivalently, (23.14) can be rearranged to determine the frequency of replenishment, i.e.

$$n = \frac{(AC_m)^{\frac{1}{2}}}{k}$$

The use of this approach is known as lot size inventory management. In practice it is used to ensure consistency of the numbers of replenishments, and hence set-ups, in the multi-item case where common facilities are used. The results in practice have been good – the technique has brought real cost reductions and has widened the area in which EOQ methods can be used.

Where a finished product consists of components manufactured and brought together in a multi-stage production process, the material requirements planning (MRP) method can bring substantial reductions in stockholding. Demand for components is derived from forecast demand for the final product and is projected over time. With these stated requirements, stocks of components, materials and work in progress can be reduced substantially and for some items can be eliminated altogether if the production plan shows significant periods in which an item is not required.

For MRP to be effective, a detailed production schedule is required along with estimates of lead times for bought-out components. The computer-based MRP package derives orders for sub-assemblies, components and materials from the production schedule, level by level. This operation, a requirement generation run, might be performed at monthly or perhaps weekly intervals.

For **demand-dependent** items such as components, MRP can bring 30% or better reduction in inventories and considerable staff savings. Changes in the master production schedule or a separate demand for spare parts still call for a component inventory. MRP has become central to manufacturing resource planning (MRP II), a more comprehensive, systems oriented, package taking in production, marketing and finance in companies manufacturing high-volume complex products such as cars. Procurement of components is based on information on orders for finished products and spares. Implementation of MRP II means that timings for delivery of bought out components or those produced in house are derived from orders for finished products and spares.

The cost of complexity

The number of component parts that a motor vehicle manufacturer needs to stock depends crucially on the number of possible permutations in the company's range of models. Where there are a large number of variations, vehicle assembly is less efficient, there are difficulties in sustaining an even workload and too much, or too little, inventory is on hand with parts tending to arrive too early or too late.

Appropriate curtailments in the number of combinations on offer – **complexity reduction** – can bring very substantial savings in inventory costs as well as quality improvements which in turn mean more satisfied customers and dealers. International consultants Bain and Co. (1989) studying best practices in major manufacturers throughout the world, showed that the total vehicle costs of a major US manufacturer could be slashed by $880. Of these enormous savings $450 were due to lowered stock costs alone.

In general, Japanese companies typically have more parts made outside the company from comparatively fewer suppliers with whom they have long term, value-managed relationships. Assembly and distribution economies yielded the remaining $430 and the complexity reduction still left the consumers with a possible 5000 model combinations.

An amazing statistic produced by Bain was a table of comparisons across six manufacturers, three US and three Japanese, of the lengths of time it would take each company to build all possible permutations of the model range at the time at the normal operating rate in one plant. The results were:

Company	Time taken
Japan Company A	45 minutes
Japan Company B	8 hours
Japan Company C	16 hours
US Company X	220 000 years
US Company Y	2 billion years
US Company Z	7800 trillion years

The potential for complexity reduction in the US companies as revealed by these figures was therefore considerable. In the case of Company Z the entire lifetime of the universe to date would have been enough to construct only 0.002% of the possible permutations! Not surprisingly the report was a catalyst for change.

MRP II implemented as part of a computer-integrated manufacturing (CIM) program usually also has the objective of higher product quality. An appropriate MRP software package is selected and adapted to meet the requirements of the user company. As with any complex exercise there can be difficulties with implementing MRP II which can mean increased costs (for as long as two years) before the substantive benefits are realized in what can be a five-year implementation programme for CIM. Considerable managerial reorganization may also be needed.

MRP II represents a **just-in-time** (JIT) philosophy of production and materials control for which reliable systems and accurate data are essential. JIT was developed initially in Japan and has brought considerable efficiency gains when implemented selectively on key parts.

JIT is a managerial strategy rather more than a set of techniques. Cheng and Podolsky (1993) describe JIT as 'a Japanese management philosophy applied in manufacturing which involves having the right items of the right quality and quantity in the right place and at the right time'. It is a customer-led, production to order approach that has the objective of eliminating idle resources throughout the company. It is the antithesis of 'just in case' management which calls for stock to be held in case something goes wrong. The JIT view is that low or non-existent stock levels show up problems and areas of weakness that had been covered up by inappropriate use of inventory.

JIT is a philosophy that extends beyond the individual company. The need for suppliers to deliver quality-assured components to match the production schedules of the purchasing JIT company will require improved inter-company information flow and has organizational consequences for the suppliers. There may even be negative externalities, for example if the supplying company resorted to higher stock levels to be able to guarantee delivery. The supplier may even physically relocate plant closer to the purchasing company.

Inventory is the first target of JIT and ideally would result in **no** component stock of key items being held before they were needed for production. In the production process JIT is implemented by a card system where the cards (called *kanbans* – from the Japanese for 'signal' – by Toyota which has been using the system since 1981) follow parts through the system and are returned to trigger more supply when the parts are used up. The approach is particularly suitable for costly, bulky or high-usage components.

The situations of companies differ widely, for example in the extent to which the management policies of other companies in the manufacturing chain can be influenced to accommodate a JIT strategy. An MRP approach is indicated in organizations making durable products containing many parts. An EOQ-based approach is indicated for a stockholder with a 10 000 product range. The two approaches can each contribute to effective inventory management within the same organization. The relationship can be complementary as well as competitive. For a company making a range of products of varying complexity, those products with independent demand would be controlled adequately with an EOQ-based system such as re-order level or periodic review. Even for raw materials inventory a re-order level or similar system may still be best if the final product is not unduly complicated and has a fairly stable pattern of demand. However, a predominantly MRP-JIT approach is indicated for products with complex production processes and a consequent need for a large number of demand-dependent items.

Stock-control models based on the economic order quantity are very amenable to computer solution. There follows a Basic program for the classical model of section 23.2. The program should run in most versions of Basic (such as QBasic as supplied with MS-DOS version 5 or later and, with the addition of line numbers, in the earlier GW Basic) and could be modified to include buffer stock, lead time, production for stock or other variations.

```
CLS

PRINT "Classical Static Model for Single Item Inventory."

PRINT
PRINT "C = (q/2)iCm + Co(A/q)"
PRINT

PRINT "Where C = annual inventory costs"
PRINT " iCm = holding cost per unit per annum"
PRINT " Co = re-order cost per re-order"
PRINT " A = Annual demand (withdrawal from stock)"
PRINT " q = order quantity (of which optimum value (EOQ) is sought)"

PRINT STRING$(65, "-")

PRINT
PRINT "Please input data as requested . . ."

PRINT
INPUT "Holding cost per item per annum"; iCm

PRINT
INPUT "Re-order cost per re-order"; Co

PRINT
INPUT "Annual demand"; a

q = (2 * a * Co / iCm) ^ .5

anncost = (q / 2) * iCm + Co * a / q

length = 52 * q / a

reorders = a / q

CLS

PRINT "Problem data"
PRINT STRING$(12, "-")
PRINT

PRINT "Holding cost ="; iCm
PRINT "Re-order cost ="; Co
PRINT "Annual demand ="; a
PRINT

PRINT "So annual inventory costs are:"

PRINT
PRINT "C = "; iCm / 2; "q +"; Co * a; "/q"
PRINT

PRINT "Optimal values"
PRINT STRING$(14, "-")
PRINT
```

```
PRINT "Economic Order Quantity ="; USING "######.##"; q
PRINT "Minimum annual cost of inventory ="; USING "######.##"; anncost
PRINT "Number of re-orders per annum ="; USING "######.##"; reorders
PRINT "Cycle length ="; USING "######.##"; length;
PRINT " weeks"

PRINT
PRINT STRING$(68, "-")

END
```

23.16 Conclusions

The importance of efficient stock control to overall company financial performance has been emphasized. In this chapter we have seen something of the range of EOQ-based stock-control methods and how they are adaptable to a wide variety of circumstances. There are also a number of more specialized models and more broad-brush approaches. An example of a less detailed approach is the use of financial ratios. This can at times prove to be of value. Improved computer hardware and software at much reduced cost has not only allowed the development of MRP and related methods but has also benefited smaller firms using EOQ-based PC packages. Computing developments have also benefited the whole range of methods by improved forecasting packages. For example, with ABC classification, category A items will require good short-term demand forecasting with monitoring. Category B items may have a less sophisticated adaptive forecasting method.

In multi-plant organizations the consequences of poor management of inventory are often experienced centrally at headquarters. The pressure on capital that is tied up in needlessly high levels of stock is not always felt by the individual plant but by the organization as a whole. This kind of situation can be addressed by **coverage analysis**, where the object is to reduce capital tied up in inventory throughout the whole enterprise. This is usually subject to the provision that the number of replenishment orders placed by the firm remains the same (a number not determined by EOQ methods).

Coverage analysis is often viewed as an alternative to LIMIT which tries to deal with similar multi-item situations. Coverage analysis has the advantages of speed and simplicity and the production of useful estimates of possible reductions in working capital. However, it has the drawback that in singling out a particular aspect of finance for special treatment some of the overall economies that might have been achievable with EOQ methods will be lost. As we have seen, MRP and JIT provide a complementary range of management methods from which companies can select according to their situation.

23.17 Key concepts

In the classical economic order quantity (EOQ) model the **square root rule** shows the economic order quantity as a function of annual demand A, holding costs iC_m and fixed costs per re-order C_o:

$$EOQ = \left(\frac{2AC_o}{iC_m} \right)^{\frac{1}{2}}$$

The EOQ is increased by a factor $P/(P - A)$ when production occurs at the rate P units per annum each run.

The **lead time**, L, is the delay between the ordering and arrival of stock and is allowed for by setting a **re-order level** R according to:

$$R = LW + B$$

where W is demand (say per week), L is the lead time and B is the buffer stock, the optimal level of which minimizes uncertainty costs comprising buffer stock holding cost (BSHC) and stock-out costs (SOC):

$$U = BSHC + SOC$$

Sensitivity analysis can be conducted on the model parameters. A **service-level** approach sets the re-order level so as to provide a given probability that customer orders can be satisfied from stock. In:

$$R = LW + z\sigma\sqrt{L}$$

the buffer stock is $z\sigma\sqrt{L}$ where σ is the standard deviation of (say weekly) demand and the z value is selected from tables to give the required probability.

In **periodic review** models, continuous monitoring is replaced by periodic stock-takings at which re-orders of fixed size are placed if and only if stock is at or below the re-order level. Information costs are reduced, at the expense of increased average stock level or stock-out costs.

In the **re-order cycle** model a replenishment of $S - I$ is ordered at each review where S is the stock level and I is the maximum level. Stock-out costs are reduced in comparison with the periodic review but increased re-order or holding costs are incurred.

The s, S model has periodic review with re-order only when stock is below s at review. In this event, the re-order quantity is $S - I$. Of the periodic review models, the s, S model generally gives best results.

In the **ABC classification** approach, high-turnover category A items justify more sophisticated forecasting and stock control, category B items rate simpler methods and category C items require a basic approach such as the two-bin re-order level.

Lot size inventory management, **LIMIT**, recasts the square root rule to give the number of stock replenishments as:

$$n = \frac{(AC_m)^{\frac{1}{2}}}{k}$$

where k is set by the company.

Coverage analysis seeks to reduce capital tied up in inventory in multi-plant organizations.

Manufacturing resources planning, **MRP II**, bases procurement on precise information on orders and synchronizes material supply with production requirements, reducing or ideally eliminating inventory for high usage, costly or bulky items. Both MRP and EOQ approaches can be used within the same organization.

.18 Revision questions

1. Distinguish the main types of inventory and the purposes for which each is held.
2. Describe the classical static model and state the square root rule. How are the different components of cost best balanced?
3. Explain why the addition of a unit cost for stock re-ordered does not affect the EOQ.
4. Show how, with a constant rate of demand, constant lead time affects the timing but not the size of stock re-orders.
5. Show how the EOQ model can be adapted to determine the number of production runs needed per annum.
6. Explain the functions of buffer stock and how a best balance is sought between buffer stock-holding and stock-out costs.
7. Describe the service level concept.
8. Explain how random demand and lead time can be taken into account when both have discrete distributions.
9. Describe the periodic review, re-order cycle and s, S models.
10. Set out the ABC classification system.
11. What advantages are offered by the lot size inventory management approach?
12. What are MRP methods and how does a JIT management approach complement them?

Buchanan, R.W. and Howell, C.D. (1989) *Improving Performance by Using Best Demonstrated Practices*, Fellowship of Engineering, London.

Cheng, T.C.E. and Podolsky, S. (1993) *Just-in-Time Manufacturing: An Introduction*, Chapman & Hall.

Lewis, C.D. (1981) *Scientific Inventory Control*, 2nd edn, Butterworths, London.

Wilkes, F.M. and Brayshaw, R. (1986) *Company Finance and its Management*, Van Nostrand Reinhold.

This section includes books covering stock control within management science as a whole and more focused references. Bennet *et al.* contains good coverage of MRP and related methods; Cook and Russell show the use of simulation and links with accounting systems and MRP; Schniederjans reviews aspects of JIT; Littlechild and Shutler and Dear have an emphasis on application; Hillier and Lieberman, Anderson, Sweeney and Williams and Taha are first-rate management science texts; Dear introduces the just-in-time approach.

Anderson, D.R., Sweeney, D.J. and Williams, T.A. (1994) *An Introduction to Management Science*, 7th edn, West Publishing Co.

Bennett, D., Lewis, C. and Oakley, M. (1988) *Operations Management*, Philip Allan.

Cook, T.M. and Russell, R.A. (1981) *Introduction to Management Science*, 2nd edn, Prentice Hall.

Dear, A. (1988) *Working towards Just-In-Time*, Kogan Page, London.

Dear, A. (1990) *Inventory Management Demystified*, Chapman & Hall.

Hillier, F. and Lieberman, G.J. (1990) *Introduction to Operations Research*, 5th edn, McGraw-Hill.

Littlechild, S.C. and Shutler, M.F. (eds) (1991) *Operations Research in Management*, Prentice Hall.

Schniederjans, M.J. (1993) *Topics in Just In Time Management*, Allyn & Bacon.

Taha, H.A. *Operations Research*, 5th edn, Macmillan, 1992.

1. A company has annual demand for 2500 units of the one product that it stocks. The replenishment cost for inventory is fixed at £400 regardless of the size of the replenishment. Annual holding costs are £8 per unit.
   (a) Find the economic order quantity.
   (b) What is the optimum number of replenishments per annum and the corresponding length of an inventory cycle?
   (c) What is the lowest achievable level of inventory costs?

2. The annual demand for a company's only item of stock is 1000 units. It costs the company £6 to hold one unit of stock for one year. Each time that a replenishment order is made the company incurs a fixed cost of £75.
   (a) Determine the economic order quantity to two decimal places.
   (b) Find the number of re-orders per annum and the best value of costs.
   (c) Suppose that the company's supplier of stock introduces a condition of no more than five orders for stock per annum. How much would the company be prepared to pay to escape this condition?

3. A company receives a steady inflow of cash of £250 000 per annum. The cash can be invested at 12.5% p.a. Each time the company makes an investment there is a brokerage charge of £25 plus 1% of the sum invested (both sums payable at the time the investment is made).
   (a) What is the best size of investment and how many investments of cash should be made per annum?
   (b) If the brokerage charges were revised to £100 plus 0.75% of the sum invested, at what rate per annum should investments now be made?
   (c) Which scheme of brokerage charges would the company prefer?

4. A company has a 50-week working year. The demand for its one product during any week is described by the distribution:

Units demanded	Probability
0	0.03
1	0.06
2	0.07
3	0.09
4	0.11
5	0.21
6	0.17
7	0.12
8	0.08
9	0.06

Stockholding costs are £40 per unit per annum. Each time that a re-order is made there is a cost of £50 regardless of re-order size. The cost of the item is £180 per unit. There is a lead time of one week. The cost of being out of stock is estimated as £20 per unit short. The company wants to minimize inventory related costs.

(a) Find the economic order quantity and the number of re-orders per annum.
(b) Work out the expected shortages per cycle for non-negative values of buffer stock.
(c) Find the optimal size of buffer stock and re-order level.
(d) For what range of values of the shortage cost figure would the re-order level found in (b) remain optimal?

5. A company faces a variable lead time of L weeks and demand averaging W per week is also variable. L and W follow the discrete distributions:

L	Probability
1	0.5
2	0.5

W	Probability
20	0.5
40	0.5

(a) If $C_o = £24$, $iC_m = £5$ and $T = £2$ per unit short, and assuming a 50-week year, find the possible levels of lead-time demand, the average lead-time demand, the optimal re-order level, the level of buffer stock to which this corresponds and the minimum level of uncertainty costs.
(b) For what range of values of the cost per unit short would the re-order level of (a) remain optimal?

6. A company is examining its inventory policy for a lightweight car wheel that it stores. Demand for the wheel runs at the average rate of 1000 units per quarter. It costs £8 to hold one wheel for one year. When a re-order is necessary, the company has fixed administrative costs of £40 irrespective of order size. The manufacturer charges £12 per wheel supplied plus a charge of £120 no matter how large the order.

(a) Find the economic order quantity and the number of inventory cycles per annum.

(b) An alternative scheme of charges would give total costs per annum (including the £12 per wheel) of £52 000. Should the company switch to this scheme?

(c) Assume a 50-week working year and a lead time of four weeks. The variance of demand in any week is 156.25 units. Demand in each week is normally distributed about the weekly average and is independent of demand in other weeks. Find the re-order level that would produce a 97.5% service level.

(d) Management is considering a reduction of the service level to 80%. Each stock-out is estimated to cost £120. Is this reduction in service level advisable? For what range of values of the stock-out cost figure is your conclusion valid?

7. A firm has setup costs of £600 each time that a production run is started and variable production costs are £20 per unit. The company operates a 50 week working year. When a production run is in progress, 500 units per week are made. Demand for the product is at the steady rate of 200 units per week throughout the working year. Stock holding costs are £5 per unit held per annum.

(a) What is the economic lot size?
(b) How many production runs should be made each year?
(c) For how long does each production run last?
(d) What is the maximum level to which stocks will rise?
(e) What is the minimum level of inventory costs per annum?

8. A company operates a lot size inventory management (LIMIT) approach. The following data apply: $C_o = 50$ $i = 0.25$ $C_m = 4$ $A = 2500$.

(a) Using the data above, find the value of k.
(b) Use k to determine the optimal number of re-orders per annum.
(c) What is the economic lot size in this case?

9. Electropoint Ltd has expanded the production of its domestic robots and now requires each year, and at a constant rate, 200 000 positronic circuits which it obtains from an outside supplier. The cost of placing each order for the positronic circuits is £32. For any circuit in stock it is estimated that the annual holding cost is equal to 10% of its cost. The circuits cost £8 each. No stock-outs are permitted.

(a) What is the optimal order size, and how many orders should be placed in a year?
(b) What are the ordering and holding costs and hence what is the total relevant inventory cost per annum?
(c) If the demand has been underestimated and the true demand is 242 000 circuits per annum, what would be the effect of keeping to the order quantity calculated in (a) above and still meeting demand, rather than using a new optimal order level?
(d) What does your answer to (c) tell you about the sensitivity of your model to changes in demand?

(CACA)

10. In an assembly process your company consumes 125 000 small screws annually at an even rate of 2500 per week. The cost of the screws is £4 per 1000. The cost of placing an order irrespective of the quantity ordered is £5. The risk of obsolescence is negligible and the cost of storage has been estimated at £1 per 1000 screws per year. The company's minimum required rate of return on capital is 20%.

(a) Calculate the order quantity and state the optimum ordering policy from a supplier who can guarantee immediate delivery.
(b) State the change required in the re-ordering policy if there were a lead time of two weeks.
(c) Calculate the optimum production policy if the company decided that it could make the screw for £2 per 1000, plus an order cost of £5 and a set-up cost of £10, at a rate of 25 000 per week.
(d) State the considerations that should be taken into account if requirements fluctuated owing to changes in demand for the assembly.
(e) State the re-ordering considerations that should be taken into account if demand

varies within the range of 1000 to 4000 screws required per week. A general stocking policy has now been agreed to ensure there is no problem if demand is 50% higher than average. A stock-out owing to demand being 100% higher than average will be tolerated.

(Chartered Institute of Management Accountants)

24 *Mergers and acquisitions*

24.1	Introduction	855		24.8	Win at what price? a case study	893
24.2	Merger and takeover activity	857		24.9	Key terms	895
24.3	Motives for individual mergers	860		24.10	Revision questions	896
24.4	Management motives	866		24.11	References	896
24.5	Takeover tactics	867		24.12	Further reading	897
24.6	Financing acquisitions	879		24.13	Problems	897
24.7	The results – who wins?	885				

There are many aspects to mergers and acquisitions. One can examine them from the point of view of each of the parties directly involved, i.e. the two groups of shareholders, the two groups of managers and the two groups of employees. One can examine them from the point of view of the economy: Do they lead to an increase in efficiency? Do consumers benefit? From the point of the financial community they are exciting – they bring action to all and fees to some.

We shall look at the evidence on the results of mergers and acquisitions. Before that, however, we look at the motives for one company's wishing to control another company. There has developed what has been called the market for corporate control. We shall look at the tactics adopted in this market. How do buyers and sellers behave?

24.1 Introduction

There is a great deal of interest in the subject of mergers and takeovers. It is the area of corporate finance that attracts the most publicity. The media, including even the 'popular' press, give considerable coverage to the large takeover battles. The financial community, the investment bankers and others are involved with tactics, and receive large financial rewards for their own involvement whether their client companies win or lose. The managers and workers in the companies involved await the outcome of the bid with concern.

Academics and other researchers are fascinated by the subject, as there are so many questions about mergers and takeovers that remain unanswered. These questions include the following.

1. If the stock market is efficient, why is it that acquiring companies are prepared to pay such a high premium above the pre-bid share price in order to obtain control?
2. Do mergers and takeovers lead to an increase in the net wealth of the economy?
3. If mergers and takeovers do lead to gains, who is it that benefits from them: the

shareholders, the managers, the workers in the acquiring company or the workers in the victim company?

4. Are there waves of mergers over time and, if so, why do they occur? What are they associated with?

5. What are the motives of those involved in mergers and takeovers? What are they hoping to achieve as a result of bringing companies together?

These and other questions are considered in this chapter. In section 24.2 we consider the level of merger and takeover activity. The number of mergers appears to vary from one period to another. Why is this? In section 24.3 we examine the motives for mergers and takeovers. Why does one group of managers attempt to obtain control of the assets of another company? There are many reasons that can be put forward to justify a merger. Indeed, with every merger and takeover what appears to be a rational justification is advanced by those representing the bidding company. However, in contested takeover bids those representing the defending company put forward reasons why the acquisition would not be rational.

A merger or a takeover

In this chapter the terms 'merger' and 'takeover' are used interchangeably. This is because in many instances it is not clear whether one or the other is occurring. However, for certain purposes it is necessary to distinguish between the two forms of business combination.

When two or more companies come together under common ownership, this is referred to as a 'business combination'. Not all combinations are similar in nature. For business, legal and accounting purposes it has become necessary to differentiate between the forms of combination.

At the extremes, it is easy to decide what is a merger and what is a takeover. When two companies of approximately equal size come together, with the shareholders and directors of the two companies supporting the idea of the combination and continuing to have an interest in the combined business, it is a merger. However, when a large company makes a cash bid for the shares of a smaller company, the directors of the small company advise their shareholders not to sell but the shares are sold anyway and neither the pre-bid shareholders nor the directors of the purchased company have any continuing interest in the enlarged business, it is clearly an acquisition or takeover.

In the first situation, what is known as merger accounting is considered to be appropriate, and in the second situation the acquisition accounting method would be used. Unfortunately, few cases are as clear cut as the two described.

With the merger accounting approach, the purchase of shares in one company by another is seen as the coming together of two businesses, the creation of a single group. The emphasis is on the continuity of ownership, the continuing interest in the business of both sets of shareholders. In the USA this is referred to as a 'pooling of interests'.

With the acquisition accounting approach one business is seen as having been purchased by the other just as if a set of assets and liabilities had been purchased, with the previous owners – the selling shareholders – giving up their interest in the business. This approach stresses the lack of continuity of ownership, with one group of shareholders ceasing to have an interest and the other group taking over their interests. This is a takeover.

The main differences resulting from the two accounting techniques arise over the treatment of (1) goodwill, (2) the value of the shares exchanged and (3) any preacquisition profits. Ignoring possible complications, the differences can be summarized as follows.

1. Acquisition: goodwill must be disclosed if acquired.
   Merger: as no real change in ownership occurs, the merger should produce consolidated accounts that do no more than combine the existing balance sheets, i.e. assets remain at the value at which they appear in the

separate company accounts and goodwill is not recognized since none is effectively acquired.

2. Acquisition: shares issued to acquire another company are recorded at market value.

   Merger: shares issued to acquire another company earned prior to the acquisition are recorded at nominal value, i.e. no share premium is recognized.

3. Acquisition: the undistributed profits of any acquired company earned prior to the acquisition are frozen and are not normally available for distribution by the group.

   Merger: the reserves of each company are merged, i.e. those that were distributable before the merger may be distributable after the merger.

The differences in the accounting treatment are therefore important and significant. If the preparer of accounts wishes to create a favourable impression, merger accounting offers considerable advantages.

An accounting standard (FRS 6) was issued in the UK in 1994 which stipulated when merger accounting should be used [1]. The new rules were designed to limit to a very few situations when it was possible to use merger accounting. It is only in the case of group reconstruction and in the rare case of a genuine merger where it is permitted. Business combinations when one company acquires control of another company should be accounted for as an acquisition.

The criteria that must be met before the coming together of two companies can be classed as a genuine merger include:

- No party to the combination can be seen as the acquirer or the acquired.
- The parties to the combination jointly participate in establishing the management structure of the combined entity and in selecting the management personnel. The decisions on these issues are made on the basis of consensus rather than on the exercise of voting rights.
- The relative size of the combining entities is similar.
- The equity shareholders of the companies coming together receive consideration which is primarily equity shares in the combined business. Securities issued as consideration which can be converted into equity are regarded as equity for this purpose.

Failure to meet any of these criteria should be regarded as evidence that a genuine merger has not taken place, and so merger accounting would not be allowed. It is important to take into account all evidence relating to the combination in forming an opinion.

The other situation in which merger accounting is allowed is in certain group reconstructions. It can be used with the following arrangements:

- the transfer of a shareholding in a subsidiary from one group company to another;
- the combing of two or more companies that before the combination had the same shareholders;
- the transfer of a subsidiary of a group to a new company that has the same shareholders as the group's parent.

It can be seen from the above that the accounting standards setting body intends to limit the opportunities for companies to use merger accounting procedures.

24.2 Merger and takeover activity

Table 24.1 shows the number of acquisitions of industrial and commercial companies in the UK over the period from 1969 to 1993, and the expenditure incurred on them. As can be seen, there were peaks of activity in the early 1970s and again in the middle and late 1980s. Since 1982 there has been a phenomenal increase in activity. In 1981 the total expenditure was £1.1 billion, and this rose to £22.1 billion in 1988. The extent of the activity is considerable. It was estimated that in 1985 in the UK the assets changing hands through acquisitions represented 6% of the total capital stock. This is a very significant turnover of the capital stock, and 1985 was not the high point of that particular takeover boom.

We shall examine who benefits from all this activity later in this chapter. It should be remembered that the vast majority of mergers and takeovers are not contested. The parties are happy with the arrangements. The few well-publicized takeover bids do tend to give the wrong impression. Less than 5% of takeovers and mergers involve a 'battle'.

The figures in Table 24.1 do not represent all the acquisitions and mergers that have taken place in the UK between 1969 and 1993; they only cover those which have been reported in the financial press. It is possible that the sale of a small private company or the merger of two private companies is not reported. There is little reason why it should be reported as it does not necessarily concern the public. However, figures clearly indicate the trend in the number of acquisitions and mergers and, with all the major deals and transactions included, the expenditure figures accurately reflect the extent of these activities.

One noticeable feature of the boom between 1984 and 1989 was the relative importance of a small number of large acquisitions. The larger takeovers, those involving expenditure of over £25 million, accounted for 81% of the total expenditure during this period. It is these that attract the publicity.

The growth in expenditure on acquisitions since the mid 1980s has coincided with a general increase in capital expenditure by industrial and commercial companies. It has been estimated that in 1986, 1987 and 1988 over 50% of the corporate spending on new fixed assets was in the form of mergers and acquisitions. The increased takeover activ-

Table 24.1 *Acquisition and mergers by industrial and commercial companies within the United Kingdom*

				Method of payment	
Year	Number acquired	Total expenditure (£million)	Cash (£million)	Ordinary shares (£million)	Pref. shares and loan stock (£million)
1969	846	1 069	296	552	221
1970	793	1 122	251	596	275
1971	884	911	285	437	189
1972	1210	2 532	493	1459	580
1973	1205	1 304	691	466	147
1974	504	508	347	114	47
1975	315	291	173	93	25
1976	353	427	302	118	7
1977	481	824	512	304	8
1978	567	1 140	654	463	23
1979	534	1 656	933	515	208
1980	469	1 475	760	669	46
1981	452	1 144	775	338	31
1982	463	2 206	1 283	701	222
1983	447	2 343	1 026	1261	57
1984	568	5 475	2 946	1837	690
1985	474	7 090	2 857	3708	525
1986	696	14 934	3 823	8642	2472
1987	1125	15 364	4 945	9579	839
1988	1224	22 122	15 426	4852	1846
1989	1337	27 250	21 356	3520	1374
1990	779	8 329	6 402	1533	393
1991	506	10 434	7 278	3034	121
1992	432	5 941	3 772	2122	47
1993	524	6 846	5 461	1155	230

ity may therefore be partly related to a period of general expansion by companies. It was also a period when companies were profitable, their liquidity was high and larger amounts of funds were available within the financial system for those wishing to use them. Takeover activity was strong from the mid-1980s not only in the UK but also in the USA, West Germany and France. As can be seen takeover activity declined in the 1990s.

What causes the so-called waves of takeover activity?

Undoubtedly there are some periods in which there is more merger and takeover activity than in others. One takeover wave occurred in the 1960s, another in the early 1970s and another in the 1980s. There were similar waves in earlier periods.

What are the economic factors that explain the patterns? Why do these waves occur? One explanation for one of the booms, that of the 1960s, was that 'conglomerate' mergers became fashionable. One popular explanation for the late 1980s boom was that UK industry was preparing itself for the single European market in 1992, but a similar boom has occurred in the USA where the same motive would not apply. These are one-off explanations given to explain individual waves of activity.

There are a number of theories of mergers which attempt to offer a general explanation for these waves of activity. One of the most commonly cited theories is that mergers are associated with booms and slumps in the economy and in stock market prices. A number of studies have provided evidence that movement in economic activity, interest rates and securities prices are positively related to merger activity.

One basis for the theory is that at certain times shareholders have differing opinions as to the true value of a share because of imperfections in the information available and how it is assessed. These differences are greater at times of dramatic change such as rapid movements in share prices, changes in technology and changes in the relative price of energy. This is referred to as the 'economic disturbance theory of mergers' [2].

One recent study based on US data found a strong positive relationship between the level of what is known as Tobin's q and the level of merger activity. This would support the economic disturbance theory. Tobin's q will be explained more fully in the next section. It is a measure of the difference between the stock market value of a company and the replacement value of its assets. It indicates whether the company can be purchased at a bargain price.

The theories of merger waves being associated with periods of high economic performance remains unproven, and indeed the justification for the theory does not seem strong. The 1980s were a time of a sluggish economy and a depressed stock market, and yet of great takeover activity. The stock market collapse of 1987 did not halt activity. In the first quarter after the collapse takeovers were greater than in any quarter in 1987. In fact when we go on to examine the motives for individual mergers, for example to remove inefficient management or to avoid bankruptcy, these reasons are as valid during times of poor economic performance as during boom periods.

Therefore there are no agreed reasons why each of the individual motives should lead many companies to act in a particular way during one period rather than another. There is much debate on these points but no agreed conclusions. For example, it has been argued that when the stock market booms, the price of some shares lags behind their true value, perhaps because of less financially aware managers, and these companies are good takeover targets. However, if the stock market is efficient this should not happen.

We still do not understand the economic forces underlying the pattern of merger activity. There is some support for the economic disturbance theory, with slumps as well as booms leading to activity. In fact the reasons for the 'waves' may not be economic but behavioural.

The 1990s have seen a modest level of merger and takeover activity. It should be appreciated that not all mergers and acquisitions are contested. Often the companies involved are in agreement; the coming together is friendly. In fact the vast majority are what is called 'friendly', with only the minority 'hostile'. This has been the case particularly in the 1990s.

As mentioned, it is difficult to explain why there are waves of merger and takeover activity. A number of explanations have been offered, but none of them is entirely satisfactory. The explanations include:

1. High activity when stock market prices are low, because it is possible to find bargain purchases.
2. High activity when stock market prices are high, when the market is bullish. This is because the firms with high prices find it easier to pay for the purchase through an equity offer. Or alternatively, if the economy is bullish the directors of the acquiring firm will be able to raise money easily.
3. High activity in certain economic situations. This applies particularly on an industry-by-industry basis. Changes in the technology or demand in an industry might mean it is rational for firms in the industry to merge or for one firm to acquire another.

24.3 Motives for individual mergers

The first point that should be made is of course the obvious one that it is not a company that decides to merge with another or to attempt to take over another. It is the managers of the companies, the top directors, who make the decision. These decision-makers should be acting in their shareholders' interests. In this section we shall look at situations in which a merger or takeover can benefit the shareholders. In a later section, we shall consider the managers' own position in a merger situation, because this is not always identical with that of the shareholders.

One company X would wish to merge or take over another company Y if it believes either that the two firms together are worth more than the value of the two firms apart or that it can purchase company Y at a price below the present value of its future cash flow in the hands of new management.

The first of these two explanations is referred to as synergy. This is usually expressed by the relationship $2 + 2 = 5$. It refers to the combining of complementary resources, and implies that using the resources of the two firms together increases total value. The combined firms increase the potential for growth and profit. It makes possible the greater utilization of each firm's relative advantage. The financial theory of mergers and takeovers would indicate that a merger or takeover would be justified if

$$PV_{XY} = PV_X + PV_Y + \text{gain}$$

i.e. the present value (PV) of X and Y as a combination, i.e. PV_{XY}, is greater than the sum of the PVs of the two companies working independently. An interesting question arises as to who benefits from the gain: it could be the shareholders of one or both of the companies.

If company X has to bid for company Y (the target company) it could finish up paying a price above PV_Y, in which case the shareholders of company Y would receive some of the gain. Let us say that $PV_{XY} = £1\,000\,000$, $PV_X = £500\,000$ and $PV_Y = £300\,000$. Then

$$1\,000\,000 = 500\,000 + 300\,000 + \text{gain}$$

If, however, in order to acquire company Y, £400 000 is paid to their shareholders, then half the gain is being received by the shareholders of Y. This is a cost of acquisition and it reduces the gain available to other parties. We shall return to this point later in the chapter.

We shall now consider the economic theories and business situations that would indicate the situations in which gains from mergers and takeovers could occur.

Economies of scale

This topic is well covered in the literature. Economies of scale can arise in the production process, where larger machines produce at a lower cost per unit than smaller machines. They can arise in marketing, with advertising costs for example. They can arise in distribution, where fleets of vehicles and large warehouses can bring down the cost per unit of transport and storage. They can arise in finance where administrative costs per unit raised are less with large issues of finance than with small.

Internalization of transactions

This can occur in the case of vertical integration. Such integration can either be backwards with the acquisition of firms that supply raw materials or earlier stages of production, or forwards with the acquisition of firms nearer the selling of the product. Its importance is that it eliminates transaction costs when firms have to deal with each other at arm's length. It certainly reduces the uncertainty of supply and having to deal with a firm that may have considerable bargaining power in the short run. It may result in cost savings because dealings between divisions or companies within a group may be more efficient than dealings conducted at arm's length between two independent businesses. This has to be balanced with the possible extra costs resulting from lack of competition between suppliers.

Market power

It has been estimated that 3% of the assets that changed hands in the UK during the period 1979–85 were in the form of vertical integration, and 57% were horizontal in nature. The Office of Fair Trading which is interested in mergers that might reduce competition states that two-thirds of the proposed acquisitions that they considered between 1985 and 1988 involved horizontal integration. Horizontal means that the firms concerned are in the same stage of the production process; a merger or takeover leads to control of a larger share of output in a particular market. It could lead to economies of scale with the new combination operating fewer and more efficient plants. However, the coming together of two such firms by definition increases concentration. This is attractive to the firms, as it has been shown that the higher the level of concentration in an industry, the greater is the level of profits. However, it reduces consumer choice; hence the interest of the Office of Fair Trading.

Entry into new markets and into new industries

Acquisitions often provide the quickest way of entry into new markets and new industries. Entry into areas where the expanding firm initially lacks the right know-how or, say, an adequate distribution system will be both risky and costly. Because growth through acquisition is rapid, it can provide almost immediately the necessary critical size for a firm to become an effective or even formidable competitor.

The single market-place in the EU provides opportunities for companies to expand, but also creates threats to a company's market share as foreign competitors move in. This has led to a certain amount of so called rationalization, and consequently to mergers and takeovers. It has been argued that it is necessary to increase the size of the organization to cope with the larger market.

Because of the diffuse and uneven distribution of managerial skills and technical competence among firms and industries, firms in declining industries seek to remedy their weaknesses by moving into new technologies to improve their growth prospects. The uncertainties of applying advanced technologies successfully are great even for an established firm: a newcomer to an industry will find it even more risky involving large outlays and negative cash flows for a long period of time. The acquisition of an established company offers an increased chance of success to such large high-risk investments.

Elimination of inefficient and misguided managements

Inefficient managements can exist for a limited period of time, but over the longer period, if the market is efficient, they will be identified and the market mechanism should ensure that they are replaced. It might not simply be that the firm is badly managed, rather than the interests of the managers are different from those of the shareholders. This is referred to as the agency problem. Managers only owning a small percentage of shares can tend to pursue perquisites. The cost of these are passed on indirectly to shareholders. This can be seen as a misdirection of resources.

Takeovers serve as a control mechanism that limits the departure by managers from the maximization of their shareholders' wealth. If the managers of company Y are inefficient or neglect their shareholders' interests, then the managers of another company (say X) might well make a takeover bid for company Y. The managers of X may need to persuade their shareholders that if they managed the assets of company Y then returns would be greater than at present. Therefore it is worth company X offering a higher price than the current market price for the shares of Y. To avoid this possibility, with the probable loss of their jobs, the managers of company Y will need to look after their shareholders' interests and will need to utilize the assets efficiently.

Free cash flow and trapped equity

Jensen [3] has suggested that managers with cash flows in excess of that required to finance new investments within the firm will use them to finance acquisitions. If profitable organic growth opportunities (within the firm) are limited, then rather than return the surplus funds to the shareholders the managers would prefer to acquire other firms. In this way the managers keep control of the funds, whereas to return them to shareholders means that they lose control.

Another motive for using these 'surplus' funds for acquisition purposes might be based on shareholders' interests and not simply on a wish of managers to control larger corporate 'empires'. King [4] has shown that the tax system in the UK can influence the level of acquisitions. Two ways to provide benefits to the shareholders from the cash 'trapped in the company' are share re-purchases and acquisitions. Share re-purchases have been permitted in the UK since 1985. If capital gains taxes are less than income tax on dividend income, then the shareholder would prefer cash to be used to make acquisitions or to re-purchase shares, leading to gains in share prices rather than to receipt of the cash as dividends.

If money distributed to shareholders as dividend, rather than being reinvested, suffers an additional burden, for example payment of advance corporation tax, then again it may be in the shareholders' interest for the funds to be used for investment. This is known as the trapped equity theory. According to the theory, if free cash flow is used to purchase another company the stock market value of the shareholders' investment will increase more than their wealth would increase if the 'surplus' funds were to be returned to them. The evidence does not provide strong support for this model.

Undervalued shares?

It might be thought that the companies taken over are less efficient, i.e. those wasting valuable scarce resources. One difficulty in this approach is deciding in practice which firms are inefficient. Unfortunately, accounting profits are not necessarily good guides. One reason for an acquisition can arise when the stock market is underestimating the real value of a company. If the company is not too conscious of its stock market valuation, and its stock market price is low in relation to its potential, it is an ideal victim for a takeover bid. The purchaser may be of the opposite type: keenly conscious of its stock market valuation, which it is anxious to keep high, and always reporting to show the best short-term position. A merger or takeover between two such companies does not automatically result in real gains for the economy. The point being made is that the victims in takeovers and mergers are not necessarily the firms failing to make the best use of their resources. The victims could be firms using their assets to their best advantage, but their stock market price does not reflect the true value of the company, perhaps because of lack of knowledge.

A question that can be asked is: if the stock market is efficient, how can a company's share be undervalued? The definition of efficiency is that the stock market price fully reflects all available information. This was discussed in Chapter 13.

It has been found that the UK and US stock markets are to some extent efficient in that the prices reflect all publicly available information. However, this does not mean that there are not undervalued companies. It has not been found that share prices reflect all privately available information. There are certain types of investors who can make excess profits through trading in the market. It has been shown that security analysts have superior information on companies, and if used properly this can give them above average returns [5]. Again, it has been shown that 'insiders' have superior knowledge and one company can have inside information about another.

Therefore it is possible for an acquiring company itself to have superior information, perhaps new information that has not yet reached the market, or to have access to superior knowledge about opportunities available and to be able to use this to purchase the shares of a company at below their 'true' value. The acquiring company, because of its entrepreneurial alertness in discovering new information or in seeing new opportunities, makes a bid. When it does so, it discloses its new information to the market, and since the market is efficient it reacts to this now publicly available information. New information may be available to one group, either before a merger or during the negotiations, that indicates that the existing share price is undervalued and therefore the shares are worth purchasing.

One group of insiders are the management of a company: the information that they have access to can become particularly important at the time of a management buyout. This point will be returned to later.

It must be recognized that it is perfectly possible to find a company's shares correctly priced or even overpriced, with the current expectations of future returns, and for it still to be a good purchase for a takeover bidder. If the prospective purchaser can use the assets of the company, including the management, more profitably, then it may be prepared to purchase shares which in terms of present market knowledge are classed as overpriced. In bidding this price higher than might be expected, the purchasing company is showing a more optimistic view of the future, perhaps based on expectations of its own ability to manage the new subsidiary.

It can be argued that any company is worth purchasing if it can be obtained at a 'bargain' price. One indication of a 'bargain' can be obtained by comparing the price paid for the company with the value of the assets obtained. If the assets are to be continued in use in the combined business for the same purposes, then it is the replacement costs that give the relevant value. If the assets are to be sold by the combined business, then it is the realizable value.

One popular ratio is Tobin's q. This compares the market value of the firm with the replacement cost of the firm's assets. The lower the ratio, the greater is the bargain. The further that q falls below unity, the greater is the bargain and the greater is the likelihood that the firm will be the subject of a bid. Of course it is difficult to determine the replacement cost and the realizable value of a firm's assets. In the years when companies were required to produce current cost balance sheets, it was possible for an outsider to gain some idea of the Tobin q factor. The normal balance sheets of a company usually have assets valued on a mixture of bases, some at historic costs and some revalued, but on a variety of dates. It is here where inside information can give those involved in a takeover bid an advantage, with either the bidding firm knowing something that the existing shareholders do not know, or alternatively the management of the victim company knowing whether the bid price offers a 'true' premium.

Tax advantages

In the USA the tax treatment of losses has been an important factor in a number of mergers. However, it was never so important in the UK. The crucial factor is whether or not the losses of one company can be used to offset the profits of another company in the group and so reduce the total amount of taxation that has to be paid.

In the UK the losses of one company incurred prior to that company's becoming a member of the group cannot be offset against the profits of another member of the group. Losses can only be offset against future profits of the same company, and even then only if it is continuing to operate in the same line of business. In the USA the laws with regard to carry-over are not so restrictive, with the result that some mergers lead to tax savings to the group. In the UK tax savings might result from a merger if the capital structure of the group is changed. Debt servicing costs are of course tax deductible. This possible advantage is discussed elsewhere in this section.

Use of high price-to-earnings ratios

This particular motive for acquiring other companies was of considerable importance during the conglomerate merger boom of the 1960s. If one company possesses a high stock market rating relative to the other company, it is able to purchase on advantageous terms. The conglomerate companies were making use of their high stock market ratings. As soon as their share price fell they were not in such a strong position to take over other companies.

The reason can be seen in the following simple example. If a potential acquisition is valued at £10 000 and the present market price of the purchaser's shares is £5, then 2000 shares will have to be exchanged to take over the company. If the market price falls to £2.50, then 4000 shares will have to be transferred. It is obviously better for the existing shareholders of the purchasing firm to acquire the new assets by exchanging the smaller number of shares.

The key to the position of the shareholders lies in the earnings per share. The stock market attaches considerable importance to this variable. As can be seen in the following example, it is possible for a company to increase its earnings per share, not by the normal manufacturing, trading and selling cycle, but simply by purchasing companies. Assume that two companies, A and B, each have 1000 shares outstanding. The relevant financial details are as follows.

	Company A	Company B
Total earnings	£250	£250
Earnings per share	£0.25	£0.25
Share price	£4	£2.50
Price to earnings ratio	16:1	10:1

The reason that company A commands a higher price-to-earnings ratio than company B is because it is assumed to have greater growth prospects. Company A purchases company B. The market value of company B is £2500 (1000 shares at £2.50); 625 shares of company A will need to be offered in exchange. The position of company A after the purchase is as follows.

Total earnings	£500
Number of shares	1625
Earnings per share	£0.3077

The earnings per share have increased, purely because of the purchase of company B. If the stock market keeps the same price-to-earnings ratio for the company as it had before the purchase, the share price will be £4.92, showing a gain for the shareholders of company A. The wealth of the shareholders of company B will have increased. Before the merger they held 1000 shares priced at £2.50 each, a value of £2500. After the merger they hold 625 shares priced at £4.92 each, a value of £3077. This is because they now hold shares in a company with higher growth prospects. This technique is sometimes known as bootstrapping.

This example is an extreme case in which the stock market keeps the same price-to-earnings ratio for the company after the purchase as it had before. One justification for this course of action could be that the management of the purchasing firm is expected to use its abilities to achieve a similar growth rate on the assets of the purchased company as they are expected to achieve on their own assets. The other extreme is where the stock market attaches the price-to-earnings ratio of the acquired company to company A: then the share price of company A would be at a lower level after the merger than before.

Logically, once an acquisition has been made the stock market should adjust the price-to-earnings ratio of the purchasing company. If no changes are expected in the immediate earnings performance of the two companies, or now the two divisions, the new price-to-earnings ratio would logically be a combination of the two pre-merger price-to-earnings ratio – perhaps an average weighted by the respective earnings levels. For example, in the above case, where the two price-to-earnings ratios are 16:1 and 10:1 and both companies contributed equal earnings, the logical price-to-earnings ratio of the enlarged company A would be 13:1. This would give a share price of £4.00: as no extra value is anticipated this would seem to be a rational response. Even if the price-to-earnings ratio of the combined company A falls from its previous level, the shareholders of the company can still benefit provided that the new ratio is greater than 13:1. For example if the price-to-earnings ratio falls to 14:1 it still gives a price of £4.31.This use of a high price-to-earnings ratio to benefit one's own shareholders by an acquisition policy is well known and has helped many firms to build up their empires. However, the long-term benefit to the shareholders must be questioned. As will be seen later in this chapter, a surprising number of mergers and acquisitions have turned out to be unsuccessful and to have failed to achieve the anticipated profit and growth.

Risk diversification

Despite a fading reputation, it has been estimated that 40% of assets transferred in the UK during the period 1979–85 were through conglomerate-type mergers and takeovers. The rationale for such mergers is said to be diversification, which will lead to a more stable cash flow. Firms in different industries experience different levels of profitability and cash flow during the various periods of an economy's booms and slumps. Therefore bringing together firms in different industries, which is the result of conglomerate mergers and takeovers, could reduce the volatility of the combined cash flow. From a company's point of view this reduces risk.

It has been argued that the more stable earnings of the company appeal to lenders, leading to lower borrowing costs or even increased debt capacity. The benefits to those investors who provide debt finance can be demonstrated with a simple example. Let us assume that two companies X and Y merge, their cash flows are not related and the correlation coefficient between the cash flows is zero. The expected cash flow for each of the companies is given in Table 24.2.

Table 24.2

Possible economic situations	Probability P	Expected annual cash flow C available for interest payments
1	0.2	£100
2	0.2	£250
3	0.6	£600

If we assume that the annual debt service costs of both companies are £200, the probability that company X will be unable to meet this annual cost is 20%. The probability is the same for Y. The probability $P(D)$ that one or both firms will not be able to meet its interest obligations is

$$P(D) = P(C_X < 200) + P(C_Y < 200) - P(C_X < 200, C_Y < 200)$$
$$= 0.2 + 0.2 \times (0.2 \times 0.2) = 0.36$$

If the two companies merge the distribution of their joint returns is as follows:

$C(X + Y)$	P
£200	0.04
£350	0.08
£500	0.04
£700	0.24
£850	0.24
£1200	0.36

The combined interest charge is now £400 and the probability of default now drops to 0.12. This is based on zero correlation between the cash flows of the two companies. If the two companies are in different industries such that when the return of one company is declining the other is rising, then the probability of default is even less.

The above indicates advantages to providers of loan finance. Furthermore Galai and Masulis [6] argue that bondholders receive more protection since the shareholders of the combined firms have to back the bondholders of both the firms. Stapleton [7] points out however that even some bondholders could lose, since the maturity dates of some bondholders will be earlier than others and some will find that as a result of the combination 'new' bondholders in the group will have earlier claims to repayment than their own.

The advantages to equity shareholders are less clear. If the shareholders want diversification they can achieve this through diversifying the investments in their own portfolio. The theory of portfolio management deals with investors reducing their own risks; they do not need companies to do it for them. This is certainly the case with other than small investors. In the context of the capital asset pricing model covered in Chapter 10 diversification *per se* would not increase shareholder wealth or reduce risk because investors are assumed to hold fully diversified portfolios. However, as discussed below, managers could benefit from a reduction in the variability of a firm's cash flow. There is considerable disagreement in the literature on whether diversification by a company does reduce shareholders' risk. Stapleton [7], using the option pricing model, concludes that even if a conglomerate can increase its debt capacity as a result of mergers and acquisitions, this can benefit the providers of debt finance more than the shareholders. However, if the extra debt capacity is utilized, the shareholders can obtain some benefit owing to tax savings on the interest payments.

The case for mergers and takeovers of the conglomerate type is far from clear. As a result of a generally poor performance by such groups over the last decade, using diversification as an argument for justifying an acquisition has fallen from favour.

24.4 Management motives

In the traditional theory of mergers and takeovers discussed above it is assumed that one company (the bidding company) seeks to acquire the shares of another company (the target company). This is, of course, the technical position. However, it is not the shareholders of the bidding company that initiate the move and actually make the bid to purchase the shares of the target company. It is the managers, the directors of the bidding company, that are seeking to acquire the shares on their shareholders' behalf.

In other words it is the managers of the bidding company who seek to appeal to the shareholders of the target company. They make an offer to the target company's shareholders, with or without the agreement of the target company's managers. Jensen and

Ruback [8] refer to the takeover market as a market for corporate control in which alternative managerial teams compete for the rights to manage corporate resources. This is a shift from the traditional view. With this approach it is managers who are the primary activists, with shareholders playing a relatively passive role.

Of course, the shareholders have the final say. It is the target company's shareholders who, through their decision on whether or not to accept the offer, finally decide whether the takeover bid is successful. The bidding company's shareholders, although not consulted about individual bids, can decide whether on balance the managers are acting in their own interests or the shareholders' interests and, if they feel that it is necessary, can remove managers and directors.

The bidding company's managers cannot diverge too much from the shareholder wealth maximization model, but they can and do take their own interests into account. One group who, on average, benefit from a successful takeover bid is the management team of the bidding firm. They finish up managing a larger business which gives them increased status and higher remuneration. One group who, on average, lose in a successful takeover is the management team of the victim firm. They therefore have a vested interest in fighting a takeover bid. If they act in their own interests they will contest the bid, whether or not it is in the interest of their own company's shareholders.

These points will be returned to later in this chapter. The point being made here is that managers' motives have to be taken into account when considering takeovers and mergers. It is not simply the division of gains between one group of shareholders and another.

As was mentioned when discussing agency theory, if managers only own a small proportion of the equity, they may have different objectives from those of the shareholders. Over time theories of the firm have been advanced that suggested that managers might well pursue profit-maximizing, growth-maximizing or even revenue-maximizing objectives. To these can be added private objectives such as power, prestige and empire building. This is one reason why share option schemes are introduced: to try to obtain goal congruence, to give the managers rewards directly tied to shareholders' rewards.

One other management motive might be survival, i.e. reduced risk of being replaced. Managers, unlike shareholders, cannot diversify to spread their risks. They are tied to one company. If that company is taken over, the managers have a high probability of losing their jobs. By acquiring other companies, the business that they operate becomes larger and so they themselves become less likely to be victims of takeovers. With conglomerate mergers, the risk diversification benefits the managers, increasing their security. However, as explained, the theory of portfolio analysis suggests that conglomerate mergers to reduce risk are not in the shareholders' interests.

We have already suggested that the private interests of managers can take precedence over the interests of their shareholders. For example, when managers of target firms decide to fight a takeover, they are not always doing so in the shareholders' interests. 'Golden parachute' contracts compensating managers who are displaced can be provided for in the event of a takeover. These are in their own interests, and not necessarily those of shareholders, as they may accept a bid rather than fight knowing that they will receive compensation if displaced.

The rules

24.5 Takeover tactics

The rules to be followed are both self-regulatory and statutory. First we shall consider the self-regulating rules of the City. These are detailed rules that have to be followed by both the bidding company and the target company at the time of a takeover. They are given in what is known as 'The City Code on Takeovers and Mergers'.

These rules were introduced to protect shareholders, and they have to be frequently modified as new bidding and defence practices are brought to light. For example, it became known after the Guinness–Argyll–Distillers takeover battle that the directors of Distillers, the target company, had agreed to cover the costs of a bid from Guinness, who were initially seen as a 'white knight' against the bid from Argyll. When this became known after the takeover battle, the Code was altered to prevent such 'poison pill' tactics happening again without the approval of the target company shareholders. It was a poison pill because if Argyll had been successful it was something they would have had to swallow; they would have not only had to pay their own costs but also those of their rival bidder.

The Code does not have the force of law, but those who wish to operate through the securities market have to follow it. The Code is administered and enforced by the Panel on Takeovers and Mergers, a body representative of those using the securities markets. It applies to listed companies: it is also relevant to unlisted public companies but not to private companies. The Panel's role is to act as a referee in a takeover and merger situation and in particular to ensure that all shareholders are treated fairly.

Within the Code itself it is described as:

> the collective opinion of those professionally involved in the field of takeovers on a range of business standards. It is not concerned with the financial or commercial advantages or disadvantages of a takeover, which are matters for the company and its shareholders, or with those wider questions which are the responsibility of the government, advised by the Monopolies Commission.

One problem with the Code is that it cannot reverse what has already happened. It cannot impose sanctions after the event. All that it can do is change the rules to make sure that what it considers to be unfair practices cannot be repeated in future.

We now turn to the legal rules which consist of some provisions in the Companies Act, the Fair Trading Act and the Monopolies and Mergers Act.

An Office of Fair Trading was established in 1973, with a Director of Fair Trading as its head. It is the Director's job to keep himself informed about prospective mergers and acquisitions and to advise the Secretary of State for Trade and Industry whether a proposed merger should be investigated by the Monopolies Commission. When a merger or acquisition is referred, the Commission have up to six months to conduct their investigation. They then report to the Secretary of State on whether or not they consider that the merger operates against the public interest. If they find that it *is* against the public interest, the Secretary of State can prohibit the merger or acquisition or can impose conditions that have to be met before it can go ahead.

A 'qualifying merger', i.e. one that is to be investigated, is based on either size or monopoly power. If the gross assets being taken over exceed £30 million it qualifies, as it does if the companies involved control at least 25% of the UK market in a product.

In making a recommendation to the Minister the Monopolies Commission does not have to find that the combined companies will be beneficial in order to give it their blessing; they only need to find that it does not operate against the public interest. In the Monopolies Commission report on Scottish and Newcastle Breweries–Matthew Brown proposed merger it was stated: 'We discern no material advantages to the public interest arising from the proposed merger, but the question before us is whether the merger may be expected to operate against the public interest and in our view there are no sufficient grounds for such an expectation.'

Public interest is judged mainly on the grounds of the effect on competition. The object of the monopolies and merger policy is to promote competition, and to prevent mergers and acquisitions that would reduce competition through the exercise of market power. A merger which may therefore be in the interests of the firms concerned may be against the public interest. This explains the need for a Monopolies Commission.

One result of the move to a Single Market in Europe will be a considerable amount of industrial reorganization. There will be a rise in the level of cross border mergers and acquisitions as markets become more homogeneous, and as the barriers to acquisitions in some countries are removed. UK companies are the most acquisitive in Europe. In the late 1980s nearly 75% of all takeovers and mergers in Europe involved UK companies. In 1988 they were involved in £35 billion worth of cross border mergers and takeovers.

There are barriers to a true free market in corporate control in the EU particularly in some countries. These barriers include:

1. the methods of corporate control. For example the departure, in some countries, from the principle of one share, one vote. This means in some countries minority shareholders are able to maintain control against the wishes of the majority;
2. the automatic casting of proxy votes;
3. differences in defence techniques that can be employed;
4. the opportunity for managers to defend against a bid without consulting shareholders.

If all barriers in the way of a Single Market are to be removed, the European Commission will need to introduce directives on these and other points.

There are Community rules that apply to cross border mergers and acquisitions, but these are mainly concerned with the rules of competition – with the wish to prevent monopolies. Plessey in defending itself against a takeover bid from GEC and Siemens claimed that the predators were breaking the competition rules of the Union by making their bid through a joint venture. The EU has the power to examine mergers with an EU dimension.

What still needs to be developed, if the so-called level playing field is thought desirable (that is providing the same opportunities for companies in all member states), is an EU 'Takeover Code' and a harmonization of company law. A number of issues are under discussion dealing with these matters. For example, in 1989 a proposed directive included the requirements that:

- A publicly quoted company that has acquired a third of the shares in another quoted company must launch a public offer for the remaining shares.
- In its bid document the bidding company will have to declare its intentions for the target company, especially with regard to its assets and workforce.
- The bid document must include the terms of the offer, the financial conditions and the reaction of the target company's management to the offer.
- Once a bid has been launched the target company will only be able to make special capital issues or absorb subsidaries if it obtains shareholders' approval at a general meeting.
- Member States will have the freedom to block a bid from a non-EU company if EU companies are barred from making takeovers in the bidding company's home country.

These are only proposals but they are indicative of the thinking of the Union, and the possible new rules.

Bidding tactics

When making a bid it is necessary to employ the services of financial advisers. With some of the larger bids more than one group of advisers may be used. The bidding company and its advisers will work out tactics.

Having decided to attempt to purchase a particular company, the next problem is to value the company and to decide how to pay for the purchase. The ordinary shares of the target company have to be acquired, and the purchasing company's equity shares, its debentures, its cash or some other security can be offered in exchange. The object is to make the offer attractive to the shareholders of the selling company at the least cost to the purchasing company.

The existing stock market price of a target company's shares is generally assumed to set the lower limit on the price which will have to be paid. The logic of this is that in order to encourage the shareholders to sell, they must be offered at least the equivalent of the present market price. This amount is often referred to as the capitalized market value of the company, i.e. the number of shares multiplied by the market price. It is by no means certain, however, that this valuation would be the same as that arrived at on a cash flow or assets basis as the stock market price at a particular time can be determined on the basis of only a small number of shares being traded in the market and a possible large demand for these. If a company is closely controlled, a high market price will not necessarily draw more shares on to the market. Alternatively, an investor may be willing to pay a high price for a small number of shares, but if all the issued shares were unloaded in the market, they would not necessarily command the same high price. The share price is determined at the margin by the buyers and sellers dealing in the market at one time. If more sellers come on to the market, the price should fall.

Nevertheless, if the existing market price is £x, and a prospective purchaser offers shareholders £x – 1, it is unlikely that they will sell. Each shareholder will expect to be offered at least £x. However, if one shareholder owns, say, 40% of the shares, he would probably have to accept an average price of less than £x if he tried to sell them all at once. For a closely controlled company, it may be possible to purchase the controlling interest at a price per share less than the market price. Another situation in which it may be possible to purchase a controlling interest in a company at a price less than the existing market price is where the market price is unrealistic. The price on a particular day may not be representative of the normal price level of the shares. It could, for example, be inflated by rumours of an impending takeover bid. The share price on the day would then reflect the expected bidding price, but the actual bid could be less than expected and yet still be successful.

Almost always the bidding firm does have to offer a premium: this is the difference between the value of the cash or securities being offered and the pre-merger market price of the target company. Empirical studies have shown that the size of the premium with the final offer can vary from 20% to over 100% of the pre-merger market price. The average premium with successful bids is in the region of 50%, although with contested takeover bids a premium of this level can be unsuccessful.

The factors that have been found in the empirical research to influence the size of the premium include, not surprisingly, whether or not there is competition to purchase the acquired firm, the level of cash flow of the target firm relative to the size of its assets and the size of the acquired firm relative to the size of the purchasing firm.

The Companies Act requires any person who acquires an interest of 5% or more of the voting share capital of a listed company to notify the company of that fact within five days of acquiring the interest. This disclosure requirement is necessary in order to enable a target company to know who it is who is buying its shares, and to give it advance notice of a possible takeover raid. These requirements became necessary in the 1960s and 1970s when there were a number of takeovers where the target company had been kept in ignorance of significant changes in the ownership of its shares until it was too late for it to be able to act.

Market raids

Market raids arise when a person or company acts with such speed in buying the shares of a target company that the 'raider' has achieved his objective before he is required to notify the company of his acquisition. 'Dawn raids' are market raids that take place in the minutes or hours immediately after the Stock Market has opened. One well-publicized case occurred on Tuesday, 12 February 1980. At the close of the market on the previous day, the price of shares in Consolidated Gold Fields stood at 525p. Early on 12 February, brokers acting for Anglo American – De Beers, the large South African multi-national, informed clients and jobbers that they would be in the market for substantial purchases of Consolidated Gold Fields shares. By 10 a.m. brokers acting for De Beers had purchased 16.5 million shares of Consolidated Gold at a price of 616p. The amount of shares purchased obviously satisfied Anglo–De Beers because they then stopped purchasing and within minutes the price of the Consolidated Gold shares fell to 510p. In fact this particular raid was also an example of buyers acting in concert (i.e. a 'concert party'). This raid is of particular interest because eight years later Anglo American–De Beers through Minorco, a subsidiary in Luxembourg, made a bid to purchase all the shares of Consolidated Gold Fields. They failed.

What is unfair about such a market raid is that the high price is not being offered to all the shareholders of the target company. It is only the large institutional shareholders easily in touch with the brokers who can benefit from the early offer. By the time that the smaller shareholders, the private individuals, find out about the purchaser, the offer has closed. There is not equality in the treatment of shareholders.

In 1981 and 1982 the City Code was revised to strengthen the restrictions on acquisitions prior to the announcement of an offer. The rules now state that where 'any person acquires, whether by a series of transactions over a period of time or not, shares which (taken together with shares held or acquired by persons acting in concert with him) carry 30% or more of the voting rights of a company . . . such person shall extend the offer to any other holders of the voting shares.' This offer price must be not less than the highest price paid for the shares within the preceding 12 months. The offer must include a cash alternative. The rules state that a person (including persons acting in concert with him) who does not hold shares which in aggregate carry 30% or more of the voting rights may not, prior to the announcement by him of a firm intention to make an offer, acquire any shares carrying voting rights in that company which, when aggregated with any shares or rights over shares which he already holds, would carry 30% or more of the voting rights.

In summary, if a person or persons acting in concert purchases 5% or more of the shares of a company he has to notify the company. He can continue to purchase shares in the market and is not required to make an offer for all the shares until his shareholding reaches 30%. When he does make an offer, if he has purchased 15% or more of shares within the offer period or within 12 months prior to the offer, then the offer price should be not less than the highest price paid for such shares during the offer period and within the 12 months prior to its commencement. A similar rule regarding paying the highest price applies if the offeror holds 30% or more of the voting rights at the time of making the bid.

Concert parties

A 'concert party' occurs where several persons act in concert to buy shares in a particular company. They do so in such a way that no one individual owns or has an interest in more than 5% and so becomes liable to notify the target company of this shareholding. The provision applies to all public companies whether or not their shares are listed on the Stock Exchange. The disclosure requirements extend to groups of persons acting together – in concert – who in aggregate have interests exceeding the 5% level. The City Code requires all persons with notifiable interests to disclose any relevant event not later than 12 noon on the dealing day following any such event.

The Companies Act defines an 'interest in shares'. It sets out eight circumstances in which a person is said to have taken an interest in shares even though he does not actually own them himself. These include shares owned by other members of a family, shares owned by a company of which the interested party is a director, shares held in trust and shares held by another person where they are both parties to the same concert party agreement.

The offer

When intending to make an offer, notice of the fact should in the first instance be communicated to the board of the company to be acquired or to its advisers. When this board receives notice that an offer is to be made, they must immediately inform the shareholders of their company by press notice, and following this they must send a copy of the notice or a circular dealing with the matter to each of the shareholders. The offer document should normally be posted within 28 days of the announcement of the terms of the offer. The acquiring company, therefore, first announces its intention to make an offer disclosing its terms and, then, within a certain number of days, posts the offer to each of the shareholders of the offeree company. The board of the offeree company must circulate its views on the offer to its shareholders as soon as possible after the dispatch of the offer document.

When the offer is announced, the terms of the offer and the identity of the offeror must be disclosed. The offeror must also disclose any existing shareholding that it has in the company that it wishes to acquire. It must also disclose any shareholding over which it has control or which is owned or controlled by any company or person acting in concert with the offeror.

The statements contained in the offer document must be treated with the same standards of care as those in a prospectus. The document must state whether or not there is any agreement, arrangement or understanding existing between the offeror or any person acting in concert with the offeror and any of the present or recently past directors, or present or recently past shareholders of the offeree company. In other words, any agreement or relationship between any relevant parties connected with the two companies must be disclosed. This is necessary as the shareholders of the offeree company must be in possession of all the facts necessary to help them make an informed judgement on the advantages and disadvantages of the offer. The board of the offeree company, in making their views on the offer known to the shareholders, must also bear in mind the accuracy requirement in any statements they make, particularly those concerning profit forecasts and asset valuations.

The offeror, the bidding company, may have to obtain the approval of its shareholders before it can go ahead with the bid. The Stock Exchange listing requirements (the Yellow Book) state that, for what are known as Class 1 transactions (these are major transactions), shareholders must be circulated when assets, bought or sold, represent more than 15% of the bidding company's total assets. Further, a shareholders vote is required when a company proposes to buy or sell assets representing more than 25% of its total. Also, of course, if shares or securities are to be issued in numbers greater than the difference between the already authorized capital of the company and the already issued capital, then the bidding company has to go to its own shareholders. It would have to seek approval from its shareholders if, in order to pay for the acquisition, it was necessary to increase the authorized capital of the company. The existing shareholders would then have an opportunity to express their views on the reason why new shares were being authorized.

An offer must initially be open for at least 21 days after the posting of the offer. If it is revised, it must be kept open for at least 14 days from the date of posting a notice of the revision of the offer. No offer shall become unconditional as to acceptances after the sixtieth day following the posting of the offer. After an offer has been declared unconditional as to acceptances, the offer must remain open for acceptances for not less than 14 days. After that date, the offer will have expired.

'Unconditional' means that the shareholders of the offeree company must now either 'take it or leave it': no better offer is to follow. The offer can only become unconditional when the offeror has acquired, or agreed to acquire by the close of the offer, shares carrying over 50% of the voting equity shares. Making the offer unconditional means in effect that the bidder has won: he has now obtained control of the offeree, and the shareholders who have not already sold to him should either do so within the next few days before the offer has expired or keep their shares and become minority shareholders in the company.

No offer which, if accepted in full, would result in the offeror having voting control of the company shall be made unless it is the condition of such an offer that it will not become unconditional unless the offeror has acquired or agreed to acquire shares carrying over 50% of the votes. After the offer has expired or it has become unconditional or it is revised, the offeror shall announce the position with respect to the offer, namely what percentage of acceptances have been received.

Classes of non-equity capital need not be the subject of the offer. When a company to be bid for has more than one class of equity share capital, a comparable offer must be made for each class of share. Normally, an offer is for all the equity shares of the company.

Partial offers are allowed, however, but with reservations. The Takeover Panel's consent is always required. In the case of a partial offer which would result, if accepted in full, in the acquiring company holding shares in excess of 50% of the voting rights of the company, the Panel's consent will not normally be given. It will not normally be given if an offer for the whole of the equity capital has already been announced, perhaps by another company, or if the offeror or persons acting in concert with them have acquired selectively or in significant numbers shares in the company that it is seeking to acquire during the 12 months preceding the application. Even if such an offer is allowed, it must be approved of by over 50% of the shareholders with voting rights not held by the offeror or persons acting with them.

In the case of an offer which would result in the offeror's holding shares carrying not less than 30% and not more than 50% of the voting rights, the consent of the Panel would be granted only in exceptional circumstances and, in any event, not unless the board of the offeree company recommends the offer. As above, the offer must be approved by shareholders in respect of over 50% of the voting rights that are not already held by the offeror. The majority of the remaining independent shareholders must be happy with the partial offer going through.

In the case of an offer which would result in the offeror's holding shares carrying less than 30% of the voting rights of the company, consent will normally be granted. Partial offers must be made to all shareholders of the class and arrangements must be made for those shareholders who wish to do so to be able to accept in full for a particular percentage of their holdings. Therefore, if the company wishes to buy 25% of the shares of another company, all the shareholders of the selling company that wish to dispose of their shares are entitled to sell 25% of their shares.

Failing to acquire all the shares

The usual takeover tactics are for the bidder to purchase some of the target company's shares in the market before making a formal offer. He then makes an offer and hopes to obtain acceptances in sufficient numbers to give him ownership of more than 50% of the shares. The offer must initially be open for at least 21 days after its posting, and the bidder is hoping to be able to announce within that 21 days that he owns shares and has acceptances that together take him above the 50% figure. He then declares the offer unconditional. Prior to this position the offer to the target company's shareholders was conditional on the bidder obtaining this 50% ownership.

Once the offer is declared unconditional the target shareholders are not entitled to withdraw their acceptance; prior to this point they could have changed their minds. Similarly, if the offer period has lapsed and the acceptances received have not taken the bidding company's holdings over 50%, the bidding company does not have to take up what acceptances it has received. Usually, once the offer has been declared unconditional many of the target company's shareholders who had been unsure whether to accept, make up their minds and sell their shares to the bidding company at the offer price.

The takeover may be successful in securing for the purchaser a controlling interest in the target company but fail to obtain all the ordinary shares of the company. The shareholders of the purchased company who did not wish to sell their shares will hold a minority interest in the purchased company. This minority interest will be recognized in the consolidated accounts of the group.

The minority shareholders are entitled to receive dividends on their shares, and these will continue to have to be paid either in perpetuity or until the holders eventually sell their shares to the holding company. The cost of these dividend payments will have to be allowed for in the valuation of the company. The assumption that all the assets are being acquired, or that all the earnings will accrue to the purchasing company, is only valid if 100% of the shares are acquired. If it is likely that a minority of the shareholders will not sell, then the value of the purchase has to allow for the liability of paying future dividends to this outside interest.

It might be thought that a proportion of the future earnings belong to the minority interests, but it can be argued that as long as the company remains in business the minority shareholders have a claim only to the part of earnings that are declared as dividends.

Where a takeover takes place and the shares of one company are being exchanged for the shares of another company, it is possible under certain conditions to buy out any dissenting minority of the shareholders of the selling company. If, within four months of making the offer, nine-tenths in value of the shares whose transfer is involved, which means that any shares already held at the date of making the offer are excluded, have been acquired, then the purchasing company can give notice to any dissenting shareholders that it wishes to acquire their shares. The purchasing company is then entitled to acquire those shares under the terms on which the other shares had been transferred.

Defence against a takeover bid

The directors of a company that is the subject of a takeover bid should act in the best interests of their shareholders. The City Code on Takeovers and Mergers specifies certain general principles that must be observed. The Code does not apply to private companies although they are wise to follow what is in it. The board should normally seek competent independent advice when they receive a bid. The directors should disregard their own personal interest in the offer and in advising their shareholders act in the interests of all the shareholders.

In most cases the independent advisors are closely involved in the preparation of the documents containing the views of the board of the target firm. Where there is any divergence of view between the board and their independent advisors, it is important that shareholders should be informed of this and given details. Usually merchant bankers are used as advisors.

If the directors decide to fight the takeover there are a number of tactics open to them. However, they must carefully consider their motives for recommending the rejection and put all the facts to the shareholders necessary for them to make up their minds: such facts must be accurately and fairly presented and be available to the shareholders early enough to enable them to make a decision in good time.

Information must not be given to some shareholders that is not available to all shareholders.

If the directors of the offeree company decide to fight a bid that appears to be financially attractive to their shareholders then they should try to convince their shareholders of the truth of either of the following.

1. The current market price of the offeror's shares is unjustifiably high and will not be sustained, which would happen if there was expected to be heavy selling of the shares allocated to shareholders of the offeree company.
2. The price of the offeree's shares is too low in relation to the real value and earning power of the assets that the offeror company is trying to acquire.

If the directors decide on course 2, then assets need to be revalued and possibly even sold and profit forecasts prepared to support this line of defence. In addition, there may be promises of higher future dividends and management changes to improve efficiency and profitability.

The City Code makes the following points about such a defence:

1. All defending circulars must be prepared with the same standards of care as if a prospectus within the meaning of the 1948 Companies Act was being prepared, whether issued by the offeree company or its advisers.
2. The bases and assumptions on which any profit forecasts are prepared by the directors must be stated. It would not be sufficient just to say 'profits will be higher than last year'. The accounting bases and calculations for the forecasts must be examined and reported on by the auditors or consultant accountants. The latest unaudited profit figures must be given together with comparable figures for the previous year for any period covered by the forecast. If they are not available this fact should be stated.

3. When revaluation of assets is given in connection with an offer, the board's valuation should be supported by the opinion of an independent valuer and the basis of the valuation clearly stated.

Directors should be able to detect that another company is interested in their company before any formal announcement of a takeover bid is made. The management can detect movements in the share ownership; it can see signs of share accumulation by certain holders or nominees. Perhaps the company will obtain advance warnings through close relationship with stockbrokers or investment analysts. Further, it should know from either changes in the structure or technology of the industry or from its own past performance in profits and dividends or by its share price in relation to the true value of its assets whether or not it is the type of company that somebody would wish to buy. The earlier that it knows of a possible takeover attempt, the more time it has to discourage a bid or fight off an offer. A well-managed defensive campaign would include aggressive publicity on behalf of the company, preferably starting before a bid is received. Investors could be told of any good research ideas within the company and of the management potential, or merely made more aware of the name of the company and any of its achievements. An announcement might be made about a proposed increase in divided payments.

We shall now consider some of the more glamorous defensive tactics that have been employed. It should be appreciated, however, that although it might be possible to fight off a bid from an unwelcome suitor, it does not mean the company will necessarily be able to maintain its independence. Sometimes the defence technique employed means finding a more acceptable partner. Sometimes as a result of the methods adopted in the defence the company makes itself vulnerable to another acquirer. In the USA fewer than one in four publicly quoted companies eventually remain independent after receiving a hostile bid. In the UK a company has a better chance of remaining independent, but even then it is only two out of four that survive.

White knights

One defensive tactic that has been used with success is for the directors of the offeree company to offer their company to a more friendly outside interest, i.e. a defensive merger. The friendly acquirer is referred to as a 'white knight'. It is a tactic to be adopted only in the last resort, for it means that the company is being taken over, but the directors decide they would rather work within one group than another. This tactic is acceptable to the City Code, provided that certain rules are observed. Any information, including particulars of shareholders, given to a preferred suitor should, on request, be furnished equally and as promptly to a less welcome but bona fide potential offeror. Of course, in addition, the directors must always ensure that they are acting in the interests of their shareholders as a whole, and not acting in the interests of their own personal future or out of spite.

One version of this technique which has been adopted in the past, but which has been made a lot more difficult following revisions in the Code, is for the directors of the offeree company to issue new shares to a friendly investor who it is known will not sell to the bidder. One of the most famous (or infamous) cases in which this happened occurred when Metal Industries were engaged in fighting off a merger with Aberdare Holdings. The directors of Metal Industries favoured a bid by Thorn Electrical. Aberdare were proving successful in their bid: they had acquired 53% of the capital of Metal Industries, when the Metal Industries directors, without the consent of the shareholders, issued 5 million new shares to Thorn Electrical in exchange for one of Thorn's subsidiary companies. This one act meant the Aberdare holding in Metal Industries dropped to only 32% of the new total of shares. Thorn then put in a higher bid for the remainder of the equity of Metal Industries and won control of the company.

In this case the directors of Metal Industries did not act in the interests of the majority of their shareholders. At the time of the issue of the new shares the majority shareholder was Aberdare Holdings, the company trying to take them over. These events happened in 1967, at a time before any attempt at an effective City Code. Therefore the directors were not breaking any formal rules of conduct. At the time the action was justified as being 'for the greatest good of the greatest number'. If Thorn had not made this new bid, shareholders would have had to take a lower offer from Aberdare.

The City Code now makes clear its attitude to this type of defensive tactic. It states: 'During the course of an offer, or even before the date of the offer, if the board of the offeree company has reason to believe that a bona fide offer might be imminent, the board must not, except in pursuance of a contract entered into earlier, without the approval of the shareholders in general meeting, issue any authorized but unissued shares, or issue or grant options in respect of any unissued shares, create or issue or permit the creation or issue of any securities carrying rights of conversion into or subscription for shares of the company, or sell, dispose of or acquire or agree to sell, dispose of or acquire assets of material amount or enter into contracts otherwise than in the ordinary course of business.'

The position of the directors is now clear; they need approval of the shareholders of the company in a general meeting before they can fundamentally alter the position of a company during a takeover battle. The directors of Metal Industries could not now carry out the actions that they did without shareholders' approval.

Poison pills

Reference has already been made to poison pills in the section on takeover rules. This refers to the case of an acquirer finding itself having to pay the costs of a rival bidder. With this approach a company takes steps before a takeover has been made to make itself less attractive to a potential bidder. One such method is for existing shareholders to be given rights to buy in future loan stock or preference shares. If a bid is made for the company before the date by which the rights have to be exercised, the terms of the arrangement are that the rights are to be automatically converted into ordinary shares. Of course, these new shares have to be purchased by the bidder. This adds to the cost of the acquisition.

Crown jewels

The tactic of selling off certain highly valued assets of the company subject to a bid is referred to as selling the crown jewels. The intention is that the target company without the crown jewels will be less attractive to the bidding company. This tactic is more common in the USA than in the UK, where Rule 38 of the City Code makes it clear that once the board of the offeree company believes that an offer is imminent this defence is not feasible. However, the offeree is allowed to state that if the bid fails an asset will be sold in the future.

The latter tactic can mean that the offeree shareholders are less likely to sell their shares to the bidder. This would be the case if the future sale brought in needed cash on disposal of assets that were pulling down the value of the company. A variation on this approach is that, once the company knows it is being bid for, it purchases assets which it knows that the bidder will not want.

Golden parachutes

Another defence is the golden parachute. This is a policy of introducing attractive termination packages for the senior executives of the offeree company. It clearly makes defeat in the takeover less painful for the victim company's executives, but it also makes it more expensive for the bidding company to make the acquisition. These termination payments have to be made when the acquiring company takes over. The City Code makes clear that details of service contracts have to be made known in any documents sent to shareholders of the companies involved, including any details of amendments within the last six months.

Pac-Man strategy

This is a defensive tactic, that has often been used in the USA, and occasionally in the UK. It involves the target company trying to take over the bidding company. The name is based on the famous computer game in which the object being chased turns the tables on the pursuer.

Greenmail and arbitrageurs

Arbitrageurs are investors who speculate on takeovers and mergers. They know that if a company is to be the subject of a takeover bid the price of its shares will increase dramatically. They therefore purchase shares of companies that they expect to be the subject of a takeover bid. When the bid materializes the shares will rise in value and they can sell at a profit. This would seem to be an interesting but not controversial type of stock market activity. The arbitrageur is taking a risk; if the company is the subject of a bid, he gains.

Unfortunately in the late 1980s the activities of a number of arbitrageurs became discredited. The leading player in the USA was Ivan Boesky who, it turned out, was reducing his risks by buying information from merchant bankers on which companies were to be the subject of a bid. He was obtaining information illegally and acting before the offer was publicly announced. What he was doing was disclosed, and he was tried and sent to jail.

Arbitrageurs when acting legally can have an important influence on the outcome of a bid. The block of shares that they hold in a company which is the subject of the bid can take on a crucial importance. If they sell to the predator the bid can succeed; if they hold or sell to someone other than the predator the bid can fail. Hence, we have the expression 'greenmail', where 'green' refers to the colour of the US dollar. They can try to obtain 'rewards' from the bidding company in return for their support, or alternatively 'rewards' from the company that is the object of the bid for not selling. A question arises as to whether such tactics by the arbitrageurs are legitimate.

An infamous takeover battle in the US took place in 1984 when Mesa Petroleum, a company known as a corporate raider, tried to purchase a block of shares in Phillips Petroleum. Mesa already held 6% of the shares and bid for a further 15%. As part of its defence, Phillips responded to greenmail. It agreed to buy back the 6% holding, giving Mesa a profit of $89 million on its transaction. In fact a few weeks later another corporate raider made a bid for Phillips, and in doing so acquired 5% of its shares. To defend itself Phillips made yet another greenmail payment.

Referral to the Monopolies Commission

It is generally believed that if a target company can have the takeover bid referred to the Monopolies Commission it either means that the bid immediately dies, as the predator will withdraw it, or there will be a delay, possibly of up to six months, while the Commission listens to all the arguments. Two cases will illustrate the influence of the Monopolies Commission in bid situations.

In 1985 Hanson PLC was attempting to takeover the Imperial Group but was worried that the Office of Fair Trading would refer the bid to the Monopolies Commission. Another bid in that year, namely Imperial's bid for Allied Biscuits, had been referred to the Commission because the two companies were heavily involved in the same industry, namely the food industry. The Office of Fair Trading was worried about the monopoly position that would result in the segment of the market concerned with 'snacks'. With the referral the Imperial bid for Allied was allowed to die. Allied Biscuits reversed the position; they now announced that they would bid for Imperial, adopting a Pac-Man strategy except that in this case the first bid was already dead. To overcome the possible monopoly problem Allied announced that they would, if successful, sell off the part of Imperial that was strong in the snack market, namely Golden Wonder. Through the sale they would be selling off the activities that had worried the Monopolies Commission. Hanson and Allied Biscuits were both bidding for Imperial. The Hanson bid was not referred to the Commission. The board of Imperial supported the Allied

Biscuits bid, but they did not obtain the result that they sought. It was Hanson who took over Imperial.

In the second case the UK company Consolidated Gold Fields adopted this tactic when Minorco, the Luxembourg arm of the South African owned Anglo American – De Beers gold mining operation, bid for them. Consolidated Gold were hoping that the increased concentration resulting from the acquisition would be judged to be against the public interest. There was also the question of whether the resulting South African control of the smaller UK company was in the UK's national interest. The Monopolies Commission investigated the bid but did not think that it would be against the national interest if the bid went ahead. However, some of the shareholders of Consolidated Gold Fields were residents of the USA. The bid was investigated by the US Securities and Exchange Commission on behalf of the shareholders in that country. They found that if the bid was successful it would be against the interest of Americans who would be involved. Even though neither company involved was a registered US company this decision effectively ended the bid.

The view of the US Securities and Exchange Commission was not based on whether the target company had substantial business interest in the USA but whether the US shareholders in the target company were in any way affected. The Securities and Exchange Commission believe that if there is a sufficiently large shareholding by Americans in the company concerned in the bid, then they have jurisdiction even if the takeover offer is not being made in the USA.

Producing a revised profit forecast

A classic defensive technique is to produce profit forecasts that indicate that the future will be very much better than investors in the market place had been expecting. If these forecasts are accepted by the market as realistic, it will naturally force up the price of the target company's shares and make the offer price relatively less attractive. It is of course one thing to make a forecast and quite another to achieve the results. How these higher profit figures are to be achieved could be the result of improved efficiency, a management shake-up or changed methods of accounting.

A novel version of this form of defence was produced in 1989 by the board of Consolidated Gold Fields in its defence against the bid by Minorco. Consolidated Gold Fields guaranteed to deliver a certain level of profit, but if for any reason it did not meet the level it would pay a very generous cash dividend to its shareholders. One might wonder how it could fund large cash dividend payments if it did not achieve the planned profit level. The answer was that it would finance the dividend by the sale of assets. The target Consolidated Gold Fields set itself was to produce an earnings per share figure of 400p over the following three years. The target represented the equivalent of an increase of 20% per annum in earnings per share. If this target was not met, the shareholders would receive a cash dividend of £6 per share at the end of the three years. In order to help achieve this target the top management in the group were to be paid bonuses related to the growth in earnings per share. This would overcome the 'agency' problem, i.e. the shareholders and the top management receiving their rewards based on the same indicator. Consolidated Gold Fields were the first company to attempt to tie themselves to the profit forecast that they produced at the time of an unwelcome takeover bid.

Other tactics

Other defensive tactics include encouraging a company's own pension funds to purchase shares in the company and introducing employee share option schemes. These approaches are based on the idea that existing employees and their representatives are not likely to sell to a potential acquirer but to remain loyal to their existing employer.

Employee share option plans (ESOPs) have been used as a means of placing shares in friendly hands. There are considerable tax advantages with such schemes in the USA and less so in the UK, but nevertheless the defence has been used in the UK.

The way in which the tactic works is for the company concerned to borrow funds from a bank, insurance company or other financial institution. The proceeds of the loan are used to buy the company's own shares, which are then put in a trust for eventual purchase by the employees. The shares purchased are in fact used as a security for the loan. As the employees contribute to the ESOP the money collected is used to repay the loan. The shares under the scheme are allocated to employees. The result is that not only are the shares placed in friendly hands, but also funds have been borrowed at a less expensive rate than normal. This technique can be used to finance a management–employee buyout. In the USA, the car hire company Avis was bought by its employees in 1987 for $1.75 million through an ESOP approach.

The colourful names that are introduced for defensive tactics suggest that many players regard takeovers as a form of game. Clearly not all can regard takeovers in a light-hearted manner, as many people can lose their jobs as the result of a change in company ownership.

The most popular methods of paying vary from one period of high takeover activity to another. The boom based on the conglomerate mergers of the late 1960s and early 1970s was paid for mainly by the exchange of equity shares; about 50% of the total consideration was met by this means. Again, in the three year period up to the stock market collapse of 1987, half the expenditure was met by the exchange of equity shares. However, perhaps not surprisingly, following the collapse in share prices this method of settlement became less popular. As can be seen from Table 24.1, in 1988 over 70% of the total consideration was paid for in cash. The shareholders of the target firms were seeking cash settlements.

These figures illustrate the importance of the capital market in financing takeover activity. Even when a takeover is paid for in cash, that cash has often been raised by the acquirer from a new equity issue prior to the takeover bid. The Bank of England found that about half the new funds raised on the stock exchange through equity issues in 1986–7 were disbursed within six months to pay for the acquisition of companies [9].

In the UK there is a high proportion of mixed bids, with only half of all bids being either all equity or all cash. These mixed bids can be partly explained by the fact that many bids provide for a cash alternative to the equity offer. Cash tends to be used more than equity in bids that are contested or are being opposed by the managers of the target firm. Evidence has also been found that cash tends to be used in high-value acquisitions. Underwriters are particularly important in cash bids, helping with the financing arrangement if the bidder is short of cash.

Methods of payment

Cash offers

An offer is made to purchase the shares of the target company for cash. The acquiring company may, prior to the bid, have been purchasing up to 30% of the target company's shares on the stock market as and when they become available. Finally, it offers to buy the remainder of the shares at a specified price. As previously explained, the same offer must be made to all the target company's shareholders; it is a breach of the City Code to offer a higher price to one group of shareholders than is available to another group.

A cash offer has two advantages from the point of view of the target company's shareholders.

1. The price that they will receive is obvious. It is not like a share-for-share offer, where the movement in the market price will alter their wealth. A share-for-share offer increases the number of shares in the purchasing company, and the effect on the share price of the increase in the supply of shares on the market price is uncertain.
2. A cash purchase increases the liquidity of the selling shareholder who is then in a position to alter his or her investment portfolio to meet any changing opportunities.

If a shareholder receives shares, until steps are taken to sell these they will not be in a position to take advantage of other opportunities.

A disadvantage to individual shareholders in receiving cash is that if the price that they receive on sale is in excess of the price paid in purchasing the shares, they may be liable to capital gains tax. This would not be the case if they received shares in exchange. The receipt of cash brings the share transaction to an end, and so the tax assessment can be made. The exchange of one share for another does not bring the transaction to an end; capital gains tax does not arise until the exchanged share is sold.

If the individual shareholder receives cash for his shares then he is subject to capital gains tax on the increase in the amount that he receives for the share above the price that he originally paid. The first tranche of capital gain in any one tax year is free from taxation. However, for the large individual investor who has a large portfolio of shares many of the transactions in a year will incur tax on any capital gain. In addition, capital gains tax is payable at the taxpayer's marginal rate of income tax. This obviously reduces the acceptability of cash offers to such shareholders. The individual investor with only a small portfolio may be able to sell shares and avoid paying any capital gains tax. Thus a cash payment for his shares could be more attractive for him. However, small individual investors collectively have little control over large companies.

The Finance Act of 1982 introduced a scheme whereby the prices of shares would become index linked for capital gains purposes. This in effect means that only an increase above the rate of inflation in the share price is liable for capital gains tax when the shares are sold.

The tax position of institutional shareholders is very different from that of individual shareholders, with the result that cash offers are more attractive to the institutions. Prior to April 1980 investment trusts and unit trusts paid capital gains at a rate lower than the standard rate. Since April 1980 authorized unit and investment trusts have been exempt from capital gains tax. Authorized pension funds have always been exempt.

The taxation position is a critical factor is determining whether a shareholder in a takeover bid situation will accept a cash payment or will want a share exchange deal. A cash payment may embarrass an individual shareholder with a large capital gains tax bill. He would prefer a share-for-share exchange. However, a cash payment gives institutional investors the opportunity to reinvest their funds in any area they see as suitable. They could be attracted by a cash offer.

From the point of view of the bidding company's shareholders a cash offer has a number of advantages.

1. It represents a quick easily understood approach when resistance is expected. If it is reasonably priced it stands a fair chance of being successful.
2. A straight cash offer will not affect the equity of the bidding company. It is often important for the bidding company's shareholders that their control over their company is not diminished. However, the gearing position of the bidding company is almost certainly going to alter unless the takeover can be financed out of existing cash funds.

It can be important to the bidding company that it does not change the balance of the different types of shareholders that it has attracted. The shareholders are critical to the power and control that the directors possess. As an example, the character of a company which has many individual small shareholders who are loyal to the existing board may be changed if a takeover is completed with a share exchange deal. Such a deal may bring into the shareholders' ranks large institutional investors who may, in the end, carry more effective power than the numerous small investors. The board of the bidding company may therefore prefer to pay for the takeover in cash and maintain the status quo.

Borrowing to obtain cash

Of course with an acquisition of any size it is unlikely that a company will have enough cash available to be able to pay fully for the purchase by this method. It could also be unable to offer a cash alternative to a share price offer or able to rely on its own cash. In such situations the purchasing company will need to borrow or at least obtain a standby line of credit. To be able to do this depends to some extent on its pre-bid level of gearing. Does the purchasing company have enough borrowing capacity? Are its bankers and advisers willing to bring together a group of backers to guarantee that loans will be available if the bid is successful and if the selling shareholders choose the cash alternative that is offered to them?

In the 1980s leveraged takeovers became relatively common. These are discussed elsewhere in this chapter. They involve the purchasing company borrowing and obtaining much higher levels of gearing than are usually thought acceptable. The cash raised from the borrowing is used to finance the purchase. Usually the intention is to reduce the gearing levels to an acceptable level as quickly as possible following the acquisition. This is achieved by selling off some of the assets acquired.

The dangers of using borrowing to finance acquisitions was demonstrated in the UK in two similar cases in 1989. Both involved companies in the furniture industry and both in the end resulted in a need for a re-financing arrangement.

In 1989 interest rates rose to surprisingly high levels. The result was that, with the resulting rise in mortgage rates and the fall in activity in the housing market, sales of furniture and kitchen and bedroom goods dropped dramatically. The chairman of MFI, one of the companies that needed to re-finance, stated that 'management buyouts are risky. If we had not been in such a high leverage situation we would have ridden this out.' The company had borrowed £500 million at the end of 1987 to buy itself out from its then owner and to take over another company that supplied it with furniture. In 1989, with the higher interest rates, not only were consumers discouraged from buying MFI's goods but also the cost of financing the borrowings of the company increased dramatically. MFI realized that it would have to raise more money in order to pay the interest payments on its existing debts. The re-financing arrangement had to be agreed with the group's 40 bankers and with the original parents of the company, namely ASDA, who had retained a 25% equity stake at the time of the management buyout. The re-financing arrangement involved a £35 million rights issue and a £60 million deferral of debt payments. The City's reaction to the re-financing deal was that it was a good one from MFI's point of view. No penalties were inflicted and the interest margins remained unchanged. No shareholder refused to take up the rights issue, although some venture capital funds were unable to do so for technical reasons. The directors and managers involved in the buyout needed to subscribe extra funds to take up the rights issue offer.

The second re-financing deal was with Lowndes Queensway PLC. Again, the company's bankers did not increase the interest margin on the debt or charge high administrative fees. This deal also involved a rights issue. One of the covenants that the 20 banks in the lending syndicate had attached to loans to Lowndes prior to the restructuring was that 90% of any cash raised from asset disposals would belong to the banks. Clearly this was a way of helping to reduce the high levels of leverage if and when the assets acquired with the funds borrowed at the time of an acquisition were sold. Lowndes proposed to raise £40 million by the sale of assets. Under the terms of the covenants £36 million of this would be paid to the bankers to repay loans. Lowndes managed to re-negotiate with the bankers for an £18 million deferment of this repayment. This meant that upon selling the assets the bankers received only £18 million, leaving Lowndes with £22 million. There were various other aspects of the re-financing involving interest rate swaps and the use of 'caps' on the interest rates being paid. Lowndes' lenders also agreed to accept substantially weaker protective covenants with respect to the net asset ratios and net interest coverage than had been spelt out in the original loan documentation.

The world's largest takeover battle (as of the end of 1988) was for the purchase of the well-known RJR Nabisco, the US food and tobacco group, which was eventually sold by its shareholders for $25 billion to a private firm. Kohlberg, Kraves and Roberts (KKR), which was almost unknown outside financial circles but was a pioneer in arranging leveraged buyouts. It might be asked how a little-known private firm can finance such an acquisition. The answer is that it was backed by large international investing institutions who were prepared to lend it cash to financing the purchase of Nabisco shares. Therefore a comparatively small company, with only a small amount of equity, was able to purchase a huge company through high levels of borrowing. This is an extreme example of a leveraged buyout.

Why are (or were) banks prepared to lend large sums to a business with little equity backing? They do so because the loans are secured by the assets of the company that is to be purchased. If need be some of the assets of the acquired company can be sold to pay off the borrowing. This practice is called 'asset stripping'.

In fact KKR did not have an easy time with the acquisition. To begin with there was a danger that the managers of Nabisco would sell off some of the crown jewels before KKR could acquire ownership. Finally, having obtained acceptances to the offer from a sufficient number of Nabisco shareholders, KKR had difficulty in obtaining the necessary borrowings to complete the takeover. A political backlash was developing against such leveraged buyouts, and the size of the bid meant that more than 100 banks were needed to provide the finance. To 'encourage' banks to participate it was necessary to offer the banks very large fees. Banks who purchased the junk bonds being issued by KKR to finance the acquisition were being asked not to sell them for at least six months so as not to flood the secondary market with such paper.

Borrowing to finance acquisitions has proved to be very popular. High levels of gearing can be achieved at such times. However, as the above cases show, with a downturn in economic activity and looking at the worst-case situations, high levels of leverage can, as theory would indicate, turn out to be very risky.

Vendor placing and vendor rights

For a merger (as opposed to an acquisition) to take place, the shares in one company have to be exchanged for the shares in the other company. Sometimes, however, the shareholders in the company to be purchased do not want shares in the acquiring company; they want cash. This should mean that a merger is not possible, although an acquisition is.

The wording of the Accounting Standard on the subject provided a loophole: 'Merger accounting is considered to be an appropriate method of accounting when two groups of shareholders continue, or are in a position to continue, their shareholding as before but on a combined basis.'

The words 'or are in a position to' permitted a technique to develop whereby the selling shareholders (the vendors) could receive cash for their shares, but still be in a position to continue their shareholding as before. This is made possible by vendor placing and vendor rights. A share-for-share exchange takes place between the shareholders of the company being purchased and those of the acquiring company, but arrangements are made for the shares received by the vendor to be placed with institutional investors, if this is what the vendor wants. The shareholders in the company being acquired are therefore in a position to receive cash in payment for their shares in the acquired company. The scheme is usually set up by the acquiring company's merchant bank, which arranges for the shares to be placed with a third party. Merger accounting conditions have thereby been met, and the shareholders of the acquired company are in a position to continue their shareholding if they so wish; they do not have to sell for cash. If, however, they do not want to continue to be shareholders in the new merged business, they have a guarantee that they can sell their shares for cash at a price known by them.

Vendor rights are a variation on vendor placing. With vendor placing the shares received by those selling off their business are placed, usually with institutional shareholders. This means that the shares of the acquiring company can become widely dispersed. With vendor rights, if the shareholders of the target company do not want to retain the shares that they receive in consideration, then the acquiring company will again arrange through its brokers to have them placed. With this approach, however, the shares will first be offered to other shareholders of the acquiring company, who will have a right to buy them before they are placed with institutions. From the point of view of the acquiring company's shareholders, it is like a rights issue. But with vendor rights, the existing shareholders pay out cash not to the acquiring company but rather to those who were once shareholders of the company that has been purchased.

Share-for-share exchanges

One advantage of a share-for-share exchange has already been discussed, namely the effect of the relatively high price-to-earnings ratio of the bidding company on the earnings of the target company. Two other advantages of a share-for-share exchange, from the point of view of the shareholders of the target company, are as follows.

1. Capital gains tax is delayed.
2. The shareholders will still have a financial interest in the fortunes of the company that they have sold. They will still be able to share in any profits that are earned. They will normally have lost control of the company, but if they considered their original company a worthwhile investment and are not disillusioned with the managers of the purchasing company, they can still expect a satisfactory return.

The disadvantages to the purchasing company of an exchange of shares are as follows.

1. Equity shares are being issued, and this is a comparatively expensive form of capital.
2. Share exchange may reduce the gearing of the group company at the time of purchase. Whether it does so or not depends on the gearing of the acquired company. It may be possible to use the asset base acquired to increase the amount of borrowing, but this cannot be done immediately; it will take time. The position of the liabilities of the purchased company needs consideration. The financial obligations need to be settled, creditors will have to be paid and certain other liabilities will have to be satisfied. Bank overdrafts, debentures, and redeemable preference shares may have to be paid; whether there is an obligation to pay at the time of purchasing the company depends on the details of the particular agreements. If they do not have to be satisfied, and the purchasing company does not wish to end the arrangements, then this will affect the gearing of the group company.
3. The effect on the share price of the increase in the number of shares of the purchasing company is uncertain. If the share price falls or is expected to fall, this would have to be taken into account by the purchasing company in deciding whether the acquisition is advantageous to its own shareholders.
4. A share-for-share exchange deal causes a dilution in the power of the bidding company's original shareholders. Thus for the takeover bid to be popular with the bidding company's shareholders there needs to be clear evidence that the bid is for the long-term benefit of the company. The dilution of the equity will in some cases cause the bidding company's share price to fall. This is partly because, by offering its shares to others, there is a likelihood that soon after the acquisition or merger has been completed many of the bidding company's shares may come onto the market for sale. The law of supply and demand suggests that this will induce a tendency for the share price of the bidding firm to fall.

Perhaps one of the main advantages of share-for-share exchanges to the bidding company is that the initial cost of this method, from the point of view of cash flow, is comparatively small as no money passes to the shareholders of the company being taken over, although in the long run dividends have to be paid out to these additional shareholders. In the long run equity is the most expensive form of capital.

Debentures, loan stock and preference shares

Very few mergers today use debentures, loan stock or preference shares as methods of payment. The main problems with loan stock and debentures for the offeror are that firstly there is a difficulty in knowing at what rate to fix the interest payment to attract the shareholders of the target company. Secondly, at times of high interest rates, issuing a fixed-interest stock can be an expensive long-term commitment which in later years, if interest rates fall, will be unnecessarily onerous on the company.

Floating-rate loan stock is occasionally offered to the offeree shareholders, but it can be difficult to entice them to accept such a security. The shareholders would have the disadvantage of indefinite returns without the advantages of their stock's being marketable or having any voting power and so having influence in the way that the company is run.

Convertible loan stock is sometimes used in acquisitions. This gives the offeree the chance to have fixed interest payments for a given period and on the expiry of this period to decide whether to receive full ordinary shares in the bidding company. To the bidding company convertibles postpone the diluting of the equity.

The main advantage to the bidding company of using loan stock is that, unlike dividend payments, all interest payments made are tax deductible. If the offeror firm can persuade the target company's shareholders to accept loan stock for their shares then this would be a very satisfactory method of payment. The offeror does not have to offer any equity shares and, with the loans not having to be repaid until a date well in the future, has a much longer period of time to collect the finance together to pay for the takeover bid. During the period of life of the loan stock, the successful bidder will have the time to build up reserves to pay out on the redemption of the stock. Hopefully, the increased profits of the new larger organization will be the major contributor in the build-up of the capital redemption reserve fund.

Preference shares are used even less frequently than loan stock. The two main disadvantages of preference shares are firstly that the dividend payments are fixed (although in certain circumstances dividends can be postponed) but not tax deductible for the company and secondly that the preference shareholder has no voting power. It is thus unlikely that a shareholder in the offeree firm who has a significant voting block will be enticed to exchange his shares for preference shares in the offeror firm.

Earn-outs

This is one way of making it easier for the acquiring firm to pay for the acquired firm. The payment is satisfied in part by an initial payment and in part by subsequent payments that are dependent upon the future profit levels of the acquired business.

Such arrangements were particularly popular in the late 1980s. Saatchi & Saatchi made extensive use of them when acquiring other advertising companies.

The percentage of the total purchase price to be paid at the time of acquisition, and the target profit levels that need to be achieved are a matter of negotiation between the parties.

The advantages of this approach to financing an acquisition are as follows.

- It reduces the initial financial outlay.
- The total profits of the new subsidiary earned after acquisition can be added to those of the parent company even though the total purchase price has not been paid. This helps the profit to asset (capital employed) ratios.
- An earn-out encourages the management team (who own shares) of the acquired company to continue with enthusiasm. The overall purchase price received depends on future performance. In the advertising industry profitability depends very much on the performance of individuals. An acquisition is not the purchase of assets but of the skills of individuals. The same occurs in some other industries.
- It reduces the risks of the acquiring firm. They are less likely to be paying more than the purchased company is worth, because the price is limited by future performance.

Such earn-out agreements can be very complicated. The agreement has to consider all possible issues that can arise in order to avoid future problems. The formula for determining profit has to be agreed. Usually the total consideration is subject to a 'cap', an upper limit. This is necessary to protect the purchaser. Usually the earn-out period is between three and five years. This is not too long to expect key individuals to remain in the acquired firm.

When Saatchi & Saatchi acquired the Rowland Company in 1985, the purchase price was ten times the average of Rowland's annual after-tax earnings in the five years to the end of 1989. This included a down-payment of $10 million in cash. Rowlands was one of the largest public relations firms in the USA.

When Saatchi & Saatchi acquired the Hay Group in 1984, the considerations paid included a cash payment of $100 million, with an additional payment of $25 million payable on condition that the group achieved average pre-tax profits of at least $21.5 million for the three years to 1987, the pre-tax profits in the year they were taken over being $12.1 million. The Hay Group was at the time the world's largest management consultancy organization.

Junk bonds

In the USA junk bonds have been issued to enable smaller companies to purchase larger companies. The smaller company uses the bonds to raise cash in the market-place. The cash is used to purchase the larger company. As a result of issuing these bonds, the acquiring company finishes up with a very high level of gearing. It often plans to sell off some of the assets that it has acquired to repay the cash that it has borrowed.

In fact the junk bond market in the USA became discredited in 1988. The leading investment banker in the US junk bond market, Drexel Burnham and Lambert, got into considerable trouble. In 1988 they agreed to pay the US government $650 million to avoid criminal and racketeering charges. In the settlement, the bank admitted insider dealing, stock manipulation, parking of bonds and shares in outside accounts to conceal true ownership and keeping false records. The individual at the bank most closely identified with junk bonds, Michael Milken, personally received a criminal indictment on the same charges. It is alleged that he directed an enormous conspiracy centred on the junk bond market. Milken and his associates personally traded heavily in junk bonds.

Of course, whether a merger or acquisition is a success or not depends on the circumstances of each case. It is one thing to have the conditions for synergy to arise; it is quite another to manage the enlarged organization to deliver the extra returns.

All mergers and acquisitions are portrayed at the time they take place as being good for the shareholders involved and for the economy in general. Presumably the directors involved would not be proposing the new acquisition if they did not believe it to be beneficial to them. It is surprising therefore that studies show that on average, mergers and acquisitions do not result in higher profits or greater efficiency. It is one thing to talk of synergy and economies of scale, it is another thing to deliver.

A large amount of research has been undertaken in the attempt to prove or disprove the existence of economies of scale. Theoretically there are economies of production, marketing, research and finance. Economies should mean that the larger the organization, the lower are the unit costs and the greater the proportional returns. The reasons put forward to justify many mergers can be interpreted as attempts to obtain increased economies of scale. However, there is no automatic reason why economies should emerge when two companies are brought together. There may be possible advantages from large-scale operation, but this does not mean that all large organizations can achieve them.

Synergy does not automatically arise. The success of the merger or takeover depends upon the management's ability to take advantage of opportunities to realize the potential economies. The type of acquisition is one factor determining the success or failure of an acquisition. Research into post-merger performance emphasizes the fact that success depends on planning and management. Profits are not produced by machinery, buildings or products. It is people who give life to these otherwise dormant assets. The key to the success of a merger or takeover turns out to be the amount of thought and planning that has gone into it and the ability of the people involved.

Diversification typically leads to basic changes in the nature of a firm's management problems. The firm may move into product areas where the research, design and production technologies may be quite new, and where the marketing, financial and economic problems involved may differ significantly from those encountered previously. Therefore, diversification often brings on substantial extra costs and financial risks, and for that reason should not be undertaken unless the firm has carefully analysed the motives for diversification and proceeds only after it has carefully reviewed opportunities.

It is in fact very difficult to decide whether a merger or takeover results in gains for the parties involved. In fact any such attempt to determine gains or losses depends on assumptions. It depends on the assumption of what would have happened if the firms involved had not come together. Nobody knows this.

It is hard to predict which mergers and acquisitions will be successful and which will not. It is hard to determine which parties will gain and which will lose. Success clearly depends on a number of factors including the following.

- The price paid for the acquisition. If the price is 'too' high, it will be hard for the acquiring shareholders to obtain gains. On the other hand the selling shareholders will benefit.
- The quality of the management and their capacity to take on extra work. Bringing two companies together takes time and means less time is available for other duties.
- The objectives of the merger or acquisition.

As has been mentioned a number of times in this chapter, there are a number of motives for a merger. There are the motives based on the concept of shareholder wealth maximization and motives based on managerial goals. Consequently, if a company is taken over because the directors of the acquiring company wish to run a particular prestigious enterprise, with a high public profile, it does not mean that the shareholders of the acquiring company will necessarily benefit.

We shall consider the evidence as to who in fact does gain from mergers and acquisitions. The interested parties, any one or more of which could gain (or lose), are as follows: the economy – a social gain; shareholders of the bidding firm; shareholders of the target firm; directors of the bidding firm; directors of the target firm; employees of the two firms; the financial institutions involved in the acquisition.

The position of each of these interest groups will now be considered.

The economy – a social gain

There have been numerous studies of mergers and takeovers in the UK which attempt to ascertain their economic impact. As long ago as 1969 the Monopolies Commission concluded that, on the evidence that they had seen, the effect of mergers and takeovers on the economy was at best neutral [10]. In another study into the takeovers and mergers that took place in the period 1954–60, Singh [11] concluded that it is on balance very unlikely that the reshuffling of economic resources which takes place as a result of the takeover process leads to any more profitable utilization of these resources. The weight of evidence indicates that the takeover process is at best neutral in this respect. This conclusion relates to the economy-wide effects of mergers and takeovers.

Other studies show that mergers and takeovers seldom live up the expectations expressed at the time that the companies come together. The true motives for mergers are often to be found outside economics, and yet the statements made at the time of a merger or takeover usually seek to justify it in economic terms. Firth [12] found that the gains to some parties in the transaction were equally offset by the losses of the others. A similar conclusion was reached in a very detailed study by Cowling *et al.* [13]. These researchers attempted to determine whether the increased efficiency resulting from the economies of scale and improved management compensated for the consumer welfare loss resulting from the increased concentration. They saw the issue as one of cost–benefit analysis: comparison of the costs in the form of increased monopoly power with the gains in the form of increased efficiency. The only way to attempt such analysis is through detailed case studies, and consequently they investigated a large number of cases of acquisitions in the engineering and other manufacturing industries. They concluded that it is difficult to sustain the view that merger is a necessary or sufficient condition for efficiency gains. In many cases efficiency has not improved above the increase that could have been expected if the firms had not merged. They found that many mergers in the UK have been horizontal and have therefore resulted in an increase in the degree of monopoly. On balance, therefore, given the low level of efficiency gains realized relative to what could have been expected and the potential social costs generated by increased market power and the lack of any other benefits, they believe that the evidence argues against mergers and acquisitions, especially those that result in the creation of very large firms. Of course, they did find that some mergers had resulted in social gains; they are simply stating that on balance, taking the good acquisitions with the bad, it is not the economy that gains.

To assess the overall impact of a merger upon the economy involves comparing the merger-related efficiency gains with society's losses arising from increases in market power. This involves trading off the potential gains against the potential losses, which are not easy variables to measure.

In a recent review of the US research on the subject Lev [14] concludes that 'there is no study I know of that found a strong, statistically significant increase in profitability due to acquisition'. He failed to find on balance any empirical support for the classical economic model that mergers and acquisitions are undertaken to maximize economic value. Of course, to repeat, some mergers are successful and undoubtedly some participants do benefit from mergers; we are referring now to the overall impact on the economy – the effect on producers and consumers.

Society could benefit from acquisitions if they were a way of removing assets from the control of less efficient managers and putting them in the hands of more efficient managers, and then passing on these benefits to consumers. However, we do not have clear evidence that the market for corporate control and the laws of competition are functioning well enough to ensure that this happens. This neutral conclusion should not be a surprise, for it should be remembered that not all the motives for mergers and acquisitions are based on overall economic gains.

Even though there are no overall gains to the economy, a takeover can result in some parties gaining and others losing. The size of the cake might not increase, but some parties will obtain a larger share at someone else's expense. The stock market may be efficient in responding rapidly to information that becomes available, but there is plenty of opportunity for investors to make gains out of takeovers and mergers. Differences of opinion and not just the identification of opportunities for increasing efficiency, can lead to a takeover. Therefore mergers and takeovers can result in some parties winning and some losing, without overall gains to the economy.

Let us now consider who does benefit.

Shareholders of the firms involved

The first problem to consider is how to evaluate the effect of a merger or acquisition on the wealth of an individual shareholder. We shall first consider the case of the shareholder of the victim firm. We can observe the pre-bid price and the price at which the share is sold to the bidding firm. The difference represents the gain or loss resulting from the bid. However, it can be argued that we do not know what would have happened to the value of that share if the victim company had not been acquired.

Empirical studies on shareholders' gains or losses usually base their calculations on the share price a certain period before the bid (and rumour of the bid) and the price following the first public announcement of the offer. We know that, if the bid is eventually unsuccessful, the target firm's share price will usually fall from this post-bid price. The shareholders of the target firm who do not sell to the bidder might not actually receive the potential gain, but they did have the opportunity.

It might be argued that the post-announcement price is not the correct measure because the target firm's share price might rise in the period following the first announcement of the offer. This might well happen if there are competing bids or the same bidder comes back with higher offers. However, the theory of modern finance indicates that the target firm's share price should adjust at the time of the first offer to reflect the probability of higher competing bids. In some cases the market anticipates correctly and in other cases it does not, but on average this post-bid market price is the correct measure if the market is efficient with respect to pricing. The share price used to measure gains or losses, the post-announcement price, should reflect the market's unbiased assessment of the outcome of the bid.

The same theory can be used to counter the argument of those who say that we need to wait a number of years to see how successful the merger turns out to be before we can measure the long-term gain or loss of the participating shareholders. This is not necessarily the case. From the point of view of the shareholders of the victim firm, they undoubtedly had the opportunity at the time of the bid to receive cash or shares which could be converted to cash, and so a gain or loss can be established at that time.

From the point to view of the bidding shareholders, the share price immediately following the bid will reflect the expected value of the acquisition. It is possible that, with hindsight, the market's initial response will not turn out to be correct, but with an efficient market we would not expect it to overestimate the future returns any more than underestimate them. The price change immediately following the announcement of the bid is therefore a good estimate of the future economic consequences of the takeover for the shareholders of the bidding firm. Therefore we can use this short-term price change to determine whether the shareholders can be expected to gain or lose in the long run as a result of the merger.

Shareholders of the bidding firm

The evidence of the effects of acquisition on the shareholders of bidding firms is inconclusive. The results are conflicting, with studies showing the average abnormal returns to the shareholders of bidding firms ranging from small to close to zero.

A study into the position in the breweries and distilleries industry in the UK between 1955 and 1972 found that on average the shareholders of the victim firm gained 26% over the three month period prior to the announcement of the acquisition [15]. The bidding shareholders gained 2.5% over this period. In the study the gains were adjusted to allow for general price movements in the stock market. The above figures relate to gains over and above the general market movements.

The numerous US studies on this subject up to 1982 have been summarized by Jensen and Ruback [8]. They show average above normal percentage share price gains of 30% to the target shareholders associated with a successful takeover bid, whereas the gains to the bidding company shareholders are only 4%. The calculation of the above normal price changes are the result of adjustments made to the actual price change that occurred in order to be able to eliminate the effects of market-wide price changes. The authors differentiated between takeovers and mergers, with the latter being defined as where negotiations take place between the two sets of directors before going to a vote of target shareholders for approval. Jensen and Ruback's results, which come from analysing the numerous studies on the subject, are shown in Tables 24.3 and 24.4.

Clearly, one group that gains from a successful takeover bid is the victim shareholders, as these are the target shareholders in the acquisitions that are successful. The figures in Tables 24.3 and 24.4 illustrate a dilemma for the directors of the target company. If they fight the takeover bid successfully, they are not benefiting their own

Table 24.3 *Abnormal percentage share price change associated with successful company acquisitions*

	Target shareholders (%)	Bidder's shareholders (%)
Takeovers	30	4
Mergers	20	0

Table 24.4 *Abnormal percentage share price change associated with unsuccessful takeover bids*

	Target shareholders (%)	Bidder's shareholders (%)
Takeovers	−3	−1
Mergers	−3	−5

shareholders. It may benefit the directors to remain independent, but it would not seem to benefit their shareholders. Clearly, they should try to obtain the best possible price for their shareholders, and this might mean recommending rejection of the first bid, with the hope that the bidding firm will come back with an improved offer. They have to be careful, however, that they act in their shareholders' interests and not their own. To recommend to their shareholders that they accept the first bid might help their own employment prospects, but not their shareholders' wealth. To put up some fight, but eventually lose, will benefit their shareholders but not them. This takes us back to the earlier section of the chapter, where the managerial explanation of takeovers was discussed.

Often the share price of the bidding firm declines following the announcement of a proposed acquisition. This has been found to be the case in the USA with over 40% of the bidding companies' shares. There can therefore be initial negative returns to bidding shareholders; this results from the market's not seeing the proposed merger or acquisition as being in the interests of this group. Indeed, Dodd [16] has shown that this decline in share price can begin before the public announcement of the bid, with even the insiders not seeing the bid as being in the best interests of the bidding company stockholders. The problem could well be that the acquiring firms are on average having to pay too high a premium in order to complete the acquisition.

Shareholders of the victim firm

The bidding firms almost always have to offer a premium to the shareholders of the victim firm. This clearly leads to a gain to the shareholders of the target firm. Indeed, the empirical evidence on this fact is quite consistent. Reference to some of it has been made above. The price of the target shares usually rises dramatically even on the basis of rumours of an intended bid. Mandelker [17] examined a number of mergers in the USA and found that large gains were made, in terms of share price increases, during the eight month period up to the announcement date of the acquisition. The shareholders of the victim firm gained on average 18% over this period, and the shareholders of the bidding firm gained 3.5%.

The studies by Jensen and Ruback [8] and by Dodd [16] came up with another interesting result. They showed that over medium to longer periods of time leading up to the bid, on average the shares of the target firms had shown abnormal negative returns. These firms had not performed as well as the average market performance. In contrast, the shares of the bidding firms had shown above average performance. *A priori*, therefore, one group of managers had not demonstrated that they could use their assets to achieve normal levels of profitability whereas the others had. Therefore, in supporting the bids, the market is transferring assets from situations which they see at the time as being less profitable to those that are more profitable.

Overall, even though the shareholders of the bidding firm on average experience little if any gains in share price resulting from the merger or acquisition, the overall impact is an increase in the wealth of shareholders. In the typical merger, the total losses to the bidding firm's shareholders are less than the gains to the target firm's shareholders.

It has to be remembered that many big institutional shareholders own shares in both the acquiring firm and the victim firm. They may therefore be happy to lose on the shares in the acquiring firm and take gains on shares in the victim firm. The gains on the one outweigh the losses on the other.

It is perhaps not surprising that in percentage terms target company shareholders do better than bidding company shareholders. Apart from the obvious point of having to pitch the offer above current market value, on average bidders tend to be larger than targets. Hence benefits by bidders have to be shared between more shareholders with a larger capital base. If a company valued at, say, £100 million takes over a company valued at £10 million creating synergy of £6 million, and the target is acquired for £13 million a gain of 30% is made. However, if the acquiring company's share price reflects the expected benefits, a gain of only 3% will be shown.

Directors of the bidding firm

It seems to be generally agreed that the directors of an acquiring company gain from a successful acquisition policy. They receive increased status and power from running a larger business, and there is evidence that at the same time they receive increased financial rewards.

There are financial incentives to managers who have little or no ownership interest in a company to pursue rapid growth, possibly at the expense of profitability. This could explain the desire to grow through acquisition rather than through organic growth.

Directors of the victim firm

There is a need for research on this topic. The folklore of the subject is that the directors of the victim company lose. They are likely to be dismissed from their jobs, either because they are judged to be inefficient or because they have fought the acquisition and so cost the bidding firm a lot of money. This is the overall impression, but of course there are exceptions. A number of managing directors of larger firms have come into those firms as a result of being a director of a victim firm.

Employees

Again, more research is needed. Often, however, a number of the employees of the victim firm will lose. Following the takeover certain parts of the victim firm might well be closed down with resulting redundancies. Sometimes assurances are given during a takeover battle that redundancies will not follow the acquisition.

However, if the situation is looked at when the excitement of the battle is over it will often be found that, despite the assurances, redundancies have followed. In fact, in many cases, it is the employees of the target firm who are anxious to fight the takeover bid, as they realize that they have much to lose. But it must be recognized that in order for a merger or takeover to be a financial success it may be necessary to create redundancies. There could be duplication of functions and processes within the combined business. It could be that the victim firm had more employees than was necessary, and it was this inefficiency that had made them a takeover target.

Financial institutions

One group who certainly benefit from takeovers and mergers are the financial institutions – the merchant bankers, the financial public relations firms and other City institutions involved in the negotiations and any resulting battles. These professionals have to be used both by the bidding firm and the target firm. Their expertise is considerable, and there is no hope of being successful either in bidding or in defending unless good advice is obtained. Of course the fees of these professionals have to be paid whether or not their advice leads to success.

A company's merchant banker is involved with mergers and takeovers in a number of ways.

1. Merger broking: they can advise companies on likely target companies. They have lists of companies who wish to be purchased and they will help to find suitable target companies to purchase if a company wishing to expand is looking for opportunities to diversify.
2. They can help to plan an acquisition, giving advice on the value of the company and the 'best' tactics to be followed either with an agreed merger or a takeover bid.
3. Defence: they will advise target companies on the 'best' ways to resist a takeover bid.
4. Merchant banks buy and sell shares of companies as part of their normal activities. However, they are not supposed to buy and sell shares of companies which they are advising clients to buy. There is an interesting question as to how far they, and/or other banks with which they are involved, should go in purchasing their clients' shares to support the price during the bid. We shall return to this point in the next section where the Guinness–Distillers case is discussed.

A merchant bank is not just expected to give advice; often it is expected to assist with the provision of finance. If they are advising on a defence that involves a financial restructuring, they could be expected to make loans and organize other banks to make loans to increase the level of gearing. If they are working with the bidding company, again they could be expected to make loans available, this time to provide the cash to purchase the shares.

In every takeover battle one group of advisors wins and another group loses. One banker might be advising a bidding firm in one takeover battle and advising a target firm in another. They all win some and lose some. The costs of a takeover battle are considerable and have to be paid by the companies involved. The more spectacular battles involve large amounts of advertising expenditure and costs of preparing and circulating many circulars. Undoubtedly financial institutions gain from a lively takeover and merger scene.

In general therefore we have identified three groups who gain from mergers and takeovers and two groups who lose. The winners in successful acquisitions are the victim shareholders, the bidding directors and the financial institutions. The losers are the directors and employees of the victim firms. The position of society and the bidding company shareholders seems on balance to be neutral – with some acquisitions they win, and with others they lose. Of course, these are generalizations, but they do give some clue as to why the motives involved in mergers and takeovers are so complex.

Strategic alliances

Companies can of course work together without merging or without one acquiring another. A strategic alliance is an arrangement between two or more companies for their mutual benefit. An alliance might be formed in order to exploit new markets, to share new ideas or technology or to cut costs of production or research. The alliance could result in a joint venture or companies becoming associates. An alliance falls short of one company becoming a subsidiary of the other; it is an alternative to a merger or acquisition.

Such alliances have become popular amongst medium-sized firms. The firms may wish to enter into global markets but the costs of doing so are too great for each individual firm. They have also proved useful in overcoming political barriers when governments restrict foreign ownership in certain activities to a certain level. A local partner is found for the joint venture.

The terms of the alliance will need to be negotiated and will vary from case to case. The issues to be considered include:

- how much each party is to invest in the joint venture, and the form the investment will take;
- the balance of risk and reward for the parties: how will profits be shared? what happens if there is a loss?;
- the roles and responsibilities of each party;
- the mechanism for developing future policy, and for the taking advantage of future opportunities;
- the mechanism for dealing with disputes.

Alliances between companies in different countries can be particularly complex and the taxation issues need to be considered, as do the possible differences in management style. Cultural differences can be important and lead to future difficulties if not properly understood.

The most common legal form for two companies working together is a joint venture, although it could be a partnership.

From an accounting point of view it has been proposed that joint ventures should be treated in the same way as associate companies. This means that the equity method is employed if the joint venture is a company, and the proportional consolidation method used if it is a partnership. This means that the appropriate percentage share of the profits/losses and of the net assets are brought into the consolidated accounts of each of the investing companies.

If Company S has a 45% interest in a joint venture, then 45% of the profits and net assets of the joint venture are brought into the accounts of company S. This is obviously one way of reflecting the financial results of the interest in the strategic alliance.

This method has been referred to as 'one-line consolidation'. The profits of the joint venture appear as one line in the profit and loss account, and the net assets as one line in the balance sheet. Full consolidation would not be appropriate as the investing company does not control the joint venture. (If it did so it would not be a joint venture, but a subsidiary.)

Proportional consolidation, in which the percentage ownership of each asset and each liability in the joint venture is added to each asset and each liability of the investing company, has been judged to be inappropriate. It is felt to be misleading to add assets together in this way when control is not exercised.

The criticism of accounting for joint ventures by the equity method is that the information provided to the shareholders of the investing company is very limited.

Companies working together can result in either

1. a subsidiary company;
2. a joint venture;
3. a strategic alliance;
4. a strategic minority stake. This is an agreement to purchase and maintain a minority shareholding in another company, which it is thought will be useful. The benefits could be future business passing between the two companies or an exchange of technology.

Honda had a minority shareholding in the Rover Car Company, before Rover was sold to BMW. Honda were happy with a strategic minority stake in Rover, which resulted in an exchange of technology and shared production. For strategic reasons Honda did not want such a link with BMW, and so sold their shareholding when the majority holding in Rover was sold by British Aerospace to the German car manufacturer.

Economic interest groups (EIGs)

One form of strategic alliance that has been encouraged by the European Union is an EIG. This is a form of business venture similar to a partnership. Two or more firms agree to work together for a particular purpose.

The situations in which it might be advantageous to form such a group include:

- to combine research and development activities;
- to form a joint selling or distribution network;
- to tender for a major public works contract.

The first official EIG came into operation in 1989, although there is a history of such groups existing in Europe before this date. These European EIGs are designed to benefit the smaller sized firms. The EIG itself must not employ more than 500 people, although of course the member companies forming the partnership can be bigger than this.

The profits of the EIG are divided between the participating firms according to an agreed formula. The members act collectively in making decisions.

The takeover boom of the 1960s was brought to an end partly as a result of disillusionment. The tactics adopted to win by Jim Slater and others caused a reaction. A similar wave of criticism arose in the late 1980s, when it became known that the success of the US takeover star Ivan Boesky was based on breaching the law. Concern about takeover activities arose in the UK at the same time when the practices that the directors of Guinness had adopted in order to acquire Distillers became known – a scandal developed.

Ernest Saunders became Managing Director of Guinness in 1981. The company had not been doing well; the sales of the company had been falling, and its share of the British beer market had halved in ten years. Its profits had fallen for three consecutive years. Saunders transformed Guinness. When he took over the management the capital value of the company was £90 million. He moved quickly. In the first two years he spent £500 million on acquisitions. In the summer of 1985 he made a successful takeover bid for Bells, the scotch whisky company, paying £340 million. The takeover was referred to by *The Economist* as one of the best-planned deals of the year. The takeover battle was vicious. A white knight was brought in as a defence by Bells, but in the end the Guinness team won easily.

Also in 1985 Sir James Gulliver of Argyll Food made a £1.9 billion bid for Distillers, a company which had a reputation as being a conservatively managed company, a sleeping giant. At the time it was the largest bid that had been made in the UK. Argyll's market value at the time that the bid was made was £0.7 billion. Gulliver had spent a long time carefully analysing Distillers, working out tactics and seeking supporters. Gulliver (as did Saunders in connection with the Bell bid) made a great effort to convince the Scottish establishment that he was worthy to run a leading Scottish enterprise. It was proposed that one-third of the acquisition price would be paid for in cash financed by a loan and two-thirds would be paid for by equity shares in Argyll. If Distillers shareholders had accepted the bid they would have finished up owning more shares in the enlarged Argyll Food than those held by the Argyll shareholders at the date of the bid.

Distillers' board decided to fight the Argyll takeover; one of the tactics that they adopted was to find a white knight, namely Guinness led by Ernest Saunders. Initially, Saunders did not intend to make a full-scale offer for Distillers; he intended to form a new holding company to which both companies would belong. In 1985 Guinness had to pay the considerable cost of taking over Bells. If they were to bid for Distillers and lose, it was estimated that it would cost them another £50 million. The pre-tax profits of Guinness were only £80 million. If Distillers wanted Guinness to bid as a white knight, they would have to cover the costs of the bid. Therefore it was proposed that Distillers would cover Guinness's costs. This was a new type of arrangement, and Distillers' board agreed to it. In agreeing to this arrangement, Distillers were in fact introducing a 'poison pill', making them less attractive to a suitor. If Argyll were successful in the takeover, they would have to cover their own costs and Distillers' defence costs which included Guinness's costs. It was estimated by Sir James Gulliver that the total cost of the bid, if it were successful, would be £160–£170 million, making it a very expensive takeover.

Before agreeing to act as a white knight Guinness made a further demand, which has been referred to as a 'crown jewel lock-up'. Guinness could not be sure that it could defeat Argyll. If it did not, it wanted something for its services. It was therefore proposed that part of the Distillers business, that concerned with the sale of brandy, would be sold to Guinness at a bargain price whether they were successful in the bid or not. In the end Distillers did not agree to this. There was a limit to how much they would pay to obtain a white knight. Many members of the Distillers board were unhappy with the idea that this once great company was now having to rely on a company half its size to protect its future.

Guinness made a bid for Distillers, offering £0.35 billion above the Argyll bid of £1.89 billion. There was still talk of a joint group and questions of who would be its chief executive. Argyll's first action in trying to fight off the rival bid was to attempt to have it referred to the Monopolies Commission. Argyll also raised the value of its bid to £2.3 billion. This raised the value of Distillers to double its pre-bid value. The Office of Fair Trading referred the bid to the Monopolies Commission. However, Saunders could not wait the months that it would take for the Commission to decide – it would mean that Argyll would have won.

Saunders came up with a strategy to withdraw the first bid and make a second one. The second bid would avoid the monopoly problem by agreeing to sell off some of Distillers and Bells brands if the bid was successful. This would reduce the share of the new group's brands in each part of the market to about 25% so that it would not have a dominant position. This was a similar solution to that proposed by United Biscuits in its bid for Imperial Group. These approaches introduced a new element into takeover tactics in the UK. A legal dispute followed as to whether the revised Guinness bid was permissible. The case went to the Court of Appeal. The repackaged bid was found acceptable and allowed to proceed.

The battle for Distillers then moved to the stock market, but it later became apparent that the contest was not exactly fair. Morgan Grenfell, one of the merchant bankers working for Guinness, purchased £70 million of shares on its own account in Distillers. The scale of this activity was surprising; even more so was the fact that Guinness indemnified Morgan Grenfell against any loss on this purchase. If the bid was successful Morgan Grenfell would buy brands from Distillers and Guinness to help them avoid the monopoly problem. They were taking similar steps to help United Biscuits in their bid for Imperial. The Bank of England criticized the merchant bank for adopting this practice and introduced new rules to prevent it happening again in the future. It limited the extent to which banks could use their capital to assist the takeover activities of their clients.

The price of Guinness's shares began to rise. A support operation was being organized to push up the price of Guinness's shares. Individuals and institutions were being encouraged to purchase the shares. This was not illegal; it had happened in other takeover situations. It is not against the takeover code. Argyll was encouraging its supporters to do the same thing. It just seemed that Guinness was being more successful. Although the Argyll cash offer was higher – £6.30 per Distillers share as against a £6.00 offer from Guinness – the rising price of the Guinness shares meant that at the close of the bid its equity offer was 50p higher than that of Argyll.

Guinness and their supporters were creating the demand for the Guinness shares. This was part of a normal attacking policy. The problem was that Guinness, determined to win, broke the accepted rules. Gerald Ronson, the wealthy owner of Heron International, invested £25 million in Guinness shares. The trouble was that Guinness agreed to cover Ronson against any loss that he would suffer if the Guinness shares fell in price. They also agreed that in the event of the bid being successful he would receive a fee of £5 million. The fee was for the help given, although he was not in fact risking anything. Later, when the scandal about the activities of Guinness came to light Ronson returned £5.8 million to Guinness; the £5 million fee plus £0.8 million he had received as compensation for the loss in share value. He expressed regret at being involved in the support of Guinness shares. It later transpired that a number of other people received large fees for assisting Guinness. A subsidiary of S. & W. Berisford, commodity dealers, received a fee in the region of £1.5 million for 'work in connection with the acquisition of Distillers'. A £5.2 million fee was paid to a Jersey-based consulting firm.

All the support worked. Around the crucial time when decisions needed to be made, the Argyll share price showed only a little movement, but Guinness shares climbed from 281p to reach a peak of 353p at the climax of the bid. Guinness took over Distillers in April 1986. The share price fell back to 280p later in 1986.

When the extent of the support operation was eventually exposed, Guinness had paid invoices totalling over £25 million that were not easily explained. It was estimated that Guinness had used about £200 million of its own money to support its share price. Much of this was paid as fees to 'advisers' that Guinness used and to those who 'supported' the bid. There is also the suggestion that Guinness indirectly used its own money to buy its shares. Bank Leu in Switzerland held £50 million of Guinness money on deposit, and it also held 5% of Guinness shares. Had Guinness money been used to buy the shares? The bank was also a large purchaser of Distillers shares in its own right. Even Ivan Boesky was involved. He purchased shares in Distillers. At one time he offered to sell these to Argyll. Of course, this was part of his normal greenmail activity. He would deal with whoever offered him the highest price. Argyll was not interested. Boesky later bought more Distillers shares, as well as Guinness shares. In turn, Guinness invested just under $100 million in one of the Boesky's funds. This of course only came to light later.

A month after Guinness took over Distillers the troubles began to emerge. Sanders decided to appoint himself as Chairman and Chief Executive, in doing so upsetting a number of the other directors of the group and a number of banks and advisers who had helped him with the bid. The Boesky affair broke in the USA. The Department of Trade and Industry sent inspectors into Guinness to investigate the Distillers bid. Saunders explained that the reason for the investment in Boesky's operations was not to support the Distillers bid but to obtain his support for a future Guinness bid which would be in the USA. A number of Saunders' close advisers and directors of Guinness resigned and insisted that Saunders knew of the arrangements that had been made to support the share price. Saunders denied any knowledge of wrongdoing.

Saunders and certain associates were tried on a number of technical issues. They were found guilty on a number of charges and given short prison sentences.

24.9 Key terms

Acquisition
Arbitrageurs
Bootstrapping
Cash bids
City Code
Combination
Concert parties
Crown jewels
Earn-outs
Economic interest groups
Economies of scale
Free cash flow
Golden parachutes

Greenmail
Joint ventures
Market for corporate control
Market raids
Merger
Monopolies Commission
Poison pills
Risk diversification
Strategic alliances
Synergy
Takeover
Trapped equity
Vendor placing

24.10 Revision questions

1. What is the difference between a merger and a takeover?
2. Why are there waves of takeover activity? Why is there more activity in the market for corporate control in some periods than in others?
3. 'The management motives for acquisition are more important than economic reasons.' Discuss.
4. 'If the stock market is efficient it does not make sense to refer to the shares of a company as being undervalued, and so being a good buy.' Discuss.
5. If shareholders want to diversify against risk, they can do so themselves and so they do not need the companies in which they hold shares to diversify for them.' Discuss.
6. The City Code on Mergers and Takeovers only responds after the event. It has not been effective in eliminating unfair practices.' Discuss.
7. What are concert parties?
8. What are the advantages and disadvantages of a cash offer as opposed to a share-for-share exchange?
9. What defensive tactics can you suggest for a small company that has just received a bid from a large multinational firm?
10. Who wins in a merger and takeover?
11. What can a firm do to make itself less likely to receive a takeover bid?
12. What effect does an acquisition have on the debenture holders of the firm acquired?
13. What are the accounting differences between a merger and a takeover?

24.11 References

1. Accounting Standards Board (1994) *FR6, Acquisitions and Mergers*.
2. Marris, R. (1964) *The Economic Theory of Managerial Capitalism*, Macmillan, London.
   Gort, M. (1969) An economic disturbance theory of mergers, *Quarterly Journal of Economics*, November.
3. Jensen, M.C. (1986) Agency costs of free cash flow, corporate finance and takeovers, *American Economic Review, Papers and Proceedings*, May, 323–9.
4. King, M. (1989) Takeover activity in the UK. In *Mergers and Merger Policy* (eds J. Fairburn and J. Kay), Oxford University Press, Oxford.
5. Dimson, E. and Marsh, P. (1984) An analysis of brokers' and analysts' unpublished forecasts of UK stock returns, *Journal of Finance*, **39** (5), 1257–92, December.
   Elton, E., Gruber, M. and Kleindorfer, P. A close look at the implications of the stable Paretian hypotheses, *Review of Economics and Statistics*, **57** (2), 231–5, May.
6. Galai, D. and Masulis, R.W. (1976) The option pricing model and the risk factor of stock, *Journal of Financial Economics*, **3**, 53–81.
7. Stapleton, R.C. (1982) Mergers, debt capacity, and the valuation of corporate loans. In *Mergers and Acquisitions* (eds M. Keenan and L.J. White), Chapter 2, D.C. Heath, Lexington, MA.
8. Jensen, M.C. and Ruback, R.S. (1983) The market for corporate control, the scientific evidence, *Journal of Financial Economics*, April.
9. Takeover Activity in the 1980s (1989). *Bank of England Quarterly*, **29** (1).
10. Monopolies and Mergers Commission (1969) *Report on the Proposed Merger of Unilever Ltd and Allied Breweries Ltd*, HMSO, London.
    Monopolies and Mergers Commission (1969) *Report on the Proposed Acquisition of De La Rue Ltd by the Rank Organisation*, HMSO, London.
11. Singh, A. (1971) *Takeovers*, Cambridge University Press, Cambridge.
12. Firth, M. (1980) Takeovers, shareholders' returns and the theory of the firm, *Quarterly Journal of Economics*, March.
13. Cowling, K., Stoneman, P., Cubbin, J. *et al.* (1980) Cambridge University Press, Cambridge.
14. Lev. B. (1986) Observations on the merger phenomenon. In *The Revolution in Corporate Finance* (eds J.M. Stern and D.H. Chew), Basil Blackwell, Oxford.

15. Franks, J.R., Broyles, J.E. and Hecht, M.J. (1977) An industry study of the profitability of mergers in the United Kingdom, *Journal of Finance*, 1513–25.
16. Dodd, P. (1986) The market for corporate control: A review of the evidence. In *The Revolution in Corporate Finance* (eds J.M. Stern and D.M. Chew), Basil Blackwell, Oxford.
17. Mandelker, G. Risk and return: the case of merging firms. *Journal of Financial Economics*, **1**, 303–35.

24.12 Further reading

Two books dealing with mergers in the UK are:
Cooke, T.E. (1988) *International Mergers and Acquisitions*, Basil Blackwell.
Fairburn, J. and King, J.A. (eds) (1989) *Mergers and Merger Policy*. Oxford University Press.
An interesting article summarizing the takeover activity in the UK is:
Bank of England Quarterly (1989) Takeover Activity in the 1980s, **29** (1).

A special edition of the *Journal of Financial Economics*, April 1983 dealt with many aspects of mergers and takeovers, and included the review article by M.C. Jensen and R.S. Ruback entitled:
The Market for Corporate Control, the Scientific Evidence.

Other significant publications include:
Cowling, K., Stoneman, P. and Cubbin, J. *et al.* (1980) *Mergers and Economic Performance*, Cambridge University Press.
Dodd, P. The Market for Corporate Control: A Review of the Evidence, in *The Revolution in Corporate Finance, op. cit.*
Franks, J.R., Harris, R.S. and Mayer, C. (1988) Means of Payment in Takeovers: Results for the UK and US. In *Corporate Takeovers: Causes and Consequences* (ed. M.J. Avernack), University of Chicago Press.
Lev. B. (1986) Observations on the Merger Phenomenon. In *The Revolution in Corporate Finance*, J.M. Stern and D.H. Chew (eds), Blackwell, Oxford.
Mitchell, M. and Lehn, K. (1990) Do bad bidders become good targets? *Journal of Political Economy*, **2**.
Mueller, D. (1992) Mergers, *The New Palgrave Dictionary of Finance*, Macmillan.

Shleifer, A. and Vishny, R. (1990) The takeover wave of the 1980s, *Science*, August.

24.13 Problems

1. Your company is subject to an unexpected takeover bid by a rival company. Your board of directors proposes to reject the bid, but believes that increased bids might follow.

   Discuss the policies that your company might adopt to defend itself against the takeover bid(s), and comment upon the significance of the City Code on Takeovers and Mergers in this process.

   (ACCA, Dec. 85)

2. The Uni-Tours PLC is in the service sector and is considering merger to achieve more favourable growth and profit opportunities. After an extensive search of a large number of companies, it narrowed the candidates to a company in the same sector, Poly-Travellers PLC. As the treasurer of Uni-Tours you are investigating the possible acquisition of Poly-Travellers. You have the following basic data to start from:

	Uni-Tours PLC	Poly-Travellers PLC
Earnings per share	£5.00	£1.50
Dividend per share	£3.00	£0.80
Share price	£90.00	£20.00
Number of shares	1 000 000	600 000

Further investigations lead you to estimate that investors currently expect a steady compound growth of about 6% each year in Poly-Travellers' earnings and dividends. Under Uni-Tours' control this growth should increase to about 8% each year, without any additional capital investment and without any change in the riskiness of operations.

Required:

(a) Compute the increase in value resulting from the merger. (5 marks)

(b) What are the gains or losses likely to be to the shareholders in the two companies, assuming Uni-Tours pays £25 in cash for each share in Poly-Travellers. (3 marks)

(c) What will be the gains or losses if Uni-Tours offers one of its shares for every three shares of Poly-Travellers. (5 marks)

(d) Calculate the gains or losses on the assumption that the market does not expect Poly-Travellers' increased growth rate to materialize. Discuss the theoretical and empirical implications of (d) with respect to (a), (b) and (c) above. (10 marks)

3. Killisick PLC wishes to acquire Holbeck PLC. The directors of Killisick are trying to justify the acquisition to the shareholders of both companies on the grounds that it will increase the wealth of all shareholders.

The supporting financial evidence produced by Killisick's directors is summarized below:

	£000	
	Killisick	Holbeck
Operating profit	12 400	5800
Interest payable	4 431	2200
Profit before tax	7 969	3600
Tax	2 789	1260
Earnings available to ordinary shareholders	5 180	2340
Earnings per share (pre-acquisition)	14.80 pence	29.25 pence
Market price per share (pre-acquisition)	222 pence	322 pence
Estimated market price (post-acquisition)	240 pence	
Estimated equivalent value of one old Holbeck share (post-acquisition)		360 pence

Payment is to be made with Killisick ordinary shares, at an exchange ratio of 3 Killisick shares for every 2 Holbeck shares.

Required:

(a) Show how the director's of Killisick produced their estimates of post acquisition value and, if you do not agree with these estimates, produce revised estimates of post-acquisition values.

All calculations must be shown. State clearly any assumptions that you make. (10 marks)

(b) If the acquisition is contested by Holbeck PLC, using Killisick's estimates of its post-acquisition market price calculate the maximum price that Killisick could offer without reducing the wealth of its shareholders. (3 marks)

(c) The board of directors of Holbeck PLC later informally indicate that they are prepared to accept a 2 for 1 share offer.

Further information regarding the effect of the acquisition on Killisick is given below:

(i) The acquisition will result in an increase in the total pre-acquisition after tax operating cash-flows of £2.75 million per year indefinitely.

(ii) Rationalization will allow machinery with a realizable value of £7.2 million to be disposed of at the end of the next year.

(iii) Redundancy payments will total £3.5 million immediately and £8.4 million at the end of the next year.

(iv) Killisick's cost of capital is estimated to be 14%.

All values are after any appropriate taxation. Assume that the pre-acquisition market values of Killisick and Holbeck shares have not changed.

Required:

Recommend, using your own estimates of post-acquisition values, whether Killisick should be prepared to make a 2 for 1 offer for the shares of Holbeck.

(6 marks)

(d) Assuming no increase in the total post-acquisition earnings, assess whether this acquisition is likely to have any effect on the value of debt and equity of Killisick PLC.

(6 marks)

(25 marks)

(ACCA, 1988)

4. Smith Locks PLC manufactures cylinder locks for the European market. The company's turnover and profits for the past three years and the expected results for the current year are as follows:

Year ended 31 December	Turnover £ million	Net profit after tax £ million
1984 (actual)	23.0	2.1
1985 (actual)	24.0	2.3
1986 (actual)	21.0	2.0
1987 (estimate)	20.0	2.0

The balance sheet at the end of the current year (31 December 1987) is expected to be as follows:

	£ million
Fixed assets	14.0
Net current assets	6.0
	20.0

	£ million
Financed by:	
Ordinary share capital (10 million fully paid ordinary shares of £1 each)	10.0
Reserves	5.0
	15.0
Debentures (15%)	5.0
	20.0

The present market price of the shares is 220p and the price has not fallen below this level since 1983.

The company's directors are concerned about the lack of growth in turnover and profit and are considering ways of improving profitability. The directors feel that there is unlikely to be any significant growth in the construction industry in the foreseeable future and that, in order to improve profitability, the company must either diversify or increase its share of the market. The directors are reluctant to diversify and are exploring the possibility of acquiring a smaller lock manufacturing company as a means of increasing the company's market share. They are particularly interested in Dead Locks PLC, which manufactures mortise locks, and are considering making a bid for its entire share capital. Dead Locks PLC is a publicly quoted company which has in issue 5 million fully paid ordinary shares of 50p each. These shares currently have a market price of 100p per share.

The company's results for the past three years and its expected results for the current year are as follows:

	Turnover £ million	Net profit after tax £ million
1984 (actual)	5.4	0.42
1985 (actual)	6.5	0.54
1986 (actual)	7.8	0.65
1987 (estimate)	9.0	0.75

The balance sheet of Dead Locks PLC has reserves of £3 million but does not have any preference share capital or long term debt.

The directors of Smith Locks PLC have estimated that, if they acquire Dead Locks PLC, the combined turnover of the two companies would be £30 million and after tax profit would be £3 million. In addition they consider that some of the fixed assets of Dead Locks PLC would no longer be required and could be sold for £500 000. The financial director has suggested that a bid for the shares in Dead Locks PLC be made at 120% of their current market price and that, as regards payment of that price, the following three options should be considered:

(a) A new issue of ordinary shares in Smith Locks PLC in exchange for the ordinary shares of Dead Locks PLC.
(b) An issue of 15% convertible debentures, with £100 of debentures convertible into 125 ordinary shares at the option of the holders in 5 years' time.
(c) An issue of 16% debentures with warrants attached. Each £100 of debentures would give the holder a warrant to purchase 10 ordinary shares at a price of 275p per share in 3 years' time.

Required:

(a) Calculate the maximum price that Smith Locks PLC should be willing to pay for shares in Dead Locks PLC. (4 marks)
(b) Briefly discuss the advantages and disadvantages of financing a takeover by an issue of convertible debentures. (5 marks)
(c) Assuming that the takeover of Dead Locks PLC is agreed at the price suggested by the financial director and takes place on 1 January 1988, advise the directors of Smith Locks PLC of the effect on the company's future earnings per share of each of the alternative financing methods and state, with reasons, which method you would recommend. Assume a corporation tax rate of 50%. (16 marks)
(25 marks)
(ACCA, Dec. 87)

5. You have been asked by the directors of Giants PLC, a large conglomerate which is involved in a wide range of different activities, to report on the price to be paid for the possible purchase of Oriole Ltd. Oriole Ltd is a private company which makes and sells fashion garments – a business which is not currently included among Giants PLC's activities. Oriole Ltd has recently experienced substantial trading

difficulties and, if successful in its proposed purchase, Giants PLC will replace the existing management of Oriole Ltd.

The directors of Giants PLC are unsure as to how the business of Oriole Ltd should be valued. They understand that two possibilities exist – either the value of the assets of Oriole Ltd or its past earnings could constitute the basis of the purchase price.

You are required to:

(a) explain the rationale underlying the assets and the earnings bases of valuation (8 marks).
(b) discuss the practical difficulties which might exist in applying each of the two methods (10 marks), and
(c) explain how the individual circumstances surrounding the purchase of Oriole Ltd might determine your choice of method in this case (7 marks).

(25 marks)

(*ICAEW*, Dec. 1983)

6. The directors of three manufacturing companies, Johnson PLC, Boswell PLC and Garrick PLC, are considering a merger, with a view of rationalizing the combined businesses and strengthening their competitive power. The three companies' balance sheets (summarized) at 31 December 1983 are shown below.

Balance sheets at 31 December 1983

Net assets	Johnson PLC £000	Johnson PLC £000	Boswell PLC £000	Boswell PLC £000	Garrick PLC £000	Garrick PLC £000
Fixed assets						
Intangible:						
Goodwill – cost	50		—		—	
– amortization	(30)	20				
Tangible:						
Freehold land – cost valuation		3 000		1500		900
Freehold buildings – cost valuation	8 000		6 000		3000	
– depreciation	(4 000)		(2 500)		(900)	
		4 000		3500		2100
Plant – cost valuation	20 000		12 000		8000	
– depreciation	(8 000)		(9 000)		(3200)	
		12 000		3000		4800
Investments:						
In related company – cost	2 000		—		—	
Other investments – cost	—		2 980		—	
		2 000		2 980		
		21 020		10 980		7800
Current assets						
Stocks	4 000		2 000		1500	
Trade debtors (net)	7 000		2 800		2000	
Owed by related company	200		—		—	
Bank and cash balances	20		2 040		2369	
Prepayments	100		80		50	
	11 320		6 920		5919	
Current liabilities						
Bank overdraft	(1 196)		—		—	
Trade creditors	(2 000)		(1 500)		(1000)	
Accruals	(130)		(100)		(60)	

Corporation tax less ACT	(1 614)	—	(743)
Proposed dividends	(1 000)	(400)	(360)
ACT on proposed dividends	(429)	(171)	(154)
	(6 369)	(2171)	(2317)
Net current assets	4 951	4749	3 602
	25 971	15 729	11 402
Financed by:			
Debenture loans less discounts	4 900	3 000	3416
Provisions			
Deferred taxation	591	329	246
Capital and reserves			
Cumulative preference shares (£1)	1 000	200	—
Ordinary shares (£1)	10 000	8000	6000
	11 000	8200	6000
Share premium account	2 000	1000	500
Revaluation reserve	6 000	3000	—
Profit and loss account	1 500	200	1240
	9 500	4200	1740
	20 500	12 400	7 740
	25 971	15 729	11 402

You are required, on the basis of these balance sheets and of the additional information given below, to draw up a scheme of amalgamation of the three companies under the name of Georgian PLC. The scheme must be fair and reasonable, and likely to be seriously considered by all three boards of directors. A consolidated balance sheet as at 1 January 1984 (the assumed date of the merger) is to be included.

Notes

(a) Johnson PLC holds 2 000 000 £1 ordinary shares in Boswell PLC, acquired at a cost of £2 000 000. Since acquisition, Boswell's post-tax profits have totalled £700 000, and its dividends £400 000. Johnson PLC has a seat on Boswell's board of directors.

(b) Boswell PLC, conversely, holds 1 000 000 £1 ordinary shares in Johnson PLC. The corresponding amounts to those in Note (a) are: the cost was £2 000 000; and since acquisition Johnson's post-acquisition post-tax profits are £1 000 000, and its post-acquisition dividends, £600 000.

(c) Boswell PLC also holds £1 000 000 nominal of Garrick PLC's debentures, acquired at a cost of £980 000 (the value in Boswell's books).

(d) The cumulative preference shares carry dividend rates of: Johnson, 10%; Boswell, 12%. There are no arrears of dividend.

(e) The debentures of Johnson PLC, £5 000 000 nominal, were issued on 1 January 1976 at 90, carry interest at 12½% per annum, and are redeemable at par on 1 January 1986. The corresponding information for Boswell PLC's debentures is: £3 000 000 nominal, issued on 1 January 1975 at par, interest 14%, redemption at par on 1 January 1985. For Garrick PLC's debentures, the information is respectively: £3 500 000 nominal, on 1 January 1980 at 96; 15%; 1 January 1990. Discount on all debentures is amortized by the straight-line method. Market prices at 1 January 1984: Johnson, 98; Boswell, 104; Garrick, 100.

(f) Johnson's tangible assets were last revalued at 1 January 1983, and Boswell's at 1 January 1981. Garrick's fixed assets have not been revalued. Current values (professionally appraised) for Johnson are: freehold land, £3 300 000 (market value in present use); buildings, £9 000 000 (replacement cost new); plant, £21 000 000 (as for buildings). For Boswell, the values are, respectively: £2 000 000; £10 000 000; and £15 000 000. For Garrick, the values are: £1 800 000; £5 500 000; and £12 000 000.

(g) Johnson PLC's purchased goodwill is being amortized by the straight-line method over 5 years.

(h) Depreciation rates in all three companies (straight line) are: buildings, 5% per annum; plant, 15% per annum.

(i) It is agreed that if the merger is effected one of Boswell PLC's factories will close and be disposed of. The book values of the fixed assets (all revalued at 1 January 1981) are: land, £300 000; buildings – gross £2 000 000, depreciation provision £1 000 000; and plant – gross £4 000 000, depreciation provision £3 500 000. The corresponding appraised values at 1 January 1984 (see Note (f)) are: land, £400 000; buildings – gross, £3 000 000; and plant – gross, £4 500 000. It is estimated that on sale the land will realize its full current value, the buildings only half their depreciated replacement cost, and the plant (which is obsolescent) only one-fourth of its depreciated replacement cost. Redundancy payments to the workers, and other shutdown costs, are estimated at £500 000.

(j) At 1 January 1984 the market prices of the £1 ordinary shares are: Johnson PLC, 150p; Boswell PLC, 80p; and Garrick PLC, 110p. The preference shares are unlisted, and held by the directors of the two companies concerned.

(k) Net trading profit projections (before interest and taxation), on the assumption that there is neither merger nor revaluations, are:

	1984	1985	1986
	£000	£000	£000
Johnson	2000	2250	2500
Boswell	1000	800	500
Garrick	900	1100	1200

No allowance for inflation has been included in these estimates. Bank overdraft interest is expected to average 10% per annum. Corporation tax is to be taken as 50% of profits after interest.

(l) It is forecast that, if the merger is effected after revaluation of assets, the net trading profits (before interest and taxation) will be:

	£000
1984	3500
1985	4300
1986	5000

(m) In any discounted cash flow computations, the discounting rate is to be 10% per annum before tax.

(ACCA, Financial Accounting, Dec. 1984)

7. The directors of Compro plc and Vendo plc consider that a merger of the two companies would be beneficial. The proposed merger would involve the issue of new ordinary shares in Compro plc which would be given in exchange for the existing ordinary shares of Vendo plc. The directors are now concerned with the question of the ratio in which new shares of Compro plc should be offered for shares of Vendo plc.

Both companies are totally equity financed and you have the following information about the ordinary shares currently in issue:

	Number of shares in issue (millions)	Current share price
Compro plc	600	£5.00
Vendo plc	300	£4.00

The cost of equity of both companies is 20% and it is expected to remain the same after the merger. It is expected that the merger will generate post-tax cost savings of £40 million in the first year and that the level of these post-tax cost savings will rise at 10% per annum thereafter in perpetuity. Additionally, the immediate sale of assets rendered redundant by the merger is expected to realize post-tax proceeds of £200 million which will be invested to produce a return equal to the current cost of capital.

You may treat the post-tax cost savings as though they result in annual cash inflows commencing one year after the merger.

Required:

(a) What should be the ratio of new shares in Compro plc issued in exchange for existing shares in Vendo plc in order that all of the benefits of the merger will accrue to:

  (i) the pre-merger shareholders of Compro plc; or
  (ii) the pre-merger shareholders of Vendo plc? (12 marks)

(b) What other factors will influence the level at which the directors of Compro plc pitch their bid for Vendo plc, assuming they act solely in the interests of their shareholders? (3 marks)

(c) Discuss what other motives might be involved in the decision to merge or acquire companies, addressing in particular:

  (i) the role of diversification;
  (ii) the observation that shareholders of acquirer companies tend to lose as a result of takeovers;
  (iii) the implications for corporate governance. (10 marks)

(25 marks)
ICAEW, June 1993

8. 'The fact that the majority of companies which collapse or fall into financial difficulties have not previously been qualified on a going concern basis is frequently cited by critics of the auditing profession as evidence that it is failing in its duty toward the investing public.'

Discuss, reaching a conclusion, why shareholders are only infrequently forewarned of financial failures and how they could be better informed.

(12 marks)
ICAEW, June 1993

9. Jetspray Ltd, a company which manufacturers speed boats at its yard in Cornwall, is an audit client of your firm. Its managing director, Mr Bond, has had preliminary discussions with his counterpart at Topdraw Ltd concerning Jetspray Ltd acquiring that company.

Topdraw Ltd is a design company which Jetspray Ltd has employed for most of its models in recent years, and Mr Bond is impressed by its expertise in advanced design, materials and testing technology.

It has been indicated to Mr Bond that the purchase price will need to be substantial to reflect Topdraw Ltd's reputation and high level of profitability.

Your firm was asked to conduct a brief initial review on Topdraw Ltd from its published accounts for the year ended 31 December 1992 and a brief meeting with its managing director.

You have completed this work, and your main findings are as follows:

(a) The shares in Topdraw Ltd are held equally by its managing director and its design director, who is acknowledged to be among the best boat designers in the country.

(b) The company capitalizes, as research and development, direct costs and proportionate overheads on all design work not undertaken on contract. This is justified on the grounds that almost all ideas are eventually incorporated into some final product, and the costs are then amortized against the income arising.

(c) Included in 'Provisions for liabilities and charges' in the balance sheet at 31 December 1992 is an amount set aside to cover investigation work into the causes of an accident in which one of the company's designs overturned during a race.

You have been told that expenditure to date has utilized most of this provision, and the indications are that the cause was not a design fault.

Mr Bond requires the conclusions from your review, with any impact they may have on the structure of the offer that should be put to the shareholders of Topdraw Ltd.

Required:

From your review as specified by your client, draft a report to the board of Jetspray Ltd containing your initial conclusions and their effect on the structure of the offer that the company might make. List in your report the other factors that it should consider before reaching a decision.

(15 marks)
ICAEW, June 1993

10. SMB Ltd is considering an all share offer to take over WBS Ltd. Relevant financial information is as follows:

	SMB	WBS
Present earnings (£000)	40 000	10 000
Ordinary shares in issue (000)	20 000	8 000
Price/earnings ratio	12	8

If SMB plans to offer a premium of 20% over the current market value for WBS shares:

(a) what are the earnings per share and current market share value of SMB and WBS?
(b) what is the ratio of exchange for the shares and how many new SMB shares will have to be issued to acquire all of WBS's shares?
(c) what are the earnings per share of the new combined group?
(d) if the P/E ratio stays at 12, what is the market capitalization of the new group?
(e) what would the P/E ratio have to adjust to to hold the merged group value equal to the sum of the two pre-merger entities?
(f) why would SMB have a higher P/E ratio than WBS? Comment on any issues that this may have for future performance of SMB.

11. Outline the operation of any **three** anti-takeover devices with which you are familiar. Assess the advantages and disadvantages of restricting the effectiveness of hostile takeover bids through these mechanisms.

12. Briefly discuss the nature and purpose of the City Code on Takeovers and Mergers. (Discussion of detailed rules is not required).

13. Discuss and illustrate how the City Code might influence the behaviour of a financial manager defending a company against an unwelcome takeover bid.

14. Axmine plc has been contacted by Traces S.A., a mining company based in a South American country. Traces has proposed a four year joint venture to mine copper, using a new technique developed by Axmine. Axmine would supply machinery at an immediate cost of 800 million pesos and ten supervisors at an annual salary of £40 000 each at current prices. Additionally, Axmine would pay half of the 1000 million pesos per year (at current prices) local labour costs and other expenses in the South American country. The supervisors' salaries and local labour and other expenses will be increased in line with inflation in the United Kingdom and the South American country respectively.

Inflation in the South American country is currently 100% per year, and in the UK 8% per year. The government of the South American country is attempting to control inflation, and hopes to reduce it each year by 20% of the previous year's rate.

The joint venture would give Axmine a 50% share of Traces' copper production, with current market prices at £1500 per 1000 kilogrammes. Traces' production is expected to be 10 million kilogrammes per year, and copper prices are expected to rise by 10% per year (in pounds sterling) for the foreseeable future. At the end of four years Axmine would be given the choice to pull out of the venture or to negotiate another four-year joint venture, on different terms.

The current exchange rate is 140 pesos/£. Future exchange rates may be estimated using the purchasing power parity theory

Axmine has no foreign operations. The cost of capital of the company's UK mining operations is 16% per year. As this joint venture involves diversifying into foreign operations the company considers that a 2% reduction in the cost of capital would be appropriate for this project.

Corporate tax is at the rate of 20% per year in the South American country and 35% per year in the UK. A tax treaty exists between the two countries and all foreign tax paid is allowable against any UK tax liability. Taxation is payable one year in arrears and a 25% straight-line writing down allowance is available on the machinery in both countries.

Cash flows may be assumed to occur at the year end, except for the immediate cost of machinery. The machinery is expected to have negligible terminal value at the end of four years.

Required:

(a) Prepare a report discussing whether Axmine plc should agree to the proposed joint venture. Relevant calculations must form part of your report or an appendix to it.

State clearly any assumptions that you make. (16 marks)

(b) If the South American government were to fail to control inflation, and inflation were to increase rapidly during the period of the joint venture, discuss the likely effect of very high inflation on the joint venture. (4 marks)

(c) Explain whether you consider Axmine's proposed discount rate for the project to be appropriate. (5 marks)

(25 marks)

ACCA, Dec. 1991

15. In a recent meeting of the board of directors of Rayswood plc the chairman proposed the acquisition of Pondhill plc. During his presentation the chairman stated that: 'As a result of this takeover we will diversify our operations and our earnings per share will rise by 13%, bringing great benefits to our shareholders.'

No bid has yet been made, and Rayswood currently owns only 2% of Pondhill.

A bid would be based on a share for share exchange, which would be one Rayswood share for every six Pondhill shares. Financial data for the two companies include:

	Rayswood £m	Pondhill £m
Turnover	56.0	42.0
Profit before tax	12.0	10.0
Profit available to ordinary shareholders	7.8	6.5
Dividend	3.2	3.4
Retained earnings	4.6	3.1
Issued ordinary shares[1] (£m)	20	15
Market price per share	320 pence	45 pence

[1]Rayswood 50 pence per value, Pondhill 10 pence per value.

Required:

(a) Explain whether you agree with the chairman of Rayswood when he says that the takeover would bring 'great benefits to our investors'.

Support your explanation with relevant calculations. State clearly any assumptions that you make. (11 marks)

(b) On the basis of the information provided, calculate the likely post acquisition
   share price of Rayswood if the bid is successful.   (3 marks)
(c) Discuss what alternative forms of payment are available in a bid and what factors a bidder should take into account when deciding the form of payment.
                                                              (11 marks)
                                                              (25 marks)
                                                      ACCA, Dec. 1992

25 Company restructuring, refinancing and liquidation

25.1	Divestment	909
25.2	Sell-off	911
25.3	Spin-off (demerger)	912
25.4	Management buyout	913
25.5	Going private	918
25.6	Buy-in	919
25.7	Increase the amount of borrowing	920
25.8	Share re-purchase	920
25.9	Reverse takeover	921
25.10	Business failure	921
25.11	Refinancing	923
25.12	Insolvency/liquidation	925
25.13	Key terms	929
25.14	Revision questions	929
25.15	References	930
25.16	Further reading	930
25.17	Problems	930

In the previous chapter we considered a number of aspects of mergers and acquisitions. In fact mergers and acquisitions are only one form of company restructuring. They are usually the aspect of company change that makes the headlines. However, during the 1980s and 1990s another trend has been in evidence, namely a move towards demerger or divestment. This came about partly as a result of a greater emphasis in the strategic planning processes within companies on concentrating on 'core' business activities. By divestment or, to give it yet another name, divestiture is meant the sale of a subsidiary, division or product line by one business to another.

We give below a number of forms of company restructuring, and in this chapter we shall examine the motives and methods behind divestment and other methods of introducing change.

1. Expansion
   (a) Mergers
   (b) Takeovers/acquisitions
   (c) Joint ventures
2. Divestment
   (a) Sell-offs
   (b) Liquidation
   (c) Spin-offs
   (d) Management buyouts
3. Other forms of change
   (a) Going private
   (b) Buy-ins
   (c) Increase the amount of borrowing
   (d) Share re-purchases
   (e) Premium buybacks
   (f) Reverse takeovers

Unfortunately during the late 1980s yet another form of change occurred in many companies: namely liquidation. Due to changes in the economic situation record numbers of companies were forced out of existence. For the first time in the 25 year history of this book we have felt it necessary to introduce a section on liquidation.

We will briefly consider the causes of failure, and then consider what can happen to companies when they get into financial difficulties.

The reasons given by companies to justify a restructuring exercise include the following.

The sum of the parts of a business is worth more than the whole

The individual parts of a business can be worth more than the whole when the shares of a company are selling at a price below their potential value. Some of the assets of the company are worth more than is appreciated, or some could be put to better use. Selling off a part or parts of the business brings in cash, and the resulting increase in company wealth is greater than any fall in share value resulting from an expected reduction in future cash flow. This is sometimes expressed at $5 - 1 = 5$.

Selling off parts of the business can be seen as similar to 'asset stripping', although this term is usually reserved for describing the practice of selling unwanted parts of a business following an acquisition. Divestment can occur whether or not a company has been engaged in takeover activity.

But why should the sum of the parts of a business be greater than the whole? It is sometimes claimed that the financial community does not always understand the true nature and structure of certain companies. For example, a company can be classified as a manufacturing business when some of its activities are in merchandising or mining. Investors and their advisors believe that a certain share price is appropriate based on the classification of a company in one industry; this can result in an undervaluation. If the company sells off its non-core interest and obtains a true value for it, the sale results in the recognition and revaluation of a previously undervalued asset. The result is that the value of the company after the sale, which is the cash collected plus the true value of the core business, can be greater than the value of the company before the sale.

However, it can be argued that this should not happen. If the stock market is efficient, the share price should reflect all publicly available information on the company's future cash flows. Some people will know of the true nature of the investments in non-core activities and their value, and so this should be reflected in the actual day-to-day share price. Therefore in an efficient market $5 - 1$ should equal 4.

The argument that $5 - 1$ can equal 5 is not just based on stock market inefficiency. It can be argued that some assets may be worth more in the hands of one set of managers than in the hands of another set. The buyers of the assets in a divestment situation see themselves as being able to make better use of them than the seller can. Therefore they are worth more to the buyer than to the seller. Thus the buyer offers a higher value than that based on their future cash flow in existing hands. In this situation the market is correctly valuing the assets in existing hands before the sell-off; it just values them more highly in the hands of a different set of managers.

Selling off unwanted parts

During the 1970s many conglomerates sold off assets they had acquired that were unprofitable to them. However, the sell-off spree of the 1980s was different. Disillusion with the concept of conglomerates developed from both a company management and a financial community point of view. Rather than simply dumping the bad parts, companies started to spin off and scale down healthy businesses to concentrate on what they could do best. In a number of cases these divestments have been accomplished by means of management buyouts or spin-offs.

At times of considerable change in the economy, constraints put on management become more explicit. The lack of time available to manage and the level of uncertainty can lead to diversified companies facing extreme difficulties in keeping up with market trends. The result has been a move towards the creation of more independent decision-making units in order to obtain better and quicker decisions.

A situation developed in which large conglomerates were seen as being risky and also less efficient from a management point of view. The increasingly competitive environment forced companies to take a long hard look at the group structure. A company was not likely to be profitable, i.e. not likely to be competitive, in all its markets. More specialization was therefore seen as desirable.

An increasing belief in the virtues of small businesses

The attitude of financial institutions to lending to small businesses has changed over time. There is now much more support. Governments have also made noises indicating that they wish to encourage small businesses. Therefore in the 1980s it has become easier for small businesses to survive when they have been spun off from large companies. In Chapter 27 on small businesses a number of reasons are given as to why they have advantages over large firms in certain situations.

Divestment as a crisis response

In a relatively stable environment the organization structure of the firm and its accompanying control systems may be able to absorb incremental development and associated problems. In a turbulent and uncertain environment where, at the extreme, survival is threatened, a quantum change in the organization may be required.

Rapid and uncertain environmental change may break down the traditional affinities between product areas within an organization, so that the original synergistic benefits from integration or conglomerate risk-spreading no longer apply. It may thus become difficult to control across these integrated processes. Integration in different markets may now be required, or alternatively different markets may now need to be entered for effective conglomerate risk-spreading. Ownership mobility provided by divestment helps to overcome the barriers.

Where crisis involves financial problems further control issues arise. A parent facing a severe financial constraint is limited in its ability to operate an internal capital market. Not only may the company be unable to act as 'lender of last resort' to its divisions/subsidiaries, but it may not be able to finance worthwhile projects. In extreme cases, the company's survival itself may be threatened – either by bankruptcy or by an unwelcome takeover bid. Hence crisis conditions may lead to divestment.

Under conditions of capital rationing some units may be designated as 'cash cows' and deliberately starved of investment funds whilst being 'milked' to finance priority developments elsewhere. This treatment is likely to impair operating efficiency and innovation in the division concerned, the more so where the 'cash cow' division is supporting divisions with crisis performance problems. Divestment may be necessary to rescue its long-run performance. For the divesting parent the lump sum proceeds of sale may better help restructuring.

There are problems in attempting to evaluate the results of divestment. Most of the published studies of divestment have adopted an efficient market methodology and examined abnormal share price behaviour about the time of the announcement to sell off a division or subsidiary. This approach parallels that taken in the extensive merger evaluation literature. However, it is not necessarily the case that divestments can be treated in a symmetric fashion using a share price framework. Firstly, in the merger literature the typical study examines the acquisition of public limited companies whose stock market quotations ensure that the market has sufficient information to place a value upon them. Secondly, as noted above, disinvestment may occur as a result of a variety of firm circumstances. It is necessary to distinguish these separate reasons for sales. As the reasons for divestment differ, the effects on shareholder wealth may also be expected to vary.

One reason for a management buyout (MBO) and for going private is to obtain the benefit of combining ownership and control. It is usually believed that, as part-owners, managers will have greater incentives to achieve good results as they will benefit directly from the profitability. 'Agency costs' are reduced. Of course some of these benefits can be achieved without reorganization through share option and employee share ownership schemes.

The mechanics of divestment involve a number of important behavioural issues. A change of ownership will increase the insecurity of managers and may provoke intense resentment if the division was not a relatively poor performer. Moreover, where the future of a division is in doubt, divisional management have to assess their own prospects. The traditional choice was either a transfer to another division or redundancy. The buyout option that now exists allows subsidiary management to weigh their risk-reward preferences, which with the ability to turn informational asymmetrics to their advantage may cause their behaviour to diverge from that which is in the parent's interest. The problem is further exacerbated when a significant element of the value of the subsidiary derives from the specific contribution of employees so that a 'management walk-out' is a credible threat.

Where a disposing corporate management envisage having a continuing trading relationship with a former division, it is in their interests to avoid alienating the divisional managers. In these circumstances a management buyout would appear particularly appropriate. With managers directly involved in the transaction, their co-operation in divorcing the division from its parent should be assured. Furthermore, the creation of an independent business may be preferable to the sale of the unit to an existing firm, perhaps thereby increasing this other firm's monopolistic or monopsonistic power.

25.2 Sell-off

A sell-off is the sale of part of the original company to a third party. Assets are sold to the third party, most probably another company, and cash is usually received in exchange. A company may take this course of action under the following circumstances.

1. It is short of cash.
2. It has carried out a strategic planning exercise and has decided that it wishes to concentrate its management efforts on certain parts of its business and not on other parts. It wishes to restructure.
3. It wishes to protect the rest of the firm from takeover by selling a desirable area of its activities that it knows is attractive to the bidder. It is selling the crown jewels in order to make itself less of a target.
4. It has a loss-making activity; by removing the loss from the consolidated accounts, it will improve the year's profit performance.

Duhaime and Grant [1], in an examination of the reasons for divestment, found that sell-offs were likely to involve the less profitable and more peripheral business units of a multi-product firm and also to be related to the profitability of the parent. Such findings are consistent with the view that the sale of divisions/subsidiaries can ease control problems (by reducing complexity as peripheral units are sold off) and that divestment represents a plausible response to financial difficulties.

Sell-offs should be undertaken as an investment decision by management. If management are interested in wealth creation, such a decision should have a positive effect on total net present value (NPV) and accordingly this should provide a signal to investors which results in an upward movement in the share price.

The rate of sell-off activity in any economy varies with the level of mergers and acquisitions taking place. This is not really surprising, as one of the reasons for a sell-off is an acquiring company quickly selling off parts of an acquired business that it does not want. When making an acquisition, a company probably knows that there are parts of the purchased business that it does not really want and so it has plans to sell them off. A further reason is that the purchasing company may need to sell some of the newly acquired business in order to obtain cash to pay off loans obtained to finance the acquisition. This is often the case with leveraged takeovers. It is also possible that, following the acquisition, it is found that some of the parts of the purchased business do not fit in with current plans and will be worth more in other hands.

Liquidation

Liquidation is the most extreme form of divestment: the sell-off of the entire business. The owners might decide to close the whole business down, sell off the assets piecemeal and use the funds raised to pay off shareholders. The situation being referred to is a voluntary dissolution, not a compulsory liquidation.

When part of the business is sold off, the funds received are reinvested in the firm or used to pay off borrowings, but this is not the case with a liquidation. This step would be taken if a firm was worth more 'dead than alive'. This situation could arise if for some reason the current organizational structure was not leading to the best use being made of the firm's assets and the business was no longer seen as a viable concern. It would arise if the current owners lost interest in the business. Although such a voluntary liquidation might be in the shareholders' interest, it is not necessarily in the managers' interests. Of course, with owner-managers there could be goal congruence. A voluntary liquidation involves making a decision to sell off all the assets of the business rather than spinning them off or selling them off as individual parts.

25.3 Spin-off (demerger)

With a spin-off there is no change in ownership of assets. A new company is created and the shares in the new company are owned by the shareholders of the company making the distribution of the assets. The result is to create two or more companies whereas previously there was one. Each company now owns some of the assets of the former single company. The shareholders own the same proportion of shares in the new company as in the original company. The assets are transferred to the new company and not sold. The new company will usually have different management from that of the continuing company. Over time the new company might well develop different policies from those of the continuing company. As a separate entity it might in time even be sold independently of the original continuing company. From a shareholders' point of view the spin-off is similar to a scrip dividend (stock dividend). The shareholders are given new shares, in this case in a new company.

An extreme version of the spin-off is where the original company is split up into a number of separate companies. The entire original company is broken up, in which case there are a number of spin-offs. The original company ceases to exist.

There are three main methods of achieving a spin-off, or what is sometimes called a 'listed demerger'. The simplest is a 'dividend in kind'. This means that shares in the subsidiary to be disposed of are distributed to company shareholders as a non-cash dividend.

There are two ways of handling this 'dividend in kind'. If the shares in the company being demerged are distributed directly to the shareholders, it is treated as a sale for tax purposes and tax may have to be paid. An alternative version is for the shares in the company being disposed of to be distributed to a newly formed company. It is this newly formed company that distributes its shares to shareholders. This second approach delays the payment of tax.

An alternative demerger method is through a 'scheme of arrangement'. This requires a court order. The third approach is through a 'scheme of reconstruction'. This arises when two or more new companies are established. The original company is liquidated. The liquidator distributes the assets of the old company to the new companies. The shares in the new companies are distributed to the shareholders of the old company. This is clearly much more of a demerger than a spin off. Everything is in fact, in this case, being 'spun off'.

The spin-off, with its separation of management but continuation of shareholders, usually results in a positive response from the stock market. The reasons put forward to explain this response include the following.

1. The changes result in a clearer management structure. The managers of the activity that has been separated are expected by the market to do a better job with the assets than when they were managed in the larger group. The assets are worth more in the

hands of the new management than in the hands of the previous management. It is thought that there will be an improvement in efficiency.

2. The change could result in making it easier in the future for a merger or takeover of the spun-off part to take place.

3. It is a way of protecting the crown jewel from a predator.

4. It allows the market to see the true value of a business that was hidden within the larger conglomerate structure. This refers back to the discussion of sell-offs. If there are hidden assets whose potential is not appreciated, they need not be sold off; they could be placed in a separate company.

5. It avoids offending regulatory agencies. In the past this reason has been more relevant in the USA than in the UK, but with the privatization programme in the UK and the resulting need for regulatory agencies it could become more significant in the UK. With business activities separated, price increases might be allowed in some activities but not in others.

6. Shareholders may benefit from an increase in the opportunity set as they are able to adjust the proportions of their investment in the demerged entities.

7. Shareholders may benefit at the expense of bond-holders where equity in the spun-off company is distributed solely to shareholders of the parent corporation, leaving the debtholders with no claim on the assets of the new entity.

A number of studies have reported significant positive abnormal returns, which were particularly pronounced in larger spin-offs. It has not been found that this results from a transfer of wealth from bond-holders. The available evidence on spin-offs appears to support the view that shareholders' gains are attributable to an improvement in the efficiency of the new structural arrangements.

Alexander *et al.* [2] found some evidence of positive announcement effects. An examination of abnormal returns in the period prior to divestment suggested an important difference between sell-offs and spin-offs. Sell-offs appear to be announced after a period of generally negative abnormal returns – a result consistent with the views of divestment as either a response to poor performance or as a cash-generating exercise. Spin-offs are likely to be preceded by generally positive returns. Miles and Rosenfeld [3] found that spin-offs outperformed sell-offs in terms of market reactions on the day of the event. Miles and Rosenfeld also found that the economic gains to shareholders of the selling and buying firms were almost identical. However, Jain [4], while confirming the positive effects, found that gains to buyers were smaller than those to sellers. This difference may be related to the effects of asymmetries of information on the valuation of the traded entity. By definition a purchaser must value an acquisition more highly than the vendor. The purchaser might expect that he can obtain better performance for an entity than the vendor because of improved prospects for synergistic benefits and because he is able to manage it more efficiently. However, where only the vendor possesses the 'true' information on the entity's performance potential, the acquirer may suffer the adverse effects of an asymmetry of information and place an unwarrantedly high valuation on his acquisition. The evidence on the past performance resulting from mergers generally supports this view.

25.4 Management buyout

Table 25.1 shows the increase in the number and the size of management buyouts. Table 25.2 illustrates the number and size of buyouts in certain well-known UK companies.

Management buyouts vary greatly in scale and method. They can be defined as a transaction through which the management of a business acquires a substantial stake in, and frequently effective control of, the business which it formerly managed. The buyout team may consist of only one individual or a whole team of directors and employees, together with external associates. In some management buyouts some equity ownership is offered to employees below the level of top management. In rare cases the offer is to all employees. An example of this latter approach was that of the National Freight Consortium. This was the sale of a publicly owned company to the

Table 25.1 *Estimate of total UK management buy-outs*

	Number	Value (£m)	Average size (£m)
1980	100	40	0.4
1981	180	130	0.7
1982	200	550	2.8
1983	220	240	1.1
1984	200	270	1.4
1985	250	1 070	4.3
1986	300	1 300	4.3
1987	350	3 230	9.2
1988	400	5 070	12.7
1989	500	6 530	13.0
1990	550	2 850	5.2
1991	500	2 600	5.2
1992	520	3 020	5.8
1993	510	2 810	5.5
	5080	31 110	6.1

Source: KPMG Corporate Finance.

management and employees. It was privatization. It was hoped that an equity involvement by all employees would increase motivation. In the majority of cases, however, it is just the top group of managers who are involved in the equity purchase.

It will become clear below that management buyouts take place under all sorts of circumstances and that consequently every buyout is different. For example, there are seller-motivated buyouts in which the selling company decides that the financial and management resources spent on a peripheral activity are not sensible. They require a greater involvement than the group is willing to commit to its non-core activity.

Alternatively, the management of a division may feel that they are isolated from the group's main decision-making process, thereby feeling frustrated in their abilities to obtain sufficient funds. This is an example of what becomes a buyer-motivated buyout. With this situation the buyer has the advantage of buying a business which is already in existence. It does not have to move up through a learning-curve process. This cuts down starting costs and running-in times.

The reasons behind a seller-motivated management buyout are similar to those listed earlier in the chapter as reasons for divestment:

1. sale of a subsidiary giving financial problems;
2. sale of a subsidiary that does not fit in with the new strategic plan for the group;
3. sale of unwanted parts to raise cash to fund an acquisition;
4. in a family-controlled business the owners might be happy to sell to the managers as it avoids publicity and should result in a speedy sale, and they may feel that they are helping to preserve the jobs of staff who have been loyal to them.

One aspect of a management buyout that has concerned some people is the use of inside information. Nobody knows more about the business being bought than the managers themselves; they know its potential and also its weaknesses. They probably know more about the business than the directors of the main company that is making the sale. Therefore the managers are in a good position to be able to buy at an 'advantageous' price. If they do so, it is the shareholders of the selling company that lose.

In fact managers of a subsidiary are sometimes in a position where they can produce reports that will make a management buyout more likely and on terms favourable to the buyers. It is the managers who can 'create' the impression that they want to give by controlling the information released. Clearly the group (the parent company) should have a good internal control system so that they always know the 'true' position, but this is not always the case. Wright and Coyne [6] have found that in some cases manipulation of figures has taken place in order to affect the buyout price.

The market for corporate control was referred to in Chapter 24 on mergers and takeovers. The management buyout is also a part of this corporate control system. If the managers and directors at group level do not perform to the satisfaction of shareholders, they can be threatened from outside the company. If they do not meet the expectation of interest groups within the company they can be threatened from within.

The buyout allows incumbent managers to exploit informational asymmetries in entering a transaction which will give them a substantial equity stake. Once they have committed themselves to the deal, the investment would be expected to act as a powerful incentive towards maximizing the value of the new entity. This pressure may be further strengthened by the bonding of the newly independent management team to their financiers, since any deviation from agreed financial targets could lead to loan default and failure. The buyout restores to the managers of the newly formed independent

Table 25.2 *Buy-outs in a sample of major British companies*

Group		Company sold	Size (£m)	
Hanson	Sep-83	Timpson	42	
	Oct-83	Collier Holdings	47	
	Dec-88	Lowfield Distribution	11	
	Apr-89	Elizabeth Shaw	25	
	May-89	Allders	260	
	May-89	Barbour Campbell	19	
	Jul-92	Kier Group	54	——
	Dec-93	SLD Holdings	91	549
Thorn EMI	Jul-87	AVO Megger Instruments	15	
	Sept-89	Kenwood Appliances	68	
	Jul-91	Data Sciences	103	
	Aug-93	Thorn Lighting Group	200	
	Jan-94	Electron Technologies	13	
	Apr-94	GB Glass	25	——
	Jun-94	Thorn Security Group	65	489
Grand Metropolitan	Nov-85	Mecca Leisure	98	
	Jul-87	Compass Group	160	
	May-89	London Clubs	125	
	Feb-90	Wimpy Restaurants	20	
	Feb-91	Bright Reasons	18	——
	Nov-92	Express Foods	116	537
British Rail	Jun-81	Gleneagles	14	
	Jan-87	BTA	50	
	Oct-87	RFS Industries	10	
	Dec-88	Travellers Fare	21	——
	Apr-89	BREL	14	109

Source: KPMG Corporate Finance.

business the threat of the bankruptcy sanction which is arguably absent where a corporate headquarters can act as 'lender of last resort'.

The funding of a management buyout can be very complicated. Venture capitalists are usually needed to assist with the provision of the equity funds. They usually finish up holding a certain percentage of the equity in the new business for what they hope will be a relatively short period of time. To begin with they might have to purchase a larger proportion of the equity than the management carrying out the buyout. It is their hope, however, that they will be able to sell these shares at a healthy profit in, say, three to five years' time. That length of time could elapse before the company can be launched on the stock market or the managers can accumulate enough finance themselves to be able to buy the shares of the venture capitalist or the company is successful enough for other investors to be interested in purchasing the shares. These are the possible exit routes for the venture capitalists.

The finance to acquire the assets from the selling company will come from a mixture of debt and equity. Usually relatively high levels of debt finance are required. Hence buyouts are sometimes called 'leveraged buyouts'. In a normal management buyout gearing (leverage) levels of 5:1 may be necessary, but in leveraged buyouts the level can rise to 20:1 (this is the ratio of debt to equity). Ratios of 10:1 are quite common. To support the resulting high levels of interest payments requires an extremely strong cash flow and the capacity to move quickly to create a market for the sale of the company's shares.

The use of leveraged buyout techniques has paved the way for many new entrepreneurial efforts. Because only a small proportion of equity finance is required, leveraged buyouts make it much easier for managers plus possible outside investors to try to run a business on their own. In a leveraged management buyout it may not be possible to raise all the finance required from the equity investment and the secured debt usually taken up by a leading bank. Hence mezzanine finance, or as it is sometimes called 'strip' finance, is required, as are specialist advisors.

A bank that specializes in buyouts is usually needed to put a suitable financial package together. The buyout specialist will purchase some of the equity. It will also arrange the loans required. The buyout specialist could well initially control the board of directors. It would of course leave the day-to-day running of the company to the managers, but it would be involved in setting strategic plans and long-range goals.

There are many banks who will assist with the raising of finance to fund a management buyout. Possible sources include the following:

1. The clearing banks.
2. Dedicated buyout funds. Many merchant bankers have set up subsidiaries specifically to deal with such situations.
3. Overseas bankers. The USA led the UK in the introduction of management buyouts. Their banks have therefore considerable expertise and finance available for this purpose. They in fact brought mezzanine finance ideas (discussed below) to the UK, to assist with management buyouts.

It is always possible, but difficult, for the managers wishing to buy a business to avoid heavy borrowing. They could try to arrange a deferred purchase scheme, i.e. to purchase the assets slowly over time. Another approach is a sale and leaseback: acquire the assets, sell them quickly and use the money raised to pay for the purchase.

Mezzanine finance

Mezzanine finance can be considered as a source of funds coming between the equity shares and the secured debt of a company. It is more risky than secured debt, but less risky than equity. It offers higher expected returns than senior debt issues but lower returns than equity. The yield it offers is high by the standards of debt, with interest rates of 4%–5% above the London Interbank Offered Rate (LIBOR). Often an equity warrant is attached which only becomes convertible if and when the company is floated on the stock market. If the company issuing mezzanine finance were liquidated, the securities issued would rank for repayment below other forms of debt. Mezzanine finance is an expression much used in the USA. It includes preference shares, convertible loans and loans which are subordinate to the secured debt. It also includes less well-known forms of finance such as vendor notes with an equity 'kicker'.

Because of its subordinate nature and the fact that in the USA it has tended to be used by companies who are not well established, mezzanine level debt issue is usually of a high-risk nature. However, a market for such high-yield high-risk securities has developed in the USA. The securities issued are not far removed from junk bonds.

The domestic corporate debt market, whether for first-class company debt, mezzanine debt or junk bonds, is not as well developed in the UK as in the USA.

Example – financing an MBO

It is easier to arrange a leveraged buyout for a company with cash flows that are expected to show a relatively stable growth over time. The example below illustrates this and shows how a leveraged buyout can work.

The new company purchases net assets of £1 million, half of which are depreciable. The fixed assets have a life of ten years. The company finances the purchase with £100 000 equity and £900 000 of debt finance. Its earnings before interest and tax (EBIT) in the first year is £200 000 and is expected to grow at 20% per annum. It pays corporation tax at a rate of 25%. Interest on the debt is at 15% per annum.

Profit and loss account (£000)

	Years				
	1	2	3	4	5
EBIT	200	240	288	346	415
Interest paid	135	125	111	92	63
	65	115	177	254	352
Tax payable	16	29	44	64	88
Earnings available	49	86	133	190	264
Sources and uses of funds					
Earnings	49	86	133	190	264
Depreciation	50	50	50	50	50
	99	136	183	240	314
Repayment of loans	70	90	130	190	270
Dividends	10	12	15	20	25
Increase in working capital	19	34	38	30	19
	99	136	183	240	314

Balance sheet

		Years				
	Opening	1	2	3	4	5
Equity	100	139	213	331	501	740
Debt	900	830	740	610	420	150
	1000	969	953	941	921	890
Assets	1000	1000	950	900	850	800
Less depreciation		50	50	50	50	50
		950	900	850	800	750
Working capital/opening balance/			19	53	91	121
increase during year		19	34	38	30	19
	1000	969	953	941	921	890

The resulting profit and loss account, sources and application of funds statement and balance sheet are shown above.

Basically what is happening is that the company, which is highly profitable, is using the funds generated each year to pay off the loans. It is only paying a small percentage of the funds earned to shareholders as dividends. The shareholders will in time receive their rewards in terms of capital gains. The funds retained in the business each year are not quite adequate to cover the loss in value of the fixed assets, and hence the total value of the assets slowly declines over the five years. The equity increases each year by the earnings available for distribution less the actual dividends paid. The year 1 figure is the initial equity of £100 000 plus the £49 000 profits, less the £10 000 dividend payment. A major change is that at the beginning of the period only 10% of the assets belonged to the shareholders, but at the end of the five years 83% of the assets belong to them. In book terms the value of the equity investment has increased sevenfold over the period. It is this increase that will lead to substantial capital gains for the original investors, i.e. the managers and any venture capital company that backed them.

Divestment may enable the subsidiary disposed of to improve its performance, as a study of management buyouts has shown [6]. Of 111 management buyouts studied, 62 per cent were bought from parents still trading. Reorganization after buyout involved changes to the management structure, changes in employee levels, improvements in cash and credit control systems, and movements into new product areas which had previously been difficult to achieve. These kinds of development were generally found to have been necessary as a result of problems which arose from being part of a parent organization or from the impossibility of resolving such difficulties within a group structure. Hence such entities may only be poor performers in a group context, and may be highly viable under an independent existence.

There has been criticism of the levels of gearing that have developed in leveraged buyouts. It means that almost any company is capable of being taken over if so much debt finance can be obtained by an acquirer. This in itself is not bad.

25.5 Going private

With this a small group of individuals, who might include existing shareholders and/or managers with or without institutional support, between them purchase all the shares of a public company. The small group end the public status of the company. It could result in the shares of a company no longer being dealt in on a stock exchange and so no longer being subject to whatever regulations applied. This type of restructuring is quite common in the USA.

On occasions a group of existing shareholders in the company purchase the shares of all the other shareholders. They would do this because the small group involved prefer private company status. An example of this occurred in the UK with the Virgin Company. Richard Branson, the founder of the company, built it up and then launched it as a public company. He later decided to revert to private company status and did so by buying back shares from the public and financial institutions.

The reasons for going private include the following.

1. The administrative burden and costs of meeting listing requirements are reduced.
2. The independence of a company that is financially attractive and vulnerable to a takeover bid is protected.
3. A company that is having financial problems that would result in a falling share price, with whatever that may bring about, is protected.
4. Agency costs are reduced; the small group of shareholders are more likely to be close to the managers than in a public company and there should be greater goal congruence.
5. The owner/manager does not wish to maximize short term performance.

It has been found that existing shareholders benefit from a 'going private' buyout situation. Their shares are purchased and this could well result in a capital gain. The reward situation is similar to that of shareholders in a company takeover; the vendor shareholders show gains. However, as mentioned above, in a normal management buy-out situation, the sale price can sometimes benefit the purchasers who have inside information and opportunity to control information to affect the purchase price.

It might be difficult for the small group to fund the acquisition, so that the assistance of a venture capital company or another third party might be required. If a large proportion of borrowed funds are required, it resembles a leveraged buyout. If the management of the original company are involved in the group making the acquisition it is a form of management buyout, with the buyout being for the whole of the assets of the selling company.

Leveraged management buyouts do however differ from going private in a number of ways. One of the key differences is that third party equity participation is usually necessary in the buyout. Another difference is the amount of borrowing required. A going private deal usually does not need so much outside finance.

Going private

SAGA, the tour operators for the over 50 year olds, changed its status from public to private in 1990. The family that owned 63% of the shares made a bid to buy the remainder of the shares. The family raised the finance to purchase the shares by bank borrowing.

The company had been launched on the stock market in 1978. As a public company it was not willing to take advantage of one of the most important benefits of being quoted, namely using its shares to fund acquisitions, because the family did not wish to dilute its controlling interest. The fear was that if the family lost control there was a risk that the successful company would be vulnerable to a hostile bidder.

A public quotation gives the opportunity to expand by acquisition. It also overcomes the problems that can be faced by many family companies of having to sell shares in order to meet death duties. The danger of the public quotation is, as mentioned, the possibility of a hostile takeover bid and a possible conflict between the long-term interests of the 'business' and satisfying outside minority shareholders' short-term expectations.

The Chairman of the company pointed to this last pressure as a reason for going private. The family on occasions wished to make medium- and longer-term investments in the business but were conscious of the need to pay dividends to meet the short-term aspirations of the City. The financial institutions owned in the region of 50% of the shares not held by the family.

As a private company the majority shareholders can now take decisions in what they see as the long-term interests of the company and be free from the short-term pressures that the City institutions are alleged to exert.

25.6 Buy-in

In a buy-in a group of managers who have, or who believe that they have, the necessary skills to run a particular type of business look around for such a business to purchase. They hope to find a company that has considerable potential but that has not been run to its full advantage, perhaps because of poor existing management. Having found a suitable company they will then work with a financier, usually a venture capitalist, to put together a deal to buy the target business from its existing shareholders. The target could be the whole of the company, or just a part of it. They will make an offer to either the managers or the existing owners of the business, and hope that the target company will be prepared to sell off part of its business or that the shareholders will sell off the whole of the business.

It is the opposite of a buyout, in which existing managers of a business attempt to buy the assets that they already manage. In a buy-in a group of outside managers attempt to take control of the target assets from the existing owners and to take over management from existing managers. With a buy-in, unlike a management buyout, there is no advantage of insider knowledge.

The financial backer – the venture capitalist – is crucial in such buy-ins. Usually the managers who are planning to run the business have limited resources of their own and so high levels of borrowing or mezzanine finance are required. In a number of buy-ins it is in fact the venture capitalist who initiates the deal. A financial institution might notice that the managers of a business are not making the best use of opportunities and so they seek a team of managers whom they would be willing to support to run the business.

25.7 Increase the amount of borrowing

Increasing the amount of borrowing is a defensive policy that is sometimes adopted at the time of a takeover bid or in a situation where a company feels vulnerable to a takeover bid. The idea is that increasing the amount of debt makes the company over-geared and so less attractive to a predator. The danger is that if a company has a low debt-to-asset ratio it is attractive to a predator; this is because its assets can be used as a base to increase borrowing. Therefore, as a defence tactic, the company can bloat itself with debt.

Of course, it is reducing the interest and asset cover that exists on any borrowings or on loan stock that has been issued. The question might also be raised as to why anyone would buy the new securities or lend to a company pursuing such a policy. In fact merchant banks advising companies on their defensive tactics at the time of a takeover bid will often buy such newly issued bonds themselves and/or syndicate them to other banks.

25.8 Share re-purchase

Since the Companies Act 1981, it has been possible for companies in the UK to re-purchase their own shares. This is a form of capital restructuring. For a company to do this it is necessary for its articles of association to give it the right to do so. There must be approval by the shareholders for a general power to buy in the market or specific approval for an off-market purchase. Own shares purchased by a UK company must be cancelled; there is no provision for them to be held for subsequent resale, as there is in the USA.

GEC was one of the first UK quoted companies to obtain and use this power. In the accounts for the year ended 31 March 1985, the Directors' Report gave a summary of the transactions in which 73 million shares of 5p each (nominal value £3.6 million) were purchased for £156 million.

A company may wish to re-purchase its shares in the following circumstances.

1. It has cash available and, rather than paying it out to shareholders as dividends, it purchases some of its shares in the market-place. The continuing shareholders should benefit as the share price should rise. The total supply of the company's shares has fallen and there is no reason to believe that the total demand for the shares will have changed.
2. A major shareholder may wish to dispose of his or her shares and the shareholders agree that the company should use its funds to buy these shares and cancel them.

Although the possibility of re-purchase is comparatively new in the UK, it has existed for a long time in the USA. It has been seen in that country as a an alternative to paying a dividend. It has been discussed in this book in Chapter 17 in connection with dividend policy. In theory, if the capital market is efficient and there are no commission and taxation problems, the company and the shareholders should be indifferent between a dividend payment and a share re-purchase.

One result of the re-purchase is an increase in earnings per share, and it is sometimes suggested that this will benefit the shareholders because it leads to an increase in share price. However, if the company had retained the cash and reinvested, this should have led to an increase in earnings, and so in share price, and if it had paid the cash out as a dividend a shareholder could have invested the cash to increase his or her returns.

The opportunity to repurchase shares has not proved to be very attractive to companies in the UK. Only a handful of publicly quoted companies have bought their own shares. In 1988 the City Capital Markets Committee suggested that company managements and shareholders should open their minds to share re-purchases. They suggested that they give greater consideration to share re-purchase as a component of financial strategies.

Reverse takeover occurs when one company X takes over another company Y that is larger than itself. If the purchase was paid for just in shares, the situation would finish up with the original shareholders of Y owning more shares in the amalgamated company than the original shareholders of X. The shareholders of X would finish up with a minority interest in their 'own' company. This situation can be avoided if some of the payment is in the form of cash. X could raise the cash through a rights issue or by borrowing.

An attempt at a reverse takeover occurred in the UK when the Australian brewing company Elders IXL attempted to take over the much larger UK company Allied–Lyons. Elders planned to finance the acquisition by borrowing from a consortium of banks. The bid was eventually withdrawn.

One result of a reverse takeover financed by borrowing is to raise dramatically the level of gearing of the company making the bid. It becomes like a leveraged buyout. The banks funding the acquisition need to be assured that the acquirer will be able to service the debt taken on.

A reverse takeover bid requires the agreement of the shareholders of the bidding firm. This technique can be used in situations where a private company wishes to go public. It needs to be organized such that it is the public company X, the smaller company, that takes over the larger private company Y. X would issue its shares to the shareholders of Y. The original shareholders of Y will now be the majority shareholders in a public company. The public company, which may or may not have a listing, will be much larger following this reverse takeover.

Asset swaps

These arise when one company swaps some of its assets for assets in another company. Such swaps often arise in cross-border deals. A British company may have a certain asset (say a factory) in the UK it does not want. It may be looking for a factory in France. If it can find a French company that wishes to dispose of a factory in France and to obtain one in the UK then a deal can be struck.

An example arose in the case of the British company Powergen. The company was required to dispose of certain generating plant in the UK. The disposal was necessary because of an arrangement it had come to with the Regulator of the electricity industry. Rather than sell the generating plant to a purchaser, and so obtain cash, Powergen preferred to swap the assets for assets in another country.

The earlier sections in this chapter were concerned with positive aspect of restructuring. We now turn to negative reasons for change. There can be many different reasons why a company might encounter financial difficulties and fail. There is evidence that the percentage of companies that fail in any year is highly correlated with macro-economic factors, such as changes in interest rates and changes in the level of economic activity. Other significant factors outside the firm's control can be changes in technology and changes in consumer demands. Changes in technology mean that the firm's production methods become obsolete, and changes in consumers' tastes and habits mean that the demand for the product or service produced quickly disappears.

The main reason, however, why a particular business fails is inadequate management. It can be argued that even if there are changes in macro-economic factors, in technology or in consumer habits a management that thinks ahead should have been ready for these events. They should have been able to anticipate these changes. A management with a strategy, with a plan, should be sufficiently diversified to be able to withstand all but the most dramatic crises.

The sequence of events leading to the typical failure can be summarized as follows:

1. Bad management: leads to
2. Poor management information (including poor accounting information): leads to
3. Mistakes: including one of the following
   (a) not responding to change in the market place, in technology or in society;
   (b) overtrading – rapid expansion;
   (c) the launch of a big project or making a large acquisition – either the growth is too much for the management to handle, or the timing is wrong;
   (d) allowing financial gearing to rise – poor financial structure;
   (e) overdependence on a small number of customers or suppliers.
   Difficulties resulting from one of these policies leads to:
4. Financial ratios deteriorating and/or creative accounting techniques being utilized.

We will briefly look at each of these 'stages'.

Bad management

There is some agreement in the literature on the management characteristics which can be dangerous and result in bad decisions. We list some of these characteristics below. It is not being suggested that all companies that experience one or more of these characteristics will fail. All that is being pointed out is that in a high proportion of companies that do fail there is one or more of these characteristics present. There are, for example, companies that are successful and have been successful for a long time that are dominated by one individual. This is not being denied. But there are also a high proportion of firms that fail that are dominated by one person.

Worrying characteristics
1. one-man (or one-woman) rule;
2. combined position of chairman of board of directors and chief executive of the company;
3. unbalanced board of directors;
4. unbalanced top management team;
5. lack of depth in management team;
6. weak finance function in the company;
7. a board of directors with too few (non participating) non-executive directors.

Most of these items are self-explanatory. The Cadbury Report on Corporate Governance commented on a number of the same issues. They had been discussed in the literature of corporation failure for a long time. The Cadbury report was more concerned with the abuse of power, that is the top management team acting in their own interests rather than in the interests of their shareholders. It is intriguing that the same factors which can lead to an abuse of power can also lead to business failure.

Inadequate management information systems

It is important that a company's decision-makers have certain up-to-date information on such items as turnover, cash flow, rate of gross profits and levels of creditors and borrowing. When failed companies are analysed after the event it is often found that they have:

- poor cost accounting data, therefore lack of information of true costs;
- there is poor budgetary control;
- there are inadequate cash-flow forecasts;
- the decision-makers are not aware of the true value of the assets;
- there is poor control of working capital.

Mistakes

The weakness in management combined with poor information leads to mistakes. Certain of the more common are mentioned above. Other mistakes include:

- badly directed research and development programmes;
- inappropriate diversification.

On the subject of an acquisition or capital expansion programme that is too large, Sir Kenneth Cork, a leading UK liquidator, has expressed the opinion that a company should not undertake an investment which if it fails could not be written off and the company still remain a viable business. 'Too large' is of course a function of the size of the company. All that is being suggested is that a company 'should not bite off more than it can chew'. There is a danger that some management teams that have done well during a boom period think they can achieve anything. This tempts them into undertaking big projects relative to their size or into making a major acquisition. It only requires a small change in the macro-economic situation to prove that the management team has its limitations.

Financial accounts

It is only some time after management mistakes have been made that this will become apparent from the published accounting numbers. The annual report and accounts is mainly an historical document. Through the use of techniques for smoothing accounting profits and losses and through creative accounting techniques, recognition of the actual financial position of a company may be delayed. Directors in companies that have something to hide will adopt a policy involving the 'management of earnings disclosure'. In the end of course, the true position will become apparent.

It is precisely because of this time lag between a company's getting into financial difficulties and it being possible to detect this from annual accounts that superficial financial ratio analysis is of limited use. There are, of course, many models based on financial ratios that are used in practice to identify companies in financial difficulties. (These are discussed in Chapter 3.)

The point being made in this section is that anybody interested in the credit standing of a company or in valuing the company's shares needs to look for the symptoms and possible causes of failure in a company. These are of course subjective but it does not mean they can be ignored. It is dangerous to wait until the financial problem can be identified objectively through the annual reports of accounts.

When a company is experiencing financial difficulties steps need to be taken to try to save the company from liquidation. The steps can be initiated by the managers themselves, the bankers or possibly the shareholders.

Managers will (or should) be the first to be aware that a company is having financial problems. The steps they can initially take which it is hoped will improve the situation include:

25.11 Refinancing

- layoff of some employees;
- plant closure;
- sale of assets;

- reduction of expenditure on research and development;
- begin to negotiate with banks for either extra finance and/or rescheduling of existing debts.

The banks may become aware of a company's difficulties as a result of increasing borrowing requirements or they may become aware that a company is near to breaking its borrowing covenants. The banks should be monitoring the company's cash-flow position. Shareholders may become aware of difficulties as a result of falling profits, of boardroom disputes, of creative accounting techniques being adopted. The shareholders (the legal owners) could well be the last to know of the financial problems.

The first step in the UK in saving a company is a 'standstill agreement'. This means that the company's bank or bankers agree to continue to provide banking facilities for a period of time in order to allow the company to work out proposals for the future. Standstill agreements are usually short: usually only a month or two is allowed.

There has been much ill-feeling over this matter. It has been argued that the banks in the UK have been too quick to close down the smaller company. It is argued that the larger the company, the bigger the debts, the more likely it is that banks will give a company time in which to be saved.

In the UK it was certainly the case in the late 1980s and early 1990s that the larger the company the greater the chance of survival once the company became insolvent. Only 13% of insolvent companies with a turnover of less than £1 million were saved and only 28% of those with a turnover between £1 million and £5 million. This contrasts with 36% of insolvent companies with a turnover of between £5 million and £15 million being saved and 64% of companies with a turnover of £15 million or more being saved.

It can be seen that for the vast majority of companies with a turnover of less than £15 million, once they are insolvent that is the end. Of course there is a stage between financial difficulties and insolvency. The Bank of England in the early 1990s tried to encourage debate among the various stakeholders who become involved with companies in financial difficulty. They were responding to the criticism that banks seek to close companies down too early. They launched what is known as the 'London approach', the main points being that

- banks should be initially supportive of insolvent companies and not rush to appoint receivers;
- consideration should be given to a standstill agreement to enable proper analysis to take place;
- decisions about a company's future should be made on the basis of reliable information which is shared among all the parties involved – banks should not rush in to save their investment at the expense of all other interested parties;
- banks and other creditors should work together to reach a collective view on whether and how a company should be given financial support.

It should be appreciated that the aim of the 'London approach' is not to prevent receivers and administrators being appointed where necessary, 'but to avoid the unnecessary collapse of potentially viable businesses as a result of disagreements amongst creditors'. The Bank of England wishes to encourage the stakeholders to formulate 'workout proposals', but only if it maximizes value for creditors; the Bank has no power however to enforce the rules.

Once a standstill agreement has been agreed upon, it is usual to appoint a firm of accountants to provide a view on the future prospects of the company. Hopefully a rescue plan is proposed. This plan will be concerned with operational matters, such as ceasing to trade in certain areas, and with financial matters.

The financial plan will have to take into account the interests of shareholders, bondholders, banks, managers and creditors. All could well have conflicting views as to whether, and how, the company should be saved.

The lenders, whether bondholders or banks, might well be reluctant to invest any further money, but might well have to put up with the restructuring of the existing loans. The restructuring could involve

- extension of the period before the loan is repaid;
- agreement to defer the payment of interest on the debt;
- agreement to roll up interest into future periods;
- the swapping of debt for an equity stake in the company.

The giving up of debt in return for an equity stake by banks was once uncommon in the UK, but it has now become more widespread. It had for a long time been a common practice in Continental Europe. British banks have argued that they are there as lenders not as investors. They see debt swaps only as a last-resort solution.

In a restructuring the interests of ordinary and preference shareholders need to be considered. In fact their position is usually very weak. They are usually unwilling to invest new money in a company in a poor financial condition.

A high-profile company that needed to restructure was Laura Ashley. In 1989 the company had high debts and trading conditions were very poor. The company was using a multiple currency option facility to enable it to borrow short term up to a certain level. The agreement contained a gearing covenant. The level of gearing was approaching the limit. It should be appreciated that the banks are in a position to monitor the level of gearing of a company at any time; they require regular cash-flow information to be supplied by the company as a condition of a loan.

Managers of Laura Ashley had a meeting with the bankers. The company wanted additional short-term lines of credit. They were worried that the need for short-term facilities would exceed the limits. It was reported in the press that some banks wanted to withdraw previously agreed commitments. They were worried Laura Ashley would default.

The company complained that they had paid 'commitment fees for years and when the funds were needed they were not there' – the commitment fee being payable to provide for a line of credit as and when needed.

The banks eventually agreed (in 1990) to make more short-term finance available, but it was reported that the terms were 'excessively punitive'. The company also had high fees to pay to lawyers, accountants and bankers for arranging the refinancing. To obtain a long-term financial solution to its problems the company in the end did a deal with a Japanese company who paid cash for shares in the company.

One hopes that as a result of the study of how to manage the financial affairs of a business the reader of this book will never experience his or her own business becoming insolvent. One hopes that the closest the reader will come to a business liquidation is that of a company supplying goods or services moving in to the hands of a receiver or of a debtor becoming bankrupt or being liquidated. It has to be appreciated, however, that sometimes the reason companies are liquidated is through little fault of their own. Changes in patterns of trade, in technology, in government economic policy, or as a result of political actions can all lead to a company's becoming insolvent. Figure 25.1 illustrates the number of liquidations in the UK in recent years.

25.12 Insolvency/liquidation

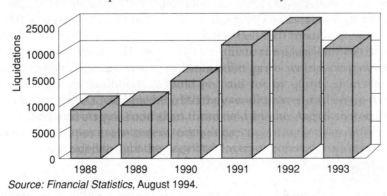

Source: Financial Statistics, August 1994.

Figure 25.1 Liquidation in the UK, 1988–93

We will briefly explain the meaning of the terms involved in this, the ultimate form of business reorganization. Insolvency arises when a business or an individual does not have enough assets to cover the debts. Insolvency of course differs from being illiquid. In the latter case a company merely does not have the cash available to pay its debts; it does not mean that if the company realized its fixed assets or sold its inventory it would not have the cash it needs.

Insolvency does not necessarily lead to liquidation. There are a number of actions that can be taken that will avoid the ultimate end of the business. Insolvency is a fact. Either the company has enough assets to cover its debts or it does not. It is the responsibility of the directors of a company to know whether or not a company is insolvent. There are very heavy fines that directors (executive and non-executive) may have to pay if they allow a company to continue trading when it is insolvent. For them to do so is known as 'wrongful trading'. It is no excuse that they did not know the company was insolvent – it is their job to know.

When a company announces it is insolvent, or it fails to pay a debt on time, there are a number of procedures the banks and creditors involved with the company and the courts can follow. We list below five of these procedures in which the court or creditors or bankers are involved:

1. company voluntary arrangement (CVA);
2. administrations;
3. receivership (administrative receiverships);
4. creditors' voluntary liquidations;
5. compulsory liquidations.

Most insolvencies result in the company going into administration. A CVA is the second most common. The third most common is receivership, followed by creditors' voluntary liquidation.

With a company voluntary arrangement, the creditors ask the court to appoint an insolvency practitioner to be an administrator with the task of attempting to rescue the company. The company management work with the administrator in an attempt to save the business – the company management and the administrator jointly run the business. Such arrangements have had mixed success and on occasions they can be unworkable.

An example will illustrate the type of complicated situation that can arise. One large UK company, Heron International, became technically insolvent in 1992. The insolvency was triggered by default on a £7 million interest payment to bondholders. The interest was not paid on the date it was due. To apply for a receivership the bondholders would have needed to obtain support from the holders of 25% of the bonds.

The company was very highly geared. Heron asked the bondholders to allow payment of the interest to be deferred. The holding company Heron International had debts of over £1.0 billion, of which £260 million was owed to bondholders, £90 million to banks, and £650 million to an associated company Heron Corporation. Most of the assets of Heron International were in shares of Heron Corporation, the other assets of the company only being £40 million. It was Heron Corporation that owned the main assets of the group.

29 banks had lent to Heron International, of which 24 also lent to Heron Corporation. In contrast the bondholders were only involved with Heron International. The bondholders claimed the bankers knew more about the operation and financial condition of the group than they did. It was not clear whether the bondholders had recourse, in the event of default by Heron International, to the assets of Heron Corporation.

The debts of Heron were rescheduled. It was the second time that rescheduling was necessary within one financial year. This large company was not put into receivership.

Administration

This is a procedure designed to allow a business to continue while plans are developed either to rescue the business or to attempt to maximize its asset value. Its aim is to give a business time to breathe. It is not necessarily beneficial for a company to cease trading the moment it becomes insolvent. It might be possible to rescue the company, or to improve the value of the assets of the business prior to disposal.

For a company to go into administration, it is necessary to obtain permission from a court. Either the representatives of the company that is insolvent or creditors of that company can seek from the court an administrative order. The court before granting such an order will wish to see some evidence that allowing administration now could lead to greater benefits than proceeding immediately to liquidation.

If the court grants an administrative order, the day-to-day running of the company is put in the hands of an administrator who is appointed by the court. While the administrator is running the company the creditors cannot take steps to recover assets or to interfere with the running of the business. This means that administrations are not always popular with banks and other creditors. The banks and creditors are concerned because the administration process can be costly and time-consuming, and does not necessarily rescue the business or lead to an improvement in the value of the assets of the business.

Receiverships

These are officially called administrative receiverships. With this process a receiver is appointed by a bank or another institution which has lent to the insolvent company and which has a fixed charge, a floating charge or a debenture over a substantial part of the company's assets. A major difference between a receivership and an administration is that with a receivership it is a lending institution or institutions that make the appointment of the person to run the affairs of the insolvent company whereas with an administration it is the court that makes the appointment. The receiver is often seen by the insolvent company as simply a debt collector for the banks and other lending institutions, whereas the administrator is seen as a person trying to save the company in a restructured form.

Technically, the receiver acts in the best interests of all creditors not just of the institutions that made the appointment. They frequently keep a business running for a period after their appointment in order to make it easier to find a buyer for the whole business. They do not necessarily sell off the individual assets in order to obtain funds to pay off the major creditors. The Society of Practitioners of Insolvency estimate that receivers in fact manage to save 45% of insolvent companies in their care.

Banks prefer receiverships to administrations, because with the latter process they are not in a position to interfere with the administrator while he or she is trying to save the business. With a receivership it is the banks who appoint the person to run the business. If and when a receiver finds it not possible to find a buyer for the business a liquidator is appointed to take over and the assets are sold, and what cash is realized is distributed to creditors.

It is sometimes claimed in the UK that when a company is experiencing financial difficulties banks frequently call in a receiver far too quickly. It is claimed that if the banks were to give a company a little more time to solve its problems the company could be saved.

Creditors' voluntary liquidations

This is a procedure for winding up insolvent businesses. It involves selling off a company's assets and distributing what cash is available. With a creditors' voluntary liquidation the shareholders of the company, on realizing that the company is insolvent, appoint a liquidator. This is followed by a creditors' meeting at which the person proposed by the shareholders as a liquidator will be confirmed or another liquidator appointed. The liquidator is expected to act in the best interest of all creditors.

The appointment of a liquidator almost always means the end for a company; it almost always means the company ceases trading.

Compulsory liquidation

This is a form of liquidation, in which an individual creditor can take steps that will lead to the winding up of a company. Compulsory liquidation is the last step of a creditor or group of creditors who cannot obtain the co-operation of the management and shareholders of a company when there are debts unpaid. The creditors petition the court for a winding-up order.

This procedure differs from creditors' voluntary liquidation, in that with the voluntary process the company shareholders agree to go into liquidation. With the compulsory process the company's wishes do not matter. If the court is satisfied that a creditor is owed money and that the company is insolvent, it will order that the company be wound up.

Members' (shareholders') voluntary liquidation

This is a winding-up process initiated by a company. It differs from the five methods mentioned above in that it occurs not when a company is insolvent, but when a company is in a position to pay its debts in full. The members, that is the shareholders, wish to have the company's assets turned into cash, to have the creditors paid and for the balance to be returned to them. They wish to cash in their investments. They may wish to do this when they believe the company has fulfilled the objectives set when it was formed, or because they no longer wish to be involved in the business venture.

Practices within the European Union

Since the time the European Economic Community was formed attempts have been made to harmonize the insolvency laws of the different states. None of the attempts has been successful, the main reason being that the results one country wishes to achieve from its insolvency laws differ from the results another country wishes to achieve. For example the French put greater weight in their insolvency laws to protecting the rights of the employees of the insolvent company than do the British. The pecking order in which the different types of creditor of the company are repaid varies from one country to another.

The attitude towards an undischarged bankrupt also varies from country to country. The term bankruptcy of course applies to individuals. In the UK a person who is bankrupt is nearly always automatically discharged two or three years after being declared bankrupt. When the person is discharged from bankruptcy this means that any unpaid balance of debts is written off. The person involved can then enter into another business venture. This is not the case in most other countries in the European Union, where the practice is that a person remains bankrupt until able to pay fully the outstanding debts. The British seem keen to give a person another chance even though the bankrupt person may have large amounts of outstanding debts. Unfortunately, it is not uncommon for an individual having been given another chance to fail yet again with a new list of creditors unable to be paid.

The differences in insolvency and bankruptcy laws within the European Union are so far apart that it will be a long time before any degree of harmonization can be achieved.

USA Chapter 11

There has been much criticism of the banks in the UK for allegedly withdrawing financial support too quickly from companies in financial difficulties. The result is that the company goes into receivership. The argument is that if the bank that had lent money to the company continued to provide support the company would survive. For the bank the decision on whether to continue support or to appoint a receiver is often finely balanced. The bank has to decide whether if it allows the company to continue to trade it could result in even greater future losses for the bank and the other creditors of the company. The bank can argue that their primary responsibility is to their own shareholders, and not in attempting to preserve jobs and maintain levels of employment.

Critics of the UK banks point enviously to the system that exists in the USA. Chapter 11 of the US Bankruptcy Code is geared more to assisting a company to survive than to protecting the creditors. If a company in the USA in financial difficulties applies to the courts for protection under Chapter 11, it is given time in which to try to solve its financial problems. The company is given the time in which to work with its creditors in an attempt to come up with a rescue package. Usually this means the business is restructured – it is reconstructed. Perhaps parts of the business will be sold, perhaps the debt repayments will be retimed. The creditors are prevented from moving in quickly and closing the business down. The company is given breathing space.

This US procedure has had some speculator successes, but its critics claim it is expensive to administer, and is only successful with larger companies. It is claimed that not more than 12% of Chapter 11 cases result in a successful reorganization. The management of a company in difficulties in the UK would not surprisingly favour US Chapter 11 type legislation, as it gives them an opportunity to continue to control the business, which would not happen in receivership. It keeps the company out of the hands of the banks at least for some time.

25.13 Key terms

Administration	Liquidation
Asset swaps	Management buy-out
Bankruptcy	Mezzanine finance
Buy-in	Receivership
'Chapter 11'	Refinancing
Demerger	Reverse takeover
Divestment	Scheme of arrangement
Going private	Sell-offs
Insolvency	Share repurchase
Junk bonds	Spin-offs
Leveraged buy-out	

25.14 Revision questions

1. Why did spin-offs, sell-offs and buyouts become so popular in the 1980s?
2. What are the advantages to shareholders of a spin-off?
3. What is mezzanine finance?
4. The advantages of leveraged buyouts were oversold in the late 1980s, and they will result in financial distress for many companies. Discuss.
5. What are the conditions attached to share re-purchases in the UK?
6. Why would a company that has gone to the trouble of obtaining a public quotation decide to reverse the process and 'go private'?
7. 'Management buyouts are popular because a group with inside information are able to use this information to purchase at an advantageous price.' Discuss.
8. What is the difference between a buyout and a buy-in? Does it make any difference to shareholders?
9. What is the difference between an administrator, a receiver and a liquidator?
10. When the directors of a company find that the company is insolvent what steps could they take if they wish the company to continue in existence?

25.15 References

1. Duhaime, I.M. and Grant, J.H. (1984) Factors influencing divestment decision-making: evidence from a field study, *Strategic Management Journal*, **5**, 301–18.
2. Alexander, G.J., Benson, P.G. and Kampmeyer, J.M. (1984) Investigating valuation effects of announcements of voluntary corporate sell-off, *Journal of Finance*, **39**, 503–17.

   Jain, P.C. (1985) The effect of voluntary sell-off announcements on shareholder wealth, *Journal of Finance*, **40**, 209–24.

   Miles, J.A. and Rosenfield, J.D. (1983) The effect of voluntary spin-off announcements on shareholder wealth, *Journal of Finance*, **38**(5), 1597–606.

   Montgomery, C.A., Thomas, A.R. and Kamath, R. (1984) Divestiture, market valuation and strategy, *Academy of Management Journal*, **27**.
3. Miles, J.A. and Rosenfield, J.D., *op cit.*, 830–40.
4. Jain, P.C., *op cit.*
5. Wright, M. and Coyne, J. (1985) *Management Buyouts in British Industry*, Croom-Helm.

25.16 Further reading

For a selection of interesting articles on the subject see:

Deangelo, H., Deangelo, L. and Rice, E. (1986) Going Private: a study of the effects of changes in corporate ownership structure, in *The Revolution in Corporate Finance*, J.M. Stern and D.H. Chew (eds), Blackwell, Oxford.

Franks, J.R. and Harris, R.S. (1989) Shareholder wealth effects of corporate takeovers: the UK experience 1955–1985, *Journal of Financial Economics*, **23**.

Jensen, M.C. (1989) Eclipse of the Public Corporation, *Harvard Business Review*, Sept./Oct.

Rybczynski, T. (1989) Corporate Restructuring, *National Westminster Bank Quarterly Review*, August.

Wright, M. (1986) Demergers, in *Divestment and Strategic Change*, J. Coyne and M. Wright (eds), Philip Allan.

Wright, M., Robbie, K. and Thompson, S. (1989) On the finance and accounting implications of management buyouts, *British Accounting Review*, September.

25.17 Problems

1. Management buyouts have become popular in UK industry since 1980, and accountants play a part in appraising the viability of such schemes.

   (a) State what you understand by the term 'management buyout', and outline three situations in which such an operation might be attempted. (11 marks)

   (b) As an accountant advising a management buyout team, set out the main matters covered by your reports:
   (i) to the members of the team
   (ii) to a financial institution which is requested to provide capital for the venture
   (14 marks)
   (25 marks)
   ACCA, June 1987

2. (a) In recent years there has been a large increase in the number of management buyouts, often when a company is in financial distress. What are the possible financial advantages to the seller of a management buyout relative to a liquidation?

   (b) Five managers of Leivers Ltd are discussing the possibility of a management buyout on the part of the company that they work for. The buyout would require a total of £700 000, of which £525 000 would comprise the purchase cost and £175 000 funds for a small expansion in activity, and for working capital. The managers believe that they could jointly provide £70 000.

(i) Discuss possible sources of finance that the managers might use to raise the required funds.

(ii) What are likely to be the major factors that a potential supplier of finance will consider before deciding whether to offer finance? What type of security or other conditions might providers of finance specify?

ACCA, June 1988

3. A large retail store decides to spin off one of its subsidiaries that produces shop fittings. You are one of the directors of this subsidiary and with other colleagues you decide that you would like to acquire it. Between you it is possible to produce £500 000 of capital, but the parent company hopes to obtain £5 million from the sale. The current level of earnings of the subsidiary before tax is £300 000. The corporation tax rate is 30%. Put together a financial proposal to purchase the subsidiary that might appeal to financial backers and to the parent company.

4. It has been argued that leveraged buyouts are self-limiting, short-term organizations, which are likely to produce significant adverse effects on corporate investment. To what extent do you agree or disagree with this view?

5. Analyse the case for requiring the parties to a merger to show that it would produce positive benefits before allowing it to proceed. To what extent do you consider that 'divestment deals' may have a positive role to play in allowing the market for corporate control to function?

6. The senior management of the plastics division of Kram plc is planning a 'leveraged' buyout of the division. The division will become an unlisted public limited company after the buyout. Recent financial details of the division are summarized below:

Plastics division: Summarized profit and loss account for:

	Last year £000	Two years ago £000
Turnover	8500	8100
Earnings before interest and tax	946	958
Interest[1]	520	466
Attributable taxation[2]	206	187
Earnings after tax	220	305

Plastics division: Summarized balance sheet as at the end of:

	£000	Last year £000	£000	Two years ago £000
Land and buildings[3]		880		840
Plant and machinery (net)		1336		1440
		2216		2280
Stock	1830		1440	
Debtors	1160		940	
Bank	40	3030	87	2467
Less:				
Creditors	720		680	
Attributable taxation	206		187	
Bank overdraft	320	(1246)	—	(867)
		4000		3880
Financed by:[4]				
Equity		2800		2720
Debt		1200		1160
		4000		3880

Notes

[1] This represents an annual payment to the group for the total amount of long-term finance provided, plus interest on the bank overdraft. The cost of the long-term finance provided by the group is based upon the group's weighted average cost of capital of 12% per year.

[2] The division is charged taxation by the group according to the percentage of group earnings before interest and tax that are generated by the plastics division.

[3] The land and buildings are estimated to have a market value 30% higher than the book value.

[4] Financing is based upon the same proportions as the book value of the group's equity and debt. The group has provided all external financing for the division, with the exception of the bank overdraft.

The managers of the plastics division have been told that the division may be purchased for the cash sum of £5 million. The bank overdraft would be repaid by the group prior to any purchase and there would be no outstanding long-term liabilities or tax liability at the time of purchase.

The managers would contribute a total of £500 000 in return for 500 000 £1 ordinary shares. Grow-Venture plc would provide the other £4.5 million, £400 000 in ordinary shares, £1.5 million in fixed rate bonds at a fixed annual interest rate of 13%, £1 million in subordinated debt at an annual interest rate of 14% and the remainder in 9% convertible loan stock. Conversion is at the rate of 50 shares for every £100 loan stock, and may occur at any time after six years.

A condition imposed by Grow-Venture is that the £1.5 million 13% debt and the £1 million 14% debt are both repaid by a series of equal annual payments (including interest and principal) over five years.

Grow-Venture plans to dispose of its shareholdings (but not convertible loan stock) in a little over five years' time when it is hoped that the company will be listed on the USM with a market value of equity at least as great as the book value of equity at that time.

Corporate tax is payable at the rate of 35% in the year that profit is earned. No further capital issues are planned, nor major purchases or disposals of fixed assets during the next five years. Annual dividends are expected to be 20% of available earnings for the forseeable future, and the division's cost of equity is estimated to be 22% per year. The average price-earnings ratio of small listed companies in the plastics industry is 14.1:1.

Earnings before interest and tax are expected to increase by 8% per year.

Required:

(a) Estimate the minimum annual compound percentage increase in the book value of its equity holding that Grow-Venture plc hopes for over a five-year period. State clearly any assumptions that you make. (10 marks)

(b) Explain what is meant by a 'leveraged' (geared) management buyout and estimate how gearing is expected to alter during the first five years after the management buyout. (6 marks)

(c) Discuss, showing any relevant calculations whether you think that the price of the buyout of £5 million is a fair price, too high or too low. (9 marks)

(25 marks)

ACCA, June 1990

7. An entrepreneur wishes to undertake a buy-in of Endess Ltd. The entrepreneur will have 60% ownership of the share capital and other investors (including some existing management) 40%.

Endess's accountant has recently read the valuation chapter in a finance textbook and suggests two valuations using methods in the book.

(a) Based upon a version of the Berliner method.

This is the *average* of:

(i) the realizable value of the net tangible assets of the company;

(ii) the estimated maintainable profits of the company capitalized at a rate of 16%.

Maintainable profits are to be based upon the average pre-tax profit of the last two years.

(b) Based upon the super-profit approach.

This requires an agreed normal pre-tax rate of return, in this case 15%, to be applied to the realizable value of net tangible assets to establish normal profits. These profits are then compared with the expected average annual pre-tax profits over the next two years. If expected profits are higher, this difference is regarded as a super-profit, and the price to be paid will be the net assets price plus three years of superprofits.

Endess has supplied the following summarized financial data to the entrepreneur.

Profit and loss accounts, year ending 31 March (£000)

	1992	1993
Turnover	1940	2175
Cost of goods sold	1410	1550
Gross profit	530	625
Distribution costs	85	100
Administrative expenses	120	140
Interest payable	84	78
Profit before tax	241	307
Taxation	70	92
Profit after tax	171	215

Balance sheets as at 31 March (£000)

	1992		1993	
Fixed assets:				
Land and buildings		340		340
Plant and equipment (net)		580		540
		920		880
Current assets:				
Stock	410		560	
Debtors	570		785	
Cash	20		15	
		1000		1360
Creditors:				
Falling due with one year				
Trade creditors	340		430	
Overdraft	250		320	
Tax payable	50		110	
		640		860
		1280		1380
Financed by:				
Ordinary shares (25 pence)		300		300
Reserves		630		730
		930		1030
Term loan (five years)		350		350
		1280		1380

Additional information

(i) Profit before tax is expected to grow at approximately 10% per year.

(ii) The existing directors who own 95% of the shares declared dividends of £115 000 in the latest financial year, and £71 000 in 1992.

(iii) The average earnings yield of USM listed companies in the same industry as Endess is 12% per year, and average earnings per share 20 pence.

(iv) The value of freehold land and buildings (never revalued) has fallen by 25% since purchased due to the recession.

(v) The entrepreneur hopes to be able to pay off all of the company's existing loans.

(vi) Endess's cost of equity is estimated to be 18%.

(vii) The replacement cost of plant and equipment is £600 000 but its current realizable value is £450 000.

(viii) £75 000 of stock is obsolete and could only be sold for £3000 as scrap.

Required:

(a) Estimate the purchase price of Endess Ltd using **each** of these two methods.

(7 marks)

(b) Acting as an adviser to the entrepreneur, prepare a short report discussing the advantages and disadvantages of each of these two methods. (6 marks)

(c) Prepare, and critically discuss **two** additional valuations of Endess for your client, and give a reasoned recommendation as to what value the entrepreneur should be prepared to pay. (12 marks)

(25 marks)

ACCA, Dec. 1993

26 *International financial management*

26.1	The international (global) financial markets	935
26.2	Sources of funds for overseas subsidiaries	951
26.3	The cost of capital	957
26.4	The foreign investment decision	963
26.5	Managing risk	967
26.6	Internal hedging techniques	971
26.7	Political risk	976
26.8	Taxation	978
26.9	Key terms	985
26.10	Revision questions	986
26.11	Further reading	986
26.12	Problems	986

A company might produce all its goods in one country, but sell some of its goods in other countries. If the foreign sales are invoiced in the currency of the buyer, it will be exposed to exchange rate risk which is known as transaction exposure. As the company grows it might set up an office in the overseas country, even if just for marketing purposes. It now has assets in that country. What will happen to the value of those assets if the currency of the host country moves against the currency of the home country?

When a company invests overseas, it may only be setting up a branch or an agency. But in many cases it is setting up a company – a subsidiary. It is becoming a multinational – a transnational – business. A multinational enterprise can be defined as a combination of companies of different nationality connected by means of shareholdings, contractual arrangements or managerial control, or some combination of these links. The setting up of an overseas subsidiary, with or without a foreign partner, clearly makes the enterprise a multi-national business. The country where the investment takes place is referred to as the host country. The country where the company which ultimately has control of the investment is registered is referred to as the home country. The UK is the second-largest home country for multinationals.

If the company is a multinational, the following question arises: should its subsidiaries borrow in the local markets or should they borrow in international capital markets and convert the borrowed funds into the currency of the country in which the subsidiary is located?

This and other problems will be considered in this chapter. As business has become more international, and as money and capital markets have become global, these international financial management issues have become of increasing importance.

26.1 The international (global) financial markets

The sources of finance available to small and medium-sized enterprises are usually limited to those available within their own domestic market. Larger companies are in a position to obtain funds in international and foreign financial markets. These funds are sometimes obtained not to finance overseas investment but to bring back to the home country to finance needs for fixed and working capital at home. Therefore involvement in global and foreign capital markets is not just limited to those companies concerned with overseas expansion.

From a company's point of view financial markets can now be divided into three groups:

1. their own domestic 'national' market;
2. national markets in other countries that are open to foreigners;
3. international capital and money markets.

The fact that large internationally known companies can obtain funds from any of these three markets puts them at a competitive advantage over smaller companies. If interest rates and the cost of capital are comparatively high in the domestic market, the larger firm will move to the global markets to keep costs down.

There is nothing new about the idea of markets in some countries being open to foreigners who wish to obtain the currency of that domestic market. The London market has for centuries been open to foreign governments and companies who wish to obtain pounds sterling. Similarly New York has been open to foreign borrowers for many decades, and those UK companies who have been in a position to do so have often taken advantage of this opportunity. What has changed in recent years is that with the 'deregulation' of monetary and legal controls more countries have opened up their markets to foreigners, and have also allowed their own nationals to purchase securities in foreign markets. Japan, a major financial power, only opened up its markets in the 1980s.

Reasons for the growth in the use of financial markets outside a company's and investors' home country include the following:

1. Motives of firms to obtain funds outside home country:
   (a) growth of transnational companies, operating around the world;
   (b) access to funds – sometimes the domestic capital markets of a firm are not large enough to raise the amounts of funds required;
   (c) funds raised can be cheaper: the funds are raised in large amounts and there is an absence of regulations in international markets;
   (d) natural hedge to international investment;
   (e) becoming known internationally.
2. Motives for investors to invest outside home country:
   (a) diversification;
   (b) high potential returns from investing in growth economies of the world;
   (c) possible gains from exchange-rate movements.

The growth of global markets

There is nothing new about the international capital market. True international markets can be described as those that are not based in any one country and which consequently do not come within the regulations of any one country. What has changed is the opportunities available within these international markets and within some national markets.

We now have what are referred to as 'global markets'. These consist of both the true international financial markets, with no national base, and the foreign aspects of national financial markets. We shall examine each of these in detail, but we shall begin this section by examining the growth of global markets in general.

There is nothing new about international trade and international borrowing. For centuries nations have traded with each other. Bankers in one country have lent to borrowers in another country. The centre of such trade and commerce has changed over time from one part of the world to another. These centres were not originally seen as global markets, but national markets open to international business. The changes that have occurred over the last two decades have, however, changed this. What has changed is the speed and manner in which money moves around the world, and the organization of the financial system to facilitate this movement. These markets are now all interlinked

Euromarkets

In order to demonstrate how the international markets developed, we shall first consider what are referred to as the Euromarkets. These are the major international financial markets, but it is important to appreciate that other international markets operate out of a number of centres around the world. It is only those that operate out of European centres that are referred to as the Euromarkets. There are markets in Asia and, with the emergence of Japan as the leading trading nation, these could provide competition with the Euromarkets.

The Euromarkets grew out of foreign bond issues in national markets. A government may have wished to borrow. It may not have wished to raise the money in its own domestic market and so it went to one of the large financial centres such as New York or London. The money raised would of course be dollars in the former and pounds sterling in the latter. This type of business fits the definition of an international financial market; it is the raising of domestic currency for a non-resident borrower.

For many years the US capital market was a world market. Issuers from any country in the world could offer securities in New York and obtain the dollars they required. These were called foreign bond issues, and they were treated on an equal footing to issues by US residents. Companies from outside the USA did not in fact make great use of this source of finance; it was mainly of service to national governments.

There were a number of reasons why foreign firms did not use New York, of which one was that the Securities and Exchange Commission was comparatively demanding in the information that it required from companies offering securities in the USA. For many years companies registered in European countries, with the possible exception of those in the UK, were very sensitive about disclosing certain information.

In the 1960s, with the expansion of national economies and multinational companies, the demand for finance was growing. Many national capital markets were inadequate and not particularly trusted. Therefore companies, as well as public authorities and governments, needed an international capital market, or at least a market in some form, that could supply them with large amounts of money without requiring too much information.

The global integration of the financial markets began therefore in the 1960s with the development of the Euromarkets. It received a major boost in the 1970s with the dramatic increases in oil prices. This resulted in a few oil rich countries having large balance of payments surpluses that they needed to invest. The Euromarkets offered the opportunity for these funds to be invested in other countries. Many countries, particularly in the Third World, needed finance to support their economic development and to cover their balance of payments deficits. As is known they borrowed heavily in the international market-place. The international money and capital markets helped recycle funds.

The next major boost to the growth of these markets came in the 1980s with changes in communication techniques, deregulation, companies seeing themselves as transnational, developing countries in the market-place to borrow and new centres of financial power emerging. The money and capital markets became truly global.

We shall briefly look at these contributing factors.

Deregulation

The political climate in many countries in the 1970s and 1980s moved towards supporting the ideology that decisions should be made in the free market-place and hence that controls and regulations should be ended. From a finance point of view deregulation means removing restrictions on the import and export of currency. If a UK investor, financial institution or company is prevented by law from moving funds out of the UK to invest in a foreign country, there are restrictions. The UK ended such restrictions in 1979. Prior to that, in 1974, the USA ended its restrictions on the movement of capital.

Two further major boosts to the flow of funds from one part of the world to another came with the ending of restrictions in Germany in 1981, and the beginning of the ending of restrictions in Japan in 1984. The move in Japan was particularly important, because, as well as that country being a major industrial nation, the Japanese people save large amounts of money. With the ending of restrictions the Japanese financial institutions, such as pension funds and banks, were able to move these savings out of Japan and invest them around the world.

Of course the other side of the removal of restrictions on the outflow of funds is that foreigners are given access to the domestic markets of a country. Thus, in the case of Japan, UK and US investors, whether companies, individuals or financial institutions, became able to invest or borrow in Japan's 'domestic' markets.

This process can be referred to as the globalization of national financial markets.

Technological change

It became technically possible for various agencies to provide computer networks that allowed trading to be conducted so that buyers and sellers could complete bargains anywhere in the world at any time. The trading could be in shares, bonds, commodities or foreign exchange. When New York is closing Tokyo is opening; when Tokyo is closing, London opens, and so on. Funds in London at 5.00 p.m. local time, as offices are closing, can be invested at overnight rates, and that money can be moved around the world, through New York and Tokyo, and be back in London plus interest at 8.00 a.m. the next morning as offices are re-opening. Of course the money does not physically move; it is just that various accounts are being debited and credited.

There was a time when buying and selling of shares was a face-to-face activity. A broker acting for a buyer would find a jobber who was willing to sell, and a price was agreed. The Stock Exchange in London, which grew out of coffee houses in the City in the eighteenth century, had as its code: 'My word is my bond'. Now there are no words. Buying and selling does not involve face-to-face contact. The buyer sits in front of one computer terminal, and the seller in front of another. Computers are not limited by distance; they can be activated around the world. The buyer could be in London, and the seller in Japan. Computer trading therefore made global markets technically possible.

Other factors

Other factors that boosted the growth of global markets were as follows.

1. There was a move to flexible exchange rates between currencies.
2. Banks became multinational businesses. Some banks, e.g. Barclays, always had a large multinational operation, but a boost came in the 1980s with the expanding multinational role of the Japanese banks and security houses. Most of the largest banks in the world are now Japanese.
3. Financial innovations were made, including securitization, an increase in currency and interest swap methods, and a growth in the financial futures and options markets.

The growth of global markets is not without its problems, which include the following.

1. Interdependence: a slump in a domestic market in one country can have repercussions in many other markets around the world. This could be seen following the collapse in Wall Street on 19 October 1987. On that day the Dow-Jones index fell by a record amount, in both absolute and percentage terms. In one trading session it fell by 23%, a larger fall than that in the Wall Street crash of 1929. The immediate cause of the crash is said to be the publication of the US trade deficit figures for the month of August, which were an all-time record. There were other factors such as share prices being at very high levels on Wall Street, despite a weak economy. There was also evidence that many computers in dealers' offices had been programmed to produce sell orders when certain events happened; they therefore all acted together when the poor trade figures

were announced. The collapse in New York led to falling prices in stock markets around the world. As so often happens, dealers in the markets over-reacted; there was panic. Why a trade deficit in the USA is bad for other countries is far from clear. It was the interdependence in the financial market that led to the global collapse. The same people selling in New York were selling around the world.

2. Another problem resulting from the growth of multinational banking is the danger that it will lead to a situation in which a few very large banks dominate the world banking scene.

3. Money now moves quickly around the world looking for growth opportunities. Large amounts can move from one centre to another, thereby increasing the volatility of security prices, interest and exchange rates in any one centre.

4. Companies who have access to global markets will be able to obtain less expensive funds than those who can only use domestic markets. This gives an advantage to big business, possibly leading to increasing concentration.

Sources and uses of funds

Where do these funds in the global financial market come from? The market in its early years had largely been a market for dollars. So where did these dollars, available outside the USA, come from? Four sources are discussed below.

1. The central bank reserves of various countries: as a country builds up a trade surplus with other countries, particularly with the USA, part of its growing reserves are in dollars. The balance of payments deficits of the USA have been partly due to the costs of US government foreign aid, partly to the outflow of dollars caused by US companies investing directly abroad and partly by the large US trade deficit. These dollars could be invested in the European markets to earn interest which, as the risks were slight, was preferable from a central bank's point of view to just hoarding the reserves. The German government, with its large trade surplus, made considerable use of the Euromarkets.

2. Commercial investors: the high interest rates that have sometimes been offered for Eurodollar deposits have attracted investors from around the world who have dollars available.

3. A certain amount of dollars have at certain times left the USA, attracted by the higher returns possible from investing them in Europe rather than on Wall Street. With deregulation investors are free to invest outside their own national markets. With the free movement of funds, currency can move from any country to a market which can offer a higher return on that currency than the domestic market. A wealthy Kuwaiti might have had dollars on deposit in Citibank in New York (this would be classified in New York as a non-resident owned dollar). Citibank in London is in need of dollars and offers a higher interest rate than that being paid in New York. Therefore the Kuwaiti moves the money to London and it then becomes a Eurodollar, part of the Eurocurrency market.

4. US companies and commercial banks have at times had dollars available outside the USA and have at times found it more profitable to invest this money in the Euromarkets rather than return it to the USA.

The international financial markets, in particular the Euromarkets, became a vital element in the recycling of the large amount of funds that resulted from the oil price adjustments of the 1970s. Some countries finished up with huge balance of payments surpluses and needed investment opportunities; other countries finished up with huge balance of payments deficits and needed to be able to borrow.

The Euromarkets are now very active in currencies other than dollars. One reason why there has been a large demand in the Euromarkets is because the national capital and money markets of Europe have sometimes proved to be inadequate. The amount of borrowing and new debt issues and equity issues raised in the national markets of Europe have not been large. It is doubtful if together the markets could have provided the amount of money that has been raised in the Euromarkets or been able to handle the size of some of the issues. One other attraction of the Euromarkets to borrowers is that they have fewer rules and regulations to accommodate than the national money and capital markets.

For one reason or another, therefore, there are borrowers who find it more convenient or essential to use the Euromarkets and other parts of the international market-place. They include the following.

1. Companies who need dollars for investment in the USA may find it easier to obtain the required dollars in Europe rather than trying to raise them in the USA.
2. Companies wishing to borrow large sums of any currency may find it easier and less expensive to obtain the currency in the Euromarkets than in the national markets of the country to which that currency belongs.
3. Unit trusts and investment trusts wishing to invest part of their portfolio in foreign securities may obtain the funds necessary for the purchases on the Eurodollar market.
4. The US banks have at times been heavy borrowers of dollars on the European market. There have been a variety of reasons for this, including lower costs.
5. National governments, bodies associated with national governments, local authorities and international agencies may, because of the large amounts involved or because of costs, prefer to use these resources when available rather than their own national markets. National governments, particularly those of the developing countries, have been borrowers.
6. Banks have been both borrowers and lenders. The markets are used for interbank activity. A bank in one country may be short of a particular currency for a few days; another bank may have cash in that currency to spare for a few days. There has always been interbank lending within countries. The existence of Euromarkets means that it can now be carried on at an international level.

The Euromarkets began as short-term markets, but since about 1970 they have extended into the provision of medium- and long-term finance. There are many reasons for this change in the length of the lending period, including the fact that not all the money flowing into the market could be used in the short-term market. In total there was not a large enough short-term demand for funds. Also, the tight credit policies of many European countries forced companies to look for longer-term finance outside their own domestic markets.

What makes investors, i.e. bankers and companies, want to invest in a currency in an account outside its country of origin? Four reasons can be suggested.

1. They want to spread their risks. Some depositors will be anxious not to leave all their balances in a given currency within the same jurisdiction. The earliest Eurodollar deposits were made in the 1950s by Communist bloc countries seeking to avoid the possible sequestration of their funds in New York. Subsequent moves by the US authorities to freeze Iranian, Libyan and Iraqi assets are likely to strengthen the resolve of many governments to maintain part of their dollar balances outside the USA. The UK High Court has determined that Eurodollar deposits held with the London branch of a US bank cannot be frozen by the US government.
2. They want to earn more interest. The rate of interest in the Eurodollar market tends to be slightly higher than that in New York, largely reflecting the absence of reserve requirements on Eurodollar deposits.
3. They want to trade in a convenient market. It is easier to trade Eurodollars in Frankfurt and London than domestic dollars within the USA (domestic dollars are available for only half of the European working day).
4. They want to avoid penalties. From time to time, some of the European countries have made it difficult (by imposing negative interest rates) or impossible (by imposing exchange control barriers) for foreigners to hold their currencies within that country.

What makes operators want to borrow in foreign currency? Two reasons can be suggested.

1. First, they want to obtain foreign exchange (this is true of governments financing a balance of payments deficit or companies financing overseas investment).
2. Second, they want to compensate for an inadequate supply of domestic credit and capital (this is true for many developing countries).

Companies will borrow in the Euromarket rather than in the corresponding domestic market (i.e. the Eurodollar market rather than New York) for one or more of the following reasons.

1. They want to avoid discrimination by lenders in the relevant domestic market.
2. They want to raise larger sums than are available in the same currency in its domestic market.
3. They want to borrow a given currency at a lower interest rate than in the domestic market.
4. They want to avoid exchange control barriers in the relevant domestic market.

International money (banking) market

The international financial markets can be divided by the activities they undertake into the international money markets, sometimes called the international banking market, and the international securities markets. We will consider the securities markets in the next section.

The money market is concerned with the short to medium-term end of international activity and is by far the largest element of the international financial markets. Suppliers of funds to the market are able to place their money on deposit with a bank for periods of time varying from overnight to a number of years. Borrowers in this market usually only want funds for short periods of time, although loans can be arranged for periods of three years or even more. Because there are so many interbank transactions, it is difficult to be precise about the size of the international banking market. When securities are involved it is possible to count the value of the securities. However, in the case of bank lending, there can be a considerable amount of double counting with the same money changing hands several times. Most of this involves cross-border lending and borrowing by banks.

The largest part of the interbank business in the Eurocurrency market is in overnight to three months money. The Eurocurrency market is one part of the international money market, and the dollar is the currency that is most often used in transactions. A Eurodollar arises when a bank physically outside the USA receives a deposit of dollars. We have given details of the possible source of such dollars. The receiving bank, which of course can be an overseas branch of a US bank, wishes to make use of such a deposit. It lends it to somebody, say a company or a government. The initial deposit of dollars can lead to the creation of much more purchasing power than its actual value. The receiver of the first loan could well deposit all or part of the dollars received in another bank. This other bank would then feel free to lend part of the sum involved again. Each bank through which the money flows may wish to maintain a reserve ratio between the amount of Eurodollars it lends and the amount of Eurodollars deposited with it.

An example of how the chain of borrowing and lending might commence would be a European company selling to the USA, receiving payment in dollars and deciding to deposit these with its European bank. The bank may lend the funds to another bank, which in turn lends them to another company that wishes to invest in the USA and so needs dollars. The money or credit allowed could change hands many times.

Because most banks avoid having a position in Eurocurrencies, they tend to lend out funds that they receive to other banks as deposits for different periods of time. This is where double counting can cause difficulties in estimating the size of the market. This interbank depositing is a profitable business for the banks and is usually relatively easy to handle. The international money market is in fact defined to include the external claims in domestic currencies. This would include, for example, dollars owned in New York by a non-resident Kuwaiti.

The banks using the international market act as both borrowers and lenders; they supply funds to the market and take funds out. The market has the following roles for banks.

1. The banks, depending on the economic situation in their particular country, use the market as an outlet for surplus funds, for surplus liquidity or as a source of funds when their liquidity position is tight.
2. The market is used as a channel for the movement of funds from countries that have low interest rates to countries that have relatively high interest rates.
3. Funds can pass through a number of hands, through a number of banks, on their way from the original supplier to the original user. Banks along the way make use of the Euromarkets. This is interbank depositing.

Companies do use the Eurocurrency market. For smaller loans of, say, between $1 million and $10 million, it is possible for one bank itself to have sufficient Eurocurrency to lend to a company. For larger loans, usually a syndicate of banks will be needed to provide the funds, although one bank will usually organize this for the company. Perhaps surprisingly, larger loans can be obtained in the Eurocurrency market than in the Eurobond market.

If a borrower wishes to borrow a certain amount of Eurodollars, he can telephone a bank in, say, London, Frankfurt, Paris, Brussels or Amsterdam. If the amount required is more than that bank can handle, then the bank will telephone other banks dealing in Eurocurrencies, perhaps a bank in the same country or in another European country. Further banks will be contacted until a syndicate has been formed that can handle the loan. The bank in London that is asked for the Eurodollars does not, of course, have to be a UK bank. There are now hundreds of foreign banks with offices in the City of London; most of them are there to attract some of the large Euromarket business.

Interest rates charged are usually based on the London Interbank Offered Rate (LIBOR). This is the rate at which most interbank transactions take place. A non-bank borrower in the Eurocurrency market will be quoted an interest rate above LIBOR. There is a considerable variation, called spread, in the rates charged to borrowers above LIBOR. The actual spread depends of course on the risks involved. The spread charged on credits to some developing countries, for example those from Latin America, increased considerably following the repayment problems that became apparent in the 1980s

Nearly all such borrowing is on floating rates of interest. The borrowing may be rolled over from one period to the next, but this is accompanied by interest rate reviews. International money market operations can be conducted from many centres; London, New York and Tokyo are the leaders.

Other centres include the offshore banking centres in the Caribbean, Singapore and Hong Kong. As mentioned, the major part of global money market activity is still centred around the Euromarkets. It is the largest deposit and funding market in the world.

Syndicated credits

These are usually included in the 'International Banking market' classification rather than the 'International Securities market' because there are no securities resulting from the borrowing and lending. There are no securities to be traded in the market-place.

Syndicated credits are medium-term credits with the borrower being allowed to draw on funds as required up to an agreed upper limit. A loan is different from a credit. A loan can be identified by the actual movement of a specific sum of money from the lender to the borrower at a particular time. The full amount of the loan is known from the outset and interest has to be paid on it for the entire period of the borrowing. With a credit the borrower can borrow funds when required, and might never draw the total amount agreed as the upper limit.

Syndicated Eurocredits are an important source of finance in international markets. Because large amounts may be required by individual borrowers the lenders often work as a group to provide the funds; they work as a syndicate. They provide medium-term finance for periods usually in the region of from three to five years. Usually, the interest rates are variable over time and are tied to some basic market rate such as LIBOR.

Large companies frequently use this market when engaged in takeover activity. They can obtain standby credit, which they will use to fund the purchase if the takeover bid is successful. The market has seen a growth in merger-related credits. Companies also use this market to re-finance debts incurred in earlier acquisitions, when they have not been able to obtain other funds to pay off the debts. Highly geared companies frequently use this market, and as a result they can be charged relatively high margins above LIBOR by the lenders.

International securities (capital) markets

There are markets in

- short- and medium-term notes;
- bonds;
- derivative instruments;
- equities.

Short- and medium-term notes

This is a very large market. As at 31 December 1993 the actual stock of notes outstanding was equivalent to $256 billion. Of the new notes issued during 1993, 60% were in currencies other than the US dollar. By far the most popular form of note issue was the Euro medium-term note (EMTN). The medium-term note market far exceeds in size the market for short-term notes (including Euro-commercial paper).

Short-term Euronotes

This covers the short-term end of the securities market. The notes are sometimes called European commercial paper (ECP). A company writes a note promising to pay to the holder of the note a certain sum of money at a certain date or dates in the near future. This note is then sold in the market and subsequently can be traded. The note is not usually underwritten. It may be written in respect of one currency, or it can be a multiple-component facility which enables borrowers to draw funds in a variety of forms and a number of currencies. The market is mainly limited to leading companies, who are referred to as prime borrowers.

Euronotes have been issued with interesting features. One of the Japanese security houses has issued ECP with which the return offered is linked to a Japanese government bond futures contract. Holders of such ECPs would benefit if the value of the futures contract rises.

Euro-medium-term notes

To some extent the medium-term Euronote market is competing with the Eurobond market. It fills a gap between short-term notes and long-term bonds. The medium-term notes are continuously issued notes, which are usually unsecured, with maturities ranging from nine months to ten years. They allow the borrower flexibility with respect to maturity profiles and the size and timing of issues.

Some companies see this form of medium-term borrowing as a way of matching the time period of the sources of finance with the time period of the loans they make available to customers. For example, these medium-term loans are a useful tool of treasury management for a company selling cars and allowing two to three years for the customer to pay, as they allow the cash inflow and outflow to be matched.

There is a large US domestic market in MTNs and in its early years this was cheaper than the equivalent Euromarket notes. However few non-US investors take part in the US market. The Euro-MTN market grew up to attract the funds of non-US investors; the Swiss and Germans were initially the most interested. The borrowers, i.e. the issuers of the notes, include sovereign governments as well as large companies and financial institutions.

The market has a lower minimum size requirement than the Eurobond market and in the market there are investors who are prepared to lend to borrowers with a slightly lower credit rating than needed for Eurobonds; for example, they would issue the notes of a company with BBB rating whereas the Eurobond market looks for AAA borrowers.

Bond market (including floating-rate notes)

There are two aspects of the international bond market. One is the traditional bond issues in the capital market of a country to a non-resident borrower. The other is the Eurobond, which is part of the Euromarkets. The type of security being issued, in addition to fixed rate bond issues, also includes floating-rate note issues.

The most common currency of issue is the US dollar, with the next three most popular being the Swiss franc, the yen and the Deutschmark. There are also issues in pounds sterling and the ECU. The borrowers in the market include large multinational companies, national governments and international institutions such as the World Bank and the EU.

Many Eurobond and FRN issues have novel features such as zero coupon rates, convertibility into equity and bonds with warrants attached. National Westminster Bank have issued a perpetual (irredeemable) floating-rate bond with LIBOR as the reference rate for interest and the spread over LIBOR being reset periodically. Most FRN issues have a call option which gives the issuer the right to redeem the note prior to maturity. Some issues offer a put option which gives the buyer of the note the option to obtain repayment prior to the maturity date.

The technique of making an issue through the Eurobond market is not similar to that of a public issue in the UK; it is more similar to the technique of placing. The bank or consortium of banks who are managing the issue invite a large number of other banks and institutions each to take up a part of the issue. These banks and institutions who are approached by the issuing bank or banks can then, if they accept the offer, either keep the bonds themselves or sell them to their clients. Underwriters are appointed by the issuing bank or banks in case the issue is not taken up through these private placings. A number of interesting features can be linked to the underwriting. These include a revolving underwriting facility which allows the issue and the underwriting to be spread over time.

The funds raised by the borrower are in a specific currency; if the borrower wishes to use that particular currency he need take no further action. If, however, the borrower wishes to obtain, say, pounds to invest in the UK and the loan obtained is in Deutschmarks, he will have to convert the currency. He has to repay the loan in the currency of issue, which means that he runs the risk of an exchange loss (or even an exchange gain) if significant movement in either of the currencies occurs between the time of the borrowing and the time of repayment. This, in fact, happened with certain of the borrowings of Deutschmarks by UK borrowers; the upward movement of the Deutschmark and the downward movements of the pound mean that it will now be more expensive for the borrowers to buy the Deutschmarks to repay the loan than it would have been before the currency adjustments took place.

The market in Eurobonds grew during most of the 1980s, but fell away towards the end of the decade. Issues in 1980 amounted to $20 billion and rose to $185 billion in 1986. Issues began to fall in 1987, particularly those denominated in US dollars. One reason for the fall was increasing competition, in particular the appearance of new opportunities for borrowers and investors following deregulation in the national markets of Japan and the European countries. Deregulation meant that foreign investors could move their funds into domestic markets, such as those in Tokyo, and buy the securities issued by Japanese companies. Also borrowers could move to these national markets to obtain funds. Many new securities were being offered to investors, with a wide choice of yield and maturity. In 1988 the Eurobond market was facing criticism in that it was expensive to use, partly because of outdated technology, and that because of the absence of adequate regulations some bad trading practices had developed. The market responded by taking steps to improve its trading methods and cut its costs.

Table 26.1 *Type and currency structure of international bond issues*

Sectors and currencies	Announced issues*				Net issues*				Stocks at end-1993
	1990	1991	1992	1993	1990	1991	1992	1993	
				in billions of US dollars					
Total issues	241.7	317.6	343.8	481.1	132.1	170.5	119.3	183.8	1 849.8
Straight fixed rate issues	166.2	256.2	276.7	373.1	80.8	142.0	115.3	193.7	1 389.9
of which: US dollar	52.2	75.0	90.9	113.1	16.0	27.9	41.2	63.8	455.1
Japanese yen	30.2	39.1	39.6	49.2	24.8	20.7	3.6	14.3	233.6
Deutschmark	7.3	12.2	29.2	50.2	1.3	4.8	17.1	27.0	142.0
Floating rate notes	42.5	19.0	42.9	68.5	28.2	3.5	23.7	44.7	263.3
of which: US dollar	15.0	4.4	25.1	43.0	7.6	–5.1	14.8	31.7	157.1
Pound sterling	10.8	7.6	5.4	8.6	6.9	4.6	3.0	3.5	44.3
Deutschmark	8.2	2.8	3.5	3.9	7.3	2.7	1.9	2.7	25.2
Equity-related issues	33.1	42.4	24.2	39.6	23.1	25.0	–19.8	–54.6	196.7
of which: US dollar	19.5	24.9	12.9	19.5	15.9	15.1	–20.0	–54.8	110.0
Swiss franc	8.2	7.0	5.3	9.8	4.1	2.3	–2.8	–3.6	43.8
Deutschmark	1.9	4.7	2.1	2.3	0.7	3.7	1.5	–2.0	16.9

* Flow data at current exchange rates.
Sources: Bank of England, ISMA and BIS.

Table 26.1 shows the issues in the market in the 1990s. It also shows the different features of the bonds, including the bonds that offer an equity involvement. Net issues mean announced issues less repayments

There is a secondary market for the Eurobonds with a number of market-makers. This secondary market has in the past been criticized for its lack of liquidity; this means that there is a shortage of funds attracted to the secondary market to buy bonds. As a result sellers could not always obtain the price that they expected and often found it necessary to spread a large sale of bonds between a number of market-makers.

Dealers are located all around the world. It is very much a telephone market. As with all Euromarkets there is no central market-place – dealers communicate with each other by telephone, telex and fax. In order to improve the liquidity almost all Eurobond public issues are listed on at least one major stock exchange.

Euroequity

These are equity issues sold simultaneously in a number of stock markets. They are designed to appeal to institutional investors in a number of countries. The shares will be listed and so can be traded in each of these countries.

The reasons why a company might make such an issue rather than an issue in just its own domestic markets include:

- larger issues will be possible than if the issue is limited to just one market;
- wider distribution of shareholders;
- queuing procedures which exist in some national markets may be avoided;
- to become better known internationally.

In the early days of the Euromarket, attempts were made to place in Europe large blocks of shares of US companies; of course, these were offered in exchange for payment in Eurodollars. These placings did not work because of the arbitrage opportunity of selling these shares back in the US stock markets. The Japanese company shares that were issued in Europe also had a rather unsuccessful history. Many of these shares issued in Europe were eventually sold in the domestic Japanese market. The difficulty is that there is not really a large independent market for such equity shares in Europe. Dealings in such shares in Europe tend to be dominated by what is happening in the large home stock market for the same shares. It is the weakness of the lack of a secondary market in Europe for such Euroequity issues that limits this method of corporate finance. Only a strong secondary market could ensure that blocks of Euroequity shares would remain-in Europe, rather than returning to their home market.

The equity shares issued in the international market that flow back to the market in the home country of the issuer is known, not surprisingly, as flowback. Despite the flowback problem there are each year a number of so called Euroequity issues. Often the equities are issued as part of a convertible Eurobond issue or an issue of a Eurobond with a warrant attached. This means of course that the bond does not have to be surrendered if the holder wishes to use the share warrant to obtain equity. The warrants, which can be converted into equity shares, can be detached from the bond and traded separately. There have also been conventional equity issues.

It is to make the issues attractive to investors that 'sweeteners' are added in the form of equity shares. United Biscuits issued £110 million of convertible preference shares in March 1988. The company raised the funds to finance an acquisition. To make it more attractive than a straight convertible issue, the shares carried a 'rolling put option'. It will be remembered that a put is the right to sell a share at a predetermined price. This particular security gave the purchasers the right to sell the convertible preference share back to the company at any time between five and ten years after the issue. The price at which it could be sold was within a range, which would mean that the redemption yield of dividends plus capital gain amounted to a fixed 9% whenever it was sold.

A conventional true Euroequity issue usually means that the shares are sold in a number of countries simultaneously. This means the shares must be listed on the domestic market in each of the countries in which it is sold. It is the individual domestic markets that provide the secondary market for trading in such shares. The issuing company hopes the shares will not all flow back to the national stock exchange of the issuer.

Because the shares need to meet the listing requirements of a number of countries such issues can be very expensive. For the reasons given at the beginning of this section many companies do however find such issues worth while.

Market for derivate instruments

There has been a rapid growth in the markets for financial futures and options. Many of the markets are outside the USA. Many of the instruments are related to interest rates in, and currencies of, European countries.

As well as this level of activity in organized derivative exchanges, there has been a rapid growth in activity in the over-the-counter derivative markets. These developments are discussed elsewhere in the book.

Example 26.1

Glomerall is a multinational company with manufacturing subsidiaries in eight different countries. It also owns a holding company subsidiary in a leading tax haven in order to attempt to minimize global tax liability, especially on dividend remittances. The company wishes to double the size of operations in two subsidiaries in France and the USA at a total cost of the equivalent of £100 million for each subsidiary.

Summarized financial data for the two subsidiaries and Glomerall (group consolidated data) are presented below.

	Glomerall £m	French subsidiary FFm	US subsidiary $m
Turnover	4200	2200	680
Pre-tax earnings	560	340	75
Fixed assets	1200	700	250
Current assets	1800	800	210
Current liabilities[1]	1100	700	200
	1900	800	260

Financed by:			
Ordinary shares	400	100	20
Reserves	900	250	130
	1300	350	150
Medium and	600	450	110
long-term debt			
	1900	800	260

[1] including overdrafts and short-term loans, Group £400m, France FF300m, USA $120m.

Suggested alternative financing sources

(a) Euroequity issue (approval by existing shareholders has been given for Glomerall to make such an issue). Finance would be provided to the foreign subsidiaries from this issue.

(b) 15 year fixed rate 11% Eurobond issue denominated in US$.

(c) 280 million ECU floating rate syndicated bank loan of five years' maturity at ECU base plus 1%. ECU base is currently 8% per year.

Required:

1. Discuss the advantages and disadvantages of each of the suggested financing sources for the two subsidiaries.
2. Suggest alternative financing sources that Glomerall might consider.

ACCA, Dec. 1993

Answer

1. The answer should include the following points:

(a) Glomerall will be attempting to minimize the after-tax cost of its funds. Using international markets (such as the Euromarkets) helps to achieve this. Usually the cost of finance in international markets is cheaper than the cost of finance in domestic markets.

(b) The company needs French francs and US dollars to finance its investments. It can however borrow in other currencies and hedge against the FOREX risk.

(c) The company is making use of a 'holding company subsidiary in a leading tax haven'. It will be doing this in order to be able to move funds between subsidiaries without tax complications and so as to be able to borrow free from restrictions.

Euroequity

(a) These have been discussed earlier in this section.

(b) Such international issues can be expensive. It is necessary to have the shares listed on several stock exchanges. Complying with the regulations of each market and producing the annual reports in many languages can be expensive.

(c) Flowback (referred to in this chapter) can be a problem. When the initial purchasers sell, and subsequent purchasers sell there is a tendency for the shares to flow back to the domestic stock market of the company.

(d) Balance sheets are provided; they are inviting gearing ratios to be calculated. The gearing ratios of individual subsidiaries are not very important. The Glomerall company should be judged on its overall level of gearing – that is what determines its financial strength.

In fact the gearing level appears to be a little high:

$$\frac{\text{Total debt}}{\text{Total assets}} = \left[\frac{600 + 1100}{1200 + 1800} \right] = 56.7\%$$

This ratio is based on the consolidated balance sheet. It includes the loans to the subsidiaries, which either will be covered by a parent company guarantee, or there will be an implicit understanding that the parent company would repay if a subsidiary fails.

It also includes in the numerator items other than debt. Included in current liabilities would be creditors but we do not know the amount. We can assume the multinational is UK-based, as the balance sheet is in £ sterling. In some other countries the ratio might not be considered high.

At some time new equity will be needed.

(e) The Euroequity issue can be used to obtain different currencies, including probably dollars and francs. If pounds sterling were raised this would need to be exchanged into dollars and francs at the spot rate. With pounds raised there would be no transaction FOREX risk as the equity would not need to be repaid. The payment of future dividends should not cause exchange problems because the amounts involved would not be great.

Eurobonds

(a) The issue is in US dollars, which would mean some of the funds raised would need to be immediately exchanged into French francs. In 15 years the dollars would need to be repaid. There is a foreign exchange transaction risk with regard to the interest and capital payments because some of the earnings are in francs and the debt in dollars. The company could hedge against this risk.

(d) There is also an (accounting) translation risk in that some of the assets will be in French francs and the liability is in US dollars in the subsidiary companies' accounts and pounds in the consolidated accounts. The company would probably not hedge against this risk.

(c) A fixed rate loan is referred to. This is risky, especially as 11% seems high. Perhaps a floating rate loan could be negotiated, or an interest rate/currency swap arranged.

(d) A new loan will raise the debt/total asset ratio to 59.4%, i.e.

$$\left[\frac{600 + 200 + 1100}{1200 + 200 + 1800} \right]$$

(e) To calculate interest cover two assumptions have to be made. First, what proportion of current liabilities are creditors? Second, what is the interest rate payable on the existing debt?

ECU (European Currency Unit) floating rate debt

(a) This is currently costing 9% per annum, so appears to be cheaper than the Eurobond loans. However we do not know the future direction of interest rates.

(b) In calculating the cost of the borrowing we also have to take into account the possibility of losses (or gains) on exchange rate movement. The loan is in ECUs, and if either (or both) the dollar and franc fall in value against the ECU this will increase the cost. This is the risk with 'foreign' borrowing.

There will also be translation risk, with the borrowing in ECU and the consolidated balance sheet in pounds sterling.

The Exchange Rate Mechanism (ERM) restricts the range of movements of certain currencies to a narrow band around an agreed central parity. The French franc is in the ERM so the movement of the French franc against the ECU is limited. The US dollar and the pound sterling are not in the ERM and so could experience wider fluctuations. These currencies could be hedged against transaction exposure.

(c) This floating rate borrowing is only for a five-year period. The maturity of the fixed rate Eurobond is 15 years. Five years seems a short period in which to complete the investment required to double the size of the French and US operations. It is doubtful if sufficient funds would have been generated from the new capacity to be able to repay the loan within five years. It is likely the syndicated loan would need to be renegotiated after five years.

(d) The issue costs of a syndicated loan are a lot less than those of a Eurobond (or Euroequity) issue.

2. Other sources of finance include:
(a) parent company finance, either internally generated funds, or funds raised from new issues in the
    UK domestic market;
(b) the French and US subsidiaries could raise funds in their own domestic markets;
(c) funds provided by other foreign subsidiaries of Glomerall – it could be that other subsidiaries are
    either cash rich, or have access to cheap borrowing;
(d) the holding company in the tax haven is probably used to collect dividends and interest from the
    subsidiaries around the world. These funds could be channelled to France and the USA. This
    would mean the earnings were not sent to the UK and so any tax liability on this worldwide income
    would be deferred.

Foreign issues in national markets

Many markets in the world are open to security issues by foreigners who wish to raise funds in the currency of that market. They are also open to foreigners who wish to invest funds and buy domestic securities. This applies to both bond issues and equity issues. Many foreign (non-domestic) companies and governments have issued securities in both London and New York.

As the Euromarkets developed, companies and governments seeking funds initially moved away from issuing bonds in those national markets that were open to them. Their principal source of foreign finance was based on either issuing securities in the Eurobond market or borrowing in the international banking market. In total the amount of foreign bonds issued in national capital markets continued to increase year after year, but the amounts raised were not as large as the amounts being raised in the Euromarkets.

The position changed again in the late 1980s when, with deregulation and changes regarding the method of taxing foreign borrowers introduced in many countries, the national markets again began to compete effectively with the Euromarkets. Clearly a company can go to whichever market offers the best terms – the international markets or various national markets.

Foreign debt issues

In a foreign debt issue a foreign borrower raises funds on the domestic capital market of another country. The borrower obtains funds in the currency of that market. The market jargon for a foreign issue in the US domestic market is a 'Yankee bond'. Issues by foreigners of yen securities in Tokyo are referred to as samurai issues, and issues of bonds by foreigners in London for sterling are known as bulldog issues.

The other side of the picture, i.e. investors investing funds in foreign markets, has grown remarkably during the 1980s. As is well known, Japanese investors have helped to fund the US budget deficit. During the mid-1980s Japanese institutions were purchasing annually over $30 billion of US government dollar debt. This was a change in the direction in which finance flowed. In earlier years it had been US investors sending funds out of the US for direct and portfolio investment in other countries. In the 1980s it was Japanese and European investors buying up US companies and government debt.

Foreign equity issues

Many multinational companies have found it an advantage to be quoted on at least one stock exchange outside their home country. The seeking of a quotation and the issuing of equities or convertibles in foreign markets has grown in popularity.

In the region of 20% of the total number of companies quoted on the major stock exchanges of the EU countries are foreign companies, i.e. they are not registered in the country in which they are being quoted. Of these foreign companies, approximately

25% are based in the USA. There is a certain amount of double counting with some companies being quoted in more than one market; for example, Du Pont, General Motors and Occidental are all quoted in three or more exchanges.

Why are foreign listings for a share attractive? One reason is, of course, that it can enable the company to raise finance in another market place. Another reason is that a company seems less foreign when it has a domestic listing, and there will be an opportunity for nationals of the country to buy shares in the company. It will improve the company's image. Once a foreign company is accepted in a country, and it discloses all the information in the form required in that country, then there is an increasing likelihood that it will continue to expand. There is little point in obtaining such a foreign listing unless a company already trades in the country where it wishes to be listed. However, once a large company is established in a country there can be political advantages from a listing. A third advantage arises in that a listing can create a wider market for a company's shares. It may well be that only a small secondary market develops initially, but as the company name becomes better known it can attract a wider group of shareholders. It will broaden the shareholder base. A listing will also allow a company to use its shares in the country's national capital market to make share-for-share acquisitions of other companies in that country or to enter into, say, a joint venture with a local company. Shares can be offered to nationals in exchange for shares in a domestic company, and these new shares will be acceptable as they can be traded in the domestic market. Finally the listing of a company's shares will simply help to make that company better known amongst the financial community of the country; it is a form of promotional exercise. The prospectus or other documents presented at the time of the listing will help the foreign company to become more understood.

For many years there were administrative and tax problems in the way of US residents who wished to purchase non-dollar securities. For example, it was difficult for them to purchase shares of UK companies quoted on the London Stock Exchange. If the company shares were quoted in dollars in New York there was no problem, but if not there were difficulties. The UK company might have liked US investors to take an interest in their pound sterling shares quoted in London as it would increase the potential demand. However, they might not have wanted to go to the trouble of obtaining a full listing on a US exchange.

A way around the problem was found by the introduction of American depository receipts (ADRs).

Many UK companies now have their ADRs listed in the USA. This policy and the policy of issuing Euroequities or convertibles was not always popular with UK financial institutions. If shares are placed with foreign investors it dilutes the percentage holding of a UK institution. If the shares had been issued in the UK, the institution would have had the option to buy shares and maintain its existing percentage level of share ownership.

This is what is referred to as a pre-emptive right – the right of a shareholder to first refusal on any new issue of shares for cash in the UK. It only applies to issues of shares for cash; a share-for-share exchange at the time of a takeover is not covered by such rights. This right is a requirement of the Companies Act 1985, although the Act does permit the rights to be waived if the shareholders give such a proposal their approval. The directors do not always receive the support of their shareholders for such a waiver.

Fisons proposed to place £110 million of equity in Europe and Japan, but the move was blocked by its institutional shareholders. The proposed issue represented a 5.5% increase in issued capital. Representative groups of institutional shareholders have at times issued guidelines recommending to members that support to waiving pre-emptive rights should normally only be given if the proposed issue in overseas markets does not exceed a certain percentage of the issued capital of the company. The percentage guidelines have varied from 5% to 2.5%.

Some institutions would prefer the companies to make rights issues in the London market, so that if they wished they could maintain their percentage holding. It is argued that if overseas investors want to buy the shares, they can purchase them in the London market. The argument against this is that often it is possible to raise money more cheaply in overseas markets than in London and, as explained above, there are other reasons for widening a company's list of shareholders. Of course, not all UK shareholders object to cash issues on overseas markets.

ADRs

These are negotiable receipts recognizing a claim on a foreign security. Within the USA they are treated for ownership and transfer purposes in the same way as the share certificates of a US company. The ADRs are issued by a US bank which receives, and usually keeps, the foreign shares. The ADR is a receipt that the bank issues to the US investor. The bank holds the shares on behalf of the US investor. The ADR holder, the investor, has the right to obtain delivery of the actual shares if he or she should so wish, although usually they would not do so, being satisfied with the ADR. The bank takes on the responsibility for passing on dividends declared as well as matters relative to rights issues and proxies. When the ADRs are traded it is the certificates that change hands, not the shares. Technically therefore the shares are not being traded in the USA.

US investors like ADRs because they are easily tradable, they are quoted in dollars, with dividends on the shares held against the certificates being paid in dollars. The transaction costs on trading ADRs is less than if the underlying shares needed to be transferred, and there are not the delays that would occur in the USA if a foreign security needed to be transferred.

To a UK company issuing such ADR certificates the advantages include:

1. the opportunity to raise dollar capital in the USA;
2. the corporate image of the company in the USA should improve, with its name becoming better known;
3. it is possible to improve the marketability of the company's shares without satisfying the listing requirements of the SEC.

A non-US company can go through a number of stages with its ADR certificates being traded in the USA before needing to obtain a full listing. First the ADRs can be traded unsponsored. All that is required is to find an investment bank in the USA willing to make a market in the company's equity. A fast-growing UK company might believe it has to appeal to US investors. At this stage only the minimal amount of information has to be filed by the company with the SEC. The costs are not high. The ADRs are being traded in the over-the-counter market.

The second stage which a company might take is to move to obtaining sponsorship with a view to a future listing on an exchange in the USA. This stage requires the company to meet increased costs and to begin to satisfy the SEC listing requirements.

The final step is to obtain a fully sponsored listing of the ADRs on one of the US stock markets. This usually involves either a placement or a public offer of new shares in the company to US investors. A foreign company that wishes to have ADRs traded in the USA has to file records with the Securities and Exchange Commission.

Table 26.2 gives a list of some of the UK companies whose ADRs are listed in the USA.

The overseas operation can be financed as follows.

1. Funds generated by the subsidiary: retained earnings and depreciation.
2. Funds transferred within the group: equity and loans from the parent company; loans from other subsidiary companies; leads and lags in the payment for intercompany transactions.
3. Funds from outside the group: borrowing from host country sources or international financial markets; local equity.

In practice most investment in foreign subsidiaries is initially financed by a mixture of parent company equity (either in the form of cash or the transfer of equipment) and

26.2 Sources of funds for overseas subsidiaries

Table 26.2 *Turnover and value of (some) UK-listed ADRs*

	Value (£m)	Jan.–Sept. 1993 Total turnover No. of Bargains	Jan.–Sept. 1993 Total turnover Shares traded (m)
Glaxo Holdings	3 474.2	6 114	279.4
Grand Metropolitan	259.0	1 110	15.2
Guinness	170.4	578	7.3
Hanson	1 201.2	2 593	97.9
Imperial Chemical Industries	2 173.7	2 893	63.4
Kingfisher	1.8	9	0.1
Marks & Spencer	11.5	125	0.6
Medeva	71.4	788	10.3
National Westminster Bank	72.6	165	2.6
PowerGen	21.4	56	0.6
RTZ Corp'n	127.3	416	4.6
Reuters Holdings	1 373.5	2 010	31.4
Saatchi & Saatchi Co	31.4	434	6.1
Shell Transport & Trading Co (The)	1 296.5	1 312	39.3
SmithKline Beecham	41.6	385	1.9
SmithKline Beecham	971.8	3 515	49.8
THORN EMI	15.7	81	1.8
Tate & Lyle	2.9	31	0.2
Unigate	2.2	21	0.6
Unilever	16.7	155	0.4

foreign currency borrowing. As the subsidiary grows, the additional finance is usually obtained through local borrowing and internally generated funds.

Local finance

One approach to investing in a foreign country is to borrow as much as possible in local markets. There are two advantages of this approach. One is that it would reduce the adverse effects if nationalization of the subsidiary's assets were to take place. With nationalization the local loans would not be repaid. A second advantage is that if the interest and repayments can be covered by revenue earned in the local currency, then it will not affect the parent company cash flows. Any movements in exchange rates would be immaterial. The alternative of borrowing from sources in other countries can lead to exchange losses if the local currency is depreciating against the currency in which the borrowing is made.

The parent company should not automatically borrow as much locally as it can. The cost of borrowing in the host country should be compared with the costs of borrowing outside the country. It could be that it would be cheaper to borrow in international money markets or in the home country. The possible rate of devaluation of the host country currency would then have to be compared with the interest savings resulting from borrowing in a foreign currency and transferring the money into the host country. The resulting earnings from the investment will probably mostly be in the currency of the host country. If this currency falls in value it will make the repayment of the foreign currency loan more expensive.

As has been explained, most multinational companies borrow in the international financial markets. They borrow in the Eurocurrency and Eurobond markets and make bond issues in national markets.

The effective cost of foreign borrowing is given by the formula

effective cost = interest rate on borrowing
   ± appreciation/depreciation in exchange rates between home and host country

For example, if the cost of borrowing in the UK is 10% and the Kenyan shilling is expected to depreciate against the pound by 10% per annum, the effective cost to a company of raising funds in London, converting these to shillings in order to invest in Kenya and using the cash flow earned in shillings to service the debt, is approximately 20%. If the cost of borrowing in Kenya is less than 20% it would pay to borrow locally. However, if the cost of borrowing in Kenya is above 20% it would pay to borrow in London and convert the funds to the required shillings.

This is demonstrated in the following example. We borrow, say, £1000 in London, have to pay £100 interest at the end of each of two years and repay the debt at the end of the second year. The pounds sterling are converted into shillings and the debt is serviced from Kenya. At the time of converting the loans into shillings and investing in Kenya the rate of exchange is £1 = 12 shillings. With the 10% devaluation of the shilling per annum the rates of exchange at the end of the next two years becomes £1 = 13.2 shillings and £1 = 14.52 shillings. The cash flows are as follows:

Years	London Interest	Loan	Kenya Interest	Loan
0		+£1000		+12 000
1	−£100		−1320	
2	−£100	−£1000	−1452	−14 520

To obtain the effective cost of servicing the loan we need to solve the following equation (representing the cash flow in shillings) and find r:

$$+12\,000 = \frac{1320}{1+r} + \frac{15\,972}{(1+r)^2}$$

Hence r is just under 21%. As mentioned above, adding together the nominal interest rate and the percentage devaluation/appreciation gives an approximate solution.

Another way of raising finance locally is through the issue of shares. Such shares could either be sold to local individuals or institutions or could be exchanged with partners in a local joint venture. Shares can be issued with or without a quotation on a local market. There are many reasons why a sale of some equity shares in the host country can be advantageous. Apart from providing access to additional sources of finance, it should mean that the company is better accepted locally. This subject is discussed in the section on foreign issues in national markets.

Movement of funds within a group

When setting up a subsidiary abroad, it needs to be remembered that at some future date it will be necessary to repatriate funds to the parent. The remittance could be in the form of dividends, royalties, interest, management fees, inflated transfer prices or loans. The incidence of tax on each of these ways of fund transference should be examined closely, as should the question of whether there is an absolute or proportional limit for each type of payment. When, finally, the exchange risk and any other legislative regulations about remittances have been taken into account, it will be possible to make decisions on such issues as from where in the group funds should be transferred and indeed who should own the new subsidiary. For example, suppose that the UK does not have a double taxation agreement with country X, but France, Holland or the Bahamas, say, does. A UK company which has a subsidiary in one of these latter countries may find it cheaper for that subsidiary to set up the new subsidiary in country X. Remitting its dividends, interest etc. via, say, the subsidiary in France, Holland or the Bahamas could be cheaper than remitting its earning directly to the UK.

Royalties, fees and transfer prices for goods offer ways in which a company can control its flow of funds. They constitute payment for specific goods or services which do not always have an easily determined market value. They are pre-tax charges against profit which may or may not be the subject of withholding tax.

The intracompany transfer of funds is a very important part of multinational financial management. A multinational also aims to produce an optimal relationship between its monetary assets and monetary liabilities. Its assets and liabilities are in many different currencies, some hard, some soft, some within the group, some external. Wherever possible a company tries to have its debts in hard currencies and its liabilities in soft currencies in order to minimize the exchange risk.

The timing of the company transfer of funds is very important, and it can be achieved without the constraint of the legal onus of payment that a normal third party debtor works under. For example, if devaluation is a possibility in the country where a subsidiary is based, or at least the spot price (in the currency to be paid) seems likely to decline, then the multinational can withhold payment to its subsidiary until such time as it feels it is safe to pay, or until the financial needs of the subsidiary cannot be satisfied by any cheaper means.

Another example arises when a company is making an investment in, say, Egypt: the parent company may arrange for, say, its Danish subsidiary to buy the equipment from a third party and resell it to Egypt on longer than normal credit terms. This may be because of the fear of political upheaval, or the possibility of devaluation or the imposition of exchange control. If Egypt finds herself in difficulties it is unlikely that foreign exchange will be available for foreign payment of trading debts. If the Egyptian company has movement of funds problems, this arrangement will help them because the terms of the deal from the Danes could be for as long as, say, two years.

To conclude our discussion, the movement of funds between the parent and the foreign subsidiary, or in fact between any members of a group, will be based on the group's financing plans, and will be influenced by the following factors:

1. the needs of the parent company for funds;
2. the needs of the various subsidiaries for funds;
3. the sources and costs of funds available to the various subsidiaries including those funds generated internally;
4. the taxation effect on the various types of payments that could be made and on the timing of the payment;
5. relative rates of inflation in the various economies in which the subsidiaries are located;
6. exchange rate and other foreign environmental risks;
7. the degree of local autonomy in the subsidiary, e.g. minority shareholdings;
8. remittance regulations and restrictions on dividends, royalties, fees, interest and management charges payable to the parent company;
9. the availability of safe tax-free collection havens for overseas funds awaiting repatriation or further use in another subsidiary

The weighting to be accorded to each of these factors depends on the company itself and its own circumstances at the time of the policy decision.

Currency swaps

One way of obtaining borrowed funds in a foreign currency is by way of a currency swap. This involves the exchange of debt from one currency to another. Swaps comprise contracts to exchange cash flows relating to the debt obligations of the two counterparties to the agreement. Although swaps are contracts between the two parties, they do not alter the direct responsibilities that each party has for the debt obligation that it has personally incurred.

Let us assume that a well-respected UK company wants to borrow French francs, but is not well known in France. If there is a company in France that wishes to borrow pounds sterling but is unknown in the UK, there is the possibility of a swap. If the UK company borrowed in France it would have to pay a relatively high interest rate, reflecting its poor credit rating. Similarly, the French company would have to pay a relatively high interest rate on its borrowing in the UK. From an interest rate point of view it is better if the French company borrows the francs and the UK company borrows the pounds sterling. The two companies then swap currencies and the payments related to them. The UK company pays the interest and eventually repays the French loan and vice versa.

The simplest method of servicing the loans would be for the UK company to pay the interest on the French franc loan and for the French company to pay the interest on the sterling loan. In fact each counter-party is paying interest on the other's loans as if it were the borrower. In fact they are both paying lower interest charges than if they themselves had borrowed the currencies they needed.

The French company has borrowed francs and the UK company has borrowed sterling. They swap the currencies, and the simplest basis of doing this is at the spot price at the time of making the deal. When it comes to repayment, again the easiest method is for the currency to change hands at the spot rate. The French company has to repay in francs, and the UK company makes the appropriate amount of francs available to the French company by selling sterling at the spot rate.

An example of a simple cross currency swap is shown in Figure 26.1. The UK company wishes to finance a subsidiary in Germany. The German company wishes to have pounds sterling to invest. Both companies are better known in their own country than in the other country.

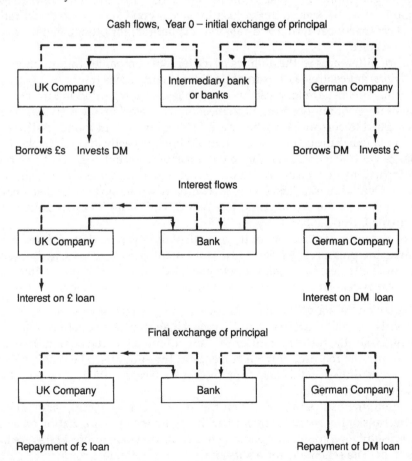

Figure 26.1

Under the agreement, the UK company contracts to pay the interest on the Deutschmark borrowing and the German company pays the interest on the sterling borrowing. The UK company passes on the proceeds of the sterling loan to the German company, which agrees to service the debt and repay the debt at the appropriate time. The companies agree in advance the appropriate exchange rates for the transactions.

A currency swap can be constructed as a series of forward exchange contracts. If it reduces exposure it is a form of hedging. The term of currency swaps can vary. The swap document should clarify the rate of exchange that will be used. Normally one currency is recorded as the fixed principal amount, with an agreed rate of exchange for calculating the amounts in the second currency.

One of the objectives of the currency swap is to take advantage of lower interest rates; another objective is to restructure the currency base of a company's liabilities. If a UK-based multinational found that nearly all its borrowing were in sterling, it would become worried if the pound was becoming stronger against the currencies in which it was generating its earnings. Therefore it might attempt to swap some of its sterling debts into debts in other currencies. It would be attempting to reduce its risks due to exchange rate exposure.

In restructuring the debts to balance its exchange rate exposure, the company could also take the opportunity to alter the structure of its interest rate liabilities. If many of its loans were at fixed interest rates and it was believed that interest rates would fall in the future, at the same time as swapping currencies it could move from fixed-rate obligations to floating-rate commitments. As implied above we can have three types of currency swaps: a cross currency fixed to floating; a cross currency fixed to fixed; a cross currency floating to floating. The reasons why a very large swap market has developed over recent years include the following.

1. Different constraints are placed on market access for different companies. Some companies may be seen in the market to have a good short-term credit rating, but their access to longer-term fixed-rate loans is limited; for other companies the position is reversed.
2. There are differences in the abilities of individual companies to raise money in different financial centres. For example, some US companies might be highly rated in the US markets but are less well known and less well regarded in Europe. An interesting example of this occurred in connection with World Bank activities. The World Bank wished to borrow Deutschmarks and Swiss francs but found itself at a relative disadvantage in European markets. It could borrow easily and relatively cheaply in the large US dollar markets. These circumstances meant that the Bank became a counterparty to European companies which could either borrow easily in Swiss francs or Deutschmarks. The European company would borrow Deutschmarks, say, and lend these to the World Bank. The World Bank would borrow dollars and lend them to the European company.
3. A third and important reason for the growth of the swap market occurred because of demand-side pressures. As part of treasury management many companies wanted to obtain a better less risky balance between fixed-interest and floating-interest debts, and between debts in one currency and those in another currency.

A variation on the above is a 'back-to-back' loan or what is sometimes called a 'credit swap'. This is a simultaneous spot and forward loan transaction between the company and a bank. Basically, the company lends a sum of money to the bank in the UK which converts it into the required foreign currency at the spot rate. The company's foreign subsidiary then draws on this loan from the bank's foreign office or the office of one of the banks in its consortium.

There are numerous permutations on this type of currency swap and back to back deal. Arbi-loans or international interest arbitrage financing is a variation on a currency swap. It is useful for a company operating in a country where interest rates are high and credit is tight. The scheme is for a subsidiary in a low-interest country to borrow the required amount and convert it at the spot rate into sterling, say, and then the UK parent signs the document promising to repay in the foreign currency at the end of the term. The parent then purchases a forward contract which will provide the right foreign currency for repayment at the repayment date. Therefore the lender, in addition to his promissory note, has the forward foreign currency purchase contract which gives the lender additional security.

One variation on the currency swap theme is a **swaption**. This as the name implies integrates features of a swap with those of an option. It is referred to as a hybrid derivative product.

The buyer of a swaption has the right to enter into a swap contract (a currency swap or an interest-rate swap) at any time within a specified period, at a rate of exchange and/or under terms agreed when the swaption deal is agreed. The buyer of the swaption has to pay to the writer of the contract an up-front premium.

These contracts are not available on the established option exchanges, but are available in the over-the-counter market.

The first point to make is that it is difficult to calculate the cost of capital for a domestic project. It is even more difficult to calculate a figure for a foreign project. An estimate can, and should be made, but it is only an estimate.

There are a number of issues that need to be considered, these include:

- *Issue A*
  Should the decision to invest be based on cash flows received by the parent company or project cash flows?
  Answer
  Parent company cash flows should be the most important factor. The company will not normally undertake a project which is profitable in host country terms, but which, because of remittance restrictions, tax or other problems, is unprofitable to the parent.
- *Issue B*
  Should the discount rate used for the parent country analysis be the parent country cost of capital or the host country cost of capital?
  Answer
  It should be the parent country cost of capital adjusted for certain factors.

The parent company will want a return on its equity investment in a project in a foreign country which is at least equal to its opportunity cost of capital. This opportunity cost for a multinational company will be based on the risk-free rate of return available in its home country plus a premium to cover risk. If the foreign project or subsidiary is in a developed country then the premium could well be similar to the premium in the home country. If the foreign subsidiary is in a developing country then the premium would probably be higher.

If the home country and the host country are similar, then the opportunity cost of equity could well be more or less the same in the two countries. This might be the situation if a UK company were investing in the USA. However, if a UK company was investing equity funds in, say, Thailand, then the opportunity cost of equity capital would be different between the two countries, and it is the UK cost (adjusted for risk) that would be used to evaluate an investment proposal in Thailand.

- *Issue C*
  A related question is: should the cost of capital be calculated based on the capital gearing of the group or of the subsidiary undertaking the project?
  Answer
  It should be based on the capital structure of the overall group.

The gearing of a foreign subsidiary may be much higher than is considered normal in the home country. This could be because of subsidized loans provided by the host government in order to encourage foreign investment into the country. The MNC will wish to obtain the cheapest sources of finance available. But in calculating the cost of capital

26.3 The cost of capital

to use in a subsidiary, the subsidized finance should be allowed for, not by taking a distorted gearing ratio, but by allowing credit in the cash-flow calculations for the saving in interest costs. This can be achieved using the adjusted present value (APV) technique.

Another reason why a high gearing level of a subsidiary should not be used as a basis for a cost of capital calculation is because often the high level of borrowings are only obtained because of parent company guarantees. The balance sheet of the subsidiary is therefore misleading. The borrowings have been obtained not on the strength of the subsidiary's asset base but on the strength of the group's assets.

Another reason why a foreign subsidiary may have a high level of gearing is because the equity of the subsidiary is not listed on the local stock exchange. It may not wish to raise local equity funds. The decision may have been reached to borrow as much as possible locally; this of course has foreign exchange advantages.

The MNC should aim to achieve an optimal capital structure on its consolidated operations. As explained above the capital structure of a subsidiary may deviate from this overall optimal. It is the global capital structure that is important to creditors and investors in determining the financial strength of a company. It is also this global structure that should be used as a base for determining the cost of capital.

The MNC should not worry about its local debt equity ratios. It should borrow wherever it can as cheaply as possible. However it has to be aware of its consolidated position. So if it has high levels of gearing in some countries (for example, those offering interest rate subsidies) it will need to have low levels of gearing in other countries.

- *Issue D*
  What are the factors that need to be taken into account when evaluating a foreign investment that make it different from evaluating a domestic investment?
  Answer
  1. foreign exchange risk;
  2. political risk, ranging from loss of assets to restrictions on dividend remittances and on other forms of repatriating income;
  3. host government subsidized loans;
  4. host country levels of capital gearing;
  5. host country tax incentives.

All these factors need to be allowed for in the investment appraisal exercise.

- *Issue E*
  Should these complex factors be allowed for by adjusting the discount rate or by adjusting the cash flows?
  Answer
  There are at least two approaches to this problem:
  1. The simplest approach is to take the overall cost of capital of the group and add on a single premium, the size of which depends on where the project is to be located. For example, a UK company with a cost of capital in the UK of 20%, before tax, might add on a 3% premium if it invests in Zambia and a 5% premium if it invests in Turkistan. The cash flows of the project are discounted by this simple risk-adjusted rate.
  2. The above approach is theoretically incorrect. An alternative often suggested in the international finance literature is to make some adjustments for risk through the parent company's cost of capital and some adjustments through the cash flows.

     The adjustment to the parent company's cost of capital is to allow for the business risk associated with the project. The business risks involved in some business activities are greater than in others (i.e. a retail store versus a coal mine).

     With foreign investment there is a major problem in deciding on the size of the risk premium to be added for business risk. It should be appreciated that it is only the systematic component of total risk that needs to be taken into account (based on the project β). The risks of investing in foreign countries due to economic factors associated with individual countries can cancel themselves out. If a company invests in a number of countries, when some countries are doing badly others will be doing well. Following a diversification argument the business risks of a well-diversified MNC are less than those of a company dependent on one country. The presence of international diversification should therefore, other things being equal, reduce the cost of capital.

Having determined a suitable discount rate, all other factors that characterize an overseas project can be allowed for either by adjusting the cash flows or through employing sensitivity analysis. This means adopting the APV technique for evaluating foreign investment projects. As was explained in Chapter 4, the APV first calculates the value of the project as if it was all equity financed, and then adds or deducts amounts from this value to allow for the actual method of financing the project.

It is particularly important to take the intricacies of the financing package into account for overseas projects. The decision on whether to go ahead with the project will depend on parent company cash flows, and these depend on the method of financing the project.

The factors to be allowed for in the cash flow calculations include:

1. different tax rates in home and host countries;
2. the contribution of the project to the borrowing capacity of the group;
3. the value of concessionary loans in foreign currencies (interest-rate subsidies).

The APV approach is based on calculating the PV as if the project were financed entirely by equity and then adjusting for these factors. It can be expressed in an equation as:

$$\text{APV} = (-)\text{ PV of cost investment outlay} + \text{PV of remittable cash flows}$$
$$+ \text{PV of interest tax shields} + \text{PV of subsidies on project}$$
$$+ \text{PV of effect of project on debt capacity of group}$$

Certain other factors affecting cash flow can be introduced to extend the equation. The different components in the equation may need to be discounted at different rates to reflect their different levels of risk. It is the remittable cash flow stream that is discounted at the appropriate cost of equity capital.

It should be noted that we have not allowed for foreign exchange risk and political risk in the above APV equation. The reason is that these are probably best taken into account using sensitivity analysis. Questions such as 'What if exchange rates move against the home currency by 2% per annum more than expected?' or 'What if remittances cease after five years?' can best be handled by sensitivity analysis.

In fact the overall impact on a group of companies of political risk and foreign exchange risk can also be reduced somewhat by diversification.

As mentioned at the beginning of this section computing the cost of capital for an individual foreign investment is very difficult. There are still many unresolved issues. The project will not have been repeated many times so it is difficult to estimate a risk premium to use in determining the equity cost. It is difficult to estimate a measure for systematic risk. In addition decisions on hedging against exchange-rate risk and decisions on the management of political risk will affect the cost.

It is difficult to allow for such factors as political risk in a single discount figure. As suggested one approach to this problem is to undertake sensitivity analysis to determine the impact on cash flows of different levels of political interference at different times. An alternative approach is to take out insurance. Yet another approach is to ignore such risk arguing that the company has a well-diversified international portfolio of investments.

- *Issue F*
  Should the decision whether or not to undertake the project be based solely on the parent company returns and the parent company cost of capital?
  Answer
  The evaluation is a two-stage process – first the cash flows in the host country, and

then the cash flows that are to be remitted to the home country. In practice companies do take into account, in the decision-making process, the returns earned in the host country.

A company is judged in the short run by its reported earnings. In consolidated company accounts the earnings of all companies in a group are added together. A project undertaken by a foreign subsidiary can therefore either add to group profits or reduce group profits. Clearly the group would prefer the former. This is why the profitability or otherwise of the project in the host country is important.

It should be noted that the answer above is in terms of profitability in the host country. Profitability is not the same thing as cash flow. Profitability is important in the host country, and remittable cash flow is important to the parent company.

We will now show two worked examples. The approach adopted to answer the questions illustrates two of a number of possible ways of arriving at an estimate of the cost of capital. The first example only considers one part of the total picture. The second example considers additional factors.

Example 26.2

One approach to estimating the cost of capital is to use the CAPM model. Let us say a major MNC based in the UK is considering undertaking a large capital investment project in Indonesia. The MNC will invest equity. It will appraise the project using the APV approach.

It is necessary therefore to calculate the project cost of equity. The systematic risk β of the project is estimated to be 1.635. This is not necessarily the same systematic risk measure as would be used on domestic projects; it reflects any additional business risk of investing in Indonesia. The risk-free rate of return available from investing the parent company's funds is 7%. The market expected rate of return on equity is 15%.

The CAPM model indicates the cost of equity on the Indonesian project is

$$7\% + (15\% - 7\%)\,1.625 = 20\%.$$

This is the discount rate that would be used to discount returns earned on the parent equity investment. In arriving at the cash-flow stream available to equity, deductions would have been made for taxation (in home country and in Indonesia) and interest payments on debt. The cash-flow stream would have been converted into pounds sterling at the expected spot rates of exchange or possibly at agreed forward rates.

Using this cost with the APV approach means that the cash flow stream would be adjusted to reflect the level of gearing. The cash benefits resulting from the tax shield on interest payments would be added to the cash flow from operations.

Political risk could be allowed for by using sensitivity analysis.

Example 26.3

In the example that follows a weighted-average cost is obtained. It is emphasized that this is a cost for a major investment proposal that has important financial implications elsewhere in the group. For minor investments, the cost of capital for the project would not be gone into in this amount of detail.

Tockham International PLC is evaluating a major investment that has been proposed by its Norwegian subsidiary. The company has estimated the cash flows associated with the project, but is unsure as to the appropriate discount rate to use to calculate the project's net present value.

The investment will cost 400 million Norwegian kroner, of which 125 million will be borrowed locally by the subsidiary at a fixed interest rate of 8%. A further $25 million will be raised through a 15% Eurobond issue guaranteed by the parent company. Fifty million kroner will be available from the subsidiary's retained earnings and the remainder will be provided by the parent company in the form of a loan to the Norwegian subsidiary.

After the announcement of the proposed investment the parent company's equity shares have stabilized at a price of 330p and its issue of 9% debentures at £75.

Tockham has purchased up-to-date estimates of its equity and debt betas from the London Business School; these are 1.25 and 0.67 respectively. The market return is estimated to be 14.5% and the treasury bill yield 7%.

A summary of Tockham's consolidated balance sheet is shown below. The company considers its current market weighted capital structure to be optimal.

Summarized balance sheet as at 31 March 19X2

		£m
Fixed assets		250
Current assets	195	
Less current liabilities	110	85
		335
Financed by		
50p ordinary shares		50
Reserves		175
		225
9% debentures 1990–3		110
		335

Corporation tax (at the time) is at 52% in both the UK and Norway, and a full bilateral tax treaty exists.

Foreign exchange rates

	Krone/£	$/£
Spot	10.89–10.96	1.8520–1.8530
1 year forward	9.80–9.86	1.9446–1.9456

The krone is expected to appreciate relative to the pound, and the dollar to depreciate relative to the pound, at a steady rate for the foreseeable future.

Calculate the discount rate that should be used to evaluate the proposed investment.

Suggested solution

The funds to finance the project will be as follows:

Local retained earnings	50 million K
Local debt	125 million K
Eurobond	147 million K ($25 million)
Parent company loan	78 million K
	400 million K

At the spot rates of exchange these equal in pounds sterling:

Local retained earnings	£ 4.591 million
Local debt	£11.478 million
Eurobond	£13.499 million
Parent company loan	£ 7.162 million

The existing capital structure of Tockham is considered optimal. This, based on market value weightings, is 80% equity and 20% debt, i.e.

	£million	
Equity (100 million × £3.3)	330	(80%)
Debt (1.1 million × £75)	82.5	(20%)
	412.5	

A problem arises in that following this new major investment the capital structure of Tockham will no longer be optimal. This has to be taken into account in calculating the cost of capital for the project; the cost will be higher because it has moved the whole company away from its optimal level of gearing.

Local capital structures may be very different from the parent company's optimal capital structure. This problem affects the cost of capital. If the parent company has £1 million equity and £1 million debt, but its overseas subsidiary which has been geared up has £0.5 million equity (all owned by the parent) and £1.00 million debt, the consolidated balance sheet would show £1 million equity and £2 million debt. This may not be the optimal level of gearing in the home country. The way in which this problem can be handled analytically is illustrated below.

The impact of the new investment in Tockham International and the adjustment required is as follows:

	Before project (£m)	Impact of project (£m)	Optimal gearing required (£m)	Adjustment needed (£m)
Equity	330	334.591	359.384	+24.793
Debt	82.5	107.477	89.846	−17.631
Loan from parent		7.162		
	412.5	449.230	449.230	

The second column reflects the impact of the project – the retained earnings are added to the equity and the Eurobond plus local borrowing added to the debt. The third column shows the desired division between debt and equity if the 80:20 relationship is to be maintained with a total capital of £449.23 million.

We can easily work out the cost of capital for three of the sources of finance for the project. The difficulty is to decide on the cost of the loan of £7.162 million from the parent company. What is being reflected in the fourth column is that this investment has moved the company away from its optimal level of gearing. The cost of capital should reflect this. It can be handled by treating the cost of the parent company loan as the cost of £24.793 million equity less the cost of £17.631 million parent company debt.

We shall now calculate the costs of the individual sources of finance and combine them to obtain an overall project cost. Based on the capital asset pricing model, we obtain the following:

Parent company's
equity
$$= 7\% + (14.5\% - 7\%) \times 1.25 = 16.375\%$$

Parent cost
of debt (pre-tax)
$$= 7\% + (14.5\% - 7\%) \times 0.67 = 12.025\%$$
$$\text{(or 5.772\% after tax relief at 52\%)}$$

(This gross cost of debt figure can be estimated based on the yield figure: 12% = £100/75 × 9%.)

Because the tax rates are the same in Norway as in the UK and a full tax treaty exists, the subsidiary's cost of retained earnings is the same as the cost of equity of the parent = 16.375%.

Cost of local debt	$= 8\% (1 - 0.52) \, 1.1 + 10\%$
(from parent viewpoint)	$= 14.224\%$
	(the latter variable allows for the fact that the kroner is appreciating by 10% per annum)
Cost of Eurobond	$= 15\% (1 - 0.52) \, 0.95 - 5\%$
(from parent viewpoint)	$= 2.2\%$
	(dollar is depreciating by 5% per annum)

This approach illustrates one way of calculating the total cost of borrowing in a foreign currency. Namely, the percentage interest charge is added to or deducted from the expected percentage change in the exchange rate of the home country and the country of borrowing.

Therefore the overall cost with adjustment is as follows:

Subsidiary

Retained earnings	£ 4.591m @ 16.375% =	751 776
Local debt	£11.478m @ 14.224% =	1 632 631
Eurobond	£13.499m @ 2.2% =	296 978
Parent equity ⎫ adjustment	£24.793m @ 16.375% =	4 059 854
Parent debt ⎭	−£17.631m @ 5.772% =	(1 017 661)
	£36.730m	5 723 578

The project's cost of capital is therefore

$$\frac{£5\,737\,578}{£36\,730\,000} = 15.62\%$$

A UN study (World Investment Report, UNCTAD) published in 1994 highlighted how a small number of multinational companies dominate the world economy. It was found that transnational corporations (TNCs) account for one-third of global output. This global network of TNCs consists of 37 000 parent companies who control 200 000 foreign affiliates.

Within these TNCs there is an elite group. The largest 100 (which includes eleven UK firms) controls about one-third of the world stock of foreign direct investment. In the early years of the 1990s US companies were the largest foreign investors, with UK companies being second highest. Surprisingly Japan slipped from being first in the 1980s to fifth in the early 1990s. The USA was the biggest recipient of foreign direct investment.

Clearly many major investment decisions are made despite all the problems involved in estimating the cost of capital, forecasting future returns, and the risks associated with exchange rate movements and political uncertainties.

Investment decision-making, particularly involving foreign investments, is a mixture of strategic decision-making and detailed financial analysis. From a strategic point of view the company first has to decide whether or not it wishes to become multinational. Having decided it does, it has to decide in which parts of the world it wishes to operate.

The cash flows that will be returned to the parent company have to be discounted at the opportunity cost of capital of the parent company. The multinational company does not have to invest its funds in any particular country. It will only be tempted to do so if the returns that it can earn in that country, after taking account of risk, are at least as high as those that it can earn elsewhere.

Risk is a complicating factor. Investing in a foreign country is one form of diversification. It is quite likely that there will be low levels of correlation between cash flows on home investments and those from overseas investments. Investing internationally is therefore one way of reducing risk relative to the overall expected return. The investing company needs to consider whether the particular overseas investment is in fact a good form of diversification. From a financial point of view the decision on whether or not to invest in a particular project in a foreign country is based on exactly the same theory and techniques as a home country investment decision. The cash flows need to be forecast and discounted at the appropriate rate. However, there are certain complications. Cash flows with international aspects will be affected by such factors as movements in exchange rates, the local financial arrangements for the project, the tax position in the host and home country, and repatriation policies.

The foreign investment decision is a two-stage process. The first stage is to ascertain whether or not the cash flows in the host country justify the project – this is the cash flow generated in the currency of the host country. The second stage is to determine whether the cash flow that is returned to the home country justifies the cash invested from the home country. If, for example, a UK company moves funds from the UK to a subsidiary in Kenya, is the cash flow returned to the UK in the form of dividends, management fees etc. sufficient to justify the outflow?

This second stage, as described, is based on the company undertaking the investment seeing itself as a UK company. It is ultimately judging its performance in terms of its group accounts produced in pounds sterling in the UK and on the impact of these results on shareholders. It could be argued, however, that if a company is truly multinational, it would not see itself in terms of its performance summarized in the currency of one country. It could be argued that many multinationals now have shareholders in many countries of the world. Companies such as Philips have far more of their shareholders outside Holland, the country in which the parent company is registered, than inside that country. In some cases therefore the 'home country' concept may no longer be relevant.

Although legally a multinational is registered in one country and needs to produce its group accounts in the currency of that country and according to the rules of that country, it might also produce alternative group accounts in the currency and according to the rules of other countries in which its shares are quoted. From a management point of view the company might therefore not be trying to maximize its performance in the country in which it is registered. It could be judging its performance in terms of its world-wide position, with a portfolio of assets valued in different countries and different currencies.

The conventional technique for analysing foreign country investment decisions is still the two-stage process, however. The worked problem below will illustrate this traditional approach.

Example 26.4

Zappo Ltd, a UK chemical company, is considering opening a manufacturing plant in the South American country of Volatilia to supply the growing local demand for industrial cleaning fluids. All refining plant can be purchased from Volatilian suppliers at a total cost of 24.2 million Volatilian pesos. A site close to the country's main industrial area is available and can be purchased from the government for 5 million pesos. The project will require an initial investment of £360 000 of working capital which can be reclaimed at the end of the project life. The funds to purchase the equipment, the site and the working capital are transferred from the UK.

Refining capacity for the cleaning fluid is expected to be as follows:

Year	19X3	19X4	19X5	19X6
Barrels	100 000	200 000	400 000	650 000

Year	19X7	19X8	19X9
Barrels	800 000	800 000	650 000

The plant has a seven year life, with no salvage value at the end of this period, and Zappo Ltd intends to sell the land at its market value at the end of the project. The cleaning fluid will have an initial selling price (in year 1) of 150 pesos per barrel and variable costs of 90 pesos per barrel. Fixed costs of the refinery are expected to be 5 million pesos per year. Inflation has been a persistent problem of the Volatilian economy and Zappo Ltd expects costs to rise by 20% per annum; however, the government restricts price increases for industrial products to 15% per annum and for land to 5% per annum. As a consequence of high domestic inflation the Volatilian peso is expected to fall by 5% per year from its current exchange rate of 5.5 Volatilian pesos = £1.

The present government of Volatilia do not discourage foreign direct investment; however, at the end of 19X5 elections are due to be held, and the leading opposition party Volatilia Nationala are known to be in favour of expropriation of all foreign direct investment. Zappo's political adviser believes that there is a 25% chance of Volatilia Nationala taking power and, if so, an 80% chance of Zappo's investment being expropriated at the start of 19X6. After this time the refinery is considered 'safe' because of the limited life of the plant. Volatilia Nationala believe in compensating foreign investors in the event of expropriation and have declared their intent to pay 70% of the present value of future peso cash flows of the project discounted at a rate of 25% per annum and to repurchase land at the original sale price.

Zappo Ltd intends to repatriate all surplus cash flows annually to the UK. In the event of expropriation it is believed that any compensation will be repatriated at the end of 19X6. Corporate tax rates are 50% in both countries and a full bilateral tax treaty exists. Volatilian corporation tax is based on accounting profit, allowing straight-line depreciation on fixed assets, and is paid one year in arrears. Zappo Ltd's cost of capital for projects of this nature is 18%.

Prepare a report advising the company whether it should proceed with the investment.

Suggested solution

Table 26.3 gives the projected cash flows if there is no expropriation. The problem is made easier by the fact that a cost of capital is given and the funds provided are all from one source. The problem illustrates the effects of exchange rate movements and possible 'loss' on the investment.

The cash flow to the parent company (line 13) includes the after-tax profits and the annual depreciation provision, both of which, it is assumed, can be repatriated. In many situations there would be additional cash flows moving from the subsidiary to the parent company arising out of such items as management charges and royalties. These do not arise in this question.

The figures in Table 26.3 show a positive net present value (NPV) and so indicate that the project should be undertaken, based on the assumption that there will be no expropriation.

We now have to consider whether the project would still be worth undertaking if the elections bring into government the party that favours expropriation of foreign companies' assets. There is then a 20% chance of expropriation. If takeover occurs then cash flows from 19X6 will be as follows:

	19X6	19X7	19X8	19X9	19X0
Cash flow to parent (excl. land)	30.38	32.53	26.43	14.73	(16.22)
25% discount factor (to 19X6)	0.8	0.64	0.512	0.410	0.328
Discounted cash flow	24.3	20.82	13.53	6.04	(5.32)

Total × % to be paid   = 59.37 × 0.7   = 41.56
                         + Land value   5
                                              ─────
                                              46.56 million pesos
Converted at   6.69 exchange rate
                                              = £6.96 million
Discount factor   0.516 (to bring to 19X3)
PV   = £3.59 million

Therefore PV of project if expropriated equals flows before takeover plus compensation

$$-(5.669) + 3.59 + 0.147 + 0.812 + 1.894 = £0.774 \text{ million}$$

and expected NPV is

$$(0.8 \times \pounds3.211m) + (0.2 \times \pounds0.774m) = \pounds2.724 \text{ million}$$

This analysis suggests that the project should be undertaken.

Whether or not a major overseas investment is profitable often depends on the financing package that can be put together. As explained in the previous section this requires an estimate to be made of the cost of capital. In the above example we were told that the cost of capital for projects of that particular nature was 18%.

Table 26.3

	19X3	19X4	19X5	19X6	19X7	19X8	19X9	19X0
(1) Sales (units)	100 000	200 000	400 000	650 000	800 000	800 000	650 000	—
Sales price (+15%) (million pesos)	150	172.5	198.4	228.1	262.4	301.7	346.9	
Variable cost (+20%)	90	108	129.6	155.2	186.6	223.9	268.7	
(2) Contribution per unit	60	64.5	68.8	72.9	75.8	77.8	78.2	
(3) *Total contribution* *(1) × (2)* *(million pesos)*	6.0	12.9	27.5	47.4	60.6	62.2	50.8	
(4) Fixed cost	5	6	7.2	8.6	10.4	12.4	14.9	
(5) Depreciation	3.46	3.46	3.46	3.46	3.46	3.46	3.46	
(6) Taxable profit ((3) − (4) − (5))	(2.46)	3.44	16.84	35.34	46.74	46.34	32.44	
(7) Tax	—	—	0.49	8.42	17.67	23.37	23.17	16.22
(8) *Profits after tax*	(2.46)	3.44	16.35	26.92	29.07	22.97	9.27	(16.22)
Add back:								
(9) Depreciation	3.46	3.46	3.46	3.46	3.46	3.46	3.46	
(10) Working capital							2	
(11) Sale of land							7.04	
(12) Tax on sale of land								(0.61)
(13) *Cash flow to parent company (million pesos)*	1.0	6.9	19.81	30.38	32.53	26.43	21.77	(16.83)
Exchange rate	5.78	6.06	6.37	6.69	7.02	7.37	7.74	8.13
£ million	0.173	1.138	3.11	4.541	4.634	3.586	2.813	(2.07)
Factors for PV at 18%	0.847	0.718	0.609	0.516	0.437	0.370	0.314	(0.266)
PV (£ million)	0.147	0.812	1.894	2.343	2.025	1.327	0.883	(0.551)

Total PV   £8.88

Initial investment   29.2 million pesos divided by 5.5
       = £5.309 million
       + £0.360 million
       = £5.669
    NPV = £3.211 million

Probability of takeover in 19X6
0.75   Volatilia Nationala lose ———————————————— 0.75 No expropriation
0.25   Volatilia Nationala win   0.8 Expropriate   0.20 Expropriation
                      0.2 No expropriation   0.05 No expropriation
                                                     1.00

All companies are exposed to business risk. The cash flows of all companies will depend on economy-wide effects such as economic growth, changing tastes and changes in technology. All companies are also exposed to financial risks which depend upon how the company is financed.

Multinational businesses are exposed to two further types of risk, foreign exchange risk and political risk. Foreign exchange risk can be divided between transaction risk, accounting risk and economic risk. We have already considered transaction risk in Chapter 21 (the actual exchange of one currency to another) and shall now move to the other two exchange risks.

Accounting (translation) risk

Accounting exposure arises not as a result of conversion of currencies but as a result of financial data denominated in one currency needing to be expressed in terms of another currency. Such translation of currencies occurs at the end of each accounting year when the accounts of all subsidiaries have to be expressed in the currency of the parent company in order to present the consolidated accounts of the group. The important question that arises is at what rate of exchange the accounts should be translated. There are a number of possibilities, one being the rate of exchange at the balance sheet date, another the rate of exchange at the time that the asset was acquired or the liability incurred and a third being the rate of exchange mid-way through the trading year.

To illustrate the problem, let us say that on 31 December 19X8 a UK company acquired the net assets of a French company. The assets in France were worth FF1 000 000; the rate of exchange at the time was £1 = FF10 so that the British company acquired net assets which it consolidates in its 19X8 accounts as being worth £100 000. The exchange rate at the end of 19X9 is £1 = FF12.5. To prepare the consolidated accounts for 19X9, translating at the current rate of exchange now gives net assets worth only £80 000. The UK company has suffered because the French franc has fallen in value against the pound. The fall in value of the assets results either in a charge to the profit and loss account of £20 000 or a charge to the reserves of the company of this amount; it is the result of a loss on foreign currency translation.

The company has not made a transaction loss; no conversion of French francs to pounds has taken place. The company may or may not have the intention of selling its French assets, which are of as much worth in 19X9 within France as when they were acquired (subject to depreciation). Nevertheless in this case adopting a closing-rate method of translation results in a book loss occurring, which could reflect badly on the company when analysts consider its performance. It might be argued it is not a real (cash) loss, but the net effect of it in the accounts is the same as if it were.

Clearly companies need to be aware of their accounting exposure and to try to minimize its impact. It should be noted in the above example that if, in 19X9, the French assets had been translated into pounds sterling at the rate of exchange at the date they were acquired no translation loss would have occurred. If a company adopts such a policy it is using what is called the temporal method. Which method of translation is recommended by the accounting profession?

The possible translation methods are as follows.

1. *Current – non-current method*: generally, this translates current assets and liabilities at the current rate (at the date of the balance sheet) and non-current assets and liabilities at applicable historical rates.
2. *Monetary – non-monetary method*: generally, this refers to the translation of monetary assets and liabilities at the current rate and non-monetary assets and liabilities at applicable historical rates. For translation purposes, assets and liabilities are monetary if they are expressed in terms of a fixed number of foreign currency units; all other balance sheet items are classified as non-monetary.
3. *Temporal method*: assets, liabilities, revenues and expenses are translated at the rate of exchange ruling at the date on which the amount recorded in the financial statements was established. At the balance sheet date, any assets or liabilities that are carried at current values are retranslated at the closing rate.

4. *Closing-rate method*: assets and liabilities denominated in foreign currencies are translated using the closing rate. Revenue items are translated using either an average or the closing rate of exchange for the period.
5. *Net investment*: the net investment that a company has in a foreign enterprise is its effective equity stake and comprises its proportion of such a foreign enterprise's net assets; in appropriate circumstances, intragroup loans and other deferred balances may be regarded as part of the effective equity stake.
6. *Closing-rate – net investment method*: this recognizes that the investment of a company is in the net worth of its foreign enterprise rather than as a direct investment in the individual assets and liabilities of that enterprise. The amounts in the balance sheet of the foreign enterprise should be translated into the reporting currency of the investing company using the closing rate, i.e. the rate at the balance sheet date. Exchange differences will arise if this rate differs from that at the previous balance sheet date or at the date of any subsequent capital injection (or reduction) and should be dealt with in the reserves. Revenue items should be translated at an average rate for the year or closing rate. Where an average rate is used which differs from the closing rate, the difference should also be dealt with in the reserves.

The accounting profession has struggled in an attempt to achieve some degree of standardization in the translation method to be used by companies.

The current accounting view on the subject is that the closing-rate – net investment method should normally be used. The different methods adopted for translation do affect the level of accounting exposure, as the following example will show.

Example 26.5

A wholly owned subsidiary of a UK company is registered in a foreign country and prepares its accounts in accordance with UK standards, but they are expressed in the local monetary unit Zs. The shares were acquired at the beginning of the year by the parent company at a nominal value of Z1500 when the rate of exchange was £1 = Z3. The financial statements recently prepared are summarized as follows.

Balance sheet

	Z000		Z000	Z000
Share capital	1500	Fixed assets net		1620
Reserves	30	Long-term advance		300
	1530	Current assets		
Long-term liability	900	Stock	450	
Current liabilities	360	Debtors	420	870
	2790			2790

Profit and loss account

	Z000
Sales	720
Cost of sales	690
Profit	30

The rate of exchange at the end of the year on the balance sheet date was £1 = Z5. These statements need to be translated into pounds sterling so that they can be incorporated into the group accounts.

Solution

To begin with we will use the closing-rate method which in this case equals the net investment method. This example requires that all items in the balance sheet, apart from the share capital, should be translated into sterling using the ratio 5:1. This gives the following.

	£000		£000	£000
Share capital	500	Fixed assets net		324
Loss on translation	(200)	Long-term advance		60
Reserves	6	Current assets		
	——	Stock	90	
	306	Debtors	84	
			——	174
Long-term liability	180			
Current liabilities	72			
	——			——
	558			558

For the profit and loss account we have, using either (a) the closing rate or (b) the average rate (say, £1 = Z4), the following.

	(a) £000		(b) £000
Sales	144	Sales	180
Cost of sales	138	Cost of sales	172.5
Profit	6	Profit	7.5

If the average rate is used for translating the profit and loss account, then the profit of £7500 has to be retranslated using the closing rate before incorporation in the balance sheet and the difference of £1500 is deducted from reserves. The advantage of the closing-rate method is that the traditional ratios from the accounts are unaltered; profit is still 4.2 per cent of sales, current assets are still 2.42 times current liabilities and this stability is considered useful. As far as the parent company is concerned, the net asset value of the subsidiary is now £306 000 compared with £500 000. The profit of £6000 (or £7500) has been more than offset by the loss arising on the translation of the share capital Z1 500 000 (the net assets at the beginning of the year) at £1 = Z5 instead of £1 = Z3. The two components of the result for the year should be treated differently, with the gain or loss on trading being part of the normal trading results and the exchange difference arising from the retranslation of the opening net investment dealt with through reserves.

If the temporal method is implemented, then further information is needed. It is necessary to determine the rate of exchange appropriate to the dates being used as the basis of measurement of particular assets and liabilities. These rate will be those appropriate to the historical cost for fixed assets – long-term advances and stock valued at cost – and the closing rate for all other items.

The practical implication of this method is that fixed assets are translated by reference to the rate of exchange when they were acquired, which retains their effective historical cost in terms of sterling. Automatically, the depreciation charge would be based on this historical translated amount. In times of relative rising prices (declining value of Zs in relation to pounds) in the overseas country, the depreciation charge based on historical cost represents a higher proportionate expense; for example, if the fixed assets costing Z1 800 000 had been acquired when £1 = Z3, they would be translated to £600 000 less depreciation for one year of Z180 000 (or £60 000) to net £540 000 instead of the £360 000 less £36 000, net £324 000, when using the closing rate of £1 = Z5. The difference in the depreciation charge would be reflected in the profit for the year: £24 000 lower when using the closing rate. The treatment of stock can be significant in particular cases (and examination problems), but in most practical situations the rate of stock turnover in relation to changes in exchange rates means that there is only a small difference between stock translated at the closing rate and stock translated at the historical rate.

The closing-rate – net investment method is normally used for translation purposes.

Accounting risk has been illustrated using a consolidated accounts example. It can also occur when any transaction has not been completed at a year end. For example, if a UK company has purchased plant and machinery from France but has not paid for it at the accounting year end, the rate of exchange appropriate at the time that the asset was acquired could be different from the rate of exchange at the year-end date. A translation gain or loss could therefore arise.

Economic exposure

The economic value of an asset, or collection of assets, is based on the present value (PV) of the future cash flows that such assets will generate. This approach was discussed in Chapter 4. A company is an asset; therefore in theory its value as a going concern is the PV of its future cash flows. However, for a multinational the question arises of the cash flows in which currency? The owner of an overseas subsidiary will usually wish at some time to be able to convert the cash flows generated in the host country currency into home country or some other currency. If the subsidiary company is sold locally, taking the cash out of the country will involve an exchange. If it is sold to another foreign company, the sale price will need to be in a hard currency. Therefore the value of the future cash flows is not just influenced by business risks, but also by exchange rate risks. The value of the business at any time depends upon the future cash flows and the expected future exchange rates.

The net present value NPV_0 of the foreign investment at time zero is given by

$$\text{NPV}_0 = \frac{\text{CF}_1 \times \text{ER}_1}{1+i} + \frac{\text{CF}_2 \times \text{ER}_2}{(1+i)^2} \cdots \frac{\text{CF}_N \times \text{ER}_N}{(1+i)^N}$$

where CF is the expected cash flow in the host country, i is the appropriate cost of capital and ER denotes the exchange rate between the appropriate currencies.

It is one thing to expect the future cash flows in the host country currency to show good growth, but if this is counterbalanced by movement of the expected value of the host country currency against the home country currency (or other hard currencies) then the PV of the investment is not necessarily increasing. Economic exposure represents the potential loss in the total value of a business due to exchange rate movements. It should be noted that accounting exposure is concerned with book values and economic exposure with market values.

The actual level of economic exposure depends on the policies pursued by the company. The more independent the subsidiary the less influence the exchange rate has on its actual cash flow. If all its sales and purchases are in the domestic currency, then the exchange rate has less influence than if there is much intercompany trade. If the foreign subsidiary is financed mainly by local borrowing, then the level of economic exposure will be less than if it is financed by parent company loans. Repayments of local borrowing (which affects the annual domestic cash flow) are not affected by movements in exchange rates, but repayments of foreign borrowing are. Other factors that can affect the operating cash flows and hence the economic exposure of a subsidiary include the following.

1. The export component of sales and the responsiveness of export sales to changes in exchange rates: if the subsidiary invoices in the currency of buyers, it clearly has a different impact to invoicing in home country currencies.
2. If a country devalues it could affect the overall level of economic activity within the host countries and so affect sales levels.

The ways in which a company can manage its operation to minimize the effect of economic exposure include the following.

1. With intercompany accounts, if a devaluation is expected, speed up payments out of the currency to be devalued and delay payments into the devalued currency.
2. Increase debts to third parties in the currency prone to downward valuation – stretch suppliers' terms of credit.

3. Reduce receivables from third parties in the currency prone to downward valuation – temporarily reduce sales.

4. If the local currency is expected to depreciate against the parent company's currency, the policy should be to rely on as little equity from the parent as possible and as much local borrowing as possible. Decisions on such factors will affect the level of economic exposure.

5. The management of economic exposure can be through financial markets as well as through the operating policies of the parent and subsidiary. For example, the value of a foreign subsidiary can be covered in the forward exchange market and the money market as illustrated in Chapter 21 on the subject of managing foreign exchange risk. However, it is more complex to cover for economic exposure than transaction exposure.

If the parent forecasts certain levels of cash flow but is worried about the exchange rate, it can lock into existing exchange rates through the forward market – if, of course, such a market exists in the currency being considered. Alternatively, if it knows that it will be receiving local currency over time, if it is permitted, it can borrow in the local currency and immediately convert the borrowed funds into its own currency at the spot rate. In future it can repay the borrowed money out of the local cash flow that it receives.

The problem is uncertainty about the actual cash flows that it will receive. With transaction exposure the amounts to be paid and received are known. With economic exposure they are based on estimates. If the company is wrong in its measures of future cash flows it is converting paper profits and losses into real exchange gains or losses.

Company disclosure

It is becoming increasingly common for large MNCs to make a statement in their accounts on their policy towards hedging foreign exchange risk.

SmithKline Beecham in the financial review appearing in their 1992 accounts explain that, as normal practice, they do hedge to protect 'the translation of its overseas profits'. They also explain that they also hedge to minimize exposure, arising 'on the translation of the Company's balance sheet'. They mention that options and forward contracts are used to limit the impact of exchange rate fluctuations on overseas profits. The company does not tell us what techniques are used to protect the balance sheet, it just refers to hedging arrangements. Matching the currency of assets with the currency of loans is clearly one such arrangement.

Tomkins plc in their Annual Report and Accounts point to a danger in this 'natural hedge' of borrowing in the same currencies as the non-sterling assets the company owns. They indicate that it can distort the balance sheet. The solution they adopt is a currency swap, which as they point out can also have a positive interest-rate effect.

De La Rue refer to the fact that the currency of their earnings is 50% in US dollars, 30% in sterling and 20% in Deutschmarks. They provide numbers to indicate the sensitivity of cash flow and earnings to changes in exchange rates. This is of course indicative of economic risk.

Cadbury Schweppes explain in their 1992 accounts that changes in exchange rates have reduced reported profits for the year. They also refer to the effect of exchange rate movement on the current year's exports and imports. Coats-Viyella in their 1992 financial review mention that 'The significant devaluation by 19% of sterling between year-end 1991 and year-end 1992 increased the value of net dollar assets by £26.8 million. The overall exchange effect on the balance sheet was an increase in net assets of £43.2 million.'

26.6 Internal hedging techniques

The external techniques for hedging against transaction risks were dealt with in Chapter 21 on foreign exchange markets. There are in addition a number of steps a MNC can itself take to reduce the risk of foreign exchange loss. These are techniques which do not involve using the foreign exchange markets, the money markets or financial derivatives. They are techniques internal to the company. They include the following.

Netting

This is the principal method of internal hedging. It reduces the number of transactions that a multinational company needs to make in the foreign exchange markets and so reduces risk. It requires the company to structure its business in such a way that cash is managed centrally. Central management is being used in this context to mean that foreign currency flows between subsidiaries or overseas branches are grouped together so that all opportunities are taken to offset inflows and outflows in the same currency.

There is bilateral netting where the flows between two subsidiaries are netted to just one amount that needs to pass from one to other. There is multilateral netting, which is more complex, and which results in just a few net transfers of cash, rather than a large number of bilateral settlements.

Bilateral netting occurs when a pair of subsidiaries net out their own positions with each other. There is no attempt to introduce the net positions of other group companies. Consider a US parent company which has two subsidiaries, one in Germany and one in the UK that have trade flows between them (as illustrated in Figure 26.2). The German subsidiary will invoice the UK subsidiary in Deutschmarks for the equivalent of US$100 000 at the end of the month. At the same time, the UK subsidiary is billing the German subsidiary in pounds sterling for the equivalent of US$180 000. Through the netting process, the German subsidiary would only owe the UK subsidiary the equivalent of US$80 000.

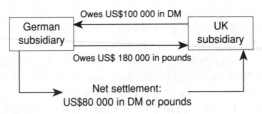

Figure 26.2 *Bilateral netting*

As seen in the above example, netting has reduced the number and the amount of the cross-border transactions and the related fees and commissions. Bilateral netting is fairly straightforward to operate as long as the participants can decide on the currency denomination of the net remittance and on a reconcilliation and settlement schedule. A centralized control system is not necessary in this form of hedging.

Multilateral netting, or inter-currency netting, can take place whenever affiliates both import from and export to companies within the same multinational company. All the payables are offset against all the receivables of the group, leaving the remaining net figures as the only items to be transferred (as illustrated in Figure 26.3). It reduces a series of cross-border fund flows to a bilateral flow between each subsidiary and the netting centre. In order to achieve successful implementation of the netting process, a netting centre is needed to co-ordinate participants' activities and to ensure that all subsidiaries are acting on the same predetermined schedule.

The calculation of the net flows is (i.e. a summary of the first part of Figure 26.3) is as below (in US dollars):

	Pays	*Receives*	*Net to/from centre*
UK	130 000	100 000	− 30 000
Swiss	220 000	340 000	+120 000
Germany	380 000	120 000	−260 000
US	120 000	290 000	+170 000
			0

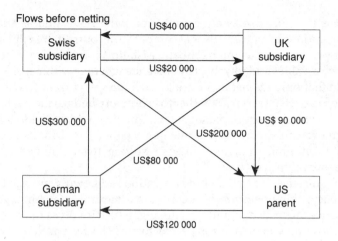

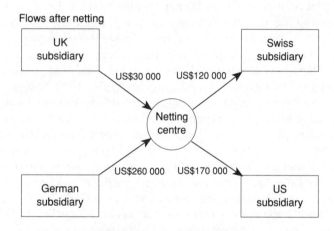

Total obligations : US$850 000 (payments)

Amount of obligations offset :
(US$850 000 – US$290 000) = US$560 000 = 56%

Figure 26.3 *Multilateral netting*

If it is decided that funds should not be paid into a netting centre, an alternative approach is for one company to settle directly with another. The payment/receipts balances can be settled by just three transactions.

UK pays to Switzerland	$30 000
Germany pays to Switzerland	$90 000
Germany pays to US	$170 000

Netting systems clearly reduce bank transfer charges and commissions. It can also assist a company in obtaining competitive foreign exchange quotes because of the centralized bargaining. It does not however reduce currency exposure up to the date at which the netting is performed.

An important aspect of a multilateral netting system is the collecting centrally of information. All subsidiaries must report all intercompany positions at the end of a given period, and the centre then advises the subsidiaries of the net amount which needs to be paid or received at a certain date. This requires a centralized communication system and discipline on the part of each subsidiary.

Matching

The terms 'netting' and 'matching' are often used interchangeably but in fact they are different. Netting, as illustrated above, refers to the netting out of **group** receipts and payments. It is typically used only for intercompany flows and as such is applicable only to the operations of a multinational company. In contrast, matching can be applied to both third-party as well as intercompany cash flows. In essence, matching is the off-setting of all receivables and payables by currency whether within a group or with other companies so that only the net exposure to each foreign currency is hedged externally or left exposed to exchange risk. Whether the company hedges the net position depends on its policy towards exposure management. The firm which seeks to maximize profit in the foreign exchange markets is termed an 'aggressive' firm: its counterpart which aims merely to minimize potential losses resulting from changed exchange rates is termed a 'defensive' firm.

The basic requirement for a matching operation is the two-way cash flow in the same foreign currency; this operation is regarded as 'natural' matching. Another type of matching operation is called 'parallel' matching, which involves the match between two currencies whose movements are expected to run closely parallel. For example, the Deutschmark and Swiss franc. In the 'parallel' matching situation, gains in one currency, say appreciation of Deutschmark receivables, is expected to be offset by losses in another, say appreciation of Swiss franc payables. Obviously, with parallel matching there is always the risk that the exchange rates will move contrary to expectations, so that both sides of the parallel match lead to exchange losses or gains.

Matching can be profitably applied to both an individual company as well as a group of companies. These two situations will be discussed. First of all, consider an individual company. Let us say that a dollar-based company with a 100% hedging policy is able to identify offsetting sterling payables and receivables three months forward; the need for individual forward contracts for both the payables and receivables is therefore eliminated. Furthermore, if the sterling payables and receivables can be managed out of a sterling account, then both the forward points and spot spread can be saved as no conversions into dollars take place. Typically, if individual currency accounts are operated by a company the offsetting of cash flows with significant timing differences is feasible.

A group situation is basically the same as that of an individual company except in terms of scale and in the extra accounting and tax complexities. Typically, the central treasury will manage the group matching. The centre can identify the net exposure and hedge according to group policy. Individual group companies deal purely on a spot basis with currency gains and losses attributable to each subsidiary being booked into inter-company accounts and settled on, say, an annual basis.

Alternatively the central treasury can be a clearing centre which facilitates a reduction in currency conversions by the group either by having subsidiary cash flows pass through a common set of currency accounts, or by assuming responsibility for all external currency cash flows.

The example for a clearing centre matching system is illustrated in Table 26.4. A multinational company has subsidiaries in the US, UK, France and Germany. The clearing centre takes the responsibilities for all the external fund flows from the subsidiary companies regardless of the nationality of the company.

Therefore, the total currencies flows are summarized as shown in Table 26.4.

Table 26.4

| | Currency (millions) | | |
Receivables/(Payables)	US$	£	DM
US company	—	(1.5)	(12)
UK company	(2)	5	3
German company	1.5	(3.5)	4
French company	5	2	—
Unmatched totals for hedging	4.5	2	(5)

The flows can be matched resulting in three total residual amounts which are unmatched and which can then be hedged.

There are at least three advantages of matching. The first one is that it reduces currency flows. Second, only the unmatched values are hedged. Third, where matching is centralized, co-ordination of the group's exposure allows greater management control including tax planning.

Of course, there are some disadvantages. Firstly matching requires accurate cash flow forecasts of the timing and amount of foreign currency settlements. Secondly, where centralized, intercompany account reconciliation must be accurate and to a previously agreed time schedule. Also the timing of currency flows in and out of a company are complicated due to inclusion of third parties in the calculations.

Leading and lagging

Leading and lagging is the process of adjusting the timing of payments and receipts. Leading refers to making payments early while lagging involves delaying payment. This is primarily a technique internal to the company since it can easily be applied to intercompany transactions. In third-party trade, there is a clear conflict of interest between seller and buyer if flows are lagged.

Multilateral netting systems usually incorporate a facility to permit leading and lagging of intercompany payments. This allows for the possibility of group companies with cash surpluses helping reduce the need for short-term financing of fellow group companies which are cash-poor. Besides, intercompany leading and lagging can be used as part of either a risk-minimizing strategy, say, to facilitate matching, or an aggressive strategy to minimize expected exchange gains. In either case, a central treasury is usually required to ensure that the timing of intercompany settlements is effective from a group's point of view rather than a purely local one. The centre may also co-ordinate intercompany interest charges where lagging has caused additional costs at an operating unit.

There are many benefits of using the leading and lagging technique. For example, leading and lagging is a useful tool for shifting intercompany funds for the purpose of liquidity management. It also facilitates the use of netting and matching. It allows fine-tuning of group tax management in the way that it takes advantage of different tax rates in different countries. It means that if the currency of a creditor is expected to fall in value, lagging the payment will reduce the real cost.

Multicurrency billing system

Foreign exchange exposure can be transferred from a sales subsidiary to a manufacturing subsidiary level via a change of the intercompany billing arrangements. This can be accomplished by a replacement of a specific currency as the billing currency with the currencies, normally the local currency, in which the individual sales subsidaries bill their customers. Therefore, the sales subsidiaries are no longer involved in currency conversions, and the manufacturing units now have a positive cash flow in a multitude of currencies.

Most companies express their intercompany transfer prices in a base currency, usually the parent company's currency. If billings are made in a variety of currencies, a centre is needed for the adjustment of the transfer prices in the individual currencies for significant exchange rate movements and to ensure that all sales subsidiaries are supplied at essentially identical transfer prices. In most cases, the transfer price is arrived at by using a current exchange rate which may be the spot or a forward rate. The transfer prices are adjusted after a period of time. Some companies adjust it monthly, some follow the short- to medium-term planning cycles.

Reinvoicing is a well-known and widely used technique for the centralization of currency exposures. Under reinvoicing, the manufacturing subsidiaries ship directly to the sales subsidiaries but bill to a separate entity, the reinvoicing company. The reinvoicing company bills the sales subsidiaries in turn (as illustrated in Figure 26.4). As a result, the currency conversion exposure is now concentrated in the reinvoicing company. Usually the reinvoicing company operates in a low tax location.

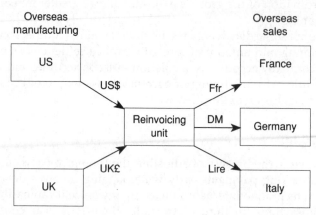

Figure 26.4 *Reinvoicing*

26.7 Political risk

There are a number of ways in which the host government of a country can interfere with the operations of a company. These range from non-discriminatory interference to wealth deprivation.

1. Non-discriminatory interference is usually comparatively mild and might be aimed at all companies in a country, not just those that are foreign owned. It would include interfering in transfer pricing arrangements and making the host country currency not freely convertible.
2. Discriminatory interference is the next step up. It is aimed at foreign firms and includes insisting on joint ventures, with a certain percentage of the shares in the company to be held by nationals. It also includes special taxes on the profits of foreign-owned firms or on dividend and interest remittances.
3. Discriminatory sanctions are more serious than the previous level of interference. They are not outright nationalization on indigenization, but they make it so difficult for the multinational to operate profitably that it might decide to close down. The sanctions would include ending the right to remit profits.
4. Wealth deprivation is the takeover of the multinational, with or without compensation.

The multinational can take certain steps to prevent or minimize the effect of such interference. Management strategies can be divided between those taken prior to making the investment, the operating strategies and those to be followed after the event. One step in the management of such risks is to try to anticipate them. Forecasting political interference is part of any multinational company's investment planning exercise. This has to take place prior to the decision to move into a country, and must continue after moving in so as to be able to anticipate any changes.

Prior to undertaking the investment the company should negotiate to try to obtain the best terms possible from the host government. What terms can be obtained depend of course on the strength of the government and its political attitudes. Prior to investment the arrangements should be settled with regard to such items as remittance of dividends, management fees, transfer prices, access to host country capital markets and provisions for local equity participation. Another possible pre-investment strategy might be planned disinvestment. This should make it clear to the host government how it will benefit from the investment in the short and long run. It might also be possible to obtain investment insurance.

The operating strategies to minimize political risk would cover such issues as local supply of goods and materials, the location of the investment, the control of transportation arrangements, the control of marketing, including brand names, methods of financing the subsidiaries using local banks and selling shares in the host country, labour policy, employment, promotion and management contracts. Decisions can be taken on each of these issues which could increase or reduce the possibility of host government interference.

Are developed countries risky?
Case study: The overseas investment of Kuwait in the British Petroleum Company PLC

Although the term 'political risk' appears frequently in the literature, there is no general agreement about its meaning. The narrow meaning of political risk confines it to an expropriation event. However, the wider meaning of political risk is any government's action that has a negative affect on a foreign investor's future cash flows. In the past the foreign investor who invested in developing countries required the rate of return to cover the business, financial and political risk borne by his investment. The same foreign investor, investing in the developed countries, usually requires the rate of return to cover only business and financial risk and ignores political risk. Governments in the developed countries have shown that their countries can also be risky for foreign investors. For example, in 1980 the US Government froze investments by Iranians in the USA; they also froze investments by Libya in 1986. Another example occurred in October 1988 when the UK Government ordered the State of Kuwait to reduce its shareholding in the British Petroleumn Company PLC (BP) from 21.65% to 9.9% within 12 months.

Kuwait is a wealthy politically independent country. Its wealth comes from two main sources, oil and overseas investment, with the latter becoming of increasing importance to the country.

In October 1987 the UK Treasury offered for sale in the UK and overseas 2194 million BP ordinary shares for a fixed price of 330p per share, of which 120p was payable immediately, 105p payable on 30 August 1988 and 105p payable on 27 April 1989. The New York stock market crash on 19 October 1987 led to a fall of share prices around the world. This, of course, affected the price of BP shares. Therefore investors lost the desire to acquire the BP shares at a price fixed before the world-wide fall. The Kuwait Government, however, adhered to a commitment it had made to buy about 13 million of the shares at 330p per share. It was also able to buy an additional 1 315 750 000 BP shares between 21 October 1987 and 11 March 1988, taking advantage of both the low market price of BP shares and its own liquidity position.

On 4 October 1988, the Secretary of State for Trade and Industry in the UK ordered Kuwait to reduce its shareholding in BP from 21.6% of the total to 9.9% within 12 months. The UK Government justified its action with the following reasons.

1. The Kuwaiti Government could influence BP's voting rights to defeat ordinary and special resolutions at BP's general meeting either alone or in combination with other shareholders.
2. The Kuwaiti Government could influence BP's management to take decisions and actions different from those that it would take without the existence of the Kuwaiti voting power.
3. The size of the Kuwaiti Government's shareholding could be used to influence BP's research and development programme to find an alternative source of energy.
4. Although the Kuwaiti Government provided a deed of covenant stating that it would not influence BP's decisions and actions, it was not certain how Kuwait would need to adapt to future changing circumstances and on occasions it would need to place its own national interest first.
5. Conflicts of interest between Kuwait and BP would be even more likely to occur if a future Kuwaiti government was less well disposed towards the West in general and the UK in particular.
6. The prospect of the sale of a large block of shares overhanging the market would have a depressing effect on the share price and would restrict the management's freedom of action at times when it wanted to raise capital or issue shares for acquisition purposes.

Each of these reasons is debatable. The first four reasons concern the ability of Kuwait to influence BP's decisions and actions to achieve its own interests or to act in a way that affects the public interests of the UK. Logically, a small friendly country would not act in a way that adversely affects a large strong country. Moreover, the State of Kuwait had provided a deed of covenant whereby it committed itself not to use its voting shares to achieve any interest of the State of Kuwait other than its interests as an investor. The fifth reason was concerned with UK fears of a future change in the Kuwaiti Government (of interest in the light of future events!). The sixth reason is debatable. Logically, Kuwait would not behave in a way that affects the value of its own investment in BP.

Whatever the arguments the case illustrates political risk. Most books on the subject write in terms of the risk when investing in Third World countries. Clearly there are risks when funds flow the other way.

26.8 Taxation

All companies wish to minimize their tax bill. MNCs have more opportunities than domestic companies to be able to do so. Domestic taxation is complicated, international tax is even more difficult. There are many ways in which an MNC can organize its affairs so as to reduce its total tax bill. Before looking at such methods, we will briefly explain certain principles of international taxation.

Taxation of profits

A company is usually taxed in the country where it is regarded as being controlled; this will establish the company's residence for tax purposes. In addition a company will usually be taxed in countries where it operates.

A subsidiary operating in a foreign country is established in that country and is subject to corporation tax in that country. A subsidiary in say Thailand pays taxes in Thailand. A parent company established in say the UK is subject to the taxation rules of the UK.

That could be the end of the story but it is not. There are two issues. One is what happens if the Thai subsidiary pays a dividend to its UK parent? The usual procedure is for the Thai government to levy an additional tax, called a withholding tax, on the dividends leaving the country. The UK tax authorities will allow the withholding tax paid to be offset (a tax credit) against the corporation tax that will have to be paid by the UK parent on its income.

The second question is whether or not the UK parent should be taxed on the basis of the total profits earned worldwide by the companies in the group (that is the income earned by all the subsidiaries) or whether it should just be taxed only on the income received as dividends (or other forms of transfer) in the UK. Should the company be taxed on earnings that are not repatriated?

The usual principle is to tax MNCs in their home country on world-wide income but to allow a credit for tax paid on such income in foreign countries. There are however ways in which the impact of this principle is reduced. These include what is known as tax deferred, which can result in either no tax being levied in the parent country on foreign income, or the payment being delayed. Tax can be deferred on income which is not repatriated.

Tax neutrality

The basic principle as explained above is that an MNC is taxed in its home country on its world-wide income. A question that arises is: should the company be taxed on this worldwide income at the tax rate that would have been paid if all the income had been earned domestically? One can either have this so-called 'domestic' neutrality or what is called 'foreign' neutrality.

Foreign tax neutrality means the profits are taxed at the rate that applies to the country in which the company earns the income. Companies would usually prefer this approach as they argue that it means they compete on equal terms with the companies in countries in which they operate. The most usual approach in practice is domestic neutrality.

Double-taxation treaties

This is concerned with the taxation position on cross-border activities. If for example a payment, say dividends or interest, is made by a company in one country to a company in another country, the source of income country may wish to tax the money before it leaves their country. The receiving country may also wish to tax the income received. This could result in the income transferred being taxed twice. To eliminate this, many countries enter into double taxation agreements.

There are two ways in which the double-tax problem is overcome. One way is to adopt a version of the 'foreign neutrality' principle and the receiving country does not tax the income received (if it has already been taxed in the source country). The second approach is where the receiving country gives a credit against domestic tax for the amount of tax paid in the foreign country. A double-tax treaty between two countries can also lead to lower rates of withholding tax on payments between the two countries, than on payments between two countries with no treaty.

Branch versus subsidiary

Whether or not a commercial activity in a country is subject to local taxes is also an issue dealt with in double-taxation agreements. The usual practice is not to tax locally an enterprise unless it has established a permanent presence. The selling of goods or just providing services to local residents is not a form of permanent establishment. The setting up of a branch or subsidiary is a permanent establishment. The way in which a company is taxed in the countries in which it operates will affect how it organizes its foreign operations.

The tax treatment of a branch usually differs from that of a subsidiary. The profits of both will usually be taxed at the same rate, but the profits of the branch when remitted to the head office will not incur withholding tax. The payment of dividends of a subsidiary to its parent company will be subject to withholding tax.

Losses of a foreign subsidiary cannot usually be used to offset profits of a parent company.

If a foreign operation is expected to make losses for a number of years it could be advantageous to the MNC to set the activity up as a branch so that the negative earnings abroad may be used to offset profits at home. Both UK and US tax laws allow foreign branch income to be consolidated in this way. If an MNC expects to earn income from its foreign activities which it intends not to repatriate, then there may be tax advantages in setting up a foreign subsidiary. As explained, unlike branches, foreign subsidiaries of UK and US parent companies do not pay taxes in their respective home countries until the income is repatriated.

Foreign tax credits

Double taxation could arise if the host country and the home country both taxed the earnings of multinational companies at domestic rates of tax. To avoid this problem it is usual for the home country to allow its MNCs to claim the amount of tax paid in foreign countries as a credit against home country tax.

Example 26.6

Rowington plc has an operating subsidiary located in Turkey which pays dividends to the parent company in the UK. Suppose that corporate tax rates in Turkey are 50%, and there is a 10% withholding tax. The Turkish subsidiary earns 1000 million lire and the exchange rate is 50 lire equals £1. We will calculate the after tax dividend (in pounds) received by Rowington.

Solution

		(million)
Before tax earnings	Lire	1000
(50 Lire = £1)		£20
Turkish corporation tax paid (50%)		£10.00
After tax earnings		10
Withholding tax (10%)		1
After tax dividend received		9
UK tax on Turkish profits (33%)		£6.60
Tax paid in Turkey		£11.00
Foreign tax credit		
(used)		£6.6
(unused)		£4.4

In the UK foreign tax credits must be taken source by source. This means that it would not be possible in the above example to use the £4.40 million credit to reduce tax on profits earned by a subsidiary in another country. In contrast the USA allows unused credit to be pooled; it can also be carried back two years or carried forward five years. In the UK it is not possible to carry credits forward or backwards.

Tax deferral

Countries in fact differ in the way their tax authorities treat the foreign earnings of their multinational companies. The differences include the way they treat tax deferral. This is a method for granting credit to the MNC for taxes paid to host country tax authorities on foreign earnings.

The choice for the home country is basically between taxing foreign earnings when they are earned or when they are remitted to the home country. In the UK, the home country MNCs are usually asked to pay UK tax only when the earnings are remitted to the UK in the form of dividends and interest. The same is the situation with US-based MNCs and the payment of US tax.

The same treatment applies to chargeable gains on the disposal of foreign assets. UK tax is only payable on the actual amounts received in the UK.

The MNC earns profits in a particular country: it pays tax on those profits in the host country. As mentioned above, with home country tax neutrality, there may be additional taxes to pay in the parent country. However, the payment of these additional taxes may be delayed. The additional taxes will only have to be paid on foreign source income remitted to the parent country.

This deferral is in fact only relevant if the taxation rates in the host country are less than those in the parent country. In the Rowington example above, more tax was paid in Turkey than needed to be paid in the UK. If the profits had not been repatriated, there would have been no advantage from tax deferral.

Tax haven affiliates

As mentioned above tax payment can be deferred on income earned until the time it is remitted to the parent country. Some tax will usually have been paid of course in the country where the profits were earned. It is any additional tax that is deferred. If the profits of the subsidiary are remitted to a tax haven affiliate it will not be subject to additional parent country tax. A typical company structure is therefore as shown in Figure 26.5.

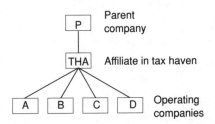

Figure 26.5

All transfers of funds, whether dividends, interest, royalties or management fees are channelled to the tax haven affiliate. The additional parent country tax can be delayed, perhaps postponed indefinitely if the finance is first pooled in the tax haven subsidiary, and then channelled to subsidiaries as and when needed.

The significance of tax credits to high and low tax rates in host countries can be illustrated with a further example. The example is also used to illustrate how (tax rules permitting) an MNC can use transfer pricing arrangements to reduce its total tax bill.

Example 26.7

Let us suppose a parent company (P) has two subsidiaries, one in a high tax country (H) and the other in a low tax country (L). The reporting currency of the group is dinars. The tax rates are as follows:

	P	H	L
Corporation tax	30%	50%	20%
Withholding tax	10%	10%	0%

Subsidiary L manufactures components and exports them to Subsidiary H. The subsidiaries are involved in many other activities but for the purpose of this example we are only interested in the taxation impact of this intercompany trade. In one year L sells 1 000 000 units to H at a transfer price of D20 per unit. L's cost per unit is equivalent to D15. Subsidiary H undertakes certain work on the components and then sells them all to customers at a price equivalent to D40 per unit. H's add-on costs are equivalent to D10 per unit.

Both subsidiaries remit all their profits to the parent company at the end of each year. The tax authorities in the home country adopt a policy of domestic neutrality.

The earnings and tax position of the two subsidiaries is as below:

	L (000s)	H (000s)
Sales	20 000	40 000
Costs	15 000	30 000
Profits	5 000	10 000
Corporation tax	1 000	5 000
Dividend	4 000	5 000
Withholding tax	0	500
Dividend received by parent	4 000	4 500

The tax position of the parent company on transactions concerned with these two particular transfers is:

	L (000s)	H (000s)
Earnings	5000	10 000
Tax at domestic rates	1500	3 000
Maximum tax credits available (paid in host country)	1000	5 500
Tax credits used	1000	3 000
Tax paid in home country	500	0
Total tax paid on earnings in home and host country	1500	5 500

As can be seen there is an unused possible tax credit from the subsidiary in the high tax country.

If a different transfer price had been used the total tax bill of the group could have been reduced. We will now assume the transfer price of the components is D25 per unit. All other costs remain the same.

The tax position of the two subsidiaries is now:

	L (000s)	H (000s)
Sales	25 000	40 000
Costs	15 000	35 000
	10 000	5 000
Corporation tax	2000	2 500
Dividends	8 000	2 500
Withholding tax	0	250
Dividend received by parent	8 000	2 250

The tax position of the parent is:

	L (000s)	H (000s)
Earnings	10 000	5000
Tax at domestic rates	3 000	1500
Maximum tax credits available	2 000	2750
Tax credits used	2 000	1500
Tax paid in home country	1 000	0
Total tax paid	3 000	2750

The total tax bill of the group is now D5750 as opposed D7000 under the previous transfer pricing arrangements.

Tax authorities do have rules to determine what is an acceptable transfer price. Companies are not completely free to set their own transfer prices simply with the object of reducing group tax bills. The rules are however not perfect and there is some disagreement between the tax authorities in different countries on what is acceptable. The rules tend to be based on accepting a transfer price based on what would be the market price in a deal between two independent companies at arm's length. Other factors looked at by some tax authorities include what would be a company's normal profit mark-up on items produced and sold to third parties.

Taxation of FOREX gains and losses

Foreign exchange transactions create profits or losses when the value of the home currency relative to the currency in which the transaction is denominated changes between the contract date and the date of payment. Gains or losses on foreign transactions may affect the tax charge of the company at home or abroad. The international taxation differences that exist between countries create market imperfections which MNCs can exploit by locating foreign exchange gains and other income in countries with low tax rates for this kind of revenue. Similarly foreign exchange losses can be channelled into high tax rate countries in which they are allowable as a deduction against profits and in which the MNC already has taxable income.

The management of taxation

Having considered certain of the basics regarding international taxation we will now examine briefly some of the techniques and opportunities available to the MNC to help minimize its tax bill.

1. Establish cost centres (subsidiaries) in high tax countries. These provide sufficient expenses to ensure that net taxable profits are not earned. Research and development centres should be set up in high-tax countries as opposed to low-tax countries.
2. Locate subsidiaries earning high profits in, or channel gains and other income through, countries with low taxes.
3. Locate a finance subsidiary in an offshore financial centre (tax haven). This issue will be dealt with separately below.
4. Adopt transfer pricing policies such that low profits are recorded as being incurred in high-tax countries and high profits in low-tax countries. An intermediary country can be used to purchase the goods from the producing country at a low price (near cost) and then to sell these at a high price to the ultimate destination. This is called re-exporting. Most of the profits are shown as being earned in the intermediary country, which is one chosen because of low taxes.
5. Take advantage of tax holidays, and other tax incentives on new investments offered by some countries.
6. Raise debt in countries with high tax rates in which the company is earning profits on other activities.
7. *Dividend mixer company*
   This is a company set up in an offshore financial centre with the object of being able to influence the timing of, and source of, flows of dividends and interest to the parent company. The objective is to pay the lowest possible level of total tax. High rates of dividends can be channelled into the mixer company from high tax rate subsidiaries such that the tax credits resulting in the home country compensate for the planned lower dividends received by the mixer company from subsidiaries in countries with low tax rates.
8. *Dividend cleaner company*
   Dividend cleaner companies are another mechanism by which MNCs can manage tax liabilities in their home country. Dividend cleaning companies are normally based in the home country and have the objective of maximizing the opportunities for double-tax relief from foreign subsidiaries before the tax charges on the income of the UK parent are determined. If cleaning companies did not exist there may be an insufficient UK tax charge to be covered by double-tax relief. This might result from the parent company incurring trading losses.
   In some instances the double-tax relief of the dividend cleaning company may not be exactly comparable to the tax liability on the dividend income. In this case the cleaning company can transfer to the parent company the exact amount of group relief necessary to eliminate the tax charge without producing excess double-tax relief.
9. *Intermediate holding companies*
   Dividends from foreign subsidiaries are sometimes channelled through intermediate holding companies who accumulate the funds. The intermediate company

would retain dividends from subsidiaries in low tax countries. The intermediate company would plan to take advantage of tax treaties in order to reduce withholding taxes. This form of tax planning is, however, subject to anti-avoidance tax legislation in both the UK and USA.

10. *Coordination centres*

   MNCs have been attracted by the tax efficient features offered by certain countries to set up financial subsidiaries. Such features include:

   - favourable tax laws;
   - no exchange controls;
   - low capital taxes;
   - good banking infrastructure;
   - good tax treaty network.

   In this context, Belgium, Luxembourg, the Netherlands and Switzerland have become popular with European MNCs for the location of financial subsidiaries. Belgium in particular has become very popular since major tax incentives were provided for MNCs which centred their co-ordination activities in Belgium. This legislation allows MNCs to establish centres designed to meet their own financial needs. Such centres are permitted to carry out a variety of financial and managerial services on a virtually tax free basis.

11. *Currency management centres*

   Given the complexity of the subject of foreign exchange dealings, most companies set up a currency management centre so that currency transactions can be controlled in ways which are tax efficient. There are sometimes problems convincing tax authorities that such centres outside the normal operating territories are legitimate business ventures. The centres are established in favourable locations from a tax point of view.

Offshore financial centres (tax havens)

The name OFC is in fact a misnomer. The centre does not need to be off any shore. Two of the best known OFCs are Luxembourg and Liechtenstein, which are both well away from any sea. Others centres are however islands, for example the Cayman Islands, Bermuda, the Isle of Man, the Channel Islands and Gibraltar.

OFCs are also known as tax havens for obvious reasons. Some have zero levels of corporation tax (Bahamas and the Cayman Islands), others very low levels of corporation tax (the Channel Islands 20%, and Hong Kong 16.5%). Most have zero levels of withholding tax, which is one of their particular attractions to MNCs. They can be used to collect and distribute dividends and interest without having tax deducted.

The demand to have OFCs established arises from the needs of companies, investors and politicians. The reasons include the following.

1. For companies to use as a base for financial subsidiaries: they can issue bonds from such centres, and pay interest around the world without having withholding tax deducted. They can be used as a centre for banking within a group of companies.
2. *Secrecy* The money of investors and companies can be hidden away: it is very difficult for foreign authorities to find out who owns what. This secrecy is needed for illegal purposes such as capital flight, smuggling, fraud, money laundering and tax evasion.
3. Low rates of income tax, corporation tax and capital gains tax payable.
4. Used by investors to buy and sell shares – avoiding regulations, such as insider trading rules, and other security laws.
5. Used by governments to support undercover activities, such as supplying arms to freedom fighters (or rebels). Also for bribery purposes.

The reason why there is a 'supply' of OFCs is:

1. It is beneficial for the country that is the OFC, generating income, creating employment.
2. Countries differ in what is considered acceptable behaviour. What is criminal activity in one country might not be against the law in another. Secrecy is seen as a virtue in some countries and a cause for concern in other countries.

Conditions necessary for a country to be an OFC:

- secrecy and lack of disclosure requirements;
- low rates of taxation;
- absence of foreign exchange control;
- freedom from international regulations and agreements;
- international banking separated from local commercial banking;
- political stability;
- good communications system.

Money laundering

A certain amount of the money that is moved around the world is secret money. This can arise in the following ways.

1. Individuals place money in secret bank accounts to avoid tax or public criticism.
2. Companies and governments wish to have slush funds that they can use to pay for certain services or assistance. They would rather not have such payments known about.
3. Criminal money that is the result of illegal activities. Fraud and drug dealing are well-known examples. Before money that is obtained from crime can be spent in needs to be laundered. That is it needs to be made clean. This is necessary because if an individual was seen to be enjoying a very expensive life-style, and there was no obvious way in which he obtained this money, he would arouse suspicion. The tax authorities would be interested in the source of the income, as would the police.

Businesses in which receipts are in a cash form, and in which the level of activity is not obvious are vehicles through which money to be laundered can be channelled. Many criminal organizations now employ accountants, lawyers and bankers who are experts on the subject of international finance. The money can be quickly moved around the world through different bank accounts, so that it is very difficult to establish how the money was initially earned.

The top criminals' organizations cannot spend all the money they generate so they become investors in legitimate companies. Financial centres, such as London and Frankfurt, are centres where illegally acquired money is invested in equities and bonds of legitimate companies. Criminal groups are becoming stronger.

The criminal groups make use of nominee names, multiple bank accounts, back-to-back loans, and cross guarantees. Very often the movement of funds gained from illegal activities involves cross-border transactions. Although the police authorities and other anti-crime organizations co-operate across borders there can be difficulties. For example there are practices which are illegal in some countries but not in others, a case being insider dealing.

Accounting exposure	Dividend mixer companies
American depository receipts (ADR)	Eurobonds
Asian dollar market	Euroequities
Back-to-back loans	Euromarkets
Cost of capital	Euro-medium term notes (EMTN)
Currency swaps	Exchange Rate Mechanism (ERM)
Deregulation	Foreign branches

26.9 Key terms

Foreign equity	Matching
Foreign tax credits	Money laundering
Global markets	Netting
Intermediate holding companies	Offshore financial centres
International banking market	Securities and Exchange Commission (SEC)
International taxation	Tax deferral
Lagging	Tax havens
Leading	Tax neutrality

26.10 Revision questions

1. What is the difference between a Eurobond and a foreign bond issued in a national market?
2. What is an EMTN?
3. Why might the market for Euroequity issues be less successful than the market for Eurobonds?
4. Should the cost of capital for a foreign investment be based on the gearing in the subsidiary undertaking the investment or the parent company gearing? Why?
5. What is the difference between netting and matching?
6. What is tax credit and tax deferral?
7. What advantages can an offshore financial centre offer to an MNC?
8. What are the problems faced in the appraisal of overseas investment projects that are not faced in appraising domestic projects?
9. How can a company minimize the impact of political risk?
10. What is the difference between accounting exposure and economic exposure?

26.11 Further reading

In Chapter 21 a number of books were listed in the further reading section. These are books on international financial management and so are relevant to this chapter. Other books and articles that are helpful are:

Euromoney (1992) *The 1992 Guide to Offshore Financial Centres*, Euromoney Publications, London.

Fatemi, A.F. (1984) Shareholder benefits from corporate international diversification, *Journal of Finance*, December.

Lee, C.K. and Kwok, C. (1988) Multinational corporations v domestic corporations: international environmental factors and determinants of capital studies, *Journal of International Business Studies*, Summer.

26.12 Problems

1. Describe and discuss the advantages and disadvantages of the internal hedging techniques available to avoid foreign exchange exposure.
2. The degree of political risk experienced in foreign direct investment projects is determined solely by sovereign government action and is therefore impossible to predict. The best policy for the multinational company is to diversify its interests geographically and hope that the worst does not happen. Discuss.
3. Describe the main features of the Eurocurrency, Eurobond and Euroequity markets.
4. What factors might be important to the financial manager of a multinational company when deciding whether to borrow funds on the domestic bond market or the Eurocurrency or Eurobond markets.

5. Discuss and illustrate the significance of bilateral tax treaties to multinational companies.

6. Explain how multinational companies might use tax havens in their tax management strategies.

7. Discuss the conflicts of interest that might exist between a multinational company and a host country government and critically appraise how a multinational company might attempt to protect itself from political risk.

8. 'The decision to finance in international capital markets involves considerable additional complexities for the corporate treasurer.'

    Discuss with particular reference to the Europaper and Eurobond markets.

9. The Multinational Company has a considerable capacity to transfer funds and profits through a wide range of internal channels. Describe the major characteristics and uses of such internal financial transfer systems, and outline the constraints under which they operate.

10. Discuss the conditions under which a multinational business is exposed to foreign exchange risk, and outline appropriate managerial strategies for such problem situations.

11. What are the key issues a bank must consider when lending overseas to corporations and governments?

12. In the 1980s international banks have switched from international bank lending to financing corporations via securities. Discuss the impact of such securitization on the multinational bank.

13. Calvold plc has a one-year contract to construct factories in a South American country. At the end of the year the factories will be paid for by the local government. The price has been fixed at 20 million pesos, payable in the South American currency.

    In order to fulfil the contract Calvold will need to invest 1000 million pesos in the project immediately, and a fixed additional sum of 500 million pesos in six months' time.

    The government of the South American country has offered Calvold a fixed rate-fixed rate currency swap for **one year** for the full 1500 million pesos at a swap rate of 20 pesos/£. Net interest of 10% per year would be payable in pesos by Calvold to the government.

    There is no forward foreign exchange market for the peso against the pound.

    Forecasts of inflation rates for the next year are:

Probability	UK	South American country	
0.25	4%	and	40%
0.50	5%	and	60%
0.25	7%	and	100%

    The peso is a freely floating currency which has not recently been subject to major government intervention.

    The current spot rate is 25 pesos/£. Calvold's opportunity cost of funds is 12% per year in the UK. The company has no access to funds in the South American country.

    Taxation, the risk of default, and discounting to allow for the timing of payments may be ignored.

    Required:

    Evaluate whether it is likely to be beneficial for Calvold plc to agree to the currency swap.

    (15 marks)

    ACCA, Dec. 1992

14. Two firms to which you act as adviser are concerned about their overseas operations.

    North is about to enter the export market but is uncertain whether its policy should be to invoice export sales in its own domestic currency or the currency of the purchaser.

South, a UK based manufacturing company, is about to set up an overseas subsidiary to deal with local manufacturing and sales. South has decided to finance the overseas subsidiary largely by fixed-interest debt finance using its own large equity base and small level of existing leverage to justify the large borrowing required for the new subsidiary. South will either borrow the required finance itself or will require its subsidiary to undertake the required borrowing. The Finance Director is uncertain whether South's strategy for financing its foreign subsidiary should be:

(i) for South to borrow in the UK for all financing needs, and for the subsidiary to be financed by South;

(ii) to require the subsidiary to borrow in the country, and currency, of its operations;

(iii) for South to borrow in whatever country, and currency, has the lowest annual interest rate at the time of taking out the loan, and for South to finance the subsidiary;

(iv) some combination of the above three approaches.

(a) Advise North on the matters to be considered in deciding on the currency in which to invoice export sales. (8 marks)

(b) Advise South on the factors to be considered in deciding on the financing of its foreign subsidiary. Explain the main merits and disadvantages of each of the financing strategies mentioned. (12 marks)

(20 marks)

ACCA, Dec. 1983

15. Potel plc is a large UK-based company that has recently decided to invest £15 million in a greenfield expansion of its main business, the manufacture of mobile telephones. The company has sought the advice of three consultants as to the best way to finance the investment and its managing director is somewhat confused by the suggestions. These are:

(a) Use a zero coupon 10 year bond, with an issue price of £50 and nominal value of £100 convertible into preference shares at any time up to the year 2000 at the rate of 60 shares for every £100 nominal value of the bond.

(b) A placing of new ordinary shares via an issuing house to institutional investors, at a discount of 10% on the current market price of the company's shares.

(c) A 4% Swiss franc 10-year loan stock with warrants to purchase ordinary shares at any time during the next ten years at a price of 200 pence per share. One share may be purchased for every 100 Swiss francs nominal value of loan stock held.

The company's summarized accounts are shown below:

Balance sheet as at 31 December 1993

		£m
Fixed assets (net)		90
Current assets		
Stock	40	
Debtors	42	
Cash	2	84
Less current liabilities		
Overdraft	31	
Short term loans	10	
Dividend payable	18	
Tax payable	12	(71)
Long term debt		
13% debenture 1999		(25)
Term loan (floating rate)		(15)
		63

Shareholders' funds

Issued ordinary shares (25p par)	20
Preference shares (25p par)	5
Reserves	38
	63

Profit and loss account for the year ended 31 December 1993

	£m
Turnover	176
Operating profit	30
Profit before tax and interest	22
Interest	10
Profit before tax	12
Taxation	4
	8
Dividend	3
Retained earnings	5

The company's current ordinary share price is 126 pence, and preference share price 75 pence. The company's loans, and interest rates, have remained approximately constant during the last financial year.

The Swiss franc spot rate is SF2.10/£, and one year forward rate SF2.05/£.

Required:

Discuss the advantages and disadvantages of these suggested means of financing. Where relevant support your discussion with calculations.

16. You are the incoming treasurer to a multinational company with subsidiaries spread across the world. There is a high volume of trade between subsidiaries, of components and finished goods, and you are presented with the schedule below. Currently the credit period is left up to the individual companies, and each company handles its payments and receipts individually. You decide to introduce a netting system.

(a) Describe the system you will set up and show the net payment schedule for May 1994.
(b) What financial benefit will you derive from the new system if a software package costs £1000 and you have an idle PC (and an idle treasurer!)?
(c) What additional benefits will you hope for and what problems might you face?
(d) At a future date how might you extend the system?

Schedule of inter-company settlements: May 1994

			Receiving co.				
	UK	France	Germany	USA	Japan	Taiwan	
Paying Co.							
UK	0	13 324	589	112	130 822	39 577	184 424
France	500	0	–	–	334 582	47 492	382 574
Germany	–	–	0	1038	167 291	–	168 329
USA	750	–	–	0	133 833	22 361	156 944
Japan	20	7 995	162	–	0	15 831	24 008
Taiwan	350	–	–	748	112 921	0	113 019
Total	1620	21 319	751	1898	879 449	125 261	1 030 298
$ Equivalent	2424	3 590	429	1898	7 865	4 735	$Total 20 941

Notes
   (i) Figures are in 000s of receiving country's currency.
  (ii) Transfer costs are $12.00 per transaction on average.
 (iii) US$ interest rate 3.5% p.a.
 (iv) Bid/Offer spread average 0.001% (0.1 of 1 per cent).
  (v) It is estimated that, due to some payments being made by cheque, there is an average of 3 days' float.
 (vi) FX rates. Spot vs $ mid rate

    £   1.4960
    FFr   5.9377
    DM   1.7504
    Yen 111.825
    T$ 26.455

(vii) Work in round 000s and in dollars.

17. Stoppall plc specializes in the construction of dams. The company has an excellent reputation and has been contacted by the representatives of a water authority in Scotland and a developing country, Bargonia, as each wishes to have a large new dam constructed. Stoppall has a full order book, but with the use of sub-contractors, could undertake one further project only. Both the Scottish and the Bargonian projects would take five years to complete.

The estimated cash outflows associated with the two projects are presented below:

Scottish project

Year	0	1	2	3	4	5
	£m	£m	£m	£m	£m	£m
Plant and machinery	20	5	3	1		
Vehicles	5	5	3	1		
Materials		25	24	26	28	14
Labour		12	14	15	16	17
Other expenses		11	10	12	14	16
Interest payments		35	42	42	42	42

Bargonian project

Year	0	1	2	3	4	5
	£m	£m	£m	£m	£m	£m
Plant and machinery	10	7	6	1		
Vehicles	5	3	4	2		
Materials		28	26	29	23	25
Labour		17	16	18	22	26
Other expenses		16	17	16	16	14
Interest payments		38	49	50	50	50

All expenses are payable in pounds sterling at the end of the year concerned with the exception of the initial outlays which are payable at the commencement of the projects.

Payment would be received in stages for both projects. The Scottish water authority would make an initial payment of 15% of the total price of £420 million, with a further 20% payable at both the start of year 2 and year 3, 25% at the end of year 4 and the remainder on completion of the project.

The Bargonian government has offered to make payment in either the local currency, the Dowl, or in $US.

Stoppall has indicated that, because of uncertainty about the future strength and convertibility of the Dowl, a 50% initial payment would be required with a further 20% at the end of year 2 and the balance on completion. The total price of the Bargonian project is 140 250 million Dowl or $US 900 million.

Payment in $US would require a 20% initial payment, with the remainder in equal annual instalments, the last being on completion of the project.

UK taxation, at the rate of 35% on worldwide net operating receipts, is payable one year in arrears. Tax allowable depreciation exists on all fixed assets at 20% per year on a straight-line basis. The fixed assets are expected to have a negligible value at the end of the five year projects. Stoppall has other taxable income besides these proposed projects. No foreign taxation would be payable in connection with the Bargonian project.

Stoppall bases its estimates of future foreign exchange rates on projections of inflation.

Projected annual inflation levels

	UK	USA	Bargonia
Year 1	5%	5%	20%
2	5%	5%	30%
3	5%	7%	30%
4	5%	7%	30%
5	5%	7%	30%
6	5%	7%	30%

The systematic risk of the Scottish project is estimated to be 1.5 and the Bargonian project 1.625. The risk free rate is 7% per year and market return is 15% per year.

Cash flow estimates already include the effects of projected inflation.

Current exchange rates are:

$/£	Dowl/£
1.60	25.0

Required:

(a) Evaluate whether Stoppall should construct the dam in Scotland or in Bargonia. If Stoppall selected Bargonia should it request payment in Dowl or $US?
State clearly any assumptions that you make. (20 marks)

(b) What other factors might be important to Stoppall when considering which project to select? (5 marks)

(25 marks)

ACCA, Dec. 1988

27 *Small business finance*

27.1	Introduction	992		27.8	Loan finance	1008
27.2	The small business sector	994		27.9	Conclusions	1012
27.3	Financing problems of small firms	995		27.10	Key terms	1012
				27.11	Revision questions	1012
27.4	The life-cycle of a firm	998		27.12	References	1012
27.5	Company failures	999		27.13	Further reading	1013
27.6	Equity finance	1002		27.14	Problems	1013
27.7	Specialist institutions	1007				

The small and medium-sized enterprise faces problems that are not faced by larger businesses. One particular difficulty concerns the provision of finance. We shall concentrate in this chapter on the sources of finance available to smaller businesses.

Governments have been aware for many decades of the importance of the small business sector. Many statements have been made over time, expressing good intentions, but unfortunately actions taken by politicians do not always live up to the statements made.

Changing technology and economic conditions gave a boost to small businesses in the second half of the 1980s. Unfortunately some of the advantages were cancelled out in the UK towards the end of the decade by the high levels of real interest rates and the downturn in the level of economic activity. This led to record levels of failures in the 1990s.

The life-cycle of the firm is discussed, together with the reasons why so many small firms fail.

27.1 Introduction

There has been an increasing interest in small and medium-sized companies in the UK and in the European Community in recent years. This has been partly due to the realization of their potential in the job creation process.

The evidence shows that, following a steady decline up to the early 1970s in the small business sector's share of total employment, the position was reversed with small businesses accounting for an increasing share of the total employment each year during the 1980s. There was evidence of a significant relationship between increases in net job creation and the size of firms. It is an inverse relationship: the smaller the size group, the more jobs being created in total.

It should be appreciated that small and medium-sized enterprises (SMEs) tend to be most prevalent in the primary and service sectors of the economy. When they are engaged in manufacturing it is usually either in the traditional type of industry or in areas of new technology, e.g. software engineering. It should also be appreciated that although there is net job creation by SMEs there is also a very high failure rate among this size of enterprise. This became evident during the early 1990s. Politicians are keen to push the virtues of the enterprise culture, but it is not always pointed out that the risks are high and the difficulties faced by small companies considerable.

In this chapter we shall be emphasizing the financial aspects of SMEs. Before doing this, however, we shall look at a number of reasons for their changing role.

Recession push

Large companies faced an increasingly competitive environment in the 1980s and needed to rationalize many of their operations and to reduce their levels of employment in order to increase their productivity. As they rationalize this reduces the opportunities for promotion of employees and this, with actual redundancy and the threat of redundancy, provided an impetus for many experienced employees to leave large organizations and establish their own firms. The withdrawal of large firms from many marginal areas of their operations also provides opportunities for former employees. This change in opportunities can be said to be due to the recession push – the downturn in world trade makes large firms look for greater efficiency.

Income growth

One further explanation for the resurgence of SMEs is that as a result of increased income levels consumer tastes have changed. The higher incomes have enabled consumers to look for varied and specialized products. This has meant that an opportunity has been created for small firms to produce items which are perhaps more expensive than those produced by the larger firms but which are different and have an appeal to a particular section of the market. Customer-specific requirements and fashion goods have created opportunities for small firms. The flexible and relatively labour-intensive characteristics of SMEs have enabled them to take advantage of changing consumer taste.

There is also danger in this, of course: the SMEs are vulnerable to small changes in taste.

Externalization

There is an increasing tendency for large firms to place a part of their work outside the organization. This involves sub-contracting and there is evidence that an increasing number of stages of production are being placed in the hands of small firms. This is the opposite of internalization, which is what happened a few years ago when large companies took on an increasing number of the stages of production themselves in order to avoid the risks of the market-place.

The current way of thinking is that placing work in the hands of sub-contractors means that labour problems are passed on to others. It means that activities that involve high levels of technical expertise can be decentralized, i.e. passed on to small firms, as can a certain amount of research and development work. There has also been a tendency to increase the amount of franchising operations.

The evidence is that an increasing amount of non-core business activities are being subcontracted or spun off into separate companies. The move to 'rationalize' company structures also creates smaller units.

Technological change

A number of recent technological innovations have resulted in considerable changes in the organization of the workplace. Clearly the microchip technology means that work can be undertaken in small units and even at home. There is evidence that small firms can adapt rapidly to new technologies and are willing to accept higher levels of risk. The result is that they now produce a disproportionate share of significant innovations. The high level of risk of course partly explains why there is a high failure rate in this sector.

Government policy

Governments in many countries have taken steps in recent years to make life easier for smaller firms. There are now advice centres for small businesses, loan guarantee schemes and a certain amount of tax relief. In the UK during the 1980s there was talk of creating an 'enterprise' culture, by which was meant encouraging people to set up their own businesses.

In the UK in 1971 the Bolton Committee drew attention to the fact that although the decline in the small business sector had occurred in most industrialized countries since the Second World War, the decline had gone further in the UK than in other countries. Table 27.1 shows that small firms have been an important source of employment, particularly in Japan. It is often claimed that it is because of the significance of the small firm sector in Japan that there is always a race to respond quickly to changes in the economic environment.

In the UK the importance of the small firm sector declined after the 1920s. The Bolton Committee and later the Wilson Committee were particularly concerned whether the decline in small businesses was the result of the financial problems they faced. It was found that this did provide part of the explanation.

Table 27.1 *Distribution of employment by establishment size, 1981 (%)*

	Establishment size (number employed)			
	Very small (1–19)	*Small* (20–99)	*Medium* (100–499)	*Large* (500+)
Austria[a]	33.6	27.9	23.1	15.4
Belgium[b]	22.2	22.6	26.0	29.0
France[b]	32.1	28.0	23.4	16.5
Italy	43.4	30.4	14.2	12.1
Japan	49.4	27.7	14.6	8.2
Great Britain	26.1	22.6	26.1	25.2
United States	26.1	28.4	24.0	21.5

The first two bands for Italy and Great Britain are 1–9, 10–99 and 1–24, 25–99 respectively.
[a] Wage and salary earners.
[b] 1983.
Source: OECD Employment Outlook, September 1985, p. 71.

27.2 The small business sector

There is no agreed definition of a 'small firm'. The 1971 Committee of Inquiry on Small Firms (The Bolton Committee) stated: 'it became clear that a small firm could not be adequately defined in terms of employment or assets, turnover, output, or any other arbitrary single quantity, nor would the same definition be appropriate throughout the economy' [1].

This 1971 Committee did find it necessary, however, to provide a definition of a small firm. They produced a definition which varied from industry to industry. The definition for a number of industries is shown in Table 27.2.

In fact a simple definition that has often been used is that a small firm is one that employs less than 200 people. It is this simple definition which is usually applied when statistics on small firms are produced. It must be remembered, however, that the definition is far from perfect. In some new high technology firms, say a firm producing

Table 27.2 *Bolton Committee definitions of small firms*

Industry	Statistical definition of small firms adopted by the Bolton Committee (turnover at 1963 prices)	Revised definition to allow for inflation[a] (turnover at 1978 prices)
Manufacturing	200 employees or less	—
Retailing	Turnover £50 000 p.a. or less	Turnover £185 000 p.a. or less
Wholesale trades	Turnover £200 000 p.a. or less	Turnover £730 000 p.a. or less
Construction	25 employees or less	—
Mining/quarrying	25 employees or less	—
Motor trades	Turnover £100 000 p.a. or less	Turnover £365 000 p.a. or less
Miscellaneous services	Turnover £50 000 p.a. or less	Turnover £185 000 p.a. or less
Road transport	5 vehicles or less	—
Catering	All excluding multiples and brewery-managed public houses	—

[a]Estimated by applying the change in the general index of retail prices between the average for 1963 and mid-1978 and rounding the result to the nearest £5000.

anti-sera, it would be a very large firm in terms of sales that employed 200 people. The sales would be high, as would be the value added.

The EU has shown considerable concern for the role of the smaller-sized business and in particular for the future of the small company following the move to a 'single market' in 1992. They employ a simple definition. They are interested in the SME and define it as an enterprise employing less than 500 people.

27.3 Financing problems of small firms

The Macmillan Report of 1931 [2], the first major report into the financing of industry, found that at that time the growth of small firms may have been held back because they did not have access to the financial resources available to larger firms. The point was made to the Committee that great difficulty had been experienced by the smaller and medium-sized businesses in raising the capital that they needed at various times, even though the security they offered was sound.

What became known as the Macmillan Gap was identified. The difficulty of raising sums of money up to, 'say, £200 000 or more' was highlighted. The Committee recommended that a financial institution be established to devote itself particularly to the needs of the smaller commercial and industrial firm. It was accepted that the existing financial institutions 'do not look with any great favour on small issues which would have no free market and would require watching closely'.

As a result of the Macmillan Committee report, several new financial institutions were established that were concerned with the provision of finance for small firms. The 1930s, however, were difficult economic times, and in general these specialist institutions were not particularly successful.

Towards the end of the Second World War the problems of financing post-war reconstruction and development became an important issue. One result was the establishment in 1945 of the Industrial and Commercial Finance Corporation (ICFC) and the Finance Corporation for Industry.

In 1959 the Radcliffe Committee [3] reported on the state of the financial system in the UK. It believed that much had been done to overcome the problem of the Macmillan Gap, but did point to other problem areas. It proposed the setting up of government-supported institutions which would provide financial resources for the commercial exploitation of technical innovation. It also recommended that the large commercial banks should make more term loans available. If implemented, both these proposals would have benefited small firms. One institution, Technical Development Capital Ltd, was created which did a little to help the financing of the 'technological gap'.

The Bolton Committee was given the specific task of investigating the problems of small businesses. They found a 'widespread belief that the financial institutions were failing to meet the legitimate capital requirements of the small firm sector'. Apparently the changes that had taken place in the 40 years following the Macmillan Report were not sufficient to meet the needs of small firms. The Bolton Committee found that some external sources of finance were not available to small firms, and other sources were very expensive for small firms compared with the cost to larger firms. The cost difference could be explained by what were said to be the greater risks of lending to smaller firms and the fixed administrative cost element which had to be covered, whatever the size of the loan.

The Bolton Committee was somewhat critical of small firms, pointing out that often they did not make use of those funds that were available. This was on some occasions because they were unaware of what was available, on other occasions because of poorly presented cases and sometimes because the businessmen themselves did not believe in borrowing.

Between 1971 and the time that the Wilson Committee [4] reported in 1979, a number of changes in the financial system took place, but the Committee nevertheless found that many of the financial problems of small firms still applied. The Committee stated that:

There is no doubt that, compared to large firms, small firms are at a considerable disadvantage in financial markets. Loans are more expensive and security requirements are generally more stringent. External equity is more difficult to find and may only be obtainable on relatively unfavourable terms. Venture capital is particularly hard to obtain. Some Government support schemes specify minimum qualifying levels which smaller businesses cannot hope to attain, and some export credit facilities also exclude small firms. Finally, proprietors of small firms do not always have the same financial expertise as their larger competitors, and information and advice about finance may not always be easily accessible.

The Wilson Committee did not find that a bias existed against small firms. From the point of view of cost, the Committee felt that the higher charges could be justified because 'the cost of providing finance to small firms is higher and the risk may be more difficult to assess'. However, the Committee did feel that there could be a bias in the banks' assessment of risk in the sense of excessive caution, particularly in the case of customers with little capital of their own.

The Committee pointed out that one reason for the banks' hesitation in lending to small firms is the lack of security. The banks believe that lending to small firms is more risky than lending to large firms and that consequently loss ratios are higher.

The Governor of the Bank of England returned to this theme in 1994. He accepted the fact that there was a great deal of resentment directed against banks by businessmen and women from small firms.

He pointed out that

between 1982 and 1991 firms with less than 20 employees created nearly 2½ million jobs, whereas larger firms actually reduced their number of jobs by ¼ million. That is a measure of how important small businesses are to the economy – and why the problems facing small businesses are, quite rightly, attracting increasing attention.

The tragedy is – and it is a human tragedy for the small business men affected as well as a tragedy for the macroeconomy – the tragedy is that tens of thousands of small firms have gone out of business in recent years. Of course not every business venture can succeed – there will always be a large number of failures. But Dun and Bradstreet calculate that through the recession – from 1991–93 – the number of business failures rose to around 55,000 a year compared with a more normal rate through the 1980's of less than 20,000 a year.

The Bank of England in 1993 held a series of discussions on the subject of the relationship between banks and small businesses. They were particularly concerned with whether there was a shortage of bank finance for smaller businesses. A number of problems were recognized by those taking part in the discussions. For example, banks accepted the need to improve their understanding of small businesses and that there should be less reliance on the secure overdraft. The firms accepted that there was a reluctance by many small business owners to dilute their equity ownership.

The Governor came out of the consultations 'reasonably confident that small firms will not be constrained (in future) by any general lack of availability of bank finance' [5].

Undoubtedly for many years there have been gaps in the provision of equity funds, venture capital and longer-term loans to small firms. Over time the position has improved.

There are many people who oppose the idea of a finance gap and instead argue that the deficiency is in the management of small firms and in particular in information and communication. Many entrepreneurs do not realize the scope of financial assistance available to them and therefore frequently the only place that they will apply for a loan is at the local branch of their bank, which does not always provide the specific service needed. Also the bank manager's judgement of viability is based on the information presented to him by the applicant. Specialist advice for new businessmen on which places to approach for a loan and how to prepare a sophisticated business plan could perhaps increase their chances of acceptance. But the supply of debt finance is not a sufficient condition for growth.

Both the firms and the investors need encouragement, for neither demand or supply for equity-type finance is very great. Only a few firms contemplate the idea of any outside equity participation and so it is hardly surprising that several have not even sought this type of finance. Information on sources of equity finance are available. Firm owners should realize that equity finance does not necessarily mean reduced control or reduced flexibility, especially if they establish a broad shareholder base with a number of small investors. With recent government policies that permit firms to buy back their own shares, external equity capital does not necessarily have to be a permanent feature.

But small businesses still face a number of financial problems. This is despite the fact that over the last decade governments and banks have tried to make things a little easier. It is still correct to say that banks are the servants of large companies but the masters of small companies. It is still the case that bank managers are reluctant to stick their necks out because their success within the bank is defined in terms of lack of failure. It is safer for them to say no for a loan request for a risky situation than to say yes with the possibility that the company is successful but with a high probability that it fails. There is also still an equity gap, despite the existence of venture capital companies. There are institutions that are willing to invest small amounts in equity, but it is very difficult to raise equity finance in sums in the range £50 000 – £200 000.

From an investor's point of view it can be shown to be high risk to help finance small businesses. Estimates vary but the failure rate amongst business start-ups tends to be in the region of four out of five. Much of this failure is due to poor management.

A study by the 3Is [6] concluded that most small business start-ups were

- under-capitalized,
- under-geared,
- burdened with the wrong mix of short- and long-term debt,
- ignorant of sources of finance open to them and
- ignorant of the real need for adequate cash planning and financial control.

A National Economic Development Office study [7] on lending to small firms identified small firm failure as usually the result of inadequate management or management inefficiency. These management failures may well be reflected in many ways, e.g. in lack of financial control and financial records.

A study by Robson Rhodes [8] on the operation of the Loan Guarantee Scheme presents a picture of financial naivety by small business managers. The managers were conscientious but too often they were optimistic and financially inept. They had little idea of the finance their businesses needed, either the amount or the appropriate type.

Studies have shown that financial management skills are of prime importance in determining the success of a small business.

27.4 The life-cycle of a firm

It is useful to be able to identify the life-cycle of the typical firm, as the financial needs usually vary at the different stages of a firm's life. Figure 27.1, plotting sales against time, shows a typical pattern. It is possible to identify five stages. The first is the experimentation period, the introductory period. The second is the exploitation period, the take-off. The third is the slow-down – the dynamic stage is now over. For a well-managed company, the fourth stage is the move into maturity with either a steady (but not spectacular) growth in sales or static sales. It is hoped that the company does not move into the next stage indicated in the figure, namely the decline.

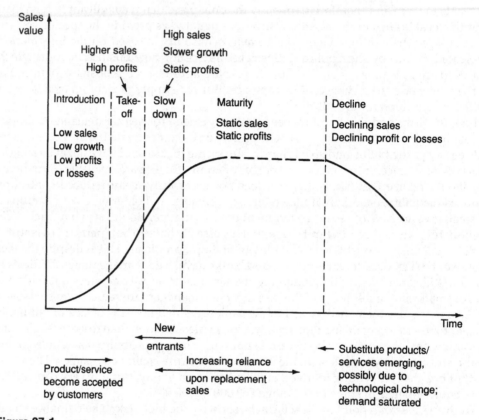

Figure 27.1

Figure 27.2 shows the cash flow position for the same firm during the life-cycle. In the first stage the company needs start-up capital, which usually means the personal savings of the proprietor and possibly some venture capital. Once the source of equity investment can be identified the company can approach the banks for loans. Some form of guarantee will usually be required on such loans; in many cases it will need to be a personal guarantee, but in some cases these loans may be covered by government guarantees. The new firm will usually be dependent not only on the banks for finance but also on trade credit from suppliers. During this start-up phase there are other financing possibilities which include leasing, hire purchase and factoring. There are also a few private and public sector financial institutions which can and do provide funds for some newly launched firms.

During this early stage in the life cycle of the firm it is essential to introduce an adequate system of financial planning and control. Cash budgets must be produced and the actual cash flows must be carefully monitored. The large accounting firms have now

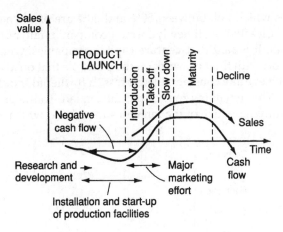

Figure 27.2

moved into the market, offering financial advisory services to small businesses in this first stage of growth. They offer to produce business and financial plans, to keep the books and to help control the financial position of the small business.

During the second phase of the company's life, the rapid growth phase, finance will continue to come from the sources indicated for the first phase and in addition from retained earnings, further trade credit and bank loans, and specialist financial institutions and government schemes. The larger small business will be able to approach merchant banks and the venture capital companies.

As the firm approaches maturity it may be thinking of selling shares to the public or to financial institutions and raising further equity through this means. In addition, it will be in a position to obtain medium- and long-term loans from the banks and the other financial institutions.

In the remaining sections of this chapter we shall concentrate on the funds that are available to firms in the first two phases of the life cycle; it is in these stages that the company can be classed as small.

The rate of failure is very much a function of company size. As Table 27.3 shows, the failure rate amongst small firms is very much greater than amongst large firms.

27.5 Company failures

Table 27.3 *Failure rates by size of turnover*

Turnover size in 1980 (£ thousand)	Number of businesses	Failures	Failure rates (%)
1–13	172 976	43 321	25.0
14	19 870	3 209	16.1
15–49	424 106	50 955	12.0
50–99	237 230	17 185	7.2
100–499	277 239	12 299	4.4
500–1999	64 769	2 306	3.6
2000+	22 389	871	3.9

Source: Ganguly, 1985.

Argenti [9] distinguishes three paths to company failure. One path is that applicable to a newly formed small company. The second path relates to a dynamic company, the company which starts small and grows quickly. The third path relates to an established company. In this section we shall concentrate on the first two paths.

Of all companies which fail, between 50% and 60% are of the newly formed small company category. Clearly not all newly formed companies fail, but the success rate is comparatively small. It is said that venture capital companies, when assessing which companies to support with finance, work on the principle that on average only two out of ten companies achieve any considerable success. A further four out of ten survive but do not really grow. The remaining four out of the ten fail. To the professional investor the problem is identifying which of the ten will succeed and which will fail.

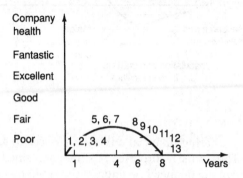

Figure 27.3

Argenti's research indicates that the maximum life for the small companies that follow his first path to failure is eight years. The path is illustrated in Fig. 27.3. Over the life-span of these companies, certain pointers to their eventual failure, certain indicators, can be identified. Clearly not all these points apply to a particular company that fails, although Argenti does believe that points 1–5 appear in all that do fail. In fairness it must be said that some of the points that suggest future failure can also be found in some small companies that are successful.

Argenti's paths to failure are an attempt to put into sequence what he feels are the characteristics present in most company failures. These patterns are subjective, but they indicate points that should be looked for in trying to identify at an early stage those companies that may experience failure or financial distress.

The key to the numbered points on the path to type one failure is as follows.

1. Launch of the company: the founder is the only manager and he or she knows little about business in general, only about the goods or services that are to be offered by the company.
2. No accounting information is available within the business, no budget, no cash flow plans, no costing system – in fact no financial yardsticks at all.
3. The company obtains a bank loan or acquires equipment on a hire purchase or lease scheme. The result is high gearing from the start.
4. A large project is launched, usually with an over-estimate of the sales revenues and an under-estimate of the costs.
5. At this point it becomes obvious that the proprietor was too optimistic.
6. Cash flows are probably bad; financial ratios also look poor.
7. Creative accounting is begun because the proprietor needs more money from the bank.
8. The proprietor begins to succumb to stress; non-financial indications of failure appear.
9. A normal business hazard, such as a large bad debt or an economic turn-down occurs.
10. The proprietor takes panic action such as cutting prices to increase sales. This leads to overtrading.
11. Further loans are obtained. At this point the liabilities exceed the assets.
12. Profit is not enough to service the loans.
13. The receiver is called in.

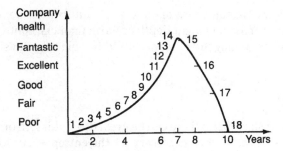

Figure 27.4

The second path to failure identified by Argenti is that followed by a dynamic company. Such companies are spectacular performers from the start, but they end with an equally spectacular finish. The points on the second path to failure as shown on Fig. 27.4 are as follows.

1. The same management defects are present as in type one companies except for one very prominent difference: the proprietor of this company has a highly extrovert personality.
2. The personality of the proprietor ensures that the company gets off the ground, satisfactorily.
3. Progress is so good that the press becomes interested.
4. Sales continue to expand rapidly.
5. New capital is required. As profit margins are high and the proprietor's powers of persuasion are considerable it is not long before it is obtained. Depending on what size the company has reached the money may come from the banks or from an issue to the public.
6. No overgearing or overtrading occurs and new offers of finance are received.
7. Sales and profits continue to rise.
8. For most good and promising companies, the growth would continue at a modest to good rate, but for this company it keeps rising dramatically.
9. Progress is so good that it continues to receive good press coverage. The company has to keep getting better as the public expect it to.
10. The company is so large that any normal firm would implement a formal management structure.
11. The proprietor is now very wealthy and his name is known throughout the country; the pressures are therefore for the fantastic results to continue.
12. Turnover grows again, but profits do not. This is the turning point.
13. Creative accounting begins.
14. Some of the decisions and actions are beginning to look absurd. This is being done to keep the backers, employees and public happy.
15. A normal business hazard shatters the dreams, ideas and public relations stories. From now on the only way is down.
16. The bankers refuse further advances.
17. The press have now got the scent of something and they inform the general public. It is merely a matter of time before the receiver is called in.
18. The receiver is appointed.

These two paths to company failure both apply to a business which collapses within ten years from its start. We shall not deal in detail with the third path to failure as it relates to an established firm. This path to failure begins when such a firm finds itself in difficulties and, as a result of decisions it then makes, the situation becomes worse and leads to bankruptcy. The things that can go wrong for the established firm include overtrading, sudden loss of a major market, the failure of an important project and a major acquisition that does not work out. For such events to lead to failure there must be something wrong with the management team, e.g. an autocratic chief executive, an unbalanced top team, lack of management depth or weak financial control. A well established company with a good management team should be able to avoid such shocks.

Start-up finance

For a small business starting up there can be great difficulties. In order to be able to raise a loan from a bank, it will first be necessary for the entrepreneur to show that he or she has some equity funds. The bank will wish to see that they are sharing the financial risks, not taking them all.

The traditional sources of equity finance for the small business were the savings of the founder or the savings of his family. With the relative decline in the importance of the private investor and the channelling of personal savings into financial institutions, it is now unlikely that many entrepreneurs with worthwhile projects will have access to sufficient capital, even on a limited scale. Because of this equity gap for small firms, undoubtedly a number of businesses fail to get off the ground.

There are only a few venture capital companies that will invest in starting up businesses. The 3Is, the largest venture capital operation in the UK, will invest funds from £5000 up to £2 million. A large proportion of its clients receive relatively small amounts, i.e. less than £50 000. On occasion it will invest this money without personal guarantees. Other sources of start-up capital include schemes operated by major companies. Some of these provide equity, and some loans. Other schemes that enable individuals to obtain start-up capital include the Enterprise Allowance Scheme. This is a sum of money, an allowance, given by the State for one year to an unemployed person if he or she sets up a business.

Venture capital

The Bank of England use the expression venture capital investment to mean a form of investment in which 'investors support entrepreneurial talent with finance and business skills to exploit market opportunities, and thus obtain long-term capital gains'.

The important points about venture capital investment are as follows:

1. it is high risk investment – it is not investing in listed companies;
2. it is not passive portfolio investment but involves a close working relationship between the venture capital company and the company receiving the funds;
3. it is not a short-term investment in which the shares will be sold in a matter of months, nor is it a very long-term investment. The venture capital company will be hoping to realize the equity shares it has acquired at a profit in five or so years after it first purchased the shares. It is hoping that either the company will go public or the shares will be bought out by another company or by the other shareholders.

Small companies usually need three different rounds of finance. The term venture capital can apply to satisfying the needs at any of these three stages of development.

1. Seed capital or start-up capital: the finance that a new or young company needs during what can be a lengthy period of research and development. It can also apply to a start-up situation in which the product or idea has been developed and it is thought that it will only be a short period before the firm's cash flow is positive.
2. A second round of finance is needed for young companies who have successfully started up and now need additional capital to allow them to begin to grow.
3. The third situation, referred to as the development capital situation, is when an established company with a good trading record needs an injection of capital for further expansion.

When a company is referred to as a start-up company it can be a new company or a very young company. In all three situations it is the same type of capital that is needed by the company, namely risk capital. It is just the risks to the venture capital company that vary between the three situations.

Undoubtedly some venture capital is available in the UK for the second and third situations mentioned above, namely finance for the exploitation of products and ideas that have already been researched and developed. It is difficult, however, to obtain finance in the seed capital situation. There are only a few institutions who offer such seed fund support. It was estimated that in 1987 just 24 seed investments were made by British venture capital funds. This represented only 0.2% of total venture capital activity in Britain.

The British Venture Capital Association that represents more than a hundred of the largest venture capital companies has recognized the problem and tries to encourage more of its members to provide such funds. The European Commission also recognized that this is a problem, not just in Britain but across the EU. In 1989 the Commission announced that it would back a number of seed capital funds. This support took the form of reimbursable interest-free advances of up to 50% of the operating costs of these funds over their first three to five years plus a contribution of up to 25% of their capital needs.

It should be appreciated that not only are the risks high from running a seed capital fund because of the high failure rate, but the operating costs are also high because the investigation and administration costs tend to be at a more or less fixed level whatever the amount borrowed.

In a 1988 survey of new companies that had opened up in Science Parks in the UK, it was found that only 3% had managed to find venture capital funds as their primary source of finance (even though 45% of them had tried to obtain it). About 55% used personal savings to start up, and 17% obtained funds from the major clearing banks. The companies located on Science Parks are usually of a high technology nature.

Venture capitalists are usually looking for an average return of 35% per annum on their investments. An important question is over what period they are looking for this return. Usually they talk about such average returns on their funds over a three to five year period. Unfortunately in high technology, with a long development stage, it can take more like seven to eight years to achieve this desired level of return. Clearly there is still a gap between those seeking funds and the type of funds that investors will make available.

Another problem from the point of view of the venture capitalist is that small businesses can take up a great deal of their management time. The company will need monitoring and much advice during the early stages of its life.

Venture capitalists are often involved in assisting with the financing of high risk projects. These companies might not produce profits in the early years of the venture. The financial backers expect a high rate of return to compensate for the risk. They are not always prepared to wait for dividends based on profits, and so sometimes negotiate an annual 'dividend' based on the level of sales.

The venture capital funds

The way in which independent and institutional venture capital companies raise the money that they invest is either through going public and raising the money in the capital markets, by attracting wealthy investors who are taking advantage of tax concessions or by attracting funds from pension funds, investment funds and insurance companies. There are also state-owned agencies who operate such funds, e.g. the Welsh Development Agency and English Estates.

Sock Shop

In May 1987 the shares of Sock Shop International were offered to the public; they were oversubscribed by a factor of 53. The offer price valued the company at £27.5 million. A week later when dealings in the shares officially began, the company was valued at over £50 million. Yet four years earlier in 1983 when they set up the company, the two founders had been unable to sell 49% of the equity in the company for £45 000.

The two founders, Sophie Mirman and Richard Ross, came up with the idea of a chain of shops specializing in socks, tights and stockings whilst they were working for Tie Rack. As with all good businesses they produced a detailed business plan but faced a problem with raising finance. They could only raise small amounts of finance personally (£2000) and with their most modest plans needed a further £45 000 in equity and £15 000 overdraft. They found it difficult. They were willing to sell equity but wished to retain control. At Barclays Bank the founders suggested that a loan might be made available with the bank taking as its return a commission (of approximately 2%) based on sales. It was to be a five year loan. With the phenomenal growth of Sock Shop over the next five years, this would have resulted in a huge return for the Bank. Unfortunately for Barclays they turned down the application for this type of loan on the grounds that it was too risky; they obviously did not think sales would be very high.

A second proposal to Barclays was for a loan under the government's Small Firms Loan Guarantee Scheme. This was successful. Barclays lent £45 000 for five years under this scheme and provided overdraft facilities of up to £15 000.

The funds were used to lease premises, to provide working capital and to pay the founders' expenses. At the end of their first trading period (September 1984) they had three shops and had earned pre-tax profits of £43 000. They were in a position to repay the loan, but initially Barclays refused to let them do so, arguing that it still had four years to run. It took 18 months of negotiations before the bank agreed. They were then allowed to repay the loan and replace it with an overdraft facility.

By September 1985 they had eight shops, before tax profits of £0.25 million and sales of over £2 million. They did not resort to franchising, a path followed by many fast-growing retailing operations. They preferred to keep control over all aspects of their branches. By September 1986 the number of shops was 22, sales were over £6 million and profits £0.75 million.

In 1987 they went public, floating their shares in the USM. They were then able to obtain access to more finance and continued to grow dramatically, including opening up overseas operations. In 1988 Sophie Mirman was voted USM Entrepreneur of the Year and Businesswoman of the Year.

The period 1983–8 had been one of dramatic growth in the high street. Many retailing companies showed very impressive performances. Troubles began to appear in 1989, with high interest rates and cuts in consumer expenditure.

Sock Shop suffered from this general decline in the retail sector. On 7 May 1987 the shares were offered to the public at 125p per share. A week later they touched 295p per share. In 1990 the company went into liquidation.

There are a number of financial institutions and banks in the UK who operate venture capital funds and who are willing to invest venture and development capital in the 'right' companies. They are prepared to purchase equity shares in such companies. They are not all, however, prepared to invest in start-up companies. Some are looking for investments in special situations, such as biotechnology, but many will invest in any industry. There are a few examples of what is known as corporate venturing, in which large companies provide funds to small businesses.

What a venture capitalist looks at when considering a company for a possible investment is the following:

1. the management team;
2. the product;
3. the markets for that product;
4. a well-developed business plan, covering all aspects including finance;

5. the commitment of the management team – how much of their own money they have
   invested and how much time they are putting into the venture;
6. the exit routes.

We shall now consider point 6 because of its financial implications.

Exit route

A key question that any venture capitalist has to consider is how he or she is to exit, at a profit, from the investment in the company. How is the investor going to be able to dispose of the shares? The possibilities are as follows:

1. the company has its shares floated on a stock exchange;
2. 'a trade sale', i.e. the company is sold to a corporate buyer;
3. a management buyout;
4. refinancing by a new team of backers (investors or new venture capitalists) probably on more favourable terms to the management and entrepreneurs so that the original venture capitalist is replaced;
5. a management buy-in;
6. liquidation.

In the latter half of the 1980s a trade sale, the purchase of the whole company by another company, was the most common. One problem with a trade sale or any approach that involves finding a replacement investor is agreeing on an appropriate price for the sale. An exit/entry price that pleases both sides and also the continuing equity owners/managers is not easy. The original venture capitalist wants as much profit as possible; the other parties are thinking of the returns and risks in the future.

Although much talked about, the public flotation has declined in popularity. This has been partly due to the volatile state of the stock market and to the publicity given to the financial difficulties that some newly floated companies have faced shortly after being floated.

Corporate venturing

Corporate venturing occurs when a large company, with cash surplus to its needs for the immediate future, purchases a minority equity stake in a small business. The large company would usually only do this in a business with whom it has contacts, because it is a customer, engaged in related technology or selling in similar markets. On occasion if the large company has the management resources available it will also provide management assistance.

Business Expansion Scheme

In 1981 the UK government introduced a Business Start-Up Scheme, the intention being to promote investment in new businesses. Income tax relief was given at an investor's highest marginal rate for money that the investor used to subscribe for new shares. For high rate taxpayers this could have proved very attractive. The idea was to encourage wealthy investors to invest directly in smaller businesses rather than to invest their funds through financial intermediaries. Unfortunately the scheme that was introduced was not particularly well thought out. There were problems with the position when the shares were sold and became liable to capital gains tax.

The start-up scheme was replaced in 1983 with the Business Expansion Scheme, which proved to be very popular. This scheme removed some of the complexities of the previous scheme and the restriction that investment only qualified if it was in new ventures or start-up situations. The new scheme applied to an investment in an unquoted trading company no matter how long it had been established. The scheme was ended in the early 1990s.

Quite often the businesses receiving money through the scheme were unable to acquire risk capital by other means because, without the tax incentives, few investors would put their money into them. It has been estimated that over 50% of firms receiving Business Expansion Scheme funds would have had trouble in acquiring finance without this scheme.

Investment could be made directly by the investor himself, through an intermediary such as a stockbroker or through an approved investment fund. With a maximum investment of 20% in any one company by any one fund, and with a preference for broad portfolios across several companies, most of the amounts invested in one company were relatively small compared with those made by venture capitalists.

The Business Expansion Scheme did not provide very much funding for the more high risk ventures, typically new businesses. Instead investors preferred to opt for the safer investments in well-established companies.

It was good that the new scheme was successful in attracting funds but it was unfortunate that many of the business expansion funds that were set up in the UK as a result of the scheme explicitly excluded investments in start-up companies. The scheme was being used to provide second-stage finance, i.e. expansion money once a business has become established. Clearly, the risks to the investors are less in this stage.

The Business Expansion Scheme was designed to encourage individuals to invest in small unquoted companies who were engaged in certain business activities. The businesses were either a trade or a business specializing in developing and letting residential properties.

As explained the scheme started in 1982. The high point for investment occurred in 1988/89 when £345 million was raised. It was undoubtedly successful in encouraging the development of privately owned rented property. Of the £345 million raised in 1988/89 only £10 million was for companies engaged in trade, the rest was for developing rented accommodation. The scheme was not successful in providing venture capital for companies engaged in trade and manufacturing.

Business angels

This is an expression that originated in the USA. It refers to wealthy individuals who are prepared to help smaller companies by purchasing an equity stake in the company. As is well-known many small companies are over-dependent on loan finance, and find it difficult to attract equity. A 'business angel' is a man or woman that comes to their help.

To venture capital companies, such as 3Is, investing amounts below a certain size is uneconomic. Hence the need for the providors of small amounts of equity capital. Some doubt that 'business angels' really exist in the UK.

In the USA they have made a contribution to the success of many companies particularly those based on new technology. They often provide technical or managerial support to the companies, not just finance.

The Business Expansion Scheme was designed to encourage wealthy individuals to invest in smaller companies. It gave investors under such a scheme tax advantages. The only trouble was that under the terms of the scheme the advantages ceased the moment the investor offered more than financial support. It prevented investors from contributing knowhow. It did not therefore encourage the business angel.

One problem is how to bring together companies who need support and the business angels. Often this is best done at a local level through regional offices of banks or accounting firms.

The London Stock Exchange

In 1994 the Exchange announced a package of measures designed to promote the interests of smaller companies. These initiatives were to help smaller companies whether or not they were quoted on the Exchange. It should be remembered it is possible for companies to have their shares traded by members of the exchange even if they are not quoted.

These initiatives included:

1. The relaunch, with increased publicity to the trading facility under rule 535.2 (later renumbered). As was explained earlier in the book this rule allows for trading in unquoted companies.
2. In 1992 the Stock Exchange Alternative Trading Service (SEATS) was introduced. This was designed to provide an efficient trading system for the less liquid shares, typically shares which had fewer than two market-makers. It was announced in 1994 that this system would be technologically enhanced.
3. A specialist Smaller Companies Group was established to champion smaller company security issues.

The Stock Exchange is keen to emphasize that they do cater for smaller companies. In 1994 over half of the quoted companies had a market capitalization of less than £50 million. In 1993 five companies joined the official list with under £5 million capitalization.

The high street banks

The seven major banks involved in lending to small businesses account for about 80% of the total lending to this sector. The banks are Barclays, National Westminster, Lloyds, Midland, TSB, Bank of Scotland and the Royal Bank of Scotland.

From the 1970s the banks have made long and medium term loans available to companies in addition to the basic overdraft, some banks being willing to lend for periods up to 10 years. In the region of 80% of lending is floating rate, with the rate charged being related to the base rate. About 15% of the loans are fixed rate and 5% managed rate. In 1992 the average level of a loan made to a firm with turnover of less than £1 million was £20 000. At the other extreme banks are willing to invest over £200 000 in the more established medium-sized firm.

There has been much criticism of the charges made by banks for loans to small and medium sized firms. Figure 27.5 shows dramatically how the interest rate charged varies by size of firm.

Unfortunately lending to the small–medium sized businesses is both a risky and costly business. As far as the costs are concerned, it has been estimated that in assessing and administering loans to the small business costs may be ten times higher compared to those involved in loans to bigger companies. Regarding the risks involved, British government statistics regarding small businesses suggest that up to 80% of all 'start-ups' either fail or withdraw from the market within the first two years.

However this criticism of the level of costs can be levelled particularly against UK banks lending to UK firms. Gray found that the cost of loans to small–medium businesses in the United Kingdom was approximately 46% above that of the four lowest cost countries in the European Community [11].

PEP

Another possible source arises as a result of the Personal Equity Plan. This scheme was introduced in 1987. As at 1 January 1994 it allowed an investor to invest up to £6000 per annum in shares and then to reinvest the dividends and to receive any capital gains on this investment free of tax. The investment must be according to a plan.

The scheme is designed to encourage savers to invest in equity shares, particularly those of smaller businesses. The tax system is being used to give incentives because it is recognized that the market is not good at channelling funds to such businesses. As explained above, those who operate in the market believe that such investments are risky and the expected returns are not high enough to justify the risk. By reducing the tax bill of the investor, the government is attempting to make the return justify the risk. Of course, as the marginal rate of income tax is lowered, and with it the capital gains tax rate, the incentive available through the scheme becomes of less value. The top rate of

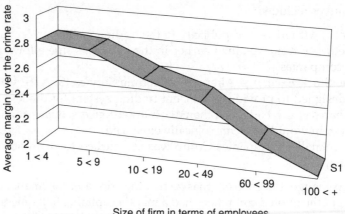

Source: Bannock and Morgan 1988 [10]

Figure 27.5 *Average interest rates on loans in the United Kingdom (late 1980s)*

tax was lowered from 60% to 40% in 1988, which reduced the value of the incentive. Nevertheless the elimination of the capital gains tax liability is an incentive.

27.8 Loan finance

For the vast majority of small businesses, borrowing from a bank is the most important source of external finance. The banks now provide not just the traditional overdraft finance but also a variety of medium- and long-term loans. The interest rate charged on overdrafts is usually between 2% and 4% above base rate. Rates on short-term loans, i.e. up to three years, are usually 3%–5% above base rate.

Most banks offer loans to small businesses. National Westminster have a Business Development Loan Plan, for a minimum of £2000 and a maximum of £250 000, for periods of from 1 to 20 years.

Midland Bank offers a loan package which requires recipients to undertake a management training scheme. Loans are available for sums up to £15 000 and with loan periods of from six months to ten years. The rate of interest is fixed at the time of the agreement.

Barclays offer an overdraft of up to £2000 to new or existing small businesses with an expected annual turnover of up to £100 000. New businesses can also obtain a business starter loan of up to £15 000 for a loan period of from one to five years.

The loan guarantee scheme

In an attempt to alleviate some of the problems of raising finance by new small businesses, successive governments have introduced various schemes aimed at increasing the availability of debt and equity capital.

In 1981 the government launched the Loan Guarantee Scheme to boost the amount of debt finance. Its aim was to help those firm founders who had exhausted other methods of raising funds but nevertheless seemed to have a viable proposition. It was perhaps insufficient security or lack of a track record which prevented their applications for funds from being accepted. When it was first introduced the government guaranteed payment of 80% of any approved loan to the institution lending the money, usually a clearing bank. In return the borrower would pay the government a premium of 3% as well as the interest charge to the lender. In this way it was hoped that any claims on the government due to business failure would be covered by the premiums collected and so, in effect, the scheme would finance itself. In the first four and a half years of the scheme over 16 000 firms obtained loans totalling £500 million.

However, the scheme did not resolve many of the difficulties of small firms and, in addition, it created new ones for the government. Many of the first recipients failed and by November 1984 it was claimed that 44% of the guarantees had been claimed against. Thus the objective of a self-financing scheme had not been achieved. Many firms experienced the same difficulties as before the scheme and the premium meant that they were still at a cost disadvantage. This discouraged many entrepreneurs from even applying. Also the scheme had a minimum loan level of £5000 and so firms which required less than this amount did not qualify.

Various revisions of policy were undertaken to try and cut down on losses. In June 1984 the guaranteed part of the loan was reduced by 10% to 70% and the borrower had to pay a premium of 5% instead of 3%. This was to ensure a tighter selection policy but what it also meant was a greater burden of debt for those using the scheme. At the end of the 1984 it was announced that the Loan Guarantee Scheme would not be available for those applicants who possessed personal assets but were unprepared to put them forward as security for a normal loan. This would then allow those without any security to be given priority. In consequence even more firms were excluded from the scheme. These changes nearly killed it. However, despite its many critics the scheme continued and the government was forced to make even further changes in an attempt to attract borrowers. Simplified administration was introduced for loans of up to £15 000: banks could make the decisions. The premium was reduced to 2.5%, the guarantee rate was increased to 85% for small companies in inner city areas and the ceiling was raised to £100 000.

In 1993 further changes were introduced to the scheme. These:

- increased the guarantee level for all loans from 70% to 85% and the maximum loan size from £100 000 to £250 000 for established businesses that had been trading for two years or more;
- reduced the premium paid to the DTI by all new borrowers, from 2.5% a year on the guaranteed portion of the loan to 0.5% a year on the whole loan for fixed interest rate loans;
- reduced the premium paid to the DTI by all new borrowers, from 2.5% a year on the guaranteed portion of the loan to 1.5% a year on the whole loan for variable interest rate loans;
- reduced the premium paid to the DTI by borrowers trading from an address within an Inner City Task Force or City Challenge area, from 1% a year on the guaranteed portion of the loan to 0.5% a year on the whole loan for both fixed and variable interest rate loans.

The Loan Guarantee Scheme was an attempt to fulfil the objectives of 'additionality' and 'viability': additional in that it was to help firms which could not have obtained funding by the more conventional means such as bank loans; viable in the sense that it was to help the potentially prosperous companies. However, identifying which firms are eligible under these preconditions is difficult and subjective. Thus young businesses are still affected by the usual selection policies of financial institutions and their avoidance of high risk. If the borrower has low risks it has been claimed that the bank will grant the loan itself. It is only for the riskier projects, by the bank's definition, that they insist on government guarantees before a loan can be granted.

Despite the criticism the scheme has been a success. The Government were able to announce that lending under the scheme was in 1994 at a higher level than at any time since 1984.

In the period 1 April 1993 to 31 March 1994 3886 loans were guaranteed at a value of £155m. This compares with 2342 loans and £52m value over the same period in 1992–93.

Investors in industry

As previously mentioned, the 3Is are the largest financial institution specializing in the provision of finance to the smaller business. The Bank's background and organization were discussed in section 19.12.

3Is invest in companies that they believe have a long-term growth potential. In assessing a company they are particularly concerned with the qualities of the management of the venture. If they were willing to support the company an equity involvement is normally sought. They are not looking for control but just a minority stake. The equity investment is usually accompanied by a medium-term loan. Interest on the loan is charged at commercial rates with the repayments of the principal spread over an agreed period.

The day-to-day running of the business is left to the managers of the company but appropriate guidance is usually offered. Sometimes a non-executive director is appointed to the Board.

The Bank's efforts are usually concentrated in the high growth fields such as microelectronics, computers, telecommunications, biosciences and industrial automation. They will consider proposals in other fields, however, if such proposals offer unique market prospects with rapid growth potential.

They are seeking new and young companies and will invest between £200 000 and £2 million in such companies. They hope to be able to realize their equity investment between five and ten years after purchase. Loans can be for periods of up to 15 years, however.

British Technology Group

The British Technology Group came into existence in 1981 when the government brought together the National Research Development Corporation (NRDC), the National Enterprise Board (NEB) and certain other funds that they controlled.

The NRDC was founded in 1949 to undertake the development and exploitation of inventions that were assigned to it. These inventions have traditionally been mainly those that have resulted from government-financed sources such as those undertaken at universities and government-owned research establishments. In addition there have always been a small number of inventions from private individuals and companies that NRDC attempt to launch commercially.

In 1983 the government announced changes in the role of BTG. In the past the corporation had first refusal rights on the inventions that had been funded by government. This position changed. The owner of the intellectual property rights from the government supported research is now able to seek finance to exploit the invention from sources other than BTG. The invention need not be offered to BTG first; private companies and venture capital companies in particular, can compete to exploit the fruits of publicly funded research.

BTG has therefore to compete. It has become a self-financing organization. It obtains its income from the licensing of new scientific and engineering products. It is still interested in the commercial exploitation of developments resulting from research in public sector organizations such as universities and polytechnics. It is also involved in providing financing for new technological developments. It will help fund the development of research ideas, the intention being that eventually the ideas will be licensed to industry.

As well as being involved in the public sector, it will now also assist in the financing of research ideas in private sector business. Under an industrial project finance scheme it will provide up to 50% of the funds needed to develop and then to launch a new product commercially. It obtains its returns on the basis of a percentage royalty payment on sales of the product.

Council for Small Industries in Rural Areas

The role of the Council for Small Industries in Rural Areas (COSIRA) is to improve the prosperity of small business in the rural areas of England. It encourages industrial development in these areas by giving technical and managerial guidance and by providing a limited amount of financial aid.

COSIRA can provide loans from its own comparatively limited resources, the maximum amount advanced being £50 000. For loans on buildings the repayment period is up to 20 years, and, for loans on plant, equipment and working capital, up to five years. COSIRA work closely with the 3Is and can help a small business in making a claim to this corporation. They also have an arrangement with the Midland Bank, which means that companies seeking help from COSIRA can also apply for this Bank's funds. COSIRA in fact expect the major part of funding for the companies it helps to come from the banks and other lenders. COSIRA has been in existence for over 60 years and has helped over 12 000 companies.

Scottish Development Agency

The object of the Scottish Development Agency (SDA) is to promote economic development in Scotland. It provides equity funds, loans, factories and management advisory services. It has a special Small Business Division to assist the smaller firms. This division deals with companies employing up to 100 people and is willing to consider applications for amounts from £500 to £50 000.

Other government agencies deal with the Highlands and Islands of Scotland, with Wales and with Northern Ireland.

The Department of the Environment and the Department of Trade and Industry encourage the setting up of enterprise agencies. These are a group of firms in a particular area who pool their resources for certain purposes in an attempt to stimulate development in the area. The agencies are usually staffed by people seconded from the firms involved, possibly the larger firms. Much of the help is directed at stimulating small business, giving them help with preparing financial and marketing plans and trying to match them with investors who have available funds.

Local enterprise agencies

These local enterprise agencies or corporations advise entrepreneurs on setting up business and try to dissuade them from embarking on projects which appear to have a poor chance of success. They also help existing firms. Most local enterprise agencies try to be independent of the public sector. They are companies limited by guarantee that consist of a board of directors with members drawn from industry and commerce as well as from local authorities. They typically employ an executive manager and have assistance from seconded staff from local firms including banks and accounting firms. The financial support for the agencies comes from both private and public sectors.

Many local authorities and regional councils have taken their own steps to encourage industry, including small companies. These are the schemes that cover a wide regional area, e.g. the Greater London Enterprise Board, the Greater Manchester Economic Development Corporation and the West Midlands Development Corporation. The Boards generally offer loans for periods of up to 20 years to help cover the cost of building or adapting premises for industrial activities.

In addition, most cities and towns now operate economic development corporations designed to encourage job creation in the region. Most of these either themselves provide some form of finance or are linked up to venture organizations.

Local venture capital funds

A number of local authorities, either individually or collectively, have set up venture capital funds in attempts to encourage local industry.

One, the Birmingham Venture Capital Fund, has already been referred to in Chapter 16. Brief details of one more will now be given to indicate the type of business the funds are designed to help, and the conditions attached to the financial support.

The 'Lancashire Rosebud Fund' was set up in 1986. Between 1986 and 1994 the Fund has invested over £0.5 million in 67 businesses. The Fund is able to invest small amounts (normally up to £10 000) of risk finance on a commercial basis in a business. The money is lent on an unsecured basis, with interest fixed at a rate just above the current bank base rate. As well as receiving interest on the loans, the Fund usually receives a small royalty on sales once the company is profitable. The Fund normally allows a one-year repayment holiday on loan capital.

27.9 Conclusions

Small companies have attracted a great deal of attention for many years. Much has been done to overcome the difficulties they face in raising finance. There are advice bureaux provided by both the public and the private sectors.

Despite the help they receive, and the political support in the 1980s for an 'enterprise' culture, at the end of the 1980s and in the 1990s there was a very high failure rate amongst small firms.

27.10 Key terms

Bolton Committee
Business angels
Business Expansion Scheme
Corporate venturing
Exit routes
Externalization
Life-cycle
Loan Guarantee Scheme

Recession push
Small medium-sized enterprises (SME)
Start-up finance
The 3Is (Investors in Industry)
Under-capitalized
Under-geared
Venture capital

27.11 Revision questions

1. Why do the financial needs of SMEs require special attention?
2. Why is there such a high failure rate amongst small firms?
3. What is venture capital? How does it differ from normal equity capital?
4. Why is it necessary for high street banks to require a guarantee before making loans available to smaller firms?
5. What are the typical difficulties faced by an SME as it grows?
6. What are 'exit routes'?
7. What is 'seed corn' capital?
8. What is 'overtrading'? Why is it a problem for fast growing companies?

27.12 References

1. Committee of Inquiry on Small Firms (The Bolton Committee) *Report* (1971) Cmnd. 4811, HMSO, London.
2. Committee on Finance and Industry (*Macmillan Report*) (1931) Cmnd. 3897 HMSO, London.
3. Committee on the Workings of the Monetary System (The Radcliffe Committee) *Report* (1959) Cmnd. 827 HMSO, London.
4. Committee to Review the Functioning of Financial Institutions (The Wilson Committee) (1980) *Report*, Cmnd. 7937, HMSO, London.
5. 'The financing of small firms' (1994) *Bank of England Quarterly Bulletin*, February.
6. ICFC Small Firm Survey (1983) London.
7. NEDO (1986) *Lending to Small Firms: A study of appraisal and monitoring methods*, London.
8. Rhodes, R. (1981) *A Study of Business Financed under the Small Business Loan Guarantee Scheme*, London, DTI.
9. Argenti, J. (1976) *Corporate Collapse: the causes and symptoms*, McGraw-Hill, London.
10. Bannock, G. and Morgan, E.V. (1988) Banks and small business: an international perspective, *The Forum of Private Business*, August.
11. Gray, A. (1988) *Impact of Competing: the Internal Market in Financial Services*, Industry Association.

A selection of books dealing with small business finance is given below.

Ganguly, P. (1985) *UK Small Business Statistics and International Comparisons*, Harper and Row, London.

Lorenz, T. (1989) *Venture Capital Today*, Woodhead Faulkner.

Storey, D., Keasy, K., Watson, R. and Wynarczyk, P. (1987) *The Performance of Small Firms*, Croom Helm, London.

Woodcock, C. (1989) *Raising Finance: The Guardian Guide for the Small Business*, 3rd edn, Kogan Page, London.

Bank of England Quarterly Bulletin (1990) Venture capital in the United Kingdom, February.

1. Explain what is meant by venture capital. Give examples of the main providers of venture capital in the UK and assess the importance of venture capital to small companies

   ACCA, Dec. 1986

2. (a) Prepare a report advising a small company of the criteria that a bank is likely to use when considering a request for a loan. (7 marks)

   (b) The chairman of a company with a turnover of £5 million has stated that it is impossible for a company of this size to raise finance for a period of 15 years or more.

      Briefly discuss how it might be possible for the company to raise funds for the desired period. (5½ marks)

      ACCA, Dec. 1987

3. Critically assess the actions available to a venture capitalist in dealing with an investee company which is:

   (a) a start-up and

   (b) a management buy-in,

   and which fails to meet its targets.

4. 'Venture capitalists should base their decisions on whether to invest in a new venture solely on the previous venture experience of the entrepreneur.' Discuss.

5. Analyse the potential role of 'business angels' in the provision of venture capital. To what extent would one expect the entrepreneur's relationship with the 'business angel' to be different from that with a venture capitalist?

6. To what extent is it possible to distinguish between different types of entrepreneur? Explain why the ability to make such distinctions may be important to venture capitalists.

Tables and Programs

In this section, tables needed for discounted cash flow and other calculations in the text are provided. We also list Basic programs that will generate the values given in the tables. These programs should run under Microsoft QBasic (provided as part of MS-DOS versions 5 or higher) QuickBasic, Visual Basic and other forms of Basic with the possible need to add line numbers in some cases (e.g. GW-basic). Minor modifications to appropriate programs would enable similar tables to be generated for continuous compounding or other compound interest formulae.

TABLES

There follow tables for:

1. The future value of £1 at 100r% compound interest:

$$(1 + r)^n$$

2. The present value of £1 at 100r% compound interest:

$$(1 + r)^{-n}$$

3. The present value of an immediate annuity of £1 for n years at 100r% compound interest:

$$\frac{1 - (1 + r)^{-n}}{r}$$

4. The future value of an immediate annuity of £1 for n years at 100r% compound interest:

$$\frac{(1 + r)^n - 1}{r}$$

5. The sinking fund for £1 after n years at 100r% compound interest:

$$\frac{r}{(1 + r)^n - 1}$$

6. The annual equivalent annuity for £1 with n years and 100r% compound interest:

$$\frac{r}{(1 - (1 - r)^{-n}}$$

7. The area under the normal curve up to t standard deviations above the mean:

$$[1/\sqrt{(2\pi)}] \int_{-\infty}^{t} e^{-x^2/2} \, dx$$

Table 1: Future value of £1 at 100r% compound interest: $(1 + r)^n$

Years	Discount rate as percentage (100r)					
n	1	2	3	4	5	6
1	1.0100	1.0200	1.0300	1.0400	1.0500	1.0600
2	1.0201	1.0404	1.0609	1.0816	1.1025	1.1236
3	1.0303	1.0612	1.0927	1.1249	1.1576	1.1910
4	1.0406	1.0824	1.1255	1.1699	1.2155	1.2625
5	1.0510	1.1041	1.1593	1.2167	1.2763	1.3382
6	1.0615	1.1262	1.1941	1.2653	1.3401	1.4185
7	1.0721	1.1487	1.2299	1.3159	1.4071	1.5036
8	1.0829	1.1717	1.2668	1.3686	1.4775	1.5938
9	1.0937	1.1951	1.3048	1.4233	1.5513	1.6895
10	1.1046	1.2190	1.3439	1.4802	1.6289	1.7908
11	1.1157	1.2434	1.3842	1.5395	1.7103	1.8983
12	1.1268	1.2682	1.4258	1.6010	1.7959	2.0122
13	1.1381	1.2936	1.4685	1.6651	1.8856	2.1329
14	1.1495	1.3195	1.5126	1.7317	1.9799	2.2609
15	1.1610	1.3459	1.5580	1.8009	2.0789	2.3966
16	1.1726	1.3728	1.6047	1.8730	2.1829	2.5404
17	1.1843	1.4002	1.6528	1.9479	2.2920	2.6928
18	1.1961	1.4282	1.7024	2.0258	2.4066	2.8543
19	1.2081	1.4568	1.7535	2.1068	2.5270	3.0256
20	1.2202	1.4859	1.8061	2.1911	2.6533	3.2071
21	1.2324	1.5157	1.8603	2.2788	2.7860	3.3996
22	1.2447	1.5460	1.9161	2.3699	2.9253	3.6035
23	1.2572	1.5769	1.9736	2.4647	3.0715	3.8197
24	1.2697	1.6084	2.0328	2.5633	3.2251	4.0489
25	1.2824	1.6406	2.0938	2.6658	3.3864	4.2919
26	1.2953	1.6734	2.1566	2.7725	3.5557	4.5494
27	1.3082	1.7069	2.2213	2.8834	3.7335	4.8223
28	1.3213	1.7410	2.2879	2.9987	3.9201	5.1117
29	1.3345	1.7758	2.3566	3.1187	4.1161	5.4184
30	1.3478	1.8114	2.4273	3.2434	4.3219	5.7435

	7	8	9	10	11	12
1	1.0700	1.0800	1.0900	1.1000	1.1100	1.1200
2	1.1449	1.1664	1.1881	1.2100	1.2321	1.2544
3	1.2250	1.2597	1.2950	1.3310	1.3676	1.4049
4	1.3108	1.3605	1.4116	1.4641	1.5181	1.5735
5	1.4026	1.4693	1.5386	1.6105	1.6851	1.7623
6	1.5007	1.5869	1.6771	1.7716	1.8704	1.9738
7	1.6058	1.7138	1.8280	1.9487	2.0762	2.2107
8	1.7182	1.8509	1.9926	2.1436	2.3045	2.4760
9	1.8385	1.9990	2.1719	2.3579	2.5580	2.7731
10	1.9672	2.1589	2.3674	2.5937	2.8394	3.1058
11	2.1049	2.3316	2.5804	2.8531	3.1518	3.4785
12	2.2522	2.5182	2.8127	3.1384	3.4985	3.8960
13	2.4098	2.7196	3.0658	3.4523	3.8833	4.3635
14	2.5785	2.9372	3.3417	3.7975	4.3104	4.8871
15	2.7590	3.1722	3.6425	4.1772	4.7846	5.4736
16	2.9522	3.4259	3.9703	4.5950	5.3109	6.1304

17	3.1588	3.7000	4.3276	5.0545	5.8951	6.8660
18	3.3799	3.9960	4.7171	5.5599	6.5436	7.6900
19	3.6165	4.3157	5.1417	6.1159	7.2633	8.6128
20	3.8697	4.6610	5.6044	6.7275	8.0623	9.6463
21	4.1406	5.0338	6.1088	7.4002	8.9492	10.8038
22	4.4304	5.4365	6.6586	8.1403	9.9336	12.1003
23	4.7405	5.8715	7.2579	8.9543	11.0263	13.5523
24	5.0724	6.3412	7.9111	9.8497	12.2392	15.1786
25	5.4274	6.8485	8.6231	10.8347	13.5855	17.0001
26	5.8074	7.3964	9.3992	11.9182	15.0799	19.0401
27	6.2139	7.9881	10.2451	13.1100	16.7386	21.3249
28	6.6488	8.6271	11.1671	14.4210	18.5799	23.8839
29	7.1143	9.3173	12.1722	15.8631	20.6237	26.7499
30	7.6123	10.062%w	13.2677	17.4494	22.8923	29.9599

	13	14	15	16	17	18
1	1.1300	1.1400	1.1500	1.1600	1.1700	1.1800
2	1.2769	1.2996	1.3225	1.3456	1.3689	1.3924
3	1.4429	1.4815	1.5209	1.5609	1.6016	1.6430
4	1.6305	1.6890	1.7490	1.8106	1.8739	1.9388
5	1.8424	1.9254	2.0114	2.1003	2.1924	2.2878
6	2.0820	2.1950	2.3131	2.4364	2.5652	2.6996
7	2.3526	2.5023	2.6600	2.8262	3.0012	3.1855
8	2.6584	2.8526	3.0590	3.2784	3.5115	3.7589
9	3.0040	3.2519	3.5179	3.8030	4.1084	4.4355
10	3.3946	3.7072	4.0456	4.4114	4.8068	5.2338
11	3.8359	4.2262	4.6524	5.1173	5.6240	6.1759
12	4.3345	4.8179	5.3502	5.9360	6.5801	7.2876
13	4.8980	5.4924	6.1528	6.8858	7.6987	8.5994
14	5.5348	6.2613	7.0757	7.9875	9.0075	10.1472
15	6.2543	7.1379	8.1371	9.2655	10.5387	11.9737
16	7.0673	8.1372	9.3576	10.7480	12.3303	14.1290
17	7.9861	9.2765	10.7613	12.4677	14.4265	16.6722
18	9.0243	10.5752	12.3755	14.4625	16.8790	19.6733
19	10.1974	12.0557	14.2318	16.7765	19.7484	23.2144
20	11.5231	13.7435	16.3665	19.4608	23.1056	27.3930
21	13.0211	15.6676	18.8215	22.5745	27.0335	32.3238
22	14.7138	17.8610	21.6447	26.1864	31.6293	38.1421
23	16.6266	20.3616	24.8915	30.3762	37.0062	45.0076
24	18.7881	23.2122	28.6252	35.2364	43.2973	53.1090
25	21.2305	26.4619	32.9189	40.8742	50.6578	62.6686
26	23.9905	30.1666	37.8568	47.4141	59.2696	73.9490
27	27.1093	34.3899	43.5353	55.0004	69.3455	87.2598
28	30.6335	39.2045	50.0656	63.8004	81.1342	102.9666
29	34.6158	44.6931	57.5755	74.0085	94.9270	121.5005
30	39.1159	50.9502	66.2118	85.8499	111.0646	143.3706

	19	20	21	22	23	24
1	1.1900	1.2000	1.2100	1.2200	1.2300	1.2400
2	1.4161	1.4400	1.4641	1.4884	1.5129	1.5376
3	1.6852	1.7280	1.7716	1.8158	1.8609	1.9066
4	2.0053	2.0736	2.1436	2.2153	2.2889	2.3642
5	2.3864	2.4883	2.5937	2.7027	2.8153	2.9316
6	2.8398	2.9860	3.1384	3.2973	3.4628	3.6352
7	3.3793	3.5832	3.7975	4.0227	4.2593	4.5077
8	4.0214	4.2998	4.5950	4.9077	5.2389	5.5895

9	4.7854	5.1598	5.5599	5.9874	6.4439	6.9310
10	5.6947	6.1917	6.7275	7.3046	7.9259	8.5944
11	6.7767	7.4301	8.1403	8.9116	9.7489	10.6571
12	8.0642	8.9161	9.8497	10.8722	11.9912	13.2148
13	9.5964	10.6993	11.9182	13.2641	14.7491	16.3863
14	11.4198	12.8392	14.4210	16.1822	18.1414	20.3191
15	13.5895	15.4070	17.4494	19.7423	22.3140	25.1956
16	16.1715	18.4884	21.1138	24.0856	27.4462	31.2426
17	19.2441	22.1861	25.5477	29.3844	33.7588	38.7408
18	22.9005	26.6233	30.9127	35.8490	41.5233	48.0386
19	27.2516	31.9480	37.4043	43.7358	51.0737	59.5679
20	32.4294	38.3376	45.2593	53.3576	62.8206	73.8641
21	38.5910	46.0051	54.7637	65.0963	77.2694	91.5915
22	45.9233	55.2061	66.2641	79.4175	95.0413	113.5735
23	54.6487	66.2474	80.1795	96.8894	116.9008	140.8311
24	65.0320	79.4968	97.0172	118.2050	143.7880	174.6306
25	77.3881	95.3962	117.3908	144.2101	176.8592	216.5420
26	92.0918	114.4754	142.0429	175.9363	217.5368	268.5121
27	109.5892	137.3705	171.8719	214.6423	267.5703	332.9549
28	130.4112	164.8447	207.9650	261.8636	329.1115	412.8641
29	155.1893	197.8136	251.6377	319.4736	404.8072	511.9515
30	184.6753	237.3763	304.4816	389.7578	497.9128	634.8198

	25	26	27	28	29	30
1	1.2500	1.2600	1.2700	1.2800	1.2900	1.3000
2	1.5625	1.5876	1.6129	1.6384	1.6641	1.6900
3	1.9531	2.0004	2.0484	2.0972	2.1467	2.1970
4	2.4414	2.5205	2.6014	2.6844	2.7692	2.8561
5	3.0518	3.1758	3.3038	3.4360	3.5723	3.7129
6	3.8147	4.0015	4.1959	4.3980	4.6083	4.8268
7	4.7684	5.0419	5.3288	5.6295	5.9447	6.2749
8	5.9605	6.3528	6.7675	7.2058	7.6686	8.1573
9	7.4506	8.0045	8.5948	9.2234	9.8925	10.6045
10	9.3132	10.0857	10.9153	11.8059	12.7614	13.7858
11	11.6415	12.7080	13.8625	15.1116	16.4622	17.9216
12	14.5519	16.0120	17.6053	19.3428	21.2362	23.2981
13	18.1899	20.1752	22.3588	24.7588	27.3947	30.2875
14	22.7374	25.4207	28.3957	31.6913	35.3391	39.3738
15	28.4217	32.0301	36.0625	40.5648	45.5875	51.1859
16	35.5271	40.3579	45.7994	51.9230	58.8079	66.5417
17	44.4089	50.8510	58.1652	66.4614	75.8621	86.5042
18	55.5111	64.0722	73.8698	85.0706	97.8622	112.4554
19	69.3889	80.7310	93.8147	108.8904	126.2422	146.1920
20	86.7362	101.7211	119.1446	139.3796	162.8524	190.0496
21	108.4202	128.1685	151.3136	178.4059	210.0796	247.0645
22	135.5253	161.4924	192.1683	228.3596	271.0027	321.1838
23	169.4066	203.4804	244.0538	292.3003	349.5934	417.5390
24	211.7582	256.3853	309.9483	374.1444	450.9756	542.8007
25	264.6978	323.0454	393.6343	478.9048	581.7585	705.6409
26	330.8722	407.0372	499.9156	612.9981	750.4684	917.3332
27	413.5903	512.8669	634.8928	784.6376	968.1042	1192.5331
28	516.9878	646.2123	806.3138	1004.3361	1248.8545	1550.2931
29	646.2347	814.2275	1024.0186	1285.5503	1611.0222	2015.3810
30	807.7935	1025.9266	1300.5037	1645.5043	2078.2188	2619.9951

Table 2: Present value of £1 at $100r\%$ compound interest: $(1 + r)^{-n}$

n	1	2	3	4	5	6	7	8	9	10
1	0.9901	0.9804	0.9709	0.9615	0.9524	0.9434	0.9346	0.9259	0.9174	0.9091
2	0.9803	0.9612	0.9426	0.9246	0.9070	0.8900	0.8734	0.8573	0.8417	0.8264
3	0.9706	0.9423	0.9151	0.8890	0.8638	0.8396	0.8163	0.7938	0.7722	0.7513
4	0.9610	0.9238	0.8885	0.8548	0.8227	0.7921	0.7629	0.7350	0.7084	0.6830
5	0.9515	0.9057	0.8626	0.8219	0.7835	0.7473	0.7130	0.6806	0.6499	0.6209
6	0.9420	0.8880	0.8375	0.7903	0.7462	0.7050	0.6663	0.6302	0.5963	0.5645
7	0.9327	0.8706	0.8131	0.7599	0.7107	0.6651	0.6227	0.5835	0.5470	0.5132
8	0.9235	0.8535	0.7894	0.7307	0.6768	0.6274	0.5820	0.5403	0.5019	0.4665
9	0.9143	0.8368	0.7664	0.7026	0.6446	0.5919	0.5439	0.5002	0.4604	0.4241
10	0.9053	0.8203	0.7441	0.6756	0.6139	0.5584	0.5083	0.4632	0.4224	0.3855
11	0.8963	0.8043	0.7224	0.6496	0.5847	0.5268	0.4751	0.4289	0.3875	0.3505
12	0.8874	0.7885	0.7014	0.6246	0.5568	0.4970	0.4440	0.3971	0.3555	0.3186
13	0.8787	0.7730	0.6810	0.6006	0.5303	0.4688	0.4150	0.3677	0.3262	0.2897
14	0.8700	0.7579	0.6611	0.5775	0.5051	0.4423	0.3878	0.3405	0.2992	0.2633
15	0.8613	0.7430	0.6419	0.5553	0.4810	0.4173	0.3624	0.3152	0.2745	0.2394
16	0.8528	0.7284	0.6232	0.5339	0.4581	0.3936	0.3387	0.2919	0.2519	0.2176
17	0.8444	0.7142	0.6050	0.5134	0.4363	0.3714	0.3166	0.2703	0.2311	0.1978
18	0.8360	0.7002	0.5874	0.4936	0.4155	0.3503	0.2959	0.2502	0.2120	0.1799
19	0.8277	0.6864	0.5703	0.4746	0.3957	0.3305	0.2765	0.2317	0.1945	0.1635
20	0.8195	0.6730	0.5537	0.4564	0.3769	0.3118	0.2584	0.2145	0.1784	0.1486
21	0.8114	0.6598	0.5375	0.4388	0.3589	0.2942	0.2415	0.1987	0.1637	0.1351
22	0.8034	0.6468	0.5219	0.4220	0.3418	0.2775	0.2257	0.1839	0.1502	0.1228
23	0.7954	0.6342	0.5067	0.4057	0.3256	0.2618	0.2109	0.1703	0.1378	0.1117
24	0.7876	0.6217	0.4919	0.3901	0.3101	0.2470	0.1971	0.1577	0.1264	0.1015
25	0.7798	0.6095	0.4776	0.3751	0.2953	0.2330	0.1842	0.1460	0.1160	0.0923
26	0.7720	0.5976	0.4637	0.3607	0.2812	0.2198	0.1722	0.1352	0.1064	0.0839
27	0.7644	0.5859	0.4502	0.3468	0.2678	0.2074	0.1609	0.1252	0.0976	0.0763
28	0.7568	0.5744	0.4371	0.3335	0.2551	0.1956	0.1504	0.1159	0.0895	0.0693
29	0.7493	0.5631	0.4243	0.3207	0.2429	0.1846	0.1406	0.1073	0.0822	0.0630
30	0.7419	0.5521	0.4120	0.3083	0.2314	0.1741	0.1314	0.0994	0.0754	0.0573

	11	12	13	14	15	16	17	18	19	20
1	0.9009	0.8929	0.8850	0.8772	0.8696	0.8621	0.8547	0.8475	0.8403	0.8333
2	0.8116	0.7972	0.7831	0.7695	0.7561	0.7432	0.7305	0.7182	0.7062	0.6944
3	0.7312	0.7118	0.6931	0.6750	0.6575	0.6407	0.6244	0.6086	0.5934	0.5787
4	0.6587	0.6355	0.6133	0.5921	0.5718	0.5523	0.5337	0.5158	0.4987	0.4823
5	0.5935	0.5674	0.5428	0.5194	0.4972	0.4761	0.4561	0.4371	0.4190	0.4019
6	0.5346	0.5066	0.4803	0.4556	0.4323	0.4104	0.3898	0.3704	0.3521	0.3349
7	0.4817	0.4523	0.4251	0.3996	0.3759	0.3538	0.3332	0.3139	0.2959	0.2791
8	0.4339	0.4039	0.3762	0.3506	0.3269	0.3050	0.2848	0.2660	0.2487	0.2326
9	0.3909	0.3606	0.3329	0.3075	0.2843	0.2630	0.2434	0.2255	0.2090	0.1938
10	0.3522	0.3220	0.2946	0.2697	0.2472	0.2267	0.2080	0.1911	0.1756	0.1615
11	0.3173	0.2875	0.2607	0.2366	0.2149	0.1954	0.1778	0.1619	0.1476	0.1346
12	0.2858	0.2567	0.2307	0.2076	0.1869	0.1685	0.1520	0.1372	0.1240	0.1122
13	0.2575	0.2292	0.2042	0.1821	0.1625	0.1452	0.1299	0.1163	0.1042	0.0935
14	0.2320	0.2046	0.1807	0.1597	0.1413	0.1252	0.1110	0.0985	0.0876	0.0779
15	0.2090	0.1827	0.1599	0.1401	0.1229	0.1079	0.0949	0.0835	0.0736	0.0649
16	0.1883	0.1631	0.1415	0.1229	0.1069	0.0930	0.0811	0.0708	0.0618	0.0541
17	0.1696	0.1456	0.1252	0.1078	0.0929	0.0802	0.0693	0.0600	0.0520	0.0451

18	0.1528	0.1300	0.1108	0.0946	0.0808	0.0691	0.0592	0.0508	0.0437	0.0376
19	0.1377	0.1161	0.0981	0.0829	0.0703	0.0596	0.0506	0.0431	0.0367	0.0313
20	0.1240	0.1037	0.0868	0.0728	0.0611	0.0514	0.0433	0.0365	0.0308	0.0261
21	0.1117	0.0926	0.0768	0.0638	0.0531	0.0443	0.0370	0.0309	0.0259	0.0217
22	0.1007	0.0826	0.0680	0.0560	0.0462	0.0382	0.0316	0.0262	0.0218	0.0181
23	0.0907	0.0738	0.0601	0.0491	0.0402	0.0329	0.0270	0.0222	0.0183	0.0151
24	0.0817	0.0659	0.0532	0.0431	0.0349	0.0284	0.0231	0.0188	0.0154	0.0126
25	0.0736	0.0588	0.0471	0.0378	0.0304	0.0245	0.0197	0.0160	0.0129	0.0105
26	0.0663	0.0525	0.0417	0.0331	0.0264	0.0211	0.0169	0.0135	0.0109	0.0087
27	0.0597	0.0469	0.0369	0.0291	0.0230	0.0182	0.0144	0.0115	0.0091	0.0073
28	0.0538	0.0419	0.0326	0.0255	0.0200	0.0157	0.0123	0.0097	0.0077	0.0061
29	0.0485	0.0374	0.0289	0.0224	0.0174	0.0135	0.0105	0.0082	0.0064	0.0051
30	0.0437	0.0334	0.0256	0.0196	0.0151	0.0116	0.0090	0.0070	0.0054	0.0042

	21	22	23	24	25	26	27	28	29	30
1	0.8264	0.8197	0.8130	0.8065	0.8000	0.7937	0.7874	0.7813	0.7752	0.7692
2	0.6830	0.6719	0.6610	0.6504	0.6400	0.6299	0.6200	0.6104	0.6009	0.5917
3	0.5645	0.5507	0.5374	0.5245	0.5120	0.4999	0.4882	0.4768	0.4658	0.4552
4	0.4665	0.4514	0.4369	0.4230	0.4096	0.3968	0.3844	0.3725	0.3611	0.3501
5	0.3855	0.3700	0.3552	0.3411	0.3277	0.3149	0.3027	0.2910	0.2799	0.2693
6	0.3186	0.3033	0.2888	0.2751	0.2621	0.2499	0.2383	0.2274	0.2170	0.2072
7	0.2633	0.2486	0.2348	0.2218	0.2097	0.1983	0.1877	0.1776	0.1682	0.1594
8	0.2176	0.2038	0.1909	0.1789	0.1678	0.1574	0.1478	0.1388	0.1304	0.1226
9	0.1799	0.1670	0.1552	0.1443	0.1342	0.1249	0.1164	0.1084	0.1011	0.0943
10	0.1486	0.1369	0.1262	0.1164	0.1074	0.0992	0.0916	0.0847	0.0784	0.0725
11	0.1228	0.1122	0.1026	0.0938	0.0859	0.0787	0.0721	0.0662	0.0607	0.0558
12	0.1015	0.0920	0.0834	0.0757	0.0687	0.0625	0.0568	0.0517	0.0471	0.0429
13	0.0839	0.0754	0.0678	0.0610	0.0550	0.0496	0.0447	0.0404	0.0365	0.0330
14	0.0693	0.0618	0.0551	0.0492	0.0440	0.0393	0.0352	0.0316	0.0283	0.0254
15	0.0573	0.0507	0.0448	0.0397	0.0352	0.0312	0.0277	0.0247	0.0219	0.0195
16	0.0474	0.0415	0.0364	0.0320	0.0281	0.0248	0.0218	0.0193	0.0170	0.0150
17	0.0391	0.0340	0.0296	0.0258	0.0225	0.0197	0.0172	0.0150	0.0132	0.0116
18	0.0323	0.0279	0.0241	0.0208	0.0180	0.0156	0.0135	0.0118	0.0102	0.0089
19	0.0267	0.0229	0.0196	0.0168	0.0144	0.0124	0.0107	0.0092	0.0079	0.0068
20	0.0221	0.0187	0.0159	0.0135	0.0115	0.0098	0.0084	0.0072	0.0061	0.0053
21	0.0183	0.0154	0.0129	0.0109	0.0092	0.0078	0.0066	0.0056	0.0048	0.0040
22	0.0151	0.0126	0.0105	0.0088	0.0074	0.0062	0.0052	0.0044	0.0037	0.0031
23	0.0125	0.0103	0.0086	0.0071	0.0059	0.0049	0.0041	0.0034	0.0029	0.0024
24	0.0103	0.0085	0.0070	0.0057	0.0047	0.0039	0.0032	0.0027	0.0022	0.0018
25	0.0085	0.0069	0.0057	0.0046	0.0038	0.0031	0.0025	0.0021	0.0017	0.0014
26	0.0070	0.0057	0.0046	0.0037	0.0030	0.0025	0.0020	0.0016	0.0013	0.0011
27	0.0058	0.0047	0.0037	0.0030	0.0024	0.0019	0.0016	0.0013	0.0010	0.0008
28	0.0048	0.0038	0.0030	0.0024	0.0019	0.0015	0.0012	0.0010	0.0008	0.0006
29	0.0040	0.0031	0.0025	0.0020	0.0015	0.0012	0.0010	0.0008	0.0006	0.0005
30	0.0033	0.0026	0.0020	0.0016	0.0012	0.0010	0.0008	0.0006	0.0005	0.0004

Table 3: Present value of an immediate annuity of £1

at $100r$% compound interest: $\dfrac{1 - (1 + r)^{-n}}{r}$

Years — Discount rate as percentage ($100r$)

n	1	2	3	4	5	6	7	8	9	10
1	0.9901	0.9804	0.9709	0.9615	0.9524	0.9434	0.9346	0.9259	0.9174	0.9091
2	1.9704	1.9416	1.9135	1.8861	1.8594	1.8334	1.8080	1.7833	1.7591	1.7355
3	2.9410	2.8839	2.8286	2.7751	2.7232	2.6730	2.6243	2.5771	2.5313	2.4869
4	3.9020	3.8077	3.7171	3.6299	3.5460	3.4651	3.3872	3.3121	3.2397	3.1699
5	4.8534	4.7135	4.5797	4.4518	4.3295	4.2124	4.1002	3.9927	3.8897	3.7908
6	5.7955	5.6014	5.4172	5.2421	5.0757	4.9173	4.7665	4.6229	4.4859	4.3553
7	6.7282	6.4720	6.2303	6.0021	5.7864	5.5824	5.3893	5.2064	5.0330	4.8684
8	7.6517	7.3255	7.0197	6.7327	6.4632	6.2098	5.9713	5.7466	5.5348	5.3349
9	8.5660	8.1622	7.7861	7.4353	7.1078	6.8017	6.5152	6.2469	5.9952	5.7590
10	9.4713	8.9826	8.5302	8.1109	7.7217	7.3601	7.0236	6.7101	6.4177	6.1446
11	10.3676	9.7868	9.2526	8.7605	8.3064	7.8869	7.4987	7.1390	6.8052	6.4951
12	11.2551	10.5753	9.9540	9.3851	8.8633	8.3838	7.9427	7.5361	7.1607	6.8137
13	12.1337	11.3484	10.6350	9.9856	9.3936	8.8527	8.3577	7.9038	7.4869	7.1034
14	13.0037	12.1062	11.2961	10.5631	9.8986	9.2950	8.7455	8.2442	7.7862	7.3667
15	13.8651	12.8493	11.9379	11.1184	10.3797	9.7122	9.1079	8.5595	8.0607	7.6061
16	14.7179	13.5777	12.5611	11.6523	10.8378	10.1059	9.4466	8.8514	8.3126	7.8237
17	15.5623	14.2919	13.1661	12.1657	11.2741	10.4773	9.7632	9.1216	8.5436	8.0216
18	16.3983	14.9920	13.7535	12.6593	11.6896	10.8276	10.0591	9.3719	8.7556	8.2014
19	17.2260	15.6785	14.3238	13.1339	12.0853	11.1581	10.3356	9.6036	8.9501	8.3649
20	18.0456	16.3514	14.8775	13.5903	12.4622	11.4699	10.5940	9.8181	9.1285	8.5136
21	18.8570	17.0112	15.4150	14.0292	12.8212	11.7641	10.8355	10.0168	9.2922	8.6487
22	19.6604	17.6580	15.9369	14.4511	13.1630	12.0416	11.0612	10.2007	9.4424	8.7715
23	20.4558	18.2922	16.4436	14.8568	13.4886	12.3034	11.2722	10.3711	9.5802	8.8832
24	21.2434	18.9139	16.9355	15.2470	13.7986	12.5504	11.4693	10.5288	9.7066	8.9847
25	22.0232	19.5235	17.4131	15.6221	14.0939	12.7834	11.6536	10.6748	9.8226	9.0770
26	22.7952	20.1210	17.8768	15.9828	14.3752	13.0032	11.8258	10.8100	9.9290	9.1609
27	23.5596	20.7069	18.3270	16.3296	14.6430	13.2105	11.9867	10.9352	10.0266	9.2372
28	24.3164	21.2813	18.7641	16.6631	14.8981	13.4062	12.1371	11.0511	10.1161	9.3066
29	25.0658	21.8444	19.1885	16.9837	15.1411	13.5907	12.2777	11.1584	10.1983	9.3696
30	25.8077	22.3965	19.6004	17.2920	15.3725	13.7648	12.4090	11.2578	10.2737	9.4269

n	11	12	13	14	15	16	17	18	19	20
1	0.9009	0.8929	0.8850	0.8772	0.8696	0.8621	0.8547	0.8475	0.8403	0.8333
2	1.7125	1.6901	1.6681	1.6467	1.6257	1.6052	1.5852	1.5656	1.5465	1.5278
3	2.4437	2.4018	2.3612	2.3216	2.2832	2.2459	2.2096	2.1743	2.1399	2.1065
4	3.1024	3.0373	2.9745	2.9137	2.8550	2.7982	2.7432	2.6901	2.6386	2.5887
5	3.6959	3.6048	3.5172	3.4331	3.3522	3.2743	3.1993	3.1272	3.0576	2.9906
6	4.2305	4.1114	3.9975	3.8887	3.7845	3.6847	3.5892	3.4976	3.4098	3.3255
7	4.7122	4.5638	4.4226	4.2883	4.1604	4.0386	3.9224	3.8115	3.7057	3.6046
8	5.1461	4.9676	4.7988	4.6389	4.4873	4.3436	4.2072	4.0776	3.9544	3.8372
9	5.5370	5.3282	5.1317	4.9464	4.7716	4.6065	4.4506	4.3030	4.1633	4.0310
10	5.8892	5.6502	5.4262	5.2161	5.0188	4.8332	4.6586	4.4941	4.3389	4.1925
11	6.2065	5.9377	5.6869	5.4527	5.2337	5.0286	4.8364	4.6560	4.4865	4.3271
12	6.4924	6.1944	5.9176	5.6603	5.4206	5.1971	4.9884	4.7932	4.6105	4.4392
13	6.7499	6.4235	6.1218	5.8424	5.5831	5.3423	5.1183	4.9095	4.7147	4.5327

14	6.9819	6.6282	6.3025	6.0021	5.7245	5.4675	5.2293	5.0081	4.8023	4.6106
15	7.1909	6.8109	6.4624	6.1422	5.8474	5.5755	5.3242	5.0916	4.8759	4.6755
16	7.3792	6.9740	6.6039	6.2651	5.9542	5.6685	5.4053	5.1624	4.9377	4.7296
17	7.5488	7.1196	6.7291	6.3729	6.0472	5.7487	5.4746	5.2223	4.9897	4.7746
18	7.7016	7.2497	6.8399	6.4674	6.1280	5.8178	5.5339	5.2732	5.0333	4.8122
19	7.8393	7.3658	6.9380	6.5504	6.1982	5.8775	5.5845	5.3162	5.0700	4.8435
20	7.9633	7.4694	7.0248	6.6231	6.2593	5.9288	5.6278	5.3527	5.1009	4.8696
21	8.0751	7.5620	7.1016	6.6870	6.3125	5.9731	5.6648	5.3837	5.1268	4.8913
22	8.1757	7.6446	7.1695	6.7429	6.3587	6.0113	5.6964	5.4099	5.1486	4.9094
23	8.2664	7.7184	7.2297	6.7921	6.3988	6.0442	5.7234	5.4321	5.1668	4.9245
24	8.3481	7.7843	7.2829	6.8351	6.4338	6.0726	5.7465	5.4509	5.1822	4.9371
25	8.4217	7.8431	7.3300	6.8729	6.4641	6.0971	5.7662	5.4669	5.1951	4.9476
26	8.4881	7.8957	7.3717	6.9061	6.4906	6.1182	5.7831	5.4804	5.2060	4.9563
27	8.5478	7.9426	7.4086	6.9352	6.5135	6.1364	5.7975	5.4919	5.2151	4.9636
28	8.6016	7.9844	7.4412	6.9607	6.5335	6.1520	5.8099	5.5016	5.2228	4.9697
29	8.6501	8.0218	7.4701	6.9830	6.5509	6.1656	5.8204	5.5098	5.2292	4.9747
30	8.6938	8.0552	7.4957	7.0027	6.5660	6.1772	5.8294	5.5168	5.2347	4.9789

	21	22	23	24	25	26	27	28	29	30
1	0.8264	0.8197	0.8130	0.8065	0.8000	0.7937	0.7874	0.7813	0.7752	0.7692
2	1.5095	1.4915	1.4740	1.4568	1.4400	1.4235	1.4074	1.3916	1.3761	1.3609
3	2.0739	2.0422	2.0114	1.9813	1.9520	1.9234	1.8956	1.8684	1.8420	1.8161
4	2.5404	2.4936	2.4483	2.4043	2.3616	2.3202	2.2800	2.2410	2.2031	2.1662
5	2.9260	2.8636	2.8035	2.7454	2.6893	2.6351	2.5827	2.5320	2.4830	2.4356
6	3.2446	3.1669	3.0923	3.0205	2.9514	2.8850	2.8210	2.7594	2.7000	2.6427
7	3.5079	3.4155	3.3270	3.2423	3.1611	3.0833	3.0087	2.9370	2.8682	2.8021
8	3.7256	3.6193	3.5179	3.4212	3.3289	3.2407	3.1564	3.0758	2.9986	2.9247
9	3.9054	3.7863	3.6731	3.5655	3.4631	3.3657	3.2728	3.1842	3.0997	3.0190
10	4.0541	3.9232	3.7993	3.6819	3.5705	3.4648	3.3644	3.2689	3.1781	3.0915
11	4.1769	4.0354	3.9018	3.7757	3.6564	3.5435	3.4365	3.3351	3.2388	3.1473
12	4.2784	4.1274	3.9852	3.8514	3.7251	3.6059	3.4933	3.3868	3.2859	3.1903
13	4.3624	4.2028	4.0530	3.9124	3.7801	3.6555	3.5381	3.4272	3.3224	3.2233
14	4.4317	4.2646	4.1082	3.9616	3.8241	3.6949	3.5733	3.4587	3.3507	3.2487
15	4.4890	4.3152	4.1530	4.0013	3.8593	3.7261	3.6010	3.4834	3.3726	3.2682
16	4.5364	4.3567	4.1894	4.0333	3.8874	3.7509	3.6228	3.5026	3.3896	3.2832
17	4.5755	4.3908	4.2190	4.0591	3.9099	3.7705	3.6400	3.5177	3.4028	3.2948
18	4.6079	4.4187	4.2431	4.0799	3.9279	3.7861	3.6536	3.5294	3.4130	3.3037
19	4.6346	4.4415	4.2627	4.0967	3.9424	3.7985	3.6642	3.5386	3.4210	3.3105
20	4.6567	4.4603	4.2786	4.1103	3.9539	3.8083	3.6726	3.5458	3.4271	3.3158
21	4.6750	4.4756	4.2916	4.1212	3.9631	3.8161	3.6792	3.5514	3.4319	3.3198
22	4.6900	4.4882	4.3021	4.1300	3.9705	3.8223	3.6844	3.5558	3.4356	3.3230
23	4.7025	4.4985	4.3106	4.1371	3.9764	3.8273	3.6885	3.5592	3.4384	3.3254
24	4.7128	4.5070	4.3176	4.1428	3.9811	3.8312	3.6918	3.5619	3.4406	3.3272
25	4.7213	4.5139	4.3232	4.1474	3.9849	3.8342	3.6943	3.5640	3.4423	3.3286
26	4.7284	4.5196	4.3278	4.1511	3.9879	3.8367	3.6963	3.5656	3.4437	3.3297
27	4.7342	4.5243	4.3316	4.1542	3.9903	3.8387	3.6979	3.5669	3.4447	3.3305
28	4.7390	4.5281	4.3346	4.1566	3.9923	3.8402	3.6991	3.5679	3.4455	3.3312
29	4.7430	4.5312	4.3371	4.1585	3.9938	3.8414	3.7001	3.5687	3.4461	3.3317
30	4.7463	4.5338	4.3391	4.1601	3.9950	3.8424	3.7009	3.5693	3.4466	3.3321

Table 4: Future value of an annuity of £1 for n years

at $100r$% compound interest: $\dfrac{(1 + r)^n - 1}{r}$

Years	Discount rate as percentage ($100r$)					
n	1	2	3	4	5	6
1	1.0000	1.0000	1.0000	1.0000	1.0000	1.0000
2	2.0100	2.0200	2.0300	2.0400	2.0500	2.0600
3	3.0301	3.0604	3.0909	3.1216	3.1525	3.1836
4	4.0604	4.1216	4.1836	4.2465	4.3101	4.3746
5	5.1010	5.2040	5.3091	5.4163	5.5256	5.6371
6	6.1520	6.3081	6.4684	6.6330	6.8019	6.9753
7	7.2135	7.4343	7.6625	7.8983	8.1420	8.3938
8	8.2857	8.5830	8.8923	9.2142	9.5491	9.8975
9	9.3685	9.7546	10.1591	10.5828	11.0266	11.4913
10	10.4622	10.9497	11.4639	12.0061	12.5779	13.1808
11	11.5668	12.1687	12.8078	13.4864	14.2068	14.9716
12	12.6825	13.4121	14.1920	15.0258	15.9171	16.8699
13	13.8093	14.6803	15.6178	16.6268	17.7130	18.8821
14	14.9474	15.9739	17.0863	18.2919	19.5986	21.0151
15	16.0969	17.2934	18.5989	20.0236	21.5786	23.2760
16	17.2579	18.6393	20.1569	21.8245	23.6575	25.6725
17	18.4304	20.0121	21.7616	23.6975	25.8404	28.2129
18	19.6147	21.4123	23.4144	25.6454	28.1324	30.9057
19	20.8109	22.8406	25.1169	27.6712	30.5390	33.7600
20	22.0190	24.2974	26.8704	29.7781	33.0660	36.7856
21	23.2392	25.7833	28.6765	31.9692	35.7192	39.9927
22	24.4716	27.2990	30.5368	34.2480	38.5052	43.3923
23	25.7163	28.8450	32.4529	36.6179	41.4305	46.9958
24	26.9735	30.4219	34.4265	39.0826	44.5020	50.8156
25	28.2432	32.0303	36.4593	41.6459	47.7271	54.8645
26	29.5256	33.6709	38.5530	44.3117	51.1135	59.1564
27	30.8209	35.3443	40.7096	47.0842	54.6691	63.7058
28	32.1291	37.0512	42.9309	49.9676	58.4026	68.5281
29	33.4504	38.7922	45.2188	52.9663	62.3227	73.6398
30	34.7849	40.5681	47.5754	56.0849	66.4388	79.0582

	7	8	9	10	11	12
1	1.0000	1.0000	1.0000	1.0000	1.0000	1.0000
2	2.0700	2.0800	2.0900	2.1000	2.1100	2.1200
3	3.2149	3.2464	3.2781	3.3100	3.3421	3.3744
4	4.4399	4.5061	4.5731	4.6410	4.7097	4.7793
5	5.7507	5.8666	5.9847	6.1051	6.2278	6.3528
6	7.1533	7.3359	7.5233	7.7156	7.9129	8.1152
7	8.6540	8.9228	9.2004	9.4872	9.7833	10.0890
8	10.2598	10.6366	11.0285	11.4359	11.8594	12.2997
9	11.9780	12.4876	13.0210	13.5795	14.1640	14.7757
10	13.8164	14.4866	15.1929	15.9374	16.7220	17.5487
11	15.7836	16.6455	17.5603	18.5312	19.5614	20.6546
12	17.8885	18.9771	20.1407	21.3843	22.7132	24.1331
13	20.1406	21.4953	22.9534	24.5227	26.2116	28.0291

14	22.5505	24.2149	26.0192	27.9750	30.0949	32.3926
15	25.1290	27.1521	29.3609	31.7725	34.4054	37.2797
16	27.8881	30.3243	33.0034	35.9497	39.1899	42.7533
17	30.8402	33.7502	36.9737	40.5447	44.5008	48.8837
18	33.9990	37.4502	41.3013	45.5992	50.3959	55.7497
19	37.3790	41.4463	46.0185	51.1591	56.9395	63.4397
20	40.9955	45.7620	51.1601	57.2750	64.2028	72.0524
21	44.8652	50.4229	56.7645	64.0025	72.2651	81.6987
22	49.0057	55.4568	62.8733	71.4027	81.2143	92.5026
23	53.4361	60.8933	69.5319	79.5430	91.1479	104.6029
24	58.1767	66.7648	76.7898	88.4973	102.1741	118.1552
25	63.2490	73.1059	84.7009	98.3471	114.4133	133.3339
26	68.6765	79.9544	93.3240	109.1818	127.9988	150.3339
27	74.4838	87.3508	102.7231	121.0999	143.0786	169.3740
28	80.6977	95.3388	112.9682	134.2099	159.8173	190.6989
29	87.3465	103.9659	124.1354	148.6309	178.3972	214.5827
30	94.4608	113.2832	136.3075	164.4940	199.0209	241.3327

	13	14	15	16	17	18
1	1.0000	1.0000	1.0000	1.0000	1.0000	1.0000
2	2.1300	2.1400	2.1500	2.1600	2.1700	2.1800
3	3.4069	3.4396	3.4725	3.5056	3.5389	3.5724
4	4.8498	4.9211	4.9934	5.0665	5.1405	5.2154
5	6.4803	6.6101	6.7424	6.8771	7.0144	7.1542
6	8.3227	8.5355	8.7537	8.9775	9.2068	9.4420
7	10.4047	10.7305	11.0668	11.4139	11.7720	12.1415
8	12.7573	13.2328	13.7268	14.2401	14.7733	15.3270
9	15.4157	16.0853	16.7858	17.5185	18.2847	19.0859
10	18.4197	19.3373	20.3037	21.3215	22.3931	23.5213
11	21.8143	23.0445	24.3493	25.7329	27.1999	28.7551
12	25.6502	27.2707	29.0017	30.8502	32.8239	34.9311
13	29.9847	32.0887	34.3519	36.7862	39.4040	42.2187
14	34.8827	37.5811	40.5047	43.6720	47.1027	50.8180
15	40.4175	43.8424	47.5804	51.6595	56.1101	60.9653
16	46.6717	50.9804	55.7175	60.9250	66.6488	72.9390
17	53.7391	59.1176	65.0751	71.6730	78.9791	87.0680
18	61.7251	68.3941	75.8364	84.1407	93.4056	103.7403
19	70.7494	78.9692	88.2118	98.6032	110.2846	123.4135
20	80.9468	91.0249	102.4436	115.3797	130.0329	146.6280
21	92.4699	104.7684	118.8101	134.8405	153.1385	174.0210
22	105.4910	120.4360	137.6316	157.4150	180.1721	206.3448
23	120.2048	138.2970	159.2764	183.6014	211.8013	244.4868
24	136.8315	158.6586	184.1678	213.9776	248.8076	289.4945
25	155.6196	181.8708	212.7930	249.2140	292.1048	342.6035
26	176.8501	208.3327	245.7120	290.0883	342.7627	405.2721
27	200.8406	238.4993	283.5688	337.5024	402.0323	479.2211
28	227.9499	272.8892	327.1041	392.5027	471.3778	566.4808
29	258.5834	312.0937	377.1697	456.3032	552.5120	669.4474
30	293.1992	356.7868	434.7451	530.3117	647.4391	790.9479

	19	20	21	22	23	24
1	1.0000	1.0000	1.0000	1.0000	1.0000	1.0000
2	2.1900	2.2000	2.2100	2.2200	2.2300	2.2400
3	3.6061	3.6400	3.6741	3.7084	3.7429	3.7776
4	5.2913	5.3680	5.4457	5.5242	5.6038	5.6842
5	7.2966	7.4416	7.5892	7.7396	7.8926	8.0484

6	9.6830	9.9299	10.1830	10.4423	10.7079	10.9801
7	12.5227	12.9159	13.3214	13.7396	14.1708	14.6153
8	15.9020	16.4991	17.1189	17.7623	18.4300	19.1229
9	19.9234	20.7989	21.7139	22.6700	23.6689	24.7125
10	24.7089	25.9587	27.2738	28.6574	30.1128	31.6434
11	30.4035	32.1504	34.0013	35.9620	38.0388	40.2379
12	37.1802	39.5805	42.1416	44.8737	47.7877	50.8950
13	45.2445	48.4966	51.9913	55.7459	59.7788	64.1097
14	54.8409	59.1959	63.9095	69.0100	74.5280	80.4961
15	66.2607	72.0351	78.3305	85.1922	92.6694	100.8151
16	79.8502	87.4421	95.7799	104.9345	114.9834	126.0108
17	96.0217	105.9305	116.8937	129.0201	142.4295	157.2533
18	115.2659	128.1167	142.4413	158.4045	176.1883	195.9942
19	138.1664	154.7400	173.3540	194.2535	217.7116	244.0327
20	165.4180	186.6880	210.7583	237.9893	268.7853	303.6006
21	197.8474	225.0256	256.0176	291.3469	331.6059	377.4648
22	236.4384	271.0307	310.7813	356.4432	408.8753	469.0563
23	282.3618	326.2368	377.0454	435.8607	503.9166	582.6298
24	337.0105	392.4842	457.2249	532.7501	620.8174	723.4609
25	402.0424	471.9810	554.2421	650.9551	764.6054	898.0916
26	479.4305	567.3773	671.6329	795.1652	941.4646	1114.6335
27	571.5223	681.8527	813.6759	971.1016	1159.0015	1383.1456
28	681.1116	819.2233	985.5478	1185.7439	1426.5718	1716.1005
29	811.5228	984.0679	1193.5128	1447.6075	1755.6833	2128.9646
30	966.7121	1181.8815	1445.1505	1767.0812	2160.4905	2640.9160

	25	26	27	28	29	30
1	1.0000	1.0000	1.0000	1.0000	1.0000	1.0000
2	2.2500	2.2600	2.2700	2.2800	2.2900	2.3000
3	3.8125	3.8476	3.8829	3.9184	3.9541	3.9900
4	5.7656	5.8480	5.9313	6.0156	6.1008	6.1870
5	8.2070	8.3684	8.5327	8.6999	8.8700	9.0431
6	11.2588	11.5442	11.8366	12.1359	12.4423	12.7560
7	15.0735	15.5458	16.0324	16.5339	17.0506	17.5828
8	19.8419	20.5876	21.3612	22.1634	22.9953	23.8577
9	25.8023	26.9404	28.1287	29.3692	30.6639	32.0150
10	33.2529	34.9449	36.7235	38.5926	40.5564	42.6195
11	42.5661	45.0306	47.6388	50.3985	53.3178	56.4053
12	54.2077	57.7386	61.5013	65.5100	69.7800	74.3270
13	68.7596	73.7506	79.1066	84.8529	91.0161	97.6250
14	86.9495	93.9258	101.4654	109.6117	118.4108	127.9125
15	109.6868	119.3465	129.8611	141.3029	153.7500	167.2863
16	138.1085	151.3766	165.9236	181.8677	199.3374	218.4722
17	173.6357	191.7345	211.7230	233.7907	258.1453	285.0139
18	218.0446	242.5855	269.8882	300.2521	334.0074	371.5180
19	273.5557	306.6577	343.7580	385.3227	431.8696	483.9734
20	342.9447	387.3887	437.5726	494.2130	558.1118	630.1654
21	429.6808	489.1097	556.7172	633.5927	720.9641	820.2150
22	538.1011	617.2783	708.0309	811.9986	931.0437	1067.2795
23	673.6263	778.7706	900.1992	1040.3583	1202.0464	1388.4634
24	843.0329	982.2510	1144.2529	1332.6586	1551.6399	1806.0024
25	1054.7911	1238.6362	1454.2013	1706.8029	2002.6154	2348.8030
26	1319.4889	1561.6816	1847.8356	2185.7078	2584.3738	3054.4441
27	1650.3611	1968.7189	2347.7512	2798.7058	3334.8423	3971.7771
28	2063.9514	2481.5857	2982.6440	3583.3435	4302.9463	5164.3105
29	2580.9392	3127.7981	3788.9580	4587.6797	5551.8008	6714.6035
30	3227.1738	3942.0254	4812.9766	5873.2300	7162.8232	8729.9844

Table 5: Sinking fund of £1 for n years

at 100r% compound interest: $\dfrac{r}{(1 + r)^n - 1}$

Years	Discount rate as percentage (100r)									
n	1	2	3	4	5	6	7	8	9	10
1	1.0000	1.0000	1.0000	1.0000	1.0000	1.0000	1.0000	1.0000	1.0000	1.0000
2	0.4975	0.4950	0.4926	0.4902	0.4878	0.4854	0.4831	0.4808	0.4785	0.4762
3	0.3300	0.3268	0.3235	0.3203	0.3172	0.3141	0.3111	0.3080	0.3051	0.3021
4	0.2463	0.2426	0.2390	0.2355	0.2320	0.2286	0.2252	0.2219	0.2187	0.2155
5	0.1960	0.1922	0.1884	0.1846	0.1810	0.1774	0.1739	0.1705	0.1671	0.1638
6	0.1625	0.1585	0.1546	0.1508	0.1470	0.1434	0.1398	0.1363	0.1329	0.1296
7	0.1386	0.1345	0.1305	0.1266	0.1228	0.1191	0.1156	0.1121	0.1087	0.1054
8	0.1207	0.1165	0.1125	0.1085	0.1047	0.1010	0.0975	0.0940	0.0907	0.0874
9	0.1067	0.1025	0.0984	0.0945	0.0907	0.0870	0.0835	0.0801	0.0768	0.0736
10	0.0956	0.0913	0.0872	0.0833	0.0795	0.0759	0.0724	0.0690	0.0658	0.0627
11	0.0865	0.0822	0.0781	0.0741	0.0704	0.0668	0.0634	0.0601	0.0569	0.0540
12	0.0788	0.0746	0.0705	0.0666	0.0628	0.0593	0.0559	0.0527	0.0497	0.0468
13	0.0724	0.0681	0.0640	0.0601	0.0565	0.0530	0.0497	0.0465	0.0436	0.0408
14	0.0669	0.0626	0.0585	0.0547	0.0510	0.0476	0.0443	0.0413	0.0384	0.0357
15	0.0621	0.0578	0.0538	0.0499	0.0463	0.0430	0.0398	0.0368	0.0341	0.0315
16	0.0579	0.0537	0.0496	0.0458	0.0423	0.0390	0.0359	0.0330	0.0303	0.0278
17	0.0543	0.0500	0.0460	0.0422	0.0387	0.0354	0.0324	0.0296	0.0270	0.0247
18	0.0510	0.0467	0.0427	0.0390	0.0355	0.0324	0.0294	0.0267	0.0242	0.0219
19	0.0481	0.0438	0.0398	0.0361	0.0327	0.0296	0.0268	0.0241	0.0217	0.0195
20	0.0454	0.0412	0.0372	0.0336	0.0302	0.0272	0.0244	0.0219	0.0195	0.0175
21	0.0430	0.0388	0.0349	0.0313	0.0280	0.0250	0.0223	0.0198	0.0176	0.0156
22	0.0409	0.0366	0.0327	0.0292	0.0260	0.0230	0.0204	0.0180	0.0159	0.0140
23	0.0389	0.0347	0.0308	0.0273	0.0241	0.0213	0.0187	0.0164	0.0144	0.0126
24	0.0371	0.0329	0.0290	0.0256	0.0225	0.0197	0.0172	0.0150	0.0130	0.0113
25	0.0354	0.0312	0.0274	0.0240	0.0210	0.0182	0.0158	0.0137	0.0118	0.0102
26	0.0339	0.0297	0.0259	0.0226	0.0196	0.0169	0.0146	0.0125	0.0107	0.0092
27	0.0324	0.0283	0.0246	0.0212	0.0183	0.0157	0.0134	0.0114	0.0097	0.0083
28	0.0311	0.0270	0.0233	0.0200	0.0171	0.0146	0.0124	0.0105	0.0089	0.0075
29	0.0299	0.0258	0.0221	0.0189	0.0160	0.0136	0.0114	0.0096	0.0081	0.0067
30	0.0287	0.0246	0.0210	0.0178	0.0151	0.0126	0.0106	0.0088	0.0073	0.0061

n	11	12	13	14	15	16	17	18	19	20
1	1.0000	1.0000	1.0000	1.0000	1.0000	1.0000	1.0000	1.0000	1.0000	1.0000
2	0.4739	0.4717	0.4695	0.4673	0.4651	0.4630	0.4608	0.4587	0.4566	0.4545
3	0.2992	0.2963	0.2935	0.2907	0.2880	0.2853	0.2826	0.2799	0.2773	0.2747
4	0.2123	0.2092	0.2062	0.2032	0.2003	0.1974	0.1945	0.1917	0.1890	0.1863
5	0.1606	0.1574	0.1543	0.1513	0.1483	0.1454	0.1426	0.1398	0.1371	0.1344
6	0.1264	0.1232	0.1202	0.1172	0.1142	0.1114	0.1086	0.1059	0.1033	0.1007
7	0.1022	0.0991	0.0961	0.0932	0.0904	0.0876	0.0849	0.0824	0.0799	0.0774
8	0.0843	0.0813	0.0784	0.0756	0.0729	0.0702	0.0677	0.0652	0.0629	0.0606
9	0.0706	0.0677	0.0649	0.0622	0.0596	0.0571	0.0547	0.0524	0.0502	0.0481
10	0.0598	0.0570	0.0543	0.0517	0.0493	0.0469	0.0447	0.0425	0.0405	0.0385
11	0.0511	0.0484	0.0458	0.0434	0.0411	0.0389	0.0368	0.0348	0.0329	0.0311
12	0.0440	0.0414	0.0390	0.0367	0.0345	0.0324	0.0305	0.0286	0.0269	0.0253

13	0.0382	0.0357	0.0334	0.0312	0.0291	0.0272	0.0254	0.0237	0.0221	0.0206
14	0.0332	0.0309	0.0287	0.0266	0.0247	0.0229	0.0212	0.0197	0.0182	0.0169
15	0.0291	0.0268	0.0247	0.0228	0.0210	0.0194	0.0178	0.0164	0.0151	0.0139
16	0.0255	0.0234	0.0214	0.0196	0.0179	0.0164	0.0150	0.0137	0.0125	0.0114
17	0.0225	0.0205	0.0186	0.0169	0.0154	0.0140	0.0127	0.0115	0.0104	0.0094
18	0.0198	0.0179	0.0162	0.0146	0.0132	0.0119	0.0107	0.0096	0.0087	0.0078
19	0.0176	0.0158	0.0141	0.0127	0.0113	0.0101	0.0091	0.0081	0.0072	0.0065
20	0.0156	0.0139	0.0124	0.0110	0.0098	0.0087	0.0077	0.0068	0.0060	0.0054
21	0.0138	0.0122	0.0108	0.0095	0.0084	0.0074	0.0065	0.0057	0.0051	0.0044
22	0.0123	0.0108	0.0095	0.0083	0.0073	0.0064	0.0056	0.0048	0.0042	0.0037
23	0.0110	0.0096	0.0083	0.0072	0.0063	0.0054	0.0047	0.0041	0.0035	0.0031
24	0.0098	0.0085	0.0073	0.0063	0.0054	0.0047	0.0040	0.0035	0.0030	0.0025
25	0.0087	0.0075	0.0064	0.0055	0.0047	0.0040	0.0034	0.0029	0.0025	0.0021
26	0.0078	0.0067	0.0057	0.0048	0.0041	0.0034	0.0029	0.0025	0.0021	0.0018
27	0.0070	0.0059	0.0050	0.0042	0.0035	0.0030	0.0025	0.0021	0.0017	0.0015
28	0.0063	0.0052	0.0044	0.0037	0.0031	0.0025	0.0021	0.0018	0.0015	0.0012
29	0.0056	0.0047	0.0039	0.0032	0.0027	0.0022	0.0018	0.0015	0.0012	0.0010
30	0.0050	0.0041	0.0034	0.0028	0.0023	0.0019	0.0015	0.0013	0.0010	0.0008

	21	22	23	24	25	26	27	28	29	30
1	1.0000	1.0000	1.0000	1.0000	1.0000	1.0000	1.0000	1.0000	1.0000	1.0000
2	0.4525	0.4505	0.4484	0.4464	0.4444	0.4425	0.4405	0.4386	0.4367	0.4348
3	0.2722	0.2697	0.2672	0.2647	0.2623	0.2599	0.2575	0.2552	0.2529	0.2506
4	0.1836	0.1810	0.1785	0.1759	0.1734	0.1710	0.1686	0.1662	0.1639	0.1616
5	0.1318	0.1292	0.1267	0.1242	0.1218	0.1195	0.1172	0.1149	0.1127	0.1106
6	0.0982	0.0958	0.0934	0.0911	0.0888	0.0866	0.0845	0.0824	0.0804	0.0784
7	0.0751	0.0728	0.0706	0.0684	0.0663	0.0643	0.0624	0.0605	0.0586	0.0569
8	0.0584	0.0563	0.0543	0.0523	0.0504	0.0486	0.0468	0.0451	0.0435	0.0419
9	0.0461	0.0441	0.0422	0.0405	0.0388	0.0371	0.0356	0.0340	0.0326	0.0312
10	0.0367	0.0349	0.0332	0.0316	0.0301	0.0286	0.0272	0.0259	0.0247	0.0235
11	0.0294	0.0278	0.0263	0.0249	0.0235	0.0222	0.0210	0.0198	0.0188	0.0177
12	0.0237	0.0223	0.0209	0.0196	0.0184	0.0173	0.0163	0.0153	0.0143	0.0135
13	0.0192	0.0179	0.0167	0.0156	0.0145	0.0136	0.0126	0.0118	0.0110	0.0102
14	0.0156	0.0145	0.0134	0.0124	0.0115	0.0106	0.0099	0.0091	0.0084	0.0078
15	0.0128	0.0117	0.0108	0.0099	0.0091	0.0084	0.0077	0.0071	0.0065	0.0060
16	0.0104	0.0095	0.0087	0.0079	0.0072	0.0066	0.0060	0.0055	0.0050	0.0046
17	0.0086	0.0078	0.0070	0.0064	0.0058	0.0052	0.0047	0.0043	0.0039	0.0035
18	0.0070	0.0063	0.0057	0.0051	0.0046	0.0041	0.0037	0.0033	0.0030	0.0027
19	0.0058	0.0051	0.0046	0.0041	0.0037	0.0033	0.0029	0.0026	0.0023	0.0021
20	0.0047	0.0042	0.0037	0.0033	0.0029	0.0026	0.0023	0.0020	0.0018	0.0016
21	0.0039	0.0034	0.0030	0.0026	0.0023	0.0020	0.0018	0.0016	0.0014	0.0012
22	0.0032	0.0028	0.0024	0.0021	0.0019	0.0016	0.0014	0.0012	0.0011	0.0009
23	0.0027	0.0023	0.0020	0.0017	0.0015	0.0013	0.0011	0.0010	0.0008	0.0007
24	0.0022	0.0019	0.0016	0.0014	0.0012	0.0010	0.0009	0.0008	0.0006	0.0006
25	0.0018	0.0015	0.0013	0.0011	0.0009	0.0008	0.0007	0.0006	0.0005	0.0004
26	0.0015	0.0013	0.0011	0.0009	0.0008	0.0006	0.0005	0.0005	0.0004	0.0003
27	0.0012	0.0010	0.0009	0.0007	0.0006	0.0005	0.0004	0.0004	0.0003	0.0003
28	0.0010	0.0008	0.0007	0.0006	0.0005	0.0004	0.0003	0.0003	0.0002	0.0002
29	0.0008	0.0007	0.0006	0.0005	0.0004	0.0003	0.0003	0.0002	0.0002	0.0001
30	0.0007	0.0006	0.0005	0.0004	0.0003	0.0003	0.0002	0.0002	0.0001	0.0001

Table 6: Annual equivalent annuity of £1 after *n* years

at 100*r*% compound interest: $\dfrac{r}{1 - (1 + r)^{-n}}$

Years				Discount rate as percentage (100*r*)						
n	1	2	3	4	5	6	7	8	9	10
1	1.0100	1.0200	1.0300	1.0400	1.0500	1.0600	1.0700	1.0800	1.0900	1.1000
2	0.5075	0.5150	0.5226	0.5302	0.5378	0.5454	0.5531	0.5608	0.5685	0.5762
3	0.3400	0.3468	0.3535	0.3603	0.3672	0.3741	0.3811	0.3880	0.3951	0.4021
4	0.2563	0.2626	0.2690	0.2755	0.2820	0.2886	0.2952	0.3019	0.3087	0.3155
5	0.2060	0.2122	0.2184	0.2246	0.2310	0.2374	0.2439	0.2505	0.2571	0.2638
6	0.1725	0.1785	0.1846	0.1908	0.1970	0.2034	0.2098	0.2163	0.2229	0.2296
7	0.1486	0.1545	0.1605	0.1666	0.1728	0.1791	0.1856	0.1921	0.1987	0.2054
8	0.1307	0.1365	0.1425	0.1485	0.1547	0.1610	0.1675	0.1740	0.1807	0.1874
9	0.1167	0.1225	0.1284	0.1345	0.1407	0.1470	0.1535	0.1601	0.1668	0.1736
10	0.1056	0.1113	0.1172	0.1233	0.1295	0.1359	0.1424	0.1490	0.1558	0.1627
11	0.0965	0.1022	0.1081	0.1141	0.1204	0.1268	0.1334	0.1401	0.1469	0.1540
12	0.0888	0.0946	0.1005	0.1066	0.1128	0.1193	0.1259	0.1327	0.1397	0.1468
13	0.0824	0.0881	0.0940	0.1001	0.1065	0.1130	0.1197	0.1265	0.1336	0.1408
14	0.0769	0.0826	0.0885	0.0947	0.1010	0.1076	0.1143	0.1213	0.1284	0.1357
15	0.0721	0.0778	0.0838	0.0899	0.0963	0.1030	0.1098	0.1168	0.1241	0.1315
16	0.0679	0.0737	0.0796	0.0858	0.0923	0.0990	0.1059	0.1130	0.1203	0.1278
17	0.0643	0.0700	0.0760	0.0822	0.0887	0.0954	0.1024	0.1096	0.1170	0.1247
18	0.0610	0.0667	0.0727	0.0790	0.0855	0.0924	0.0994	0.1067	0.1142	0.1219
19	0.0581	0.0638	0.0698	0.0761	0.0827	0.0896	0.0968	0.1041	0.1117	0.1195
20	0.0554	0.0612	0.0672	0.0736	0.0802	0.0872	0.0944	0.1019	0.1095	0.1175
21	0.0530	0.0588	0.0649	0.0713	0.0780	0.0850	0.0923	0.0998	0.1076	0.1156
22	0.0509	0.0566	0.0627	0.0692	0.0760	0.0830	0.0904	0.0980	0.1059	0.1140
23	0.0489	0.0547	0.0608	0.0673	0.0741	0.0813	0.0887	0.0964	0.1044	0.1126
24	0.0471	0.0529	0.0590	0.0656	0.0725	0.0797	0.0872	0.0950	0.1030	0.1113
25	0.0454	0.0512	0.0574	0.0640	0.0710	0.0782	0.0858	0.0937	0.1018	0.1102
26	0.0439	0.0497	0.0559	0.0626	0.0696	0.0769	0.0846	0.0925	0.1007	0.1092
27	0.0424	0.0483	0.0546	0.0612	0.0683	0.0757	0.0834	0.0914	0.0997	0.1083
28	0.0411	0.0470	0.0533	0.0600	0.0671	0.0746	0.0824	0.0905	0.0989	0.1075
29	0.0399	0.0458	0.0521	0.0589	0.0660	0.0736	0.0814	0.0896	0.0981	0.1067
30	0.0387	0.0446	0.0510	0.0578	0.0651	0.0726	0.0806	0.0888	0.0973	0.1061

	11	12	13	14	15	16	17	18	19	20
1	1.1100	1.1200	1.1300	1.1400	1.1500	1.1600	1.1700	1.1800	1.1900	1.2000
2	0.5839	0.5917	0.5995	0.6073	0.6151	0.6230	0.6308	0.6387	0.6466	0.6545
3	0.4092	0.4163	0.4235	0.4307	0.4380	0.4453	0.4526	0.4599	0.4673	0.4747
4	0.3223	0.3292	0.3362	0.3432	0.3503	0.3574	0.3645	0.3717	0.3790	0.3863
5	0.2706	0.2774	0.2843	0.2913	0.2983	0.3054	0.3126	0.3198	0.3271	0.3344
6	0.2364	0.2432	0.2502	0.2572	0.2642	0.2714	0.2786	0.2859	0.2933	0.3007
7	0.2122	0.2191	0.2261	0.2332	0.2404	0.2476	0.2549	0.2624	0.2699	0.2774
8	0.1943	0.2013	0.2084	0.2156	0.2229	0.2302	0.2377	0.2452	0.2529	0.2606
9	0.1806	0.1877	0.1949	0.2022	0.2096	0.2171	0.2247	0.2324	0.2402	0.2481
10	0.1698	0.1770	0.1843	0.1917	0.1993	0.2069	0.2147	0.2225	0.2305	0.2385
11	0.1611	0.1684	0.1758	0.1834	0.1911	0.1989	0.2068	0.2148	0.2229	0.2311
12	0.1540	0.1614	0.1690	0.1767	0.1845	0.1924	0.2005	0.2086	0.2169	0.2253

13	0.1482	0.1557	0.1634	0.1712	0.1791	0.1872	0.1954	0.2037	0.2121	0.2206
14	0.1432	0.1509	0.1587	0.1666	0.1747	0.1829	0.1912	0.1997	0.2082	0.2169
15	0.1391	0.1468	0.1547	0.1628	0.1710	0.1794	0.1878	0.1964	0.2051	0.2139
16	0.1355	0.1434	0.1514	0.1596	0.1679	0.1764	0.1850	0.1937	0.2025	0.2114
17	0.1325	0.1405	0.1486	0.1569	0.1654	0.1740	0.1827	0.1915	0.2004	0.2094
18	0.1298	0.1379	0.1462	0.1546	0.1632	0.1719	0.1807	0.1896	0.1987	0.2078
19	0.1276	0.1358	0.1441	0.1527	0.1613	0.1701	0.1791	0.1881	0.1972	0.2065
20	0.1256	0.1339	0.1424	0.1510	0.1598	0.1687	0.1777	0.1868	0.1960	0.2054
21	0.1238	0.1322	0.1408	0.1495	0.1584	0.1674	0.1765	0.1857	0.1951	0.2044
22	0.1223	0.1308	0.1395	0.1483	0.1573	0.1664	0.1756	0.1848	0.1942	0.2037
23	0.1210	0.1296	0.1383	0.1472	0.1563	0.1654	0.1747	0.1841	0.1935	0.2031
24	0.1198	0.1285	0.1373	0.1463	0.1554	0.1647	0.1740	0.1835	0.1930	0.2025
25	0.1187	0.1275	0.1364	0.1455	0.1547	0.1640	0.1734	0.1829	0.1925	0.2021
26	0.1178	0.1267	0.1357	0.1448	0.1541	0.1634	0.1729	0.1825	0.1921	0.2018
27	0.1170	0.1259	0.1350	0.1442	0.1535	0.1630	0.1725	0.1821	0.1917	0.2015
28	0.1163	0.1252	0.1344	0.1437	0.1531	0.1625	0.1721	0.1818	0.1915	0.2012
29	0.1156	0.1247	0.1339	0.1432	0.1527	0.1622	0.1718	0.1815	0.1912	0.2010
30	0.1150	0.1241	0.1334	0.1428	0.1523	0.1619	0.1715	0.1813	0.1910	0.2008

	21	22	23	24	25	26	27	28	29	30
1	1.2100	1.2200	1.2300	1.2400	1.2500	1.2600	1.2700	1.2800	1.2900	1.3000
2	0.6625	0.6705	0.6784	0.6864	0.6944	0.7025	0.7105	0.7186	0.7267	0.7348
3	0.4822	0.4897	0.4972	0.5047	0.5123	0.5199	0.5275	0.5352	0.5429	0.5506
4	0.3936	0.4010	0.4085	0.4159	0.4234	0.4310	0.4386	0.4462	0.4539	0.4616
5	0.3418	0.3492	0.3567	0.3642	0.3718	0.3795	0.3872	0.3949	0.4027	0.4106
6	0.3082	0.3158	0.3234	0.3311	0.3388	0.3466	0.3545	0.3624	0.3704	0.3784
7	0.2851	0.2928	0.3006	0.3084	0.3163	0.3243	0.3324	0.3405	0.3486	0.3569
8	0.2684	0.2763	0.2843	0.2923	0.3004	0.3086	0.3168	0.3251	0.3335	0.3419
9	0.2561	0.2641	0.2722	0.2805	0.2888	0.2971	0.3056	0.3140	0.3226	0.3312
10	0.2467	0.2549	0.2632	0.2716	0.2801	0.2886	0.2972	0.3059	0.3147	0.3235
11	0.2394	0.2478	0.2563	0.2649	0.2735	0.2822	0.2910	0.2998	0.3088	0.3177
12	0.2337	0.2423	0.2509	0.2596	0.2684	0.2773	0.2863	0.2953	0.3043	0.3135
13	0.2292	0.2379	0.2467	0.2556	0.2645	0.2736	0.2826	0.2918	0.3010	0.3102
14	0.2256	0.2345	0.2434	0.2524	0.2615	0.2706	0.2799	0.2891	0.2984	0.3078
15	0.2228	0.2317	0.2408	0.2499	0.2591	0.2684	0.2777	0.2871	0.2965	0.3060
16	0.2204	0.2295	0.2387	0.2479	0.2572	0.2666	0.2760	0.2855	0.2950	0.3046
17	0.2186	0.2278	0.2370	0.2464	0.2558	0.2652	0.2747	0.2843	0.2939	0.3035
18	0.2170	0.2263	0.2357	0.2451	0.2546	0.2641	0.2737	0.2833	0.2930	0.3027
19	0.2158	0.2251	0.2346	0.2441	0.2537	0.2633	0.2729	0.2826	0.2923	0.3021
20	0.2147	0.2242	0.2337	0.2433	0.2529	0.2626	0.2723	0.2820	0.2918	0.3016
21	0.2139	0.2234	0.2330	0.2426	0.2523	0.2620	0.2718	0.2816	0.2914	0.3012
22	0.2132	0.2228	0.2324	0.2421	0.2519	0.2616	0.2714	0.2812	0.2911	0.3009
23	0.2127	0.2223	0.2320	0.2417	0.2515	0.2613	0.2711	0.2810	0.2908	0.3007
24	0.2122	0.2219	0.2316	0.2414	0.2512	0.2610	0.2709	0.2808	0.2906	0.3006
25	0.2118	0.2215	0.2313	0.2411	0.2509	0.2608	0.2707	0.2806	0.2905	0.3004
26	0.2115	0.2213	0.2311	0.2409	0.2508	0.2606	0.2705	0.2805	0.2904	0.3003
27	0.2112	0.2210	0.2309	0.2407	0.2506	0.2605	0.2704	0.2804	0.2903	0.3003
28	0.2110	0.2208	0.2307	0.2406	0.2505	0.2604	0.2703	0.2803	0.2902	0.3002
29	0.2108	0.2207	0.2306	0.2405	0.2504	0.2603	0.2703	0.2802	0.2902	0.3001
30	0.2107	0.2206	0.2305	0.2404	0.2503	0.2603	0.2702	0.2802	0.2901	0.3001

Table 7: Area under the normal curve up to t standard deviations above the mean

$$\text{Area} = [1/\sqrt{(2\pi)}] \int_{-\infty}^{t} e^{-x^2/2} \, dx$$

t	0.00	0.01	0.02	0.03	0.04	0.05	0.06	0.07	0.08	0.09
0.0	.5000	.5040	.5080	.5120	.5160	.5199	.5239	.5279	.5319	.5359
0.1	.5398	.5438	.5478	.5517	.5557	.5596	.5636	.5675	.5714	.5753
0.2	.5793	.5832	.5871	.5910	.5948	.5987	.6026	.6064	.6103	.6141
0.3	.6179	.6217	.6255	.6293	.6331	.6368	.6406	.6443	.6480	.6517
0.4	.6554	.6591	.6628	.6664	.6700	.6736	.6772	.6808	.6844	.6879
0.5	.6915	.6950	.6985	.7019	.7054	.7088	.7123	.7157	.7190	.7224
0.6	.7257	.7291	.7324	.7357	.7389	.7422	.7454	.7486	.7517	.7549
0.7	.7580	.7611	.7642	.7673	.7704	.7734	.7764	.7794	.7823	.7852
0.8	.7881	.7910	.7939	.7967	.7995	.8023	.8051	.8079	.8106	.8133
0.9	.8159	.8186	.8212	.8238	.8264	.8289	.8315	.8340	.8365	.8389
1.0	.8413	.8438	.8461	.8485	.8508	.8531	.8554	.8577	.8599	.8621
1.1	.8643	.8665	.8686	.8708	.8729	.8749	.8770	.8790	.8810	.8830
1.2	.8849	.8869	.8888	.8907	.8925	.8944	.8962	.8980	.8997	.9015
1.3	.9032	.9049	.9066	.9082	.9099	.9115	.9131	.9147	.9162	.9177
1.4	.9192	.9207	.9222	.9236	.9251	.9265	.9279	.9292	.9306	.9319
1.5	.9332	.9345	.9357	.9370	.9382	.9394	.9406	.9418	.9429	.9441
1.6	.9452	.9463	.9474	.9484	.9495	.9505	.9515	.9525	.9535	.9545
1.7	.9554	.9564	.9573	.9582	.9591	.9599	.9608	.9616	.9625	.9633
1.8	.9641	.9649	.9656	.9664	.9671	.9678	.9686	.9693	.9699	.9706
1.9	.9713	.9719	.9726	.9732	.9738	.9744	.9750	.9756	.9761	.9767
2.0	.9772	.9778	.9783	.9788	.9793	.9798	.9803	.9808	.9812	.9817
2.1	.9821	.9826	.9830	.9834	.9838	.9842	.9846	.9850	.9854	.9857
2.2	.9861	.9864	.9868	.9871	.9875	.9878	.9881	.9884	.9887	.9890
2.3	.9893	.9896	.9898	.9901	.9904	.9906	.9909	.9911	.9913	.9916
2.4	.9918	.9920	.9922	.9924	.9927	.9929	.9931	.9932	.9934	.9936
2.5	.9938	.9940	.9941	.9943	.9945	.9946	.9948	.9949	.9951	.9952
2.6	.9953	.9955	.9956	.9957	.9959	.9960	.9961	.9962	.9963	.9964
2.7	.9965	.9966	.9967	.9968	.9969	.9970	.9971	.9972	.9973	.9974
2.8	.9974	.9975	.9976	.9977	.9977	.9978	.9979	.9979	.9980	.9981
2.9	.9981	.9982	.9982	.9983	.9984	.9984	.9985	.9985	.9986	.9986
3.0	.9986	.9987	.9987	.9988	.9988	.9989	.9989	.9989	.9990	.9990
3.1	.9990	.9991	.9991	.9991	.9992	.9992	.9992	.9992	.9993	.9993
3.2	.9993	.9993	.9994	.9994	.9994	.9994	.9994	.9995	.9995	.9995
3.3	.9995	.9995	.9995	.9996	.9996	.9996	.9996	.9996	.9996	.9996
3.4	.9997	.9997	.9997	.9997	.9997	.9997	.9997	.9997	.9997	.9998
3.5	.9998	.9998	.9998	.9998	.9998	.9998	.9998	.9998	.9998	.9998
3.6	.9998	.9998	.9999	.9999	.9999	.9999	.9999	.9999	.9999	.9999
3.7	.9999	.9999	.9999	.9999	.9999	.9999	.9999	.9999	.9999	.9999
3.8	.9999	.9999	.9999	.9999	.9999	.9999	.9999	.9999	.9999	.9999
3.9	1.0000	1.0000	1.0000	1.0000	1.0000	1.0000	1.0000	1.0000	1.0000	1.0000
4.0	1.0000	1.0000	1.0000	1.0000	1.0000	1.0000	1.0000	1.0000	1.0000	1.0000

PROGRAMS

The Basic programs that were used to generate these tables now follow. Once again, the method of programming employed is very straightforward. A more sophisticated programming style could have been used. But an important objective here is to produce simple and relatively readable programs that will do the job and which should be relatively easy to understand and to develop further.

For Table 1 (future values) the program used was:

```
PRINT "Table 1: Future value of £1 at 100r% compound interest: (1 + r)^n"
PRINT "------------------------------------------------------------------"
PRINT
PRINT "Years";
PRINT TAB(30); "Discount rate as percentage (100r)"
PRINT
PRINT " n ";

FOR a = 0 TO 24 STEP 6

    FOR r = 1 + a TO 6 + a

        PRINT TAB(2 + 10 * (r - a)); r;

        IF r = 6 + a THEN PRINT

    NEXT r

    FOR n = 1 TO 30

        PRINT n;

        FOR r = 1 + a TO 6 + a

            x = (1 + .01 * r) ^ n

            PRINT TAB(10 * (r - a)); USING "####.####"; x;

            IF r = 6 + a THEN PRINT

        NEXT r

    NEXT n

PRINT

NEXT a

END
```

Note that in this and the following programs, in order to print the output, the PRINT statement should be replaced with:

LPRINT

In order to send the output to a text file (for incorporation into a word processor for example) add near the beginning of the program the line:

```
OPEN "c:\table1.txt" FOR OUTPUT AS #1
```

and replace the PRINT statements with:

```
PRINT #1,
```

including the comma. A plain text file named table1.txt will be created in the root directory of the C drive when the program is run.

For Table 2 (present value factors) the program used was:

```
PRINT "Table 2: Present value of £1 at 100r% compound interest: (1 + r)^-n"
PRINT "--------------------------------------------------------------------"
PRINT
PRINT "Years";
PRINT TAB(30); "Discount rate as percentage (100r)"
PRINT
PRINT " n ";

FOR a = 0 TO 20 STEP 10

    FOR i = 1 + a TO 10 + a

        PRINT TAB(7 * (i - a)); i;

        IF i = 10 + a THEN PRINT

    NEXT i

    FOR r = 1 TO 30

        PRINT r;

        FOR i = 1 + a TO 10 + a

            x = (1 + .01 * i) ^ -r

            PRINT TAB(7 * (i - a)); USING "#.####"; x;

            IF i = 10 + a THEN PRINT

        NEXT i

    NEXT r

PRINT

NEXT a

END
```

For Table 3 (present value of an annuity) the program used was:

```
PRINT "Table 3: Present value of an immediate annuity of £1"
PRINT "                                      1 - (1 + r)^-n"
PRINT " at 100r% compound interest:       ———————————"
PRINT "                                           r"
PRINT "---------------------------------------------------------"
PRINT

PRINT "Years";
PRINT TAB(30); "Discount rate as percentage (100r)"
PRINT
PRINT " n ";

FOR a = 0 TO 20 STEP 10

    FOR r = 1 + a TO 10 + a

        PRINT TAB(7 * (r - a)); r;

        IF r = 10 + a THEN PRINT

    NEXT r

    FOR n = 1 TO 30

        PRINT n;

        FOR r = 1 + a TO 10 + a

            x = (1 - (1 + .01 * r) ^ -n) / (.01 * r)

            PRINT TAB(7 * (r - a)); USING "##.####"; x;

            IF r = 10 + a THEN PRINT

        NEXT r

    NEXT n

    PRINT

NEXT a

END


For Table 4 (terminal value of an annuity) the program used was:


PRINT "Table 4: Future value of an annuity of £1 for n years"
PRINT "                                      (1 + r)^n  -  1"
PRINT " at 100r% compound interest:       ———————————"
PRINT "                                           r"
PRINT "---------------------------------------------------------"
PRINT

PRINT "Years";
PRINT TAB(30); "Discount rate as percentage (100r)"
```

```
PRINT
PRINT " n ";

FOR a = 0 TO 24 STEP 6

    FOR r = 1 + a TO 6 + a

        PRINT TAB(2 + 10 * (r - a)); r;

        IF r = 6 + a THEN PRINT

    NEXT r

    FOR n = 1 TO 30

        PRINT n;

        FOR r = 1 + a TO 6 + a

            x = ((1 + .01 * r) ^ n - 1) / (.01 * r)

            PRINT TAB(10 * (r - a)); USING "####.####"; x;

            IF r = 6 + a THEN PRINT

        NEXT r

    NEXT n

PRINT

NEXT a

END


For Table 5 (sinking fund) the program used was:


PRINT "Table 5: Sinking fund of £1 for n years"
PRINT "                                              r"
PRINT " at 100r% compound interest:  ——————————————"
PRINT "                                      (1 + r)^n  -  1"
PRINT "----------------------------------------------------------"
PRINT

PRINT "Years";
PRINT TAB(30); "Discount rate as percentage (100r)"
PRINT
PRINT " n ";

FOR a = 0 TO 20 STEP 10

    FOR r = 1 + a TO 10 + a

        PRINT TAB(7 * (r - a)); r;

        IF r = 10 + a THEN PRINT
```

```
        NEXT r

    FOR n = 1 TO 30

        PRINT n;

        FOR r = 1 + a TO 10 + a

            x = .01 * r / (((1 + .01 * r) ^ n) - 1)

                PRINT TAB(7 * (r - a)); USING "#.####"; x;

                IF r = 10 + a THEN PRINT

        NEXT r

    NEXT n

    PRINT

    NEXT a

    END


For Table 6 (annual equivalent annuities) the program used was:


PRINT "Table 6: Annual equivalent annuity of £1 after n years"
PRINT "                                                r"
PRINT " at 100r% compound interest:   ——————————————"
PRINT "                                         1 - (1 + r)^-n"
PRINT "----------------------------------------------------------"
PRINT

PRINT "Years";
PRINT TAB(30); "Discount rate as percentage (100r)"
PRINT
PRINT " n ";

FOR a = 0 TO 20 STEP 10

    FOR r = 1 + a TO 10 + a

        PRINT TAB(7 * (r - a)); r;

        IF r = 10 + a THEN PRINT

    NEXT r

    FOR n = 1 TO 30

        PRINT n;

        FOR r = 1 + a TO 10 + a

            x = .01 * r / (1 - (1 + .01 * r) ^ -n)
```

```
            PRINT TAB(7 * (r - a)); USING "#.####"; x;

            IF r = 10 + a THEN PRINT

        NEXT r

    NEXT n

PRINT

NEXT a

END
```

Table 7 was the table of areas under the normal curve up to given numbers of standard deviations above the mean. The program uses Simpson's Rule to find areas for the standard normal curve (mean of zero, variance one). In the program, 'coeff' is the value of $1/\sqrt{(2\pi)}$. It will be seen that, for simplicity, the program evaluates the integral from the mean upwards and adds 0.5. The program is:

```
DEF fnf (x) = (EXP(-(x ^ 2) / 2))

steps = 10

coeff = .3989423

CLS

PRINT "Table 7:"
PRINT "Area under the normal curve up to t standard deviations ";
PRINT "above the mean."
PRINT "                    t"
PRINT "                   ⌠"
PRINT " Area = [1/√(2π)]   ⌡  exp(-(x^2)/2)  dx"
PRINT "                   -∞"
PRINT "------------------------------------------------------------------";
PRINT "------"
PRINT

FOR i = 0 TO .09 STEP .01

    PRINT TAB(8 + 700 * i); USING "#.##"; i;

NEXT i

PRINT

PRINT " t"

FOR h = 0 TO 4 STEP .1

    PRINT USING "#.#"; h;

    FOR i = 0 TO .09 STEP .01
```

```
upper = h + i

breadth = upper / steps

sum = fnf(0) + fnf(upper)

FOR j = 1 TO steps - 1 STEP 2

    temp = 4 * fnf(j * breadth)

    sum = sum + temp

NEXT j

FOR j = 2 TO steps - 2 STEP 2

    temp = 2 * fnf(j * breadth)

    sum = sum + temp

NEXT j

S = (breadth / 3) * sum

Area = .5 + coeff * S

IF Area < .99995 THEN

    PRINT TAB(7 + 700 * i); USING ".####"; Area;

ELSE

    PRINT TAB(7 + 700 * i); USING "#.####"; Area;

END IF

NEXT i

PRINT

NEXT h

END
```

Programs have been provided for the seven tables printed. Only relatively minor modifications to the appropriate programs would be needed to produce similar tables for continuous compounding or for other circumstances as may be required.

Index

ABC Classification Policy 844
Abnormal Return 280
Acceptance Credits 567
Accepting Houses 559
Accountancy 39–65
Accounting Exposure (Risk) 788, 967–70
Accounting Information 393–4, 513–17
Accounting Rate of Return 163
Adjusted Present Value (APV) 645–8
Administration 926–7
Advance Corporation Tax (ACT) 32–3, 617–19
Advanced Manufacturing Technology 218 ff
Agency Theory 4, 662, 867
Aharony, J. 626
Allen, D. 248, 272
Allied Lyons plc 789, 921
Alpha, see Abnormal Return
Alternative Investment Market 335
Altman, E. 63–4
American Depository Receipts (ADR) 325, 909–52
Amortization 108
Annual Equivalent Annuities 108
  Method 109
  Tables 1027
Annuities 103, 142
  continuous 125
  with growth 112
  tables 1020
Anticipated Inflation 118
Arbitrage 650
Arbitrageurs 877
Arbitrage Pricing Model 289
Argenti, J. 998–1001
Arithmetic Progressives 139
Arithmetic Series 138
Asquith, P. 662
Asset Swaps 921
Asymmetric Information 405, 661
Auction Market Preferred Stock (AMPS) 374–5

Babiak, H. 627
Backlogged Demand 831
Bad Debts 561, 799–802
Barclays Bank 600
Balanced Score Card 4
Ball, R. and Brown, P. 393–4, 515
Bank Borrowing 432–4, 558–66
Bank of England 65, 329, 542, 924, 996
Baskin, J.B. 662
BAT Industries plc see British American Tobacco

Baxter, N. 659
BCCI 15
Bearer Securities 433
Berliner Method 529
Beta Books 273–80
Beta Coefficient 262, 271, 280
  asset beta 283
  determinants 286
  industry 280, 281
  measurement 274
  stability 280
  ungearing 282
Beta of Portfolios 264
Benefit-Cost Ratio 147
Big Bang 16–17, 327
Bills of Exchange 567
Black, F. 625
Bodyshop plc 499–500
Boston Consulting Group Model 214
Blue Arrow Case 11–12, 15, 337
Boesky, I. 893–5
Bolton Committee 994–6
Bonds 428–30, 434–47
Borrowing Ratios see Gearing Ratios
Brands 59
Branson, R. 918
Brealey, R. A. 248, 249, 272
Brennan, M. J. 625
British American Tobacco (BAT) 623
British Petroleum plc 977–8
British Technology Group 1010
Buffer Stocks 830
Business Angels 1006
Business Combinations 855–93
Business Expansion Scheme 1005–6
Business Risk 650
Business Statistics 26–7
Buy Backs (Equity Shares) 343–4
Buyer Credits 579
Buy-Ins 919–20

Cadbury Committee Report 10–13
Capital Asset Pricing Model 261–96, 388–90, 507–12, 543
Capital Decay 226
Capital Gains Tax 35–6
Capital Markets 13–17, 320–38, 568–9
Capital Market Line (CML) 259, 260
Capital Rationing 144 ff
Capital structure 634–75
  financial distress 658–60
  Modigliani and Miller 649–53
  taxes 653–8
  traditional view 648, 649

CAPS 732
Cash Budgets 714–20
Cash Cycle 721–2
Cash Discounts 570–2, 804–8
Cash Flow – Acquisitions 862
Cash Flow Accounting 47–50, 512–13, 696–700
Cash Flow, Discounted 74 ff
Cash Flow Ratios 61–3
Cash Flow Statements 722–7
Cash Management 708–50
Cash Management Models 758–65, 827
Cash Transmission Techniques 713–14
Certificates of Deposit 727
Chapter 11 (USA) 928–9
Chartists 415–16
Chen, N. F. 289
City Code on Takeovers and Mergers 867–78
Clarkham, J. 7
Classical Model of Stock Control 823
Clientele Effect 548
Coefficient of Variation 187
Collars 732, 738–41
Collection Cycle 712–13
Company Failures 921–3, 999–1002
Commencement Date: Optimum 120
Commercial Paper 435
Commitment Fee 568
Committee of London Clearing Banks 564
Common Ratio 142
Complexity Reduction 846
Compound Interest 74
Computer Integrated Manufacturing 218
Computer Programs 96, 131, 208, 848, 1030
Concert Parties 871
Conglomerates 909–10
Consolidated Gold Fields 870, 878
Consols 103, 143
Continuous Compounding 124
Controlled Non Subsidiaries 454–6
Convertible Euro Bond 468–9
Convertible Loan Stock 468–77
Cooper, G. M. 280
Corporate Governance 7–10, 869
Corporation Tax 31–4
Correlation Coefficient 192, 244, 245, 253
Corridors 746
Cost of Capital see Cost of Finance
Cost of Finance 443–4, 540–9
  marginal cost of capital 643–5, 957–63
  weighted average cost of capital 639–42
Council for small Industries in Rural Areas (COSIRA) 1010–11

Countertrade 581
Covariance of Security Returns 192, 244, 245, 252
Covenants 429, 660, 662
Coverage Analysis 849
Covered Warrant 480–3
Cowling, K. 887
Creative Accounting 411–13, 513–17
Credit Cards 123
Credit Insurance 573, 580, 811
Credit Policy 797–811
Creditors 711–14
Credit Terms 803–8
Creditors Voluntary Liquidations 927
Crown Jewels 876
Currency Swaps 954–6
Current Ratio 55, 158
Currency Futures Contracts 784–8

Dawn Raids 870–1
Declining Balance Depreciation 142
DCF Methods 74 ff
DCF Rate of Return, see Yield
Debentures 428–30
Debt-Equity Swaps 464
Debtors 711–14, 797–814
De La Rue plc 789, 971
Deep Discounted Bonds 445–7
Deferred Annuities 103
Deferred Tax 574
Demerger 912–13
Depreciation and DCF Methods 74, 139, 117, 142
Deregulation 937–8
Derivatives 297–300, 400–83, 946
  see also interest rate futures; interest rate swaps; foreign currency futures; foreign currency swaps
Development Grants 598
Dimson, E. 248, 272, 284
Directional Policy Matrix 215
Discount Houses 559
Discount Factors 76
Discounting 74 ff
Disintermediation 569
Distillers plc 893–5
Divestment 908–11
Dividend Controls 620
Dividend Cover 352
Dividend Policy 610–33
  foreign income dividends 619, 623
  irrelevancy 612–14
  national expectations 616
  practical issues 619–22
  and taxation 611, 617–19, 621
Dividends and Shareprices 614
  clientele 616
  information 616
Dividends 494–504, 546
Dividend Yield 349–50
Dodd, D. L. 614
Donaldson, G. 661
Double-Taxation Agreements 979
Downside Variation 180
Dun and Bradstreet 802, 996
Duration 741–2

Earnings per Share 350–2
Earnouts 884–5
Earnings Management (Manipulation) 411–13, 513–17
Economic Exposure 788, 970–1
Economic Interest Groups 893
Economic Lot Size 825

Economies of Scale 861
Earnings Yield 547
Economic Order Quantity 825
Efficient Market Hypothesis 8, 385–420
Efficient Portfolios 256, 258
EOQ 825
Equity Kicker 436
Eurobonds 944–45
Eurocurrency Market 941–2
Euroequity 945–9
Euromarkets 937–41
Euronotes 943
European Union 869, 928, 992–5
European Coal and Steel Community 601
Euro Disney S.A. 236
European Investment Bank 599
Eurotunnel plc 62–3, 236, 497
Exit Routes 1005
Expected Net Present Value 175
Expected Return 238
Extended Yield Method 83
Export Finance 576–82

Factoring 572–4, 581
Fads and Bubbles 399–400
Failure Prediction 63–5
Fair Game 388–9
Fama, E. 627
Farlly, G. E. 627
Financial Distress 658–60
Financial Objectives 2–5, 676–8
Financial Planning Models 145, 158 ff, 680–4, 689–91
Financial Gearing Structure see Capital Gearing
Financial Reporting Review Panel 514
Financial Services Act 14–15
Financial Times 353, 440–2, 734 , 768
Finished Goods Inventory 821 ff
Finite Horizon Method 112, 163
Finite Series 140
Floating Rate Notes 431
Flexible Monetary Systems 218 ff
Flow of Funds 21–30
Foreign Exchange Options 779–84
Foreign Exchange Risk Management 708–10
Foreign Exchange Futures 784–8
Foreign Exchange Markets 766–89
Foreign Exchange Rates 768–77
Forfeiting 581
Forward Interest Rate Agreements 731 , 738–41
Forward Exchange Market 767–8, 777–9
Forward Forward Loans 730
Functional Fixation 413
Fundamental Analysis 415–16
Funds flow Statement 696–700
Futures see Interest Rate Futures; Foreign Exchange Futures
Future Value 74, 76
  tables 1015

Gearing 475–7
Gearing Ratios 58–61, 535–638, 648–9, 660
General Electric Corporation (GEC) 844, 920
Geometric Progressives 139, 142
Glaxo plc 789
Global Financial Markets 322–5, 935–51
Goal Congruence 3
Going Concern Concept 41
Going Private 918–20
Golden Parachute 867–76
Gordon, M. J. 615
Government Guaranteed Loans 574

Graham B. 614
Greenmail 623, 877
Gregory-Allen, R. 281
Gross Present Value 77ff
Grouping Methods 844
Guinness plc 43–7, 51–60, 337, 497, 867, 893–5

Hanson plc 877, 915
Hard Capital Rationing 145
Hedging 777–88, 971–6
Heron Corporation 926
Hire Purchase 582–4
Holding Costs 823

Ibbotson, R.G. 248, 272, 541–3
Immediate Annuity 103
Imputation Tax System 32–3
Implied Yield 157
Income Smoothing 42
Incremental Yield Method 85 ff
Indifference Curves 94, 192, 243, 257
Inflation and DCF Analysis 118, 169, 198
Initial Outlay 76
Initial Public Offers 517–21
Innovation 217
In-Process Inventory 821
Inside Information 394–404
Insider Dealing 400–4
Insolvency 925–6
Interest Cover 635, 638
Interest Rate Futures 733, 748
Interest Rate Guarantees 731, 738–41
Interest Rate Parity 771–5
Interest Rate Risk Management 730–48
Interest Rate Changes and NPV 90, 106, 139
Interest Rate Swaps 434, 461–4, 743–9
Interest Rates 455–6, 466
International Business Finance 935–85
International Money Market 733–4
Institutional Shareholdings 5, 6
Internal Rate of Return, see Yield
Interpretation of Yield 81
Inventory Management 821 ff
Investment Appraisal 73 ff
  in AMT 218 ff
  in multinational companies 963–6
Investment Opportunity Line 94
Investors in Industry (3 i's) 433, 575–6, 600–1, 997, 1002, 1010
Invoice Discounting 573
IRR see Yield
Irredeemable Bonds 439

Jensen, J. 662
Jensen, M.C. 9, 404, 660, 866, 888–9
Joint Ventures 891–2
Junk Bonds 436–7, 885
Just In Time Approach 224, 822, 847, 849

Kaplan, R. 4, 512
KPMG 914, 915
Kuwait Investment Office 624, 977–8
Kwan, C. 626

Leading and Lagging 975
Lead Time 828
Leasing 585–97
Lev B. 887
Leverage see Gearing Ratios
Liars Poker 435
Licensed Dealers 338–9
Life cycle of Firm 998–9
Liquidation 912, 926–30
Liquidity Ratios see Gearing Ratios

Lintner 262, 626
Litzengerger, R.H. 625
Loan Guarantee Scheme 432, 997–8, 1004, 1008–9
Loan Stock 428–30
Local Authority Debt 727
Local Authority Financial Support 599
Local Enterprise Agencies 1011
London International Financial Futures Exchange (LIFFE) 299, 733–4
London Stock Exchange 325–39, 434 ff
London Traded Options Market (LTOM) 299
Long, J. B. 626
Lorie-Savage Problem 151
Lot Size Management 845
Lowest Common Multiple Method 112
Lowndes Queensway plc 881

Macmillan Gap 995
Majluf, N. 661
Make or Buy 115
Management Buy-Outs 436, 910, 913–18
Marginal Value of Funds 149
Market Portfolio 259
Market Risk see Systematic Risk
Markowitz, H. M. 252, 266
Marsh, P. 284
Matching 973–4
Material Requirements Planning 846 ff
Maxwell, R. 412
Mean-Variance Analysis 195
Mean-Variance Efficiency 256, 257
Meckling, W. 662
Medium Term Notes 420–31
Merchant Banks 559, 574–6
Merger Accounting 856–7
Mergers and Takeovers 394–5, 855–95, 908
Merton, R. C. 312
Mezzanine Finance 436, 916–18
Milken, M. 885
Miller, M. H. 288, 611, 649
Minority Shareholders 873
MIRR 88
Mission Statement 677
Modified Internal Rate of Return 88
Modigliani, F. and Miller, M. H. 504, 611, 649–53
Modigliani, F. 611, 649
Money Laundering 985
Monopolies and Mergers Commission (MMC) 272, 877, 886
Morgan Grenfell 894
Mortgages 465, 585
Mossin, J. 262
MRP Methods 822, 846 ff
Multicurrency Billing System 975–6
Multiple Yields 83 ff
Mullins, D. W. 662
Mutual Recognition 329
Myers, S. C. 661

Net Future Value 79
Net Present Value 76 ff
  Decision rule for single project 77
  Decision rules under capital returning 146
  Expected 175
  Interest Rate Changes and 90
  Theoretical justification for 92
Netting 972–3
New Equity Issues 517–21
Non-Executive Directors 10–11
Normal distribution 240

Normative models 158
NPV see Net Present Value
Net Terminal Value 79, 91

Objective function 152
Off Balance Sheet Finance 513–17
Office of Fair Trading 861, 877, 894
Offer for Sale 345–6
Offshore Financial Centres 402–4, 981–6
Operating Cycle 694–6
Operating Exposure see Economic Exposure
Opportunity Costs 78, 109, 223
Optimists Diagram 182
Options 299 ff
  American and European 300, 312
  Applications 315, 316
  Binomial valuation 312, 313
  Black-Scholes valuation 313–15
  calls 300
  Foreign Exchange 779–84
  futures 308, 309
  Option delta/hedging ratio 313, 315
  put/call parity 311
  puts 301
  strategies 306
  traditional 299, 306
  valuation 309–11
Ordinary Shares 341–3
Overtrading 692–3
Overdrafts 559–62
Over the counter market 338
Overseas investment 26–7

Pareto Analysis 844
Payback Method 160 ff, 218
Payment Cycle 712–13
Pecking Order 661
Performance Bonds 580
Perpetuities 103, 126
Periodic Review Model 842
Personal Equity Plans (PEP) 1007
Personal Investments 24–5
Personal Savings 24–5
Pessimists Diagram 182
Pettit, R. R. 626
Philips 412, 964
Planning 676–700
Plessey plc 869
Poison Pills 876
Political Risk 976–8
Pooling of Interests 856
Porterfield, J.T.S. 611
Portfolio Theory 251, 252
Portfolio Return 243, 244
Portfolio variance 244, 256
Pre-emption Rights 372
Preference Shares 343, 373–5
Pre-production Inventory 821
Present Value 75
  Tables 1018
Price Earnings (PE) Ratios 352–4, 505, 527, 864–5
Private Companies 339–41
Product Life Cycle 721–2
Profitability Index 148
Profitability Ratios 52–5
Project Finance 581
Prospectus 332
Public Sector 28–30
Purchasing Power Parity 770

Ramaswamy, K. 625
Random Walks 389–92
Rate of Return: Accounting 163

dcf see Yield
  internal see Yield
  modified interval 88
Ratio Analysis 50–65
Real discount Rate 118
Real returns 273
Receivership 927
Redeemable Preference Shares 373–4, 453
Redemption Yield 106
Refinancing 923
Regional Enterprise Grants 598
Regulations (Stock Exchange) 13–16, 331, 339
Reinvoicing Centres 975–6, 983
Relevant Costs 74, 223 ff
Reorder Policy 842
Reorder Level 828
  Model 842
Research, Development and Technology Support 598, 601
Restructuring 908–26
Returns on Equity 541–2
Return, Single period 237
Reverse Takeover 921
Revolving Underwriting Facility 566
Rights Issue 359–71
Risk Adjusted Discount Rate 165
Risk Premium Approach 165
Risk Profiles 177, 182
Risk Free Rate of Interest 258, 271
Risk in Capital Budgeting 235, 236, 264
Risk Measurement Service 239, 274
Risk Premium 236, 237, 272, 273
Risk Shifting 662
Robson Rhodes 997
Roll, R. 288
Ronson, G. 894–5
Ross, S. A. 289
R Squared in Risk Measurement 280
Rule 4.2 336–7

Saatchi and Saatchi plc 884
SAGA 919
Sale and Lease-Back 584–5
Saunders, E. 893–5
Scenarios 158, 169 ff
Science Parks 1003
Scholes, M. 288, 625
Scottish Development Agency 1011
Scrip Dividends 354–8, 622–4
SEAQ (Stock Exchange Automatic Quotation) 327–8, 337
Securities and Exchange Commission 878
Securities and Investment Board 14–15, 339
Security Market Line (SML) 262, 263, 282
Securitization 447–8
Self Regulation 13–15
Sell Off 911
Semi-derivatives 180
Semi-variance 240
Sensitivity Analysis 166 ff
Separation Theories 94 ff, 260
Serious Fraud Office 15–16
Series 140
Service Level 839
Set-up Costs 224, 830, 845
Share Option Schemes 344
Share Price Anomalies 405–10
Share Prices 353–4, 387–9
Share Price Valuation 492–521, 862–4
Share Repurchase 622–4, 920–1
Sharpe, W. F. 262, 280
Sigma Rotation 77
Simple Interest 139

Simulation 173 ff, 198 ff
Sinking Funds 106
    Tables 1025
Sinquesfield, R. A. 248, 272
Size Effect 284
Skewness 197
Small Business 910, 992–1012
Small companies – Taxation 33–5
Smith, T. 412
Sock Shop International 1003–4
Soft Capital Rationing 145
Special Purpose Transactions 452–5
Specific Risk 222, 247, 261, 270
Spin Offs 912–13
Spreadsheets 198
Square Root Rule 825
Stags 348
Standard Deviation of Return 238, 239
Standard Deviation of NPV 176
Standard Error of Betas 280
Start up Finance 102
Starting Date: Optimum 120
Strategic Alliances 891–2
Strategic Business Units 213, 676–700
Strategic Planning 213 ff
Stock Control 821 ff
Stock Exchange Alternative Trading
    System (SEATS) 1007
Stock Market 320–38
Stock Market Efficiency 385–420
Stock-Out Situation 830
Stock Splits 358–9
Subjective Probability 238
Systematic Risk 222
Super Profits 530
Swaps 298
Swaption 957
Swary, I. 626

Syndicated Credits 942
Synergy 860–1, 885
Systematic Risk 247, 261, 270

Tables for DCF 1014 ff
Takeovers 855–93
Taurus 329
Taxation and Corporate Profits 29–37
    capital gearing 653–8
    dividend policy 617–19
    overseas investment 978–86
Taxation and DCF 116
Tax Havens 981–6
Tax Neutrality 978–9
Technical Analysis 415–16
Tenders 347–8
Term Loans 464–5
Term Structure of Interest Rates 455–6
Terminal Rate of Return 88
Terminal Value 74
    of annuity 106
Termination Date: optimum 121
Total Quality Management 225
Third Market 335
Tobins 'q' Ratio 859, 863
Tompkins plc 971
Trade Credit 570–3
Transfer Pricing 975–6, 983
Trapped Equity 862
Trafalgar House plc 514
Transaction Exposure 777–89
Translation Exposure (Risk) 788, 967–70
Treasury Management 708–65
Treasury Organisation and Control 748–50
Two Bin System 842, 844

Unanticipated Inflation 118
Uncertainty 160, 235

Underwriters 348
Unique Risk see Specific Risk
United Biscuits (Holdings) plc 636, 637
Unsystematic Risk see Specific risk
USM (Unlisted Securities Market) 326,
    332–4, 337, 1004
Utility Index 196, 242, 257

Valuation–Assets 43–6, 528
Valuation–Companies 521–40
Valuation–Shares 492–520
Variance of NPV 179 ff
Vendor Placings 349, 882–3
Vendor Rights 882–3
Venture Capital 375–6, 1002, 1007, 1011

War Loan 103
Warner, J. P. 659
Warrants 477–83
Watts, R. 626
What-if Analysis 198
White Knights 875–6, 893
Wilson Committee 996
Winners Curse 521
Working Capital 55–6, 117, 687–93
Work in Progress 821
Writing Down Allowance 117

Yellow Book (London Stock Exchange Rule
    Book) 331–2, 336, 372, 872
Yield 79 ff.
    Decision rule for many projects 85 ff.
    Decision rule for single project 80
    Implied 157
    Interpolation Method 81
    Multiple 83 ff.
    to maturity 105
Yield Curve 455–6